D0225401

SENSIBLE POLITICS

SENSIBLE POLITICS

THE VISUAL CULTURE OF NONGOVERNMENTAL ACTIVISM

Edited by

Meg McLagan and Yates McKee

ZONE BOOKS · NEW YORK

2012

ZONE BOOKS
1226 Prospect Avenue
Brooklyn, NY 11218

Printed in the United States of America.

Distributed by The MIT Press,
Cambridge, Massachusetts, and London, England

Library of Congress Cataloging-in-Publication Data

Sensible politics : the visual culture of nongovernmental activism / edited by Meg McLagan and Yates McKee.
p. cm.
Includes bibliographical references.
ISBN 978-1-935408-24-6 (alk. paper)
1. Arts—Political aspects. 2. Visual communication—Political aspects. 3. Non-governmental organizations—Political activity. 4. Politics and culture. I. McLagan, Meg, editor. II. McKee, Yates, editor.

NX180.P64S45 2012
700.1'03—dc23

2012004106

Contents

PART FOUR: EXPANDED ARCHITECTURES

PART FIVE: MULTIPLYING PLATFORMS

Taryn Simon, *Transatlantic Sub-Marine Cables Reaching Land, VSNL International, Avon, New Jersey*, 2006/2007 (© Taryn Simor
Courtesy Gagosian Gallery).

Introduction

Meg McLagan and Yates McKee

Politics revolves around what can be seen, felt, sensed. Political acts are encoded in medial forms—feet marching on a street, punch holes on a card, images on a television newscast, tweets about events unfolding in real time—by which the political becomes manifest in the world. These forms have force, shaping people as subjects and constituting the contours of what is perceptible, sensible, legible. In doing so, they define the terms of political possibility and create terrain for political acts. Following Jacques Rancière, we are interested in how various orderings of social relations become "sensible" as viable sites of contestation by nongovernmental activists. Pursuing this line of questioning requires two interconnected levels of analysis. First, it requires close attention to the formal, aesthetic, rhetorical, and affective dimensions of the images, performances, and artifacts that make up what George Marcus has called "the activist imaginary."[1] Second, it requires an examination of the processual aspect of this imaginary, which is to say, the whole network of financial, institutional, discursive, and technological infrastructures and practices involved in the production, circulation, and reception of the visual-cultural materials with which this volume concerns itself. By bringing these realms together into one complex we examine the political fields constituted by images, the practices of circulation that propel them, and the platforms on which they are made manifest.

The conjunction of visual culture and nongovernmental politics in this volume's subtitle could be presumed to refer to two distinct realms: the representational world of visual culture that somehow encodes and represents the political, on one side, and the domain of the political, on the other. The works in this book refuse this opposition and instead analyze their mutual imbrication. Of particular concern to us here are the ways in which images are tied to "making things public," to the relational processes through which particular relations of social power are reinscribed as issues of political concern and concrete transformation.[2] A photograph displayed in a newspaper is not the same object when it is displayed in an art gallery. The networks in which the image circulates and the platforms by which it is manifest rest upon differing epistemologies and infrastructures. These different modes of circulation address distinct publics and make possible varying forms of political action, enabling particular claims to be made while foreclosing others.

The emergence of new forms of nongovernmental politics in the last few decades rests upon practices of mediation whereby social movements constitute particular publics, advance claims in the world, and seek to intervene politically. Images circulate in specific institutional and discursive networks, anchored by the specificity of their form of mediation and attentive to the aesthetic and generic demands of their particular platforms. These platforms can be concerts, human rights reports, magazine photojournalism, graffiti, legal cases, documentary films, online videos, or a thousand other such domains. Each one demands its own modes of address, it own techniques of soliciting attention, its own supporting discourses whereby it claims truth, authority, and legitimacy. Attending to political aesthetics means attending not to a disembodied image that travels under the concept of art or visual culture or to a preformed domain of the political that seeks subsequent expression in media form. It demands not just an examination of the visual forms that comment upon and constitute politics, but analysis of the networks of circulation whereby images exist in the world and the platforms by which they come into public prominence.

Diverse activists of all ideological stripes are involved in these projects. This book was conceived prior to the emergence of demonstrations around the world, from the Arab Middle East, to Europe, to the United States, in which protesters are occupying everywhere, including the abstract place known as Wall Street, coming together to locate, reify, and contest performatively the usually vague nonspace of capital or authoritarian rule. Although these movements are in many cases regionally specific, internally fractious, and distinguished from one another through a whole range of highly specific, contingent situations, they have in common a characteristic identified by Michel Feher, following Foucault, in the predecessor to this volume: "a shared determination not to be governed *thusly*."[3]

NONGOVERNMENTS

The premise of nongovernmental politics—organized political action separated from the state—is sometimes mapped onto a simplistic assumption that nongovernmental politics are progressivist and frequently *opposed* to the work of the state. This view has come under challenge in recent years in two main ways.

The first has been a growing scholarship devoted to analyzing the work of NGOs, including aid and humanitarian movements, as forms of what Mariella Pandolfi refers to as "mobile sovereignties."[4] This scholarship has made clear that NGOs, through interventions in the name of disaster relief, care, or humanitarianism, are frequently engaged in what Didier Fassin terms "humanitarian government." By this he refers to the measures, initiatives, and techniques of government engaged in by both states and nongovernmental actors and brought into operation to manage precarious populations.[5] Through the biopolitical care of vulnerable people, aid apparatuses, religious movements, and medical relief organizations enter into territories for particular periods of time and come to take on the de facto status of a government through the act of administering welfare. Operating on similar terrain, NGOs take on tasks that were previously the prerogative of the state.

The assumption that nongovernmental politics are opposed to the work of the state also fails to take into account the ways in which the state, as the object of contest, is configured differently in a neoliberal age in which the hegemonic norm is to deny the legitimacy of state responsibility for the quality of life of its citizens. We can see this not only in the rise of new populist movements such as the Tea Party, with its antigovernment ideology, but also more generally in the common devaluation in countries such as the United States and the United Kingdom of state intervention in favor of the privatization of public services. Whether under the cloak of austerity or that of deficit reduction, the dismantling of subsidies for public education, health care, and housing is at the same time an eradication of the legitimacy of the term "public" itself. The initiatives of the postwar period that strove to make welfare, education, and social equality a democratic right freely available to all were the outcome of a series of political claims that were made upon the state in the name of the public and that have now become increasingly difficult to make in an era that exalts the logic of the market and the "responsibilization" of citizens. It is precisely because so many of the protests of 2011 were staged in order to call attention to the state's failure to perform its customary function (from public education to the regulation of the financial industry, or what Lauran Berlant describes as the place of the state in the production of the "good life") that we cannot adopt any simplistic dichotomy between the state and the nongovernmental.[6] Their relations are not structurally opposed, but tactical and shifting, at times close and at others bitterly contested.

The nongovernmental is a form of politics that involves a reorientation of political analysis away from the dichotomy often drawn between myopic reformism, on the one hand, and antisystemic radicalism, on the other. As Feher points out, nongovernmental politics entails an engagement with the political on the part of the governed "without aspiring to govern, be governed by the best leaders, or abolish the institutions of government altogether."[7] The politics of the governed is not organized around the "who" of government—the state, for instance—but rather targets the "how" of a particular means of being governed. The claim of the governed is therefore "not to be governed *thusly*," rather than to not be governed at all, on the one hand, or to be governed perfectly, on the other.[8] For Feher, this displaces a "representational" paradigm of the political that would still posit some implicit ideal of adequation between government and governed and thus a potential termination of politics. Far from the abandonment of grand political designs, the structurally incomplete dimension of the political is what keeps the condition of being governed alive as a matter of contestation, rather than of acquiescence to sheer governmental administration or of spontaneous self-determination.

Nongovernment is thus premised on a constitutive split between government and the forms of politics that operate outside of it while at the same time recognizing that this split is not fixed, but mutable, constantly in dynamic interaction. At certain times, the nongovernmental may be aligned with the state and at other times opposed to it. The rise of progressive political figures—Barack Obama's emergence as a presidential candidate, for instance—may produce a situational alignment, but as Feher stresses, the nongovernmental is fundamentally about a politics of the governed that in the last instance will exceed and trouble the practice of government.

In this volume, our focus is on the techniques for sensing the political and on its mediation through infrastructures of circulation and display. The visual culture of nongovernmental politics is about proliferating platforms. It is not about the image, but the image complex, the channels of circulation along which cultural forms travel, the nature of the campaigns that frame them, and the discursive platforms that display and encode them in specific truth modes. This involves form-sensitive analysis of the specificity of differing platforms that chart the imbrication of aesthetic form, medial practice, and political intent into one assemblage.

POLITICAL AESTHETICS

In the most general sense, the rubric of visual culture conceives "vision" not as a naturally given optical faculty, but rather as an historical, shifting assemblage of technical and social forces that shape—without mechanically determining—the perceptual, cognitive, and psychic lives of subjects in their relation to the world.[9] Theories of visual culture have necessarily concerned themselves with questions of power, situating themselves in a broad lineage of critical, skeptical, or even iconoclastic analysis of the hegemonic organizations of visual experience put forth by corporations, governments, and various collusions thereof. While indebted to Marxist analyses of the relations between media systems, ideology, and subjectivity put forth in the postwar era under the rubrics of "the culture industry" (Theodor Adorno), "the society of the spectacle" (Guy Debord), "ideological state apparatuses" (Louis Althusser), "the consciousness industry" (Hans Magnus Enzensberger), or "the manufacture of consent" (Noam Chomsky), visual-culture discourse has gradually attempted to distinguish itself from approaches that would posit a self-evident transition from ideological mystification to visual enlightenment. Instead of a unilateral, top-down flow of visual manipulation, visual-culture discourse has concerned itself with the complex dynamics of audience reception, suggesting the ways in which the consumers of hegemonic corporate and governmental visual materials might variously refuse, resist, or recode those materials for their own purposes.[10]

Rather than examine this or that form of nongovernmental political work as a self-evident sociological object, the essays in this book retrace mediatic articulation, thus calling attention "to the way in which what had hitherto been considered accessory and intermediary—the program, its transmission, reception, storage, recycling, retransmission—infiltrates the inner integrity of the work, revealing it to be inscribed in and as a network."[11] Though not overtly concerned with the political in this passage, Samuel Weber's sense of the mediatic is germane to our current project in that it treats media as both a general condition of existence and as a specific set of technical devices and practices that define "a relational process which depends as much upon what it is not as upon what it is."[12]

Weber's conception of the mediatic is deeply informed by Walter Benjamin's 1936 essay "The Work of Art in the Age of its Technological Reproducibility," which remains startlingly pertinent to the contemporary world. Of particular resonance is Benjamin's suggestion that photographic media and their avatars involve a general dynamic of displacement, deterritorialization, and dissemination that opens "a vast and unsuspected field of action" and with it a new range of potential agents for whom the "distinction between author and public is about to lose its axiomatic character."[13] Benjamin was not of course a techno-utopian who would assume the inevitable benevolence of any particular technology in and of itself. Alarmed by the successful mobilization of newspapers, radio, and especially film by corporations and governments in constructing reactionary patterns of "simultaneous collective reception,"[14] Benjamin called for progressive movements to make the economies, infrastructures, and competencies involved in mass-media systems a matter of urgent political concern in its own right.

Benjamin's essay, it should not be forgotten, was nominally concerned with the fate of "art" as a specialized category of cultural production and spectatorial experience when confronted with the "world-historical upheaval"[15] of technological reproducibility. Unlike his interlocutor Theodor Adorno, Benjamin was enthusiastic about the liquidation of the traditional principle of aesthetic autonomy—*l'art pour l'art*—and indeed saw its monstrous dialectical counterpart in what he called the "aestheticizing of politics" by fascism, which is to say, its transformation of collective sociopolitical experience into a spectacular harmonious totality of intensified sensory experience.[16] Against both bourgeois autonomy and the fascist *Gesamtkunstwerk*, Benjamin famously called for "politicizing art" qua counterpropaganda in which the disjunctive principles of photomontage (as in the work of Dziga Vertov or John Heartfeld) would play a crucial role in activating the critical acumen and political consciousness of its audience.[17] Despite Benjamin's own complex philosophical dialogue with Romantic aesthetic theory throughout his career—culminating in the messianic figure of the "dialectical image"—his polemical derogation of aestheticization has long functioned as a kind of taboo concerning the category of the aesthetic *tout court* for left-oriented thinkers, artists, and media practitioners.

Without reneging on Benjamin's insights, the recent work of Jacques Rancière has involved a highly generative revisiting of the relation between aesthetics and politics in which aesthetics ceases to be an esoteric philosophical subfield, an indulgent appreciation of art for its own sake, or an ecstatic experience of consensual fusion. Drawing on Schiller's Enlightenment concern with the artwork as the locus of an undecidable negotiation between autonomous play of the subjective imagination and the heteronomous molding, training, or education of the citizen, Rancière's aesthetic emerges as a general inquiry into the volatile role of sensory experience in the organization of relations of power and resistance:

> a delimitation of spaces and times, of the visible and the invisible, of speech and noise, that simultaneously determines the place and the stakes of politics as a form of experience. Politics revolves around what is seen and what can be said about it, around who has the ability to see and the talent to speak, around the properties of space and the possibilities of time.[18]

In this approach, aesthetic techniques—including, but not limited to those occurring within the institutionally sanctioned realms of literature, art, or film, for instance—do not simply create unreal fantasies or, conversely, expose hidden truths in an already constituted public sphere or political realm whose rules are determined in advance. Rather, they challenge and reconfigure what Rancière calls the "distribution of the sensible," which "parcels out places and forms of participation in a common world by first establishing the modes of perception within which these are inscribed." This includes, paradoxically, those in society "who have no part," the surplus or remainder of the population whose conditions, concerns, and claims do not register as legitimately political for those agencies responsible for governing them. For Rancière, democratic politics—as opposed to the "police order" of the status quo—involves the "challenging of governments' claims to embody the sole principle of public life and in so doing to be able to circumscribe the understanding and extension of public life. If there is a 'limitlessness' specific to democracy," it lies "in the movement that ceaselessly displaces the limits of the public and the private, the political and the social."[19]

Rancière often fixates, with little elaboration, on exemplary figures or events, such as the civil disobedience of Rosa Parks, as metonymic signs for the political as such. In its privileging of exemplary figures and events, such an approach calls out for supplementation with a semiotic perspective that understands the formal devices whereby the figure of Parks, for example, is envisioned and circulated, as well as with an ethnographic perspective that understands the life of the particular, individual intervention as it travels in space and time. Both perspectives call for attention to the processes, practices, and techniques involved in the design, staging, circulation, and aftermath of activist campaigns and media events such as that undertaken by Parks. Her intervention, though often described as the spontaneous act of a courageous individual, was in fact meticulously designed as part of a long-term and multilevel arsenal of media tactics then being developed by civil rights organizers and legal advocates and was thus structured in advance by the cameras, coverage, and eventually, the legal proceedings that it would undoubtedly call forth. The refusal to change seats for a white person was one platform of political display involving the media of body and bus. This moment was rapidly added to by her arrest and booking photograph, which produced a different medial form with its own formal devices, its own capacities for circulation and remediation, its own affectual address to a spectator. The production of pamphlets, the boycott, Parks's legal trial, and the news-media coverage of the events all represent differing sorts of platforms weaving together the semiotic and the ethnographic, the political and the poetic, in a total campaign.

How did Parks's intervention register mediatically? What forms of transmission and retransmission did Parks's media event undergo as it reverberated in time and space at local, national, and global scales in variously contested discursive frames from newspapers, radios, televisions, and courtrooms to activist manuals and eventually to history books and museums? When we look at the iconic image of Rosa Parks on the bus, itself a retrospective staging undertaken with a sympathetic white journalist from the day after the Supreme Court ruled against the State of Alabama, or at Parks's famous mug shot—only one among several hundreds made of bus dissidents a year after her initial intervention—what we are not seeing are the historical processes, practices, and techniques that made that image speak politically.[20] The point here is not to encourage cynicism regarding the performative force of the event in the reconfiguration of the order of the sensible, but rather to remain vigilant in our attention to the enabling conditions and relational processes that make such an event possible without exhausting the singularity of what Alain Badiou would call "the hole it punches in the order of constituted knowledge."[21]

CIRCULATION AND PLATFORMS

The essays in this book focus primarily on activisms of the recent past. Central to our analysis is the argument that images do not move by themselves, but are trafficked along material networks and embedded in platforms. One way to understand the relationship between the image and its political contexts is to examine the modes of circulation that affect the way an image is allowed to exist in the world and comes to make claims. Benjamin Lee and Edward LiPuma adopted the term "culture of circulation" to move away from the idea of circulation as something that simply transmits meanings to examining it as a constitutive act in itself. "Circulation is a cultural process with its own forms of abstraction, evaluation, and constraint which are created by the interactions between specific types of circulating forms and the interpretive communities built around them."[22] In order to circulate, images must conform to aesthetic and formal modes that allow them to be recognized by the discursive norms of the world in which they travel and to become politically visible. Writing about human rights activism, for instance, Meg McLagan has argued similarly that rights claims are not simply "'something out there' waiting to be realized legally or philosophically," but rather come into being through a process of encoding or "formatting" into cultural forms such as testimony that are legible as political-ethical claims in the international arena.[23]

More recently, Thomas Keenan and Eyal Weizman have advanced this idea through the concept of what they term "forensic aesthetics," the medial form through which truth claims are made and political claims advanced in courts of law. They are particularly interested in what they term "forums" (and we term "platforms"): the performative context in which a circulating object stages its public presence, so to speak, so that its claims can be made. It is the point at which it becomes public. Keenan and Weizman argue that objects can make claims only via the forums in which they are manifest and that to do so, objects must be interpreted and translated by the experts most associated with the aesthetic form of the object that circulates:

> Forensics is not only about the science of investigation but rather about its presentation to the forum. Indeed there is an arduous labor of truth-construction embodied in the notion of forensics, one that is conducted with all sorts of scientific,

rhetorical, theatrical and visual mechanisms. It is in the gestures, techniques, and turns of demonstration, whether poetic, dramatic, or narrative, that forensic aesthetics can make things appear in the world.[24]

Platforms are not neutral spaces, but sites that produce the image politically. These platforms demand particular representational forms, are coded with their own epistemological norms, and employ their own modes of address. Many accounts of the relation between visual culture and political transformation have tended to isolate images or to focus on individual acts of "do-it-yourself" cultural repurposing of corporate icons. Political agency in this mode of analysis is often considered in terms of episodic and opportunistic acts of tactical sabotage on the part of disempowered citizen-consumers and cultural activists vis-à-vis monolithically conceived systems of domination. But this image-centered analysis obscures the embeddedness of cultural forms in broader campaigns that facilitate and build (though never contain) the architecture of circulation.

One example can be found in Ariella Azoulay's analysis of the political consequences of a photograph taken by an Israeli soldier of an indoor scene at a Palestinian house in Ramallah. The image shows four soldiers seated, eating, watching television. "This photograph, like many others taken by Israeli soldiers, found its way into private family albums and was circulated through various family and social networks."[25] Azoulay uses this photo as a basis of a broader critique of the sharp distinction between the aesthetic and the political. But the ground of her analysis is the specificity of a mode of circulation tied to snapshot souvenirs. The image is encoded into the platform of the family album, making it likely that any viewer would know one of the subjects depicted, who perhaps had the album passed on by another family member or friend. This mode of circulation constitutes an intimate public, making the image visible within a discrete interpretive regime. Once encoded in a particular medial form, the image becomes publicly available and capable of being diverted into other circulatory modes, of being made visible in differing forums. Azoulay points out that the indexical nature of the snapshot taken as a casual souvenir "became the document of a crime, of an event to be denounced, to be shared in public" by one of the soldiers in the image, who recognized its political implications.[26] To be resignified from souvenir to evidence, however, means to traffic along different communicative infrastructures, to be made visible on other platforms—a newspaper, a courtroom—with their own discursive norms, their own aesthetic forms, and their own modes of generating visibility and invisibility.

Material networks are important because they shape the nature of the cultural forms that travel along them, but also because, like platforms, they are political actors themselves. Politics does not lie within an image, as if the only political exchange at stake is lodged in the hermeneutical ability to decode a meaning that inheres in a text. Rather, the modes of circulation and of making public are forms of political action in and of themselves. From the elaboration of publicity campaigns that surround human rights media to the human microphone used in Occupy Wall Street, attention to images, their modes of circulation, and the platforms on which they are made public instantiate a different relation between the aesthetic and the political in which the two are seen as mutually active on the constitution of political subjects.

THE POETICS OF CAMPAIGNS

In citing the example of Rosa Parks above and the issues involved in reading the images that were generated by and around her intervention, we draw attention to the question of the historical legacies and inheritances that mark contemporary nongovernmental activism. The essays collected here are diverse in terms of region, topic, and field and include historical examples as well as contemporary activisms. It has been beyond the scope of the current volume to attempt an intensive historical survey of the image-complexes produced by the visual cultures of nongovernmental politics, but a recognition of the historical depth of the practices we identify retards the supposition that the centrality of visual-cultural practices to political action is an aftereffect of the emergence of modern mass-mediated societies. We hope that the current volume can encourage historically oriented scholars in many fields to consider this dimension of the activisms they study. Although recent activisms have become more intensively engaged with and dependent on images and image-oriented media in both qualitative and quantitative terms, the thought and action of nongovernmental activisms have been, from the beginning, marked by a wide variety of aesthetic repertoires, media networks, and visually oriented publicity techniques. To put it another way, the intensification of mediatic concerns on the part of contemporary activisms retroactively throws into relief similar concerns in the past in a kind of historical parallax.

Feher notes in *Nongovernmental Politics* that the origins of a politics based on the determination "not to be governed *thusly*" can be traced as far back as abolitionism, when activists appealed to the universality of the rights of man to critique and combat the exclusive national sovereignty claimed by governments sanctioning the practice of slavery, whether directly or indirectly. Indeed, the transatlantic abolitionist movement largely constituted itself through technologically reproduced and illustrated reports, books, broadsheets, posters, banners, and eventually photographs designed to call forth an antislavery public with the will to pressure the governments in question into ending the practice. An exemplary image for the purposes of the present volume is the so-called "Brookes image," a shipbuilder's diagram demonstrating the optimal design of a ship for the purpose of "tight-packing" a vessel with slaves. As recounted by Marcus Rediker, this diagram, originally designed for functional and promotional purposes within the slaving industry, was appropriated, reinscribed, and recirculated by abolitionists as evidence of the profit-driven brutality of slavers. Through a close reading of the image and its social life across time and space, Rediker shows how the image became an important node of conflict and advocacy in the eventual abolition of slavery in Britain in 1807 and subsequently in the United States.[27]

Throughout the abolitionist era, an image such as the Brookes diagram would have moved alongside a range of other visual and textual forms, ranging from proto-viral images such as William Blake's drawing *A Negro Hung by the Ribs to a Gallows* and the unattributed seal *Am I Not a Man and a Brother?* to illustrated testimonial literatures by former slaves such as Olaudah Equiano and Frederick Douglass. The abolitionist movement was also the first to mobilize photography deliberately for activist purposes, exemplified by the image of "Private Gordon," an escaped slave who joined the Union Army. Gordon displayed the scars of the multiple whippings he endured in captivity for the photographic firm McPherson and Oliver in 1863. The photograph was immediately circulated as both an annotated *carte-de-visite* and as a lithographic engraving in popular periodicals such as *Harpers Weekly* and the *New York Independent*, which opined: "This card photograph should be multiplied by the 100,000 and scattered over the states. It tells the story in a way that even Mrs. Harriet Beecher Stowe cannot approach, because it tells the story to the eye."[28]

"It tells the story to the eye." The journalist here foregrounds the medial effect of the photograph and its mode of address as it is encoded in the platform of a *carte-de-visite*. It is because the form is iconic that it can be remediated as a lithograph and thus circulated to a broader public in an era when the mass reproduction of photographs in magazines was expensive. The photograph, as a reproduction made by a machine, carries with it an evidentiary truth value that the lithograph, as a drawing of the photograph, yet still made by a human, does not (except as a reflection of the originary photograph). Both make an affectual address to audiences, attempting to mobilize sentiments of anger, shame, and outrage by displaying the scarred body of a slave.

To express such faith in the optical veracity of the photographic image does not derive solely from the medium, of course, but from an epistemology of truth that lies outside of the medium and that remains constant in much activist visual media today. The "eye" here is understood not simply as an optical faculty, but as a locus of reception itself endowed with an interpretative power and implicitly ethical structure of witnessing. Yet the attribution by the text to the image of a story-telling capacity belies the actual muteness of the visual image in question. In other words, the text both calls for and performs the "multiplication" of the image and the becoming story of the violated body that appears before the audience, setting up what Azoulay would call an unforeseeable "civil contract" between the photographer, the photographed subject, the unforeseeable mediatic contexts of the image, and the reception process of those who ultimately encounter the image in its various mediations.[29]

The indissoluble relationship of the photograph—as medial form, aesthetic device, and epistemology—to the broader campaign that constitutes and is constituted by the image is echoed in Thomas Keenan's groundbreaking critique of the paradigm of "mobilizing shame" underlying much human rights activism in the 1980s and 1990s.[30] This paradigm posited an automatic "if/then" relation between the visual exposure of governmental abuses or negligence and an ameliorative result on the part of the offending governing agency due to the "humiliation" it would presumably experience were its dirty deeds brought into the light of public scrutiny. Informed by the relative indifference on the part of Western publics and governments during the 1990s to the genocides in Bosnia and Rwanda, despite intensive visual and textual documentation by both media organizations and nongovernmental activists, Keenan's analysis suggests the inadequacy of the strategic tropes of exposure and revelation invoked by many activists. Rather than bringing this or that abuse into self-evident presentation, Keenan suggests the "relevance of aesthetic categories" to how human rights activists might redesign their discursive and mediatic techniques in attempting to call into being publics with the passion and will to address the crises in question.

Another paradigmatic instance combining these techniques can be found in the work of the AIDS Coalition to Unleash Power (ACT UP).[31] Established in 1987 to publicize and challenge the forms of biopolitical neglect and cultural stigmatization to which people with AIDS (PWAs) were subjected by urban, state, and federal governments, ACT UP developed a remarkable visual-cultural repertoire capable of operating in a number of registers.[32] The movement drew upon and hybridized the legacies of previous U.S. social movements, especially the mediagenic techniques of nonviolent civil disobedience pioneered by the civil rights, antiwar, and environmental activists such as Greenpeace, as exemplified by the tactic of the "die-in," in which demonstrators would use their bodies to block pedestrian and vehicular traffic in specifically targeted sites in anticipation of the media coverage such interruptive events would garner. Laid out prone like so many accumulating corpses, demonstrators put forth their own bodies as both memorials to those who had already died due to governmental neglect and to those living PWAs perishing in the present—a group that includes the majority of the demonstrators themselves. While often discussed in terms of "direct action"—and celebrated as such by later generations of activists availing themselves of civil disobedience—such activities were anything but direct, because such bodily-based activities were irreducibly mediated at every level.

First, as noted, the very bodily techniques in question were themselves inherited from the protest forms of earlier activist traditions—traditions that were themselves oriented toward the creation of media events and photo opportunities for both mainline news organizations and activist documentarians. Furthermore, the bodies in question were always supplemented by a variety of signage combining a rich array of iconic and textual signification through which critiques of and demands upon governing agencies were made. In many cases, the design of such "demo-graphics," as Douglas Crimp famously described them, were informed by earlier histories of visual politics. Most famous in this regard is the inverted pink triangle accompanied by the injunction "Silence=Death."[33]

AIDS activists, like civil rights activists and abolitionists before them, staged their claims via strikingly different platforms, traversing mainstream and alternative media; celebrity, fashion, and advertising culture; legal and policy arenas; direct action, and the artistic and academic worlds. Their work poses a series of questions that continue to inform the current volume, including those relating to affect, such as how cultural forms create structures of feeling that are not yet articulated by politics, how desire and belief shape circulation and what gets taken up, and the vexed criteria of how to gauge the scale and quality of the transformation that a campaign might foment.

Although movements have long sited forms of representation in broader architectures of activism, this is only now being analyzed in its full complexity. One ambivalent consequence, for instance, of the emergence of new forms of political art and media has been an inverse concern with "impact," a term that has become dominant as a result of the entry of a new set of actors into the nongovernmental arena, namely, newly rich social entrepreneurs who are interested in deploying their vast wealth to help solve society's most pressing problems. As believers in investment, rather than in charity, these individuals have brought with them a commitment to the "double bottom line"—the potential of their philanthropy to produce financial as well as social returns—along with a concern for accountability and measurable results.

Nowhere has the interest in tangible metrics of political efficacy by funders been more prominent than in the independent documentary film arena, which, over the past decade, has attained a level of mainstream attention and influence arguably unmatched since the era of the Great Depression. The success of films such as Michael Moore's *Fahrenheit 9/11* and *Sicko*, Morgan Spurlock's *Super Size Me*, and especially Davis Guggenheim's *An Inconvenient Truth* inaugurated a new structure of documentary filmmaking that has trickled down from commercial successes such as these to smaller independent films.[34] *An Inconvenient Truth*, funded by social entrepreneur Jeffrey Skoll's film-production company Participant Media, was at once a film and a dispersed cultural process in which the material conditions of its public appearance and circulation took on paramount importance, from the presentation of the project to funding institutions, to the advertising campaign and screenings at festivals, theaters, and television, to the long-term aftermath of the film on DVD and its widespread use by educators, activists, and legislators in spatial contexts including living rooms, classrooms, courtrooms, and Congressional hearing rooms.

An Inconvenient Truth's wildly successful outreach campaign became a model for other social entrepreneurs interested in producing social change through film. "Impact" quickly shifted from being an aftereffect of a film's release to being a condition for funding itself, with filmmakers having to imagine their work's circulation and its potential impact before it even exists or is created. Not only has this rendered the boundary between the inside and the outside of the work increasingly porous, it has meant that films that do not conform to the mode of visibility demanded by this logic of impact find it harder to receive funding. It also pushes the demarcation of what counts as a "political" film away from projects that are more aesthetically challenging and not as easily incorporated into broad outreach campaigns.

Our aim in this volume is to further extend the analytical protocols of visual culture by drawing on the vocabularies of art history, anthropology, film studies, and political theory to argue for the recognition and interpretation of the image complex via a double sense of vision, one that treats vision as a metonym for perception, cognition, and aspiration in general and that takes account of the specific configurations of visuality enabled—but never completely determined by—the various image-based technologies through and to which nongovernmental actors address themselves. The concept of the image complex allows us to take realms often treated separately—aesthetics, mediation, political movements—and see them as mutually constitutive. For instance, we are interested in the continuing evolution of digital and social media in which cultural forms such as film, photography, and art have found themselves reinventing structures of display and circulation to take into account wider and proliferating platforms. It is a technophilic commonplace to locate innovation within the realm of technologies and to interrogate the emergence of new cultural forms in relationship to them. But we are also interested in the evolution of political movements, from the Iranian Green Revolution, to the Arab Spring, to Occupy Wall Street, that are themselves just as generative of new modes of communication, new aesthetic acts, that demand novel platforms and technologies to make their movements public. The nongovernmental realm more broadly has in turn seen the emergence of new legal forums such as truth and reconciliation commissions and the International Criminal Court. These demand forms of evidence—testimony, forensics, visual and written documents of abuses—and they themselves constitute performative platforms in which those modes of evidence are remediated, framed, and entered into new circulations. The creation of these new platforms means that politically oriented cultural producers—and by this we mean artists, filmmakers, and photographers, but also funders, activists, and journalists—have come to shape their works with these new platforms in mind.

Cumulatively, there is a continual feedback loop whereby political actions, cultural forms, and technologies of mediation interact with each other, each with their own dynamics of innovation, but in mutual interdependence. In her contribution, Judith Butler argues that media do not merely report the street scenes, but are part of the scene and action. Media participate in the delimitation and transposability of the scene, constituting it in a time and place that includes and exceeds their local instantiation. Media require bodies on the street to have an event, even as those bodies on the street require media to exist in a global arena. Similarly, Eyal Weizman argues that the increased importance of forensics in legal forums has transformed the communicative capacity and aesthetic life of the objects that circulate within those forums as evidence. But the presence of objects—from DNA samples to forensic analyses of building ruins—also brings about the demand for new forums to be able to amplify, interpret, and publicly perform their significance. All cultural forms bring publics into being, just as publics demand cultural forms in order to exist as publics. In order to circulate, those objects must conform to the infrastructures of the media technologies that distribute them, be transposed into the discursive norms of the platforms in which they appear, yet retain, as Mikhail Bakhtin famously argued about heteroglossic speech, their own stubborn aesthetic autonomy, never fully submitting to transposition.

This volume attempts to make sensible this competitive interaction by bringing together artists and activists, filmmakers and academics, to write short case studies, interviews, and essays. It is why we moved beyond the usual disciplinary distinctions and their particular specialties. This is not because disciplines do not offer specialization—indeed, it is important to draw on specific technical inquiries, theoretical histories, and lineages of argument that each discipline brings to bear. Rather it is because we wish to trace a broader image-complex whereby politics is brought to visibility through the mediation of specific cultural forms that mix together the legal and visual, the hermeneutic and the technical, politics and aesthetics. In many respects, then, the book is more than the sum of its parts, arguing that while many of its contributors address various aspects of this image-complex, in toto they address the thickly constituted and dynamic spaces of contemporary aesthetics and politics.

NOTES

The authors would like to thank Brian Larkin and Liza Johnson for their helpful comments on earlier drafts of this text.

1. George Marcus, *Connected: Engagements with Media* (Chicago: University of Chicago Press, 1996), p. 6.
2. Here the ambition of the current volume overlaps with certain of the terms put forth in Bruno Latour and Peter Weibel (eds.), *Making Things Public: Atmospheres of Democracy*, trans. Robert Bryce (Cambridge, MA: The MIT Press, 2005), though the current volume adheres to a much stricter focus on political activism and its associated visual and mediatic forms.
3. Michel Feher, "The Governed in Politics," in Michel Feher (ed.), with Gaëlle Krikorian and Yates McKee, *Nongovernmental Politics* (New York: Zone Books, 2007), p. 14.
4. Erica Bornstein and Peter Redfield (eds.), *Forces of Compassion: Humanitarianism between Ethics and Politics* (Santa Fe: SAR Advanced Seminar Series, 2011); Didier Fassin and Mariella Pandolfi (eds.), *Contemporary States of Emergency: The Politics of Military and Humanitarian Intervention* (New York: Zone Books, 2010); Ilana Feldman and Miriam Ticktin, *In the Name of Humanity: The Government of Threat and Care* (eds.), (Durham: Duke University Press, 2010).
5. Didier Fassin, *Humanitarian Reason: A Moral History of the Present* (Berkeley: University of California Press, 2011), p. 5.
6. Laurent Berlant, *Cruel Optimism* (Durham: Duke University Press, 2011).
7. Feher, "The Governed in Politics," in Feher (ed.), *Nongovernmental Politics*, p. 12.
8. Feher derives this formulation from Foucault's discussion of the "arts of government" and Kant's definition of enlightenment as the release of the subject from heteronymous power into full self-determination. See Michel Foucault, "What Is Critique?" (1979), in Michel Foucault, *The Politics of Truth*, ed. Sylvère Lotringer, trans. Lysa Hochroth and Catherine Porter (Los Angeles: Semiotext(e), 2007).
9. For general introductions to the concept of visual culture, see Nicholas Mirzoeff, *An Introduction to Visual Culture*, 2nd ed. (London: Routledge, 2009) and Marita Sturken and Lisa Cartwright, *Practices of Looking: An Introduction to Visual Culture*, 2nd ed. (New York: Oxford University Press, 2009), p. 3.
10. See the subchapter "History of Media Critiques," in Cartwright and Sturken, *Practices of Looking*, pp. 236–42.
11. Samuel Weber, "Introduction: Where in the World Are We?" in *Mass Mediauras: Form, Technics, Media* (Stanford: Stanford University Press, 1996), p. 3. For a further consideration of this dual sense of media as both a shifting assemblage of technological devices systems and practices, on the one hand, and as a "quasi-transcendental" condition of human life in general, see Mark B. N. Hansen, "New Media," in W. J. T Mitchell and Mark B. N. Hansen (eds.), *Critical Terms for Media Studies* (Chicago: University of Chicago Press, 2010).
12. Weber, "Introduction: Where in the World Are We?" in *Mass Mediauras*, p. 3.
13. Walter Benjamin, "The Work of Art in the Age of Its Technological Reproducibility," third edition, 1936, trans. Harry Zohn and Edmund Jephcott, in Howard Eiland and Michael Jennings (eds.), *Selected Writings, Volume 4, 1938–1940* (Cambridge, MA: Harvard University Press, 2003), pp. 262 and 265.
14. *Ibid.*, p. 264.
15. *Ibid.*, p. 258.

16. *Ibid.*, p. 270.
17. *Ibid.*
18. Jacques Rancière, *The Politics of Aesthetics: The Distribution of the Sensible*, trans. Gabriel Rockhill (New York: Continuum, 2004), p. xi.
19. Jacques Rancière, *Hatred of Democracy*, trans. Steve Corcoran (London: Verso, 2007), p. 61.
20. For an important recent study that resonates deeply with the concerns of the current volume, but which curiously neglects Rosa Parks, see Maurice Berger, *For All The World to See: Visual Culture and the Struggle for Civil Rights* (New Haven: Yale University Press, 2010). Berger's excellent study, which accompanied an exhibition of visual-cultural artifacts at the International Center for Photography, dwells somewhat inordinately on the racist visual cultures of popular entertainment against which civil rights activists defined their own visual imagery, as well as the post–civil rights imaginary of black power. The civil rights movement in the strict sense actually receives only relative treatment. For a nuanced analysis of the pedagogical framing of Rosa Parks and the images generated around her intervention, see Herbert Kohl, *She Would Not Be Moved: How We Tell the Story of Rosa Parks and the Montgomery Bus Boycott* (New York: New Press, 2007).
21. See Rosalyn Deutsche, "Not Forgetting: Mary Kelly's *Love Songs*," *Grey Room* 24 (Summer 2006), pp. 26–27, for a discussion of Badiou's understanding of the event as what "presents hitherto unknown possibilities that put an end to consensus or dominant opinion in the order it disrupts; its course is uncertain, and it compels the subject to decide a new way of being.... After Schoenberg, for instance, I do not go back to writing Romantic music" (p. 29).
22. Benjamin Lee and Edward LiPuma, "Cultures of Circulation: The Imaginations of Modernity," *Public Culture* 14.1 (2002), p. 192. See also Dilip Gaonkar and Elizabeth A. Povinelli, "Technologies of Public Forms: Circulation, Transfiguration, Recognition," *Public Culture* 15.3 (2003), pp. 385–97; Brian Larkin, "Making Equivalence Happen: Commensuration and the Grounds of Circulation," in Patricia Spyer and Mary Steedly (eds.), *Images That Move* (Santa Fe: SAR Press, forthcoming); Michael Warner, *Publics and Counterpublics* (New York: Zone Books, 2005).
23. Meg McLagan, "Human Rights, Testimony, and Transnational Publicity," in Feher (ed.), *Nongovernmental Politics*, p. 306. See also Meg McLagan, "Circuits of Suffering," *Political and Legal Anthropology Review* 28.2 (2005), pp. 223–39.
24. Thomas Keenan and Eyal Weizman, *Mengele's Skull: The Advent of a Forensic Aesthetics* (Berlin: Sternberg Press, 2012).
25. Ariella Azoulay, "Getting Rid of the Distinction between the Aesthetic and the Political," *Theory, Culture, and Society* 27.7 (2010), p. 240.
26. *Ibid.*, p. 242
27. Marcus Rediker, *The Slave Ship: A Human History* (New York: Viking, 2007).
28. "The Scourged Back," *New York Independent*, May 28, 1863.
29. See Ariella Azoulay, "Regime-Made Disaster: On the Possibility of Nongovernmental Viewing" in this volume. See also Azoulay, *The Civil Contract of Photography* (New York: Zone Books, 2008).
30. Thomas Keenan, "Mobilizing Shame," *South Atlantic Quarterly* 103.2/3 (Spring–Summer 2004), pp. 435–49.
31. See Ann Cvetkovich, "*Sex in an Epidemic* as AIDS Archive Activism: An Interview with Jean Carlomusto," in this volume.

32. See Douglas Crimp (ed.), *AIDS: Cultural Analysis/Cultural Activism* (Cambridge, MA: The MIT Press, 1989), and Douglas Crimp and Adam Rolston, *AIDS Demo-Graphics* (Seattle: Bay Press, 1990).
33. The pink triangle was originally the graphic marker physically affixed to the prison uniform of homosexuals in the Nazi concentration camps.
34. See Meg McLagan, "Imagining Impact: Documentary Film and the Production of Political Effects," in this volume, along with Barbara Abrash and Meg McLagan, "*Granito*: An Interview with Pamela Yates" and Barbara Abrash and Meg McLagan, "*State of Fear* and Transitional Justice in Peru: A Case Study," also in this volume.

PART ONE

THE PERSISTENCE OF PHOTOGRAPHY

FIGURE 1 The King Abdullah Bridge (unknown photographer, 1967).

Regime-Made Disaster: On the Possibility of Nongovernmental Viewing

Ariella Azoulay

"Heartbreaking convoys of refugees have started their journey across the Jordan River. They seem helpless and their eyes are crying for assistance. The soldiers immediately have given them water and helped them carry their children and cross the river on the half-drawn Abdullah Bridge," wrote Brigadier General Uzi Narkiss, military commander of the Southern Region, who in 1967 was responsible for the destruction of the bridges over the Jordan, for the forced displacement of the Palestinian refugee population from Jericho, for the destruction of three Palestinian villages in the Latrun enclave, and for the displacement of thousands of Palestinians in their own land.

This quote contains the intricate conditions in which nongovernmental politics emerges in disaster situations that occur under a democratic regime (fig. 1). By discussing the Israeli/Palestinian context, I'll analyze this particular type of disaster, which I call a "regime-made disaster," a disaster that takes place as a structural part of democratic regimes.

Regime-made disasters not only are produced by democratic regimes, but in some cases constitute them. Regime-made disaster can occur without being acknowledged and recognized as disasters. One reason for this is that many of the acts that constitute regime-made disasters lack the common characteristics of violence: spontaneous eruption, arbitrariness, and randomness. Instead, they are a part of an organized, well-ordered, and well-grounded system of applied force that feeds on the institutions of the democratic regime and that is safely anchored in them.

The first half of the twentieth century saw several regime-made disasters par excellence that were not grounded in democracies,[1] but the second half of the twentieth century has produced disasters that take place within and as a part of the structure of democratic governance itself.[2] In *The Origins of Totalitarianism*, Hannah Arendt analyzed the various elements that constitute a totalitarian regime. In the disaster landscape of the second half of the twentieth century, however, such elements were commonplace around the world, and not just in totalitarian regimes. Today, rather than judging that "this is not a totalitarian regime," we need to be alert to the ways in which all regimes, including democratic regimes, produce such disasters.

To recognize a regime-made disaster, a necessary, albeit not a sufficient condition, is to focus on the entire governed population and not only, as is often done, on the population that suffers immediately from the disaster. A regime-made disaster can be recognized by attention to what I propose calling a "differential body politic." By a "body politic" one usually refers to a homogeneous group of citizens, but by a "differential body politic," I refer to the entire governed population under one regime, a nonhomogeneous population whose forms of being governed by that regime—as citizens, as noncitizens, or as flawed citizens—are different. Regime-made disasters usually target those elements of a population that do not partake in governance at the time of the disaster or that are distanced from access to the governing power by the disaster itself.[3] A differential body politic consists of uncounted populations or, to use the Arendtian term, "superfluous" populations.

A very long tradition of viewing photographs from regime-made disasters leads our gaze only to its victims. Instead, with the notions of regime-made disaster and a differential body politic, I propose to change the field of vision and reconstruct in each and every photograph beside the presence of the victims in the frame the traces of the citizens or other populations involved in the production of the regime-made disaster, even if outside the frame.

A regime-made disaster can be identified by its visibility, its temporality, the form in which it occurs, the tools used to bring it about, and its goal—that is, preserving the existing form and differentiation of the differential body politic. A regime-made disaster also can be identified by the way in which it is represented, the purpose for which it is carried out, and the ways in which responses to the regime-made disaster deflect attention away from the disaster's actual causes and ends.

A regime-made disaster does not take place in the dark, but is fully visible, although normal citizens are trained not to regard it as disaster. It is not a one-time event, but develops according to various steps and phases over time. Most importantly, the occurrence of a regime-made disaster is not an incidental event, and its traces enable the reconstruction of the planning principles and/or management models by which it was brought about, the tools and modes of action that its perpetrators employ, its limits and margins, the levels of intensity with which it is managed, and the identity of the target population, a population that is considered external to what is usually thought of as "the body politic." A regime-made disaster is represented as a nondisaster, or it is represented as a disaster only from the point of view of its victims or as a necessary or justified effect of an external purpose. But beyond any contingent purpose, from the persistence of a disaster managed by the governing power we can learn that one of its typical features is reproducing the differential relations between governed groups in a way that enables the reproduction of the regime based on such differential relations. Finally, the means used by the regime to deal with the disaster or to cope with its aftermath do not offer a sweeping solution to end the disaster, but instead focus on side issues and/or are aimed at individual cases.

Regime-made disasters are usually not conceptualized within democratic regimes as being part of them. The citizens within the differential body politic draw the contours of the regime so as to determine what is part of the regime and what is external to it, thus differentiating between those who are vulnerable to regime-made disaster and those who are not. Subsequently, disaster itself is differentiated into acknowledged disasters that affect one part of the differential body politic and nondisasters, or "disasters from their point of view," that affect another part. These two differentiations enable such regimes to erase the permanent disaster they produce from their self-representations. Regime-made disasters are considered to be external to the regimes that produce them, although they are actually inherent in them and organize their entire civil space.

The words of Narkiss with which I opened here reveal three related, characteristic strategies that make regime-made disasters possible within democratic regimes. The perpetrators observe the disaster from the outside, as if it were not their own doing, unable to recognize themselves as perpetrators. The disaster-struck population is considered outside the body politic and an object of humanitarian intervention. And finally, the perpetrators of the disaster and their official representatives, senior and junior alike, use a language and gestures that enable them to demonstrate a universal moral intention toward the population that they have harmed.

In a regime-made disaster that occurs as part of a democratic regime, such moral intentions are said to be manifested both in actions that the ruling power carries out directly and in the activity of many nongovernmental organizations that the regime encourages through outsourcing. This split in the way the regime-made disaster is shaped by its perpetrators and perceived by the citizens who support such a regime enables these spectators to see themselves a priori—and to continue seeing themselves a posteriori—as citizens of a democratic regime that does not practice spontaneous, capricious, random, and arbitrary violence.

The degree to which claims to moral intention are embedded in regime-made disaster was clearly evident in a conversation I had in 2002 with two officers at the Bureau of the Government Coordinator in the Occupied Territories. The head of the Economics Department answered my questions about humanitarian organizations thus:

> No, they [the humanitarian organizations] are not subsidizing the Occupation. They don't see it like that. They're helping the Palestinian population. In addition to offensive missions and to eliminating or capturing of a specifically wanted terrorist, there is also the humanitarian element incorporated within the operational orders given to the units in the field. Now, we don't instruct them, but we fully cooperate with them. We don't tell them: "Get to a specific point." We don't say: "Go to a different spot. How much food is needed?" They do it all on their own.

This attitude was confirmed by the head of the Foreign Relations Department at the same bureau:

> At seven o'clock in the morning we received calls. An UNRWA representative in the district, a Red Cross representative in the district, an MSF representative in the district, an MDM representative in the district, representatives from all organizations that operate in the district told the representatives of these organisations: "Good morning in Jenin. The IDF entered the town to fight against terror. From now until the end of the operation our humanitarian efforts are such and such, come to our offices."

Concern for the Palestinian population thus expressed is actually a concern for the maintenance of the disaster, a constant effort to contain it below a certain threshold, thus preventing it from erupting in ways that are not controlled and managed and preventing the regime-made disaster from becoming a disaster that can no longer be denied as such.

A search in the Government Press Office's archives for photographs since the onset of the Occupation in 1967 yields a great number of photos in which visual expression can be found for the Narkiss quote above. What is involved here is not a single, insignificant photograph I ran into incidentally, but rather extensive, systematic documentation (figs. 2 and 3). Those photos revolve around the humanitarian gesture par excellence of food distribution or offering water to the disaster-struck population. At times, such a gesture is performed by government representatives, while at other times, representatives of foreign or local NGOs are at the fore.

In both instances, the regime, far from being reluctant to perform this gesture, favors, encourages, and endorses it. The universal moral intention expressed in this gesture is a necessary condition for the preservation of the regime under which the regime-made disaster takes place. Without this condition, the disaster would appear as a disaster, and the regime that perpetrated it might not win the support of its citizens as a worthy regime. Thus, for decades, Israeli Jews have

FIGURE 2 Qalqiliya, 2001 (photo: Nir Kafri).

FIGURE 3 The official caption reads: "Israeli soldier offers water to a Palestinian suspected of terrorism, Defensive Shield Operation," (unknown photographer, Government Press Office, 2002).

been able persistently to avoid any acknowledgment of an existing Palestinian disaster—the Nakba—and altogether ignore their regime's responsibility for the existence of millions of Palestinian refugees expelled from their country for the sake of creating a Jewish body politic. They also perceive the 1967 occupation as a temporary disturbance taking place in territories outside the borders of their state, a project separate from their regime, and they can continue not to regard "their" regime as a dark regime.[4]

For the sake of simplicity, I use the current Palestinian appellation for the catastrophe of 1948, the Nakba, for Palestinians are the ones bearing the heaviest brunt as a result. Characterizing the disaster as Palestinian, however, is part of a way in which the disaster is structured as external to the regime, affecting only the population intended to be its victim. Viewing disaster from the point of view of all the governed, however—citizens and noncitizens alike—it becomes clear that regime-made disasters necessarily strike all the governed, even if they do not all pay a price measurable in life and property.

The differentiations that democratic regimes produce in populations and between different kinds of disasters are prerequisites for the preservation of the regime's democratic nature in the eyes both of its citizens and the international community that regards democracy as its preferred form of governance worldwide. These differentiations, always invaded by other forms of relationships, constantly require supremacy over the differential body politic and usually attain it through the sovereign power that is exerted in order to maintain these differentiations and to make sure that disaster itself will not erupt and appear as it is—a structural part of these same sovereign democratic regimes.

For decades, these differentiations have affected the models for the production and dissemination of photographs and have shaped the discourses that have developed around them. The discourse of photography revolves around the sovereign photographer, who also is the acknowledged owner of the goods—the photograph—produced in the midst of the act carried out in public with the participation of others in a common space.

That process, too, has assumed a series of differentiations in a sovereign act of inclusion and exclusion—between the photographer and the photographed; between the photographer and the spectator; between the viewer and the viewed; and between what was, in an instant (the photographed event) and what remains of it, allegedly unchangeable (the photograph). What is included is what the photographer (or those who set the limits of his or her field of vision) wished to situate within the frame. Usually it is the disaster event, the extent of which is actually established by the regime that perpetrated it, even if its local limits can still be negotiated on a regular basis. What is included is thus the disaster perceived as occurring in a designated area and experienced as such by a specific population that the regime does not recognize—at least not fully—as equal to all governed.

Photographers, and with their mediation, distant spectators, as well, consequently have become, even if virtually, a privileged population apart: observing "the disaster" of others—others who are governed with them as part of the same differential body politic, yet who are not one of them—the gaze of the photographers and spectators having been shaped by similar differentiations as those shaping the photograph. They are the ones observing a disaster that befalls others. The disaster takes place elsewhere. Others are conceived as a natural object of disaster and of photographs that portray it, and the event they are observing has already occurred and become a fait accompli, an instant in the past, captured on film or in digital media. Because those spectators are usually citizens of similar democratic regimes who wish to preserve them, these citizens are likely to view the disaster population just as the citizens of the particular disaster-perpetrating regime do. The photograph is perceived as a product of whoever holds the camera. What is inscribed in it is regarded as an expression of his or her worldview, position, and perspective on an external reality.

The discourse that has developed from gazing at photographs from disaster zones has been articulated mainly by those usually belonging to the population viewing the disaster. It concentrates mostly on photographs as closed units of information. Although they differ on many other levels, both the hegemonic discourse of the media and politics and the discourse of photography, influenced by the discourse of art, focus on photographs "by" photographers. Both discourses tend to attribute to the photographer the way in which what is photographed is seen in the photograph. They establish whether the photographer proposed—or failed to propose—a proper or more just way of viewing "the disaster," presented it to the world, and caused the larger international community to take interest in it. The hegemonic discourse of the media and of politics tries in various ways to control which photographs will be taken in disaster zones—if any are allowed to be taken at all—and which are allowed to be seen, delegitimizing photographs coming from sources that escape its control.[5] A recent example of the collaboration between the hegemonic media and the powers that be in replacing various possible points of view with a single, authorized point of view involves what happened on the Gaza Freedom Flotilla carrying humanitarian aid and construction materials with the intention of breaking the Israeli-Egyptian blockade of the Gaza Strip. The Israeli Defense Forces actually erased the magnetic cards of the cellular phones and digital cameras of the activists on board, while the media continued to publish and broadcast images coming from the army, including images that were reframed and enhanced to support the point of view that the army and government tried to establish.

Critical discourse, for the most part, has not overcome these types of differentiation and has continued to sort and characterize photographs according to the position attributed to their maker. It usually evaluates photographs of disaster areas as being "critical," "subversive," "political," "collaborative," or "embedded."[6] The information inscribed in the photograph is valued as being a precise or false representation, as biased one way or another, depending on the photographer's ethnic or national and professional identity or explicit position.

Claims as to the success of photographers in capturing with their lenses the disaster befalling others and claims as to the regime's success in repressing the horror it perpetrates for the sake of documenting its humanitarian gestures are examples of two common claims made about photographs of disaster areas. The two claims take what is seen in the photograph to be an expression of the side that has the means to produce the photograph. Such claims based solely on the photographer's identity and position dismiss the civil potential of the photograph's ontological nature.

Here is a photograph, for instance, of the expulsion of the women inhabitants of Al-Tantura from Fureidis, where they had been staying as internally displaced

FIGURE 4 The official caption written by the photographer on the original contacts reads: "Arab women from Tantura going to Jordan" (photo: Beno Rothenberg. Israel State Archive, 18.6.1948).

persons (IDPs) for several months until the present expulsion—the one we view in the photograph—determined their fate as refugees outside their country. A long bus convoy transported them about thirty kilometers away from Fureidis to Tul Karm. Even those who would eventually deny that mass expulsions from Palestine were indeed carried out between 1947 and 1949 did not—at the time—find it necessary to conceal what we can now recognize in the photograph as an expulsion (fig. 4). The photograph reveals no signs of violence, and no one is using force to load the women onto the buses. It is easy and even tempting to disqualify this photograph as evidence that the ruling power uses such photographs to present itself in a positive light, brandishing its humanitarian gestures for the photographers' sake. In the middle of the frame, a Palestinian woman holds out a small tin to the soldier on her right, and while looking into the camera, he provides her with water for the long ordeal ahead. Conversely, it is easy and even tempting to criticize the photographer as "embedded," to say that he echoes the ruling power's words, and to ignore all the information that is held in the frame, whether or not the photographer is the one who chose to include it. Such disqualifications of the photograph are possible only when it is perceived as a product of the photographer or other agents involved in its production or dissemination and on the assumption that the photograph is a closed unit of information completed at the time the photograph was taken—that what is shown in the photograph is a subject such as "water distribution" or "refugees" chosen by the photographer and which we are viewing after this event has been concluded.

Ontologically, however, a photograph is never a finished product of whomever has been established as its owner and wishes to impose sovereign control over it. Whatever is inscribed in the photograph always exceeds what its owner wished to put in it. In other words, the photograph is not a document belonging to a photographer, to a ruling power, or to any governmental or nongovernmental body. Its identification as any of these things undermines its civil potential. Instead, it is open at all times to additional participants who will not only interpret what is seen in it as a given, but will also reshape the seen that is to be read.

The photograph, then, is a very special kind of document. Even when it bears its creator's unique "handwriting," it is always drawn out of the relationship within which and from which it is produced. Furthermore, it is equally so, whether we talk about the relationship within which it was produced—between photographers, the photographed, and others who took direct or indirect part in its design—or about the relationship in which it is viewed at present, in which the viewers, too, take part in its constitution as a document.

The photograph is a shared political document, but not one agreed upon by the various sides involved in its production and seeking to influence—sometimes in opposite ways—what is shown in it. While a ruling power can use photography among other means of shaping its public image, what is inscribed in a photograph is never merely what the ruling power wishes to inscribe in it or the way in which that power aspires to represent the regime in which it is elected to rule.[7] On the contrary, the photograph is a preferred place in which to read the image of the regime not as it is represented on the paper that defines its institutions and their interrelations, but in the forms of relations layered between governmental power and the governed, including not only those who took part in the act of photography, but also those who take part in the act of viewing.

Understanding a photograph from a disaster area as a document bearing the seal of the regime, one comprehends the limited nature of common categories such as "compassion," "pity," "empathy," "rage," "concern," "empowerment," and "victimization," which in fact describe only a single axis of relations between the photographer and the photographed while erasing all other relationships that were inscribed in the photograph.

Let us return to the photograph of the expulsion of the Palestinian women from Palestine. Obviously, the government has obliterated all traces of the eruptive violence that was needed in order to expel these women from their homes and homeland—women who had been separated from the male population of

Al-Tantura, who had witnessed the massacring of many of them, and who had then spent several months away from their homes. This violence was replaced, as I said, by a human scene that, in the photograph, looks staged especially for the camera—what would later be called "photo opportunity." One might say that this photograph does not instruct us about the horror of expulsion. But is that really so? Viewing the photograph as a document enables us to learn from this frame, for example, not merely about the nature of this specific expulsion, but rather about the actual existence of expulsion as a premeditated act by the regime at the time. In this photograph, one can clearly read that the uprooting of Palestinians from their homes was by no means an improvised or spontaneous escape on their part, but rather the result of a precise military action perfectly administered, from the provision of trucks to the supply of water for the journey.

The historians' debate about the expulsion from Palestine in the late 1940s is motivated by the need to locate the ultimate archived textual document—an explicit "order"—that would determine whether expulsion was planned, whether it was a part of a comprehensive master plan, or simply took place here and there spontaneously and capriciously, with no official orders from the higher echelons. Such a document, if it exists, is still buried in an archive, awaiting governmental ruling whether—and when—to make it accessible.[8]

Historians are usually indifferent to photographs and to the unique type of information they contain, due to their ontological nature as documents that do not express the position of their "author," but rather contain an excess of heterogeneous information. With a photograph such as this, for example, one can clearly reconstruct several modes of action used by the democratic Jewish regime constituted in the area. Such photographs are kept in state archives and available to the public, since—like historians—government officials regard them with a certain disrespect. They see them as the mere presentation of what officials wished them to present—the "topic" or the "representation"—and thus do not treat them as documents to be filed away for forty years and even then perhaps not exposed to the public eye. Their accessibility to all and sundry, like the bussing of a lengthy procession of refugees in broad daylight through a civilian community, enable us to trace the limits of the regime's constituent violence,[9] that is, what the ruling power perceived as necessary and proper for the constitution of a Jewish democratic regime and its expectations of what would be required for the citizens to recognize it as such.

By viewing photographs, we reconstitute time and again what has been inscribed in them. Therefore, the act of viewing photographs from disaster areas can function either as an act ratifying law-preserving violence—the law of the regime-made disaster—or as an act disapproving the constituent violence inscribed in the photograph by reconstructing the disaster that the constituent violence seeks to erase in order to prevent it from appearing as such out of the traces recorded in photographs. Here we see women who had been forced out of their homes several months previously. They, their children, and their fathers were separated from the younger, healthy men, some of whom—nearly two hundred—were then massacred in front of their eyes. The woman in the middle of the frame, the children scurrying around, all the women seated inside the bus are not yet refugees. The soldier who pours water into the tin that the woman holds, like the soldier standing aside and looking on, are now taking an active part in turning her into a refugee and in making refugeeness a trait of her being. She is not yet a refugee, but they are already treating her as if she is obviously a refugee. They are already a part of the regime being constituted that very moment, while the Arab inhabitants of the land are being expelled. They do not see their expulsion as an act of violence or a crime that they commit, but rather as a project to be completed while preventing excessive suffering that might result from it, such as the refugees' death of thirst—which, however, did occur in certain places.

The photograph, then, shows us the limit of law-constituting violence, a limit within which three-quarters of a million of the land's Palestinian inhabitants became refugees so that a new regime would be constituted in the area. Any reading of the photograph from the point of view of the ruling power, reducing its richness as a document to the humanitarian gesture that was framed in its foreground and remaining blind to the traces of constituent violence is in fact an act ratifying the law-preserving violence of the regime and contributes to its preservation. The ontological nature of the photograph enables one to enact a civil reading, a viewing that one can call "nongovernmental viewing," a viewing that will turn the traces of constituent violence that became the law—the sovereign law of the state of Israel—into traces of disaster and that will show the expanded field of the disaster. It will point out that this disaster has also affected those the regime has maimed by virtue of the loss of their ability to see disaster and recognize it as such. Nongovernmental viewing should expand the focus from the population of victims—the usual subjects of "human rights" discourse—to include those who made them victims, thus restoring the effaced presence of the regime that governs all participants in the events of photography—the event that took place when the photo was taken and the one taking place now, in front of the photograph with the participation of the spectator. This can be done only when the spectator no longer looks at photographs as "showing" what is inscribed in them, but rather as a participant in the event that can be seen through them. Such a spectator will replace the description "These are refugees," as if this were their "natural" trait, with "This is a photograph of citizens transforming others into refugees."

These photographed persons continue to be produced as refugees by the constituent violence of regime-made disasters, but through her gaze in the photograph, the spectator can refuse to contribute to the ongoing transformation of this violence into supposedly respected law. Photographs never show "refugees." The term "refugees" does not constitute a visual category, although the people it denotes might have visual characteristics. It is a political category at the heart of the regime that imposes it upon those people.

Translated by Tal Haran

NOTES

1. This type of disaster was called a "man-made disaster" by Hannah Arendt. See *The Origins of Totalitarianism* (Boston: Houghton Mifflin Harcourt, 1973).
2. I will not refer here to regime-made disasters that took place in the first half of the twentieth century, although some of the characteristics of the conditions for the appearance of regime-made disasters may also be applicable to this type.
3. As was the case of the Palestinians in 1948.
4. On the Israeli regime and the occupation, see the book I cowrote with Adi Ophir, *This Regime Which Is Not One: Occupation and Democracy between the Sea and the River (1967–)* (Stanford: Stanford University Press, forthcoming).
5. This delegitimization occurred with the censorship and orchestrated delegitimization of photographs taken by dozens of Palestinian photographers in Gaza during the latest Israeli assault in December 2008 – January 2009, when the army forbade entry of Israeli and international photographers. For more on photography during the Gaza assault, see www.aperture.org/humanrights/azoulay.php.
6. For more on the problematics of the judgments of political taste, see my *Civil Imagination: A Political Ontology of Photography* (London: Verso, 2012).
7. For more on the distinction between a ruling power and a regime, see *This Regime Which Is Not One*.
8. See Ilan Pappe's discussion of "Plan D" in *The Ethnic Cleansing of Palestine* (New York: Oneworld Publications, 2006).
9. For more on this, see Ariella Azoulay, *From Palestine to Israel: A Photographic Record of Destruction and State Formation, 1947–1950* (London: Pluto Press, 2011), an English translation of *Constituent Violence, 1947–1950: A Genealogy of a Regime and "A Catastrophe from Their Point of View"* (Tel Aviv: Resling, 2009), and Ariella Azoulay, "Declaring the State of Israel: Declaring a Warring State," *Critical Inquiry* 37.2 (Winter 2011), pp. 265–85.

Trevor Paglen, *Keyhole/Improved Crystal Optical Reconnaissance Satellite Near Scorpio* (*USA 129*), 2007 (courtesy Altman Siegel, San Francisco; Metro Pictures, New York; and Galerie Thomas Zander, Cologne).

Disappearances: On the Photographs of Trevor Paglen

Thomas Keenan

Thus I hurl
My dazzling spells into the spongy air,
Of power to cheat the eye with blear illusion,
And give it false presentments.
—John Milton, *Comus*

The geographer and artist Trevor Paglen has made it his project of late to take pictures of things that are very hard to see, whether because they are very far away, or because they are hidden in secrecy or beyond the pale of recognition, or because they do not officially exist. In a series of projects, he has tracked the flight paths of the CIA's clandestine fleet of private jets, photographed U.S. military and intelligence installations in Afghanistan, captured the orbits of American spy satellites, and reproduced the signatures of the fictitious people operating some of this country's intelligence apparatus.

In Paglen's work, photography confronts a shadow world. There are "ghost detainees" in American detention camps, detainees who have sometimes been deposited there by aircraft owned by "ghost" companies. "You find nonexistent people here who are somehow designed to disappear others," he told me in a 2006 conversation published in the journal *Bidoun*.[1] Paglen is interested in how people have been made to disappear and in what can be done to make them appear. His project, though, is less one of restoration or recovery than of identifying the mechanisms and the visual texture of disappearance itself.

In an article of May 13, 2004, the *New York Times* quoted a "former intelligence official" going public about "disappearance": "After the Sept. 11 attacks, the [Central Intelligence] agency began to search for remote sites in friendly countries around the world where Qaeda operatives could be kept quietly and securely. 'There was a debate after 9/11 about how to make people disappear,' a former intelligence official said. The result was a series of secret agreements allowing the C.I.A. to use sites overseas without outside scrutiny."[2] But when that former official tells the reporter about making people disappear, and when the newspaper publishes his words, what becomes of that disappearance? The bodies have not been produced (no *habeas corpus* yet), and many of the prisoners in question have not been presented to the public; still, the facts of their disappearance—and of what is being done to them in detention—are by now well known. Thanks to such officials, "disappearances"—along with "waterboarding" and "rendition," among other phenomena—have become open secrets. Something important has transpired, and the secrets are no longer simply secret. But challenging these practices by merely exposing them, bringing them into the light of public scrutiny, seems to be insufficient. So what is the status of this information? What shall we do with it?

In the introduction to his *Torture and Truth: Human Rights after 9/11*, Mark Danner draws our attention to what he calls the "peculiarity" of the Abu Ghraib incident: "It is not about revelation or disclosure but about the failure, once wrongdoing is disclosed, of politicians, officials, the press, and, ultimately citizens, to act. The scandal is not about uncovering what is hidden, it is about seeing what is already there—and acting on it. It is not about information: it is about politics."[3] This is true, and important, but the line between information and politics, sight and action, may not be as clear as Danner suggests. If it were, then the issue would be purely and simply political, a matter only of force and persuasion, and it is not. The Abu Ghraib images and the publicity they received were part of the politics. Danner rightly indicates that the problem is not that we don't know enough or that we are in need of further enlightenment before anything might happen. We can, in fact, see (almost) everything. But images, even if they are graphic, are not self-evident. They do not lead irrevocably to particular or obvious conclusions. If, today, actions in the political realm are rarely unaccompanied by images, the force and import—the gravity—of those images cannot simply be taken for granted. That is the enigma.

When we look at what is *already there*, even if it has only just emerged into the realm of visibility, what do we see? Paglen has been investigating the landscapes of disappearance, and especially the enigma of the open secret, in a number of ways over the last few years, with compelling results. He suggests that the outcome is, in more ways than one, blurry.

The English word "blur" seems to come from the same root as "blear." It signifies that something has happened to our vision: we see, but as if through tears. With

Trevor Paglen, *Chemical and Biological Weapons Proving Ground, Dugway, Utah, Distance: 42 miles, 11:17 a.m.*, 2006; *Workers, Gold Coast Terminal, Las Vegas, Nevada, Distance: 1 mile, 8:58 a.m.*, 2007 (courtesy Altman Siegel, San Francisco; Metro Pictures, New York; and Galerie Thomas Zander, Cologne).

blurs, the basic question is one of resolution—which is, on the one hand, a matter of determination, fixing, and deciding, and on the other a matter of the reduction of something complex into its constituent parts, into simpler elements. But when speaking about blurs, we are also talking about images and their quality, about clarity and hence about light. There are blurs of motion and blurs of focus, but they share the trait of indistinctness. The blurry image is difficult to resolve, make out, reduce: it is not clear, but dim, not sharp, but dull. The blur challenges our habits of looking. We blink or squint, try again to see something that is somehow out of alignment with itself. We always look twice, more than twice, when things get blurry.

In many of Paglen's images, blurring is not something that befalls an otherwise crisp image. It is not something secondary or accidental, not the sign of a failure to capture what is there to be seen clearly. The image begins and persists in a haze. If it is blurry, that is because it has to be. It would not be the same were clarity to be achieved.

Thus, Paglen's photographs of secret military installations and equipment, taken at very great distances with very long lenses, are dominated by the haze of all that air between the camera and the object, by the sheer fact of remoteness. The distance bends and warps a faraway air-traffic-control tower, and the faces of the workers leaving their plane are blobs. An enormous interval separates camera and hangar, and although the camera's sensors are capable of traversing that space, to some extent, they also respect and acknowledge it visually. In the blurry image, the distance itself is evident—perhaps more evident than the subject. The places that Paglen photographs are meant, somehow, not to be seen: they are designed for secret missions, for operations that take place in the dark; in rendering them visible Paglen's images take care to preserve that element of the covert.

Faced with something obscure—something essentially dark—it is radically insufficient merely to shine the light of publicity. It misses the point: to turn on the lights tells us nothing about the dark itself. Paglen is in search of something as he takes these pictures. Confronted by something unknown, or barely known, but still accessible to the senses, he employs his instruments of remote discovery to learn about it. He attaches telescopes, some with focal lengths of up to 7,000 millimeters, to a digital SLR camera, and (as he puts it in a project description) takes pictures across "upwards of forty miles of thick atmosphere between an observer and the sites depicted." (He also shoots on 35-millimeter and 4-by-5 film.)

In Paglen's project on the CIA's "extraordinary rendition" program, documented in *Torture Taxi: On the Trail of the CIA's Rendition Flights*,[4] he tracks the CIA's fleet of private planes, discovers their registration numbers, maps their flight paths, and records the names of many of the passengers on them. Over great distances, Paglen resolves things, analyzes and synthesizes the constituent parts of the structure into a coherent pattern. There is a quest for knowledge in his work and a method that aims at the greatest possible reduction of uncertainty.

Of his work with those extremely long lenses, Paglen says: "Limit-telephotography involves photographing landscapes that cannot be seen with the unaided eye."[5] The idea is at least as old as Walter Benjamin's 1936 essay "The Work of Art in the Age of Mechanical Reproduction," in which he wrote: "The enlargement of a snapshot does not simply render more precise what in any case was visible, though unclear: it reveals entirely new structural formations of the subject. . . . Evidently a different nature opens itself to the camera than opens to the naked eye—if only because an unconsciously penetrated space is substituted for a space consciously explored by man."[6]

So we look, with the aid of the usual instruments—and some unusual ones—and what do we see? Something entirely new, something to which we would ordinarily have no access. And strangely, things are not bleak, but bright, once seen in this other light. The images constitute a provocation, a question for us . . . or, actually, a question about us. Our ability to read and interpret what we see with their assistance is put into question. The announcement that the image makes, before any reading starts, is that the reading will be difficult, somehow beyond our control—but still we have to do it.

Exploring this new unseen space of blurs is an effort that takes us in at least two directions: our loss of orientation is simultaneously the overcoming of limiting boundaries and the disappearance of the markers of certainty. Both erasures and stains, blurs take us apart, put us in motion. The experience, if it is one, is by definition illegible, at least in part. And the effects of our own actions and encounters remain obscure: Did we make something happen? And if the effects are blurry, what about the causes? Blurs put us, our agency and our resolution, into question.

Looking toward political theorists such as Jacques Rancière and Hannah Arendt, Paglen wonders how we might extend their "notions of political speech into the realm of images. Certainly images 'do things,' but they are without guarantees." Is this work evidence? Yes, of a sort, Paglen told me recently. Or perhaps it is more like evidence of evidence, an effort simply to establish the possibility that some of these things might exist in the public realm. He notes that lawyers for Guantánamo detainee Majid Khan used Paglen's images of CIA "black sites" (secret prisons) as evidence in their filings, but in an unexpected way: "Their argument," he said, "had to do with trying to establish that there was enough unclassified 'evidence' in public to construct a 'grammar' for courtroom proceedings." The evidence was not about what was exposed in the images, but about the mere existence of such images. The advocates, Paglen says, were "simply trying to establish that something *could* be spoken about 'politically.'"[7]

In this sense, he continues, "Photography—and this is especially true after September 11—is a performance." Not fundamentally a statement, a document, or a record of how things are, but an activity, an event. And so, he says, we need to face up to the fact that, today, for some of us, at least, "to photograph is to exercise the right to photograph. Nowadays, people get locked up for photographing the Brooklyn Bridge."[8]

Paglen's work does not simply expose what is hidden, or render the invisible visible, or establish certainties. It does those things and marks their insufficiency. It announces that cameras, lenses, maps, data and databases, publicity, and even beauty are not enough. Why make photographs, then? In the name of what? These are all questions left open. Perhaps the knowledge is produced for something like its own sake: because we ought to know, in general. Perhaps the work takes the responsibility of calling us to *our* responsibilities: we cannot say, now, that we didn't know. Perhaps the knowledge is instrumental as a pathway, however unreliable, toward action.

Or perhaps not. Paglen seems careful to be modest—or blurry. As he told Rene Gabri in a 2006 interview for the 16beavergroup blog: "It's a fact, in my opinion, that we have access to more and better information than ever before." But "the dynamics that shape public opinion, the dynamics of an 'informed public,' and the dynamics of change are extremely messy."[9]

The mess, like the blur, is not going away. We stand a slightly better chance of getting oriented in it, though, thanks to these pictures.

NOTES

This essay is a reprint of Thomas Keenan, "Disappearances: The Photographs of Trevor Paglen," *Aperture* 191 (Spring 2008).

1. Trevor Paglen and Thomas Keenan, "Fog of Wars," *Bidoun* 1.8, "Interviews" (Fall 2006), pp. 36–39.
2. James Risen, David Johnston, and Neil A. Lewis, "Harsh C.I.A. Methods Cited in Top Qaeda Interrogations," *New York Times*, May 13, 2004, p. A1.
3. Mark Danner, *Torture and Truth: America, Abu Ghraib, and the War on Terror* (New York: New York Review Books, 2004), p. viv.
4. Trevor Paglen and A. C. Thompson, *Torture Taxi: On the Trail of the CIA's Rendition Flights* (Hoboken: Melville House, 2006).

5. See Trevor Paglen, "Limit Telephotography," http://www.paglen.com/pages/projects/nowhere/photos_images.htm.
6. Walter Benjamin, "The Work of Art in the Age of Mechanical Reproduction," in *Illuminations*, ed. Hannah Arendt, trans. Harry Zohn (New York: Schocken, 1969), p. 236.
7. Trevor Paglen, "RE: Aperture," comments to author on an earlier draft via e-mail, January 17, 2008.
8. *Ibid*.
9. See Rene Gabri, "Introview," Rene—Journalisms—Interview with Trevor Paglen—The Black World of the Military—08.15.05—09.02.05, *16beaver*, http://www.16beavergroup.org/journalisms/archives/001612.php.

Fazal Sheikh, *Neela Dey* (*"Saphhire"*), Vrindavan, India.

Of Veils and Mourning: Fazal Sheikh's Widowed Images

Eduardo Cadava

for Gayatri Chakravorty Spivak

> We have been turned away from the face, sometimes through the very image of the face, one that is meant to convey the inhuman, the already dead, that which is not precariousness and cannot, therefore, be killed; this is the face that we are nevertheless asked to kill, as if ridding the world of this face would return us to the human rather than consummate our inhumanity. One would need to hear the face as it speaks in something other than language to know the precariousness of life that is at stake. . . . We would have to interrogate the emergence and vanishing of the human at the limits of what we can know, what we can hear, what we can see, what we can sense.
> —Judith Butler, *Precarious Life*

Each time it is a story of what the eye can see and what it cannot—of what the camera can capture and of what eludes it. To say this, however, is simply to say that our experience of these photographs is always an experience of the eye—of an eye that seeks to see where it does not see, where it no longer sees, or where it does not yet see. At every moment, we are asked to respond to a certain play of light and darkness—the light and darkness without which the eye would have no story—and we respond to the muteness of this play by inventing stories, by relating each of these shifting images to several possible narratives. We will never know, however, if the stories we tell—about what we think we see as we look—will ever touch or engage the images before us.[1]

But what happens when—as is so often the case in the images that compose Fazal Sheikh's remarkable series of photographs, *Moksha*—a photograph gives the experience of the eye over to blindness, when it leads the line of our sight toward a light or shadow that prevents us from seeing? What happens when our eyes meet what they cannot see or when they encounter what cannot be encountered? What might this experience of blindness and shadows have to do with what makes photography photography? In what way do these images tell us that sight is essentially linked to an experience of mourning, an experience of mourning that mourns not only experience, but sight itself? As Sheikh would have it, as soon as a technology of the image exists, sight is already touched by the night. It is inscribed in a body whose secrets belong to the night. It radiates a light of the night. It tells us that the night falls on us. "But even if it were not to fall on us, we already are in the night," Derrida explains,

> as soon as we are captured by optical instruments that have no need for the light of day. We are already ghosts. . . . In the nocturnal space in which this image of us, this picture we are in the process of having "taken," is described, it is already night. Moreover, because we know that, once taken, once captured, such an image can be reproduced in our absence, because we know this already, we already know that we are haunted by a future that bears our death. Our disappearance is already there.[2]

What does it mean to read an image or a photograph? What would it mean to assume responsibility for an image or a history, to respond to the claims they make on us? How can we respond, for example, to the images and histories inscribed within the photographs that compose Fazal Sheikh's *Moksha*, the first part of his exhibition *Beloved Daughters*? How can we begin to read them? Each detail of the photographs has its force, its logic, its singular place. A condensation of several histories, each photograph remains linked to an absolutely singular event and therefore also to a date, to a historical inscription. What the photographs ask us to think about, then, is the relation between these several histories and the set of traces that has been preserved for us by Sheikh's camera. They belong to a series of photographs taken by Sheikh in the first few months of 2004 in the holy city of Vrindavan, also known as the "city of widows." They therefore must be read in relation to the history of the city (and, in particular, to the sacred history of the city, a history that includes its being the birthplace of Krishna), but also in relation to the way in which, "as more temples and shrines were built in Krishna's name, the city became the holy place of refuge for India's thousands of dispossessed widows," who, worshipping Krishna, "meditate on his name at the end of their lives in the hope of achieving *moksha* [salvation or heaven], and joining him forever."[3] As part of Sheikh's effort to expose the plight and circumstances of the widow's lives, the photographs also belong to his longstanding focus on the rights of displaced and dispossessed populations, from his efforts within the last fourteen years to document and record the mass phenomena of the refugee—in Afghanistan and Pakistan, but also in Somalia, Kenya, Brazil, and beyond—to his more recent projects on the systemic oppression, displacement, and discrimination against women in India, *Moksha* and *Ladli*. His work has been exhibited at, among others, the Tate Modern in London, the Henri Cartier-Bresson Foundation in Paris, the International Center of Photography and the United Nations in New York, and the Museum of Contemporary Art in Moscow. It has garnered him the International Henri Cartier-Bresson Grand Prize, the Infinity Award from the International Center of Photography, and the Leica Medal of Excellence. He has received fellowships from the Fulbright Foundation and the National Endowment of the Arts and, in 2005, he was named a MacArthur Fellow. In addition, in 2000, he established the International Human Rights Series, which, in collaboration with international galleries, institutions, and human rights organizations, uses publications, exhibitions, and the Internet to bring these issues to a broad public audience. This increased visibility has helped Sheikh bring the plight of the world's displaced people into greater focus, an outcome also legible in the innumerable articles and reviews that have appeared everywhere from the *New York Times* to *ArtForum International* and in the fact that all of his publications have been distributed, mostly free of charge, throughout global institutions concerned with human rights and, in particular, through cultural and nongovernmental organizations. (In the fall of 2008, for example, the NGO Action Aid distributed a set of thirty of the images from *Moksha* to more than one thousand organizations across India—including schools, women's organizations, humanitarian organizations, and libraries—and especially in rural areas of India that lack access to the Internet.)

In each instance, Sheikh's photographs seek to evoke what Walter Benjamin famously referred to as the "tradition of the oppressed"[4]—a tradition composed of the silence of the displaced and marginalized and the unspeakability of the traumas of the dispossessed. Like Benjamin, Sheikh seeks to enable those whom violence has deprived of expression to articulate their claim to justice—silently perhaps, but in the name of a judgment of history itself. As Shoshana Felman would have it, these are the "expressionless" of the "tradition of the oppressed," those who,

> on the one hand, have been historically reduced to silence, and who, on the other hand, have been historically made faceless, deprived of their human face—deprived, that is, not only of a language and a voice but even of the mute expression always present in a living human face. Those whom violence has paralyzed, effaced, or deadened, those whom violence has treated in their lives as though they were already dead, those who have lived (in life) without expression, without a voice and without a face, and have become—much like the dead—historically (and philosophically) expressionless.[5]

Like Benjamin's writings, Sheikh's photographs seek to cast light on the historical injustices and acts of violence that constitute history and to call forth the Judgment Day that might enable "even the expressionless of history (the silence of the victims, the muteness of the traumatized)" to "come into historical expression."[6]

If Sheikh's photographs begin in a kind of muteness, then, they also convey a silence that seeks to be heard, a silence that—in presenting us the traces of violence, deprivation, oppression, and effacement in relation to which these widows exist—attests to the necessity and responsibility of producing photographs, but also of making them speak. What is at stake is not only the possibility of casting a light on those whom history has sought to reduce to silence, whom history has deprived of a voice and a face, but also the chance that the inexpressibility of the traumas they have experienced can be given expression. What is implied here is that a photograph can never be thought solely in terms of what is printed on its surface: it always bears the traces of a photographic event, and if we are obliged to reconstruct this event, this act of reconstruction requires more than simply identifying what is exhibited in the photograph. It requires an act of engagement, an act of interpretation, which responds to the several histories that form the photograph's conditions. This is perhaps especially the case when—because we may be viewing a woman who has suffered some form of injury, a woman who, because of this injury, now lives as if, even in life, she were already dead—the relation between what is visible and what is invisible is no longer certain. We know, for example, that numerous visual and textual expressions might be able to testify to the woman's injuries, even while still enabling the most visible signs of the trauma to remain unseen, and this because in the world of the photograph, what is visible always threatens to become invisible, and what is presently invisible is what needs to be read.[7]

To read these photographs therefore means to give an account of the several histories and contexts sealed within them, to respond to the innumerable experiences commemorated, displaced, and ciphered by them, to seek to reconstruct the circumstances in which they were produced, or better, of those they name, code, disguise, or date on their surfaces, circumstances that include the trauma of violence and loss, of dispossession and death. But precisely because the circumstances or contexts in which a photograph is produced can never be fully given (since they are interwoven within an entire network of historical and social relations), how can we respond to what remains invisible, to what can never be seen directly within the images? If the structure of an image is defined as what remains unseen, this withholding and withdrawing structure is what prevents us from experiencing the image in its entirety, or to be more precise, encourages us to recognize that the image, bearing as it always does several memories at once, is never

Parchment with drawings of Krishna and his life with the *gopis* made by a Bengali widow, Vrindavan, India.

closed. It perhaps also tells us, if it can tell us anything at all, that it is in relation to this invisibility, to this departure from sense and understanding, that our capacity to bear witness may indeed begin to take place.

Let us return to these women, or at least to the question of what it might mean to see them. Although Sheikh seeks to present to us a series of images of Indian women who have been left widows, another characteristic distinguishes them even more: they are widows who live in Vrindavan. Abandoning what was left of their lives after the death of their husbands, they have come to this holy city in order to overcome the cycle of reincarnation, to be converted into brides of Krishna, and in this way to achieve *moksha* and salvation. Before we can even see these women, though, Sheikh evokes the iconography of Krishna and his women. Recalling the story that justifies their presence in Vrindavan, these images delay our encounter with the widows: because we should not rush here, because we should not imagine ourselves able to view these women directly, without the many mediations that we must pass through and that Sheikh places between these women and our eyes. As in the "anatomy lesson" that doctors encounter in a book before they confront the naked body on the dissection table, here, the photographer suggests that we cannot understand the images that follow without first encountering and reading the images that precede them, the story (a necessarily visual story) that serves as a lens through which to read the conjunction of contradictions and ambivalences that we will see in each of the photographed women: women marked by loss, but also by the utopia of an encounter with Krishna, women who have been displaced, dispossessed, and expelled from the world, but who are in Vrindavan because they believe they are at the threshold of Heaven.

Sheikh's work distances itself from ethnographic or documentary photography at the very moment in which he destroys the fictions that sustain ethnography: first, the idea that a direct encounter between the camera and the photographic subject is possible and, second, the fiction that the photographic mediation disappears in order to facilitate a direct encounter between our eyes and what the image shows us. Our encounter with the widows of Vrindavan is delayed not only by the iconographic images of Krishna that open the book, but also because Sheikh emphasizes the entry into the city. To enter *moksha*, he seems to suggest, is to enter the imaginary that sustains the city, to enter the city and the stories and legends that belong to its representation. Indeed, it is not possible to view the widows without passing through a series of mediations: we must look at them with eyes that bear the iconography of Krishna, the images of utopia, or the religious beliefs that promise happiness and Heaven and that view the city in which they

Fazal Sheikh, *Commemorative plaques; Passageway at dawn; Dawn along the Yamuna River* [BOTTOM], Vrindavan, India.

Fazal Sheikh, *Bhajan Ashram; Dawn along the Yamuna River; Tupasi's icons*, Vrindavan, India.

now live. We must look at them knowing that we are not looking only at a particular subject, a woman, an Indian woman, a Hindu woman who has been left a widow. To view the other is nearly impossible, Sheikh seems to suggest, since we always must look at her through something else, through the images that precede her, through the stories that justify her presence here and even at the very moment in which the photograph is taken.

The person who wishes to encounter these women should follow the path of Sheikh's camera: to go in search of them and to enter the city, to trace the path of these women who, after their experience of loss, seek shelter and refuge in this holy city, and enter this city in the same way that they have been promised entry into Heaven—because *moksha* is achieved by crossing "across the waters of sorrow to the farthest shore from darkness." And this is also the entry into *Moksha*, Sheikh's book. It is necessary to cross the waters, to pass through the sorrow, and to arrive on the other side of darkness. After the images of Krishna, after the images that tell us why these women have made their journey into this holy city, we enter the city, but without being able to see anything clearly. Unlike his other images, these images are blurry, unclear, and uncertain. They are dominated by obscurity; it is difficult to discern what is in front of us. They are images that emphasize the relation between light and obscurity, between seeing and not seeing. We cannot see clearly; we do not know what we are seeing: rather than select a fragment of reality for us, the camera instead seems to have taken these pictures by itself. At moments, it would seem that it is a question of a river and that we perhaps are crossing the waters that will carry us, too, to *moksha;* at other moments it would seem that we can make out a flight of steps, perhaps a door, perhaps a column. We are confronted with an urban landscape, with an entry into a city that is deliberately like a river, like the waters that separate the sorrow and darkness of the world in order to transport us into light. After crossing this river that is also a city, after looking at a city that is also a river, we can look at Sheikh's widows. And yet the first illumined image, the first high-definition image, as it were, the first portrait of this book of portraits, is the image of a woman whose identity is occulted, since we can see her only from behind, hidden by a shawl that covers her body and that seems to bind her, to hold her tightly, to keep her in place.

We will return to this later—to the many widows who remain unseen by us—but let us stay a little longer in this passage, in this suspended moment created by Sheikh, in this very delay, in this ensemble of images that we should see before seeing this entirely covered subject. In order to see, he suggests, we must pass through darkness; to see an image, we must open our eyes, but, much more importantly, we must keep them closed first. It is not so much that darkness is a condition of light, but rather that the shadow, the blurred and uncertain vision, is a condition of vision. Sheikh reinforces this in his description of his initial entry into Vrindavan, when he tells us

> our journey had been slowed by intermittent bands of mist and as we approached the town a dense pall of fog reduced our visibility to only a few feet. . . . Though it was only a few hours since we had left Dehli, it felt as if we had descended through time to another era. Late that night, walking through the town still shrouded in fog . . . I stumbled along the passageways. . . . Next morning I woke very early to be out on the streets at what Hindus refer to as one of the "threshold" times—the moments after sunset and just before dawn. In this mysterious twilight the streets of Vrindavan are like an empty stage, from which the boy-god Krishna and his *gopis* have only just retired.[8]

Within this uncertain twilight zone, what is to be seen cannot be seen unless we can begin to see that this uncertainty and indeterminacy is precisely the point. Just as we cannot see the city clearly and directly, we can never see the widows directly, since they must be seen through eyes touched by at least the history of Krishna, the history of Vrindavan as a sacred city and refuge for widows, and through the apparatus of infinite mediation that we call "photography." This is why Sheikh's work is, before anything else, a reflection on the conditions of possibility of the gaze in general and on the conditions of possibility of the gaze of the camera in particular. But what are the conditions for seeing? Under what conditions can we see the other or the other's image? Or better yet: under what conditions can we see the other as what she necessarily is: an image, a construction of the gaze or of the camera that permanently prevents us from viewing her directly?

What Sheikh suggests here is that the experience of the photograph is always associated with a kind of delay or belatedness, and not only with the interval of time necessary for memory to activate the life arrested and sealed within it. No matter how instantaneous the action of a camera might be, there is always some measure of delay, always some interval of time, between the click of the camera and the taking of a photograph. This delay structures the photograph that, emerging with the click of the shutter, corresponds to the transit between light and darkness, to the duration that arrests what we call an image, even if this image can become a photograph only later, when it is developed. This is why the delay that he inserts into the beginning of his book—into the space and time between the moment in which we open it and the moment in which we first can view the widows—becomes not only an allegorical meditation on the delay built into every photograph, but also a first suggestion that sight can take place only through a series of mediations, that our eye requires these mediations in order to see, even if they also prevent us from ever seeing what is before us directly and in all its immediacy.[9]

Fazal Sheikh, *Yamuna Dasi* (*"Servant of Yamuna"*), Vrindavan, India.

How are we to understand the vertigo of this series, and especially when it signals an endless reflexivity? And, indeed, Sheikh's photographs are extremely self-reflective. They often are traversed by different mirror effects: from the images cast upon reflective surfaces, to the mirrors in which objects and persons are reflected, to the several images that cite or replicate other images, even if at times in displaced forms, to the various modes of representation represented within the images—writing, photographs, statues, stones with inscriptions, buildings, posters, portraits within various kinds of frames, signs on windows or walls, dioramas, and coins with writing and images on them. These reflections operate in his photographs as a means of photographing photography itself. These are photographs, in other words, that tell us something about photography, and not only because, within a photograph, everything is representation.

When Sheikh's preliminary photographs lure us into their world, when they invite us to pass through the threshold of his book in order to display their capacity to preserve the broken pieces of the past, they also suggest the ways in which these memories are held in reserve, sometimes put away and forgotten until, one day, we happen upon them and view them under the light of our own eyes—or to be more precise, amid the shadows and recesses of our memory's eye. Drawing us into their space, these photographs tell us that in order to see them from the outside, we must already—or still—be in them. In order to bring the truth about the photograph to light, we must be ready to bring it into the light of the photograph. To say this, however, is to say that we can speak about the photograph only from its threshold. And the photograph is itself perhaps nothing other than a threshold—like the camera's shutter, an opening and a closing—and this is why the photographs that compose *Moksha* are so often traversed by thresholds and passages, doors and windows, streets and alleys, but also by cloth of different kinds that serves as the threshold between what we can see and what we cannot.

In Pankaj Butalia's 1993 documentary on the widows of Vrindavan, also entitled simply *Moksha*, we hear the voice of an unseen woman recite the lines of a poem that, written by Butalia himself and fragmented across the length of the film, punctuates it at various key moments. The first fragment we hear is recited during the film's opening scene, as we watch a woman going downriver on a boat, alone and in white, and seated with her back facing the viewer. As we watch the woman crossing the waters, we hear the unseen woman say:

> Conjure up time
> mirror the ancient story
> for the past is here
> searching

the streets mingled with dust
concentrated ash and sorrow in by-lanes strewn
spewed
like bones from marrow.

She later adds the command and question:

Inscribe, O Mother
with the ink of poverty
this story of yours etched so long ago.
What could you write that was not for you written?

The film opens with an evocation of the journey "across the waters of sorrow to the farthest shore from darkness" and then, like Sheikh, suggests that in order to understand the widows of Vrindavan, we should link the city and its dispossessed inhabitants to the "ancient story" of Krishna, which survives not only in the lives of the widows—inscribed as they are within it—but also in the streets and by-lanes of the city itself. Suggesting that the widows are following a script they have inherited, the disembodied voice asks us to read the relation between this ancient script and the lives of these impoverished and dispossessed women.[10]

While there are innumerable versions of the Krishna story, circulated in sacred poems as well as in folkloric traditions, one of the most important sources for the history of Krishna is the *Bhagavata-Purana*, a collection of narratives, genealogies, epic stories, prayers, and hymns of praise. This celebrated Sanskrit work—probably produced in South India between the seventh and tenth centuries—was central to medieval devotional theism and to Krishnaism in particular. What is singular about the work, and something that is entirely pertinent to the reading I wish to pursue here, is that it is composed of a series of narratives that are told to someone who is about to die.[11] Having been told he will die in seven days, King Parikshit spends his last days listening to the sage Suka tell him what a person on the point of death should hear and remember: Krishna's names, forms, and stories. Organized around a meditation on death and dying, then, the *Bhagavata* seeks to think about how we should regard death and about the relations between death, loss, and love.

The composition of the *Bhagavata* is itself framed by death, since it takes its point of departure from the death of Krishna and therefore begins with the passing of an era. This background of death is essentially linked to the myth of the text's composition and to how the *Bhagavata* views itself in relationship to dying and to its own narrative movement. It is a narrative organized around death, composed of death, and of a death that begins with birth, that is inseparable from birth. The portrayal of death in the *Purana* is so pervasive that nothing or no one is untouched by it. Beyond its many scenes of literal death, the *Bhagavata* is filled with figurative deaths, all of which confirm separation as an essential component of both Indian literature and religion. These instances of separation emphasize the anguish that comes from being apart from one's beloved or from one's own nature. This separation often is described as more anguishing than "mere death," and it includes the distance between the human and the divine, as well as the separation from loved ones. As E. H. Rick Jarow has noted, "Fathers are constantly losing sons, wives lose husbands, parents lose children, and lovers lose their beloved. The entire *Purana* may be read as a sustained meditation on loss, and this perhaps is its force."[12] Rather than seeking to avoid loss, the *Bhagavata* not only celebrates it, but also transforms it into an agent of change. This is most clearly legible in the climactic story of Krishna and the cowherd women whom he seduces along the river, the *gopis*, in relation to which the poem explores the relations between love and loss and the human and the divine. In the story, the *gopis* had prayed to the goddess Katyayani that Krishna would become their husband, and their prayers were answered when, after stealing their clothes while they were bathing in the river, Krishna asks them to come out of the river and approach him if they want their garments returned. Seeing the *gopis* without clothes, he is said to have become their husband. All of this takes place within a scene that exceeds ordinary conceptions of time and space, since it suggests that within this particular night, there already are many nights. That the story of Krishna and the *gopis* leads to darkness (we can recall here that "Krishna" literally means "dark" or "black") brings us back to the story of Krishna's birth, a story that is entirely a photographic one.

As we learn in an earlier *Bhagavata* narrative, Krishna's birth is predicted by a star,[13] and as we know, the history of photography (from Baudelaire to Valery to Proust to Benjamin to Kracauer and to Barthes) can be said to begin in the interpretation of stars.[14] Within this photographic context, then, Krishna is born on a moonless night at midnight in the Mathura prison and under the threat of execution.[15] He is born in a photographic space, in other words, in a dark room, in a kind of *camera obscura* in which, appearing in his majestic four-armed form, he is begged by the only mortal who witnesses his birth to assume a more usual appearance and, in a flash, the blinding light of divinity both strikes and blackens Krishna, who now appears as an infant. This link between Krishna and the realm of photography is suggested by Sheikh in this remarkable image of an imagistic altar to the little Krishna. Surrounded by darkness, inserted into and emerging from out of this photographic space, his representation seems situated within the aperture of a camera, but also within a kind of womblike environment. That mothers are always another name for photography—like the camera, they, too, are a means of reproduction—suggests that the little Krishna, this little offspring of a principle of reproduction, will himself become a principle of reproduction, something that is confirmed when he is presented as a force of multiplication when he multiplies himself to be available with equal intimacy to every *gopi* he summons.[16] A force of reproduction, he also becomes a mechanism for the production of distance and separation when he leaves the *gopis* behind. Like the photograph, which is always organized around the absence of the photographed, Krishna is another name for mourning, if not for photography itself. Indeed, it is perhaps no accident that the widows whom Sheikh photographs believe, as he tells us in the text that accompanies *Moksha*, that his photographs will be an offering to Krishna.[17]

Returning to the story of Krishna and the *gopis*, the next verse begins with the first of many references to the moon. Setting up the theme of separation and return, the rising moon is compared to the long-awaited sight of a beloved one. As Krishna tells the cowherd girls: "Love for me comes from hearing me . . . meditating on me, and reciting my glories, not by physical proximity. Therefore, please return to your homes" (p. 127: 10.29.27). Suggesting that the strongest experience of the absolute occurs through separation, Krishna disappears, and in doing so inaugurates the great separation.

Of all the words that could have been used for this disappearance, the *Bhagavata* uses a word that also suggests "merging into" or, more literally, to "place within": *antar-dha*.[18] In other words, Krishna does not really go anywhere, since he inhabits everything and everyone. The experience of loss instead inaugurates a transformation. The disappearance is sudden, and it overwhelms the cowherd women. They begin to exhibit various symptoms and degrees of loss, the first being the imitation of his activities. Becoming absorbed with him, the *gopis* begin to identify with him and declare, "I am He." The verse reads as follows:

> When *Bhagavan* suddenly vanished, the women . . . were filled with remorse at his disappearance . . . .
>
> Intoxicated by the pleasing gestures, playfulness and words, as well as by the quivering glances, smiles of love and movements of Krishna . . . their minds were overwhelmed. They acted out each of those behaviors, their hearts [dedicated] to him.
>
> Those beloved women were so bewildered by Krishna's pastimes that their bodies imitated their beloved in the way they moved, smiled, glanced, spoke, and so forth. With their hearts [dedicated] to him, the women declared "I am He." (p. 130: 10.30.1–3)

We will return to this assertion of an identity that finds itself in another, but for now, I simply wish to stress that Krishna orchestrates his separation in order to induce the *gopis* to follow him. He explains that even as he has remained hidden, he actually has been reciprocating. Some critics have reasonably argued that such "reciprocity" appears to be "rather sadistic at times, and that going to the extreme of denying all of one's relations and even destroying one's life to love God is not love at all, but an exaggerated form of divinely coated slavery (with slavery to a husband and a social order being displaced with slavery to God)."[19] But the *Bhagavata-Purana* is not bound by reason.

In the *Bhagavata*'s version of the story, Krishna never returns to Vrindavan, and the cowherd women are obliged to spend the rest of their mortal lives remembering and mourning him. Indeed, the distancing effect of loss transforms emotion into a mode of remembrance. We might even say that Krishna is another name for this distancing effect. While Krishna never returns to Vrindavan, however, he does encounter the cowherd women once more at the pilgrimage site of Kuruksetra. The occasion is a total eclipse of the sun—another moment of sheer darkness—but this time the kind that augurs the world's dissolution. Sorrow turns into verse, poetic utterance again begins in loss, and the songs of the *gopis* are throughout touched by separation and longing. If Krishna is born under the sign of photography—if his story is a tale of stars and moons, light and darkness, distance and separation, correspondence and withdrawal, and life and death—the *gopis* complain of their own photographic plight: they suggest that the creator of their eyes has erred, since blinking eyelids hinder their contemplation of Krishna's face: "When you, Lord, go to the forest during the day, a moment becomes an eternity for those who do not see you. He who created eyelids is dull-witted, from the perspective of those beholding your beautiful face, with its curled locks of hair" (p. 136: 10.31.15).[20] Within the *Bhagavata*, it is left to the philosopher-king Nimi—who, after giving up his body, speaks from beyond the grave to resist the transmigration of his self into another body, saying that he does not wish to reenter his body, because, he claims, he dislikes birth as much as he does death, and responding to his request, the gods offer him the chance to live without a body by enabling him to take up residence in the bodies of all beings through the opening and closing of their eyelids—through, that is, the opening and closing of the body's own camera shutter.[21]

In *Provincializing Europe*, Dipesh Chakrabarty identifies "a certain will to witness and document suffering . . . for the interest of a general reading public" and claims that this will has "embedded itself in modern Bengali life." "Both this will and the archive it has built up over the last hundred years are part of a modernity that British colonial rule inaugurated in nineteenth-century India," he goes on to say.

> What underlay this will to document was an image of the Bengali widow of upper-caste Hindu families as a general figure of suffering . . . . It is not that every Bengali upper-caste widow has suffered in the same way or to the same extent throughout

history or that there have been no historical changes in widows' conditions. Many widows earned unquestionable familial authority by willingly subjecting themselves to the prescribed regimes and rituals of widowhood. Many also have resisted the social injunctions meant to control their lives. Besides, factors such as women's education, their entry into public life, the subsequent decline in the number of child brides, and the overall increase in life expectancies have helped reduce the widows' vulnerability.[22]

Yet there is no question that widowhood exposes women to several difficulties and trials in the patrilineal, patrilocal system of kinship of upper-caste Bengali society. The prescribed rituals of widowhood suggest that it is regarded as a state of inauspiciousness. The rituals take the form of extreme and lifelong atonement on the part of the widow: celibacy, dietary restrictions, unadorned bodies that carry familiar defining marks—a lack of jewelry or other decorative accoutrements, a shaved head or cropped hair, white saris that signal both a relation to death and an absence of desire, white ash on the forehead—aim not only to make widows unattractive and to set them apart from others, but also to control their sexuality. Stories recounted since the nineteenth century reveal the torture, oppression, and cruelty that often, if not always, have accompanied the experience of widowhood. As Uma Chakravarti has noted, among the upper castes, widowhood is a state of sexual and social death.[23]

Nevertheless, widowhood was not registered as a problem in Bengali society until the arrival of colonial rule, and indeed, the problems of widowhood rarely, if ever, received any attention. Colonial rule erased this inattention as it began to write the history of modern widowhood with the help of Bengali social reformers such as Rammahoun Roy, who worked to make *sati* illegal in 1829, and Iswarchandra Vidyasagar, who actively worked to give widows the legal right to remarry through the 1846 Act for the Remarriage of Hindu Widows. As Chakrabarty notes:

> The capacity to notice and document suffering (even if it be one's own suffering) from the position of a generalized and necessarily disembodied observer is what marks the beginnings of the modern self.... The archives of the history of the widow-as-sufferer eventually came to include the subjectivity of the widow herself. The widow became both the object and the subject of the gaze that bore witness to oppression and suffering.... To build an archive of the widow's interiority, to see her self as deep and stratified, to hear her own voice, as it were, required the development of a set of observational techniques for studying and describing human psychology. This was a role performed primarily by the novel.... To delve into the interior world of the widow, whose innermost feelings were denied recognition by society, was to write the desire for freedom and self-expression into the very structure of the new Bengali subject.[24]

Fazal Sheikh, *Asha Rajak ("Hope")*, Vrindavan, India.

What Chakrabarty suggests is that Bengali modernity, with its delineation of a subject who can bear witness to the problems of widowhood, arose in relation to European narratives of the modern observing subject. While Sheikh also seeks to bear witness to the plight of dispossessed widows, his work exceeds this colonialist gaze not only by including and multiplying the many perspectives of the women he photographs, but also by contextualizing their lives in relation to, among others, the story of Krishna and the history of Vrindivan. Moreover, as I have argued, his insistence on the mediatory character of vision in general suggests that however much his work may wish to present the widows to us, to expose their vulnerability and distress so that these might be ameliorated by enforcing legislation and collective action, it never can capture or expose its subjects fully, since to do so would require its being able to incorporate the entirety of the network of mediations through which we must view the widows. This is to say that in producing a series of photographs that, because of the order in which they are presented to us (an order that emphasizes the network of mediations through which we must pass even to begin to approach the widows), points to the widows, even as it indicates that they can never be revealed to us transparently or immediately, Sheikh seeks to remain faithful to the widow's simultaneous appearance and disappearance, life and death, presence and absence, and subjecthood and objecthood. This relation between the widow as object and the widow as subject replicates the internal division of the widow's subjectivity, a subjectivity that, as it seeks its own form of agency, nevertheless remains linked to a script in which she must follow her husband, even in death, like the body its shadow. It is to this complicated and contradictory subjectivity to which I now wish to turn in order to delineate the widow's paradoxical and permanent exile from herself, even before her widowhood.

What we register as we read the texts that accompany Sheikh's images is that the widows seem to experience "more and more of less and less," perhaps especially because, being widows, they are no longer who they were before their husband's death. But if these women have lost their identity, can we say that they are dead or alive? If identity is the condition of possibility for mourning, how, then, can those who have lost their identity mourn? If identity is the condition of possibility for memory, how can those who do not have an identity memorialize anything? What kind of temporality constitutes their strange, nonsubjective lives—what is the past of the life that does not belong to any identity? Or to put it differently, by what life do those who lost themselves live? Can they bear witness to that loss even though they themselves are no more? Is it possible that a witness can witness his or her death while dead, while alive but dead? And, finally, is it by chance that all such questions are most profoundly and precisely addressed in the medium of photography?

What is exposed in Sheikh's photographs is the paradox of a face that is not a face, a face that can never be seen directly as the face of the woman at whom we are looking.[25] This is a face that exists, in the wording of Branka Arsic, as "the negative of the face: it is the face that is not, it is the visibility of the effacement in the moment of its effacement."[26] This is why, paradoxically, since Sheikh was not present at the moment of the widow's "death," at the moment of the death that makes her who she now is, who she now is not or no longer, he can witness only what he did not witness by allowing the other, the one who died, but remains "alive," to speak through him. He desubjectivizes himself and thus becomes—through his work, through his photographs, through his texts, and through his effort to listen to and see this or that woman who is no longer—the survival of the other who did not survive. Testimony to the desubjectivation of the victim is thus a labor of the desubjectivation of the witness. In the wording of Giorgio Agamben, "Testimony takes place where the speechless one makes the speaking one speak and where the one who speaks bears the impossibility of speaking in his own speech, such that the silent and the speaking . . . enter into a zone of indistinction . . . . This also can be expressed by saying that the subject of testimony is the one who bears witness to a desubjectivation."[27] This means that a witness always witnesses a desubjectivation of the other, but also of himself.

This series of photographs, however, attempts the impossible: to produce the witness who would testify to her own nonsurviving. This is the paradox of a testimony that would bear witness to the moment of a death and to the testimony of this death, which is to say to a moment in which life is at the same time dead and alive. This is why the photographs bear witness to a different temporality of witnessing, a temporality in which the past is contemporaneous with its present and in which the widow is therefore always in a moment of exile.

But what does it mean to be in exile? What precisely is exile? For Freud, this question touches upon the fundamental, defining experience of subjectivity. As he suggests in "The Uncanny," what is homelike already is inhabited by what is unhomelike.[28] To be in one's own home is precisely never to be in it, always to be outside it. To put it another way, one can truly only be "in" one's home when one is outside it, when one no longer inhabits it. One can only be "in" one's home, that is, when one has left it. In our context, this means that the widow is a subject because she leaves herself, because she is always already in exile: she is a subject only insofar as she is homeless. This point already is made in the *Bhagavata*. There, in book 10, the *gopis* become so absorbed in Krishna that they cannot find their own homes: "Their minds absorbed in Krishna, the *gopis'* conversations focused on him, their activities centered on him, and they dedicated their hearts to him. Simply by singing about his qualities, they forgot their own homes" (p. 134: 10.30.43). But as Arsic notes, this homelessness, this exile, "produces an exile different from that of the exile."

> In one case, it is a question of exile as the overcoming of identity into a new identity that keeps within itself or shelters within itself the "former," sublated identity. In the other case, it is a question of a total interruption of identity. Interruption means: what constituted an identity is not sublated but gone, vanished so that there is nothing left that could assume another identity, so that what is left is only the pure outsideness of an impersonal life. This outsideness is exile. In other words, exile is the unbearable space in between in which there is nobody who can assume what has to be assumed in order for a new identity to be born.[29]

This is where the disturbing paradox of these photographs lies: what is photographed is not a subject anymore, but it is not yet an object. The photographs are taken at the moment when the photographed subjects are exposed to their desubjectivation while still preserving traces of their subjectivity. The fact that this process is staged in the medium of photography once more asserts its importance. For there is no photograph that does not expose the photographed while also subjecting it to objectivation. As Roland Barthes would have it: "The Photograph . . . represents that very subtle moment when, to tell the truth, I am neither subject nor object but a subject who feels he is becoming an object: I then experience a micro-version of death (of parenthesis)."[30] The widow is a subject only when she does not have a self. This is why we can say that the "I" of devotion identifies with itself (with the other) through the process of identification, or as we might say, by giving itself to another. The identity acquired through love is the effect of an identification that separates. The passionate passivity that characterizes so many of Sheikh's widows defines a life of the wound, the living wound, the body that lives off of wounds so wounding, so avid, that they exhaust all life and turn the life of this passive existence into perpetual dying, neither life nor death, but a life that is lived by dying.

Nevertheless, it is the widow's survival, her living on, even after her death, her social death, that indicates that things pass, that they change and transform, and minimally, because this survival asks us to think not of the impossibility of a return to life, but of the impossibility of dying—not of life or death, but of life and death, or perhaps even more precisely, of "life death." It is this ghostly survival—as a metonym for all such survivals—that defines the madness of the photograph, too, since it is there, within the medium of photography, that we simultaneously experience the relation between life and death, between testimony and its impossibility, between the self and an other, and between the past, the present, and the future. Indeed, whether or not the widow is already dead, literally dead, she already will have experienced (a kind of) death. This point is confirmed—less abstractly perhaps, but not at all less rigorously—when Neela Dey, one of the widows whom Sheikh photographs, tells us that "in Vrindavan we are so determined in our devotion that everything else in the world is dead to us. We ourselves are dead and living with Krishna."[31]

That this experience of living at the threshold of death and life is another name for the experience of love—for what takes place in our relation to the one we love, even if our beloved is Krishna—is confirmed when, in *A Lover's Discourse*, Barthes confesses: "I have projected myself into the other with such power that when I am without the other I cannot recover myself, regain myself: I am lost, forever."[32] While he suggests that this loss of self occurs especially in relation to the absent other, he also implies that it happens even when the other is presumably "present," since the very relation between a self and an other means that because each already inhabits the other, because each is defined in relation to the other, neither the self nor the other can return to himself (or, in the case of the widow, to herself): the self and the other deconstitute one another precisely in their relation. The widow is already a widow, even before her husband's literal death.

What are we to do with the many hands that appear in Sheikh's work, not only within *Moksha* and *Ladli*, in which there are many, but especially in *The Victor Weeps*, his record of Afghan refugees along the border between Afghanistan and Pakistan in the winter of 1997? In each instance, whether the hands are holding something, whether they are holding each other or resting on this or that part of a body, they imply an effort to keep and to hold, to carry and hand over, to hand down, like a kind of legacy or inheritance, a fragment of the past. In this way, these hands tell us what a photograph desires: it, too, wishes to offer, to keep, to convey and hand over a fragment of our memory. Like the hand, it comes to us as a mode of transmission—but a mode of transmission that asks us to think about what it means to transmit or communicate, to bequeath something, to leave behind a legacy or inheritance through which a future might become possible. The photographs are about what it means to pass something down, to hand something over—a memory, a story, a death, a past, present, or future—and not only because they confirm, in however an interrupted manner, a story of inheritance and lineage, a story of the relations between mothers and daughters. Emphasizing the singularity of a single displacement—and we should never forget that what is ineffaceable about displacement is that no matter how many thousands, hundreds of thousands, or even millions of displaced persons there may be, these displacements are each time singular ones—they also suggest that like photography itself, inheritance is a matter of both singularity and repetition, a matter of the singularity of a memory and of the repetition without which there could be neither memory nor inheritance. This association between inheritance and photography also suggests that what these hands surrender to us is what is given to us by every photograph: an image. We can never remind ourselves enough that the photograph gives us an image, rather than what is photographed. We could even say that every photograph turns the photographed into a kind of widow. Tearing it from its context and displacing it to another place and moment, these photographs tell us that every image is widowed, insofar as its existence is the best indication that what we have before us, what we have in our hands, is not the photographed. This is why, like Sheikh's widows, photography exists in perpetual mourning for the referent in relation to which it emerges.

This bereavement acknowledges what takes place in any photograph—the return of the departed, of the one who is no longer here. This is why the return of what was once there takes the form of a haunting. The possibility of the photographic image requires that there be such things as ghosts and phantoms. This is confirmed not only by the fact that one widow after another dreams of her dead husband and sees him in her dreams, time and time again, as if he were alive, but also by the shadow lives that the widows themselves lead. It is perhaps precisely in death that the power of the photograph is revealed, and revealed to the very extent that it continues to evoke what can no longer be there. In photographing someone, we know that the photograph will survive her—it begins, even during her life, to circulate without her, figuring and anticipating her death each time it is looked at. This means that there is no photograph, no image, that does not consign the photographed to ashes. As Man Ray wrote in 1934, in an essay entitled "The Age of Light," images are the "oxidized residues, fixed by light and chemical elements, of living organisms. No plastic expression can ever be more than a residue of an experience.... [It is rather] the recognition of an image that has survived an experience tragically, recalling the event more or less clearly, like the undisturbed ashes of an object consumed by flames."[33] Benjamin makes a similar point in his essay "The Storyteller" in a passage that identifies flame with the reader. The reader is said to "annihilate" and "devour" the "stuff" or "subject matter" of a novel "as fire devours logs in a fireplace." What sustains this reader-flame is no longer just wood and ashes—even if these are now transformed into a text—but a question that keeps the reader's interest burning: how to learn that death awaits us? As Benjamin notes, that "the 'meaning' of a character's life is revealed only in death" means that in order to read, the reader must know "in advance, no matter what, that he will share [this] experience of death."[34] The living reader-flame burning over the logs of the past and the ashes of past experience learns to read by learning of its mortality. Reading means: learning to die.

What Sheikh's photographs tell us is that the earth is not a place where humanity or rights are shared—and this despite their respective and repeated claims to universality. It is instead a place of inequality and injustice, a place of loss and death, a place where every day there are more women and young girls who are abandoned and abused, who are displaced and dispossessed, who starve, who are mutilated and raped, who are marginalized and exiled, and who live without the full exercise of political and civic rights. It is a place where, because of the inequality and injustice often written into the very formulations and definitions of humanity and rights—and, again, despite their associations with a certain rhetoric of universality—the task of defining and realizing human rights is infinite and therefore permanently urgent and necessary. As Sheikh notes in *Ladli*,

> in India's main cities, every six hours, a young married woman is burned to death, beaten to death, or driven to suicide by emotional abuse from her husband. According to the United Nations Population Fund, two-thirds of Indian women between the ages of fifteen and forty-nine have been beaten, raped, or forced to provide sex.... The fact remains that Indian society traditionally subordinates women and its treatment of them amounts to a cultural prejudice as ingrained as any racial or religious divide.... What India suffers from is apathy—it is clearly not for lack of legislation that women and children are still abused, but because of the unwillingness of the police, the courts and the government to enforce the laws made to protect them.[35]

That India can evoke the universalism of human rights at the same time that it continues to contribute to the regime it condemns (and here it is no different from every other nation, including ours) is only one indication that what it means to be "human" by no means always counts with the same force—in invocations of human rights, but also in their absence. This is why the question of human rights is a question that remains at the heart of any politics or ethics that concerns itself not only with who we are, but also with what it means to live in a world in which the call for human rights and humanitarian intervention is not always made in the name of preventing the dispossession of rights that so often defines the conditions of our human existence. If Walter Benjamin were alive today, he might remind us that there is no document of humanitarianism that is not at the same time a document of inhumanity, inequality, and violence and that the human rights activist should therefore dissociate himself or herself from it as much as possible. If the projects and discourses of human rights do not wish to neglect this counsel, they will have to define themselves continuously against the inhumanity, inequality, and violence that threaten them from within, as well as from without. Always and at once motivated by humanitarianism and democracy—but a humanitarianism and democracy that corresponds to other and more just forms of humanitarianism and democracy than those we have with us today—they would thus begin in an aporetic praxis, one that would take its point of departure from the "perplexities" of human rights.[36] They would seek to inaugurate a world in which displacements, racisms, nationalisms, class ideologies, sexisms, and economic oppressions of all kinds would no longer exist and would ask us to imagine what the world has never offered us: absolute freedom, justice, equality, and rights. If this world can ever be inaugurated, if there can ever be a future that will not simply be a repetition of the past, it may well be enabled by work like that of Fazal Sheikh.

NOTES

1. I would like to thank Fazal Sheikh for his initial invitation to have me write on *Moksha* in relation to his exhibition, *Beloved Daughters*, at the Princeton Art Museum at Princeton University in the fall of 2007, and for everything his work has permitted me to invent and say. All of the photographs in this piece are reproduced courtesy of the artist and are © Fazal Sheikh.

   I also would like to thank Pankaj Butalia for so kindly responding to my queries about his film, *Moksha*, and Gayatri Chakravorty Spivak, to whom I have dedicated this essay, for her inspiration and ongoing friendship. She remains, as always, a "beautiful daughter."

   This essay is a companion piece to "Palm Reading: Fazal Sheikh's Handbook of Death," which has appeared in abbreviated form in Spanish in *Acta Poetica* 28.1–2 (Spring–Fall 2007), pp. 15–47, in *Confines* 21 (December 2007), pp. 25–41, and in *Parallax* 16.4 (2010), pp. 117–35, and which will appear in full in English in *Of Mourning and Politics*, which is forthcoming from Harvard University Press in 2013. It stages its relation to this earlier essay by citing (in Benjaminian mode, "without citation marks") certain sentences from it, as in these opening paragraphs. In this way, it seeks to suggest the way in which my reading of Sheikh's *Moksha* project is mediated by my earlier encounters with his work, but also the way in which reading always begins elsewhere. As I will argue in what follows, Sheikh suggests that any encounter—for example, our encounter with his images of Vrindivan and its widows—is always mediated and therefore never immediate, transparent, or direct.
2. Jacques Derrida, *Échographies de la television: Entretiens filmés* (Paris: Éditions Galilée, 1996), p. 131 (my translation).
3. See Fazal Sheikh, "Across the Waters of Sorrow: The Widows of Vrindivan," in *Moksha* (Göttingen: Steidl, 2005), p. 258. There are approximately forty million widows in India and roughly twenty thousand widows at any given time in Vrindivan, many (although by no

means all) from West Bengal. Even though the Hindu Succession Act of 1969 made women eligible to inherit equally with men, and some individual states have legislated equality provisions into inheritance law, in actual practice, widows often are deprived of their legal rights. Local interpretations of caste customs, for example, can determine whether or not a widow will be granted some permanent or temporary share of the family's land or property, and because of this, a widow's rights often are violated. Indeed, the common restrictions on property, residence, remarriage, and employment destine most widows to a life of economic, social, and even physical distress. Moreover, because the widows who move to Vrindivan come from different caste and economic backgrounds, their living conditions there differ greatly, with some of the widows living in government homes, but most living in tiny alcoves in the streets or in small old-age homes to be found throughout the town. What needs to be explored, however, is the extent to which their decision to come to Vrindivan truly offers them the solace they come to secure, however pressed they might have been, and for whatever heterogeneous reasons—including the nature of the relations they have or do not have with their families, their age, their economic status (it should be noted, however, that many upper-caste widows, who could be supported by their relatives, also are reduced to poverty because they are cast out of the household), and the fact that, at times, rural widows are more likely to remarry than widows from higher castes, since the latter are more strictly bound to celibacy. Sheikh provides a measure of this solace by including passages from his interviews of several of the widows he photographed during his stay in Vrindivan.

4. See Walter Benjamin, "On the Concept of History," trans. Harry Zohn, in *Selected Writings, Volume 4, 1938–1940*, ed. Howard Eiland and Michael W. Jennings (Cambridge, MA: Harvard University Press, 2003), p. 392.
5. See Shoshana Felman, *The Juridical Unconscious: Trials and Traumas in the Twentieth Century* (Cambridge, MA: Harvard University Press, 2002), p. 13.
6. *Ibid.*, p. 15.
7. I am indebted on this point to Ariella Azoulay's delineation of what she calls "the civil contract of photography," a contract that, for her, takes into account all of the participants in a photographic act, "camera, photographer, photographed subject, and spectator," and approaches "the photograph (and its meaning) as an unintentional effect of the encounter between all of these." "None of these," she adds, "have the capacity to seal off this effect and determine its sole meaning." See Ariella Azoulay, *The Civil Contract of Photography* (New York: Zone Books, 2008), p. 23.
8. Sheikh, "Across the Waters of Sorrow: The Widows of Vrindivan," p. 257.
9. As Yates McKee has noted in a discussion of the role and place of the technical media in NGOs and of the mediated character of vision in general: "if vision acquires an inflated metaphorical privilege because of the centrality of technologies such as cameras, camcorders, television, satellites, the Internet, and PowerPoint presentations in contemporary politics, it is only insofar as they prevent vision from ever simply being itself. It is not that these technologies distort the immediacy typically associated with the optical faculty; rather, they magnify and exacerbate the general point that every visual artifact and experience is always already marked by an unforeseeably mediated network of histories, interpretations, and contexts that, strictly speaking, are not visually evident as such. In this sense, every image is a kind of text that requires both looking and reading, or rather looking *as* reading, regardless of whether an image contains or is accompanied by text in the narrow sense of the word." See

Yates McKee, "'Eyes and Ears': Aesthetics, Visual Culture, and the Claims of Nongovernmental Politics," in Michel Feher (ed.), with Gaëlle Krikorian and Yates McKee, *Nongovernmental Politics* (New York: Zone Books, 2007), p. 330.

10. Emphasizing the relation between the embrace of this ancient script and the difficulties of a life that at the same time is "chosen" by the widows, Gayatri Chakravorty Spivak suggests—in reference to Butalia's film, in particular—that the widows cannot be seen simply as victims. As she puts it: "It is too easy to have a politically correct interpretation of these widows, although the denunciation of the predatory male establishment of moneylenders and petty religion-mongers is altogether apt. These women, who would seem decrepit to the merely sophisticated eye, speak with grace, confidence, and authority, not as victims.... They have come to Vrindivan for freedom, such as it is.... As old-age homes for... widowed female relatives, these dormitories are harsh indeed. But they are transformed into a space of choice and performance by the gift for theater of these near-destitute widows, ready to inhabit the *bhakti* scripts that are thrust upon them. There is everything to denounce in a socio-economic sex-gender system that will permit this. But the women cannot be seen as victims, and theater of *bhakti* cannot be seen as orthodoxy pure and simple. The contrast between the sentimental voiceover of the documentary and the dry power of the women is itself an interpretable text." See Gayatri Chakravorty Spivak. "Moving Devi," *Cultural Critique* 47 (Winter 2001), pp. 154–55.
11. As far as I know, the most extensive and elaborate treatment of this structure—of this series of narratives organized around several kinds of death—can be found in E. H. Rick Jarow's *Tales for the Dying: The Death Narrative of the Bhagavata-Purana* (Albany: State University of New York Press, 2003). Much of my discussion of this collection of narratives is indebted to Jarow's own analysis and, at certain moments, I in fact incorporate a kind of miniaturized photograph in prose of this analysis. In the same way that Sheikh suggests that our encounter with the Vrindivan widows is mediated by, among other things, the story of Krishna, my own reading of the *Bhagavata-Purana* has been mediated by Jarow's.
12. *Ibid.*, p. 11.
13. Indeed, at the time of Krishna's birth, "the constellations and the stars were all favorable." See *Krishna: The Beautiful Legend of God (Srimad Bhagavata Purana Book X)*, trans. Edwin F. Bryant (New York: Penguin, 2003), p. 19. All further references to book 10 of the *Bhagavata* are to this edition and will be cited parenthetically within the essay by page number, then 10, chapter number, verse number.
14. I have made this argument in my *Words of Light: Theses on the Photography of History* (Princeton: Princeton University Press, 1997), pp. 26–41.
15. Krishna was born in the Mathura prison, where his parents, Devaki and Vasudeva, were being held by Devaki's brother, King Kamsa. They had been imprisoned because their eighth son, Krishna, was prophesied to kill his maternal uncle, King Kamsa. The king fully intended to kill the infant upon his birth, but, when Krishna was born, the prison guards fell asleep, and the doors of the prison magically opened. Vasudeva walked out of the prison and took Krishna across the Yamuna River to Gokul, where he was cared for by his foster parents, Nanda and Yasoda, in Vrindavan, just fifteen kilometers from Mathura.
16. If we accept Rimbaud's suggestion that the entry into a photographic space always corresponds to the "advent of [the self] as an other," always implies a transformed version of our "self," then Krishna's appearance as one of Vishnu's ten avatars—his appearance as a

transformed double of Vishnu—confirms his photographic status.

17. As Sheikh notes, "On my last evening visit to the ashram the widows asked why I had never photographed the altar in the temple. In fact, it was because I felt too conspicuous standing in the middle of the mass of chanting women. But at their request I set up my camera in the central aisle and began to work. The widows' chanting quickened and some of the women let out ululations of a kind I'd never heard before. I found out later that this was because they considered the making of the photographs as an offering to Krishna." See *Moksha*, p. 274.
18. On this point, see Jarow, *Tales for the Dying*, p. 105.
19. *Ibid.*, p. 113.
20. This point is repeated later in the *Bhagavata*, when Sri Suka continues his narrative: "The *gopis* obtained their beloved Krishna after such a long time. Gazing at him, they cursed the person who had created eyelids on their eyes" (p. 349: 10.82.40).
21. The story of Nimi is relayed in book 9 of the *Bhagavata*. See especially chapter 13, verses 1–11, in *The Bhagavata Purana*, trans. Ganesh Vasudeo Tagare (Delhi: Motilal Banarsidass, 1976), pp. 1193–95.
22. Dipesh Chakrabarty, *Provincializing Europe: Postcolonial Thought and Historical Difference* (Princeton: Princeton University Press, 2000), p. 117. Much of what follows is indebted to Chakrabarty's incisive historico-theoretical reflections on Bengali widowhood.
23. See Uma Chakravarti, *Everyday Lives, Everyday Histories: Beyond the Kings and Brahmanas of "Ancient" India* (Delhi: Tulika Books, 2006), pp. 156–82.
24. Chakrabarty, *Provincializing Europe*, pp. 119, 129, 133.
25. I develop this idea of a face that is not a face from Judith Butler's discussion in *Precarious Life* of the way in which the giving of a face at the same time can "derealize" the face. As she puts it: "It is important to distinguish among kinds of unrepresentability. In the first instance, there is the Levinasian view according to which there is a 'face' which no face can fully exhaust, the face understood as human suffering, as the cry of human suffering, which can take no direct representation. Here the 'face' is always a figure for something that is not literally a face. Other human expressions, however, seem to be figurable as a 'face' even though they are not faces, but sounds or emissions of another order. . . . In this sense, the figure underscores the incommensurability of the face with whatever it represents. Strictly speaking, then, the face does not represent anything, in the sense that it fails to capture and deliver that to which it refers." See Judith Butler, *Precarious Life: The Powers of Mourning and Violence* (New York: Verso, 2004), p. 144.
26. See Branka Arsic, "The Home of Shame," in Eduardo Cadava and Aaron Levy (eds.), *Cities Without Citizens* (Philadelphia: Slought Books and the Rosenbach Museum, 2003), p. 40. I am indebted in this section—and in some of my formulations here—to Arsic's discussion in her essay of the face's negativity and of desubjectivization and exile.
27. See Giorgio Agamben, *Remnants of Auschwitz: The Witness and the Archive*, trans. Daniel Heller-Roazen (New York: Zone Books, 2002), pp. 120–21.
28. See Freud, "The Uncanny," in *The Standard Edition of the Complete Psychological Works of Sigmund Freud*, vol. 17, trans. James Strachey (London: Hogarth Press, 1955), pp. 217–56.
29. Arsic, "The Home of Shame," p. 46.
30. Roland Barthes, *Camera Lucida: Reflections on Photography*, trans. Richard Howard (New York: Farrar, Straus, and Giroux, 1981), p. 14.
31. Quoted in Sheikh, *Moksha*, p. 118.

32. Barthes, *A Lover's Discourse: Fragments*, trans. Richard Howard (New York: Farrar, Straus, and Giroux, 1978), p. 49.
33. Man Ray, "The Age of Light," in *Photography in the Modern Era: European Documents and Critical Writings, 1913–1940*, ed. Christopher Phillips (New York: Metropolitan Museum of Art / Aperture, 1989), p. 53.
34. Walter Benjamin, "The Storyteller," trans. Harry Zohn, in *Selected Writings, Volume 3, 1935–1938*, ed. Howard Eiland and Michael W. Jennings (Cambridge, MA: Harvard University Press, 2002), p. 156.
35. Fazal Sheikh, *Ladli* (Göttingen: Steidl, 2007), pp. 143 and 187–88.
36. It is of course Hannah Arendt who famously wrote about the "perplexities of the rights of man" in her 1951 book *The Origins of Totalitarianism*. See Arendt, *The Origins of Totalitarianism* (New York: Schocken, 2004), p. 290.

FIGURE 1 Lewis Hine, *Young Russian Jewess at Ellis Island*, 1905 (photo: New York Public Library/Art Resource, NY).

Making Human Junk

Jaleh Mansoor

In 1905, Lewis Hine produced a photograph of a young woman entitled *Young Russian Jewish Immigrant at Ellis Island* (fig. 1). The title, operating as a caption to locate the object in time and place, provides the information necessary to map one's relationship to the girl. She is alien and therefore subject to our gaze. This "our" is, through the subject-object axis that characterizes so much photography, the availability of the other to be seen and the power of the viewer to see, the consolidated "we" of power. That this caption notes her ethnicity and nationality marks her, and beyond the marking operation, marks her as other.

The specific photograph, in tension with the condition of nonreciprocal visibility specific to the medium, nonetheless makes any such rationalization impossible. The woman's torso is situated within the frame in the triangular composition of a notable individual. The figure of her body occupies its ground in the classical proportions of Renaissance painterly portraiture,[1] which provided the common format for nineteenth-century photographic portraiture, starting roughly with Nadar's portraits of geniuses and Mathew Brady's heroicized images of the Civil War, notably the portrait *Ulysses S. Grant*. The literature of art history has established the relationship between Hine's cropping strategies and the *longue durée* of portraiture. John Tagg, for instance, traces the compositional structure of Hine's photographs of single subjects to early modern (eighteenth-century to nineteenth-century) academic portraiture, from Charles Le Brun's treatise on the language of gestures through Hogarth's and Daumier's critical social caricature. However, Hine draws on a much earlier tradition of aggrandizing the subject, one dating to Raphael's inauguration of a form of portraiture, as in the portrait *Baldassare Castiglione* (1515), that quickly became a standard conceit of the genre, mediated through many centuries of painterly portraiture. *Mona Lisa Visits Ellis Island,* also taken in 1905 (fig. 2), which demonstrates a clear preoccupation with

FIGURE 2 Lewis Hine, *Mona Lisa Visits Ellis Island,* 1905 (photo: New York Public Library/Art Resource, NY).

framing and the history of single-point perspective that organizes the family portrait, suggests that Hine thought about the conventions of portraiture dating back to the genre's inception. It also evidences Hine's consciousness of the entanglement of framing and power, centering the mother under the vanishing point. Photography here is situated as anything but neutral or naive.

This brief essay acknowledges Hine's awareness of the conditions of the photographic frame, or rather of photography as a function of cropping and the decontextualizing cut, doubled as an interrogation of the way in which social conditions frame subjectivity, assigning humanity to some and dehumanizing others. His work doubles the operations of subjection and simultaneously undermines those very operations.

The eponymous immigrant of *Young Russian Jewish Immigrant of Ellis Island* is framed by first a head scarf and, beyond it, in the background, by a metal lattice. Both repeat the photographic frame, qualifying how the young woman may be read. Yet each contradicts the other. The head scarf denotes tradition; she is from elsewhere, informed by a set of practices impervious to modernity. By contrast, the metal bars form a grid, that ur structure of modernity, which encloses her on her arrival to America, processed by the bureaucratic machinery of Ellis Island.

Hine's attention to historical and ideological frames is concretized by these formal framing devices. At stake in his attention to historical and ideological frames, in other words, is a modality of visualization that is neither dependent on a naive notion of an ontologically guaranteed, materially self-evident object of documentary practices nor simply an insistence on the opacity of the subject as object. Hine demonstrates the opacity of the person he presents as a form of antagonism in relation to the opacity of the operations of the frame itself, that is, in relation to a set of discursive and historical phenomena that shape the subject who remains in excess of those frames.

Just as the woman's accoutrements oppose her environment and betray the dialectic of a modernity textured from within by tradition and uneven development, her posture and expression contradict the cagelike structure of the grid from which she appears to emerge. She is purposive, her eyes intense and focused somewhere outside the frame. These contradictions become a function of the multiple framing devices put in play in Hine's image. Posed within the conventions of a privileged compositional structure and presented in a moment of severity and concentration, the woman generates a sense of willful subjectivity that exceeds the limit conditions of her context: the scarf, the grid. That she is visually striking—beautiful, even—also acts in excess of the coordinates set by the title. Hine's camera records the geopolitical, historical, and cultural frames in which she is to be seen, and yet she, through the irreducible quality of her gaze, is in surfeit of those conditions, resisting them. These challenges to the entities that limit the woman's subjectivity make it difficult finally to objectify her, let alone to aestheticize her.

Four years later, Hine made an image in a rather different context—the steel and coal belt of Appalachia. The title, *Pittsburgh Steel Worker's Child* (fig. 3) presents a toddler dressed in a filthy smock, its gender indeterminate, face smudged with dirt and presumably with the toxic materials that ensure its father's wage and therefore its survival. The child is in focus against a blurred background in which one makes out industrial forms. This photograph decidedly negates hegemonic images of childhood, a genre established during the Victorian era in the work of David Octavius Hill and Robert Adamson. Such photographic oeuvres frame childhood as a space prior to and free of ideological and class determinations. And yet in Hine's image, the toddler's gesture guarantees it an expressive interiority richer than the sum of the details that denote poverty. The toddler waves at someone who is somewhere beyond the frame, an expression of humor and joy on its face. Poverty, it seems, is not a condition of internal lack or a symptom of moral decrepitude about which to feel shame, but finds its locus in a specific set of historical conditions. Hine's choice to frame a joyful child, rather than a pitiable urchin, denaturalizes class relations and defamiliarizes Victorian conventions

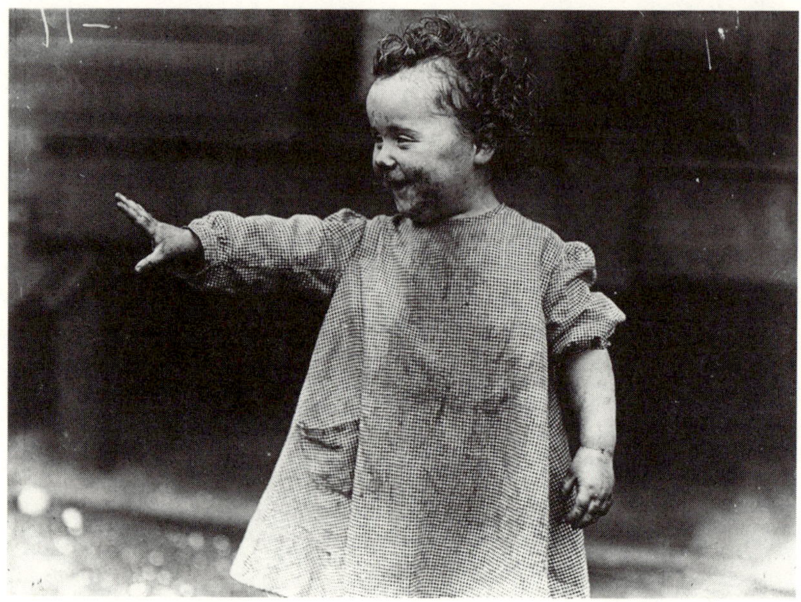

FIGURE 3 Lewis Hine, *Pittsburgh Steel Worker's Child*, 1909.

of representing poverty, to which I will return, that border on reifying the state of victimization as a function of fate.[2] The child's subjectivity is clearly mediated by class, history, and ideology, but cannot be reduced to it. This refusal to rationalize suggests a model of subjectivity that is just that, *subjectivity* (rather than objecthood) that confronts the instrumentality of industrial capital that surrounds the child and of which the child could be a mere symptom. As such, the child's subjectivity stands in defiance of the objectifying force of the camera. At the same time, and needless to say, it is clear that subjectivity is subjection to social and ideological coordinates. We have no idea why the child is happy, given the filth in which it is enmeshed. And because we have no information within the frame to satisfy our inquiry into the child's smile, this expression is also a point of excess, a surplus that, like that of the Jewish immigrant, overflows the objectivity of the photograph and insists on subjectivity as both a function of a set of social and ideological frames and as something irreducible to them. Hine's work suggests the mutual imbrication *and* agonistic tension among visual and ideological frames.

Lewis Hine's photographic practice takes its place in the canon of twentieth-century photography as exemplar of the social documentary, a genus of photographic practice in which the image is to act in an illustrative register within a larger discursive framework, frequently a goal-driven mission such as the land survey or social work, often elaborated within the broader project of assisting/controlling an other, whether the socially "less fortunate" or the geopolitically colonized. This understanding of documentary photography as fulfilling an evidentiary role suggests a degree of transparency and the assignment of a fixed end to which photography is the means.

From the medium's inception, the notion of evidence has been connected to the issue of power. Europe's nineteenth-century colonial project meshed with the drive in the late nineteenth and early twentieth centuries to construct archival banks of information, understood as repositories of objective, empirically grounded knowledge in the photographic medium. The metaphor of photography as a stream of light penetrating darkness—the unknown—dovetails with age-old metaphors of light as redemption, or, in secular terms, as enlightenment and justice. Assigning to the indexically produced image the instrumental burden of supplying legible information delivered in a matrix of light drove the Enlightenment project and its dialectical twin, disenchantment, forward. The document, in other words, finds its meaning assigned by the discursive structure, or archive, within which it is situated. That discursive frame, in turn, purported to be a neutral repository of data, but was anything but.

Recent discourse has emphasized photography's managerial role.[3] John Tagg, for example, has argued for the medium's disciplinary function. Situating his argument against Roland Barthes's use of the term "studium" to refer to the intended narratival meaning of a photograph, or its "content," and Barthes's coinage of the term "punctum" to articulate the irreducible materiality of the image, Tagg argues that photography both constitutes and delivers a mythological "real" to power in a way that supports its interest in maintaining its hegemony. Tagg's argument hinges on the problem of, or rather the misreading of, the "real" in discourses on photography. He insists that dominant readings of the medium, emblematized by Roland Barthes's *Camera Lucida*, rely on an unmediated notion of "the real." However, Barthes's insistence on the materiality of the image does not amount to saying that the photograph is an unmediated, ontologically guaranteed presentation of the referent. If anything, any such ontological guarantee makes the image ultimately illegible and utterly opaque, obfuscating the referentiality of the referent and thereby shattering its claim to objective status or to offering evidentiary "truth." Hine works with the problem of legibility in relation to materiality by emphasizing the mediating presence of the frame via internal frames that double back to emphasize the frame as such.[4]

Most accounts of Lewis Hine's specific project—as opposed to generalizations about the medium—place him decidedly in the genre of documentary photography and therefore within the larger *épisteme* of empirical evidence able to be mobilized for social progress. Thus, Tagg sees Hine as naively participating in the idea that photography could be a form of unmediated representations offering the "truth" of the object and supports his reading of Hine with the anecdotal account of Hine's assertion that "if he could have told the story in words, he would not have needed to lug a camera around." Tagg argues that Hine "saw the camera as a means to vivify empirical, scientific facts, to flesh them out, to prove them. The camera, for Hine was ultimately a source of truth. The photograph was an unmediated reflection of the world 'outside,' a true record of the subject stood before it. Technique, therefore, was an intervention which only falsified."[5]

However, Hine's best-known work suggests otherwise. Hine works with the problem of legibility in relation to materiality by emphasizing the mediating presence of the photographic frame that symbolizes ideological frames producing subjectivity in a given time and place. Internal frames double back to emphasize the medium's frame and, broadly, social frames as such. His photographs make clear an awareness of the fact that by the late nineteenth century, photography was intimately bound up with biopolitical control. It regulated the distribution of bodies, categorizing some as normative and others pathological within the self-legitimating institutions of law, medicine, psychology, and education. Photography provided a map on which to locate the coordinates of identity.

Hine is best known for his work for the National Child Labor Committee, founded in 1904 to lobby for national laws regulating the exploitation of children in industry. While the NCLP was initially successful in having a law passed, the Supreme Court overturned it in 1907 for violating a child's right to seek employment. Hine had begun work for the National Child Labor Committee in 1906 and had allied his interests with this private political organization, which did not have a clear aesthetic agenda. He began to produce work specifically for NCLC, and in 1909, Hine published the first of many photo essays depicting working children at risk. Among those, *Jennie Is 51 Inches Tall*, taken in 1908 (fig. 4), shows his understanding of the frame as a social condition prior to the moment of photographic capture, a moment that, in turn, can challenge or reify the social and ideological determinants or frames producing the subject. In his accompanying article for the NCLC, Hine embedded the cotton mill worker's image in the following text: "One of the spinners in Whitnel Cotton Mill. She was 51 inches high. Has been in the mill one year. Sometimes works at night. Runs 4 sides—48 cents a day. When asked how old she was, she hesitated, then said, 'I don't remember,' then added confidentially, 'I'm not old enough to work, but do just the same.' Out of 50 employees, there were ten children about her size. Whitnel, N.C."

While the text acts as a caption that brackets the basic message to be communicated, that is, that the girl is not physically up to the demands of work, the

FIGURE 4 Lewis Hine, *Jennie Is 51 Inches Tall, December 1908. North Carolina* (photo: New York Public Library/Art Resource, NY).

image exceeds it, not only positing the disciplinary existence of child labor, but making a bid for a model of disidentificatory subjectivity that negates the commonplace tendency to see an example of marginal society as expendable, as locked in a morass of hopeless inevitability. In the text, the girl is keenly aware of her situation, but in a turn, attempts to master it, rather than having it own her. On the one hand, her self-conscious insistence on her right to work symptomatizes the nefarious way in which disciplinary power subjugates, lending the girl her meaning to herself and expropriating any other self-definition to which she may lay claim. She identifies with the power that dispossesses her and assists in her own exploitation disguised as independent agency. On the other hand, her capacity for any self-assertion belies her self-objectification.

And the photograph itself works in excess of this tautological operation of power. In the image, a set of contradictions and condensations break the circular logic of power within which the girl is caught. Concretely, towering in the foreground, the woman dwarfs the background, the framing forces, that enclose her. An expression of will and potential exceeds the classical system of perspective, which, far from rejected, reaches its apotheosis in modernity's emblem, the grid. She is in sharp focus against the blurring perspectival recession of the industrial machinery she works and against the receding bank of windows to her left.

In this sense, Hine's way of framing the problem of poverty, and indeed of defining what constitutes poverty (a self made to recognize itself only in reification, while exceeding, consciously or unconsciously, its terms) contrasts sharply with classic humanist perspectives as exemplified by Jacob Riis's *How the Other Half Lives*. The immediate message of Riis's *Italian Rag Picker* (1880s) (fig. 5), assisted by the title, is that the existence of poverty is irreducible and, above all, elsewhere. Riis frames that social problem, however, through a thinly veiled evocation of one of the most recognizable and overdetermined tropes in Western representation, the Madonna and Child. The woman's gaze, directed skyward, underscores the transcendental quality of Riis's vision of her experience, the bags of rags around her framing a modern manger. Her suffering becomes ahistorical, independent of social and geopolitical coordinates. The rag picker as Madonna becomes a mythical image of poverty as destiny, and worse, as a medium of grace and endurance. The title of the folio of photographs, *How the Other Half Lives*, both problematizes and supports the single image's sweeping humanist message. The other confirms the essential alterity of the subject, opaque, inaccessible, yet managed within the economy of the image.

Hine's *Jennie Is 51 Inches Tall*, by contrast, presents an interior that contains the girl. This interior discloses a set of historical shifts within which the girl is located. Historical, geopolitical, economic, and ideological interests are inscribed in the spatial construction, making it impossible to essentialize the girl's status. She is situated along the perspectival recession structured by the machinery she operates, on her right, and by the wall of windows that enclose, even as they illuminate her, on her left. The burden of perspectival space as a metaphor for transcendental futurity and redemption is truncated. On the picture's left, the grid of the cotton-mill machinery that contains her suggests equivalence and exchange, abstract advanced forms of production and distribution—that is, industrialization. On the right, Hine brackets the child with the bank of windows, the symbolic form of a humanist culture and its concomitant belief in the transcendence of man, while the wall they define encloses and anchors the receding sense of space, the empirical underpinning of Renaissance spatial construction, becoming the dominant structure in the form of the grid as a concrete, material determinant within which the young spinner becomes a piece of machinery.

The photographic frame then functions as a secondary frame that estranges the existent social frame. Because of the way that Hine monumentalizes and heroicizes his subjects, the frame restores to the expropriated subject her agency

FIGURE 5 Jacob Riis, *Italian Rag Picker*, 1880s (photo: The Art Archive at Art Resource, NY).

in an antagonistic relation to the social, industrial, and ideological framework within which she is entrenched. This operation of the frame is not merely a result of bringing the unrepresented into representation, an act of visual colonization characterizing much photographic presentation of the other, but produces the terms through which to recognize the human.

Indeed, recognizing the human as such is the primary thrust of Hine's project, which both situates it within and problematizes the documentary category. Hine, at the turn of the last century and in its first few decades, precisely located the need to constitute the human subject in a contemporary historical matrix dependent on its erasure for labor power.[6] As Judith Butler notes: "if one is to respond ethically to the human face, there must first be a frame for the human. . . . But given how contested the visual representation of the 'human' is, it would appear that our capacity to refer to a face as a human face is conditioned and mediated by frames of reference that are variously humanizing and dehumanizing." Consequently, "The possibility of an ethical response to the face . . . requires a normativity of the visual field; there is not only an epistemological frame in which the face appears, but an operation of power as well."[7]

The human face is not universally guaranteed or even representable in the mimetic logic of representation. Photography as moving beyond mimesis and into the evidentiary guarantee of the ontological veracity of the referent is beside the point, because "human" and "subject" are themselves functions of discursive frames. In other words, the "real" putatively captured by the camera is an eternally receding horizon of the already inscribed, the "real" itself nothing but an inscription. Within the labor conditions of turn of the last century in the United States, the "real" putatively captured by the camera was a highly mediated inscription of inequity.

Beyond the parameters of the human for whom "human rights" are a set of guarantees, the question of which forms of the human are grievable and which are not surfaces as a function of the frame, social and ideological, and within photographic representation, the decontextualizing cut.[8] Hine's awareness that the category "human" was far from a self-evident given is evidenced in many of his captions in posters for the National Child Labor Committee. In a montage poster entitled "Making Human Junk" published in the *Child Labor Bulletin* in 1914–1915, Hine presents something of a flow chart in which photographs of healthy children are linked to a factory from which a second line issues linked to underweight, unhappy, and injured children. But the term "human junk" is interesting for the way in which it qualifies the human as industrial waste as anything but human in the humanist sense. It concretizes Marx's dictum that capital turns objects into subjects and subjects into objects. Hine's project, again, revolves around the notion that the human needs to be framed, produced even, as human within the realm of representation in order to be awarded the rights of the human. However, the lines linking each term to the other replace the frame, translating the embedded sociality articulated by the frame into rationalized terms denotatively diagramming the symbiotic quality of ideology.

Hine appears to have been aware of the internal contradiction characteristic of indexical forms of representation: its understanding in the nineteenth century as a form of re/presentation finally capable of delivering facts and, simultaneously, its failure to convey a fixed message due to the polysemy of the physical trace.[9] This sensitivity to the infinite regress of the referent motivated Hine to anchor photographic meaning by recourse to captions and by carefully situating the individual image in an archival or institutional context: the parameters of the survey, the space of the courtroom, the page of a flyer.

Hine was aware that no photograph could act as an unmediated entity capable of supplying either objectivity or truth. By contrast, photography for Hine was first and foremost an interruption into the existing operations of power that frame and thereby performatively produce some people as subjects and others as objects. Given that photography was a foundational instrument in determining what and who could be assigned the privilege and responsibilities of hegemonically valid subjectivity through the elaboration of medical and juridical archives, it was the medium through which to argue for the dignity and civil rights of the marginalized. In other words, precisely because of its implication in regulative biopolitics that circumscribe norm and pathology, photography was a necessary medium for reframing the other as fully subject. Hine argued for the rights of the other from within the parameters, the frame, of the disciplinary social order.[10] Hine's strongest formal strategy, an attenuated emphasis on the operation of the photographic frame, draws attention to the social and political processes of division, fragmentation, cutting, and framing that produce subjectivity. While power frames some lives as human, as subjects, as citizens, and as privileged lives and others as expendable objects, Hine's photographic framing functioned to reframe those deemed to be lesser lives as full and equal subjects.[11]

Nonetheless, a remainder—beyond the irreducible materiality of the medium and beyond the bracketing by a politically motivated project—haunts Hine's images. This remainder, owing much to Hine's manipulation of photography's particular condition as a function of the cut or the crop, characterizes Hine's photographs as much as their putative legibility owing to the discursive framework in which he placed them. In other words, Hine found a way to manipulate framing and cropping to carve out an aesthetic that was itself always already political and a politics shown to be always already aesthetic.

This remainder preserves an impenetrability that emerges as the crux of Hine's project. This irreducible trace is not a reinvestment of aura, which would be impossible by the time Hine was working, given the developments of the medium.[12] Nonetheless, this deliberate opacity or excess informs Hine's insistence on subjectivity in an industrial matrix expropriating the subject as object and achieving a form of dehumanization that rendered its laborers invisible, less than human.

Hine does not pose the question common to early twentieth-century photography: How can we gain access to the other via the medium of photography? Rather, having begun with an acknowledgment of the absence of any unmediated sight, the impossibility of vision unassisted by the frame, and concomitantly with a model of the subject unassisted by social, historical, and ideological framing devices, Hine asks after photography's ability to resist the objectifying gaze historically fundamental to industrial modernity and structurally fundamental to reification. Hine suggests that the person is only ever already the result of mediation, a mediation that must be renegotiated via a medium emerging as yet another form of mediation.

The political therefore lies in the endless renegotiation of the terms in which politics is staged and its subjects are determined. Politics exists when the hegemonic order is disrupted by those who have no part in the exercise of that power. I have argued that Hine established a formal idiom as singular as those of his contemporaries associated with a more apolitical and strictly aesthetic project, such as Edward Weston, Alfred Stieglitz, and Paul Strand. This idiom, in turn, was part of the construction of a historically specific subjectivity on which Hine's political aspirations rested. Hine did not simply rely on the presumed patency of the photographic document to bring the marginalized into visibility and thereby into representation. His work demonstrates the way in which he thought about how to construct and mediate this visibility through meticulous attention to issues of framing.

NOTES

1. See John Tagg, *The Burden of Representation: Essays on Photographies and Histories* (Minneapolis: University of Minnesota Press, 1993), pp. 195–96.
2. In *Regarding the Pain of Others* (New York: Picador, 2003), Susan Sontag has argued that images of suffering on continuous offer in a variety of media run the risk of numbing the viewer into a state of passive receptivity and a sense of helplessness in the face of world-historical events. The media exposure of suffering, Sontag claims, inadvertently begins to discourage engagement by overwhelming the viewer. While recent works, most notably Ariella Azoulay's extraordinary *The Civil Contract of Photography*, have critically addressed and argued against Sontag's points, I would speculate that Hine was aware of such a possibility and made a concerted effort to ward off any sense of the subjects he photographed as utterly victimized and incapable of asserting their own will to assist themselves.
3. Alan Sekula, "The Body and the Archive," in Richard Bolton (ed.), *The Contest of Meaning: Critical Histories of Photography* (Cambridge, MA: The MIT Press, 1989), pp. 343–89. The panopticism of the nineteenth-century photographic archive is also the premise of Tagg's *The Burden of Representation*.
4. Tagg, "Introduction," *The Burden of Representation*.
5. Tagg, *The Burden of Representation*, p. 195. Hine works with the problem of legibility in relation to materiality by emphasizing the mediating presence of the photographic frame that symbolizes ideological frames producing subjectivity in a given time and place. Internal frames double back to emphasize the medium's frame and, broadly, social frames as such.
6. Hine also worked for The Pittsburgh Survey, a sociological study of urban industrial life in the United States that took the city of Pittsburgh in 1907 and 1908 as representative of industrial centers in general. Paul Kellog, the project director, hoped to mobilize what he believed to be "scientific tools," an objective gaze in constructing an archival body of empirically verifiable evidence in the service of reformist legislation and corporate policy making in the region and nationally. He chose Pittsburgh because of the way it emblematized the intersection of several of modernity's negative effects: poverty, corporate greed, and the effects of industrialization on health and on the environment. Although Kellog never grasped the structural visual tactics that Hine employed in manipulating the possibilities of the photographic

medium to articulate a model of subjectivity through which to specify the otherwise abstract demographics on whose behalf he worked, Kellog's forward to one of the six volumes of The Pittsburgh Survey, entitled *Women and the Trades*, conducted by Elizabeth Beardsley Butler, evidences a similar desire to reintroduce the human into the mechanical forms of empirical information gathering. Kellog arrives at this inflection of the project—the wish to convey industry's dependence on human energy, rather than on machinery: "Yet there was human machinery, more delicate, more sensitive, of finer metal than his propeller shaft. And of this he [the engineer] was ignorant." Paul Kellog, "Director's Foreword," in Elizabeth Beardsley Butler, *Women and the Trades: Pittsburgh, 1907–1908* (Pittsburgh: University of Pittsburgh Press, 1984). Kellog participated in a logic that would insert the human into a broader machinery generative of efficient industrial production. At the same time, he emphasized the precariousness of the human, eager to remind the reader that laborers are entitled to be included in the category "human" and, as such, to protections and rights.

7. Judith Butler, *Giving an Account of Oneself* (New York: Fordham University Press, 2005), pp. 29–30.
8. See Judith Butler's discussion of "what counts as a livable life and a grievable death" in her introduction to *Precarious Life* (London: Verso, 2004), pp. xv–xxi.
9. On the problem of indexicality and the myth of facticity in nineteenth-century photography, see Carol M. Armstrong, *Scenes in a Library: Reading the Photograph in the Book, 1843–1875* (Cambridge, MA: The MIT Press, 1998). See also Molly Nesbit's discussion of the document as a guarantor of meaning in a positivist framework and simultaneously as the site of drainage of intrinsic meaning, placing it instead in context or discursive frame, in *Atget's Seven Albums* (New Haven: Yale University Press, 1992). Rosalind Krauss addresses the dependency of the photographic message on its placement in a discursive and institutional framework in "Photography's Discursive Spaces," in Bolton (ed.), *Contest of Meaning*, pp. 287–302.
10. Far from participating in "a new structure of documentation whose institutionalized effect was to reverse the political axis of representation, making it no longer a sign of power and prestige to be recorded but a sign of subjection," as John Tagg argues, Hine attempted to take a system that worked to guarantee subjection and carve a space for countersubjection within it. Tagg goes on to say that the "effect of this argument, of course, is to disrupt the liberal, reformist story of documentation, documentary, and the benevolent progress of truth." Tagg, *The Burden of Representation*, p. xxxi.
11. Tagg argues to the contrary: that Hine's work, although harnessed to an immediate project that sought to ameliorate conditions for the unrepresented—children, immigrants—ultimately participates in a structure of representation, of social documentary as evidentiary, that "appropriates dissent, and re-secures the threatened bonds of social consent" in his images of workers, on the one hand, while his images of women and children evidences a sense of disenchantment: "The others—children, women, immigrants from peasant economies—seemed entirely dependent upon enlightened reformers who might 'rescue' them. In themselves, these groups were represented as entirely helpless." *Ibid.*, p. 193.
12. Walter Benjamin attributes an effort to simulate auratic presence to some late nineteenth-century photographic portraiture. See Walter Benjamin, "Little History of Photography" (1931), trans. Edmund Jephcott and Kingsley Shorter, in Michael W. Jennings, Howard Eiland, and Gary Smith (eds.), *Selected Writings, Volume 2, 1927–1934* (Cambridge, MA: Harvard University Press, 1999), p. 517.

FIGURE 1 Gideon Mendel, AIDS educators, Hlabisa, South Africa, from *A Broken Landscape: HIV & AIDS in Africa* (Barcelona: Blume, 2001; courtesy of the artist).

Photojournalism, NGOs, and the New Media Ecology

Roger Hallas

The international success of Emmanuel Guibert and Didier Lefèvre's graphic novel *The Photographer: Into War-Torn Afghanistan with Doctors Without Borders*, which recounts Lefèvre's 1986 assignment to document a Médecins Sans Frontières field hospital in Soviet-occupied Afghanistan, has highlighted a well-established, but recently intensifying tendency in contemporary photographic practice: the collaboration between photojournalists and nongovernmental organizations.[1] Some more recent examples include Tim Hetherington's work with Human Rights Watch on the Liberian civil war, the Afghan photographer Zalmai's UN High Commissioner for Refugees project on the return of Afghan refugees, Sebastião Salgado's commission with the World Health Organization to document its global campaign to eradicate polio, and Amnesty International's collaboration with five photo agencies on a historical account of two decades of war and genocide in Darfur.[2]

The reasons for this increasing collaboration are multiple and complex. First of all, photographers, editors, and critics have argued for the past decade or more that photojournalism is in a state of crisis, in terms of both its ethics and its political economy. The critique of classical photojournalism, which began in the 1970s with the work of photographer-critics such as Martha Rosler and Allan Sekula, intensified in the following two decades, thus transforming how photojournalism is taught, practiced, and curated.[3] But even more significant than the demand for greater critical reflexivity are the economic, technological, and cultural transformations in our contemporary media ecology, especially the exploitation of new digital media, which have ushered swift and radical changes that many in the profession perceive as a fundamental crisis. Photographers and agencies have thus approached collaborations with NGOs as an important strategy in overcoming this crisis.

The new media ecology has also profoundly affected how NGOs communicate and advocate through media. As the established media institutions of twentieth-century mass media—specifically, national newspapers, news magazines, and broadcast news—lose their hegemony over news culture, NGOs must develop new strategies of media advocacy. As Meg McLagan explains in her analysis of the human rights organization WITNESS, the notion that NGOs' single most important communicative strategy must be to garner as much public attention to an issue by capturing and disseminating powerful images is now understood to be naive and, at times, potentially counterproductive.[4] NGOs such as WITNESS have shifted their organizational emphases from "documentation to strategic communication," which entails both exploiting the decentered social networking tools of Web 2.0 to "summon witnessing publics" and tailoring messages through "smart narrowcasting" to specific policy-making audiences.[5] In addition, as Yates McKee argues, NGOs have responded to the critical insights of visual studies and contemporary art practice over the past several decades by engaging in what Jacques Rancière calls "the politics of aesthetics."[6] This turn to aesthetics does not involve "mere ornamental embellishments layered on a set of preexisting political objectives or, in a slightly different register, as secondary means for the accomplishment of ends that would exist outside the sphere of means, mediacy, or media."[7] Rather, it is, in Rancière's words, "a delimitation of spaces and times, of the visible and the invisible, of speech and noise, that simultaneously determines the place and the stakes of politics as a form of experience."[8] Aesthetic techniques thus construct the frames within which politics may be constituted, not merely on the representational level of image texts produced by NGOs, but also in how they are produced, distributed, and used.

Here, I examine the collaboration of photojournalists and NGOs in a number of projects addressing the global AIDS pandemic, specifically, the work of South African photographer Gideon Mendel and the multimedia project *Access to Life*, which was produced by the Magnum Photos agency and the Global Fund to Fight AIDS, Tuberculosis and Malaria. Focusing on the global politics of HIV/AIDS proves particularly useful, because the imperatives of AIDS activists and AIDS-related NGOs were changing at precisely the time when the new media ecology was rapidly transforming public culture in the early twenty-first century. The development and approval of effective antiretroviral drugs (ARVs) against HIV brought about an increasing discourse of normalization concerning HIV/AIDS in the late 1990s in the Global North, where access to such antiretroviral treatment generally became standard care. The fight to provide ARVs for the Global South, where the pandemic was largest and fastest growing, invigorated and globalized AIDS activism, creating networks of solidarity and collaboration that necessarily transcended local and national struggles.[9] Global treatment activism increasingly framed its struggle with national governments, international agencies, and transnational pharmaceutical corporations in terms of the right to health as a universal human right. However, AIDS activists and NGOs faced a major communicative challenge countering the dominant iconography of "global AIDS," which continued to replicate the figure of the impoverished "AIDS victim" from earlier discourses of "African AIDS" in the 1980s, a trope deeply embedded in the ideological construction of the Third World as a site of intractable poverty, chronic hopelessness, and recurrent human disaster.

A cover story in the *New York Times Magazine* from January 2001 entitled "How to Solve the World AIDS Crisis" aptly demonstrates the enduring ideological hold of such iconography, even amid progressive discourse of the universal right to antiretroviral treatment.[10] While the article by Tina Rosenberg provided a well-researched analysis of the economic and geopolitical obstacles preventing the Global South from gaining affordable access to ARVs, the accompanying photojournalism persisted in a singular focus on the person with AIDS as hopeless, poverty-stricken victim. The front cover presented a high-contrast black-and-white photograph of an African man with AIDS close to death, while the first page of the article was accompanied by a photomontage of twenty emaciated "AIDS victims" from around the world, each identified only by their country. In replicating the dominant iconography of "global AIDS," this photo spread elided any attempt to visualize the tenacious local and global AIDS activism and the progressive institutional initiatives that the article actually describes and affirms.[11] Magnum and the Global Fund's *Access to Life* and Mendel's photographic projects demonstrate how aesthetic techniques—several of them afforded by the new media ecology—can reframe the discursive context in which a politics of "global AIDS" may be constituted.[12] Before I discuss these projects in detail, it is important to consider more closely the transformations in photojournalism that have facilitated these collaborations with NGOs.

PHOTOJOURNALISM IN CRISIS

Like "documentary," "photojournalism" is a widely used term that has never been pinned down to a single categorical definition. Photojournalism can be used to describe a profession, a practice, and a photographic form. Arguably, one of the most important conceptions of photojournalism has been the idea of the photographer as witness. Despite the incursion of postmodern skepticism about the truth value of photographic representation, this idea continues to pervade the discourses of photojournalists, critics, photographic historians, and educators.[13] Cornell Capa's concept of the "concerned photographer," which he coined for his now-legendary 1967 exhibition, illuminates the ambiguous position of the photographer-witness. This notion of concern points in two directions: to the objective validation of the photographer's perspective as outsider and to the subjective investment of the photographer's commitment to the plight of his or her subjects. This constitutive tension in fact derives from the very duality of the term "witness," which draws from two Latin roots: the *testis*, who is the third-party eyewitness observer, and the *superstes*, who is the embodied witness of the survivor.[14] Indeed, we may thus come to recognize the gendered discourse of the "heroic photojournalist" as the displacement of the witness-survivor from the photographed subject to the photographer himself.

In terms of approaching photojournalism as a specific medium, multiple definitions abound, even just among the magazine and newspaper editors who have long overseen the profession. Harold Evans, the former editor of the London *Sunday Times*, defined photojournalism merely as "pictures on a page," whereas Wilson Hicks, a photo editor at *Life* magazine, insisted that it constitutes the combination of "words and pictures." Dan Mich, another photo editor at *Life*'s lesser-known rival, *Look*, characterized photojournalism in far more precise terms as "storytelling . . . done by related pictures arranged in some form of continuity" and accompanied by subordinate text.[15] Moreover, some have defined photojournalism by attempting to differentiate it from other categories, such as press photography or documentary photography.[16] This endeavor is often an attempt to strengthen or weaken the cultural capital of photojournalism. In its complex combination of images (and text) in order to generate a narrative or argument, photojournalism is understood by some to exceed the allegedly illustrative function of the single press photograph. Conversely, the art world has often dismissively compared photojournalism with documentary photography in terms that pit information, commerce, and spectacle against critique, independence, and sobriety. Although we cannot ultimately disentangle photojournalism from the histories of documentary and the press, I concentrate my attention in this essay on the specific practices of photojournalism that produce photographic or picture essays.

Since the photo-essay develops an idea, narrative, or argument precisely through aesthetic techniques—namely, the combination, arrangement, and sequencing of its photographs and accompanying words—it potentially has much to benefit from the functional enhancement provided by multimedia software. The impact of such new digital media on photojournalism constitutes a process that media scholars Jay David Bolter and Richard Grusin have called "remediation." Bolter and Grusin argue that new media are best understood through the ways in which they "honor, rival, and revise" existing media forms. Moreover, they contend that "what is new about new media comes from the particular ways in which they refashion older media and the ways in which older media refashion themselves to answer the challenges of new media."[17] For example, video games have appropriated and reworked many conventions from narrative cinema, such as point-of-view shots, voice-overs, and continuity editing, while cinema has responded to video games by experimenting with nonlinear narratives, split screens, and shifts in representational form. This two-way conception of remediation focuses attention on the complex and interrelated dynamics of continuity and discontinuity at work in media transformation. It resists the tendencies of either a technological fetishism that uncritically champions any such change or a nostalgic skepticism that merely eulogizes the death of old media. The development of multimedia software such as Flash has permitted photojournalism to translate existing modes of presentation such as the slide show, the gallery wall display, the photo book, and the magazine spread into the digital environment. But it has also, more importantly, provided new functionalities, principally sound, moving images, and cinematic editing. Digital photojournalism thus remediates both print photojournalism and the documentary film. In fact, Bjarke Myrthu and Brian Storm, two of the pioneers of multimedia photojournalism, have both articulated its potential primarily in terms of creating a "cinematic" experience.[18]

To comprehend the specific aspects of such remediation fully, we need first to examine the institutional and economic context in which it is taking place. Photojournalism has undergone substantial transformations in the last several decades. News publications have increasingly outsourced more and more of their daily photographic needs to commercial photo agencies, which have also dwindled in number as the industry moves closer and closer toward a duopoly of Getty Images and Corbis. These two corporate giants have pushed through substantial changes in how photojournalists are paid and who owns the intellectual property of the photographs they take.[19] Furthermore, the shrinking advertising revenues of print media have massively reduced the purchasing power of photo editors, who are commissioning fewer and fewer photojournalist assignments and paying far less for the completed work than in previous decades. Digital technologies have changed not only photographic production, but also the mechanisms of delivery and sales. Massive online archives give customers immediate access through databases with tag-based search functions. Furthermore, amateur photographers armed with multimedia smart phones can now provide cheap and frequently free images of news events only seconds after they have been shot. Establishment news operations such as the BBC have increasingly turned to such sources of information and images in an attempt to offset the growing circulation of news through nontraditional circuits of communication such as Web 2.0 social networks. The impact of such citizen journalism on photojournalism has been both swift and deep.

Photojournalists have also felt squeezed out of contemporary media culture because of larger technological and cultural changes that antedate the digital revolution. As Liz Jobey points out about the transformation of photojournalism, "The changes were no different in degree from those that many other labour markets—print journalism included—have had to cope with. But what made them harder to bear in this case was that, in its purest sense, photojournalism was connected to the belief that it could improve the world."[20] The ascendency of television in the 1950s led to the waning of photojournalism's mass audience by the 1960s as that audience turned increasingly to television for access to current events. The emergence of a continual and instantaneous flow of twenty-four-hour news delivery on cable television in the 1980s was only amplified by the rise of news reporting on the Internet in the following decade. The visual and narrative complexities of images produced by photojournalism render them more and more incompatible with the demands of such omnipresent news flow. The rise of celebrity-driven publications such as *InStyle* and *People* has also had an effect across broad sections of news media, including the demise of *Life* magazine, the quintessential and much-loved icon of the postwar illustrated press, as well as the growing incursion of celebrity reporting in even the most serious-minded of news institutions.

Even at the fabled Magnum Photos agency, its select and prestigious members are increasingly having to turn to high-paying corporate work to finance their own "personal projects" of photojournalism, which circulate more and more in fine-art institutions rather than in news contexts. As Thomas Hoepker, former president of Magnum, has noted, the agency used to make 80 percent of its revenue from magazine work, whereas by 2003, 60 percent of its money came from fine-art sales.[21] But much of those sales come from Magnum's commercial exploitation of its massive archives, which include over four hundred thousand photographs. While there is a strong market for fine-art prints by classic Magnum photographers such as Robert Capa, Henri Cartier Bresson, Eve Arnold, and Elliott Erwitt, the work of many current Magnum photographers, such as Gilles Peress and Thomas Dworzak, has found less of a market in the art world, primarily due to their photographs' highly contemporary and thus deeply politicized subject matter. The turn to the art market has itself proven highly controversial among photojournalists, especially within Magnum, which has long sustained tensions between the discourses of fine art and social commitment.[22]

In light of these multifaceted transformations in the profession, many photojournalists are increasingly turning to NGOs for opportunities to work on new projects.[23] The funding structures for such projects are usually complex for two reasons. First, the NGOs are reluctant to divert their own funds away from direct aid. Thus, most of these projects are funded through sponsorship from private foundations and corporations. The collaboration between a renowned photographer or agency and a well-regarded NGO can synergize the reputation of each party, creating "a kind of gravity that attracts further collaborators, often from the business or private sector."[24] Second, the projects rely on synergistic modes of promotion and distribution, tying together web-based presentations, newspaper and magazine publications, book publications, and gallery exhibitions. The kind of support that NGOs can provide photojournalists varies greatly, ranging from fully paid commissions to cover an emergent crisis to assistance in providing access to and security within a particular place. In return for such logistical support, NGOs usually negotiate permission for exclusive use of a number of photographs for a limited period of time. Photojournalists also highly value the deep knowledge that NGOs have of the environments and events they are interested in shooting. NGOs, in turn, benefit from access to high-quality documentation of their work and their causes, as well as from the cultural capital accrued from the authorial or brand-name recognition of the photographer or agency. NGO campaigns often incorporate such brand value into the branding of the campaign itself through the development of a graphic identity that resonates with aesthetics of the particular photographer(s) involved.[25] Since newspaper and magazine publications are still eager to publish photojournalism, but not willing to fund the initial assignments, photographers can now turn their former primary market into a secondary market. In his twenty-year commitment to documenting HIV/AIDS, photographer Gideon Mendel has built up not only long-standing relationships with a wide range of NGOs, but also an adept capacity to position his work in both traditional and emergent venues for photojournalism.

GIDEON MENDEL: FROM PHOTOJOURNALISM TO VISUAL ACTIVISM

A self-taught photojournalist who began his work within the so-called "struggle photography" of the late apartheid years in South Africa, Gideon Mendel has been documenting the HIV/AIDS pandemic in southern and eastern Africa since the early 1990s. His interest in the AIDS pandemic began in 1990, when he was assigned by his British photo agency, Network Photographers, to a project documenting people living with HIV in the UK, titled *Positive Lives: Responses to HIV—A Photodocumentary*.[26] The agency subsequently sent him in 1993 to document the impact of AIDS at the Matibi Mission Hospital in rural Zimbabwe. When the exhibition of *Positive Lives* traveled to the South African National Gallery (SANG) in Cape Town that same year to help stimulate local media interest in the pandemic, its British NGO sponsor, the Terence Higgins Trust, provided funds for Mendel to document local responses to the pandemic at a time when little of the South African AIDS crisis was being documented either by the press or in photojournalism. His award-winning photography on HIV/AIDS has subsequently circulated in a range of publications around the world, including the *Guardian* (UK), the *Mail and Guardian* (South Africa), *National Geographic*, MSNBC's website, numerous books, and publications produced by NGOs such as Action AID, Médecins Sans Frontières, and the Global Fund.[27]

A Broken Landscape: HIV and AIDS in Africa, his 2001 book publication, which collects eight years of his work on the subcontinent, reveals the profound influence of his earlier years within struggle photography.[28] The black-and-white photographs engender a particular mode of politicized realism in which the brutality of suffering and the power of collective organizing are rendered through a high-contrast documentary aesthetic. They frequently capture the kind of poignant scene that Henri Cartier-Bresson famously described as "the decisive moment" in photography: "the simultaneous recognition, in a fraction of a second, of the significance of an event as well as the precise organization of forms which gives that event its proper expression."[29] For example, the photograph titled *AIDS Educators. Hlabisa, South Africa* captures a fleeting moment of the intersection of multiple gazes upon the condom demonstration in the foreground of the image (see fig. 1). Framed most prominently in the center of the photograph, the gaze of Jabu Shezi, a young female AIDS educator, becomes our principal focus of attention as she looks upon the demonstration along with the other women behind her. Her testimonial text on the facing page of the book explains how she became an AIDS educator: "A nurse spoke to me and asked whether I wanted to see other people with HIV, so that I would not be alone with this disease. Six of us met at Hlabisa hospital. We found that we gained strength just from knowing each other. I was trained as an AIDS educator with the other members of the group."[30] The design of the book challenges the hegemony of the image within photojournalism through the prominence granted to the testimonial texts, which always precede the images and which are given equal visual emphasis in the layout of the book. Such texts specify, individualize, and give voice to the documentary subjects in the frames. This text further narrativizes an already narratively rich image, fleshing out both its individual and social context. Jabu's husband, Jaconia, appears on the next page spread, which allows both Jabu and Jaconia not only to be named, individualized documentary subjects, but to appear as people embedded in social relationships and networks that the project explicitly recognizes and foregrounds. The significance of these strategies should not be underestimated in a contemporary context where the "victim tradition" of documentary representation, to borrow Brian Winston's phrase, continues to present documentary subjects as anonymous embodiments of social and political disasters or metonyms of the human condition.[31]

As with *Positive Lives, A Broken Landscape* also produced a touring exhibition. When it came to SANG in 2002, Mendel collaborated with the institution and the

Treatment Action Campaign (TAC), South Africa's leading AIDS activist organization, to produce what he called "a live documentary space" in which people living with HIV/AIDS could be actively involved in the political and aesthetic processes of representation, rather than merely be their subjects.[32] The exhibition integrated the monochrome photographs of *A Broken Landscape* with four other elements: a new color photographic series of portraits in which Mendel invited his subjects to determine how they were framed by the camera; memory boxes made by HIV-positive women who fill them with objects and photographs by which they wish their children to remember them; a notice board for displaying testimonies, community notices, press clippings, visitor comments, and new photographs taken by Mendel during the course of the exhibition; and a website that updated documentation of the exhibition on a daily basis. This explicit politicization of the exhibit and the institutional gallery space was particularly important at that historical moment—when AIDS had quickly become the "new struggle" in South Africa as activists fought the AIDS denialism of Thabo Mbeki's government, specifically, its refusal to provide HIV-positive pregnant women with antiretrovirals to prevent mother-to-child transmission.[33] At the book launch for *A Broken Landscape* at SANG in June 2002, Supreme Court Justice Edwin Cameron's opening remarks gained national media attention:

> The acts and words of the deniers for some time paralysed our national response to the epidemic. They confused our planning and befuddled our strategies. They confounded our insights, sapped our energies and dispirited our determination to act. And most significantly, they silenced all too many voices amongst those who are experiencing the epidemic in their own bodies and their own families and in their own communities. The deniers re-created shame, and re-imposed silence, in an epidemic where the struggle for twenty years has been to create voices and to defeat shame.[34]

Mendel's new color portrait series in the show addressed this question of giving voice raised in Cameron's speech by reframing of the relationship between photographer and documentary subject of AIDS representation. Mendel had developed a new mode of portraiture in Mozambique on September 11, 2001, then had continued it with TAC on his return to South Africa. Oxfam had arranged for him to take portraits of members of a local AIDS organization in rural Mozambique, but when it became clear that the photographs would be used locally in HIV awareness campaigns, the members of the group raised serious concerns about disclosure and confidentiality in a social context in which the stigma of infection was very high. Forced to rethink the assignment, Mendel pulled out some black duct tape, created a rudimentary rectangular frame on a bare blue wall, and asked the members of the group to think of the rectangle as their frame and to consider how they might want to fill it. He would return a few days later and photograph whatever they put in the frame. He asked only that they tell him their reasons for what they chose to place, or not to place, in the frame. Words consequently became as significant as the image itself. As Mendel himself admits, he had inadvertently empowered his subjects on two levels: by handing over a substantial degree of power to frame their visual representation and by giving them a voice to bear witness to their experience and the conditions of their own social visibility as a person living with HIV/AIDS.[35] These portraits perform a variety of different relationships with visibility: some subjects chose to obscure their face or place it outside of the frame, while others extend a hand into the frame holding an object, such as HIV medication or a mobile phone. Many present themselves proudly and defiantly in the center of the frame, returning the camera's gaze.

In one of the portraits, titled *Anonymous (member of Kindlimuka): Maputo, Mozambique*, the duct-tape frame remains empty; nothing has been placed before it. The accompanying testimonial text reads:

> I do not want to be alone within this frame. I would like to leave my space empty because there are so many who should be joining me. So I wish to use this opportunity to dedicate this empty frame to all the people on this continent who are living with HIV or AIDS—although many don't know it. I would also like to fill this frame with the millions of orphans who will have to grow up without their parents. I want to leave this frame open for all those who are tormented by the fear of stigma, those who have been abandoned or isolated, those suffering discrimination from their family, friends, colleagues, and those suffering from lack of money to buy drugs or food. This frame is for those who lost their loved ones in silence. This frame is also for all the ones who care.[36]

This image-text moves between the two modes of bearing witness that Paul Farmer describes in *Pathologies of Power: Health, Human Rights, and the New War on the Poor*.[37] The first mode aims to break the imposed silence on the suffering of the poor and disenfranchised. It is the notion of giving voice to those who have been denied any opportunity to speak. The second mode, Farmer argues, is "a more freighted form of knowing," a "second silence" that he argues is worth maintaining, for it helps to mitigate against the "victim tradition" and the spectacle of pain within the documentary representation of suffering.[38] There is a visual silence in this photograph, an act of resistance and refusal as powerful as the act of stepping into the frame and being seen.

These images subsequently circulated globally in print and web publications under the title *Looking AIDS in the Face* and locally in South Africa under the title *Treatment Access*, reproduced as large canvas prints that were used in community spaces and carried as banners in TAC demonstrations. As Mendel began to identify more as "a visual activist than a photojournalist" during this period, his photographic practice demonstrated more and more flexibility as it moved across local, national, and global contexts, embedding itself within a range of media technologies, from web pages, to print articles, to canvas posters.[39] This mobility of his images thus mirrored the social mobilization of TAC, which similarly operated on local, national, and global levels.[40]

THE HARSH DIVIDE: REMEDIATING THE PANORAMA

In the dynamics between its testimonial and visual aspects, the *Looking AIDS in the Face* treatment campaign would lay the foundation for Mendel's initial experimentation with digital multimedia after he joined the Corbis Images agency in 2003. Brian Storm, a commissioning editor at Corbis and a fervent advocate of the use of sound by photojournalists, encouraged Mendel to experiment with sound and provided some seed money and audio equipment for *The Harsh Divide*, his subsequent project, another collaboration with TAC about the need for and viability of antiretroviral treatment programs in South African townships. Mendel's former assistant, Guilhem Alandry, had gotten him interested in experimenting with the panoramic images that could be produced with Quicktime VR software. With Alandry's training, Mendel traveled to Khayelitsha, a township outside Cape Town where Médecins Sans Frontières had initiated the first pilot antiretroviral program in South Africa. Mendel initially intended to contrast the lives of one HIV-positive TAC member in treatment with a member who was not in the program. This plan changed once the local TAC chapter insisted that far more people be represented in the project, both individually and collectively.[41] On two trips to Khayelitsha, Mendel made numerous sound recordings and panoramic image sets, which require the use of a single-lens-reflex camera mounted on a special tripod that allows it to take the eighteen vertical shots needed for one 360-degree panoramic photograph. On returning to London, Mendel realized the larger potential of the project and brought in filmmaker Tessa Lewin and web designer Andy Brockie to help him and Alandry develop the project for a number of different media platforms. *The Harsh Divide* was subsequently realized as a series of short films for Channel 4 in the UK, a video installation in several group exhibitions, photo essays for the *Guardian* (UK) and the *Mail and Guardian* (South Africa), an interactive microsite on the *Guardian* website, and a series of archival fine-art prints (see color plates).

Mendel is not alone among photojournalists in developing multimedia projects that come to be realized across several different media platforms. In the same year as *The Harsh Divide*, Mendel's Corbis colleague Ed Kashi produced *Aging in*

America as a microsite for MSNBC,[42] a book, a documentary video, and a set of archival fine-art prints. Kashi's project exemplifies the kind of conventional remediation of documentary film that has become standard practice for mainstream news sites such as MSNBC and the *New York Times*. The website for *Aging in America* performs a seamless montage of sound, text, and image through dissolves, intertitles, and voice-overs. Although the site realizes the database logic of new media through the nonlinear option of the sidebar menu organized thematically, once you start a section, the software will automatically roll over into the next section if you take no action when the first selected section ends. The linear and integrative logic of documentary film returns. As accomplished and complex as the images and narration are, such remediation of documentary film produces a comparatively passive user.

By contrast, Mendel's microsite for *The Harsh Divide*, which the *Guardian* renamed Salvation Is Cheap, consistently demands interactive engagement by its viewer.[43] The site is structured as a horizontal scroll in which you can navigate left or right. In addition, a numbered database of the pages of the site is permanently visible at the bottom of the screen, allowing you to jump to any page of the site. Each page presents a photographic frame that permits horizontal navigation of a 360-degree panoramic image alongside written testimony of the subject in the frame and a media player that permits the viewer to listen to the voice of the documentary subject. As you move through the different numbered images, you begin to recognize a narrative progression. The earliest panoramas present courageous individuals in their homes with their families as they struggle to survive without medication. These then give way to group portraits at a memorial ceremony, in a health clinic, and at a TAC meeting. The final panoramas present people whose lives and health have substantially improved due to their access to antiretrovirals in the pilot program. The narrative telos becomes apparent: from courage, to collective mobilization, to treatment.

Although panoramic photography has been used for documentary purposes since the nineteenth century, Quicktime VR, with its navigable functionality, has largely been overlooked by photojournalists and other documentarists. Outside of contemporary new-media art, its most common application has been within the tourist and real estate markets, where it produces virtual panoramas of cityscapes and virtual tours of hotels and luxury homes for sale. As media historian Oliver Grau contends, the panorama has a long history as a medium that generates a visual experience that is illusory and increasingly immersive. However, Mendel's use of the panoramic capabilities of Quicktime VR is not wholly subsumed into an immersive logic, but instead exemplifies the tension between immediacy and hypermediacy that consistently structures the logic of new digital media, according to Bolter and Grusin. Whereas immediacy frames a medium in terms of a transparency that disavows the very act of mediation, hypermediacy emphasizes the density and complexity of mediation.

Mendel's panoramas do produce several elements of immediacy. They provide the user with the perspectival sensation of standing in the space of the township. The cursor control facilitates a virtual mobilized gaze that further enhances the illusory and immersive effect of the image. Moreover, users are given time to explore the space at their own pace. But the aspects of hypermediacy are, I would argue, even more emphatically embedded in the structure of the site. The size and shape of the panoramic frames vary, but they are always elements within the larger frame of the scroll-like visual design of the site. The virtual mobilized gaze of the panorama is consciously produced by the tactile interaction of the user with the cursor controls. The time that users have to explore the space depicted in the image also allows them to become aware of their ability to frame and reframe the image on the screen. But perhaps most importantly, and unlike most multimedia photojournalism, Salvation Is Cheap maintains a clear separation of sound and image functionality. The interactive invitation to "Start" the panoramic functionality of the image is distinct from the "Start" function of the sound file. In a kind of Brechtian separation of the elements, the testimonial voice and text supplement not just the image, but also each other. Their redundancy does not lessen their testimonial effectiveness, but rather pushes users to be more active in their engagement with the work. Thus, the tension between immediacy and hypermediacy in Salvation Is Cheap becomes crucial to fostering a mediated ethical encounter between user and documentary subject. The multimedia aspects of the work provide a powerful sense of the presence of both the user and the subject, but the encounter is self-consciously understood to be produced by the user's active response to the address of the interface.[44]

In sum, Salvation Is Cheap remediates a highly spatialized technology of vision within new-media software that permits the user varying degrees of interactive navigation. Yet rather than enhance the presumed transparency and completeness of the visual evidence that these images constitute, such spatial navigation of the images potentially pushes the user to recognize their degrees of opacity and partiality. The image fails to give us the full picture—the totalizing perception that its technology promised. Moreover, it begs us to acknowledge the magnitude that exceeds the images, texts, and voices made available to our interactive engagement.

The significance and value of Mendel's collaborative work with NGOs lies precisely in the adaptability of this practice both to the changing role of photojournalism within the continually shifting media ecology of our globalized present and to the exigency of the local, where his images become embedded within community-organized initiatives on HIV prevention and treatment. Moreover, Mendel's commitment to producing images that function in the context of "visual activism" on the local level challenges one of the most enduring shibboleths of photojournalism—that the primary function of the profession must be to bring the suffering of the world into the public gaze, that is, that the camera acts as the world's witness.

ACCESS TO LIFE: THE FRAME OF AESTHETICS/THE AESTHETICS OF THE FRAME

The *Access to Life* project also challenges the foundational conception of photojournalism, but from quite a different angle, namely, the use of photojournalism by NGOs in forms of strategic communication. Recognizing the need to produce visual documentation of its rapidly expanding antiretroviral treatment programs against HIV/AIDS around the world, the Global Fund launched an open submission process in 2007 to select a photographic agency to document the successes and challenges of its programs in resource-poor countries. On winning the commission, Magnum managing director Mark Lubell convinced the Global Fund to seek external funding to develop the project into a multimedia campaign that would send eight of its photographers to nine different countries around the world to document people living with HIV/AIDS before and four months after their antiretroviral treatment began.[45] The photographers included some of the agency's biggest current stars, several of whom took the assignments in order to return to countries in which they had previously worked: Jonas Bendiksen (Haiti), Jim Goldberg (India), Paolo Pellegrin (Mali), Alex Majoli (Russia), Gilles Peress (Rwanda), Eli Reed (Peru), Larry Towell (South Africa and Swaziland), and Steve Curry (Vietnam). With a budget close to $1.4 million, the project subsequently produced a travelling exhibition, a book publication, numerous print and online feature articles, and a dedicated website of Flash photo essays. The strategic launch of each element of the campaign sought to maximize its impact. The exhibition debuted at the Corcoran Gallery in Washington, D.C., in June 2008, shortly before the U.S. Senate was scheduled to vote on renewing the President's Emergency Plan for AIDS Relief (PEPFAR), which the House of Representatives had approved earlier in the year.[46] The exhibition then subsequently opened at the International AIDS Conference in Mexico City in August and on World AIDS Day in Paris. Given the high priority for retaining global health-funding commitments in the aftermath of the economic crisis, the Global Fund launched the book in Italy during the G8 Summit in July 2009 by presenting each of the G8 leaders with a copy.

The Global Fund understood the audience of the campaign to be twofold. It was primarily to address politicians and policy makers, given that 75 percent of the organization's funding came from national governments. The general public constituted a secondary, but significant audience, since domestic public pressure is often a crucial factor in getting national governments to commit funding to global inequity issues such as poverty, education, and health. Rather than devote its principal effort to generating the broadest possible public consciousness of the issue through the traditional avenues of photojournalism (that is, news publication), the project exploited the shifting economy of photojournalism by maximizing the substantial brand value of the Magnum agency in the art world. Carla Bruni-Sarkozy's decision to become a spokesperson for the Global Fund after visiting the *Access to Life* exhibition in Paris demonstrated to the organization that the high-art cultural realm could provide an effective alternative route to accessing policy makers and their networks of influence. Lubell acknowledges the reciprocal benefits of Magnum's collaboration with the Global Fund: the agency accesses new sources of project funding, in part thereby replacing vanishing press commissions while the NGO benefits from the brand value of the agency's aesthetic reputation and editorial respectability. The former helped to place the stories of *Access to Life* in media outlets such as *Time* and MSNBC, which can justify featuring a story produced by an external party due to the aesthetic framing of its production by Magnum photographers.

Although each photo essay addresses the specificities of the pandemic in each national context and articulates the particular visual style of each individual photographer, together, the essays retain three key continuities. First, they all focus on a small number of individual stories; second, they incorporate the voices of their photographed subjects on the sound track, with subtitled translations appearing over the photographs; and third, they intercut between photographs and video footage of their subjects. Combined with many of the essays' frequent attention to frames (both internal and external to the image), this oscillation between stasis and movement produces an unsettling self-consciousness about the dynamics of representation. The project exhibition would create a similar effect in real space through several curatorial strategies, including mixing radically different print sizes, integrating flat-screen video into photographic wall displays, and experimenting with unconventional display methods, such as Jim Goldberg laying a scroll of photographs across a table and onto the floor (fig. 2).

Larry Towell's photo essay on HIV treatment in Swaziland exemplifies the project's recurrent self-conscious concern with the process of representation.[47] The essay opens with color video footage of a rural highway shot from the front passenger seat of a moving vehicle. The image dissolves to monochrome video and then to a black-and-white panoramic photograph of a man carrying a child across a gateway on the road. These images provide visual tropes of travel, entrance, and arrival. The secondary frame provided by the vehicle's windshield registers Towell's

FIGURE 2 *Access to Life* (2008), installation, Corcoran Gallery of Art, Washington, D.C. (courtesy of Magnum Photos).

and our position as outsiders looking through an aperture. Framing becomes a central visual strategy of the essay, inscribed in the use of multiple images within the frame, the repeated focus on the photograph of mother and child hanging on the wall in Siphiwe Tfumbatsi's home, the preoccupation with doorways and apertures in the photographs, and the persistent reframing movement of the video footage. Towell's voice-over, which opens and closes the essay, functions as a testimonial frame, providing both contextualizing exposition of Swaziland's AIDS crisis and insight into his photographic practice. At the end of the essay, he concludes: "As a human being I'm really much more interested in the patient's emotional state of mind, in their quality of life and in their reasons for living, especially their reasons for living. Because I was given that rare honor of being part of that. So that's really what the pictures are all about." Although Towell's voice-over bookends the recorded voices of the photographic subjects who make up the majority of verbal testimony in the essay, the decision to subtitle Towell's voice-over mitigates the discursive privilege and naturalization of the photographer's voice, drawing it into the same doubling structure of speech and text that frames the voice of his photographic subjects.

The combination of still photographs and voice-over testimony has long been a staple strategy of documentary film, normally performed through the so-called

"Ken Burns effect," which uses camera movement to animate the still photograph. The visual movement of pans and zooms adds a temporal dynamic to the photograph, thus facilitating the tight suture of voice and image. In this way, documentary film forces the photograph to displace stasis with movement. Towell's multimedia essay, however, resists such dynamic alignment, preferring instead to fracture and multiply the temporalities of sound, image, and text. Towell combines in a single frame still photographs and moving images of Siphiwe shot during the same period. The movement of the video image unsettles the stasis of the photographic image, but the reverse is equally true. Each haunts the other as its uncanny double, implying the representational limit of each. Towell's essay thus doubles both words and images, not in the service of a deconstructive critique of photojournalism, but rather as something closer to Trinh T. Minh-ha's notion of "speaking nearby." In contrast to the representational positions of "speaking about," "speaking for," or "speaking as," Trinh champions "speaking nearby" as "a speaking that does not objectify, does not point to an object as if it is distant from the speaking subject or absent from the speaking place. A speaking that reflects on itself and can come very close to a subject without, however, seizing or claiming it. A speaking in brief, whose closures are only moments of transition opening up to other possible moments of transition."[48]

CONCLUSION

Collaborations between photojournalists and NGOs will continue to grow for economic, political, and practical reasons. Like other long-established institutions of media culture, photojournalism still finds the new media ecology difficult to monetize directly, thus making NGO support and collaboration in all its various forms all the more important. But the new media ecology has also engendered new possibilities for aesthetic experimentation, as I illustrated in my discussion of *The Harsh Divide* and the *Access to Life* projects. Such aesthetics of politics build as much upon the limits, aporias, and silences of representation as they do upon its differing capacities to render visible and give voice. As Magnum photographer Paolo Pellegrin contends, "It's about asking questions, really. I'm interested in unfinished work, work that leaves space open for the viewer. There is very good photography that doesn't allow that because it's too composed, advocating for one point of view. For me, it's never clear. It's much more complex."[49] Thus, as NGOs develop increasingly sophisticated visual strategies, they find more common ground with many photojournalists in the profession, such as Pellegrin, Mendel, and Towell, who are questioning both the specific visual styles of classical photojournalism and its abiding assumptions about the profession's political functions and ethical values.

NOTES

1. Emmanuel Guibert and Didier Lefèvre, *The Photographer: Into War-Torn Afghanistan with Doctors Without Borders*, trans. Alexis Siegel (New York: First Second, 2009).
2. Tim Hetherington, *Long Story Bit By Bit: Liberia Retold* (Brooklyn: Umbrage, 2009); Zalmai, *Return, Afghanistan* (New York: Aperture, 2005); Sebastião Salgado, *The End of Polio: A Global Effort to End a Disease* (New York: Bulfinch Press, 2003); Leora Kahn (ed.), *Darfur: Twenty Years of War and Genocide in Sudan* (Brooklyn: Powerhouse, 2008).
3. See Martha Rosler, "In, Around, and Afterthoughts (On Documentary Photography)," originally published in 1981, reprinted in *The Contest of Meaning*, ed. Richard Bolton (Cambridge, MA: The MIT Press, 1989), pp. 303–41; Allan Sekula, "Dismantling Modernism: Reinventing Documentary" (1978), reprinted in Allan Sekula, *Photography against the Grain* (Halifax: The Press of Nova Scotia College of Art and Design, 1985), pp. 53–76.
4. Meg McLagan, "The Architecture of Strategic Communication: A Profile of WITNESS," in Michel Feher (ed.), with Gaëlle Krikorian and Yates McKee, *Nongovernmental Politics* (New York: Zone Books, 2007), pp. 318–25.
5. *Ibid*. Web 2.0 refers to the development on Internet applications that transform the World Wide Web from a platform for the dissemination and passive reception of information by making possible information sharing, collaboration, and the interoperability and user-centered design of websites.
6. Yates McKee, "'Eyes and Ears': Aesthetics, Visual Culture, and the Claims of Nongovernmental Politics," in Feher (ed.), *Nongovernmental Politics*, p. 329.
7. *Ibid*.
8. Jacques Rancière, *The Politics of Aesthetics*, trans. Gabriel Rockhill (London: Continuum, 2004), p. 21, quoted in *ibid*.
9. For an activist perspective on these transformations, see Alexander Irwin, Joyce Millen, and Dorothy Fallows, *Global AIDS: Myths and Facts* (Boston: South End Press, 2003); and the documentary, *Pills Profits Protest: Chronicle of the Global Aids Movement*, by Anne-Christine d'Adesky, Shanti Avirgan, and Ann T. Rossetti (Outcast Films, 2005).
10. Tina Rosenberg, "How to Solve the World AIDS Crisis," *New York Times Magazine*, January 28, 2001, pp. 26–31, 52, 58–63.
11. For more discussion of these contradictions in relation to documentary films about global AIDS, see Roger Hallas, "The 'Face' of AIDS: Commodity Compassion and the Global Pandemic," in Amy Schrager Lang and Cecelia Tichi (eds.), *What Democracy Is Like: A New Critical Realism for a Post-Seattle World* (New Brunswick: Rutgers University Press, 2005), pp. 88–101.
12. In my *Reframing Bodies*, I argue that discursive and aesthetic processes of reframing have been central to the complex acts of witnessing performed by queer AIDS media. See Roger Hallas, *Reframing Bodies: AIDS, Bearing Witness, and the Queer Moving Image* (Durham: Duke University Press, 2009).
13. As one popular photojournalism textbook asserts, "Photography, as witness to history, gives testimony in the court of public opinion. Photojournalists are the bearers of that witness." Howard Chapnick, *Truth Needs No Ally: Inside Photojournalism* (Columbia: University of Missouri Press, 1994), p. 13.
14. See Giorgio Agamben, *Remnants of Auschwitz: The Witness and the Archive*, trans. Daniel Heller-Roazen (New York: Zone Books, 1999), p. 17.

15. All quotes from Mary Panzer, "Introduction," *Things as They Are: Photojournalism in Context Since 1955* (New York: Aperture Foundation, 2005), p. 9.
16. See Martin Parr and Gerry Badger, *The Photobook: A History*, vol. 1 (London: Phaidon, 2004), pp. 117–23.
17. Jay David Bolter and Richard Grusin, *Remediation: Understanding New Media* (Cambridge, MA: The MIT Press, 1999), p. 15.
18. See Bjarke Myrthu, "Magnum In Motion: The Philosophy behind the Story," Magnum Photos, http://blog.magnumphotos.com/2007/10/magnum_in_motion_the_philosophy_behind_the_story.html; and Brian Storm, "About MediaStorm," http://mediastorm.org/about.
19. See Glen Mutel, "Picture Pac-Men," *Campaign*, July 29, 2005, p. 29, http://www.campaignlive.co.uk/news/488748/Photography-Picture-Pac-Men.
20. Liz Jobey, "In the Age of Celebrity Journalism," *New Statesmen*, May 30, 1997, p. 42.
21. Peter Lennon, "Magnum Force," *The Guardian*, July 31, 2003, p. 12.
22. See Gerry Badger, "Mission Impossible: 60 Years of Magnum," *Aperture* 187 (Summer 2007), pp. 68–83. These tensions notoriously erupted in 2003 over the $15,000 sale of Luc Delahaye's large-scale photograph *Taliban Soldier* (2001) in a New York art gallery. The combination of the photograph's content, scale, price, and exhibition context radically unsettled the categories of both photojournalism and photographic art. Shortly after the controversy, Delahaye left the Magnum agency and began to disidentify his work with the practice of photojournalism.
23. See Edgar Allen Beem, "The State of the Art Report: Photojournalism Survival" *Photo District News*, August 2008, pp. 34–39; David Walker, "How NGOs Work with Photographers: Doctors Without Borders," *PDN Online*, September 16, 2009, available (subscription required) at http://www.pdnonline.com/pdn/content_display/features/pdn-online/e3i813900b0f9f5febdea6d048210332c6e; Conor Risch, "How NGOs Work with Photographers: Human Rights Watch," *PDN Online*, September 17, 2009, available (subscription required) at http://www.pdnonline.com/pdn/content_display/esearch/e3i59191706a17f2192ef516ba218f6a900.
24. Judith Gelman Myers, "NGOs to the Rescue," *American Photo*, May–June 2007, p. 91.
25. For a discussion of branding in such campaigns, see Meg McLagan, "Human Rights, Testimony, and Transnational Publicity," in Feher (ed.), *Nongovernmental Politics*, pp. 311–15.
26. Stephen Mayes and Lyndall Stein (eds.), *Positive Lives: Responses to HIV—A Photodocumentary* (New York: Cassell, 1993).
27. Mendel's awards include the Eugene Smith Award for Humanistic Photography in 1996 and the Amnesty International Media Award for Photojournalism in 2003.
28. Gideon Mendel, *A Broken Landscape: HIV and AIDS in Africa* (Barcelona: Blume, 2001).
29. Henri Cartier-Bresson, *The Decisive Moment* (New York: Simon and Schuster, 1952), n.p.
30. Mendel, *A Broken Landscape*, p. 152.
31. Brian Winston, *Claiming the Real: The Documentary Film Revisited* (London: British Film Institute, 1995), pp. 40–47.
32. Gideon Mendel, quoted in Marilyn Martin. "HIV/AIDS in South Africa: Can the Visual Arts Make a Difference?" in Kyle D. Kauffman and David L. Lindauer (eds.), *AIDS and South Africa: The Social Expression of a Pandemic* (Houndmills, UK: Palgrave Macmillan, 2004), p. 124.
33. See Steven Robbins, "'Long Live Zackie, Long Live': AIDS, Activism, Science and Citizenship after Apartheid," *Journal of Southern African Studies* 30.3 (2004), pp. 651–72.
34. "Remarks by Mr Justice Edwin Cameron, Supreme Court of Appeal," TAC E-Newsletter, June 25, 2002, available at http://www.tac.org.za/newsletter/2002/ns25_06_2002.txt.

35. Gideon Mendel, personal interview, February 27, 2006.
36. This image-text was reproduced in Gideon Mendel, "Looking AIDS in the Face," *Virginia Quarterly Review* 82.1 (Winter 2006), p. 51.
37. Paul Farmer. *Pathologies of Power: Health, Human Rights, and the New War on the Poor* (Berkeley: University of California Press, 2003), pp. 25–28.
38. *Ibid*., p. 25.
39. Gideon Mendel, personal interview, February 27, 2006.
40. Steven Robbins summarizes: "TAC's mode of social mobilisation operated at a number of levels: global, national and local. At the global level, it challenged the intellectual property regime and drug pricing protocols and regulations imposed by the pharmaceutical industry; at the national level, it posed a fundamental challenge to the South African government's AIDS treatment policies; at the local level, it mobilised working-class black communities, creating the conditions for the articulation of forms of health/biological citizenship as well as new gendered identities and subjectivities that challenged 'traditional' and patriarchal ideas and practices." Robbins, "'Long Live Zackie, Long Live,'" p. 671.
41. Gideon Mendel, personal interview, February 27, 2006.
42. See http://www.msnbc.msn.com/id/29055812.
43. Gideon Mendel, "Salvation Is Cheap," *The Guardian*, October 18, 2003, http://www.guardian.co.uk/flash/mendel.swf.
44. Although Mendel has not used Quicktime VR in his subsequent projects, he has continued to experiment with the separation of elements within a new-media platform. For example, *Eight Women, One Voice*, his web project for ActionAid's G8 campaign in 2006, included regular panoramic photographs, Quicktime video files, and sound files of music and voice, as well as written testimony—all given their own functionality within the interface.
45. Mark Lubell, personal interview, June 5, 2009. My account of the conception and production of the project is drawn from Lubell's comments in this interview. The principal funding for the project came from Hewlett-Packard, Chevron, the Rockefeller Foundation, the Ford Foundation, and Friends of the Global Fund.
46. Every U.S. Senator was personally invited to the opening of the exhibition on June 14, 2008. A month later, the Senate voted to renew PEPFAR with a five-year commitment of $48 billion, including $2 billion allocated to the Global Fund for the following year.
47. Larry Towell, Swaziland, http://inmotion.magnumphotos.com/essay/access-life-swaziland. The project's dedicated website on the Global Fund's server is now defunct.
48. Nancy N. Chen and Trinh T. Minh-ha, "Speaking Nearby," in Lucien Taylor (ed.), *Visualizing Theory: Selected Essays from V.A.R., 1990–1994* (New York: Routledge, 1994), p. 443.
49. Paolo Pellegrin, quoted in Edgar Allen Beem, "Towards a New Language of Photojournalism," *Photo District News*, August 2008, p. 38.

PART TWO

DISOBEDIENT BODIES, CIRCULATING IMAGES, ARCHIVAL TRACES

Demonstrators hold giant replica textbooks as they protest outside the University of London, on December 9, 2010, as thousands of students prepare to take part in protests against government proposals to let universities triple tuition fees (photo: Leon Neal/AFP/Getty Images).

Bodies in Alliance and the Politics of the Street

Judith Butler

In the last months there have been, time and again, mass demonstrations on the street, in the square, and though these are very often motivated by different political purposes, something similar happens: bodies congregate, they move and speak together, and they lay claim to a certain space as public space. Now, it would be easier to say that these demonstrations or, indeed, these movements, are characterized by bodies that come together to make a claim in public space, but that formulation presumes that public space is given, that it is already public and recognized as such. We miss something of the point of these public demonstrations if we fail to see that the very public character of the space is being disputed, and even fought over, when these crowds gather. So though these movements have depended on the prior existence of pavement, street, and square and have often enough gathered in squares, such as Tahrir, whose political history is potent, it is equally true that the collective actions collect the space itself, gather the pavement, and animate and organize the architecture. As much as we must insist on there being material conditions for public assembly and public speech, we have also to ask how it is that assembly and speech reconfigure the materiality of public space and produce, or reproduce, the public character of that material environment. And when crowds move outside the square, to the side street or the back alley, to the neighborhoods where streets are not yet paved, then something more happens.

At such a moment, politics is not defined as taking place exclusively in the public sphere distinct from a private one, but it crosses those lines again and again, bringing attention to the way that politics is already in the home, or on the street, or in the neighborhood, or indeed in those virtual spaces that are equally unbound by the architecture of the house and the square. So when we think about what it means to assemble in a crowd, a growing crowd, and what it means to move through public space in a way that contests the distinction between public and private, we see some ways that bodies in their plurality lay claim to the public, find and produce the public through seizing and reconfiguring the matter of material environments; at the same time, those material environments are part of the action, and they themselves act when they become the support for action. In the same way, when trucks or tanks are rendered inoperative and suddenly speakers climb on them to address the crowd, the military instrument itself becomes a support or platform for a nonmilitary resistance, if not a resistance to the military itself; at such moments, the material environment is actively reconfigured and refunctioned, to use the Brechtian term. And our ideas of action then need to be rethought.

In the first instance, no one mobilizes a claim to move and assemble freely without moving and assembling together with others. In the second instance, the square and the street are not only the material supports for action, but they themselves are part of any account of bodily public action we might propose. Human action depends upon all sorts of supports—it is always supported action. We know from disability studies that the capacity to move depends upon instruments and surfaces that make movement possible and that bodily movement is supported and facilitated by nonhuman objects and their particular capacity for agency. In the case of public assemblies, we see quite clearly the struggle over what will be public space, but also an equally fundamental struggle over how bodies will be supported in the world—a struggle for employment and education, equitable food distribution, livable shelter, and freedom of movement and expression, to name a few.

Of course, this produces a quandary. We cannot act without supports, and yet we must struggle for the supports that allow us to act or, indeed, that are essential components of our action. It was the Roman idea of the public square that formed the background for Hannah Arendt's understanding of the rights of assembly and free speech, of action and the exercise of rights. Hannah Arendt surely had both the classical Greek *polis* and the Roman Forum in mind when she claimed that all political action requires the "space of appearance." She writes, for instance, "the *polis*, properly speaking, is not the city-state in its physical location; it is the organization of the people as it arises out of acting and speaking together, and its true space lies between people living together for this purpose, no matter where they happen to be." The "true" space then lies "between the people," which means that as much as any action takes place in a located somewhere, it also establishes a space that belongs properly to alliance itself. For Arendt, this alliance is not tied to its location. In fact, alliance brings about its own location, highly transposable. She writes: "action and speech create a space between the participants which can find its proper location almost anywhere and anytime."[1]

So how do we understand this highly if not infinitely transposable notion of political space? Whereas Arendt maintains that politics requires the space of appearance, she also claims that space brings politics about: "it is the space of appearance in the widest sense of the word, namely, the space where I appear to others as others appear to me, where men [sic] exist not merely like other living or inanimate things but make their appearance explicitly."[2] Something of what she says here is clearly true. Space and location are created through plural action. And yet, in her view, action, in its freedom and its power, has the exclusive capacity to create location. Such a view forgets or refuses that action is always supported and that it is invariably bodily, even, as I will argue, in its virtual forms. The material supports for action are not only part of action, but they are also what is being fought about, especially in those cases when the political struggle is about food, employment, mobility, and access to institutions. To rethink the space of appearance in order to understand the power and effect of public demonstrations for our time, we will need to consider more closely the bodily dimensions of action, what the body requires, and what the body can do,[3] especially when we must think about bodies together in a historical space that undergoes a historical transformation by virtue of their collective action: What holds them together there, and what are their conditions of persistence and of power in relation to their precarity and exposure?

I would like to think about this itinerary by which we travel from the space of appearance to the contemporary politics of the street. Even as I say this, I cannot hope to gather together all the forms of demonstration we have seen, some of which are episodic, some of which are part of ongoing and recurrent social and political movements, and some of which are revolutionary. I hope to think about what might gather together these gatherings, these public demonstrations. During the winter of 2011, they included demonstrations against tyrannical regimes in North Africa and the Middle East, but also against the escalating precaritization of working peoples in Europe and in the Southern Hemisphere, the struggles for public education throughout the United States and Europe and, most recently, in Chile, and struggles to make the street safe for women and for gender and sexual minorities, including trans people, whose public appearance is too often punishable by legal and illegal violence. In public assemblies by trans and queer people, the claim is often made that the streets must be made safe from the police who are complicit in criminality, especially on those occasions when the police support criminal regimes or when, for instance, the police commit the very crimes against sexual and gender minorities that they are supposed to prevent. Demonstrations are one of the few ways that police power is overcome, especially when those assemblies become at once too large and too mobile, too condensed and too diffuse, to be contained by police power and when they have the resources to regenerate themselves on the spot.

Perhaps these are anarchist moments or anarchist passages, when the legitimacy of a regime or its laws is called into question, but when no new legal regimen has yet arrived to take its place. This time of the interval is one in which the assembled bodies articulate a new time and space for the popular will, not a single identical will, not a unitary will, but one that is characterized as an alliance of distinct and adjacent bodies whose action and whose inaction demands a different future. Together they exercise the performative power to lay claim to the public in a way that is not yet codified into law and that can never be fully codified into law. And this performativity is not only speech, but the demands of bodily action, gesture, movement, congregation, persistence, and exposure to possible violence. How do we understand this acting together that opens up time and space outside and against the established architecture and temporality of the regime, one that lays claim to materiality, leans into its supports, draws from its material and technical dimensions to rework their functions? Such actions reconfigure what will be public and what will be the space of politics.

I push against Hannah Arendt even as I draw upon her resources to clarify my own position. Her work supports my action here, but I also refuse it in some ways. Arendt's view is confounded by its own gender politics, relying as it does on a distinction between the public and private domains that leaves the sphere of politics to men and reproductive labor to women. If there is a body in the public sphere, it is presumptively masculine and unsupported, presumptively free to create, but not itself created. And the body in the private sphere is female, ageing, foreign, or childish, and always prepolitical. Although she was, as we know from the important work of Adriana Cavarero, a philosopher of natality, Arendt understood this capacity to bring something into being as a function of political speech and action. Indeed, when male citizens enter into the public square to debate questions of justice, revenge, war, and emancipation, they take the illuminated public square for granted as the architecturally bounded theatre of their speech. And their speech becomes the paradigmatic form of action, physically cut off from the private domicile, itself shrouded in darkness and reproduced through activities that are not quite action in the proper and public senses. Men make the passage from that private darkness to that public light and, once illuminated, they speak, and their speech interrogates the principles of justice it articulates, becoming itself a form of critical inquiry and democratic participation. For Arendt, rethinking this classical scene within political modernity, speech is understood as the bodily and linguistic exercise of rights. Bodily and linguistic—how are we to reconceive these terms and their intertwining here against and beyond that presumption of a gendered division of labor?

For Arendt, political action takes place on the condition that the body appear. I appear to others, and they appear to me, which means that some space between us allows each to appear. One might expect that we appear within a space or that we are supported by a material organization of space. But that is not her argument. The sphere of appearance is not simple, since it seems to arise only on the condition of a certain intersubjective facing off. We are not simply visual phenomena for each other—our voices must be registered, and so we must be heard; rather, who we are, bodily, is already a way of being "for" the other, appearing in ways that we can neither see nor hear; that is, we are made available, bodily, for another whose perspective we can neither fully anticipate nor control. In this way, I am, as a body, not only for myself, not even primarily for myself, but find myself, if I find myself at all, constituted and dispossessed by the perspective of others. So, for political action, I must appear to others in ways I cannot know, and in this way, my body is established by perspectives that I cannot inhabit, but that, surely, inhabit me. This is an important point because it is not the case that the body only establishes my own perspective; it is also what displaces that perspective and makes that displacement into a necessity. This happens most clearly when we think about bodies that act together. No one body establishes the space of appearance, but this action, this performative exercise, happens only "between" bodies, in a space that constitutes the gap between my own body and another's. In this way, my body does not act alone when it acts politically. Indeed, the action emerges from the "between."

It is both problematic and interesting that, for Arendt, the space of appearance is not only an architectural given: "the space of appearance comes into being," she writes, "wherever men are together in the manner of speech and action, and therefore predates and precedes all formal constitution of the public realm and the various forms of government, that is, the various forms in which the public realm may be organized."[4] In other words, this space of appearance is not a location that can be separated from the plural action that brings it about; it is not there outside of the action that invokes and constitutes it. And yet, if we are to accept this view, we have to understand how the plurality that acts is itself constituted. How does a plurality form, and what material supports are necessary for that formation? Who enters this plurality, and who does not, and how are such matters decided?

How do we describe the action and the status of those beings disaggregated from the plural? What political language do we have in reserve for describing that exclusion and the forms of resistance that crack open the sphere of appearance as it is currently delimited? Are those who live on the outside of the sphere of appearance the deanimated "givens" of political life? Are they mere life or bare life? Are we to say that those who are excluded are simply unreal, disappeared, or that they have no being at all—shall they be cast off, theoretically, as the socially dead and the merely spectral? If we do that, we not only adopt the position of a particular regime of appearance, but ratify that perspective, even if our wish is to call it into question. Do such formulations describe a state of *having been made* destitute by existing political arrangements, or is that destitution unwittingly ratified by a theory that adopts the perspective of those who regulate and police the sphere of appearance itself?

At stake is the question of whether the destitute are outside of politics and power or are in fact living out a specific form of political destitution along with specific forms of political agency and resistance that expose the policing of the boundaries of the sphere of appearance itself. If we claim that the destitute are outside of the sphere of politics—reduced to depoliticized forms of being—then we implicitly accept as right the dominant ways of establishing the limits of the political. In some ways, this follows from the Arendtian position that adopts the internal point of view of the Greek *polis* on what politics should be, who should gain entry into the public square, and who should remain in the private. Such a view disregards and devalues those forms of political agency that emerge precisely in those domains deemed prepolitical or extrapolitical and that break into the sphere of appearance as from the outside, as its outside, confounding the distinction between inside and outside. For in revolutionary or insurrectionary moments, we are no longer sure what is the space of politics, just as we are often unsure about exactly in what time we are living, since the established regimes of both space and time are upended in ways that expose their violence and their contingent limits. We see this when undocumented workers gather in the city of Los Angeles to claim their rights of assembly and of citizenship without being citizens, without having any legal right to do so. Their labor is supposed to remain necessary and shrouded from view, and so when these laboring bodies emerge on the street, acting like citizens, they make a mimetic claim to citizenship that alters not only how they appear, but how the sphere of appearance works. Indeed, the sphere of appearance is both mobilized and disabled when an exploited and laboring class emerges on the street to announce itself and express its opposition to being the unseen condition of what appears as political.

The impetus for Giorgio Agamben's notion of "bare life" derives from this very conception of the *polis* in Arendt's political philosophy and, I would suggest, runs the risk of this very problem: if we seek to take account of exclusion itself as a political problem, as part of politics itself, then it will not do to say that once excluded, those beings lack appearance or "reality" in political terms, that they have no social or political standing or are cast out and reduced to mere being (forms of givenness precluded from the sphere of action). Nothing so metaphysically extravagant has to happen if we agree that one reason the sphere of the political cannot be defined by the classic conception of the *polis* is that we are then deprived of having and using a language for those forms of agency and resistance that focus on the politics of exclusion itself or, indeed, that operate against those regimes of power that maintain the stateless and disenfranchised in conditions of destitution. Few matters could be more politically consequential.

Although Agamben borrows from Foucault to articulate a conception of the biopolitical, the thesis of "bare life" remains untouched by that conception. As a result, we cannot within that vocabulary describe the modes of agency and action undertaken by the stateless, the occupied, and the disenfranchised, since even the life stripped of rights is still within the sphere of the political and is thus not reduced to mere being, but is, more often than not, angered, indignant, rising up, and resisting. To be outside established and legitimate political structures is still to be saturated in power relations, and this saturation is the point of departure for a theory of the political that includes dominant and subjugated forms, modes of inclusion and legitimation as well as modes of delegitimation and effacement.

Luckily, I think Arendt did not consistently follow this model from *The Human Condition*, which is why, for instance, in the early 1960s, she turned her attention to the fate of refugees and the stateless, and came to assert in that context the right to have rights. The right to have rights is one that depends on no existing particular political organization for its legitimacy. Like the space of appearance, the right to have rights predates and precedes any political institution that might codify or seek to guarantee that right; at the same time, it is derived from no natural set of laws. The right comes into being when it is exercised, and exercised by those who act in concert, in alliance. Those who are excluded from existing polities, who belong to no nation-state or other contemporary state formation, may be deemed "unreal" only by those who seek to monopolize the terms of reality. And yet even after the public sphere has been defined through their exclusion, they act. Whether they are abandoned to precarity or left to die through systematic negligence, concerted action still emerges from their acting together. And this is what we see, for instance, when undocumented workers amass on the street without the legal right to do so, when squatters lay claim to buildings in Argentina as a way of exercising the right to livable shelter, when populations lay claim to a public square that has belonged to the military, or when the refugees take part in collective uprisings demanding shelter, food, and rights of sanctuary, when populations amass, without the protection of the law and without permits to demonstrate, to bring down an unjust or criminal regime of law or to protest austerity measures that destroy the possibility of employment and education for many. Or when those whose public appearance is itself criminal, transgendered people in Turkey or women who wear the *niqāb* in France, appear in order to contest that criminal status and assert the right to appear.

Indeed, in the public demonstrations that often follow from acts of public mourning, as in Syria in recent months, where crowds of mourners became targets of military destruction, we can see how the existing public space is seized by those who have no existing right to gather there, who emerge from zones of disappearance to become bodies exposed to violence and death in the course of gathering and persisting publically as they do. Indeed, it is their right to gather free of intimidation and the threat of violence that is systematically attacked by the police, the army, hired gangs, or mercenaries. To attack those bodies is to attack the right itself, since when those bodies appear and act, they are exercising a right outside, against, and in the face of the regime.

Although the bodies on the street are vocalizing their opposition to the legitimacy of the state, they are also, by virtue of occupying and persisting in that space without protection, posing their challenge in corporeal terms, which means that when the body "speaks" politically, it is not only in vocal or written language. The persistence of the body in its exposure calls that legitimacy into question and does so precisely through a performativity of the body. Both action and gesture signify and speak, both as action and claim; the one is not finally extricable from the other. Where the legitimacy of the state is brought into question precisely by that way of appearing in public, the body itself exercises a right that is no right; in other words, it exercises a right that is being actively contested and destroyed by military force and that, in its resistance to force, articulates its way of living, showing both its precarity and its right to persist. This right is codified nowhere. It is not granted from elsewhere or by existing law, even if it sometimes finds support precisely there. It is, in fact, the right to have rights, not as natural law or metaphysical stipulation, but as the persistence of the body against those forces that seek its debilitation or eradication. This persistence requires breaking into the established regime of space with a set of material supports both mobilized and mobilizing.

Just to be clear: I am not referring to a vitalism or a right to life as such. Rather, I am suggesting that political claims are made by bodies as they appear and act, as they refuse and as they persist under conditions in which that fact alone is taken to be an act of delegitimation of the state. It is not that bodies are simply mute life forces that counter existing modalities of power. Rather, they are themselves modalities of power, embodied interpretations, engaging in allied action. On the one hand, these bodies are productive and performative. On the other hand, they can persist and act only when they are supported, by environments, by nutrition, by work, by modes of sociality and belonging. And when these supports fall away and precarity is exposed, they are mobilized in another way, seizing upon the supports that exist in order to make a claim that there can be no embodied life without social and institutional support, without ongoing employment, without networks of interdependency and care, collective rights to shelter and mobility. Not only do they struggle for the idea of social support and political enfranchisement, but their struggle is its own social form. And so, in the most ideal instances, an alliance begins to enact the social order it seeks to bring about by establishing its own modes of sociability. And yet that alliance is not reducible to a collection of individuals, and it is, strictly speaking, not individuals who act. Moreover, action in alliance happens precisely between those who participate, and this is not an ideal or empty space. That interval is the space of sociality and of support, of being constituted in a sociality that is never reducible to one's own perspective and to being dependent on structures without which there is no durable and livable life.

Many of the massive demonstrations and modes of resistance we have seen in the last months not only produce a space of appearance, they seize upon an already established space permeated by existing power, seeking to sever the relations between the public space, the public square, and the existing regime. So the limits of the political are exposed and the link between the theatre of legitimacy and public space is severed; that theatre is no longer unproblematically housed in public space, since public space now occurs in the midst of another action, one that displaces the power that claims legitimacy precisely by taking over the field of its effects. Simply put, the bodies on the street redeploy the space of appearance in order to contest and negate the existing forms of political legitimacy—and just as they sometimes fill or take over public space, the material history of those structures also works on them, becoming part of their very action, remaking a history in the midst of its most concrete and sedimented artifices. These are subjugated and empowered actors who seek to wrest legitimacy from an existing state apparatus that depends upon the regulation of the public space of appearance for its theatrical self-constitution. In wresting that power, a new space is created, a new "between" of bodies, as it were, that lays claim to existing space through the action of a new alliance, and those bodies are seized and animated by those existing spaces in the very acts by which they reclaim and resignify their meanings.

Such a struggle intervenes in the spatial organization of power, which includes the allocation and restriction of spatial locations in which and by which any population may appear, which implies a spatial regulation of when and how the "popular will" may appear. This view of the spatial restriction and allocation of who may appear—in effect, of who may become a subject of appearance—suggests an operation of power that works through both foreclosure and differential allocation.

What, then, does it mean to appear within contemporary politics, and can we consider this question at all without some recourse to the media? If we consider what it is to appear, it follows that we appear to someone and that our appearance has to be registered by the senses, not only our own, but someone else's. If we appear, we must be seen, which means that our bodies must be viewed and their vocalized sounds must be heard: the body must enter the visual and audible

A man associated with Occupy Wall Street relaxes in Zuccotti Park on November 4, 2011 in New York City (photo: Spencer Platt/Getty Images).

field. But is this not, of necessity, a laboring body and a sexual body, as well as a body gendered and racialized in some form? Arendt's view clearly meets its limits here, for the body is itself divided into the one that appears publically to speak and act and another, sexual and laboring, feminine, foreign, and mute, that generally is relegated to the private and prepolitical sphere. Such a division of labor is precisely what is called into question when precarious lives assemble on the street in forms of alliance that must struggle to achieve a space of appearance. If some domain of bodily life operates as the sequestered or disavowed condition for the sphere of appearance, it becomes the structuring absence that governs and makes possible the public sphere.

If we are living organisms who speak and act, then we are clearly related to a vast continuum or network of living beings; we not only live among them, but our persistence as living organisms depends on that matrix of sustaining interdependent relations. And yet, our speaking and acting distinguishes us as something separate from other living beings. Indeed, we do not need to know what is distinctively human about political action, but only finally to see how the entrance of the disavowed body into the political sphere establishes at the same time the essential link between humans and other living beings. The private body thus conditions the public body in theories such as Arendt's, but in political organizations of space that continue in many forms. And even though the public and private body are necessarily the same, the bifurcation is crucial to maintaining the public and private distinction and its modes of disavowal and disenfranchisement.

Perhaps it is a kind of fantasy that one dimension of bodily life can and must remain out of sight, and yet another, fully distinct, appears in public. Is there no trace of the biological in the sphere of appearance? Could we not argue, with Bruno Latour and Isabelle Stengers, that negotiating the sphere of appearance is, in fact, a biological thing to do, one of the investigative capacities of the organism? After all, there is no way of navigating an environment or procuring food without appearing bodily in the world, and there is no escape from the vulnerability and mobility that appearing in the world implies, which explains forms of camouflage and self-protection in the animal world. In other words, is appearance not a necessarily morphological moment where the body risks appearance not only in order to speak and act, but to suffer and move, as well, to engage others bodies, to negotiate an environment on which one depends, to establish a social organization for the satisfaction of needs? Indeed, the body can appear and signify in ways that contest the way it speaks or even contest speaking as its paradigmatic instance. Could we still understand action, gesture, stillness, touch, and moving together if they were all reducible to the vocalization of thought through speech?

This act of public speaking, even within that problematic division of labor, *depends upon* a dimension of bodily life that is given, passive, opaque, and so excluded from the conventional definition of the political. Hence, we can ask: What regulation keeps the given or passive body from spilling over into the active body? Are these two different bodies, and if so, what politics is required to keep them apart? Are these two different dimensions of the same body, or are these, in fact, the effect of a certain regulation of bodily appearance that is actively contested by new social movements, struggles against sexual violence, for reproductive freedom, against precarity, for the freedom of mobility? Here we can see that a certain topographical or even architectural regulation of the body happens at the level of theory. Significantly, it is precisely this operation of power—the foreclosure and differential allocation of whether and how the body may appear—that is excluded from Arendt's explicit account of the political. Indeed, her explicit account of the political depends upon that very operation of power that it fails to consider as part of politics itself.

So what I accept from Arendt is the following: Freedom does not come from me or from you; it can and does happen as a relation between us, or, indeed, among us. So this is not a matter of finding the human dignity within each person, but rather of understanding the human as a relational and social being, one whose action depends upon equality and articulates the principle of equality. Indeed, there is no human, in her view, if there is no equality. No human can be human alone. And no human can be human without acting in concert with others and on conditions of equality. I would add the following: The claim of equality is not only spoken or written, but is made precisely when bodies appear together, or, rather, when through their action, they bring the space of appearance into being. This space is a feature and effect of action, and it works, according to Arendt, only when relations of equality are maintained.

Of course, there are many reasons to be suspicious of idealized moments, but there are also reasons to be wary of any analysis that is fully guarded against idealization. There are two aspects of the revolutionary demonstrations in Tahrir Square that I would like to underscore. The first has to do with the way a certain sociability was established within the square, a division of labor that broke down gender difference, that involved rotating who would speak and who would clean the areas where people slept and ate, developing a work schedule for everyone to maintain the environment and to clean the toilets. In short, what some would call "horizontal relations" among the protestors formed easily and methodically, alliances struggling to embody equality, which included an equal division of labor between the sexes—these became part of the very resistance to the Mubarak regime and its entrenched hierarchies, including the extraordinary differentials of wealth between the military and corporate sponsors of the regime and the working people. So the social form of the resistance began to incorporate principles of equality that governed not only how and when people spoke and acted for the media and against the regime, but how people cared for their various quarters within the square, the beds on the pavement, the makeshift medical stations and bathrooms, the places where people ate, and the places where people were exposed to violence from the outside. We are not just talking about heroic actions that took enormous physical strength and the exercise of compelling political rhetoric. Sometimes the simple act of sleeping there, on the square, was the most eloquent political statement—and even must count as an action. These actions were all political in the simple sense that they were breaking down a conventional distinction between public and private in order to establish new relations of equality; in this sense, they were incorporating into the very social form of resistance the principles they were struggling to realize in broader political forms.

Second, when up against violent attack or extreme threats, many people chanted the word *silmiyya*, which comes from the root verb *salima*, which means "to be safe and sound," "unharmed," "unimpaired," "intact," and "secure"; but also "to be unobjectionable," "blameless," faultless"; and yet also "to be certain," "established," "clearly proven."[5] The term comes from the noun *silm*, which means "peace," but also, interchangeably and significantly, "the religion of Islam." One variant of the term is *hubb as-silm*, which is Arabic for "pacifism." Most usually, the chanting of *silmiyya* comes across as a gentle exhortation: "peaceful, peaceful." Although the revolution was for the most part nonviolent, it was not necessarily led by a principled opposition to violence. Rather, the collective chant was a way of encouraging people to resist the mimetic pull of military aggression—and the aggression of the gangs—by keeping in mind the larger goal: radical democratic change. To be swept into a violent exchange of the moment was to lose the patience needed to realize the revolution. What interests me here is the chant, the way in which language worked not to incite an action, but to restrain one: a restraint in the name of an emerging community of equals whose primary way of doing politics would not be violence.

Finally, then, to what extent was the revolution a media revolution, and how does that make actual bodies less central to the political action? How important was the locatedness of bodies to the events that took place? Of course, Tahrir Square is a place, and we can locate it quite precisely on the map of Cairo. At the same time, we find questions posed throughout the media: Will the Palestinians have their Tahrir Square? Where is the Tahrir Square in India? That's to name but a few. So it is located, and it is transposable; indeed, it seemed to be transposable from the start, though never completely. And of course, we cannot think the transposability of those bodies in the square without the media. In some ways, the media images from Tunisia prepared the way for the media events in Tahrir, then those that followed in Yemen, Bahrain, Syria, and Libya, all of which took different trajectories and take them still. As you know, many of the public demonstrations of these last months have not been against military dictatorships or tyrannical regimes. They have also been against the monopoly capitalism, neoliberalism, and the suppression of political rights and in the name of those who are abandoned by neoliberal reforms that seek to dismantle forms of social democracy and socialism, that eradicate jobs, expose populations to poverty, and undermine the basic right to a public education.

The street scenes become politically potent only when and if we have a visual and audible version of the scene communicated in live or proximate time, so that the media does not merely report the scene, but is part of the scene and the action; indeed, the media *is* the scene or the space in its extended and replicable visual and audible dimensions. One way of stating this is simply that the media extend the scene visually and audibly and participate in the delimitation and transposability of the scene. Put differently, the media constitute the scene in a time and place that includes and exceeds its local instantiation. Although the scene is surely and emphatically local, those who are elsewhere have the sense that they are getting some direct access through the images and sounds they receive. That is true, but they do not know how the editing takes place, which scene conveys and travels and which scenes remain obdurately outside the frame. When the scene travels, it is both there *and* here, and if it were not spanning both locations—indeed, multiple locations—it would not be the scene that it is. Its locality is not denied by the fact that the scene is communicated beyond itself and so constituted in global media; it depends on that mediation to take place as the event that it is. This means that the local must be recast outside itself in order to be established as local, and this means that it is only through globalizing media that the local can be established and that something can really happen there. Of course, many things do happen outside the frame of the camera or other digital media devices, and the media can just as easily implement censorship as oppose it. There are many local events that are never recorded and broadcast, and some important reasons why. But when the event travels and manages to summon and sustain global outrage and pressure, which includes the power to stop markets or to sever diplomatic relations, then the local will have to be established time and again in a circuitry that exceeds the local at every instant.

And yet, there remains something localized that cannot and does not travel in that way, and the scene could not be the scene if we did not understand that some people are at risk, and the risk is run precisely by those bodies on the street. If they are transported in one way, they are surely left in place in another, holding the camera or the cell phone, face to face with those they oppose, unprotected, injurable, injured, persistent, if not insurgent. It matters that those bodies carry cell phones, relaying messages and images, and so when they are attacked, it is more often than not in some relation to the camera or the video recorder. It can be an effort to destroy the camera and its user, or it can be a spectacle for the media produced as a warning or a threat. Or it can be a way to stop any more organizing. Is the action of the body separable from its technology, and is the technology not helping to establish new forms of political action? And when censorship or violence is directed against those bodies, are they not also directed against their access to media and in order to establish hegemonic control over which images travel, and which do not?

Of course, the dominant media are corporately owned, exercising their own kinds of censorship and incitement. And yet, it still seems important to affirm that the freedom of the media to broadcast from these sites is itself an exercise of freedom and so a mode of exercising rights, especially when they are rogue media, from the street, evading the censor, where the activation of the instrument is part of the bodily action itself. This is doubtless why both Hosni Mubarak and Michael Cameron, eight months apart, both argued for the censorship of social media networks. At least in some instances, the media not only report on social and political movements that are laying claim to freedom and justice in various ways; the media also are exercising one of those freedoms for which the social movement struggles. I do not mean by this claim to suggest that all media are involved in the struggle for political freedom and social justice (we know, of course, that they are not). Of course, it matters which global media do the reporting and how. My point is that sometimes private media devices become global precisely at the moment in which they overcome modes of censorship to report protests and in that way become part of the protest itself.

What bodies are doing on the street when they are demonstrating is linked fundamentally to what communication devices and technologies are doing when they "report" on what is happening in the street. These are different actions, but they both require the body. The one exercise of freedom is linked to the other, which means that both are ways of exercising rights and that, jointly, they bring a space of appearance into being and secure its transposability. Although some may wager that the exercise of rights now takes place quite at the expense of bodies on the street, that Twitter and other virtual technologies have led to a disembodiment of the public sphere, I disagree. The media requires those bodies on the street to have an event, even as those bodies on the street require the media to exist in a global arena. But under conditions when those with cameras or Internet capacities are imprisoned or tortured or deported, the use of the technology effectively implicates the body. Not only must someone's hand tap and send, but someone's body is on the line if that tapping and sending gets traced. In other words, localization is hardly overcome through the use of media that potentially transmit globally. And if this conjuncture of street and media constitutes a very contemporary version of the public sphere, then bodies on the line have to be thought as both there and here, now and then, transported and stationary, with very different political consequences following from those two modalities of space and time.

It matters that it is public squares that are filled to the brim, that people eat and sleep there, sing and refuse to cede that space, as we saw in Tahrir Square and continue to see on a daily basis. It matters, as well, that it is public educational buildings that have been seized in Athens, London, and Berkeley. At Berkeley, buildings were seized and trespassing fines were handed out. In some cases, students were accused of destroying private property. But these very allegations raised the question of whether the university is public or private. The stated aim of the protest—to seize the building and to sequester themselves there—was a way to gain a platform, indeed, a way to secure the material conditions for appearing in public. Such actions generally do not take place when effective platforms are already available. The students there, but also at Goldsmiths College in the UK more recently, were seizing buildings as a way to lay claim to buildings that ought properly, now and in the future, to belong to public education. That doesn't mean that every time these buildings are seized it is justifiable, but let us be alert to what is at stake here: the symbolic meaning of seizing these buildings is that these buildings belong to the public, to public education, and it is precisely the access to public education that is being undermined by fee and tuition hikes and budget cuts. We should not be surprised that the protest took the form of seizing the buildings, performatively laying claim to public education, insisting on gaining literal access to the buildings of public education precisely at a moment, historically, when that access is being shut down. In other words, no positive law justifies these actions that oppose the institutionalization of unjust or exclusionary forms of power. Can we then say that these actions are nevertheless an exercise of a right, a lawless exercise that take place precisely when the law is wrong or the law has failed?

Let me offer you an anecdote to make my point more concrete. Last year, I was asked to visit Turkey on the occasion of the International Conference against Homophobia and Transphobia. This was an especially important event in Ankara, the capital of Turkey, where transgendered people are often served fines for appearing in public, are often beaten, sometimes by the police, and where murders of transgendered women in particular have happened nearly once a month in recent years. If I offer you this example of Turkey, it is not to point out that Turkey is "behind"—something that the embassy representative from Denmark was quick to point out to me and that I refused with equal speed. I assure you that there are equally brutal murders outside of Los Angeles and Detroit, in Wyoming and Louisiana, or even in New York. It is rather because what is astonishing about the alliances there is that several feminist organizations have worked with queer, gay/lesbian, and transgendered people against police violence, but also against militarism, against nationalism, and against the forms of masculinism by which they are supported. So on the street, after the conference, the feminists lined up with the drag queens, the genderqueer with the human rights activists, and the lipstick lesbians with their bisexual and heterosexual friends—the march included secularists and Muslims. They chanted, "We will not be soldiers, and we will not kill." To oppose the police violence against trans people is thus to be openly against military violence and the nationalist escalation of militarism; it is to be against the military aggression against the Kurds, but also to act in the memory of the Armenian genocide and against the various ways that violence is disavowed by the state and the media.

This alliance was compelling for me for all kinds of reasons, but mainly because in most Northern European countries, there are now serious divisions among feminists, queers, lesbian and gay human rights workers, antiracist movements, freedom-of-religion movements, and anitpoverty and antiwar mobilizations. In Lyon, France, last year, one of the established feminists had written a book on the "illusion" of transsexuality, and her public lectures had been "zapped" by many trans activists and their queer allies. She defended herself by saying that to call transsexuality "psychotic" was not the same as pathologizing transsexuality. It is, she said, a descriptive term and makes no judgment or prescription. Under what conditions can calling a population "psychotic" for the particular embodied life they live not be pathologizing? This feminist called herself a materialist, a radical, but she pitted herself against the transgendered community in order to maintain certain norms of masculinity and femininity as prerequisites for a nonpsychotic life. These are arguments that would be swiftly countered in Istanbul or Johannesburg, and yet these same feminists seek recourse to a form of universalism that would make France, and their version of French feminism, into the beacon of progressive thought.

Not all French feminists who call themselves universalists would oppose the public rights of transgendered people or contribute to their pathologization. And yet, if the streets are open to transgendered people, they are not open to those who wear signs of their religious belonging openly. Hence, we are left to fathom the many universalist French feminists who call upon the police to arrest, detain, fine, and sometimes deport women wearing the *niqāb* or the *burqa* in the public sphere in France. What sort of politics is this that recruits the police function of the state to monitor and restrict women from religious minorities in the public sphere? Why would the same universalists (such as Elisabeth Badinter) openly affirm the rights of transgendered people to appear freely in public while denying that right to women who happen to wear religious clothing that offends the sensibilities of die-hard secularists? If the right to appear is to be honored "universally," it would not be able to survive such an obvious and insupportable contradiction.

Perhaps there are modalities of violence that we need to think about in order to understand the police functions in operation here. After all, those who insist that gender must always appear in one way or in one clothed version rather than another, who seek either to criminalize or to pathologize those who live their gender or their sexuality in nonnormative ways, are themselves acting as the police for the sphere of appearance, whether or not they belong to any police force. As we know, it is sometimes the police force of the state that does violence to sexual and gendered minorities, and sometimes it is the police who fail to investigate, fail to prosecute as criminal the murder of transgendered women or fail to prevent violence against transgendered members of the population.

If gender or sexual minorities are criminalized or pathologized for how they appear, how they lay claim to public space, the language through which they understand themselves, the means by which they express love or desire, those with whom they openly ally, choose to be near, engage sexually, or how they exercise their bodily freedom, what clothes they wear or fail to wear, then those acts of criminalization are themselves violent, and in that sense, they are also unjust and criminal. In Arendtian terms, we can say that to be precluded from the space of appearance, to be precluded from being part of the plurality that brings the space of appearance into being, is to be deprived of the right to have rights. Plural and public action is the exercise of the right to place and belonging, and this exercise is the means by which the space of appearance is presupposed and brought into being.

Let me return to the notion of gender with which I began, both to draw upon Arendt and to resist Arendt. In my view, gender is an exercise of freedom, which is not to say that everything that constitutes gender is freely chosen, but only that even what is considered unfree can and must be claimed and exercised in some way. I have, with this formulation, taken a certain distance from the Arendtian formulation. This exercise of freedom must be accorded the same equal treatment as any other exercise of freedom under the law. And politically, we must call for the expansion of our conceptions of equality to include this form of embodied freedom.

So what do we mean when we say that sexuality or gender is an exercise of freedom? To repeat: I do not mean to say that all of us choose our gender or our sexuality. We are surely formed by language and culture, by history, by the social struggles in which we participate, by forces both psychological and historical—in interaction, by the way with biological situations that have their own history and efficacy. Indeed, we may well feel that what and how we desire are quite fixed, indelible or irreversible features of who we are. But regardless of whether we understand our gender or our sexuality as chosen or given, we each have a right to claim that gender and to claim that sexuality. And it makes a difference whether we can claim them at all. When we exercise the right to appear as the gender we already are—even when we feel we have no other choice—we are still exercising a certain freedom, but we are also doing something more.

When one freely exercises the right to be who one already is and one asserts a social category for the purposes of describing that mode of being, then one is, in fact, making freedom part of that social category, discursively changing the very ontology in question. It is not possible to separate the genders that we claim to be and the sexualities that we engage from the right that any of us has to assert those realities, in public, or in private, or in the many thresholds that exist between the two, freely, that is, without threat of violence. When, long ago, one said that gender is performative, that meant that it is a certain kind of enactment, which means that one is not first one's gender and then one decides how and when to enact it. The enactment is part of its very ontology, is a way of rethinking the ontological mode of gender, and so it matters how and when and with what consequences that enactment takes place, because all that changes the very gender that one "is."

To walk on the street without police interference is something other than assembling there en masse. And yet, when a transgendered person walks there, the right that is exercised in a bodily form does not only belong to that one person. There is a group, if not an alliance, walking there, too, whether or not they are seen. It is a person there who walks, who takes the risk of walking there, but it is also the social category that traverses that embodied movement in the world, and the attack, when it comes, is clearly on both at once. Perhaps we can still call "performative" both this exercise of gender and the embodied political claim to equality and protection from violence so as to be able to move with and within this social category in public space. To walk is to say that this is a public space in which transgendered people walk, that this is a public space where people with various forms of clothing, no matter how they are gendered or what religion they signify, are free to move without threat of violence. But this performativity applies more broadly to the conditions by which any of us emerge as bodily creatures in the world.

If we are thinking well, and our thinking commits us to the preservation of life in some form, then the life to be preserved takes a bodily form. In turn, this means that the life of the body—its hunger, its need for shelter and protection from violence—all become major issues of politics. Even the most given or nonchosen features of our lives are not simply given; they are given *in* history and *in* language, in vectors of power that none of us chose. Equally true is that a given property of the body or a set of defining characteristics depends upon the continuing persistence of the body. Those social categories we never chose traverse this given body in some ways rather than in others, and gender, for instance, names that traversal as well as its transformations. In this sense, those most urgent and nonvolitional dimensions of our lives, which include hunger and the need for shelter, medical care, and protection from violence, natural or humanly imposed, are crucial to politics. We cannot presume the enclosed and well-fed space of the *polis*, where all the material needs are somehow being taken care of elsewhere by beings whose gender, race, or status render them ineligible for public recognition. Rather, we have not only to bring the material urgencies of the body into the square, but to make those needs central to the demands of politics.

In my view, a shared condition of precarity situates our political lives, even as precarity is differentially distributed. And some of us, as Ruthie Gilmore has made very clear, are disproportionately more disposed to injury and early death than others. Racial difference can be tracked precisely through looking at statistics on infant mortality, for example. This means, in brief, that precarity is unequally distributed and that lives are not considered equally grievable or equally valuable. If, as Adriana Cavarero has argued, the exposure of our bodies in public space constitutes us fundamentally and establishes our thinking as social and embodied, vulnerable and passionate, then our thinking gets nowhere without the presupposition of that very corporeal interdependency and entwinement. The body is constituted through perspectives it cannot inhabit; someone else sees our face in a way that none of us can and hears our voice in a way that we cannot. We are in this sense, bodily, always over there, yet here, and this dispossession marks the sociality to which we belong. Even as located beings, we are always elsewhere, constituted in a sociality that exceeds us. This establishes our exposure and our precarity, the ways in which we depend on political and social institutions to persist.

After all, in Cairo, it was not just that people amassed in the square: they were there; they slept there; they dispensed medicine and food; they assembled and sang; and they spoke. Can we distinguish those vocalizations emanating from the body from those other expressions of material need and urgency? They were, after all, sleeping and eating in the public square, constructing toilets and various systems for sharing the space, and thus not only refusing to disappear, refusing to go or stay home, and not only claiming the public domain for themselves—acting in concert on conditions of equality—but also maintaining themselves as persisting bodies with needs, desires, and requirements: Arendtian and counter-Arendtian, to be sure, since these bodies who were organizing their basic needs in public were also petitioning the world to register what was happening there, to make its support known, and in that way to enter into revolutionary action itself. The bodies acted in concert, but they also slept in public, and in both these modalities, they were both vulnerable and demanding, giving political and spatial organization to elementary bodily needs. In this way, they formed themselves into images to be projected to all who watched, petitioning us to receive and respond and so to enlist media coverage that would refuse to let the event be covered over or to slip away. Sleeping on that pavement was not only a way to lay claim to the public, to contest the legitimacy of the state, but also quite clearly, a way to put the body on the line in its insistence, obduracy, and precarity, overcoming the distinction between public and private for the time of revolution. In other words, it was only when those needs that are supposed to remain private came out into the day and night of the square, formed into image and discourse for the media, did it finally become possible to extend the space and time of the event with such tenacity as to bring the regime down. After all, the cameras never stopped; bodies were there and here; they never stopped speaking, not even in sleep, and so could not be silenced, sequestered, or denied—revolution happened because everyone refused to go home, cleaving to the pavement as the site of their convergent temporary, awkward, vulnerable, daring, revolutionary bodily lives.

NOTES

1. Hannah Arendt, *The Human Condition* (Chicago: University of Chicago Press, 1958), p. 198.
2. *Ibid*., p. 199.
3. "The point of view of an ethics is: of what are you capable, what can you do? Hence a return to this sort of cry of Spinoza's: what can a body do? We never know in advance what a body can do. We never know how we're organized and how the modes of existence are enveloped in somebody." Gilles Deleuze, *Expressionism in Philosophy: Spinoza*, trans. Martin Joughin (New York: Zone Books, 1992), pp. 217–34. This account differs from his in several respects, but most prominently by virtue of its consideration of bodies in their plurality.
4. Arendt, *The Human Condition*, p. 199.
5. Hans Wehr, *Dictionary of Modern Written Arabic*, 4th ed., ed. J. Milton Cowan (Ithaca: Spoken Language Services, 1994), s.v. "salima."

FIGURE 1 A Palestinian woman thrusts forth olive leaves as she shouts at Israeli soldiers during a demonstration against the separation barrier in the village of Al-Zawiya near the Israeli settlement of Ariel, south-southwest of Nablus, Wednesday, June 9, 2004 (photo: AP Photo/Nasser Ishtayeh).

Circulating the Stances of Liberation Politics: The Photojournalism of the Anti-Wall Protests

Amahl Bishara

Mariam Mustafa Daoud sits down in front of an Israeli demolition machine, her arms stretched skyward as she calls out in protest. An Associated Press photographer is there to snap a photo of this elderly Palestinian woman in a vibrantly embroidered dress. Another picture, apparently from a few minutes later, shows five soldiers forcibly removing her from the scene, holding her by each limb (fig. 2). The caption says this is occurring in Beit Dukou, a village about ten kilometers north of Jerusalem, and that the Separation Barrier will be built here. The verdant green of the grass says this is Palestinian springtime.

The Separation Barrier, also known as "the Wall," is a system of walls and fences to the west of most Palestinian cities and villages in the West Bank. The barrier separates these areas from Israel and many West Bank Israeli settlements. Under construction since 2002, the barrier restricts Palestinian movement and population expansion and, many opponents believe, constitutes a permanent Israeli land grab. Israeli officials assert that the barrier was built as a defense against suicide bombers.[1]

Palestinian NGOs of different scales and histories have been on the forefront of the struggle to bring down the barrier. The anti-Wall NGO mobilization distinguishes itself by being manifestly political, an exception to evidence that many NGOs have depoliticizing effects, even when NGOs are directly concerned with human rights issues. Indeed, anti-Wall NGOs have gone against the trend toward depoliticized NGOs in the Israeli-occupied West Bank and Gaza.[2] To a large extent, anti-Wall politics and antioccupation politics are the same.

There are at least three aspects of this movement that indicate its overtly political orientation. First, there is the context of governance. In contradistinction to many arrangements of NGO activism that strive for better governance, rather than changes in leadership,[3] NGO activism can become a politics of liberation when

FIGURE 2 TOP Palestinian Mariam Mustafa Daoud protests the building of the separation barrier near the village of Beit Dukou, about 10 km northwest of Jerusalem on Sunday, March 7, 2004 (photos: AP Photo/ Lefteris Pitarakis).

many activists perceive that there is no legitimate, functioning government. This has been the case for Palestinians in the West Bank and Gaza, both before the establishment of the Palestinian Authority (PA) in 1994 and during the second intifada, which began in 2000, when both the power and the legitimacy of the PA came into question for some activists. Second, defining the Separation Barrier as a concern of human rights or humanitarian law or as a topic relevant to discussions about Palestinian statehood, as these activists have done, is tantamount to challenging politically Israel's claim that the barrier was erected purely for security reasons. Finally, in this movement against the Wall, activists have employed tactics of popular protest from the first intifada,[4] and, as I will demonstrate, these tactics themselves index antioccupation politics.

These tactics of popular protest have a prominent visible dimension. Protesters such as Mariam Daoud have been represented frequently in the mainstream news medium of wire service photographs. The meanings of these photographs, like any others, are polysemic, politically complex, and contextually specific. Nonetheless, I will show here that such images of protests against the barrier display Palestinian cultural and political traditions. In these images, Palestinians perform their relationship to the Israeli army and assert their right to self-determination.

Manifold media, including editorials, human rights reports, maps, documentaries, feature films, political cartoons, and artwork, have been employed to critique the barrier. Each of these mediums has its own distinct logics and mechanisms for calling people to action.[5] Though photographs are often perceived as auxiliary to written media, photojournalism is probably the medium in which the barrier most frequently appears. These photographs follow a market logic as photographers seek out spectacular images. Many photojournalists are paid by the day or the image, and wire service agencies seek a variety of material that will work for different clients around the world. In this environment, even relatively small protests have received photojournalists' coverage from international wire services,[6] but most of these protests have not warranted a news article from these same news agencies. So it is that many images of the Wall or of protests against it often appear in Yahoo! slideshows of the Middle East conflict, where, unlike in printed media, editorial space is not a pressing issue and dozens of photographs can be published in a single day.

Palestinians pictured in the protests certainly do not have control over the contents of these images. Yet they are important to the anti-Wall movement. During the second intifada, photojournalism has more often directed its attention to the dramas and sufferings of everyday people,[7] allowing for an expansion of "who or what can be seen or heard as political."[8] Protest photography establishes protesters as political actors worthy of a place in the public sphere alongside officials and spokespeople photographed at meetings and press conferences. Moreover, photojournalism asserts a status of objectivity,[9] and this, too, can be politically effective, especially when the messages themselves are affectively charged.[10] Much like eyewitness testimony to a crime in court, the ideology of objectivity in news photography seems to confirm that these dramatic events actually happened. Professional photographs are often of better quality than those activists take, and they circulate more widely. Palestinians can monitor these images, since they are available online and since Palestinian newspapers publish a large amount of material from international wire services,[11] including images of these protests. For all of these reasons, these photographs might be considered "a new way to reconcile political goals and capitalist aims using a pervasive and influential medium,"[12] one that is as well suited to the "hot" issue of the Israeli-Palestinian conflict as logos, commercials, and flashy websites have been for other political issues.

In part because the PA was slow to mobilize,[13] NGOs have been at the forefront of Palestinian opposition to the barrier. One of the most prominent organizations is Stop the Wall, the Anti-Apartheid Wall Campaign, a network of NGOs and village-based and district-based popular committees that was established in 2002, just months after Israeli prime minister Ariel Sharon revealed the plan for the barrier. It coordinates grassroots campaigns and conducts research about the effects of the barrier. Other organizations that have organized protests against the separation barrier include the Bethlehem-based Holy Land Trust, the International Solidarity Movement, and the Israeli groups Ta'ayush, Gush Shalom, and Anarchists Against the Wall. Many community-based organizations have also independently protested against the barrier in their own villages, camps, and cities.

All of these organizations also oppose Israel's occupation of the West Bank and Gaza. Stop the Wall's mission statement underscores the relationship between eliminating the barrier and Palestinian self-determination. After listing four goals of the campaign concerning the dismantling of the barrier and the reversal of the damage it has already done, the mission statement continues: "These calls are firmly grounded in the context of the struggle against Israeli Colonization, Apartheid and Occupation, and for Palestinian rights and self-determination."[14]

Notably, among all of these organizations, even the locally prominent Stop the Wall is seldom represented directly in U.S. mainstream news about the barrier. In conducting a LexisNexis search of major U.S. and world publications, I found only a few references to the organization or quotes from its director, Jamal Juma', in U.S. newspapers. From a reporter's perspective, Jamal Juma' is neither a good expert for a news-analysis story nor a good victim for a human-interest story. Yet photographs of demonstrations against the barrier have for years been staples of wire service photojournalism, often appearing on Fridays, when many demonstrations are held. Protests are dramatic visual events, while coverage of NGO movements is more complicated. Protests happen every week and require a few hours of work to cover, while articles on land claims or the everyday losses of people who live next to the barrier require intensive labor and could never be published with the same frequency as photographs.

In other locations, scholars of journalism have noted that there can be a tension between journalists' (institutionally situated) proclivity to view protests as spectacles or sites of potential disorder and protest organizers' will to communicate a political message.[15] For example, Mark Pedelty analyzes the coverage of a march in Guatemala that brought together indigenous, black, and working-class delegations. U.S. photojournalists sought out women who were wearing recognizably indigenous clothing and who appeared unsullied by markers of global consumerism. They covered the protesters in a way that essentialized indigenous culture and flattened out the political message of solidarity across groups.[16] Though some of the photographs of Palestinian protests are visually similar to those of the Guatemala protest, they carry very different meanings, due to each respective context.

Many of the photographs from the West Bank consist of wide shots of protest: Palestinian flags unfurled against a blue sky, men and boys lined up in prayer on a construction site, a mountainside olive grove clouded in tear gas where hundreds of protesters are gathered. Other photographs depict participants on either side executing their typical protest actions: Israeli soldiers wielding guns or lobbing sound grenades or Palestinians holding signs or throwing stones. Some suggest ambiguous messages about Palestinian politics. Another photograph from Beit Dukou by the same photographer who photographed Mariam Daoud shows a woman and a girl standing boldly in front of an Israeli demolition machine—while in the foreground, a man in a *kaffiyah* smokes a cigarette, looking off in another direction. The photograph could suggest his apathy, fractures in Palestinian solidarity, or even his abandonment of the pair.

But I am most interested here in photos that depict protesters actively engaging with Israeli soldiers or weapons. These photographs point well beyond the precise struggle against the barrier by representing icons of Palestinian culture in ways that are novel for the mainstream Western media.[17] These icons also reinforce for Palestinians the cultural stakes of their struggle and, perhaps most importantly, make plain a Palestinian view of power relations under occupation and a Palestinian will to resist. These are not new messages for Palestinians, yet in times of political crisis, their repetition is powerful.

Such photographs exemplify how photographs of protest can communicate messages about Palestinian heritage and the Israeli occupation that are powerful to both Palestinian and Western audiences. Although NGOs' names do not appear in these images or their captions, and although NGOs do not play a major role in circulating these images, these images are linked to NGO organizations in that the protests, especially the weekly protests that occurred in rural areas, were generally organized by village popular committees in coordination with larger networks such as Stop the Wall. The AP photographs I described at the opening of this essay, of the elderly woman refusing to leave village land to be confiscated by the army, taken on March 7, 2004, by Lefteri Pitarakis near the village of Beit Dukou is a classic image of civil disobedience, showing an unarmed woman passively resisting an armed soldier. Another AP photo taken by Nasser Ishtayeh depicts a young woman in an olive grove outside Al-Zawiya village on June 9, 2004, thrusting forth small olive branches as she calls out to a helmeted, armed soldier standing less than two meters away (see fig. 1). It is evident from her expression and their postures that in this case, the olive branches are something other than a symbol of peace.

Photographs like this one contain icons of traditional Palestinian culture that likely have slightly different meanings for Western and Palestinian audiences. The older woman in front of the demolition machine is wearing a vivid red-and-black cross-stitched Palestinian dress. Dresses like this have been exhibited as symbols of Palestinian culture around the world. Even outsiders unfamiliar with Palestinian culture would recognize the dress as charming non-Western clothing, just as they would the Guatemalan women's attire. Palestinians see these dresses as treasures of the Palestinian heritage; they are also social markers of rural, poorer, and older women.

In the photograph from Al-Zawiya, a young woman holds out olive branches as though for display. For Western audiences used to seeing Palestinians in refugee camps or cities, the olive branches and rural context in these images might reveal a new side of Palestinian culture. Palestinian viewers would know that these women are calling attention to an urgent economic and cultural issue. Tens of thousands of trees have been destroyed during the second intifada, many as a result of the construction of the Wall.[18] In Palestinian society, olive trees symbolize a shared agricultural legacy and an age-old connection to the land. For external audiences, unlike in the example of Guatemala, focusing on Palestinian culture does not depoliticize Palestinians. "Humanizing" Palestinians, more than in other cases, has political effects, because Palestinians have often been characterized as a group with a pathological "culture of violence." For Palestinians, these photos highlight elements of Palestinian cultural continuity—olive trees, embroidery—upon which concepts of cultural survival and self-determination have been built.

These protesters also perform their relationship with state power on a dangerous stage, like ACT UP protesters of the 1980s and 1990s who advocated for AIDS care and research with "die-ins" and the Tiananmen Square protesters who confronted the Chinese military in 1989. These and other images of protest illustrate a fundamental Palestinian political truth, that Palestinians are the weaker party that is oppressed by the state of Israel. Yet rather than exhibiting Palestinians as indistinguishable and passive victims, as is all too common in photographs of human rights victims,[19] these photographs are also tableaux of an assertive and even articulate brand of nonviolent resistance. In the Al-Zawiya picture, the woman calling out to the soldier seems to be showing something to him that is patently obvious to her. This is one of the essential dynamics of Palestinians' antioccupation activism, for Palestinians live intimately with what they identify as the injustices of the occupation. Moreover, for Western audiences, these photographs represent women as activists, the opposite of popular images of Arab women as passive victims of patriarchy.

Finally, these protesters' physical stances mark a vital intersection between NGO politics under the Palestinian Authority and the popular politics of the first intifada in the pre-Oslo period, when poets wrote paeans to the "Children of Stones" who confronted Israeli soldiers with nothing but rocks. The photographs exhibit Palestinian techniques of the body, behaviors and gestures that are acquired as one lives in a particular culture.[20] These techniques have been developed and fostered over decades of antioccupation activism. Palestinian women famously confronted soldiers during the first intifada, often in efforts to prevent arrests of youth. Other time-honored demonstration skills that also express these fundamental dynamics of occupation and resistance include kicking back tear gas canisters that the army throws at demonstrators and, of course, throwing stones at much more heavily armed military positions.

In recent years, Palestinians have lamented that their liberation struggle has been reduced to negotiating for the reversal of incremental losses—for the removal of checkpoints, the release of prisoners, the ceasing of the Wall construction—as opposed to pressing for large-scale political change. They have also decried the diminishing role of popular politics during a militarized intifada[21] and during a period in which NGOs are often seen to be answering more to international donors than to local needs. Yet in popular protests against the Wall, NGOs and activists have drawn strength from a vigorous history of popular protest and, felicitously, from the dissemination of photographs by wire service journalists looking for powerful images. Paradoxically, the NGOs behind these images are rarely represented. Nevertheless, through a convergence of NGO politics and boldly staged acts of individual resistance, activists have elevated a potentially narrow campaign against the Separation Barrier into a broad campaign against the occupation. To grasp the significance of these images, it is helpful to examine them from both an insider Palestinian perspective and an outsider one. Even though these categories are overly broad, this approach accounts for the way such news agency images circulate on the Internet. These images are potentially politically effective both for Western audiences, who see Palestinians and Israeli occupation in a new light, and for Palestinians, who renew popular politics and reassert the importance of key cultural symbols in a highly public forum.

NOTES

1. The Wall is 708 kilometers long, more than twice the length of the Green Line that it is meant to approximate—the line that marks Israel's borders prior to the 1967 Six-Day War. The extra length of the barrier accommodates Israeli settlements in the West Bank, and only 15 percent of the barrier will actually be constructed on the Green Line, with 9.4 percent of West Bank land isolated west of the Wall, cut off from the remainder of the West Bank. Current plans would leave 25,000 Palestinians living in this area, not including Palestinians who hold East Jerusalem ID cards. As of 2011, 61.8 percent of the barrier has been completed, and 8.2 percent is under construction. See United Nations Office for the Coordination of Humanitarian Affairs, Occupied Palestinian Territory, "Barrier Update: Seven Years after the Advisory Opinion of the International Court of Justice on the Barrier," July 2011, available at http://www.ochaopt.org/documents/ocha_opt_barrier_update_july_2011_english.pdf.
2. During the period in which the Oslo Accords were in effect (1993–2000), the Palestinian Authority's repressive tendencies weakened critical NGOs, and the influx of international funding to Palestinian civil society led to the reshaping of Palestinian NGOs' priorities and modes of action. These two trends diminished the role of the popular antioccupation organizations that had led the first Intifada from 1987 to 1993. See Sari Hanafi and Linda Tabar, *The Emergence of Palestinian Globalized Elite: Donors, International Organizations, and Local NGOs* (Jerusalem: Institute of Jerusalem Studies, 2005); Penny Johnson and Eileen Kuttab, "Where Have All the Women (and Men) Gone?: Reflections on Gender and the Second Palestinian Intifada," *Feminist Review* 69.1, pp. 21–43.
3. Michel Feher, "The Governed in Politics," in Michel Feher (ed.), with Gaëlle Krikorian and Yates McKee, *Nongovernmental Politics* (New York: Zone Books, 2007), pp. 12–27.
4. Julie Norman, *The Second Palestinian Intifada: Civil Resistance* (London: Routledge, 2010). The first intifada, which started in 1987, was a popular and mostly unarmed uprising that consisted of mass protests, stone-throwing demonstrations, strikes, refusal to buy Israeli goods, and other forms of civil disobedience. It indirectly led to the signing of the Oslo Accords in 1993 and the formation of the Palestinian Authority the following year.
5. Meg McLagan, "Introduction: Making Human Rights Claims Public," *American Anthropologist* 108.1 (2006), pp. 191–95.
6. Amahl Bishara, "Covering the Barrier in Bethlehem: The Production of Sympathy and the Reproduction of Difference," in S. Elizabeth Bird (ed.), *The Anthropology of News and Journalism: Global Perspectives* (Bloomington: Indiana University Press, 2010), pp. 54–70.

7. Michelle Woodward, "The Depiction of Israeli-Palestinian Conflict since 1948," *Jerusalem Quarterly* 31 (Summer 2007), http://www.jerusalemquarterly.org/ViewArticle.aspx?id=48.
8. Yates McKee, "Eyes and Ears": Aesthetics, Visual Culture, and the Claims of Nongovernmental Politics," in Feher (ed.), *Nongovernmental Politics*, p. 329.
9. Dona Schwartz, "Objective Representation: Photographs as Facts," in Bonnie Brennen and Hanno Hardt (eds.), *Picturing the Past: Media, History, and Photography* (Urbana: University of Illinois Press), pp. 158–81; Susan Sontag, *On Regarding the Pain of Others* (New York: Farrar, Straus, and Giroux, 2003).
10. Didier Fassin, "The Humanitarian Politics of Testimony: Subjectification through Trauma in the Israeli-Palestinian Conflict," *Cultural Anthropology* 23.3 (2008), pp. 531–58.
11. The Palestinian Initiative for the Promotion of Global Dialogue and Democracy MIFTAH, Media Monitoring Unit, "Public Discourse and Perceptions: Palestinian Media Coverage of the Palestinian-Israeli Conflict" (2005), http://www.keshev.org.il/FileUpload/Miftah%20report%201%20Eng.pdf.
12. Meg McLagan, "Human Rights, Testimony, and Transnational Publicity," in Feher (ed.), *Nongovernmental Politics*, p. 313.
13. Peter Lagerquist, "Fencing the Last Sky: Excavating Palestine after Israel's 'Separation Wall,'" *Journal of Palestine Studies* 33.2, p. 535.
14. The Grassroots Palestinian Anti-Apartheid Wall Campaign, "Introduction: Palestinian Grassroots Anti-Apartheid Wall Campaign," http://stopthewall.org/news/1.shtml.
15. Todd Gitlin, *The Whole World Is Watching: Mass Media in the Making and the Unmaking of the New Left* (Berkeley: University of California Press, 1980); Mark Pedelty, "News Photography and Indigenous Peoples: An 'Encounter' in Guatemala," *Visual Anthropology* 6.3 (1993), pp. 285–301; Gadi Wolfsfeld, Eli Avraham, and Issam Aburaiya, "When Prophecy Always Fails: Israeli Press Coverage of the Arab Minority's Land Day Protests," *Political Communication* 17.2 (2000), pp. 115–31.
16. Pedelty, "News Photography and Indigenous Peoples."
17. While the category of "Western media" contains tremendous diversity, it accounts for the way in which news agency photographs circulate in many different countries.
18. Michele K. Esposito, "Various Organizations, Losses on the Five-Year Anniversary of the Al-Aqsa Intifada, Comparative Statistical Table," *Journal of Palestine Studies* 35.2 (2006), p. 196.
19. Lori Allen, "Martyr Bodies in the Media: Human Rights, Aesthetics, and the Politics of Immediation in the Palestinian Intifada," *American Ethnologist* 36.1 (2009), pp. 161–80; Liisa Milky, "Speechless Emissaries: Refugees, Humanitarianism, and Dehistoricization," *Cultural Anthropology* 11.3 (1996), pp. 377–404.
20. Marcel Mauss, "Techniques of the Body," *Economy and Society* 2.1 (1973), pp. 70–88.
21. Johnson and Kuttab, "Where Have All the Women (and Men) Gone?"

FIGURE 1 Allan Sekula, *Waiting for Tear Gas (White Globe to Black)*, 1999–2000 (courtesy of the artist).

On Strike: Allan Sekula's *Waiting for Tear Gas*

Benjamin J. Young

> And then there was the question of space: the police line represented one kind of order, the union stewards another. And between the two of them, a space. A space that had to be filled.
>
> — Chris Marker, *Grin without a Cat*

A jagged, silver gash breaks up the dark mass of people standing shoulder to shoulder in the street. The figures are wrapped in deep blues and blacks, their scarves, hats, and hair blown by the wind. Shot from below, they seem to fill the corridors of the city, reaching to the top of the buildings in the background, even the sky above. They stand two or three or more deep and occupy the full width of the photograph's frame, eclipsing the horizon and the receding depth of the street. Bright faces limn the top of the picture. Some people chant, some clap, some stand silently with folded arms. The pair in the middle look off calmly, solemnly, in opposite directions. With their heads tilted obliquely in the damp, radiant air, their gazes are drawn away from each other to the edges of the frame; their bodies are drawn together in quiet intimacy. This young man and woman also hold between them, at the center of the picture, a makeshift, three-quarter-length mirror. Light splashes across its surface, piercing the indigo huddle of bodies and tracing another picture: in the reflected image, gray buildings across the way highlight a staggered line of police clad in black uniforms, their faces unrecognizable behind the glare of plastic visors, their bodies thickly padded with armor, their truncheons raised. Enfolded by a picture that seems to project forward into the street and backward through the mirror at once, the viewer is caught between the demonstrators stretched out ahead and the police stationed to the rear—and is cast into the open, virtual space of the street (fig. 1).

This picture belongs to a sequence of color photographs titled *Waiting for Tear Gas* (*White Globe to Black*) (1999–2000) taken by Allan Sekula during protests against the World Trade Organization (WTO) in Seattle in 1999. Made with the customary photojournalistic means of a portable film camera and available light, the project exists both as a slide installation and in book form.[1] The photos record the emergence of a resistance to neoliberalism and corporate globalization within the cities of the Global North that had already been building in the Global South during the previous decade. By documenting this new political formation, *Waiting for Tear Gas* helps constitute it as visible and historically significant in the face of its dismissal and trivialization in the mass media. In this sense, the project functions as a kind of "anti-photojournalism."[2] At the same time, the emphasis that *Waiting* places on describing the sensations and experiences of these people as they assemble in the street suggests that the form of their collective appearance is fundamental to the makeup of this new politics. In other words, it suggests that the ways in which these participants occupy and thereby transform the space of the street may be just as important for politics as the goals or ends that this new movement aims to pursue.

The project also provides an occasion to reexamine some aesthetic issues raised by Sekula's artistic practice, emerging as it does not only from a tradition of documentary photography, but also from that of conceptual art. Since the 1970s, Sekula's work has cannily combined the serial format and photo-text pairings of photoconceptualism with the investigative photo essay, seeking to register the facts of everyday life while questioning the naturalness and transparency of the documentary image.[3] While Sekula's practice is most often understood within the framework of ideology critique and of Brechtian aesthetics more narrowly, *Waiting for Tear Gas* troubles some of the premises that undergird this framework. Many of the devices familiar to this approach—self-reflexive acknowledgement of the constructedness of the artwork, a text or script that determines the production of the image, theatricality, pedagogy, and didacticism—often abandon aesthetic inquiry to point to a social or political truth presumed to lie beyond images. However, Sekula's photographs also deserve to be examined as pictures and attended to at the phenomenological level of their surfaces, surfaces that are consistently positioned within a field of bodily intersubjectivity. The persistence of the portrait, especially—which retrospectively illuminates the indispensability of the human figure to Sekula's previous work—presents issues of identification and absorption often assumed to be alien to his approach. The depiction of people gathered in the street provided by *Waiting for Tear Gas* troubles the oppositions between identification and estrangement and between absorption and theatricality that underpin ideology critique and modernist criticism, respectively. The reliance on the group portrait and what Sekula calls "a simple descriptive physiognomy of the crowd" develops certain absorptive themes without denying the existence of the beholder in a broader social realm.[4] In place of absorption or estrangement, proximity and exposure prove to be key dynamics animating the photos.[5]

Although the rise of the photographic portrait coincided with the flowering of bourgeois individualism in the nineteenth century, one important thread in the history of twentieth-century art and photography is the disappearance of this bourgeois subject.[6] Not only overcome by the large-scale crowds of mass society in the 1920s and 1930s, the individuals who have gone missing from the empty streets of Atget's old Paris will find no home in the vacant postwar industrial, suburban, and urban spaces of photoconceptualism, whether in its pop (Ed Ruscha's *Thirty-Four Parking Lots*) or agitational (Martha Rosler's *Bowery in Two Inadequate Descriptive Systems*) modes. Sekula's photography and his critical writing register the challenge this crisis in portraiture poses to humanist tenets of liberal social documentary, in which the photographer or viewer confers a compensatory beauty, innocence, or dignity on the unfortunate individual in the face of broader exploitation, impoverishment, or violence. Yet Sekula still insists on picturing human figures, especially as they are found at the margins of typical work, home, and social spaces. In *Waiting for Tear Gas*, Sekula responds to the absence of a world-historical political subject neither by dogmatically reasserting, against all odds, the presence of a coherent class subject nor by romantically celebrating the anticapitalist revolutionary. Instead, he records the simultaneously singular and plural existence of the people in the street, linking them to each other and their surroundings through the careful sequencing of images.

As Sekula points out, the demonstrations assert the materiality of the body over and against the abstraction of commodity exchange, global trade, and finance capital flows.[7] However, as my opening reading suggests, the street is also a virtual space—not in the limited sense of digital technology, but in the sense of images and appearances, capacities and potentialities—albeit one that accommodates a certain kind of collective embodiment. And while the street is a space for collective action, that action is here recast as patient waiting or as the militant refusal to act that is the strike. In these photographs of the street, the oppositions between activity and passivity, materiality and virtuality, human and inhuman, particular and universal are quickly complicated by the dynamics of appearance, visibility, and representation, beginning with the mirror.

The mirror held by the demonstrators in the photograph enacts a reflexive use of images to arrive at a truth that lies if not wholly outside the image, then just at its edge—the protestors use the mirror to point out the threatening violence of the police. As an allegory of critical documentary work in general, the estrangement that results is expected to provoke a more self-conscious, knowledgeable, and even enlightened grasp of the political situation; this reflexive meditation on the external, often invisible social conditions that limit and direct the construction of the image and the viewing subject reveals the ways state power constrains who can appear and assemble in public. But perhaps more importantly, the photograph also contrasts two different ways of facing and encountering others. Although it appears in the middle of the sequence, I take this photo as a starting point because of the contrast it stages between two different kinds of lines, lines that organize different postures, attitudes, and looks. Despite the apparent symmetry of their lines as they occupy public space, the two formations differ in their stance: the declarative frontality of the demonstrators is firm, but open; the police are crouched back on one foot, both defensive and ready to advance on command. Each policeman clenches a nightstick, advertising its combative use; the demonstrators clap with empty hands, hold signs, or prop up the mirror, whose flimsy reflection seems ill suited to shield against physical violence.

Deep shadow engulfs the crowd, dissolving the contours of their bodies and making palpable the free space that fuses them together. The atmospheric light that draws individual faces from the shadow gives them a rounded, fragile, haptic quality. Meanwhile, the silhouettes of the police remain only dark outlines in the glare; their armor leaves no patch of skin showing. The standard uniform and helmet makes each police officer identical and unidentifiable. Unlike the resolute exteriority of those blank statues, the pair of demonstrators at the center strike a subtle balance of inwardness and outwardness. Their bodies merge in the darkness behind the mirror, yet their faces remain distinct. Although they stand close enough to be touching, they regard not each other, but what lies beyond the frame. Have they just met? Are they lovers? Do they remain anonymous and unknown to each other? Their momentary proximity is unbroken by word or look. Wrapped in their closeness, they do not look directly at the viewer or the police; at the same time, the world around them draws out their looks, as the sides of their faces, angled toward the viewer, are offered up to the gaze of others.

In contrast, the demonstrators cannot see the police, who have tried to make themselves invisible, untouchable, and spectacularly so.[8] Any reciprocity between the two lines has been cut off by the visors of the police, who attempt to conduct surveillance without being seen and whose gaze cannot be returned, or rather is always reflected by their armor.[9] As a picture of sovereignty, this photograph of absent, commanding bodies recalls that exemplary painting of another era, Velázquez's *Las Meninas*. Although *Waiting for Tear Gas* stands on the other side of modernity from the classical model of representation identified in *Las Meninas*—a separation that can be summed up by the word "biopolitics"—these two works share a similar composition. They both markedly superimpose sovereign, artist, and viewer in the same viewing position, exterior to the surface of the picture, and consequently use a mirror image to circuitously reflect the sovereign back into the picture. Of course, the differences are instructive: in the photograph, the figure of the creator-painter is eclipsed and elided with the figure of the spectator-demonstrator; there is less play with the means of representation (the unfinished canvas, the finished portraits hanging on the wall, and the light-filled window in Velázquez's painting are all condensed in the mirror and visor); the figure of the sovereign has joined the anonymously plural and monolithic ranks of the police; in a new willingness to appear in the open, the couple has switched sides to join the ranks of spectators and attendants; and the viewer now occupies the less fixed, more vertiginous terrain of the street. And yet we may still learn something from the description of the sovereign couple in *Las Meninas* as the invisible "center" and "essential void" whose image reflected in the looking glass is nonetheless: "the palest, most unreal, most compromised of the painting's images: movement, a little light, would be sufficient to eclipse them."[10] Looking again at Sekula's photograph with these words in mind, the viewer may be more inclined to notice the woman's fingers lightly pinching the corner of the mirror, creating an indentation in the plastic sheeting and releasing a puddle of silver whose deformation of the image threatens to spread across the scene.

The pair at the center seem to register this armored invisibility of the police and so look beyond the police line, beyond the immediacy of the scene, even as they are aware of—can feel—the threat confronting them. Nor do they look at the mirror, which they display for others to see. Instead, the mirror serves to publicize this image of the police and to expose what was previously hidden: the violence necessary to enforce the law and maintain the rule of the state. And since the police are there to keep the demonstrators from blocking the streets and disrupting the WTO meeting, the violence that backs the prerogatives of the state also stands in for the reigning order of economic governance and the normally invisible, systemic violence of exploitation and uneven development it involves. Seen in this context, the armored police instantiate the unaccountable, nontransparent, and closed nature of the ministerial meeting that protects from scrutiny the imperative of trade and profit—rather than economic, social, or environmental justice—motivating the economically powerful nations who dominate the organization. This asyndeton, which superimposes structural economic violence and spectacular police violence, is the strength and weakness of the demonstration. In this rhetorical gambit, the state serves as the nexus of both economic governance and sovereign law. One of the risks of making this argument in this way is that it loses sight of the broader field of government operating beyond the nation-state.[11]

The mirror serves first of all to reflect the ways in which the equipment and task of the police dehumanize their appearance and their senses, or—if "dehumanize" assumes too much of a human essence only secondarily lost or corrupted—to deaden their ability to touch, to feel, to be affected by others. (They retain, presumably, the ability to feel the hardness of the inside of their armor, the warmth then chill of their sweat underneath it.) Confronting the police with their own image might force them to confront their place in a scenario of domination. However, it remains doubtful that the police will recognize this image of themselves or in recognizing it find it so countervailing to their own self-image that they would be compelled to drop their weapons or refuse their orders. In this case, the mirror is also aimed at anyone who passes by, at a broader public who in disapproval of this violent stance would shame the police and those responsible for their conduct.[12] In publicizing this image of the police, the mirror functions as a means of persuasion, a trope: an apotropaic deflection that turns the image of violent conduct into one that exposes and by implication denounces or counteracts that violence.[13] A visual equivalent of the well-worn chant "The whole world is watching"—a phrase that entered the public lexicon during the television broadcast of police beating demonstrators and passersby outside the 1968 Democratic National Convention in Chicago—the mirror points to bearing witness as an important function of protest, as well as exemplifying its reliance on media and mediation.[14] (In this way, the mirror serves as a metonym of the different media that might reproduce the event, Sekula's photographs included.) A similar kind of demonstrative showing occurs in other photographs where an outstretched hand cups a rubber bullet or a pair of them carefully holds a spent smoke grenade for the camera to examine, even as the demonstrator's face is sometimes cropped from the frame. These hands serve a dual function: first, as testimony, that I was here and witnessed someone being attacked; second, as evidence, a record of what happened that draws on the photographic index, that this was here. This deictic gesture appeals to an unseen viewer who is interpellated, and so partially created and imagined, through the act of demonstration. The gesture seeks to assemble a public, if not a court of judgment, beyond that already found in the street.

Yet it may be that publicizing or exposing is not enough; exposure does not automatically lead to understanding nor understanding to action. After all, nothing guarantees that the world will watch without changing channels or that in watching, viewers will make sense of the images in the same way as the demonstrators. And because the viewer of the mirror, and by extension of the photograph, remains structurally undetermined—positioned in the same viewing position or just to the side of that enjoyed by the police—this exposure does not guarantee viewers will see the scenario from the standpoint of the demonstrators, thereby siding with them and their cause.

There is, however, another kind of exposure at work in the image—that of the viewer. This image exposes not only the actions of the police, but also the look of the viewer. At first, the viewer seems to approach the scene from the vantage point of the police. But the mirror also troubles the fantasy of security embodied by the police. As the viewer gazes at the demonstrators, the mirror points out the viewer's blind spot, creating the sensation of being looked at and approached from behind. This vulnerability intimated in the viewer would seem to ruin the ideal of a simultaneously fortified and panoptic vision figured by the police. The loss of an invulnerable, all-seeing standpoint subverts any facile notion of perfect security. Discomfited, exposed, and no longer safe in the anonymity of looking, the viewer is caught between the two lines, perpetually suspended between them *and* urgently asked to choose sides.

The photograph certainly seems inclined toward one side: although they face off against the viewer, the broad scale, openness, and intimacy of the demonstrators in the foreground overshadow the figures of the police. For some viewers already inclined to the demonstrator's cause, the imbalance in weaponry will automatically confirm the moral rightness of the activists. However, this moral feeling cannot trump a broader struggle over the uncertain politics of the image, a struggle over how others not already committed to the activists' ideals will understand the events. And there may be good reasons to linger suspended between the lines. First, as much as the photograph invites identification with the demonstrators, viewers who discover in the mirror an uncomfortable confrontation with the police in place of their own image may also be called to reflect on their own place in the economy of violence for which the police serve as placeholders. Second, when considered within a broader climate of fear, the attraction of this fantasy of invulnerability personified by the police cannot be discounted. Such a fantasy, no matter how impossible or irrational, may not be dispelled, but rather can be strengthened by any discomfort, vulnerability, or threat with which the public is confronted.

Despite the clear asymmetry between the two groups in their inclination and capacity for violence, the image of confrontation risks a specular doubling. Depending on the viewer's preconceptions about who is entitled to speak and act in the name of the people, about legitimate and illegitimate forms of public conduct, the police response is liable to be justified as protective of a larger public, as a preemptive strike construed as defense against anticipated—or imagined—violence originating from the other. After all, the years following the Seattle protests have repeatedly reminded us of the ways in which the rhetoric of defense can serve to justify all manner of aggression.

In another photograph, a young man in the center of the frame wears a gas mask over his face (see color plates). The segmented tube that protrudes from the mouth of the apparently World War II–era gas mask snakes across his torso and is tucked into a gray satchel hanging off the shoulder of his chestnut-brown leather jacket. He lightly holds a video camera in one hand; the other hand is held up to his face, gingerly touching the gray plastic that forms a second skin, as if he were adjusting it, still uncomfortable with its fit and feel. Cast-offs of the military-industrial complex are recycled and turned against the nexus of corporate and government interests that produced them. The obsolete, army-surplus tech repurposed for civilian defense gives him the look of a retrofuturistic citizen superhero or a posthuman media vigilante. Mixed in with some steelworkers sporting T-shirts, ball caps, and the occasional backward hard hat, a larger group of young men with kerchiefs and gas masks over their faces mills about behind him, also equipped to defend themselves against police violence. At first glance, the center figure's gas mask mimes those of the police. The key difference is that he holds in his hand neither a club nor a gun, but a camera. Like the mirror previously, the gas mask and video camera are technological supplements to human vision. While the mirror exhibited the dehumanization of the armored police, the masked videographer enacts the reflexive dehumanization of the demonstrator. The camera and insulating, protective gear intervene in the field of vision, displacing existing human faculties precisely in the service of recording, publicizing, and exhibiting the police attempt to disable those same senses by overloading them.

In this encounter, both police visors and the gas masks and kerchiefs worn by demonstrators disturb the ideal of a liberal public sphere in which parties recognize each other as interlocutors in a rational dialogue. Even as the camera promises to promote enlightenment, it is deployed within a public sphere structured by antagonism. The footage that results may be used as a tool for refining protest tactics, as a document in a history told from below, or as evidence in a search for legal accountability; more immediately, the camera also serves as the means by which government violence might be portrayed as unjustified and illegitimate.[15] This agonistic struggle over the meaning and significance of the events takes place not only in the media, but also in the streets, in a struggle over the ability to be seen and heard in public space. In this struggle, the camera, unlike the tools of the police, is not likely to inflict bodily harm; the improvised, militant defense staged here must be distinguished from the willingness and capacity of the police to inflict bodily injury. However, even given these important differences, the masking and pose of these demonstrators still partially mirror those of the police, forming their militant if defensive complement. The specular doubling persists. When public space is occupied by those with no authorization or prior right to do so—an appropriation signaled by the demonstrators' chant "Whose streets? Our streets!"—it is often justified with reference to the sovereignty of the people. It is worth asking to what extent this embodiment of the

FIGURE 2 Allan Sekula, *Waiting for Tear Gas (White Globe to Black)*, 1999–2000 (courtesy of the artist).

people occurs in the mode of the fictional "as if," the contingent, or the provisional, like the performative contradiction of claiming a right—in this case, to occupy public space—precisely at the moment in which it is being forcefully denied. However, rather than meeting police sovereignty with popular sovereignty, it may be instead a question of relinquishing the pose of sovereignty altogether.

Perhaps for this reason, *Waiting for Tear Gas* largely sidesteps the iconic images of confrontation familiar to photojournalism. The mirror photograph, although it appears roughly in the middle of the sequence, does not lead to an ensuing battle with the police. Instead, it is followed by another line of demonstrators cloaked in tans, browns, and grays arrayed frontally across the frame, with the camera positioned just off center from the double yellow line that leads the way down the center of the street (fig. 2). The couple at the middle each tread on the line with alternate legs, and their contrapuntal step leads the whole front row, holding hands, mouths open in chant or song, in a syncopated march down the street. Proceeding through lateral moves, Sekula investigates what it looks like to stand alongside the demonstrators, replacing the head-on address of the mug shot or forensic photo with both frontal portraits of demonstrators surrounded by others on the street and sidelong glances down their horizontal lines as they link arms. As the crowds become dense, each individual is no longer oriented on his or her own vertical axis and spaced out across a horizontal row. Instead, the scale shifts away from the individual as bodies start to overlap, giving a contour to the group. Then, as the demonstrators begin to disperse, the camera returns again to the free space that links smaller groups, couples, and singles. But the sequence does not proceed chronologically, by imposing a narrative of dramatic actions with beginning, middle, and end.[16] Instead, the photos track an ongoing process of alliance or—after the term "affinity group," designating a unit assembled for direct action—affinitization, elaborating a repeated crescendo and diminuendo as individuals gradually fill up and drain out of the frame.

With the exception of the opening and closing shots of globes taken in a library, which I'll discuss later, nearly all the photos in *Waiting for Tear Gas* are taken in the street. The sequence begins with close-up portraits, moving to full-length shots of individuals picked out of crowds as the assembly grows, switching to a line of police with weapons drawn, then to a number of isolated demonstrators, some injured, as they mill about in the gas-filled night. Some delegates, surrounded by police guards, watch and wait from within an illuminated glass entryway, monitoring the events in the street that have waylaid them; returning to a day-lit scene, other delegates with conference badges and business suits enter and exit their hotels. (The account is not without moments of levity: as one delegate tosses his head over his shoulder to speak with a colleague, his tie—the top half battened down by a tie pin, the bottom half blown upward by the wind—comically juts upward, threatening to poke him in the face once he turns back toward the camera. The image suggests that at least once they leave their glass cocoon, some things lie outside the bureaucrats' control, and everyone is subject to the weather.) In the middle of the sequence are paired the two pictures of lines of demonstrators in daylight, those with the mirror followed by those marching with clasped hands. They lead to a climax of two other photographs shot from just over the heads of crowds who move across the picture plane diagonally, each frame in the opposite direction (fig. 3). Each line is now a thick mass filling the depths of the city: chilled, wet, tired, festive. In both pictures, the tangle of bodies blots out the horizon line, and the diagonal composition further upends their orientation and perspectival stability; onlookers are denied any fixed viewing position, as if the ground were giving way beneath their feet. Moving away from the static lines of confrontation shown earlier, the crowds have slipped from their moorings. Evening settles in with a set of half-length portraits, and it becomes more difficult to separate the protestors from passersby, especially after a number of residents were caught downtown after work or holiday shopping and others, hearing the news, rushed there from surrounding neighborhoods to join the scene.[17] The anarchists and hippies and steelworkers with their hard hats mix with more ordinarily dressed folk, some white, some black, some Latino.

FIGURE 3 Allan Sekula, *Waiting for Tear Gas (White Globe to Black)*, 1999–2000 (courtesy of the artist).

A woman in a red jacket stands at the center of the frame, facing the camera. In an apparent call for peace, she holds both hands up with fingers in a V, a gesture directed outward to a threat on the other side of the photographer. She steps into the open to intervene between that beyond and the out-of-focus row of black-clad activists who hover a few steps behind her, everyone backlit with yellow light streaming from the windows of a nearby store. In another shot, a messenger in a blue jacket, with shoulder bag and radio, fills the frame and lifts his head to gaze past the viewer as he walks by, with a scattering of people in the empty street and sidewalk behind him. In another, a young man dressed in cargo pants, sweatshirt, and knit cap pushes his bike as he walks out of frame, his back turned to the viewer; at the same moment, a bald cop strides across the frame, reaching out to stop him by fastening onto the man's backpack with a gloved hand. In the middle of an empty street, a man strums an electric guitar plugged into the amplifier apparently being tugged along in the cart beside him; his hands, face, and long hair are a blur as he plays. In an interior scene awash in the same reddish light from the street, a young woman in profile grins slightly as she gazes out from the white cocoon of a chemical-protection suit (fig. 4). Behind her sits a stack of broken-down computer parts and the edge of a window that opens out onto the orange-colored cityscape. Having taken temporary refuge in an artist's studio that had been raided earlier by the police, she has donned a cast-off hazmat suit left

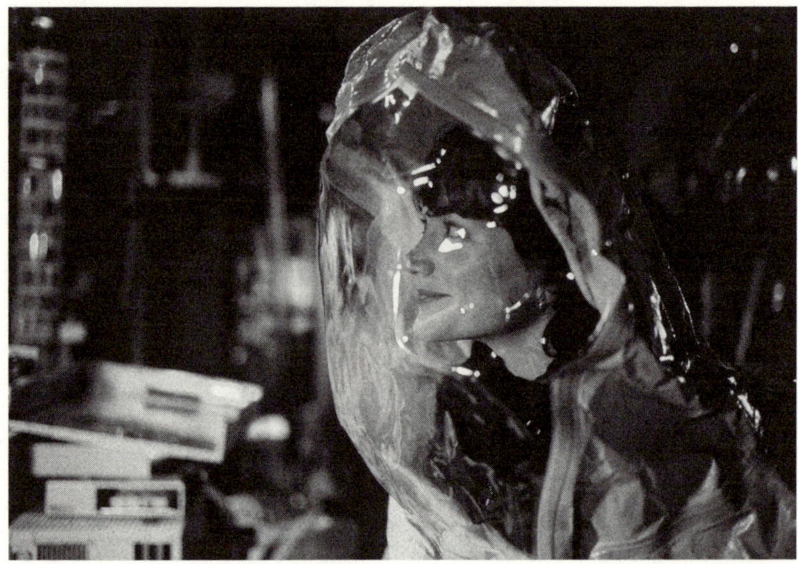

FIGURE 4 Allan Sekula, *Waiting for Tear Gas (White Globe to Black)*, 1999–2000 (courtesy of the artist).

behind by the authorities.[18] Her look of wonder overflows the protective shell. The highlights that play across the clear, crinkled plastic of her hood resemble stars glinting off an astronaut's visor, hinting at some unseen vastness. The defensive armor is transformed into a vehicle for space travel. Then an armored truck streaks by with a helmeted cop in riot gear hanging off the back. Later, two women appear in the entryway to an all-night sex shop, apparently the "live girls" featured in the ad for "peep shows" and "fantasy booths" posted on the wall behind them. Performing for the camera a parody of arrest, one woman in high heels and a bright, scarlet-red dress leans with hands against the wall, legs spread, her behind to the viewer; the other playfully administers a spanking. As cops-and-robbers turns into sex play, business is never far off. It isn't easy to tell whether this free show is a ludic break from work or a preview meant to advertise the commodity sold inside. Acknowledging the erotics of urban voyeurism from behind the enclosed, windowed doorway, these working women also remind the viewer that not everyone can afford to take the day off. The final figure, a masked man in a red devil suit, turns to face the viewer as he carries an oversized chainsaw crudely fashioned out of cardboard.

The photographs in *Waiting for Tear Gas* trace an arc of events through the alternating emptiness and density of the streets as they fill with people. By attending to the way these figures inhabit the space of the street, the photographs in the sequence question the terms in which nongovernmental politics is conventionally understood. The term "protest" too often connotes a merely symbolic message of discontent that fails to challenge the material and discursive framework of government, and "direct action" too often suggests an allegedly unmediated physical force that will prove effective in altering or abolishing government. It thus becomes important to challenge some of the key assumptions on which these terms rely, starting with the implicit distinction between symbolic speech and physical act.[19] Of course, as the mirror photograph from *Waiting for Tear Gas* has already made clear, protest often requires the physical occupation of public space, and direct action requires mediation in order for it to be tied to any larger political universe. However, the images in *Waiting for Tear Gas* focus less on the messages communicated or on the acts committed by those assembled in the street. Instead, they concentrate on people as they gather together and drift apart in the sometimes anxious, sometimes quiet intervals between events—as they march and stand and wait.

As the photographs capture people lingering at the edges of the crowd, picked out on a street emptied of daily traffic, paused as they clasp hands in a march, or halted before a line of police, stillness infuses the scene. The photographs abet this stillness, and in each single frame, duration reigns outside of time. As a sequence, the intervals between frames then assemble the images and release them back into time. By attending to the "lulls, the waiting, and the margins of events" and integrating those pauses into the sequential form of the work, *Waiting for Tear Gas* marks another time apart from the impatient, immediate rhythm of politics. This conduct is best understood in terms of the *strike*, an event that troubles many of the conceptual oppositions that structure conventional accounts of politics, such as the oppositions between protest and direct action, speech and act, mediacy and immediacy, violence and nonviolence, manifestation and withdrawal.[20]

In contrast with the rhetoric of protest, the strike is more than the "expression" by individuals of previously held political opinions or the exercise of free speech. While government loudly proclaims the right to free speech, it often simultaneously seeks to limit the right to assemble, for example, by restricting the time, place, and size of demonstrations, by confining demonstrators in "protest pens," or by excluding them from public space when declaring "protest-free zones."[21] In this framework, protest is reduced to a merely symbolic activity by an aggregate of rights-bearing individuals that may be conducted anywhere, preferably apart from legitimate government activity and without disrupting the normative uses of space dedicated to an atomized public. As a collective manifestation of dissent that exceeds this framework of individualized speech, the strike appears as a contest over the use of public space. In the strike, the withdrawal from the specialized spheres of life and work may become a paradoxical retreat into public space. Like the secession of the plebs from Rome, this retreat is also a gathering that may constitute other discourses, social relations, and spaces of politics. However, unlike the retreat to Aventine Hill, it need not occur only as an escape from the city, but also as the convergence on and occupation of the public square.[22] In the process, the street is transformed from a space of commerce into something other than the channel for the efficient transport of people and goods toward their predestined ends—thus the importance of the economic strike by dockworkers and taxi drivers in Seattle that accompanied the WTO demonstrations.

In contrast with the rhetoric of activism and direct action, the strike appears here as an anomalous suspension of action: a withdrawal of the body from the workplace; from the empty, segmented time of wage labor; from the familiar rhythm of shopping and consumption; from the spaces and routines of domestic life; as well as the withdrawal of consent and participation from the normal operation of government. As a form of abstention that does not seek to govern events as they unfold or to impose an order on the world, the strike may remain nonviolent; as a work stoppage, its disjunctive force threatens to annul the ruling order.[23] This withdrawal realizes itself as manifestation when people, often unknown to each other, find themselves standing together in the street.[24]

By documenting this manifestation, *Waiting for Tear Gas* undertakes the group portraiture of an emerging political collective and the individual actors who make it up, granting visibility to those often demonized or simply ignored by mainstream journalism. In an age of individuals the group portrait is a neglected genre, but Sekula does not return to it by taking as his models the great twentieth-century images of masses sutured together through photomontage.[25] The rows of figures, who when arranged on vertical axes maintain their individuality, do not settle onto a single plane or into a single image; meanwhile, the atmospheric, free space between them puts them into close bodily contact. The figures exhibit a "coordinative attentiveness" somewhere between activity and passivity as they stand and wait and look—they are drawn to each other and the world without imposing their will on it.[26] They maintain this attentiveness as openness even in the face of violence: while the phrase "waiting for tear gas" suggests the certainty that repression will meet such a gathering, another kind of expectation emerges from that experience of waiting, one oriented to the as yet unseen or unknown.[27] Giving equal time to each image in sequence, the regular intervals at which the photos click through the slide projector also invite a similar attentiveness from the viewer. Refusing to subordinate any individual composition to a larger whole, or the sequence to a single action, narrative, or subject, the work does not provide a unified picture of the group. Instead, Sekula assembles this picture over time, working slowly and recurrently, at different scales and moments, first approaching individuals to catch their faces, drawing back to show them interacting with others, then finally surrounded in a crowd, coordinating singular and plural views in the same nonhierarchical way that the demonstrators gather themselves.

After the introductory picture of two globes, the initial photographs of the demonstration are two head-and-shoulder portraits of women, each shown in profile, but facing opposite directions, with their heads slightly raised to meet the sunlight cast across them (figs. 5 and 6). In the first picture, a young woman faces to the left and sports a black sweater and cropped, bright red hair; an equally red jacket contrasts with the long, black hair of the rightward-facing middle-aged woman in the following frame. Although they are pictured individually in separate frames, the similar pose and inverted red and black colors begin to twine them together.[28] Another photograph shows a woman seen from the side as she steps forward down the street, simultaneously pivoting on her heel to laugh and talk with a man behind her, her blue jacket rhyming with the blue background of the union banner held by the man as he marches with a line of dockworkers across the frame. Not absorbed by the group, her pivot nonetheless articulates the free space between them as a kind of bond.

As a meditation on the importance of the bodily occupation of public space for dissent and democratic politics, *Waiting for Tear Gas* nonetheless does not champion the vitalism of the multitude.[29] Rather, the sequence emphasizes the provisional appropriation of public space and the precariousness of the life that occupies it. The demonstration emerges as the shared exposure and vulnerability of those bodies—to the warmth and glare of light, to the damp and chill of the weather, to the possibilities and constraints of the city, and to the force and violence of armed police. After a number of introductory portraits set off against the assembling crowd, a woman appears in close-up (fig. 7). She turns back toward the camera with a look of grace and composure as her silver-gray, shoulder-length hair falls neatly around her head. Behind her, an out-of-focus young policeman stands with a drawn visor, stern look, and wooden club across his chest. Turned away from him, she registers his presence as a few strands of hair blow across her face, hinting at the other kinds of force that threaten her. Yet her poise absorbs all this with equanimity; resolved to wait in defiant openness, she does not move.

Shortly afterward, the viewer is faced head-on with a line of police in complete riot gear, shin guards and visors gleaming in the yellow streetlight, alternately holding truncheons and oversized tear gas launchers, blocking the way. This is followed by an image of a street flooded with the same pale mustard hue of light where two young people crouch at the center of the frame. The camera is also low to the ground, and only the blurred legs of the oblivious crowd are visible in the

FIGURES 5–6 Allan Sekula, *Waiting for Tear Gas* (*White Globe to Black*), 1999–2000 (courtesy of the artist).

FIGURE 7 Allan Sekula, *Waiting for Tear Gas (White Globe to Black)*, 1999–2000 (courtesy of the artist).

background. One young woman, frightened and bleeding at the mouth, has knelt down and clasps her hands together in front of her torso, as if in prayer, her gloves carefully laid on the ground before her knees. The neatly stacked gloves, stark and small in their deliberateness, provide a meager anchor against the chaotic blur that threatens to overtake her. Her companion perches on one knee beside her and strokes her hair. Of all the images in the project, this one most risks sanctifying the righteousness or innocence of the injured demonstrator. Too often civil disobedience is justified only through a sacrificial moralism, through the purity of the individual who willingly endures suffering. As if to prevent such monumentality, a second image appears, with the camera now moved in a ninety-degree arc, showing the same scene from the side. As the woman begins to cry with her companion's hand on her back, this lateral move brings the viewer closer to her, making her less a fixed, moral icon than a picture of creaturely life, another person vulnerable to injury to whom we might respond. The second image reinserts her into the time and space of assembly, into a world of others. No longer an exalted symbol, she is a person who is approached and touched, in a responsive situation with others.

In another frame, a young man in a black sweater, tan kerchief, and ball cap tilts his head back to the night sky, his face lost to the viewer as his wet hand rubs the chemicals from his eyes; this gesture of defacement paradoxically allows the camera to draw nearer to him than it would otherwise (fig. 8). Approaching,

FIGURES 8–9 Allan Sekula, *Waiting for Tear Gas* (*White Globe to Black*), 1999–2000 (courtesy of the artist).

almost touching his torso, as if to reach out in aid, viewers encounter him less as an identifiable actor or type than as someone whose injury demands care. Distant regard is replaced by bodily proximity. Dispensing with the moralization of suffering seems to require a certain blindness to identity and to the recognizable boundaries that structure the social order.[30] This disidentification also entails suspending judgment about the guilt or innocence of the actors. What remains is a situation in which the viewer may approach or be approached by anyone at all, as if anyone at all could step into this space and be seen.[31]

As a young woman runs toward us with a handkerchief over her mouth and others scatter from the empty street behind, the whole scene goes out of focus, and even our vision begins to blur. A lone man dressed in white shoes, white poncho, and straw hat flinches as a concussion grenade flashes behind him, and he clutches his placard and folds his chin to his chest as five policemen run to encircle him. An older woman, also in white, reclines on a park bench; apparently injured, she holds a towel over her right eye, covering the side of her face (fig. 9). The yellow light cast across the scene draws together the cream-colored glove, towel, scarf, and blanket in which she is wrapped, almost allowing us to take comfort in her susceptibility. While it is an anticapitalist commonplace to oppose lived, embodied experience to the deathly abstraction of capital, we are here reminded of the way in which life remains inherently exposed to injury and death. Instead of seeking to transcend the body's limits through collective revolutionary action, the viewer is enjoined simultaneously to prevent injury and to affirm the vulnerability that allows us to be affected by others.[32] Part of the political force of the assembly lies in the way, at least for the duration of the demonstration, it carves out a counterpublic of care, responsiveness, and collective action apart from the state. However, rather than simply celebrating a spontaneous, vital freedom, the photos depict the experience of collective assembly as dependence on others. And what began as an operation of enlightenment and increased visibility transforms into an exposition of blindness. As artificial tears mix with real ones, they blur the dividing lines between life and technics, nature and culture.[33] As we move among these injured and blinded figures, this blurring also forces us to negotiate with the inhuman conditions that augment life—that discipline and control life, but that also support and maintain it—including not only the instruments, means, and tools required to care for others, but also capital, the state, law, and the varied prosthetic institutional and civic bodies on which we have come to rely.

The final, parting figure of the sequence occupies a netherworld between the realms of human and inhuman, life and death. He appears alone on the sidewalk, outside the existing *socius* of other demonstrators, or delegates, or police, covered head to toe in flame red: a grinning demon who wields a chainsaw with wickedly pointed teeth (see color plates).[34] At first glance, this devil serves as a stark symbol of the evil wrought by profit-based exploitation of natural resources without regard to environmental destruction, sustainability, or social justice. But this moral equation does not fully account for the strangeness of this figure. His otherworldly nature provokes a response somewhere between terror, bathos, and glee. If he seems a not thoroughly convincing embodiment of evil, it is due not only to the outlandish sight of a grown man with a slight paunch in bright red pajamas alone on the street. If his figure continues to unsettle the viewer, it may also be that the ghostly embodiment enacted here also precisely figures the fate of labor under capitalism, for capital not only drains "living labor" from the body of the worker, congealing it in the dead value of the commodity and its universal form, money. Once transmuted into the form of capital, that dead labor apparently comes to life again when capital seems to go on generating value out of itself, like an "animated monster."[35] Thus, disembodied labor suffers a paradoxical reincorporation when it appears in abstract-sensuous form, in a demonic body, as if possessed by life, in a life that is not life.[36] Apprehending this devil and the fate he portends may provoke a sense of terror. However, this feeling is also accompanied by an unexpected joy at seeing his garish luminance cut through the dreary equivalence of his surroundings, the officious khaki and dull gray of passing traffic, the drab tan of surrounding concrete. Not just serving as an allegory of alienation, he may also provoke a flash of recognition on the viewer's part, for the figure also serves as a reminder of the ways the forces of creative destruction escape the capitalist's control, often in monstrous ways.[37] Some of those forces may return here in the disruptive protestor who haunts his world. In short, the viewer might be forgiven a little sympathy for this devil, the red disrupter of heaven's order. As sharp moral division gives way to the ambiguity of this figure—the difficulty of deciding whose side he is on—it again turns out that life cannot be lived without encountering death. The issue quickly shifts from moral denunciation of limitless exploitation to the political question of how to reappropriate and redistribute these forces justly. This question of appropriation is further broached by the two images that begin and end the work.

As I've noted, *Waiting for Tear Gas* opens with a close-up of a pair of globes sitting on top of a filing cabinet in the Seattle public library, into which Sekula had retreated during the day (see color plates). In the left foreground stands a globe whose empty seas are rendered in white; behind it stands its out-of-focus twin, whose multicolored patchwork of countries is set off against black seas. The sequence closes by reiterating that shot, although this time the white globe has fallen away and the black globe occupies the foreground, standing in the center of the frame (fig. 10). The pairing suggests, as the artwork's subtitle points out,

FIGURE 10 Allan Sekula, *Waiting for Tear Gas* (*White Globe to Black*), 1999–2000 (courtesy of the artist).

a movement from white globe to black, from one vision of the globe to another. What has transpired in the intervening sequence amounts to something more like counterglobalization, rather than the reductive, simple-minded antiglobalization for which so many pundits would castigate the demonstrators.

White or black, the globe already figures a certain relation to the world: it is an artifact of a certain kind of appropriation, a grasping of the world as a map. With the globe, the world is turned into an object, its surface produced through standardized measurement that presumes one continuous, uniform space, grasped as if no longer standing on Earth.[38] Not just a product of science, the globe is also the tool of explorers, princes, and merchants and a symbol of the reach of geographic, political, and economic power. Yet this repetition of shots of the globe uncovers a kind of latency in the interval between the two objects. Like photography itself, the movement from white globe to black registers an image that, when developed, yields a reversal of values. However, the reversal signaled in the shift from white to black is not divorced from another sense of revolution, that of the daily turning of the Earth, "the rhythm of this eternally transient worldly existence," and of nature's "eternal and total passing away."[39] This ceaseless passing lends an urgency to waiting, producing a sensitivity to what is at every moment lost and suggesting that any revolutionary political transformation must stay in touch with the mundane rhythms of earthly life. This rhythm is also built into the constant passage of images through the slide projector and the looped structure of the work, where the final image returns viewers to the beginning of the sequence.

This turning also recalls the turning of the Earth and highlights the aspectual character of the globe: one part of the Earth is always in shadow. In the black globe, it is as if this shadow has begun to spread from the far side over the entire surface. Attention to these aspects of the globe make it less a picture of totality than a body existing in time and space and seen from a particular, embodied standpoint. Running counter to the reduction of world to picture, this shadow globe might give way to a more expansive attempt to imagine a world of variable light and shadow, of passing time and of contiguous, but not necessarily continuous, spaces—and therefore of a world with a plurality of others spread across it.[40] Insofar as this shadowed globe figures another world, it is a world whose contours are sketched out in the interim between the globes that open and close the *Waiting for Tear Gas*, in the moments of equality, solidarity, democratic organization and participation, care, and dependency on unknown, anonymous others witnessed in the demonstration. Combined with the experience of waiting explored throughout the work, the black globe also figures a certain relation to the future. It seems, however, that darkness clouds this picture, so that it is oriented not toward foreseeable ends that unfold through historical progress, but toward ends that cannot be fully prefigured or pictured.[41] A kind of impossible image, the black globe adumbrates something like the unfigurable, the incalculable, or the not yet possible. Part of its disjuncture with the present, globalized world seems to come from the darkness in the image that resists knowledge or calculation—like the shadow of an unknown future cast across the present.

By figuring the passage from light to dark, the turning of the globe from day to night, and the spread of shadow over the world, the photo also questions the new visibility enjoyed by these demonstrators in the Global North as compared with the relative invisibility, at least from the vantage point of the United States, of those actors from the Global South with whom they may seek to collaborate.[42] The challenge of linking the WTO meeting in Seattle with systemic violence and exploitation elsewhere is inscribed in the international division of labor and the global geographical division between the Global North and the often postcolonial or neocolonial Global South.[43] An expanded, more capacious sense of the world would start to link those resisting neoliberalism and corporate globalization in the center and on the periphery. If something like a global general strike seems unthinkable today, it is not only because of the double bind that Engels identified in the strike: the proletariat needs enough resources to sustain the strike long enough to overthrow the ruling class, and if the working class had these resources, it wouldn't need to strike.[44] Compounding this problem is the double bind that as global capital becomes ever more mobile, linking far-flung locations, it simultaneously reinforces borders restricting the rights and movement of labor, preventing the development of the world community that it establishes materially. In addition to those who appear in Sekula's photos, it becomes crucial to acknowledge those who cannot afford to take a day off work or travel to confront the global financial elite. In this sense, the shadow that falls across the globe also marks the limit beyond which lie those others excluded from the realm of visibility and appearance. Even as the spread of light over the surface of the globe suggests the ideal of a world community, its drop off into shadow points to those who fall outside its range.

In the penultimate shot of the sequence, just prior to the appearance of the black globe, day has passed and night settles in (see color plates). Darkness surrounds an empty, rain-slicked street. Every surface under the streetlight glistens. The only trace of the previous events is the red scrawl of an anti-WTO graffito set adrift on the nondescript, gray metal of a municipal utility box, the sort of anonymous street fixture that houses traffic-signal controls or telecommunication cables. It stands upright at the edge of the sidewalk like a lone sentry. The red inscription quietly unsettles the usually invisible order of the urban infrastructure; it is as if all the objects of the world were still in place, but with the relations between them slightly altered. The street has emptied out and the people have gone. The responsibility for attentively waiting and watching over this space has passed to the viewer. While *Waiting for Tear Gas* is devoted to picturing those who rush into the space opened between the police line and union line, it closes by marking their withdrawal from the scene.[45] Rather than ending by grounding the protestors in the earth, it is as if the air that had so palpably linked them before—the atmospheric free space between the figures—has itself become visible. The space of the street is not completely or permanently filled. Instead, this concluding photograph seems to hold this space open, as a space whose light falls evenly on every object it touches, a space that awaits whoever next steps into its amber glow.

NOTES

I would like to thank Walter Johnston, Erica Levin, and Andrew Weiner for reading and helpfully commenting on earlier drafts; Meg McLagan and Yates McKee for their encouragement and perseverance; Katie Shapiro for her help with images; and especially Allan Sekula for discussing his work with me.

1. The slide show includes eighty-one images projected in a fourteen-minute-long loop. The complete set of images is reproduced in Allan Sekula, *TITANIC's Wake*, exh. cat.

(Cherbourg-Octeville, France; Le Point du Jour Éditeur, 2003), pp. 87–104; a smaller selection of thirty-two images is reproduced in Alexander Cockburn, Jeffrey St. Clair, and Allan Sekula, *Five Days That Shook the World: Seattle and Beyond* (London: Verso, 2000). Here I largely follow the sequencing of the latter publication, not only because of its wider availability, but also because its reproduction of a single photograph per page resembles the "flow" of the single-channel slideshow. While the facing pages of the book format lend themselves to paired, contrasting and grouped images, the slide show emphasizes the rhythm of passing time between each image.

2. Allan Sekula, untitled preface to *Waiting for Tear Gas*, in Cockburn, St. Clair, and Sekula, *Five Days That Shook the World*, p. 122.
3. See Benjamin H. D. Buchloh, "Allan Sekula: Photography between Discourse and Document," in Allan Sekula, *Fish Story* (Rotterdam: Witte de With, 1995), pp. 189–200.
4. Sekula, untitled preface to *Waiting for Tear Gas*, in Cockburn, St. Clair, and Sekula, *Five Days That Shook the World*, p. 122. Sekula is well aware of the scientistic and racist history of physiognomy as a pseudoscience, which he carefully recounts in "The Body in the Archive," *October* 39 (Winter 1986), pp. 3–64; he also uses physiognomy to link photographic portraiture to the mug shot in "Walker Evans and the Police," in *Walker Evans and Dan Graham*, eds. Jean-François Chevrier, Chris Dercon, and Mat Verbekt, exh. cat. (Rotterdam: Witte de With; Marseille: La Direction des Musées de Marseille; Münster: Westfälisches Landesmuseum für Kunst und Kulturgeschichte; New York: Whitney Museum of American Art, 1992), pp. 193–96. Without erasing photography's historical role in this violent operation of power, he is also echoing Walter Benjamin's positive use of the term "physiognomic" to describe a method of materialist criticism. Although Benjamin's widespread use of this fraught concept deserves more intensive treatment, he explicitly applies it to photography when approving of the "social functions" inherent in photographs like August Sander's catalog of German society. For Benjamin, Sander's photographs, like Soviet film of that era, are no longer portraits, but instead a scientific, "physiognomic gallery" of social and "facial types." Walter Benjamin, "Little History of Photography," trans. Edmund Jephcott and Kingsley Shorter, in *Selected Writings, Volume 2*, 1931–1934, ed. Michael W. Jennings, Howard Eiland, and Gary Smith (Cambridge, MA: Harvard University Press, 1999), p. 520. If I cling to the term "portrait," it is partly because *Waiting for Tear Gas* pursues something other than such a functional typology.
5. "In photographing the Seattle demonstrations my working idea was to move with the flow of protest, from dawn to 3 a.m. if need be, taking in the lulls, the waiting, and the margins of events. The rule of thumb for this sort of anti-photojournalism: no flash, no telephoto lens, no gas mask, no auto-focus, no press pass, and no pressure to grab at all costs the one defining image of dramatic violence." Sekula, untitled preface to *Waiting for Tear Gas*, in Cockburn, St. Clair, and Sekula, *Five Days That Shook the World*, p. 122. That Sekula eschews the journalistic apparatus that would distance him, as a privileged observer, from the protestors and the bodily dangers they face is pointed out in Kaja Silverman, "Disassembled Movies," *Synopsis 3: Testimonies: Between Fiction and Reality*, ed. Anna Kafetsi (Athens, Greece: National Museum of Contemporary Art, 2003). Philip Armstrong presents a compelling reading of *Waiting for Tear Gas* that emphasizes the experience of exposure, with particular reference to the work of Jean-Luc Nancy. Since I encountered his article after finishing mine, I can only second the impressive constellation of contemporary political theory he brings to the work, with which I hope my account of the strike resonates. One remaining point of disagreement would be with his claim for the "untechnical matter-of-factness" and "banal, almost dumb

facticity" of the photos, which seems contradicted by color, sequencing, and the scale of half-length or three-quarter-length views of individuals—elements further magnified when presented in an exhibition context that projects them as slides. Philip Armstrong, "Seattle and the Space of Exposure," in *Reticulations: Jean-Luc Nancy and the Networks of the Political* (Minneapolis: University of Minnesota Press, 2009), pp. 185–244. In his excellent reading, Steve Edwards helpfully addresses some of the formal aspects of *Waiting* with the concept of "horizontal montage" that creates, alongside works by Chris Marker and Joel Sternfeld, "an alternative vision of multitude from below." Steve Edwards, "Commons and Crowds: Figuring Photography from Above and Below," *Third Text* 23.4 (July 2009), pp. 447–64. See also Zanny Begg, "Recasting Subjectivity: Globalisation and the Photography of Andreas Gursky and Allan Sekula," *Third Text* 19.6 (November 2005), pp. 625–36, and Daniel Hoffman-Schwartz, "Empire/State: Artists Engaging Globalization," *Afterimage* 30.2 (September–October 2002), p. 13.

6. See Benjamin H. D. Buchloh, "Residual Resemblance: Three Notes on the Ends of Portraiture," *Face Off: The Portrait in Recent Art*, ed. Melissa E. Feldman, exh. cat. (Philadelphia: Institute of Contemporary Art, 1994), pp. 53–69. As Buchloh observes, this crisis also continually provokes attempts to reassert a unified, hieratic subject.
7. Sekula, untitled preface to *Waiting for Tear Gas*, in Cockburn, St. Clair, and Sekula, *Five Days That Shook the World*, p. 122.
8. Walter Benjamin touches on this curious invisibility of the police when he denounces the "spectral mixture" of law-making and law-preserving violence in the police because it is not open to critical evaluation, as is written, sanctioned law. When the police not only apply existing law, but suspend written law—as during the state of emergency declared in Seattle—thereby instituting new, unwritten law, "its [the police's] power is formless, like its nowhere-tangible, all-pervasive, ghostly presence in the life of civilized states." Walter Benjamin, "Critique of Violence" (1921), trans. Edmund Jephcott, in *Selected Writings, Volume 1, 1913–1926*, ed. Marcus Bullock and Michael W. Jennings (Cambridge, MA: Harvard University Press, 1996), p. 243.
9. For an account of the asymmetry of the "visor effect"—the experience of not being able to see who looks at us—in the ghost of the king, in the figure of the father, and in the law; as a call to justice; and as a general condition of ethics and politics, see Jacques Derrida, *Specters of Marx*, trans. Peggy Kamuf (New York: Routledge, 1994), esp. pp. 6–8.
10. Michel Foucault, *The Order of Things: An Archeology of the Human Sciences* (New York: Vintage Books, 1994), pp. 14 and 16.
11. See, for example, the distinction between an "art of government" that manages goods and populations, and the "problem of sovereignty" and juridical rule over a territory in Michel Foucault, "Governmentality" (1978), in *Essential Works of Foucault, 1954–1984, Volume 3, Power*, trans. Robert Hurley et al., ed. James D. Faubion (New York: New Press, 2000), pp. 201–22.
12. See Thomas Keenan's analysis of "mobilizing shame" as an axiom of human rights discourse, especially his interrogation of the Enlightenment model of reason underpinning such a tactic, which assumes an automatic transfer from shameful public exposure to guilty knowledge and corrective action. Thomas Keenan, "Mobilizing Shame," *South Atlantic Quarterly* 103.2/3 (Spring–Summer 2004), pp. 435–49.
13. A corollary to this exposure of police violence is an opposition between the mirror as non-violent means of persuasion and the club as instrument of physical violence. But while it

remains ethically necessary to distinguish bodily harm from other kinds of violence, the force at work in persuasion may not be so simply or completely disentangled from violence, for the club is already a sign, a threat of what awaits those who do not obey the police. And like Perseus's shield, the blinding glare of the mirror can have its own disorienting, if not dangerous, physical effects. Setting aside the perennial debate about whether and to what extent property damage should be considered violence, we might consider how the strange, bloodless violence of light is mobilized in contrast to the "less lethal" weapons of the police, which mark the body with bruises from rubber bullets or the tears and coughed-up blood from tear gas.

14. This slogan is also linked to this photo in Philip Armstrong, "Seattle and the Space of Exposure," p. 210.

15. The demonstrations in Seattle also saw the debut of the Independent Media Center (IMC), to which unpaid, freelance contributors—often demonstrators themselves—posted to a website live reporting on the demonstrations, including photos, video, and audio. Although locally run IMCs have since spread across the world, they are now largely supplanted by user-generated uploads to social-media sites. This archiving cuts both ways, however: since Seattle, the video camera has also passed to the cops, as well, who often conduct blanket surveillance of demonstrations.

16. Most stories about Seattle contain the following: in the early morning of the opening day of the conference, November 30, hundreds blockade the conference center and Paramount Theater, soon reinforced by thousands in a mobile demonstration and roving occupation of intersections downtown. The Seattle Police respond with tear-gas and pepper-spray assaults in an attempt to clear lines of access to the conference and take control of the streets. In the early afternoon, tens of thousands participate in a rally with organized labor and environmental nongovernmental organizations (NGOs). The subsequent protest march is diverted away from the demonstrations near the convention center, despite which thousands break off from the march to reinforce those engaged in civil disobedience downtown. With delegates still unable to reach the meeting, officials announce that the WTO opening ceremonies are cancelled. Under pressure from the federal government to clear the streets, Seattle mayor Paul Schell declares a state of emergency, prohibiting everyone except WTO delegates, business people and employees, and residents from entering downtown. (The order is revised to include journalists and City Council members.) The police soon enforce it as a blanket ban on any otherwise lawful speech or activity critical of the WTO or government and police response. Reinforced with more chemical weapons and extra officers from surrounding areas, police again move to clear the area. Black-bloc activists vandalize some downtown businesses, focusing on banks and multinational corporations. Pushed from downtown, demonstrators retreat to the nearby Capital Hill neighborhood, where police continue gassing and attacking demonstrators, onlookers, and residents into the late evening. The next day, police use indiscriminate force, including tear gas and less-lethal munitions such as wooden dowels, bean bags, and rubber bullets, to keep protestors out of downtown, in the process ejecting, attacking, or arresting demonstrators, residents, city officials, journalists, and individuals passing out flyers on the sidewalk. The open-air Pike Place Market is gassed and the assault on demonstrators and residents in Capitol Hill is repeated a second night. After the police make mass arrests, demonstrators switch to protesting at the jail to have detainees released and charges dropped. The WTO meeting gets underway and is addressed by President Clinton. The talks

collapse at the end of the week with no agreement among the most economically powerful nations on a framework for further trade negotiations and with strident protest from delegates from developing countries, who were locked out of crucial meetings. (The Doha Round of negotiations, begun at the 2001 meeting in Qatar, remains stalled). Eyewitness accounts include Jeffrey St. Clair, "Jeffrey St. Clair's Seattle Diary: It's a Gas, Gas, Gas," in *Five Days That Shook the World*, pp. 13–52; and Chris Dixon, "Five Days in Seattle: A View from the Ground," in Rebecca Solnit and David Solnit (eds.), *The Battle of the Story of the Battle of Seattle* (Oakland: AK Press, 2009), pp. 73–107. For an overview of key actors and events, see Paul de Armond, "Netwar in the Emerald City: WTO Protest Strategy and Tactics," in John Arquilla and David Ronfeldt (eds.), *Networks and Netwars: The Future of Terror, Crime, and Militancy* (Santa Monica: RAND, 2001), pp. 201–35. For a comprehensive account of the widespread police violence, see *Out of Control: Seattle's Flawed Response to Protests against the World Trade Organization* (Seattle: American Civil Liberties Union of Washington, 2000). For an attempt to dispel the false claims repeated in major newspapers that demonstrators threw Molotov cocktails, engaged in arson, or attacked police with excrement, see Rebecca Solnit, "The Myth of Seattle Violence: My Battle with the *New York Times*," in *The Battle of the Story of the Battle of Seattle*, pp. 56–71.

17. Some accounts emphasize a split between those engaged in direct action and those in the labor rally and ensuing permitted march and construe it as the division between those committed to abolishing the WTO and those looking to reform it. Thus, tactics come to symbolize the division between liberals and anticapitalists, reformers and revolutionaries. (Cockburn and St. Clair attack mainstream environmental NGOs and organized labor, with some exceptions for local dockworkers' and steelworkers' unions—without addressing the presence of WTO delegates from the Global South also trying to attend the meeting—for demanding a "seat at the table.") To these political divisions could be added those between the labor and environmental movements, advocates of protectionism and internationalism, the metropole and the countryside, and, perhaps most importantly, the Global North and the Global South. Such divisions are difficult to perceive in Sekula's photos. Without claiming to have transcended these differences, the photos nevertheless open onto other dimensions of affective and bodily life. On the split between those engaged in direct action and the labor march, see Cockburn, St. Clair, and Sekula, *Five Days That Shook the World*, pp. 22 and 29–30. Sekula himself began the day at the labor march before making his way downtown and later up to Capitol Hill. Sekula, interview with author, May 1, 2010.
18. Sekula, interview with the author.
19. Of course, "protest" may signify not only negative opposition or dissent, but also a more neutral act of announcing, declaring, or testifying publicly. For a definition of "direct action" that includes as examples "street manifestations, blockades, trespass, sit-ins, banner hanging, squatting, sabotage, croptrashing, piethrowing," as well as a mordant overview of some of the other keywords of anticapitalist struggle, see Ian Boal, "Glossary," in Eddie Yuen, Daniel Burton-Rose, and George Katsiaficas (eds.), *Confronting Capitalism: Dispatches from a Global Movement* (New York: Soft Skull Press, 2004), pp. 389–403. For more on the Direct Action Network (DAN), the Ruckus Society, and others who helped carry out direct action in Seattle, see the entry s.v. "Direct Action Network" in *ibid*. and John Sellers, "Raising a Ruckus," in Tom Mertes (ed.), *The Movement of Movements: Is Another World Really Possible?* (New York: Verso, 2004), pp. 175–91. On DAN and direct action after Seattle, see David

Graeber, *Direct Action: An Ethnography* (Oakland: AK Press, 2009).

20. This opposition between protest and direct action could also be mediated by a third term, "civil disobedience," a form of collective action that violates unobjectionable laws (such as traffic regulations) to protest indirectly other unjust laws or policies. By concentrating on the political character of this group action and the collective appearance it requires, Hannah Arendt rightly extracts civil disobedience from the individualistic and moralizing framework that justifies it only with reference to moral conscience, higher spiritual law, or suffering and self-sacrifice as guarantees of sincerity and commitment. For reasons I hope will become clear, I prefer to conceive of what she calls the "art of associating together" not in terms of action, but of its suspension in the strike. Hannah Arendt, "Civil Disobedience," in *Crises of the Republic* (San Diego: Harcourt Brace, 1972), pp. 49–102.

21. Although the plans for direct action to shut down the meeting had been publicized widely and also openly announced in dialogue with the police, the Seattle demonstrations largely took the authorities and the country by surprise. Since then, local governments have learned how better to control demonstrations by limiting in advance the ability to assemble publicly, using the rationale of security or other normative uses of the city. (In one notorious example, New York City officials denied an antiwar rally the right to assemble on the Great Lawn of Central Park during the 2004 Republican National Convention for the allegedly nonpartisan—but nonetheless biopolitical—reason that they needed to protect the health of the grass.) These "time, manner, and place" restrictions are largely accepted as within the law. In addition to permit requirements, unfounded predictions of violence are often circulated, which also serve to discourage attendance. The use of direct physical force and less lethal weapons to clear the streets, as in Seattle, has largely been replaced by a governmental apparatus that also mobilizes increased surveillance, a greater number of police, and miles of temporary, sometimes mobile barricades to prevent or circumscribe public assembly. And when the movements or actions of certain groups can no longer be controlled, overwhelming numbers are used to make indiscriminate mass arrests, often on pretextual grounds, sometimes followed up by prolonged detainment without charge or on trumped-up charges that are later dropped. This is to say nothing of the willful abrogation of the rights to speech and assembly through surveillance, provocateurs, and preventive arrest and detention. Those in government seem increasingly willing to make the cynical calculation that it is worthwhile in the long run to break up demonstrations, illegally arrest and detain protestors, and then pay for court costs and damages in the post facto legal battle than to allow the disruption of official or authorized events as they occur. Of course, these struggles must also be understood in the context of the post–9/11 dismantling of limits formerly placed on police conduct during the Church Committee era and new measures legitimized by security concerns amid the so-called War on Terrorism. For an overview of the increasingly restrictive preemptive regulation of public assembly in the United States, see Tabatha Abu El-Haj, "The Neglected Right of Assembly," *UCLA Law Review* 56.3 (2009), pp. 543–89. For another view that holds that "freedom of action" will never be adequately covered under the First Amendment and may not finally be legally justifiable, see Arendt, "Civil Disobedience," p. 101. For a comprehensive index of post-Seattle police tactics used to disrupt demonstrations, see Heidi Boghosian, *The Assault on Free Speech, Public Assembly, and Dissent: A National Lawyers Guild Report on Government Violations of First Amendment Rights in the United States* (Barrington, MA: North River Press, 2004). Some specific examples of post-Seattle policing

can be drawn from New York City: see Christopher Dunn et al., *Arresting Protest: A Special Report by the New York Civil Liberties Union on New York City's Protest Policies at the February 15, 2003 Antiwar Demonstration in New York City* (New York: New York Civil Liberties Union, 2003); and Christopher Dunn et al., *Rights and Wrongs at the RNC: A Special Report about Police and Protest at the Republican National Convention* (New York: New York Civil Liberties Union, 2005).

22. On the plebeian secession, see Jacques Rancière, *Disagreement*, trans. Julie Rose (Minneapolis: University of Minnesota Press, 1999), pp. 23–27. These struggles should also be considered as part of a broader "right to the city" theorized by Henri Lefebvre in *Le droit à la ville* (Paris: Éditions Anthropos, 1968); see also Rosalyn Deutsche, *Evictions: Art and Spatial Politics* (Cambridge, MA: The MIT Press, 1996), pp. 73–79.

23. For Benjamin, "an omission of actions, a nonaction, which a strike really is, cannot be described as violence [*Gewalt*]. . . . The moment of violence, however, is necessarily introduced, in the form of extortion, into such an omission, if it takes place in the context of a conscious readiness to resume the suspended action under certain circumstances that either have nothing whatever to do with this action or only superficially modify it." While the second form of interruption of work is violent, the first, "as pure means, is nonviolent," whatever its allegedly violent effects may be, since "it takes place not in readiness to resume work following external concessions and this or that modification of working conditions, but in the determination to resume only a wholly transformed work, no longer enforced by the state, an upheaval that this kind of strike not so much causes as consummates." Walter Benjamin, "Critique of Violence," pp. 239–40 and 245–46.

24. In his reading of the "Critique of Violence," Werner Hamacher writes that "for Benjamin, the strike is the social, economic, and political event in which nothing happens, no work is done, nothing is produced, and nothing is planned or projected." As a "severing of relations," it "does not permit itself to become effective in any form other than as the bare minimum of its existence, the manifestation of the social *tout court*. . . . in it the sheer mediacy of all social relations opens up, and all the formal and especially juridical restrictions of these relations are suspended." Werner Hamacher, "Afformative, Strike: Benjamin's 'Critique of Violence,'" trans. Dana Hollander, in Andrew Benjamin and Peter Osborne (eds.), *Walter Benjamin's Philosophy: Destruction and Experience* (London: Routledge, 1994), p. 121. The politics of pure means—analogous to Benjamin's account of the "immediate mediacy" of language in "On Language as Such"—proves an important contrast with the anarchist account of direct action as the unity of means and end: that is, as a form of action that immediately embodies the political end it seeks. Taking groups such as DAN as a "model of consensus-based, decentralized direct democracy," David Graeber defines direct action as an ideal "form of action in which means and ends become, effectively, indistinguishable . . . the form of action—or at least, the organization of the action—is itself a model for the change one wishes to bring about." Graeber, *Direct Action*, p. 210. In contrast, the politics of pure means refuses to take for granted those common ends, whether prefigurative or otherwise; nor does it imagine the end of representation or mediacy as such. As a refusal to work, the strike might instead be thought of as manifestation without end(s) or as participation in the common without commonality. That we cannot act without orienting ourselves toward some end or presupposed common ground—that the politics of pure means cannot simply be implemented or practiced—does not absolve us from attending to its occurrence.

25. The foundational study of the group portrait as a genre is Aloïs Riegl, *The Group Portraiture of Holland*, trans. Evelyn M. Kain (Los Angeles: Getty Research Institute, 1999). While many of the formal aspects of the group portrait discussed in this paragraph are drawn from Riegl, he ties the group portrait to the emergence of a bourgeois-democratic political order and its accompanying subjectivity and describes a careful balance between the individual and collective in both new civic institutions and the business corporation. The question is what of this genre survives in picturing subjects at the margins of that order. On modernist photomontage of the masses, see Benjamin H. D. Buchloh, "From Faktura to Factography," *October* 30 (Autumn 1984), pp. 95–119.
26. Riegl, *Group Portraiture*, pp. 74–86. Compare also the treatment of physical activity and a certain neutralization of the hands "as a manifestation, so to speak, of nonactivity" (p. 103).
27. Discussing a series of photographs by Anthony Hernandez, Sekula remarks that "by and large waiting is what poor people do, for the bus, for the next meager paycheck, for the welfare check; waiting is an instrument of humiliation, worsened only by the condition of no longer having anything to wait for. Waiting is for people for whom time is little money, or no money at all." And yet in Hernandez's photos of welfare offices, in the smear of a cigarette put out on the wall of the waiting room, emerge "veiled propositions that attentive esthetic impulses can emerge from waiting, that waiting in line can lead one to step out of line." After all, "waiting is also what photographers do." Allan Sekula, "Waiting for Los Angeles," in Anthony Hernandez, *Waiting for Los Angeles* (Tucson, AZ: Nazraeli Press, 2002), pp. 5–6. See also the discussion of waiting in Philip Armstrong, "Seattle and the Space of Exposure," pp. 190-91.
28. Kaja Silverman has emphasized the importance of color in the photographs. In her generative reading, she draws on Roland Barthes to contrast the manufactured "average affect," the emotional solicitation made by government as its interpellates subjects (literalized by the forced crying produced by tear gas), with another kind of affect exhibited by the protestors in Sekula's photographs as they "invent a new political relationality." Pointing out that *Waiting for Tear Gas* is arranged chromatically, she observes that as it moves through red, blue, and yellow passages, the colors are increasingly divorced from the properties of objects, so that "they pulse with human affect" and suffuse the scene, thereby "connecting the demonstrators so firmly to the earth" and affirming their presence in the world. Silverman, "Disassembled Movies."
29. A theory of the multitude is advanced in Michael Hardt and Antonio Negri, *Empire* (Cambridge, MA: Harvard University Press, 2000); their concept is brought to bear on *Waiting for Tear Gas* in Zanny Begg, "Recasting Subjectivity." For a critique of the vitalism underpinning their argument and Marxism more broadly, see Pheng Cheah, *Spectral Nationality: Passages of Freedom from Kant to Postcolonial Literatures of Liberation* (New York: Columbia University Press, 2003), pp. 178–208.
30. In this scenario, the kerchief no longer signifies the threat of a disguised terrorist or violent opportunist, as it so often does in the news. In addition to establishing anonymity or screening out tear gas, the kerchief also signifies a collective solidarity verging on radical substitutability: it could be assumed by anyone at all. This still leaves the task of differentiating it from the state-issued police visor—another of the sweeping emergency ordinances in Seattle made wearing gas masks illegal and later had to be amended to carve out an exception for law enforcement. Although anonymous speech is constitutionally protected, when masking is treated as conduct it can be outlawed. A number of cities and states passed "mask laws"

prohibiting masks in public demonstrations before and after the WTO demonstrations. On recent uses of the New York State mask law against demonstrators as well as its long history—it was passed during the mid-nineteenth-century Rent Wars to prevent tenant farmers, dressed and masked as "Indians," from physically resisting eviction by landlords—see Clare Norins, "Mask Law Memo," National Lawyers Guild, New York Chapter, 2004. See also L. M. Bogad, "Facial Insufficiency: Political Street Performance in New York City and the Selective Enforcement of the 1845 Mask Law," *The Drama Review* 47.4 (Winter 2003), pp. 75–84.

31. On the peculiar equality that is not predicated on identity or the parting out of common lots, but rather the "equality of anyone at all with anyone else," see Rancière, *Disagreement*, esp. pp. 15–19 and 28–42.
32. Here I draw on the ethics and politics of vulnerability outlined in Judith Butler, *Precarious Life* (London: Verso, 2004) and *Frames of War* (London: Verso, 2009); see also her essay in this volume.
33. The forced crying produced by tear gas has a mythical precedent in the tears of Niobe, whose prideful boasting about her numerous children offended the goddess Leto (Latona), who sends her only children Apollo and Artemis to slaughter Niobe's progeny. In Ovid's fable, although Niobe is spared, her grief-stricken body turns to stone, even as her tears of mourning continue to flow. Benjamin takes this tale of fate as the very paradigm of law. According to Benjamin, while the gods kill the loved ones closest to her, they leave Niobe's life intact "as an eternally mute bearer of guilt and as a boundary stone on the frontier between men and gods." Touched not simply by anger or revenge, she is the victim of an inaugural legal violence, for the violence of fate, in laying down political frontiers, marking out the borders of the world, and fixing life with guilt, "brings to light a law." Struck mute, Niobe can no longer respond to the gods or other people, but must silently and eternally bear her guilt. The ethics of responsibility are replaced with the timelessness of a moral norm, with culpability. Her fixed body, the representation of what Benjamin later calls "mere life," figures as the ground on which law imposes itself. Benjamin, "Critique of Violence," pp. 294–95. We witness in Niobe an arrest that codifies a certain arrangement of bodily life and the world of things. The photographs of *Waiting for Tear Gas* allow for a duration in each instant that runs wholly counter to this specious eternity of arrest. They perform a kind of reverse magic that seeks to turn stone back into flesh.
34. The longer version of *Waiting for Tear Gas* that appears in *TITANIC's Wake* positions this devil figure at the beginning of the sequence; the last figure to appear is instead the woman in the hazmat suit discussed above. In both versions the concluding two photographs are the same: the empty street and globe discussed below.
35. "As the capitalist turns money into commodities which serve as the building materials for a new product or as factors in the labor process, as he incorporates living labor into their dead objectivity, he simultaneously transforms value—i.e., past, objectified, dead labor—into capital, value which can perform its own valorization process, an animated monster [*beseeltes Ungeheuer*] which begins to 'work,' 'as if its body were by love possessed.'" Karl Marx, *Capital: A Critique of Political Economy, Volume I*, trans. Ben Fowkes (London: New Left Review, 1976), p. 302 (translation modified). This formulation was developed earlier in the *Grundrisse* in the context of machinery and automation. The final phrase, a quote from Goethe's *Faust*, is the chorus of a drinking song about the contortions of a rat poisoned by a free lunch apparently left out by the cook possibly as an allegory about the temptations of the devil. For

discussions of the monstrous, ghostly, and vampiric in Marx's text, see among others, Thomas Keenan, "The Point Is to (Ex)Change It: Reading 'Capital,' Rhetorically" in *Fables of Responsibility* (Stanford: Stanford University Press, 1997), pp. 103–104 and 114–22; Derrida, *Specters of Marx;* and Cheah, *Spectral Nationality*, pp. 197–200.

36. Derrida, *Specters of Marx*, pp. 125–26.
37. "Modern bourgeois society... has conjured up such gigantic means of production and of exchange, [it] is like the sorcerer who is no longer able to control the powers of the nether world whom he has called up by his spells." Karl Marx and Friedrich Engels, *The Communist Manifesto*, in Robert C. Tucker (ed.), *The Marx-Engels Reader*, 2nd ed. (New York: W. W. Norton, 1978), p. 478.
38. Although speed has conquered space and united the Earth in a "continuous whole" whose space has "become small and close at hand," this bringing close of the immense in the globe simultaneously distances humankind from its earthly surroundings. "It is in the nature of the human surveying capacity that it can function only if man disentangles himself from all involvement in and concern with the close at hand and withdraws himself to a distance from everything near him." Thus, the globe grasps the Earth as if from a groundless outside, from the "Archimedean point" of outer space. Here the globe is only one part of a larger process that also includes the Protestant Reformation and the development of modern science, that leads to "world alienation," the "twofold flight from the earth into the universe and from the world into the self." Hannah Arendt, *The Human Condition*, 2nd ed. (Chicago: University of Chicago Press, 1958), pp. 250–51, 254. Arendt is silently drawing on Martin Heidegger, "The Age of the World Picture" (1938), in *The Question Concerning Technology and Other Essays*, trans. William Lovitt (New York: Harper & Row, 1977), pp. 115–54.
39. Walter Benjamin, "Theological-Political Fragment," trans. Edmund Jephcott, in *Selected Writings, Volume 3, 1935–1938*, ed. Howard Eiland and Michael W. Jennings (Cambridge, MA: Harvard University Press, 2002), p. 306. The date of this text is contested. Although Gershom Scholem maintained it was written in 1920–1921, in the early period of the "Critique of Violence," Theodor Adorno held it was from late 1937 or early 1938. See Benjamin, "Theological-Political Fragment," p. 306 n. 1.
40. Implicitly in dialogue with Arendt, Pheng Cheah traces a certain conception of the world back to Goethe and Marx and highlights an important distinction between globe and world. "The world is a form of relating or being-with. The globe, on the other hand, the totality produced by processes of globalization, is a bounded object or entity in Mercatorian space.... The globe is not the world." Pheng Cheah, "What Is a World?: On World Literature as World-Making Activity," *Daedalus* 137.3 (Summer 2008), p. 30. See also the important engagement with Arendt and the opening onto a world in Kaja Silverman, *World Spectators* (Stanford: Stanford University Press, 2000).
41. Once the immense or gigantic is so wholly surveyed and quantified that it undergoes a qualitative shift, "what can seemingly always be calculated completely, becomes, precisely through this, incalculable. This becoming incalculable remains the invisible shadow that is cast around all things everywhere when man has been transformed into subiectum [i.e., the subjective ground of what is] and the world into picture. By means of this shadow the modern world extends itself out into a space withdrawn from representation, and so lends to the incalculable the determinateness peculiar to it, as well as a historical uniqueness." It is then a question of thinking this invisible shadow, not as lack of light, but as "that which, withdrawn

from representation, is nevertheless manifest in whatever is." Heidegger, "The Age of the World Picture," pp. 135–36; 154, appendix 13.

42. Gayatri Spivak rightly cautioned against focusing only on the Seattle protests and in turn on activists from the Global North, as well as on the often middle-class, migrant activists of the Global South who appeared there. Doing so risks romanticizing global social movements to the neglect of the long-term formation from below of subaltern collectivities, which, for her, should take education as its model. Gayatri Chakravorty Spivak, "A Note on the New International," *Parallax* 7.3 (2001), pp. 12–16.

43. As Sekula and other critics have noted, Seattle was a significant locale for the meeting because of its status as a port city and node in the global economy, home to both Boeing and Microsoft. This intersection of industry and digital services in Seattle links *Waiting for Tear Gas* with two of Sekula's other works: *Fish Story* (1990–1995), the long-term project documenting seafaring, ports, and international containerized shipping, and *Dear Bill Gates* (1999), a meditation on art, the sea, and the watery metaphors that link it to the digital economy. Sekula was visiting Seattle partly because *Fish Story* was on exhibit at the Henry Art Gallery, an exhibition cosponsored by the labor center at the University of Washington, which also enabled the creation of *Dear Bill Gates*. See Allan Sekula, "Between the Net and the Deep Blue Sea (Rethinking the Traffic in Photographs)," *October* 102 (Fall 2002), pp. 3–34.

44. Rosa Luxemburg recounts Engels's objection and argues that he is mistaken because he applies it only to the anarchist theory of the strike, which treats the strike only as a tool—that is, a technical means that can be intentionally employed—for triggering revolution. In contrast, she argues that the mass strike is not a "pocketknife" to be unclasped when needed, but should be understood as a historically produced contributor to daily political struggle, including parliamentary politics. Despite the deterministic metaphors that govern her account of historical struggle, Luxemburg also stresses the convertibility between the economic and the political strike. Rosa Luxemburg, *The Mass Strike, The Political Party, and the Trade Unions,* trans. Patrick Lavin (New York: Harper, 1971), pp. 10–17.

45. The "question of space" cited in my epigraph is raised by one of the narrators of Chris Marker's essay film *Grin without a Cat*. He describes footage of protests in 1967 in France and elsewhere, detecting "a new attitude in the demonstrations" that marked the rise of the New Left, which rushed in to occupy the open space between the police and the unions. The narrator remarks that this "new kind of confrontation" with government and the institutional left was marked by an increased militancy, but suggests that this occupation was not its only legacy. Even as the space of the street between the police and union lines calls out to be filled, those who enter it may do so less as its rightful proprietors than as stand-ins: when the film cuts to another shot showing demonstrators surging into such a space, a pan across the banner they carry reveals that they trusted "the workers will take the flag of struggle from the fragile hands of the students," prompting the narrator to add that "those fragile hands have left us the mark of their fragility." *Grin without a Cat* (*Le fond de l'air est rouge*), directed by Chris Marker, DVD (1977/1993; Brooklyn: Icarus Films, 2001).

A man photographs on his mobile posters depicting pictures of the late former PPP leader Benazir Bhutto, at the site where former opposition leader died, on February 17, 2008 in Rawalpindi, Pakistan (photo: John Moore/Getty Images).

The Convergence of Old and New Media during the Pakistan Emergency

Huma Yusuf

On March 13, 2007, a few days after Pakistan's president General Pervez Musharraf suspended the chief justice of the Supreme Court, an online petition condemning the government's abuse of the independent judiciary was circulated via mailing lists and blogs.[1] But over the course of several weeks, the petition attracted only 1,190 signatories. Less than a year later, however, in February 2008, Dawn, the country's leading English-language media group, launched a citizen journalism initiative, inviting Pakistanis to submit images, ideas, news reports, and analyses that they wanted to share with the world. In a matter of months, the Pakistani media landscape thus had evolved from a point where a politically relevant online petition failed to gain momentum to one where a prominent mass-media group felt the need to include citizen journalists in the process of news gathering. In less than a year, a public sphere had emerged where none had existed before.

In *The Wealth of Networks: How Social Production Transforms Markets and Freedom*, Yochai Benkler argues that the networked information economy produces a public sphere because in the new media, "the cost of being a speaker . . . is several orders of magnitude lower than the cost of speaking in the mass-mediated environment." He adds, "the easy possibility of communicating effectively into the public sphere allows individuals to reorient themselves from passive readers and listeners to potential speakers and participants in a conversation."[2] This evolution is precisely what occurred in Pakistan, facilitated by both old and new media, and it had a significant impact on the political process and civic engagement there. As many Pakistanis—for example, university students—came to use digital technologies and new-media platforms in the spring of 2007 to organize for political action and report on matters of public interest, they began to participate, reciprocate, and engage in many-to-many, rather than one-to-many communications. The Arab Spring, which was spurred by Facebook and chronicled tweet by tweet, and Iran's

2009 Green Movement have made new media and political activism synonymous. The use of new media in political protest in Pakistan as early as 2007 foreshadows this trend and provides important insights into how online movements gain—and maintain—momentum.

Pakistan's networked public sphere emerged during a time of heightened political instability that has been colloquially termed "the Pakistan Emergency."[3] Digital technologies that were harnessed during this time for political advocacy, community organizing, and hyperlocal reporting included cell phones, camera phones (mobile-connected cameras), SMS (short message service) text messages, online mailing lists, and Internet broadcasts (live audio and visual streams). Meanwhile, popular new-media platforms utilized during the Pakistan Emergency included blogs (live blogging), YouTube, Flickr, Facebook, and other social-networking or sociable-media sites.[4]

Writing about mass-mediated markets that are slowly inundated with new-media tools, Benkler points out that a transition occurs "as the capabilities of both systems converge, to widespread availability of the ability to register and communicate observations in text, audio, and video, wherever we are and whenever we wish."[5] During the Pakistan Emergency, a similar convergence of old—that is, traditional broadcast—and new media occurred. In a time of turmoil and censorship, Pakistanis were driven by the desire to access information and thus turned to multiple media sources when the mainstream media were compromised. One could say the media landscape became hydra-headed during the Pakistan Emergency: if one source was blocked or banned, another one was appropriated to get the word out.

The combined use of digital technologies and new-media tools also helped bridge the digital divide in a country where only 17 million people have Internet access and the literacy rate is less than 50 percent. In "Democracy and New Media in Developing Nations: Opportunities and Challenges," Adam Clayton Powell describes how the Internet can help open up developing democracies:

> Many argue that in much of the world, the Internet reaches only elites: government officials and business leaders, university professors and students, the wealthy and the influential. But through Net-connected elites information from the Internet reaches radio listeners and newspaper readers around the world, so the Internet has an important secondary readership, those who hear or are influenced by online information via its shaping of more widely distributed media, outside of traditional, controlled media lanes of the past.[6]

No doubt traditional broadcast media relay information from the Internet to the Pakistani public, but the national secondary readership was established in a far more dynamic and participatory way during the Pakistan Emergency, thanks to the prevalence of cell phones and the popularity of SMS text messaging. Citizen reporting and calls for organized political action were distributed through a combination of mailing lists, online forums, and SMS text messages. E-mails forwarded to net-connected elites containing calls for civic action against an increasingly authoritarian regime inevitably included synopses that were copied as SMS text messages and circulated well beyond cyberspace. This two-tiered use of media helped inculcate a culture of citizenship in Pakistanis from different socioeconomic backgrounds. In other words, old and new media technologies converged in the media landscape, a convergence that also led to widespread civic engagement and greater connection across social boundaries.

Despite such multivalent uses, the overall impact of digital and new-media tools in Pakistan remains limited. After all, General Musharraf's dictatorial regime retained control over access to the Internet and other elements of the communications infrastructure throughout the period of widespread civic engagement. The only antidote to the government's control of digital and new-media tools was the widening of the networked public sphere to include Pakistanis in the diaspora and global media sources. For example, when the government blocked news channels and jammed cellular networks in November 2007, young Pakistanis across the globe continued to plan and organize protest rallies via the social networking site Facebook.

Ultimately, the means of communication in Pakistan became dispersed, accessible, and decentralized, leading to a freer flow of information during the Pakistan Emergency. Users adopt and adapt tools in a way that responds to local needs. As Benkler puts it, "the networked public sphere is not made of tools, but of social production practices that these tools enable."[7]

MEDIA VACUUM

President Musharraf's declaration of a state of emergency on November 3, 2007, may have had a greater impact on Pakistan's media landscape than on its political history. During emergency rule, a media vacuum was created that allowed for the rise of new-media outlets as viable alternatives for information dissemination and community organizing, and the mediated practices that facilitated civic engagement and citizen journalism during the six-week-long emergency have continued to be widely adopted and refined. The manner in which the government handled media outlets during the emergency, which ended on December 15, 2007, demonstrated the vulnerability of mainstream media and created an opportunity for the systematic, sustained, and nationwide use of new-media platforms. Indeed, barely five years after independent television stations were established as the go-to medium for news and infotainment for one-third of Pakistan's population of 150 million,[8] Musharraf's crackdown on news channels during the emergency demonstrated how easily the boom could go bust.

On November 3, soon after proclaiming emergency rule in a televised address, Musharraf demanded that cable television operators block the broadcasts of all local and foreign news channels, except those of the state-owned Pakistan Television Corporation. Nearly thirty privately owned channels were promptly taken off the air. The next day, policemen raided the Islamabad offices of Aaj TV, an independent news channel, and attempted to confiscate the channel's equipment. The telephone lines of Pakistan's first independent news channel, Geo TV, were cut, and their broadcasters were threatened with long jail terms.[9] The crackdown on the television channels was in some ways more remarkable than Musharraf's emergency announcement. The general's decision to block television channels reveals how powerful the medium had become since 2002.

Ironically, the very media freedom that Musharraf thus stifled was one of the hallmarks of his rule until the emergency declaration. After coming to power in 1999, he increased freedom for the print media and liberalized broadcasting policies to mitigate the perception that military rulers are authoritarian. In March 2002, the Pakistan Electronic Media Regulatory Authority (PEMRA) was established to induct the private sector into the field of electronic media. Geo TV became Pakistan's first private news channel in 2002. Fifty-six privately owned television channels were licensed in Pakistan, and forty-eight were fully operational as of May 2008.[10]

The proliferation of independent television channels was a marked departure for the Pakistani media landscape, which had been dominated by the state-owned channel Pakistan Television (PTV) until the early 1990s. In the previous decade, access to international satellite television channels via illegal satellite dishes had many Pakistanis tuning in to Indian channels such as Zee TV and other regional offerings via Star TV, the Asian news and entertainment network owned by News Corp. These illegal channels gained popularity because they circumvented the censorship and religiosity that defined Pakistani media throughout the 1990s.

Since 2002, independent news channels had been operating with unprecedented freedom, as per Musharraf's directives. Cable television thus became the fastest-growing media property in Pakistan: subscribers increased from 1.5 million to 32.7 million from July 2004 to July 2007, meaning that one-third of all Pakistanis had access to private news channels in 2007.[11] News content was increasingly investigative and often openly critical of the government. However, signs that the mainstream media remained vulnerable to the government's whims began appearing well before the emergency declaration of November 2007.

On March 16, 2007, government forces raided the offices of the most popular news channel, Geo TV, after it broadcast live coverage of a rally for Chief Justice Chaudhry, who had been dismissed by Musharraf the previous week. When security forces broke into Geo TV's offices, they shattered windows, fired tear gas, and harassed the channel's employees. But the channel defied orders to stop the transmission and later received an apology from Musharraf.[12] On June 3, 2007, the channel was again taken off the air for broadcasting a public-affairs show on the chief justice's suspension.[13] These initial attempts to stifle the broadcast media were acknowledged by online communities—for example, the Karachi-based *Teeth Maestro* blog, which a dentist, Dr. Awab Alvi, launched in 2004, originally as an online diary,[14] ran a post about the March 16 interrupted transmission.[15] The blogger protested the "media gag," but did not suggest that blogs might increasingly have to play the role of media watchdogs if government censorship became a trend.

After failing to rein in Geo TV, Musharraf promulgated the amended PEMRA Ordinance, a new regulation that imposed curbs on media freedom, in June 2007. The new laws restricted live coverage, empowered the government to interrupt broadcasts that were deemed inappropriate, and gave government regulators the power to seal buildings and seize privately owned equipment.[16]

Significantly, Musharraf's emergency order expanded on the June 2007 PEMRA amendments and increased restrictions on the media. As he announced the broadcasting ban, he also declared that broadcast journalists were banned from covering live incidents of violence such as suicide bombings and militant activity. It also outlawed the expression of opinions that might undermine the "ideology . . . or integrity" of Pakistan and any statements defaming the president, the military, or state offices.

These new regulations alerted members of the broadcast media that their freedoms were being significantly curtailed, and they prepared to counter the government's attempt at control and censorship. After most channels were blocked during the emergency, two independent news channels made every effort to continue live broadcasts. Geo TV and ARY One World, another independent station, transmitted live broadcasts from their bureaus in Dubai. The news that some independent news channels were continuing to broadcast prompted Pakistanis across the country to obtain illegal satellite dishes—which had declined in popularity since the 1990s—so as to continue receiving independent coverage of the unfolding political crisis from their favorite news anchors and broadcast journalists. Despite a prompt government ban on the purchase of satellite dishes, they sold like hotcakes.[17]

The fact that Pakistanis resorted to satellite dishes in the wake of the government ban indicates that broadcast media were considered the most important form of news delivery in Pakistan. (The English and Urdu-language print media were not censored during the emergency, nor did they see an increase in sales.)

Interestingly, it was this desire to seek out live television broadcasts that also drove many Pakistanis to the Internet, in many cases for the first time.

Geo TV, ARY One World, and Aaj TV live-streamed their coverage on the stations' websites.[18] As soon as Geo TV initiated live streams, its website registered three hundred thousand simultaneous users, up from one hundred thousand before the emergency. Through November, the site received as many as seven hundred thousand hits after breaking news.

News broadcasts featuring important updates were also uploaded by both station producers and users to YouTube to allow for easy circulation.[19] Moreover, websites such as Pakistan Policy compiled streaming audio and video content from the independent news channels to allow users across the country and in the diaspora to enjoy uninterrupted news reporting on political events.[20] Initially, then, broad Pakistani interest in finding news online was an example of old and new media colluding: content was produced by traditional media outlets and intended for consumption along the one-to-many model. But the distribution of that content was diffuse and collaborative.

On November 8, most international and local news channels were allowed to resume broadcasting on cable networks, but only after agreeing to adhere to guidelines laid down by the government. But Geo TV and ARY One World remained off the air, hoping to provide genuinely independent coverage via satellite and the Internet. On November 16, however, Musharraf's government escalated its attempts to block the electronic media and convinced the emir of the United Arab Emirates to cease the transmission of Geo TV and ARY One World from Dubai.[21] In an attempt to maintain good diplomatic relations, the emir complied with Musharraf's request, and the last two independent news broadcasts in Pakistan were completely silenced. It was not until November 30 that the government of the UAE allowed Geo TV and ARY One World to resume broadcasting.

The weeks during which all independent electronic news outlets were completely shut down or censored by the government marked a significant turning point in the transformation of the Pakistani media landscape. Other alternatives began to fill this media vacuum and began to flourish: the public realized that to fulfill its hunger for news in a time of political crisis, it had to participate in both the production and dissemination of information.

DISCONNECTED: JAMMING CELLULAR NETWORKS

As the public adopted alternative media platforms, the government escalated its efforts to control communication and news dissemination. In the first few days of the emergency, sporadic efforts to cut telephone lines and jam cell-phone networks were common, even though the telecommunications infrastructure in Pakistan is privately owned. Mobile connectivity at the Supreme Court, protest sites, and the homes of opposition politicians and lawyers who were placed under house arrest was jammed at different times. In off-the-record interviews, employees at telecommunications companies explained that the government had threatened to revoke the companies' operating licenses in the event that they did not comply with jamming requests.

The government's attempts to jam cell-phone networks during the emergency demonstrates that much like television, cell phones had become an integral medium of information dissemination and community organizing across Pakistan. This is not surprising, given that cell phones have been the most rapidly adopted—and adapted—technology in Pakistan's history.

Between late 2002 and August 2007, the number of cell phone users in Pakistan increased from 2.4 million to an unprecedented 68.5 million.[22] Months before the emergency declaration, in August 2007, 60 percent of the total potential cell phone market in Pakistan was equipped with a mobile connection.[23] Given Pakistan's leapfrog into the era of wireless communications, it is not surprising that the authorities were intimidated by the public's unprecedented and instantaneous access to connectivity during a time of political instability. Indeed, citizen journalists and activists harnessed this connectivity in subsequent protest rallies, as well as during the February 2008 general election.

SMS text messaging also played a large role in helping communities organize protests during the emergency. Owing to the low literacy rate and the nonavailability of mobile platforms in local languages, SMS traffic has remained low. That said, 2007 saw a marked increase to 8,636 million text messages exchanged, up from 1,206 million in 2006.[24] In the absence of independent news channels, text messaging emerged as an instantaneous way for people to update each other on developments such as protest rallies and the numerous arrests of lawyers, journalists, and activists. In the early days of the emergency, SMS text messaging was lauded across the Pakistani blogosphere as the savior of communication in a time of crisis.

STUDENT ACTIVISM/DIGITAL ACTIVISM: *THE EMERGENCY TIMES*

In the media vacuum created by the censorship of television channels, Pakistani university students turned to new-media platforms such as YouTube, Flickr, Facebook, and blogs to facilitate hyperlocal reporting, information dissemination, and community organizing against emergency rule. As such, student activism during the Pakistan Emergency was synonymous with digital activism.

On November 7, over one thousand students of the privately owned Lahore University of Management Sciences (LUMS), Pakistan's most prestigious business school, gathered to protest the imposition of emergency rule. Students at universities across Pakistan had begun protesting and organizing vigils immediately after Musharraf's televised emergency announcement on November 3, but the gathering at LUMS was among the largest of the civil movements launched by lawyers, journalists, and students against the emergency. (By contrast, about ninety students attended a protest the same day at Lahore's National University of Computer and Emerging Sciences, FAST-NU, a federally chartered university.)

The protest took place amid a heavy police presence. Prior to the gathering, policemen warned LUMS students that they would be attacked with batons and arrested in the event of civil agitation. On the morning of the scheduled protest, police surrounded the campus, while plainclothes officers patrolled its grounds. Still, students managed to march through the campus grounds and eventually staged a sit-in at the main campus entrance, in front of the dozens of police officers.

Broadcast journalists for Geo TV and other stations that were continuing to provide live coverage of emergency-related events via satellite and Internet streams were present to cover the LUMS protest. However, police officials successfully prevented media personnel from entering the LUMS campus and eventually confiscated their cameras and other recording equipment. After successfully removing all journalists from the premises, the police ramped up their presence on the campus grounds.

Once LUMS students realized that major Pakistani news networks had not been able to cover their protest, they took it upon themselves to document the authorities' intimidation tactics and their own attempts at resistance. Midway through the day-long protest, a student narrated the morning's events in a post on *The Emergency Times* blog,[25] which had been established to help students express their opinions about democracy and organize against emergency rule. This post was then linked to by other blogs, such as *Metroblogging Lahore*, that are frequented by Pakistani youth.[26] *The Emergency Times* blog also featured pictures of the protest.

Within an hour of the LUMS protest commencing, a Karachi-based blogger, Awab Alvi, who runs the *Teeth Maestro* blog, also helped those behind *The Emergency Times* blog set up an SMS2Blog link, which allowed students participating in the protest to post live, minute-by-minute updates to several blogs, including *Teeth Maestro*, via SMS text message.[27] Students availed themselves of this setup to report on police movement across campus, attempts to corral students in their hostels, the deployment of women police officers across campus, and the activities of LUMS students to resist these actions. On the night of November 7, students posted video clips of the protest that were shot using handheld digital camcorders or cell phone cameras to YouTube.[28]

Some students uploaded their video footage of the protest, shot on cell-phone cameras, to CNN's iReport website, which solicits contributions from citizen journalists across the globe in the form of video, photos, or blog posts.[29] Footage from iReport was then used in a regular CNN broadcast about the student protests. That CNN broadcast was then posted to YouTube for circulation among Pakistanis who no longer had access to the channel because of Musharraf's blanket ban on news programming.[30] Through this confluence of citizen reporting and the international broadcast media, Pakistanis—and a global audience—were informed about the LUMS protest.

Interestingly, between November 3 and November 6, video clips of protests and gatherings at LUMS had been posted to YouTube, but none of these were as well produced or well contextualized as those uploaded on November 7. In the days after the emergency, posted videos up to ten minutes in length were not clearly titled for easy searchability, nor did they provide any explanation of the events portrayed in the footage.[31] In contrast, November 7 video clips were clearly titled and tagged. In many cases, the clips included captions that dated the event, identified the location, and contextualized the students' activities.[32] This difference suggests that university students were aware within days of the beginning of the emergency that their collectively generated coverage of the campus protests was the primary source of information for those looking for coverage of responses to the political crisis, including local and international journalists. For example, Dawn News, Pakistan's first English-language news channel, first broadcast news of the student protests on November 10 in a clip that was made available via satellite and YouTube.[33]

It is worth nothing that university students became savvier in their use of new media platforms over the course of the emergency. On December 4, policemen and intelligence agents once again surrounded and barricaded the LUMS campus to prevent students and faculty from attending a daily vigil for civil liberties. As soon as police appeared at the LUMS campus, a post warning students that traffic in and out of the university was being inspected appeared on *The Emergency Times* blog.[34] Once again, an SMS2Blog link allowed students protesting against the barricade to post live updates to the *Teeth Maestro* blog. This time, the live updates were used to identify particular members of the security agencies[35] so that students could remain on guard and included messages from political parties advising students on how to conduct themselves during the protest.[36] This content indicates that students were using them as a dynamic resource for community organizing during the protest, not merely for archival and documentation purposes.

In all emergency-related demonstrations between November 3 and December 15, university students posted images from the events to Flickr.[37] However, security forces soon began using these images to identify student activists and subsequently arrest them. In an attempt to one-up the authorities, students began blurring the faces of protestors in images before uploading them to Flickr and other blogs.[38] The fact that the authorities were monitoring new-media platforms such as Flickr is an indication of how quickly alternative resources gained influence in the media vacuum created by the television ban.

Meanwhile, young Pakistanis who were unable to join university protests and youths across the diaspora turned to the social-networking site Facebook to express solidarity and oppose emergency rule. Within three days of the emergency declaration, a Facebook group titled "We Oppose Emergency in Pakistan" boasted over five thousand members.[39] The group's home page featured links to online petitions, up-to-date news reports from the Pakistani print and broadcast media, and blogs with original news content, such as *The Emergency Times*. Embedded video clips of messages by detained opposition leaders were also uploaded to the Facebook site. The group's discussion board quickly became the scene of lively discussion, with teenagers and twentysomethings—who previously did not have a voice in the Pakistani public sphere—debating the implications of Musharraf's decision. As the emergency dragged on and the movement to restore the judiciary gained momentum, Facebook was harnessed by diaspora communities as a tool for organizing protests.

The Internet also allowed students outside Pakistan to play key roles. For example, Samad Khurram, an undergraduate at Harvard University, helped mobilize the protesters in Pakistan from his dorm room in Cambridge, Massachusetts, by maintaining an online newsletter and mailing list.

It is not surprising that university students were among the first Pakistanis to turn to the Internet as a venue for information dissemination in the wake of the television ban. Owing to low literacy rates and high service costs, the Internet has not been as widely adopted in Pakistan as cell phones. In December 2007, there were seventy Internet service providers covering 2,419 cities and towns in Pakistan, but only 3.5 million Internet subscribers. Owing to the popularity of cybercafés, however, the total number of Internet users was estimated by the PTA to be closer to 17 million. Pakistani universities are among the few venues where Internet saturation is high: by 2005, over 80 percent of all university libraries had Internet access. And in July 2007, the Higher Education Commission of Pakistan enhanced bandwidth fourfold at public-sector universities—at private universities, bandwidth was doubled—to facilitate videoconferencing and other online communications. Private institutions such as LUMS boast two Internet access nodes in each double-occupancy or triple-occupancy room.

The Emergency Times blog and newsletter exemplify the collision and collusion between old and new media that helped shape civic action against increasingly authoritarian rule. What began as an informative on-campus handout quickly evolved to become the mouthpiece and major news resource for the Student's Action Committee (SAC), the umbrella organization that rallied student activists across Pakistan and the diaspora against Musharraf and his policies.

Launched online on November 5, 2007, *The Emergency Times* described itself as "an independent Pakistani student information initiative providing regular updates, commentary, and analysis on Pakistan's evolving political scenario." An early experiment in youth citizen journalism and digital activism, *The Emergency Times* became one of the most regular and reliable sources of information about the Pakistani civil society's movement against the government between November 2007 and June 2008. At its height, the blog claims to have reached over one hundred and fifty thousand people in over one hundred countries.

Although many students were involved in generating the blog and its accompanying online mailing list, Ammar Rashid, a LUMS student who served as editor in chief for the blog, and Samad Khurram, the undergraduate at Harvard University who managed the mailing list, led the initiative. Khurram explains that Musharraf's crackdown on news channels during the emergency motivated his and Rashid's work: the blog was conceptualized as a daily newspaper, while the mailing list was meant to emulate the one-to-many distribution model of traditional broadcast media. "Providing these were important to us," says Khurram, "since all the private TV channels were banned, and the print media faced serious curbs." The choice of a blog and mailing list was further motivated by the fact that these media are "simple, reliable, and cost-effective."[40]

Khurram and Rashid determined that the combination of a blog and mailing list would be the most effective ways of disseminating information. While Rashid compiled and edited news, Khurram focused on coordinating and mobilizing different groups that included lawyers, journalists, and politicians, in addition to students.

As the SAC movement gained momentum, the blog became the go-to website for information about the campaign, upcoming meetings and protests, and related events, such as a lecture series featuring leading activists. Politicians and lawyers hoping to woo, inspire, or advise student activists also used *The Emergency Times* blog as a communications platform. Moreover, students who had the opportunity to meet or speak with leaders of the movement for democracy, such as deposed judges, detained lawyers, or opposition politicians, would share notes from their conversations with the SAC community at large through the blog.

Significantly, *The Emergency Times* blog was one of the few resources for original reporting on the government crackdown on student activism. Reports of students being harassed or arrested were regularly posted.[41]

After emergency rule was lifted and Musharraf surrendered his post as chief of army staff, the blog shifted its focus to campaign for the restoration of an independent judiciary. Broadening the mandate of *The Emergency Times* in this manner kept it relevant and timely in the context of the unfolding political crisis, but resulted in a reduction of original content. Since most students were not directly involved in what came to be known as the "lawyers' movement"—a campaign to restore the independent judiciary that was in office on November 3 under Chief Justice Chaudhry—*The Emergency Times* blog increasingly featured news articles and opinion pieces from the mainstream print media, both Pakistani and international. Other online resources also began posting to *The Emergency Times* blog to generate traffic. For example, *Parliament Watch*, a political blog, announced its launch on *The Emergency Times*.[42]

To its credit, *The Emergency Times* blog did maintain its link to the students' movement by emerging as a mouthpiece for the SAC. The blog became a venue for stating and clarifying the goals and political agenda of the movement, both for the SAC's members and for the activist community at large.

The mailing list, meanwhile, gathered momentum and gained credibility as it expanded to serve the activist community, particularly in the context of the lawyers' movement. By March 2008, during Black Flag Week, a week-long protest against the dismissal of the judges, the mailing list reached over fifty thousand people. Khurram explains that he initially pushed his e-mails to prominent journalists, columnists, bloggers, newspaper editors, and political-party leaders. The list was then forwarded by these "influentials" to wide networks that were eventually incorporated into the original mailing list.

Thanks to the regularity of updates and its distribution of original content—posts from *The Emergency Times* blog or forwarded correspondence from high-profile lawyers, activists, and politicians—the mailing list of *The Emergency Times* came to be seen as a credible news source by most of its recipients. In a big moment for alternative news sources, Chief Justice Chaudhry chose to circulate a letter responding to allegations against him by Musharraf's government via the mailing list of *The Emergency Times*. Indeed, news items and statements originally circulated on *The Emergency Times* list were eventually cited by publications such as the *New York Times* and the *Washington Post*. The mailing list's credibility also allowed it to function as a fund-raising resource: "When I made a call for donations for the SAC long march [in June 2008], we were able to raise over U.S. $1,000 with one e-mail," says Khurram.[43]

Interestingly, both *The Emergency Times* blog and the mailing list relied on their audience's use of SMS text messaging to push their content and community-organizing efforts well beyond the limited online audience. For example, the blog coordinated a "mass contact campaign": readers were asked to forward protest messages and campaign demands to politicians via SMS text message. The coveted cell-phone numbers of relevant recipients, including top-level politicians, diplomats, and army personnel, were posted to the blog.[44] For his part, when forwarding e-mails with logistical details about protest marches, Khurram would also make sure to circulate SMS text messages containing the same information. "We had a few key people in each segment of the population on an SMS list: a couple of lawyers, a couple of students, a few civil-society activists, and some journalists," he explains. "They would then [forward the message] and inform others [in their network]. Text messaging was a primary source of communication and the mailing list was a close second."[45]

Despite its success during the Pakistan Emergency, *The Emergency Times* blog suspended operations on June 25, 2008. In his final post, Rashid indicated a lack of time and resources to maintain the blog. The fate of *The Emergency Times* blog raises questions about the sustainability of new-media platforms beyond times of emergency. Can young Pakistanis overcome the participation gap and use new-media platforms to enact democratic and participatory practices on an everyday basis and not only as tools for community organizing during crises?

CITIZEN JOURNALISM: REDEFINING MEDIA AND POWER

In the developed world, a single event often triggers the widespread realization that citizen journalism has forever changed a nation's media landscape. For example, within six hours of bombs exploding on London subway trains and a bus on July 7, 2005, the BBC received over one thousand photographs, twenty amateur videos, four thousand text messages, and twenty thousand e-mails. This influx of citizen reporting prompted Richard Sambrook, director of the BBC's World Service and Global News Division, to write: "We know now that when major events occur, the public can offer us as much new information as we are able to broadcast to them. From now on, news coverage is a partnership."[46] In Pakistan, the assassination of former prime minister Benazir Bhutto on December 27, 2007, redefined Pakistani news media as a hybrid product generated by professional and amateur reporters and disseminated via old and new media sources.

Bhutto's death shocked and enraged Pakistanis, as well as the international community, heightening the sense of political instability across the country. By the time of Bhutto's death, Musharraf had lifted his ban on news channels, and the incident received twenty-four-hour news coverage for several days. And yet the assassination marked a turning point in the transformation of Pakistan's media landscape and ushered in a new era of citizen journalism. The circulation of an amateur video and images by one blogger catapulted citizen journalism to the center of the Pakistani media landscape and earned the work of nonprofessional reporters unprecedented credibility. The following case study illustrates how media coverage of the investigation into Bhutto's assassination transformed the course of citizen journalism in Pakistan.

Soon after Bhutto's death had been verified, its cause was contested. Eyewitnesses in Rawalpindi had reported hearing gunshots, then an explosion. Members of Bhutto's entourage and her colleagues in the Pakistan People's Party (PPP) claimed that the leader had been shot. In the immediate wake of the attack, a team of doctors examined her body and stated in a report that she had an open wound in her left temporal region. A day after the assassination, however, government officials claimed that Bhutto had died when her head hit the lever of the sunroof of her car as she ducked to avoid an assassin's bullet and/or in response to the sound of a blast caused by a suicide bomber. The question of whether Bhutto died of gunshot wounds or a head injury riveted the nation, because the truth would have implications on allegations about lax security and government complicity in the assassination.

An important piece of evidence to help settle this debate came in the form of images and an amateur video generated by a PPP supporter at the rally where Bhutto was killed and subsequently circulated by a popular Karachi-based blogger. By making the footage and images available to the mainstream media and public at large, these citizen journalists sparked an accountability movement that eventually forced the Pakistani government to revisit its account of Bhutto's death.

The blogger who initially circulated the key images and video clip is Dr. Awab Alvi, who runs the *Teeth Maestro* blog.[47] During the emergency, *Teeth Maestro*—motivated much like *The Emergency Times* by the media vacuum created by Musharraf—emerged as a go-to blog for information about the students' activist movement. At the time of Bhutto's assassination, Alvi was arguably the most prominent Pakistani blogger. This is evidenced by the fact that on the day of Bhutto's death, he made four posts on *Teeth Maestro*, including live updates via SMS. The next day, he posted twelve times: his own updates from the streets of Karachi and links to important news items and to insightful commentary from the global print media were supplemented by contributions from other bloggers and citizen journalists. For example, he posted an eyewitness report of the violent response across Karachi to Bhutto's death that he received via e-mail.[48]

Two days after the assassination, someone contacted Alvi claiming to have obtained images and a video clip that confirmed that Bhutto was shot by an assassin and therefore did not succumb to an accidental head wound, as government officials were suggesting. These images and video footage had been posted by a PPP supporter on his home page on the social-networking site Orkut. However, after being inundated with questions and comments about the new evidence, the original source removed the images and clip from Orkut. Luckily, Alvi's contact was able to grab screen shots of those uploaded images before they were taken down.

Alvi then contacted the original source, the PPP supporter, and convinced him to share the images and video. Soon after, Alvi had obtained four images indicating that Bhutto had indeed been shot. However, the video clip proved harder to obtain. The PPP supporter was based in Islamabad and had access only to a dial-up Internet connection. Since the video was a fifty-six megabyte file, he was having trouble uploading and electronically forwarding it to Alvi. At that point, Alvi contacted two employees at Dawn News, an independent English-language Pakistani news channel, and arranged from them to collect the video from the PPP supporter's house the next morning. The goal, after all, was to make the images and video clip available to the public as soon as possible, whether via the *Teeth Maestro* blog or a mainstream media broadcast. After a late-night phone call with Alvi, the PPP supporter agreed to share the video clip with the Dawn News team. But the next morning, the original source could not be reached on his cell phone, and the handoff of the video clip did not occur.

In the meantime, by the end of the day on December 29, Alvi had posted the four images he received from the PPP supporter to his blog (fig. 2).[49] *Teeth Maestro* was thus the first media outlet to circulate images of Bhutto's assassination that could help clarify whether she died of gunshot wounds or a fatal head injury. "The moment I saw these images, I knew I had to get them out publicly as soon as possible," says Alvi. "I quickly edited the posts, published them online on my blog, and circulated the link far and wide, letting the dynamics of the free and open Internet protect me and the [original] source."[50]

The images were soon cross-posted on other Pakistani blogs, such as *The Emergency Times*.[51] Alvi also contacted CNN iReport with his story about fresh evidence and forwarded the images to the Dawn News channel. But these mainstream media outlets were slow to pick up on the story. Dawn News first broadcast the images in the context of an interview with a security analyst at 3:00 p.m. on December 30. Meanwhile, *CNN iReport* did not contact Alvi until the next day.

On December 31, the UK-based public-service channel, Channel 4, first broadcast the video clip of Bhutto's assassination that Alvi was not able to obtain from the PPP supporter.[52] This video was then endlessly circulated within the Pakistani blogosphere and on YouTube.[53] Interestingly, Channel 4's analysis of the video clip borrows heavily from the annotation on the pictures uploaded by Alvi. The

FIGURE 2 Screen grab from *Teeth Maetro*'s blog from December 29, 2007. This video cell phone image was taken just after the gun shots which were fired from the left but moments before the bomb blast. Here we see Benazir Bhutto not on the sunroof of the car but most likely already shot and injured slumped inside.

similarity indicates that the citizen journalists' interpretation of Bhutto's assassination set the tone for international mainstream media coverage of the "cause of death" controversy.

The wide circulation and analysis by the global mainstream media of this video and the four images that accompanied it eventually caused the Pakistani government to retract their statement about Bhutto succumbing to a head injury. According to the BBC, this amateur video and the related images proved that security provided for Bhutto by the Pakistani government was indeed lax.[54]

It remains unclear how Channel 4 obtained the video clip that eluded Alvi and reporters for various independent Pakistani news channels. Alvi explains that the PPP supporter—who may have been part of Bhutto's security team on the day of the assassination—first showed his video footage and images to other members of the PPP. Apparently, at the time of this initial screening, he saved the video clip to the hard drive of a computer in a PPP office in Islamabad. PPP officials then instructed the supporter not to share this evidence with the media. However, sensing the importance of the evidence, the supporter returned home and uploaded his images to Orkut, thereby drawing Alvi's attention. The original source for the video footage and images has not been heard from since he spoke with Alvi on the night of December 29. For that reason, Alvi believes that a PPP official who knew that the video was available on a PPP office computer sold the footage to Channel 4 for a hefty sum. This, however, remains unconfirmed.

Alvi's involvement in the circulation of such key evidence regarding Bhutto's assassination helped revolutionize the role played by citizen journalists in Pakistan. Soon after Bhutto's death, the Dawn Group of Newspapers, Pakistan's leading news and media entity, launched a "citizen journalism unit." A section on their website encourages contributions by nonprofessional reporters to be showcased on the Dawn News television channel and on the group's site.[55] This opening up to collaboration by the most traditional and therefore most respected news outlet in Pakistan underscores how much citizen journalism and the credibility of information available on new-media platforms matured between the imposition of emergency rule on November 3 and Bhutto's death on December 27, 2007.

NEW MEDIA AND CITIZENSHIP

After Bhutto's assassination, general elections, initially scheduled for January 2008, were postponed until February 18, 2008. It was widely understood that the outcome of the elections would be pivotal for restoring democratic norms in Pakistan. While Pakistanis struggled to imagine who could possibly replace Bhutto—a shoo-in to be elected to her third term as prime minister—they were adamant that the decision be theirs alone, as reflected in a free and fair election.

However, in the run-up to the election, it became clear that election rigging and campaign misconduct were rampant. On February 12, the New York–based Human Rights Watch reported that the Pakistani election commission charged with managing polling was under the control of pro-Musharraf officials.[56] Opposition politicians across the country complained that the police and representatives of Musharraf's governing party were harassing them, illegally removing their billboards and banners, and obstructing their campaign rallies. Citizens demonstrating support for any other than the ruling party were either being intimidated by police into changing their vote or bribed.

After being subject to new restrictions during emergency rule, the mainstream media were in no position to expose these dire circumstances. Journalists, particularly those in rural areas, reported that they were being prevented from covering news stories and campaign rallies, threatened with arrest, and regularly having their equipment confiscated. The mainstream broadcast media, meanwhile, were prohibited from covering election rallies and protests and from airing live news broadcasts, live call-in shows, or live talk shows.[57] Moreover, the government kept specific restrictions on election coverage deliberately vague in order to put the onus of caution and restraint on media outlets.

To drive home the point that the Pakistan Electronic Media Regulatory Authority would be scrutinizing the appropriateness of election coverage, cable operators in the Punjab province, Pakistan's most populous, were asked to block broadcasts of the independent news channel Aaj TV for almost twelve hours on February 6. This censorship took effect after a talk show broadcast by the channel featured a journalist who had been banned by Musharraf from appearing on television in the wake of the emergency. As a result of these measures, Pakistanis were aware that the media would not be able to report promptly on whether proper voting procedures were followed on election day.

In this environment, citizen journalists took it upon themselves to monitor the elections, armed with little more than camera phones. According to the *Wall Street Journal*, the Free and Fair Election Network (FAFEN), an independent coalition of nongovernmental organizations, enlisted over twenty thousand civilians to observe polling stations and preelection campaigning in more than two hundred and fifty election zones. Such recruitment was unprecedented in FAFEN's history. No doubt Musharraf's actions in the months leading up to the election motivated much of this civic engagement, but an active online movement coordinated and implemented via new-media platforms played a vital role in mobilizing Pakistanis in record numbers.

Mailing lists became the main form of communication between activists and Pakistanis in the days before the election. To lay the groundwork, messages circulated on mailing lists encouraged voters to beware rigging. The following is the text of an e-mail circulated by the Concerned Citizens of Pakistan, a "non-partisan, non-political group" on February 16: "Be vigilant against rigging. Find your polling station and your name in the voters' list a day before the election. Arrive early, cast your vote yourself according to your conscience for honest candidates who promise to restore the judiciary and to work for a peaceful, democratic Pakistan." Messages containing Human Rights Watch and FAFEN updates about the extent of election rigging were also forwarded through mailing lists.

Closer to the election, democracy advocates circulated specific requests for volunteer monitors that included calls for action as well as logistical details about how, where, and when to monitor polling. An e-mail explained that the SAC was compiling a twenty-page paper documenting "electoral irregularities as well as the impressions of various students about the electoral process of 2008" and asked that volunteers submit one-page reports on their findings. The message also included a list of "irregularities" of which youth monitors should remain aware and pointed those interested to external websites managed by nongovernmental organizations and the official election commission that detailed Pakistani voting protocol.

It is important to note that activist groups did not rely on mailing lists alone to mobilize Pakistanis on election day. Each e-mail included a cell-phone number that volunteers could contact via SMS text messages with questions and to indicate the specific time slots during which they were available to monitor polling. In most cases, e-mails included short messages that were meant to be copied and further circulated via SMS text message. The parallel use of SMS text messages allowed activists to reach a wider audience while continuing to keep information about their monitoring activities restricted to trusted recipients.

On the day after the election, activist groups and volunteer monitors used the mailing lists to distribute their observations from the polling booths. First-hand accounts of election rigging at specific polling stations were widely circulated by civilian monitors. For example, on February 19, Ahmed Mustafa, a student at the Sindh Muslim Law College in Karachi, sent out the following e-mail with the subject "100% rigging at polling station NA250 and NA24": "I was... on my field visits [at] polling station of SM Law College NA250. Presiding officer stamped 400 fake ballot papers in favor of [political party] MQM in front of our team.... When we approached NA 242 in Federal B. Area, people said that when they entered the polling booth to cast votes, a person with a badge of the MQM blocked everyone and snatched [their] ballot papers." Mainstream media journalists and nongovernmental organizations such as Human Rights Watch used such brief e-mails to evaluate the prevalence of election rigging.

CIVILIANS WITH CAMERA PHONES

On February 21, 2008, a civilian monitor posted on YouTube a video documenting blatant election rigging. The clip shows a woman in charge of conducting polling at the NA250 station in Karachi marking several ballots in favor of the MQM political party with her own thumbprint (owing to low literacy rates, this is a common way of casting a vote). The angle from which the video is shot, its quality, and its duration indicate that the civilian monitor used a concealed camera phone to capture the incriminating footage.

By February 22,[58] the link to the YouTube clip was distributed via the mailing lists that had been established in the run-up to the election and posted on a handful of blogs. But the same day, users began to complain that they could not access the YouTube domain. Blogs such as *PKPolitics* and *Adnan's Crazy Blogging World* reported that YouTube had been banned in Pakistan.[59] These reports prompted a range of responses from Internet users nationwide: some claimed that they could still access the video-sharing site, while others were convinced that the Pakistan Telecommunications Authority had in fact banned YouTube. Eventually, it was determined by several bloggers that users relying on Internet service providers that utilized the infrastructure—primarily phone lines—of the government-run Pakistan Telecommunications Limited were being prevented from loading the YouTube domain.

Since the Pakistani government had not officially announced a ban on the video-sharing site, bloggers began to speculate as to why access to YouTube was being limited. Adnan Siddiqi, who maintains *Adnan's Crazy Blogging World*, wrote: "I . . . don't know what's the actual reason [for the YouTube ban] but . . . [people] say that there were some videos published on YouTube which were singing praises of free and fair election in Pakistan."[60]

Similarly, with reference to the YouTube election-rigging clip, Awab Alvi blogged on *Teeth Maestro*: "Sadly the release of these videos appear[s] too suspiciously close to the YouTube blocking, which came barely a day after these videos become public."[61] Pakistanis posting to online chat forums such as Shiachat also linked the government's attempt to block YouTube to the clips documenting election rigging.[62] Indeed, news of the government's attempts to suppress evidence of election rigging sparked a vibrant conversation throughout the Pakistani online community about the transparency of the 2008 elections, the frequency of polling violations, and the significance of rigging. The political party whose officials can be seen improperly marking ballots in the video was also maligned.

On February 23, 2008, the Pakistani government officially blocked access to the YouTube domain, claiming that the popular website hosts blasphemous content. No mention of the election-rigging videos was made in the announcement. The BBC reported that the PTA had instructed Pakistani Internet service providers to block the site because it featured the controversial Danish cartoons depicting the Prophet Muhammad as well as a trailer for a Dutch film that negatively portrays Islam.[63]

News of the official ban prompted quick efforts against censorship throughout the Pakistani blogosphere. Bloggers alerted users that one major Internet service provider relying on foreign routers had not banned YouTube and that the election-rigging video was still available for viewing. To ensure wider access, the blog *NaiTazi* uploaded the election-rigging clip in an embedded format that did not require access to YouTube for viewing purposes. Links to this embedded version of the clip were widely forwarded via the mailing lists of several bloggers, *The Emergency Times* blog, and the Student Action Committee. It is significant that bloggers were not convinced by the government's allegations about blasphemous content and instead focused their efforts on preventing the election-rigging videos from being suppressed.

It is interesting to note that if the government had not blocked YouTube, the election-rigging video would have been viewed only by activists, students, and volunteer monitors who subscribed to mailing lists. The YouTube block, however, created a buzz in the blogosphere and curiosity about the government's motivations, thereby attracting more attention to the election-rigging clip and ensuring its broad circulation.

The incident also prompted an interesting collaboration between old and new media. Soon after reports about the YouTube ban surfaced online on February 22, the leading independent news station, Geo TV, broadcast the original video uploaded by the civilian monitor. However, as it became increasingly clear that the government was making an effort to suppress the video, the news channel, which had already been banned during the 2007 emergency, ceased broadcasting the clip.

Instead, the channel took a cue from the clip's content and, emboldened by the online response to the YouTube video, began broadcasting other footage that revealed irregularities at polling stations. Although Geo TV reporters had captured this footage on election day, February 18, they did not compile and broadcast it as an investigative report focusing on election rigging until February 22, the day the YouTube video was being circulated online.[64] The channel made sure to include any footage captured on hidden cameras in an effort to mimic the tactics of citizen journalists and civilian monitors who mobilized for the election.

While it cannot be explicitly documented, the fact that Geo TV did eventually broadcast the YouTube clip must have boosted the perceived credibility of citizen journalism. More importantly, the fact that Geo TV shifted the focus of its programming to accord with a civic-media artifact indicates that the Pakistani media are moving toward a hybrid model, where professional journalists take the work of citizen journalists seriously while citizen media rely on the mainstream media for dissemination and legitimacy. Another lesson highlighted by the fate of the YouTube clip is that new-media platforms are not utilized by the public alone. Officials of the Pakistani government were obviously tracking the coverage of the elections by citizen journalists and understood the reach and influence of the video-sharing site.

On February 24, the Pakistani government's attempts to block YouTube led to a worldwide shutdown of the website for several hours. A Pakistani Internet service provider complying with the ban routed global traffic to YouTube using erroneous Internet protocols, preventing users from accessing the site.[65] This error prompted a global condemnation of the Pakistani government's attempts at censorship and fueled a debate within the Pakistani blogosphere about the PTA's readiness to enforce domain-wide censorship. For example, a guest blogger on the *Teeth Maestro* site wrote: "It seems illogical for the government of Pakistan to hinder their own people from using one very important tool of the modern era. Pakistan Internet Exchange is also advised to upgrade its filtering/censorship systems which can cater to URL-specific blocks and not take the entire country down a roller coaster of censorship."[66]

Owing to the global ramifications of the YouTube block, the Pakistani government was forced to lift the ban on February 27. Clips showing election rigging—those posted by the civilian monitor as well as subsequent broadcasts from independent news channels—continue to be available on the website.

EPILOGUE

Once a democratically elected government came to power in February 2008, the urgency with which new-media technologies were being used for citizen journalism and community organizing lessened. Certain influential blogs, such as *The Emergency Times*, shut down in June 2008—the editor explained that the blog no longer served what he called the "exemplar purpose" it did during emergency rule.

Overall, however, the number of bloggers and Facebook users continues to increase dramatically. There are currently about seven thousand Pakistani blogs, many of which boast a wider readership than print magazines. Blog aggregator sites such as PakPositive and Bloggers.Pk have also been established to help an increasing number of Internet users navigate the local blogosphere. In addition to political, activist, or technology-related blogs, posts on everyday life, food, and culture are proliferating. Social networking and microblogging are also popular: in August 2011, the number of Pakistani Facebook users crossed the 5-million mark,[67] while over 1.9 million people turned to Twitter to critique or mock the state.[68] In March 2012, Twitter launched an Urdu-language site interface.

The growth of the Pakistani blogosphere has also consolidated the hybrid model of news gathering and opinion making that brings together professional and citizen journalists. Indeed, until the February 2008 election, citizen journalists believed they were working at a tangent to the mainstream media. In 2011, however, many see themselves as an integral part of a diversified media landscape.

Many full-time journalists are blogging for their media groups or on private sites, and increasingly contributing guest posts on popular blogs. In turn, the *Dawn* blog, the multiauthor blog of the largest English-language Pakistani newspaper, which launched in February 2009, regularly features posts by popular bloggers.

In some cases, citizen journalists have also helped set the news agenda. In September 2009, a Pakistani citizen was killed while competing in a reality television show that was sponsored by a multinational company. The company managed to kill the story in the mainstream media, but several Karachi-based bloggers posted the news on their sites. It was only after details began to circulate online that journalists reported on the story for mainstream publications.

More importantly, citizen journalists have stepped up to provide news coverage of major events that have been overlooked by the mainstream media. In the summer of 2009, over three million people from Pakistan's northwestern and tribal areas had been displaced by military operations against Taliban militants—the largest displacement and humanitarian crisis in recent times. The mainstream media was focused on covering the conflict and the escalation of militant attacks in Pakistan's major urban centers. Luckily, bloggers united to address the information vacuum from the many refugee camps housing internally displaced persons (IDPs).

Bloggers initially highlighted the few news reports that were published on the extent of the IDP crisis. Soon, however, many citizen journalists began traveling to the various refugee camps, from which they posted evocative descriptions of the conditions in which IDPs were forced to live, along with photos, audio clips, and lists of relief goods that were urgently required. Writing in *The Huffington Post*, Mona Sarika stated that Pakistani bloggers had become "the voice of the voiceless." Indeed, prominent blogs such as *Teeth Maestro* and *CHUP!—Changing Up Pakistan*—have offered the best documentation of Pakistan's IDP crisis. While the November 2007 emergency sparked the political consciousness of online Pakistanis, the IDP crisis added a fillip to the blogosphere's social consciousness. Similar citizen journalism initiatives were aimed at documenting the widespread suffering resulting from devastating floods that occurred in the summers of 2010 and 2011.

That said, the Pakistani blogosphere remains connected to its activist roots. In June 2008 and March 2009, lawyers, students, and activists participated in countrywide protests—known in the vernacular as "long marches"—to demand the reinstatement of senior judges deposed during the 2007 emergency rule. (In the first instance, protestors were also calling for the resignation of President Pervez Musharraf.) As one young blogger, Faisal Kapadia, who posts at *Deadpan Thoughts*, put it: "We now have a standing army of online activists, ready to mobilize for a cause when needed."

During the March 2009 long march, student activists widely distributed an "official" protest anthem via YouTube and posted live updates from rallies to several blogs as well as a "Seen Report" using SMS2Blog. For the first time in an activist context, a Twitter feed was also created to allow those participating in the long march to upload bite-sized updates from rallies and the streets of Lahore and Karachi, as well as news as it broke on private news channels.

Twitter came into wide use amongst net-connected Pakistanis in 2009. After the long march, young activists and bloggers coordinated relief drives for the IDPs via Twitter. Those who traveled to and volunteered at refugee camps also regularly tweeted updates on the plight of IDPs, riots within refugee camps, and delays in aid delivery.

As a testament to Twitter's increasing popularity, in July 2009, the online community organized its first "tweet up" (a meeting organized through tweets), where over eighty microbloggers gathered to brainstorm ideas on how best to use Twitter for citizen journalism and community organizing. No doubt young Pakistanis had been inspired by the powerful use of Twitter by young Iranians during the June 2009 elections in the neighboring Islamic republic.

In another case of the mainstream media adopting the use of new-media technologies, Naveen Naqvi, an anchor on the private television station Dawn News, began tweeting with her audience during her daily morning news show. Naqvi would share information about guests on the show via Twitter, and while the show was screening, she would pose questions tweeted in by her viewers to those guests. This was the first instance of social media helping to make a traditional, one-to-many medium more interactive.

Robust online energy has not escaped the Pakistani authorities' attention, however. Admittedly, the Pakistan government has not harassed, intimidated, or detained bloggers, as has become common in Egypt, China, Iran, and Saudi Arabia. Nor is the government restricting online free expression by filtering or blocking content or monitoring activity. But this may change.

In July 2009, President Asif Ali Zardari promulgated the Prevention of Electronic Crimes Ordinance, legislation that aims to curb cyberterrorism, but that employs vague language that could be invoked to bring serious charges against anyone who owns a computer. The promulgation of this cybercrime ordinance can be read as a sign of the growing power of the blogosphere. Why else would a civilian, democratically elected government promulgate an ordinance that was drafted in 2007 during the reign of an increasingly paranoid military dictator, General Musharraf?

Under the cybercrimes bill, the Pakistan Telecommunication Authority can arbitrarily invoke hazy definitions of what constitutes spamming, spoofing, stalking, "terroristic intent," or a terrorist act and put someone behind bars for years. Indeed, the act is peppered with words such as "lewd," "obscene," and "immoral," which are not legal terms and are highly subjective. In other words, it is up to the authorities' discretion to determine what is unacceptable online.

With the act in place, the PTA has slightly increased the frequency with which it blocks Pakistani websites. In February 2010, links to certain YouTube videos showing President Zardari in an unfavorable light were blocked. Websites with antigovernment content and those run by ethnic Baloch separatists are also sporadically blocked. In October 2009, websites hosting a video that showed a Pakistan Army major interrogating people suspected of harboring terrorists was blocked—the clip revealed that the major ordered his team to beat the suspects. And in August 2008, the PTA blocked links to a video alleging the misuse of power by the naval chief, Admiral Afzal Tahir. Notably, it is not only Pakistani websites that face censorship. In May 2010, a Pakistani court ordered Facebook to be banned for two weeks for hosting blasphemous content. The ban followed the launch of a Facebook page called "Everybody Draw Mohammed Day," which invited caricatures of the Islamic prophet and therefore sparked protests across several Pakistani cities.[71]

There are now calls for the Prevention of Electronic Crimes Act to be redrafted and brought in line with international legal standards for cybercrime and with the International Covenant on Civil and Political Rights and the Universal Declaration of Human Rights. For new media to continue shaping Pakistani politics and society, those calls must be backed up by international press freedom groups and ultimately heeded by the government of Pakistan.

NOTES

1. "Pakistanis Condemning the Mockery of the Judicial System in Pakistan," *Proud-Pakistani.com*, http://proud-pakistani.com/2007/03/13/sign-the-petition-now.
2. Yochai Benkler, *The Wealth of Networks: How Social Production Transforms Markets and Freedom* (New Haven: Yale University Press, 2006), p. 213.
3. At this time, when the military ruler, General Musharraf, dismissed the Supreme Court's chief justice, Iftikhar Muhammad Chaudhry, thereby undermining the country's independent judiciary, he continued to serve simultaneously as the country's president and chief of army staff, thus blurring the distinction between democracy and dictatorship. Between November 2007 and February 2008, Pakistanis learned just how rocky the road to democratic rule can be. In that time, General Musharraf imposed a state of emergency and suspended the constitution, opposition parties called for elections, a popular politician—former prime minister Benazir Bhutto—was brutally assassinated, and general elections were held. Moreover, press freedom was drastically curtailed during this time—amendments promulgated by General Musharraf in the summer of 2007 made it impossible for the media to report on elections or to investigate matters relating to the government or the Pakistan Army.
4. Pakistani blogs are primarily written in English, but discussion in the comments section

features a mixture of English and romanized Urdu-language posts. Since English remains the official language of the state, most semiliterate Pakistanis have a reading knowledge of the language. Communication via SMS, Twitter, on Facebook, or on YouTube largely occurs in a mixture of Urdu and English. Messages may be in English with keywords in romanized Urdu or vice versa. Inspirational messages or those containing jokes or poetry are often entirely in romanized Urdu. On a few occasions, text messages forwarding information about protest rallies included both an English and an Urdu-language version. As the Arabic script (in which Urdu is written) becomes more widely available on mobile phones, Urdu-language messages that are not romanized are also circulated.

5. Benkler, *The Wealth of Networks*, p. 219.
6. Adam Clayton Powell, "Democracy and New Media in Developing Nations: Opportunities and Challenges," in Henry Jenkins and David Thorburn (eds.), *Democracy and New Media* (Cambridge, MA: The MIT Press, 2003), p. 173.
7. Benkler, *The Wealth of Networks*, p. 219.
8. Shahan Mufti, "Musharraf's Monster," *Columbia Journalism Review*, November–December 2007, http://www.cjr.org/feature/musharrafs_monster.php?page=1.
9. "Musharraf Imposes Tough Curbs on Pakistani Media," *VOA News*, November 4, 2007, http://www.voanews.com/english/news/a-13-2007-11-03-voa20.html.
10. "Eight TV and 10 Radio Channels Issued Licenses," *The Daily Times*, May 23, 2008, http://www.dailytimes.com.pk/default.asp?page=2008%5C05%5C23%5Cstory_23-5-2008_pg7_29.
11. Precise television viewership statistics for Pakistan are not available. For a list and pie chart compiled by MediaTrek Pakistan showing advertising time shares on different private channels and the state-owned PTV that is a good indicator of the relative popularity of different channels, however, see "Pakistan TV Medium Statistics," *Travel & Culture*, http://www.travel-culture.com/pakistan/media.
12. Mufti, "Musharraf's Monster."
13. Declan Walsh, "Musharraf Closes TV Stations as Democracy Calls Grow," *Guardian*, June 5, 2007, http://www.guardian.co.uk/media/2007/jun/05/pakistan.television.
14. Awab Alvi, in discussion with the author, December 31, 2007.
15. "Govt Bans Kamran Khan's Geo.TV show," *Teeth Maestro*, March 16, 2007, http://www.teeth.com.pk/blog/2007/03/16/govt-bans-kamran-khans-geotv-show.
16. Zulfiqar Ghuman, "Musharraf Gags Media," *Daily Times*, June 5, 2007, http://www.dailytimes.com.pk/default.asp?page=2007%5C06%5C05%5Cstory_5-6-2007_pg1_1.
17. "Top Judge Attacks Musharraf's Rule," *BBC Online*, November 6, 2007, http://news.bbc.co.uk/2/hi/south_asia/7080433.stm.
18. Robin McDowell, "Pakistan TV Fights Back," Associated Press, November 8, 2007, http://www.internews.org/articles/2007/20071108_ap_pakistan.shtm.
19. "Pakistan Emergency Geo News," YouTube, November 3, 2007, http://www.youtube.com/watch?v=BqbJj2ZKDYM.
20. Live Pakistani television feeds are available via *The Pakistan Policy Blog* at http://pakistan-policy.com/pakistan-television-live.
21. "Two Pakistani Television Channels Broadcasting From Dubai Ordered Off the Air," *IFEX, the International Freedom of Expression Exchange*, November 19, 2007, http://www.ifex.org/en/content/view/full/87779.
22. Pakistan Telecommunications Authority, *PTA Annual Report 2007*, Ch. 2, "Mobile Cellular

Services" pp. 53–55, www.pta.gov.pk/index2.php?option=com_content&do_pdf=1&id=1033. In the 1990s, three telecom operators (Paktel, Ufone, and Mobilink) were present in Pakistan. However, exorbitant connection fees, airtime charges, and billing on incoming calls kept mobile penetration low until the end of the decade. The Pakistan Telecom Authority (PTA), a government agency founded in 1997 to regulate the telecom industry, introduced a calling party pays (CPP) policy in 2001, which resulted in industry competition that helped increase mobile penetration to 8.3 percent in 2004. The introduction of two new telecom operators in early 2005 led to fiercer competition, cheaper connections, and affordable handsets. By July 2006, overall teledensity in Pakistan stood at 46.9 percent, of which only 3.3 percent was due to fixed-line services.

23. *Ibid*. According to the PTA, the total target market for cell phone users—excluding those living well below the poverty line and children under the age of eight—was about 97 million people. In other words, over 60 percent of the potential Pakistani market was using cell phones when Musharraf suspended the constitution. Since 2003, telecom companies have invested over U.S. $8 billion in Pakistan, with the mobile sector accounting for 73 percent of that expenditure. In the 2007 fiscal year alone, the mobile sector invested U.S. $2.7 billion. And the market is expected to grow: China Mobile has acquired one cellular network and contracted U.S. $500 million to companies such as Ericsson, ZTE, and Alcatel to roll out new networks. Meanwhile, existing mobile service providers were investing heavily in the industry. For example, Mobilink, the largest local network, invested U.S. $500 million in the 2008 fiscal year to improve the quality of its service and expand infrastructure.
24. *Ibid.*, p. 58.
25. "Details of the LUMS Rally and Police Response," *The Emergency Times*, November 7, 2007, http://pakistanmartiallaw.blogspot.com/2007/11/details-of-lums-rally-and-police.html.
26. "Protest at LUMS," *Metroblogs Lahore*, November 7, 2007, http://lahore.metblogs.com/2007/11/07/protest-lums-november-7th-2007.
27. "Update @ 13:40: Police Outside LUMS Lahore," *Teeth Maestro*, November 7, 2007, http://www.teeth.com.pk/blog/2007/11/07/update-1340-police-outside-lums-lahore. SMS2blog is a software application that publishes text messages sent to a particular, preassigned number to a blog in real time. The application is ideal for providing real-time updates on an evolving situation. New software applications that allow users to broadcast text messages as tweets and vice versa also started coming into use in 2009.
28. "2nd Major Protest Rally at LUMS," YouTube. November 7, 2007, http://www.youtube.com/watch?v=FbfD_xyN7Dw&feature=related.
29. "About CNN iReport," CNN iReport, http://www.ireport.com/about.jspa.
30. "LUMS Protest on CNN," YouTube, November 7, 2007, http://www.youtube.com/watch?v=5zobFeyJ2Uc&feature=related.
31. See, for example, "LUMS Protest," YouTube, November 5, 2007, http://www.youtube.com/watch?v=oVg_dHsghpI.
32. See, for example, "2nd Major Protest Rally at LUMS," YouTube, November 7, 2007, http://www.youtube.com/watch?v=FbfD_xyN7Dw&feature=related.
33. "LUMS Student Protests in Pakistan—Newseye, Dawn News," YouTube, November 10, 2007, http://www.youtube.com/watch?v=fJYp-jPEPgU.
34. "LUMS Besieged by Police," *The Emergency Times*, December 4, 2007, http://pakistanmartiallaw.blogspot.com/2007/12/lums-beseiged-by-police.html.

35. "Update @ 13:43: LUMS Besieged, Important Information for Islamabad," *Teeth Maestro*, December 4, 2007, http://www.teeth.com.pk/blog/2007/12/04/update-1343-lums-besieged-important-information-for-islamabad.
36. "Update @ 16:00: PTI Information Secretary Sends Activism Message for Students," *Teeth Maestro*, November 8, 2007, http://www.teeth.com.pk/blog/2007/11/08/update-1600-pti-information-secretary-sends-activism-message-for-students.
37. "Essamlums Photostream," Flickr, November 7, 2007, http://flickr.com/photos/essamfahim/page2.
38. See, for example, "Update @ 21:13: Images from Today's Peace Rally at LUMS," *Teeth Maestro*, November 9, 2007, http://www.teeth.com.pk/blog/2007/11/09/update-2113-images-from-todays-peace-rally-at-lums.
39. The Facebook page is now titled "We Want Independent Judiciary in Pakistan," http://www.facebook.com/group.php?gid=5772092761. This is because the end of emergency rule in Pakistan on December 16, 2007, did not coincide with the reinstatement of the deposed chief justice. Activism opposed to the emergency quickly morphed into a movement to restore an independent judiciary. That struggle continued until March 2009, when a democratically elected government that came to power during elections in February 2008 finally upheld its campaign promise of reinstating the chief justice.
40. Samad Khurram, telephone interview with the author, July 9, 2008.
41. See, for example, "SAC Lahore Members Harassed and Beaten Up," *The Emergency Times*, February 2, 2008, http://pakistanmartiallaw.blogspot.com/2008/02/sac-lahore-members-harassed-and-beaten.html.
42. "Parliament Watch," *The Emergency Times*, February 6, 2008, http://pakistanmartiallaw.blogspot.com/2008/02/parliament-watch.html.
43. Khurram, interview with the author, July 9, 2008.
44. "Force MMA to Boycott!!" *The Emergency Times*, December 2, 2007, http://pakistanmartiallaw.blogspot.com/2007/12/force-mma-to-boycott.html.
45. Khurram, interview with the author, July 9, 2008.
46. Richard Sambrook, "Citizen Journalism and the BBC," *Neiman Reports* (Winter 2005), http://www.nieman.harvard.edu/reportsitem.aspx?id=100542.
47. Alvi is aware of the trajectory of his blogging career: "It started with me keeping an online diary. Then it became a serious hobby." Awab Alvi in discussion with the author, December 31, 2007. Since playing a significant role in the coverage of Bhutto's death, Alvi describes himself as a citizen journalist.
48. "Was Yesterday's Carnage in Karachi All PPP's Doing or Did MQM Have a Hand In It?" *Teeth Maestro*, December 28, 2007, http://www.teeth.com.pk/blog/2007/12/28/was-yesterdays-carnage-in-karachi-all-ppps-doing-or-did-mqm-have-a-hand-in-it-an-eyewitness-report.
49. "Updated: Mobile Pictures—Benazir Was Definitely Shot Dead before the Blast," *Teeth Maestro*, December 29, 2007, http://www.teeth.com.pk/blog/2007/12/29/mobile-pictures-benazir-was-defintely-shot-dead-before-the-blast.
50. Awab Alvi in discussion with the author, December 31, 2007.
51. "Mobile Phone Pictures Reveal Benazir Was Shot before the Blast," *The Emergency Times*, December 31, 2007, http://pakistanmartiallaw.blogspot.com/2007/12/mobile-phone-pictures-reveal-benazir.html.
52. "More Video Evidence Bhutto Did Not Die in Bomb Blast," YouTube, December 30, 2007, http://www.youtube.com/watch?v=Mc-ICcefi48.

53. "Video of Benazir's Last Seven Seconds Released," *Teeth Maestro*, December 31, 2007, http://www.teeth.com.pk/blog/2007/12/31/video-of-benazirs-last-seven-seconds-released.
54. Ilyas Khan, "Bhutto Murder: Key Questions," *BBC Online*, February 8, 2008, http://news.bbc.co.uk/2/hi/south_asia/7165892.stm.
55. See, for example, "Become a Citizen Journalist," *Dawn News*, http://dawnnews.tv/citizen-journalists.
56. "Pakistan: Election Commission Not Impartial," Human Rights Watch, February 12, 2008, http://hrw.org/english/docs/2008/02/11/pakist18034.htm.
57. "Pakistan: Media Restrictions Undermine Election," Human Rights Watch, February 16, 2008, http://hrw.org/english/docs/2008/02/16/pakist18088.htm.
58. "Rigging by PPP in NA 250 Karachi Elections 2008," YouTube, February 21, 2008, http://www.youtube.com/watch?v=r693adEEGhQ.
59. "YouTube Banned in Pakistan," PKPolitics, February 22, 2008, http://pkpolitics.com/2008/02/22/youtube-banned-in-pakistan; "YouTube Banned in Pakistan," *Adnan's Crazy Blogging World*, February 22, 2008, http://kadnan.com/blog/2008/02/22/youtube-banned-in-pakistan.
60. "YouTube Banned in Pakistan," *Adnan's Crazy Blogging World*, February 22, 2008.
61. "Vote Rigging Videos in Karachi: Could This Be Why YouTube is Blocked?" *Teeth Maestro*, February 22, 2008, http://www.teeth.com.pk/blog/2008/02/22/vote-rigging-videos-in-karachi-could-this-be-why-youtube-is-blocked.
62. "YouTube Blocked in Pakistan by PTA's Orders, after Vote Rigging Videos Show Up???" Shia-Chat, February 22, 2008, http://www.shiachat.com/forum/index.php?showtopic=234941366.
63. "Pakistan Blocks YouTube Website," *BBC Online*, February 24, 2008, http://news.bbc.co.uk/2/hi/south_asia/7261727.stm.
64. "MQM Rigging in Karachi," YouTube, February 22, 2008, http://www.youtube.com/watch?v=zqvXOkD5HYQ.
65. "Pakistan Lifts YouTube Ban," ABC News (Australia), February 27, 2008, http://www.abc.net.au/news/stories/2008/02/27/2173501.htm?section=world.
66. "TWA Internet Backbone Link Blocks Only Blasphemous Video URL," *Teeth Maestro*, February 24, 2008, http://www.teeth.com.pk/blog/2008/02/24/twa-internet-backbone-link-blocks-only-blasphemous-video-url.
67. Aamir Attaa, "Facebook crosses 5 million users from Pakistan." ProPakistani, August 9, 2011, http://propakistani.pk/2011/08/09/facebook-crosses-5-million-users-from-pakistan.
68. Catriona Luke, "Pakistan's Tweeters Take On the State." *The Staggers: The New Statesman Rolling Blog*, June 22, 2011, http://www.newstatesman.com/blogs/the-staggers/2011/06/9608-quetta-pakistan-isi.
69. Habibullah Khan, "Facebook Banned in Pakistan," ABC News, May 19, 2010, http://abcnews.go.com/Technology/International/facebook-banned-pakistan-prophet-muhammad-sketch-competition/story?id=10688625#.TraOC3EtjyM.

Holocaust in Your Face

Hugh Raffles

In the spring of 2000, I was teaching an undergraduate lecture course at the University of California on the connections between people and other animals. I asked each of the forty-odd students to make an individual or group presentation of their choosing. One group wrote and performed a play, a couple of students made short videos, most gave talks, and one explained the ecological effects of European colonialism using finger puppets.

If the course had an argument, it was the unsurprising one that the boundary between human and nonhuman animals is variable, historical, and largely indeterminate; that despite the self-evident differences between beings, every universal line of demarcation—whether consciousness, cognition, language, affect, morality, pain, whatever—crumbles in the face of animal capacity; and that rather than looking to establish more reliable criteria, we might think instead about the motivation and effects of the line itself. At times, the course was simply an argument for difference without hierarchy, for the ethical equivalence of ontologically distinct forms of life, a counterclaim to Martin Heidegger's famous order of being (a stone is worldless, the animal is poor in world, man is world-forming; humans and nonhumans, he wrote, are separated not merely by capacity, but "by an abyss of essence").[1]

One student used her fifteen minutes to take the class through a slide show. With little introduction or commentary, she projected a series of images, alternating scenes of industrial animal slaughter with views of the Nazi death camps. The class sat in silence as she switched between black-and-white photographs of heaped animal bodies—massed corpses whose arrangement could have been achieved only by forklifts and bulldozers—and eerily similar, but more familiar photographs that showed piles of naked human bodies.

The student was on topic with her presentation. She understood the logic of the course and assumed a sympathetic audience. But something wasn't right. The room was full of discomfort and hostility. After a lengthy silence, I spoke up. My comments took me by surprise: something human kicked in, and I found myself pushing back against the equivalences she was proposing and that she had every reason to suppose I shared. And it wasn't just me who was surprised. Had she identified the limit case for liberal animal love?

When the class was over, I told myself that it was the superficiality of the student's presentation that had upset me. I told myself that the problem wasn't so much the cross-species equivalences she had drawn as the historical ones. And I also told myself that I was reacting to her methodological claim that the images spoke for themselves and would do the work of arguing, that what bothered me was the way she had allowed the visual analogy to substitute for speech.

But none of this was very convincing. It was true that she didn't say much. But her images had spoken. In the world of words, they said, even in the densely factual world of Holocaust words, there is a gap, a violent gap, between the rationality of liberal speech and the excess facticity of the image. Through the flesh of these photographs and by their crude juxtaposition, she had raised some of the most difficult questions about death, its commensurabilities, and its representations.

Two years later, in February 2002, PETA (People for the Ethical Treatment of Animals) launched a traveling exhibition called *Holocaust on Your Plate*. The campaign consisted of a series of giant square panels in high-contrast black and white. Each panel was equally divided between an image from a Nazi death camp and an image from an industrial animal farm or slaughterhouse. It was the student's presentation scaled up: a starving man next to a starving cow; children gazing blankly through barbed wire fencing alongside pigs staring emptily through metal bars; prisoners packed onto camp bunks crammed up against chickens squeezed into factory pens. Predictably, the campaign had a polarizing effect. But three years later, when Ingrid Newkirk, the founder and president of PETA, announced the exhibit's abrupt cancellation, she chose Holocaust Remembrance Day to issue a somewhat bewildered apology in which she managed to make everything worse with her simple-minded stress on the prominence of the organization's Jewish staffers in the campaign's development.[2]

Neither PETA nor my student invented this dreaded comparison. In her apology, Newkirk suggested that the connection between the killing of Jews and the killing of animals was a natural one, pointing out that Jewish intellectuals, acutely sensitive to mass hygienics, had secured the link long before she did. At a climactic moment in his story "The Letter Writer," Isaac Bashevis Singer's deathly sick central character has time to pity the fate of those even weaker than himself: "In relation to [the animals]," Herman Gombiner says, "all people are Nazis; for the animals, it is an eternal Treblinka," thus providing Charles Patterson with the title for his widely circulated book, the one sustained treatment of this parallel and the source that animal rights campaigners routinely use to bolster the comparison's scholarly legitimacy.[3]

Patterson's book is a bit scattershot. The Nazis themselves are the more authoritative and complicated source. Not only did they—like Henry Ford—closely study the assembly-line mass killing of the early twentieth-century Chicago stockyards, not only did they transport Jews in cattle trucks and kill them with pesticide, not only did they, as J. M. Coetzee put it in an op-ed piece in *The Sydney Morning Herald* in 2007, "treat human beings like units in an industrial process," but, dedicated taxonomic engineers that they were, one of their first actions following Hitler's appointment as chancellor in 1933 was to introduce new animal-cruelty laws to outlaw kosher slaughter.[4]

Is there anybody—even in the meatpacking industry—who is comfortable with what we do to food animals these days? Maybe it's not everyone who feels, as Coetzee does, that there is "something deeply, cosmically wrong" here, but Timothy Pachirat and others have shown the vast amount of design, management, and linguistic work that goes into hiding what happens inside a slaughterhouse (even from the people working there) and into more generally disguising the animality and multiple exploitations that are prime ingredients of our food.[5] Pachirat doesn't share journalist Michael Pollan's confidence that making publically visible the treatment of animals (and people) in slaughterhouses would turn everyone into ethical reformers.[6] It might equally—as another of my students recently suggested—create a whole new class of popular spectacle.

Animal rights people are right to argue along with Coetzee that it's a crime "to treat *any living being* like a unit in an industrial process," to point out that the industrialization of animal killing is related to the extermination of people not simply by analogy, but by rationality, by aesthetics, and by the direct transfer of technology and practice. They are right to worry that the ethical morass that enables mass brutality against animals also makes other ethical catastrophes, including those against people, more possible. And they're right to insist that the dehumanizations that underwrite human genocide (Jews are vermin, Tutsis are cockroaches) are possible only because the nonhuman avatars are not only nonhuman, but subhuman and killable.[7]

Some of the people who opposed PETA's campaign argued that unlike the Jews, Roma, Poles, sexual noncomformists, political activists, and others dragged from their everyday lives to the fascist camps, the animals in the photographs are raised to die, are likely incapable of independent existence, are dead even before they are born. They were right to insist that this difference matters, that the differences between the many forms of "lives not worth living" are real, that the culture, history, and transgenerational kinships that perish (or somehow persist) along with people are profoundly human. They are right to insist that human dead live on in a different way from animal dead. And they are right that the offense they feel as custodians of the human dead is far from trivial.

Why should anyone be forced to, claim to, or feel the need to arbitrate the unspeakable? Why should horrors be made to compete? Depending on your commitments, making these impossibilities apparent is either the fullness or the emptiness of the comparison, its depth or its shallowness.

I'm far from alone in believing that images of the dead and of the soon to die, both human and animal, have a sacredness, albeit an uncertain sacredness that speaks to us in a language we barely understand. It's too obvious and too European to call it an "uncanniness." The images speak of the thing that has happened and that will happen. They speak of the loss of something unknowable and the doubtful status of the lifeless substance that remains, like us, but not like us, like we will be when we lose the vital thing that is temporarily ours, when we become the thing we can never imagine or understand, the thing we are always becoming. If nothing else, the dead and dying body demands dignity. Yet what is less dignified than the anonymous photograph of anonymous death? Maybe only the anonymous photograph of collective anonymous death, the heaped corpses, awkward, exposed, spilled every which way.

As a form of reason, analogy can be too easy—visual analogy even more so. In this case, it misunderstands both of the stories it hopes to bring together as one. During the Holocaust, Jews and cokilled were not only butchered like domesticated animals, they were turned into those animals. As much as the fact of killing, it is this fact of ontological destruction—the fact that made killing possible—that remains so raw and incalculable. During our present age of industrialized animal slaughter, cows, sheep, pigs, chickens, and their cokilled are born, raised, and killed as the animals they currently are. In the world in which we live, to be able to be killed (in this and other more casual ways) is what it means to be an animal.

As in Auschwitz, there is no confusion here, either ethical or ontological. In this respect, the two stories are both identical and fundamentally distinct.

There is no controlling these images. They reveal a truth invisible to the campaign. The campaign says: Look, the killing of these animals is the same as the murder of these people. The destruction of the Jews was an unconscionable evil and so, therefore, is the killing of the animals. The images say: Look, the killing of these animals is the same as the murder of these people. The Jews died as animals, and so do the animals.

NOTES

Many thanks to Clive Dalton, Meg McLagan, and Sharon Simpson for very helpful comments on earlier versions of this essay.

1. Martin Heidegger, *The Fundamental Concepts of Metaphysics: World, Finitude, Solitude*, trans. William McNeill and Nicholas Walker (Bloomington: Indiana University Press, 1995), p. 177; and *What Is Called Thinking?* trans. John Glenn Gray (New York: Harper & Row, 1968), p. 16.
2. Ingrid Newkirk, "Apology for a Tasteless Campaign," May 5, 2005, http://web.israelinsider.com/Views/5475.htm.
3. Isaac Bashevis Singer, "The Letter Writer," trans. Alisha Sherwin and Elizabeth Shrub, *The New Yorker*, January 13, 1968, pp. 26–54; Charles Patterson, *Eternal Treblinka: Our Treatment of Animals and the Holocaust* (New York: Lantern Books, 2002).
4. J. M. Coetzee, "Exposing the Beast: Factory Farming Must Be Called to the Slaughterhouse," *The Sydney Morning Herald*, January 22, 2007, http://www.smh.com.au/news/opinion/exposing-the-beast-factory-farming-must-be-called-to-theslaughterhouse/2007/02/21/1171733846249.html?page=fullpage#contentSwap1. On this, see also my "Jews, Lice, and History," *Public Culture* 19.3 (2007), pp. 521–66.
5. Timothy Pachirat, *Killing Work* (New Haven: Yale University Press, forthcoming); Noëlie Vialles, *Animal to Edible* (Cambridge: Cambridge University Press, 1994).
6. Michael Pollan, *The Omnivore's Dilemma: A Natural History of Four Meals* (New York: Penguin, 2007).
7. "Perhaps the commandment should read 'Thou shalt not make killable,'" says Donna Haraway in *When Species Meet* (Minneapolis: Minnesota, 2007), p. 80.

FIGURE 1 Image of Mahmoud Asgari and Ayaz Marhoni being prepared for their execution by hanging.

Iran in Pictures: Social Suffering and Three Sets of Images

Negar Azimi

In July of 2006, a series of curious, jarring images began popping up on various gay-oriented websites around the Internet. One of the images, of two young men in blindfolds—they do not look much older than sixteen—nooses being placed around their necks by ominously hooded interlocutors, had the words "Iran Executes Two Gay Teens in Public Hanging" writ large as a headline (fig. 1). In another image, the young men are visibly shaken and in tears as they are interviewed by journalists en route to their public hanging in a location identified as the northeastern Iranian city of Mashhad's Edalat Square. Their crime, announced the various websites, was being homosexual. Later, we would learn that the ill-fated teenagers were named Ayaz Marhoni and Mahmoud Asgari. "Edalat," as it happens, means "justice" in Farsi.

Some seven years earlier, the cover of the July 17, 1999 edition of the *Economist* magazine carried an image of a young man holding a blood-stained T-shirt up over his head. He had a fiercely defiant look about him, a bandana wrapped around his forehead held back his thick, wavy dark hair, and a ribbon was tied around his left arm, like a badge. Just below him one could make out an image—perhaps taken from the page of a newspaper—of a veiled woman looking aghast. The *Economist*'s headline read, in bright green letters: "Iran's Second Revolution?"

Move forward ten years, to June, 2009, and Iran once again found itself embroiled in tumult, the result of competing visions as to what the country's future should look like. On June 12, the tenth Iranian presidential elections under the Islamic regime were carried out. On the night of the election, an official announced that the primary opposition candidate, a former prime minister, architect, and sometime painter of abstractionist bent named Mir Hossein Moussavi had taken the election on the strength of a tremendous campaign effort collectively referred to as the "Green Movement"—probably because of its abundant, not to mention telegenic—use of the color green. The following day, the state media announced that the incumbent, President Mahmoud Ahmadinejad, had in fact won—and in a dramatic landslide, no less—with 63 percent of the total votes cast. The streets erupted in anger, producing the largest popular protests the country has known since the revolution of 1979. As images of the demonstrators and an ensuing crackdown streamed in from ordinary digital cameras, cell-phone cameras, video cameras perched atop rooftops, and so on, one particular phone video—or perhaps it was two—captured the last minutes on earth of a twenty-six-year-old protester named Neda Agha-Soltan who had been shot in the chest, presumably by a member of the paramilitary Basij force. It didn't take long for that video, all forty or so grainy seconds of it, to go viral, and by extension, to take the world by storm.

What follows will provide a space to begin to think about these images and their particular trajectories and fates in the media. All three sets of images are documents of human rights abuses of one sort or another, and each was—following its initial circulation—disseminated en masse in the print press, but even more prominently on the Internet. One image—that of the young student we would come to know as Ahmad Batebi—has assumed somewhat iconic proportions, emerging as a symbol of the moral failings of an Iranian regime that had not delivered on the promises of the revolution that brought it to power. Another set—composed of the images of the two young men in Mashhad—was equally replicated many times. And then there is Neda Agha-Soltan, the young woman who swiftly emerged as the symbol of the Iranian protesters, but also, of their fallen hopes and aspirations. Following their initial revelation, each of these photographs was appropriated in multiple ways, whether by invested individuals, human rights organizations, bloggers, the press, or policy makers. In short, the circulation of these images was central to the ways in which they were perceived and used—and there have been multiple ways in which they have been understood and appropriated.

What is at issue here is not just the content of those images, but also how the particular form of their introduction and their subsequent circulation have informed our understanding of the narratives they have purported to represent and, more broadly, our understanding of human rights abuses that may take place in distant lands. How has their materiality—their existence as snapshot images—affected our relationship to them? What role did framing—whether in the form of captioning or in the provision of context at large—play in our understanding of what they sought to represent? What is the relationship between their revelation and subsequent action (or nonaction) in the public sphere—whether in the form of inspiring the expression of public opinion (where is the outrage?), making action on particular policies possible, or mobilizing publics? How do these images in this particular form relate to the traditional human rights paradigm of shaming? And if they do not fit the neat confines of that paradigm, in which revelation leads to outrage and outrage leads to action what exactly happened along the way?

PHOTOGRAPHY AND ATROCITY

Photography has captured images of suffering almost as soon as it was possible to do so. In the late nineteenth century, photographers took images of the Plains Indians forcibly displaced in a rapidly expanding United States. Susan Sontag reminds us that our conceptions of the Crimean War, as well as of the American Civil War, are largely informed by photographs, while the Spanish Civil War may have been the first war "covered"—visually that is—in the modern sense. At the turn of the last century in Iran, public hangings were not only photographed, but also printed on postcards for mass distribution. In short, most experiences of social suffering, whether plague, the ravages of AIDS, street violence, or famine, have been mediatized. Over the past decade, the ubiquity of digital technology has made our encounters with the suffering of distant others more and more common. Saddam Hussein was hanged before all of us thanks to video taken with a small digital camera phone. Likewise, Muammar Al-Gadhafi's protracted and bloody death was rendered a spectacle, thanks to phone cameras wielded by jeering rebel forces. How we capture suffering on film defines what we come to know of the suffering of others—if we are to know anything at all; often, it will determine if we decide to care, to intervene, or to look away.

Modern history poses the question: if atrocity is not photographed, does it exist at all? Again, Sontag notes how the complete absence of images documenting the greatest famine of the twentieth century, during China's Great Leap Forward, raises questions as to how this catastrophe may or may not have been ingrained in the historical consciousness. In the case of the Ethiopian famine of 1984, two years of reports from humanitarian organizations were ignored until a highly choreographed media campaign galvanized public opinion; the story became attached to visual images of suffering, and a movement was born.[1] Likewise, prisoner abuses at Abu Ghraib became a public scandal only after the release of a series of eerily iconic amateur photographs documenting them; reports of torture had been trickling out as early as two months before the release of the now famous hooded-man image and others. Here, as in many other cases, it was images that created the story. Thomas Keenan has pointed out that most contemporary relief operations since Biafra have been "born and bathed in the light of the television camera."[2] Says Sontag, "Photographs lay down routes of reference, and serve as totems of causes: sentiment is more likely to crystallize around a photograph than around a verbal slogan."[3]

Today, the mass media have appropriated social suffering to an extent that is perhaps without precedent. Stanley Cohen has written that the media have a near monopoly in creating the cultural imagery of suffering and atrocities.[4] The mainstream American media's depictions of Hurricane Katrina's aftermath exposed the power that photographs and other standard accoutrements of the media apparatus may have in framing the terms of an event. Images of African-Americans whose homes had been lost, presented with the caption "looters," served as stark contrast to comparable images of white inhabitants of New Orleans—who were instead, for the most part, declared "victims."

In "Mobilizing Shame," Keenan briefly outlines the philosophical provenance of what we have come to understand as the traditional human rights model, what he refers to as the "lock-step" belief that "knowledge generates action." In other words, if mass violations become known, the world will react. According to Keenan, one may consider what happens before the camera as "not simply representations and references," but rather "opportunities, events, and performances." In this way, the strategic use of images and words to "mobilize shame"—in other words to perform—has become the prevailing strategy of the contemporary human rights movement today. He continues: "The pervasiveness of the consensus cannot be overstated, nor can its special relationship to the mass- and especially the image-based media. The concept gathers together a powerful set of metaphors—the eyes of the world, the light of public scrutiny, the exposure of hypocrisy—as vehicles for the dream of action, power, and enforcement."[5] If one were to place one's belief in such a formulation, the images from the Mashhad hangings, from the student protests of 1999, as well as from the unrest in Iran would likely lead to outrage, outrage to retribution, and in the end, some form of justice—however fraught and difficult any notion of "justice" may be to define.

A STRATEGIC REVELATION

With its tentacular reach, the Internet can cater to distinct, finite constituencies and interests. In this way, the images of the two hanging boys were strategically deployed by and for a particular set of constituencies, and by extension, a particular set of interests. First revealed by the Iranian Student News Agency (ISNA), an official state entity, the images seem to have subsequently been picked up by a group called the National Council of Resistance of Iran (NCRI) and its associated website, Iran Focus. Iran Focus, as it happens, is a site run by the Mujahedeen Khalq Association (MKO), a socialist-inflected Islamist group perhaps best known for its dramatic tendency toward self-immolation. It is important to note that the MKO is the most significant Iranian opposition group outside of the country; their raison d'être is to destabilize the Iranian regime in any way they possibly can. In that sense, they share many of the same interests as the greatest hawks in the U.S. administration: to depict Iran as a stark, draconian, unstable land that is unfriendly to human rights. Plainly, an image of two young men being brutally executed represented a significant opportunity to do just that. Sontag writes about the use value of photographs, "the photographer's intentions do not determine the meaning of the photograph, blown by the whims and loyalties of the diverse communities that have use for it." She continues: "But the photographic image, even to the extent that it is a trace, cannot simply be a transparency of something that happened. It is always the image that someone chose; to photograph is to frame and to frame is to exclude."[6]

Shortly after the Iran Focus story, a British gay rights organization somewhat tellingly called Outrage! drafted a press release with the headline "Iran Executes Gay Teenagers." The press release was based on a translation from the original ISNA report. It dismissed the allegation of rape, arguing that it was either a "trumped up charge to undermine public sympathy for the youths" or that the thirteen-year-old boy was a "willing participant but that Iranian law (like UK law) deems that no person of that age is capable of sexual consent and that therefore any sexual contact is automatically deemed in law to be a sex assault." Peter Tatchell, Outrage!'s outspoken campaigner, was quoted as saying "this is just the latest barbarity by the Islamo-fascists in Iran . . . the entire country is a gigantic prison, with Islamic rule sustained by detention without trial, torture and state-sanctioned murder."[7]

From there, the images would take on a life of their own. The popular conservative American blogger Andrew Sullivan posted an entry on his site titled "Islamists versus Gays" that also argued that the two teenage boys were hanged by the "Islamo-fascist regime in Iran" for "being gay." Doug Ireland, a longtime activist, carried on, making posts daily on his website, Direland. Other gay websites, such as 365gay.com, Planetout.com, and Pageoneq.com also ran stories about the boys. *Gay City News* and the *Washington Blade* did, too, and all focused on the story of the execution of two gay teenagers. The *LA Weekly* and *In These Times* ran similar stories. The two young men, in the meantime, had been taken up as gay emblems—intensely photogenic as they were. Most posts related to the photographs ignored the issue of rape entirely. Scott Long, the former director of Human Rights Watch's Lesbian, Gay, Bisexual and Transgender Rights Project, says the "implication was that people should only care about these people and these photographs if the two boys were gay lovers. The message was here they are: they are young, beautiful, gay, like us. But on the question of death, the photographs are mute."[8]

It was not too long before the human rights community at large got involved. The Human Rights Campaign (HRC), a U.S.-based gay, lesbian, bisexual, and transgender rights organization, cited Ireland's post and immediately called upon then-Secretary of State Condoleezza Rice, as a representative of "the world's greatest democracy," to condemn the hangings. The HRC letter, dated July 22, called on the State Department to issue an "immediate and strong condemnation" of the execution of "two Iranian teenagers" who were "hanged in a public square after being tortured for 14 months, simply for being caught having consensual sex." It also made no mention of the rape allegations.[9]

Soon after, the conservative right picked up the images. On July 26, a lobbying group called the Log Cabin Republicans weighed in with a statement that began in this way: "In the wake of news stories and photographs documenting the hanging of two gay Iranian teenagers, Log Cabin Republicans re-affirm their commitment to the global war on terror." The teenagers' fate seemed to fit seamlessly into a larger post–9/11 narrative about Islam and Islamic lands. Log Cabin president Patrick Guerriero said, "This barbarous slaughter clearly demonstrates the stakes in the global war on terror. Freedom must prevail over radical Islamic extremism." Their press release also ignored the allegations of rape.[10]

Though more established organizations such as Amnesty International, Human Rights Watch, and the International Gay and Lesbian Human Rights Commission (IGLHRC) were cautious in their treatment of the case, reluctant to frame it as a gay rights issue as opposed to a capital punishment question, damage may have already been done. Some activists in Iran wondered why so much attention was showered upon an isolated incident when rights abuses of this variety happen every day and very often on a larger scale. Since the incident, a wider crackdown on "loose moral conduct" has taken shape across Iran; while the Mashhad case that initiated the outcry in the first place may not have been about prosecuting homosexuality per se, it may have eventually managed to give the Iranian authorities the motivation to do so.[11] There is also little question that the incident and the attention born of it managed to lend itself to the popular perception that human rights are a mostly Western, and vaguely imperial preoccupation—and by extension, aggravated the project of human rights in Iran at large.

So how exactly did we get to this point? And how did the news of the rape get so muddled and finally lost? Writing in the *Nation*, Richard Kim traced a mistranslation that found its way into many of the blog posts. Kim argued that Outrage!—one of the primary architects of the campaign—had worked with a faulty translation, one that did not mention the charge of rape. Though a local Mashhad-based newspaper called *Quds* announced on the morning of the execution that the two had been hanged for the rape of a thirteen-year-old boy, the images combined with the compelling narrative had their effect, rendering the details of the rape charge irrelevant and finally invisible.

And the images would not go away. On the first anniversary of the hanging, Tatchell and others organized candlelight vigils for the young men around the world. Hearings were also planned in the British House of Commons on the Iranian human rights situation. And in the fall of 2007, when Iranian president Mahmoud Ahmadinejad famously passed through New York's Columbia University, the images of the young men were reproduced en masse on flyers—festooned on lampposts, bathroom stalls, and even the university gates. A not insignificant group of students came together around the university's central courtyard to protest the Iranian president's treatment of homosexuals on the day of his address. When the question of Iran's treatment of homosexuals came up during the speech, the president obliquely had this to say: "In Iran, we don't have homosexuals like in your country. We don't have that in our country. . . . We do not have this phenomenon. I do not know who's told you that we have it."[12] The ensuing outrage was considerable.

Following the Iranian president's visit, the *New York Times* reprinted the images of the two boys in a piece entitled "Despite Denials, Gays Insist They Exist, if Quietly, in Iran."[13] There was no mention of the contentious nature of the event depicted. Likewise, the *Wall Street Journal* ran a story entitled "The Queerest Denial."[14] Some months later, conservative Dutch politician Geert Wilders's 2008 film *Fitna*, a diatribe about Islam and terrorism, also featured the two young boys in its pondering what life would be like if Muslims one day ruled the Netherlands. Even Oprah Winfrey ran a segment on homosexuality in the Middle East and, not surprisingly, showed the photographs of the Mashhad two.

In the considerable sea of images from and about Iran, why did these particular images have such considerable staying power? Stripped of context, they were associated with and intersected with a number of agendas (conservative, gay, human rights). And in part because of the promiscuity of the web—with its ease of linking incongruous sites and ideas—they are not likely to leave us anytime soon. Human Rights Watch's Long notes, "the photographs seem to reappear anytime there is a surge in prowar sentiment about Iran. And the boys are dead, so different interests could get away with telling the story in any number of ways."[15]

BLOODY TIMES

In the late 1990s Tehran University was shaken by dramatic student protests, most immediately over the closure of a popular reformist newspaper called *Salaam*. A twenty-one-year-old named Ahmad Batebi was among the disgruntled students who assembled, and his image, taken by a photojournalist employed by Reuters, ended up becoming an icon of that unrest. It continues to live a long life on the Internet, in murals, on book covers, in pamphlets, and far beyond.

Let us step back a moment to look at the setting of this "crime"—for that is the essence of this photograph—of a young man holding up, quite literally, evidence of blood shed by a fellow student at the hands of Iranian authorities. Here, screams the young man, is proof of an egregious wrong, of rights trampled. Iran in the late 1990s was a place of contradictions. On the one hand, a chorus of young persons and women in particular had voted in a smiling, sweet-talking reformist president named Mohammad Khatami. Iran under Khatami experienced a mild opening up. The number of newspapers who dared to publish unsubtle critiques of the regime increased exponentially, social pressures loosened, and diplomacy blossomed under the banner of the president's celebrated "dialogue of civilizations."

But in spite of being president, Khatami was one man, a single member of a labyrinthine governmental structure characterized by multiple and dizzyingly opaque poles of power. In other words, all was not sunny and well in Iran. In the mid-1990s, for example, a series of murders of dissident intellectuals—mostly in their own homes—shook the city. Newspapers such as *Salaam* were routinely threatened and very often shut. Rights activists faced the stiffest of sanctions.

The closure of *Salaam*, one among many triggers, ignited student protests across the city of a scale unseen since the revolution of 1979. Batebi was among the unlucky students rounded up. By the time the *Economist* cover had been printed (fig. 2), he was already in prison. Tried privately by a Revolutionary Court, Batebi was convicted of "creating street unrest," "agitating people to create unrest," and "endangering national security." He and four others were sentenced to death.

Years later, in 2008, he told reporters from the *New York Times* that the first time he saw his face on the front cover of the news magazine was when a judge showed it to him. "You have signed your own death sentence,"[16] the judge reportedly told him.

While in prison, Batebi wrote of his condition: "I resisted and punched one of them in the face. At this point, they took me and ducked my head into a closed drain full of excrement. They held me under for so long, I was unable to hold my breath any longer, and excrement was inhaled through my nose and seeped into my mouth." He continued: "During the interrogations, they threatened several times to execute me and to torture and rape my family members as well as imprison them for long terms."[17]

Following an international outcry that brought together the primary protagonists of the international human rights movement, that initial sentence was reduced to fifteen years by Iran's supreme leader, Ayatollah Khamenei. Upon further appeal, it was reduced again to ten years. Batebi was spared, but each of the members of the initial group that had been arrested faced death sentences. It seems that the iconic image was both his doom and his salvation.

FIGURE 2 Image of the cover of the July 17, 1999 edition of *The Economist* (© The Economist Newspaper Limited, London 1999).

In and around March of 2005, Batebi was temporarily released from Evin in order to get married. He did not return, and on June 23, 2005 a newspaper interview reported that the former student was "currently on the run, avoiding the authorities in Iran." He was rearrested on July 27, 2006, and led back to prison. He continued to serve his ten-year sentence. In August of that year, he went on hunger strike.

At that time, Amnesty International reported that Batebi's physical and mental health were poor and deteriorating further: "He suffers from a number of medical problems as a result of being tortured and ill-treated during his previous period of detention, including stomach and kidney problems. He has lost some of his teeth, and has permanent hearing problems and poor vision."[18] In the ensuing years, he was rumored to have suffered two brain strokes, recurrent seizures, and on at least one occasion to have fallen into a coma.

In 2008, he left prison to seek medical attention, and with the help of an Iranian-American lawyer named Lily Mazehery, whose name he says he found on a Yahoo chat site and who had apparently helped other Iranians before him leave the country, he ran. Carrying only some cash drawn from an ATM, a camera, and a pocket-sized video camera, he was picked up in a busy downtown Tehran square by members of the underground Kurdish Democratic Party of Iran, who set him on a tortuous path, over much of which he was blindfolded, to Kurdish-controlled Iraq. Once he arrived in Erbil, he presented his case at the United Nations High Commissioner for Refugees, and from there it was a short route to the United States. Interviews with the likes of the *New York Times*, Voice of America and the *Guardian* followed.

THE USES OF AHMAD BATEBI

From the time of the initial dissemination of Batebi's image to the present, that photograph and the narratives tied to it have been evoked many times. In December of 1999, the website of the Green Party of Iran, a Quebec-based movement for reform in Iran, posted a press release from the Student Movement Coordination Committee for Democracy in Iran with these words: "The Hero of *The Economist* Magazine Sentenced to Death."[19]

In 2005, Batebi's case was raised before the Senate Foreign Relations Committee by Abbas William Samii, then a correspondent for Radio Free Europe / Radio Liberty (like the Voice of America, funded by the U.S. Congress), in a speech entitled "The Quest for Iran's Democratic Movement." He was cited as one of the unlucky student activists who had not managed to get out.[20]

In August of 2006, the *Guardian*'s Tehran correspondent, Robert Tait, invoked Batebi in an essay on the discouraging state of human rights within Iran, seven years after the printing of the *Economist* cover. The newspaper reprinted the original image, and Tait called Batebi "the symbol of a brave new dawn of student protest in Iran." He went on: "What Batebi represents today is not the hope of seven years ago, but growing despair. With international attention focused almost exclusively on Iran's nuclear activities, the country's small and beleaguered human rights community fears its cause is becoming more forlorn than ever. Under the cloak of national security, a fierce crackdown is underway, and Batebi's case is just the tip of the iceberg."[21] Also in 2006, the Batebi image was embedded in an Amnesty International press release calling for his release on the occasion of his hunger strike, as reprinted in the Iranian website Payvand.com.[22]

As it did with the image of the hanging boys, the American right seized upon the image of Ahmad Batebi. Writing in the journal of Middle East Forum, a conservative American think tank founded by Daniel Pipes, Suzanne Gershowitz, a research assistant at the equally conservative American Enterprise Institute, used the occasion of a short piece about Batebi to call for "democratic change." The subtext here seemed to be that the U.S. government may need a heavy hand in bringing about that change: "For this generation, Batebi—imprisoned for having his picture taken while calling for basic rights—is a cause célèbre. Unclear, though, is whether Washington will take up his plight."[23]

In 2006, an initiative known as the Iran Freedom Concert popped up on the Harvard University campus. It seemed to summon up the spirit of the anti-apartheid movement, especially with its use of entertainment to aestheticize and bring attention to a faraway human rights cause. On its promotional poster was an image of Batebi. Also included were images of a white dove, an Iranian woman with her eyes covered up by what appear to be bandages, along with assorted oppressed-looking others.

Closer inspection revealed that the concert initiative's primary backer was the New Haven–based Iran Human Rights Documentation Center, a recipient of the State Department's controversial "democracy fund."[24] An April 7, 2008 event announced that Batebi's lawyer, Lily Mazehery, would be one of the concert's featured speakers. A list of "causes" that the concert would aim to bring attention to included media censorship, gender discrimination, blocking the Internet, arresting bloggers, denying labor rights, banning members of the Baha'i sect, executing gays, and, of course, banning concerts.

That same year, a piece in the conservative magazine the *National Review* mentioned Batebi, claiming to have interviewed him via a Los Angeles contact, through a translator. The article quotes him: "What I want is international pressure for all the political prisoners who have been so horribly treated. I want all these human-rights activists, these Amnesty Internationals, to put their resources together to give more attention to the political prisoners in Iran." He continues: "Whenever the Iranian people or the government hears that the U.S. doesn't have a plan or doesn't have a policy regarding regime change in Iran, this is like fresh blood in the veins of these mullahs."[25] The message here seems to be that the United States should be "firm" about one thing only: the need for regime change. That same year, Batebi's case was raised on an international workers' solidarity website.[26] Gary Metz of the popular *Regime Change Iran* blog simply ran the Batebi image on his home page.[27]

The photograph has also had uses within Iran. Iranian human rights lawyer Shirin Ebadi, who won the Nobel Peace Prize in 2003, has publicly announced that the T-shirt held up in the image is that of Ezzat Ebrahim-Nejad, a student who was shot by security forces. Ebadi represents Ebrahim-Nejad's family. Whether the bloodied T-shirt did belong to the dead student or not is beyond the point. Connecting the dead student's fate to the iconic image of Batebi was convenient. There seemed to be no limits to the uses of Ahmad Batebi.

RELEASE

The *Economist*, which in circuitous fashion was "responsible" for putting Batebi into this position in the first place, published the following on the occasion of his release:

> Nine years ago, Ahmad Batebi appeared on the cover of *The Economist*. He was a 21-year-old student, one of thousands who protested against Iran's government that summer. He was photographed holding aloft a T-shirt bespattered with the blood of a fellow protester. Soon afterwards, he was arrested and shown our issue of July 17th 1999. "With this", he was told, "you have signed your death warrant." . . .
>
> He is cagey about how exactly he escaped. But he says he used a cellphone camera to record virtually every step of his journey, and will soon go public with the pictures and his commentary. Meanwhile, he seems to be enjoying America. He praises the way "people have the opportunity to become who they want to be." Shortly after he arrived, he posted a picture of himself in front of the Capitol on his Farsi-language blog, with the caption: "Your hands will never touch me again".
>
> Thank God![28]

In his first televised interview on Voice of America Persian TV, he was introduced by the interviewer in a manner that referenced his famous face—or *chehre* in Farsi. After the introduction, the screen cut to grim images of Evin prison, followed by the camera panning over the ominous words "House of Detention." In the meantime, the *London Sunday Times*, in a long piece on Batebi, called him "Iran's 'Johnny Depp.'"[29]

But perhaps most poignantly, Batebi—an individual reduced to an iconic image—has shown that he himself understands the power of images. After all, he did carry two cameras with him during his harrowing escape from his homeland. Excerpts of the trip were posted on the *New York Times* website as video.[30] He also hosted two blogs, one in Farsi,[31] and the other an English-language blog hosted by Yahoo!, that has since been taken down. Both prominently have featured images of him, some more Photoshopped than others.

The Yahoo! blog introduced Batebi as a university student at "Sociology University" and had dozens of snapshots of the former prisoner in Washington, D.C., standing before various monuments and often posing with his own camera. We see Batebi lustily relishing the fruits of freedom: skiing, strumming presumably lyrical notes on a guitar, and so on. There are also images of birds on a wire and, inexplicably, scissors.

Around the same time, another Iranophile blog announced that Batebi had come to America. In the comments section, someone wrote: "Ahmad Batebi has a page on Facebook. If you aren't already on Facebook, please join so you can wish him a welcome to the U.S.!"[32]

THE IMAGE

We will never know how important the *Economist* cover and its associated visibility was in defining Batebi's case with the Iranian authorities. We do know that the authorities went so far as to try to get him to deny the veracity of the image, to offer that the red was in fact paint or animal blood. To erase the truth of the blood would be to alter the image—in other words, to attach new meaning to it. In this sense, Batebi's biggest crime was not being a student activist. Rather, it was the crime of showing, of revelation.

At the same time, his credentials as a student activist, which many have lingered over and questioned, are beside the point. It is true that at the time of his arrest, he was a student without a significant history of agitating against university authorities or the state at large. In a 2003 interview with the *New York Times*, he recognized the responsibility that has been thrust upon him: "Whether I want it or not, I am in prison as a representative of the student movement, and I will have to carry this burden as honorably as I can," he said. "There is not a second that I don't wish I was a free man."[33]

Since coming to the United States, Batebi has been writing articles in the Iranian press—including one for *Rooz Online* about the plight of the Baha'i community in Iran. Once an object of the human rights machinery, he is now a protagonist within its workings.

When interviewed by the *New York Times* upon his release, he had this to say about his arrival at Dulles: "When I entered the airport [in the United States], I saw that everybody had a different clothing on, in Iran, people are forced to wear what the government tells them."[34] Even after his harrowing journey, the image—here one that evokes the freedom to wear what one wants—is of utmost import.

Aesthetically effective, these images were seen by millions. They were re-created on websites, posters, and beyond as symbols of Iranian abuses. Let us return for a moment to Keenan, who offers that the "dark side of revelation is overexposure." He poses this question: "In the age of the generalized photo opportunity—whether the suicide bomber's videotape, made-for-television ethnic cleansing, or embedded reporters and videophones—what role can publicity, the exposé, and shame [still] play?" He points to two moments in the last decade—the debacles of Somalia and Kosovo, respectively—in trying to understand some of our collective assumptions surrounding media and the traditional human rights model. The collapse of Somalia, which seems to have entered the annals of history as an uncontested debacle, underlined the importance of cameras in framing the intervention. First, the images of starving children mobilized an international outcry, then the images of U.S. soldiers being dragged through a Mogadishu street inspired the eventual pullout that would be memorialized in the film (and book) *Black Hawk Down*.[35]

Still, in this case, the fact that the images in question tended to be circulated in digital format, that they were not originals, that they had been cropped, and, in a sense, affected by the peculiar medium of the Internet must all be taken into account. Walter Benjamin, in "The Work of Art in the Age of its Technological Reducibility," ponders the loss of what he terms "the aura" of the work of art when it is reproduced.[36]

Here, the digital image, cropped, pasted, repasted, and rearticulated through the medium of the Internet, is rendered perhaps the most auraless of images. But what of its photogenic nature, what of its appropriation and associated captioning? Could the Internet in fact leave us with cause to rethink Benjamin's conception of "aura?" Could the Internet even accentuate this mysterious thing called "aura?" In the case of the two hanging boys, it was too late. But could the fact that the Batebi image refused to go away have played a part in galvanizing support for him and finally put pressure on the Iranian authorities to spare him from an early death?

NEDA: THE ANGEL OF IRAN

Like Ahmad Batebi, Neda Agha-Soltan was unknown to the world before her encounter with a camera. We know this about her: a recent graduate of the Philosophy Department at Tehran's Islamic Azad University, she worked at her parent's travel agency and took singing and violin lessons in her spare time. She hoped to become a professional musician, she loved to travel, and had saved up money to travel to Thailand, Turkey, and Dubai. It was in Turkey that, two months earlier, she had met a thirty-seven-year-old photojournalist named Caspian Makan. They had been engaged at the time of her death.

We know this, too: on June 20, 2009, just after 6:00 p.m., Neda Agha-Soltan was driving her Peugeot 206 along downtown Tehran's Kargar Avenue as the day's demonstrations were in progress. With her was her music teacher and two unidentified others. At one point, so the reports go, she got out of the car to view the road ahead and ostensibly to get some air (the Peugeot's air conditioner was not working). It was shortly after that she took a bullet in the chest—allegedly from a Basiji militant on a nearby roof. She fell to the pavement. There were calls of "She has been shot! Someone come and take her!" One man hovering over her, probably the music teacher, said, "Don't be afraid." Another said, "Don't die!" over and over again. One account says that her last words were simply "I'm burning! I'm burning!" A doctor who was on the scene of the killing, Dr. Arash Hejazi, later told news reporters that she died within two minutes of taking the bullet. Other accounts offered that she died en route to Tehran's Shariati Hospital.

As Agha-Soltan fell to the ground, at least two cell phone cameras hovered above and around her, capturing her last minutes on earth (fig. 3). One shows her collapsing to the ground, while another moves toward her, first focusing on the two and then three men who rush to her aid, then zooming in and focusing on her face as she bleeds to death. A few seconds into the cell-phone video, her eyes roll up, almost as if they are addressing the cameraman, and then blood starts to pass out from various orifices in eerily straight lines. By now, her regard at the cameraman is terrifyingly vacant, and a man in a white shirt implores, "Don't die." His voice is desperate.

Within hours, the video made the rounds of the television networks and the blogosphere. A version of the video was the single most viewed news video of the week on YouTube. One CNN segment entitled "Neda: Face of a Movement," first showed a different video, capturing a crowd of people, and spotlighting one figure—hardly perceptible—offering that it was Agha-Soltan. The rest of the segment featured close-ups of stills taken from the original video, creating a silent montage for a full forty seconds, finally ending the program with a screen shot of the Twitter home page revealing the legions of mentions of "#neda."

Neda Agha-Soltan's life and image immediately took on a dramatic life of its own. She was dubbed "The Angel of Iran." Her face was reproduced en masse on T-shirts, websites, and banners. A Facebook group called "We Are Neda" was erected, and the domain http://weareallneda.com was occupied, too, filled with all manner of eclectica in her memory. The Iranian-born visual artist Shirin Neshat compared her to the principal character in her new film, *Women without Men*, while a variation of the successful Iranian graphic novel *Persepolis*, renamed *Persepolis 2.0*, recreated her death. There was an HBO documentary made and, of course, a multitude of vernacular YouTube remixes laid over by DIY graphics and music. Neda Agha-Soltan's death inspired demonstrations in the United States, Egypt, Poland, and many other places.

Speaking at a press conference on June 23, 2009, U.S. president Barack Obama said: "We've seen courageous women stand up to brutality and threats, and we have experienced the searing image of a woman bleeding to death on the streets."[37] Former presidential candidate and Senator John McCain also had this to say: "She had already become a kind of Joan of Arc." He continued: "Today, I and all America pays tribute to a brave young woman who was trying to exercise her fundamental human rights and was killed in the streets of Tehran."[38]

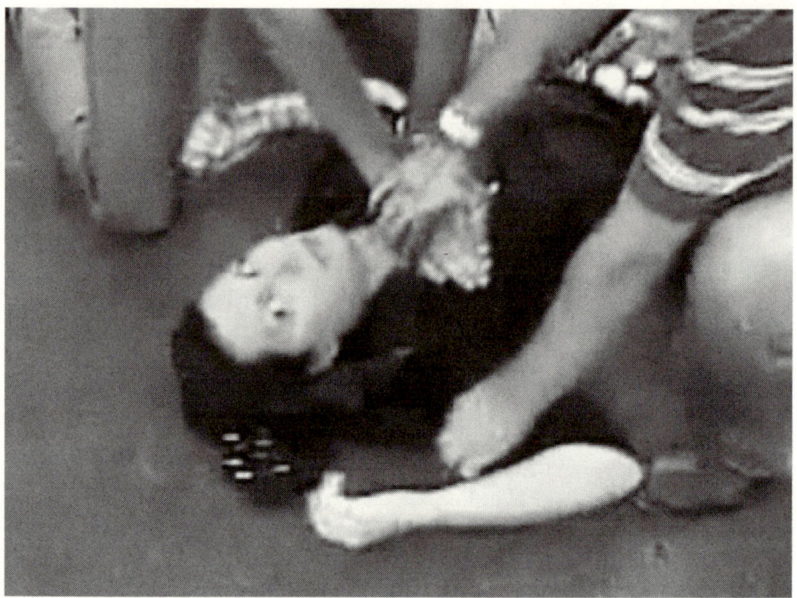

FIGURE 3 Still from uploaded video of Neda Agha-Soltan's last minutes on earth.

Plainly, it would not be easy for the Iranian regime to deny her existence or her passing. They concocted countless explanations for her death—each more creative than the last. The state-run *Jomhouri Islami* newspaper blamed her shooting on snipers from the Mujahedeen Khalq. Another regime-oriented paper, *Javan*, blamed an even more unlikely source in the form of the expelled BBC correspondent Jon Leyne. Days later, in an interview with CNN's Wolf Blitzer, the Iranian ambassador to Mexico, Mohammad Hassan Ghadiri, pointed his finger at the CIA. And then there was a hard-line cleric speaking at Tehran's Friday prayers who claimed that she was killed by demonstrators, not by security forces. President Mahmoud Ahmadinejad called her death "suspicious," eventually calling for an investigation of the media accounts of her passing: "The massive propaganda of the foreign media, as well as other evidence, proves the interference of the enemies of the Iranian nation who want to take political advantage and darken the pure face of the Islamic republic," the president said in a letter to Seyyed Mahmoud Hashemi Shahroudi, head of the judicial system, according to various state news agencies.[39]

The letter came a day after Iran's state-run English-language news channel, Press TV, announced that Agha-Soltan did not die in the way that the opposition—

and by this point, the world—claimed. Two witnesses told Press TV there were no security forces in the area when she was killed, while another "expert" told the station that the bullet that killed her was not the kind used by Iranian security forces. And that was that.

What had come to be known as the "opposition" or the "Green Movement," in the meantime, adopted Agha-Soltan as a symbol of their struggle. Both Moussavi and fellow failed presidential candidate Mehdi Karroubi called for public memorials for her death. Both were also officially banned from visiting her grave site in Tehran's sprawling Behesht Zahra Cemetery, where, in spite of a massive security presence, some three thousand protesters gathered to honor her. On the eve of the fortieth day after her death, Karroubi visited the slain girl's family. Moussavi, in the meantime, called for a memorial service in Tehran's Moussala Mosque, a gigantic venue still under construction that will eventually come to house the city's official Friday prayer gatherings.

Iranians agitating against the regime were perhaps most eager to make Neda Agha-Soltan theirs. The weekly antiregime protests at the Capital Building on Los Angeles's Wilshire Boulevard featured a sea of Neda posters and T-shirts, banners, and more. Iranians in Silicon Valley staged a hunger strike in her memory. In Paris, Maryam Rajavi, the enigmatic leader of the exiled Mujahedeen Khalq Association, stood before a poster of the fallen angel in a speech in which, as usual, she eviscerated the regime. And even moderate Islamic groups that advocate reform from within the faith, such as Muslims against Sharia, were swift in invoking her killing as evidence of the Iranian regime having strayed from the true essence of Islam.

Predictably, the American right appropriated news of the brutal death as evidence of the Iranian regime's brutality. The conservative Fox News Channel, for example, aired dozens of features devoted to Agha-Soltan. Her fiancé, the photojournalist Caspian Makan, became a fixture on news shows, giving interviews to the BBC, Al Jazeera, and well beyond. By March, he had gone so far as to visit Israeli prime minister Shimon Peres in Tel Aviv. Peres, for his part, spoke of the Israelis' "historic connection to the Iranian people" and alluded to the struggle of the Iranian people to restore their ancient honor. "Neda was a brave soldier in that struggle," he remarked.[40]

Writing in the *Guardian*, the British writer Martin Amis offered that Agha-Soltan personified "the modern." It was a short route from there to his (rather pat) thesis: "the Islamic Republic is also doomed by modernity (in the form of instant communications) and by demographic destiny. Persia, one of the oldest nations on earth, is getting younger and younger."[41]

And of course, women's groups had a field day. In the aftermath of her death, countless articles were written about how women were at the forefront of the so-called Green Revolution. Most of these articles mentioned Agha-Soltan along with a usual suspect in the form of Nobel Prize–winning human rights advocate Shirin Ebadi. The British newspaper the *Telegraph* asked in a headline "What Will Become of Iran's "'Stiletto Revolution' Now?"[42] Very few of these articles acknowledged or even seemed to know about some of Iran's most impressive and substantive women's rights movements, like the "One Million Signatures Campaign," a grassroots project that has been ongoing in relative media obscurity since its inception some years ago.

And then there were some Iranians—probably trying to raise their own visibility—who eagerly associated themselves with the "fallen angel." One Iranian blogger, for example, who goes by the name "Khoshnya," announced that he had "escaped" to Pakistan, but not before taking a photo of Agha-Soltan as she fell.[43] Having captured her death would surely be his claim to fame.

Recognizing the power of images—or perhaps experiencing a peculiar sort of déjà vu—the Iranian authorities fought back. Four days after the election, Iran banned foreign media journalists from filming or taking photos of protests. On July 17, Reuters reported the systematic arrests of photographers in the streets. The Paris-based watchdog Reporters Without Borders said in a statement: "The Tehran regime is scared of images. The authorities have launched a real hunt on visual reporters so that no professional photo or video of sensitive subjects will leave the country."[44]

While preventing the creation of another Neda Agha-Soltan was one goal of the regime, blocking the technology that brought her image to the world—more precisely, Twitter and the Internet—was equally critical to their strategy. Iranian officials hustled to shut down the barrage of spontaneous tweeting, imposed Internet filters, and lowered bandwidths to obstruct the flow, while the U.S. State Department worked with Twitter to expand access to its website in Iran. It seemed that a sort of proxy war was taking shape between the two nations in the technological domain.

Much has been made of the Twitter Revolution in Iran. A July 2009 editorial in the *Christian Science Monitor* went so far as to call for a Nobel Prize to go to the technology. The author wrote: "Her name was Neda Agha-Soltan, and without Twitter we might never have known that she lived in Iran, that she dreamed of a free Iran, and that she died in a divided Iran for her dreams. Neda became the voice of a movement; Twitter became the megaphone."[45] A July 20 editorial in the *Wall Street Journal*, equally rhapsodizing about citizen activism, invoked Neda, announcing in its headline "Let's Help Iranians Beat the Censors." The article's author even suggested smuggling satellite phones into the country to help activists.[46] And then, in December of 2010, the prestigious George Polk Award was given to the anonymous person who uploaded the footage of Neda's death onto the Internet.[47]

There is little question that the image of Neda Agha-Soltan, like that of the hanging boys or that of Ahmad Batebi, was an aesthetically effective one. Immensely photogenic as she was—even as she gruesomely bled to death for all the world to see—she was a symbol of life lost too soon, of the excesses and hypocrisy of a regime that had lost any legitimacy it may have once enjoyed. It was as if the video announced "Here they go again, killing their own."

Still, some pointed out that the image received disproportionate attention, given its seductive nature—at the expense of other, worthwhile causes. Writing in *The Huffington Post*, for example, Max Blumenthal pointed out that while American cable networks replayed the video of Agha-Soltan 's death over and over and over again, they would never dare to exhibit the strife in the West Bank in the same manner:

> These videos are no less outrageous than the video of Neda's death. However, to my knowledge, no outlet from the mainstream American media has ever broadcast them. And as far as I know, no cable news program, including liberal-leaning shows like Olbermann and Maddow, have never even mentioned the non-violent protests in Bi'lin and Ni'ilin, or Israel's brutal response. The videos remain unseen by American eyes. The struggles of Bi'lin and Ni'lin do not even play in Peoria.[48]

Just weeks after Agha-Soltan's blood was spilled, another young life was lost that may provide a valuable counterpoint to our story. On July 1, a thirty-two-year-old Egyptian-born pharmacist living in Germany named Marwa El Sherbini was stabbed to death eighteen times with a seven-inch blade inside a courtroom in the city of Dresden, Germany—right in front of her three-year-old son. El Sherbini, who was three months pregnant with her second child, had just won a verdict against a German man who had verbally assaulted her in a children's playground, calling her an Islamist, a terrorist, and a slut. Her husband, an Egyptian scientist, leaped to her rescue and was also stabbed some sixteen times. In the midst of the scuffle, he was shot by a policeman who mistook him for the attacker, but survived. Marwa died on the scene.[49] Still, her death was not reported by any Western news media until protests erupted in her native Egypt. Though she was as photogenic as Agha-Soltan, there was no iconic image, no video disseminated en masse associated with the event. El Sherbini was modest, studious, and veiled. (Note that many images of Agha-Soltan that circulated in the days after her death show her with makeup and without the requisite veil—evidence that she loved freedom, and by extension, was a victim of a repressive regime.) In an interesting turn of events, the Iranian president, of all people, Mahmoud Ahmadinejad, attacked the German government in the aftermath of El Sherbini's death, calling for international condemnation. Although the British press was relatively vociferous in bringing attention to Marwa El Sherbini's death, and some took to referring to her as "the head-scarf martyr," her death created little of the echo that Agha-Soltan's did.

But if Marwa El Sherbini's case provides evidence as to Neda's tremendous success as an image, two other deaths cum media events during the summer of the Iranian elections, those of Farrah Fawcett on June 25 and then Michael Jackson's on the very same day, reveal that image's limitations. During the week of June 22 to 26, discussions of Michael Jackson and of Iran in general combined to make up almost half (47 percent) of the links on blogs and social media as measured in the New Media Index by the Pew Research Center's Project for Excellence in Journalism. Jackson's death—inspiring five thousand tweets per minute at peak—quickly surpassed the Iranian elections, swine flu, or President Obama's ongoing health-care debacle on Twitter.[50] Like other iconic events that have played out in the city of Los Angeles, from the Rodney King riots in 1992 to the bizarre freeway pursuit and eventual trial of football hero O. J. Simpson, Jackson's death and its mourning were mediated by television—but also, and here was evidence of the difference that the new media made in 2009—on Twitter. A *New York Times* blog cited one tweeter by the name of toomarvelous: "I don't recall where I was when Buddy Holly died. But I'll recall where I was when Michael Jackson died. I was on Twitter."[51] Biz Stone, one of the founders of Twitter, said of Jackson's passing and its immediate legacy: "We saw more than double the normal tweets per second the moment the news broke—the biggest increase since the U.S. presidential election."[52]

END

When the Internet was first launched, there was much talk of the "democratic possibilities" it would afford citizens. The same language was summoned up when speaking of digital snapshots—particularly because growing numbers have cameras attached to their phones or computers. When blogging became de rigeur, the romance surrounding the technology was further amplified. Suddenly, ordinary citizens were self-styled journalists. Images of police abuse taken by ordinary citizens with their camera phones and uploaded onto blogs during the 2004 Republican National Convention led to some accused of vandalism or disturbing the public peace being exonerated. In Egypt, in 2007, police officers guilty of torturing citizens were prosecuted for the first time in history after images of abuse ended up on the Internet, posted by a number of intrepid bloggers. Thanks to the dramatic impact of small and tactical media on the human rights field, everyone is suddenly a witness, a would-be revolutionary, a polemicist, and perhaps most fundamentally, an editor.

Similar claims for the revolutionary democratic possibilities of the technology were once made about the printing press, as documented by Michael Warner in his book *The Letters of the Republic*. Warner reminds us that the likes of John Adams and Benjamin Franklin waxed eloquent about the democratic possibilities that the printing press had created for translating Enlightenment principles into practice. Revolutionaries such as Adams believed that a "history of reflection takes the form of a history of letters" and "a history of letters can be a history of emancipation," as Warner puts it. It was therefore the printing press that gave birth to this republic, he argues: letters became "a technology of publicity whose meaning in the last analysis" was "civic and emancipatory." He continues, "it will be recalled that the struggles leading to the colonial revolution were largely undertaken by writers."[53]

But in the same book, Warner goes on to challenge the popular assumptions of technological determinism, which tend to posit technology as a singular driving force that enables change. He chronicles the birth of notions such as "the people," "the individual," "reason," and "democracy," and shows how they are inextricably wrapped up in certain interests. All technologies, argues Warner, serve specific interests, whether repressive or emancipatory in nature. In the same way, the Internet can be hijacked to serve interests that are both emancipatory (mounting a critique of repressive regimes) or not (as, for example, a means of surveillance or a means to identify dissidents or reinforce hegemonic stereotypes linked to class or skin color).

Indeed, it is perhaps especially the Internet's considerable ceding of control over framing and context or over the question of "origin" to particular interests that may have trumped its democratic promise. And so we return to the three sets of images we began with. In Tehran, was Batebi a leading student activist? A martyr to the democratic cause? In Mashhad, did a violent rape take place? Were the two young men just lovers? Was Neda Agha-Soltan driving toward the demonstrations that day or driving away? The truth is, it may not matter. Or rather, at some point, the truth ceases to matter. The Internet, after all, is ruled by the logic of the hyperlink. With every click of the mouse, one gets further from the realm of representation, and deeper into what Hito Steyerl has referred to as a culture of "spam" or the "negative image."[54] Robbed of their status as individuals with distinct lives, stories, and associations, these images and their inhabitants assume meanings and follow trajectories that are not determined by anything to which the images might be said to refer. Writes Sontag about images of suffering in particular: "Harrowing photographs do not inevitably lose their power to shock. But they are not much help if the task is to understand."[55] In the case of the hanging boys, for example, photos of execution by hanging have become—thanks to Google—synonymous with homosexuality in Iran. The image of handsome Ahmad

Batebi is synonymous with an exalted vision of student activism, and that of Neda Agha-Soltan with a vaguely defined Green Revolution and calls for regime change in Iran. Set free from any control over the provision of context and set loose on the Internet, digital images are likely to confuse—even manipulate—us even more.

But if we can agree as to the iconic, shocking nature of the photographs in question, were they "effective" in bringing about change? How does one measure efficacy, anyway? In "Publicity and Indifference (Sarajevo on Television)," Keenan traces a case that may be enlightening for the purposes of the case studies at hand. He opens with what he refers to as the most frequently cited lesson on Bosnia's troubles in the 1990s: "that a country was destroyed and a genocide happened, in the heart of Europe, on television." He continues, "If the lesson of Somalia was that cameras made things happen and sometimes too quickly, Bosnia seems to tell the opposite story: a brutal combination of overexposure and indifference. Somalia was hyperactivity; Bosnia inactivity, just watching."[56]

So what happened? How did the Enlightenment axiom, that revelation leads to public outrage, and public outrage leads to action, fail? Keenan asks, "what if the belief in this public was part of the failure?" He admonishes us as to the dangers of putting too much faith in the power of images to raise consciousness. "If we continue to think that images by virtue of their cognitive contents or their proximity to reality have the power to compel action, we miss the opening of new fields of action that they allow."[57] He continues, pondering the "conceit or fantasy of this kind of public sphere"—here specifically thinking about the Bosnian case that inspired a humanitarian response, but not the needed political response. He writes, "no image speaks for itself, let alone speaks directly to our capacity for reason. Images always demand interpretation, even or especially emotional images. There is nothing immediate about them." He ends with these somewhat depressing words: "Images, information, and knowledge will never guarantee any outcome, nor will they force or drive any action. They are, in that sense, like weapons or words: a condition, but not a sufficient one."[58]

In the case of the Mashhad hangings, the case of Batebi, as well as that of Neda Agha-Soltan, the content of the images managed to fit seamlessly into existing narratives about Iran. They were convenient and, in their own ways, extremely effective in confirming certain stock ideas and narratives about Iran as a place. They were furthermore effective in raising awareness about the plight of the abused: in this case, persons understood to be homosexuals or democracy activists or students who simply wanted a better life. Whether the gratuitous publicity born of the images was in fact detrimental to the cause of human rights at large in Iran is a subject for another investigation. But there is little question that as rallying points for various and multiple causes, these images were very successful.

In the end, this is a story about three crimes. It is also a story about the promiscuity of the Internet, the usefulness of images, and the ways in which they inform, inflect, and hijack how we understand suffering in faraway places. These particular images became totems by virtue of their iconicity and performative power, swiftly eclipsing and even erasing the details surrounding their "capture" in the first place.

NOTES

1. Stanley Cohen, *States of Denial* (London: Polity Press, 2000), p. 175; Jonathan Benthall, *Disasters, Relief and the Media* (London: I. B. Tauris, 1993), p. 8.
2. Thomas Keenan, "Mobilizing Shame," *The South Atlantic Quarterly* 103.2/3, (Spring–Summer 2004), pp. 435–49.
3. Susan Sontag, *Regarding the Pain of Others* (New York: Farrar, Straus & Giroux, 2003), p. 85.
4. Cohen, *States of Denial*, p. 168.
5. Keenan, "Mobilizing Shame," p. 438.
6. Sontag, *Regarding the Pain of Others*, p. 39.
7. Peter Tatchell, "Gay Teens Executed in Iran—Ayatollahs Have Murdered 100,000 People," Peter Tatchell, July 27, 2005, http://www.petertatchell.net/international/iran/iranexecution.htm.
8. Interview with Scott Long at Human Rights Watch headquarters, December 3, 2007.
9. Press release, "Secretary Rice Urged to Condemn Execution of Gay Iranian Teens," *Human Rights Campaign*, July 22, 2005, http://www.hrcatlanta.hrc.org/1945.htm.
10. Quoted in Richard Kim, "Witnesses to an Execution," *The Nation*, August 15, 2005, http://www.thenation.com/article/witnesses-execution?page=0,1.
11. Human Rights Watch, "Iran: End Arrests on Immorality Charges," May 17, 2007, http://www.hrw.org/en/news/2007/05/16/iran-end-arrests-immorality-charges.
12. See http://www.youtube.com/watch?v=zAel96pxGeI.
13. Nazila Fathi, "Despite Denials, Gays Insist They Exist, if Quietly, in Iran," *New York Times*, September 30, 2007, http://www.nytimes.com/2007/09/30/world/middleeast/30gays.html.
14. Bret Stephens, "The Queerest Denial," *Wall Street Journal*, October 2, 2007, http://online.wsj.com/article/SB119129023259045999.html.
15. Interview with Scott Long at Human Rights Watch, December, 2, 2007.
16. Scott Shane and Michael R. Gordon, "Dissident's Tale of Epic Escape From Iran's Vise," *New York Times*, July 13, 2008, http://www.nytimes.com/2008/07/13/world/middleeast/13dissident.html.
17. Student Movement Coordination Committee for Democracy in Iran (Information Service), "The Public letter of Ahmad Batebi (Hero of *The Economist*) to the Special investigation team of the Islamic Judiciary," June 29, 2000, http://www.daneshjoo.org/article/publish/printer_88.shtml.
18. Amnesty International, "Document—Iran: Further Information on Fear for Safety/Medical

Concern/ Incommunicado Detention: Ahmad Batebi (M)," September 20, 2006, http://www.amnesty.org/en/library/asset/MDE13/103/2006/en/3d077c80-d3f2-11dd-8743-d305be-a2b2c7/mde131032006en.html.

19. Student Movement Coordination Committee for Democracy in Iran, "The Hero of *The Economist* Magazine Sentenced to Death," December 12, 1999, http://www.iran-e-sabz.org/news/students7.html.

20. Abbas William Samii, "The Quest for Iran's Democratic Movement," May 19, 2005, http://www.iranwatch.org/government/US/Congress/Hearings/sfr-051905/us-congress-sfr-samii-051905.pdf.

21. Robert Tait, "A Cause without Effects," *Guardian*, August 23, 2006, http://www.guardian.co.uk/world/2006/aug/23/worlddispatch.iran.

22. Payvand Iran News, "IRAN: Former Student Activist Ahmad Batebi on Hunger Strike, August 10, 2006, http://www.netnative.com/news/06/aug/1111.html.

23. Suzanne Gershowitz, "Dissident Watch: Ahmad Batebi," *Middle East Quarterly* 12.1 (Winter 2005), pp. 87–88, http://www.meforum.org/article/697#_ftnref10.

24. In 2006, then secretary of state Condoleezza Rice requested $85 million from Congress for the promotion of democracy in Iran. What ensued was a crackdown in Iran of individuals and organizations suspected of being tied to the fund.

25. Rachel Zabarkes Friedman, "Youngbloods: Meet a Key to a Golden Iranian Future," *National Review*, August 3, 2005, http://old.nationalreview.com/comment/friedman200508030817.asp.

26. Workers' Liberty, "Keep Up the Pressure to Free Ahmed Batebi!" October 22, 2006, http://www.workersliberty.org/node/7119.

27. See http://www.regimechangeiran.com.

28. "Silent No More," *Economist*, July 10, 2008, http://www.economist.com/node/11707464.

29. Sarah Baxter, "Ahmad Batebi'—Iran's 'Johnny Depp'—Flees into Exile," *London Sunday Times*, July 20, 2008, http://www.timesonline.co.uk/tol/news/world/middle_east/article4364196.ece?Submitted=true.

30. The video is available accompanying Shane and Gordon, "Dissident's Tale of Epic Escape From Iran's Vise."

31. See http://www.ahmadbatebi.us.

32. See http://www.solomonia.com/blog/archive/2008/07/iranian-ahmed-batebi-makes-it-to-america/index.shtml.

33. Nazila Fathi, "After 2 Visits to the Hangman, More Horror for Iran Dissident," *New York Times*, December 14, 2003, http://www.nytimes.com/2003/12/14/world/after-2-visits-to-the-hangman-more-horror-for-iran-dissident.html.

34. Shane and Gordon, "Dissident's Tale of Epic Escape From Iran's Vise."

35. Keenan, "Mobilizing Shame," p. 438.

36. Walter Benjamin, "The Work of Art in the Age of its Technological Reproducibility: Third Version," trans. Harry Zohn and Edmund Jephcott, in *Selected Writings, Volume 4, 1938–1940*, ed. Howard Eiland and Michael W. Jennings (Cambridge, MA: Harvard University Press, 2003), p. 254.

37. "Barack Obama on Iran—the Full Text," *London Sunday Times*, June 23, 2009, http://www.timesonline.co.uk/tol/news/world/middle_east/article6564551.ece.

38. "McCain 'Neda Speech' Blasts Obama's Weakness on Iran (Full Text)," *Hawai'i Free Press*, June 23, 2009, http://www.hawaiifreepress.com/main/ArticlesMain/tabid/56/articleType/

ArticleView/articleId/837/McCain-quotNeda-Speechquot-blasts-Obamas-weakness-on-Iran-full-text.aspx.

39. Brian Kates, "Ahmadinejad Calls Iranian Martyr Neda's Death 'suspicious,'" *New York Daily News*, June 29, 2009, http://articles.nydailynews.com/2009-06-29/news/17926114_1_guardian-council-neda-agha-soltan-recount.
40. "Israel: Iranian Exile linked to Neda Meets with President Shimon Peres," *Los Angeles Times*, March 23, 2010, http://latimesblogs.latimes.com/babylonbeyond/2010/03/israel-nedas-fiance-meets-with-israeli-president-shimon-peres.html.
41. Martin Amis, "The End of Iran's Ayatollahs?" *Guardian*, July 17, 2009, http://www.guardian.co.uk/world/2009/jul/17/martin-amis-iran.
42. Con Coughlin, "What Will Become of Iran's 'Stiletto Revolution' Now?" *Telegraph* (UK), June 27, 2009, http://www.telegraph.co.uk/news/worldnews/middleeast/iran/5651664/What-will-become-of-Irans-stiletto-revolution-now.html.
43. "Iranian Blogger Tells of Escape from Tehran," *Mathrubhumi*, August 5, 2009, http://www.mathrubhumi.com/english/story.php?id=21386#.
44. "Seven Photographers and Franco-Iranian Cameraman Arrested," *Reporters Without Borders*, July 17, 2009, http://en.rsf.org/iran-seven-photographers-and-franco-17-07-2009,33864.html.
45. Mark Pfeifle, "A Nobel Peace Prize for Twitter?" *Christian Science Monitor*, July 6, 2009, http://www.csmonitor.com/Commentary/Opinion/2009/0706/p09s02-coop.html.
46. Jeremy Rabkin and Ariel Rabkin, "Let's Help Iranians Beat the Censors," *Wall Street Journal*, July 20, 2009, http://online.wsj.com/article/SB124779708428055757.html.
47. "2009 George Polk Award Winners," Long Island University, George Polk Awards, http://www.liu.edu/About/News/Polk/Previous.aspx#2009.
48. Max Blumenthal, "Neda In Palestine, Senntenced to Die Alone," *Max Blumenthal*, July 3, 2009, http://maxblumenthal.com/2009/07/page/2.
49. See, for example, Wikipedia s.v. "Murder of Marwa El-Sherbini," http://en.wikipedia.org/wiki/Murder_of_Marwa_El-Sherbini#cite_ref-bild20090724-dpa_26-0.
50. "The Deaths of Michael Jackson and 'Neda' Grip the Blogosphere," *PEJ New Media Index*, June 22–26, 2009, http://www.journalism.org/index_report/deaths_michael_jackson_and_%E2%80%9Cneda%E2%80%9D_grip_blogosphere.
51. Jenna Wortham, "Michael Jackson Tops the Charts on Twitter," *New York Times*, June 25, 2009, http://bits.blogs.nytimes.com/2009/06/25/michael-jackson-tops-the-charts-on-twitter.
52. *Ibid*.
53. Michael Warner, *The Letters of the Republic: Publication and the Public Sphere in Eighteenth-Century America* (Cambridge, MA: Harvard University Press, 1990), pp. 1 and 3.
54. Hito Steyerl, "The Spam of the Earth: Withdrawal From Representation," *e-flux journal* 32.
55. Sontag, *Regarding the Pain of Others*, p. 89.
56. Keenan, "Publicity and Indifference (Sarajevo on Television)," p. 109.
57. *Ibid*., p. 113.
58. *Ibid*., p. 114.

HIV Prevention Justice Alliance Rally, National HIV Prevention Conference, Atlanta, Georgia 2007. From Jean Carlomusto, *Sex in an Epidemic* (2010).

Sex in an Epidemic as AIDS Archive Activism: An Interview with Jean Carlomusto

Ann Cvetkovich

As a longtime AIDS activist and mediamaker, Jean Carlomusto has been at the forefront of a movement noted for its innovative use of video as an integral part of activism. Cultural theorist and ACT UP member Douglas Crimp has used the term "cultural activism" to describe the video camera's ubiquitous presence at demonstrations, as well as the sophisticated use of graphic design and print culture by AIDS activists.[1] Carlomusto was a member of the Testing the Limits and DIVA-TV video collectives, which used newly available video technologies not only to document and more widely publicize direct action, but to create new forms of media activism by extending the life of a demonstration and its messages.[2] *Testing the Limits: NYC* (1987) documented early responses to AIDS activism as well as the formation of ACT UP in 1987. DIVA-TV, a collective affiliated with ACT UP, produced videos about key ACT UP actions, including *Target City Hall* (1989) and *Stop the Church* (1990), which served to publicize and promote the tactics of direct action. Carlomusto also worked at Gay Men's Health Crisis (GMHC), where she and Gregg Bordowitz produced the *Living With AIDS* cable television series, which made cultural production integral to providing health care and social services. GMHC's *Safer Sex Shorts* (1989), for example, presented safe sex in openly erotic ways that embraced pornography, S/M, and cruising. Another GMHC video, *Doctors, Liars, and Women* (1988), showcased Carlomusto's work with the ACT UP Women's Caucus by focusing on their demonstration against *Cosmopolitan* magazine for its claim that women are not at risk for AIDS through heterosexual intercourse.

Jean Carlomusto's most recent video, *Sex in an Epidemic* (2010) (with Shanti Avirgan as associate producer), draws quite literally on her longtime career as an AIDS media activist by reusing footage from this archive in order to keep it alive and sustain its meanings.[3] Using a personal archive of tapes she made for *Testing the Limits*, DIVA-TV, and GMHC (as well as from other sources such as the Lesbian Herstory

Archives collection of tapes by the video activist group the Love Collective), Carlomusto revisits early responses to the AIDS crisis in the gay male community that led to the invention of safer sex and to a remarkable AIDS activist movement in order to claim this history as central to understanding contemporary sexual politics. Especially compelling is the reminder of how frightening and devastating the early years of the health crisis were, when people were dying with no idea why and with no information about how to halt the transmission of what had not yet even been named as a virus. Carlomusto also uses the retrospective power of archival documentary to provide a broad context for this moment and to link past and present. She situates the history of safer sex in relation to the post–World War II sexual revolution in the United States and the feminist reproductive rights movement, connects the early AIDS crisis to debates over sex education and abstinence-only policies during the Clinton and Bush administrations, and explores the legacies of AIDS activism in contemporary struggles over HIV/AIDS prevention that are now global in scope. She seeks to make the history of queer sexual activism central to a politics of prevention justice that remains relevant now not only in the battle against HIV/AIDS, but in efforts to create more honest and open sexual cultures. In addition to making more visible a history that is in danger of being forgotten, she articulates a vision of a queer sexual politics in which public sex education could continue to benefit from the insights of early AIDS activism. *Sex in An Epidemic* also has a memorial function, preserving the images and the work of those who struggled to create safer sex; to this end, Carlomusto uses footage she taped for GMHC's oral history project, which includes interviews with key GMHC leaders that are especially valuable, because many of them have since died. Carlomusto's emotional investment in the archival footage contributes to its political and historical value.

Less to be expected, perhaps, is that *Sex in an Epidemic* also shows the influence of the more personal body of work that Carlomusto has produced alongside of and in dialogue with her activist media, including *L Is for the Way You Look* (1990), about lesbian visibility, *To Catch a Glimpse* (1997), about the secret of her grandmother's death from a botched abortion, *Shatzi Is Dying* (2000), about the death of her dog and burnout from AIDS activism, and *Monte Cassino* (2003), about her Italian father's experience of bombing in Italy during World War II.[4] This autoethnographic work manifests a queer commitment to the historical significance of personal experience, and Carlomusto often uses both personal and public archives in the videos, incorporating material such as family photographs because it is emotionally meaningful. The influence of Carlomusto's more personal work is present in *Sex in an Epidemic*'s efforts to keep the history of AIDS activism alive, not just as a fading or distant memory, but as a vital resource, by reusing and recirculating its substantial documentary archive. She practices a version of what

Alex Juhasz has called "queer archive activism," creating a new generation of AIDS media activism by recontextualizing and reviving earlier media.[5]

Our conversation, which took place on June 25, 2009 and is transcribed here, underscores *Sex in an Epidemic*'s argument that people having sex and then talking about it in public constitutes a form of nongovernmental politics. As a lesbian and a feminist with a pro-sex sensibility, Carlomusto describes the powerful appeal of gay male sex cultures that are open about sexuality. At the heart of *Sex in an Epidemic* is the insistence that this early moment remains relevant, that we have not yet learned how to grapple with the challenges that were faced by gay men encountering not only an epidemic, but homophobia and fear of sex, and who drew on intimate experience and semipublic sexual networks to figure out what to do in the absence of any publicly available information. Men such as Richard Berkowitz, one of the early advocates of how to have sex in an epidemic, were hustlers and club goers who figured out that there is lots of sexual activity that is not dangerous sex, and that promiscuity and sex are not the same thing. (In 1983, Berkowitz coauthored with Michael Callen and Joseph Sonnabend the pamphlet *How to Have Sex in an Epidemic* that provides crucial inspiration for Carlomusto.) *Sex in an Epidemic* chronicles the grassroots efforts through which they were able to take this message to others, forging a cultural activism in which pornography met social work in support groups where men could reclaim sex at a time when it seemed to be taken away from them. They used forms of cultural activism—safer-sex comics, film screenings, and media that Carlomusto herself produced—in order to make a public culture out of the knowledge derived from their intimate lives. Carlomusto uses the documentary history of *Sex in an Epidemic* to suggest that these lessons created by gay men in stigmatized and vulnerable social positions remain relevant to the present, when ordinary people continue to make significant interventions to change people's daily sexual practices. She creates a queer version of what sexual knowledge and education might look like.

A key concept promoted by Carlomusto in the video is prevention justice, the rallying cry of CHAMP (Community HIV/AIDS Mobilization Project), one of the organizations influenced by ACT UP that Carlomusto documents in the closing section of *Sex in an Epidemic*. "Prevention justice" is a broad term for the complex systemic changes required fully to address and eliminate AIDS, including a politics of safer sex that acknowledges the messiness of sex, rather than trying to eradicate it, and that continues to find ways to create media that are sexy and affectively meaningful. CHAMP shows the influence not only of AIDS activism of the late 1980s and early 1990s, but also of the global AIDS activist movement of 2000 and beyond, which was catalyzed by the World AIDS Conference in Durban in 2000 and the United Nations Special Session on HIV/AIDS in 2001, both of which inspired new transnational coalitions dedicated to making treatment for HIV/AIDS and health care available across global economic divides.[6] At a 2007 demonstration in Atlanta, CHAMP held up puzzle pieces that named the interlocking elements of a program for HIV/AIDS prevention, including free condoms, syringe exchange, racial justice, housing for all, equity for women, drug policy reform, economic justice, honest sex ed, prevention in prisons, valuing LGBT lives, health care for all, a national AIDS strategy, research, harm reduction, and immigration rights. *Sex in an Epidemic* performs the important work of remembering a lineage of queer AIDS activist work that aims to destigmatize sex and that continues to have relevance now, even as it must be transformed by work in a range of different communities, including people of color, prisoners, and those outside the U.S.

I was delighted to interview Carlomusto in order to let her speak for herself, just as she has enabled others to speak and be witnesses and in order to create another form of activist archive. Presenting Carlomusto's newest work in this format also seemed especially appropriate because it was an opportunity to follow up on my previous interviews with her as part of an oral history project on lesbians in ACT UP.[7] In that earlier project, I wanted to create an archive of lesbian participation in ACT UP so as to prevent the loss of that history, and I also wanted to suggest the ongoing legacies of activism by asking Carlomusto and others how their work and lives continued to be affected by their involvement in AIDS activism into the following decade. The genre of the interview allowed me to explore the personal and affective investments in activism that might not be apparent in more public forums, such as demonstrations and documentary media. Interviewing Carlomusto about *Sex in an Epidemic* provided an opportunity to continue that conversation by exploring how she continues to make use of AIDS activist media some twenty years after some of the footage was originally filmed, not only in order to make history, but in order to make new activist interventions.

ANN CVETKOVICH: Why did you want to make *Sex in An Epidemic* [*SE*], and how does it emerge from your history as an AIDS media activist?

JEAN CARLOMUSTO: I always wanted to do a piece about the early safer-sex movement. In 1986, I started volunteering for GMHC [Gay Men's Health Crisis]. I was the projectionist for *Chance of a Lifetime*, an early safer-sex video produced by Ray Jacobs in 1985 for GMHC, which eroticized safer sex and drew on pornography for inspiration. I had so much fun projecting the film for weekend workshops in the auditorium of the High School for the Humanities, where the projector screen felt like a locus of all the sexual fear, anxiety, and hope of the moment. People were talking about sex, and in a very loving way. They were saying we can do this, this isn't going to end our sex lives, we can still be sexual, we just have to think about ourselves and each other. We have to talk about sex and find ways to make it safer. It was an amazing achievement.

I learned about all these sexual practices that I didn't know before. Part of the men's process was to think about all the things you can do that aren't sucking and fucking. All of a sudden, they would talk about shrimping... do you know what that is? [*Laughter.*] Sucking on toes. There were all these great practices, and it was just so cool to be honest about them. I felt like I owed a debt to that kind of thinking.

I also wanted to witness what went on. Joey Leonte, who was the director of publications for GMHC, was the one who hired me. He was one of three bosses I had at GMHC who died eventually of AIDS. He was always very special to me, because he recruited me out of NYU when GMHC had no equipment, no anything. [*Sex in an Epidemic* includes footage of Leonte talking about GMHC's low-cost production and distribution of safer-sex comics and of Jesse Helms condemning them on the floor of the Senate.]

The debates within the community in the beginning of the epidemic were intense. The conflicts between people who wanted to close the bathhouses or keep them open or the differences in politics between Richard Berkowitz and GMHC were at some points very acrimonious. [Berkowitz is a hustler turned safer-sex activist who features prominently in *Sex in an Epidemic* and whose pamphlet *How to Have Sex in an Epidemic* was one of the first publications to promote the idea that abstinence was not the only way to prevent HIV.] I tend not to want to get involved with the internal politics. I wanted to tell the story and bring out the differences, but not to judge anybody harshly, because, frankly, I think they're all heroes. I think in that atmosphere anyone who came to the forefront and offered comfort or help to people who were scared shitless, who's to judge them?

SE emerges from my life in the context of the epidemic; it's a collection of material from the period during which I was really active in AIDS activism. But I also wanted to bring this historical material into dialogue with current politics and activism around HIV prevention. I can't believe it's 2009 and we have only just perhaps shrugged off the yoke of abstinence policies. The last segment of *SE* looks at prevention justice in a more honest way. Prevention justice is the big net that takes in comprehensive health education, abstinence, talking honestly about sex, the fact that if people don't have access to condoms, the advice to use them is impossible. If people don't have a home, they are not going to come up with the resources to practice safer sex, if part of their ability to sleep somewhere on any given night is dependent on their ability to trade sex. I see current discussions around HIV prevention as part of a larger continuum of discussion around social-justice issues.

AC: One of *SE*'s important points is the connection between early HIV/AIDS activism, especially safer-sex activism, and contemporary abstinence policies. When people debate comprehensive versus abstinence sex education in schools, they don't necessarily bring queer activism or HIV/AIDS activism into those discussions, and the fact that you're linking them is important.

JC: We always get left out as the nutty aunt who can't be trusted in public.

AC: For example, as you tell it, the history of sex education in the 1990s and following under Clinton and Bush, such as the forced resignation of Jocelyn Elders from the position of surgeon general in 1994, has important precursors from the 1980s.

JC: So few people have ever seen the clip of the statement in support of masturbation as part of sex education that led to Elders's resignation. I really wanted to get the actual clip of her remarks, which were made at the United Nations on World AIDS Day. Shanti Avirgan [Carlomusto's associate producer] is the one who got it from the UN. I had been trying to assemble the clip of what she actually said from fragments (it's not on YouTube) in order to show how Elders was completely undermined and unfairly treated by the media. [Following the clip, *Sex in an Epidemic* includes a collage of the media coverage in which the word "masturbation" is repeated over and over, suggesting how Elders's comments were wrenched out of context in sensationalizing ways.] What she was talking about is just as important today, since only 5 percent of sex education programs are comprehensive.

AC: In addition to trying to capture an important moment in the history of the HIV/AIDS epidemic and gay men's responses to it, *SE* also does a great job of contextualizing that history and connecting it to other issues, such as feminist reproductive politics and contemporary sex-education politics. Can you elaborate on why this early safe-sex activism is so important to other forms of sexual politics?

JC: That's one reason I wanted to begin *SE* with some landmarks of the sexual revolution and political issues that have always caused consternation around people's sexuality, such as the Kinsey Report, women's access to abortion, and Masters and Johnson talking about people having sex. The subtext of the whole film is our society's reluctance to talk honestly about sex—they won't deal with it. George Bush didn't want to talk about sex, he wanted to talk about abstinence. He thought the problem is that people have too much sex outside of the confines of marriage. This view negates the sexual lives of so many people.

I wanted to show the continuity between this problem and the early battles we had to fight around AIDS and safer sex. For example, GMHC decided that a great way to reach men was through safer-sex porn. They came up with a very cheap way to do this with eight-page comic books featuring an eroticized fantasy cartoon. Jesse Helms hit the Senate floor three days after over eight hundred thousand queers marched to Washington for rights. He came out with a bill prohibiting any federal money going to anything that promotes sodomy or a homosexual lifestyle and it passed ninety-two to two. This was in 1987, when HIV/AIDS was going through the roof, and we could have saved so many lives if we could have just allowed people to speak honestly to their communities. I'm not saying we're trying to put pornography out everywhere, but the model here was that community-based education works, and it needs to be specific for the populations that are affected. We needed general discussions, but we needed other things, too. This has been the political landscape for talking about sex. No one in government wants to talk honestly about sex or about what it's going to take to lessen drug use in this country.

AC: *SE* suggests that this earlier history remains relevant to the present and what you call "prevention justice." It remains counterintuitive to most people that pornography might be a model for safe-sex education or that the experiences of someone such as Richard Berkowitz working as a hustler might be an important source of knowledge that can feed into our public-health programs.

JC: Yes, there are many people out there, making low or no salaries, who come from communities that have come up with great interventions. Waheedah Shabazz-El [a member of ACT UP Philadelphia who is one of the current AIDS activists featured toward the end of *Sex in an Epidemic*] tells the story of how she was not feeling well one day and went to the doctor and was told she had full-blown AIDS. She looked around her community—she is Muslim—and wondered about the rise in HIV rates and started to think about intervention. One of the things she knew is that a lot of people in prison have HIV, and she wanted to make sure that people in the Philadelphia jail system would have condoms provided to them, because there was an ordinance passed in 1987 that condoms should be available. It was awful that this very ordinance was being ignored by law enforcement.

AC: I'd like to hear more about how this project continues the work of your other video projects, including not just the activist ones, but the more personal ones, and particularly about how you use your own video archive to make *Sex in an Epidemic*.

JC: I just spent the entire day moving my archive, which consists of tapes in white cardboard boxes. It makes me aware of the preciousness of archival material, because as I get older and the tapes get older, there's a lot of history that I don't think should ever be lost. That's why I try to make use of archival materials, especially if I feel the preciousness of their passing.

SE has my sensibility in it, even though I'm less present than in some of my other videos. The way I used the archival footage to go back and forth between

Larry Mass and Larry Kramer reminds me of *L Is for the Way You Look* and the story about Dolly Parton at the Reno show. [In *L Is for the Way You Look* (1991), Carlomusto investigates new forms of lesbian visibility and queer fandom by documenting her friends' responses to seeing Dolly Parton in the audience at a performance by the lesbian comic Reno at P.S. 122 in New York.] One person's story either validates or contradicts the next person's, and a kind of narrative is made.

It's also present in the montages, such as the one in which Richard Berkowitz is talking about it being the end of the world. (I think it's 1982.) He has just had a lump biopsied, and he is miserable, and he puts on Nina Simone's great rendition of "Everything Must Change" from her album *Baltimore*. It's the saddest song of impermanence. I wanted to use archival material from the LOVE collective, which was a fabulous lesbian collective from late 1970s and early 1980s that documented life as it was in New York City at that time. It's a great collection that is housed at the Lesbian Herstory Archives, but a lot of the tapes have never been transferred from three-quarter-inch (which is also known as Umatic tape), and they are in archival danger. I thought it was apropos to use that footage in a segment about fear of mortality.

AC: In an earlier conversation, you mentioned "the desire to relive a time through the sadness of its passing."

JC: For many of us who were coming of age during that time (or perhaps coming to a late coming of age), there was a real happiness and joy we felt about being honest and out there about who we were. This was such an important time in our lives for coming to an awareness of the power of community, but that power and joy got tied into a lot of grief and sadness when we saw many of our friends die. When you go back and look at some of these images of people in their prime, you can't help but know that so many of the guys in this footage aren't alive. It becomes like watching ghosts of the past. There's a ghostly feeling that is inherent in the moving image. That's why horror films are such a popular genre. There is a ghostliness when you see someone move and speak and you know they're dead. In *To Catch a Glimpse*, I used the comment made by one of the first people to see Lumière's cinema in 1885—"When this device is made available to the public, everyone will be able to photograph those dear to them, not just in their static form, but with their movements and with speech on their lips; then death will no longer be absolute."

AC: How does *SE* serve a memorial function? In the closing credits, for example, you dedicate the work to AIDS educators who have passed, with additional clips of some of those who have been featured earlier in the video: Joey Leonte, Bob Cecchi, Michael Callen, Jed Mattes, Ray Jacobs, Ortez Alderson, Richard Dunne, Michael Shernoff, and Rodger McFarlane.

JC: I've been making this tape for over ten years. I've wanted to make this piece for a long time because so many fabulous AIDS educators that I knew who were dead had struggled up until they got sick to try to prevent people from getting HIV. And they were doing something really amazing because they were trying to do that without making anybody feel bad about themselves. That to me was the magic of what they did. They changed a lot of behavior because they went out into the community and they were who they were and they had a message that was relevant to the men they were speaking to. They had some innovative things that they tried because they knew these guys—they were these guys. They figured guys grew up on porn, so let's make some safer-sex porn.

AC: I think that conception of safer sex activism as emerging from everyday practices is one way that *Sex in an Epidemic* implicitly defines nongovernmental politics. In our earlier conversation, you said that filling the streets with public emotion is the first step in any radical change—that it isn't going to happen in a government office. You talked about showing the power of people gathering in the streets in the GMHC archival footage from a 1987 candlelight vigil in New York, which you described as emotionally charged material for you.

JC: I keep going back to that footage—I've used it in *Shatzi Is Dying* and some other tapes. These vigils were being held everywhere; that was not the only candlelight vigil where people were standing on the streets with candles in their hands at dusk. I keep on going back to that footage because I found that so moving. The footage that I took that day in New York of that candlelight vigil in 1987 was emblematic of the kinds of mass grief that we took into the street as part of what would boil over that year into activism.

AC: The focus on safe-sex intimacy in *SE* suggests that change begins with ordinary people and their daily practices, more so than in government policies.

JC: I think about the demonstration against *Cosmopolitan* magazine by the women in ACT UP and how we were shocked by how much of an impact we had. We were four or five lesbians in ACT UP who were having dinner, and one person walked in and said isn't this an awful article [about how heterosexual women are not at risk of HIV transmission through vaginal intercourse], and we started organizing. Maxine Wolfe [one of the founders of the ACT UP Women's Caucus, who is interviewed in *Sex in an Epidemic*] had an important role here, because she was such an experienced activist. Through her leadership, she provided really strong ideas about what was good in terms of organizing. We were going to talk to the doctor first before we ever protested to see if he would publish a retraction. We would have been really happy with that, but he wouldn't budge. So then the next step was planning this action, and all of a sudden, the media happened to pick it up, and then the next thing you knew it was on *Nightline* and it was on *Donahue*, and it became a national issue and change happened. Eventually, a retraction was printed, and we had a lot of time to talk about women and AIDS and risk. That was a good action, because it wasn't just about protest, it was about raising awareness.[8]

AC: You made an interesting point about people being able to make a difference even when they were scared, such as gay men inventing safer sex in the early days of the AIDS crisis or Waheedah Shabazz being willing to speak out, despite being in a vulnerable position.

JC: The fear and stigma of the early days was so pervasive. It's amazing that people such as Michael Callen and Steven Berkowitz and Joseph Sonnabend had the guts even to put a theory forward and say you can still have sex but care for one another. And use condoms.

I noticed people in ACT UP who were often doing truly outrageous things would talk about fear beforehand or having nothing to lose. The transition from having the emotion to actually doing something is very liberating. I remember someone getting up at an ACT UP Oral History videotaping, and he spoke about how he went to the governor's office and picked up the phone and he couldn't believe he was speaking from the governor's office.

AC: What are your goals for the distribution and reception of *Sex in an Epidemic*? I like how you use Maxine Wolfe's statement at the end of the film to put forward the idea that we don't need to be living with AIDS and that we could be imagining a world without AIDS.

JC: I would like *Sex in an Epidemic* to be a companion piece to a growing movement of people who want to reignite a discussion around HIV prevention in this country. We must get HIV prevention back on the agenda. It's really important that we bring down the numbers. Over fifty-six thousand people a year are getting newly infected with HIV and it's not necessary. I think it would be great if we could finally find a cure and stop the disease from spreading.

I hope this video becomes a resource for universities to use. I've been teaching now for a long time, over twenty years, and I don't see that many students are really informed on the issues or have a knowledge of the history of HIV. We need to have something less superficial so that they feel invested, so that it's not just "Use a condom," so that they understand it a little more deeply. It's not just about HIV, it's about being able to talk honestly about sex . . . and about not having sex. It's really important to be more open and honest about a variety of expressions.

NOTES

1. For a foundational discussion of the importance of cultural activism, including video and other media, to AIDS activism, see Douglas Crimp (ed.), *AIDS: Cultural Analysis / Cultural Activism* (Cambridge, MA: The MIT Press, 1988), as well as Douglas Crimp and Adam Rolston (eds.), *AIDS DemoGraphics* (Seattle: Bay Press, 1991), which documents ACT UP's distinct visual graphics. Other important discussions of AIDS media activism include Alexandra Juhasz, *AIDS TV: Identity, Community, and Alternative Video* (Durham: Duke University Press, 1995), and Roger Hallas, *Reframing Bodies: AIDS, Bearing Witness and the Queer Moving Image* (Durham: Duke University Press, 2009). For a discussion of the distinctive role of affect in AIDS activism, see Deborah Gould, *Moving Politics: Emotion and ACT UP's Fight Against AIDS* (Chicago: University of Chicago Press, 2009).
2. These videos and many others are archived in the Royal S. Marks AIDS Activist Video Collection at the New York Public Library.
3. *Sex in an Epidemic* (2010) is distributed by Outcast Films, http://www.outcast-films.com. It had its world premiere at the NewFest in New York City in June 2010, followed by a screening at Frameline in San Francisco, also in June 2010.
4. For more on Carlomusto's work, see Ann Cvetkovich, *An Archive of Feelings: Trauma, Sexuality, and Lesbian Public Cultures* (Durham: Duke University Press, 2003), and Julianne Pidduck, "Queer Kinship and Ambivalence: Video Autoethnographies by Jean Carlomusto and Richard Fung," *GLQ* 15.3 (2009), pp. 441–68.
5. Alexandra Juhasz, "Video Remains: Nostalgia, Technology, and Queer Archive Activism," *GLQ* 12.2 (2006), pp. 319–28.
6. See, for example, the video by Anne-Christine D'Adesky, Shanti Avirgan, and Ann T. Rosetti, *Pills, Profits, and Protest: Chronicle of the Global AIDS Movement* (2005) and the work of Health GAP (Global Access Project) (http://www.healthgap.org), and, in South Africa, Treatment Action Campaign (http://www.tac.org.za).
7. See *An Archive of Feelings*. Carlomusto has also been interviewed for the ACT UP Oral History Project (http://www.actuporalhistory.org), which now includes over one hundred interviews with AIDS activists that are available online and itself constitutes an important new activist media project for preserving and mobilizing the history of AIDS activism.
8. For this section of *Sex in an Epidemic*, Carlomusto uses footage from *Doctors, Liars, and Women: AIDS Activists Say No to Cosmo* (1988), the video she made with Maria Maggenti for the GMHC Living With AIDS series. She also showcases the work of the ACT UP Women's Caucus by including video documentation of the Shea Stadium action, in which, during a baseball game, they held up signs promoting safer sex. Carlomusto thus includes material that is drawn directly from her own experience as an AIDS activist, particularly experience that focuses on lesbian involvement in AIDS activism. For more on this aspect of ACT UP's history, see my *An Archive of Feelings*.

Still from Liz Garbus's *The Execution of Wanda Jean* (2002).

Envisioning Abolition: Sex, Citizenship, and the Racial Imaginary of the Killing State

Kendall Thomas

For most of its history, the academic literature on the U.S. system of capital punishment has concerned itself with policy analyses of death penalty law and its administration. In recent years, however, the traditional policy paradigm has been supplemented (if not displaced) by scholarly investigation of the *cultural* register of death penalty jurisprudence and the regime of "state killing"[1] of which it is a part. At the center of this "cultural turn"[2] in death penalty scholarship is an interest in the symbolic dimension of capital punishment. In the words of one of its most accomplished proponents, the cultural study of the death penalty attends to the ways in which the death penalty "create[s] social meaning and thus shape[s] social worlds."[3]

If the death penalty is part of a larger cultural imaginary that it helps shape, contemporary advocates for the abolition of the death penalty cannot hope to transform our national conversation about race and capital punishment without first taking the full measure of the *cultural* challenge that the abolitionist movement faces. That challenge, in a word, is this: because the death penalty serves important symbolic functions in the wider culture of the twenty-first-century United States, the continuing, if conflicted civic consensus in favor of state killing is no longer responsive (if it ever was) solely to the logic of the better argument and the persuasive power of empirical proof. If we are honest with ourselves, we have to reckon with the fact that the current terms of the discourse of civil society in this country on race and the death penalty throw us up against the limits of liberal political legalism, with its faith in the well-ordered rhetoric of reason and rule-governed rationality, and above all, in the American political theology of individual constitutional rights.

The popular American discourse on the death penalty operates through cultural mechanisms that do their work at the level of the unconscious, or more specifically, at the level of what might be called the "racial unconscious." If we are to envision abolition of the death penalty, what we need, then, is a critical conceptual vocabulary that places the cultural phenomena of racial desire and racial fantasy at the heart of popular American discourse on capital punishment.

To work toward that end, this essay examines the production and circulation of cultural "meanings and symbols and representations"[4] in the capital case of Wanda Jean Allen. Allen, poor, black, mentally impaired, and lesbian, was put to death by the State of Oklahoma on January 11, 2001. The essay pursues two overlapping concerns. The first is an interpretive account of the trial and appellate records in Allen's case, together with a documentary film about the final three months of her life, *The Execution of Wanda Jean*.[5] I argue that the project of social meaning and social world making in the Allen case proceeded largely through the state's strategic manipulation of the psychic or "subjective side of social relations,"[6] above all through the deft, unspoken appeal to fantasy and the mobilization of the politics of racial and sexual enjoyment.

The essay's other mission is methodological. Here, I advance the following propositions. First, the Allen case demonstrates the limits of the "rationalist" or "reformist" understandings of and arguments against capital punishment that have thus far characterized the cultural study of the death penalty. Second, a critical cultural analysis of the "irrational rationality" of the death penalty system should be seen as a crucial task for those of us who are trying to map the complex relationship between race and state killing at the beginning of the twenty-first century, a moment some have argued will be remembered as the dawn of a new era of "postracial" racism. Between and alongside these two, I develop a third argument, which has to do with the productive possibilities of staging an encounter in this theater of analysis between critical race theory, queer theory, and a political conception of psychoanalytic theory.

On December 2, 1988, Wanda Jean Allen shot her lover, Gloria Leathers, during an argument in the parking lot of a suburban police station just outside Oklahoma City, Oklahoma. Four days later, Allen was arrested in connection with the shooting. Shortly afterward, Gloria Leathers died from her wounds. Allen was eventually tried and convicted under Oklahoma law of murder in the first degree and the felonious possession of a firearm after former conviction of a felony. After deliberating for only two hours, the jury recommended that Allen be sentenced to death for the murder of Gloria Leathers and given a ten-year prison sentence for the felonious possession of a firearm. After exhausting her state and federal appeals, Allen sought and was denied clemency by the Oklahoma Pardon and Parole Board. On Thursday, January 11, 2001, Allen was killed by lethal injection at the Oklahoma

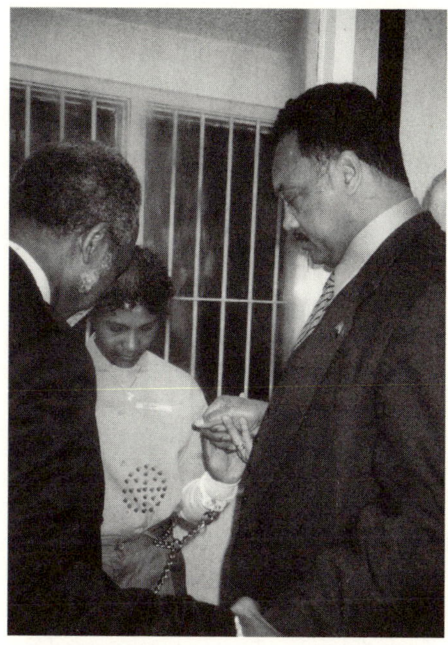

Still from Liz Garbus's *The Execution of Wanda Jean* (2002).

State Penitentiary in McAlester. Wanda Jean Allen was the first woman to be executed by the State of Oklahoma and the sixth woman to be executed in the United States since the administration of the death penalty was resumed in 1977. Allen was the first black woman executed in the United States since 1954, the year the U.S. Supreme Court rendered the landmark *Brown* decision, a fact that, as I will argue, should not be ignored.

In the briefs filed with various courts during the appellate process, a number of arguments were offered on Allen's behalf. Relying on evidence that Allen had been found as a teenager to have an IQ of 69, Allen's counsel argued that she was mentally retarded and thus unable to control her actions. The appeals briefs charged, further, that her trial attorney, who had never represented a client in a capital case, had improperly been forced to remain on the case despite his request to have competent counsel appointed. Finally, Allen's appellate counsel argued that her initial conviction and the jury's recommendation of the death penalty at the sentencing hearing were the result of prosecutorial misconduct. The briefs placed particular emphasis on what they characterized as the prosecution's continual "distortion" of evidence regarding the relationship between Allen and Leathers, who had met and become lovers while they were both serving time in prison. These distortions, argued Allen's lawyers, included the depiction of Wanda Jean as the "dominant" person in the relationship, testimony by Gloria Leathers's mother that Allen was the "man" in the relationship, the introduction of testimony about greeting cards Wanda Jean had given Gloria on which she had signed her name "G-e-n-e" and other characterizations that, in the words of Allen's counsel, "unduly emphasized that [Allen] was engaged in a homosexual relationship with Leathers" and "tended to humiliate [Allen] in the eyes of the jury."[7]

The tone of Oklahoma Court of Criminal Appeals was typical of the opinions issued by both the state and federal courts that reviewed Allen's conviction. After stating that the first issue before it was "whether the sentence of death was imposed under the influence of passion, prejudice or any other arbitrary factor,"[8] the Court of Criminal Appeals concluded, inter alia, that the lower court committed no error in allowing presentation of "evidence [that Allen] was the 'man' in her homosexual relationship with the decedent.... It was used to show [Allen] was the aggressive person in the relationship, while the decedent was more passive." In the words of the presiding judge, "The evidence would help the jury understand why each party acted the way she did both during the events leading up to the shooting and the shooting itself.... Under these circumstances, its probative value was not substantially outweighed by its prejudicial effect...and the evidence was properly admitted."[9] The Court of Criminal Appeals did not address the argument of the lone dissenting opinion, which took exception to the notion that

> the majority finding the appellant was the 'man' in her lesbian relationship has any probative value at all. Were this a case involving a heterosexual couple, the fact that a male defendant was the 'man' in the relationship likewise would tell me nothing. I find no proper purpose for this evidence, and believe its only purpose was to present the defendant as less sympathetic to the jury than the victim.[10]

In *The Execution of Wanda Jean*, an assistant Attorney General for the State of Oklahoma, Sandra Howard, defended the verdict and sentence imposed on Allen. After summarizing Oklahoma law on the concept of premeditation, Howard offered the following remarks about Allen:

> Wanda Jean was just a very domineering person. Their relationship was very turbulent over the years. Police had been called out numerous times and, you know, there was really no doubt from the testimony at trial that Miss Allen was the dominant person in the relationship. The state introduced into trial two different cards that Wanda Jean had sent to Gloria that were very threatening. One of them looks very innocent on the front, shows someone talking about, you know, being in Wanda's prayers and says also, you're also in most of my confessions. But then Wanda Jean puts the P.S. on the card, "I'm the type of person who will hunt someone down I love and kill them. Do I make myself clear Gloria?" and it's signed "Gene." And then

a second card shows a gorilla on the front, it says, "Patience, my ass, I'm gonna kill something" and when you read the back, Wanda has written to Gloria, "Try and leave and you'll understand this card more. Dig, for real, no joke. Love, Gene" and she signed it "G-E-N-E," Gene. Wanda would sign her name sometimes sign "G-E-N-E." That's when she considered herself to be the male figure in the relationship, if there is such a thing in these types of relationships.[11]

Media accounts, particularly in the gay and lesbian press, seized on Allen's case as evidence of a pattern in capital prosecutions of men and women who are gay or lesbian. In this perspective, the conviction and sentencing of Wanda Jean Allen are a blatant example of homophobia in the criminal justice system generally and in capital cases specifically. In a representative article entitled "Queer on Death Row," journalist and social critic Richard Goldstein lists the Allen case as one of a number of recent capital murder convictions of gay men and lesbians in which "stereotypical beliefs about homosexuals... may have sealed their fate."[12]

Although Goldstein concedes that "race, class, and reduced mental capacity all play a major role in capital punishment," the heart of his discussion of Wanda Jean Allen centers on the ways in which "Allen's sexuality was never far from the case."[13] While I agree that the Allen prosecution is a textbook example of the legal uses of homophobia in capital murder cases, I also believe that a standard "lesbigay studies" (to use a term coined by William Eskridge, Jr.) perspective minimizes or risks altogether ignoring another, equally meaningful aspect of the case. This is the obvious, though unacknowledged, significance in the Allen prosecution of race and racism, which, if we hope to understand it, demands a more complex interpretation of the case than is possible through the language of lesbian and gay studies. However, what I have said about the limited value of a conventional lesbigay studies framework also holds true for any approach to the Allen case that uncritically relies on standard post–civil rights understandings of race and racism in U.S. death penalty law. Racial inequality is alive and well throughout the criminal justice system: in the composition of the bench and prosecutorial bar, in the demographics of grand and petit juries, and in the incidence and severity of punishment. Nonetheless, the now regnant ideology (both in and outside the courts) that racism may be said to exist only when consideration of race is explicit and purposeful (and not always then) has all but knocked the political wind out of standard race-based critiques of the criminal justice system, generally, and the administration of the death penalty, in particular.

Given the enfeebled state of the mainstream discourse, then, we can expect little traction in a simple shift of critical attention from something called "sexuality" or "sexual orientation" to something called "race" or vice versa. The intellectual challenge, rather, is to think the questions of race and racism raised by the case around, or, if you prefer, *inside* the axes of sex, sexuality, and sexual orientation.

In the words of Wahneema Lubiano, we might say that the story of Wanda Jean Allen's trial and execution is a story of the "places where race no longer talks about race" precisely and paradoxically by talking about it through something else and elsewhere. "What," asks Lubiano, "might race help us think about that race does not name, but to which it is nonetheless connected?"[14]

Jacques Derrida once famously argued that there is "no racism without a language. The point," he goes on to insist, "is not that acts of racial violence are only words but rather that they have to have a word."[15] My question is this: Does that "word" have to be the word "race"? Are there circumstances in which racial meaning making takes place through recourse to other words or, indeed, through the language of image and symbol, without the use, that is, of any words at all? What does the Allen case tell us about the ways in which race and racial representation figure in the U.S. legal and political discourse on capital punishment in our putatively "postracial" age?

THE RACIAL IMAGINARY

The interpretive strategy toward which I am gesturing is suggested in part by Paul Kahn in a brief, but brilliant polemic, *The Cultural Study of Law*.[16] Kahn's stated goal is to outline the program of a scholarly legal method that abandons the reformist ambitions that have historically guided the practice of legal criticism. "The legal academic is the captive of law. If a discipline is to emerge that actually studies law as an object for theoretical description and elaboration, the scholar must first free herself from the law."[17] Kahn issues a call for legal scholarship that undertakes the systematic study of the language and logic of "law's rule." This "cultural discipline of law" aims to elaborate the "genealogy" and "architecture" of law whose chief object is a critical understanding of the "legal imagination": "To understand the power of law," Kahn argues, "we must stop looking so much at the commands of legal institutions and start looking at the legal imagination."[18]

Kahn's urged investigation of the "legal imagination" is provocative and potentially productive. Nonetheless, a thick description of the implication of law and culture in the trial of Wanda Jean Allen demands a more radical and a more radically interdisciplinary understanding of what we mean by the idea of "imagination" than Kahn himself provides. The cultural study of how legal actors and institutions "imagined" the trial and execution of Wanda Jean Allen must find a language to describe the burden of representation that was borne in the Allen case by the "racial imagination" or the racial imaginary.

A first step in the effort to specify the relationship between the legal and racial imaginations might be consider the ways in which the racial imaginary occupies a region or site in the broader constellation that philosopher and social theorist Charles Taylor has denominated the "social imaginary."[19] For Taylor, the term is meant to capture the ways in which people imagine "their social existence, how they fit together with others, how things go on between them and their fellows, the expectations that are normally met, and the deeper normative notions and images that underlie these expectations."[20] Taylor notes that the work of the social imaginary "is not often expressed in theoretical terms," but is rather conveyed and "carried in images, stories, and legends."[21]

We might say that the raw material of the social imaginary consists of pictures, rather than propositions. This imaginary field reflects and refracts the "largely unstructured and inarticulate understanding of our whole situation, within which particular features of our world show up for us in the sense they have." This understanding "can never be expressed in the form of explicit doctrines because of its unlimited and indefinite nature. That is another reason for speaking here of an imaginary and not a theory."[22]

Although he does not discuss the idea of race, Taylor's concept of the "social imaginary" takes us a step further in mapping the movement of the modern racial imaginary. Extrapolating from Taylor, I would emphasize two distinctive modal dimensions of the social imaginary that is "race." First, the racial imaginary differs from other social imaginaries in the way it emerges from, indeed, may be said only to exist in, a field of vision and visualization that exceeds the boundaries of language and discourse. Second, the racial imaginary operates in and through mental mechanisms that are not only unstructured and inarticulate, but *unconscious*. No deep understanding of the work of the unconscious in and on the racial imaginary is impossible without serious, sustained engagement with psychoanalysis. The psychoanalytic account of "how we acquire our heritage of the ideas and laws of human society within the unconscious mind"[23] offers an indispensable resource for a critical cultural study of the psychic life of race in law.

My point of entry into the intersection of the legal and racial imagination via the psychoanalytic approach is the idea of "racial castration," which David L. Eng has elaborated in a book by the same name. Eng's study offers a sophisticated revision of Freud's theory of fetishism. According to Freud's classic account, fetishism is a story about the trauma of sexual difference. The male fetishist, as it were, disavows what in Freud's theory is thematized as female castration. Instead, he "[sees] on the female body a penis that is not there to see."[24] From the Freudian perspective, this imagined penis is a fetish—a surrogate penis, projected onto the female body or symbolically displaced onto a substitute object, such as a lock of hair, a pair of undergarments, a shoe.

In a probing psychoanalytic reading of David Henry Hwang's play *M. Butterfly*,

Eng offers an account of this psychic process when it is faced with the trauma of racial difference. In Hwang's drama, a French diplomat falls in love with a Chinese opera male diva/transvestite/spy. Instead of seeing on the female body a penis that is not there to see, the French diplomat refuses to see on his lover's male Asian body a penis that most definitely is there. In Eng's account, this "racial castration" of the lover's body "suggests that what is being negotiated in this particular scenario is not just sexual but racial difference." It is a psychic operation that unfolds under the jurisdiction of Orientalist law: an Asian man "could never be completely a man." As Eng reads it, *M. Butterfly* thus demonstrates "the impossibility of thinking about racism and sexism [and I might add homophobia] as separate discourses or distinct spheres of analysis."[25]

As Rey Chow has similarly reminded us, "Race and ethnicity are . . . coterminous with sexuality, just as sexuality is implicated in race and ethnicity. To that extent, any analytical effort to keep these categories apart from one another may turn out to be counterproductive, for it is their categorical enmeshment—their categorical miscegenation, so to speak—that needs to be foregrounded."[26] The challenge is to elaborate a concept of the erotic that remains alert to the social fantasies that animate the psychic life of racial and gender violence. If writers such as Rey Chow and David Eng are right about the need to attend to the "categorical miscegenation" of race, sexuality and ethnicity, we must be prepared to come to grips with the possibility that political fantasies are indistinguishable from psychic realities of the sexual imagination.

Two further points must be emphasized straightaway. First, the acting out of the violent racial and sexual fantasy on whose erotic kernel I have been insisting need not find its aim and end in the experience of pleasure we associate with sex. To the contrary. At its extremity, sexual and racial violence can find satisfaction only in a realm of psychic pain that lies, as it were, "beyond the pleasure principle."

The second point returns to the problem of the death penalty, to a consideration of the ways in which the relationship between *eros* and *thanatos* underwrites the political imaginary of the state and of the law that legitimates state power. The erotic economy is not limited to the social enactment of racial and gender violence commonly categorized as crime. The history of Africans in America is replete with instances in which sex and sexuality have been deployed as tools in the arsenal of racial violence. In this context, the death penalty, particularly, calls for an analysis that seeks to understand how the production of death that is state-sanctioned killing is a kind of "political erotics," a triangulated affair between the state, the citizen, and the condemned.

A critical account of cases such as that of Wanda Jean Allen must place the question of the erotics of racial power and violence at the very center of its analysis. How does the Wanda Jean Allen case implicate social values and psychic investments in a libidinal economy that is not merely similar to, but parasitic on those we ordinarily associate with the political economy of sex?

In the Allen case, the prosecution pursued a strategy of "lesbian fetishism" (the term comes from Elizabeth Grosz, although I use it in a quite different sense here).[27] Over the course of the trial, Allen's body became the imagined site of a penis "that [was] not there to see." From this perspective, Allen was subjected to a psychic (and cultural) mechanism of social homophobia. Allen's lesbian identity and desire were "masculinized": she was the "dominant figure" in her relationship with Leathers; she was the "husband" to Leathers as wife; she was the woman masquerading as a man who dared to walk around the house with her breasts bared in the company of men, who defiantly refused her given (feminine) name.

I do not mean to deny the force in Allen's case of the prosecutorial uses of the figure of the murderous lesbian, a stock stereotype with an infamous and long pedigree. My intention rather is to indicate why the act of "legal imagination" that animated the prosecution's strategy in the Allen case was not merely or primarily the homophobic projection of lesbian body. It was already also a racist projection, a fantasy of the *black male* body in which Allen's masculinized lesbian body was conscripted to serve as a screen for the dangerous, deadly hypermasculinity that remains the iconic image of the black presence in white America: "She is a hunter when she kills," as the prosecutor put it at Allen's trial. "She hunts her victims down and then she kills them."[28] By the end of the trial, Allen had been remade into the apotheosis of the figure of black "female masculinity," to use Judith Halberstam's phrase.[29] Allen's rage (which the prosecution recounted so frequently during her trial that it became virtually identic) was insistently invested with racial meanings the prosecution never had to articulate explicitly. One might say that the state effectively played the race card; what the prosecutor did in fact was to make racist use of a homophobic hand.

Stereotypical representations of homosexuality operated freely in the Allen trial as a simultaneous point of transfer for psychic processes of sexual and racial fetishism. Sexuality became the site of a kind of surplus semantic value, which made race and racial meanings available as technologies of state power while silently masking the latter's operation. What a reading of the record suggests was a scrupulous adherence to the formal protocols of a putatively color-blind criminal law regime was, in the event, not color-blind at all. In this respect, the Allen trial fits seamlessly into the critical framework of Slavoj Žižek's notion of "ideological fantasy," whose basic logic is disavowal.[30]

I suggested earlier that the field of vision and visibility is an important theater of racial representation. As Kalpana Seshadri Crooks has reminded us, "although race cannot be reduced to the look," it is nonetheless "fundamentally a regime of looking" or visualization.[31] This visualization is not strictly epidermal or corporeal.[32] In the United States, the fetishistic regime of the racial gaze has long been part of the metaphysical, deep structure of our law. A few examples will suffice to underscore the centrality of this cultural form in the political unconscious of American legal thought. Seen in visual terms, the law of hypodescent (more colloquially known as the "one drop of blood" rule) ascribed a power to the specular field of whiteness, a power that could see past the folds of flesh that cover the black body; Article I, Section 2, clause 3 of the U.S. Constitution could visually amputate three-fifths of the black slave body and ignore the unrepresented remainder; and we are all familiar with the masterful projection of scopic power (I am thinking of Harlan's dissent in *Plessy v. Ferguson*) that declared that the "eyes of our Constitution" could be "color-blind" precisely because "every one knew" that the "dominance" of the "white race" was secure "for all time."

In *The Execution of Wanda Jean*, the continued refusal of the "racial solipsistic"[33] among us to see and thus to know the intersubjective relationship of racial equality is poignantly evident in the clemency hearing granted to Wanda Jean Allen a few months before her death. A viewer of the documentary cannot help but be struck by the defining silence that follows Allen's statement to the clemency board at the end of the hearing. On the standard account, the purpose of a clemency hearing is to provide representatives of the state who are not judges or lawyers to consider the human costs and consequences of the decision to execute a convict who has been sentenced to death.[34] The hearing is not the place to engage in adversarial legal argument (for example, about race-based or sexual-orientation-based discrimination in the administration of capital punishment—arguments that, as I have noted, the U.S. Supreme Court has effectively foreclosed). Rather, its purpose is to stage a performance of abjection by the convicted felon: in short, the purpose, meaning and effects of the contemporary clemency hearing are all directed at the production of affect and emotion (in this regard, they are the flip side of the victim-impact statement that, in recent years, has witnessed such a lively resurgence). With the loss of her voice—a literal loss—Allen is deprived of the communicative means necessary to convey her humanity to the parole board. The progressive and quite literal phonic dematerialization of her voice perversely affirms her infrahumanity, to use Paul Gilroy's term.[35]

The Allen clemency hearing reveals another aspect of the racial politics of capital punishment in the United States: the death penalty is not merely about the literal liquidation of the black body, but about its antecedent reduction to the mere biological existence that Giorgio Agamben has called "bare life." The body of the death row inmate stands in effect as a specific instance of the more general figure of the black civic condition in the contemporary U.S. political order. From this perspective, Negro citizenship is not the active, robust political personhood of Madisonian republicanism, but a species of what Russ Castronovo has aptly denominated "necro citizenship,"[36] a civic status in which political life and identity are constructed on an ideological foundation of death. Again, this death is not always literal: the racial thanatopolitics of the modern "postracial" era concerns not only the actual biological death of black citizens, but the strategic subjugation of living black bodies through the mode of discipline that Michel Foucault has called biopower. The biopolitical practices that consign African-Americans to the liminal sphere of civic half life or virtual death are not primarily material, but symbolic. This is a form of political death dealing that proceeds primarily through the exercise of semiotic state power, for example, the "racist color blindness" that holds that official affirmative reference to or recognition of race in the contemporary postracial moment is by definition racist.

RACE, STATE, *JOUISSANCE*

It would be a mistake, however, to see the Allen prosecution solely as a public staging of the psychic and physical degradation that awaits the bodies of those black and brown ethnic irritants who refuse, in Randall Kennedy's approving phrase, to "the established moral standards of white, middle-class Americans."[37] The suffering and death inflicted on Wanda Jean Allen's imagined male body operates simultaneously as a conduit for organization and the expression of racial and sexual enjoyment.

By "enjoyment," I refer to the English rendering of *jouissance*, a term introduced into the psychoanalytic literature by Jacques Lacan. However, while at one level of meaning, *jouissance* is a cognate of the English word "enjoyment," both in the ordinary language "sense of deriving pleasure from something, and in the legal sense of exercising certain property rights,"[38] for French speakers, *jouissance* conveys a second, specifically sexual connotation, since it is also an idiomatic expression for orgasm. The substance of what I am calling "racial sexual enjoyment" and of the violent political and social fantasies that underwrite it are in many ways indistinguishable from the psychic realities that inform the sexual imagination.

What do the trial and state killing of Wanda Jean Allen tell us about the politics of racial enjoyment? Reading the transcript and opinions in the Allen case or watching the documentary film on her execution, one is struck by the smug, but barely concealed delight Oklahoma officials seemed to take in the abjected figure of Wanda Jean Allen as a "dead citizen" (to adapt Lauren Berlant's vivid phrase).[39] Before she is actually killed, Allen is conscripted to play the role of "dead citizen walking" in a bureaucratic spectacle that enacts her social and civic annihilation.

Slavoj Žižek's account of the "ethnic moment" of the nation as the "surplus" or "leftover" of the universalizing project of the nation is particularly pertinent here. For Žižek, nationalism is "the privileged domain of the eruption of enjoyment into the social field," a materialization of *jouissance* as a collective political fantasy:

> What is at stake in ethnic tensions is always the possession of the national Thing: the "other" wants to steal our enjoyment (by ruining our "way of life" and/or it has access to some secret, perverse enjoyment. In short, what gets on our nerves, what really bothers us about the "other," is the peculiar way he organizes his enjoyment (the smell of his food, his "noisy" songs and dances, his strange manners, his attitude to work—in the racist perspective, the "other" is either a workaholic stealing our jobs or an idler living on our labor). The basic paradox is that our Thing is conceived as something inaccessible to the other and at the same time threatened by him; this is similar to castration which, according to Freud, is experienced as something that "really cannot happen," but whose prospect nonetheless horrifies us.[40]

That prospect also fascinates us. This "package deal" of horror and fascination goes some way toward explaining the persistently high level of support for the death penalty in this country. Wanda Jean Allen is the projected representation of the specter of the dangerous black masculinity that threatens the political utopics of a harmonious, "more perfect" (if not perfectible) union. She embodies, by proxy, the long nightmare that haunts the phantasmatic dream of our criminal justice system as an enlightened exercise in rational participatory democracy: the ugly arc of racial antagonism without which there would be no "national Thing."

The trial and execution of Wanda Jean Allen demonstrate that contemporary racism in the United States is characterized by a number of the features David Halperin has observed about American homophobia: it has no fixed propositional content and no determinate discursive form. In the Allen case, the mobilization of homophobia as an alibi for racism ought not obscure the degree to which racial fantasy and the psychic politics of racial enjoyment will remain a critical pillar in the architecture of the emerging "postracial" state. In mapping the relationship in the Allen case between the death penalty and the politics of enjoyment, I align myself with writers such as Michael Taussig, who has called for critical attention to the symbolic economy of state fetishism: "Like the Nation-State, the fetish has a deep investment in death—the death of the consciousness of the signifying function. Death endows both the fetish and the Nation-State with life, a spectral life, to be sure. The fetish absorbs into itself that which it represents, leaving no traces of the represented. A clean job."[41]

Without specifying the role of the racial imaginary in the collective psychic processes by which the U.S. nation-state binds its subjects to the political fantasy of a "postracial" multicultural citizenship, the play of life and death to which Taussig refers can be only partially understood. The "death of the consciousness of the signifying function" of race in no way entails the death of race itself. To borrow the words of Daniel Patrick Moynihan, the execution of Wanda Jean Allen stands as a case study in "semantic infiltration," a linguistic operation by which racial meanings are secreted through the interstices of language that has nothing to do with race. In order to describe this "splitting off" of racial signifiers and racial signifieds, we must move beyond an abstract, general account of the formal *"figure* of state fetishism"[42] to consider the "politics and historicity of *jouissance*"[43] that is its material social ground.

In a discussion of the publication by Benetton of a January 2000 book of photographs and interviews of U.S. death row inmates, *We, on Death Row*, Austin Sarat suggested that the Italian clothing company's catalog of portraits of condemned prisoners "misses the mark." Sarat argues that in thinking about the death penalty, "the faces we should be looking at are our own. The question to be asked about state killing is not what it does for us, but what it does *to* us." For Sarat, to pose this question is to reckon with "the cost of state killing to our law, our politics, our culture." On Sarat's account, "state killing diminishes us by damaging our democracy, legitimating vengeance, intensifying racial divisions, and distracting us from the challenges that the new century poses for America."[44]

Sarat is surely right. The costs of the death-dealing market in capital punishment are great indeed. Yet this rationalist reckoning of the price we pay to have the death penalty tells only part of the story. In making the case for the fundamental irrationality of capital punishment, Sarat's analysis overlooks the political, cultural, and psychic *benefits* of the dance of state death for the U.S. racial and sexual polity. In the Allen case, the production of death that is state killing involves a fetishistic transubstantiation of value. The Allen case involves an irrational rationality in which values are reversed, costs become benefits, and the laws of objective interest and rational calculation give way to the transvaluative law of an irrational, but by no means illusory enjoyment.[45] David Cole has noted that the American criminal justice system "affirmatively depends on [the exploitation] of inequality. Absent race and class disparities, the privileged among us could not enjoy as much constitutional protection of our liberties as we do; and without these disparities, we could not afford the policy of mass incarceration that we have pursued over the past two decades."[46]

The claim that state killing is at odds with America's enlightened democratic self-image is both true and beside the point. A thick-descriptive or normative account of the dance of state death must attend to the libidinal economy of capital punishment, to the miasmatic politics of a racial and sexual enjoyment that eludes the assumptive logic of rationalist policy analysis. The death penalty in the United States evokes Achille Mbembe's account of the public execution in 1987 of "two malefactors" in Douala, Cameroon. Mbembe suggests that the economy of power in the postcolonial state "is an economy of death—or, more precisely, it opens up a space for enjoyment at the moment it makes room for death, "a space in which power procedurally mediates the transformation of pleasure into a site of death."[47]

CONTESTING CRIMINAL JUSTICE AS A RACIAL PROJECT: *MCCLESKEY V. KEMP*

The case of Wanda Jean Allen not only highlights the fetishistic character of state killing and its perverse, peculiar pleasure in the projected figure of the murderous, masculinized, black, lesbian body, the operation of state power in the "post-racial" state in which a growing number of commentators in and outside law have begun to say we now live or must aspire to live. It demonstrates the relevance in understanding the operation of racial power in the "postracial" state of the question "What does the practice of capital punishment do for (some of) us?" Answering that question should remain an urgent task for anyone who is committed to contesting this nation's necrophilic romance with the death penalty.

In my view, abolitionist activists cannot afford to ignore the lesson we should have learned from Justice Antonin Scalia's now infamous memorandum to the Conference in *McCleskey v. Kemp*,[48] a 1987 case that has been described as "the Dred Scott decision of our time."[49] In *McCleskey v. Kemp*, the U.S. Supreme Court was asked to rule on a federal constitutional claim by Warren McCleskey, an African-American who had been convicted and sentenced to die by a Georgia jury for the murder of a white police officer. Relying in part on statistical evidence of systemic interracial and intraracial disparities in the state's administration of the death penalty, McCleskey maintained that Georgia was using capital punishment in a racially discriminatory fashion in contravention of the equal protection clause of the Fourteenth Amendment to the U.S. Constitution.

Replying to an early draft of what would become the majority opinion in the case, Justice Scalia wrote:

> I disagree with the argument that the inferences that can be drawn from the Baldus study are weakened by the fact that each jury and each trial is unique, or by the large number of variables at issue. And I do not share the view, implicit in [Justice Lewis Powell's draft language], that an effect of racial factors upon sentencing, if it could be shown by sufficiently strong statistical evidence, would require reversal.[50]

"Since it is my view," continues the memorandum, "that the unconscious operation of irrational sympathies and antipathies, including racial, upon jury decisions and (hence) prosecutorial [ones], is real, acknowledged by the [judgments] of this court and ineradicable, I cannot honestly say that all I need is more proof."[51]

Much might be said about this extraordinary document. The first and most important observation has to do with Scalia's "breathtaking"[52] admission that race and racism are constituent components of our criminal justice regime. In conceding that racism is an "ineradicable" and (by a strange twist of logic) constitutionally inconsequential fact defining who and how we criminally punish, the Scalia memorandum in effect concedes the extent to which, in Stephen Bright's words, our criminal courts "are the institutions in the United States least affected by the civil rights movement that brought changes to many American institutions in the last forty years."[53] Criminal justice is a racial project; the United States is a racial state.

What chiefly interests me here, however, is the passage in which Justice Scalia traces the roots of these "race effects" to "the *unconscious* operation of irrational sympathies and antipathies."[54] In raising the question of the "unconscious" and "irrational" determinants of the death penalty, Scalia's analysis puts its finger on the very heart of the problem with which opponents of capital punishment must reckon. How might attention to the unconscious and irrational dimensions of the popular discourse on race and the death penalty help the abolitionist movement fashion a strategy to break the current consensus in favor of capital punishment?

First, the Scalia memorandum directs our attention to the way in which, at its core, the question of the relations between race, crime, and capital punishment must be approached from at least two distinct, but related directions: as a legal question, but also as a *political* question. The continued consensus in favor of the death penalty rests on the state's manipulation of racial anxiety and animus in the service of a project that has very little to do with the actual perpetrators or the actual victims of crime. Its central object is to entrench and extend the technology of modern state power that Jonathan Simon calls "governance through crime."[55] We would do well in this regard to remember the legal realist insight that law is the continuation of politics by other means. The fact that the popular public discussion of the death penalty and racial justice continues to be framed with reference to law and the rule-of-law state does not divest that discourse of its political character and consequences.

Moreover, it should be said straightaway that the political dimension that concerns us here is most emphatically *not* the formal institutional politics of reasoned debate and deliberation. This brings me to a second implication of Scalia's argument. To say that the public discourse on and the state practice of capital punishment is riven by unconscious and irrational forces is to argue for a distinctively *cultural* conception of death penalty politics. In its cultural register, political mobilization against or in favor of the death penalty is not only or not primarily about penal policy and practice. The production and circulation of "meanings and symbols and representations"[56] of crime and punishment addresses the "subjective component of political being"[57] or the "psychic life" of politics.[58] In insisting on the presence and power of the "unconscious" and "irrational," Justice Scalia is in effect arguing that capital punishment is a political field of image, identification, and association. Like politics generally, the popular politics of the death penalty is a politics "in which the way that people 'imagine' themselves occupies a crucial place."[59]

A number of recent studies have noted the extent to which "the statistical overrepresentation of African Americans among violent offenders and victims provides much less of a basis for white fear than the images of black criminality fostered by the media and other sources."[60] In the words of one commentator, the U.S. news media has come to play a decisive role in "increasing fear of crime," in "instilling and reinforcing racial stereotypes," and in "linking race to crime,"[61] not least through the sensationalist specularization of the black male body. Despite falling crime rates, the media's racialization of violent crime at the level of the image (despite falling crime rates) has fueled the shift to more punitive policies that has characterized our criminal justice system in the last couple of decades.

The task of the abolitionist movement is to break the imagined connection between black Americans and crime (a connection, I might note, to which African-Americans themselves are by no means immune). The goal, as I see it, is to "manufacture dissent"—to contest the deadly ideological fantasy that underwrites the racial thanatopolitics of the popular discourse on capital punishment. If they are to meet the resistance to abolition on its own ground, activists opposing the death penalty must begin to take political fantasy seriously. Put another way, the strategy of this abolitionist movement should be to produce new images and identifications that, on the one hand, deracialize crime and, on the other, decriminalize race.

Stephen Duncombe comes very close to the argument I am advancing here in his *Dream: Re-imagining Progressive Politics in an Age of Fantasy*. Although he does not explicitly address the politics of capital punishment, Duncombe urges progressive political activists to learn how to "build a politics that embraces the dreams of people and fashions spectacles which give these fantasies form—a politics that understands desire and speaks to the irrational; a politics that employs symbols and associations; a politics that tells good stories."[62]

Given what I have said about the links between the phantasmatic representation of black masculinity as the very embodiment of the problem of crime and the imagined danger it poses to a U.S. body politic that, more often than not, is figured as white, it seems to me that one of the crucial tasks of abolitionist activism is to mobilize its constituency around a new corporal (punishment) politics.

NOTES

1. I take this phrase from Austin Sarat, *When the State Kills: Capital Punishment and the American Condition* (Princeton: Princeton University Press, 2001).
2. Benjamin Fleury-Steiner and Victor Argothy, "Lethal 'Borders': Elucidating Jurors' Racialized Discipline to Punish in Latino Defendant Death Cases," *Punishment and Society* 6.1, (2004), p. 67; Austin Sarat and Jonathan Simon, "Beyond Legal Realism?: Cultural Analysis, Cultural Studies, and the Situation of Legal Scholarship," *Yale Journal of Law & the Humanities* 13.1, (2001), p. 8.
3. Sarat, *When the State Kills*, p. 22, quoting David Garland, "Punishment and Culture: The Symbolic Dimensions of Criminal Justice," *Studies in Law, Politics, & Society* 11 (1991), p. 191. See also Austin Sarat (ed.), *The Killing State: Capital Punishment in Law, Politics and Culture* (New York: Oxford University Press, 1999).
4. Garland, "Punishment and Culture, p. 193.
5. Liz Garbus, *The Execution of Wanda Jean* (2002).
6. Richard Johnson, "What is Cultural Studies Anyway," *Social Text* 16.1 (Winter 1986–1987), p. 39.
7. *Allen v. State* 1994 ok cr 13 871 P.2d 79, case number: F-89-549, decided: 02/15/1994. *Wanda Jean Allen, Appellant, v. the State of Oklahoma, Appellee*, Oklahoma Court of Criminal Appeals, An Appeal from the District Court of Oklahoma County; Bana Blasdel, District Judge. [871 P.2d 85] http://law.justia.com/cases/oklahoma/court-of-appeals-criminal/1994/11496.html.
8. *Allen v. State of Oklahoma*, 871 P. 2d 79 (Okla. Crim. Ct. App. 1994), p. 87.
9. *Ibid.*, p. 95.
10. *Ibid.*, p.105.
11. Garbus, *The Execution of Wanda Jean*.
12. Richard Goldstein, "Queer on Death Row," *Village Voice*, March 20, 2001, p. 38.
13. *Ibid.*, p. 40.
14. Wahneema Lubiano, "For Race," keynote address presented at Color, Bone, and Hair: The Persistence of Race in the Twenty-First Century, a conference at Bucknell University, September 25, 2002.
15. Jacques Derrida, "Racism's Last Word," trans. Peggy Kamuf, in Peggy Kamuf and Elizabeth Rottenberg (eds.), *Psyche: Inventions of the Other*, vol. 1 (Stanford: Stanford University Press, 2007), p. 379.
16. Paul W. Kahn, *The Cultural Study of Law: Reconstructing Legal Scholarship* (Chicago: University of Chicago Press, 1999).
17. *Ibid.*, p. 30.
18. *Ibid.*, p. 135.
19. Charles Taylor, *Modern Social Imaginaries* (Durham: Duke University Press, 2004).
20. *Ibid.*, p. 23.
21. *Ibid.*
22. *Ibid.*, p. 25.
23. Juliet Mitchell, *Psychoanalysis and Feminism: Freud, Reich, Laing, and Women* (New York: Vintage Books, 1974), p. xiv.
24. David L. Eng, *Racial Castration: Managing Masculinity in Asian America* (Durham: Duke University Press, 2001).
25. *Ibid.*

26. Rey Chow, *The Protestant Ethic and the Spirit of Capitalism* (New York, Columbia University Press, 2002), p. 7. Chow develops this point as part of an argument for the relevance for critical race theory of Michel Foucault's notion of "biopower." Biopolitical logic uses death (or the threat of death) as a form of governance; state killing comes to be seen as a "productive, generative activity" undertaken to preserve and protect the life of collective body politic. *Ibid.*, p. 9. Foucault's innovation lies in the recognition that for biopower, the human body is not merely an instrument or object of governance, but one of its central resources.
27. Elizabeth Grosz, "Lesbian Fetishism?" in Emily Apter and William Pietz, (eds.), *Fetishism as Cultural Discourse* (Ithaca: Cornell University Press, 1993), p. 101.
28. Ron Jenkins, "Wanda Jean Allen Described as a 'Hunter' Who Would Kill Again," Ardmore, OK, *Daily Ardmorite*, no longer available at http://www.ardmoreite.com/stories/100800/new_allen.shtml.
29. Judith Halberstam, *Female Masculinity* (Durham: Duke University Press, 1998).
30. Slavoj Žižek, *The Sublime Object of Ideology* (London: Verso, 1989), p. 33.
31. Kalpana Seshadri-Crooks, *Desiring Whiteness: A Lacanian Analysis of Race* (London: Routledge, 2000), p. 7.
32. This draws upon Frantz Fanon, *Black Skin, White Masks* (New York: Grove Press, 1967), p. 111.
33. Maurice O. Wallace, *Constructing the Black Masculine: Identity and Ideality in African American Men's Literature and Culture, 1775–1995* (Durham: Duke University Press, 2002), p. 31.
34. The U.S. Supreme Court has held that the Fourteenth Amendment requires that minimal due process rights be accorded capital convicts in clemency proceedings. Ohio Adult Parole Authority v. Woodard, 523 U.S. 272 (1998). The *Woodard* Court did not conclude that state capital punishment systems must make clemency available. For a discussion of *Woodard* in the context of women's capital cases see Elizabeth Rapaport, "Staying Alive: Executive Clemency, Equal Protection, and the Politics of Gender in Women's Capital Cases," *Buffalo Criminal Law Review* 4.2 (2001), pp. 967–1004.
35. Paul Gilroy, *Against Race: Imagining Political Culture beyond the Color Line* (Cambridge, MA: Harvard University Press, 2000).
36. Russ Castronovo, *Necro Citizenship: Death, Eroticism, and the Public Sphere in the Nineteenth-Century United States* (Durham: Duke University Press, 2001).
37. Randall Kennedy, *Race, Crime, and the Law* (New York: Pantheon, 1998), p. 17.
38. Dylan Evans, "From Kantian Ethics to Mystical Experience: An Exploration of Jouissance," in Dany Nobus (ed.), *Key Concepts of Lacanian Psychoanalysis* (New York: Other Press, 1999), p. 1.
39. Lauren Berlant, *The Queen of America Goes to Washington City: Essays on Sex and Citizenship* (Durham: Duke University Press, 1997), pp. 59–60.
40. Slavoj Žižek, *Looking Awry: An Introduction to Jacques Lacan through Popular Culture* (Cambridge, MA: The MIT Press, 1991), p. 165.
41. Michael Taussig, "*Maleficium:* State Fetishism," in Apter and Pietz (eds.), *Fetishism as Cultural Discourse*, pp. 216 and 246. Taussig shows how Genet's *Thief's Journal* "writes with clarity and beauty the endless story of [the state and its sexuality], its seductive bodily prowess and the sensuous trafficking between rationality and violence as writ into the Law itself." *Ibid.*, p. 246. Taussig argues that Genet "brought the fetish character of the modern state into a clear and sensual focus." *Ibid.*, p. 240.
42. *Ibid.*, p. 218. "It is to the peculiar sacred and erotic attraction, even thralldom, combined with disgust, which the State holds for its subjects, that I wish to draw attention in drawing the figure of State fetishism. . . . By state fetishism I mean a certain aura of might,

aesthetic-moralistic rendering of the social structure of might."

43. Fredric Jameson, "Pleasure: A Political Issue," in Fredric Jameson, *The Ideologies of Theory, Essays 1971–1986*, vol. 2, *The Syntax of History* (Minneapolis: University of Minnesota Press, 1988), p. 73.
44. Sarat, *When the State Kills*, p. 250.
45. For a useful line of argument in these terms, but in a different context, see Todd McGowan, *The End of Dissatisfaction?: Jacques Lacan and the Emerging Society of Enjoyment* (Albany: State University of New York Press, 2004).
46. David Cole, *No Equal Justice: Race and Class in the American Criminal Justice System* (New York: New Press, 1999), p. 5. "While our criminal justice system is explicitly based on the premise and promise of equality before the law, the administration of criminal law—whether by the officer on the beat, the legislature, or the Supreme Court—is in fact predicated on the exploitation of inequality. My claim is not simply that we have ignored inequality's effects within the criminal justice system, nor that we have tried but failed to achieve equality there. Rather, I contend that our criminal justice system affirmatively depends on inequality." *Ibid.*
47. Achille Mbembe, *On the Postcolony* (Berkeley: University of California Press, 2001), pp. 112–13, 115, 126.
48. 481 U.S. 279 (1987).
49. Anthony G. Amsterdam, "Race and the Death Penalty before and after McCleskey," *Columbia Human Rights Law Review* 39.1 (Fall 2007), pp. 34 and 37.
50. Memorandum to the Conference from Justice Antonin Scalia in No. 84-6811-McCleskey v. Kemp of January 6, 1987. *McCleskey v. Kemp* File, Thurgood Marshall Papers, The Library of Congress, Washington, D.C.
51. *Ibid.*
52. Dennis D. Dorin, "Far Right of the Mainstream: Racism, Rights, and Remedies from the Perspective of Justice Antonin Scalia's McCleskey Memorandum," *Mercer Law Review* 45.3 (Spring 1994), pp. 1035 and 1039.
53. Stephen B. Bright, "Discrimination, Death and Denial: Race and the Death Penalty," in David R. Dow and Mark Dow (eds.), *Machinery of Death: The Reality of America's Death Penalty Regime* (New York: Routledge, 2002), p. 47.
54. Emphasis supplied.
55. Jonathan Simon, *Governing through Crime: How the War on Crime Transformed American Democracy and Created a Culture of Fear* (Oxford: Oxford University Press, 2009).
56. Garland, "Punishment and Culture," p. 193.
57. Jacqueline Rose, *States of Fantasy* (Oxford: Oxford University Press, 1993), p. 10.
58. See Judith Butler, *The Psychic Life of Power: Theories in Subjection* (Stanford: Stanford University Press, 1997).
59. Jacqueline Rose, "Margaret Thatcher and Ruth Ellis," in *Why War?—Psychoanalysis, Politics, and the Return to Melanie Klein* (Oxford: Blackwell, 1993), p. 45.
60. Darnell F. Hawkins, "The Nations Within: Race, Class, Region, and American Lethal Violence," *University of Colorado Law Review* 69.4 (1998), p. 910.
61. Sara Sun Beale, "The News Media's Influence on Criminal Justice Policy: How Market-Driven News Promotes Punitiveness," *William and Mary Law Review* 48.2 (2006), p. 398.
62. Stephen Duncombe, *Dream: Re-imagining Progressive Politics in an Age of Fantasy* (New York: New Press, 2007), p. 9.

FIGURE 1 The Langenort, a ship rented for use by Women on Waves, with the mobile clinic aboard, in the Netherlands just before embarking to Poland, 2003 (photo: Willem Velthoven © Women on Waves Foundation).

Women, Waves, Web

Carrie Lambert-Beatty

Squint, and you can see the boat as sculpture. Its base is a workaday tugboat, to which a single shipping container—the kind usually found stacked on much bigger ships—is conjoined. Contrast is the formal principle of this large-scale assemblage. The boat has a dented hull and bristles with utilitarian antennae and railings. But the box perched on its deck—a striated block in a very pale blue—has the stripped-down gleam of contemporary design. It also has design's communicative savvy. Its side is emblazoned with a purple spot on which, in turn, floats an orange shape outlined in pink: a squared cross of the kind that symbolizes humanitarian and medical aid, turned into a boat and sent to sea.[1]

Of course, as the emblem suggests, the hybrid object photographed in the Netherlands in 2002 is no sculpture, but the vessel of an activist human rights initiative (fig. 1). In fact, viewing the boat aesthetically might seem beside the point, for its mission was literally a matter of life and death: to offer safe, legal abortions to women who might otherwise be among the sixty-eight thousand who die each year from unsafe attempts to terminate pregnancies.[2] The boat was operated by a nongovernmental organization founded in 1999 by Dutch physician Rebecca Gomperts. Called Women on Waves, the NGO's first action was to transform a shipping container into a fully functional mobile gynecological clinic. In 2001, Gomperts began strapping the unit to rented ships and sailing to countries that criminalize abortion. The plan: to dock, take aboard local women, and sail them twelve miles out to sea. Twelve miles is, in most cases, the limit of a nation's territorial waters. Beyond that invisible line, Gomperts had realized, the ship's doctors could legally offer all the advice and treatment available in a liberal nation such as the Netherlands—including abortion, for it is Dutch law that governs a ship registered in the Netherlands afloat in international waters. In the years following, Women on Waves boats embarked for Ireland (2001), Poland (2003), Portugal (2004), Ecuador (2008), and

Spain (2008), bringing the Netherlands to the shores—or at least to twelve miles from the shores—of countries where abortion, information on abortion, and even contraception were difficult to access.[3]

For Gomperts and Women on Waves, abortion is a human rights issue, and the project is powered by its urgency. Studies make it clear that criminalizing abortion does not eliminate the practice or even significantly reduce its rate; what it does accomplish is to increase unsafe abortions.[4] Every year, at least two million women sustain lasting injury in what writers in the medical journal the *Lancet* dubbed "the preventable pandemic." The majority of these casualties are poor women in impoverished parts of the world who can afford neither quality illegal care at home nor "abortion tourism" to more liberal countries.[5] No statistic gives a better sense of what is at stake for Women on Waves, however, than the stories told by the women who called its hotline during each of its voyages: the Polish woman who could not afford the next day's meals for the two children she had already and who had been jumping off furniture in hopes of miscarrying; or the woman, still bleeding as she talked on the phone, who had taken an unknown drug in an attempt to self-abort and whose doctor only offered to sew shut her cervix to stop the miscarriage; or the less dramatic, but no less distressing stories of the many women who left messages like this one: "You are my last chance to live as I've planned.... I'm still counting on you. Help me please, I'm desperate."[6]

Inspired by Doctors Without Borders and Greenpeace (for which Gomperts was for a time a ship's medic), Women on Waves responded to such calls with a fully functional medical clinic, two physicians and a nurse, an almost entirely female ship's crew, and networks of local volunteers, all backed by years of planning and research. In port, in addition to running a local hotline for women to call for advice and help, it offered legal and medical workshops, sex education, and contraception. On the way out to sea, it offered sonograms and counseling, and in international waters, it provided the abortion pill to women who wanted it. The group's missions were controversial enough to earn its doctors and volunteers not only bombardment with eggs and paint, but also court cases and death threats. Women on Waves was radical enough in its challenge to national sovereignty to move the Portuguese government in 2004 literally to launch warships to protect its populace from the feminist invasion.

I've said it might seem absurd to approach this lifesaving and health-saving mission in aesthetic terms. But to show that it isn't, in the particular case of Women on Waves, and that it shouldn't be, as the lesson of Women on Waves shows—these are the goals of this essay. Women on Waves is as much an expressive as a political act. Outraged critics call Women on Waves "just a publicity stunt," and they are not altogether wrong. With its photogenic ship, daring feminist heroines, and nearly guaranteed counterdemonstrations, each campaign is a media intervention on a grand scale. Gomperts speaks movingly of the help provided to individual women during her ventures, but she doesn't hide the boat's essentially communicative function. In fact, Women on Waves is a perfect example of what Daniel Boorstin famously called a "pseudo-event," something, like a press conference or a "grand opening" ceremony that happens in order to be reported upon. That Women on Waves missions are events of this kind became particularly clear in 2008, when a Women on Waves ship bound for Ecuador was beached by a tropical storm. The main question on everyone's mind, according to the campaign's online diary, wasn't how they would provide the promised abortions without a boat, but "how can we launch the hotline without the attention that the ship would bring?"[7]

Élise Vallois gave a vivid and useful description of Women on Waves in *Nongovernmental Politics*, detailing its means and ends.[8] What I'd like to add in this companion volume is an exploration of what its means mean. To consider this case within the rubric of the media of nongovernmental politics does two nearly contradictory things: it counters the sense that an NGO must be measured by its efficacy and at the same time insists on the efficacy of work done at the level of the image. Some commentators have treated Women on Waves as a humanitarian relief organization that innovatively provides abortions for women whose other alternatives would be unsafe. Others have assumed the abortions provided are merely bait to draw protesters and press. But Women on Waves is a complicated knot of image and efficacy, and it is as such that it is important for a discussion of the media of nongovernmental politics. Simply put, Women on Waves demonstrates the inadequacy of a certain set of oppositions: "actually doing," and "just talking," activism and representation, physicality and information, politics and media. This has become increasingly evident since 2006, when, as I'll discuss below, the Internet began to replace the sea as the project's primary arena for action. But it was true from the earliest days of Women on Waves and the group's inception at what might seem an unlikely intersection: of feminism, humanitarianism, seafaring, and conceptual art.

ART MATTERS

In founding Women on Waves, one of Rebecca Gomperts's first steps was to commission a well-known Dutch artist named Joep van Lieshout to design and build the shipping container/clinic she planned to use at sea. No run-of-the-mill designer, Lieshout was an enfant terrible of the international art world, whose work took form, variously, as munitions factories, plumbing, and sex chambers. These last were sometimes constructed out of trailers and shipping containers, making him a practical choice for Gomperts. (Lieshout was likely attracted to the project's flouting of national law—his most ambitious work is AVL-Ville, a compound in Rotterdam he declared a "free state.") Following Gomperts's instructions, Lieshout outfitted the container with an ultrasound machine, stirruped examining table, and vacuum aspirator. His design also met her requirement that the space be as pleasant and comfortable as possible, with a private consulting area and an interior washed in a soothing blue. The design for the clinic—he called it the A-Portable—soon had its debut, not at sea, but in an exhibition at the Witte de With Center for Contemporary Art.[9] The grant that then provided the bulk of the money to construct it—and thus seed money for the project as a whole—did not come from the Dutch Health Ministry, the World Health Organization, Ipas, or Planned Parenthood. It came from the Mondriaan Foundation.[10]

But the engagement with art did not stop there. While in port, Women on Waves held workshops aboard the "abortion boat" for local professionals whom Gomperts felt were essential for the politics of reproductive rights: lawyers and doctors, artists and writers. Curators and art critics quickly seized on the project, featuring it in exhibitions such as Ute Meta Bauer's *Women Building* in Portugal and in a dedicated show at the Mediamatic art space in Amsterdam. It was featured in *Artforum* magazine and counted by art critic Claire Bishop among notable examples of recent political art.[11] In 2001 it even made an appearance in what is arguably the art world's most prestigious venue, bobbing in the waters at the Venice Biennale.

These intersections with the modes, traditions, and institutions of art are not coincidental. While she was in medical school and before the stint as a ship's doctor for Greenpeace during which she came up with the idea for Women on Waves, Gomperts, a polymath (she is also a published novelist), completed a four-year art degree at Amsterdam's Rietveld Academie, studying conceptual art.[12] Gomperts no longer identifies herself as an artist, but in 2003, she and her partner, the artist and critic Willem Velthoven, began exhibiting a series of multimedia installations that document the abortion boat trips.[13] In a video projection called *Sea*, for instance, the voices of women who called the boat's hotline in 2001 play over images of the open ocean. Other projects used the language and spaces of contemporary art to promote Gomperts's vision of a normalized and safe abortion policy for all women. For instance, minidresses designed by Dutch-Brazillian artist Renata Andrade were displayed on hangers (fig. 2). Each dress bears on one side a red circle and on the other the text "I had an abortion" in one of the twenty-three official languages of the European Union. Savvy in terms of art and design history, the display nods to

FIGURE 2 *I Had an Abortion* (2003). Installation designed by Willem Velthoven, at the Macedonian Museum of Contemporary Art, Thessaloniki, Greece (photo: Willem Velthoven © Women on Waves Foundation).

the modernist Man Ray, who made and photographed a mobile of coat hangers in 1920–21; to pro-choice agitprop in which the hanger symbolizes illegal, back-alley abortions; and to the history of open letters such as the famous 1971 French "Manifesto of the 343" in which prominent women fought stigmatization by publicly proclaiming "I had an abortion."[14]

All of this of course raises the question: Is Women on Waves art, itself? Boorstin famously borrowed the then-new art category of the Happening as a synonym for the "pseudo-event," and Women on Waves certainly lends itself to interpretation of the kind more usual for performance, theater, or films than for an NGO. Start with the act of radical imagination at the core of the project: the idea that the dominion of one nation-state over the bodies of its female population could be evaded by a short trip on a boat registered in another. It is outrageous in its simplicity as well as in its implications. (What's next, one wonders: cannabis cruises? Euthanasia yachts?) But using international waters as a refuge for women's rights, in particular, unfurls further, into a poetic series of associations. It literalizes the metaphor of waves used to describe generations of feminism and links it to ancient images that associate dangerous female power and the sea, from sirens and mermaids to female pirates Ann Bonny and Mary Read. Meanwhile, it takes on the traditional associations of women and ships, invariably referred to as "she." To mention a ship's "berth" in this context may only be a weak pun, but not the connection between the female body, defined in terms of its reproductive capacity, and a seagoing vessel, both expected to "deliver." In the eighteenth century, in fact, shipwrecks were sometimes called miscarriages.[15] (The beached Women on Waves boat on the way to Ecuador was certainly accidental—but perfectly in keeping with the project's poetics.)

To define Women on Waves as art, one could claim, pragmatically, that it is not the essence of an object that determines what is and isn't art, but its context (following the lesson of Duchamp's infamous *Fountain*—a commercially manufactured urinal submitted to an art exhibition in 1917). One could also turn to Joseph Beuys's model of "social sculpture," introduced in the mid-1960s and encountered by Gomperts as an art student. Beuys, a combination of sculptor, shaman, and showman, proposed that by a kind of conceptual alchemy, anything already is art, and he used this notion to encourage creative solutions to social and political problems. One could also slip Women on Waves into the special category of activist art, which has been used, since it began to be theorized by critics such as Lucy Lippard in the 1980s,[16] to hold open a space for the fusion of work that is symbolic with work that is social. Activist art was explicitly the topic of the workshop for artists held aboard the Women on Waves ship in Ireland in 2001,[17] and it is likely the rising interest in this category at the time that allowed so many arts organizations and institutions to support Women on Waves: while geopolitically, the early 2000s was a period of political retrenchment and imperialist incursion, art-historically, it emerged as a thriving period for socially and politically engaged art.

Yet I am not arguing that Women on Waves "is art," even art of this special kind. For one thing, the term "activist art" depends on a contrast with "political art": the latter is supposed to represent political subject matter, while the former tries actually to create change. But Women on Waves, I'm arguing, rejects the distinction between representation and action. Moreover, as important as it has been for legitimating, theorizing, and promoting politically engaged practice, the category of activist art may obscure the nature of many of the most productive and provocative practices at the crossing of its terms: projects that do not hybridize art and activism so much as they play on their ambiguous separation or arrange provisional encounters between them—a provisionality to which the visual mismatch of Women on Waves's boat and the container atop it give visual form. Women on Waves is not art, nor is it not art. Nor does it "blur the boundaries," as clichéd discussions of "art and politics" would have it. Rather, like light as wave and particle, it is both, but never quite at once. It tacks between art and politics in much the same way that it moves between a human rights mission and a media-political campaign, legality and piracy, fact and myth.

PERFORMATIVITY AND PLAUSIBILITY

"Under the cobblestones, the beach," read the graffito on the streets of Paris in May 1968. "Twelve miles from the beach, the Netherlands," Women on Waves might respond, for the project is driven by a similar determination to replace what is with what could be. But understanding Women on Waves in terms of its media, or even in terms of what we might call its aesthetics, depends on its difference from the 1960s vision. Instead of the vague image of liberation, it imagines something concrete: a world in which women have access to safe and legal abortion, no matter where they live. Rather than symbolically promoting change, the project's method is to make it so: to use maritime law and the concept of international waters actually to create—however temporarily and provisionally—the dreamed-of situation. This, the "performative" quality of Women on Waves, was captured in 2001 by critic Jennifer Allen. The project "does not thematise, represent, nor illustrate the problem of abortion," she wrote, "it imposes a new geo-political reality that challenges [the] status quo in ways that cannot be fathomed, let alone controlled."[18]

In this sense, Women on Waves's missions do not only generate speech, they are speech—speech of a particular kind. In speech-act theory, a "performative" is a statement such as "I christen this ship." It is nonrepresentational: such a statement doesn't so much describe something as do something. A performative, in this sense, is a kind of bridge concept between representation and action—not unlike Women on Waves itself.

A performative can't be judged to be true or untrue. It must be judged to be successful or unsuccessful. J. L. Austin, the philosopher who first proposed this category, called a failed performative utterance "unhappy."[19] An example of an unhappy performative is a bet made within a play or, closer to the current case, the notorious act of media infiltration in which, during a live cable newscast in 2004, an activist pretending to be a spokesperson for Dow Chemical took legal responsibility in the name of the corporation for the twenty-year-old disaster at Bhopal. Just as a wager agreed to within a play would not bind the actors offstage, the performative utterance "Dow takes responsibility" is "unhappy" in the mouth of an imposter—in this case, a member of the Yes Men, brilliant pranksters of the movement opposing corporate globalization.

Women on Waves calls its operations "campaigns": the Yes Men call theirs "hijinks." And it would at first seem that their versions of the performative are similarly opposed: When Women on Waves conjures the condition of safe and legal abortion for women in a particular country, it is "successfully" or "happily" performed. (The pregnancies are terminated, safely and legally.) But of course, it is more complicated than that. While they do not have the authority to make real the changes they announce on behalf of a corporation, the prankster Yes Men nevertheless have real effects—on Dow's stock price that day in 2004, for example, and residually, on the kind of attention given to corporate speech. Though a performative uttered by an imposter or within a play might be "infelicitous," it can also put into question its "happier" counterparts: it helps us recognize the normal newscast and corporate spokesmanship as also a kind of theater—much as the boat's crossing of an invisible border reveals the arbitrariness of national sovereignty.[20]

Women on Waves lists toward the unhappy performative more than one might think. In its role as an NGO, it aims to help women by giving them the option of safe, legal abortion. But the fact is that its campaigns to provide legal abortions have often been thoroughly thwarted. Licensing and other technicalities kept them from giving any abortion-related treatments during the pilot program's voyage to Ireland.[21] Later, with its claim that the ship posed a threat to national security worthy of deploying its navy, the government of Portugal was able to prevent Women on Waves from coming ashore at all.[22] Even the clinic displayed at the Venice Biennale turns out to have been a functionless decoy, because in summer 2001, the actual container was on its way to Ireland.

Recognizing the limits of currently available options, politicians often quote Otto von Bismarck's quip that politics is the "art of the possible." In quite another register, global justice and anticorporate activists have united under the World Social Forum's motto "another world is possible."[23] Between these two senses of possibility—the resignation to current conditions and the imagination of utterly different ones—the Yes Men and Women on Waves meet. Call it "the art of the plausible." By providing opportunities for belief, however fleeting and no matter how often stymied, tactics of plausibility provide especially rich, emotional experiences of "What if." It is always possible that Dow will have a change of heart; what the Yes Men did is make us, for a moment, believe it had happened. And this politics or aesthetics of plausibility is also the function of the handful of abortion pills that Gomperts and her crew have actually managed to dispense.

The bodily care that Women on Waves provides anchors its representational work. At the same time, the space it opens for imagination inflates that bodily care with belief-changing potential. To put it another way, in the art of the plausible, imagination takes on a measure of responsibility.

WAVES AND WEB

"Pirate abortionists," the leader of a right-wing American antiabortion group labeled Women on Waves activists in 2000.[24] Despite the fact that it was lobbed within an inflammatory statement—not a ship had yet sailed—and that the NGO's seafaring campaigns were in fact scrupulously, technically legal, it is not surprising that this epithet has had sticking power among both critics and supporters of Women on Waves. To call Gomperts a "pirate" is to call attention to the simultaneously political and poetic significance of her project as a maritime adventure. It's not just because they are picturesque that the Women on Waves boats draw attention, after all, but because of the nerve they strike in crossing the invisible line of sovereignty, in evading, even negating national jurisdiction. As warlike acts committed on the high seas by nonstate actors, piracy is the image for the maritime as the nonjurisdictional. Though technically Women on Waves boats only passed from Polish or Irish jurisdiction to Dutch, the concept of international waters that allows that transfer of sovereignty is both central to and destabilizing for a global order oriented toward deregulation and transnationality, on the one hand, and security and policing, on the other.

Piracy is also the quintessential crime of the Internet, whose transnationalism and fluidity lend themselves so well to maritime images, such as nets or surfing. The World Wide Web's indeterminate borders, uncertain jurisdiction, and manifold opportunities for hiding, hijacking, and disguise—not to mention rumor and romanticization—have encouraged a transfer of pirate imagery from the high seas to high technology. (In fact, the equation of informational theft and maritime crime dates back to the early eighteenth century.) The first legal challenge faced by Women on Waves was to protect themselves from a version of Internet piracy: the hijacking of their URL by an antiabortion group that linked it to inflammatory images of aborted late-term fetuses. Winning the case, Women on Waves went on to use the Internet skillfully, with a website full of press-quality photographs, up-to-date, detailed accounts of the group's exploits, and links to related news stories. But it was in April 2006 that a new cultural synapse linking the Internet, piracy, the ocean, and abortion was fired with the appearance of a new entity: Women on Web.

Distinct from but linked to Women on Waves, Women on Web is an entirely online operation. It has a bifurcated home page, asking the viewer to identify with one of two subject positions: the title "I had an abortion" appears on one side, "I need an abortion" on the other.[25] Not surprisingly, the latter has received the most attention, for it opens onto an online counseling and referral service for women in early pregnancy who don't have access to legal, safe services. Women on Web essentially practices telemedicine, using an interactive form to give women information about medical abortion and to determine their eligibility for the procedure (less than nine weeks gestational age, no history of bleeding disorders, and so on). After further communication online or by phone, if the woman is a candidate for medical abortion, but can't obtain the drugs mifepristone and misoprostol from local pharmacies, Women on Web sends them the pills in a package.

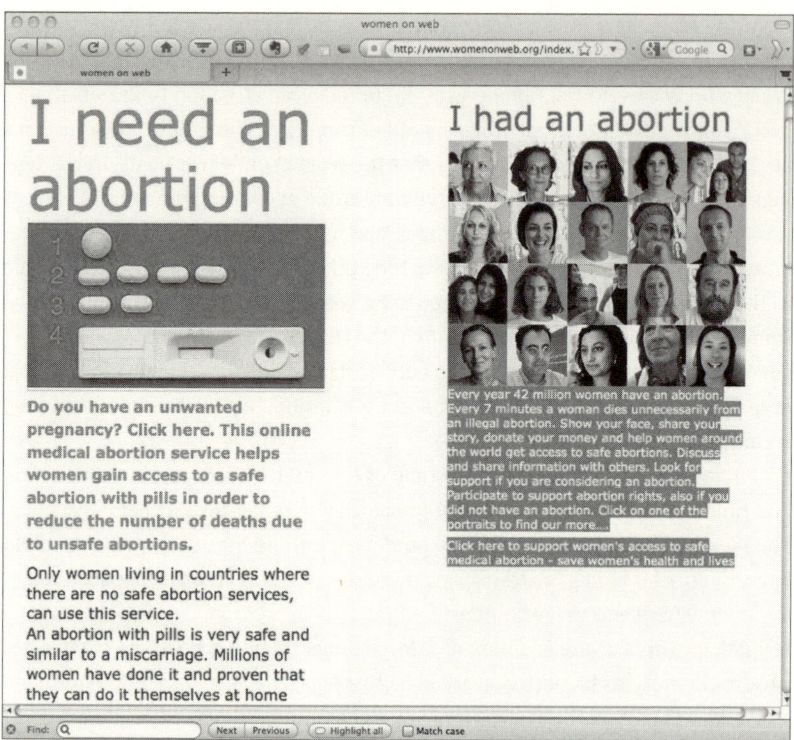

FIGURE 3 Women on Waves website (http://www.womenonweb.org/).

Previously, it could be said that Women on Waves used the real space of bodies and borders to do representational work; now the seemingly disembodied, representational space of the Internet allows Women on Web to give actual care (fig. 3). In fact, both WOW projects recognize that the increasingly prevalent practice of terminating pregnancy with drugs, rather than surgery, draws the educational and the medical closely together. More and more, abortion becomes a matter of information. One of the group's simplest, but most incisive projects is a sticker downloadable in fifteen languages from the Women on Waves website and designed to be surreptitiously left in public places. It contains the complete directions for inducing a miscarriage with the ulcer drug misoprostol.

"I had an abortion" would seem far less scandalous. It is a continuation of a gallery installation Gomperts refers to as the *Portrait Collector*, in which women are invited to post a photograph of themselves, along with descriptions of their abortion experiences and their feelings about them. (If they choose not to post a photograph, a fashionably modeled image of one of Andrade's T-shirts appears, instead.) Viewable as either a mosaic of faces or a database, the *Portrait Collector* invites women to join the legacy of "the 343" and to forward its still-unattained goal: a shift in the perception of abortion from an aberrance and tragedy to a common life experience. (It is, after all, among the most prevalent medical procedures on earth.) This was a stated part of the mission of Women on Waves from the beginning, but as Jennifer Doyle has pointed out, like much pro-choice discourse, the project may have undercut this goal. Surely there is nothing ordinary about a service provided by the "abortion boat," surrounded by demonstrations and counterdemonstrations, if not by naval ships or motorboat vigilantes. Moreover, the women who avail themselves of the service are perhaps unavoidably cast as victims—"I'm desperate"—in need of protection and disguise. (From another point of view, they may be heroines, but this characterization reverses the victim role without undermining it.)

The word "portrait" puts the emphasis on the artistic aspect of "I had an abortion." Indeed, the *Portrait Collector* fits in the lineage of the history of photography: as a collection of photographic portraits, it plays on the accusatory, classifying, and collating function of the photographic archive—think police mug shots—that has accompanied photography since its invention.[26] But it also is in the legacy of conceptual art, from Douglas Huebler's *Variable Piece #70 (In Process) Global*, consisting of the attempt "to photographically document the existence of everyone alive," to a project such as Carla Williams's *How to Read Character*, which involves rerendering objectifying ethnographic photographs of racial "others" as honorific self-portraits. But the accomplishment of the *Portrait Collector* as art is inseparable from its siting at Women on Web: searchable by the nationality, religion, or even type of emotional response, the collective project is a source of information and support for women whose relation to abortion is more present than past tense.

There's one detail about the *Portrait Collector* that bears special mention. Among the portraits—and included in the mosaic that is the project's immediate public image—there are several photographs of men. What happens when someone who appears male occupies the subject position in the sentence "I had an abortion"? One function is to be something of a decoy, not unlike Women on Waves volunteers who covered their hair and wore sunglasses to board the boat during missions so that it was impossible to tell who was staff and who was there to undergo an abortion. Male faces in the *Portrait Collector* raise the possibility that anyone in the collection might be lying about their past experience, providing cover for those who might feel fearful about this pubic gesture. But more significantly, the male faces visibly raise the possibility that the meaning of the terms "had," "abortion," and even "I" might be more complicated than they seem, for when they record their stories, the men who add their faces to the *Portrait Collector* are generally sincere in feeling that they have had an abortion, that it was an experience they shared with their partner. They thus announce and perform a shift in the understanding of the subject of abortion from singular to plural and from unproblematically "female" to something more complex. If on the one hand this shift could be taken in troubling legal directions (like paternal consent), it also instantiates a different culture around abortion—and therefore maternity, gender, and subjectivity itself. As Jennifer Doyle has argued, Women on Waves stops short of "queering abortion discourse," staying largely within patterns of liberal humanism as it grounds the struggle against punitive antiabortion law in concepts of human rights and privacy, in a woman's self-determination, and thus in a fundamentally autonomous, humanist model of subjectivity. Doyle offers, as an alternative, Mary Poovey's call for an alternative abortion politics, veritably pictured by Women on Web, that "would emphasize not the ways in which subjects are isolatable, autonomous, centered individuals, but the ways in which each person has conflicting interests and complex ties to other, apparently autonomous individuals with similar (and different) needs and interests."[27]

ART, ACTIVISM, AND AUTONOMY

The category of activist art starts from the belief that the aesthetic is not a retreat from the real, but is in and of it.[28] It is peculiar, then, that in the most striking crossings of art and activism, the idea of art's imbrication in the world meets an opposing model: that of art's autonomy.[29]

Consider the case of the Austrian collective WochenKlausur, which beginning in the mid-1990s used art exhibitions as opportunities to develop creative forms of civic service. In 1995, the group took on the problem of Austria's strict and quota-driven immigration law and managed to provide seven refugees legal residency in the country by getting them new professional identities as artists—an employment category for which there was no quota.[30] This project recalls the attitude of van Lieshout, the Dutch artist who designed the Women on Waves clinic and whose own practice has culminated in the founding of his own city—that is, in reworking the idea of art's autonomy in the register of separatism, or even survivalism. Allen paraphrases him this way: "Since the state usually respects the autonomy of aesthetics, why not use art to take over the world?"[31] WochenKlausur might not use the same kind of language, but its members, too, trade on the fact that art's special status leaves it less regulated than other forms of employment or production.

Less regulated than seafaring, for example—as occurred to Gomperts and her crew in a moment of crisis during the abortion boat's pilot mission. Almost immediately upon setting sail for Ireland in 2001, the crew was radioed from their Dutch port to stop and unload the shipping container because adding a medical clinic to the ship had voided its inspection certificate. Thinking quickly, Women on Waves explained to the officials that the container was not a medical facility, but a work of art. Calls were made and documents faxed to confirm the artistic pedigree, and the boat was allowed to continue to Ireland. I started this article considering the abortion boat, rather tendentiously, as a kind of sculpture, and Women on Waves here did the same. What's crucial, however, is that as opposed to the activist-art model of expanding art's reach to include action in the world, here, art is tactically configured as a space apart: a not quite real and thus somewhat extra-legal sphere that provides activism a safe harbor.

We want to eat our cake and have it, too, those of us who believe in a political or activist art. We do not accept that art is an apolitical space apart from worldly pressures, and yet we want it to be a zone of special freedom. This is either an embarrassing lapse or, as Jacques Rancière would suggest, a structuring paradox for art today. According to Rancière, there is a constant tension in modernity "between the logic of art that becomes life at the price of abolishing itself as art, and the logic of art that does politics on the explicit condition of not doing it at all."[32] But consider a corollary: the possibility that the category of activist art is not just defined against, but actively requires a nonactivist counterpart—it needs borders around art so that it might sail through them or so that, as Rancière puts it, "the border be always there yet already crossed."[33] Women on Waves is fascinating because it embodies both sides of the paradox. If one lesson of Women on Waves is that aesthetics does not equate with frivolity—that to look and think aesthetically is to look and think politically—another is that precisely to ensure this power, a distinction between art and nonart must be maintained. Even as it demonstrates the inadequacy of the opposition between activism and art, between action and representation, it requires them to be distinct. It opens art to real action in the world, but does so precisely by using art, and thus constructing it, as a space apart.[34] Indeed, one of the striking things about Women on Waves is the parallel between the boat as a place that provides temporary escape from a nation's law and the art world as a place where normal regulations do not quite apply.

From the model of seafaring it deploys to the model of the temporary autonomous zone it makes use of; from its heuristic use of art's spaces, funding, and legal status to its epistemological strategy of plausibility; from its strapped-on clinic to its repurposing of misoprostol, Women on Waves is based on tactics—one could almost call them "formal choices"—of the temporary, the expedient, and the mobile. But this very taste for the provisional—which is also a worldview—is what allows Women on Waves to trade on and thus to reinforce the model of art as a separate sphere that it would seem designed to oppose. Women on Waves is a border exercise in many senses. It treats the border between art and political action much the way it treats the invisible line between Polish territory, say, and international waters: as both fictional and consequential.

FREE FLOATING

This suggests one final aspect of the art and politics of Women on Waves.[35] Critics have been quick to identify colonialist undertones in the project's central image: a Dutch ship sailing to foreign lands to promote social and cultural change. It took an antiabortion Dutch health minister to accuse Women on Waves of treating Poland like a "banana republic," but even the staunchest pro-choice partisan may find disturbing symbolism in its mission.[36] It should be noted that Women on Waves comes to a country at the invitation of local pro-choice groups and that to provide an option is not the same as to enforce an ideology or take possession of a territory.[37] But the real weakness of the colonialist critique is that it misidentifies the ideological implications of a basic assumption underlying the project: that violent invasion, occupation, and enforcement are not necessary when invitation, transportation, and provision of options will do instead.

If the project has a political unconscious, it is not colonialist, but neoliberal. There is an uncomfortable rhyme between the strategic retreat to international waters to escape local laws and the offshoring by which corporations evade taxes and national laws. Aren't the hallmarks of globalization precisely the weakening of national sovereignty and the ability to shake off regulation, as in the concept of the free trade zone, where bits of land are freed from the law of the countries to which they belong, as if themselves set afloat? And isn't there something very much of its time in the realization that for maximum flexibility and efficiency, an abortion clinic could be housed in a shipping container, that steel box so indispensable to the post–World War II reorientation of trade that Allan Sekula dubbed it "the very coffin of remote labor power"?[38]

It might be said, then, that Gomperts's project makes use of old maritime law while partaking of a newer model of sovereignty. But let me be clear: to recognize such parallels is not to call the women who have risked their safety and freedom in this attempt to better the lives of their sisters neoimperialists. If anything, they might be said to wear the forms of economic globalization—from container shipping to legal loopholes—the way pranksters use the dominant system to their own progressive ends. Nevertheless, while Women on Waves works on the politics of reproductive rights, it works within the politics of globalization.

The axes on which this project makes its multiple turns have emerged as some of the most important for the new century. Information access and epistemology; national sovereignty and globalization; secularism and religion; aesthetics and activism. Each of these becomes, here, literally a matter of life and death. The very need for a project like Women on Waves gives the lie to the image of free-flowing information and fluid borders that characterizes globalization ideology: when you cannot tell a woman how to get an abortion without fear of imprisonment because of the side of the border on which you sit, or when you cannot afford a trip from Ireland to Britain or from Poland to Germany to avail yourself of more liberal abortion laws, the idea that national sovereignty and geographical boundaries are no longer primary determinants of power seems a ludicrous abstraction. What interests me, however, is that globalization's modes and rhetoric themselves might be a condition for the project's central innovation, in which a way around national sovereignty aboard a free-floating piece of territory was imagined—and mobilized—as a solution. Here again, politics and aesthetics tangle, for the underlying logic of the otherwise regulated space links not only free-trade zone and abortion boat, but the spheres of art and politics, as well.

NOTES

This is a substantially revised version of my article "Twelve Miles: The Borders of Art and Activism," *Signs* (Winter 2008). It has been updated in light of the ways the Women on Waves project has changed in the subsequent years. I'm grateful to the many interlocutors who have responded to talks I've given on this subject, to the editors of *Signs*, and especially to the students who have explored these questions with me.

1. The logo was designed by Kees Ryter in 2001.
2. The number is from UNFPA (United Nations Population Fund), "Contraception: Reducing Risks by Offering Contraceptive Services," United Nations Population Fund, n.d., http://www.unfpa.org/public/home/mothers/pid/4382. See also Susan A. Cohen, "Envisioning Life without Roe: Lessons without Borders," *The Guttmacher Report on Public Policy* 6.2 (May 2003), pp. 3–5; World Health Organization, *Unsafe Abortion: Global and Regional Estimates of the Incidence of Unsafe Abortion and Associated Mortality in 2000*, 4th ed. (Geneva: World Health Organization, 2004), http://whqlibdoc.who.int/publications/2004/9241591803.pdf; and David A. Grimes, Janie Benson, Susheela Singh, Mariana Romero, Bela Ganatra, Friday E. Okonofua, and Iqbal H. Shah. "Unsafe Abortion: The Preventable Pandemic." *Lancet* 368.9550 (November 2006), pp. 1908–19, 2006.
3. All the nations visited were those in which abortion was illegal or extremely limited. Portugal was among the most restrictive countries—one of the few in Europe actually to prosecute women for having abortions—when Women on Waves attempted to visit, but a new government in February 2007 passed by 59 percent a referendum legalizing abortion if performed

during the first ten weeks of pregnancy. (The cutoff in other European countries ranges from twelve to twenty-four weeks). Although low voter turnout was considered to invalidate the referendum, in March 2007, parliament voted to enact the new, more liberal abortion regulation.

4. According to the United Nations Population Fund, comparative statistics show that criminalizing abortion has little effect on the prevalence of the practice: "More than one quarter of pregnancies worldwide, about 52 million annually, end in abortion. This is the proportion in Latin America, where abortion is generally illegal, as well as in the United States and China, where the procedure is legally available." UNFPA, "Contraception." See also Cohen, "Envisioning Life without Roe"; World Health Organization, *Unsafe Abortion*, and Grimes et al., "Unsafe Abortion." The Netherlands, with free access to contraception and abortion on request, has had one of the lowest abortion rates in the world. Stanley K. Henshaw, Susheela Singh, and Taylor Haas, "The Incidence of Abortion Worldwide," *International Family Planning Perspectives* 25, supplement (January 1999), pp. S30–S38.
5. Grimes et al., "Unsafe Abortion." See also Cohen "Envisioning Life without Roe"; and World Health Organization, *Unsafe Abortion*.
6. Women on Waves, "Quotes and Emails," Women on Waves, http://www.womenonwaves.org/article-1020.284-en.html, n.d.; see also Women on Waves, "Calling: What the Locals Say on the Phone," Women on Waves, June 21, 2003. http://www.womenonwaves.org/article-1020.134-en.html, and "Kremlin, Acropolis, Eiffel Tower, Langenort! Abortion Boat Latest Tourist Attraction," Women on Waves, July 2, 2003. http://www.womenonwaves.org/article-1020.442-en.html. Many of the women who tried to make use of Women on Waves's services were poor. Though the majority of deaths from unsafe abortions occur in the Global South, the lack of options for poor women even in countries such as Ireland, where middle-class and wealthy women can access abortion relatively easily by traveling outside their national borders, is one of the crucial facts Women on Waves was able to publicize through its campaigns. There are more quotations from the hotline on the Women on Waves Web site, http://www.womenonwaves.org, and in Rebecca Gomperts, *Women on Waves* (Amsterdam: Women on Waves, 2002).
7. Women on Waves, "Ecuador Diary: Trainings and Preparations, June 15, 2008," http://www.womenonwaves.org/article-1625-en.html. Note that even here, the question of "getting attention" and providing service remain intertwined: the hotline would be the means for Ecuadorian women to avail themselves of advice and assistance.
8. Élise Vallois, "Naval Battle: A Profile of Women on Waves," in Michel Feher (ed.), with Gaëlle Krikorian and Yates McKee, *Nongovernmental Politics* (New York: Zone Books, 2007), pp. 482–85.
9. *Play-use*, at the Witte de With Center for Contemporary Art Rotterdam, Netherlands, July 9–September 24, 2000.
10. The Feminist Majority later contributed to the project by sending experts to provide security during the Poland trip. The Mondriaan Foundation (named for the most famous modern Dutch painter) is a national funding agency for visual arts and design.
11. Claire Bishop, "The Social Turn: Collaboration and Its Discontents," *Artforum International* 44.6 (2006), pp. 178–83. See also Jennifer Allen, "Up the Organization," interview with Joep van Lieshout, *Artforum International* 2001 39.8, pp. 104–11.
12. Telephone interview by the author with Rebecca Gomperts, December 19, 2006; Rebecca Gomperts, e-mail to the author, December 21, 2006.

13. These installations have been shown at the Macedonian Museum of Art in Thessaloniki, Greece; at Mediamatic in Amsterdam; and at the gallery Modelarnia in Gdansk, Poland. The exhibition in Thessaloniki was © *Europe Exists*, curated by Rosa Martinez and Harald Szeemann. (Szeemann was also the curator of the 2001 Biennale that included the van Lieshout/Women on Waves project.) An additional intersection with visual art is the multimedia documentation project, titled *Waves*, commissioned by Gomperts from Sascha Pohflepp and Jakob Schillinger, based on footage shot during the Poland campaign, exhibited at Mediamatic, Amsterdam, in 2003 and selected for the new-media competition at the Stuttgarter Filmpreis, January 2004.
14. "Un appel de 343 femmes" [Manifesto of the 343], *Le Nouvel Observateur* 334, April 5–11, 1971, p. 5. Following the example of the "Manifesto of the 343," the first issue of *Ms.* magazine in 1972 included a list of fifty-three prominent U.S. women willing to proclaim that they had had an abortion. "We Have Had Abortions." *Ms.* (Spring 1972), pp. 34–35. The strategy was picked up again in 2006, with a new petition from *Ms.*, this one specifically intended to address the problem of unsafe abortion in developing nations and the U.S. contribution to the problem through the global gag rule and its restriction of sex-education funding to abstinence-only programs. See "We Had Abortions," *Ms.*, Fall 2006, p. 38.
15. Toby L. Ditz, "Shipwrecked; or, Masculinity Imperiled: Mercantile Representations of Failure and the Gendered Self in Eighteenth-Century Philadelphia," *Journal of American History* 81.1 (June 1994), pp. 51–80. Thanks to Jennifer Roberts for this reference.
16. See Lucy Lippard, "Trojan Horses: Activist Art and Power," in Brian Wallis (ed.), *Art after Modernism: Rethinking Representation*, pp. 341–58 (New York: The New Museum, 1984).
17. Telephone interview with Rebecca Gomperts by the author, December 19, 2006. Artists involved in the workshop included Louise Walsh, Mick O'Kelly, and Pauline Cummins. See Valerie Connor, "C97 Review: Dublin," *Circa* 97 (Autumn 2001), pp. 5–53.
18. Jennifer Allen, "AVL/ Joep van Lieshout 1963," in Harald Szeemann, Cecilia Liveriero Lavelli, and Lara Facco (eds.), *Biennale di Venezia: 49. Esposizione internazionale d'arte: platea dell'umanità*, 2 vols. (Milan: Electa, 2001), 1:158–59. Theorist of tactical media David Garcia privileges Women on Waves as an exemplar of a second wave of tactical media, one that has the creativity and communicational savvy of earlier 1990s culture jamming and its goal of promoting discourse, rather than simply agitating for a belief, but that forgoes the fleetingness of earlier work, demonstrating longer-term commitment and deeper engagement. He cites, in particular, the way it actively assists women and describes its use of art and design in the campaign as a reminder that the very idea of cultural politics in its contemporary sense came from the women's movement. David Garcia, "Learning the Right Lessons," *Mute*, January 25, 2006, http://www.metamute.org/en/Learning-the-Right-Lessons.
19. J. L. Austin, *How to Do Things with Words: The William James Lectures Delivered at Harvard University in 1955*, 2nd ed., ed. J. O. Urmson and Maria Sbisà (London: Oxford University Press, 1976), p. 14.
20. See Barbara Johnson on the fictionalizing function of the performative in "Poetry and Performative Language," *Yale French Studies* 54 (1977), pp. 140–58. Johnson's essay, like writings by Jacques Derrida and Judith Butler, helped radicalize the implications of Austin's speech-act theory.
21. See Sara Corbett, "The Pro-Choice Extremist," *New York Times Magazine*, August 26, 2001, p. 26, and Gomperts, *Women on Waves*, n.p.
22. The project first became known internationally through a rumor-based report that it was

going to Malta, published by an antiabortion group in 2000. The portable clinic is equipped for surgical abortions, but except perhaps in the very earliest moments of the project's imagining, there was no intent to perform invasive procedures at sea. Where the project has been stymied has to do with the point at which it is authorized to perform medical abortions—that is, to offer abortifacient medication. Because the Dutch government has approved its medical facility, but not granted it an abortion clinic's license, Women on Waves is limited to providing the abortion pill in very early pregnancies—before forty-five days—because this use of the medication does not require a special clinic license.

23. "The art of the possible" generally is attributed to Otto von Bismarck in conversation in 1867. See *The Concise Oxford Dictionary of Quotations*, ed. Elizabeth Knowles (Oxford: Oxford University Press, 2003). "Another world is possible" is the motto of the World Social Forum, which began meeting in 2001.
24. "Calling the group 'pirate abortionists,' Judie Brown, president of American Life League said Women on Waves is 'circumventing the sovereign rights of nations by carrying women offshore to kill their children. The human rights of poor women of color who want and need basic health care, are being plundered. The international community should be outraged by these shark abortionists.'" PRNewswire, May 25, 2000. This statement from the leader of a right-wing antiabortion group in the United States was one of the first to call Women on Waves "pirates," but the image has been taken up by more sympathetic writers, as well, for example, Matthew Fishbane "The Pro-choice Pirate," Salon.com, July 20, 2007, http://www.salon.com/life/broadsheet/2007/07/20/women_waves.
25. See Women on Web, http://www.womenonweb.org.
26. See Allan Sekula, "The Body and the Archive," in Richard Bolton (ed.), *The Contest of Meaning: Critical Histories of Photography* (Cambridge, MA: The MIT Press, 1992), pp. 343–89.
27. Jennifer Doyle, "Blind Spots and Failed Performance: Abortion, Feminism, and Queer Theory," *Qui Parle: Critical Humanities and Social Sciences* 18.1 (Fall–Winter 2009), p. 30; Mary Poovey, "The Abortion Question and the Death of Man," in Judith Butler and Joan Scott (eds.), *Feminists Theorize the Political* (New York: Routledge, 1992), p. 252.
28. More than twenty years ago, Lucy Lippard distinguished political art from activist art. Both have political intent and may deal with the same topics or issues, but while political art represents political subject matter, activist art does politics. "Although 'political' and 'activist' artists are often the same people," she wrote, "'political' art tends to be socially concerned and 'activist' art tends to be socially involved.... The former's work is a commentary or analysis, while the latter's art works *within* its context, *with* its audience." Lippard, "Trojan Horses," p. 349.
29. In theoretical terms, this corresponds to what Sarah Kanouse calls the "tactical irrelevance" of art, a concept writers influenced by Jacques Rancière have begun to articulate. Kanouse writes that "the blithe irrelevance of art through most of Euro-American history ends up serving a tactical purpose: art can become a relatively safe and 'conveniently sequestered' space not for obscuring or aestheticizing capitalism but within which people might play with new forms of agency and enhance their expectations for participation in the politics routinely encountered in everyday life." Sarah E. Kanouse, "Tactical Irrelevance: Art and Politics at Play," paper presented at the Conference of the Union for Democratic Communication, Boca Raton, May 20, 2006, http://journals.fcla.edu/demcom/article/view/76476/74107, p. 9.
30. Grant H. Kester treats WochenKlausur in depth in *Conversation Pieces: Community and Communication in Modern Art* (Berkeley: University of California Press, 2004). On this project

in particular, see Pascale Jeannée, "WochenKlausur: Art and Sociopolitical Intervention," in Ken Ehrlich and Brandon LaBelle (eds.), *Surface Tension: Problematics of Site*, pp. 255–64 (Los Angeles: Errant Bodies, 2003), and the in-depth description of the project at http://www.wochenklausur.at/projekte/04p_lang_en.htm.

31. Allen, "AVL/ Joep van Lieshout 1963," p. 105.
32. Jacques Rancière, "Problems and Transformations in Critical Art," in Claire Bishop, (ed.), *Participation* (Cambridge, MA: The MIT Press, 2006), p. 83.
33. *Ibid.*, p. 85. Such a formulation might also help address a tension in the discourse on activist art between its theoretical dimension, in which arguments are put forward regarding the inherent nonseparation of the artistic and the political, and the curatorial and art-historical dimension, in which activist art is distinguished from other forms of cultural production. The tension between these—between the urge to argue for the inherent interrelation of the artistic and the political, on the one hand, and to identify and defend a specifically artistic kind of activism, on the other—is not often remarked, but surfaces in the tactical use of the conventional separation of art and real-world politics in projects such as those of WochenKlausur and Women on Waves. As I see it, there are two ways of viewing these tactical uses of art's autonomy: a negative way of looking at them as cynical use and a positive way of looking at them as protecting—by deploying—art as a free, unregulated sphere for imagination.
34. Though I think they have a great deal of complexity and interest, the more or less conventional form of multimedia installations by means of which Women on Waves is usually represented in art museums and galleries fits a conventional understanding of the value of the art world—as a space for representation, rather than action.
35. Jennifer González and Adrienne Posner remind us that, in addition to doing politics, any given activist-art project also has a politics: its own "political character which produces and is produced by its historical moment and subsequent reception." (p. 213). It is this dimension of Women on Waves's politics that may be most problematic, at least for those of us who start from a position of support of its pro-choice mission. Jennifer González and Adrienne Posner, "Facture for Change: US Activist Art Since 1960," in Amelia Jones (ed.), *A Companion to Contemporary Art since 1945*, pp. 212–29 (Malden: Blackwell, 2006).
36. The Dutch health minister is quoted in "Open Ship: For More Information," Women on Waves, July 1, 2003, http://www.womenonwaves.org/article-1020.440-en.html. Around the same time, a U.S. antiabortion writer described the campaign as an invasion and also interpreted the project in terms of colonial imposition of culture. Michael S. Rose, "Mission Aborted: The Failed Dutch Invasion of Poland," *The American Conservative*, September 8, 2003, http://www.amconmag.com/2003/09_08_03/article1.html.
37. Telephone interview by the author with Rebecca Gomperts, December 19, 2006.
38. Allan Sekula argues that the traditional relation of land and sea has been reversed under conditions of neoliberal trade and the globalization of capital: "Sites of production become mobile, while paths of distribution become fixed and routine." The containerization of cargo—a process invented in the United States in the 1950s—is the condition for globalized manufacturing, and as such, to Sekula, the boxes bear "the hidden evidence of exploitation in the far reaches of the world." Allan Sekula, *Performance under Working Conditions*, exh. cat. (Vienna: Generali Foundation, 2003), p. 279. It should be noted that shipping containers have become quite ubiquitous in contemporary art and design, but this interest in rehabilitating and exploring the modular, transport-ready structure is also itself symptomatic.

Kristen Johnson, Guantánamo Bay Naval Base, journalists' sleeping quarters, 2008. See Kristen Johnson, "All Eyes," pp. 349–71.

Fazal Sheikh, *Sarla Goraye* ("*Simple*"), *Seva Sasi* ("*Service*"), *Phulmala Rai* ("*Garland*"), and *Chapala Dhar* ("*Electric*"), Vrindavan, India. See Eduardo Cadava, "Of Veils and Mourning," pp. 51–79.

Gideon Mendel, Treatment Action Campaign (TAC) members in Johannesburg, from the series *The Harsh Divide: AIDS Treatment in Africa*, 2003 (courtesy of the artist). See Roger Hallas, "Photojournalism, NGOs, and the New Media Ecology," pp. 95–114.

HIV
POSITIVE

TREATMENT NOW!!
ARV's CAN REMOVE
STIGMA
TREATMENT FOR
ME
TREATMENT FOR
US
HIV IS NOT
DEATH SENTENCE
GIVE US
TREATMENT PLEASE

FR
K

Allan Sekula, *Waiting for Tear Gas* (*White Globe to Black*), 1999–2000 (courtesy of the artist). See Benjamin J. Young, "On Strike," pp. 149–81.

HOLLYWOOD VIDEO

A building destroyed by controlled explosion by engineers, Rafah, Gaza Strip, 2009 (photo: Kai Wiedenhoefer).
See Yates McKee and Meg McLagan, "Forensic Architecture," pp. 429–51.

R1009-31

DAAR, a map of the Beit Surik area with the different walls drawn on it (Bimkom, 2004). See Alessandro Petti, Sandi Hilal, and Eyal Weizman, "The Morning After," pp. 453–69.

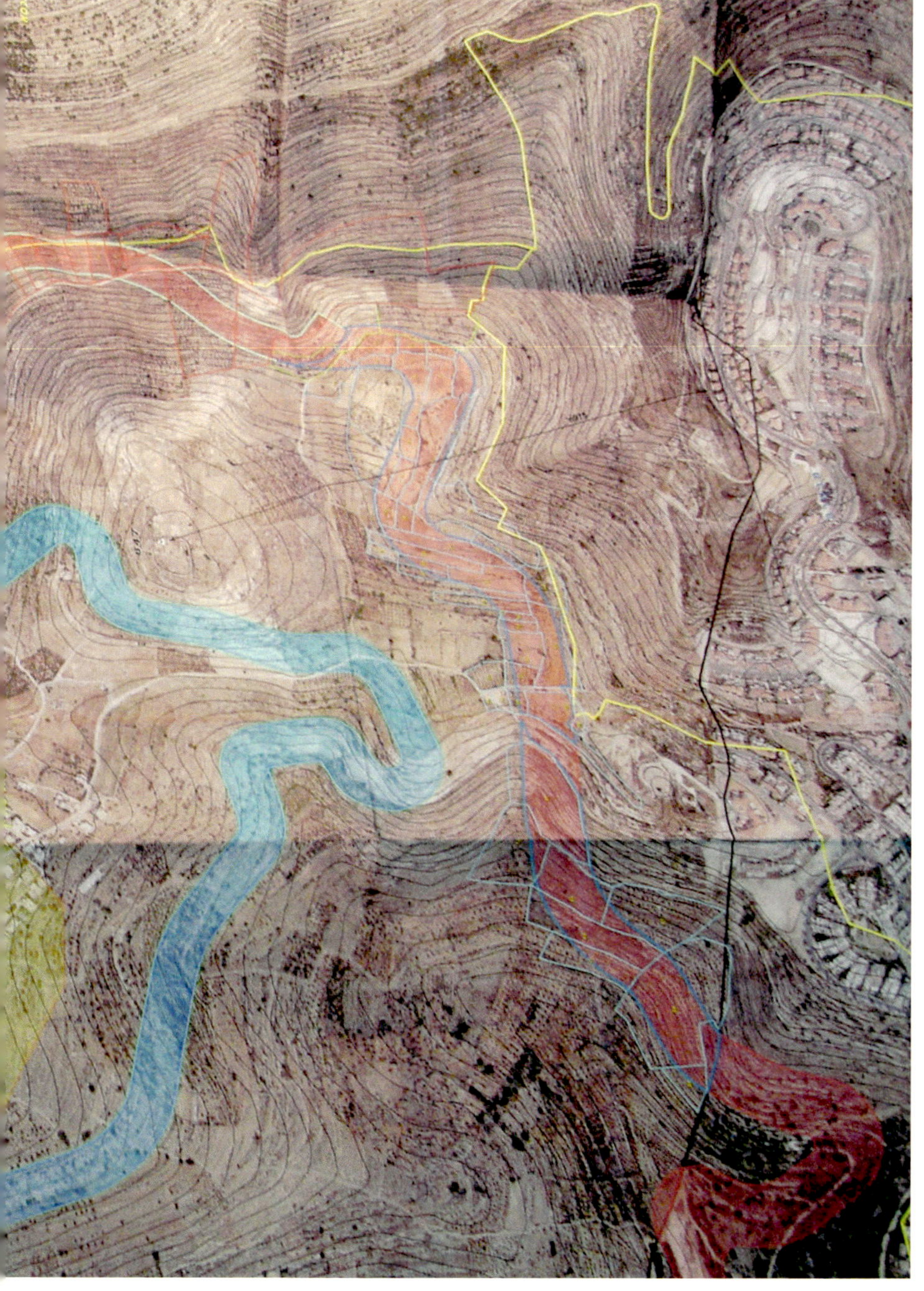

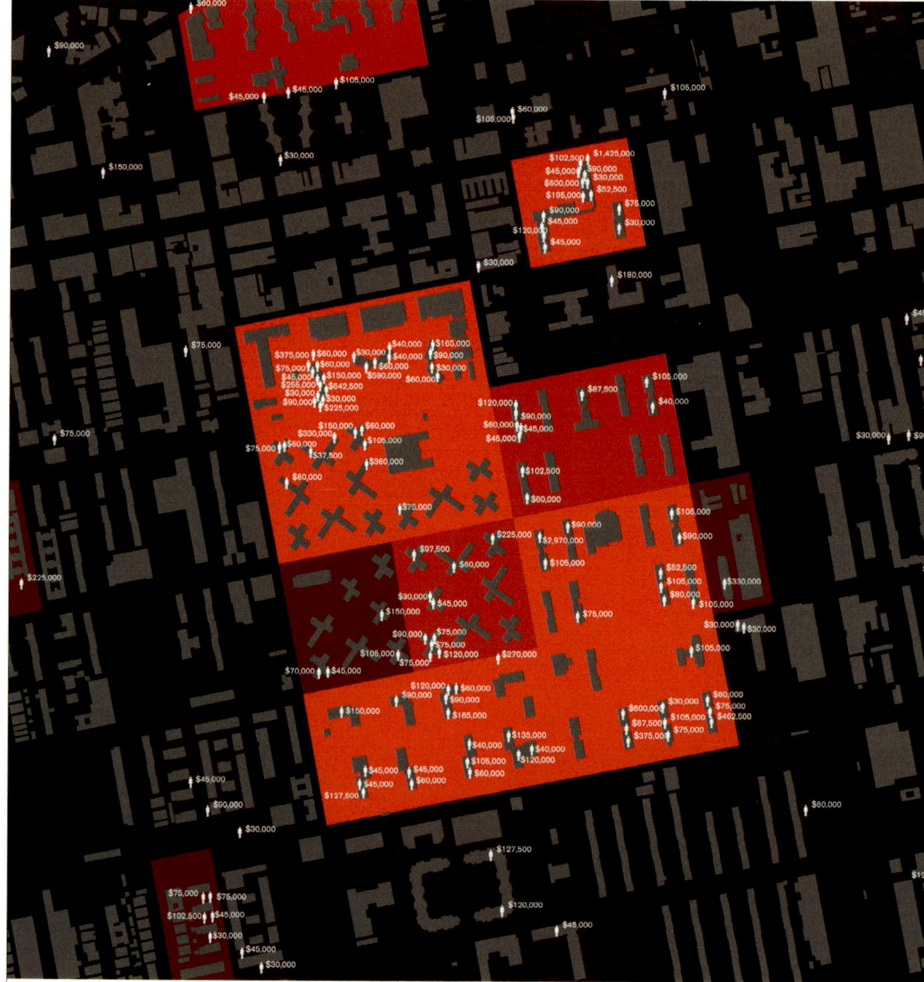

BROWNSVILLE, BROOKLYN

IT COST 17 MILLION DOLLARS TO IMPRISON 109 PEOPLE FROM THESE 17 BLOCKS IN 2003. WE CALL THESE MILLION DOLLAR BLOCKS. ON A FINANCIAL SCALE PRISONS ARE BECOMING THE PREDOMINANT GOVERNING INSTITUTION IN THE NEIGHBORHOOD.

Image part of Million Dollar Blocks. Project Directors: Laura Kurgan, Eric Cadora. Research Associates: Sarah Williams, David Reinfurt (courtesy Spatial Information Design Lab, GSAPP Columbia University). See Yates McKee, "How to Do Things with Space," pp. 491–514.

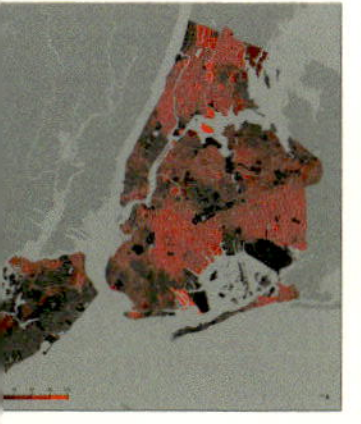

Persons of Color, 2000.

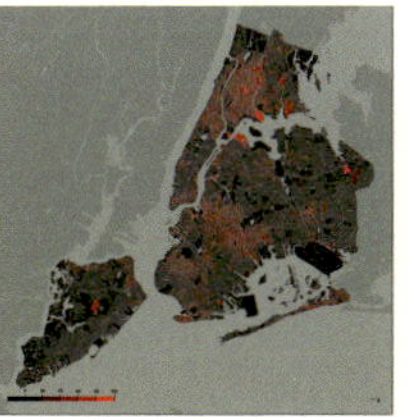

Percent Persons Below Poverty Level, 2000.

Percent Adults Admitted to Prison, 2003.

BROOKLYN COMMUNITY DISTRICTS	% POPULATION	% POVERTY	% ADMISSIONS
BROOKLYN CD 1	6.51 %	9.08 %	5.37 %
BROOKLYN CD 2	4.03 %	3.58 %	4.64 %
BROOKLYN CD 3	5.63 %	8.10 %	16.51 %
BROOKLYN CD 4	4.24 %	6.34 %	9.34 %
BROOKLYN CD 5	7.04 %	9.30 %	14.45 %
BROOKLYN CD 6	4.23 %	2.60 %	3.08 %
BROOKLYN CD 7	5.02 %	5.03 %	3.82 %
BROOKLYN CD 8	3.78 %	4.15 %	9.46 %
BROOKLYN CD 9	4.26 %	4.14 %	4.43 %
BROOKLYN CD 10	4.96 %	2.79 %	0.91 %
BROOKLYN CD 11	7.05 %	5.54 %	1.35 %
BROOKLYN CD 12	7.39 %	8.54 %	1.32 %
BROOKLYN CD 13	4.23 %	4.94 %	3.41%
BROOKLYN CD 14	6.76 %	6.22 %	3.79 %
BROOKLYN CD 15	6.48 %	4.42 %	1.20 %
BROOKLYN CD 16	3.48 %	5.92 %	8.43 %
BROOKLYN CD 17	6.75 %	5.40 %	5.29 %
BROOKLYN CD 18	7.96 %	3.91 %	3.20 %
BOROUGH TOTAL	100.00 %	100.00 %	100.00 %

Comparisons Expressed as Percent of Borough Total.

Migration with Expenditures by Block, 2003.

ROOKLYN, EW YORK CITY

ADDED UP BLOCK BY BLOCK, IT COST $359 MILLION DOLLARS TO IMPRISON PEOPLE FROM BROOKLYN IN 2003, FACILITATING A MASS MIGRATION TO PRISONS IN UPSTATE NEW YORK. 95% EVENTUALLY RETURN HOME.

Michael Rakowitz, *Return*, Babylon dates box designed by Al Farez, 2006; and *Headless Male Figure* (Kh. IV 112) from *Recovered, Missing, Stolen* series, 2007 (courtesy the artist and Lombard-Fried Gallery). See Liza Johnson, "The Market Is the Medium," pp. 627–56.

Kristen Johnson, Guantánamo Bay Naval Base, journalists' sleeping quarters, 2008. See Kristen Johnson, "All Eyes," pp. 349–71.

PART THREE

CINEMA, DOCUMENTARY, POLITICAL EFFECTS

FIGURE 1 Still from Jean-Luc Godard, *Histoire(s) du cinéma* (1988–98).

Jean-Luc Godard, *Histoire(s) du cinéma*

Jonathan Crary

In a segment of Jean-Luc Godard's 2003 film *Notre musique*, we see the filmmaker meeting with students in post–civil war Sarajevo. After Godard pauses in his reflections on the image and the imagination, an audience member asks him: "Do you think the new little digital cameras will save the cinema?" The film cuts to Godard's face, holding it, almost invisible in deep shadow; the audience waits, but he makes no reply. Godard's self-dramatized silence is of course his response to a wrongly conceived question, and certainly he has nothing against mini-DV equipment, which he has used creatively in numerous projects. Also, he would have been acutely aware of the many possible uses of such digital tools, for witnessing, for documentation in the immediate social context of Bosnia. But as his monumental *Histoire(s) du cinéma* makes clear, the fate of cinema for him has never primarily turned on questions of technology or media. Also, Godard's concern now is not about "saving" cinema, but to invent a form through which it can be remembered, and in remembering it, to locate what in it might yet be redeemable.

Godard worked for well over ten years on *Histoire(s)*, but spent many more years, beginning in the 1970s, pondering and planning for it. He began showing sections of it in the early 1990s, and even before its first completed exhibition in 1998, it was already an object of critical focus. Its initial reception coincided with widespread discussions in the 1990s around notions of the death of cinema, the end of film, and the obsolescence of the analog film image and its material support. At the time, Godard's work seemed to many to be consonant with the melancholic obituaries of film in the writings of Susan Sontag, Serge Daney, Peter Greenaway, and many others. But now, a decade and more since those hyperbolic debates of the nineties, Godard's film has proved to be enduringly relevant for very different reasons, above all for its exemplary demonstration of alternate narrative and historical practices, for its status as an unprecedented set of experiments with word, sound, and image. Although Godard has said many times that one of his goals was to tell the history of cinema through cinema itself, the obvious fact is that *Histoire(s) du cinéma* is a video work that relies on an array of technologies that fully postdate the time frame of cinema that he purports to narrate. While much of its visual texture is made up out of extracts of over five hundred films, the work is fundamentally unlike any kind of "compilation" movie. Obviously, the rich history of the film-essay, which of course includes Godard, stands behind *Histoire(s)*, and of particular significance for its conception would have been the work of Chris Marker, Syberberg's *Our Hitler*, and the elegiac *In girum imus nocte* . . . of Guy Debord, to mention a few.

Godard's work, ever since the 1960s, has depended on a range of "citational" practices, but he rarely makes a quotation, whether of text or image, without modifying it in some substantive fashion. Thus, almost all the cinematic fragments in *Histoire(s)* are never shown as film-clip segments, but as images (still or moving) that have been subjected to a wide variety of metamorphoses and processings. The fleeting shards of films we see are second-or third-generation images, treated with effects of flickering, oversaturation, repetitive oscillations, flashings, extreme slow motion, and many more. They are operations achieved deliberately without the appearance of refinement or technical finesse even though undoubtedly many of his dissolves in fact have been painstakingly worked out with the digital and other means that were at his disposal. Nonetheless, the vast citational fabric or layering of the work has led many critics to associate its scope with canonical earlier twentieth-century works, such as Pound's *Cantos*, Musil's *Man without Qualities*, Joyce's *Finnegans Wake*, and Benjamin's *Arcades Project*. And there is no question that Godard has drawn deeply on the accumulated experiments of twentieth-century avant gardes and modernisms (whether as collage, montage, stream of consciousness, surrealist automatism) in the creation of an unprecedented syntactical organization of spoken word, graphic text, music, and image (as artwork, film, or photograph), what Jacques Rancière has discussed as Godard's "image-sentence." But if these are reference points for Godard, they are not simply an inventory of heterogeneous formal strategies, as they might have been for him in the 1960s. Rather, they are embedded in the very histories he is attempting to relate. His particular account of cinema is heavily weighted to the 1920s and 1930s, and much of the spoken textual content of *Histoire(s)* is from these two decades, for example, Virginia Woolf's *The Waves*, Denis de Rougemont's *Penser avec les mains*, Hermann Broch's *The Death of Virgil* (begun in 1938), and many other works that pose various counterstrategies to traditional narrative or historiography.

As many critics have indicated, the French word *histoire* does not translate easily into English, and the plural sense of this word is crucial to Godard's aims: its

FIGURE 2 Still from Jean-Luc Godard, *Histoire(s) du cinéma* (1988–98).

overlapping of the English notions of history, story or tale; the matter, affair, or business of something; and even the sense of a lie or fib. Thus, there is a mobility and a contingency to the proposition that Godard poses as the building blocks of his particular storytelling. As many have noted, if taken at face value, his account lacks nuance, it is often rhetorically exaggerated, and it presumes a universality when in fact he is looking at a very limited European and American framework. But as they are developed in the larger audiovisual fabric of the work, his themes all acquire far more complicated shadings and associations: the immense loss that occurred with the introduction of sound, the dominance of Hollywood and its imperatives, the destruction or colonization of the national cinemas, the failure of film with regard to the Holocaust, and the final devastation of cinema by television and Spielbergism. What is primary are his mobile constellations of sound, image, and text that explode any linear development of ideas, that unfold in a quasi-musical structure, composed rhythmically out of disparate speeds and temporalitites. Godard's ambition, which he has insisted on, was not a project of thinking about images, but a project in which images themselves would operate like thought, would become, in his words, "a form that thinks."

Godard and Gilles Deleuze share a related sense of the historical importance of the early to mid-1920s as a moment when cinema seemed to have opened a stunning and revelatory field of possibilities in which thought itself might be reinvented and endowed with unprecedented, unbounded capacities. But in this view, the tentative experiments of Gance, Epstein, Vertov, and Eisenstein were never taken up, and the moving image became, in Deleuze's words, "linked to the organization of war, state propaganda, ordinary fascism, historically and essentially."[1] Thus, the fate of cinema in the 1920s and 1930s, when its very best and worst prospects were realized, is in part what led Godard to his conflation of the history of cinema with the history of the twentieth century. No other medium or art form ever had the capacity to fabricate images and myths that subsequently became social and political reality. Walter Benjamin sought to disclose the images and spaces that constituted a dream world of emerging capitalism in the nineteenth century; Godard has attempted to account for some the catastrophes and consequences that were inseparable from the dream world created by cinema in the twentieth century.

In interviews, Godard has mentioned how the history of art was of little value in providing models or starting points for his history-of-cinema project. He stressed, however, that there were two exceptions: the works of Elie Faure and André Malraux, and both of them figure in crucial ways in *Histoire(s)*. Malraux, in particular, provided Godard with the example of a historical project with important parallels to his own undertaking. Many people forget or are ignorant of the fact that the text that finally took shape in the 1950s as *Les voix de silence* had its intellectual genesis in the antifascist struggles of the 1930s. Like Walter Benjamin, Malraux meditated on the consequences of both the modern museum and the effects of photographic reproduction on our relation to artworks. Malraux, with even less nostalgia than Benjamin, saw the deracination of art from its original meanings and uses as irrevocable and unlamentable. At the same time, he refused to accept that artifacts of the past thus had become only mute, inert traces of lost and alien cultures. In the 1930s, the idea of discovering new and unforeseen commonalities and resonances between historically disparate objects was a means of opposing pervasive Spenglerian notions that saw civilizations as inescapably insular and noncommunicating with each other. Thus, the guiding impetus of Malraux's art history was to counter the fascist and racist implications of Spengler's hierarchies and segregations, but also to reject the ominous cultural prohibitions he simultaneously saw expanding in the Soviet Union. Even as he made one of the greatest of all political films, *L'espoir* (1937), in the midst of the Spanish Civil War, he was insistent on the comparable political importance of his notion of the imaginary museum and the cultural affirmations that were possible because of it.

Obviously, there are enormous differences between these projects, and Godard is hardly making an uncritical affiliation of his own work with Malraux's. But

Godard is clearly cognizant that cinema, within a far briefer time span, has undergone an irreversible loss of its origins and conditions of possibility. Just as artworks were uprooted and recreated as photographic images, the entire universe of cinema is either chemically disintegrating or has been transubstantiated into digital formats of various kinds. Just as Malraux believed there was no way to recover an originary relationship to artworks, Godard would reject the possibility of recuperating an innocent relationship to historical cinema.

Godard's *Histoire(s)* instead asks whether the ghostly remains of what had been cinema could become pieces of new creative or critical practices or even new models of thought itself. His assumption is that the spectral persistence of film, in whatever ruined or mutated forms of afterlife, can be deployed in ways that unsettle the amnesias and evasions of the present. If cinema is to be an object of memory, it can be only to ensure the survival of historical trauma, of unfulfilled emancipation, of victims lost in historical oblivion. And *Histoire(s)* foregrounds the specific historical circumstances that surround its making, with pointed references to civil conflict and genocide in Rwanda and the Balkans reverberating back through the earlier disasters of the twentieth century. Just as technologies such as cinema, television, and now the Internet have been crucial in forming the illusion of universalizable and simultaneous audiences and a homogenized time of the present, counterpractices of the audiovisual, even if powerless politically, might at least affirm that modes of seeing and listening (and thus of inhabiting time) can be created and sustained in spite of all the ubiquitous imperatives of current information and communication systems.

NOTE

1. Gilles Deleuze, *Cinema: The Time-Image*, trans. Hugh Tomlinson and Robert Galeta (Minneapolis: University of Minnesota Press, 1989), p. 165.

FIGURE 1 Jennifer Arnold pitches her film *A Small Act* at the Good Pitch UK 2010. The Good Pitch is an international forum created by Channel 4 BRITDOC Foundation that brings together selected funders, NGOs, social entrepreneurs, broadcasters, and potential corporate and brand partners to listen to pitches by independent filmmakers seeking support for their films and associated outreach campaigns (photo: Channel 4 BRITDOC Foundation).

Imagining Impact: Documentary Film and the Production of Political Effects

Meg McLagan

The structural transformation of long-form documentary in the last decade has reshaped its capacity for political intervention, the types of claims it makes, and the forms through which it makes them. One can see this as part of the broader reconstitution of politics and media that has taken place across a variety of domains, driven in part by developments in digital technologies. I have been interested in this transformation in two ways.

First, as a scholar, I have written about architectures of activism and the processes of mediation through which a subject matter gets turned into an object of politics. Drawing on ethnographic research on the transnational Tibet movement and human rights advocacy, I have analyzed how nonstate and nongovernmental actors stage their claims using an array of representational means and how their rhetorical dimensions condition the forms of publicity mobilized.[1] This work is premised on the idea that claims do not just exist in the world; they have to be relayed, remediated, and reframed in order to be able to circulate, a process that entails social labor.[2] At the same time, circulation is not neutral, but is grounded in a network of financial, institutional, technological, and discursive infrastructures that have a determining effect on the shape of the objects that travel through their channels.[3]

Second, as a filmmaker, I have participated in these processes of mediation firsthand. In 2008, I codirected *Lioness* (82 minutes), a feature documentary about American servicewomen who were sent into direct ground combat in Iraq. The experience gave me immediate insight into the role cultural forms can play in constituting things as sites of public debate, struggle, and advocacy. Nonfiction film has been a cinema of social engagement, dating back to the 1920s and 1930s, when it emerged as a distinct form through the works of individuals such as Dziga Vertov, John Grierson, and Pare Lorentz. As many scholars have noted, there is something inherent in documentary codes that produces a network of effects as seemingly real and that gives documentary the potential to operate with concrete consequences in the world. This power has always been a part of the documentary form.[4]

Recently, however, the conceptual and practical architecture that comprise what we call "documentary" has begun to unravel, and in its place has emerged a proliferation of new platforms and interfaces that have reshaped the form, along with its potential to produce political effects. This transformation in the technical apparatus of production and distribution occurred at the same time as the entry of funders seeking to use film, especially documentary, to promote social change. Both of these innovations occurred over the period I was making *Lioness*. My codirector and I began the project in 2005 with the aim of following a long-established model in which a filmmakers' major effort went into raising funds and producing and directing a film. Distribution and exhibition, by contrast, received far less attention, in part because distribution options were fairly limited and straightforward.[5] By the time we finished in 2008, the conventional structures of filmmaking were collapsing, and new digital technologies were raising the possibility of alternative forms of distribution.[6] Meanwhile, socially conscious funders were becoming a notable presence in the indie film space, a shift reflected in the industry's growing reliance on new marketing and business models and new partnerships with nongovernmental organizations. Together, these trends created the conditions for a new focus that coalesced under the term "impact." Consequently, like other filmmakers, we found ourselves forced to reconceptualize the way we thought about creating and disseminating our projects.

The depth of these changes, which I analyze below, pushes us to recognize that no longer a single inviolate text, documentary is now structurally presumed to have different forms of life, to exist in different modalities, extended across multiple platforms and networks. From a film's outreach plan to its crowd-sourced online funding campaign, from its Facebook page to community screenings, where the filmmaker and film subjects are present, from its mobile app to interactive video games, these different modalities present a challenge to our understanding of the ontology of film by rendering the boundary between the inside and outside of a work increasingly porous.

THE CHANGING ECONOMY OF THE LONG-FORM DOCUMENTARY

Contemporary long-form nonfiction film is an increasingly important global art form and critical cultural practice. It occupies a zone that is totally commodified, yet it claims something beyond that; its mission is its value added. In an era of mass-media consolidation, long-form documentaries constitute an alternative space of investigation, debate, and active questioning of traditional channels of knowledge production and validation. Deploying a methodology of discovery and immersion in a social world or problem, they seek to describe the dynamics of an unfolding present. What gets created formally comes out of an experience of something and a belief that it is worth knowing about. Thus, built into the form is a contract with the audience that it seeks to engage or address viewers as public actors.

Documentary's status as a commodity grew in the 1990s and 2000s following the theatrical release of films such as Michael Moore's *Fahrenheit 9/11* (2004), a critical look at the Bush presidency that grossed $119 million at the box office, *Supersize Me* (2004), Morgan Spurlock's first-person documentary about fast food that took in $11 million domestically, and Davis Guggenheim's *An Inconvenient Truth* (2006), a film about Al Gore's film about global warming that grossed over $24 million in the United States.[7] The success of these films dramatically raised expectations for documentaries to function both as commercially successful entertainment and as political tools. Many of those who saw *Fahrenheit 9/11* subsequently subscribed to his website and become active in related causes. Six weeks after *Supersize Me*'s debut in theaters, McDonald's dropped its supersize portions.[8] *An Inconvenient Truth*,[9] released two years later, reached millions and has been widely credited with igniting debate over climate change, setting press agendas, and influencing politicians, companies, and environmental activists.[10] It was at once a film and a dispersed cultural process from the advertising campaign and numerous screenings at film festivals, in theaters, and on television, to the long-tail aftermath of the work on DVD and its widespread use by educators, activists, legislators, and many others in living rooms, classrooms, courtrooms, and Congressional hearing rooms.

At the other end of the economic scale, a different mode of financially successful and politically engaged filmmaking was pioneered by Robert Greenwald, whose grassroots socially networked documentary practice centered on his house-party model, in which audiences of like-minded viewers were invited to view the films. The emergence of digital outlets, along with the DVD format, meant that filmmakers such as Greenwald could eschew traditional film screenings altogether and use domestic dvd consumption as both a viable financial mechanism and a new political tool. This represented a dramatic reshaping of the possibilities for documentary funding. The retail strategy that Chris Anderson termed "the long tail," by which profit can be made from small sales over a long period of time by marketing directly to a targeted segment of consumers, highlighted the Internet's ability to create a platform for niche goods.[11] Greenwald was one of the first filmmakers to apply this strategy and his success led it to become a standard option for documentarians.[12]

The success of nonfiction works such as *Fahrenheit 9/11*, *An Inconvenient Truth*, and *Supersize Me*, as well as *Uncovered: The Whole Truth about the Iraq War* and *Outfoxed: Rupert Murdoch's War on Journalism*, inaugurated a new structure of filmmaking that has become a model for other independents, one based on the expectation that their work should not just *represent* political conditions, but actually *change* them. In ways that echo the early years of cinema, a film is just one part of a far broader array of activities, and "documentary" should now properly refer to the dispersed cultural texts and practices within which a film lives a socially diverse life—spread across a variety of screens in a networked media environment.

One extreme example of the diffusion of a film into a broader campaign took place in March 2012 with the release of the viral documentary *Kony 2012*. Developed by the Christian evangelical nongovernmental organization Invisible Children, *Kony 2012* was designed, depending on whose point of view you take, either to bring visibility to human rights atrocities in Uganda or to use human rights atrocities in Uganda to build a mass movement in the United States.[13] As several analyses have shown, the film was the outcome of a sedimented activist infrastructure which is thematized within the film itself.[14] In this sense it becomes what the anthropologist Christopher Kelty terms a "recursive public," a public that foregrounds its own communicative infrastructure.[15] The film portrays the experiences of an ex-child soldier from the Lord's Resistance Army and then goes on to show scenes in which it deploys that interview in public lectures designed to build a campaign. From there, it instructs viewers on how to join this campaign and offers clear information about the architecture of relay and dissemination by which the campaign is spread. It is a remarkable text in that it so thoroughly collapses the distinction between film text and media campaign as to make the two indissoluble.

SOCIAL ENTREPRENEURS AND THE DOUBLE BOTTOM LINE

About a decade ago, a new set of social actors appeared on the independent film scene who had made a significant amount of money in the technology sector.[16] Many of these individuals created private foundations with the aim of deploying their considerable wealth to help solve society's most pressing problems. Unlike most of the arts, which were given a short shrift by the new philanthropists, documentary film was viewed as a cultural genre well suited to their goal of addressing deep-seated global issues such as the AIDs pandemic, poverty, discrimination, lack of access to education and healthcare, and human rights abuses. Consequently, they made social issue filmmaking a priority.

Led by individuals such as Jeff Skoll, former president of eBay, social entrepreneurs began investing heavily in documentaries. While philanthropic organizations such as the Ford and MacArthur Foundations have long underwritten public media projects, until recently their spending on social issue documentaries has been relatively modest. In contrast, the "filmanthropists"—a phrase coined by former AOL executive and creator of SnagFilms, Ted Leonisis—quickly energized the indie film sector with their deep pockets and passion.

As believers in investment rather than charity, the filmanthropists brought with them a commitment to the "double bottom line"—the potential of their philanthropy to produce financial as well as social returns and a belief that making the nonprofit world responsible to financial discipline would create a more sustainable practice.[17] This approach, known as "impact investing," challenged the assumption in the traditional grant-making world that creating financial value and social value are necessarily different pursuits.

The concept of impact as used by social entrepreneurs merges two dissimilar things.[18] On the one hand, it refers to demonstrable political effects something can have in the real world, such as, for instance, helping to raise money for new schools in the developing world, as the film *A Small Act* did in Kenya in 2010.[19] On the other hand, the term refers to the institutionalization of audit practices through the introduction of a set of concrete performance criteria by which such change can be imagined and then assessed. In other words, for social entrepreneurs, much like money managers, the key issue is to invest in socially valuable projects that can provide quantifiable returns. They place great emphasis on measuring their investments' effectiveness using valuation tools such as algorithms to help them in their calculations. In this their approach differs from the political culture of grant making by old-money private foundations such as Rockefeller, Ford, and Carnegie, which were large, opaque institutions with huge endowments that focused on social and scientific problems requiring the expenditure of funds over a period of years without expectation of financial return.

The vision behind the new philanthropists' change agenda is exemplified by the mission statement of Skoll's film production company, Participant Media:

> The company seeks to entertain audiences first, then to invite them to participate in making a difference. To facilitate this Participant creates specific social action campaigns for each film and documentary designed to give voice to issues that resonate in the films. Participant teams with social sector organizations, non-profits and corporations who are committed to creating an open forum for discussion, education, and who can, with Participant, offer specific ways for audience members to get involved. These include action kits, screening programs, educational curriculums and classes, house parties, seminars, parties and other activities and are ongoing "legacy" programs that are updated and revised to continue beyond the film's domestic and international theatrical, DVD and television windows.[20]

One of the striking things about the new philanthropists' approach is the commitment to strategic partnerships with nongovernmental organizations and other stakeholders in an issue with whom filmmakers are expected to consult during the filmmaking process and the social-action campaign (see fig. 1). The idea is that by consulting with partners during the production process, filmmakers ensure that their projects will reach target audiences and that their messages will fit into the needs of the activists who hope their cause will benefit from the film's circulation.

A key example of this can be seen in a report by the Fledgling Fund, a private foundation that funds innovative media projects and that was one of the first organizations to codify the practices underpinning the emergent social-issue film-funding model.[21] Once a film is in distribution, the report notes, the task is to let people know that the film is available and to get them interested in watching it:

> This phase of outreach and strategic communication is largely determined by how the film fits into the social movement, how the movement itself has connected with the film, embraced it and worked with the filmmaker to understand the message it conveys, how it fits into the needs of the social movement and how the members of this movement can see it. In order to do this effectively, film teams (made up of filmmakers, outreach and engagement coordinators, movement builders and/or leaders/organizers) have to think critically about how and where the film's message should be conveyed.[22]

The moment after a film ends, when "audience emotions are tangible," the filmmaking team, with the support of its partners, "has a real opportunity to move the audience from passive to active."[23] "Audience engagement" is the term used to describe when the film team attempts to maximize this energy by suggesting specific actions that people can take, having them sign up for e-mail lists, connecting them to potential local partners working on the issues, and so on. According to Fledgling, these "asks" should be generated in collaboration with the partners to help them energize their base, raise money, and educate more people about the issue in the film, among other things. In other words, audience engagement is what happens after audiences see the film and want to use their energy, resources, ideas, connections, or time to make a difference.[24]

While the idea of outreach and audience engagement is not new, the institutionalization of the concept and its associated practices through the creation of a number of funding organizations and nonprofit initiatives between 2006 and 2011 was unprecedented.[25] Entities such as Working Films, the Fledgling Fund, Chicken & Egg Pictures, Active Voice, BRITDOC, the Good Pitch, and Just Films, to name just a few, provided significant funding, mentoring, and pitching opportunities, as well as outreach and audience-engagement advice and support. Together, they provided the scaffolding for a dramatic elaboration of this particular subgenre of documentary.

The influence of these funders' functionalist orientation is evident in the criteria that applicants are generally expected to meet in order to secure funding. In their proposals, social-change filmmakers must be ready to define the processes that might lead to "outcomes" and be able to outline social change goals that are "tangible, realistic, and measurable" (fig. 2). Questions that filmmakers need to ask themselves now include "what is the goal? Who are the target audience(s)? What are the goals for these target audiences? What is the best way to reach and activate those audiences during both outreach and audience engagement?"[26] Answering such questions as a way of envisioning "strategic outreach" involves thinking pragmatically about how a film will circulate.[27] Of course, once a film finally makes its encounter with the world, its effects cannot be controlled—like any aesthetic form, its horizon is open.

We discovered the need for planning strategic outreach while making *Lioness*. For us, the filmmaking process entailed the usual steps: developing the story idea, researching characters, shooting, and editing. However this time around, it included an additional step—the creation of a plan for how to maximize the film's impact. The inclusion of this information in our proposals, framed as our "outreach and audience engagement plan," was required in most of our funding applications. So before reaching the rough-cut stage, we had already begun to imagine the forms of circulation the film might take, who its target audience would be, which partners would help us spread the word, and what social action we might suggest viewers could take in relation to the issues represented in the film. In other words, in order to obtain funding, we were expected to imagine how our film would circulate in the future and what kind of impact on the world that circulation would have. This imagined future structured the condition of possibility for the film.

Cinema scholar Michael Renov has observed that the documentary form's ability to persuade is built first "on the ontological promise of the photographed image, its suggestion that what appears on screen once existed in the world."[28] This appearance, based on indexical verisimilitude, produces a network of effects as seemingly real that allows certain claims to be made. However, the effects take on a facticity as they circulate through networks patterned in ways that imbue them with authority and relevance. Documentary practices, from preproduction to production, postproduction, distribution, exhibition, outreach, and audience engagement, form the basis of the network through which claims circulate and become sensible.[29]

David Whiteman underscores this idea when he argues that "to assess impact adequately, we must evaluate the entire filmmaking process, including both production and distribution and not just the finished product. A film's development, production and distribution create extensive opportunities for interaction among producers, participants, activists, decision makers, and citizens and thus all stages of a film can affect its impact."[30] Documentary film is at once a form of policy analysis and a node in a larger "issue network" consisting of the filmmaker, activist organizations, social movements, decision makers, and policy elites.[31] Flipping the focus from the film to the campaign in which it is embedded, in other words, reveals a film's performative power as it circulates, connecting different actors and arenas and in so doing, producing political effects.

By 2008, not only had documentary filmmakers begun to receive significant support to underwrite outreach and audience engagement around the issues represented in their work, they were in fact getting more money for outreach than they were for production, with the trend catching on with traditional funders, as well.[32]

Despite the flourishing of this corner of the documentary world, devising a metrics of impact suitable for the medium remains a challenge. In one study sponsored by Channel 4 BRITDOC, a foundation based in London, the author struggles

FIGURE 2 In an attempt to assess a film's impact, the Fledgling Fund created a visual framework organized around what it considers to be key indicators of success that are concrete and measurable. Fully aware that realizing change is a long and complex process, Fledgling uses the framework as a working model to help structure how it develops and evaluates the projects it funds. Many other funders as well as nongovernmental organizations have adopted this visualization as part of their efforts to make sense of the dynamics of film and social change (image © 2008 The Fledgling Fund).

to identify the best models and methodologies one might apply to determine the value of *An Inconvenient Truth*:

> How do we value a film like *An Inconvenient Truth* (AIT)? It is not obvious with *AIT* whose value should be measured. The value the film had to investors? Its value to audiences? Or to the nation? And *what* should we measure? The money it made? The money it saved? The damage to the planet which was avoided? The contribution to public awareness? The place it had in people's hearts? Should the film be valued as a cultural artifact? Or as an instrument of social change? And which models and methods should we employ?[33]

The questions posed above reveal the challenge of applying audit technologies—practices of measurement and evaluation in the name of responsibility and accountability—to artistic phenomenon. They also reveal the assumptions embedded in the notion of a metrics of impact: Can change be quantified? Is change linear, i.e. does it always go from story to action? Is more impact always better? How transposable are the criteria through which impact is measured in different cultural and political contexts? In other words, the notion of impact, which purports to be neutral, is in fact not. The conditions of possibility for what counts as impact have a history and a structure that makes or allows certain kinds of work to be visible and other kinds not.

THE NEW PARADIGM

As I have outlined, new funding practices and market shifts in the independent film industry came together to set up conditions for a new emphasis on social-issue documentaries in the latter half of the aughts. But the focus on change is also tied to the rise of new digital technologies that made certain things possible that were not before.

As the trend toward nonphysical media accelerated, the emergence of alternative distribution models enabled by digital media, including à la carte streaming video, video-on-demand (VOD), and social media, reconfigured the independent film economy. Various attempts to help independent filmmakers, especially documentarians, find their way in the changing marketplace were led by do-it-yourself distribution consultants such as Peter Broderick and Scott Reiss, who urged filmmakers to hold onto their sales rights and sell them off separately, instead of handing them over to one distributor.[34] Led by these self-distribution evangelists, a mini industry in DIY distribution and marketing has sprung up, a "virtual infrastructure," as one observer has called it, that doesn't compete with Hollywood, but rather is about the creation of a sustainable artist-based alternative.[35]

As a result of these changes, social-change filmmakers are now encouraged to think of themselves as entrepreneurs whose film practice is essentially a small business. Indeed, like the social entrepreneurs who fund their work, they are encouraged to strive for self-sufficiency through the creation of multiple revenue streams. To assist them in acquiring the necessary skills, many film schools and funders have integrated entrepreneurial training into their programs. For instance, Sundance Institute's new Artists Services Initiative offers tools, access, and aid to filmmakers who want to create a customized system to self-distribute their films. The Independent Filmmaker Project and other film-support organizations now offer hands-on mentorship to teach filmmakers about various forms of distribution, including theatrical release through "four-walling" or paying certain theaters directly for a week-long run.[36] Innovations in social media and data analytics, which enable tracking a film's circulation far more effectively than ever before, have allowed filmmakers to go around traditional industry gatekeepers to identify and interact directly with their audiences. This, in turn, has allowed them build a fan base, one that can be mobilized to attend local screenings and take specific actions related to issues in the film and to whom DVDs as well as ancillary products such as T-shirts, posters, hats, and soundtracks can be marketed.

Helen de Michiel captures the complexity of the new technical and business skills filmmakers must master in order to succeed within the new paradigm:

> Making an independent documentary (or any film for that matter) in these times is like conceiving, designing, and building a three-dimensional structure or system with a variety of moving parts and launching it like a startup organization. The film must be able to live in and around a variety of venues, from the Web to large theatrical screens, from disks to hard drives and mobile devices. It must appeal to the funders, who need to justify costs to their boards, and be able to be used by a variety of communities of interest. It may have to serve policy agenda, but also reveal stories from and about people who have no narrative presence in the media otherwise.[37]

De Michiel's observations encapsulate the real paradigm shift that has created a whole new world for filmmaker-entrepreneurs to navigate.

At the same time independent filmmaking is an artisanal practice in that the films are handcrafted with unique and individual qualities, as opposed to mass-produced television shows, for example. Like avant-garde film practices such as those used by the film and photo leagues of the 1930s and the newsreels of the 1940s and 1950s, the independent documentary is an artisanal mode that rejects the commercial production process that dominates Hollywood, and yet historically it has not been shielded from the exigencies of the marketplace.[38] The artisanal quality of social-issue filmmaking is most evident in outreach screenings, which are often premised on the presence of the filmmaker and sometimes the film's subjects, who in being there become a part of the work of art. These "live event / theatrical screenings" stage an encounter not just between the film and the audience, but also between the audience and the film's creator and subjects. These encounters have a performative quality in that they call communities into being around the film-viewing experience.

Although documentaries are embedded in an autonomous marketplace, they remain sensitive to philanthropic imperatives. For some, this is a worrisome fact given the predominance of funders who are focused on using film to make change. The current fixation on outreach and impact has generated considerable internal debate in the industry. It is seen as being at odds, in a way, with independent film's original mission "to make films that aren't prefabricated to hit a target audience of someone else's devising." Critics argue that the drive to fund social issue projects has affected their formal aesthetics, that the balance between storytelling and activism has tilted too far toward activism: "Keeping the artistry in documentary has been hard," noted one well known producer at a recent panel in New York. Others state their concerns about the pressure on films to make change even more directly: "is such hyperbolic politicking too much to ask of films? Should they not be free to document and observe and let audiences make up their own mind?"[39]

For those who have fully embraced the new social issue documentary funding model, there are still things to be negotiated. Artists have always had patrons, and often patrons want to be in a positive relation with artists, but sometimes the collaboration between filmmakers and their funding partners can be fraught. Indeed, Active Voice, a company that helps filmmakers, funders, and nonprofits devise strategies for the use of media in social-issue campaigns and messaging, created an online multimedia project called The Prenups to service the growing need in the social-issue documentary community for better tools to manage relations between filmmakers and funders:

> Filmmakers and funders need each other more than ever. Filmmakers spend years of their lives creating powerful stories that let viewers slip into the skins of people they don't know but come to care about, and these filmmakers need support to tell such high-impact stories. Funders bring tremendous knowledge, networks, analytical skills, money and other resources to social change efforts. They need powerful stories to put human faces on the issues they work on, because doing so helps influence public will. We didn't choose the term Prenups accidentally. We've learned that both parties need language and guidelines in order to understand each other's goals, standards, values and expectations—before they tie the knot.[40]

From the earliest days of the "documentary movement," as Basil Wright once wrote, filmmakers faced a choice between serving the needs of their "enlightened patrons" and following their own creative instinct as artists. The tension between the two paths for the form continue to shape documentary practice today, as the very existence of the Prenups demonstrates.[41]

CONCLUSION

The restructuring of documentary after the digital revolution has challenged the ontology of the form, as experience with my own film illustrates. Upon completion in 2008, *Lioness* was screened in festivals, broadcast on television, downloaded and streamed online and sold on DVD via a range of outlets. In addition to being spread across a number of platforms, the film was extended and supplemented by the creation of additional content, including material for two websites, bonus features for the DVD, a five minute video op ed, blog posts, and a study guide. *Lioness* came to exist in other semiotic modalities as well—in the responses posted by viewers of the film online and the face-to-face conversations we had with audiences around the country during our outreach campaign.

The film's circulation helped crystallize a set of concerns about military and veteran women that had not been articulated yet but was in the air and ripe for revelation. It did so by stitching together a heterogeneous range of actors from disparate realms—soldiers, veterans, military and VA medical professionals, social workers, politicians, activists—who had no inherent existence as a unified community except through the mediation of the film. My codirector and I documented the emergence of this new formation and its political effects in a nineteen page "impact" report, creating yet another form of our film's existence.[42]

Documentary film has been affected not just by the rise of new architectures of distribution and exhibition, but also by a broader process in society, one that is reshaping contemporary life, namely the migration of calculative technologies of accounting into social and cultural realms. Both private and public sector activities are increasingly structured around calculations of costs and benefits, estimates of financial returns, assessments of performance and risk, and other forms of numerical and financial representation.[43] As we know this ongoing economization of the social field, best exemplified by a shift to viewing metrics as the only legitimate tool to measure effectiveness, has raised problematic issues in arenas such as universities, schools, hospitals, and professional sports. What happens when audit practices are applied to artistic production? What does it mean to attempt to standardize unique cultural works—to make the previously incalculable calculable—through the imposition of quantifiable goals and benchmarks? The infiltration of economic reasoning into the independent film sector, as I have suggested, has been of significant consequence but much more work remains to be done on the topic.

NOTES

1. See Meg McLagan, "Human Rights, Testimony, and Transnational Publicity," in Michel Fehr (ed.), with Gazelle Krikorian and Yates McKee, *Nongovernmental Politics* (New York: Zone Books, 2007), pp. 304–17.
2. Social labor is part of the process of assembly, association, and translation through which knowledge is produced and sustained by a network of interdependent interacting agents, what Bruno Latour calls in *The Pasteurization of France*, trans. Alan Sheridan and John Law (Cambridge, MA: Harvard University Press, 1988). In my essay "Spectacles of difference: Cultural Activism and the Mass Mediation of Tibet," in Faye Ginsburg, Lila Abu-Lughod, and Brian Larkin (eds.), *Media Worlds: Anthropology on New Terrain* (Berkeley: University of California Press, 2002), pp. 90–111, I explore the role of public-relations experts as cultural brokers or translators of cross-cultural knowledge about Tibetan Buddhism in the context of transnational Tibet activism.
3. In Meg McLagan, "Circuits of Suffering," *Political and Legal Anthropology Review* 28. 2 (2005), pp. 223–39, I analyze the networks and social practices that shape the way local concerns get translated into narratives and discursive forms that register as legitimate human rights claims in an international context. For more on the architecture of circulation, see Brian Larkin, "Degraded Images, Distorted Sounds: Nigerian Video and the Infrastructure of Piracy," in *Signal and Noise: Media, Infrastructure and Urban Culture in Nigeria* (Durham: Duke University Press, 2008), pp. 217–41, and Larkin, "Making Equivalence Happen: Commensuration and the Grounds of Circulation" in Patricia Spyer and Mary Steedly (eds.), *How Images Move* (Durham: Duke University Press, forthcoming).
4. Nonfiction film, as a "discourse of sobriety," has long operated under the assumption "that they can and should alter the world or our place within it, that they can effect action and entail consequences." Bill Nichols, *Blurred Boundaries: Questions of Meaning in Contemporary Culture* (Bloomington: Indiana University Press, 1991), p. 67.
5. Traditionally, film release entailed the sale of a finished film to a distributor who guaranteed theatrical distribution and took all rights. Ceding control of her rights, a filmmaker usually saw little revenue in the end but was free to move on to her next project instead of having to put substantial time into trying to reach audiences.
6. The numbers tell a dramatic story: of thirty-eight film-financing firms that existed in 2007, only eleven remained in 2011. Wall Street invested $2 billion into independent films (fiction and nonfiction) between 2005 and 2007. That number dropped precipitously after 2008. In addition, due to the recession, the industry experienced a decline of the presale market and the DVD market, and overall returns diminished. Such developments made it difficult to construct a financial model by which a single, independently produced feature film could return

on its investment through conventional distribution channels. Alicia Van Couvering, "Slumpdays," *Filmmaker* 18.2 (Winter 2010), p. 90.

7. See "Documentary, 1982–Present," Box Office Mojo, http://www.boxofficemojo.com/genres/chart/?id=documentary.htm.
8. The company claimed its decision had nothing to do with the film, but observers have argued otherwise.
9. The film premiered at the Sundance Film Festival in 2006 and won two Academy Awards, and Al Gore went on to win a Nobel Peace Prize in 2007 for his work.
10. See Jess Search, *Beyond the Box Office: New Documentary Valuations*, Channel 4 BRITDOC Foundation, May 2011, http://www.documentary.org/images/news/2011/AnInconvenient-Truth_BeyondTheBoxOffice.pdf, for a detailed evaluation of *An Inconvenient Truth*'s "social return on investment."
11. Chris Anderson, *The Long Tail: Why the Future of Business Is Selling Less of More* (New York: Hyperion Books, 2006).
12. For a recent analysis of Greenwald's house party strategy, see Chuck Tryon, "Digital Distribution, Participatory Culture, and the Transmedia Documentary," *Jump Cut* 53 (Summer 2011), http://www.ejumpcut.org/currentissue/TryonWebDoc/index.html.
13. See Josh Kron's discussion of Invisible Children's evangelical roots, http://www.theatlantic.com/international/archive/2012/04/mission-from-god-the-upstart-christian-sect-driving-invisible-children-and-changing-africa/255626/. For information on Invisible Children's connection to conservative evangelical entities whose controversial practices include supporting anti-homosexual legislation in Uganda: http://www.talk2action.org/story/2012/3/11/145213/275/.
14. Brian Larkin, personnal communication. See also Gilad Lotan, "Kony 2012: See How Invisible Networks Helped A Campaign Capture the World's Attention." *Social Flow*, March 14. 2012, http://blog.socialflow.com/post/7120244932/data-viz-kony2012-see-how-invisible-networks-helped-a-campaign-capture-the-worlds-attention.
15. Christopher M. Kelty, *Two Bits: The Cultural Significance of Free Software* (Durham: Duke University Press, 2008).
16. In addition, the boom in hedge funds and private equity markets in the aughts created staggering amounts of wealth for the individuals involved, some of whom also invested in social-issue documentaries.
17. Ted Leonisis, "Ted Leonsis on Filmanthropy," American University Center for Social Media, August 2, 2007, http://www.centerforsocialmedia.org/blog/making-your-media-matter/ted-leonsis-filmanthropy.
18. In *Global Accountabilities: Participation, Pluralism, and Public Ethics* (Cambridge: Cambridge University Press, 2007). Alnoor Ebrahim and Edward Weisbrand argue that the nonprofit and philanthropic sector was transformed in the 1990s by a powerful mantra—accountability—and that impact is the most recent manifestation of this discourse.
19. Vincent Stehle, "How Documentaries Have Become Stronger Advocacy Tools," *The Chronicle of Higher Philanthropy*, October 2, 2011, http://philanthropy.com/article/A-Revolution-in-Documentaries/129202.
20. "Our Mission," Participant Media, http://www.participantmedia.com/company/about_us.php.
21. See Emily Verellen, "From Distribution to Audience Engagement: Social Change Through Film," The Fledgling Fund, August 2010, p. 6, http://www.thefledglingfund.org/impact/From%20Distribution%20to%20Audience%20Engagment.pdf.

22. *Ibid.*, p. 6.
23. *Ibid.*, p. 7.
24. *Ibid.*, p. 9.
25. For an example of immediate and distant antecedents to liberal public media philanthropy, see Barbara Abrash and Pat Aufderheide, "Documentary Funding at the Ford Foundation, 1970-2005," a report submitted to Ford Foundation, September 14, 2006, and see Anna McCarthy, *The Citizen Machine: Governing by Television in 1950s America* (New York: New Press, 2010).
26. Verellen, "From Distribution to Audience Engagement," pp. 14 and 15.
27. For more on American entrepreneurship and the presentification of the future through accounting technologies, see Martin Giraudeau, "Remembering the Future: Entrepreneurship Guidebooks in the US, from meditation to method (1945-75), *Foucault Studies* 13, pp. 40-66, May 2012.
28. Michael Renov, *The Subject of Documentary* (Minneapolis: University of Minnesota Press, 2004).
29. Ilana Gershon and Joshua Malitsky, "Actor-Network Theory and Documentary Studies," *Studies in Documentary Film* 4.1 (2010), pp. 65–78.
30. David Whiteman, "The Impact of The Uprising of '34: A Coalition Model of Production and Distribution," *Jump Cut: A Review of Contemporary Media* 45, www.ejumpcut.org/archive/jc4S.2002Avhiteman/uprisingtexthtml.
31. David Whiteman, "Documentary Film as Policy Analysis: The Impact of Yes, In My Backyard, on Activists, Agendas, and Policy," *Mass Communication and Society* 12.4 (2009), p. 476.
32. Elizabeth Miller, "Building Participation in the Outreach for the Documentary The Water Front," *Journal of Canadian Studies* 43. 1 (Winter 2009), pp. 59–88.
33. Search, *Beyond the Box Office: New Documentary Valuations*, p. 10.
34. Peter Broderick, "Declaration of Independence: Ten Principles of Hybrid Distribution," *IndieWire*, September 2009, http://www.peterbroderick.com/writing/writing.html; and Scott Reiss, *Think Outside the Box Office: The Ultimate Guide to Film Distribution and Marketing in the Digital Era*, http://www.thinkoutsidetheboxoffice.com.
35. Manohla Dargis, "Declaration of Indies: Just Sell It Yourself!," *The New York Times*, January 14, 2010, http://www.nytimes.com/2010/01/17/movies/17dargis.html.
36. For a detailed acccount of one filmmaker's foray into the brave new world of self-distribution, see Paul Devlin, "The Theatrical Launch," *Filmmaker Magazine* (Winter 2010), pp. 92–99, 109–11.
37. Helen de Michiel, "A Mosaic of Practices: Public Media and Participatory Culture," *Afterimage* 35.6 (May–June 2008), pp. 7–14.
38. Basil Wright, "The Documentary Dilemma," *Hollywood Quarterly* 5.4 (Summer 1951), pp. 321–25.
39. "Battle of Ideas 2010," November 6, 2010, http://www.battleofideas.org.uk/index.php/2010/session_detail/4711/.
40. "The Prenups: What Filmmakers and Funders Should Talk About Before Tying the Knot," http://www.th eprenups.org/?q=content/overview.
41. Wright, p. 324.
42. See www.lionessthefilm.com/ImpactReport_hiRes5.pdf. See also Jessica Clark and Barbara Abrash, "Social Justice Documentary: Designing for Impact," http://www.centerforsocialmedia.org/tags/impact/designing-impact for a series of documentary impact case studies, including *Lioness*.
43. Andrew Mennicken and Peter Miller "Accounting, Territorialization, and Power," *Foucault Studies* 13, pp. 4-24 (May 2012).

Indigenous women and military man, Nebaj, Guatemala, 1982 (photo: Jean-Marie Simon).

Granito: An Interview with Pamela Yates

Barbara Abrash and Meg McLagan

Pamela Yates is a filmmaker who has been making social-issue documentaries for more than two decades. Her latest project, *Granito: How to Nail a Dictator*, premiered at the 2011 Sundance Film Festival. *Granito* follows up on Yates' 1984 film, *When the Mountains Tremble*, which documented the Guatemalan civil war from the perspective of the indigenous insurgents narrated by then political refugee Rigoberta Menchú, who won the Nobel Peace Prize in 1992. *Granito* traces Menchú's efforts to bring the former Guatemalan military government leaders responsible for the genocide to justice, drawing on Yates' footage from the 1980s which now serves as evidence of war crimes for the prosecution in Spain's National Court.

MEG MCLAGAN: One of your first films, *When the Mountains Tremble*, documented the Guatemalan civil war in the 1980s. How did you come to make that film?

PAMELA YATES: I had been working in Central America with Tom Sigel. He was camera, I was sound, and we would do work-for-hire jobs together and then dream of making more of our own films with Peter Kinoy, of course. Tom was also my partner for many years and across many films. We would do the jobs, make money, and then come back to the United States and put the money into our own films. We found that it was a lot easier to hire ourselves out as crew than to apply for a two- or three-thousand-dollar grant. It took less time, and you could make more money.

We heard about this rebellion in the indigenous highlands of Guatemala against the military dictatorship. That was when we decided to go. Getting into Guatemala was tough, because the Guatemalan military was hostile to the press. They had killed about seventeen Guatemalan journalists between 1979 and 1981 for trying to report on the movement for democratic reform, and when foreign journalists came to report, they would stop them at the airport, question them, and deport them.

Pamela Yates filming *When the Mountains Tremble* in Guatemala, 1982 (photo: Newton Thomas Sigel).

The only way we got in was that there were presidential elections called in 1982 to show that Guatemala was "free" and "democratic"—of course, the only candidates were generals—so they had to let in the international press corps. They were worried about attracting and retaining foreign investment, because the military had accrued this terrible human rights record. The elections were a way of showing that the Guatemalan military rulers were democratic.

When I got there, no one would talk to me because they were so afraid. People were being killed and had disappeared, yet everything appeared normal. Death squads were operating in the open, so people were just way too afraid to talk to me. Even if you found someone whose son had disappeared, they would say he was picked up by *desconocidos*, unknown men, but everybody actually knew they were paramilitary death squads. It was really impossible. I tried to talk to the army, and they slammed the door in my face and threatened me. I tried through an intermediary to contact the guerrillas to go on a trip with them and tell their side of the story, but I got no response. I thought, "Oh this is bad. I'm a total failure on my first film."

BARBARA ABRASH: How did you finally earn trust?

PY: I started with the army. I would go down every day to the air force base and smoke cigarettes with the enlisted soldiers standing around outside. They gradually introduced me to their sergeant, and their sergeant introduced me to his colonel, and then I got to meet the head of the Guatemalan Armed Forces—this macho General Benedicto Lucas García. I did an interview with him, and then I convinced him to take me with him on a helicopter mission to the Guatemalan highlands.

MM: Clearly, you had a lot of feelings about what was going on. How did you conduct a reasonable conversation with somebody like a colonel or the head of a militia? As just a curious journalist?

PY: Yes, and at that time, military sales and aid from the United States had been cut off under Jimmy Carter. The Guatemalan military was very anxious to reopen those sales and military aid under Ronald Reagan. Reagan took office in 1981; we're talking a year later, 1982, because those things move very slowly. The Guatemalan government was petitioning and working very hard to get the United States to reopen sales, and I think they saw me or us as a megaphone to state their story. I basically just ask people about themselves. I am really interested in people. But as I got up through the ranks, I would ask people about military aid from the United States and relationships to the United States. In many ways, it was a matter of being in the right place at the right time and understanding that we could take advantage of this moment to get at the truth of what was happening there.

There were four different guerilla groups, and they formed a united front. One of the leaders of the Guatemalan National Revolutionary Unity (URNG) made the filming of *When the Mountains Tremble* possible by arranging the trips with the guerrillas. Back in the day, it was all done through intermediaries, so I couldn't know his identity. I knew only his *nombre de guerra*. I recently got to know him and the role he played in making that crucial part of the film possible. This former guerrilla is now the director of the recently discovered secret National Police Archives, which outline the Guatemalan state's system of repression and disappearance. The archives are nearly finished scanning all of the relevant documents from the worst period of violence. It is an important research repository.

When I went on that helicopter mission with the general, we went to a battle, and it was in a bowl-shaped valley, and as we were circling, there were guerrilla sharpshooters on the side of a mountain, and they shot our helicopter down. We were falling out of the sky. The bullets had gone through the windshield—all the windows shattered—out the machine gunner's door, which was open, and hit the rear rotor. And the rotor stopped, so we were falling. The copilot restarted the rear rotor and made an emergency landing on the other side of the mountain. What that meant was that this near-death experience created this bond with General Benedicto Lucas García. When we were rescued to the nearby army base, he let me film anything I wanted. I got to film a lot of other stuff. So they never suspected.

Years later, I actually found the shooter, and he's in our latest film, *Granito: How to Nail a Dictator* [2011]. His *nombre de guerra* was Rafael. Rafael shot the helicopter out of the sky. The footage I was able to film because of nearly crashing is now being used in the genocide case to indict the general. Rigoberta Menchú is [also] part of this destiny.

The conditions were harsh; you took opportunities to film wherever you could. A lot of stuff we tried to film we couldn't. We shot with civil society, we filmed the army, the guerrillas, we tried to film the whole spectrum of Guatemalan society. Tom did a really good job under tremendously dangerous conditions. Working together gave me a good sense how you imbue beauty and humanity into really difficult situations, into conflict—how to communicate our shared humanity and the value of each individual life.

After six months, we smuggled the footage out of Guatemala and came back to the United States with three hundred rolls of film, fifty hours of footage. Which is not very much. We didn't have anything to hold the film together in terms of telling a coherent story, just a lot of good scenes.

Then we got lucky. Someone brought Rigoberta Menchú to our studio. She had just escaped from Guatemala with her life and was in exile. She was speaking in front of the General Assembly at the United Nations. Our studio is across Manhattan from the UN, on West Forty-Second Street. I did a traditional interview with her, sitting down in front of a desk, and then we realized when we got back the dailies that she was really special, that she could be the storyteller, she was the voice of the voiceless Mayas.

She also brought a huge amount to the story of the film. We sat down and went through all the scenes that we had, and then she wrote the parts of her own story that were illustrated in the different scenes. It was her personal story, but it provided links with the political story unfolding in Guatemala. Then we went into a real studio for two days and filmed her speaking into the camera with a simple black background. I was influenced by the film *Reds* in those days and wanted it just like that film.

BA: How did you fund the film?

PY: The film was supported by the Corporation for Public Broadcasting (CPB), the Rubin Foundation, and a private donor who was interested in Guatemalan weaving and who could see from the war that Mayan culture was being decimated. We made a couple of presales to European television. But we owned our own equipment, and Peter Kinoy was the producer and also the editor of *When the Mountains Tremble*. He is slightly older than we are, and he said, "OK, I'll be the producer, and you be the director." We could really make films for a low cost.

MM: How was *When the Mountains Tremble* received?

PY: *When the Mountains Tremble* opened in forty U.S. cities and was distributed in twenty-five countries in Europe and Latin America. It went to the Sundance Film Festival, where it won a Special Jury Prize. Sundance was a meeting of the tribe then, principally just us filmmakers.

Even though CPB gave us the lion's share of funding for the film, PBS refused to show the film. We got the money in 1982, but the film was not broadcast until 1986. PBS dubbed the film *When the Stations Tremble* [laughs]. They made us do two different wraparounds and finally decided that they were going to have a five-minute film before the film started that basically told you everything you were about to see in the film—told in the bland *Frontline* style. Then PBS showed the film, with a half-hour panel discussion afterward about why what we said wasn't true [laughs]. They included the ambassador of Guatemala to excuse the genocide! That's what they considered to be "balanced."

Others on the panel were Harry Moses, a producer at *60 Minutes* (CBS) and Doyle McManus, the *Los Angeles Times* Washington correspondent. All white men. All attacking me, whom they reluctantly agreed to let on the panel to defend the film. People said it was like the sharks circling. Remember, it was the second Reagan administration, PBS was afraid for their survival. I have to get a copy of that tape, because we plan to use it in *Granito*.

In 1992, when Rigoberta was awarded the Nobel Peace Prize, I called PBS up and I said, "You know, you have the broadcast rights to *When the Mountains Tremble*. Would you like to rebroadcast it?" The PBS executive said, "We're in an election year—we don't have any air time."

It's wonderful to now know that the PBS series *POV* has committed to broadcasting our latest film, *Granito*.

BA: You've always had the usefulness of your films in mind.

PY: We've always been committed to doing outreach with our films. We tried hard with *Resurgence*, but there wasn't really a movement to take the film out and around in the United States. But when we released *When the Mountains Tremble*, there was a movement to stop the war and in solidarity with the people of Central America. That really took off. Peter, Tom, or I would go to every single city and do a parallel campaign. One part was to work with the grass roots, the solidarity groups in the area, and the other was to ensure mainstream press coverage. We wrote an outreach handbook, a model for other filmmakers to follow. That worked really well, and after each screening, we raised money for the solidarity committees. We raised a lot of money—on average, a dollar a person who came to the movie theaters.

MM: Could you say a few words about your continuing work with Rigoberta Menchú and how her status has changed over the years, from guerrilla activist, to Nobel Peace Prize winner, to her candidacy in the Guatemalan presidential elections?

PY: Rigoberta was a member of the Committee for Peasant Unity (CUC) in the late seventies and early eighties. It was composed of peasants organizing in cooperatives for small farms and was in the forefront in getting proper lands rights for local Mayas. She was never a guerrilla, though the Guatemalan Army didn't differentiate—all who opposed the military dictatorship, all who worked for reform, were considered "Communist subversives." After Rigoberta fled Guatemala in 1982, fearing for her life, she spent ten years tirelessly crisscrossing the globe, trying to get the international community to understand what was happening in Guatemala and to intervene politically. She and I traveled together for a few years when *When the Mountains Tremble* was showing in festivals and opening in theaters, and she had the amazing ability afterward to get the greatest potential out of each and every single audience member to work for human rights in Guatemala. If you ever want to see a true leader in action, Rigoberta Menchú is the quintessential one. I think *When the Mountains Tremble*, as well as her autobiography, *I, Rigoberta Menchú*, and her active speaking tour all contributed to putting her on the world stage. And on the five hundredth anniversary of the Europeans' arrival in the Americas, she was awarded the Nobel Peace Prize.

The Nobel Peace Prize comes with a large amount of money, and with that she created a foundation. She also invested in drugstores that dispense low-cost drugs to poor people. She's constantly fundraising for projects centered on peace and indigenous rights. We have gotten Docurama, the distributor of *When the Mountains Tremble*, to donate hundreds of DVDs to her foundation's efforts.

In 2007, Rigoberta Menchú ran for president of Guatemala. Not only was she the first woman to run for that office, she was the first Mayan to run. Because of the culture of fear that still permeates Guatemala, because the political violence has morphed into drug-trafficking violence, and because the impunity of the past was never addressed, the violence continues. A lot of people who were in the army became part of the drug mafia. Rigoberta ran her presidential campaign in a very difficult situation, security-wise. In the 2007–2008 campaign, eight people who were campaign workers or candidates in her party were killed. Young people in their twenties were gunned down.

Rigoberta ran unsuccessfully for president again in September 2011. Inspired by Obama's successful campaign for president, she's now organizing a civil rights movement in Guatemala called Winaq ("the wholeness of the human being" in Mayan). Once again, thirty years later, the cycle continues as she works to unite the Mayas of Guatemala to fight for their rights. She says, "We act like a minority, but we're actually the majority. Let's claim our civil rights."

BA: How does she stay safe?

PY: The government of Guatemala is equally concerned that she is a target, and they've issued her bodyguards. There is a liberal democratic president of Guatemala now, Alvaro Colomut, but the army and other economic interests still hold a lot of power, and change comes slowly in Guatemala. The default is to stop change by reverting to violence.

MM: Your main focus was on supporting the solidarity movement, wasn't it?

PY: Right, and twenty years later, in 2003, when we had the first public showing in Guatemala of *When the Mountains Tremble*, I came to find out that the film had been shown thousands of times clandestinely during the war. The resistance movement would get VHS copies from El Salvador and make copies of copies of copies. You see these copies now and you can barely see the image.

We made another film after *When the Mountains Tremble* called *Nicaragua: Report from the Front* [1983]. We traveled with the Contras, a covert counterrevolutionary group trying to overthrow the Sandinistas and backed by the CIA. We walked with them from Honduras into Nicaragua, maybe a hundred kilometers. We were with them for about two weeks. Then we did the same thing with the Sandinistas in the same area in Nicaragua. We tried to show the war from both sides of the front. We also released the Contra material on a series of five *CBS Evening News* reports, and we broke the story about U.S. covert aid to support the Contras. The fact of the Contras was secret in the United States, but they weren't covert in Central America.

Then we worked with an NGO in Washington called the Caribbean Basin Project on a short film that they could use to lobby Congress to extend the Boland Amendment, cutting off military aid to groups who willfully violated human rights norms such as attacking civilians. The Boland Amendment forced the Reagan administration to cut off aid to the Contras, which is why the government began to fund them covertly, and Iran-Contra was born. They had to find ways to get the funding to the Contras so they could destroy the Sandinistas.

BA: Your work has always been linked to movements, close to activists.

PY: Yes. In the 1990s, we made a trilogy called *Living Broke in Boom Times* about poor people who were left out of the largest economic boom in U.S. history. The trilogy was made with and about poor-people's movements dedicated to trying to get up and out of poverty.

"Movement" is a funny word. What actually makes a movement? Sometimes you are hopeful that a movement will arise. We were hopeful that a movement of all those hungry Americans would develop, but it didn't, really. We worked closely with the people who were trying to make it happen. What was unique about them was that they weren't advocates for the poor. They were actually the poor, the homeless.

MM: Your film *State of Fear: The Truth About Terrorism* [2005, 94 minutes] represented a shift from a focus on solidarity movements to working with transitional justice and human rights organizations. How did that launch your relationship with the International Center for Transitional Justice (ICTJ)?

PY: *State of Fear* is a documentary based on the Peruvian Truth and Reconciliation Commission's examination of their country's twenty-year "war on terror" against Shining Path insurgents. During the conflict, both the state and the insurgents carried out campaigns of terror that led to the deaths of nearly seventy thousand civilians, many of them from Quechua-speaking areas of the country. When we first met with staff of the ICTJ, it was a new NGO, born after the South African Truth Commission. They were the ones who said, "The Peruvian Truth Commission is starting up, it will have the first public audiences of any truth commission in Latin America. It would make a really great film. What if we could help you raise $20,000? Do you think you could make a film for that?" We said, "No, we don't think so, but we could start on it." They went with us to meet with the Ford Foundation, which provided seed funding and later support. That was the beginning of a fruitful relationship with the ICTJ.

ICTJ is not a funder of our recent films, but its staff members are valued advisors. ICTJ has been especially helpful with *The Reckoning* [2009, 95 minutes], our film about the International Criminal Court, in that they made it officially part of their consulting work. We could talk to any of their experts, and we could use their offices in any of the countries where we were filming; all of their expertise helped us make much more nuanced films. We were working with people working in conflict zones, day in and day out, people who know the lay of the land. We come to stories and we learn as much as we can as quickly as possible, but we had really good advisors on both *State of Fear* and *The Reckoning*.

MM: Could you talk about working with transitional justice and human rights organizations? Especially in terms of your point of view and how you approached telling the story?

PY: A lot of times when you go to make a film, especially if it is a complex film like *The Reckoning*, there are so many people who know much more about it than you do. One of the things we do is get people from the different organizations that have made their focus international justice and ask them to be on our advisory board. And then we get insight into what to read, what to look at, who else to talk to, and that forms the basis of our research. Later, the advisors become our outreach partners. While we're making the film, they come and they look at samples of the film, or they look at the film before we lock it, and they comment on it. But we have final artistic decision over every aspect of the film and educational initiative and narratively how we're going to tell the story. We're always very clear with our outreach partners about that. They also see that we are incredibly good listeners and can recognize good ideas when they are proffered.

BA: You have said that storytelling is the core of your films. Can you talk about how aesthetics play into your stories?

PY: I am an intuitive filmmaker working inside a visual language that I'm not always used to verbalizing. One of my strengths is always having worked with cinematographers who are excellent interpreters of ideas into the visual realm. This began with Tom Sigel and *When the Mountains Tremble*. And since I was a sound recordist for many years, I worked with some excellent cinematographers and learned from them as I learned from Tom. On *The Reckoning*, I worked with Melle van Essen, whom I call "the Dutch Master." He has a steadiness, a calm core. He can bring out the beauty, the humanity, the place we all inhabit that connects us as humans, by how he photographs each scene, no matter how difficult.

I think the geography of the human face is one of the most beautiful panoramas of cinema. I know we connect with faces—it's part of our limbic brain, a remnant from when we were pack animals. We look for meaning in each others' eyes.

BA: Close-ups of faces are a signature stylistic element of your films.

PY: Yes, that's what makes the individual stories universal. These are stories about the human drama, about the human condition, and then there are the faces to bring it home. These faces help create a deep emotional place for the audience. In *State of Fear* and *The Reckoning*, we took a portable green screen with us to all the locations—the sea, the Andes, the jungle, the Congo, Acholiland in northern Uganda. This is a four-by-six-foot piece of green cloth that we set up with two C stands and did portraits in front of it. Then we combined the portraits with many other background images in the editing room to create the signature look of the films.

At the center of everything I do are the victims, those most affected, those whose voice is so rarely heard, but who are crying out to be heard. So thinking about how best to help them tell their own stories has taken many different forms throughout my life as a filmmaker. Those most affected have always been the protagonists in my films. I never have experts opine. You can be an expert, but you also have to be a player in the history, not simply an observer, to be in one of my films. This led me to finding and including Rigoberta Menchú and later Luis Moreno-Ocampo, for example.

MM: Have you ever had issues where an organization has wanted you to go one direction, and you really wanted to go in a different direction?

PY: Not on major structural things, but on smaller things, we've had a lot of back and forth. Sometimes we can see their point, and we find a way to finesse putting it into the film, and sometimes we just don't. The differences more often happen when NGOs want to put something into a film because of its content, but if you put something in for content and it doesn't have a reason organically to be there, it's really not heard or felt. It doesn't touch people emotionally. Sometimes our advisors or outreach partners want to do away with certain style elements that they don't think are right, but we feel are really engaging for a general audience. So we have to be pretty clear why we've made this decision.

When we have a screening, we have a questionnaire. The first ten or fifteen minutes after a screening, we ask each person to fill it out, because once the group dynamic kicks in, it's hard to get a contribution from everyone. That's helped a lot in terms of seeing trends in how the films are viewed, but it also confronts us with recognizing what we think, why we think it, and how are we communicating the story. Especially with *The Reckoning*, the contributions of the advisors and the NGO partners were at an extremely high level, intelligent and well thought-out. It really was good for us, but it was challenging too, because everyone had his or her own idea about what the film should be.

MM: When you worked previously with solidarity movements, you didn't have rough-cut screenings or engage in that sort of practice?

PY: We actually did. We're interested in what they think. I also like to show people the films they are in before they are broadcast, because sometimes I am not always a hundred percent sensitive to what they might be sensitive to. I feel that in making nonfiction films, if they're open to it, you should show it to them.

In *When the Mountains Tremble*, the person who became my liaison to the guerrillas told me to meet her in a McDonalds in downtown Guatemala City and to bring a tourist map and *Time* magazine and sit there. We had never met in person, and this was the way she would recognize me. I was really scared. I thought I was being set up. I went, of course [laughs], but I thought this small Mayan woman was going to come in and sit down next to me and everybody was going to know exactly what was going on here. But this woman came in, and she was fair-haired and white-skinned and spoke perfect English. She told me not to be afraid and that she was there to set up a clandestine trip to film with the guerrillas. She told me that from then on, my *nombre de guerra* would be Ana María.

Twenty-five years later, she's now a practicing international justice attorney and a professor at a leading U.S. law school. She's in *Granito*. She's the kind of person I have to be sure is okay with what I'm saying and doing with her story in the film, because the way the United States is now, the guerrilla groups fighting for national liberation in the 1980s could potentially now be classified as terrorist organizations, though they never engaged in terrorist acts. I feel like it's her story, her life. She has the right to decide how that is made public for the first time in *Granito*.

BA: It must have been amazing to reconnect with people who were in *When the Mountains Tremble*.

PY: I had stayed in contact with Rigoberta Menchú all these years, though I lost contact with my guerrilla liaison, but more because she wanted to lose contact, not me. I think it is really important to go back to places, even if you are not filming there; that you should continue to have relationships that were formed during the film. It's immoral to go to a place, tell a story, and then say, "Thanks for your story, now I'm going on to the next story." It is so much deeper than that. You are changed fundamentally by the telling of it.

BA: How would you characterize *State of Fear, The Reckoning, Granito*, and the film you are working on now? How do they relate to one another?

PY: They are a transitional justice quartet—transitional justice meaning the act of redressing and preventing the most severe violations of human rights by confronting legacies of mass abuse. This holistic approach includes truth commissions, prosecutions, reparations, and memorialization. *State of Fear* is really about truth, because it's based on the findings of the Peruvian Truth and Reconciliation Commission, and *The Reckoning* is about justice, because it's about the first six years of the International Criminal Court. *Granito* is about legacy, or how a documentary film, *When the Mountains Tremble*, made twenty-five-plus years ago, becomes forensic evidence in a genocide case. Our next film, *The Future of Memory*, is about how societies create their collective memory and memorialize their history. How history is an argument. *The Future of Memory* will focus on four to six stories in different parts of the world and on places where people are actively engaged in shaping their historical narrative. Often, the debates take place over building memory museums, as in Uganda; or a monument, as in Peru, or where memory is absent, as in Russia, or where memory is forbidden, as in Spain. And there will be a story that takes place here in the United States.

MM: With solidarity movements, you are often working with people from the community, and with human rights activists, you are sometimes working with people who are representing others.

PY: Yes. Over the years I've learned how to weave more seamlessly both kinds of stories, since both are integral to finding a way forward. Our multiyear outreach campaigns create tools—because the films themselves are the flagships—for movements and for human rights defenders. The screening kits and supplemental educational materials are designed for people at the community level, and they work with us in creating them and then using them.

BA: You are still on the side of the people who are affected.

PY: It is always individuals who make history. They are often ordinary people who sacrifice enormously to make change. They endure setbacks and challenges to their integrity, and yet they keep going. This effort makes them extraordinary. Like Rigoberta Menchú, a poor Maya woman from a small village in the highlands who became a Nobel Peace laureate. It's these kinds of people who are the protagonistsin our films.

MM: In *When the Mountains Tremble*, there was no mechanism for justice—there was only the hope that the United States would stop supporting this calamity.

PY: I thought that by exposing the violence in Guatemala, the international community, including the United States, would come to the aid of the beleaguered Mayan villagers and prevent it from continuing. That was my naive belief, and it was not to be.

The anger I feel knowing that those ex-generals responsible for the Guatemalan genocide have never been brought to account and that they still lead lives of power and luxury is almost too much to bear. Yet I believe that channeling that anger into telling the story of the victims who have never given up on seeing justice done strengthens me. Their many *granitos* have inspired my sole *granito*, the tiny grain of sand we can each contribute.

BA: And now you are also directly contributing to the process of justice. Your outtakes and footage from *When the Mountains Tremble* are contributing to the forensic evidence against the Guatemalan military leaders.

PY: Exactly, that's the *granito*. That concept was part of my testimony in front of the Spanish National Court, where the Guatemalan genocide case is being adjudicated. Using *When the Mountains Tremble* and all the outtakes and complete transcripts from 1982, I entered them into evidence in the case. I ended my testimony saying, "I thought I would stop the violence by showing *When the Mountains Tremble* to the world, but now I hope that by adding my *granito*—together with all the other *granitos* that so many others have contributed—that it will bring the perpetrators of the genocide to justice and vindicate the victims."

And what I thought I was doing back then transforms itself into something completely different. It's at the core of our understanding of the importance of human rights documentation, including documentary film.

MM: Can you give us an update on how that case came about and where it is now?

PY: Rigoberta Menchú brought the case to the Spanish National Court in 1999. She was inspired by the court's arrest warrant for Augusto Pinochet and his detention in London as his extradition to Spain was pending. Enough evidence has now been gathered for Judge Santiago Pedraz to issue eight arrest warrants for generals and police officials on charges of genocide. Two of these generals are in *When the Mountains Tremble*, which is why my outtakes were so valuable to them. Because of the two minutes we used in *When the Mountains Tremble* of General Ríos Montt, for example, there are thirty or forty minutes of the interview in real time. In the outtakes, General Ríos Montt talks about how he is at the top of the chain of command. He admits to command responsibility, which is always one of the most difficult elements of the crime to prove in a genocide case.

After the arrest warrants were issued, the Guatemalan Constitutional Court decided that they would not allow anyone to be extradited from Guatemala to Spain to face justice. And the Spanish National Court cannot try the accused in absentia. So none of the alleged perpetrators now dare leave Guatemala. In *Granito*, the scene then shifts to Guatemala, where we see how the Spanish National Court case has had a profound effect on emboldening the domestic judicial system and how evidence uncovered in Spain can now be used in the Guatemalan courts. This is what's come to be known as "the Pinochet Effect." More has happened in the past year in the judicial realm in Guatemala itself than has happened in the last thirty years in terms of arrests and convictions for crimes committed by the army and the state during the years of the genocide and forced disappearances. A former president and army general, Mejia Victores, has been issued an arrest warrant for genocide, and the chief of staff of the army was arrested and charged with genocide. Special Forces officers and a lieutenant were convicted and sentenced to 6,060 years each in the Dos Erres Massacre—30 years for each person they killed in 1982. That, combined with the findings of evidence in the National Police Archives implicating the state for crimes committed during the war, has enabled the attorney general's office to open cold cases from the 1980s.

Fredy Peccerelli, Executive Director Guatemalan Forensic Anthropology Foundation at the La Verbena public cemetery exhumation (photo: Dana Lixenberg).

So whatever happens, this is *Granito*'s moment in time. I hope the film itself will contribute to this tipping point for justice in Guatemala.

Because long-form documentaries such as *Granito* are fixed in time, we have developed a digital media project that will be constantly flowing and changing. At the Bay Area Video Coalition Producers Institute, I developed a flexible media project called Granito: Every Memory Matters. The idea is to create a data bank of memories, a public archive that will contain the memories of the genocide. While filming *Granito* in Guatemala, I realized that not only was the film being used as forensic evidence, but it was awakening a whole new generation, those under thirty, to what actually happened during the war. Because that is not being taught in school. There is a culture of *el olvido*, meaning forgetting. So we want to partner with the Guatemalan Forensic Anthropology Team to build a memory team and get young people to collect memories and to interview their elders with mobile devices to upload to Granito: Every Memory Matters. This memory bank will be a repository of memories that will live on the cloud. Anyone can add to or access this memory bank—either in Guatemala or in the diaspora.

An important feature of the memory bank is a time line that starts in the present, when you can stream *Granito* for free, and then you can travel back through history, all the way back to 1982 and stream *When the Mountains Tremble*. Along the way, you can add or access memories in that time line. It could be videos, photographs, testimonials, evidence, music, or maps.

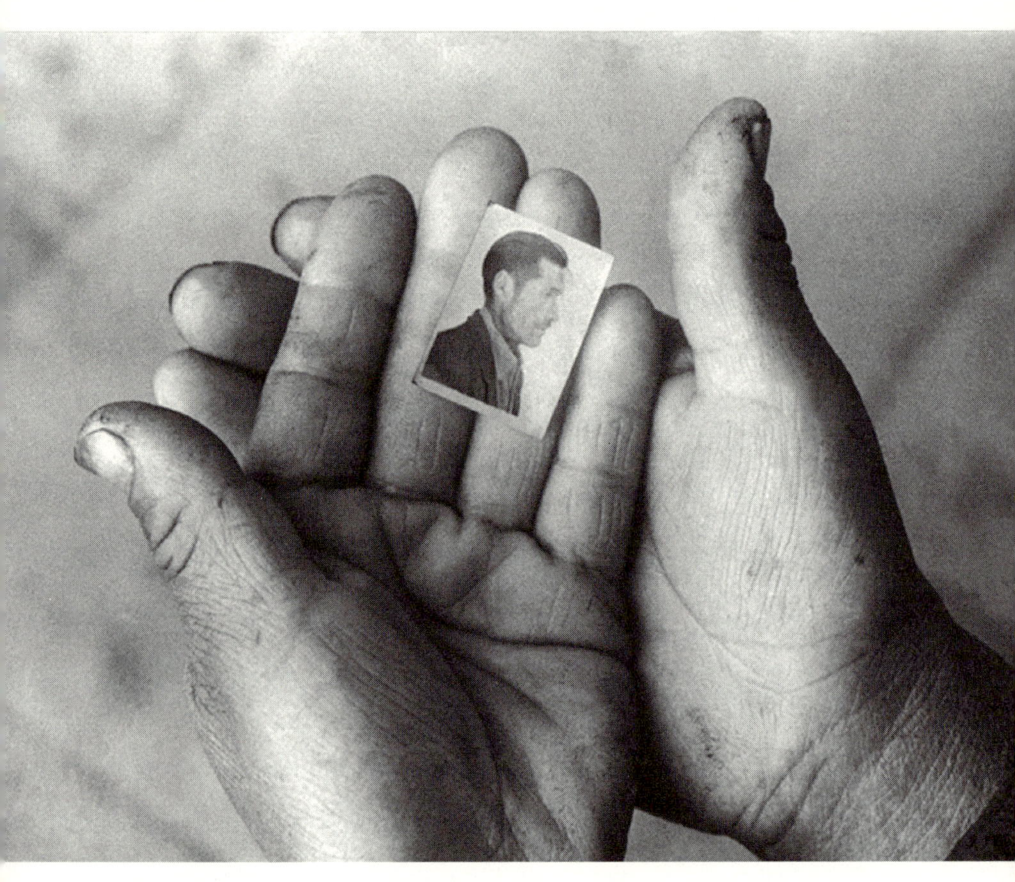

FIGURE 1 Peasant hands cradle the photo of a disappeared man in Ayacucho, Peru (photo: Vera Lentz).

State of Fear and Transitional Justice in Peru: A Case Study

Barbara Abrash and Meg McLagan

In recent years, human rights activists and documentary filmmakers together have explored the uses of old and new media technologies in order to transform the power and reach of their work. This kind of partnership is the result of the recognition of the importance of strategic communications, including documentary media, in campaigns for social change—a recognition that has reshaped the global NGO landscape as well as documentary film practice. Over time, an infrastructure of organizations, circuits, and activist networks has emerged that sustains the production and circulation of these kinds of media, bridging the gap between legal discourse based on abstract universal principles and subjective personal narratives.[1]

The following text briefly outlines the outreach campaign around *State of Fear: The Truth about Terrorism* (2005, Pamela Yates, Peter Kinoy, Paco de Onís, 94 minutes), a feature-length documentary film that portrays twenty years of repression and resistance in Peru (1980 to 2000), a period in which politicians manipulated fears of terrorist activity by Shining Path guerrillas to suspend civil liberties and unleash military and political violence (fig. 1). It tells this history through the lens of the Peruvian Truth and Reconciliation Commission (PTRC), which was established in 2001. Produced in collaboration with the International Center for Transitional Justice (ICTJ), which supports truth and reconciliation commissions worldwide, and a network of funders and human rights organizations, *State of Fear* encapsulates the transition from social-issue documentary film as text—intended to inform and enlighten—to storytelling as the core component of a long-term strategic transmedia campaign. Employing an array of media technologies and embedded in a multiplatform human rights campaign, the film project became a laboratory for new tools and practices and an important model for other social-issue filmmakers.

TRANSITIONAL JUSTICE, THE ICTJ, AND *STATE OF FEAR*

Transitional justice is a field of knowledge and theory of social change that focuses on the way societies deal with the legacy of systemic human rights violations. The approach emerged in the late 1980s and early 1990s in response to political changes in Latin America and Eastern Europe and demands in these regions for justice. As these societies transitioned to democracy, their governments adopted a number of strategies to recognize victims and promote reconciliation, including criminal prosecutions of rights abusers, truth commissions, and reparations initiatives. The International Center for Transitional Justice, a New York–based NGO, was founded by a group of lawyers who played a central role in the South African Truth and Reconciliation Commission. Their aim was to create a global clearinghouse of best practices used in societies undergoing transition. Since 2001, the ICTJ has trained human rights groups and individuals in more than thirty countries and has engaged with policy makers in numerous governments around the world.

In addition, having witnessed firsthand the valuable role of film in publicizing the work of the South African Truth Commission, the ICTJ's cofounders have recognized the value of documentary film to help broaden awareness of transitional-justice issues. As Paul van Zyl, one of the cofounders explained it: "Democratic social change requires robust public discourse and deliberation based on transparent information and the rule of law. While it is produced by institutions, rather than individual actions alone, and requires the engagement of elites, its true strength and efficacy is derived from broad-based social movements. Documentary films designed to inform, engage, and mobilize publics and linked with strategic outreach campaigns play a significant role in this process."[2]

After 9/11, Skylight Pictures (Yates, Kinoy, and de Onís) became interested in making a film about the dangers of authoritarian governments that manipulate fears of terrorism for political purposes. They approached van Zyl at the ICTJ, who immediately linked their idea with the work of the recently convened Peruvian Truth and Reconciliation Commission. Seed funding was provided by the Ford Foundation, which recognized the importance of documenting and publicizing the findings of the truth commission, but had not been successful in finding filmmakers in the region. They welcomed the project.[3]

Filmmakers bring their own experiences and sense of mission to projects like this one. Yates, Kinoy, and de Onís are passionately committed filmmakers who are knowledgeable about social-justice movements in Latin America and fluent Spanish speakers. Yates, who founded Skylight Pictures with Kinoy and cinematographer Tom Sigel in 1981, is an award-winning director. Her films include *Witness to War* (Academy Award, 1985), about an American doctor behind rebel lines in El Salvador; *When the Mountains Tremble* (Special Jury Award, Sundance, 1984), which features Nobel laureate Rigoberta Menchú; *Nicaragua: Report from the Front* (1983) about the U.S.-supported Contra War, and most recently *Granito: How to Nail a Dictator* (2011).[4]

With *State of Fear*, the Skylight team built on trusted relationships with Latin Americans that had begun with documentary films telling stories in solidarity with the Central American anti-imperialist struggles of the 1980s. These movements, which reached a high-water mark during the Reagan era, spoke to and against state power. After nonviolent reform efforts were brutally repressed by dictatorial governments, the turn to guerrilla warfare was accompanied by a fortress mentality that accepted extreme actions such as violence against civilians in the name of the cause.

Post–Cold War activism, in contrast, reaches beyond borders of nation-states to address people in terms of their common humanity and links with legal structures for achieving justice. *State of Fear* represents this historic shift. The focus on the Peruvian Truth and Reconciliation Commission places it within a human rights movement that seeks to hold states responsible for securing legal rights and obligations. The objective is to change laws that enable the persistence of intolerable modes of government and to protect rights that are threatened by government

In Peru, the filmmakers found the largest and most active human rights movement in Latin America. At the same time, the Peruvian Truth and Reconciliation Commission judiciously reported that the state and Shining Path shared responsibility for deaths and suffering. According to Yates, in this new environment, it was possible for a more nuanced, complex story to be told, one that gave an account of a specific country's process for determining and carrying out justice according to universally applicable principles.

With a small grant from the Ford Foundation's New York and Southern Cone offices and the assistance of the ICTJ, Yates and de Onís covered the PTRC's May 2002 open hearings in Lima and began to connect with local human rights activists. Once assured of the filmmakers' ability to establish relationships of trust with local Peruvians, the truth commission opened its rich archive of rarely seen films and photographs and granted permission to contact witnesses.

Full production with a Peruvian coproducer and crew began in 2003 and continued in close collaboration with both the Peruvian human rights movement and people directly affected by the conflict. As production proceeded, the elements of strategic outreach were assembled in consultation with Human Rights Watch, Facing History and Ourselves, Amnesty International, the Peruvian National Human Rights Coordinator, and other organizations ready to amplify the reach and uses of the film. Shortly after the first shoot, Skylight began to screen rough cuts of the film and discuss content, narrative strategies, and outreach plans with partner organizations. This reciprocal process, which continued throughout production, informed both the film and the strategic-outreach design. By the time the film was completed in 2005, *State of Fear* was the keystone of an ambitious outreach plan developed in collaboration with opinion leaders, stakeholders, programmers, and other social actors. It provided tools and services for organizations capable of mobilizing audiences and incorporating the film into their work.

THE FILM

State of Fear opens with sweeping views of the Peruvian landscape, upon which are imposed the faces of contemporary Peruvian men, women, and children staring directly into the camera (fig. 2). These images set the stage for the story to follow and become motifs that punctuate the film. The narrative framework is provided by the work of the PTRC, whose archives, witnesses, and findings constitute most of the content of the film. Interweaving archival film and photographs, contemporary scenes, witness testimony, and commentary by human rights activists, the film tells how terrorist attacks by members of the Shining Path provoked military occupation of the countryside, escalating violence, and widespread fears (fig. 3). In the period of corruption and virtual dictatorship thus unleashed, nearly seventy thousand people died at the hands of Shining Path guerillas and the Peruvian military and police.

The film demonstrates that powers assumed by former president Alberto Fujimori and his chief of intelligence, Vladimiro Montesinos, in the name of "national security" simply produced new state-terrorist conditions and government corruption. It was, in fact, honest police work that ultimately led to the capture of Shining Path leader Abimael Guzmán and the restoration of the rule of law.

The dramatic pivot of the film is the courage of human rights activists who documented the repression and were responsible for the creation of the truth commission. The film ends on a hopeful, but uncertain note. The commission's incontrovertible findings were presented in 2003, a reparations process has begun, and Fujimori was brought to trial in 2005. But perpetrators of past crimes remain in the military, legislature, and high office in a government eager to erase the truth of the past.

LAUNCH

Like other contemporary social-issue filmmakers, Yates, Kinoy, and de Onís created a launch strategy that intertwined distribution and outreach goals. That is,

FIGURE 2 Ayacucho, Peru (photo: Vera Lentz).

FIGURE 3 Ashanínka Indians in the Peruvian jungles form self-defense groups to defend their communities from Shining Path attacks (photo: Vera Lentz).

they rolled out the film with the aim of reaching broad audiences through festival, theatrical, and broadcast platforms and at the same time created an outreach campaign targeting niche audiences of human rights activists, policy makers, and victims of abuse through use of new technologies. This combined strategy opened multiple pathways of publicity and circulation for the film.

State of Fear was the official opening night selection of the 2005 New York Human Rights Watch International Film Festival. Shortly after, it launched National Geographic Channels International's *No Borders* series, where it reached 170 million people in 156 countries. It was the top-rated broadcast in every market during the premiere week. Following the January 2006 theatrical premiere at Film Forum in New York, a group that included Cinema Tropical, Human Rights Watch, the ICTJ, and Amnesty International organized theatrical screenings in forty-five American cities.

Favorable reviews, major awards, and wide visibility secured the film's reputation and set the stage for domestic screenings as well as screenings at international film festivals and broadcasts abroad. By the time it received the 2006 Overseas Press Club Award for Best Reporting in Any Medium about Latin America, *State of Fear* was well established on human rights circuits internationally, traveling on tours organized by Human Rights Watch and Amnesty International.

When the film screened abroad, it led to the creation of new human rights media circuits, as was the case when *State of Fear* screened at the new Brazil Human Rights Film Festival and was followed by a tour of five regional cities. The success of a Human Rights Watch tour of eight European cities encouraged organizers to expand the tour to Eastern Europe. Special screenings at the International Criminal Court in The Hague, the Human Rights Defenders Forum at the Carter Center in Atlanta, and—at the invitation of Spanish judge Baltazar Garzón—a symposium at the NYU Law School brought the film to key policy makers working in the transitional-justice arena. The film also was institutionalized, becoming part of human rights curriculum at law schools and used in ICTJ training seminars with human rights professionals and students.

Educational distribution has capitalized on the emergence of new distribution mechanisms such as digital downloads and streaming that enable filmmakers to circumvent traditional marketplace gatekeepers and deliver content directly to their customers. Here, the filmmakers have retained the freedom to screen and distribute the film on their own terms—for free, if necessary—by choosing to self-distribute *State of Fear* through the New Day Film collective, where, in addition to traditional educational distribution (DVDs sold to libraries), rights to stream the film can be purchased by institutions for use in classrooms and by individual students.

OUTREACH CAMPAIGN

State of Fear, a specific story with universal resonance, was intended to engage different audiences. The first goal was to publicize the role of truth commissions worldwide by creating awareness in a general international audience about the transitional-justice process in Peru via a cautionary tale about governments that manipulate popular fears of terrorism to amass power. The second objective was to provide a resource for human rights defenders, and the third was to draw attention to the suffering of the victims, the majority of whom were Quechua-speaking populations living in the Andean regions of Ayacucho and Apurimac.

In Skylight's view, an effective outreach campaign requires a three-year commitment. Its strength lies in relationships established during the production and editing process that forge the network of support that will amplify the message and utility of the film. For *State of Fear*, the process began with the imprimatur of the ICTJ and Ford Foundation and was fortified by gaining the confidence of the Peruvian human rights community. This global-local focus was a hallmark of a campaign strategy that continued to evolve as the filmmakers positioned the film within the human rights networks, a process in which human rights festivals played an important role.

While Skylight Pictures targeted a broad spectrum of audiences, the compelling purpose of the project was to support democracy movements in places where antiterrorism tactics threaten human rights. Broadcasts, festivals, and the Internet offer opportunities to tap into documentary films' capacity to circumvent official gatekeepers. A screening at Moscow's Stalker Film Festival, for instance, sparked discussion about Vladimir Putin's policy toward Chechnya so intense that event organizers closed the session for fear of angering officials. Russian-language DVDs continue to circulate underground through human rights networks. Another example occurred at the Barrel of a Gun festival in Kathmandu, when audience members used the film to speak indirectly about their own situation. Prodemocracy activists then requested permission to translate and duplicate the film, distributing three hundred DVDs at the height of the successful movement to depose the king and hold elections.

In Peru, *State of Fear* became an integral part of the process of transitional justice. It played a significant role in efforts to bring the Fujimori regime to justice and in public debates about the competing narratives of the nation's recent past put forth by Fujimori supporters as well as by the PTRC. In 2005, the former president, who had been living in Japan since 2000, arrived in Chile to attempt a political comeback. He was detained, following demands by human rights defenders for his extradition to Peru to face criminal charges for human rights violations.

During extradition hearings, Peru's national television station (Canal 7) aired the Spanish-language version of *State of Fear* every week to "reassert the findings of the Peruvian Truth Commission in the collective memory of the nation." Pirated DVDs of *State of Fear* circulated widely during the Fujimori trial, which began in 2007, and the filmmakers distributed hundreds of DVDs free through human rights organizations.

ESTADO DE MIEDO QUECHUA

Perhaps the greatest contribution made by the film was its critical role in the campaign to achieve justice for the Andean Indians. The Skylight team considered it essential to bring the findings of the PTRC to the Quechua-speaking communities that made up the majority of the victims of Shining Path and the Peruvian state. With funding from the Ford Foundation's Santiago office and the new Sundance Institute Audience Engagement Fund, a Quechua-language version of *State of Fear, Estado de Miedo Quechua*, was produced in collaboration with Toronja Comunicación, a Lima-based company with a track record in human rights work, the Institute of Legal Defense, and a team of translators from Ayacucho, birthplace of the Shining Path.[5] In an interview, Pamela Yates describes the translation process:

> We thought it would just take us a few days, but the first sentence took us two hours! [laughs] There is a huge cultural abyss between Spanish and Quechua. For example, the difference in the sense of time. The Quechua speakers say that the past is in front of you, because you've already seen it, and the future is behind you, because it's unknown and unseen. It's kind of like riding on a train backwards. So how to translate, "Vera persevered and made her way to the town of Socos. Because of what she photographed there, it would be twenty years before she dared return."
>
> We think of Spanish as a beautiful, musical language and English as Germanic and guttural. The Quechua speakers think that Spanish is a cold language, but Quechua is warm and affectionate. They think that the word "reconciliation" means that you bury something and you forget it. For us, reconciliation means you forgive, but not forget. There were all kinds of things like that that made it difficult, yet fascinating to translate. Then the four people who did the translation did the four voiceovers. These were great Quechua speakers, with full voices, who added so much dignity to this version.[6]

The Quechua/Spanish two-DVD set, which included a screening guide, became the centerpiece of an Andean-region campaign organized in partnership with COMISEDH (the Comisión de Derechos Humanos, the Human Rights Commission), the national human rights coordinator, and other human rights activists.

One of the most interesting things the filmmakers did was to distribute the Quechua version of *State of Fear* free of charge to anyone who provided a blank DVD. More than six hundred people showed up to get DVDs from local nonprofits, each individual representing a remote Quechua-speaking community eager to watch the film in its native language.

The filmmakers are early and eager adopters of accessible technologies, from small-format cameras to cell phones. Perhaps their boldest outreach innovation was EDMQ 2.0 (for Estado de Miedo Quechua), a multiplatform Quechua-language website (http://skylightpictures.com/edmquechua), "a hub to engage human rights activists, victims, educators and youth with the social networking power of Web 2.0." EDMQ 2.0 was designed to host news feeds, a blog, a workshop guide, and streaming. The Skylight team showed local activists how to use inexpensive Flip video cameras to capture personal stories and local events and upload clips directly to the site. Incorporating Twitter, photo sharing, Google Maps, YouTube, and other readily available social-networking tools, EDMQ 2.0 became a platform through which Quechua-speaking survivors of the regime's violence could tell their belated stories of suffering and gain social dignity.

In August 2008, screenings timed to coincide with the fifth anniversary of the release of the PTRC report took place in plazas and community centers in Andean cites (fig. 4). For Quechua-speaking Indians, whose access to information had been filtered through government controlled media, it was an opportunity to understand the work of the truth commission, as well as to take ownership of their own histories and insert Quechuan voices and issues into the public conversation about Peru's path to democracy. The screenings took place in a period of political controversy and competing national narratives. Alberto Fujimori was on trial, and the PTRC's recommendation for reparations to victims of the terror was slowly being put into motion by a reluctant government, even as it disputed the commission's findings. As Paco de Onís has written, "The impact of the Quechua-speaking population seeing their story in their own language cannot be underestimated, and it helps them enormously to understand the enormity of Fujimori's crimes and why he was put on trial."[7]

One of the central findings of the PTRC was that the atrocities committed against indigenous Peruvians could have occurred only because they were invisible in Peruvian mass media and politics. What *State of Fear*'s outreach campaign did was to show indigenous Peruvians to be citizens, both to Peruvians as a whole and to themselves. This was achieved by viewing the film in their native tongue and eliciting testimony about what they had experienced.

This transformation of indigenous Peruvians into legal social subjects with memories sharable with a community of others with similar pasts under Fujimori is

FIGURE 4 The first public screening of the Quechua language version of *State of Fear* took place in the Andean village of Socos on August 28, 2008 (photo: Paco de Onís).

perhaps *State of Fear*'s greatest outreach achievement. Throughout 2008 and into early 2009, human rights NGOs in Peru used the film to draw out memories and accounts of abuse from Quechua speakers. These were entered into the database for the Register of Victims that will receive reparations from the Peruvian state. Money for the reparations has been approved and has started to trickle out to some of the ten thousand victims.

CONCLUSION

The power of *State of Fear*'s outreach strategies across cultures and platforms makes it a model for civil-society media initiatives in the twenty-first century. Employing a range of new technologies and languages in order to reach venues as diverse as an Andean village and a Nepali film festival, it demonstrates how a deeply researched documentary film with a strong story and an informed strategic plan can be an enduring tool for transitional-justice work. By embedding in the public consciousness the narratives of a society's own transition and its inherited history, storytelling through film helps build a culture of accountability and put an end to impunity.

Meanwhile, in August 2009, Fujimori was convicted of human rights abuses and sentenced to twenty-five years in prison for his role in killings and kidnappings by death squads during his government's battles against leftist guerrillas in the 1990s. Fujimori's conviction represents the first time that an elected head of state has been extradited back to his home country, tried, and convicted of human rights violations.

NOTES

1. For more on this subject, see Meg McLagan, "Circuits of Suffering," *Political and Legal Anthropology Review* 28.2 (November 2005), pp. 223–39.
2. Interview with Paul van Zyl, January 15, 2009.
3. The Ford Foundation was an early supporter of the ICTJ; it also funded the publication and dissemination of the findings of the PTRC.
4. See the interview with Pamela Yates in this volume.
5. See Paco de Onís, "Documentary Film and Social Networking in Defence of Human Rights: Producing and Distributing a Quechua-language Version of 'State of Fear,'" *Journal of Human Rights Practice* 1.2 (June 2009), pp. 308–14.
6. Pamela Yates, interview for this volume; conducted June 23, 2010, in New York City.
7. De Onís, "Documentary Film and Social Networking in Defence of Human Rights," p. 312.

Kirsten Johnson, Guantánamo Bay Naval Base, site of the Military Commissions trial for Salim Hamdan, July 2008.

All Eyes

Kirsten Johnson

> I am growing eyes on the back side of my head. I have an eye underneath my chin. I am growing eyes on the underside of my arms.
>
> —Salim Hamdan, accused and convicted of material support for terrorism in his role as Osama Bin Laden's driver on August 21, 2008, in the first trial conducted under the Military Commissions Act of 2006, the first U.S. war crimes trial since Nuremburg

What I see and how I think about what I see are my personal obsessions. It is also an obligation of my profession as a documentary director and cinematographer. In a flippant way, I have often wished I had more eyes. The thought took on a whole new meaning when I heard Salim Hamdan's vivid words, "I am growing eyes." Hamdan's description filled me with a rush of thoughts about seeing. What made him actually imagine that he was growing eyes all over his body? Was it that he felt so confined, so watched, so interrogated, so paranoid, or just so alone? He used these words about growing new eyes in a conversation with Dr. Emily Keram, the defense-appointed psychiatrist who met with him multiple times over the course of four out of the six years he was detained at the U.S. incarceration and interrogation facility at the Guantánamo Bay naval base in Cuba. Accredited to observe the trial from the section reserved for journalists, I was sitting in the courtroom fifteen feet away from Hamdan when I heard his words. Hamdan sat at the defense table as he watched Dr. Keram, on the witness stand, describing his own thoughts. He listened to her speak through the simultaneous translation of English to Arabic provided by a court-appointed translator who sat in another room and watched the proceedings via a closed-circuit camera. Hamdan listened to the translator's words through headphones, which he wore over his traditional Yemeni headdress. From where I was sitting, most of the time I could see him only in profile. It was just close enough to imagine that I could interpret what he was thinking from the look on his face, but I sat at just an oblique enough angle that his face was often turned away from me, revealing so little information that I could not even begin to imagine what he was thinking. When the translator spoke Hamdan's words, it was one more strange glimmer of light into the experience of a man who had been held in U.S. custody since November 21, 2001, and whose thoughts were being made public for one of the few times since his capture in Afghanistan almost six years earlier. I wondered, as I did many times during the course of the trial, if the poetic nature of his thoughts had been lost or found in the translation.

I attended Mr. Hamdan's pretrial hearings in April and July of 2008 and his trial in August of 2008, which were held in a courtroom on the military base. I went to Guantánamo as a cinematographer to explore what footage I might shoot there for a project that would become the film *The Oath* with the director Laura Poitras. *The Oath* premiered at the 2010 Berlin Film Festival and the Sundance Film Festival, where it was awarded the Cinematography Award, which Laura and I shared. Laura had shot her previous film, the Academy Award–nominated *My Country, My Country*, by herself in Iraq. In her desire to make a film about a detainee returning from Guantánamo, she had gone to Yemen, where she met Hamdan's brother-in-law, Nassir al-Bahri, most often known by his nom de guerre, Abu Jandal. Abu Jandal was Osama bin Laden's former bodyguard, and Laura realized immediately that a film might emerge from following him as he worked as a taxi driver in Yemen's capital city of Sana'a. As she filmed with him, she grew curious about whether there was a way to bring together the stories of Abu Jandal in Yemen and Hamdan in Guantánamo. Knowing that it would be impossible to film Hamdan himself, we wondered whether there would be a way to communicate his presence (and absence) in the film. Between the constraints of the military's Public Affairs Office and the exploratory nature of the filmmaking process, it was clear that I would need to pay attention to how the limitations of the place might inform the aesthetics of my camerawork. Like the rest of the journalists present at Guantánamo, I was not allowed to film in the courtroom, but I was allowed to attend and observe the trial. All of my filming would have to take place outside of the courtroom, before or after the hours of the trial. I knew that it was an incredibly rare opportunity simply to be present for Hamdan's trial, but I didn't initially understand how much witnessing the trial would inform everything else I filmed while on the base. I wondered what kind of images I could possibly film that would resonate with the questions that filled the courtroom.

CENTER OF ATTENTION

In any trial, it is not rare that the accused person is the center of everyone's attention and the object of much speculation. Each moment of testimony reveals new information about what may possibly be true about the accused. In this case, the focus on Salim Hamdan was acute. He, like all of the other Guantánamo detainees, had been virtually invisible to the world since his capture and arrest in 2001. But beyond that, he was the Hamdan of *Hamdan v. Rumsfeld*, the Supreme Court case brought by Hamdan's Navy JAG (Judge Advocate General) lawyer Charlie Swift and Georgetown University law professor Neal Katyal that had temporarily shut down the possibility of any military commission trials at Guantánamo. The Supreme Court, in a five-to-three decision, found that the Bush administration did not have the authority to set up these commissions without Congressional authorization, because they did not comply with the Uniform Code of Military Justice or the Geneva Conventions. In response to the issues raised in the *Hamdan v. Rumsfeld* case, within four short months, the Bush administration had presented a new Military Commissions Act that was then endorsed by Congress and signed into law that would allow trials to move forward at Guantánamo.[1] In a significant gesture, Hamdan's was the first trial to be held under the freshly retooled Military Commissions Act of 2006, which pointedly designated "Material Support for Terrorism" as a war crime for the first time.

Hamdan's trial promised to reveal many things. Part of it was all about Salim Hamdan. For the first time, people other than just his defense team might learn the answers to questions—whether he was indeed just a "driver," just what his experiences were with Osama bin Laden, what had happened to him in Afghanistan, who had learned what from interrogating him there, what had he experienced while in confinement in Guantánamo, and whether he had been coerced (and how) to give information. The other part of it would be all about the military commissions. How would a military commission actually function in practice? Would the judge even let the process move forward? Would the trial reveal itself to be an inherently unfair process? Would the military jury be capable of judging Hamdan on the evidence as they heard it?

Hamdan's illusion of having many eyes haunted me from the moment I heard it. As I did my best to follow the procedure of the trial, the arguments of the lawyers, and the testimony about the conditions of Mr. Hamdan's confinement, I imagined how many eyes were necessary to piece together the story of what had happened to Salim Hamdan in the last seven years and what it meant about the choices the United States had made. That Hamdan's trial was being held in Guantánamo, far from the eyes of most Americans and open only to those civilians approved by the U.S. military, was an extension of the concerns about transparency and constitutionality that had been raised since the United States began detaining accused conspirators in the "War on Terror." As Hamdan's chief defense counsel, former Naval JAG officer Charlie Swift argued, "I submit to you, my fellow Americans, that the real reason the president abandoned 250 years of American jurisprudence was that doing so was the only way to use confessions obtained through physical and mental coercion, and to shield the methods being used to obtain these confessions from public scrutiny."[2]

LIGHT ON THE SUBJECT

On June 2, 2006, Deputy Secretary of Defense Gordon England issued a memorandum to the commander of the Joint Task Force in Guantánamo that "all photographs that clearly identify the face of an individual currently or formerly detained by the Department of Defense at Guantánamo are classified SECRET." He went on to conclude that the "unauthorized disclosure of these photographs reasonably could be expected to cause serious damage to the national security of the United States."[3] The code word for the clandestine or secret in the realms of the military, government, or even in certain business contexts is "black." The idea is that "black" information or operations will not be exposed to the light. Beyond the justifications of national security and protecting sources in intelligence gathering, this lack of light on the subject may also offer those involved "plausible deniability" if there are accusations of illegal behavior, because no one without security clearance is allowed to "see" what happened. When it comes to "black" operations, because nothing can be seen, it is possible to insist that nothing ever happened, or perhaps, if it is evident that something did happen, the "blackout" of redacted information, the "black box" that is erected around "black" operations, can create a situation in which it is simply impossible to conclude who was responsible. Nothing can be seen in pitch blackness. It would seem that photography and "black" operations are not compatible. For a photograph to be taken, or for a person to be filmed, there must be light.

Since Guantánamo opened in January 2002 as the site where captured suspects of the "War on Terror" would be imprisoned, the issues of visibility—who gets to see what, who gets to photograph or film what, and who gets to see which photographs or videos—have been of critical interest to all involved. One of the many reasons Guantánamo was chosen as a prison site was that its military-controlled location on an island that was not U.S. soil made it difficult for anyone other than the U.S. military to see what goes on there. I was reminded of this on my second flight to Guantánamo, which left from a commercial gate at the Baltimore/Washington International Airport. When the first boarding announcement was called over the loudspeaker, the attendant announced that the flight would soon be leaving for "An island south of here." Flying on the plane, which was chartered by the Department of Defense, were many of the people who would participate in the military commissions—the judge, lawyers, FBI agents, human rights observers, and journalists. When the airline attendant made the final boarding call, she once again succeeded in keeping our destination invisible, even though she was speaking into a loudspeaker in a crowded civilian airport. She said, "Final boarding call to... oh, you all know where you're going."

When we landed, the thick summer heat of Cuba was waiting for us right outside the airplane door. When you get off the plane in Guantánamo, you can't help but think of the people who have come before you. On January 11, 2002, the first group of detainees arrived on this same runway, after a twenty-four-hour journey from Afghanistan, during which they were shackled, wearing diapers, and not allowed to move for the duration of the flight. There were twenty of them. On that day, there were three journalists present to record their arrival. Carol Rosenberg of the *Miami Herald* was there that day and remembers thinking that because cameras were not allowed, she would try to describe the scene as if it were an image. Watching from behind a fence, she took great care to detail the taped goggles, surgical masks, headphones, and mittens they wore in addition to the orange jumpsuits and shackles. She wrote: "Marines surrounded them, shouting as they led them—stumbling and shackled at the ankles—down a steel ramp. Then, one by one, they crumpled to their knees on the tarmac in the searing Caribbean heat." It was the beginning of journalists' depictions of whatever the Joint Task Force at Guantánamo would allow them to report about what was happening there. And from the beginning, the few journalists who were there knew that their job was to strive to see more than the military wanted them to and to communicate what was invisible to so many eyes.

THE LANDSCAPE I COULD SEE

Geography is an obsession when one first arrives in Guantánamo Bay. There is a clear sense of having an opportunity to see a place where few U.S. civilians are allowed. Not only is one filled with questions, but one is all eyes. Where is the border with Cuba? Where are the detainees held? Where do the prison guards live? The landscapes that I could see and film became a way of addressing all that I was not allowed to see and film. The sky and the ocean there are beautiful, as are rock banks of fossil coral and the fields of cactus that grow along the hillsides. Igaunas occasionally stroll leisurely across the road, and cars drive at a strict forty-mile-per-hour crawl to avoid the legal ramifications of hitting them. There is an initial shock to discover the banality of the suburban world of the military base with its churches, golf course, hospital, schools, outdoor movie theater, shopping complex, and fast-food restaurants. Camp X-Ray, the initial site of the detainees' internment, is no longer in use and is now overgrown by viney plants. Journalists may visit it on a guided tour. There are many reasons cited for why the Camp X-Ray facility is no longer used—besides the fact that it was too small to house all of the detainees who came to be held at Guantánamo, it was also clear that detainees could speak to each other too freely through the chain-link fences. The military would have preferred to tear the whole structure down, but human rights groups succeeded in lobbying for it to remain intact as historical evidence. It is certainly not being maintained by the military, and the plywood rooms where initial interrogations were held are buckling and warping. Public roads lead to beautiful beaches where there are concrete bathing houses and picnic tables by the shore, frequented by both iguanas and military personnel on their days off. There is a range of housing complexes that correspond to rank—apartment buildings for marines, split-level homes in cul-de-sacs for officers, dormitories for the civilian contract workers from Jamaica and the Phillipines, prefab trailers that house two enlisted soldiers each, and eight-person army tents on the tarmac near the military commmisson buildings for journalists. Because it is a live-on-the-base military facility, the incongruities of everyday civilian life bump up against the realities of military life at every turn: an armed humvee drives past swimmers in bathing suits headed to the beach, a late-night baseball game takes place just down the road from the empty cages of Camp X-Ray, the white van carrying Hamdan to his trial waits at a stoplight as a school bus full of children passes. The only bar open to nonofficers is filled with prison guards, legal teams, and journalists. Down a road, past a gate, is the complex of functioning detention facilities frequented by the incoming and outgoing guards. The Guantánamo military base is a small world where all of the banality of life for some exists next to the extraordinary confinement of men who have lived in isolation for years. This juxtaposition of the everyday and the unprecedented brought a strange gravitas to the rhythms of daily life on the military base.

Filming in the sites I was officially allowed to film, I tried to keep in mind that only a few minutes' drive away, men were being held indefinitely in small cells. I tried to frame each shot with some element that would trouble the composition and make the viewer wonder what lay beyond the edge of the frame. Often, I would almost completely fill the frame with the sky, leaving just a slight indication of human inhabitation. The weather varied wildly, and thunderstorms were common, so often, I could fill a frame with a heavy cloud crushing the landscape.

Kirsten Johnson, picnic table at Windmill Beach, Guantánamo Bay Naval Base, July 2008.

The extraordinary thing about filming documentary images is that you cannot film something that isn't there. What you are able to film is what is there, and if it is possible to compose frames that evoke melancholy or consternation, it is because something is present in the landscape that allows it. I filmed a walkway that leads from the shore to a naval ship, framing it like a diagonal that cuts across the sky—the silhouetted image of sailors, marching with purpose up the steep ramp. I filmed vultures, spreading their wings out to dry, perched upon the empty movie seats of the drive-in. I filmed late-night baseball games from behind the chain-link fence in the same way I framed the empty cages of Camp X-Ray. With each composition, I worked to make a frame that would indicate an environment where it was possible to see and yet meaning was still hidden.

NAMELESS/FACELESS

From the initial arrival of detainees in January 2002 until the information was leaked by Lieutenant Colonel Matthew Diaz in March 2005, the official policy of the Department of Defense was that no one without security clearance could know even the names of the people being held indefinitely in Guantánamo. In early 2002, as the commanders on the base struggled to understand and prepare for the confinement of the men arriving from Afghanistan, even the terms that they were authorized to use for men whose names couldn't be used reflected the contradictions of their mission—they could not be "prisoners" or "prisoners of war," because then their Geneva Convention rights would have to be respected.[4] Using the word "detainees" to describe them would allow the legal permissibility of ongoing interrogations throughout their confinement. People would be referred to with numbers. And when it came to questions of photographing detainees, the Department of Defense position from the start allowed no images that would reveal the identities of detainees, the "worst of the worst," as Donald Rumsfeld described them.

However, this position would be completely undermined by the first images that the military authorized out of Guantánamo. Although journalists remained prohibited from photographing detainees upon their arrival at Guantánamo, the Public Affairs Office of the Joint Task Force put Navy Petty Officer Shane McCoy on the job of photographing the detainees once they arrived in Camp X-Ray. The JTF Office was confident that the identities of none of the detainees would be revealed, because they were still wearing goggles and headphones, hoods, and gloves. But to the international public, it was just these masking elements that made the images of the men so disturbing. Camp X-Ray is a series of outdoor enclosures of chain-link fences that was built in the 1980s as a prison for Haitian refugees accused of criminal behavior. Even when overgrown with vines, as the site was when I saw it, the enclosures looked startlingly like dog kennels, and perhaps if more images of Haitian refugees imprisoned there had been released to the public in the 1980s, there would have been a public outcry then, too. But what the Department of Defense hadn't anticipated was how incendiary the images of unidentifiable and hence dehumanized Guantánamo detainees in cages surrounded by Marines would be. Petty Officer McCoy's photos of detainees on their knees inside the chain-link cages of Camp X-Ray became infamous as quickly as they were released to news outlets.

The photos were released by the Public Affairs Office of the Pentagon without consulting the Office of the Secretary of Defense. The Department of Defense spokeswoman, Torie Clarke, who took responsibility for the decision to release the photos, wrote later "I felt that releasing selected images could allay some of our critics."[5] Far from "allaying" critics, the photos were published in articles with headlines such as "Inside Camp Terror," "War on Terror: Welcome U.S. Style," "Horror of Camp X-Ray," and the images of hooded men in what looked like cages fit for dogs on their knees in orange jumpsuits came to symbolize Guantánamo. Almost as quickly as the military had released the images, they were removed from the Department of Defense website, but the images had made their way into the digital public domain, and there was no putting the genie back in the bottle. When I was in Guantánamo, six years after those photos were taken and Camp X-Ray was no longer used to house detainees, almost every public-affairs officer I met bemoaned the fact that those images of detainees taken at Camp X-Ray were the only ones the public knew. From the Department of Defense point of view, the initial attempt to manage public relations with transparency had completely backfired.

Since there was so much lack of transparency at Guantánamo, in fact, any image would raise more questions about what was not being seen, and these first images set into motion just such questions: "If this is what they are willing to show us, what's going on that they won't show us?" The ongoing struggle over whether the U.S. government allows its public to confront the visual evidence of its actions indicates that images have a different kind of impact than words. The candid digital photos taken by soldiers of the physical, psychological, and sexual abuse at Abu Ghraib Prison in Baghdad, Iraq that emerged to the public in the spring of 2004 shook the entire U.S. military chain of command, as well as the international public.[6] In the context of Guantánamo, the person who photographs anything is answering to all of the photographs that cannot be taken, as well as the photographs that will be withheld from the public if someone, anyone, manages to take them.

In March 2006, the Associated Press evoked the Freedom of Information Act to sue the Department of Defense for the right to publish photos that revealed Guantánamo detainees' faces. In a statement in that litigation, Richard B. Jackson, the chief of the Law of War Branch for the Office of the Judge Advocate General, reiterated the Department of Defense policy:

> 5. I have personally reviewed a representative sample of the photographs responsive to the AP's FOIA request, and determined that they consist of identification photographs taken of individuals in the custody of U.S. forces, detained during a period of armed conflict in Afghanistan and elsewhere against the Taliban and Al Qaeda. I believe that the public release of the responsive photographs would violate long-standing DoD policy and practice, and the President's direction on the treatment of detainees. The public release of the responsive photographs would subject the photographed individuals to public insult, curiosity, embarrassment, unwanted exposure, harassment, and exploitation of their personal images. Such release would also encourage foreign governments or enemies detaining U.S. service members to subject those service members to similar treatment.
>
> 6. The United States has consistently sought to prevent the public disclosure of photographs and other public depictions and displays that identify individual detainees. . . . The Department of Defense has disciplined service members who have violated the foregoing, including U.S. soldiers who are being disciplined for committing violations of this regulation in Iraq.
>
> 7. The foregoing U.S. Government policy is also reflected in the Department of Defense's guidance concerning media embedded with U.S. military units operating in Iraq. Specifically, DoD guidance provides that "no photographs or other visual media showing an enemy prisoner of war or detainee's recognizable face, name tag, or other identifying feature or item may be taken."
>
> 11. Although the President determined on February 7, 2002, that members of Al Qaeda and the Taliban do not qualify as POWs under the GPW, the President also determined that U.S. armed forces will "treat detainees humanely and, to the extent appropriate and consistent with military necessity, in a manner consistent with the principles of Geneva.[7]

In 2002, the U.S. government had determined that it was under no obligation to grant detainees Geneva Convention rights because of their status as "unlawful combatants,"[8] yet in this Department of Defense statement, the Geneva Convention rights of the detainees are invoked and selectively applied to prevent the press from showing images of detainees that would allow them to be recognizable as individual human beings. Images are not equal in their meaning and impact. The men in the images from Abu Ghraib Prison were nameless and faceless, too, as all of their human rights were being violated.[9] When anonymity and invisibility are invoked in the name of the protection of rights, a question to ask is just who is being protected.

EYEWITNESS

The number of people who were allowed simply physically to see Salim Hamdan in the period since his capture in Afghanistan in the fall of 2001 was extremely limited. Those who were not members of the military who had seen Hamdan during his detention numbered a handful—his civilian lawyers, his translators, his psychiatric evaluator. In the courtroom, the people seeing him included the judge, the military jury of six officers, and the prosecution and defense teams. In the audience, which fluctuated each day and numbered some twenty people or so, were Department of Defense lawyers, the representatives of NGOs—Human Rights Watch, Human Rights First, and the American Civil Liberties Union—occasional lawyers for what was referred to in the courtroom as the "other governmental agency" (the "OGA," or as most people know it, the CIA), and members of the media.

My shooting day would often begin at the end of the court day, when the lawyers would come down to the press-conference room to address the other journalists. It was an extremely uncommon experience for me—to be on location and to be prohibited from filming the person who was at the center of my story. Although many courtrooms are off-limits to cameras in the United States, there is often access to filming a defendant and his family and friends. There is no notion that the person at the center of the drama should be invisible, as was the case with Salim Hamdan. "What was there to film?" everyone asked me when I returned home. I realized that I would need to become a translator of sorts myself. I could see Hamdan, but I could not film him—what images could I film that would translate his presence, evoke his experience, and draw attention to his forced invisibility?

On most days of Hamdan's trial, there were three to seven journalists there to watch in the courtroom, while our colleagues from the wire agencies were consigned to watch the trial on the closed-circuit television in the press room down the hill from the courtroom, so that they could file stories electronically as they happened. The few of us who were permitted to see Hamdan and witness his trial were also the object of his consideration. Thinking about it from Hamdan's point of view, we forty or so people were the only people out of uniform he had seen in six years. His interest in us was clear. Every day, when he was led into the courtroom by two young soldiers, one holding each of his arms, he would look around the entire courtroom, eyeing each person with intensity. Often he would turn to his defense-appointed translator, Charles Schmidtz, and consult with him about who

Kirsten Johnson, U.S. Military Defense Attorney, Lieutenant Commander, Brian Mizer in press conference at Guantamano Bay Naval Base, July 2008.

a new person in the audience might be. He clearly wanted to know who each of us was and why we were there. At one point during the pretrial hearings, according to Dr. Keram, Hamdan asked her whether the entire courtroom and all of the people in it might be complicit in an elaborate form of role playing created simply to interrogate him again. Was it, he wondered, some form of theater in which we were all playing roles in order to confuse and entrap him? The more we learned about what he had experienced in U.S. custody, the easier it was to understand such a thought. Since Hamdan had been arrested, he had been officially interrogated over forty times about the reason for his presence in Afghanistan. The other times he had been interrogated that were alluded to—how and by whom—were classified and remained known only to Hamdan and those who had done the interrogating.

OUT OF SIGHT

In the six years that Hamdan had been held captive in Guantánamo, he had experienced a handful of physical environments. He had lived inside an eight-by-six-foot outdoor chain-link cage with a concrete floor and a corrugated roof at Camp X-Ray. Then he was transferred to an eight-by-ten-foot prison cell without windows, where he lived for years with access one hour per day to an eight-by-ten-foot outdoor exercise cage. For a brief period of a few months, he was allowed to live in Camp 4, which was a communal living situation where ten detainees shared a communal room and were allowed to walk outside and eat together at outdoor picnic tables. For five and a half years, Hamdan had not seen the horizon, nor had he ever seen the ocean that lay just yards beyond where he was imprisoned.

In contrast to Hamdan's experience (and to that of the other detainees), the visiting journalist was allowed to see most everything Hamdan could not see and almost nothing of what he saw every day of his internment.

THE COURTHOUSES

From the beginning of its one hundred-plus-year-old existence, the Guantánamo military base has been a work in progress, because its purpose has been in a constant state of flux. In its latest iteration as a detention facility, which began in 2002, Guantánamo has been rebuilt and expanded, and what was an empty bluff overlooking the ocean has been transformed into a bustling prison complex.

The decision to hold war-crimes trials as extraconstitutional events at Guantánamo meant that courtrooms had to be built on the base. The entire judicial complex is built on top of and out of a 1950s infrastructure that has been in a state of decay for some time. One of the courtrooms, although it is a "state of the art" $12 million facility that can be dismantled and moved, has been built on the tarmac of an old runway, and it is surrounded by army tents that are used as housing for those who need to stay close to the courtroom. There is both evidence of no expense spared to create a functioning infrastructure and a strange, make-do ambiance. It is the undoubtedly somewhat typical atmosphere of military bases, which grow and contract over time, or the battlefield base infrastructures that make use of existing structures and add the military's tents and prefabricated structures when necessary.

Because of the attempt to conduct multiple military commission trials simultaneously when there was only one new facility, the courtroom in which Salim Hamdan's trial was held was inside a 1950s building that used to be the base's dental clinic. I am grateful that his trial took place there, because the room in which the trial happened was so small that it was easy to see everyone in the courtroom. In contrast, the lack of visibility in a new "state of the art" facility was shocking. It was virtually impossible to see the accused from the visitor's gallery, forty feet away and directly behind the first defense table. Thinking like a cameraperson, I realized that in the courtroom where Hamdan's trial was being held, I was able to see everyone in close-up. I could see Judge Allred's eyes, and I could note the smallest gestures by both the prosecution and defense teams. I could see Hamdan in three-quarter profile and know when he was crying, shaking his head, or lifting his chin in dispute. In contrast, on the one day in which I visited the new courtroom, I realized that I could see everyone only in a wide shot from behind. It was impossible to see anyone's facial expressions, and I was left to try to read the wide, vague signal of their bodily movements. This arrangement struck me as a purposeful gesture on the part of the military to make defendants even less visible to the few witnesses present.

ALLOWED TO FILM

As a member of the press in Guantánamo, one is considered an embedded journalist and must respect the rules the Joint Task Force has established. The application of these rules shifted over the weeks I spent there, but still entailed such a high level of military surveillance that journalists such as Carol Williams of the *Los Angeles Times* and Jon McChesnay of National Public Radio indicated that the level of military oversight was more acute than what they experienced as embedded journalists in Iraq. When we first arrived in the spring of 2008, the initial idea was that members of the press were to be accompanied by a military escort at every moment on the base. Very quickly it was clear that no escort was actually needed for a member of the press to walk from the press room, located inside a defunct blimp hangar, out onto the adjacent tarmac, where the sleeping quarters in six-person tents were located. That soon became one of the few places where the press was allowed unaccompanied. Otherwise, we were escorted to and from the courtroom, escorted to every meal, and always accompanied when filming. Most of the journalists present for the trial were press journalists. Television crews arrived for the opening and closing of the trial, filming at the press conferences and shooting on-camera stand-ups with reporters in front of an area designated by the military and decorated with flagpoles.

I chose to film the television journalists filming stand-up interviews with frames that revealed the mechanisms of their work—the blocks they had to stand on, the tent filled with camera gear, the microphones placed just out of their frame. I also tried to film what was outside of the conventional frame in the press conferences: shooting back at the journalists asking the questions or filming the lawyers from the side, instead of the frontal angle, which implicitly makes more official the person at the podium. By filming from different positions, the makeshift theater of the news conference and the nature of the relationship between the presenters and the journalists reveal themselves.

There were several distinct zones that I understood were completely off-limits for filming: any of the trial proceedings, any member of the security team on the perimeter of the courtroom, the white van that transported Hamdan to the courtroom from the prison, the interior of both of the two courtrooms, the exterior of SCIF (Sensitive Compartmented Information Facility) sites, the coastline, Camp 7 and Camp 8 for high-value detainees, and of course, although he was at the center of everyone's attention, it would be impossible to film Salim Hamdan himself in any way.

Then there were the places and people I hoped I might be able to film: in the detention facilities (although I knew I wouldn't be able to show men in their cells or anyone's faces), inside the press room with the journalists, in the cafeteria where the soldiers ate.

And finally, there was what I was explicitly allowed to film: the natural world that surrounds and often encroaches on the base, the press conferences, public spaces without people in them, the area around the courthouse, the now-abandoned Camp X-Ray, tents on the tarmac. ("A maximum of three in a row," said the public-affairs officer. When I asked why, as usual, the answer was "Security.")

I knew that I would always be accompanied by one of these PAOs, who would almost always check my composition of a shot: "Let me check your frame," the PAO would say over and over. All of my footage was reviewed and subject to erasure if there were any frame that might, according to a PAO, "jeopardize operational security," such as a glimpse of the barbed wire on the exterior of the courtroom, or the security station that housed the Marines next to the courtroom, or a recognizable stretch of coastline.

For one of the first times in my filming career, instead of being able to compose and create frames within the world, it felt like the world had been divided into frames for me. I could frame the field only without the orange barriers in the foreground. I could film the sky, but had to frame out an antenna. I could film a hillside, but not the outline of the SCIF site that sat on top of it. Every shot was filmed up to the edge of something deemed unfilmable by the regulations of the military. The world felt full of invisible edges and boundaries. I found myself imagining that I was filming the negative space around Salim Hamdan.

It was a great relief when the courtroom illustrator, Janet Hamlin, came for a few days and I was actually able to film her drawings of what went on inside the courtroom. Then I stepped back and filmed the journalists gathered around her drawings—all of them as eager as I was to have something to show for what we were seeing in the courtroom. Even though her drawings were quite remarkable, considering the speed and conditions in which she had done them, she agreed with us that she never quite "got" Hamdan's face as it really looked.

DETENTION FACILITIES

Of course, of the things I hoped to film in Guantánamo, what loomed largest in my imagination were the detention facilities themselves. I knew that we would be allowed to visit the facilities in a prearranged tour, escorted by military public-affairs officers and accompanied by prison guards. I had seen photographs of detainees in Camp 4, which was considered the camp for the least dangerous and most cooperative detainees. It was where Hamdan had enjoyed living for a few months before the privilege was taken away. In photographs, detainees could be seen, shot through telephoto lenses, hanging their laundry on outdoor lines, congregating at a picnic table, or praying together, always with their faces hidden by some strategically framed object in the foreground or their own hand blocking their eyes. I knew that regulations involved never photographing detainees in such a way that they could be recognized. This was also true for the prison guards themselves—no photographs could be taken that made them recognizable, either.

I had scoured the Internet for all of the images that had already been taken in the detention facilities. I was impressed with the different composition solutions some of my colleagues had found while respecting the restrictions placed on them. One photographer had captured a prison guard standing in the hallway of Camp 5—he was cropped from the chest down to his boots, and you could see the corridor disappearing behind him. Another had photographed one eye of a detainee peering through the slot in which food was slid into the cell, his hands up, palms forward, blocking the rest of his face. Other photographers had dutifully taken pictures of the display the military had laid out for them inside the model prison cells. Many pictures have been taken of the "comfort items" detainees are allowed, depending on their compliance with prison regulations. Folded neatly on a bed are the bright-orange uniforms to be worn by a combative inmate, the tan smocks and pants to be worn by the cooperative inmate, and the white uniforms to be worn by the especially cooperative. Prominent in all of the "comfort item" displays are prayer beads, skull caps, Korans, and prayer mats. Less prominent are the small tubes of "Maximum Security" toothpaste and the toothbrushes designed to prevent their co-option into weapons—just a plastic thimble-sized cup that can fit over a fingertip, with a few integrated plastic bristles. There are small squares of toilet paper. Toilet paper can be used to make ropes and potential weapons or to cover the window that the guard looks through every few minutes to check on a detainee, so a certain number of squares are counted out each day by prison guards and parceled out to detainees. I had also seen many photographs of empty rooms: the empty eight-by-ten-foot cells of Camps 5 and 6, the empty communal areas with stainless steel circular tables, the empty recreation cages, the empty rooms where detainees meet their lawyers. I also saw the many photographs of the barbed wire on the exterior of the camp and the large painted words "duty bound to honor freedom." Similarly to the way I felt about my filming restrictions, it was clear that every photographer who had visited any of the detention facilities had photographed everything he or she was allowed to shoot. I thought I would at least be allowed to film empty rooms, and I was looking forward to seeing what kind of compositions I would discover by complying with the rules being imposed on me.

On our first trip, we were told that filming the detentions facilities while the military commission trials were underway was impossible. We were told by PAOs that the level of security lockdown was extremely high when a detainee was transferred from the detention facility to a commission courtroom on the other side of the island and that the staff of the prison was overtaxed by the number of guards necessary to accompany the detainee to the courtroom. On our second trip, we again put in an early request of our desire to film in the detention facilities. We were promised that if it was possible, it would happen. Twice during our stay—once at the start of the trial and once when the verdict was declared—a larger group of media representatives arrived for brief stays. They included television and radio reporters from CNN, Court TV, Al Jazeera, Al Arabiya, and the BBC. On the day of the start of the trial, I learned that a group of camera people and photographers would be going to the prison. They would be generating images that would be available to all of the media as a pool feed. We were told there was not enough space for us, and since we would be staying for the entire duration of the trial, in all likelihood, there would be another occasion for us to film at the detention facilities on our own. When they returned, I looked at the footage the others had shot and thought about how quickly their images would flash on television screens—iconographic stand-ins for all of the life we could not film inside the prison.

Finally, in the last week of our stay, we were told that we would have the privilege of touring the facilities with the new admiral in charge of the prison. We would not be allowed to film. Within the constraints of their rules, on the tour, I saw only a handful of things I really wished I could have filmed. One was the admiral's description of how he had decided to let himself be fed for a week in the same manner as those inmates who were currently on hunger strikes. He sat in the restraining chair and held up the small can of the liquid diet that is fed through a tube into the nose. He told us that "it smelled like vanilla and didn't taste bad at all." Another was the vision of a dozen inmates out together in the exercise cages. I could have filmed the legs of the old man who was exercising, lifting his knees up to slap his outstretched hands, or the feet of the young man turning a soccer ball around and around in the eight-foot space. What I knew I would never have been allowed to film, even if my camera had been allowed in, was the glimpse I caught of Hamdan, sitting knee-to-knee with the defense translator and psychiatrist in a tiny triangular meeting room behind one-way smoked glass. Of course, Hamdan couldn't see me.

INTERROGATION VIDEO

Midway into the trial, the judge allowed the screening of video recordings of two of Mr. Hamdan's initial interrogations in Afghanistan. Hamdan himself kept his head mostly bowed throughout the broadcast of the videos, but was clearly uncomfortable, seeing for the first time images of himself at a moment in which he did not yet realize how being captured would change his life. Looking at the video from the point of view of a cameraperson, I was impressed by how the drama of the situation had been succinctly rendered by the choice of camera angle and lighting. The camera had been placed on the ground. Shackled with his hands behind his back and a bag over his head, Hamdan is kneeling on the ground. It is dark all around him and he is illuminated by a strong, directional light. The entire scene is shot in a deep black and white tinged with green. The initial sight of Hamdan on his knees with the bag over his head was breathtaking. Legs walk into the foreground of the frame. The interrogator is wearing boots and conducts himself with military efficiency. His face can never be seen. The camera is clearly on his side, protecting his anonymity and shooting a wide shot of Hamdan's entire body from the interrogator's side of the space. When the interrogator lifts the bag off

Kirsten Johnson, still from interrogation video of Salim Hamdan, July 2008.

of Hamdan's head, the transformation is immediate. What has been the troubling sight of a captured and bound human being who could be anyone—perhaps a defiant and violent enemy or a cowering victim of mistaken identity—is suddenly seeable as the specific person he is: Salim Hamdan. His hair is wild from the bag that has been over his head, and his eyes are electric with the need to bring the interrogator around to seeing his point of view. He smiles frequently. The interrogator speaks to him in Arabic, and Hamdan answers in rushes of words.

As the interrogation continues, there seem to be many ways to interpret Hamdan's answers. He is conciliatory and earnest, but also evasive and self-contradictory. He smiles and even laughs, somehow intent on getting the interrogator to concur that it is truly absurd that he is on his knees, unable to move his hands or walk away from this captivity. The interrogation goes on for some thirty minutes. The increasing frustration of the interrogator is understandable. Little that Hamdan answers offers any illumination. He could easily be lying, and his manner of answering feels like he is making up most responses on the fly. And I wonder why is he smiling so much.

Strangely, what has initially been such a shocking image of a trapped man has become monotonous to look at, once it is clear that the man will not answer the way the interrogator wants him to. The man is not making great statements of ideological resistance, nor is he pleading for his life in explicit terms. It is unlike any fictional portrait of an interrogation scene in which the captive's words are well written to convey ideas in the most dramatic ways possible. Instead, Hamdan rambles and evades and looks confused and smiles and smiles and smiles. There is surely meaning to be found in his behavior, but there is not enough context for the interrogator or the viewer to go beyond feelings of frustration and, at a certain point, even boredom, because Hamdan responds over and over again in the same unreadable manner. It struck me as more evidence that even images with synch sound cannot tell the full story of such complicated situations. The inscrutability of the video was compounded by Hamdan's presence in the room—if only we could ask the person what he was thinking, instead of staring at his recorded image and trying to make sense of it.

Twenty minutes into watching the video, Judge Allred called the court to recess for lunch and Hamdan's noon day prayers. When the court resumed in the afternoon, for our own logistical reasons, my production teams needed to stay in the press room, where we would have access to the Internet and telephones, instead of returning to the courtroom. So we watched the rest of the video on the television screen in the press room. The press room consisted of two adjoining rooms filled with rectangular formica folding tables aligned in rows. Each journalist could choose a space at the table, use the telephone positioned there, and plug his or her laptap computer into the bundled lines of blue cabling attached to the tables by clamps. Each room was being monitored by a service member—whether from the national guard, the army, or the navy—who was a public-affairs officer. The PAOs operated from a desk at the end of each small room where they could see all of the journalists and listen to any of their conversations. (At one point, a young PAO who was driving a group of us journalists to the mess hall turned around and asked journalist William Glaberson of the *New York Times* if he could repeat what he just said. The PAO hadn't been participating in our conversation before, just driving. "Why?" Glaberson asked. "Because we have to report everything you say," the PAO replied.) Each room of the press area had a flat-screen television mounted on the wall. When court was not in session, the televisions broadcast the Armed Forces Network, which besides its own programming and public-service announcements, seemed to play only CNN News or Fox News.

In the press room, the television abruptly changed from the Armed Forces Network to the frontal view camera of Judge Allred, who indicated that Hamdan's capture video would resume. In the press room, unlike the courtroom, it was no longer possible to watch the reactions of Hamdan as he watched the video images of himself. Although there were multiple cameras in the courtroom, simultaneously recording different angles, the closed-circuit television in the press room could screen only one view at a time. Carol Rosenberg, the *Miami Herald* correspondent, who is the person who has most frequently and consistently traveled to report in Guantánamo since the detention facilities opened in 2002, is known by military personnel and fellow journalists alike as a strong and persistent advocate for the journalists' access to information on the base. She repeatedly put in requests to the Joint Task Force that runs the press room for split-screen technology or multiple screens in order that journalists might monitor not only multiple views in one courtroom, but simply the two commission courtrooms scheduled to operate at the same time. Her requests were denied, and budget constraints were cited. It is thus impossible for journalists to cover any of the trials happening simultaneously in their entirety. And so it was that the video of Hamdan's capture came back on the screen, and we in the press room could no longer see the rest of the courtroom watching it. The interplay of the capture video and its spectators in the courtroom, which was giving the most information about its meaning, was now invisible.

EYE CONTACT

Every day when Hamdan entered the courtroom, he looked at all of us. On one of my first days in the courtroom, when he looked at me, I looked back at him and slightly nodded my head in recognition of his eye contact. He nodded back. Every day thereafter, when he first entered for the day, he looked around the courtroom, and he looked to me and noddded. I wondered if I was in breech of military security. I wondered if my nod might connote "material support" for terrorism. All of us were being filmed in the courtroom. Hamdan was being filmed by a military cameraperson every time he entered and leaves the courtroom. This is all secret footage and will never be seen by anyone other than members of the military with the proper security clearance.

On the day that Hamdan was declared not guilty of conspiracy and guilty of five of eight counts of material support for terrorism he hung his head and covered his eyes as he wept. The prosecution asked the military jury for a sentence of thirty years. Regardless of the sentence, JTF-GTMO still would retain the right to hold him indefinitely. The next day, when the jury slowly read out his sentence, the entire defense team gasped in shock as he was given a sentence of sixty-six months. He was given credit for time served, meaning that his sentence amounted to five months. All of the lawyers hugged each other and Hamdan. When the entire team stopped hugging and everyone was standing around looking stunned, Hamdan looked around the courtroom, searching the eyes of those in the audience. He looked at me, nodding his chin up and down, two thumbs up, and beaming.

I smiled back at him, wondering whether or not I was standing in a place where a courtroom camera would record my spontaneous grin.

NOWHERE TO BE SEEN

Six months later, and one month after Hamdan was released from Guantánamo, having served his sentence, I landed in Sana'a, the capital city of Yemen, hoping to get a chance to film Hamdan in his home. I joined Laura Poitras there, who was trying to set up filming privileges with Hamdan through the intermediary of a respected Yemeni journalist, Nasser Arrabyee, and Hamdan's brother-in-law, Abu Jandal. By this point, Laura had been filming with Abu Jandal on and off for almost two years. As evident in *The Oath*, Jandal is a voluble man, interested in talking to a wide variety of audiences about the conflicting forces that rage inside of him. But Hamdan is a different person. After ten days of waiting and filming the streets of Sana'a, Laura and I get a clear message that Hamdan doesn't want to see us and doesn't want to be filmed. I feel deeply disappointed that after a month of meeting eyes with him in the courtroom, I will not be able actually to speak to this man and learn something new about him for myself. In The *Oath*, Hamdan's feelings about how much Jandal is talking to the press are expressed in the form of a letter to Jandal in which Hamdan basically tells Jandal to mind his own business and that these matters are for Allah to see and no one else. In the film, it comes off as rather eloquent advice. In the courtroom, when Judge Allred asked Hamdan what he would do if he was released and returned to Yemen, Hamdan said that he would take some camels and disappear with his family into the desert. Here was a man who had been made both highly visible and completely invisible through his Guantánamo confinement, his Supreme Court case, and his military commissions trial. When I heard him tell Judge Allred what he would do if he were freed, I was deeply struck by the fact that if it were left up to him, Salim Hamdan wanted only to disappear.

NOTES

1. The revised Military Commissions Act of 2006 (HR-6166) passed the Senate, 65 to 34, on September 28, 2006. The bill passed in the House, 250 to 170, on September 29, 2006. George W. Bush signed the bill into law on October 17, 2006. *Hamdan v. Rumsfeld* is described in *The Challenge*, by Jonathan Mahler, who was not able to meet Hamdan before writing his book, but who did interview Nassir al-Bahri, as well as Hamdan's defense counsel and translator. See Jonathan Mahler, *The Challenge:* Hamdan v. Rumsfeld *and the Fight over Presidential Power* (New York: Farrar, Strauss, and Giroux, 2008).
2. Lt. Cmdr. Charles Swift, "The American Way of Justice," *Esquire*, March 2007, http://www.esquire.com/features/ESQ0307swift, p. 2.

3. Gordon England, Deputy Secretary of Defense, "Memorandum to Commander, Joint Task Force–Guantanamo," June 2, 2006, http://media.miamiherald.com/smedia/2008/03/27/19/englandmemo.source.prod_affiliate.56.pdf.
4. Karen Greenberg, *The Least Worst Place: Guantánamo's First 100 Days* (New York: Oxford University Press, 2009), pp. 51–57.
5. Torie Clarke, *Lipstick on a Pig: Winning in the No-Spin Era by Someone Who Knows the Game* (New York: Free Press, 2006), p. 82.
6. The accounts of abuse at Abu Ghraib prison in Iraq were first described in 2004 in the Taguba Report, as the document titled the *Article 15-6 Investigation of the 800th Military Police Brigade* is usually called. Seymour Hersh relied on the Taguba Report for his *New Yorker* article "Torture at Abu Ghraib" in the May 10, 2004 issue, which included candid digital photos of that abuse taken by soldiers. The "amateur" and "unauthorized" images would have extraordinary international impact. Also on this subject, see "Exposure: The Woman behind the Camera at Abu Ghraib," by Phillip Gourevitch and Errol Morris, *New Yorker*, March 24, 2008. Donald Rumsfeld was quoted: "We're functioning in a—with peacetime restraints, with legal requirements in a wartime situation, in the information age, where people are running around with digital cameras and taking these unbelievable photographs and then passing them off, against the law, to the media, to our surprise, when they had not even arrived in the Pentagon." *Washington Post*, May 7, 2004, http://www.washingtonpost.com/wp-dyn/articles/A9173-2004May7_3.html. The debate over the release of all of the photos that exist from that period continues to the present. In May 2009, President Obama declined to release classified images that reveal detainee mistreatment in Afghanistan, Iraq, and Guantánamo. He cited the need to avoid a backlash that might endanger U.S. troops worldwide. He added that the publication of the photos "will not add anything to our understanding of what was carried out in the past by a small number of individuals." *New York Times*, May 15, 2010, http://thecaucus.blogs.nytimes.com/2011/05/05/obama-blocks-release-of-graphic-photos-for-second-time.
7. "Declaration of Richard B. Jackson" pursuant to 28 U.S.C. § 1746, Associated Press v. United States Department of Defense, pp. 2–5, http://docs.justia.com/cases/federal/district-courts/new-york/nysdce/1:2006cv01939/281574/11/0.pdf.
8. "Humane Treatment of Taliban and al Qaeda Detainees," White House Memorandum, February 7, 2002, http://www.pegc.us/archive/White_House/bush_memo_20020207_ed.pdf.
9. The identities and faces of the Iraqi men in the Abu Ghraib photos are still much less widely known than the images themselves.

FIGURE 1 The final frame in *Coffee Futures*, playfully serving up the metaphor of EU membership as a desired, not yet attained but tantalizingly visible individual and national future.

Following *Coffee Futures*: Reflections on Speculative Traditions and Visual Politics

Zeynep Devrim Gürsel

On May 9, 1950, French statesman Robert Schuman issued an invitation to the Germans and all other European countries to manage their coal and steel industries jointly. Known as the "Schuman Declaration," it is considered to be the beginning of the supranational entity today called the European Union (EU). May 9, 2010, was the sixtieth anniversary of the declaration, an event marked by the annual celebration of Europe Day. Yet falling as it did in the midst of European officials grappling with the risks of Greece's economic crisis, the threat of its spreading wildly to other EU countries, and the necessity to create highly unpopular emergency loan funds, Europe Day 2010 was not met with great fanfare, at least, not within the eurozone. Perhaps in an attempt to demonstrate strategic savvy, EU officials instead focused their energies on celebrations at the Shanghai Expo to underline confidence in EU-China relations. Yet what fanfare was missing from Europe Day events inside the EU could be found in Europe Day events in candidate countries, which gave the impression that in the midst of the greatest economic challenge the community has faced in sixty years, the greatest supporters of the European Union were those who were not quite yet members.

The celebrations in Ankara, the capital of Turkey, were hard to miss. Perhaps this is because of all the candidate countries, Turkey has the most experience being a candidate; it has in fact been a candidate country since 1999.[1] In the preceding week banners in Istanbul and Ankara reminded the public that there was a "More Democratic, More Respectable, More Modern, Stronger Turkey en Route to the European Union."

This banner, often accompanied by a photograph of the prime minister, Recep Tayyip Erdogan, leader of the conservative Justice and Development Party (AKP), could be interpreted to mean that today, there is a more-confident-than-ever Turkey asking for EU accession—admission to the European Union and to

FIGURE 2 Official Europe Day lottery tickets being sold in Ankara, May 9, 2010 (photo: Zeynep Gürsel).

FIGURE 3 A banner bearing the logos of the Ankara municipality and the Secretariat General for EU Affairs reads "The EU is achieving higher environmental standards" at Europe Day celebrations in Ankara, May 9, 2010 (photo: Zeynep Gürsel).

participation as a full member in all of its international agreements. Implied message: Thanks to the efforts of the AKP. Or it could be taken to state that the path to EU accession has strengthened Turkey, again thanks to the AKP, which had prioritized EU membership since coming to power in 2002. In other words, yet again, the public was given the dual message that the EU is good for Turkey and Turkey is good enough for the EU. Both messages underscore the EU's desirability—an impressive claim at a moment when several EU members were said to be teetering on the brink of national bankruptcy. And both messages emphasize the centrality of Turkey's drive to EU membership in Turkey's internal politics. At least on Europe Day.

One marker of the day as a holiday was a special Europe Day national lottery ticket, an honor normally reserved for religious and national holidays. Europe Day's official celebrations are centered in the Youth Park of Ankara (fig. 2). Stands had been set up for each of the member countries. There were musical and theatrical performances for the public all day.[2] Children walked around with balloons and flags bearing the clever logo of the Secretariat General for EU Affairs; this logo prophesies Turkey's accession to the EU through a graphic integrating the star in the Turkish flag into the stars of the EU (fig. 3). Banners around the park underscored the benefits of European Union membership in many different domains: "Obstacles limiting the participation of women in social life and the workforce are being lifted with Turkey's goal of EU membership"; "Membership in the EU is the most concrete project of Turkey's goal of modernization"; "The EU is achieving higher environmental standards"; And so on. One banner bearing the Turkish EU integration logo read "Happy Mother's Day," since Europe Day 2010 happened to fall on the second Sunday of May, leaving me wondering if even mothers were better appreciated in the European Union.

Among the festivities at the park was a film screening—actually two separate screenings—of my twenty-two-minute documentary film *Coffee Futures*, each followed by Semih Kaplanoğlu's feature-length narrative *Honey*. Kaplanoğlu is an established filmmaker of international renown, and his film *Honey* won the Golden Bear award at the 2010 Berlin Film Festival. Presumably, his film was being shown to exemplify the success that Turkish artists have had in Europe, to underline that, at least in the domain of film, Europe had already accepted, supported, and honored Turkish talent.[3] My more modest film, *Coffee Futures*,[4] had not won the range of impressive awards that Kaplanoğlu's had, nor had it screened at major European film festivals. But it had been granted the EurActiv prize for Originality in a competition for projects that contribute to debates about Europe on a national scale. EurActiv is an EU information website that publishes in twelve languages. One hundred and ten projects were nominated from across Europe; five received prizes in different categories from "Media Institution" to "Individual Politician." *Coffee Futures* did not fit into any category, but the jury gave the film a Special Prize for Originality at a ceremony in Brussels. This seemed particularly appropriate for a film about Turkey and the EU. Proposals on the part of some in the EU to offer Turkey "special membership" or "privileged partnership" have been highly contested and perceived as insulting in Turkey, where such propositions are taken as offers of second-class membership based on treating Turkey as slightly different from everybody else.

Shortly after Europe Day, I received a letter from the Secretariat General for European Union Affairs thanking me for participating in the 2010 Europe Day festivities with my short documentary. I am intrigued by a particular sentence that reads: "In our accession process to the European Union, I believe that our artistic activities will make important contributions to Turkey's being more positively perceived in the European Union." It is signed by Turkey's chief negotiator for EU accession.

I'd like to reflect a little on this claim and the potential role of a film such as *Coffee Futures* in Turkey's star-crossed efforts to join the European Union. I am an academic anthropologist—or, to be more precise, a visual anthropologist just starting to produce films as well as articles and books—and have only a very limited status as a filmmaker. Hence, it may seem far-fetched to suggest that this twenty-two-minute documentary could have any political impact. But allow me to elaborate, for watching the film during its first year of circulation taught me a lot about visual politics.

COFFEE FUTURES

Coffee Futures is a short documentary about a long story. On the one hand, the film is about a long-standing cultural practice: the reading of personal futures in coffee grounds. The widespread custom of coffee fortune-telling in Turkey is an everyday communication tool.[5] Coffee fortunes are both a way of dealing with hopes, fears and worries and a way of indirectly voicing matters usually left unspoken. It is a form of communication that allows for a lot of intimacy and yet protects both fortune seeker and teller from losing face, because it is a very playful form of knowledge production. Everyone will tell you, "Don't believe your fortune, but don't be without it, either." So taking the fortune seriously is simply part of the game. Like any language, coffee fortune-telling has its protocols, rules and tropes, and yet each telling bears distinct marks of the teller's personal style and the individual fortune seeker's condition.

At the same time, the film is about the political status of Turkish citizens—as always-deferred, never-quite-realized citizens of the European Union. July 31,

2009 marked the fiftieth year anniversary of Turkey's attempts to join the ever-elusive EU. That is, *Coffee Futures* attempts to render the emotional texture of a society whose fate has been nationally and internationally debated—often in terms of its being or not being European—over a very long period of time. To that end, it weaves individual fortunes with the story of Turkey's decades-long attempts to become a member of the European Union. Promises and predictions made by politicians, both foreign and domestic, are juxtaposed with the rhetorics and practices of everyday coffee fortune-telling.

THE RHETORIC, EMOTIONS, AND POLITICS OF PROGNOSTICATION

For the English title, *Coffee Futures*, I wanted to make a reference to futures trading in the financial industry, because "futures" are profitable only when the future is uncertain, when there is risk and unpredictability involved. Many perceive Turkey's EU bid as not only a political gamble on both sides, but also as strongly connected to economics. After all, at the time of Schuman's proposal, long before all this debate about who fit into Europe culturally, the EU was essentially an economic community. The financial crisis of 2010 threatening to have dire financial consequences for the entire European Union once again underscored the economic nature of the union.

However, as an anthropologist, not an economist, I wanted to suggest that accuracy is not the only way to evaluate a practice of divination. How does the future shape the present? How can we comprehend a period of speculation itself? How can we understand the very particular forms of sociability that any particular practice of prognostication enables?

Coffee Futures is an ethnography of ways people speak about the future. In some degree, this challenges norms of ethnographic filmmaking, because it is not a film in which the viewer gets to know specific individuals well, nor is it observational cinema. In order to capture ways of everyday prognostication, I needed to find nonartificial (that is, not prompted by the anthropologist), commonplace rituals of prognostication and concrete practices of speculation on the future. Coffee fortune-telling is such a practice, as is making political speeches on the part of national and international politicians. In other words, in seeking to understand how people speak about the future, I turned to two groups who regularly and confidently make pronouncements about what lies ahead, two types of experts in seeing the future. By editing together official forms of prognostication and informal, casual forms of prognostication, by focusing not on the prognosticators, but rather on the range of prognostications available and the ways of prognosticating, I'm asking if ways of talking about the future influence one another across very different domains and registers of speech.

One of the elements I wanted to evoke in the analogy between personal futures and national futures is the effect of having one's future, regardless of content, discussed and commented upon. How does it feel for one's future to be a regular topic of speculation? Also, what does it mean politically for political futures to be understood as just as vague and dependent on whim as playful coffee fortunes? Or when certain fortunes don't change, but rather become predictable prophecies, despite never materializing, does the future begin to seem improbable or unattainable? What are the uses and abuses of vague futures?

For years, news audiences in Turkey have heard pronouncements that Turkey should or could or will be a part of Europe, but "not just yet," or "in a little while," or "as soon as it has met the following criteria." Indeed, in some ways, this is how the film started. When I was living in Paris in 2004, everyone I met wanted to talk about Turkey's application to join the European Union. Yet people had such entrenched opinions on the topic that I found it hard to be heard; those in favor of Turkey's entering the EU and those opposed both seemed to be asking me only to confirm their preexisting ideas on the matter. I longed for debates in which genuine dialogue was possible; instead, I often felt scripted into the role of a national spokesperson. Likewise, when I moved back to Istanbul in 2007, I was surprised by how the rhetoric of EU membership had seeped into everyday life. Whether the conversation was about human rights, traffic, arts, or education, every conversation seemed to return to the question of the European Union. When I listened to politicians on the topic, whether foreign or domestic, I was struck by their formulaic phrases. The rhetoric of Turkey's future relationship with the EU reminded me of the rhetoric of coffee fortune-telling. On the one hand, the topic of being evaluated for EU membership was inescapable, and yet, on the other, all conversation seemed stuck in ossified, intransigent ways of speaking. What were the social and psychological effects of these ways of speaking about Turkey's foreign affairs and national future?

After reflecting on casual fortune-telling as a creative way to address matters that are usually left unspoken, the idea for *Coffee Futures* arose from my hope that coming at "the EU question" from this lighter angle might open up the possibility for fresh dialogue, one that went beyond the well-rehearsed lines that everyone knows by heart. So in the late summer of 2008, I set out to seek my fortune: I asked around for anyone who was good at reading coffee grounds. None of the people in this film were paid to read my fortune. They are all amateurs in the sense that they read fortunes only socially. People recommended their colleagues, their ex-lovers, their friends and neighbors. Since I had been interested in coffee fortune-telling for quite some time, several of the people in the film had been reading my fortune for years—over a decade, in some cases. I flipped my cup for two dozen people, both friends and strangers. These amateur fortune-tellers all read my individual fortune as they might any other day. We drank Turkish coffee together, then I turned my cup over on the saucer to let the grounds settle, and then they read my fortune, some for fifteen minutes, some for an hour. At the very end, when it is customary for the fortune seeker to pose a question, I surprised them by asking for their opinion on a political, not a personal, matter: What did the future hold for the relations between Turkey and Europe?

It was editor and director of photography Ebru Karaca's idea to ask each of the fortune-tellers his or her opinion of Turkey/Europe relations. Initially, I worried that some might have nothing to say. Ebru laughed at me when I voiced this concern. "You have been abroad too long!" she teased. "Of course they will have an opinion!" She was right. In fact, initially, the idea was to edit in such a way as to show someone being surprised by this completely out-of-context question, but none of them demonstrated visible surprise. All of them were taken aback, but all were equally ready to answer the question. They didn't have to search for a way to talk about the issue, so thoroughly has the discourse of EU accession saturated everyday conversation and every domain of discussion in Turkey.

In other words, no one really looks into a coffee cup to read the future of Turkey's relations with the EU. Rather, my fieldwork and editing choices were intended to present an ethnography of how people speak of uncertain futures in Turkey today—and to illuminate ways in which the uncertain futures of Turkish citizens have for so long been presented to be inextricably bound up in Turkey's painfully, eternally stalled courtship with the EU. I'm asking whether looking at how people make prognostications in one domain of personal life, predictions of an intimate relationship, can hint at how the political future is constructed in a country where all kinds of people are constantly asking "What will become of us?" or "Where is this all leading?" My intention was not to make an expository documentary about either coffee fortune-telling or Turkey's EU accession process. Rather, I wanted to create a film in which the viewer is drawn into conversations and, if possible, given a sense of the unsettling experience of waiting to have one's future read in something as enigmatic as the residue of a cup of coffee—the experience of being in the vulnerable position of looking to others for clues about one's own future.

VISUAL CHOICES: LOCATING STEREOTYPES AND THE POLITICS OF IMAGES

From the beginning, I imagined *Coffee Futures* as a film for several reasons. First, coffee fortune-telling itself is a visual practice about interpreting shapes in coffee grounds. I wanted to underscore that this is a form of knowledge production that is about ways of seeing. Second, I wanted to give a sense of what it feels like to have one's future forever speculated on, and I believed I had a better chance of doing that visually. Finally, stereotypes are difficult to avoid when making visual representations, and I wanted to think about how to confront this challenge, since politics trades heavily in stereotypes.

There is a tradition of "talking heads" in documentary film in which interviews are done with experts in the field. *Coffee Futures* technically also shows a series of talking heads, though their realm of expertise is quite different, and they are certainly not the people whose political opinions we usually get to hear. I wanted to contrast these two domains of prognostication—the private, mostly feminine realm of reading coffee grounds and the public, male-dominated realm of politics. There are exceptions in both cases, of course, reflected in the film by the men reading coffee grounds and the cameo appearances of female politicians such as Tansu Çiller and Angela Merkel. I also wanted to play with the classic trope of the male colonizer and the female colonized, since here it is Turkey who is the desirer and Europe who is the pursued.

Though outside the domain of nation-state politics, there are certainly power dynamics inherent in the ritual of reading coffee grounds. Regardless of what the actual relationship is between the two people before one person picks up the cup (they might be people of different ages, one might be much less wealthy than the other, one might work for the other, one might be trying to seduce the other), as soon as the cup has been lifted, a performance begins. During this performance, the person telling the future is in a position of power, because to be seeking your fortune is a position of vulnerability.[6] However, as the fortunes reveal, the courtship is a complicated dance, rather than one lover pursuing the unyielding other.

One of the overdetermined visual elements in the film is the currently very popular cosmopolitan city of Istanbul. As we began shooting, the city itself began to be very important. I tried to find locations on the Bosphorus. This is a deeply significant body of water inasmuch as it gives Istanbul much of its personality and poetry. But it is also highly overdetermined politically and geographically, inasmuch as it is the strait separating Europe from Asia.[7]

The Istanbul vista scenes included in the film were intended to be tongue-in-cheek references to touristic views of this city: silhouettes of minarets, the view of the Rococo mosque, the symbolically laden bridge spanning two continents (fig. 4). Istanbul often becomes the only part of Turkey that is talked about when it comes to conversations about Europeanness, so by deliberately choosing postcard-like backdrops, I tried to approach that with a little irony. I wanted to include these classic backdrops, oversaturated with meanings, to capture some of the frustration of feeling as if alternative ways of looking have been foreclosed.

When the film was screened to a group of management students at Middle East Technical University in an MBA course titled Economic and Political Aspects of

EU-Turkey Relations, one of the questions the instructor asked the students to reflect on was how the film might have been different had it been shot in locations around Turkey rather than only in Istanbul. The students come from many different parts of the country, and some of them thought the film would have been very different, while others disagreed. However, one particular answer gets at precisely the stereotypes with which Istanbul gets associated, both at home and abroad:

> I thought about this while watching the film and concluded that Istanbul was the perfect choice. Istanbul is our pride and joy. It's got rich history, natural beauty, and variety. It is an aesthetic city. It has often helped me disprove European and American friends' beliefs that we are dirty nomadic tribes who ride camels. I am from a city in the Southeast that resembles India in terms of its disorderliness. I wouldn't have wanted the film to have been shot there. Maybe once we've put some things in order, then I'd be proud.

In other words, in imagining how Westerners imagine Turkey and claiming that Istanbul shatters those prejudices, the student displays a belief that only Turkey's pride and joy should be shown to Europe, despite the fact that he personally knows that Istanbul does not accurately reflect all of Turkey. (And ironically, given his critique of Western friends, he defines the disorderliness of his hometown in an equally prejudiced and geographically imagined way as "like India.") This is precisely the episteme I hoped to capture: the habit, in Turkey, of seeing Turkey through the aspirations of a European future or, to return to the language of the official thank-you letter I received, the constant necessity "to contribute to Turkey's being more positively perceived in the European Union."

In order to portray accurately the ritual of coffee fortune-telling, it was important to capture the intimacy of the practice. As an experienced filmmaker herself, Ebru Karaca, the director of photography, pointed out that if we showed people reading cups and saucers without anyone else in the frame, they would look as if they were lecturing. So with much trepidation, I agreed to be in the frame, and she shot from over my shoulder (fig. 5).

One of the unintended benefits of this is that as a result, the camera always looking over my shoulder can be read as a slight twist on Clifford Geertz's idea of the role of the anthropologist reading culture over the native's shoulder.[8] The result is a frame in which the viewer overhears my personal fortune while peering over my shoulder.[9] However, not only am I both native and anthropologist, as well as director, social scientist, and fortune seeker, but the types of cultural texts being "read" over my shoulder—rhetorics of prognostication, whether coffee readings or political aspirations and strategies—are always relational and exist only in the relations between self and other.[10]

FIGURE 4 The Bosphorus bridge that connects Europe and Asia, an Istanbul landmark present in almost all visualizations of the stereotype of "East meets West" or "the bridging of civilizations." Still from *Coffee Futures*.

FIGURE 5 Reading culture over the shoulder. Still from *Coffee Futures*.

What I personally look like and its correspondence or dissonance with others' expectations had been one of the starting points of the film in that very often, when people abroad heard I was Turkish, they would say, "But you don't look Turkish." This is (I believe) usually voiced to me as a compliment (though heard with much discomfort on my part) and most often means (I surmise) that I don't look like their mental image of a Turkish woman, whatever that might be or however it might have been formed.[11] Just as there are many Europes within Europe, there are many Turkeys within Turkey. This was why I wanted to have many different cups, many different ways of making coffee, and many different types of people in the film (without making them pedantically "representative" of all the different ethnic or religious groups in Turkey). The youngest person in the film was nineteen, and the oldest was in her seventies. The film includes people from a diverse array of ethnic, class, and educational backgrounds. This is not to say everyone in Turkey reads coffee grounds, but rather that the practice is widespread enough to transcend other important categories in society.

Coffee fortune-telling itself has its own stereotypes. The Romani woman in the film immediately confronted visual stereotypes when we started shooting. "Now watch how I transform into a fortune-teller," she teased as she put on exaggerated eye makeup and tied an electric-blue scarf around her head. She was dressing up to look like a "gypsy fortune-teller" in a way that Turkish audiences would immediately recognize. Fortuitously, the image of her as the low-class ignorant conniving gypsy is one of the stereotypes the film undermines when she makes one of the most insightful comments on the European Union accession process. Given that she didn't know I would ask about the EU, I can take no credit for this. Rather, her extremely astute answer to the EU question reflects her own keen awareness of image and how she is positioned in the eyes of others.

When asked what will become of Turkey's relations with Europe, she talks about going to visit Silivri Prison and not being let in to see her husband because she is five minutes late for visiting hours, despite the fact that she is disabled and has to walk with crutches. Objecting that there are not enough provisions for the disabled, she immediately invokes the EU as an authority and chastises the prison guard barring her entry: "You want to get into the EU. You've built EU-style prisons, but where's the EU order? Without it, the EU won't accept you or Turkey." She uses the formal second-person "you," *siz*, to address the guard. In contrast, he uses the informal second person when incredulously replying with disdain, "And they'll let you in?!" Clearly knowledgeable, not only about penal reforms as part of the negotiations for EU accession, but also about how EU provisions for the disabled might affect her personally, she replies, "They'll not only accept me, they'll even take care of me." To which he can only reply that he's merely following the law. Her response, “Well, with laws like this, they won’t accept us,” is exemplary of how she deftly negotiates her minority status (double minority actually, as both Romani and disabled) by including herself in the nation-state—“they won’t accept us”—while talking to the prison guard as representative gatekeeper. Her intelligence has not been lost on the film’s audiences, perhaps because her exaggerated appearance leads them to expect a far more cartoonish simple response, or perhaps because she is the only person who speaks not in generalities, but rather as a citizen cognizant of how EU policies will directly effect her.

Audience members also commented on the film’s inclusion of several women who wear head coverings. Women who wear head scarves are an increasingly visible part of the Turkish population. Perhaps precisely because of the visual nature of the head scarf, both domestically and abroad, women so dressed are often facilely portrayed as a homogenous group positioned against modernity and, by proxy, against Europe. I wanted to avoid such black-and-white caricatures in the film. I wanted to include women with a range of religious beliefs. Yet I faced the challenge of how to avoid reinforcing stereotypes while also including women who perhaps look like pious Muslims. Additionally, I had a hard time finding a woman who looked like a Muslim woman who was nevertheless willing to be filmed while reading my coffee fortune. Due to the politicized weight given to the headscarf, many women who dress this way, particularly younger women active in civil society, express feeling an added responsibility to uphold the religious standards to which they adhere when it comes to public displays, including being filmed. Many of the women I approached—by no means limited to those wearing head scarves—stated that only God can know the future; they therefore held that any form of fortune-telling is sinful. They worried that the audience might misunderstand their playful, casual, social practice of fortune-telling as a serious attempt to prophesy. A few proposed a number of innovative compromises. One covered the Korans that would otherwise have been identifiable in the frame. One woman was willing to read my fortune, but only if we shot her from behind as she sat with her daughters at a café. However, as luck would have it, we couldn’t include much of that scene, because the call to prayer started up in the middle of our shoot and rendered much of the recording inaudible.

In the end, I found a very articulate young woman willing to act as a film subject. This woman in some ways exemplifies the challenges facing women who choose to wear religiously inflected clothing. She studies at a university in Sarajevo because head scarves are banned in Turkish universities. Perhaps one of the reasons that she agreed was because her older sister is a well-known Islamic rapper. In other words, someone in her family has already negotiated the combination of piety with public visibility in popular culture. While editing her scenes, I sought the input of a number of prominent female commentators who weigh in on public debates on religious matters and are self-identified devout believers themselves. I did so because religion is central to many debates in Turkey, particularly around Europeanness, and I therefore felt a responsibility to try to anticipate how diverse audiences might generalize whatever position this one woman articulated. Whether these precautions were in the end necessary or not, audience members, both foreign and domestic, with a range of attitudes regarding religious dress in higher education, have remarked on this young woman's eloquence.

AUDIENCES, RECEPTIONS, AND PERCEPTIONS

The film traveled widely in its first year. The premiere took place in Istanbul on the night before the bittersweet milestone marking the fiftieth anniversary of Turkey's application to enter the EU. This first audience was composed of journalists and academics specializing in EU affairs, a few diplomats, and most of the people who were in the film, along with their families.[12] I wanted to get the film to three different types of audiences—filmgoers at film festivals, academic institutions and their students, and people directly involved with EU-Turkey politics. I have traveled with the film to screen it at Middle East centers, centers for European Studies, Turkish Studies colloquiums, and anthropology departments at over a dozen campuses in the United States, England, and Turkey, and I hope to continue these screenings.[13] The film has also been shown at a variety of film festivals, both in Turkey and internationally.[14]

The most unexpected use of the film so far has been in the sphere of politics. A few weeks after the EurActiv Awards ceremony in November 2009, I showed the film at the EU Parliament at a celebration of the seventy-fifth anniversary of Turkish women receiving the right to vote and be elected.

This anniversary was celebrated in Brussels with all of the predictable emphasis on Turkish women getting the vote before women in many European countries.[15] The film returned to Brussels without me for an International Women's Day celebration in which the Turkish ambassador's wife also participated. In fact, several viewers of different nationalities have commented that the women all seem much more articulate than the politicians, foreign or Turkish. Perhaps for this reason, many frame the film as a feminist film.

Yet with audiences who are professionally involved with politics, the film gets praised for giving a sense of how politics exists in everyday life among ordinary people, rather than as a form of elite activity or mediated ideology. In other words, political elites and others alike seem to welcome a representation of EU-Turkey relations that does not center on officials. One political scientist specializing on Turkey enthusiastically told a university audience that what was needed was more anthropology. "What we need is more of this bottom up-perspective . . . that does not take the narrow institutional approach."

Turkish government officials have also responded very enthusiastically. Several Turkish diplomats have come up to me and thanked me for making the film and asked to use it as part of a program at their embassies. Younger diplomats have stated that the film expressed what they could not say, but had felt for so long. When the Turkish prime minister's wife went to Brussels in April 2010 with more than a hundred prominent women, *Coffee Futures* was screened during the private flight from Ankara to Brussels. I was invited to attend a Salzburg Global Seminar workshop on the topic "What Turkey? What Europe?" at which most of the other attendees were Turkish and European politicians, diplomats, and bureaucrats or journalists, political scientists, or public intellectuals who specialize in EU matters.

One ambassador who attended an event where the film was screened spontaneously asked for permission to address the audience again following the film. In these unscripted comments, delivered in a tone far more personal than his earlier formal address, he insisted that official views, like his own, were not heard or listened to precisely because they are official. "Opinions directly coming from the people is what is needed. Public diplomacy is very important, and this film is a good example of public diplomacy. This film conveys the feelings, thoughts, and emotions of Turkish public opinion." Despite the diversity of views expressed in the film, he concluded his remarks by reminding the audience that the overwhelming majority of Turkish opinion is for EU membership.

Politicians and diplomats, including European bureaucrats, thus seem confident that the film has a pro-EU agenda. Or perhaps this is what they imply to me after screenings, though of course I cannot know their true feelings. Coincidentally, at a coffee break just a few minutes before the ambassador's impromptu address, four young Turkish students had gathered around me to share their fears that if Turkey joined the EU, this would result in its losing its strength or in the dilution of its national character. I don't bring up this juxtaposition to imply that the ambassador was mistaken, but rather to highlight that the film has been favorably received by people with differing opinions about the EU. In other words, the film's ambiguity allows people to interpret it in multiple ways. Where audiences with different views find common ground seems to be in an understanding of what it means always already to be thinking about these issues—what it means, in other words, to live always partly in the future.

I should perhaps mention, here, that I believe it would be irresponsible to ignore the important progress that has been made in many domains through civil-society organizations in Turkey under the rubric of EU accession. Minority rights are just one domain where there has been a lot of progress in the last decade, partly because of the EU serving as an external authority that civil-society organizations can invoke when faced with obstacles, but from which they can also receive financial support.

And yet, despite the thank-you letter from the chief negotiator with which I opened this piece, *Coffee Futures* was not necessarily intended to contribute "to Turkey's being more positively perceived in the European Union." Rather than pronounce on the economic or political benefits or disadvantages of full membership, as an anthropologist, I had wanted to draw some attention to the fact that regardless of what the future holds, that the EU has for so long been part of what is promised as a potential political future in Turkey has a weight of its own as a social fact. In other words, regardless of whether or not Turkey eventually joins the EU, during this half century, the promise of Europe has shaped Turkey, just as the debates about including or excluding Turkey have shaped the contours of contemporary Europe.

The desirer and the desired, and indeed, the very nature of desiring, change over the course of time, especially over the course of fifty years. Turkey is not what it was in 1959, in part due to the negotiations with the EU. Likewise, Europe is not what it was, in part due to its negotiations with Turkey. Europe and Turkey have served as very powerful "others" for one another, limits against which or through which to define themselves. Of course, these complex relations have a history going much further back, into the Ottoman Empire.[16] But they also inhabit the very texture of everyday experience—of the taste and experience of the simple act of sharing a cup of coffee. It is this doubleness—what it means to live day to day under the sign of longstanding international negotiations—that I hoped *Coffee Futures* might dramatize (see fig. 1).

CODA: ANOTHER DAY, ANOTHER CUP

One of the reasons people read each others' fortunes regularly is because futures, and hence fortunes, change. Indeed, since the summer of 2008, when *Coffee Futures* was filmed, there has been a sea change in public opinion about the EU in Turkey. One of the many universities in Turkey that have a department of European Union Studies did not accept applications in 2010 for fear of losing face if no students applied. The degree of the ongoing sea change and its causes are debatable. Much commentary focused on the economy. Turkey's economic strength and potential were portrayed as a sharp contrast to the economic status of Europe in the crisis that sent shock waves throughout the eurozone in the spring of 2010 and beyond. At one screening at a North American university in 2011, just after boasting of Turkey's 8.9 percent economic growth rate, the Turkish consul general who had been invited to comment on the film told the audience that public support for the EU had dropped from 73 percent in 1995 to 30 percent. European economies, on the other hand, faced troubled times. Yet, he added, this was not just about being accepted into the EU, but rather about Turkey's identity. "We are looking for acknowledgement of our Western identity. This has become more and more of a symbolic objective for us." Yet despite the economic upheavals, many say that EU membership is still not in Turkey's immediate future.

At several recent screenings of the film both inside and outside Turkey, I have been asked what incentives Turkey has to continue pursuing the EU. "The sting of unrequited love?" some surmise. Another audience member volunteered a Turkish proverb, "A wrestler who is losing cannot get his fill of beatings." Perhaps EU application has become a national habit? Or is this just another phase in the waxing and waning of Turkey's efforts or Europe's attentions? This has certainly not been a story of steady progress. In fact, there have been so many stops and starts along the way that even the origin of the process is difficult to pin down: experts give several different dates as the beginning of Turkey's efforts to join the EU.

To return to the strategically multiple message of the banners announcing Europe Day and the promise of a stronger, more democratic, more respectable, more modern Turkey en route to the European Union, perhaps one should ask why so many different groups seemed to agree that the path to the EU was the right one at a time when so many other issues were hotly contested and led to bitter polarizations in Turkish politics and society. Particularly from the end of the 1990s to the mid-2000s, membership in the EU had the significant characteristic of being a project promising a future that could gain the support of many different groups in Turkey, groups whose desired domestic futures had little in common.

Those who believe that the way to progress since the foundation of the republic in 1923 has been through relations with the West, sometimes called "Kemalists," because they see themselves defending the legacy of the nation's founder, Mustafa Kemal, support integration into the EU because they see it as the next step in Turkey's Westernization project. For Kemalists, accession to the EU is merely the next step in modernization and development. More conservative and Islamic groups see the EU project as important for Turkey's democratization. They contest the assumption that Turkey's future is in the hands of its Kemalist—or perceived Kemalist—military and bureaucratic elite. They likewise mean to disabuse them and the public of the belief that members of this small group are the sole inheritors of the country. The conservative group is also very interested in the EU as a guarantor of what they take, somewhat narrowly, to be personal freedoms: the right to organize around religious identity and the right to wear a head scarf in official public spaces such as schools and courts, for instance. Another group supporting

EU membership is the Kurdish population, and their main hope is the changes that they believe EU membership might bring about in minority rights.

The EU project also enjoys the support of the business community and workers alike. Workers give their support in hopes that they will earn higher wages, experience more of the benefits of a welfare state, and have more freedom to organize. Business communities, on the other hand, believe that Turkey's becoming a member country will result in greater market shares in Europe for Turkish products and companies. They also hold that a relatively more stable Turkey will increase the country's attractiveness in the eyes of investors.[17]

In short, there is no other alternative project in which so many diverse interests are perceived to converge. This makes it a goal from which it is not easy to turn away.[18] Perhaps aspiring for a future as a citizen of the EU is a bit like coffee fortune-telling in that the practice is widespread enough to transcend other important categories in contemporary Turkey.[19]

At the Salzbug Global Seminar, I kept hearing EU officials and European politicians emphasize that joining the EU now is not what it was before. Times have changed. And they will continue to change. One EU expert underscored this by commenting that the EU did not need to make any decisions today—that instead, there would be time to reflect along the way, because the evaluation process would still take a long time. This is a quite different sentiment from the idea that any candidate country will achieve membership once it has met all the criteria. Furthermore, it was clear that what mattered now was not at all how long a particular applicant country had desired to join the EU or how much experience it had as a candidate country. What mattered was its ability to articulate a joint future. "Turkey needs to convince the EU about what Turkish involvement in the EU would look like. What is the Turkish view of the EU role in the world?" In other words, while anything could change over time, what mattered now was the confidence with which Turkey could imagine itself as a member imagining a future for the EU in the world. A veteran British diplomat whose opinions of EU matters are taken very seriously emphatically stated: "Knowing what the applicant country's idea of the future is, is important." In other words, "the EU" was no longer a sufficient answer to the question "What lies in the future for Turkey?"

Hence, we return to the importance of futures and the confidence with which they are articulated. One thing I have learned along the way is that it is especially dangerous for young people to grow skeptical of political futures, because it can breed cynicism not only about the EU accession process, but about political processes in general. This is critical, particularly inasmuch as any democratic and peaceful future for Turkey will involve negotiations with populations with which there have been long-standing grievances, whether Armenian, Kurdish, Greek, or

Cypriot. In other words, a country with a large population of young people who have inherited several unresolved political issues with complex histories can ill afford skepticism about possibilities in the future and about projects on which diverse interest groups can converge.

So can a film play a role in Turkey's star-crossed efforts to join the European Union—especially a film that advocates taking into consideration emotional complexity when addressing long-standing international relations, rather than a particular policy decision or political act? What kind of impact could such a film have? Is its circulation itself a form of politics?[20]

As I was finishing this piece, I received an e-mail from an EU bureaucrat I had met at a screening of *Coffee Futures*: "Just to tell you that your movie cheered up a bunch of Brussels bureaucrats who work on Turkey on a daily basis this morning. . . . I'm very much looking forward to the sequel, which I hope will bring good news." When I inquired as to the context in which he'd seen the film, he told me that the director general of EU enlargement for the European Commission, to whom I had sent a copy of the film, had shown it to the unit that works on Turkey. The audience had consisted of EU nationals exercising secretarial or policy functions related to Turkey.

As for why they needed cheering up? "We tend to spend too much time on procedures or not seeing the outcome of our work or being far away from the decision centre. The fact that things don't always go the way we would wish with Turkey doesn't help either."[21] I can only speculate on why the director general chose to show the film, what, if any, impression the film left on these viewers, in what conversations, if any, it came up in later, or when, if ever, it will be remembered and reflected upon. Perhaps the very characteristics that make *Coffee Futures* an unusual piece of scholarship within traditional academic frameworks—that it is humorous, that it has a lighthearted approach, that its message is not spelled out, and that it is a visual piece that can be experienced in full in twenty-two minutes—are what made it possible for the director general to use it in a meeting with a group of policy makers. Or perhaps its political potential stems from its polyvalence, because the film's approach is similar to one expressed toward fortune-telling by one woman in the film: "I can only tell you some things, but you'll have to draw your own conclusions." Perhaps one of the ways that visual representations and their circulations can contribute politically is by enabling unexpected virtual encounters between people, registers of speech, and domains of life that do not usually intersect. The challenge is for makers of visual media to harness the power of visual representations existing, often unlike the people portrayed, in a free-travel zone.

NOTES

1. Turkey officially applied for membership in the European Economic Commission (EEC) on July 31, 1959. The EEC then became the European Community (EC). Turkey applied for membership in the EC in 1987. The EC evolved into the European Union (EU). Turkey's EU candidacy was accepted in 1999. Official membership negotiations began in 2005.
2. The National Lottery is drawn on the ninth, nineteenth, and twenty-ninth of every month and on special holidays.
3. Ayça Tunç provides an interesting comparative analysis of how Turkish media and European media portray the success of Turkish directors at European film festivals. See Ayça Tunç Cox, "Hyphenated Identities: The Reception of Turkish-German Filmmakers in the Daily Turkish Press," in Barbara Mennel and Sabine Hake (eds.), *Contemporary Turkish Cinema* (New York: Berghahn, 2012). Turkish media repeatedly emphasize the success of Turkish directors and artists abroad—even if the individuals are citizens of another country or have long lived in a European country—as "entry into the European Union," whereas arts reporters for European newspapers have not regularly tied together these awards to Turkish relations with the European Union. *Honey* was supported by the Script Development Fund of the Antalya Eurasia Film Festival and received funding from the Council of Europe Eurimages Fund, the North Rhine Westphalia Film Foundation, and the television stations ZDF and Arte. *Coffee Futures* was funded by my sister, Umut Gürsel, after failed attempts to secure funding. I kept getting asked if I was making a pro-EU or anti-EU film. When I responded that I wanted to make neither, but rather a film about the social, psychic weight of a process that has now lasted half a century, I was told no one would want to watch a film without a message.
4. *Neyse Halim Ciksin Falim (Coffee Futures)*. Directed by Zeynep Devrim Gürsel, 2009, 22 minutes, color. Distributed by Documentary Educational Resources, 101 Morse Street, Watertown, MA 02472, www.der.org.
5. Reading coffee grounds is a practice that exists not only in Turkey, but also in the Balkans, Greece, Bulgaria, Armenia, Syria, Lebanon, Yemen, and other parts of the Middle East. Anthropologists Alexandra Bakalaki and Nadia Seremetakis have both written about coffee fortune-telling practices in Greece, practices that are very similar to those I observed in Turkey, while Ana Croegaert discusses different national and international pasts and futures in relation to Bosnian refugees enjoying "Turkish coffee" in Chicago. See Alexandra Bakalaki, "Domesticated Experiences, Wild Narratives: Observations on Coffee Cup Reading," in Rika Benveniste and Theodoros Paradellis (eds.), *Narrativity, History, and Anthropology* (Mytilini: University of the Aegean, Department of Social Anthropology, 1994), pp. 90–113 (in Greek). The transliterated title is "Eximeromenes empeiries, agria afigimata: Paratiriseis gia tin cafemanteia" and the title of the collection is *Afigimatikotita, Anthropologia kai Istoria*. C. Nadia Seremetakis, "Divination, Media, and the Networked Body of Modernity." *American Ethnologist* 36.2 (2009), pp. 337–50. Ana Croegaert, "Who Has Time for *Cejf?*: Postsocialist Migration and Slow Coffee in Neoliberal Chicago," *American Anthropologist* 113.3 (September 2011), pp. 463–77.
6. Perhaps it is these power dynamics that make people extremely articulate and confident when reading coffee grounds. In fact, one concerned woman in the film showed such confidence in her own knowledge production that she whispered a gentle warning to me after we filmed her reading, in case I hadn't thought things through carefully: "But Zeynep, if you

make this film, everyone will know everything about your personal life!"

7. The Bosphorus Bridge as a trope signifying a meeting of East and West has become ubiquitous. See German filmmaker Fatih Akin's *Crossing the Bridge: The Sound of Istanbul* (2005) for an example of this trope being used to describe the plurality of musical forms in Istanbul. When Istanbul was designated by the EU as the European Capital of Culture in 2010, this trope appeared constantly, from its logo to much of the art featured.
8. Clifford Geertz, "Deep Play: Notes on the Balinese Cockfight," in *The Interpretation of Cultures* (New York: Basic Books, 1973), p. 452.
9. Perhaps this is a form of listening nearby parallel to Trinh Minh-ha's notion of "speaking nearby." See Nancy N. Chen and Trinh T. Minh-ha, "Speaking Nearby," in Lucien Taylor (ed.), *Visualizing Theory: Selected Essays from V.A.R., 1990–1994* (New York: Routledge, 1994).
10. See the review of *Coffee Futures* by Alexandra Bakalaki for a forceful discussion of social relationality in coffee fortune-telling. *Visual Anthropology* 27.1 (Spring 2011), pp. 102–103.
11. For more on the problematics around *looking* Turkish, see Zeynep Devrim Gürsel, "Biting my Tongue." *Eurozine*, October 24, 2005, http://www.eurozine.com/articles/2005-10-24-gursel-en.html.
12. Several of the individuals featured in the film confessed to having been a little bothered by my asking a political question out of the blue, but all was forgiven now that they understood why I had not asked them to prepare their answers.
13. At a few of these screenings, I have been able to collaborate with sociologist Zeynep Korkman, who has done extensive ethnography on professional fortune-tellers who work at special cafés that have sprung all over Istanbul and other metropolitan areas of Turkey in the last decade. We have jointly presented her research and *Coffee Futures* at several universities. Zeynep Kurtulus Korkman, "Gendered Fortunes: Occult Economies and Feminized Publics in Secular Turkey," Ph.D. dissertation, University of California, Santa Barbara, 2011.
14. *Coffee Futures* has shown at several international festivals, including the San Francisco International Film Festival, the International Film Festival of Ireland, the Elles Tournent Women's Film Festival of Brussels, the Verzio Human Rights Film Festival in Budapest, the Miradas-Doc Festival in Tenerife, the Cairo Documentary Film Festival, Days of Ethnographic Film in Moscow, and the Addis Ababa International Film Festival. It also screened at several festivals within Turkey and won the audience award at the Istanbul Independent Film Festival. For a full list of screenings, please see the press kit at http://www.coffeefuturesfilm.com.
15. Turkish women received the right to vote and be elected in 1934, compared with 1945 in France and 1971 in Switzerland.
16. Apparently, coffee and the integration of prophecy with policy making also have long histories in Turkey. Traders from Yemen brought coffee to the Ottoman Empire in the fifteenth century, from whence it eventually spread to Europe, giving rise eventually to the coffeehouses and café culture so characteristic of the European Enlightenment. Cemal Kafadar, "A History of Coffee," *Economic History Congress XIII* (Buenos Aires, 2002) The fifteenth century was also a time when prognosticators had significant power in the court, though they mostly relied on stars, not coffee grounds. Cornell H. Fleisher, "Ancient Wisdom and New Sciences: Prophecies at the Ottoman Court in the Fifteenth and Early Sixteenth Centuries," in Massumeh Farhad (ed.), with Serpil Bagci Falnama, *The Book of Omens* (London: Thames and Hudson, 2010). See also Ralph S. Hattox, *Coffee and Coffeehouses: The Origins of a Social Beverage in the Medieval Near East* (Seattle: University of Washington Press, 1985).

17. One well-known industrialist apparently liked *Coffee Futures* so much that he had twenty-five bootleg copies made and distributed them to other major industrialists. Unfortunately, I have not had a chance to interview him and better understand what it was about the film that so appealed to him.
18. I am grateful to Sabah Günce Eryilmaz for this sketch of domestic political interests and stakes in EU membership.
19. Like all political commentary, this brief sketch of Turkish politics presents groups as more homogenous than they really are. While *Coffee Futures* does not directly speak to any of these issues, different audiences have perceived allusions to all of them in one way or another.
20. A high-profile Turkish expert on EU affairs agreed to be the film's "EU consultant"; his work has consisted mostly in helping the film reach political actors who play a role in Turkey's EU negotiations, rather than in giving editorial direction.
21. This sentence can be interpreted to mean "Turkey does not always do things as we in Brussels would wish," or "Despite our best efforts, Turkey's membership does not advance as smoothly as we might desire."

PART FOUR

EXPANDED ARCHITECTURES

Skarpnäck police car, 1972. From Gun Zacharias, *Skarpnäck, USA: En Bok om Droger och Politik* (Stockholm: Förbunder mot Droger, 1975).

Woodstockholm

Felicity D. Scott

In "Getting Back to Earth," an article published in the *Washington Post and Times Herald* on June 25, 1972, journalist Daniel Zwerdling reflected enthusiastically upon one of the so-called alternative conferences or counterconferences that had run concurrently with the United Nations Conference on the Human Environment (UNCHE) held in Stockholm from June 5 to 16, 1972. "If living at peace with the environment begins at home," he remarked, invoking a popular ethic of personal responsibility,

> ... then the most encouraging progress in Stockholm wasn't made in the gilded parliamentary halls of the United Nations Conference but on a muddy old airport field called Skarpnäck. Here the Hog Farm, a commune which travels about America in battered old school buses, erected their Tent City–Sweden, home for the ecofreaks who flocked to Stockholm as unofficial and uninvited guests of the environmental conference.
>
> It was a model in clean environmental living: great canvas tents and an Indian teepee, a geodesic dome fashioned from wood strips and beer cans, giant bins of throwaway bottles for landfill and mounds of human excrement and garbage which would return to the earth as compost. Hog Farmers made and mended their own clothes (natural fibers, of course), repaired their own buses (25 years old, at least) and cooked with wood fuels.[1]

While we might question whether traveling the country in battered old school buses was environmentally sound, let alone transporting them along with fifty commune members to Stockholm, it is not surprising that the highly theatrical and media-savvy "lifestyle" demonstrations of the Hog Farmers at Skarpnäck might have appealed to the American journalist. Such ecotactics and counterconducts had by this time enjoyed a half decade or more of mainstream press coverage, and

Zwerdling's account in many ways fell back on well-worn mass-media portrayals of American hippie culture and the back-to-the-land environmental activism of the late 1960s. These familiar tropes were in fact precisely what the Hog Farm had been brought there to convey, invited to Stockholm under the auspices of Stewart Brand's initiative the Life Forum to, as Barry Weisberg put it, "create a better show."[2]

The Life Forum would be only one of many alternative platforms hoping to supplement and to trouble the circumscribed range of environmental issues that had been identified, synthesized, and tabled for discussion at the UN conference. Motivating the creation of Miljöforum (Environment Forum) and Folkets Forum (People's Forum), as well as the activities of groups such as Pow Wow, Dai Dong, Alternativ Stadt, and others was the recognition that missing from the UN agenda were adequate considerations of the economic and political roots of environmental distress, including the impact of defense spending, warfare, and social and distributive injustices.[3] Numerous contemporary accounts puzzled over the status and expanded range of political actors at play, trying to understand just how the claims made at the counterconferences would interface with or affect official UN proceedings. Indeed, the prospect of an encounter between governmental delegates, scientific experts, and countercultural and radical voices marked the political imaginary of this event even before it began. In a *Village Voice* article, symptomatically titled "Woodstockholm '72: The Subject is Survival," Ross Gelbspan and David Gurin speculated in the month leading up to the conference that anywhere "from 5,000 to 150,000 people—high-level government leaders, earth-concerned scientists from around the world, journalists (about three to every UN delegate), non-official environmentalists, and intellectual leaders, freaks, poets, holy men, conservationists, and revolutionaries—will converge to talk about ways to heal the planet and avert devastation for the next population-doubling generation of potentially starving and unhoused people."[4]

Newsweek's special feature, "The Big Cleanup: The Environmental Crisis '72," perpetuated this characterization of a potentially unruly, if transient mass gathering at the event itself, positing a strange hybrid outgrowth of the famous Woodstock music festival as it encountered the scientific, political, and media establishment: "At the railroad and airline terminals last week, motley groups of hippies, radicals and ecofreaks were mingling with scientists, diplomats, politicians and newsmen from 109 [sic] nations. . . . The whole scene suggested a complex cross between a scientific convention, a summit conference and rock festival—and in effect, that is precisely what this week's United Nations Conference on the Human Environment will amount to."[5] "Wags," the article reiterated, "are calling the gathering 'Woodstockholm.'" *Time* magazine would also invoke the neologism, connecting it to the Hog Farm's Tent City and activities at Skarpnäck.[6]

The reference to Woodstock was not incidental: as Brand's press release covering the commune's participation in the Life Forum announced, the Hog Farm enjoyed a certain fame from having fed, organized, and controlled the crowds of youth that descended on upstate New York in August of 1969. Brand loudly prophesied, in turn, a similar mass migration to Stockholm, estimating the arrival of "100,000 to 400,000 youth" and campaigning the Swedish authorities to allow Hog Farm to take charge.[7] Brand was in fact a driving force behind this much-anticipated population swell. As reported in the *Voice*, "Life Forum leaders are calling for a mass migration to Sweden 'to provide a living reality-model of people taking care of each other.'"[8] The Hog Farm's role at the UN conference, Brand proposed, "is to help wherever it is needed: with field kitchens in the parks, with liaison between the municipality and street populations, with free stage organization and activities, with medical and drug First Aid, with on-going recycling[,] clean-up and other ecological projects, with information dispersal, with anything that leads to people feeling good and helping each other."[9] From their adoption of alternative cooking and shelter technologies—the latter including stylized tepees, geodesic domes, and customized buses and tents—and distinctly nonnormative appearance, to their Digger-inspired free-food giveaways, free-stage, theatrical demonstrations, and nomadic and/or communal modes of living, the Hog Farm was, indeed, retracing familiar countercultural ground, this time performing "care" and "love" before a global audience in order to help them "feel good" while considering the state and fate of the environment.

According to *Newsweek*, which stressed the importance of the environmental movement "mov[ing] off the streets and into the legislatures, the courts and the corporate boardrooms," the spectacularized nature of this countercultural element came with a certain risk: "if the circus elements of Woodstockholm managed to overshadow the substance of the conference," the editors warned, "the loss would be immense."[10] The countercultural element would not, as it turns out, overshadow the UNCHE itself, but it would at times redirect attention. In the first instance, under Brand's careful management, new alliances were forged between the UN, the U.S. delegation, and the Life Forum, coming together around a "politics no, environment yes" approach that served to keep that attention on resource management.[11] In the second instance, those "circus" elements encountered hostile reactions from other environmental activists and nongovernmental actors at work in Stockholm, reactions that spoke to important political and operational distinctions. Whether understood as potentially distracting "sideshows" to the main UN events, as principled and even ethical alternatives (as with Zwerdling's account of the Hog Farm),[12] or as verification of the environmental movement's status as a powerful political constituency and hence as evidence of the growing impact of nongovernmental voices upon the UN, the multiple, conflicting, and occasionally competing outer conferences were hardly incidental to the UN's shepherding of interstate deliberations. "History may not find it clear," Frances Gendlin noted in *Science and Public Affairs: Bulletin of the Atomic Scientists*, "which was the main event and which the sideshow."[13] As suggested by the rhetoric of circuses, sideshows, and voices, the modes of communication were not unimportant—theatrical performances, demonstrations, costumes, teach-ins, exhibitions, films, publications, press releases, alternative declarations, and even built environments each operated as critical components in opening UN discussions up to other political claims.

There are many aspects to this story: here I want to follow just one as it bears on questions of territorial insecurity and what we might provisionally call its "architectural manifestation" or "residue." What I want to do here is to reconsider Zwerdling's account of the Hog Farm's Tent City by resituating it and, more briefly, the other components of Brand's Life Forum, back into the expanded set of environmental debates that marked the institutional, visual, and discursive matrix of the UN conference and both its semi-official and unaccredited "sideshows." In addition to the Hog Farm, the Life Forum sponsored three other programs: the publication of Mary Jean Haley's *Open Options: A Guide to Stockholm's Alternative Environmental Conferences*,[14] events by Black Mesa Defense Committee addressing environmental pressures on indigenous Americans, and a "salon" that was run by celebrity birth-control and overpopulation activist Stephanie Mills and that included Beat poets Gary Snyder and Michael McClure. My aim here is not to privilege the distinctly American genealogy of theatrical ecotactics within which Life Forum activities are readily legible and whose legacy surfaces at times in environmental activism today, but to ask how they might be troubled by other (equally, if differently symptomatic) paradigms of nongovernmental politics and environmental activism that were "driven by a shared determination not to be governed *thusly*."[15] While these activities depart significantly from my own field, architecture, they nevertheless speak with some precision to historical forces (not only environmental, but also social, economic, material, technological, and geopolitical forces) affecting the discipline of architecture in the early 1970s. Although these activities rarely speak to that discipline directly, my motivation in revisiting the Stockholm Conference is informed by a sense of the need to articulate then-emergent connections between environmental paradigms, architectural paradigms, and about what Michel Foucault would soon after theorize as governmentality and biopolitics as they informed, implicitly or explicitly, nongovernmental politics in these areas.

This was a critical moment in the history of environmental politics, and the UNCHE in Stockholm was itself a punctual, if not uncomplicated event. It marked at once the moment of an increased role for nongovernmental organizations

(NGOs) within the UN and of the integration of (and polemical interruptions staged by) so-called Third World voices in environmental debates. It was also characterized by the repeated mobilization of the figure of the Earth as an ecological system, not only to foster environmental awareness, but also to launch challenges to extant modes of national sovereignty upon which the UN was founded. The vulnerability of humanity's global habitat—so eloquently stated by Adlai Stevenson in a famous 1964 speech to UNESCO and for many rendered comprehensible for the first time in NASA's famous Apollo images of Earth from outer space broadcast a few years later—provided the occasion for the UN to step in and help governments develop the political and economic infrastructure through which to manage the "whole Earth" on behalf of humanity as such.[16] Along with systems-based paradigms of operations research and scientific management, this image all too seamlessly lent itself at once to an emerging countercultural environmental consciousness—as manifest most famously on the cover of the *Whole Earth Catalog*—and to advancing the institutions and mechanisms of global governance of the environment and hence, in turn, of global capitalism, the violent contours of which remain hauntingly familiar in the present. My ambition here is not to demonstrate unequivocally how this might have happened—how the very geopolitical contours of modernity could have shifted so dramatically—but to ask how the techniques at work within certain streams of environmental activism might have functioned unwittingly to serve (but also to interrupt) this logic of globalization. The events of 1972, that is, offer us some cautionary tales.

ONLY ONE EARTH

The United Nations Conference on the Human Environment took place in Stockholm under the motto "Only One Earth." Motivated by the growing recognition in the late 1960s (primarily among industrialized nations of the so-called Global North) of an impending and potentially global "ecological crisis," the conference was initiated in 1968 by the Swedish delegation to a summer session of the United Nations Economic and Social Council (ECOSOC) and ratified by the UN General Assembly on December 3, 1968.[17] Thus, although Weisberg could wryly note that "it was almost as if the carefully controlled but colorful Earth Days in the U.S. over the last two years had been dress rehearsals for what went on in Stockholm," the initial proposal in fact preceded this widespread popularization of environmental issues. Indeed, the conference's agenda seems to have been quite distinct. In December 1970, Maurice Strong, a wealthy Canadian industrialist and former oilman then overseeing Canada's external aid program to developing countries, was appointed secretary general of the conference.[18] With the ambition of forging a worldwide consensus, Strong, according to many accounts, played an active diplomatic role in an effort to bring together growing divides—not only along the familiar East-West axis characteristic of Cold War battles, but across the (to many) less expected, but increasingly evident North-South distinction between industrialized countries and their less developed counterparts.[19] The twenty-seven-nation Preparatory Committee met four times to set the official agenda, synthesizing literally hundreds of thousands of pages of national reports into a streamlined set of largely scientific and technical (and hence supposedly less controversial) concerns regarding the state of the global environment and recommendations for new legal and institutional frameworks to manage its future. These highly edited and, in one reviewer's words, "prefabricated"[20] documents served as the basis for official deliberations among the 113 nations that arrived in Stockholm.

With the introduction of voices from the Third World or Global South and other political activists working against injustice (as both delegates and nongovernmental actors), the Stockholm Conference also set the stage for the emergence of a more complex understanding of global environmental issues than that previously dominated by more traditional Euro-American environmental and conservation discourses, from that of scientific experts to the positions advocated by activists of many leanings. As American biologist and ecosocialist Barry Commoner rightly predicted, "ecological crusaders are about to clash with seekers of social justice."[21] And in the aftermath of the conference, Terri Aronson felt confident to write that "now that the first international conference on the environment is over, it will be difficult for Western environmentalists ever again to view 'the environment' in a parochial way. The developing countries of the world offered the West a new, expanded perspective on environmental issues."[22] Issues of pollution and population control and the protection of the natural environment encountered distributive-justice claims from developing nations, including an unanticipated resistance to environmental standards as a pretext for discriminatory trade policies or as potentially sponsoring "pollution havens" in developing countries; multiple calls for technology transfer as well as for reparations arising from earlier exploitation of resources and environmental damage, whether by colonial occupiers or multinational corporations; sharp political divides over the ideological underpinnings of calls for population control; and battles over the inclusion in a draft declaration on the human environment of considerations of apartheid, colonial and neocolonial aggression (or expansion), racism, warfare, and genocide, as well as the "ecocide" then being systematically wrought in Vietnam by U.S. military forces. All, various parties insisted, were forces affecting the environment and hence properly environmental concerns.

Perhaps not incidental to the emergence of those political claims, and certainly of more lasting consequence, was that under Strong's leadership, the UNCHE launched the framework for new paradigms of global environmental regulation and governance that soon were employed to manage any perceived threats to economic growth in (or the political power of) dominant Western nations as posed either by ecological crusaders or those seeking social justice. Indeed, as Commoner suggested all too presciently of the impact of this newly recognized "interconnectedness," even if his imagined resolution of the situation would not come to pass:

> The environmental crisis is a signal that we have run out of ecological credit, that it is time to pay the debt to nature or go into bankruptcy. This much is now well known. What is just beginning to become apparent is that the debt cannot be paid in recycled beer cans or in the penance of walking to work; it will need to be paid in the ancient coins of social justice—within nations and among them.
>
> In this sense, the environmental crisis has become the world's most dangerous political issue, as it wrenches back into the open view the brutality of racial competition for survival, the incompatibility between the economic goals of entrepreneur and worker, the tragic absurdity of war. . . . If nations must, on ecological grounds, become more dependent on each other's indigenous goods, how can we avoid the ancient evils of international exploitation? As these issues are brought into the view of the world at Stockholm, new steps can be taken toward making the peace among men that must precede a peace with nature.[23]

Commoner was reiterating a controversial argument made during his Earth Day speech in 1970 at Brown University and published in his 1971 book *The Closing Circle*.[24] As reported in *Time*, in Stockholm, too, Commoner had "urged a near Utopia. 'To solve the environmental crisis,' he said, 'we must solve the problems of poverty, racial injustice and war.'"[25] The response to "the world's most dangerous political issue" did not, as we are all too aware today, take the form of peace as such, either among men or with nature, or of alleviating poverty and injustice, but of new forms of control ("perpetual peace") over those global flows of resources (especially oil) now cast as an issue of national and international security. Strong, we might note, would be appointed executive director of the newly founded United Nations Environment Programme the following year; he was also a member of the important Brundtland Commission and involved in the 1987 report published as *Our Common Future*.[26] In turn, he served as secretary general of the UN Conference on Environment and Development, aka the Earth Summit, in Rio de Janeiro in 1992. If we add to this his background in the oil industry, we find a trajectory that might help us understand how failures to address environmental issues and their relation to "development" remained so hauntingly similar across two if not three and a half decades.

MASS MIGRATION

To come back, then, to the Hog Farm and the Life Forum: Brand's ambition for the UNCHE had been to transplant to European soil and to a global arena the ethos of mass transience and alternative modes of life, as well as festivities characteristic of the so-called "Woodstock Nation," replete with rock bands, street-theater companies, and countercultural celebrities, as a sort of corrective to political activities. It was to demonstrate a lifestyle aiming, in the words of his ally Allen Ginsberg, at a "transformation of world consciousness," rather than at "political action."[27] Brand's initial preparatory work, however, had led to a bitter confrontation with Swedish radical groups with whom he sought alignment. In May 1972, the *Village Voice* reported that

> a loose collection of happenings called "Household Earth" or "Life Forum" is being put together for Stockholm. Originally it was to be a part of the People's Forum planned by a coalition of Swedish leftists groups. But that alliance disintegrated when the American counter-culture contingent of Stewart Brand (compiler of the *Whole Earth Catalog*), David Padwa (a counter-culture lawyer working with the Black Mesa Defense Fund), and Melissa Savage [no qualification given] went to Stockholm to meet with organizers from Sweden's new left. Apparently Brand passed out copies of the [*Whole Earth*] Catalog at a meeting and someone opened the book to a page advertising books of grass-growing. The ideologues freaked and accused Household Earth people of being CIA plants, intending to spread drugs around Stockholm.[28]

Ever the entrepreneur, Brand had considered the Stockholm conference to be "an unusual opportunity" for gaining "world wide visibility" for the catalog's "whole earth" ideology, a giant networking event for "unprecedented exchange of environmental information."[29] Here was a global marketplace for the whole-earth faith and potentially even for its sales catalog. In addition to working with Black Mesa, Padwa was a representative of the Kaplan Fund, which in the mid-1960s had been accused of being a conduit to the CIA.[30] With Life Forum funding coming both from Brand's Point Foundation, itself a channel for profit from sales of the *Whole Earth Catalog*, and the Kaplan Foundation, the scene was set for a disastrous encounter with members of the Scandinavian left.[31]

The "mass migration to 'Woodstockholm'" paradoxically, or perhaps simply cynically, posed the threat that Stockholm would become a model in miniature of the global ecological crisis. As Brand suggested, "Stockholm can build, or destroy, a faith."[32] Management was the key, and it was here that the Hog Farm was to play a role in providing that "living reality-model of people taking care of each other." The *Voice* also reported that the Life Forum was aiming to "charter two planes—one from California and one from the East Coast—to fly Americans to Stockholm."[33] The prospect of planeloads of Americans—commune members, rock bands, street-theater companies, environmental activists, hippies, and so on—let alone tens of thousands of other youth arriving for the UN event, was alarming not only to city authorities, but to the UN and to the U.S. delegation, the latter expressing concern that on account of this mass migration the UNCHE "does not become a highly charged political atmosphere of a divisive kind."[34] Thus, beyond the specter of an environmental catastrophe like that at Woodstock (which was left strewn with garbage), Brand's alarmist claims that tens of thousands of youth were expected to show up had convinced the police of an imminent security threat,[35] to which they responded with excessive police presence. In John Lewallen's words, "The city was crawling with platoons of cops, with the Swedish National Guard on stand-by alert."[36] The "mass international invasion of hippies," as he characterized the problem, never took place, but in the meantime, Brand had successfully cast the Hog Farm's intervention in terms of "crowd control" and hence as in alignment with the security concerns of local police and other authorities, who by many accounts maintained "friendly relations" with the commune, even when faced with accusations of their promoting drug use.[37] Calling attention to the rhetoric of pacification, Weisberg noted, "In the words of the Chief of Police of Operations, 'They are nice people, they wish to cooperate. They don't intend to cause any disturbances. Instead, as far as the Hog Farm is concerned, they wish to quiet other people.'" The Hog Farm was there to keep order.

Long a disciple of R. Buckminster Fuller, Brand was unapologetic about his rejection of politics. He made his position clear as early as a 1969 conversation published in *Rolling Stone* and took care to reiterate his "non-political" position while in Stockholm. In "A Visit to the Life Forum HQ," Alfred Heller recounted a conversation with Brand at the Life Forum's downtown venue. Heller had asked Hog Farm member Calico how she felt about the UN conference, receiving the answer that she "doesn't believe in government." Savage had tried to clarify that "the politics of the Hog Farm itself are complicated." At which point Brand interjected: "I don't agree with that.... The Hog Farm is non-political. Everything we do is non-political. The 'Whole Earth Catalog' was non-political although everybody kept trying to tell me it was a political document."[38] Weisberg, too, stressed the Life Forum's apolitical stance: "the greatest contrast to the Folkets Forum was not the United Nations—where political issues were at least acknowledged," he wrote, "but a collection of Americans brought to Stockholm under the auspices of Life Forum, an organization created by Stuart [sic] Brand."[39] Although, as he indicated, the more radical Folkets Forum and Pow Wow had regarded the UN conference to be "an opportunity to educate people to the connection between politics and ecology . . . this was not the Hog Farm's intention," he clarified. "As one Hog Farmer explained condescendingly, 'Political action is representative, Hog Farm action is direct, one to one.'"[40] As many commentators noted, this was not simply a tactic of "direct action" but, more specifically, a "politics no, environment yes" ideology, one seeking to connect the pursuit of an individual's planetary "consciousness" not to international political institutions, but somehow directly to the care of Spaceship Earth.

For Weisberg, such a position had a predilection not only to usurp more familiar leftist political discourses, but also to remain blind to (or unwilling to address) questions of social and distributive justice. "Hog Farm's message, that we must return to an idyllic, less industrial way of life," he proposed, "was lost on delegates from countries struggling for simple survival."[41] What we might call the Hog Farm's "identification down," their adoption of tents, teepees, and obsolescent forms of cooking, dressing, and transportation as a form of care of the self and of the land, was very much in line with the "voluntary primitivism" operating within Open Land communes and other forms of back-to-the-land activism of the mid to late 1960s. If such practices remain highly problematic, they were perhaps not entirely lost on those struggling for survival, and I think we need to unpack their programmatic and semantic resonances somewhat further.

I have written in detail elsewhere about the way in which such practices served not to demonstrate rights claims for access to or inclusion within a dominant system, but rather as attempts to withdraw from the sites, institutions, and lifestyles through which micropolitical techniques of power proper to a post-Fordist economy interfaced with the Open Land communards' bodies and psyches in the most palpable manner.[42] These practices and structures of identification remained problematic in many regards, but we can read them not only as symptomatic, if dissident responses to a biopolitical regime, but also in turn as tactical vehicles for the production and dissemination of images of something like a counter-*dispositif*. My aim here, though, is not to rehearse my reading of such alternative modes of life and their architectural manifestations, but to ask what happens when they are detached from the sociopolitical and technological milieu of the United States from which they derived their specificity and grafted into other contexts.

POLITICAL IDEALS: CANTONMENTS

Convinced by Brand's arguments, the City of Stockholm provided the Hog Farm with a site at the abandoned airfield in Skarpnäck on the outskirts of the city, a safe one-hour subway ride away from the main UNCHE venues, along with approximately a hundred and seventy-five army tents to house the transient population. As Harold Gilliam recounted in "Eco-Trips at Hog Farm," after reaching the end of the subway system and being guided through "a maze of housing compounds and wood lots" by bemused local residents, he "found an encampment of army tents set up by Stockholm officials, a scattering of brightly colored mountain tents, a large tie-dyed teepee and some psychedelic-painted buses. The Hog Farm," he continued, "is a commune of about 50 long-haired young people and several over-30s" who specialize as "trouble shooters and crowd-coolers."[43] There he met Wavy Gravy, described by Brand as the commune's "wise fool," then busy dressing up one of the Day-Glo painted buses as a giant whale for a demonstration the following day, along with Lou Todd, the Hog Farm's so-called "straw boss."[44] "We have set up a life-support system," Todd explained to the reporter of their method of disseminating threats, "we feed everybody free, we have a free stage . . . this is our way to take the heat off and keep violence out of the streets." The commune's function, he went on to clarify, confirming the ideals of its palliative and consensual agenda, "is to effect consciousness-change among large numbers of people, to give people a living experience of a cooperative group-energy project, to show them how good that feels, to show them that sharing and cooperating is a much better approach to getting things done than competing with each other."[45] Describing the scene as "a colorful collection of Woodstock graduates, former Merry Pranksters and other assorted acid-heads, eco-freaks, save-the-whalers, doomsday mystics, poets and hangers-on," Rowland, too, commented on the idealistic mystical or New Age ethos that pervaded the group, which, he noted, "had come to Stockholm—mostly from the U.S.—to help the conference to 'get it on,' to try to imbue the historic debates with the spirit of transcendentalism and humility before nature that the American counter-culture had lately been espousing."[46]

The Hog Farm was founded around 1966 when Wavy Gravy (then Hugh Romney) and three other "dropouts" made a deal to tend a pig farm in the foothills of the San Gabriel Mountains in Southern California in exchange for free rent. It quickly became, according to the magazine *Avant-Garde*, "the grooviest hippie commune in America." Composed, as *Avant-Garde* put it, of a "motley cantonment of geodesic domes, tents, trailers, huts, and a cinderblock farmhouse," it had "assumed the proportions of a post-escape base camp. Drifters, refugees from less fortunate communes, friends, and strangers seeking a crash moved in."[47] Romney, a veteran street-theater performer,[48] played "Commissioner of Talk" for this "experiment in utopian living." They also experimented with an ad hoc appropriation of Eastern religions, which, as *Avant-Garde* suggested, "seems to work for them. They seek to live in accord with the Tao, egoless identification with a World Consciousness to which reality is a continuous change," with all decisions being made "with the help of the *I Ching*."[49] Seeking to undermine hierarchical leadership structures (though not traditional gender divisions), Hog Farm members had instituted a rotating system of daily "dance masters," who ran the farm, and "dance mistresses," who ran the kitchen, both chosen by spinning a wheel and together in charge of running the camp. Out of this had emerged the practice of a rotating "power day," playing out fantasies of being "god for 24 hours."[50]

The commune soon acquired a bus and hit the road to put on theatrical "freakshows" and, in turn, elaborate psychedelic light shows—later called "life shows"—for a wider audience. Harnessing their Merry Prankster legacy, the self-proclaimed "citizens of Earth" eventually left the farm (and their increasingly hostile neighbors) behind entirely to become a nomadic show replete with domes, teepees, tents, an inflatable house, costumes, props, generators, lights, and the cameras, projectors, microphones, loudspeakers, and other electronic equipment necessary for such theatrical generation of "whole" or "cosmic consciousness." They even took a pig, Pigasus, along as a mascot, soon to serve as the Yippee's nominee at the 1968 Democratic Convention in Chicago.[51]

The ideals pursued by the Hog Farm and the environmental and media techniques they employed to pursue them are, in retrospect, far from unproblematic, as is Brand's cynical redeployment of these ideals and techniques in Stockholm. While we can presume that *Avant-Garde*'s use of the term "cantonment" to describe the original Hog Farm commune was intended to be somewhat ironic, it nevertheless suggests the degree to which the commune remained haunted by the logics of and fallout from a militant global capitalism and its expansionist, neoimperial character, even if launched as a battle against them. The term refers both to accommodations for troops while on an extended campaign or during winter and to permanent military stations in India under British colonial rule. One needs only to look at the technologies and ideologies of survival in the *Whole Earth Catalog* to understand the extent to which these practices (in general) and their technological underpinnings formed an uncanny mirror image of and even offered new models for the forces that ostensibly were being opposed, pursuing a paradigm of global unity or consensus and the replacement of political contestation by "cooperative group energy," a domestication of the emerging neoliberal milieu for Household Earth.

In detailing the Hog Farm's "skill in serving large crowds of transients," Brand listed in addition to Woodstock a series of other "accomplishments": "their money-raising and faith-raising efforts for Earth People's Parks, their week of crowded starvation for the Hunger Show (Liferaft Earth), their peace-keeping activities on numerous battlefields such as Newark, Chicago, and Washington DC, their innumerable shows and presentations in America and Europe and their helping journey to the heart of need in East Pakistan and Nepal last year."[52] The Hog Farm was not only a group of hippie celebrities, but also an ideal vehicle for Brand's ambitions and his fear-mongering at Stockholm, as further evidenced in those precedents.

In the same vein, Earth People's Park sought to expand upon the Open Land movement ideals of LATWIDN ("land, access to which is denied no-one"), this time seeking to "free some land, and not just a little." As recalled in the "The Outlaw Area" issue of the *Whole Earth Catalog*, the "Earth People's Park idea originated largely at the Sympowowsium" organized by Hog Farmer Tom Law, which in November 1969 had "brought together organizers and promoters of festival events, particularly rock music festivals" such as Woodstock.[53] Based on the "idea of using the fantastic power and profits of rock music to free a piece of the planet," Earth People's Park entailed "the idea of acquiring and returning one small segment of Mother Earth back to herself." It was, moreover, to be a "nationLESS piece of Earth in a sectioned-off world," its inhabitants likewise identified with a new global tribe, rather than as citizens of a nation. The antigovernance ambition at Earth People's Park was described as "a sort of basic anarchism: a sociological experiment in whether a group of strangers can live under the most primitive conditions without rules or government to guide them, for there is no boss or manager here, nor any governing body."[54]

If conceived as a means of liberating land from capitalist rule, even, to reiterate, as countering neoimperialism, the idealistic project of "freeing a piece of Mother Earth," however, quickly encountered other voices that complicated this picture. "One black guy" in the preparatory group, the *Whole Earth Catalog* recounted, symptomatically eliding his name, had "thought that the Earth Park idea was *nice*, but it was running away from the real problems of hunger and oppression."[55] In March 1970, the *Los Angeles Free Press* announced that the original idea for creating Earth People's Park on large tract of land in New Mexico had been abandoned. "Recent meetings in San Francisco with New Mexican Chicanos and Indians have convinced EPP organizers that an influx of white settlers would be regarded as another land rip-off." "Most of the locals," the article added, "sympathize with or support Reles Tijerina and La Alianza in their right to regain the land stolen from them by U.S. invaders."[56] The connection to the Hog Farm's activities in Skarpnäck was direct: they had come to Stockholm in order to raise money and support for Earth People's Park. Tent City was, quite literally, to be a testing ground for the so-called Woodstock Nation's expansion beyond the United States, part of an ambition to achieve a permanent, global, post-territorial network of free spaces on Earth. "The Hog Farm may be found," Brand had indicated, at "Rainbow Junction, Earth People's Park (temporary), Stockholm."[57]

ARE YOU READY TO DIE?

In addition to envisioning and promoting a vision of global, post-territorial unity that, unfortunately, resonated with neoliberal ideals, Brand also promoted a neo-Malthusian rhetoric of population control that offers us further clues regarding his political intentions. The next precedent he cited as evidence of the Hog Farm's skills and experience, Liferaft Earth, had taken place in October 1969 and took the form of a weeklong voluntary communal fasting game to simulate famine, with a departure from the group cast as a death. "Its intent," Brand recalled, "was to make very personal the matter of population control," but to project that "personal" act into the public sphere by harnessing media attention. "The stadium," Brand acknowledged, "was the news media, so a certain amount of theater (i.e. plot) was designed in." In addition to Wavy Gravy (dressed as a hamburger and then still going by Hugh Romney) and other Hog Farmers, support had come from Stephanie Mills (famous for announcing at her commencement speech at Mills College in 1969, after reading Paul Ehrlich's *The Population Bomb*, that her contribution to the planet would be to bear no children), from other individuals dedicated to population control, and from the Friends of the Earth, and the Sierra Club. In addition to celebrity support, "Further visual interest—useful for TV and wirephotos," Brand noted, "was provided by the Earth posters, the door for the event with its sign 'Are You Ready to Die,' and a splendid model of the inflated 10,000 sq. ft. polyethylene pillow that we planned to hold the event in."[58] Filmed by Robert Frank, the Hunger Show eventually landed in the parking lot of a poverty-program office in Hayward, California, with participants numbering almost one hundred and seventy. Local fire marshals rejected the large inflatable pillow as a fire hazard, so the Southcoast Pneumads (soon to join the Ant Farm collective) stepped in to produce a "stage" ringed by a four-foot-high inflatable wall. The scene was also replete with Earth flags and a giant inflatable globe. Bearing one of NASA's Apollo images, the eleven-by-thirteen-inch Earth flags had just been added to the sales list of the Whole Earth Truck Store. "A gentleman named John McConnell came into the Truck Store a few weeks ago," an editorial note in the print catalog symptomatically recalled, "and said that since all the nations have flags, and the UN has a flag, and states and businesses have flags, maybe there ought to be a flag that's just people. . . . I don't know if I'd die for it, but it's the first flag I've seen that I don't feel it somehow excludes me."[59]

In addition to mediation, yoga, and participating in the Hog Farm's communal "gong-bong" breathing exercise, in which people would hold hands in a circle and breathe rapidly to effect a collective dizziness, entertainment included "a UN starvation movie on a sheet hung from the poverty center balcony," a recording of Franz

Kafka's "Hunger Artist," and reading *The Population Bomb*, itself a prominent sales item in Brand's *Catalog*.[60] Brand's account of the event appeared alongside that on Earth People's Park in "The Outlaw Area." It was illustrated with an Oxfam photograph of an emaciated child captioned "In case there's some question what *Liferaft Earth* was about, it was about this" and accompanied by notes on a population bibliography and entries for publications on abortion and voluntary sterilization.

It was not surprising that Ehrlich had become a key reference here. Brand had studied biology with the young professor while a student at Stanford in the late 1950s, at which point Ehrlich was still, as Fred Turner notes, "concentrating on the fundamentals of butterfly ecology and systems-oriented approaches to evolutionary biology." It was through Ehrlich that Brand had been introduced to the systems and cybernetic-based approaches to ecology that would come to characterize not only his environmental thinking, but also the networking culture of the *Whole Earth Catalog*.[61] Liferaft Earth suggests that systems thinking was not the only legacy of Ehrlich at work, however—that the neo-Malthusian population bomb thesis also haunted his approach to environmental questions, or at least his alarmist presentation of them.

MOBILIZING SHAME

The third example raised by Brand as evidence of the Hog Farm's expertise and their relevance to the media agenda of his Life Forum initiative is equally, if slightly differently, problematic. The Hog Farm's use of what might be called "parodic humanitarianism" in its journey to the "heart of need" in the East offers us a set of clues regarding the existence of uneasy slippages between the group's ideals and the visual language that they employed to promote them. Wavy Gravy offered a brief description of the trip in his 1974 book *The Hog Farm and Friends*, explaining that "the plan was to move food and doctors to East Pakistan, where the flood had just receded, killing a million and leaving the rest homeless and hungry." Their (mock) humanitarian mission was supposed both to resemble but constitutively depart from those of groups such as the Red Cross or Médecins Sans Frontières: "Our best show has always been dinner, and doctors were needed," he recalled, "but first on the menu and that [sic] we could leave, was our love. We never believed that we could feed millions, but merely our presence and the sense of the press could embarrass great countries to take care of business."[62] Hog Farm had thus, it seems, planned to deploy a key tactic of human rights activism, mobilizing shame, in which visibility afforded by exposure through public media was intended to mobilize public opinion regarding the violation of rights or mass human suffering and in turn to bring pressure on governments or intergovernmental institutions.[63]

While we might question the potential efficacy of their publicity tactic during a moment of massive overexposure of pictures of hippies (if not of humanitarian crises), the Hog Farm's would-be humanitarian actions (if we can call love that) were interrupted before they could begin: "a war beat us to it and borders were closed," Wavy Gravy explained. The group continued on instead ("next slide please") to Nepal, Wavy Gravy telling the story of their turn to hiking, of blowing bubbles for children, and of creating an Earth People's Playground.[64]

As with Liferaft Earth and even Earth People's Park, with the Hog Farm's proposed mission to mobilize shame by intervening in East Pakistan we find ourselves in a quandary regarding how to understand the relation between the idealism informing their project—whether bringing attention to hunger and suffering or attempting to provide land rent free—and the ambiguous nature of the mass-media tactics employed to do so. "So what difference does it make, for those of us who have to respond," Thomas Keenan asks of distinct instances of more recent media overexposure and a loss of distance during humanitarian actions, "when the technologies of exposure become opportunities for performance, exhibition, self-exposure? What becomes of shame?" Keenan posits that despite risking ethical uncertainties, "aesthetic categories are relevant here. The aesthetic finds itself in extreme proximity to the ethico-political now; that proximity is perhaps discomforting to some, but it is also the condition of any serious intervention."[65] The Hog Farm's parodic performance of humanitarianism and its redeployment of the visual language of dissent produces another strange convolution or complication in the political potential inhering in the aesthetic. It reminds us that even if meaning remains unstable, and even if reception cannot be, strictly speaking, controlled, this does not exempt us from seeking to articulate the conditions of a "serious intervention." This is not to oppose a serious intervention to one taking the form of parody or irony; quite the opposite. It is to suggest (as Keenan does elsewhere)[66] the need to take irony seriously; in this case, the need to distinguish between ethico-political interventions that, while harboring this risk, are also articulated with a knowing precision regarding context and their modes of dissemination and ethico-political interventions that perhaps do not.

A *Time* reporter stressed shortly after the Stockholm conference the absurdity of any thought that the "youthful environmentalists at the abandoned airport" were dangerous. "The violent demonstrations the police feared never came. Instead, the students put on gentle 'eco-skits' to dramatize 'eco-catastrophes.' In one, for example, a girl painted as a skeleton and accompanied by drums and cymbals danced a warning about the radioactive fallout from French nuclear-bomb tests in the Pacific. Total damage to property caused by such activities: one broken window."[67] Unlike the turn to violence undertaken by groups such as the

Weathermen and other advocates of militancy, this aspect of the "movement" responded to impasses in the mechanisms of participation within democratic processes by making "love not war."

Despite the nonpolitical character of "Woodstockholm," as we've seen, the conference responded with increased measures of security. "The Swedish authorities were accused of over-reaching to supposed threats," recalls Peter Stone in *Did We Save the Earth in Stockholm?* "and one day . . . outside the New Parliament Building a busload of police arrived to break up a group of hippie musicians who were playing nothing more revolutionary than a selection from *Hair*." "Security men," he added, "opened mail first and you could never get anywhere without passes." Although at the time this appeared absurd or irritating to him, that soon changed. In Stone's words: "the more recent memory of the Olympic Games and postal bombs has made one much more appreciative in retrospect."[68] The implied connection might give us pause, for as we know all too well from responses to the antiglobalization movement's attempts to interject alternative voices into global institutions such as the World Bank, the International Monetary Fund, or the World Trade Organization, it is no longer just violent terrorist acts that elicit such anxieties regarding security: civil disobedience and rights struggles have also come to be treated as terrorist threats.

TENT CITY

In "A Crying Need for Quiet Conferences," Paul Ehrlich reflected upon "the pleasantly relaxed atmosphere of the Tent City organized for nonofficial 'delegates' by the Hog Farm commune," reiterating that the atmosphere was "peaceful."[69] The psychedelic teepees, customized buses, and geodesic domes were all familiar icons of countercultural modes of life, particularly in Northern California, where Ehrlich taught. While the Hog Farm's environment proved unthreatening to Ehrlich, unlike the chaotic and crowded scene in his visit to Delhi that had motivated the biologist's neo-Malthusian crusade against overpopulation, the impression might not have struck other viewers as simply a peaceful atmosphere or refreshing contrast. Tents and geodesic domes were of course key technologies for rapid deployment during both military actions and humanitarian crises; to some they might have been hauntingly familiar not from hippie communes and Woodstock-like gatherings, but from other encampments.

In *Skarpnäck, USA*, anti-drug activist and Folkets Forum participant Gun Zacharias reproduced a range of photographs of the Hog Farm's encampment, including views of the field of tents behind cyclone fencing, as well as the geodesic domes, old buses, and people cooking with low-tech devices for hungry masses lining up to eat. Here, indeed, were images depicting those "potentially starving and unhoused people" whom Gelbspan and Gurin had identified as informing emerging environmental concerns in their article "Woodstockholm '72: The Subject is Survival." The images served, in this sense, further to desublimate Tent City's resonance with emergency shelters and temporary sites for disaster relief and the management of refugees or housing of soldiers. And they resonate all too hauntingly with images of tent cities circulating today, including (but not at all limited to) Camp Bucca in Iraq, America's largest detention facility, which houses five thousand prisoners in the "War on Terror" in the southern desert of Iraq. Along with Camp Cropper, sited on the military base attached to the Baghdad International Airport, this camp is for "security detention," for "holding without charge people believed to pose a potential risk to security," a category recognized neither by Iraqi or American law.[70] That is, the images spoke (and speak) at once to humanitarian crises and warfare, not only in Indochina (very much on the mind of activists in Stockholm), but also in other sites or camps emerging during states of emergency.

Brand understood the semantic ambiguity that the Hog Farm's camp might produce. And we might note here that following a period as an infantryman, his military service had been spent as a photographer and photojournalist.[71] In fact, he acknowledged a potential slippage, but thought it to have been solved. As Heller reported, to Brand, "Sweden is not a convincing model of environmental management. 'Sweden gives me the creeps,' he said. 'The way people think here does not coincide with natural processes. Stockholm wanted to put the tents out at Skarpnack in rows like a concentration camp. We stopped that. The Hog Farm stopped that. Now they're in a circle.'"[72] The Hog Farm had long used circular configurations in attempts to generate "whole consciousness." Domes provided the infrastructure for this function (or fiction). As Romney recalled, "We built a big dome (a domelette next to what we're into now) out of rubber hose, wooden dowels, and this enormous yellow parachute under which we would gather in circles and search for our center."[73] But Brand's connection of circular (or partially circular) organizations to "natural processes"—rather than, say, mystical or cultural ones—remains of course tenuous.

TERRITORIAL INSECURITY

I want to come back, in concluding, to Brand's invocation of Liferaft Earth and Earth People's Park as precedents for the Hog Farm's capacity to manage the makeshift environment and its itinerant population in Stockholm. Whether taking the form of a mock-humanitarian crisis zone (Liferaft Earth and its Hunger Show) or a space to be liberated from state rule and returned to an emergent tribal "humanity" (Earth People's Park), both were conceived as forms of outlaw territory, literally as spaces beyond the reach of the law. Beyond its resonance with the mythology and libertarian ethos of the nineteenth century American frontier, the term "outlaw area" had entered the *Whole Earth* lexicon from Fuller, most likely from Calvin Tompkins's 1966 *New Yorker* profile "In the Outlaw Area." In Fuller's conception of a totally unregulated Air Ocean World, environments such as the ocean and in turn outer space would exist, at least initially, in Fuller's words "outside the law"; military battles over the occupation or control of such territories, according to his argument, have been the very source of, or occasion for technological advancement. "The whole development of technology," he declared, "has been in the outlaw area, where you're dealing with the toughness of nature." It was these "weaponry arts" that, he repeatedly argued, would give rise to what he called the "livingry arts" that form industrial man's very milieu.[74] Whether derived from technologies of colonial (and neocolonial) expansion or motivated by contemporary Cold War defense, the result was the same: a thoroughgoing incorporation of military technology into the matrix of contemporary forms of life on what he called Spaceship Earth.

Such an idealization of a territory beyond the reach of law and the normalizing forces of government, and hence also beyond the reach of international legal institutions, poses the question of what sort of political space was at work in Skarpnäck, what sort of rights the Hog Farm (and Brand) imagined this "outlaw" population might retain in their "living reality model" of caring for the environment. I have pointed a number of times to the widespread ethic of taking personal responsibility adopted by the counterculture, and I think we need also to ask how the particularity and personal nature of such an ethos might (or might not) have a bearing on nongovernmental politics and the public sphere. (Recall that we are not here in the domain of the feminist challenge, "The Personal is Political," which would explicitly make an articulation with rights issues and the public realm.)

In a widely cited text "Why Tribe?" Gary Snyder, who had come to Stockholm with the Life Forum, connected this trope of personal responsibility to an emergent tribalism. "The tribe," he wrote, "proposes personal responsibilities rather than abstract central government, taxes and advertising-agency-plus-Mafia type international brainwashing corporations."[75] He dated the emergence of this phenomenon to "the increasing insanity of the modern nations" after World War I and articulated its adherents' modes of disidentification with the state within a genealogy of critiques of Western industrial civilization that began with interwar Marxism, passing through a fascination with Buddhism and Hinduism (ultimately rejecting both as too closely involved with the state) to end with the embrace of heretical, Gnostic, and esoteric movements. Together, these constituted a "Great

View of Tent City, 1972. From Gun Zacharias, *Skarpnäck, USA: En Bok om Droger och Politik* (Stockholm: Förbunder mot Droger, 1975).

Underground" whose spirit could be recognized in hippies of Golden Gate Park.

"In America of course," "Why Tribe?" begins, "the word has associations with the American Indians, which we like. The new subculture," he goes on to clarify, "is in fact more similar to that ancient and successful tribe, the European Gypsies—a group without nation or territory which maintains its own values, its language and its religion, no matter what country it may be in."[76] Snyder's model did not offer clues as to how such tribalism might interface with or otherwise produce an encounter with those "abstract central governments" at the UNCHE or with international legal codes overseeing the actions of those "international brainwashing corporations." Indeed, there is a good chance that he had little interest in so doing. His precedents for this new tribalism—Native Americans and the European Roma—might, however, offer lessons in how taking responsibility for one's actions can relate to frameworks for political participation and/or the public sphere, even if not in simple terms. The rights claims put forward under the rubric of Indian nationalism and Romani demands to be recognized by the UN as a nation without a state both explicitly involved an appropriation and "detourning" of traditional modes of governance.[77]

Snyder's examples might, however, also be productively troubled by the history of violence against these and other ethnic and cultural groups, populations for whom the decoupling of territorial organizations from the nation-state, as sought by Earth People's Park, had been not voluntary, but forced. Like Native Americans, Roma have suffered centuries of discrimination. Despite their arrival in Europe during the fifteenth century, they are, as Sean Nazerali reminds us, "still regarded by many as foreigners and strangers," as outcasts, and "the darkest period of Romani history was World War II," when, along with Jews, they were transported to concentration camps on the basis of race.[78] To understand what is at stake here I want to turn to Hannah Arendt's seminal text "The Decline of the Nation-State and the End of the Rights of Man," which addressed the plight of people forcibly "ejected from the old trinity of state-people-territory that," as she noted, "still formed the basis of European organization and political civilization." It is a philosophical text that also identified the importance of the historical period following World War I to this disruption in relations between nations, citizens, and territory, albeit in very different terms from Snyder's.[79]

Arendt traced the plights of minority groups, stateless persons, and refugees in Europe, those who were not easily assimilated during the construction of a unified political body or who, under fascism, had been forcibly denationalized. Without the right of asylum, some had become, in her words, outlaws "by definition." There are many things one could unpack from this text with regard to what Arendt identified as a "new global political situation," but here I want to turn to her recognition of the emergence of a disturbing topology for which the text is widely cited. Deprived of the trappings of civilization, "rightless people" had been "thrown back into a peculiar state of nature." Without access to a political community, they had become, in her words, "nothing but human," at once a "human being in general . . . *and* different in general, representing nothing but his own absolutely unique individuality."[80] This condition of being rightless had a disturbing spatial correlate: as she explained, "the internment camp—prior to the second World War the exception rather than the rule for the stateless—has become the routine solution for the problem of domicile of the 'displaced persons.'"[81] Given their status as "outlaw by definition," Arendt posited, "the only practical substitute for a nonexistent homeland was an internment camp. Indeed, as early as the thirties this was the only 'country' the world had to offer the stateless."[82] Ad hoc shelters such as tents, cantonments, and, in turn, their translation into permanent, if far from homely structures, we might add, had become the recognizable architectural infrastructure of those "countries."

The Hog Farm's Tent City and the Earth People's Park of which it formed a component were conceived during a different historical moment from those camps discussed by Arendt. The "unsettlement" they registered and the transient constituency for which they offered a domicile on so-called Household Earth, even a "Woodstock Nation," was not, of course, that of the forcibly displaced, but typically a group of white, educated, disenchanted people who were voluntarily seeking to withdraw not only from normative and environmentally damaging lifestyles, but from extant geopolitical organizations. While the Hog Farm's outlaw area forms an almost diametrically opposed condition to the violent exclusions of which Arendt wrote, Tent City emerged as a strange sort of semantic, spatial, even architectural residue of the territorial insecurity inscribed within the "new global political situation" of which Arendt spoke, the contours and strange topologies of which remain, as Giorgio Agamben reminds us, in a more extended form today, whether in the reuse of public spaces for detention or in gated communities. "This principle," he proposed, "is now adrift: it has entered a process of dislocation" or of a dislocating localization of spaces of exception in which, as he put it, "we can expect not only new camps but also always new and more delirious normative definitions of the inscription of life in the city."[83] As a historical artifact, the Hog Farm's Tent City was both a symptom of such territorial insecurity and an apparatus for controlling it.

Despite their radical appearance to some at Stockholm, the Hog Farm was *not*, to invoke Foucault's argument in "Confronting Governments: Human Rights," bringing "the testimony of people's suffering to the eyes and ears of governments," suffering that, as Foucault announced, "grounds an absolute right to stand up and speak to those who hold power." And indeed, this was not necessarily their aim in Stockholm. The images of nonnormative modes of life they produced resonated ambiguously with such suffering and with the insecurity for which it was a harbinger. But they did not do so either with adequate irony or in a manner that would confront governments. "It is true that good governments appreciate the holy indignation of the governed, provided it remain lyrical," Foucault explained. "Experience shows," he continued, "that one can and must refuse the theatrical role of pure and simple indignation that is proposed to us."[84] Under Brand, the Hog Farm's depoliticized appropriation of countercultural protest served as something of a red herring, a reminder of the need to pay attention not only to the captivating images of theatrical counterconducts and counterenvironments that have long operated as efficient vehicles for garnering attention, but also to the ambiguous political ends to which they are or might be deployed.

Architecture has long served both as a means of protection or defense against the environment (both "natural" and man made) and simultaneously as a discipline whose concern has been the materialization, organization, and representation of the life taking place within such a milieu, whether at the scale of the house, apartment building, institutional headquarters, or city. In the case of the early 1970s, as I have tried to trace, we are faced with a situation wherein that scale of concern had expanded exponentially, as registered in the figures of Household or Spaceship Earth or in the equally postsovereign territory sought by Strong as the domain of UN management of the environment. It was not incidental to this story of the encounter of the Life Forum and the UN that the UN became increasingly concerned not only with questions of international security and war, but also with the environmental management of populations and in turn of human settlements, as would become evident four years later with the Habitat Conference in Vancouver. With architecture now understood as inscribed within a global matrix of forces (environment, development, migration, war, poverty, and so on), the pressures on those domiciles and habitats for those "starving and unhoused people" and the conditions in which they lived rendered the appearance of this "architecture" distinctly strange. Unlike their utopian modernist forerunners in the architecture of functional planning and hygienic-housing estates, with their correlate in the International Style, these artifacts were now almost excised as a concern for the discipline proper, which soon retreated into the historical and semantic experiments of postmodernism, a call to order that itself forms an equally symptomatic, if more legible architectural response to those very same globalizing forces.

What the Life Forum and the Hog Farm rendered visible in Stockholm, whether self-consciously or not and whether cynically or simply unwittingly, was that it was indeed "life" itself that was at stake in the biopolitical paradigm of management sought by the UNCHE. The "human" in the term "human environment," they made evident, is not *necessarily* a political subject who would question laws or protest the actions of particular governments, but something closer to the "population" that Foucault recognized during the 1970s as long to have been the subject of techniques of governmentality. Trained in the life sciences, Brand might have understood very well that "life" had become, as Foucault argued, the subject of explicit calculation under a biopolitical regime, in this case directed toward management of the environment, built or otherwise, and the populations within it. Collected in the *Whole Earth Catalog* was information on alternative technologies for managing health, education, food, and shelter, offering not an opposition to this dominant logic, but something like its uncanny mirror image. In the context of the UNCHE, wherein environmental issues had taken on multiple and conflicting political casts, with business groups such as the Club of Rome announcing "limits to growth," the portrayal of "survival" in the Hog Farm's Tent City resonated all too strongly with and hence potentially fueled prevalent neo-Malthusian anxieties of population explosion and limited resources, anxieties often directed at countries recently liberated from or still struggling to gain independence from colonial rule. That is to say, the lifestyle images presented by these self-styled "refugees" from the American way of life can be read not only as attempts to withdraw from biopolitical regulation into an outlaw area, but also as vehicles, witting or unwitting, for the desublimation of the very environmental violence that characterized the global impact and neoimperial imperative of that same logic: poverty, environmental catastrophe, displacement, genocide, and warfare. It was of course, to come full circle again, these forces that many of the other alternative voices in Stockholm worked actively to interrupt.

NOTES

A version of this essay will appear in *Outlaw Territories: Environments of Insecurity / Architectures of Counter-Insurgency* (forthcoming, Zone Books). I would like to thank sincerely Mary Jean Haley for her generosity in lending me a dossier of documents related to the United Nations Conference on the Human Environment, particularly materials related to the Life Forum, from her personal archive, and for providing me with notes from her recollections of the conference. Both were invaluable. I would also like to express my enormous gratitude to the librarians and staff of the Sterling and Francine Clark Art Institute, where, as a fellow in the fall of 2008, I completed aspects of this research. I would also like to dedicate this essay to Gun Zacharias.

1. Daniel Zwerdling, "Getting Back to Earth," *Washington Post and Times Herald*, June 25, 1972, p. B3. Zwerdling's article is of course only a very minor and marginal document in the history of the politics of environmentalism. I begin with it to demonstrate a symptomatic bracketing of the issues at stake in Stockholm, a bracketing that becomes highly problematic when we consider the range of voices extending the terms of environmental debates.
2. Barry Weisberg, "The Browning of Stockholm: America Takes Its Ecology Show Abroad," *Ramparts*, September 1972, pp. 33–40. "Whole-earther Stuart [sic] Brand," Weisberg reported, "cavorted on the periphery of the proceedings with the nearly 100 people he brought to Stockholm . . . because he believed that the Conference itself would be dull and worthless and it was up to him to create a better show" (p. 34).
3. Mary Haley explained that a "matter on which there is general agreement—outside the UN at least—is that the United Nations Conference on the Human Environment is inadequate. That is why the many parallel and alternative conferences have been arranged. . . . The alternative groups say that since the UN Conference delegates are representatives of their governments, they will be bound to represent the vested interests of those governments whether or not they coincide with the interests of improving the human environment." Mary Jean Haley, *Open Options: A Guide to Stockholm's Alternative Environmental Conferences* (Stockholm: Life Forum, 1972), p. 1.
4. Ross Gelbspan and David Gurin, "Woodstockholm '72: The Subject is Survival," *Village Voice*, May 11, 1972, pp. 29 and 34. They argued additionally that "the UN is unable to touch the major underlying political and military causes of the ecological crisis, mass malnutrition and the widening gap between the world's rich and poor. That is why the UN Conference will

be surrounded by several simultaneous counter-conventions in Stockholm, bringing together non-official scientists, environmental activists, political movement groups, and counter-culture people from around the world."

5. "The Big Cleanup: The Environmental Crisis '72," *Newsweek*, June 12, 1972, p. 38.
6. Friedel Ungeheuer, "Woodstockholm," *Time*, June 19, 1972.
7. Stewart Brand, quoted in Weisberg, "The Browning of Stockholm," p. 38.
8. Gelbspan and Gurin, "Woodstockholm '72," p. 34.
9. "Hog Farm," undated press release from the Life Forum, signed "Stewart Brand." Courtesy of Mary Jean Haley.
10. "The Big Cleanup," p. 36.
11. This was most evident in their work on behalf of Project Jonah's campaign to save the whale, which remains outside the scope of this text.
12. Zwerdling recognized that the Hog Farm's Tent City was not about to solve the "world environmental crisis" and that "making peace with our environment will require massive political, social and cultural changes." He situated the commune's activities, however, as "tak[ing] up where the United Nations left off." As he recounted, the official UN delegates had talked of food shortages and famine and of the need for mass transit and better communication of environmental information while stuffing themselves on state banquets and being transported in private limousines and implicitly condoning the police barricades that under the auspices of security blocked all but the official delegates and the press from attending the conference, while the Hog Farm represented to the journalist an inverse paradigm; a model of "personal cultural transformation" and of facilitating access to alternative information.
13. Frances Gendlin, "Voices from the Gallery," *Science and Public Affairs: Bulletin of the Atomic Scientists* 28.7 (September 1972), p. 26.
14. *Open Options* was commissioned by Brand on behalf of his Point Foundation with the aim of providing information for the tens of thousands, if not hundreds of thousands of youth who were expected to appear in Stockholm. Based at the Life Forum's downtown headquarters, Pilgatan 11, Haley arrived in Stockholm in April to work on the publication. Correspondence with author. In addition to detailed outlines of the alternative groups and information on living cheaply in Stockholm, *Open Options* provided a day-by-day calendar of events. Even the harshest critics of the Life Forum, such as Barry Weisberg, acknowledged the value of this document, as would many in the mainstream press.
15. In his introduction to *Nongovernmental Politics*, Michel Feher articulates a cogent and productive map for considering what might constitute various forms of nongovernmental politics. "Rather than good intentions, limited ambitions, or insufficient means," he argues, "what distinguishes the various political involvements of the governed as such is that they are all predicated on an intolerance of the effects of a particular set of governmental practices—regardless of whether the governing agency is a state, an international organization, a public institution, or a private corporation." "Yet what these activists all have in common," he adds, "is that they are driven by a shared determination not to be governed *thusly*." Michel Feher, "The Governed in Politics," in *Nongovernmental Politics*, ed. Michel Feher, with Gäelle Krikorian and Yates McKee (New York: Zone Books, 2007), pp. 13–14. This text forms one component of a much larger study of the Stockholm Conference in which the UNCHE itself and the other outer conferences are dealt with at length and used as a platform to expand paradigms of activism beyond that of the Hog Farm and the Life Forum. In the interests of

length, I have chosen to focus here on the Hog Farm's Tent City, which, it should be stressed, formed only one component of their work at Stockholm. Focusing on the Hog Farm runs a certain risk of reiterating the displacement of attention from social and distributive-justice claims to the mediatic ecotactics of the American counterculture, but I think it is precisely at this intersection that we need to articulate the stakes of revisiting this period of environmental activism and to ask how the lifestyle demonstrations and forms of visual production deployed in Life Forum events could be (or have been) pushed further or complicated in such a manner as to be less mutually exclusive or romanticizing of alterity. Thus, if I offer more details of the Life Forum here, my aim is to recognize the importance for the present of critically scrutinizing their articulation of new forms of life or counterconducts and their highly self-conscious inscription within the mass media.

16. Stevenson remarked that "we travel together passengers on a little spaceship, dependent upon its vulnerable reserve of air and soil; all committed for our safety to its security and peace; preserved from annihilation only by the car, the work, and I will say, the love we give our fragile craft." Albert Roland, Richard Wilson, and Michael Rahill (eds.), *Adlai Stevenson of the United Nations* (Manila: Free Nations Press), p. 224.
17. With growing evidence of potentially irreversible damage to ecological systems under the impact of accelerating industrialization and urbanization and with environmental issues having gained a mass audience through works such as Rachel Carson's *Silent Spring* of 1962, environmental concern had extended from the domain of specialists and political activists to capture the attention of the general public, hence attaining an additional sense of urgency for governments within the industrialized world. The litany of concerns are all too familiar: the pollution of rivers, oceans and other waterways, the destruction of forests and other terrestrial habitats, the accelerating rate of extracting nonrenewable natural resources, unsustainable farming practices leading to salination and desertification, a reduction in biological diversity under the impact of the so-called "Green Revolution" in agricultural practices, and a growing number of species threatened with extinction.
18. Strong's story of growing up in poverty and ending up, by the age of thirty, running an oil company has been told a number of times, typically romanticizing his lack of education and hardscrabble background as the source of empathy with developing nations. See, for instance, Wade Rowland, *The Plot to Save the World: The Life and Times of the Stockholm Conference on the Human Environment* (Toronto: Clarke, Irwin, 1973), pp. 35–38.
19. Gladwin Hill, a journalist for the *New York Times*, listed among the surprises or unexpected events "the bluntness with which the newer nations taxed the advanced countries with prime responsibility for global environmental deterioration, and with an obligation accordingly to make reparations to the 'third world' in various forms, from technical assistance in pollution control to special consideration in world trade." Gladwin Hill, "Sense of Accomplishment Buoys Delegates Leaving Ecology Talks," *New York Times*, June 18, 1972, p. 14.
20. *Ibid.*
21. Barry Commoner, "Motherhood in Stockholm," *Harper's*, June 1972, pp. 49–54.
22. Terri Aaronson, "World Priorities," *Environment* 14.6 (July–August 1972), p. 4.
23. Commoner, "Motherhood in Stockholm," p. 54.
24. Barry Commoner, *The Closing Circle: Nature, Man, and Technology* (New York: Knopf, 1971). Citing Commoner, Michael Egan recalls: "'The environmental crisis, together with all of the other evils that blight the nation—racial inequality, hunger, poverty and war—cry out for a

profound revision in our national priorities,' Commoner insisted on Earth Day. 'None can be solved until that is accomplished. But, tragically, the nation remains immobilized by the cost of the Vietnam War and the huge military budget, by the talent and money-gulping space program, by the disastrous cuts in the federal budget for research support, by the reduction in funds for the cities and education.'" Michael Egan, *Barry Commoner and the Science of Survival: The Remaking of American Environmentalism* (Cambridge, MA: The MIT Press, 2007), p. 118.

25. Ungeheuer, "Woodstockholm." Commoner's words were also cited in "Man vs. Man not Man vs. Nature: Commoner Tells Overflow Crowd," *Forum: Environment Is Politics* 2, June 6, 1972, p. 1.
26. World Commission on Environment and Development, *Our Common Future* (Oxford: Oxford University Press, 1987).
27. Gelbspan and Gurin, "Woodstockholm '72," p. 34. "Allen Ginsberg, who supports the Life Forum, says what is needed—more than any political action—is a 'transformation of world consciousness.' To that end, the Life Forum will import masters in the disciplines of Buddhism, Yoga, nature-survival, and woodmanship."
28. Gelbspan and Gurin, "Woodstockholm '72," p. 34. In Rowland's account, largely derived from Weisberg, "Given the 'turn on, tune in, drop out' philosophy of the one and the intensely serious political activism of the other, it was probably inevitable that friction should develop between Life Forum and *Folkets Forum*. . . . After a series of progressively more angry meetings, *Folkets Forum* decided it would have nothing to do with what it saw as a highly-suspicious collection of American degenerates, dope addicts and ne'er-do-wells." Rowland, *The Plot to Save the World*, p. 123. Gun Zacharias reproduces sample pages of the *Whole Earth Catalog* that include information on drugs, carefully crossing out information for procurement. Gun Zacharias, *Skarpnäck, USA: En Bok om Droger och Politik* (Stockholm: Förbunder mot Droger, 1975).
29. Stewart Brand, "Stockholm Preamble," *Clear Creek* 16 (October 1972), p. 29.
30. See Foster Haley, "Kaplan Fund, Cited as C.I.A. 'Conduit,' Lists Unexplained $395,000 Grant," *New York Times*, September 3, 1964, p. 10, and E. W. Kenworthy, "Tax Case Held Up for C.I.A. Conduit: Inquiry into Kaplan Fund of New York put off 2 Years, but a Deal is Denied," *New York Times*, March 5, 1967, pp. 1 and 38.
31. For a more detailed history and description of the Point Foundation and its otherwise often important work, see Andrew G. Kirk, "On Point," in *Counterculture Green: The Whole Earth Catalog and American Environmentalism* (Lawrence: University Press of Kansas, 2007), pp. 115–55. Kirk makes only passing mention of Brand's involvement with the Stockholm events, noting that "during the spring of 1972, Point spent significant Life Forum funds on a 'misbegotten effort to liven up' the [UNCHE] in Stockholm. . . . Brand later dismissed the effort as a waste of resources, with the exception of the work of Point grantee Joan McIntyre's attempt to promote a United Nations–sponsored whaling moratorium" through Project Jonah (p. 138). Rowland, among others, notes funding from the Kaplan Foundation in *The Plot to Save the World*, p. 122.
32. Brand, "Stockholm Preamble," p. 29.
33. Gelbspan and Gurin, "Woodstockholm '72," p. 34.
34. Russell Train noted in a Senate hearing, "There also will be, as I understand it, an activity called a people's forum which will be very much larger, made up of—the last report I heard—25,000 to 30,000 participants, camping in Stockholm, of a much more political orientation,

not necessarily related to the environment, and this could be a very significant element that I think you should be aware of in your own thinking about the conference. I am personally concerned that the conference and the environment within which the Conference is held does not become a highly charged political atmosphere of a divisive kind. The environment has been one of the positive bridges to improved communication and coordination among nations." "Hearings before the Committee on Foreign Relations, United States Senate, Ninety-Second Congress, Second Session on Preparations for and Prospects of the June 1972, U.N. Conference on the Human Environment (May 3, 4, and 5, 1972)," (Washington: U.S. Government Printing Office, 1972), p. 18.

35. Weisberg also recounts that Brand then approached the Environment Forum about the threat of "crowds of young people," presenting Brand's "imaginary dialog [of] what transpired." Weisberg, "The Browning of Stockholm," p. 38.

36. John Lewallen, "Stockholm Revealed," *Clear Creek* 16 (October 1972), p. 27.

37. "The Hog Farm has offered its services to the local police to help keep order at Skarpnack and elsewhere. The police are being cooperative." Alfred Heller, "A Visit to the Life Forum HQ," *San Francisco Chronicle*, June 9, 1972, p. 21. The *New York Times* reported: "Despite some apprehension here over the influx of exotically dressed young people, the mood at Skarpnack has been good. An American traveling commune, Hog Farm, showed up, proclaimed its ability to organize campgrounds and counterculture groups, and has been cooperating with Swedish authorities to set up the tent city and make it a 'good ecological example.'" "Environment Conference Will Offer Some Sideshows," *New York Times*, June 5, 1972, p. 24. Peter B. Stone, in *Did We Save the Earth at Stockholm?: The People and Politics in the Conference on the Human Environment* (London: Earth Island, 1973), noted of the Swedish authorities, "They had helped to bring Wavy Gravy and the Hog Farm (a 'family' about fifty strong) from the United States on the strength of their reputation of being able to keep order among youth" (p. 132).

38. Heller, "A Visit to the Life Forum HQ," p. 21. The reverse side of this article included the notorious photograph of a naked girl running with napalm, later identified as Kim Phuc.

39. Weisberg, "The Browning of Stockholm," p. 38. Weisberg described Brand as "a former merry prankster of Ken Kesey's salad days and now a millionaire as a result of the Whole Earth Catalog." He noted that Life Forum's budget was $75,000, with funds coming from both Brand and the Kaplan Foundation.

40. Weisberg, "The Browning of Stockholm," p. 39. This and other citations of Brand and his group appear to have come from a taped interview undertaken by Alvin Duskin, a San Francisco environmental activist who, as noted in Heller's "A Visit to the Life Forum HQ," was present during his own visit and writing a book on the UNCHE with Dougald Sturmer, Barry Weisberg, and Anne Dowie. Weisberg, "The Browning of Stockholm," p. 21.

41. *Ibid.*, p. 34.

42. See Felicity D. Scott, "Open Land," lecture at Cykl Wykładów Archfilm at Centrum Sztuki Wspolczensnej, Warsaw, September 3, 2008. This research on Open Land communes forms part of my current book project, entitled *Outlaw Territories: Environments of Insecurity, Architectures of Counterinsurgency*, from which this research on the UNCHE also derives.

43. Harold Gilliam, "Eco-Trips at Hog Farm," *San Francisco Chronicle*, June 14, 1972.

44. Brand, in "Hog Farm," undated press release from the Life Forum. Courtesy of Mary Jean Haley.

45. Gilliam, "Eco-Trips at Hog Farm."
46. Rowland, *The Plot to Save the World*, prologue.
47. Neal White, and Peter Schjeldahl, "Living High on the Hog Farm," *Avant-Garde* 5 (November 1968), p. 46.
48. Stephen Starger recalled that beyond his time as a Beat and with the Pranksters, "the rest of Hugh Romney's pre–Wavy Gravy years took him through work with improvisational theater and comedy troupes such as the Living Theater and the Committee." Stephen Starger, "When Wavy Gravy Comes Home," *Hartford Courant*, May 10, 1970, p. 2M.
49. White and Schjeldahl, "Living High on the Hog Farm," p. 51.
50. Romney explains that with the idea of ensuring an equitable division of labor, they "instituted the dance master program. Our dance master ran the farm and the dance mistress ran the kitchen, and each day it was some different person working off this wheel with everybody's name." Under the impact of a "Fantasy Box" "into which people would place ideas of stuff the group could do," this transformed into "a power day for each Hog Farmer in alphabetical order to become god for 24 hours." Hugh Romney, "The Hog Farm," *The Realist* 86 (November–December 1969), p. 18. See also William Hedgepeth and Dennis Stock, *The Alternative: Communal Life in New America* (New York: Collier Books, 1970), pp. 77–78.
51. Romney, "The Hog Farm," pp. 1–31. For an outline of Romney's relation to Kesey and appearance in the latter half of Tom Wolfe's account of Kesey and the Pranksters, *The Electric Kool-Aid Acid Test*, see Starger, "When Wavy Gravy Comes Home." Hedgepeth writes, "'Riverwood residents wonder about recurring rumors of Communist plans for the total destruction of Los Angeles and neighboring communities by violence and fire on a magnified Watts scale. They wonder if these people are a Red Trojan Horse in their midst.' All this led to miscellaneous acts of terrorism by a local ranchers' group and another gang of Vietnam veterans, who eventually set up an armed roadblock across the Farm's sole access route. In response, the Farmers simply outfitted an old schoolbus with bunks, packed up their mascot, a hog named Pigasus, and set forth on the open highway-ultimately venturing into all parts of the country, doing good deeds and supporting themselves by operating comfort stations for 'bad trippers' and drug-zonked kids at various music festivals, such as the legendary rock-gala near Woodstock, New York," p. 78.
52. Brand, in "Hog Farm."
53. "Earth People's Park," *Whole Earth Catalog*, special issue, "The Outlaw Area," January 1970, pp. 28–29. The account described participants as "people who had cooked at Woodstock, put up an overnight sound stage at Altamont, survived *Liferaft Earth*, doctored with the Hog Farm, built domes and tilled ground at innumerable communes, dodged tear gas canisters, smoked dope, been busted" (p. 28). "The Document" accompanying the account states, "Woodstock was a moment in history. Earth Peoples Park can be the foothold for the culture and ecological development of that moment, a permanent home for those of us concerned with living and growth" (p. 29). See also Christopher McDermott, "Plans to Free a Piece of Mother Earth," *Los Angeles Free Press*, January 16, 1970, pp. 10 and 13.
54. Rodney Clarke, "Earth People's Park: 'Liberated' Land With a Mortgage," *Washington Post*, October 24, 1971, p. 178. The article is referring to the economic crisis of the Earth People's Park founded in Norton, Vermont. After noting the initial concern of the local residents, it explains that "relations were improved also by the realization by Nortonites that the political 'freaks' were more 'into' the land than they were 'into' taking over the town's governmental

structure." Noting that Romney was a "veteran of the Beat scene of the late fifties and of the writer Ken Kesey's Merry Pranksters, creators of California's psychedelic movement five or six years ago," a reporter for the *Hartford Courant* explained: "Romney's and the Hog Farm's mission now, he says, is to save the land and return it to the people. The communal group carries itself and its considerable equipment around the country in a caravan of multi-colored mural-painted buses, doing shows to raise money for the benefit of 'Earth People's Parks,' where people would be able to go and 'live the simple life.'" "Everything's Groovy Down on 'The Farm,'" *Hartford Courant*, March 13, 1970, p. 31E.

55. "Earth People's Park," *Whole Earth Catalog*, p. 28.
56. "Earth People's Park Abandons New Mexico," *Los Angeles Free Press*, March 6, 1970, p. 22.
57. Brand, in "Hog Farm," undated press release from the Life Forum .
58. "Liferaft Earth," *Whole Earth Catalog*, January 1970, pp. 23–27. On the inflatables related to this event, see Felicity Ap, *Living Archive 7: Ant Farm* (Barcelona: ACTAR Editorial, 2008).
59. The note explains that McConnell "got together with artists Norman LaLiberte and one of the Apollo Earth photographs and came up with the Earth Flag." *Whole Earth Catalog*, Fall 1969, p. 80.
60. "Liferaft Earth," *Whole Earth Catalog*, pp. 23–27.
61. Fred Turner, *From Counterculture to Cyberculture: Stewart Brand, the Whole Earth Network, and the Rise of Digital Utopianism* (Chicago: University of Chicago Press, 2006), pp. 43–44. See also Kirk, *Counterculture Green*.
62. Wavy Gravy, *The Hog Farm and Friends, by Wavy Gravy as told to Hugh Romney and Vice Versa* (New York: Links, 1974), p. 132.
63. On mobilizing shame, see Thomas Keenan, "Mobilizing Shame," *South Atlantic Quarterly* 103.2/3 (Spring–Summer 2004), pp. 435–49.
64. Wavy Gravy, *The Hog Farm and Friends*, pp. 132 and 134.
65 Keenan, "Mobilizing Shame," p. 447.
66. Thomas Keenan, "Drift: Politics and the Simulation of Real Life," *Grey Room* 21 (Fall 2005), pp. 94–111.
67. Ungeheuer, "A Stockholm Notebook."
68. Stone, *Did We Save the Earth at Stockholm*, p. 127.
69. Paul Ehrlich, "A Crying Need for Quiet Conferences," *Bulletin of the Atomic Scientists* 28.7 (September 1972), p. 30.
70. Alissa J. Rubin, "As Iraq Takes Control, Puzzle over Prisoners," *New York Times*, Sunday, October 25, 2008, pp. A1 and A8.
71. Brand had studied photography at the San Francisco Art Institute following his graduation from Stanford and returned to further his education at San Francisco State after leaving the army.
72. Heller, "A Visit to the Life Forum HQ," p. 21.
73. Romney, "The Hog Farm," p. 18. On the following page he writes, "Whole consciousness guided through the body . . . heart throat head and out to merge with other consciousness in the circle . . . getting stronger . . . becoming whole *whole* consciousness *consciousness*," ellipses in the original.
74. R. Buckminster Fuller, "Proposal to the International Union of Architects," in *Your Private Sky: Discourse*, ed. Joachim Krausse and Claude Lichtenstein (Baden, Switzerland: Lars Müller Publishers and Museum für Gestaltung, 2001), p. 248.
75. In Snyder's account, the emphasis on personal responsibility had emerged in the interwar

period, when "alienated intellectuals, creative types and general social misfits" had come "to recognize each other by various minute signals." He charted a trajectory of multiple identifications; Communism and Marxist thought in the thirties and forties; rejection of the entire Western tradition following World War II in favor of a study of Buddhism and Hinduism and in turn a rejection of all great religions as "social institutions that had long been accomplices of the State in burdening and binding people, rather than serving to liberate them"; on to "small but influential heretical and esoteric movements," "peasant witchcraft in Europe, Tantrism in Bengal, Quakers in England, Tachikawa-ryu in Japan, Ch'an in China." All were "outcroppings of the Great Subculture which runs underground through history," landing in San Francisco's Golden Gate Park. Snyder's writings, by many accounts, were an important reference for many within the counterculture. "How do they recognize each other?" he asked, "Not always by beards, long hair, bare feet or beads. The signal is a bright and tender look; calmness and gentleness, freshness and ease of manner." Such characteristics marked those following "the timeless path of love." Gary Snyder, "Why Tribe," in *Earth House Hold* (New York: New Directions Books, 1969), pp. 113–16.

76. *Ibid.*, p. 113.
77. In *détournment*, "any elements, no matter where they are taken from, can serve in making new combinations." Thus, the elements of an existing system can be used against that system. See Guy-Ernest Debord, "Method of Détournement," trans. available at http://library.nothingness.org/articles/SI/en/display/3; originally published in *Les Livres Nues* 8 (May 1956).
78. Sean Nazerali, "The Roma and Democracy: A Nation without a State," in Okwui Enwezor, et al. *Democracy Unrealized: Documenta 11, platform 1* (Ostfildern-Ruit: Hatje Cantz Publishers, 2002), p. 133.
79. Hannah Arendt, "The Decline of the Nation State and the End of the Rights of Man," in *The Origins of Totalitarianism* (San Diego: Harcourt Brace, 1966), p. 282.
80. *Ibid.*, p. 301.
81. "The survivors of the extermination camps, the inmates of concentration and internment camps, and even the comparatively happy stateless people could see," she proposed, "that the abstract nakedness of being nothing but human was their greatest danger." *Ibid.*, p. 300.
82. *Ibid.*, pp. 283 and 284. Arendt's formulation would be famously pursued by Giorgio Agamben in his theorization of "bare" or "naked life," in which the camp is precisely the space that opens up when the nation-state is in crisis, when, in his words "the political system of the modern nation-state—founded on the functional nexus between a determinate localization (territory) and determinate order (the state), which was mediated by automatic regulations for the inscription of life (birth or nation)—enters a period of permanent crisis." Giorgio Agamben, "What is a Camp?," in *Means Without End: Notes on Politics* (Minneapolis: University of Minnesota Press, 2000), pp. 42–43. In another formulation he notes that "*The camp is the space that opens up when the state of exception starts to become the rule*. In it, the state of exception, which was essentially a temporal suspension of the state of law, acquires a permanent spatial arrangement that, as such, remains constantly outside the normal state of law" (p. 39).
83. *Ibid.*, pp. 43–45.
84. Michel Foucault, "Confronting Governments: Human Rights," in *Essential Works of Foucault, 1954–1984*, vol. 3, *Power*, ed. James D Faubion (New York: New Press, 2000). See Thomas Keenan, *Fables of Responsibility: Aberrations and Predicaments in Ethics and Politics* (Stanford: Stanford University Press, 1997).

Richard Goldstone's press conference in Gaza, 2009. This image is perhaps one of the best demonstrations of the contemporary principle of forensics. Goldstone stands in front of a destroyed multi-storied building. Around him are members of the government in Gaza; before him is a bouquet of microphones belonging to international news networks.

Forensic Architecture:
An Interview with Eyal Weizman

Yates McKee and Meg McLagan

YATES MCKEE: We would like to start by asking you to talk about the broader trajectory of your career. You first gained prominence in the architectural field when the exhibition you cocurated, *A Civilian Occupation*, was withdrawn as the submission by the Israeli Architecture Association to the 2002 International Union of Architects Congress in Berlin. You were trained professionally as an architect and had a practice, but already in 2002 you were operating in relation to political and human rights activism. How did that come about?

EYAL WEIZMAN: I studied architecture at the Architecture Association School of Architecture in London and in 1996 spent my "year out" working in Tel Aviv. I wanted to volunteer for work at the Palestinian Ministry of Planning. It was the Oslo years, only a few months after [Prime Minister Yitzhak] Rabin was assassinated. The Ministry of Planning was on the seam between north Jerusalem and south Ramallah. I volunteered as a planner, but there was not much to do. The offices had large contingents of Norwegians who felt, I assume, responsible for the agreement that bore the name of their capital. I was doing all sorts of planning-assistant tasks, such as hand-rendering plans and so on, when at some point, the planners thought of a better use of my time. As an Israeli, I had access to cartographic information that was not otherwise made available to the Palestinians. In the innocence of the pre–Google Earth years, aerial and satellite imagery and maps had to be obtained at state cadastral offices, to which Israel did not provide access for Palestinians. This withholding of maps was a de facto policy.

What we had at the ministry were Russian—I think KGB-compiled—maps of the area. They were quite good topographically, but the built environment they represented was a state long gone. The settlements, for example, were simply added as dots on the map. I was sent out on "missions" to libraries and the cadastral office to obtain maps; I was a combination low-level industrial espionage agent and copyboy: photocopying maps and bringing them back to the ministry in Ramallah.

MM: So they were readily available in libraries and other places?

EW: Yes, I should therefore not overstate the importance of what I was doing. It was really about bringing maps that were available to any Israeli with a student card. It allowed the ministry to update all sorts of data, and it taught me the significance of maps; it also started a long relationship with Palestinian planners and architects. These connections became the skeleton on which I would place my later work. At the time, working in Ramallah for the ministry was relatively easy—it might have not been legal, but it wasn't criminalized. Being in Palestinian-controlled areas and in touch with Palestinian institutions became illegal for Israelis only after the second intifada began in 2000.

YM: Did you continue to work for the Planning Ministry after 1996?

EW: There were frequent exchanges. I came back to meetings later when I worked with B'tselem—the human rights center dealing with the Occupied Territories. Some Palestinian NGOs, such as ARIJ, the Applied Research Institute–Jerusalem, were doing some good mappings and we were exchanging aerial and satellite data, whatever we had. In the early 2000s, B'Tselem was receiving some satellite information from the American consulate, which was implicitly and explicitly supporting NGOs in Israel and Palestine. There's a department in the Pentagon that is in charge of geography and general statistical data; we supposed that the United States had an interest in monitoring the growth of the settlements. From them we were getting fresh satellite images that were not yet available to the public. Different people and organizations had vested interests in compiling maps and making them public, and this was reflected in the way they were doing cartography. But when we compiled the map from master plans and from some photographs from the ground and air, we were following our own agenda.

At the center of these projects was the West Bank, a territory violently reshaped by conflict. It is in reality a beautiful, fragile, and shrinking piece of landscape, almost extinct. A good account of this is given by Raja Shehadeh in his book *Palestinian Walks*.[1] This fragile landscape has gradually turned into something I understand as the "political plastic"—a territorial arrangement that is continuously shaped and reshaped by political forces. If you look at it closely, you can notice that it registers the forces that act upon it. In this conflict, or in territorial conflicts in general, you cannot say that politics "happen in space," but rather that they happen *by* space. Space is not the set of abstract coordinates on which the events of politics unfold, but something that is transformed and remade by every political action that takes place within it. So I was thinking of politics as something like "space in action" or "space in movement" and of this movement as quite a deadly thing. We can discuss later what this will mean for all sorts of legal challenges and forensic investigations brought in relation to territories and structures. The object never stands in isolation; the evidence is also constantly mutating. It is like conducting an analysis of a living body while it is twisting in pain.

YM: Did you go back to Israel/Palestine after you finished your degree?

EW: I never really left. I was living between the region and different places in Europe at the time and also started my PhD with Mark Cousins and Paul Hirst, who encouraged me to use my work in and on Palestine as the foundation for my doctoral research.

YM: So in 2001, were you contacted by B'Tselem, or did you already know the person there?

EW: I went to B'Tselem to study their archives, and they happened to stumble upon an architect at the moment they were looking for one. Yehezkel Lein, who has since moved to the UN, proposed that we do a report that would be based on an analysis of the built environment. The idea was to shift the language of critique away from one based on Article 48 of the Fourth Geneva Convention, which stipulates that an occupying state is forbidden to transfer population to or from an area it occupies. By this principle, any home that would be built even just beyond the Green Line, the border of Israel prior to the 1967 Six-Day War, would be considered illegal. True enough, but this principle was not able to capture the full extent of the planning dimension of violations—the way crimes were contemplated and produced on drawing boards. If you wanted to take issue with architecture and planning, you needed to take critique a step further and give our study a forensic dimension—do spatial forensics.

This started a new phase in our thinking in which we were interested in demonstrating what we started to call the "second order" of a crime: beyond the fact that an action—here, planning and building—was undertaken within a general zone of illegality. We wanted to engage the entire depth of invention, technology, and techniques that go into that planning, query its intentions, unpack its formal and organizational logic, and compare them to a set of legal norms. Ultimately, though it wasn't impossible at the time, we thought we had to construct a case tight enough to put an architect in the dock. And for this we needed a new type of spatial representation and analysis. By synthesizing all fragments of maps and plans into a single document, we could observe and draw some initial conclusions, in particular regarding the way in which that planning is employed to cause material damage to Palestinian communities by splintering and fragmenting the logic of their regional economy. We could also show how generic Israeli planning principles, in relation, for example, to the building of a suburb, were paradoxically compromised—which means that planners were creating less convenient built environments for settlers—in order to serve the auxiliary function of this planning in disrupting Palestinian economy. We could see how simple planning irregularities, variations in the proportion of parking lots to housing units, for example, were created because of what the layout of some settlement was asked to do—to draw a long arc that bisects Palestinian towns and villages.

By saying that a settlement was badly designed as a residential community, we were of course not protesting the way settlers were treated, although I do think that the state lured in some of these people and bears the ultimate responsibility. We were protesting what a forensic investigation of planning documents, statistics, and layout revealed: that there were other interests at play and that these folded in larger geopolitical motivations and ultimately violations of international laws. We were trying to read geopolitics in architectural and planning details.

In the frame of criminal courts, there is a potential problem, because they seek individual responsibility. But we had an extensive view of architecture, which we saw not necessarily and not always as a creation of a single author, but as a diagram of a set of forces and power relations, slowing into form. This also meant a conception of architectural crime as one grounded in diffused agency. The courts in which this study could be used were thus those in which state acts, state crimes—rather than individual ones—could be reviewed.

YM: This research was published as a widely circulated online as a PDF report with the title *Land Grab*.[2] You've mentioned that the map contained in the report actually became the matrix for work by other people with their own data sets and projects, almost like an open-source process.

EW:We saved the PDF document in a way that when it is opened, one can isolate the layers, continue working on the document, and upload it. So mapping the occupation indeed became something of an open-source project, with many participants downloading, updating, and uploading material. But this was done not only by well-meaning activists. The most disturbing thing was when we realized that the army was using this map. Somebody from B'tselem saw it hanging on the wall at the Ministry of Defense, with a sketch of the Wall on it! Indeed, we finished the mapping just as they started their planning.

MM: So the *Land Grab* report largely revolved around the map?

EW: Yes, the report was a way of framing the map in terms of international and human rights law— a forensic reading of architecture and planning. It offered a reading of the built landscape as a product of the interplay of planning decisions and forces on the ground. But the map had a larger effect. It gained autonomy beyond the report and started to be used widely, both locally and internationally. Part of the attractiveness of the map, it was later said, was its "elegance." It operated simultaneously as a map and as an image. As a map, it could be read for the navigational and relational associations that it established between things on the ground, such as bases, settlements, and villages. As an image, it could be read instantly. It had to communicate a dynamic process of expansion in one look. So there is—broadly speaking—an epistemological and an aesthetic dimension that were entangled in this map/image.

YM: A signature feature is the color gradients.

EW: The color gradient is a tool to make sense of expansion and of an ongoing process. This is what accounted for it being simultaneously a map and an image. Some maps can do that, of course. In fact, ideally, one should have been able to press "play" on this map and see how its ongoing transformation, the political plastic, continued to register and translate political processes into color and form. The map finally looks like camouflage—which is fitting, because camouflage is also an attack on form. The colonial project of the settlement is an attack on political form—on the coherence of Palestinian political space. We insisted on giving this part extra attention, and I remember that some people in B'Tselem did not understand the delay involved in the design of the map as we were endlessly reworking it.

YM: So this was not merely a matter of aesthetic appearance in the superficial sense of the word—the gradients highlight a process of growth and also indicate the dynamics simultaneously at work at various topographical levels, which has been another innovation of your research. However, there were certainly activist mapping techniques in the past, or at least an understanding of the importance of maps, no? In his article in *The New Intifada*, Edward Said talked about how one of the major disadvantages of Palestinian negotiators had been their lack of comprehensive maps.[3] Indeed, Said included in that article several maps, but as in your earlier point, they are composed basically of points and lines.

EW: The article, first published in the *London Review of Books* at the end of 2000, was about the violent beginnings of the second intifada. It is an extremely important piece, in fact formative. In it, Said calls for a spatial turn, by which he meant, I think, turning the physical mapping of the conflict into a form of evidence. You know, he wasn't very fond of the Palestinian Authority, to say the least, certainly from a certain point on, perhaps after Oslo, and he was particularly furious with the way they conducted negotiations and signed agreements without a mandate and also without being aware of the geography and without having maps of their own. The Israelis, in the meantime, fielded an array of generals and geography experts who managed to create an illusion of a "Palestinian Territories" that was actually nothing but a patchwork of spaces. It was a paradox that Said, who in his writing was one of the strongest critics of mapping as a colonial practice, pointing out the imaginary geography of the colonizers as they are registered in cartography, would himself propose cartographies or countercartographies as one of the forms of resistance.

I think that one can understand this apparent contradiction in terms of the fact that nowadays, contemporary colonialism could no longer afford to conduct its crimes in broad daylight, as it had done in the nineteenth and early twentieth centuries. They were not crimes then, because international humanitarian law was in its infancy. Now, colonial occupation needs to create a level of secrecy, covering its traces as it goes along, destroying its evidence, or at least not making the data public for all to see . . . so mapping and all sorts of techniques based on civilianized former military technology started to become a prevalent form of protest. It is strange that it was now human rights people who were conducting reconnaissance flights—we were hiring light planes to do this—or interpreting satellite images and remote sensing technologies as if we were intelligence officers in the RAF. We can discuss the problems associated with that later.

The Said article indeed inspired a generation of activists and researchers, including me. In the following years, the "spatial turn" in the discourse surrounding the occupation has extended our political understanding of the conflict to a physical, geographical reality and has led to the production of a plethora of maps, drawn and distributed by a multiplicity of political and human rights groups. Ours was only one of many.

And yes, mapping requires some rethinking. Maps are interventions in the fields of territorial visibility. This is apparent in the selections of what to show and how to draw it. What do you show and what do you hide? Obviously, showing some of the informal ways in which Palestinians use the terrain or how they bypass checkpoints, as is the case in some ill-informed art-inspired practices of countercartography, can be counterproductive. It's like revealing a productive secret. On the other hand, being able to choose what to show and how to represent it can challenge the otherwise absolute monopoly of such information by the state, even if the choice is enabled by forms of technology initially provided by the state.

After a while, I returned to thinking about Said's point about Palestinians not having maps. Maybe there is also another way of thinking about it. The

Palestinians might have used the fact they did not have maps as a negotiation strategy. They could have refused to enter the game of maps and lines altogether. Israelis would say, "We constantly offer you this compromise and that compromise, this or that line, and you have not drawn up a proposal in return; you have not shown us one single map." But geography could of course be rejected for a set of political principles or political demands, equality or single citizenship, for example. The minute you come in with other maps, you enter a zone of negotiation. In the trials prompted by the construction of the Wall, negotiations about the location of the Wall just ended by creating an arena for the participation of Palestinians in the design of their own means of incarceration. So in this sense, maps are more useful for the documentation of crimes in the past, rather than as proposals for the future. Maps, but not geographical plans! Plans in this conflict should be based on political principles, rather than on geographical solutions.

MM: So at what point did you commit yourself to this work? Can you narrate that for us?

EW: In the early 2000s, I was entering several collaborations in order to fund the research I wanted to do. The art world was rather useful for that. The banning of the *Civilian Occupation* exhibition inadvertently gained publicity for the project. At the time, I was very much in the mind-set of wanting to get the work out using different platforms. The art world provided us a great set of possibilities—it was like a laboratory for thinking about the several dimensions of the work: arenas of discussion and critique, infrastructure, and networks of dissemination that enabled the work to move into all sorts of unexpected forums, including, through this detour and using the media generated, political ones. It led to excellent collaborations.

I also found myself in the middle of an architecture discussion that had already started about politics and urban research, the meaning and methods of research and urban transformation. We did not initially intend the work to be an intervention in the architectural discipline per se, but as it happened, we found ourselves fighting two battles, so to speak, one political-contextual in relation to the area—Palestine—in which we had stakes and the other for architectural research to be considered as a form of architecture, with effects in the world, and this without having to be validated by leading to a design proposal, so this work contributed to a change of sensibility in contemporary architecture as practiced by different people.

YM: The institutions of architecture in the limited sense have been only one site or platform among many others for publicizing and extending this work, but in theoretical terms, a key point you have made is that the occupation is itself thoroughly architectural at many different levels.

EW: Yes, architecture was both the subject of research—we were studying buildings, landscapes, territories—and the methodology of research. We used the toolbox of architectural analysis to enter the political debate in a different way.

MM: How have the conditions for doing this kind of work evolved since you began?

EW: There has been an explosion of mapping that coincided with ours. Specifically, the West Bank must be the most mapped area of the world. Our project was not the first, but it took place at a moment when geography started to matter in a particularly urgent way. This explosion of activities involved the combination of mapping with visual documentation—amateur video and satellite images became much more available. At present, there is an incredible wealth of information around. People are mapping and posting their maps in real time. It seems as if any change in the territory is immediately registered in image and video form.

YM: Could you say something about your relationship with both governmental and nongovernmental actors in Palestine? Do you still work in some capacity with the Planning Ministry?

EW: In the spring of 2005, when the Israeli settlements were being evacuated from Gaza, I was invited to advise on the reuse of the settlements when the Palestinian Ministry of Planning was thinking of what to do with them when evacuated.

MM: So you were called in as a consultant?

EW: I was part of the group of planners and politicians in the Palestinian ministry. Obviously, it was rather chaotic. Nobody knew what was happening and when, because Israel did not provide any reliable information about its intentions, whether it would leave the houses standing or whether they would be destroyed, or when it all would happen. From Israel's perspective, it was an entirely unilateral operation. But still, the frame of the question was that if there is going to be an evacuation, there are going to be new sites available, properties, infrastructure, and there's going to be a lot of demand for them in an area that is extremely dense, aggravated by a land system that leaves few public lands. The Ministry of Planning was the office through which all the international organizations and politicians entered this discussion. All major geopolitical players—the United Nations, the European Union, the United States, the International Monetary Fund, the World Bank, and so on—had their own thoughts and their own proposals and optimistic fantasies, and they presented them like in a giant board meeting.

So the situation was complex, difficult, and rather frustrating. There was this assumption that the Ministry of Planning would adopt one of the plans that were largely seeking privatization of the land, but in fact, it had no power to do so.

Furthermore, the ministry, I quickly learned, had its own agenda that had much to do with internal struggles within the Palestinian Authority. Land was at the center of it all. Yet at the time, the Palestinian Authority was the only body that was, in principle, at least partially publicly accountable.

In Gaza, a large proportion of the land on which the settlements stood was a different type of public or collective land that the occupation called "state land" and used for the purposes of Jewish settlers. Some of it was fields that previously belonged to private owners. Settlement planners, whenever they could, preferred to build on public lands—it was easier, because they could better face challenges in the High Court... although in total, about half of the settlement area, Gaza and the West Bank included, is built on private property.

So it was the public land that people like the World Bank and the IMF sought to sell to investors for all sorts of uses, from industry to hotels and tourism. What we were saying was the opposite and rather simple: private land should go back to people who owned it—this is clear enough—but public land should be reserved for the public for supporting public functions where so little land was available. We resisted the idea of privatizing things in advance or by default.

Second, we did not want simply to propose the reuse of the evacuated settlement homes as private housing (we didn't know they would be destroyed), which might reproduce similar social hierarchy in space and enforce the continuity of colonial history. You know, in the history of decolonization, most buildings were reused in the very same way as before. When you have debates about reuse, they are rather robust and intense, such as the famous debate between Nehru and Gandhi about the reuse of the Viceroy Palace, which Gandhi wanted to use as a hospital for the poor. In Gaza, settlement homes were pretty good houses; our idea was to turn these suburban structures into a nucleus of public institutions. Rather than destroy them, as some wanted, or simply reproduce their use as gated communities for the elite, we recommended their transformation. We succeeded in only three cases, in what Israel calls "isolated settlements." These were outposts that were generally very close to the Palestinian urban fabric and that could be considered as part of that fabric. They were seen as "isolated" from the perspective of Israeli geography, but they were almost urban from the Palestinian perspective. They were simultaneously urban and suburban, as we later put it in the context of the work Sandi Hilal, Alessandro Petti, and I undertook in Decolonizing Architecture Art Residency.

YM: You've said that Israel has deliberately destroyed many evacuated settlements precisely to avoid the image of the potential reversibility of the occupation and the potential reusability of these structures.

EW: Yes, Netanyahu, who is very media and image conscious, was the first to realize that the power of such images—Arabs living in the homes of Jews—could designate a certain reversal and reversibility of the Zionist project. He therefore called for their destruction. He thus pointed out the relation of politics and architecture as organized by the media.

YM: What strikes me about your work is your refusal to reduce it to just Israel versus Palestine in a clear-cut opposition, even though of course you highlight and work to resist the massive unevenness of the overall occupation. But you insist on tracing the multiplicity of agents that are on the ground; you read the Wall, for instance, as a kind of political seismograph, as an index of all these heterogeneous forces that are irreducible to top-down sovereignty. Do you sometimes encounter resistance to this insistence on a kind of micropolitical analysis that departs somewhat from the idea of Israel as a monolithic oppressor? It is a different frame from what one often hears among some in the U.S. or European left.

EW: Of course there are many detractors of this mode of critique and the kind of activism that is derived from it. Some comrades claim that this type of reading makes things more complicated than necessary—that insisting on this kind of complexity gives credibility to the system, or even worse, that by according the occupation a level of complexity and sometimes sophistication, we glamorize it. I think that this is a typical postmodern confusion that can see complexity and elasticity only as inherently liberating.

I find these positions weak. It is counterproductive to create a false essentialism, which more often than not blocks, or worse, polices the boundaries of thinking and acting. Further, the micropolitical, microphysical research and the microagencies that I track in my work are the "how" of the colonization and therefore the "how" of resistance to it.

MM: Can you tell us about the work you have been doing recently?

EW: Over the last few years, together with Thomas Keenan, Susan Schuppli, and others at the Centre for Research Architecture, I have been engaged in building upon the different experiences I have had with the practice of architecture, with conflict, and with international law to think through the problems of "forensic architecture." This takes place at the Centre for Research Architecture at Goldsmiths, University of London. It includes a collaboration with a number of NGOs and cultural institutions. It is a large project, funded by the European Research Council's program of "frontier research." The term "forensic architecture" has been used in the field of property surveying for some time, but we extracted it from this context and aim to place it as a field of practice within the context of the prosecution of war crimes. This strategy is based on my previous experience in presenting architectural evidence in several international legal cases. The intention is to sketch out and theorize an emergent relation between architectural research and international law. Many possible methodologies are scattered in the fields of building conservation, archaeology, urban analysis, architectural theory, and damage-assessment engineering, but "forensic architecture" has not yet been formulated as a field with its own assumptions, problems, and propositions. Space enters the legal process as a mediatized representation: as images, drawings, films, maps, models, and the remote sensing of built structures, environments, and their ruins. It is quite evident that these types of spatial representations now often frequently appear in international courts.

Between 2002 and 2004, for example, I had the opportunity to track a series of petitions against the Wall in the Israeli High Court of Justice and at the International Court of Justice in The Hague, because I provided drawings that were presented as evidence there. And the use of spatial representations, and especially of satellite imagery, continuously increases. In September 2009, using geospatial data, high-resolution satellite imagery, and data gathered in on-site investigations into destroyed buildings, the Goldstone Fact Finding Mission for the UN Human Rights Council and Human Rights Watch (HRW) alleged that the Israeli military had deliberately destroyed homes and infrastructure in the Gaza Strip.[4] In Iraq, HRW had done something similar when it attempted to conduct a forensic analysis of rubble in order to determine how and why civilians were killed in the early stages of the U.S. invasion in 2003.

In these places, as well as in Iran and in Darfur, the inability or lack of enthusiasm to employ researchers on the ground means that international processes, whether juridical or political, increasingly rely on the interpretation of satellite imagery. This is mainly before-and-after imagery. So buildings become the resource from which political events and intentions can be read. Satellite images and other geospatial technologies are used to corroborate claims of structural damage in conflict zones. Thus, we are told Iran wants to develop nuclear capability and are shown buildings and earthworks from the air. The organization Eyes on Darfur has monitored the conflict with satellite imagery, with experts called in to interpret them.

As much as spatial representations start structuring our understanding of conflict, the courts and judges are not always very used to understanding these spatial representations. If legal claims in conflict zones have acquired a territorial and spatial dimension, then we need to think harder about the implications of this. What is the place of architecture and the built environment within the institutions and the language of international law? How does the introduction of spatial representation affect the legal process? What is the relation of these types of evidence to testimony? In a sense I can say that the project deals with the increased significance of architectural evidence and also with the way it has somewhat shifted the focus of investigations away from human testimony, so we look at the methodological, legal, political and ethical implications of this shift.

Overall, then, I can say that my interest in this project is twofold: first in developing forensic architecture as an operative concept and analytical method for probing the events and histories inscribed in spatial artifacts and in built environments—for this we need to survey the above practices and work technically—and second, simultaneously in thinking critically about this practice. What are its potentials, and what are its limits? What are its political and ethical pitfalls? The project takes neither a purely practical nor a purely critical approach, but rather combines them both. Finally, the term "forensics" is what enables architecture to become a diagnostic technique in forums different from the academic.

YM: Can you talk about your methodology? We know that destruction takes on particular forms—it is not just unreadable chaos.

EW: Yes. We see buildings as sensors of sorts. We are interested in the way by which both slow processes of transformation and abrupt events are registered in their details and materialities. Buildings are just freeze shots of a process of constant transformation. A building's skin—the first few millimeters of a building—is like a membrane that is in constant movement. It expands and contracts with temperature changes, swelling or crumbling, slowly degenerating. This transformation is not the corruption of architecture, but rather part of the process of form making. Cracks are also interesting—they connect mineral geological formations and architectural forms.

But there are also more obvious and practical implications that are more directly related to war-crime investigation. In fact, the investigation of Israel's destruction in Gaza described in the Goldstone Report represents a methodological shift in several respects. Initially, it designates a shift in emphasis from witnessing to evidence. More attention and more resources were given to scientific evidence in the general balance. Of course, there were several dozens of witnesses interviewed for the Goldstone Report, but there was an implicit assumption that the testimony of people would be hard to defend, because it would be considered to have been manipulated by Hamas, and that public opinion, mainly in the West, is too biased to understand or listen to such testimony. This is a disturbing assumption.

So autopsy reports and investigations of the ruins of buildings somewhat overshadow the testimony of the living. Human Rights Watch employed a former target specialist in their investigation of the ruins. This shows that together with the shift in emphasis from human testimony to forensic evidence, different sets of skills and different types of people have entered the human rights world. It is now no longer only the empathic and compassionate human rights workers, but scientists and ex-soldiers who have gradually become part of the investigation.

YM: Given that the military apparently also takes the legality of its procedures very seriously, does it maintain an archive of evidence to demonstrate that it has indeed followed its own professed protocols—for example, those of proportionality in violence or warning?

EW: Yes, in fact, the paradox is that Israel's attack on Gaza in the winter of 2008–2009 was both one of the most violent and destructive since the Nakba of 1948 and, crucially, also the attack in which Israeli experts in international humanitarian law were most closely involved. So we can legitimately ask whether the use of the law here helped proliferate destruction. The Israeli military, like other militaries worldwide, has become very mindful of its exposure to international legal action. And of course, as you suggested, new legal technologies were introduced to military practice, such as issuing all sorts of new "warnings," which and includes a set of warnings—by telephone or leaflets or megaphones or warning shots—ordering people to evacuate the battlefield. This seemingly humanitarian approach has ended up allowing unparalleled levels of destruction, because when receiving such a warning, people who choose to stay are unjustifiably regarded by the military as voluntary human shields and thus as legitimate targets. International law not as a static body of rules, but rather an arena in which the law is shaped by an endless series of diffused "border conflicts" over what is and is not illegal. The question is who has the political influence, the authority, or the military power to force their interpretation to become authoritative.

YM: So where does this leave you?

EW: I think that one has to work according to two principles—it is a double strategy: to work both within and outside of the frame of international law. The law can be very useful, but it can't do all the political work necessary to address injustice and rights issues. In the work I have done so far, cartography or other forms of political representation were used in the courts, but they were also used outside them. Every different forum in which spatial issues are represented has its own logic.

An interesting example is the use of the evidence of destroyed buildings undertaken by the Gaza-based and Hamas-run Ministry of Public Works and Housing. It started compiling its own "book of the destruction" in the aftermath of the 2008–2009 attack. This archive contains thousands of entries, each documenting a single building that was completely or partially destroyed, from cracked walls in houses that still stand to those completely reduced to piles of rubble. This is another instance of forensic architecture, but it is not the legal framework that it is aimed at; rather it is practical in the sense of being directed at reconstruction and political in connecting this destruction to a history of Palestinian displacement.

YM: Forensics is of course a concern for many human rights activists, especially in reading things such as mass graves, but this specifically architectural approach seems like a new avenue.

EW: In the institution of the field of forensics, the conjunction of bones and ruins makes for a good analogy. Yes, in war-crime investigations, forensic sciences started to appear in the late 1980s, mainly from within the discipline of forensic anthropology, that is, exhumations of the victims of war crimes. Bone diggers use the term "osteobiography" to refer to the attempt to read the life story—not only the moment of death—of an individual from the bones in which these events are registered. So I guess that the analogy might extend to images of ruins, cities, landscapes, even deforestations. These can reveal the longer-term political processes that are saturated in them.

A conjunction might be the forensic architecture work we undertake for the prosecution in Guatemala courts. This is reconstruction and modeling we do for the FAFG—the Guatemala Forensic Anthropology Foundation—in the context of trials undertaken in regard to the genocide inflicted on the Mayan people and in particular the Ixil in the Quiche region of West Guatemala in the early 1980s. We joined FAFG archaeologists on a trip to the forest area to find traces of villages that were completely destroyed and that became overgrown with vegetation. Finding remnants of these villages requires attention not only to possible ruins—many of the buildings were made of organic materials and were consumed by the forest—but to patterns of vegetation, because some cultivated species remain in higher densities in areas where the forest overgrew most ruins. So there are statistics, patterns, and numbers of destroyed homes that we are looking for and modeling.

MM: So buildings will provide a different kind of evidentiary function than standard conventions of documentary exposure would allow; the modeling will trace very precisely the form and trajectory of an action—of an act of destruction?

EW: Yes, we hope, but as I mentioned, forensic architecture rarely has an immediate relation to the spaces, ruins, buildings, and landscapes that it studies. It mostly approaches spaces as they are registered and recorded in different media. In this respect, you must also consider the politics of this media, whether it is satellite images, other forms of digital topographic mapping, different scanners and remote sensing technologies, cameras, videos, and mobile-phone devices. If we analyze

A boy looking at his former home in the al-Salam quater in Gaza City, which was destroyed by the Israeli army during the attack on the Gaza Strip at the turn of 2008/09 (photo: Kai Wiedenhoefer).

a space as registered in media, then we must use but also think about this media, its presentation in different forums—courts or otherwise. I will try to give you several examples.

We have done much analysis based on activist video footage—what we call "image-to-space analysis." This project, like most other complex media and technology-driven projects we undertake, we did with Situ Studio, a New York–based architectural practice. One of the cases we have researched together was based on multiple and simultaneous video documentations of the April 17, 2009, killing of Bassem Abu Rahma in Bil'in during a demonstration against the Wall. He was hit with a gas canister shot directly at him through the barrier, which is a system of fences in this area. We started by synching multiple videos together, then these with satellite images, and reconstructed from them a dynamic 3D model. There were three videos that show Abu Rahma from different perspectives, the location of the Wall, and the soldiers who shot him. With Situ, we have traced the movement of each camera on a computer terrain model. It is a dynamic process because all the people involved—the camera people, the soldiers, and Abu Rahma himself—constantly move. From this, we managed to identify the place and angle from which he was shot. The investigation was widely reported and opened a legal process against the soldier. It is a little something within a situation of almost complete impossibilities.

Now we try to apply what we learned from this and apply it to more complex scenarios, conducting image-to-space analysis of recent incidents in Syria and Egypt similarly recorded on multiple cameras from different angles. When an activist holds a camera, she or he "Hoovers" in a lot of spatial data that could be useful for spatial scene reconstruction. When you have more than one camera in a scene and both record similar things, it is easier to reconstruct a scene in 3D.

Our research also includes the work of a group of postgraduate students at the Centre for Research Architecture at Goldsmiths. They explore other incidents and the legal, spatial, and conceptual problems associated with them. In all these cases, space is a media product. Charles Heller and Lorenzo Pezzani from our group have undertaken an analysis for a petition that should ultimately be presented at the Strasbourg European Court for Human Rights. It is a case against nonintervention on the high seas, basically when vessels of European states ignore migrants in peril in the Mediterranean sea. The project seeks to turn the European surveillance of the Mediterranean against itself. If the states of the southern littoral, such as France and Italy, can monitor almost everything that happens in the sea, they are obligated to intervene when SOS calls are made. Situ Studio helped again in mapping out the changing "architecture" of the sea in relation to the path approximated by the coordinates from which SOS calls were made by a satellite phone in a particular migrant boat. They also were able to map the paths of European vessels by looking at different image sources, such as satellite images and remote sensing, as well as boat itineraries, and also from images of boats in the phone cameras of migrants themselves.

YM: While important, numbers in and of themselves do not tell the kind of forensic stories that you are interested in putting forward in legal terms. Presented in sheerly quantitative terms, such data tell us nothing about the forms, strategies, and techniques of the destruction. In a recent lecture, you made the same observation about analyses of the Battle of Jenin [2002], in which there was much emphasis placed on the number of houses destroyed while ignoring the strategic design evident in the footprint of the Israeli Defense Forces: to clear a pathway for tanks, to break up spaces of resistance.

EW: At the end of an attack, such as that of Jenin, you are left with survivors' testimonies and material ruins, and you need to build a story. For this, you need to understand the logic of military maneuvers—the logic of urban warfare as a form of urban design. Militaries often believe that to win over the city, they have to change the logic by which the city operates. Battle spaces are messy, but there are logics and patterns in them. In Jenin, the Israeli military needed to get the tanks into the center of the town. They mobilized bulldozers from all directions to cut roads through the city. It is one thing to say that four hundred out of two thousand buildings were destroyed in this process, but it is another to understand how and why you see patterns within this destruction.

YM: So even as they do not proceed seamlessly, these techniques of destruction become a kind of de facto urban planning in the manner of Haussmann in nineteenth-century Paris?

EW: Yes. Consider also the reconstruction process of Jenin, led by Red Crescent donations from the United Arab Emirates. It has in effect continued the logic of the paths cut by the IDF during the battle, widening the roads there.

MM: You've called this the "decamping" of refugees, a technique for breaking up or at least rationalizing the space of the camps.

EW: Yes, because the idea on the part of the IDF is that the camp is not simply the physical location of resistance, but also the "breeding ground" for insurgents—that is, the conditions there create resistance. Undoing these conditions is one of the aims of the destruction and of the reconstruction, which are often continuous. This is the "war on refugees"—a kind of violence that seeks not to kill all the refugees, necessarily, but to undo "refugeeness" as a political category—and it is undertaken by different states—not only Israel, but at different periods also Jordan, Egypt, and Lebanon.

Those destroying the camps can take advantage of the fact that these spaces are financed and somewhat governed by international institutions and donors—they can couple their technologies of destruction with an anticipated humanitarian "upgrade" of the camps by such institutions in the aftermath of battle.

MM: Though the Israeli public is not being exposed to the same kind of physical violence, I wonder if you could say that they are also test subjects of sorts. In other words, how far can the IDF push the parameters of what they can do to a population before they cross the threshold of accountability and liability, whether in the judgment of the Israeli polity, of the Israeli courts, or of the international media?

EW: By operating constantly on the margin of the law, "creatively" reinterpreting it, putting pressure on established norms, Israeli military lawyers have been able to push the thresholds you mentioned. It also seems as if the creative interpretation of the law has shifted from the left to the right. Critical legal studies was a post-structuralist development in the theory of law that insisted on the indeterminate, contingent, and elastic nature of the law. This was done in the search for a certain liberating potential in this elasticity, but some of these principles are now used by state agents as they look for untapped potential in the laws of war. Michael Sfrad, who is one of the most prominent human rights lawyers, called Israeli military lawyers "anarchists against the law."

MM: I have a question in response to what you are saying about the human rights groups and the territorial proximity of the court to the scene of the abuses. This is a basic point, but it seems that in having the highest court of appeal being run by Israelis, even those judges and lawyers who are committed to human rights as an abstract principle are still operating within the framework of Israeli sovereignty and Israeli law. This is distinct from the more familiar scenario in which human rights grievances are taken to the court of another country or to an international court that would presumably not have a bias built into it in favor of the state that is being accused of abuses. A lot of NGO work in the Global North entails advocating for people who are miles away and making claims in forums that are not under the jurisdiction of the offending state. Of course, the situation differs from case to case in contemporary human rights work across the world, but this seems to be an extreme situation of the court being embedded within the social and political sphere in which the abuses are taking place.

EW: Yes, universal jurisdiction is only seldom exercised. It has led to some Israeli generals and politicians not disembarking from flights to London and Spain, but not to trials. Moreover, in Israel's internal exercise of international human rights law, the proximity you mentioned means that you often meet the same people in different roles. First someone may be an officer in the army, then become a human rights lawyer, and then go into the army again on reserve duty. Sometimes people working for humanitarian organizations become humanitarian officers for the army. Civilian lawyers serve in the military courts. Some of the people who designed the Israeli military's "humanitarian policy" were former Israeli humanitarians working with the UN. If the Wall becomes an international border, it will be the first ever to have been designed together with human rights experts.

MM: I was struck by the actual inroads made by NGOs, who clearly have their own agendas and interests. How is it that Israel allows this, because by doing so, they are opening up the playing field for other actors to come in that are not fully under their control. Does it become about money, about their image on the international scene, about their embrace of human rights norms?

EW: It depends how cynical you want to be. In a press conference, an NGO person asked an IDF general, "What would happen if we all just pulled out?" And the general replied, "Then there'd be total chaos. We would not be able to govern without you." So the prospect of ungovernable chaos is a potentially powerful political option. But NGOs are drawn into generating order and sometimes inadvertently into participating in governing.

YM: To be clear, acknowledging all of these double binds and complicities does not mean taking simply a cynical approach to human rights; it is the very condition of the work.

EW: There is a problem that is structural, and we acknowledge that. Between complete refusal and tactical embrace, the difficulty of the dilemma faced by human rights people and humanitarians is equally in practicing and in avoiding it. However, the question is not about dismissing the entire field and principle of human rights, but involves asking frankly in a manner of autocritique how such a contradiction could be translated into more productive political practice.

MM: This brings to mind the case of Mohammed Dahla—the human rights lawyer who petitioned in the first case against the Wall in the Israeli High Court of Justice—whom you mentioned in a recent lecture.

EW: Yes, he was the first one to conduct a trial on behalf of villagers—those of Beit Sureik, near Jerusalem, when the Wall encroached on their lands. And he won the case in the sense of forcing the state to move the Wall closer to the Green Line so that its path better reflects the principle of proportionality between human rights violations and security issues. The problem was that the trial also meant that the path of the Wall now became the result of a legal process.

I was interested in these trials of the wall because they were not trials of people—designers or builders—but trials of a thing, meant to regulate the behavioral properties of the Wall. When a model of the Wall was called as evidence into court—and it was the first such time that a model was produced and used there—the judges had to step down to approach it, calling the lawyers from both parties to join them. There was a disruption, because the physical presence of the model disturbed the usual structure and protocols, and there was an unordered conversation. It was the "object quality" of the model, its function as evidence, that changed the choreography of the legal process and the language in which it was discussed.

When the judge asked Dahla why he had described alternative "lesser evil" routes, he answered that it was not in order to propose them, but to render illegal the line that the state actually had built by showing that there is a less drastic way to achieve a similar security objective. Furthermore, the line he had proposed crossed the Green Line into Israeli territory, as much as to say: "If you want to build a wall, build it in your own land," but this was also a way to make sure that the line he proposed could not be fully adopted by the state in practice.

Simultaneously with this trial in the Israeli High Court, Dahla helped conduct another in the International Court of Justice in The Hague. It so happened that he had to argue against the legality of the entire Wall in The Hague at the same time that he had to argue against the details of its execution in Jerusalem . . . a paradox—right? This contradiction could be explained by the fact that he operated simultaneously from inside and outside Israeli law. In many ways, his "win" in Jerusalem might have been a Pyrrhic victory, because from that moment on, in a weird process of participation in which the victims design their own prison, human rights lawyers started to design the Wall with the military.

YM: So this approach interrogates and even displaces the very parameters of the discussion from within.

EW: Dahla is also a lawyer for Balad, the Arab party in Israel, which stands for a civic, rather than a Jewish state. Lawyers working inside the state constantly face the dilemma of having to use Israeli law, on the one hand, and to protest the injustice that exists within it, on the other. Many lawyers explain their selection of cases on the ground that they constitute precedent-setting legal challenges that expose paradoxes between the state's democratic pretence and its colonial realities. But this is of course a double-edged sword, especially when the justice system has been so fully taken to be a part of the political conflict. From time to time, Israeli lawyers

Parties assemble around the model, 2008 (illustrations: Christine Cornell and Eyal Weizman).

consider alternative forms of action to that of petitioning the High Court: connecting local legal struggles to international legal action and boycotting local courts. These alternatives not yet been enacted consistently, because frankly, the sector of human rights has its own inertias, and this is also tied to the way they are financed. There has not yet been a lawyer of the stature of Jacques Vergès here—somebody who has managed to enact the "rupture strategy" in turning the law against itself or using it politically in an effective way.[5] The rupture is also of course an aesthetic moment when things that were kept out of the court or out of public visibility all of a sudden become visible. Here is another dimension of forensics. Forensics is of course not only about the science of investigation, but about the performative dimension of presentation—about the theatrics and gesture of expertise and the use of technology, about what we can call "forensic aesthetics."

MM: How would you characterize this other register? I wonder if Jacques Rancière's notion of the distribution of the senses is pertinent here—a shift in perception that destabilizes or multiplies the ossified frames of the discussion. You've said that you don't necessarily go to court and simply or immediately challenge international humanitarian law, for instance, because you still need it as a point of reference. But there is still the imperative to question both the norms that would authorize a moderating technique such as the warning and the justification for bombarding the city in the first place.

EW: The court is not only a mechanism to debate the terms under discussion, and using its language does more than affirm it. It is also a platform and a theatre in which one makes issues visible, which is always, as you mentioned, a political task. Architecture is a good frame for doing this because buildings, cities, and their representations can communicate things in different ways than human witnesses.

This is also true of forensics in general. If the political is the rearrangement of the sensible, the fact that the testimony of things, nonhuman witnesses of all sorts, enters the court in different forms reconfigures the nature of what testimony means in the first place. But this "speech of things" is not without its dangers—not only the dangers of complicity that we discussed, but those when a scientific process supersedes and replaces the human voice.

YM: What you said before about architectural proposals as future-oriented fictions also sounds very Rancièreian, as when he writes that fictions involve "the introduction of a visible field of experience, which then modifies the regime of the visible. It is not opposed to reality; it splits reality and reconfigures it as its double."[6] This brings to mind some of the experimental design projects you've been working on with Sandi Hilal and Alessandro Petti under the rubric of "decolonizing architecture."

EW: Maybe it is more interesting to call these "experiments in architectural fiction." The projection of future scenarios—as possible fictions—can sometimes activate a latent political dimension. In other words, using architectural provocations, you can put dormant situations in motion and provoke systems to enact and reveal their logic. The provocation that architectural design can achieve produces the very knowledge upon which it seeks to comment. This can actually invert the relation between research and practice. While previously we thought that research is a prerequisite of practice and that you need to know in order to act, this realization reverses this logic: you also intervene as a form of research. This is an "incitatory" action, a research that produces its own subject. It is a kind of an epistemological attack that I think can capture the nature of how we see practice—artistic, architectural, and cultural—as the production of knowledge today.

NOTES

1. Raja Shehadeh, *Palestinian Walks: Forays into a Vanishing Landscape* (New York: Scribner, 2008).
2. Yehezkel Lein, in collaboration with Eyal Weizman, *Land Grab: Israel's Settlement Policy in the West Bank*, ed. Yael Stein, trans. Shaul Vardi and Zvi Shulman (May 2002), http://www.btselem.org/download/200205_land_grab_eng.pdf.
3. Edward W. Said, "Palestinians under Siege," in Roane Carey (ed.), *The New Intifada: Resisting Israel's Apartheid* (London: Verso, 2001), p. 33.
4. See United Nations General Assembly Human Rights Council, "Human Rights in Palestine and Other Occupied Arab Territories: Report of the United Nations Fact-Finding Mission on the Gaza Conflict," A/HRC/12/48, September 25, 2009, http://www2.ohchr.org/english/bodies/hrcouncil/docs/12session/A-HRC-12-48.pdf.
5. French defense lawyer Jacques Vergès is best known for employing the "rupture strategy" or "rupture defense," in which the defense attorney accuses the prosecution of the same offenses as those with which the defendant is charged, most notably crimes against humanity.
6. Jacques Rancière, *Dis-agreement: Politics and Philosophy*, trans. Julie Rose (Minneapolis: University of Minnesota Press, 1999), p. 99.

P’sagot, DAAR, Situ Studio, 2008.

The Morning After: Profaning Colonial Architecture

Alessandro Petti, Sandi Hilal, and Eyal Weizman

In 2007, after a few years of engaging in spatial research and theory with the conflict over Palestine as our main site of investigation, we decided to shift the mode of our engagement and to establish an architectural collective based on a studio/residency program in Beit Sahour, Bethlehem. The studio/residency that we call DAAR—Decolonizing Architecture Art Residency—seeks to use spatial practice as a form of political intervention and narration. It is based on a network of local affiliations and the historical archives that we have gathered in our previous work and that we keep on assembling. The residency program has already brought together groups of leading international practitioners—architects, artists, activists, urbanists, filmmakers, and curators—to work collectively within the framework we have set up.

Our practice has had to engage continuously with a complex set of architectural problems centered on one of the most difficult dilemmas of political practice for architects: how to propose and build new structures, and yet to think, write, and act critically about the built environment in a situation in which the political force fields, as complex as they may be, are so dramatically skewed. Is intervention at all possible? How could spatial practice within the here and now of the conflict over Palestine negotiate the existence of institutions and of their legal and spatial realities? How can we find an "autonomy of practice" that is both critical and transformative?

We started by experimenting with a series of interventions that attempted to give new contents, meaning, and agency to the term "decolonization." We suggested revisiting this largely discredited term in order to maintain a distance from the current political language of a "solution" to the Palestinian conflict and its respective borders. The one-state, two-state, and now three-state solutions seem equally entrapped in their respective "top-down" expert perspective, each with its own self-referential logic. Decolonization, on the contrary, seeks to unleash a process of open-ended transformation toward the goals of equality and justice. It looks for and finds cracks where the potential for the transformation and reuse of the existing dominant structures—architectural, infrastructural, and legal, could be found. It is a sometimes confrontational, at other times cunning approach to the reality of occupation and dispossession.

Historical processes of decolonization often have reused the buildings and infrastructure left behind in the same way for which they were designed, a way that left the colonial territorial hierarchies intact. In this sense, past processes of decolonization never truly have done away with the power of colonial domination. The effect of profanation, a concept analogous to decolonization that Giorgio Agamben has proposed in relation to the domain of the sacred, is "not simply to restore something like a natural use," but he also points out that "to profane means not simply to abolish and erase separations but to learn to put them to a new use."[1] Decolonization is a counter apparatus that seeks to restore to common use, to fantasy and play, what the colonial order had separated and divided. The goal of decolonization is the construction of counterapparatuses that find new uses for the abandoned structures of domination. These uses are sometimes pragmatic and at other times ironic or provocative challenges. As such, "decolonization" is never achieved, but is an ongoing practice of deactivation and reorientation understood both in its presentness and in its endlessness.

The issues we are dealing with led us to assume that a viable approach is to be found not in the professional language of architecture and planning, or not only there, but in inaugurating a collaborative arena of speculation that incorporates varied cultural and political perspectives from a multiplicity of individuals and organizations. We concluded that an open and collaborative architectural residency program thus had to replace established modes of architectural production.

In what follows, we will elaborate on several key concepts informing the overall program of DAAR. We will then present several specific case studies that investigate and probe the political, legal, and social force fields through a series of architectural interventions. By combining discourse, spatial intervention, education, collective learning, public meetings, and legal challenges, the attempt is to open up the discipline and praxis of "architecture"—understood as the production of rarefied buildings and urban structures—into a shifting network of spatial practices that includes various other forms of intervention.

DAAR engages a less-than-ideal world. It does not articulate a utopia of ultimate satisfaction. Its starting point is not a resolution of the conflict over Palestine and the just fulfillment of all Palestinian claims; also, the project does not offer a solution and should not be thought of in terms of one. Rather, it mobilizes architecture as a tactical tool within the unfolding struggle for Palestine. It seeks to employ tactical physical interventions to open a possible horizon for further transformations.

Whatever trajectory the conflict over Palestine takes, the possibility of further partial—or complete—evacuation of Israeli colonies and military bases must be considered. Zones of Palestine that have been or will be liberated from direct Israeli presence provide a crucial laboratory to study the multiple ways in which we could imagine the reuse, reinhabitation, or recycling of the architecture of Israel's occupation at the moment this architecture is unplugged from the military/political power that charged it.

DESTRUCTION, REUSE, SUBVERSION

The handing over of colonial buildings and infrastructure is always deeply problematic, for it is torn between two contradictory desires: destruction and reuse. The popular impulse for destruction seeks to articulate "liberation" spatially from an architecture understood as a political straitjacket, an instrument of domination and control. If architecture is a weapon in a military arsenal that implements the power relations of colonialist ideologies, then architecture must burn.

The impulse of destruction seeks to turn time backward, reverse development into a virgin nature, a tabula rasa on which a set of new beginnings might be articulated. However, time and its processes of transformation can never be simply reversed: rather than the desired Romantic ruralization of developed areas, destruction generates desolation and environmental damage that may last for decades. In 2005, Israel evacuated the Gaza settlements and destroyed three thousand homes, creating not the promised tabula rasa for a new beginning, but rather a million and a half tons of toxic rubble that poisoned the ground and the water. The decontamination process has been greatly impeded by the complete closure of the Gaza Strip, which is the new form that Israel's occupation has taken.

The other impulse, reuse, seeks to impose political continuity and order under a new system of control. It is thus not surprising that postcolonial governments tended to reuse the infrastructure set up by colonial regimes for their own emergent practical needs of administration. The evacuated infrastructure and built structure were often also seen as the legacy of "modernization" and as an economic and organizational resource. A strong temptation present throughout the histories of decolonization was thus to reuse infrastructure and built structure in the very same way they were used under colonial regimes. Such repossession tended to reproduce some of the colonial power relations in space: colonial villas were inhabited by new financial elites and palaces by political ones, while the evacuated military and police installations of colonial armies, as well as their prisons, were reused by the governments that replaced them.

Reusing Israeli residential and military areas would, similarly, establish a sense of continuity, rather than of rupture and change. In the context of present-day Palestine, reusing the evacuated structures of Israel's domination in the same way as the occupiers did—the settlements as Palestinian suburbs and the military bases for Palestine security needs—would mean reproducing their inherent alienation and violence. The settlement's system of fences and surveillance technologies would thus enable their seamless transformation into gated communities for the Palestinian elite.

There is, however, a third option: subversion of the originally intended use, repurposing it for other ends. We know that evacuated colonial architecture doesn't necessarily reproduce the functions for which it was designed. There are examples of other uses, both planned and spontaneous, that have invaded the built environment of evacuated colonial architecture, subverted its programs, and liberated its potential.

Even the most horrifying structures of domination can yield themselves to new forms of life. Believing in the potential of existing forces to shape reality, we started our investigation with the most complex option of the three, which speculates on the use of colonial architecture for purposes other than those they were designed to perform. For this reason, the project seeks to spatialize a set of possible collective functions in the abandoned military structures and the evacuated houses of the colonists. What new institutions and activities can model the evacuated space, and what physical transformations do these spaces require? The guiding principle is not to eliminate the power of the occupation's built spaces, but rather to reorient their destructive potential to other aims. We believe that if the geography of occupation is to be liberated, its potential must be turned against itself.

Given the scale of Israeli construction in Palestine and the need for housing, all three approaches may need to be applied and simultaneously coexist.[2] Some areas of settlements will be destroyed, some reused, and the original uses of others subverted. Because the reuse of the colonial architecture is a general cultural/political issue, we do not seek to present a single, unified architectural solution, but rather "fragments of possibility."

Thus, rather than a single unified proposal of urban planning covering the entirety of Palestine, DAAR has presented a series of detailed transformations of different architectural sites. There are hundreds of thousands of Israeli-built structures in the West Bank, but because the number of typologies in settlements and military bases are limited—variations on the single-family dwelling in settlements and concrete prefabricated barracks on military bases—these fragments of possibility constitute a semigeneric approach that could be modified to be applied in other evacuated areas.

These projects have sought to determine to what extent the evacuated structures are adaptable to accommodate new uses and will demonstrate the various ways in which they can be transformed. These investigations were based upon a series of meetings with the stakeholders in this process, including representatives of various organizations and individuals, the local community, members of various NGOs, representatives of government and municipal bodies and academic and cultural institutions, local residents, and representatives of resident associations. Their genuine participation is the crucial factor and the only element that could guarantee the implementation of the actions proposed by these projects.[3]

Two project sites were chosen as two different prototypes of decolonization: the colony of P'sagot, which is still inhabited by colonists, and the former Israeli military base of Oush Grab, which was evacuated in 2006. The proposals that follow exemplify a variety of different approaches to the decolonialized subversion of existing structures.

CASE STUDY NORTH: THE COLONY OF P'SAGOT/JABEL TAWIL IN THE RAMALLAH REGION

Located on the hill of Jabel Tawil, 900 meters above sea level, the colony of P'sagot visually dominates the entire Palestinian area. Until the occupation, it was used as an open space for recreation. The hills of Jerusalem and Ramallah were popular with families from the Gulf, especially Kuwaitis, who traveled there to escape the summer heat (the people of Ramallah still call the hill "the Kuwaiti hill"). In 1964, the municipality of Al Quds (Jerusalem) bought the land and prepared a plan for its development into a tourist resort. The work started in early 1967 with the construction of an access road. The work was interrupted by the Israeli occupation. In July 1981, on the initiative of the Likud Party, the colony of P'sagot was inaugurated as "compensation" to right-wing Israelis for the evacuation of the Sinai Peninsula. The area designated for tourist accommodation was the first to be occupied by settler housing. The first houses set on the hill of Jabel Tawil were prefabricated structures wheeled over from Yamit, a settlement in the north of the Sinai. P'sagot is at present a religious settlement inhabited by seventeen hundred people, mainly American Jews and a minority of recent Russian and French immigrants.

UNGROUNDING: URBANISM OF THE FIRST TEN CENTIMETERS

Settlements are suburban when put in relation to the Jewish geography in the Occupied Territories—they are fenced bedroom communities fed by a growing matrix of roads and other infrastructure—but they could be understood as potentially urban when put in relation to the Palestinian cities beside which they were built. The surface of the suburb is marked by its various uses. It is inscribed extensively with the signs of the petty-bourgeois lifestyle that maintains it: an excess of roads and parking lots, private gardens, fences, sidewalks, and tropical plants. The pattern of streets in the settlements/suburbs is a folded linear structure strung by roads and sidewalks. By designating drive/walk/no-walk areas, channeling movement, and designating the different degrees of private and public space, the first ten centimeters of the urban ground surface embody most of its operational logic and also its ideology.

This surface is the primary site of our intervention. Under the category of "ungrounding," we have suggested a radical transformation of the first ten centimeters of ground. It is the logic of the surface that we seek to deactivate in order to dismantle the structures that define the internal organization of the suburb and transform its private, public, and communal functions.[4] Ungrounding is achieved by the dismantling of the existent surface—roads, sidewalks, private gardens—and replacing them with a new surface layer. The pervasive system of concentric roads and spaces for parking will be eroded, removed, or buried under new surface layers. The barriers and fences that demarcate the edges of the private lots of the single-family homes will be removed as the ground gets abstracted and "collectivized." Built structure will be suspended like pavilions on a single, unified new surface. The regrounding of the surface is a central part of a strategy that seeks to reconfigure a new figure-ground relation. The possible connection between the individual buildings will be reconceived. Connection would be undertaken across a field in which movement is not prescribed by the linear folds of the roads and the sidewalks.

Could controlled material decay become a process of place making? How can destruction become a design process that may lead to new uses? In the case of ungrounding, it is clear that the destruction of the surface by actively uprooting its elements and also by accelerating the decay of other surface elements would create the ground from which new life could emerge.

UNHOMING

The molecular level of the occupation is the single-family house on a small plot of land. Investigating ways to transform this repetitive semigeneric structure may open up ways to transform the entire geography of occupation. What are its limits of transformability? Can a single-family home become the nucleus of new types of public institutions? Which structural parts should be retained, and what are the possible ways of connecting together groups of houses? The problem is also how to transform a series of small-scale single-family houses into unified clusters of communal space to accommodate larger functions such as halls and classrooms, laboratories for a research institute, clinics, and offices.

The problem of "unhoming" is not only a technical question of transformation. A lingering question throughout the project has been how to inhabit the home of one's enemy. Within the multiple cultures that inhabited Palestine throughout the decades, rarely has one ever been the "first" or "original" occupier, but rather each is always a subsequent inhabitant. To inhabit the land is always to inhabit it in relation either to one's present-day enemies or to an imagined or real ancient civilization. This is a condition that turns the habitation of old cities, archaeological sites, battlegrounds, and destroyed villages into culturally complex acts of "cohabitation."

FOLDED VISION

We believe that any act of decolonization must include interventions in the field of vision. The settlements are organized as optical devices on a suburban scale. Their pattern of streets as concentric rings around the hilltop, the placement of each house, and the space between the houses and the organization of windows and rooms follow design principles that seek to maximize the power of vision with both ideological and strategic aims in mind.

The pastoral view out of home windows reinforces a sense of national belonging when it reads traces of Palestinian daily lives—olive groves, stone terraces, livestock—as signifiers of an ancient holy landscape. The view is also strategic in overseeing tactical roadways and surveying the Palestinian cities and refugee camps. The visual affect of the settlements on Palestinians is in generating a constant sense of being seen. From Palestinian cities, one can hardly avoid seeing a settlement, and one is most often seen by one.

Because the organization of homes is directed toward the surrounding view, the main door into each settlement home is approached from the inner areas of the settlement. Entering the home, one moves into the living areas and the main window, which opens onto the landscape. But what happens if the people that should now be arriving at these houses are those formerly "composing the view"? What if the new user could now approach the house from the view? Our response is a small-scale intervention. We propose to change the direction of the front door to face not the inner areas of the settlement, but the Palestinian cities. Changing the direction from which one enters the house also alters the spatial syntax of its interior. This small-scale intervention is "cinematic" in the sense that it is an intervention in the framing of the conditions of vision and in directing ways of seeing. It reorganizes the field of the visible, a perspective folded onto itself.

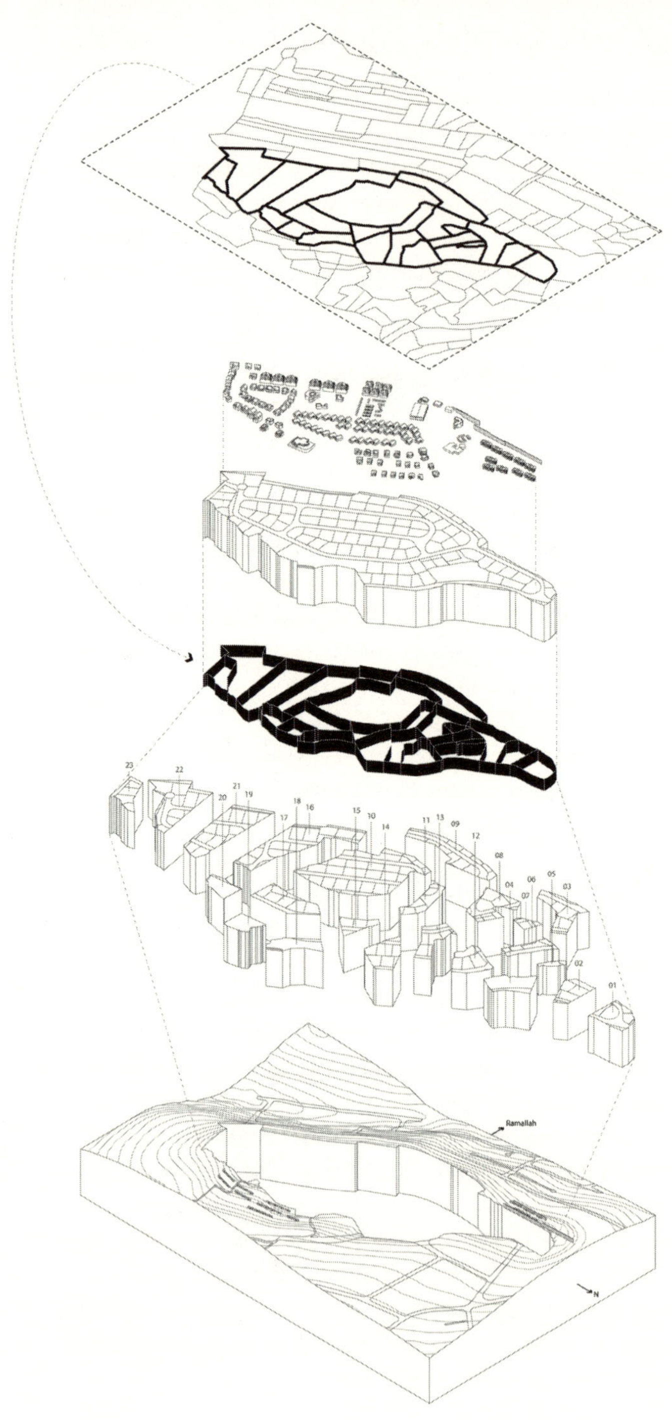

Deparcelization: the fabric of the settlement is partitioned by the boundary of fields from the period preceding the occupation.

DEPARCELIZATION

In the course of our analysis, we made use of both documentary and narrative sources to identify some of the landowners within the areas of the colonies. Jabel Tawil/P'sagot is at the gravitational center of various orbits of extraterritoriality: displaced communities, displaced individuals, migrations, and family connections. Our investigation traced some of the Palestinian landowners to the United States, Australia, Kuwait, Saudi Arabia, Iraq, and of course closer at hand in Palestine, sometimes fenced off a few meters away from their lands. Their private and family histories are the intertwined histories of Palestine and its displaced communities, forced out by the occupation and by economic and professional opportunities overseas. About half of the area occupied by the P'sagot colony belongs to private owners, with the other half registered as belonging to one of various kinds of collective lands. The fate of private lands should be decided by their owners. It is within the communal lands that we propose various types of collective uses.

We discovered a map dating to 1954 that shows the original parcelization of Jabel Tawil. We superimposed the 1954 plan onto the plan of the colony. The Palestinian demarcation lines cut arbitrary paths through the suburban fabric of the settlements, sometimes literally through the structures themselves, creating a new relationship between the houses and their parcels, between internal and external spaces, and between public and private spaces. Some of these odd lots are public lands. This archipelago of public lots forms the basis of our proposals.

CASE STUDY SOUTH: THE FORMER MILITARY BASE OUSH GRAB (THE CROW'S NEST)

In May 2006, the Israeli Army evacuated a military camp strategically located on the highest hill at the southern entrance to the Palestinian city of Beit Sahour, in the Bethlehem region. It was built as a military base by the British Mandatory Army during the Arab revolt (referred to by some as the very first intifada). After 1948, it became a military base for the Jordan Legion. After 1967, it became an Israeli military base. A menacing fortress, it overlooked the edge of the town. Most houses surrounding the camp were destroyed by tank shells and gunfire originating at the base. Floodlit during the night, with searchlights constantly scanning the area around it, the base was caught in an endless day.

The evacuation was itself a violent operation. At night, dozens of tanks rolled into the town, and in the morning, the base was found empty. Moments later, Palestinians entered the base and took away every element and material that could be recycled.[5] During the era of the Oslo Accords, an agreement was signed between the Palestinian municipality of Beit Sahour and the office of the Palestinian president,

Yassir Arafat, guaranteeing that in case of a possible Israeli evacuation, the base would not be used by the Palestinian police and be handed over to the management of the municipality as a public space. Upon the municipality gaining control of the site, a master plan designated a set of public functions, including a neighborhood with a hospital and a public park. A play area for children, a restaurant and an open garden for events have already been constructed on the slopes of the hill.

The most contentious part of the site is its summit. There, several concrete buildings formed the heart of the former camp. Surrounded by a giant earth mound running around the top rim of the hill, these buildings seem to inhabit the crater of a volcano. Although the summit is evacuated, it is still kept under the (remote) control of the Israeli military. Because it provides the most strategic views in the entire area, the military did not accept it being occupied by Palestinian eyes.

REVOLVING-DOOR OCCUPATIONS

After its evacuation, the summit and its buildings were at the centre of various contentious confrontations between Israeli settlers, the Israeli military, and Palestinian organizations. Our office has been directly engaged in this. In May 2008, protesting against President George W. Bush's visit to Israel and in anticipation of some "government concessions," settler groups sought to use the emptied buildings of the military base as the nucleus for a new settlement outpost. The topographical location of the base on the summit and its existing fortification would easily lend themselves, they thought, to their regimented and securitized way of life. The military declared the site a "closed military zone," but nearly every week settlers would come back to occupy the base, hold picnics there and conduct heritage tours and Torah lessons, and raise the Israeli flag. Israeli soldiers have been present to "protect" the settlers. Palestinian and international activists, including members of our office, also have occupied the site and have confronted the settlers. A set of competing graffiti written by one side and then obliterated by the other testifies to the revolving door nature of occupancy there. Our proposal for the reuse of this site thus became an intervention in the political struggle for this hilltop.

DESIGN BY DESTRUCTION

In the base of Oush Grab, the first stages of our architectural proposal have employed forms of destruction. Because of its revolving-door occupation, in which the danger of the place's appropriation by settlers always exists, it is important first to render the building less amenable to being used before allowing new functions to inhabit them. As a first stage of design, we have proposed to perforate the buildings of the military base by drilling holes in their walls (fig. 3). When the building is finally appropriated, these holes will transform the walls into screens.

Oush Grab, DAAR, Sara Pellegrini, 2008.

Another way to intervene within the base is to transform its landscape. The earth rampart raised around the buildings has been constantly shifting due to Palestinian contractors using the site as a dump for their unwanted rubble and other contractors taking some of the earth from the rampart as material for construction. Our intervention seeks to use the shifting nature of the rampart to reorganize the relationship between the buildings and the landscape. We will partially bury the buildings in the rubble of their own fortifications.

MIGRATION

Given the competing claims for Oush Grab, our intention was to accelerate the processes of destruction and disintegration. It was to be an architectural project of obsolescence in which the ghost town of the former military base would be returned to nature. In researching the site, we consulted with a number of local NGOs,[6] including, perhaps unexpectedly, the Palestine Wildlife Society, from whom we learned that the contested hilltop is a point of singularity within the natural environment.

More than 500 million birds on their way between northeastern Europe and East Africa navigate over the Syrian-African Crack—the Jordan Valley as it crosses Palestine—during the autumn and spring migrations. These large flocks of birds land on the high points and important grasslands. The former military base that overlooks Bethlehem is on a bottleneck of the migration navigation path in the Jerusalem Mountains.

Twice a year for a few weeks each autumn and spring, tens of thousands of these birds land on the hilltop of Oush Grab. Around them, a temporary microecology of small predators and other wildlife gathers. It is a breathtaking and terrifying scene.

Given the intense claims for the site, our intention is not to renovate and convert the base into another function, but rather to return it to nature. The buildings and the artificial landscape will stand at the center of a park in which nature will gradually take over the buildings.

Our proposed physical intervention is to accelerate this process of return to nature. As noted, the first stages of our architectural proposal involve perforating all external walls within the buildings on the summit with a series of equally spaced holes. In the next stage, our colleagues in the Palestine Wildlife Society expect that these holes will be inhabited by birds.

We also seek to transform the landscape. We intend to open up the fortified rampart enclosure to allow access and drainage. This transformation of the earth rampart will partially bury the buildings in the rubble of their own fortifications, reorganizing the relationship between the buildings and the landscape.

THE LAWLESS LINE

In addition to the strategies followed in these two case studies, events have provided the opportunity for an intervention of a different kind. In 1993, a series of secret talks held in Oslo between Israeli and Palestinian representatives inaugurated what was later referred to as the "Oslo Process." As is well known, this process defined three types of territories within the West Bank: Area A, under Palestinian control; Area B, under Israel military control and Palestinian civilian control; and Area C, under full Israeli control. When the process collapsed and the temporary organization of the Occupied Territories solidified into a permanent splintered geography of multiple prohibitions, a fourth area has suddenly been discovered. Existing between all others, it is the width of the lines separating them.

Less than a millimeter thick when drawn on the scale of 1:20,000, it measures more than five meters in real space. Our proposed project exploits the thickness of this line, following it along the edges of villages and towns, across fields, roads, fences, and terraces and through olive and fruit orchards, gardens, kindergartens, homes, public buildings, a football stadium, a mosque, and finally, a large castle recently built.

Within this line is a zone undefined by law, a legal limbo that pulls in like a vortex all the different forces, institutions, organizations, and people that operate within and around it. With Areas A, B, and C already claimed by Israel and the Palestinian Authority, the area within the thickness of this line is an extraterritorial territory, perhaps all that remains from Palestine, a thin, but powerful space for potential political transformations. Political spaces in Palestine are not defined by its legal zones, but operate as legal voids. Investigating the clash of geopolitical lines intersecting on the domestic space of a house and operating on the margin between architecture, cartography, and legal practice, we have sought to bring a court case that in effect calls for acknowledging the anarchic regime of political autonomy represented by this line. It is the extraterritorial dimension of these seam lines, small tears in the territorial system, that offers the possibility for tearing apart the entire system of division.

FORMS OF THE PRESENT RETURN TO THE COMMON

Territorially speaking, the common is different from both the public and the private domains. Both private and public lands involve relations between people and things regulated by the state. The state guarantees private property and maintains public property. By contrast, the common is a relation between people and things that is not mediated by the state.

Both private and public lands are territorial mechanisms for the governing of men and women. Sometimes this form of government operates by maintaining these distinctions and sometimes by blurring them. The endless privatization of the public space and the incessant intrusion of agents of the public into the private domain are both techniques of government control.

In Palestine, the idea of public land is particularly toxic.[7] Although prior to Zionist colonization there existed a wide multiplicity of collective lands and collective uses of land, agricultural, religious, nomadic, and so on, upon occupying the land and excluding its people, the Israeli state has reduced them all to one category—"state land"—and has seized control over it as the sovereign. This state land was once a public space, but only inasmuch as it was reserved to the only public that was acknowledged as legitimate—the Israeli Jews. The contours of public land became the blueprint for colonization. This form of sovereignty was willing to acknowledge only Palestinian individual rights and thus only private land. The state's mechanism of humanitarian balance could tolerate Palestinian presence only as individuals. In many cases, it simply took their land.

The main legal resource for this aspect of colonization was the Ottoman Land Law of 1858. This law was the result of an agrarian reform across the Ottoman Empire, which was sovereign in Palestine until 1917. It recognized a plot of land as *miri* (privately owned) if it had been continuously cultivated for at least ten consecutive years. If a landowner failed to farm the land for three consecutive years, the land changed its status to *makhlul*, land that the state could appropriate to itself or transfer to a private citizen. Farmers who did not want to pay tax for land that could not be used for cultivation therefore gave up ownership over uncultivated areas, even if these were only small patches of rocky ground that actually existed within their fields, which then in effect became islands of state land. The topographical folds, summits, slopes, irrigation basins, valleys, rifts, cracks, and streams of Palestine were no longer seen simply as mere topographical features, but as signifiers of a series of legal manipulations, generating a pattern of small, privately owned fields both within and enclosing an area of uncultivated "state land."

Today, as a result, a common exists in Palestine only in immaterial territorial form or in extraterritorial forms, scattered in a diasporic archipelago of camps. The cities and villages demolished in 1948 are now one example of a common space, and their mirror image, the camps, is another. After sixty years, the memory of a single house is now equally shared by hundreds of families. In the camp, the common is the shared history of displacement and the absence of private property.

In this respect, thinking the revolution that is "return"—the reinhabitation of Palestine by those displaced from it—means thinking a revolution in relation to property.[8] Seen in this way, the common is an action, rather than the designation of a kind of property or type of land. The return is the practice that attempts to return this land to common use.

The notion of return has defined the diasporic and extraterritorial nature of Palestinian politics and cultural life since the Nakba in 1947–48. Often articulated in the "suspended politics" of political theology, it has gradually been blurred in the futile limbo of negotiations: while the common that is a shared Palestine is under suspension, it is a common inasmuch as it is under suspension.

POSTSCRIPT: PRESENT RETURNS

Our projects dealing with the return extend the legalistic approach to the right of return with a projective strategy that aims to open the political imagination to different forms in which a return could take place. The return is today a political act that is continuously and incessantly practiced and that projects an image into an uncertain future. It connects to a varied set of practices that we would like to call "present returns," thus grounding them in present-day material realities. Present returns include a multiplicity of rites and practices. Thinking about returns necessitates the adoption of a stereoscopic vision that navigates the complex terrain between two places—the extraterritorial space of the refugee and the out-of-reach village of origin. The destroyed village and the destroyed camp are two interrelated sites in a terrain with a history of continuous destruction. But the destruction of the refugee camp does not simply mirror the destruction of the village. To destroy a camp is to destroy what is already destroyed—the destruction of destruction. Both the demolished villages and the refugee camps are extraterritorial spaces not fully integrated into the territories that surround them. The former is legally defined as absentee property and the latter as an area administered by the United Nations, a sphere of action carved out of state sovereignty. Refugee life is suspended between these two ungrounded sites, always double. A circular probe from both camp and village, our projects materially articulate the complex extraterritoriality stretched between these two sites.

Present returns also involve exploring ways in which the figure of the refugee and its associated spatial regime of dislocation reshape the political space of the present. It is between the sites of dislocation and of destruction that an architecture of the future could take place and shape. Exploring the forms of return of Palestinian refugees means also exploring ways in which the figure of the refugee and its associated spatial regime of dislocation both reshape the political space of the present and force us to image a new political space yet to come. It is in this space between the sites of dislocation and of destruction that a future extraterritorial polity could take shape.

NOTES

1. Giorgio Agamben, *Profanations*, trans. Jeff Fort (New York: Zone Books, 2007), pp. 85 and 87.
2. Although our proposals are based essentially on the third approach, we consider the possibility in some cases of also using the other two at the same time. Demolition, for example, will be necessary in cases in which colonies or military camps are constructed in particularly valuable landscape areas, just as simple reuse as residences could be proposed in areas where demand for housing is particularly urgent and in which colonial architecture is constructed on lands belonging to private Palestinians. In these cases, only the owners can decide on the future reuse of these structures.
3. We started our project by setting up a series of meetings with local NGOs—the Palestine Wildlife Society, the Women's Shelter, Save the Children, the Alternative Tourism Group, and the Alternative Information Center, among others—but also with local authorities, the University of Birzeit, local residents, and so on. Together, we developed conceptions regarding the various ways in which particular sites within the colonies and military bases could be designed. Whenever we presented and discussed our plans and models, the initial reaction of our discussants was a smile. In the beginning, we feared we were being ridiculed. Were our plans too far-fetched and outlandish in this environment of permanent impossibility? It is also true that

models are reduced worlds "under control" and that they often make people smile. But on the other hand, the smile we noticed may be the first moment of decolonization. We would like to interpret the smile as an opening up of the imagination to a different future. Decolonization starts when people regain their agency and articulate their right to plan their future.

4. Through our work in the Occupied Territories, we have started to realize that the project may form a possible laboratory for architectural actions whose reach may go beyond the local specificity of our immediate environment. It may also form the beginning of a way to think through the future of the suburban settlements, many of which are in dire crisis in other places worldwide. The ritual destruction, reuse, *redivivus*, or *dětournement* of the single-family house may suggest a possible repertoire of action for the larger transformation of other types of secluded suburban spaces.
5. The first moment of access to the colonies and to the military bases is a possible moment of transgression whose consequences are unpredictable. Although in the Gaza Strip it was the Israelis who demolished most of the buildings, those buildings left intact were mostly destroyed by the Palestinians. The morning after the military left, Palestinians destroyed the space and carried out as many remnants of building materials they could use and carry. This destruction is a spontaneous architectural moment of reappropriation, and as such, we believe that it should not be prevented or controlled. It is only after the indeterminate result of this moment of first encounter and within the possible rubble of its physical results that architectural construction may begin. This moment of first access questions the conception of architecture and urban planning. The acceptable precondition for planning is a situation of spatial and political certainty—a clear site demarcation, a schedule, a client, and a budget. The erratic nature of Israeli control and the unpredictable military and political developments on the ground render Palestine an environment of high uncertainty and indeterminacy. Planning in such conditions could not appeal to any tested professional methods.
6. The role that NGOs play in Palestinian society must be explained: Palestinian civil society was greatly strengthened during the intifada of 1987–1992. Local leaders organized resistance and a set of alternative services, such as schooling and medicine, for those denied access to them by the Israeli Army. The Palestinian Authority, whose leaders have largely come from abroad, attempted to centralize and regulate the network of self-governing institutions that developed throughout the intifada. The network of institutions locally formed during the first intifada was transformed into the infrastructural framework of contemporary NGOs in Palestine. The local leaders of the first intifada largely preferred to become directors of NGOs, rather than officials in the Palestinian Authority. Most former leaders of the leftist Popular Front are now directing leading NGOs. A good example is Mustafa Barghouthi and his health-care network. The West Bank has since been governed in parallel by the Palestinian Authority and by a series of local and international NGOs, both under the umbrella of ultimate Israeli sovereignty. In many cases, Palestinian "NGOcracy" (as the phenomenon came to be known) provided better-quality services—medical, educational, planning—than those of the Palestinian Authority, which was always "less than a government in less than a state," as the saying has gone. NGOcracy has its dangers, of course. Most NGOs, much like the Palestinian Authority, are internationally funded, and although donors are operating in support of Palestinians, they are in fact not accountable to the people of Palestine and often pursue the cultural and political agendas of the donor states. Philanthropy has thus become one of the main vehicles for Western countries to intervene in the politics and culture of Palestine. Bearing

these dangers in mind, the network of NGOs seems to us an important vehicle for developing new types of Palestinian public, social, and communal spaces, and some NGOs might be the first to occupy the evacuated and transformed spaces. We have noticed that the archives of these NGOs are also the "living archives" of Palestine. A combined archive of the hundreds of local NGOs, or access to them, would provide information about the environment, welfare, human rights, and politics throughout Palestine and thus could offer a diffused and multifocal alternative to state-centered information centers.

7. Public spaces and public institutions are generally managed by state and/or local authorities and are thus an important means by which government articulates itself. In Palestine, the long period of statelessness under colonialism has shifted the manner in which public space and the public in general functions. Until the beginning of the 1990s, Palestinian cities were directly managed by the Israeli military. Through the "Civil Administration," the military controlled planning and development permission and thus the central activities of the different municipalities. During this period, the Palestinian cities were transformed into dormitory towns with very little public space. Furthermore, the Civil Administration actively inhibited public institutions from developing. Private clubs, cinemas, schools, and universities were put under close scrutiny or forcibly shut. The military required any association of more than three persons to have a permit. But difficulty in establishing and maintaining public institutions persisted even after the Oslo Accords of 1993. The main reasons that impeded the creation of open public space in the Palestinian cities were the borders set up for Palestinian "self-administered areas." These borders where drawn tightly around the built-up area of the Palestinian cities and villages, leaving little potential land for new construction. The structure of land ownership within Palestinian cities meant that very little land was privately owned, and municipalities have had difficulty accessing lands. Most open spaces and new institutions were created by the many international organizations and NGOs.
8. The return of things to common use is of course the main condition for the general political tendency that in the last sixty-odd years was collected under the term "return" in relation to two inverse, but interdependent utopias—the Palestinian rights of return and the Jewish law of return.

FIGURE 1 Advertisement for a heritage preservation campaign, Prishtina, Kosovo, 2004 (photo: Andrew Herscher).

Political Activism in Post-Yugoslavia: Heritage, Identity, Agency

Andrew Herscher

"Preserve it. It's yours!" In Albanian, Serbian, and English, this command appeared on billboards throughout Prishtina, the capital city of Kosovo, in the summer of 2004 (fig. 1). These billboards usually advertised products such as cigarettes, jeans, beer, ice-cream novelties, and political candidates—the various goods of the neoliberal political economy whose institution constituted a major component of Kosovo's postwar reconstruction. Advertisements for these goods were designed to appeal to a postwar consumer of goods and services who was to replace a wartime consumer of history and myth and thereby secure a future of prosperity, or at least a future of shopping, in postconflict Kosovo. But this was also a consumer who had to be informed about what should *not* be consumed, about nonexchangeable possessions, about goods such as heritage, that were to be held in reserve, outside of Kosovo's newly globalized spaces of consumption.

The advertisements for Kosovo's preservation campaign depicted twelve examples of heritage, including the Roman-era Ulpiana archaeological excavations, the Byzantine-era Dečani and Gračanica Monasteries, the Ottoman-era Sinan Pasha Mosque, and the early twentieth-century Prizren League Building, birthplace of the modern Albanian nationalism. References to Serbs and Albanians, Christianity and Islam, high and vernacular culture, and antiquity and modernity each seemed to be carefully included and balanced with one another. The multiethnic branding of Kosovo's cultural heritage was unfolded in a tag line, also in Albanian, Serbian, and English, that accompanied these images: "Kosovo's cultural heritage is respected as the common patrimony of all of Kosovo's ethnic, religious and linguistic communities." These otherwise differentiated communities, that is, were supposed to have a singular identity, a cultural identity, an identity that was materialized in the forms of Kosovo's "cultural heritage." The billboard's dominant representation of this heritage was the extraterrestrial image of a Neolithic figurine, among the oldest products of human culture found in the territory that is now known as Kosovo. On the billboard, the figurine loomed over the other images of historically subsequent cultural products. Its size and position were easy to understand; as a pre-ethnic artifact, it was the only heritage object whose multiethnic credentials were impeccable or perhaps even believable.

This preservation campaign, sponsored by the Ministry of Culture, Youth, and Sports in what was at the time Kosovo's provisional government, was far more than a simple attempt to protect an objectively defined and preexisting "heritage." Rather, the campaign appropriated its objects as components of an official national culture, it deputized its subjects as that culture's custodians, and it posed the state as the space of that culture, a culture at once deethnicized and historicized. The campaign, that is, involved profoundly political performances of authority, community, identity, and, most importantly, of cultural heritage itself, which was rendered in this campaign as a site of politically compatible difference.

This rendering accurately mediated the relevant European and international conventions on heritage. At the same time, though, such a rendering had a particular salience in Kosovo, whose politics, whether before, during, or after the 1998–1999 war, revolved around the meanings, functions, and effects of ethnic, religious, and national difference. In this context, the preservation campaign recast the property of despised ethnic others as the property of all Kosovars of all ethnicities. In so doing, the campaign appealed to a subject who did not exist in Kosovo, a subjective counterpart to the cultural objects defined in European and international cultural-heritage policy. In Kosovo, this was a subject whose cultural status transcended, even contradicted, other identities—social, political and also cultural—that resulted from other identifications and that were almost all circumscribed by ethnicity. The preservation campaign, then, was an attempt by a weak postconflict state (in fact, a protostate) to position difference in cultural, rather than political terms, terms that this state could manage, rather than ones that would call it into question.

The billboards of the preservation campaign accompanied another series of signs dealing with heritage in Kosovo's visual landscape: plaques that were placed on thirty-five Serbian Orthodox churches and monasteries—or their remains—edifices that were damaged during riots a few months previously, in March 2004. These riots were responsible for initiating the preservation campaign, yet the plaques on damaged buildings displayed not an advertisement, but an ordinance, also in Albanian, Serbian, and English versions:

> This building/site is protected by law. Any act of vandalism and looting will be considered as a criminal offense of the utmost gravity. The police forces of Kosovo and KFOR will take necessary actions, including the use of force, to stop such crimes. All acts of destruction and looting will be punished in accordance with the Kosovo Criminal Law.[1]

What the preservation campaign solicited—the protection of cultural heritage—was here proclaimed as enforced. The preservation campaign, then, was an attempt not only to domesticate ethnic difference, but to naturalize this domestication as the will of the community. The ministry's campaign attempted to move heritage preservation from the domain of government to that of the governed. In the words of Jacques Rancière, the state "purport[ed] to act as the self of the community, to turn the techniques of governing into natural laws of the social order."[2] The conjunction of preservation advertisements and preservation ordinances thus registers the bifurcated status of nongovernmental agency with regard to governmental authority. This agency is at once the object of authority and potentially disruptive of it and so must be both solicited and managed. Indeed, even the directives of the preservation campaign itself—to tell Kosovo's public what "their" heritage is, what it means, and what to do with it—express the fraught relationship between heritage, agency, and collective identity, a relationship that the campaign, by contrast, poses as natural and given.

The cultural identity to which the preservation campaign referred was actually an artifact of a solicited identification. The object of this identification was "cultural heritage"; the preservation campaign solicited its addressees to recognize themselves in the injunction to preserve this heritage as their patrimony. This sort of solicited identification, famously termed "interpellation" by Louis Althusser, addressed a multiethnic collective subject appropriate to the multiethnic state that the United Nations, the European Union, and their allies were attempting to institute in Kosovo.[3] This multiethnic collectivity, that is, did not precede the campaign, but was invoked by it.

Yet as post-Althusserian theorists have observed, there are inherent oppositions to the process of interpellation. In Michel Pêcheux's words, analysis of interpellation must account for "the multitude of heterogeneous resistances and revolts which smolder beneath dominant ideology, threatening it constantly."[4] These resistances sponsor multiple subject positions in any given ideological regime.[5] Thus, the interpellation of an imagined multiethnic community around a common cultural heritage has necessarily opened up a variety of responses to that heritage, in Kosovo as in other post-Yugoslav contexts. Accepting the discourse of the state, some individual and collective subjects have performed identifications with cultural objects; these performances have both reproduced and inflected state-defined concepts and meanings of cultural heritage. As Pêcheux has described, however, interpellations have also yielded what he termed "counter-identifications" and "disidentifications," each a mode of identification that diverges from the "respect" for heritage sought by the state.

Pêcheux's reformulation of the process of identification in effect evacuates the category of ideology and opens onto what Foucault calls "subjectivization": the processes by which individuals become objects of power and fit within specified social positions.[6] The space vacated by ideology comes then to be filled and reconfigured by institutions, discourses, and practices—the various formations of governmentality. The "resistances" and "revolts" that compromise ideology establish interpellation as a fraught, contested interface between the institutions of government and the governed. Interpellation, in Pêcheux's sense, thus becomes enmeshed in what Foucault terms the "strategic reversibility" of power relations—the ways in which practices of governing can be reformulated as objects of resistance or "counter-politics" on the part of the governed.[7]

Rancière's discussion of subjectivization brings the post-Althusserian discourse on interpellation and the Foucauldian discourse on governmentality into dialogue:

> Political subjectivization ... is never the simple assertion of an identity; it is always, at the same time, the denial of an identity given by an other, given by the ruling order of policy. Policy is about "right" names, names that pin people down to their place and work. Politics is about "wrong" names—misnomers that articulate a gap and connect with a wrong. ... The place of a political subject is an interval or gap: being together to the extent that we are *in-between*—between names, identities, cultures and so on.[8]

The nongovernmental politics of cultural heritage can be understood as the articulation of such an interval or gap between the governance of this heritage and the appropriation of heritage, on the part of the governed, as a mnemonic technology, political instrument, or site of public appearance. A consideration of this politics introduces the diverse nongovernmental actors, agencies, and practices that have mobilized cultural heritage in the postwar contexts of the post-Yugoslav states and brought heritage to bear on the memorialization of war and on postwar reconstruction, reconciliation, and peace building. Attention to these mobilizations qualifies the utilization of cultural heritage as a medium of consensual postwar nation building—a utilization whose address to stable, bounded, and homogenous "ethnic communities" in the interest of postconflict reconciliation has served to reify the very political actors in whose names conflicts were carried out in the first place. This attention also poses cultural heritage not simply as a set of artifacts whose social life is defined by national, transnational, and international laws and conventions, but as a figure by means of which political claims are articulated, negotiated, and contested.

In nongovernmental politics, cultural heritage has been transformed from a set of artifacts to preserve into instruments by means of which to enter into and participate in political discourse and action. While the state politics of cultural heritage revolve around the definition and management of heritage objects, nongovernmental politics has opened up cultural heritage as a site of and means for rethinking political participation and political imagination more generally. Thus, just as postconflict states such as Kosovo have mobilized cultural heritage as an object and representation of reconstruction so, too, have political agencies in these states mobilized heritage in tension with or opposition to this mobilization. What has emerged are not simply alternatives to reconstruction, but alternative models of reconstruction—new ways of thinking about the past, the present, and their relationship that contest the typically assumed conjunctions between preservation and memory, on the one hand, and destruction and forgetting, on the other.

The interval between cultural heritage policy and nongovernmental politics is usually understood to be negotiated by nongovernmental organizations (NGOs) dedicated to heritage conservation and reconstruction. The activities of these NGOs, such as Cultural Heritage without Borders, Patrimoine sans Frontières, or the World Monument Fund, are usually focused on "heritage at risk": that is, on buildings and sites simultaneously recognized as of historical importance and in precarious physical condition. With these buildings and sites defined by state laws as elements of a "national cultural heritage" and by international conventions as, in the words of the Hague Convention, "the cultural heritage of all mankind," heritage NGOs participate in what they usually take pains to emphasize as a depoliticized humanitarian project. Yet as Kosovo's preservation campaign indicates, such projects perform precise political work as they are instantiated in particular situations and rearrange structures of power.[9] This work can be framed as the facilitation of state-sponsored identification with a cultural heritage, a facilitation that is of particular import in postconflict contexts where states typically lack resources to engage in the conservation of their cultural heritage and where the very terms "conservation" and "heritage" are dictated from without. The work of heritage NGOs, then, is frequently defined by the outsourcing of state heritage conservation and reconstruction and is thus often part of what James Ferguson and Akhil Gupta have called an emerging "transnational governmentality," particularly pronounced in states whose sovereignty is limited or challenged.[10] The particular nongovernmentality of NGOs, then, has to be interpreted, rather than assumed, and the work of nongovernmental organizations must therefore be distinguished from nongovernmental politics.

At the same time, however, the form of the transnational or global NGO also has provided a template for the definition of otherwise "local" political agencies. In the post-Yugoslav states (or "parastates," as some analysts argue in the case of Bosnia-Hercegovina and Kosovo), the NGO has been a primary instrument of postconflict governance. Transnational and international donors also sponsor NGOs as a primary mechanism to build "civil societies" in postconflict contexts. In these contexts, the NGO has thus become available to a diverse set of polities to facilitate public appearance, to enter into transnational and global networks of publicity and funding, and to participate in both national and transnational governmentalities.

In the following, I will explore the nongovernmental engagement with cultural heritage in ex-Yugoslavia via the various modes of identification that these engagements perform. To pay attention to these modes of identification is to collapse boundaries between explicitly "aesthetic" projects produced in the domain of art practice and explicitly "political" projects produced by governmental or nongovernmental institutions or organizations. I will overlook distinctions between "discipline" or "medium," then, in favor of distinctions between identificatory structures, which supply the organizing matrix for what follows. I will thus approach cultural heritage not as a preexisting object of visual representation, but rather as a species of visual culture, a form produced, circulated, and reproduced in spatial, visual, and textual representations.

IDENTIFICATION

The positing of cultural objects as heritage is both a performance of identification with those artifacts and a solicitation of collective identification with them. These identifications suggest transformations in the social status of their objects, rendering those objects as repositories of collective identity, memory, or historical significance.

These transformations, along with the discourses of identity, memory, or history that they invoke and materialize, are usually posed as agentive, as artifacts of the agency of their authors. In post-Yugoslavia, these authors have typically fashioned themselves as NGOs, the conventional broker of relations between governmental and nongovernmental domains. The labor of these NGOs is thus to identify sites deemed to be of unrecognized or transformed historical importance, an identification that has taken place alongside the efforts of new postconflict states to "inventory" and "valorize" their cultural heritages in accordance with the relevant European and international procedures.

Identification with cultural objects as heritage on the part of the governed embodies a demand for the state to recognize this identification and include those objects within the state's official list of its cultural heritage. Yet this demand is ambivalent, at once agentive and reactive, a claim on the state and a mimicry of the state's own labor. The memory, identity, or history that heritage NGOs locate or produce is each a resource for the reproduction of state hegemony. The state's acknowledgement of nongovernmental identifications with heritage thereby reaffirms the state as a custodian of heritage and cultural memory, as well as heritage itself as a locus of collective meaning and value.

The link between nongovernmental identification and governmental recognition is exemplified in many postwar reconstruction projects, such as that focused on the Avala Tower (Avalski Toranj) on the outskirts of Belgrade, Serbia. The tower was bombed and destroyed by NATO on April 29, 1999, as a component of the Serb military's communication infrastructure. The 202-meter-tall tower supported a television transmitter owned by Radio Televizija Serbija (Radio Television Serbia) and was one of twenty-five such transmitters and relays that NATO targeted during its 1999 bombing campaign (fig. 2).

During and after the war, the Serbian government protested the destruction of the tower as a destruction of "civilian infrastructure."[11] In 2001, however the Avala Tower Fans Association (Udruženje Ljubitelja Avalskog Tornja) was founded in Belgrade as an NGO in order to sponsor the tower's rebuilding. On the association's former website, the tower was posed not as infrastructure, whether military or civilian, but as cultural heritage: "a tour de force of modernist technology, the only tower in the world that had an equilateral triangle as its cross-section," and of aesthetics, "one of the most beautiful TV transmitters in Europe and the whole world." Under the transmitter, the tower supported a glass-enclosed bar and restaurant that gave onto panoramic views of Belgrade. These were framed by the association as sites of public appearance and urban memory. As it was recalled on the website of the association, "People used to say 'see you at the tower,' and now the asphalt road that leads to the tower is all covered with grass. People used to queue so that the elevator could take them to see the sight. It was a matter of prestige to have a drink at the top of the tower, to have dinner and watch the city glittering at night."

The association's initial work included a media campaign to intensify public awareness of the tower's importance and the importance of its reconstruction, as well as a fund-raising campaign. One part of the latter also included a proposal to fly a balloon of the size and form of the tower on the tower site, the sponsor of which would be identified by an enormous airborne sign.

The staging of the Avala Tower as a heritage site resonated with narratives of Serbian national victimization at the hands of NATO, the United States, and "the West," narratives that were widely circulated, especially in the waning years of the Miloševič presidency. The association's identification with the Avala Tower as heritage was, accordingly, recognized by the Serbian state. In 2004, Radio Television Serbia, the owner of the tower, began its own series of fund-raising events to rebuild the tower, in essence appropriating the project of the association. After an exhibition tennis match between Serbia's top tennis players, a benefit concert by

FIGURE 2 Avala Tower, Belgrade, Serbia, before and after destruction (photo: courtesy Avala Tower Fans Association).

Ceca Ražnjatović, turbopop singer and widow of the paramilitary leader Arkan, and other public events, the tower's reconstruction commenced in December 2006.

One of the primary cultural functions of the Avala Tower's reconstruction was to suture together prewar and postwar history and thereby neutralize the war's disruption and trauma. In other contexts, however, an identification heritage does not yield an object to reconstruct, but one to preserve in its ruined state. This preservation foregrounds the moment of ruination as a temporal fulcrum, a break in history. This has been the case in Kosovo, where, unlike in Serbia, the 1998–1999 war has been narrativized not in terms of national victimization, but national liberation. In Kosovo, one of the key artifacts of that war is a complex of buildings owned and occupied by the Jashari family in the small village of Prekaz. These buildings were destroyed by Serb forces in March 1998, a destruction that accompanied the killing of fifty members of the family and its relatives, some of whom were founders of the guerilla force that became the Kosovo Liberation Army.

In postwar Kosovo, the killing of the Jashari family has come to mark the beginning of Albanian resistance to Serbia, the resistance that would lead to the expulsion of Serbian forces from Kosovo in June 1999. Accordingly, the ruined buildings in which the family died have been preserved since their destruction (fig. 3). This preservation project emerged in the context of the municipality in which the buildings are located. After the conclusion of the 1998–1999 war, the municipal board of Skënderaj, the region in which Prekaz is located, named the site the Adem Jashari Memorial Complex—Prekaz (Kompleksi Perkujtimor "Adem Jashari"—Prekaz), after the member of the Jashari family most identified with the insurgency against Serbia. In 2000, the board formed an NGO, the Foundation for the Construction of the Commemoration Complex "Adem Jashari—Prekaz." The initial interventions at the site were to cover the ruined buildings by a roof supported by scaffolding, illuminate the buildings by spotlights at night, and arrange the grounds around the buildings with a parking lot, entrance path, cemetery, and gift shop. Each of the preceding was accomplished by an architect from Kosovo's Institute for the Protection of Monuments. A brochure available at the gift shop instructs visitors that the ruined buildings of the site "take the wounds like people."[12] The preservation of these "wounds" thus becomes a registration of otherwise invisible violence, the violence that frames the Jashari family's violence as a legitimate, necessary, even heroic resistance.

As in the case of the Avala Tower, the nongovernmental framing of the ruins of the Jashari complex as "heritage" resonated with governmental concepts of national identity and, accordingly, the Kosovo state appropriated responsibility for the complex. In 2001, the parliament of Kosovo passed a law that guaranteed state oversight, management, and funding of the complex and eventually earmarked one million euros for the further development of the complex as a site of national importance.[13] At the same time, the complex has become, for Kosovar Albanians, the key monument of the 1998–1999 war and, as such, the destination of commemorative ceremonies, cultural tourism, and school visits.[14] The heir to the KLA, the Kosovo Protection Corps, also organized an annual march, On the Path of the Future, that begins and ends at the Memorial Complex and wends through sites where significant battles took place during the 1998–1999 war.

Just as Kosovo's national government was attempting to stage a multiethnic cultural heritage in accordance with European and international standards and conventions, the Adem Jashari Memorial Complex emerged as an introjection into and critique of this formulation. The preservation of the complex suggested not the overcoming of the war, but its ongoing relevance, a relevance that acted, at the least, as a friction against the multiethnic communality that the United Nations and its emissaries in Kosovo urged. Yet this critique of a multiethnic cultural heritage took the form of cultural heritage itself; the advocates of the memorial complex identified with the state injunction to preserve cultural heritage, but in so doing, put pressure on the multicultural concept of that heritage suggested by transnational and global institutions. Indeed, the memorial complex projects a version of national culture wholly at odds with that officially sanctioned by the Kosovar state.

FIGURE 3 Preservation of damaged buildings at Adem Jashari Memorial Complex, Prekaz, Kosovo, 2010 (photo: Andrew Herscher).

The Jasharis are the model of the nationally extended family of Kosovar Albanians, rightful heirs to and defenders of the land and patrimony of Kosovo.[15]

COUNTERIDENTIFICATION

The identification of cultural objects as heritage, whether or not that heritage has already been recognized by the state, is already inscribed in the social order; it is a process that produces subjects and objects to occupy already-established social positions. An identification of heritage, then, does not transform the nation or history as much as it endows subjects and objects with extant national or historical identities—endowments that are interventions in existing systems of order, rather than changes of those systems themselves.

Yet interventions in the order of cultural heritage can be made not only by claiming or affirming an identification with heritage, but also by refusing such an identification. These refusals, or counteridentifications, contest the status of cultural objects as heritage deserving of respect, as the patrimony of specified communities, and as artifacts that it is necessary to preserve. More generally, counteridentification also frames the seemingly agentive nature of identification as itself structured into the system of order within which that identification operates. Counteridentifications with heritage can be distinguished as either underidentifications or overidentifications, with each embodying a refusal of the affective response, social action, or political effects that cultural heritage conventionally solicits. These refusals, however, are not symmetrical. Underidentification is the explicit opposite of identification; withholding, protesting, or contradicting the respect for heritage that identification engenders, underidentification is what Slavoj Žižek has termed the "inherent transgression" of heritage-preservation practice. As such, underidentification is structured into this practice insofar as it presumes resistance as part of its operation.[16]

A critical refusal of this ideology, by contrast, does not take the form of its explicit refusal, or underidentification, but rather its obsessive acceptance, or overidentification. As Žižek has argued, "In so far as power relies on its 'inherent transgression,' then, sometimes, at least, overidentifying with the explicit power discourse—ignoring this inherent obscene underside and simply taking the power discourse at its (public) word, acting as if it really means what it explicitly says (and promises) can be the most effective way of disturbing its smooth functioning."[17]

A primary form of underidentification with cultural heritage is vandalism, which aims not at the preservation of heritage, but rather at violent transformation. The destruction of the cultural heritage of ethnic others during the wars of Yugoslav succession were performances of such underidentifications. This destruction registered and reformulated the cultural status of its targets in the very act of negating that status. In the context of postwar reconstruction, vandalism constituted a highly charged aesthetic practice. In one example, the 1998 project *Black Peristyle* (*Crni peristil*), a large black circle was clandestinely painted on the stone floor of the peristyle of Diocletian's Palace in Split, Croatia (fig. 4). The peristyle was the center of the palace, itself a UNESCO World Heritage Site and one of the most historically significant cultural heritage sites in Croatia. The intervention, eventually claimed by the artist Igor Grubić, took place on the thirtieth anniversary of the *Red Peristyle* (*Crveni peristil*) intervention, when the floor of the peristyle was painted red. In the 1998 project, a note, signed "Black Peristyle," left on the door of a nearby tourist agency, read: "In honor of the group Red Peristyle, thirty years later, the peristyle, as a magic mirror, reflects the state of society's conscience."[18]

As in the case of *Red Peristyle, Black Peristyle* was classified by public authorities as an act of vandalism against a cultural-heritage monument. Grubić later described how he attempted to foment public reaction to *Black Peristyle* by calling one independent newspaper (*Stojednice*) and offering it an interview and by writing a letter to the editor of another independent newspaper (*Feral Tribune*),

FIGURE 4 Igor Grubić, *Black Peristyle*, intervention at Diocletian's Palace, Split, Croatia, 1998 (photo: courtesy Igor Grubić).

signed "Black Peristyle."[19] He later presented these and other media accounts of *Black Peristyle* in the Thirty-Third Zagreb Salon, an annual exhibition of Croatian art. *Black Peristyle* was awarded the second prize in this salon, an event that then created a second wave of media coverage. According to Grubić, "it was the intention to use all possible media channels, and media times, and gallery space, so that information about the protest would be repeated like a mantra until a critical point would be reached and some real changes would begin to take place."[20]

The object of this "real change" was the contemporary Croatian state, at the time governed by the Croatian Democratic Party, the party that had, under the leadership of Franjo Tudjman, led Croatia out of Yugoslavia and into independence. Yet *Black Peristyle* provoked the same reaction from the postsocialist state as *Red Peristyle* had from the socialist state thirty years earlier, an assertion of independent Croatia's suppressed affiliation with its prewar socialist past, the past that independence was supposed to have overcome. This assertion did not target the folkloric culture that independent Croatia privileged as its heritage. Rather, it was an intervention on a site of heritage that was already inscribed, by *Red Peristyle*, into the history of modern art; *Black Peristyle* thereby advanced a claim for modern art as heritage, even as it vandalized a heritage site. The invocation of a modernist heritage extended beyond *Red Peristyle*: the black circle painted on the palace's floor was staged by Grubić as "a legacy from Suprematism and Constructivism," and the act of public painting itself echoed related Fluxus-inspired performances in Croatia in the 1970s. The underidentification with Diocletian's Palace as a cultural heritage site in its given form thus mediated an identification with another formulation of heritage, the heritage of a modernism enmeshed in the history of socialism, also suppressed by postsocialist Croatian nationalism.

The status of an underidentification with one heritage object as, simultaneously, an identification with other heritage objects is pronounced not only in vandalism, but also in protests over the definition of cultural objects as heritage. For example, in May 2007, the Kosovar Albanian NGO Vetëvendosje (Self-Determination) protested the building of a protective wall around the Byzantine-era patriarchate in Peć, Kosovo, seat of the Serbian Orthodox Church and focal point of Kosovo's Serb cultural identity. For the Serbian Orthodox Church, the wall was an objectively necessary instrument of protection, especially important after the destruction inflicted on Serbian Orthodox churches and monuments in demonstrations in March 2004. After that violence, the low wall surrounding the patriarchate appeared wholly inadequate to block hostile actions against its buildings and grounds.

For Vetëvendosje, however, the wall was a symbolic expression of the patriarchate's status as exclusively Serb property, unavailable to both the predominantly Albanian city of Peć (Peja, in Albanian) and the predominantly Albanian state of Kosovo. In a demonstration outside the patriarchate, Vetëvendosje members built a section of a barbed-wire barricade and displayed posters proclaiming "No New Walls," "Kosovo Will Not Be Palestine," and "Peja is Not Mitrovice" (Mitrovice is a city that was divided between Serbs and Albanians in the aftermath of the 1998–1999 war).

Vetëvendosje's protest did not refuse the status of the patriarchate as a heritage site as such; rather, it refused its presumed status as a specifically Serb heritage site, managed not by the Kosovar state, but by the Serbian Orthodox Church. Yet Vetëvendosje's refusal was not made in the name of secularism or the state, but of Kosovar Albanian nationalism. Thus, the organization conjoined protests against the patriarchate's new wall with the publication of historical narratives documenting the Orthodox Church's supposedly Albanian roots and political narratives asserting Albanian sovereignty in Kosovo.[21] The protest thus constituted both a refusal of the patriarchate's status as a Serb patrimonial heritage and an assertion of its cryptic status as an Albanian heritage.

While underidentifications are inscribed in the ideological system of heritage and thus easily absorbed within it, overidentifications present such a system with a more profound challenge by presuming to take its claims and imperatives more rigorously than it is capable of doing itself. One example of such an overidentification is the piece *JBT 27.12.2004*, in which the Croatian artist Dalibor Martinis photographed himself standing on a plinth formerly occupied by a bronze statue of Josip Broz Tito, the founder of socialist Yugoslavia (fig. 5). The statue, in Tito's birthplace of Kumrovec, Croatia, was destroyed—a performance of underidentification—on December 27, 2004, a date commemorated in the title of Martinis's piece. Identification with the statue would yield either a project to reconstruct it, à la the Avala Tower, or to preserve its empty plinth, à la the Jashari Memorial Complex. But Martinis overidentified with the preservationist agenda by collapsing the distinction between the preserving subject and the preserved object; on the plinth, he became both subject and object, both preserving and preserved. In so doing, Martinis's work made manifest the distance between subject and object that "normal" identification maintains, a distance that leaves this identification partial and limited. Indeed, narrating his experience in an interview, Martinis said that "when I stood on the marble pedestal with the inscription 'Josip Broz Tito,' I realized that I was at a place where it is not possible—neither physically, politically, or symbolically—for anyone to stand except Tito himself."[22] This realization frames identification, in the form in which it is conventionally solicited and asserted, as inherently incomplete, founded on unacknowledged gaps between subject and object.

A similar registration of such gaps was accomplished by the monument to Bruce Lee erected in Mostar, Bosnia and Hercegovina, in November 2005 by the Bosnian NGO Urban Movement (fig. 6). Mostar was heavily damaged during the Bosnian war, with the city becoming divided between Bosniacs, in East Mostar, and Croats, in West Mostar. According to Nino Raspudić, the Urban Movement's cofounder and director, Mostar's division was only amplified in postwar reconstruction: "each one of the two constituent parts of the city is trying to give 'their own' space 'their own' characteristics, to 'possess' it even more by constructing their religious and cultural objects and symbols."[23] The sectarian instrumentalization of a heritage produced the possibility for that heritage to be instrumentalized as, in contrast, either multiethnic or universal. But instead of reframing local cultural objects as unifying works of heritage, as postethnic national governments have tended to do, the Urban Movement posed the hero of 1970s kung-fu movies, Bruce Lee, as this object. Lee, according to Raspudić, "was dear to all, no matter our political or ideological convictions. . . . [He] was, above all, a symbolic bridge between the East and the West." Thus, Raspudić concluded, it was quite appropriate to memorialize Bruce Lee in between the divided eastern and western parts of Mostar.

Bruce Lee, a product of late-capitalist global culture, was the object of a cosmopolitan and postethnic identification that revealed other objects of such identification as merely ideological. The universality of the cultural heritage that served as the object of "normal" identification becomes a fantasy when compared with the universality of an object of global culture such as Bruce Lee. By overidentifying

FIGURE 5 Dalibor Martinis, *JBT 27.12.2004*, performance on site of destroyed statue of Tito at Tito's birthplace, Kumrovec, Croatia, 2005 (photo: courtesy Irena Sertić).

with the universality of cultural heritage, the monument to Bruce Lee radicalizes and literalizes universality. In Mostar, the monument thus stands in sharp contrast to the city's most renowned work of heritage, the Stari Most (Old Bridge), an Ottoman-era bridge over the Neretva River. While it was held by Bosniacs in East Mostar, the bridge was destroyed by Croat Army artillery in 1993. This destruction provided a symbol of sectarian conflict in Mostar, while the bridge's reconstruction, completed in 2004, was framed by its sponsors and state officials as a sign of that conflict's being overcome. Yet the monument to Bruce Lee foregrounded the artifice of such a framing by memorializing a cultural object whose heritage was shared in a far more profound fashion between East and West Mostar.

DISIDENTIFICATION

In Pêcheux's theorization of the positions that are possible to assume in response to ideological interpellation, both identification and counteridentification confirm ideology, the former by passively accepting it, and the latter by accepting the "evidentness of [its] meaning."[24] In what Pêcheux terms "disidentification," by contrast, ideology is neither accepted nor contested as such; rather, ideology is

FIGURE 6 Ivan Fijolić, *Monument to Bruce Lee*, Mostar, Bosnia, 2005 (photo: courtesy Sarajevo Center for Contemporary Art).

problematized, that is, disidentified with, with the disidentifying subject becoming a site for the emergence of new forms of subjectivity. Disidentification, in other words, is a transformation in ideology from within.

This sort of transformation was staged in an intervention sited on either side of the reconstructed Old Bridge in Mostar. The intervention consists of two small stone blocks, recovered from the destroyed bridge, on which are painted the words, in English, "Don't Forget." After the end of the Bosnian war, the same message was often graffitied, in both Bosnian and English, on the walls of destroyed buildings in Mostar. Sometimes the message took the form "Don't Forget '93," explicitly invoking the year of the Old Bridge's destruction. But the message assumes a wholly new significance when it is read with reference to the reconstructed Old Bridge.

The stones on which are painted "Don't Forget" frame views of the Old Bridge from a distance and precede and follow passages over the bridge; the injunction against forgetting is connected both visually and experientially to the bridge, whose reconstruction was framed as a crucial recovery of cultural memory. But the message on the stones neither accepts nor rejects this recovery. Indeed, the message accommodates both acceptance and rejection: the injunction to remember could be read as a confirmation of the reconstruction of the bridge as a recovery of memory or as a contestation of this recovery. What is it that should not be forgotten? That an Ottoman bridge once spanned the Neretva River in Mostar? Or that this bridge was destroyed and is now reconstructed? Or that this reconstruction involved a destruction of the traces of destruction: a loss of loss, of the memorialization of war? The memory that "Don't Forget" enjoins is reducible to all of these memories and thus irreducible to any one of them in particular.

The intervention raises similar questions about its author and the subject whom it hails. Written in English, the message on the stones is available to both Bosniacs and Croats, to both residents of Mostar and visitors to the city. Who is authorized to ask for memory? And who is required to remember? These questions, too, are posed, but not answered. In this intervention, precisely the sort of ideological suturing of subjects and objects that is conventionally mediated through a heritage is simultaneously gestured toward, but left incomplete. Subjects are implored not to forget, but not told what not to forget. Historical objects are confirmed as repositories of memory in general, but not of a specified memory in particular. History is situated not in some heritage or another, but in the agencies that endow that heritage with meaning. These small stones around the Old Bridge, then, constitute neither "a strategic intervention in the existing order," an identification with heritage, nor the "destructive negation" of such an intervention, a counteridentification, but rather a miniature, but nevertheless decisive opening onto a "trans-strategic intervention which redefines the roles and contours of the existing order."[25]

RECONSTRUCTIONS

Reconstruction literally signifies a mimesis, the effort to replicate a once-extant condition, to reproduce the past in the present. The postconflict reconstruction of damaged heritage in post-Yugoslavia thus allows for a double gesture of return—not only a return to the past before the conflicts in the region, but also to the past represented by various forms of heritage. Yet reconstruction is only one response to damaged heritage. The responses facilitated by counteridentifications and disidentifications with heritage, some of which involve their own infliction of "damage," invoke or even initiate other versions of reconstruction, premised not on returns, but on turns: on historicity, instead of history.

Figured as a return, reconstruction suppresses historicity: the possibility of transformation, difference, and alterity. This suppression is a management of temporality, a rendering of the present not as an actively produced reality, but as a reflection of the past. The present, in whatever form, is interred in the past as its legacy. History is both the object and technology of mimetic representation.

The mimesis of reconstruction implies the mimesis of the past: history as a site of recoveries and a destination of revisits.

Counteridentifications and disindentifications with heritage are, by contrast, potential openings onto historicity. They contest the seemingly natural status of heritage as a representation of an objective, neutral past, and they explore the capacity of heritage to embody or engender different or novel pasts. In so doing, they invoke not only counterhistories, alternative pasts to those produced according to a mimetic model of inheritance, but also a counterconcept of history, the concept of an intervention or eruption of alterity. As the object of counteridentifications and disidentifications, heritage becomes not the site of actual or even contested pasts, but a mnemonic technology of unprecedented "reconstruction," a generator of new pasts for new futures: points of no return.

NOTES

1. In Anna Tsing's terms, cultural heritage is a site of friction where universal claims "are charged and enacted in the sticky materiality of practical encounters." See Anna Tsing, *Friction: An Ethnography of Global Connection* (Princeton: Princeton University Press, 2005), p. 1.
2. James Ferguson and Akhil Gupta, "Spatializing States: Toward an Ethnography of Neoliberal Governmentality," in Jonathan Xavier Inda (ed.), *Anthropologies of Modernity: Foucault, Governmentality and Life Politics* (Malden: Blackwell, 2005).
3. Federal Ministry of Foreign Affairs, *NATO War Crimes in Yugoslavia: Documentary Evidence, 25 April—10 June 1999* (Belgrade: Službeni Lasnik, 1999), p. 424.
4. Michel Pêcheux, "La langue introuvable," *Canadian Journal of Political and Social Theory* 7.1–2 (1983), p. 26.
5. Memorial Complex, *Adem Jashari: Prekaz* (Prishtina: UÇK, 2004), unpaginated.
6. Beta News Agency, "One Million Euros from Kosovo Budget for KLA Memorial," May 24, 2005; Kosovapress, "In Prekaz Set Fundament [sic] of the Memorial Complex 'Adem Jashari,'" December 4, 2006.
7. See Anna Di Lellio and Stephanie Schwandner-Sievers, "Sacred Journey to a Nation: The Construction of a Shrine in Postwar Kosovo," *Journeys: The International Journal of Travel and Travel Writing* 7.1 (Summer 2006).
8. See Anna Di Lellio and Stephanie Schwandner-Sievers, "The Legendary Commander: The Construction of an Albanian Master-Narrative in Post-War Kosovo," *Nations and Nationalism* 12.3 (2006).
9. Slavoj Žižek, "The Inherent Transgression," *Cultural Values* 2.1 (January 1998).
10. Slavoj Žižek, in Judith Butler, Ernesto Laclau and Slavoj Žižek, *Contingency, Hegemony, Universality: Contemporary Dialogues on the Left* (London: Verso, 2000), p. 220.
11. Suzana Marjanić, "Aktivizmom protiv crne mrlje na duši: razgovor s Igorom Grubićem," *Zarez* 219 (November, 29, 2007).

12. *Ibid.*
13. *Vetëvendosje!* 43 (May 23, 2007).
14. Silva Kalčić, "Strategija kušaca vina," *Zarez* 147 (January 17, 2005).
15. Nino Raspudić, "The Monument to Bruce Lee—Yes and Why?," http://www.projekt-relations.de/en/get/pressematerial/de_construction.php.
16. Michel Pêcheux, *Language, Semantics, Ideology: Stating the Obvious*, trans. Harbans Nagpal (London: Macmillan, 1982), p. 26.
17. Slavoj Žižek, *Organs without Bodies: Deleuze and Consequences* (London: Routledge, 2004), p. 81.
18. KFOR, or "Kosovo Force," is NATO's term for its "peacekeeping force" in Kosovo. This force is the military component of the United Nations Interim Administration Mission in Kosovo, or UNMIK, which has administered Kosovo since the 1998–1999 war.
19. Jacques Rancière, "Politics, Identification, and Subjectivization," in John Rajchman (ed.), *The Identity in Question* (New York: Routledge, 1995), p. 65.
20. Louis Althusser, "Ideology and Ideological State Apparatuses (Notes Towards An Investigation)," in *Lenin and Philosophy and Other Essays*, trans. Ben Brewster (New York: Monthly Review Press, 1971).
21. Pêcheux, *Language, Semantics, Ideology*, pp. 156–58.
22. For some theorists, including Pêcheux, these resistances emerge from inevitable discontinuities between conflicting discourses in a given social order; for others, they emerge in the inevitable discontinuities between ideologies and subjects. For a review of these positions, see Paul Smith, *Discerning the Subject* (Minneapolis: University of Minnesota Press, 1988). At issue in the following is not the different implications of these perspectives, however, but rather the fraught status of interpellation and its relation as such to Foucauldian models of subject formation. On this relation, see Judith Butler, *The Psychic Life of Power: Theories of Subjection* (Stanford: Stanford University Press, 1997), pp. 1–30.
23. See Mark Cousins and Athar Hussain, "The Question of Ideology: Althusser, Pêcheux, Foucault," in John Law (ed.), *Power, Action and Belief: A New Sociology of Knowledge?* (London: Routledge and Kegan Paul, 1987), pp. 158–79.
24. Michel Foucault, "Afterword: The Subject and Power," in Herbert Dreyfus and Paul Rabinow (eds.), *Michel Foucault: Beyond Structuralism and Hermeneutics* (Chicago: Harvester Press, 1982), p. 221.
25. Rancière, "Politics, Identity, Subjectivization," p. 68.

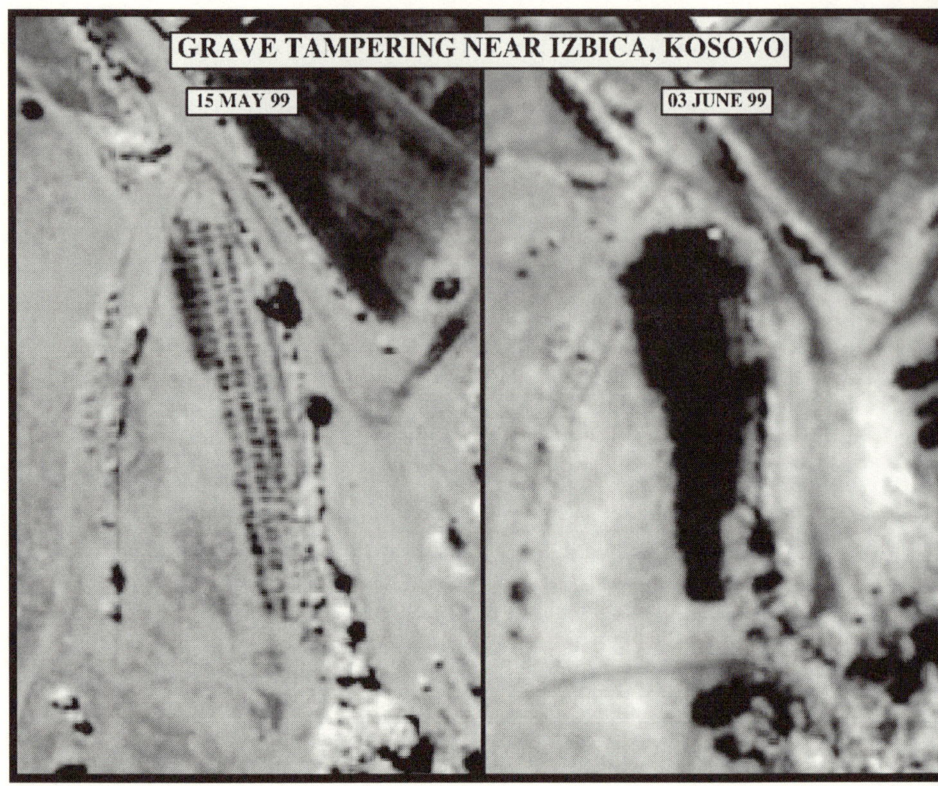

NATO image released as evidence of grave tampering. May–June 1999, near Izbica, Kosovo.

How to Do Things with Space—
Expanded Architecture and Nongovernmental Politics: An Interview with Laura Kurgan

Yates McKee

YATES MCKEE: In this interview, I'd like to discuss the broad trajectory of your work as it has developed at the intersection of architecture and nongovernmental politics. Though you were trained as an architect and direct the Spatial Information Design Lab at the Columbia Graduate School of Architecture, Planning, and Preservation, the projects for which you are best known rarely involve the design of discrete buildings. Instead, your projects have concerned satellite images, data archives, urban-policy debates, environmental monitoring, transnational financial flows, and especially forms of civic participation as they materialize spatially—or, indeed, architecturally, in a very expanded sense of the word. Before explicitly addressing the status of architecture in your work, let's begin by considering some of your most recent research, such as that concerning Google Earth as an emergent interface for activist spatial politics.

LAURA KURGAN: To begin, let me say that among my broad concerns has been that we not take our relation to new spatial technologies for granted. The very ubiquity of something like Google Earth on television, in newspapers, and in people's everyday lives tends to naturalize this new spatial interface. But consider the fact that only ten years ago, satellite imagery was a domain tightly controlled by a relatively small group of corporations and governments. What is interesting about Google Earth for our discussion is not simply the fact of sheer visual access to an expanded realm of satellite imagery—which in and of itself doesn't mean very much—but rather the new forms of reading, writing, and action that have emerged around this accessibility. People—including activists—can now make their own maps for a limitless array of purposes and concerns; there are millions of maps embedded in the Google Earth interface, but often they are difficult to read and poorly annotated, one doesn't have any idea about what the maps are actually of, and they have not been made public in broader networks of activity. As of now, it is very difficult to search this mega archive of spatial data—you are almost forced to perform what the Situationists would call a *dérive*, or open-ended spatial wandering, through this database in order to discover the spectrum of what is out there. But by simply being able to "zoom in" on this or that image—which is among the often-celebrated technical capacities of Google Earth—you are not usually going to learn much about the social and political dynamics of either the site in question or the mapping practice that has concerned itself with that site. We have been interested in how to map this map.

YM: So what is your research procedure in attempting to "map" Google Earth in order to set forth some of these dynamics and to explore their political possibilities?

LK: Mark Hansen and I are currently downloading all of the Keyhole Markup Language (KML) files of Google Earth. KML is a basic way of storing the place markers and coordinates of maps. If you use KML to search Google Earth, you get everything in a massive database. A few researchers have done "density maps" using this method, which shows us where these technologies are being used—or where their usage is being focused—but in some ways, this is the least interesting point, in that it offers up a sheerly quantitative and geographical analysis. What I want to know is what these maps are about, who is using them, and for what purposes. What heterogeneity is concealed behind this "universal" interface? Needless to say, one needs to consider issues of access to computer technologies and languages between the Global North and the Global South, rich and poor; but there is still a great democratizing potential in these new forms of map making. In terms of artists' and architects' interest in these technologies, we've come a long way since Charles and Ray Eames, for instance, who were happy to defer to the expertise of NASA scientists and then basically to aestheticize the results in their film *Powers of Ten* (1978), which shifted perspectives on the world one order of magnitude every ten seconds. We need to explore the fact that the technologies are now in the hands of nonexperts, with unforeseeable outcomes—but again, this needs to be qualified in light of global inequalities of knowledge and access.

YM: Can you give me a sense of how you might bring this mode of research to bear on a particular activist practice?

LK: At this stage, we are simply interested in mapping the content, to see what is out there, for instance, when one searches "garbage" or "environment," what comes up? It is almost like a psychogeographic *dérive*. The idea would be to create partial trajectories through the maps. It would not be an image in a typical sense; in fact, it will suggest that you cannot map this map as a visual totality, but only as a series of contingent movements and linkages without any ultimate ground plan. That said, we know that there are increasingly well-established activist usages of such spatial technologies, as when slum dwellers and their advocates map their environment and take their findings to an urban planning commission with a set of proposals or demands. We are interested in mapping the patterns of these usages, which could indeed become an interface in its own right for activist pedagogy and strategy across different contexts.

Maybe I can make a shift here to another project that has a similar strategy—looking for the local instances in the global database. The great thing about Google Earth is that almost anyone can tell a local story through a global interface—that's where the potential of heterogeneity lies, if there is any legitimate heterogeneity. But this relationship between a global condition and its local instantiation is a theme in a lot of my recent work and collaborations.

A good example of this is a research workshop that I recently ran in Barcelona concerning global remittance flows, which is to say, the dynamics of sending money home by migrant communities in the Global North. We begin with the startling fact that according to Manuel Orozco by way of the *New York Times*, in 2007, "migrants from poor countries send home about $300 billion. This is more than three times the global total in foreign aid, making 'remittances' the main source of outside money flowing to the developing world." This workshop examined the pathways, institutions, and built products of the informal global trade in money. We asked "How is the movement of money manifested locally, and in what forms, in urban centers worldwide?" The Raval district of Barcelona was our laboratory for looking at this phenomenon, and we used visual, analytic, and design tools to understand the flexible forms and institutions that emerge with informal patterns of global migration. Rather than reaffirming the common presumption that the West or the developed world establishes institutions that dominate the developing world, we sought to document and respond to the reverse trend, in which the developing world establishes new patterns in its host cities, euro by euro, person by person, often in ad hoc, makeshift, unapparent ways. As a group, we made use of new, easy-to-use web-based user-driven software, Flickr, RSS Feeds, and Google APIs, to explore the ways in which new toolkits enable nonexperts to create maps and populate them with all sorts of information and in doing this discover new possibilities for participation, interaction, critique, creation, and dissidence. The idea was to have participants ask questions about the movement of money, in the form of visualizations of the multiple cities linked through remittances to and thus in a certain sense embedded in the Raval district. What are the spatial definitions of these multiple cities—what do they look like now? What materials, networks, technologies, and programs inform or build them? How does the informal city embed itself in the formal city? How do the informal and the formal cities transform one another? And what might each look like in the future?

YM: Who were the participants in the workshop? You mentioned having been approached by migrants' advocates about creating toolkits that could be used to assist in the design of informal financial techniques that would both minimize the profiteering of remittance companies as well as potentially enable collective transnational reinvestment projects by migrant communities—right?

LK: The participants in this case were a group of international students who were living in the Raval district who had not noticed what was hidden in plain sight: dozens of remittance locations, Western Unions and the like, embedded within one of the tourist centers of Spain. The migrant toolkits would be a great future project. That idea for that comes from Orozco, whom I just quoted and who is a scholar of remittances at the Inter-American Dialogue in Washington and very generously provided his detailed data set for us to visualize in the *Terre Natale* show at the Cartier Foundation. I had known about Orozco's data through another studio I had run at Columbia in the spring of 2008, where we focused on Roosevelt Avenue in Queens—a place where there is a concentration of immigrant populations and hence remittance locations. Orozco has great plans to train migrants in financial literacy, and he has a powerful critique of conventional remittance statistics.

YM: Your interest in the political, economic, and spatial dynamics of sending money home initially took shape as part of your collaborative project with the architectural firm of Diller Scofidio + Renfro for Paul Virilio's *Terre Natale* project in 2009—correct? Can you describe this project?

LK: Yes. The overall project was conceived by Virilio and aimed to address the intensification of human migration at a global level at the beginning of the twenty-first century. Realized in collaboration with DSR, and with Mark Hansen and Ben Rubin, my contribution was in the part of the exhibit that involved an animated, large-scale, 360 degree video projection of this "blue marble" of the Earth moving around the perimeter of a darkened gallery. This figure is of course quite familiar from the early environmentalism of the sixties and seventies...

YM: ... When it functioned in things such as the *Whole Earth Catalog* as an icon of the global village—humanity unified in its fate of self-induced destruction and possible redemption.

LK: Yes, and it's been on the cover of so many environmental books and reports over the past forty years. Here, though, the globe functioned not as a flat icon, but as a kind of generative interface with huge amounts of data inscribed in it. As this globe moves around the perimeter of the gallery, every forty-two seconds, it "prints" out graphic interpretations of data pertaining to different forms of mobility: these range from the data sets on remittance flows that we've just discussed, for instance, to the drawing of a line that divides the Global North and South in terms of the geographical distribution of carbon emissions, on the one hand, and increased vulnerability to rising sea levels in places such as Bangladesh and the South Pacific, on the other. The dynamics have already given rise to the new legal and political category of the "environmental refugee," in which processes of displacement are now guided not only by economic or military planning at the local or even national scale, but by unforeseeable planetary ecological disequilibria driven by Northern consumption patterns.

YM: The data are being visually interpreted in this quasi-cinematic environment that has a certain phenomenological and indeed architectural quality—something very different from looking at charts or numbers in a UN report or a news broadcast.

LK: The installation was a matter both of storytelling and of architectural immersion. It was important for us that the data be about people—however abstracted in formal terms—rather than numbers in and of themselves. This was one way to tell a series of stories embedded in data that are typically seen or read in isolated, self-contained sets, rather than as large-scale dynamics, flows, and trajectories. And the stories in question concern the dynamics of inequality—we're not showing here the trajectories of business people, for instance, but rather those of the people least responsible for global economic disruptions and ecological crises, but who bear the brunt of their effects.

YM: Keeping in mind your reference to the relations between data, storytelling, and architectural immersion, let's segue into a brief biographical discussion of your background as an architect, a professional identity that you still embrace—albeit with certain qualifiers. How and why has an architect come to concern herself with the patterns of global remittance flows or climate-change refugees, for instance? How, if at all, does architecture still pertain to your current practice?

LK: I was trained as an architect in the days of so-called "high theory"—the late eighties and early nineties. This moment of innovative theoretical discourse, marked by Derrida, Foucault, Lefebvre, and Virilio, coincided with two other historical developments—an economic recession that reduced the opportunities for actual building commissions and the increasing introduction of computers into the design curriculum. While for many in the design field the latter development was met with a certain euphoria in terms of its novel formal or sculptural possibilities—eventually exemplified by the work of Frank Gehry in the late nineties—as an architect, I was interested in how computers and computer networks would reconfigure our sense of space and what Rosalyn Deutsche called "spatial politics." The well-publicized usage of aerial imaging systems in the Gulf War was an important point of reference in this regard. It forms a kind of prehistory to what I would go on to do in the mid-nineties with geographical positioning systems. Whereas other young architects were later concerned with GPS primarily as a drawing tool, I was more interested in the "architecture" of the computer systems themselves, such as the spatiotemporal logic of the atomic clock, which governs time keeping around the globe, as stored by satellites as they record the surface of the Earth.

YM: Your formation thus involved a reopening of questions of media technology, scale, and planetary networks that had been posed in the late sixties by experimental architects, but now without the technoutopian horizons.

LK: Teaching at an architecture school, critically investigating these new technologies of visuality, is my way of addressing the "canon." But there has always been that kind of research and experimentation at moments of social and technological change. Architectural modernism was one, but so was Renaissance perspective. But yes, I see the military and industrial technologies that emerged in the sixties and that have only intensified up through our present day as a key point of concern for architectural research—not simply as a pool of resources for formal innovation, but as an entry point into urgent matters of space, building, and politics. To return to the Eameses—until recently, new spatial technologies have been very inaccessible to nonexpert users. They were clued into the importance of the view from outer space for their architectural arguments about scale and relative size, but they had to turn to NASA and a community of elite research scientists to obtain the imagery. Now you've got experts, and citizens, and various combinations thereof operating with the same maps, sometimes with competing claims. The Situationists, to take another legacy of the sixties, are often heralded in architectural discourse as radical activists. But they were experimental activist artists. This is not to say that certain of their concepts and techniques are not of interest or use, especially to cartographers. It's just that the contemporary field of nonexpert map making takes us into terrain that requires something more than an aesthetic or art-historical approach.

YM: And also an approach to the political that would be different from the grand revolutionary rhetoric of the Situationists, defined in militant opposition to capital and the state as monolithic systems. Speaking of the ongoing pertinence of certain Situationist terms—"repurposing" is a phrase you've used to describe your relation to military imaging technologies—let's talk about your second project dealing with satellite imagery, which dealt with images of suspected mass graves in Kosovo during the 1999 war.

LK: I was unable to work with these kinds of images earlier in the 1990s, during the Bosnian war, for instance, because the satellite imagery was still all classified. 1995 was the year that satellite imagery and technology started to be declassified by the Clinton administration, thanks to the work in particular of Vice President Gore. In 1999, when the NATO campaign against Milosevic started, the Clinton administration released high-resolution satellite images showing evidence of mass graves. These forensic traces were a crucial point of reference for the administration in making its case about the crimes of the Serbian regime. But back in 1995, there still was a real controversy about whether even to admit satellite images of the mass graves near Srebrenica into a public debate about how to respond to the war in Bosnia. The images from July, when the massacres happened, were classified, and UN Ambassador Madeline Albright wanted to release them, but was blocked from doing so outside the Security Council. They have now been admitted into evidence by the Hague tribunal. In 1999, when I produced a show about the mass graves in Kosovo, I used what was publicly available: much lower-resolution imagery than what the military was releasing and annotating as imagery.

YM: So what kind of imagery did you purchase, and what did you do with it?

LK: When the images were first released by NATO, as handouts at press conferences and online JPGs, you were not actually able to obtain them at their original resolution, one meter per pixel, or even to get them as data. You couldn't actually get the original data behind the image the military had released. So I bought a lower-resolution satellite image, from a commercial satellite company, of the same place on Earth at roughly the same time—not simply an image, but the data captured by another satellite on the same day. There was a whole controversy at the time about the NATO images possibly being doctored—my interest in these images was controversial among certain people in the art world who doubted the existence of the graves and suspected me of somehow colluding with the military! I had no doubt that the graves were in fact there, but my concern was about how actually to read what was there: What exactly were we seeing, or not? The military had released these images as pictures and not as data sets.

YM: Can you explain this distinction?

LK: By "picture" I just mean something that has pixels that come together to form a more or less coherent visual shape. But a satellite image in the full sense, as a technical artifact, is not just an image, but a coordinated data set in which you can read the spectral signature of the pixels, which have latitude and longitude and different gradations of shading on the surface of the Earth—such as the freshly upturned soil at the site of the mass grave. A satellite image has a date stamp, a time stamp, and a location stamp...

YM: ...All of which had been effaced in the image released by the military...

LK: Yes, thus naturalizing it in a way and obscuring the fact that there is an art and science to satellite interpretation in which reading the data—and not simply looking at the picture—becomes an essential question, especially in terms of making evidentiary and indeed political claims with major consequences. What I wanted to do was to put the data back into the lower-resolution image that I had obtained, as a kind of memorial to the site in its specificity as both a site of violence and a site of mediatic displacement, forensic analysis, and political action. I wanted to repurpose what had been reduced to a picture into a data set for memory and witnessing and also to open questions about the politics of reading in such circumstances.

YM: So what visual form did this reintroduction of the data into the images ultimately take?

LK: This project took the relatively simple form of images on the wall of a gallery. As I noted, the only images that I was able to purchase at the time were of comparatively low resolution. So in the images I presented, I not only retrieved the data sets underlying the images, but also added tons of new pixels to make them look higher resolution—not as a form of trickery, but to foreground a certain play of resolution and irresolution, shape and formlessness, which is among the most elementary, though in itself insufficient, conditions of satellite interpretation.

YM: In the years following the Kosovo project, which saw the increasing commercial availability of satellite imagery that would have been difficult to obtain just a few years earlier, you began to explore the possibility of "tasking" satellites to take pictures of specific areas of the Earth's surface, as in your *Monochrome Landscapes* series. Of particular interest for our discussion is the image you ordered of a particular segment of the Cameroonian rainforest in which it was possible to read the trails of illegal corporate logging activity through areas that had been protected under Cameroon's sustainable-forestry legislation. I know you've recently resumed work on a related project, which we can discuss further on in the interview.

LK: Yes, in 2001, I was invited to contribute a piece to Thomas Levin's groundbreaking surveillance show, *CTRL [SPACE]*, at the ZKM in Karlsruhe. The museum gave me five thousand dollars to buy an image, and I wanted in turn to channel this opportunity to someone in the human rights field who could actually use it in their own work. By this time, more commercial satellites had been launched, and it was possible to purchase a genuinely high-resolution satellite image, the real thing, with all its associated data. At the time, none of the organizations I approached were sure they wanted to work with such images; there was a kind of squeamishness about the images having been derived from a military technology and an anxiety that they had been possibly doctored or toyed with. (Today, however, satellite images are a key tool in the arsenal of many human rights groups.) Global Forest Watch, an environmental organization that's now part of the World Resources Institute, agreed to work with me. They actually helped to draft the Cameroonian legislation on deforestation and were just beginning to utilize such technologies in their own monitoring activities. (And indeed today, the interpretation of satellite imagery is a crucial part of their activist work.) Unfortunately, the period in which I had arranged to have the photos taken was extremely overcast, so I was not able to produce the piece for the ZKM show. And then, a few weeks before the show was to open, the September 11 attacks occurred. By September 15, extremely detailed satellite images of Ground Zero were already available. I purchased one such image, enlarged it to a scale of fifty feet, and laid it out across the floor of the ZKM space . . .

YM: . . . A kind of hypercontemporary memorial to what was a still-smoldering disaster site. And you used this same image in a publically distributed folio map, as well—right?

LK: The map that I made was intended as an intervention in the controversy surrounding how and in what ways the public should have access to the disaster site in the months following the attack. I told Ed Vulliamy from the *Guardian* at the time: "Has anyone really asked what it means to build a memorial when you are still in the middle of a war? I think the site itself is the memorial. This is a mass grave—the site is what it is." For me, it was a matter of bearing witness to what was actually going on down there beyond the iconic images, documenting the temporary spaces, structures, and activities surrounding it as a disaster site—the building and planning and infrastructure involved in establishing it as a disaster site, one might say, well before any actual process of reconstruction commenced. We did the project for a year, with a new image and updated annotation every few months. Though it perhaps seems sentimental in retrospect, at the time, it seemed like the right thing to do, to try and teach people how to look at the site as a zone of postdisaster architecture, rather than primarily as a site of monumental nationalist identification. What the city initially wanted to do was to erect a forty-foot opaque wall around the site. I was also involved with the memorial committee of a group of architects called New York New Visions, and among our activities was to pressure the city to allow visual access to the site by the public with a transparent fence; but then, of course, the fence was covered in all kinds of monumentalizing texts and images.

YM: The latter thus functioned as a kind of palliating screen between the public and the site in both its traumatic and banal dimensions. As many critics have remarked, September 11 provided an unprecedented public platform for architects; the hope had been that it might reactivate earlier disciplinary concerns with how buildings in their formal and functional dimensions are related to broader questions of urban space, public planning, infrastructural networks, historical memory, civic participation...

LK: Well, yes, these debates did resurface around Ground Zero to some extent, but ultimately, it was a matter of real estate, on the one hand, and a high-profile architect concerned with building primarily as a question of symbolism or iconography—"the Freedom Tower"—on the other. It was a disappointing outcome on the part of the profession as a whole, though not entirely surprising, given the balance of political and economic forces at the time.

YM: Even in the high-profile competition, which actually highlighted some very artistically avant-garde designs that would have resisted the crass nationalist pandering of the Freedom Tower, designers primarily addressed their projects to the public as some combination of form, iconicity, and technology at the level of the discrete building or building complex. This was to some extent dictated by the parameters of the competition itself, but it leads me to ask how you would assess the response of architects to September 11 and the response to the devastation of New Orleans by Hurricane Katrina. Though it did not have the same level of high-profile visibility, architects were initially eager to participate in debates about the reconstruction. But once again, there was a privileging of the formal and the iconic.

LK: Yes, or of solving social problems through iconic buildings. To be clear though, iconicity is not unimportant—the question is how the iconic would be articulated with other levels of programs, planning, infrastructure, finance, and legislation. But in New Orleans, you did not have a large, unified, well-financed, and high-profile governmental initiative for reconstruction. It was pretty much the opposite: massive numbers of displaced people unable to return to their homes, even when the buildings had not been badly damaged by the storm. In architectural discourse, the debate played out as a contest between the conservative aesthetics of the New Urbanism, on the one hand, and a variety of "visionary" avant-garde building projects, on the other, both of which left the question of population displacement, housing rights, and equitable urban development untouched. Ironically, the New Urbanists were much more activist in orientation—within weeks of the hurricane, they had already drawn up elaborate proposals that were being shown at city council meetings and cited by legislators. Among progressive architects, at least, the politics of urban planning did not emerge as the central issue that it should have been, even as numerous comprehensive plans were put forth and debated in the two years following the disaster.

YM: This brings us to the recent work in New Orleans and other U.S. cities of the Spatial Information Design Lab (SIDL), the research center that you run with Sarah Williams at the Columbia University School of Architecture. Can you talk about the overall mission of SIDL and then bring it back to the New Orleans–related work?

LK: SIDL was started in 2004 to address a vacuum both within the architecture school in particular and in the university at large in terms of the increasing importance of spatial-information technologies to a range of research practices in disciplines from ecology, to public policy, to sociology and urban planning. The idea was to create an experimental laboratory for cross-discipilinary research and collaboration at the school, a place in which analyses and techniques of space in the broadest possible sense are a key concern and a matter of expertise. But SIDL was also conceived as a place to link university research with other groups and actors outside the university for whom spatial interpretation and design is or could be an important dimension of their work—especially in terms of urban policy. Our first project dealt with urban criminal justice, specifically in terms of what are known as "million-dollar blocks," MDBs. This is a paradigm of urban spatial analysis that tracks the disproportionate use of public money to incarcerate people from specific neighborhoods to the extent that more money is "invested" in putting people in prison than in any other service or infrastructure provided to that area by the city. Indeed, many urban neighborhoods across the country have developed extensive institutional "exostructures" of absent residents living in rural prisons. Aiming to highlight both the financial inefficiency and social dysfunction of the policies behind these patterns, this spatial paradigm was conceived by Eric Cadora after reading an article in the *New York Times* in 1992 quoting Eddie Ellis,[1] a former Black Panther and prisoner who became a criminal-justice-reform advocate upon his release in 1994.

YM: The key innovation was to use publically available data sets concerning incarceration and public spending and then to collate them with neighborhood-by-neighborhood, or indeed block-by-block urban maps—right?

LK: Yes, more or less. But it is important to emphasize that the data sets in question, although public information, are actually quite difficult to obtain—they are files assembled by the courts in tracking individuals though the prison system. Unlike the "crime maps" made available on the web by many police departments, in which color-coded crime rates for this or that neighborhood are generically superimposed onto urban maps to give an impression of overall "risk," MDB analysis displays the accumulated trajectories of specific individuals based on their residential addresses as recorded by the court. MDB mapping does not, of course, disclose the identities or precise residences of the individual cases that make up the patterns, but it does start from this individualized data, and so ethical issues of privacy are indeed a concern at a certain level. In other words, the data in question are quite sensitive and should not be publically streamed into the void of the web. The question is how to map and contextualize this data geographically in such a way as to tell a story about the policies and the people involved in this revolving door of incarceration and criminalization. Framed, annotated, and presented properly, these maps make a very compelling case that disproportionate amounts of money are going into imprisoning people, rather than to addressing socioeconomic problems (see color plate 7). What they show, at least in part, is the massive evacuation of municipal services and infrastructure that characterizes the neighborhoods they live in and the transfer not only of urban populations, but also of resources to the rural communities where prisons are located.

YM: So how did the collaboration between SIDL and the MDB activists develop?

LK: Well, when I first saw early versions of the MDB maps, my question was what does it mean when a specific area is marked as a "highest concentration area" for incarceration? What does that neighborhood look like? Who lives there—or at least has their official place of residence there? We knew that much more data needed to be considered in filling in the dynamics of these areas than were represented by the incarceration maps. Instead of putting generic splotches of color on a map representing sheer financial investment, we were interested in collating incarceration and financial data with specific buildings and in learning how much public money, per capita (that is, per prisoner), was going into incarceration at the expense of that neighborhood. The question was how to frame this data in an urban way, rather than a purely financial way. This meant intensively consulting about the best ways to communicate the ideas, analyses, and data in a clear way to a range of publics—from planners, to urban residents, to prisoners, to legislators, to museum audiences, and beyond. How could we as designers and spatial analysts assist in articulating the relatively technical, data-based research of the criminal-justice advocates into a set of actionable narratives concerning the injustice and dysfunctionality of actually existing criminal-justice spending patterns—and by extension, criminal justice and urban policy in general? The next step was then to ask, given that this money was being poorly spent in these neighborhoods by paying for their residents' incarceration in distant regions, how might that money be actually reinvested in terms of civic reentry, job training, infrastructural development, et cetera? Million-dollar blocks are understood as part of what Cadora calls "justice mapping": we describe the possibilities opened by this mode of mapping in terms of justice reinvestment.

YM: Can you talk about the multiple platforms, audiences, and publics that you and your collaborators have addressed with this work?

LK: This is actually something that I'm quite proud of with this work—it has been presented to and taken up by community members, local NGOs, city councils, museum audiences, journalists, and legislators, among others. The gradient across which the project has been able to communicate has been very impressive. Sometimes people worry that nonacademic and nonelite audiences are not going to follow these kinds of presentations, that you need to speak or visualize differently for different groups. To the contrary, my experience has been that if you have something that communicates well, it will communicate well across a broad spectrum, thus becoming a shared point of reference, debate, and proposal making. Across all the projects we've discussed so far, my underlying concern remains how to teach people to read architecture and its spatial characteristics in areas and fields and topics that apparently have little to do with architecture as we know it.

YM: Can you elaborate a bit on what it means to have an "architectural" reading of these statistical data sets? How do you as an architect relate to what Ian Hacking once called the "avalanche of numbers" characteristic of modern governmentality?

LK: In working with quantitative data, our approach at SIDL is not simply to give visual or spatial form to information that is taken for granted in advance. Without ever retreating from or dismissing the real-world power of statistical knowledge, we emphasize two key points. First, that no data set is ever neutral, either in its initial creation or in its eventual usages. And second, that data can tell compelling stories, but aren't often used that way. These forms of knowledge are out there and being mobilized in the exercise of power in various ways. Our task is to both critically question them and explore their unforeseen possibilities for making political claims about the organization and control of space.

YM: This involves a certain detour through nonquantitative methods, then. The numbers never speak for themselves. The question becomes what kinds of analyses, interpretations, or stories or narratives are told with, around, and about these data sets so that they become legible sites of public debate, rather than hermetic instruments of governmental administration by experts. This is a major concern for us in *Sensible Politics*, and it has often been undertheorized in discussions of activism and their visual cultures: How do different groups do things with data? How do data get framed and visualized so as to become the locus of a claim or a debate? Consider the ubiquity of data, numbers, and charts that are actually mobilized in NGO briefings, reports, testimonies, and so on.

LK: The collection of data is already "designed" from the beginning—this is why, in a deep sense, there are no neutral data. This is not a matter of falsification or manipulation in the typical sense—though that of course happens, and it is important to be vigilant about it—but rather, the very decisions and concerns that motivate the collection of a particular kind of data and the ways in which the data is collected and collated already have interpretive frames built into them that are all too often naturalized. This is the case, for instance, in the police crime maps that I mentioned earlier, which were an important point of reference for Cadora and Ellis in articulating million-dollar blocks as an alternative model of spatial analysis.

YM: SIDL has just published the fourth of a series of pamphlets concerning justice mapping and justice reinvestment, this one dealing with New Orleans. Can you talk about SIDL's work in New Orleans?

LK: We got a secondary grant for New Orleans on top of the original justice mapping grant; through our earlier research, we had already acquired a 2003 data set on New Orleans from the Council of State Governments, and we noticed that the criminal-justice population, which had already been in a kind of migratory pattern between rural prisons and specific urban neighborhoods, had a lot in common demographically with the populations displaced by Katrina and its aftermath. The project was to design a neighborhood plan for one of the communities that had shown high levels of incarceration-based migration prior to the disaster and to come up with a civic reentry program in concert with a range of other physical, infrastructural, and institutional initiatives in that neighborhood. Most of the planning in New Orleans was focused on rethinking housing and education, and the issue of criminal justice was really being neglected in planning discourse. On the other hand, there was a great deal of (well-founded) concern about crime increasing in these devastated areas after the flood, a reality and a perception that contributed to the sense of these areas as being somehow inevitably forsaken. So our initial task was to try to inject these concepts of justice mapping and justice reinvestment into planning discourse at various levels and to make clear that a focus on criminal justice was not simply a matter of "law and order" conservatism, but rather that the prison was already a central civic, social, and financial institution in these neighborhoods—so the question was how to reprioritize and redirect this dysfunctional public spending into sustainable urban reentry for ex-prisoners while still addressing neighborhood concerns about safety.

YM: What was the architecture of the planning process that you had to navigate?

LK: First it was a matter of communicating through the maps and acquiring new data sets with which the justice-mapping concept could be tested. We went to a lot of planning meetings at the local and city level and then had an opportunity to do a presentation for the city council. By demonstrating the disproportionate concentration of crime and criminal-justice spending in one particular area—Central City—we captured their interest. They saw our work as a comprehensive preventive strategy for the neighborhood, rather than a "crime reduction" tactic such as might typically be undertaken by law-enforcement agencies. Through the doors opened by the city council, we were able to form a network of organizations working in this one neighborhood, organizations dealing with urban development, education, and the arts. Since then, we have been working with this network to make criminal-justice and prisoner-reentry issues central to their programs, along with health, housing, education, employment, etcetera. We tried to show how in each of these sectors the issues intersect with criminal justice and the invisible centrality of the prison to the neighborhood overall. It has resulted in four pilot projects, including a mobile health clinic and a day reporting center, where offenders who are on pretrial release, probation, or parole check in with their caseworkers, but also affiliated activities, such as work with a group concerned with drug treatment, another with green-jobs training, another with teaching kids to make maps of local environmental conditions. There is also the Good Works program, which focuses specifically on job training for formerly incarcerated people. But really to make any of this work, you need an organizational person to sustain it as a pilot program—we want some of the money to go to getting an on-site coordinator, someone involved in long-term capacity building that will work outside of the rubric of SIDL. And of course also to have all of these activities be part of a system-wide evaluation. This aim of moving money away from the urban exostructure of prisons and into justice reinvestment is an element in a larger system of urban policy and political economy.

YM: So how then do the pilot projects relate to or get coordinated with larger-scale planning and policy initiatives in the city?

LK: Ed Blakely, the so-called "Recovery Czar" of the city, was aware of our initiatives, but he has had a very narrow approach to what he calls "renewing" these neighborhoods rather than rebuilding them. Based on the research and mapping that we have done with local NGOs, it is clear that a much wider sense of urban reinvestment is needed in both the private and public sectors. We have proposed a "justice-reinvestment corridor" in this area, which had historically been a site of black entrepreneurship, a network of overlapping projects and initiatives such as those we've just discussed. With very little money, you could prop up these small nonprofit groups. Things move very slowly in New Orleans. We don't have a predetermined model for how this will unfold; it's about developing the connections with the groups, securing further funding, and taking advantage of opportunities that become available with the urban administration at large.

YM: How is the project currently financed?

LK: This was initially a six-month grant from the Open Society Institute, but we've been working for much longer than that. We really rely on their network of grantees in New Orleans. We've had much more success working with the NGOs than with the community organizations.

YM: Can you explain the distinction, at least as it takes shape in New Orleans?

LK: The community groups have been long established in these areas and play an important sustaining role, but they are often very ineffectual at the level of policy. The NGOs have a relationship to these groups, but also with larger national organizations, and are embedded in a variety of scales in terms of mobilizing publicity and resources. I make this point because the way that a lot of people in the architecture and planning worlds conceive of "community design" often takes the status of the notion of community for granted, as a pregiven unity or foundation. But a community can be quite heterogeneous, with numerous goals and motivations, and it is defined in terms of relations between people without having any necessary spatial basis. Our analysis of million-dollar blocks takes the space of the neighborhood—rather than the substance of the community—as a starting point. NGOs typically have much more precisely targeted goals or missions in terms of the particular policies they aim to transform. The community groups were often not very interested in addressing questions of crime and incarceration, for instance, but rather in representing the community coming together, for example to work with business groups. While not unimportant, these efforts had little purchase on the specific needs of a high-incarceration neighborhood such as Central City. The NGOs working on criminal-justice issues across the city, but based in Central City, understood the specific needs and policy issues involved and were quite responsive to our pilot projects. Indeed, these NGOs chose to locate themselves in Central City for precisely this reason.

YM: You mention the fact that while working on very precisely targeted spaces and issues, NGOs can work within more broadly scaled and affiliated networks of activism, including at the national scale. And indeed, the SIDL *Justice Mapping* exhibition has itself been circulating nationally. Do you see the insights of justice mapping gaining any traction with the Obama administration? To what extent are these questions that can be addressed at a federal level, in any case?

LK: Actually, the Council of State Governments just presented it to Congress a few weeks ago, but of course, these processes are very slow, so we'll see what kind of response it might get from legislators. There's also the Second Chance Act, which is a proposed piece of legislation dealing with criminal records and prisoner reentry.[2] Around six hundred and fifty thousand people are coming out of prison every year, and one of the provisions of the bill would allow local-level reentry programs that have demonstrated at least 50 percent success rates to qualify for federal money. The notion of a Justice Reinvestment Act seems to make a good platform for a set of broader-ranging reforms. With the financial crisis, states are eager to cut their massive incarceration budgets, so justice mapping actually resonates in the current climate with many legislators, regardless of party affiliation.

YM: That said, even though there is a certain pragmatic bottom-line argument that justice-mapping analysis makes about the inefficiency and dysfunctionality of actually existing policy that is resonating with many urban administrations, at a deeper level, it also does call for a reorientation of the assumptions that guide much criminal-justice discourse in terms of the meaning of urban crime and the appropriate ways for society to address it.

LK: Yes. To be clear, the basic premise of this project is that incarceration is a response to economic and racial inequality, and not to crime as an isolated social problem. The work of sociologist Loïc Wacquant concerning structural processes of ghettoization in the neoliberal city and the revolving door between ghettoes and jails is quite resonant with our concerns at SIDL.[3] But we do not frame our analyses in terms of academic, theoretical, or even ideological discourse in the narrow sense, not because we disregard these in favor of some sort of naive populism—far from it—but because as I mentioned above, we are interested in developing new forms of spatial and policy literacy that will translate across and between different audiences and venues.

YM: In Foucault's terms, we might say that your concern is not to define and denounce a great "who" of power—which after all many people, ranging from Wacquant to Angela Davis, have done to convincing effect with respect to the U.S. criminal-justice system—but rather to develop techniques capable of working on the "how" of governmentality as it is exercised in this domain. To shift gears slightly, can we talk about your relation to the figure of Edward Tufte, author of

Envisioning Information and other canonical texts?[4] I ask because he is someone who had been quite influential in the fields of graphic design and architecture and who seems at first glance quite pertinent to the question of how activists visualize and mobilize data. I know that one charge made against his work is that it is primarily about aestheticizing, rather than interrogating the data in question.

LK: I like your "Foucauldian" interpretation of the project—thank you. As for Tufte, I share this view, but honestly, he is not a major point of reference for me, even negatively. Tufte's approach has been very standardized among graphic designers, with the cardinal goal being to communicate information "clearly." The information designer is thus defined as a kind of functional aesthetician who has no critical purchase on the data set in question in terms of its origins, its trajectories, its interpretation—all of the things that I am interested in excavating and tracking. My project is a much broader concern with the "communication," which is to say, the bias, that is already embedded in the data itself and about how it relates to spatial practices in the widest sense. Communication is not extraneous to preexisting data as a neutral medium through which that data set would then simply be translated or visualized—into icons, for instance. As in the *Terre Natale* project, the data builds the maps, and so what is left out of the data is absent from the map. In a satellite image, the most reduced form of the pixel, where it reveals itself as simply a block of color, is the place where suddenly you become blind to it—it is just an abstract color, and no longer recognizable as a piece of an image. None of the maps made with data that I have worked on have translated it into something pictorial that stands in for the image. Rather than Tufte, my object or my target would be more Otto Neurath, who was concerned with the translation of numbers into pictures—into icons that could be universally interpreted. If you think about GIS software, geographic information systems software, for instance, it is a constant picturing of numbers, but the images are all ready-made, because the numbers are spatially joined to a map. In some ways, GIS maps are latter-day Neurath icons. I'm interested in what the new icons of information are, and I think they're the satellite image, the pixel, and constantly updatable GIS maps.

YM: So it is not about developing a symbolic language. Neurath's project of modernist graphic design was about a kind of universal legibility based in translating numbers and pictures.

LK: Right, so one "person" icon would represent 500 people. I try to avoid that kind of language, and indeed Tufte and his followers are basically just reinventing an approach that had already been established in the 1930s. Our work is more about an updateable iconographic language that, again, is embedded in the form of the data.

YM: Perhaps we can extend this point to consider your recent revisitation of the *Monochrome Landscapes* project dealing with deforestation, which is concerned less with making a representational picture of data—this or that graphic icon standing in for a particular quantum of deforestation—than a kind of forensic image that is itself constituted as data in the very precise geographical and technical terms discussed above.

LK: I'm happy we're coming back to this, because we got sidetracked earlier. The new project is entitled *Shades of Green*. Like the earlier project, it involves the tasking of commercial satellite services, in this case Ikonos and GeoEye, to photograph very remote forest areas in Brazil and Indonesia, respectively. Ikonos now provides image data at one meter per pixel resolution, and GeoEye at 0.5 meters per pixel. According to the 2010 *Global Forest Resources Assessment* from the UN's Food and Agriculture Organization, "deforestation— mainly the conversion of tropical forests to agricultural land—shows signs of decreasing in several countries, but continues at a high rate in others. Around 13 million hectares of forest were converted to other uses or lost through natural causes each year in the last decade, compared to 16 million hectares per year in the 1990s. Both Brazil and Indonesia, which had the highest net loss of forest in the 1990s, have significantly reduced their rate of loss."[5] Nevertheless, forests continue to disappear. In these images, forest-cover loss is registered in different shades of green: dark green indicates original forest, medium green indicates recently burned and depleted forest, and light and very light green indicate pastures or crops. These chromatically graded images are annotated with the data pertaining to the moment of their being photographed and their precise geographical coordinates.

YM: How do you articulate such data-rich images with political analysis?

LK: Along with their constitutive underlying data, the images are accompanied by short captions describing the long-term patterns and dynamics at work "on the ground." Indonesia has aggressively converted its tropical forests into oil-palm plantations. These increased from 106,000 hectares in 1960 to around 18 million hectares of forests cleared for oil palms in 2006. "Clearing" may be a misleading term, of course, since what is going on is also logging. According to an intensive multidisciplinary study carried out between July 2005 and September 2006 by a group of activists and experts, it appears that loggers have been using oil-palm plantations as a justification to harvest timber. The government announced new plans, under the Kalimantan Border Oil Palm Mega-Project (April 2006), to convert an additional 3 million hectares in Borneo, of which 2 million will be in the border of Kalimantan and Malaysia. The rapporteurs of this report emphasize that the

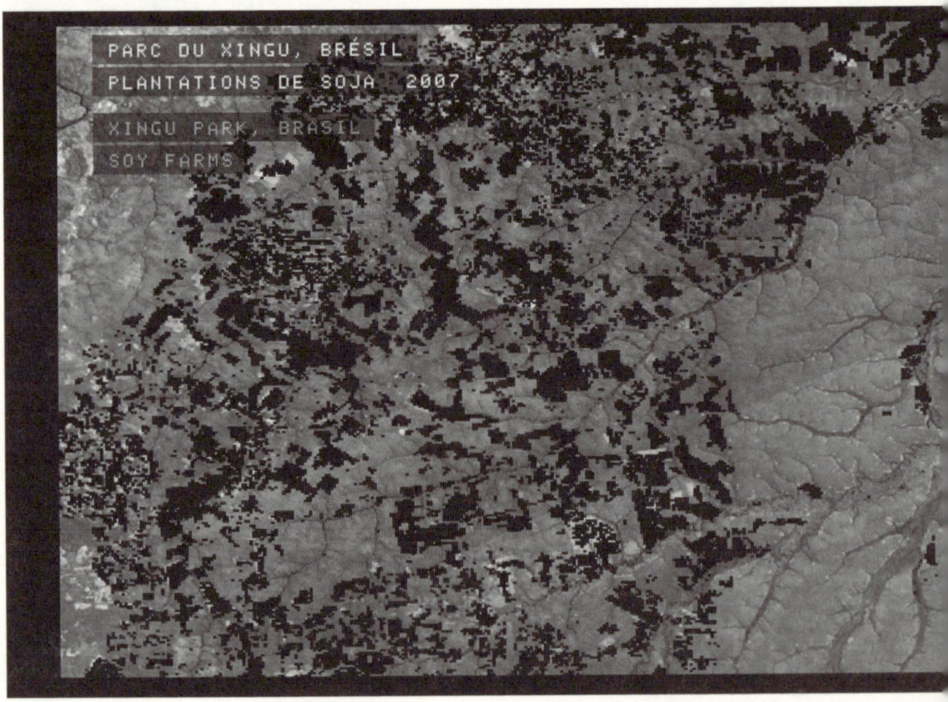

Xingu Park, Brasil, 1994–2007. Forest loss: 1,052,020 hectares. Cause of deforestation: Large-scale farming companies producing beef and growing soybeans (image: courtesy Artists Team).

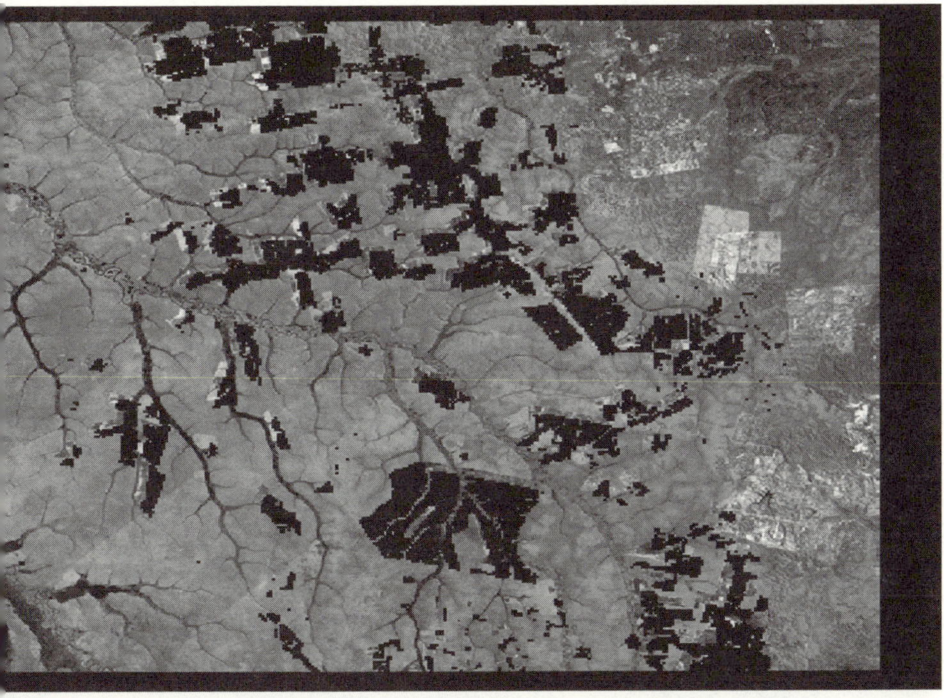

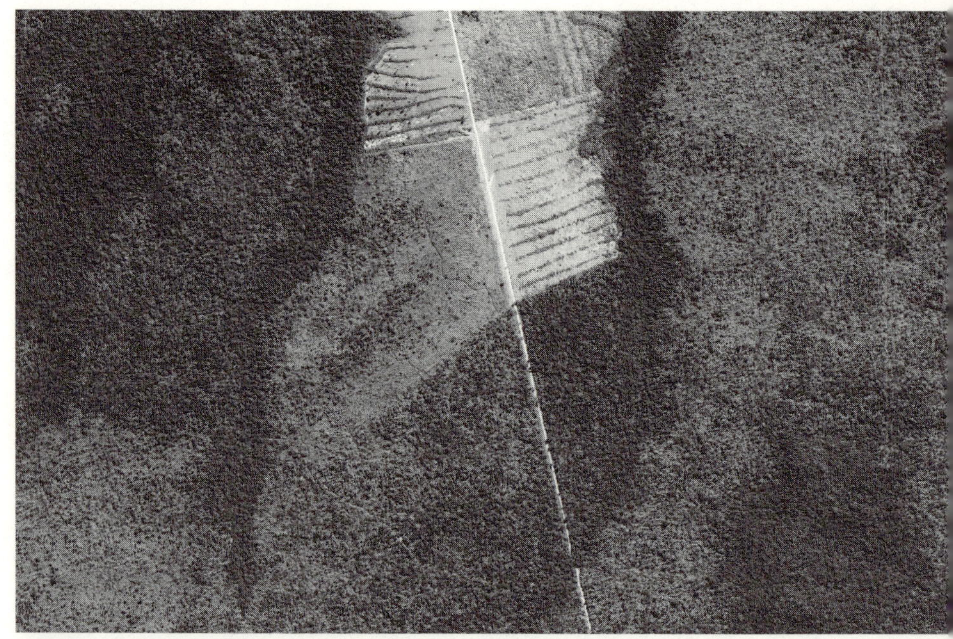

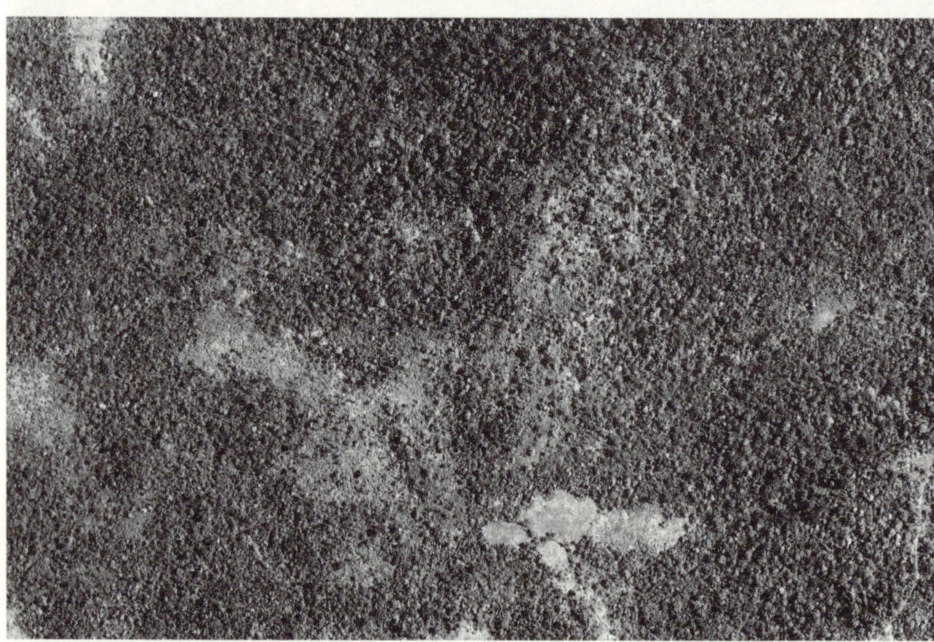

Details from "Shades of Green," Itauba County, State of Mato Grosso, Brazil. Itauba County covers about 4,500 square km, just south of the Amazon, with a population of less than 5,000 people. Agricultural lands now extend well into former forests, primarily for cattle ranching and soybean farming. Image Purchased from Ikonos Satellite, 2010, 1m per pixel, acquired February 16, 2008, 03:08 GMT (Includes material © 2008 GeoEye. All rights reserved).

area deemed suitable for oil palms includes forests used by thousands of people who depend on them for their livelihoods.[6]

YM: What do you think of the proliferation of experimental spatial and geographical practices in recent years? Some are within the disciplinary parameters of architecture, as with the work done by you and Eyal Weizman, while others emerge more specifically from art, as with the work of Trevor Paglen.

LK: Yes, I am happy to be identified with this group of practices, which are indeed coming from a diverse range of backgrounds—from Weizman and Paglen to Sandi Hilal and Alessandro Petti, Ursula Biemann, or Teddy Cruz—but they share an interest in critically addressing similar subject matter in terms of space and politics. I'm pleased this work is getting a lot of exposure lately—it definitely helps the kind of work that I do. They are all engaged with research design and crossing between research and design practice. For me, it started off as research, and it's crossing over into practice in a way that I would not have predicted. This is why I can now say with confidence that I do not have a building-design practice. For a period, I struggled with this, trying to develop a building practice in the limited sense. But I've realized that what I am most interested in doing is teaching people about spatial concepts, where and how to intervene as a catalyzing agent in spatial practices with technologies of presentation, representation, maps, and geography, overlapping with planning and also structures of participation. I see all of this as an expanded sense of what architecture can be or already does in the world.

YM: But there have been some projects in which this expanded sense of spatial analysis intersects with building practice in the limited sense, such as the projects with public schools?

LK: OK, I admit it, I have tried to build things once or twice—and I might try again. In this case, I was involved in advising architects on how to take certain spatial questions into account in terms of how physical spaces were articulated with the program of the school, how the different consultants and trades involved in the project interrelated. But I was not the architect—it was about defining how the project should be approached architecturally for everyone involved. But though I do not design buildings, I do have another kind of practice, one that operates not only in the university, but elsewhere in such a way as to have effects on things that are happening in the world... not in a grand sense, but...

YM: That brings to mind the SIDL mission statement. Alluding to Walter Benjamin, it suggests that data can open up new spaces and times of action. That is not a matter of just reflecting or communicating what's already there, but rather there is a kind of generative or inventive potential there for politics. Rather than a matter of truth or falsity, it is almost a question of the performative—"how to do things with data," to paraphrase J. L. Austin.

LK: Actually, I like to think about what I do as "how to do things with space."

YM: How about, in conclusion, some philosophical ruminations on the university institution? SIDL is a kind of experimental laboratory that in many ways is a kind of counterpoint—though not simply in opposition—to something like the Earth Institute at Columbia, which has a very unexamined technocratic agenda.

LK: For me, the university is a hugely productive place. As someone working in a nonprofit, nonbusiness mode, the university really does provide me a space in which to experiment with research and to do prolonged projects that can draw on lots of disciplines. For me, the combination of teaching and research has been hugely productive. The setup of a lab is important, because I'm not just writing—I'm not that kind of an academic. It's research that relies on actually doing things with the data, utilizing the technology that I'm writing about. The theoretical stakes are high, but the research happens by way of practice: much of what I know I have learned by doing things. Maybe the best word for this, in a not so traditional sense, is "experiment."

NOTES

1. Francis X. Clines, "Ex-Inmates Urge Return to Areas of Crime to Help," *New York Times*, December 23, 1992, http://www.nytimes.com/1992/12/23/nyregion/ex-inmates-urge-return-to-areas-of-crime-to-help.html.
2. Readers can track the current status of justice-reinvestment initiatives, legislative and otherwise, at the Council of State Governments website, http://justicereinvestment.org.
3. See, for example, Loïc Wacquant, *Punishing the Poor: The Neoliberal Government of Social Insecurity* (Durham: Duke University Press, 2009).
4. See, for example, Edward R. Tufte, *The Visual Display of Quantitative Information* (Cheshire, CT: Graphics Press, 1983), and *Envisioning Information* (Cheshire, CT: Graphics Press, 1990).
5. UN Food and Agriculture Organization, *Global Forest Resources Assessment 2010*, FAO Forestry Paper 163 (Rome: FAO, 2010), p. xiii.
6. See Marcus Colchester, Norman Jiwan, Andiko, Martua Sirait, Asep Yunan Firdaus, A. Surambo, and Herbert Pane, *Promised Land: Palm Oil and Land Acquisition in Indonesia. Implications for Local Communities and Indigenous Peoples* (2006), http://www.forestpeoples.org/sites/fpp/files/publication/2010/08/promisedlandeng.pdf.

PART FIVE

MULTIPLYING PLATFORMS

FIGURE 1 Egyptian activist filming in Tahrir Square during WITNESS video advocacy training (photo: courtesy WITNESS).

The Participatory Panopticon and Human Rights: WITNESS's Experience Supporting Video Advocacy and Future Possibilities

Sam Gregory

In testimony before the Senate Armed Services Committee May 7, 2004, in the aftermath of the revelations about torture committed by U.S. troops at Abu Ghraib Prison in Iraq, U.S. Secretary of Defense Donald Rumsfeld complained that "we're functioning . . . in the information age, where people are running around with digital cameras and taking these unbelievable photographs and then passing them off, against the law, to the media, to our surprise, when they had not even arrived in the Pentagon."[1] Rumsfeld should not have been surprised. We are in the midst of a period of tremendous growth in the use of images to document, educate, engage, and advocate issues concerned with human rights. The past twenty years have seen a progressive expansion in the participatory possibilities of audiovisual media: first, increased access to cameras and mobile technology with still and video image capability, then access to editing capacity, and most recently, the dramatic growth of online and mobile options for networking, circulating, manipulating, and sharing media. Twenty years ago, a video camera was a household novelty. Now the camera cell phone is ubiquitous. The latest statistics indicate that there are almost as many cell-phone accounts as individuals on earth, and that a third of the global population is online.[2]

This expansion in the technical capacity to gather and share media has been paralleled by increased digital media literacy, especially among youth who have access to technology and the Internet, and in a culture more and more focused on the audiovisual. Cultural expectations are changing toward a model in which it is taken for granted that anyone can create a piece of media. Via online video sharing and social networking sites and the "i-witness" appeals of media entities to send in footage, there also are apparent "amateur" and "professional" distribution venues for much of this material, venues that did not exist before. The presence of a camera in every concerned citizen's hand poses profound questions and creates powerful opportunities for the future of human rights video and human rights advocacy: issues of agency, action, and audience become even more pertinent. Across the world, human rights groups and concerned citizens are picking up cameras, utilizing new tools for collaboration, editing, and sharing, and attempting to place their footage in front of people who will act, whether these be their peers or people within formal structures of power. In many cases, the truth emerges even when repressive governments have done their utmost to suppress it—for example in Burma during the Saffron Revolution and after Cyclone Nargis, where violations documented on cell phones and digital cameras emerged from a closed society.

Yet, of course, human rights abuses continue to occur—individual acts of state violence, crimes against humanity on a mass scale, lack of state intervention to prevent egregious violations in the private sphere, as well as failures of accountability from corporations and nonstate actors, as well as the structural violations that involve denial of access to food, health care, or even basic education. This raises a question that must be addressed: As more documentation emerges and circulates, how do we ensure that increasingly ubiquitous images enable people to be more than just casual documentors, bystanders, and observers—how do we ensure that images generate more than compassion fatigue in viewers and contribute to meaningful action by all to counteract and end abuses?

Peter Gabriel, founder of WITNESS, the human rights organization where I am the program director, has talked of "Little Brothers" and "Little Sisters" watching Big Brother. This world of the "participatory panopticon," as the futurist Jamais Cascio has called it,[3] is one where rather than the visible and invisible state monitoring all, as in Jeremy Bentham's original concept of the panopticon and its subsequent use by Michel Foucault, everyone participates in "watching" each other and the state. A variety of other terms, including "sousveillance," "equiveillance,"[4] "ubiquitous sensing," have been proposed for this emerging phenomenon of the reversal of surveillance in societies that is facilitated by technological innovation employed by an empowered citizenry. The phenomenon is filled with emancipatory potential in terms of securing accountability for rights abuses. But this is only as long as we can make sure that the footage that circulates helps facilitate voice, action, and change, rather than enabling apathy, or, at worst, social control, public humiliation, and state repression.

Here, I initially focus on some of the lessons learned since its founding from WITNESS's experience enabling advocates at a local level to use video to conduct campaigns, including the development of a strategy of audience-centered video advocacy. At the center of all the shifts in approach and focus, however, has been a commitment not just to developing effective strategies and tactics, but to authenticity in storytelling, to the safety of those whose story is told and those who tell it, and to other essentially ethical issues that must perforce arise in the use of visual media for human rights advocacy. Using a series of videos as examples, I explore the growing range of creators and users of video, as well as the commercial, mass-public spaces they use for sharing and the challenges for human rights video in those sites. I then go on to explore ways in which ethical issues arise and how WITNESS has learned to deal with them, considering the new forms of emerging video documentation, including increasing quantities of witness and perpetrator-shot footage, as well as a burgeoning culture of the remix, and analyze them in relation to recurring issues of human dignity, human rights and efficacy, and the way in which we construct and share stories for advocacy and entertainment. Finally, I consider what modes of organized advocacy and action will be effective in a world of ubiquitous video production and distribution, considering the possibilities of a renewed form of targeted advocacy as well as the opportunities of distributed and collaborative production and distribution to create a new, network-centered video advocacy that will draw on an increasingly broad range of participants, not just passive viewers.

ENABLING LOCAL VIDEO ADVOCACY: LESSONS LEARNED

More than twenty years ago, a short sequence of video footage transfixed America and the world. It is a piece of video familiar to people I have trained around the globe—be they from Indonesia, Guatemala or Nigeria. Shot by George Holliday from his apartment window, the clip captured the beating of Rodney King—an African-American man—by members of the Los Angeles Police Department following a traffic stop. It was broadcast nationally and internationally, and it was a moment of visual imagery that simultaneously showed the reality of racism and discrimination to vast swathes of America and reminded many who experienced it on a day-to-day basis of its nature.

The Rodney King incident provided the impetus for the creation of WITNESS in 1992. Cofounded by Peter Gabriel and the Lawyers Committee for Human Rights, with support from the Reebok Human Rights Foundation, WITNESS was begun on the assumption that if you could place cameras in the hands of the people who chose to be "in the wrong place at the right time" and were not just accidental observers or uncommitted bystanders, that is, human rights advocates and activists around the world living and working with communities affected by violations, then you would enable a new way to mobilize action for real change.

WITNESS developed into a small organization working at an intersection of multiple professional worlds, including those of human rights (in which it primarily places itself), digital activism, video, online media, strategic communications, news media, and the world of popular entertainment. WITNESS's mission is to empower people to use video to open the eyes of the world to human rights violations and to transform personal stories of abuse into powerful tools for justice, promoting public engagement and policy change.

For the first decade of its work, WITNESS wrestled with how best to operationalize its founding idea. In the early 1990s, it focused primarily on technology, and the lessons learned as a result of that focus have shaped what we now do today. it distributed hundreds of cameras to human rights groups around the world, assuming that they would be able to gather footage that could get on television or be used as evidence—two polar extremes of usage, one very specialized and targeted at a judicial fact finder or jury, the other playing to a vast, undifferentiated court of public opinion.

As the *New York Times* described it in March 1992, "Let human-rights advocates around the world take heart. They will soon receive powerful new arms with which to wage their struggles against repression: hand-held video cameras, computers and fax machines," citing Peter Gabriel, "it's much easier for those in power to get away with murder, torture, repression and the destruction of our environment if their actions are not witnessed by the media and public."[5] It was a moment of what the anthropologist Meg McLagan has succinctly termed "1990s technophilia and [a] model of change based on the transparency of media."[6] The approach was grounded in a perhaps naive belief in the indexicality of the image—a firm conviction that "seeing is believing" and that seeing would create action in the same way that the Rodney King video had seemingly inspired mass outrage, and in the same way.

But this model was insufficient, frustrating, and ineffective. Technology in itself was not enough. In those first five to six years, WITNESS learned that without technical training, you could shoot the raw video, but you could not create the finished narratives that matter in most advocacy contexts, other than providing the raw footage directly to the news media. Similarly, in the absence of a strategic thinking for incorporation of the video into effective advocacy, even the most powerful visual evidence is potentially wasted. And the distribution venues for this type of human rights–oriented material were either absent or underutilized. Especially given the risks that human rights advocates ran to secure footage, the model required rethinking.

At the beginning we assumed—perhaps on the basis of the Rodney King experience—that most video shot would be used by the media or potentially as evidence.[7] Michael Posner, then executive director of the Lawyers Committee for Human Rights (now Human Rights First), the parent organization of WITNESS, noted "There are many countries where there is no Viznews [the international TV wire service] and the networks haven't had a reporter in years. . . . We hope that we can be a prod to international coverage, whether the networks air our footage or whether they take a look at it and decide there's a story to be done there" by their own correspondents.[8] Yet the initial assumptions about audiences and how footage would be perceived and utilized were largely not correct. In those days, before widespread online video sharing, the ways to access broad publics were ineffective. Although WITNESS focused on video in judicial processes and sharing video with the mass media—both of which are premised on the "evidentiary" value of human rights footage—both news media and evidentiary settings proved to be challenging to access.

Considered in retrospect, the Rodney King experience was anomalous. Although George Holliday's footage permeated the mass media and was used in the subsequent state and federal trials, the overwhelming majority of human rights video cannot and does not reach those venues. Furthermore, if it does, it is often presented in ways that are contradictory to the desires and intentions of the communities affected by the rights violations, as many marginalized groups have experienced in their media advocacy.

The reasons for lack of access and the failure of representation of course vary. But the results are the same. In some countries, it may be that media are under government or corporate control, or won't screen graphic imagery, or are interested in screening only graphic imagery. And in many cases, the news media focus on episodic framing that emphasizes individual actions, victims, and perpetrators and are less interested in structural violence, systemic challenges, or the ongoing problems that characterize many of the most pernicious abuses, especially violations of economic, social, and cultural rights. So, for example, a group that I have worked with in Papua, Indonesia,[9] documents the systematic, ongoing, and pervasive exclusion of indigenous Papuans in an economy dominated by migrants from other parts of Indonesia and in a justice system that rarely moves against the powerful. In seeking widespread media attention, they will face the triple barrier of government censorship, popular neglect, and an issue that is not easily reduced to the blow of a security-force baton. And indeed, for them, as for many other groups, it may be counterproductive for their concerns to be represented by thirty seconds of television footage of a popular protest in which violence erupts.

The other aspirational hope of WITNESS's founders was that video would be used as direct evidence. Yet the rules of evidence are frequently difficult to navigate, and the contested space of a courtroom is a challenging environment in which to place visual evidence.[10] Even if the evidence is admitted, we need only see how the Rodney King footage was flipped around, framed, and/or manipulated, both to prove that the Los Angeles Police Department officers were following the training they had been provided to deal with a resisting suspect and to demonstrate the grotesque abuse of power evident in the fifty-six blows delivered to Rodney King.

As a consequence of these lessons learned, WITNESS evolved a strategy of working intensely with a select smaller group of "campaign partners"—human rights groups on the ground that approach WITNESS to collaborate in helping them integrate video into specific campaigns and that it trains and supports in editing, producing, and developing a video action plan for effective storytelling, audience targeting, messaging, and distribution. WITNESS works alongside them on distribution, supporting the goals they have defined. Their footage contributes to one of the leading human rights media archives, sustained and archived at WITNESS's office. Sometimes WITNESS works with a range of groups in particular issue-advocacy areas, for example, challenging gender-based violence in conflicts and in situations of political repression, identifying how collaborative efforts and networked advocacy can enhance the effectiveness of the use of video in multiple venues in the campaign.

Alongside this, the organization offers extensive training for the growing number of human rights advocates seeking to use video, including intensive, two-week "boot camp" Video Advocacy Institutes, and it produces online training materials, such as short, shareable videos and an interactive online tool kit for developing a video action plan,as well as a regular blog dealing with what works, *Video for Change* (blog.witness.org).[11] It also edits books such as *Video for Change: A Guide for Advocacy and Activism* to promote effective ideas in the video advocacy community.

WITNESS has also engaged with how online and participatory spaces enhance human rights advocacy. First, it has done this via the development of The Hub, a participatory media site run by WITNESS from 2007 to 2010 where individuals and organizations could upload footage of abuses and finished advocacy videos, share it, learn how to deploy it in their campaigns, and present clear contexts for and links to more information, links to groups working to address the issues, and suggestions for actions that viewers and supporters could take. The Hub was also conceived as an online human rights community for knowledge sharing and networking on what has worked in using video and related tools for human rights advocacy. Subsequently, WITNESS's emphasis has shifted to a stronger focus on engagement with technology providers and broader online communities to build these values into their work, as well as on using commercial tools and spaces for video advocacy, a shift that I will discuss later.

Over the past twenty years, a number of other strategies also have come to characterize the WITNESS approach. As has been the case with many autonomous media groups and community media organizations, as well as many of its peers in the human rights movement, there has been a focus on the empowered voices of those who are closer or closest to rights violations—including victims, survivors, community members, and engaged advocates on behalf of affected communities. The agents of action are typically human rights workers and concerned citizens, in contrast to the groups such as Internews or the Crimes of War Project that improve the capacity of professional journalists to report on human rights issues.

Until recently, the approach has generally been to use "smart narrowcasting,"[12] rather than "broadcasting," that is, speaking to a particular key audience at a particular time, as the best way to seek a distinct change in policy, behavior, or practice. So, for example, the video *Bound by Promises: Contemporary Slavery in Rural Brazil*,[13] produced by my former colleague Tamaryn Nelson in partnership with the two human rights organizations Comissao Pastoral da Terra in Brazil and El Centro por la Justicia y el Derecho International (CEJIL), shares the stories of Brazilian men who are trapped in a cycle of exploitation in rural plantations, charcoal factories, and ranches, mired in increasing debt, and facing violence if they attempt to leave. The video was framed for and used in screenings to government officials and legislators in Brazil to push them to prioritize concrete programs to reduce rural slave labor.

As a consequence of the difficulties of using video in the media and as judicial evidence, WITNESS and its human rights partner groups also have looked for new advocacy audiences for visual evidence and testimony. In contrast to the human rights advocacy community's traditional view of visual media as simply providing news content or playing a "soft" promotional, fundraising, or educational role, the focus of video advocacy is as a directed campaign tool that motivates both individuals and communities to take action.

Videos are crafted for sequenced and targeted distribution and are always part of a continuum of action—and a strategy—rather than a stand-alone product or event. Primarily, the work has been in the advocacy spaces that lie in between the two framing and audience-scale extremes of direct evidence in the courts and undifferentiated mass-media attention. Several potential audiences inhabit these spaces. Beyond evidentiary settings such as a courtroom or international war crimes tribunal, where video could function as direct, contextualizing, or circumstantial evidence or can serve as material to prompt an investigation,[14] there are also quasi-judicial settings in which the potential audiences are the bodies that monitor compliance with international human rights law, but have limited enforcement power, including the UN Human Rights Committee or other UN charter and treaty bodies, as well as institutions at a regional level. For example WITNESS recently worked with an NGO in Kenya, the Centre for Minority Rights Development (CEMIRIDE), to use video as part of a successful land rights case at the African Commission on Human and Peoples' Rights, a case affecting the Endorois people of Kenya (figs. 2 and 3). Next, videos can target direct-to-decision-maker

FIGURE 2 Advocates from the Central African Republic and Democratic Republic of Congo participating in a WITNESS video advocacy training (photo: courtesy WITNESS).

FIGURE 3 WITNESS training with partner organization CEMIRIDE in Kenya (photo: Ryan Kautz).

contexts, meaning that in some cases, video needs to be shown directly to a key decision maker or decision-making body so that they can "witness" directly human rights violations or "meet" the victims. For example, our partners at the Macedonian human rights organization HOPS have brought the testimonies and experiences of sex workers who have experienced police violence directly to senior police and Ministry of Justice officials in their country as part of an effort to emphasize that no person should face illegitimate abuse.

Closer to the mass-media end of the scale are community mobilizing campaigns in which a video is shown within a community to mobilize it to take action on a specific issue or to demonstrate the capacity of individuals and communities to challenge abuses and alter the context in which these abuses happen, for example, showing a video on voluntary recruitment of child soldiers in villages across eastern Congo to stimulate community dialogue. Finally, closer still to the distribution of a video to general audiences via the mass media is its use in activist organizing of solidarity within a community or virtual community, increasingly via the Internet, integrating participatory and dispersed creation and distribution of advocacy content (fig. 4).

When WITNESS works to secure mass-media coverage of our partners' campaigns in news and mainstream documentary, it is with a recognition of the power of the mainstream media to distort the original agency and intent of the advocates who film the footage and reframe the issues and concerns in ways that will be nonproductive in a campaign context. In all these advocacy contexts, WITNESS encourages partners always to ensure that their videos provide a space for action by the audience, encouraging them to participate in solving the problem.

WITNESS's approach is thus to create videos for audiences as part of a campaign, rather than about an issue or in isolation. The videos are not just "about an issue," but "for a reason." They are constructed with an appropriate style and format in visual and storytelling languages appropriate for specific audiences, and they draw on different testimonial styles. For example, the video pushing for community debate on child soldiering in the eastern Congo will highlight conflicting opinions on the issue, will include children and parents talking about their experiences and warning others, and will be structured to lead into an in-person debate.[15] A video targeting youth organizers in California to engage them in organizing against the disproportionate incarceration of youth of color will deploy a visual style and story line that will differ markedly from the video presented to legislators, prison system officials, attorneys, and parents at a subsequent stage of the same campaign.[16] The first will feature music by the hip-hop group Dead Prez, empowered youth seen invading a Board of Corrections meeting to shut it down, and articulate teenagers explaining how they are organizing against the prison

FIGURE 4 Community screenings in the Democratic Republic of the Congo of *On the Frontlines: Child Soldiers in the DRC* (produced by Ajedi-Ka and WITNESS; photo: © Heidi Schumann, 2005).

system. The subsequent follow-up video will soberly present the vicarious experiences of parents watching their incarcerated children slide into despair and the retrospective views of former inmates, all framed by the official findings of expert reports reviewing the California Youth Authority and the counterintuitive voices for change of former officials from within the juvenile-justice system, of California senators, and even of the current director of the authority.

A premise underlying all of this audience chasing is that it is not necessarily the size of the audience that is most important, but their capacity and ability to act. Effective storytelling for action understands what combination of emotional, analytical, political, and persuasive registers or tones is needed to convince a particular audience. It generates an impetus to act—be it from shame, horror, compassion, or solidarity—and leaves a space for action by the audience. It is not a closed narrative or structure. Rather than relying on the visual evidence in and of itself or offering a high degree of interpretive openness,[17] stories provide a rhetorical framework that explains the visual evidence, and offers ways to act. Seeing may be believing, but it may also lead to pessimism and compassion fatigue in the absence of opportunities to act. WITNESS does not promote a journalistic model of studious neutrality—marginalized voices are excluded enough, without the need to balance their voices in a one-for-one ratio with the voices of authority or perpetrators. Most advocacy videos do have a point of view and an outcome in mind, but the best do this with clear respect for the facts of the situation.

WITNESS's role is often—though not always—to support its partners so that they can speak to audiences distant from themselves, often in order to generate a "boomerang"[18] effect in their home country. In these cases, you are telling transnational stories that must speak to an audience inevitably less grounded than you in the everyday realities of the oppression. So the footage in the video "Shoot on Sight: The Ongoing SPDC Offensive against Civilians in Eastern Burma" produced by one of WITNESS's campaign partners, Burma Issues,[19] working undercover in Burma, must speak not only to human rights activists within Asia, but to government officials, decision makers, and solidarity supporters in North America and Europe who operate within a different frame of reference and with a different level of knowledge and different predisposing assumptions than the human rights activists and, even more so, than the people whose stories they are telling and whose voices they are amplifying.

This transnational advocacy storytelling carries with it some distinct challenges:[20] of contextualization, of the dilemmas of moving testimony between differing advocacy and media arenas, and of the difficulties of establishing an ethical relationship, a community of witness, at a distance. Most human rights situations are embedded in contexts of structural complexity, with long histories of repression and reaction and many actors with different agendas. WITNESS tries to help its partners resist the "globalization of local images stripped of their meaning"[21] by keeping intact local voices in local contexts in a way that is faithful both to the direct visible violence of a situation as well as to the underlying structural causes. Yet as you move testimony and images between different advocacy and media arenas, it is often more effective to strip out some of the markers of specificity. For example, it may not be useful to include the details of a particular local offensive or set of local grievances related by an interviewee in a village in eastern Burma as you work to create a video that conveys a set of experiences across a whole region. From experience, I know that with many audiences, too much analysis of the particularity and nuance of a testimonial story may undermine it as an advocacy call. You are balancing the ethical demands to be true to the people who speak out, a recognition of the real complexities, and the desire to make viewers genuine ethical witnesses, on one side, against the need to convince, shame, or horrify a distant audience with a medium whose power often lies in directness, both visually and in narrative, on the other. In addition, one is wrestling with what Thomas Keenan has identified as "the paradox of rights talk: the claim is meaningless if it is not universalizable, but it is effective only if it is rooted concretely," since all rights claims are inherently a "plea on behalf of everyone, passing through someone in particular."[22] You must tell a story that is emblematic of a broader pattern, yet does not reduce it to a simple demonstration of a preconceived or overly simplistic argument. You must tell what might be termed a "paradigmatic story."[23] Frequently, you also have to make tough choices in balancing the visceral power and problems of raw visual evidence (for example, of graphic violence) with the use of testimony.

THE EMERGING HUMAN RIGHTS VIDEO ECOSYSTEM

What immediately follows are examples—videos from The Hub and other online spaces—of the emerging ecosystem of the "participatory panopticon" of human rights: what types of footage are being filmed, by whom, and how they are being used. YouTube is an example of one of the primary venues for the sharing and circulation of this material, and it thus also provides examples of the challenges faced by social-justice material in this space when competing for a mass audience or engaging a niche audience.

In Malaysia, in what has been called "Squatgate," police film the humiliation of a seminaked young woman of Chinese-Malaysian origin and e-mail it to each other. In Chechnya, a shocked woman staggers in the street after an assault by security forces.[24] In China, anonymous watchers document the scale of protest in small towns, challenging the state control of public knowledge about dissent,[25] and in Canada, First Nations protestors film their standoff with government officials, while in Madagascar footage shows security forces firing on protestors.[26] In the United States, passersby on a subway platform use cell phones to capture the shooting of an unarmed African-American man by police,[27] and in East Timor, a protestor on a beach is assaulted in front of the country's President,[28] while in Guatemala, China, and Cambodia, communities facing displacement from their land by mining and commercial development, video their moments of resistance.[29] Activists participating in a UN-affiliated mission to New Orleans take advantage of a digital camera to provide daily updates from the field to campaigners back home who were unable to be present,[30] demystifying the process, while leaders of the monks' protest in Burma speak direct to the camera to share mobilizing messages one year on from the Saffron Revolution,[31] and a survivor of a still-unpunished prison massacre in Brazil makes an impassioned call for accountability sixteen years on.[32] Campaigners for justice for crimes in Darfur share testimonies from on the ground at the Chadian border and the unexpected voices of people implicated in the crimes,[33] while hundreds of ordinary citizens add their own call for justice to a video wall of claims for action by the UN in the 24 Hours for Darfur campaign.[34] Sex-worker advocates from Southeast Asia remix and rework popular songs and images from antitrafficking campaigns into their own mobilizing films,[35] and labor activists in the Philippines use video to support hospital workers' petitioning for more reasonable work hours.[36]

As you can see from these videos, in the growing world of human rights video online, it is both the abuser and the abused, the purposeful witness and the casual observer, who are documenting what happens to them and what they do, and their outputs fall along a continuum from raw to produced and from journalistically "objective," to proudly partisan, to oblivious. They include the raw footage from the sites of tragedy, variants of which news organizations pursue through their user-generated media programs—what we might term "witness journalism." There are citizen-produced or NGO advocacy videos that are constructed and edited with a narrative or rhetorical framework, bystander witnessing, and also perpetrator-shot footage. There are also aggregative spaces for video where multiple citizen voices make a collective call for action. It is a world of remixers, commentators, and (re)purposeful users, of virtual witnesses and viral witnesses, as much as of direct observers. So where are the online spaces where this profusion of footage is shared, and how can we make them conducive to supporting human dignity, appropriate levels of transparency, and meaningful action? In terms of human rights footage being shared more broadly, rather than the voluntary sous/surveillance to which participants in social networking sites such as Facebook self-commit, the most prominent place that will come to mind for many Western creators, users, and perusers of online video is YouTube. YouTube is an example of a general, mass platform for online video and also the most prominent platform (at least in the Global North and for English-language media) for sharing video online with a broader public. For many individuals, alongside Facebook, it is the first place to put a piece of human rights video they shot or found. And many nongovernmental advocacy organizations that are trying to engage a general public either with a single video or via a channel assume rightly that YouTube is likely to be the first place that public will look. However, many of the issues I will raise concerning YouTube would be as relevant to Tudou (one of the most popular online video-sharing platforms in China), or Daily Motion (a prominent European-based video-sharing site), or indeed most of the primary commercial platforms for video sharing or most social-networking sites in general.

The initial burst of scholarship about YouTube, has highlighted the inherently contradictory nature of the site:[37] it is simultaneously a site for broadcasting by established corporate interests and a site for grassroots creativity, participation, and action. Thus, "much as the site supports broadcasting-like activities, for some users the site is as much about discussion, response and interaction with audiences and friends as it is achieving economies of scale for wide-spread distribution."[38]

It is also a useful starting point to recognize the Web 2.0 nature of YouTube or any similar mass platform for uploading: it is a pushing-out point for footage that finds homes in many other subculture-specific media systems, including human rights, where it is embedded and recontextualized in ways that may be much richer than their first home on YouTube. YouTube itself is also a series of niche communities, rather than one homogeneous site. As Michael Wesch, an astute observer of the overall online mediascape, notes, "the 'most viewed' videos on the prominent pages of YouTube may not be important, interesting, or intellectually stimulating, but social bookmarking services, memediggers, and social networks often bring the rich, stimulating, and politically important content we want to see right onto our desktops."[39] To this list, we might also add the way in which blogs embed and recontextualize video clips.

It is also important to note concerns that emerge in the use of a mass, commercial space for human rights activism, particularly for users who are engaged citizens concerned about security, looking to ensure that their footage galvanizes action, and suspicious of corporate and government surveillance. Their concerns may include the fact that they are small fish in a big pond and the opportunities that commercial sites present to create meaningful communities and to generate action.[40] Add to these the concerns about commercial exploitation of human rights imagery, the safety and security of the uploaders and the filmed, surveillance by corporations and the state, inflexibility in redistribution, downloading, and sharing, and where editorial control is vested. Against these worries users must consider the opportunity to engage an audience that goes beyond preaching to the choir and the technological capacities of a space that is backed by the creative engineering power of Google, a massive corporation.

In the interests of simplicity, it may be worth considering two types of human rights video content on YouTube: first, content that posted with the hope that it will achieve viral status or high numbers of views, and second, content that circulates within niche communities of interest and sometimes specifically within a YouTube cultural context.

Human rights video remains generally among the least-viewed content on YouTube, amid the proliferation of music videos, parodies, and commentary. A March 2007 Center for Social Media study found that public-issue videos are "small fish in a vast sea,"[41] though this was before the launch of the YouTube Nonprofit and Activism Channel, which has increased slightly the visibility of social-issue videos, and before the Citizen Tube channel and the agent change editor position at YouTube were created. The most popular social/public-issue video in the Center for Social Media study had 150 times fewer viewers than the most popular video on YouTube, and the terms on which they had to compete for the public audience were the co-optation of the characteristics of humor, celebrities, popular-culture touchstones, and music that are most common in the top-ranked YouTube videos. Even when we turn to the frequently watched witness-journalism footage, for example material from the postelection protests in Iran in 2009, viewer figures are in the hundreds of thousands for some significant videos, but remain dwarfed by the tens and hundreds of millions of hits for music and popular-culture videos.

Henry Jenkins has described an aesthetic of online videos that is comparable to that of vaudeville, in which "in a context of constant variation, the individual performer tried above all else to be memorable, which typically meant a strong reliance on spectacle and a desire to intensify emotional effects. . . . The best YouTube content is content that is so unbelievable that it has to be shared."[42] Some human rights video can play in this field. A powerful example is the "Waiting for the Guards" video developed by Amnesty UK for their Unsubscribe-me campaign, which features a recreation of the stress-position enhanced-interrogation technique used by the CIA as the centerpiece of a Web 2.0 campaign focused on action via social-networking sites.[43] But with some exceptions, much human rights material is not immediately powerful and may not be most effectively or honestly presented as "so unbelievable that it has to be shared."

Another aspect is what happens to grassroots human rights video on YouTube if it does secure a mass YouTube audience. WITNESS's own experience with YouTube has included at least two videos that were fortunate enough to be chosen as Editor's Picks and that also received a strong, continuing viewership: "Shoot on Sight,"[44] produced by partner Burma Issues documenting military attacks on ethnic minority civilians in eastern Burma, picked during the height of the crisis in that country in autumn 2007, and "Awaiting Tomorrow,"[45] highlighting lack of access to HIV/AIDS treatment in the Democratic Republic of the Congo, produced by locally based partner Ajedi-Ka Project Enfants Soldats and placed on YouTube's home page on December 10, 2007, International Human Rights Day. Both videos received reasonably high viewer levels (approximately one million, three hundred and thirty thousand for various versions of the long and short videos of "Shoot on Sight" and four hundred and thirty thousand for "Awaiting Tomorrow," as of November 2011) and significant levels of comments.[46] These levels of viewership are great in terms of reaching an audience that would know little about ethnically targeted violence in eastern Burma or access to antiretrovirals in the Congo, and the commentary is indicative at least of the interactive power of YouTube.[47] However, the comments ranged from the constructive to the racist and conspiracy-theory obsessed.[48] Many tapped into the "underground culture of cathartic pleasure" that characterizes many serendipitous encounters with footage of horror and distress on YouTube,[49] and it is unclear how the framework of the YouTube page lends itself to using individual videos to focus action of the type that WITNESS or local human rights advocates seek or to fostering sustained, meaningful discussion.[50]

Recognizing that YouTube should not be viewed solely as a single site, but as a nexus of content that circulates in more detailed, niche contexts, I should note that the most effective uses of the YouTube versions of "Shoot on Sight" were in blog postings, where the video was embedded in additional context, commentary, and recommendations for action, and in its use by venues such as the Facebook Support the Monks in Burma action group.

However, in general, from the point of view of human rights advocacy, it was very hard to turn a transitory audience into an engaged public or to measure the transition from viewing to action and on to impact. For human rights activism, one wants a community oriented toward action, recognizing also that online environments where no one "listens" to others and responds constructively are the opposite of the empowerment of voice that grounds WITNESS. As Howard Rheingold has observed in relation to youth participation online, in an analogy that could easily be extended to overstretched, marginalized human rights advocates, "it isn't 'voice' if nobody seems to be listening."[51]

In this light, it is more interesting to consider how human rights activism is taking place within niche communities and YouTube-specific subcultures. An example within a particular YouTube community is the work of the Nerdfighter vloggers, John and Hank, a pair of thirtysomething American brothers who publish a regular blog, *vlogbrothers*, subscribed to by over three hundred and sixty thousand YouTube users, including many teenagers and young adults.[52] Each year, they organize an installment of what they call the Project for Awesome that mobilizes their fan base to create videos for charity and to take over the YouTube "Most Discussed" page on a given day.[53] In 2009, they, alongside the Harry Potter Alliance (which is "dedicated to using the examples of Harry Potter and Albus Dumbledore to spread love and fight the Dark Arts in the real world"[54] and creatively combines pop culture, new media, and social action), supported the UK-based Aegis Trust's Candles 4 Rwanda Project, which memorialized the fifteenth anniversary of the Rwandan genocide, raised awareness about what happened, and raised funds to support survivors. The Aegis Trust asked people to light a candle and film it, then share it on YouTube. The Nerdfighters, on their *vlogbrothers* YouTube channel, took the characteristic indigenous format of YouTube, the vlog, and translated this appeal for action into a personal, conversational request to their own community, framed within their own understanding of YouTube's "attention economy." Hundreds of the channel's followers, as well as supporters of the Harry Potter Alliance, responded, creating videos such as that of YouTube User HEH28, who was apparently then in her late teens, living somewhere in the United States, and from a brief look at her YouTube channel page, was into vampires, the cop show *Castle* on U.S. television, and Harry Potter. Most of her uploads relate to these interests and include examples of vidding remixes (fan videos made by remixing footage from TV shows, movies, and music videos to create new narratives) from these pop-cultural touchstones, except for this one human rights video. In her video, with her eyes (or those of the young woman she filmed, though one assumes it is her) aligned with a candle on a table and a camera, she silently lights the candle in memory of Rwanda, then switches the light off, leaving her eyes illuminated in the candle's glow. Then the video ends. Hundreds of others, mainly young women, such as ZfrogGirl, HatofDoom, and TheOneEyedOwl, did this, as well, in each case watched by between fifty and two hundred of their friends. They thus spoke to a small audience, they did it with a simple act, they experienced the act themselves directly, and they reached people who would never have known about the fifteenth anniversary of the genocide. In the face of critiques that this type of activism is an example of "slactivism" or "clicktivism," it is worth considering such an act in the context of a ladder of participation that offers first opportunities for action and where participation in and of itself helps shift people from being bystanders to participants, offering an opportunity to make an active contribution to a cause.[55]

EMERGING ETHICAL QUESTIONS WITH NEW CREATORS AND NEW FORMATS

Core to all of the strategies and tactics that WITNESS has developed as a result of the lessons learned over the years has been a focus on ensuring that video usage in human rights contexts is ethical in terms of creation, storytelling, and distribution, not just effective for its advocacy usage. These concerns—also expressible in terms of issues of authenticity, efficacy for action, and safety—are brought into even sharper focus as we enter a world of dramatically increased participation in the documentation and sharing of images and testimony of human rights violations. Perpetrator-shot footage and the use of remix for human rights provide a useful entry-point into this discussion, and after sharing some key examples of both I examine the ethical issues raised by new forms of storytelling and a culture of sharing, reappropriation, and remixing.

Among the human rights video clips found online, the footage shot by perpetrators—particularly the proliferation of images of torture filmed by police, security forces, and military personnel themselves—raises a series of ethical questions related to human rights norms in this online sphere, the participants in this content generation, and the efficacy of different strategies for using videos to influence viewers.

One of the five most-viewed videos on The Hub is a redacted version of a notorious clip of cell-phone footage shot by Egyptian police in which they humiliate a Cairo bus driver by slapping him repeatedly.[56] These images—and other, more graphic videos that include the sodomization of another driver—were filmed by the police and subsequently used to humiliate the victims, for example, by sending the images to other drivers,[57] and to intimidate other people by demonstrating what would happen if they didn't follow police orders. They carry the triple humiliation of the act of assault, the act of documentation and the subsequent preservation and distribution of the material.[58]

Similar cases have galvanized debate in Slovakia, where Roma boys were forced to hit each other, kiss each other, and strip naked,[59] in Greece,[60] where similarly, two Albanian immigrants were forced to slap each other on camera (a case extensively discussed by Nelli Kambouri and Pavlos Hatzopoulos),[61] in Malaysia (the infamous Squatgate case mentioned above), and in countries on almost every continent. And of course, footage is also shot increasingly by governments to document and apprehend protestors and dissidents. In the United States, there has been a contentious suit related to the arrests of protestors at the Republican National Convention in 2004, with video accounts from police and activists contradicting each other; in the UK, there has been controversy over the so-called Forward Intelligence Units (FITs) that monitor people attending climate-change protests, and in the footage of protests from Burma, Iran, and Tibet, official cameramen can be seen documenting the events for future use in detentions, prosecutions, and/or persecutions.

Consequently, a question arises of intent. Does it matter that these videos were originally shot by perpetrators, if they succeed in generating action once they enter the public sphere? Jamais Cascio has suggested that the "Rodney King moment" of the digital camera era may have been the Abu Ghraib photos,[62] and I would argue that the analogue for cell phones was the footage of Saddam Hussein's execution. Yet both sets of images were filmed by perpetrators or by insiders, not by concerned citizens, advocates, or observers. They are about voyeurism and the exposure of powerlessness as a final humiliation. Understood in those terms, they are diametrically opposed to human rights values. Yet these videos circulate beyond the circles for which they were intended and are reascribed new meanings and new contexts and framings, and this is a characteristic of the new ecosystem in which we operate. For example in Egypt, bloggers and journalists led by Wael Abbas[63] and Hossam el-Hamalawy[64] circulated the leaked cell-phone videos to challenge repeated denials by the government of accountability for police brutality and torture. By circulating the videos and connecting online to both a local and an international audience, they were able to generate media attention and force an official response. Although the government initially tried to discredit the activists and their material, it was very hard to deny the truth of the images or the public exposure, and for the first time, there was an investigation into the conduct of police officers, the officers in two of the leaked videos, leading to a prosecution.

As Henry Jenkins has described it in *Convergence Culture*, this circulation and reappropriation of images shot by others is a key aspect of contemporary online culture, which emphasizes participation and enables "consumers to archive, annotate, appropriate and recirculate media content in powerful new ways."[65] Sometimes this will take the form of culture jamming—surfacing unexpected or hidden meanings in pop culture and footage not obviously connected to human rights issues. See, for example, the virtuoso work of Jonathan McIntosh remixing the U.S. television series *Buffy the Vampire Slayer* and the globally popular film series *Twilight* to pull apart themes of gender identity and violence[66] or the multiple remixes of the film *Avatar* with, for example, the animated film about Native Americans, *Pocahontas*.[67] Remixes of news and archival footage have made powerful political commentary in the United States about President Bush and his actions in Iraq, and in the UK, Nick Griffin, the leader of the British Nationalist Party, has been remixed to state his "true" views on race and the Holocaust.[68] Similarly, groups with which WITNESS has worked at a local and regional level around the world have used karaoke remix formats to communicate effectively about human rights issues, for example in a video from one of our Video Advocacy Institute alumni from the Asia-Pacific Network of Sex Workers.[69]

Other times, remixes can more directly use human rights footage—for example, in a much-viewed and commented-upon YouTube video entitled "Police Brutality—Police Get What They Deserve." Set to the anti-establishment song "Mr. Jack" by System of a Down, it had been watched almost two and a half million times on YouTube and with almost fifteen thousand comments before it was removed as a violation of YouTube's policy on shocking and disgusting content, or the range of videos that appropriate the Michael Jackson song "They Don't Care About Us" for commentary on the situation in New Orleans,[70] East Timor,[71] and Iran.[72]

But how does this remix ethos relate to a human rights culture that is concerned with the dignity and integrity of victims and survivors and the role of ethical witnessing and ethical reuse of individuals' testimonies and images of real individual and structural violence? I laughed heartily at remixes of George Bush, and even more so of Nick Griffin, but how do we think about the remix of images and words pulled from the sites of real trauma into the new expressive cultures of the Internet? Human rights culture emphasizes the integrity and dignity of the individual survivor of abuse on the basis of the first principle that every human being is possessed of "inherent dignity,"[73] a concept that runs through every right in the

Universal Declaration of Human Rights and that is particularly concerned with protection of the victim and survivor from physical revictimization and psychological revictimization, as can happen when an image is distributed and exploited inappropriately—the young woman in the Malaysia Squatgate scandal pleaded for her image not to be circulated anymore in public. Human rights culture also valorizes the role of the "ethical witness," who reacts with empathy to another's suffering. Consequently, we face considerable existential and practical dilemmas in a remix culture environment. (For more on these dilemmas see "Human Rights Made Visible: New Dimensions to Anonymity, Consent, and Intentionality" in this volume.)

In the YouTube video cited above on police brutality, a series of images from multiple cultures, political contexts, and longer-form documentation are genericized into a political argument stripped of meaning. The key frame image of the "Police Brutality—Police Get What They Deserve" video is the iconic image of Egyptian police torture described earlier in this essay, but in the video, that context is lost, and that individual case for justice is subsumed into a generalizing narrative, a paradigmatic story stripped of any substantive logic, just the propulsive logic of the underlying music. This point is not lost in the comments stream—amid the fifteen thousand or so comments, two sides are represented, each imposing their framing on the material. Surferknut23 notes, from one perspective, "all i saw when i watched this video was people who don't know how to listen getting their asses beaten," while SplittingSkulls from a different perspective comments: "Gota love fucking stupid people. A bunch of random photos with no way of knowing what happened and videos from around the world where the laws are completely different then here adds up to police brutality? What a fucking stupid video."

And beyond this question of authenticity and fidelity to the truth, are we adding yet a further layer of humiliation and revictimization to existing layers? Individuals in a cell-phone torture video are victimized first by what happens to them in custody, then by the act of filming, and then as the footage achieves widespread circulation and is potentially remixed and reused inappropriately or in a manner that further harms them.

This continuum of remix also extends to more purposeful projects and structures. We are in a moment of an exploding profusion of service providers (free and otherwise) enabling remixing, including YouTube Editor, Stroome.net, Kaltura, and Citizens Global Studio. This also is a time of experimentation by networks and more formal organizations with how to incorporate remixing into their practices. This impulse is driven by the recognition from social-movement theory that direct participation is at the heart of any mobilization of activity and that for the so-called "digital native" youth of today's connected societies in the Global North, the most active forms of participation are taking place in these online spaces, often by creating, remixing, and annotating visual media. And of course, beyond initial participation, there is the hope that the opportunity to be an active participant, a coproducer, rather than just a viewer or mechanical actor (writing a form letter, signing an electronic petition) may promote more thought, more insight, and sustained engagement.

WITNESS has participated in some experimental advocacy in this space, driven by this recognition of the power of participation. In one instance, we provided footage for a contest-based approach to publicizing the use of conflict minerals from the Congo in cell phones, a contest coordinated by the Enough campaign in collaboration with YouTube's Video for Change initiative. We provided a series of clips from our partner Ajedi-Ka Project Enfants Soldats in the Democratic Republic of the Congo that documented conditions in the militia camps, as well as in as a range of urban and rural settings. We debated internally how to present the material and ended up sharing it as a series of clips with title cards providing specific time and location details. Ultimately, however, it turned out that footage of the situation on the ground was little used in the leading entries in the competition, and where it was, it was often as "wallpaper" footage or emotive imagery echoing standard tropes of the "African child soldier," rather than being used in any substantive sense. For example, it is seen transposed onto a computer screen that is intercut with a young woman receiving a text on her cell phone about the campaign in a video uploaded to YouTube by user CheFoo10.[74]

In a more deliberative instance of remix advocacy—and a more bounded one, in terms of what users were asked to do and their understanding of their audience—we partnered with the student antigenocide coalition STAND on their Pledge2Protect campaign,[75] seeking more effective U.S. legislation on genocide prevention. Here, we were interested in remixing not only as a mode to secure participation, but also because of the narrative and advocacy possibilities of building on a broadening base of visual-media skills in a distributed network of peer production for thinking about how to rework a set of audiovisual material to appeal to a range of specific communities of interest.

We developed a short "template video" with STAND organizers in Washington that outlined the case for enacting into law the recommendations of the bipartisan Genocide Prevention Taskforce and that included footage from genocidal situations around the world, as well as some key interviews. We also prepared a selection of short clips from the WITNESS archive that could be used by others. Then we supported student chapters of STAND from around the United States to develop customized videos that would be targeted to their specific U.S. senators, speaking to their particular interests and incorporating material and local voices relevant to them. Here, we were attempting to combine the power of remixing with the principles of video advocacy in focused storytelling directed to specific audiences, in this case, down to the individual level. As my colleague Chris Michael described it on the WITNESS blog: "We wanted to see how video could not only be made for a group of key decision makers—but individualized for each decision maker. We wanted to integrate video into this campaign to see how a decentralized, motivated network could quickly create, share and edit multimedia content targeted to key decision makers—in this case U.S. Senators."[76] So WITNESS provided focused training resources and advice to help the participants think about video advocacy and personalized remixing. In one of the videos from Florida, students took this guidance and not only included their own voices making direct appeals and personal appeals grounded in their and their senator's Christian faith, but also identified "lost boy" refugees from Sudan who were living in Jacksonville, Florida, to speak about their own experience of genocide and persecution and to "approve this message" in a self-referential and legitimizing aside to the political campaign-ad format.

Videos from California and Wisconsin included montages of high-school and college students expressing their thanks to their respective senators for their actions to date and incorporated community figures whom they assumed their senators would know, respect, and listen to (for example, a respected academic and an award-winning humanitarian), who urged the senators on to further action. Other videos took this full-remix approach, while many took a simpler approach and incorporated intros and "outros" from students and community leaders into the template video. Of note was the way in which many of the students incorporated music and found footage from documentaries and news clips from the Internet, played with the conventions of YouTube vlogging speech to camera and its contrast with the more formalistic narrative of the template video, and how their remixes did not depend on using sophisticated software —indeed most of the remixes were done using basic tools such as iMovie and Final Cut Pro. Although the finished videos did also live online, they were narrowcast direct to the senators, shown to them personally during students' visits to their offices on a Washington, D.C. lobby day.

The possibility of remixing, reappropriation, and recirculation thus simultaneously pulls the material further and further from its source testifier and witness, even as that process of translation undoubtedly sometimes increases the chance that the footage will find its consumer, its reshaper, and its audience and be framed in ways that will be meaningful to that audience, and engaging for its re-shapers.

MOVING PEOPLE TO ACTION: IMPLICATIONS FOR HUMAN RIGHTS ADVOCACY

Such a fully participatory approach is of course only one of the many possible ways in which videos can be used to further a human rights agenda. From a practitioner's perspective, two key aspects bear thinking about with regard to how ubiquitous moving-image media, particularly online, can be used to motivate action in a human rights campaign. These are the ways in which storytelling and messaging can best be approached and how the possibilities of collaborative production, distribution, and advocacy can best be realized.

As we have discussed in the context of YouTube, the process of creation and distribution has been democratized, but the question of how consistently to find and mobilize an audience remains relatively open to experiment in the world online human rights video, particularly for human rights movements and organizations. As they reach out to communicate to and engage the unconverted and the curious, how do they cultivate an audience that has an interest in this material that goes beyond looking for the most brutal and graphic images? How can they create a dynamic of responsible witnessing? As they try not just to preach to the choir, how do they mobilize an engaged public to effective rather than token action?

As discussed earlier, I believe one of the keys to successful human rights video is the process of responsibly creating transnational stories that hold meaning and generate action. How are these meaningful and ethical stories generated, circulated, and acted upon in venues that to date have prioritized very short forms and even raw footage and that seem to value the highly postmodern characteristics of irony, humor, cynicism, and a focus on popular culture that often is extremely disconnected from a human rights agenda? In a glutted information environment where there is more of everything on everything, how is attention to be focused, and how is action to be generated?

The artist Tom Sherman, in assessing the challenge that video as the new everyman vernacular, the new "people's medium," poses to traditional video artists, notes the "vernacular video" characteristics of YouTube.[77] As he describes it, in its "noisy torrent of immense proportions . . . the people's video is influenced by advertising, shorter and shorter attention spans, the excessive use of digital effects, the seductiveness of slo-mo and accelerated image streams, a fascination with crude animation and crude behaviour, quick-and-dirty voice-overs and bold graphics that highlight a declining appreciation of written language." It also is permeated by "mediated horror" from the capturing of natural and man-made catastrophes. In a world where videomakers are a dime a dozen, Sherman observes that "video artists must introduce their brand of video aesthetics into the vernacular torrents. They must earn their audiences through content-driven messages."[78]

Human rights activists face the same challenges as they attempt to access an audience without losing their integrity in conveying stories while maintaining a message that will generate action. They also have the opportunity to engage with this "noisy torrent" in creative and effective ways that draw on the volume of the torrent, rather than fearing this bombardment of images,[79] by aggregating, curating, and contextualizing multiple images for evidentiary and advocacy purposes.

So what will work as strategy in this context? Any answer is likely to incorporate the old and the new and both controlled and unbounded approaches. Just as much as focusing on single images in the torrent, it will consider ways to give meaning and context and ways to promote action using multiple images aggregated there. It will neither assume that the digital environment of ubiquitous creation and sharing completely transforms existing models of activism or organizing nor, conversely, take for granted that nothing has really changed with the advent of increased participation and the opportunities for collaboration, creation, and re-creation offered by digital video, digital literacy, and the Internet.[80]

On the one hand, there will continue to be value in building a powerful strategic communications strategy where some of the assumptions of current video advocacy concerning smart narrowcasting for advocacy and organizing do not shift much. As discussed earlier, in this context video is created within a tightly focused communications team and strategy and distributed to a defined audience. Online distribution functions primarily as a delivery method both to a core audience and onward as the video is shared by that audience to secondary audiences. This approach particularly lends itself to mobilizing dispersed audiences who can be reached and aggregated through an online campaign, for example, mobilizing both the solidarity community of activists and the diaspora concerning the situation in Tibet, or Israel, or Burma, or engaging a transnational campaign network or movement such as sex workers, trade-union activists, or antitrafficking advocates. In these cases, campaigners need to develop an approach that finds self-contained storytelling strategies that resonate with their audience and that also work for the online video medium, then disseminate the material in ways that take advantage of the viral or community-based qualities of successful online distribution and that make the transition between viewing and acting either online or offline as seamless as possible.

However, we now operate (often, though not always, because of the continuing global digital divide in skills, access, and participation) within a networked public sphere where, as Yochai Benkler describes it, "the easy possibility of communicating effectively into the public sphere allows individuals to reorient themselves from passive readers and listeners to potential speakers and participants in a conversation."[81] So, alongside renewed opportunities for individual production and targeted advocacy, both online and offline, collaborative message generation, production, distribution, and advocacy offer powerful new possibilities for a network-centered video advocacy drawing on the diverse capacities and shared resources of a networked universe of supporters.

As Howard Rheingold has noted, "participatory media are social media whose value and power derives from the active participation of many people. Value derives not just from the size of the audience, but from their power to link to each other, to form a public as well as a market."[82] This DIWO (doing it with others) element of new forms of advocacy recognizes the advocacy possibilities of drawing on some audiences as publics collaborating both with themselves and with you and as coproducers, not just as consumers or passive distributors of advocacy video. It utilizes the creative and advocacy potential of the remixing and reappropriating strategies that characterize the new-media economy.

Collaborative message creation, production (a more formalized approach to remixing), distribution, and advocacy allow for the possibility of drawing on all the potential resources in a given advocacy community. As the environmental advocate Marty Kearns describes it, traditional advocacy involves the advocate organization picking and packaging an argument for delivery to an audience, but what he terms a network-centric approach "asks the network to find, package and select the arguments (think MoveOn Bushin30Seconds example). The network picks the message." Similarly, whereas a traditional advocacy campaign has a core communications team at its center, "managing" the campaign, a distributed-network campaign trains "many spokespeople to speak their own voice."[83] This has been seen in recent political campaigns in the United States. See, for example, the excellent analysis by Connect US, which works on network-centered advocacy in the U.S. foreign policy community, of Obama's 2008 election campaign, noting its capacity to "foster conversation between supporters," to "respond to what supporters say," and most importantly, to "put power in supporters' hands.... Messages are made more popular, more exciting and more diverse by enabling supporters to take the reins. Give constituents the basic tools and let them go!"[84]

In terms of video, this collaborative, network-centered approach includes efforts such as the video collages created by campaigns including 24 Hours for Darfur,[85] which gathered expert, citizen, and refugee voices to speak out on the situation in Sudan and join an online montage of voices, twenty-four hours of which were screened at a rally outside the UN. It also includes the YouTube and MoveOn.org approaches to user-generated or citizen-generated video contests and what WITNESS did with its partnership with STAND, described earlier, or what Greenpeace did in the environmental community, providing a stock of footage to supporters and encouraging them to "download our footage from the e-waste yards in China and India to edit and use in your video. Use it to make your own video about e-waste and how Apple should be a leader in helping tackle this problem." The "only limitations are please use the logo provided, a positive campaign message and the website URL somewhere in your video."[86]

A multisourced networked approach may also be a necessary corollary of the profusion of the number of sources available and of the evolution of our understanding of "truth" in the online media sphere. Jamais Casco has suggested that in an era of digital manipulation, truth will no longer be linked to the increasingly problematic indexical truth of one image, but will derive from the depth of images of a particular incident. We will have to rely on the collective images of multiple observers to generate and verify the truth of documentation. This is particularly true in the situation he has called the "participatory decepticon," in which the ubiquity of easy editing tools (already manifested in the culture of remix videos) will allow for the creation of falsified "verité" political videos that create their own firestorm of controversy in the next-minute news cycle before they can be proved to be false. With the torrent of images created in a livecasting society of ubiquitous recording, we will have to come up with alternative ways of understanding footage that go beyond viewing single videos in isolation.

In this context, the role of human rights organizations and affiliated technology developers, as much as doing direct documentation themselves, will be to provide tools to present in meaningful ways the variety of perspectives on a story or track the complex reality of an incident. These aggregation, mapping, and visualization approaches will likely include tools such as the Ushahidi platform,[87] which shows how a range of incidents play out across a geographical area and across time, video and social media aggregation platforms like Crowdsource and Storify,[88] as well as technologies such as the Photosynth software launched by Microsoft,[89] which composes thousands of individual 2-D images to create a panoramic 3-D image of an event. They also likely will include more curated approaches in human rights and mainstream online video sharing and in social-media spaces to show how multiple image sources relate to a particular event.

Incorporating a DIWO collaborative, multisource approach alongside other tried and tested targeted strategies is part of the future of video advocacy. To illustrate how this might work in a particular human rights situation, consider Burma. After twenty years of brutal military repression, we can see how activists and concerned citizens, both within Burma and abroad, could act collaboratively to galvanize action using moving-image media.

Inside Burma, activists on the ground can shoot—on cell phones and video cameras—documentation of the repression of citizen protests in the cities and urban areas, as well as the hidden crimes against humanity perpetrated against ethnic-minority villagers in rural areas in eastern Burma. This can be uploaded, from a mobile phone, a computer in Burma, or from a secure location, to crisis-mapping applications such as Ushahidi, blogs, and online video-sharing and social-networking sites, where a community of concerned citizens can map, tag, tweet, link, circulate, remix, and incorporate it all into both direct video blogs of material as it happens and more edited advocacy videos, then circulate it on blogs, social-networking sites, and from cell phone to cell phone via Bluetooth. With the aid of online subtitling tools and again tapping the DIWO approach, versions of videos can be translated into a range of languages. Through the tagging of images with GPS coordinates, the on-the-ground footage could even be combined with satellite imagery of emptied villages in eastern Burma or troop movements in the streets of Mandalay. The veracity of the imagery would come both emotionally in the direct evidence of cameras close to the action and as scientific "proof" from the skies. At the immersive edge of advocacy, where "Seeing is believing" moves toward questions of "Feeling is believing," the footage might be incorporated into a virtual-reality experience or virtual world, enabling the solidarity viewer to stand on the street in Mandalay as the troops enter or to imagine what a cell is like in the infamous Insein Prison.[90]

An offline component of targeted advocacy would continue to be important in this as in any campaign context—footage, crafted into advocacy videos either by organizers or by collaborative efforts, could be screened at the right time and in the right place before key governing institutions at a national and international level. Deployed by solidarity groups in the EU, across Southeast Asia, and in the United States, the videos could be used in community organizing, lobbying, and in screenings before key decision makers debating action to pressure the regime in Burma. From these settings, organizers and lobbyists can start to livecast their meetings and discussions to constituents and supporters who are unable to attend and vlog personal accounts of how the campaign is going. And approaches that draw on remixing and individualized narrowcasting can enable individual constituents to repurpose material into personalized and localized advocacy videos for particular decision makers, tapping into local power dynamics, addressing local influence brokers, and making calls for action as specific as possible, just as the STAND student groups did on the issue of genocide prevention.

For those without access online, a key organizer could download footage to DVDs or USB sticks or receive a DVD copy and coordinate physical distribution, as well as screenings and local action. Meanwhile, versions of key footage adapted for the multimedia 3GP format could recirculate back into Burma, passing from cell phone to cell phone and evading Internet blocks. Selected footage would also make its way into the mass media (just as it did during the Saffron Revolution of 2007), supporting continuing mainstream attention to an issue while the pictures lasted.[91]

These scenarios are just some among many that could spring from the innovation of an empowered citizenry and innovative human rights campaigners.[92] As we move forward into a world of the increased grassroots production and distribution of human rights video, with all its promise and perils, the aspiration of human rights organizations such as WITNESS, as well as of grassroots human rights activists and engaged citizens, is to use ubiquitous video offline and online as a tool to draw effectively on the presence of crowds, the energy and (what is often of importance) the size of crowds, as well as on the "wisdom of crowds" to generate and sustain innovative advocacy. It is an open challenge to us all to do that in a manner that protects the most vulnerable and helps set norms that permeate these online spaces, to find ways to align human rights principles and cultures with the powerful emancipatory trends that ubiquitous participatory media represent, and to make sure that moving images of human rights violations move people to create real change.

NOTES

Earlier versions of this paper benefited from feedback from WITNESS staff, Meg McLagan, Larry Alan McDowell, and participants at Visible Evidence conferences. This version benefited immensely from the time and creativity afforded by a Rockefeller Foundation residency at the Bellagio Study Center.

1. "Iraq Prisoner Abuse 'Un-American,' Says Rumsfeld," transcript, *Washington Times*, May 7, 2004, http://www.washingtontimes.com/news/2004/may/7/20040507-115901-6736r. I am indebted to Jamais Casco in a post on Worldchanging.com for highlighting this Rumsfeld quote: Jamais Casco, "The Participatory Panopticon vs. The Pentagon," May 10, 2004, www.worldchanging.com/archives/000680.html.
2. International Telecommunications Union, "The World in 2011: ICT Facts and Figures," http://www.itu.int/ITU-D/ict/facts/2011/index.html.
3. Jamais Casco, "The Rise of the Participatory Panopticon," May 4, 2005, http://www.worldchanging.com/archives/002651.html.
4. See, for example, Steve Mann on the concept of equiveillance, http://en.wikipedia.org/wiki/Equiveillance.
5. Marvine Howe, *New York Times*, Chronicle, March 20, 1992, http://www.nytimes.com/1992/03/20/style/chronicle-589492.html.
6. Meg McLagan, "Making Human Rights Claims Public," *American Anthropologist* 108.1 (March 2006), pp. 191–95.
7. It should be noted that WITNESS was founded just before the end of the California state trials on April 29, 1992, when four LAPD officers involved in the Rodney King beating were acquitted on charges of assault with a deadly weapon and assault under color of authority. Video evidence was extensively used both by the defense and the prosecution in these trials.
8. Quoted in Jane Hall, "Electronic Witness to Rights Abuses," *Los Angeles Times*, May 26, 1992, http://articles.latimes.com/1992-05-26/entertainment/ca-91_1_human-rights-abuses.

9. SKP-Jayapura. See http://www.hampapua.org/home2.html.
10. For more detail, see Bill Nichols's chapter, "The Trials and Tribulations of Rodney King," in *Blurred Boundaries: Questions of Meaning in Contemporary Culture* (Bloomington: Indiana University Press, 1994), pp. 17–42.
11. See WITNESS, "Video Advocacy Resources & Tools," http://www.witness.org/training, and "Video Advocacy Planning Toolkit," http://videoplan.witness.org.
12. McLagan, "Making Human Rights Claims Public."
13. *Bound by Promises: Contemporary Slavery in Rural Brazil* (2006, CPT, CEJIL and WITNESS), accessible in a short version at http://www.youtube.com/watch?v=qZCnPu_iJwU.
14. For example, our partners have done screenings with senior officials of the International Criminal Court to convince them of the need to prioritize the recruitment of child soldiers in the eastern Congo in their investigations.
15. An example of this video and subsequent debate is *On The Frontlines* by WITNESS partner Ajedi-Ka/Projet Enfants Soldats (see http://www.ajedika.org/news/advocacy.html) and the footage of a community screening in Priscila Néri, "DRC: Using Video to Sensitize Communities About Child Soldiers" (January 23, 2009), http://hub.witness.org/en/node/11904.
16. See *Books Not Bars* (Ella Baker Center for Human Rights and WITNESS, 2001) and *System Failure: Violence, Abuse and Neglect in the California Youth Authority* (Ella Baker Center for Human Rights and WITNESS, 2004).
17. See the discussion by John Corner in "Documenting the Political: Some Issues," *Studies in Documentary Film* 3. 2 (2009), pp. 113–29.
18. See Margaret E. Keck and Kathryn Sikkink, *Activists Beyond Borders: Advocacy Networks in International Politics* (Ithaca: Cornell University Press, 1998), pp. 12–13.
19. "Shoot on Sight: The Ongoing SPDC Offensive against Civilians in Eastern Burma," available at http://hub.witness.org/shootonsight and http://www.youtube.com/watch?v=SPSsKcpxJMk, produced by Burma Issues (http://www.burmaissues.org) in cooperation with WITNESS, 2007.
20. Discussed in Sam Gregory, "Transnational Storytelling: Human Rights, WITNESS and Video Advocacy," *American Anthropologist* 108.1 (March 2006), pp. 195–204.
21. See Arthur Kleinman and Joan Kleinman, "The Appeal of Experience; the Dismay of Images: Cultural Appropriations of Suffering in Our Times" in Arthur Kleinman, Veena Das, and Margaret M. Lock (eds.), *Social Suffering* (Berkeley: University of California Press, 1997), p. 18.
22. Thomas Keenan "Where Are Human Rights . . . ?: Reading a Communiqué from Iraq," in Michel Feher (ed.), with Gaëlle Krikorian and Yates McKee, *Nongovernmental Politics* (New York: Zone Books, 2007), p. 65.
23. "Paradigmatic story" is a term suggested by C. Sarah Soh in *The Comfort Women: Sexual Violence and Postcolonial Memory in Korea and Japan* (Chicago: University of Chicago Press, 2008), p. xv.
24. See Radio Free Europe, Radio Liberty, "Chechnya: Cell-phone Videos Reveal Abuses," http://www.rferl.org/content/Article/1071107.html.
25. See "China: Government's Video-Censorship Foiled" at http://hub.witness.org/en/node/32.
26. See "Madagascar: Dozens Killed and Injured in Pro-opposition Rallies" at http://hub.witness.org/en/node/12259.
27. See "Mobile Phone Footage Shows Police Shoot and Kill Unarmed Man in California" at http://hub.witness.org/en/node/11825.

28. See "Police Brutality in Timor-Leste," posted by user alextilman on YouTube, http://www.youtube.com/watch?v=6R7uMaOoe_4.
29. See "Violent Evictions at El Estor, Guatemala," at http://hub.witness.org/en/node/620, "Riot Police Dispatched to China Protests" at http://www.citizentube.com/2010/07/riot-police-dispatched-to-china.html, and videos by LICADHO in Cambodia, at http://hub.witness.org/en/users/licadho.
30. See Eric Tars of National Law Center on Homelessness and Poverty on the Advisory Group on Forced Evictions mission at http://hub.witness.org/NewOrleansForcedEvictionsMission.
31. See "Burma: Leader of Monks' Alliance on the Saffron Revolution—Pt. 1" at http://hub.witness.org/en/node/8864.
32. See "Brazil: Survivor of the Carandiru Massacre on 16 years of Impunity" at http://hub.witness.org/en/node/8884.
33. Both videos originate with the UK-based Aegis Trust: "Darfur—Waiting for Justice," http://vimeo.com/1111316, and "Darfur Destroyed: Sudan's Perpetrators Break Silence," http://www.vimeo.com/3161513.
34. See Darfurian Voices, www.24hoursfordarfur.org.
35. See sexworkerspresent at http://sexworkerspresent.blip.tv/#203321.
36. See "STOP! 12, 16, 24, 32 Hours Duty of Nursing Staff !—TMCEA-AHW," by Kodao Productions, at http://hub.witness.org/en/upload/stop-12-16-24-32-hours-duty-nursing-staff-%E2%80%93-tmcea-ahw.
37. See, for example, Jean Burgess and Joshua Green, *YouTube: Online Video and Participatory Culture* (Cambridge: Polity, 2009), as well as Pelle Snickers and Patrick Vondereau (eds.), *The YouTube Reader* (Stockholm: National Library of Sweden, 2009).
38. Burgess and Green, *YouTube*, p. 34, citing Patricia G. Lange, "Commenting on Comments: Investigating Responses to Antagonism on YouTube," paper presented at the Society for Applied Anthropology Conference, Tampa, Florida, 2007.
39. Michael Wesch, "Visualizing the Mediascape (Another Step Towards an Ethnography of YouTube)," http://mediatedcultures.net/ksudigg/?p=144.
40. Transmission, "Why NOT Just Use YouTube," http://transmission.cc/node/112.
41. Jessica Clark, *Big Dreams, Small Screens: Online Video for Public Knowledge and Action* (March 2007), http://www.centerforsocialmedia.org/sites/default/files/documents/pages/big_dreams_report.pdf.
42. Henry Jenkins, "YouTube and the Vaudevillian Aesthetic," *Confessions of an Aca-Fan*, http://www.henryjenkins.org/2006/11/youtube_and_the_vaudeville_aes.html.
43. See "Unsubscribe Campaign—Waiting for the Guards," October 11, 2007, http://www.youtube.com/watch?v=TZ1NYizv2sw.
44. See "Video from Burma: Shoot on Sight," produced by Burma Issues, April 8, 2007, available in two locations on YouTube: http://www.youtube.com/watch?v=SPSsKcpxJMk, and http://www.youtube.com/watch?v=z2EEJkyntV4.
45. See "Awaiting Tomorrow: People Living with HIV/AIDS in Africa," produced by Ajedi-Ka Project Enfants Soldats, December 3, 2007, http://www.youtube.com/watch?v=hzQQiCPWSYA.
46. "Awaiting Tomorrow" had almost fourteen hundred comments within a month of being uploaded, before this function was disabled, preventing further belligerent commentary.
47. This interactive power is also evident in the use of "reply videos" that often take the tone of a conversational video response; powerful examples of the range of these are the responses

to the footage showing the killing of Oscar Grant by transit police in Oakland, California on January 1, 2009.

48. Exacerbating a concern in the human rights community, given the nature of the online environment, it is unlikely that the victims and survivors in the original video would have the opportunity to respond in the online comment environment
49. Malin Wahlberg, "YouTube Commemoration: Private Grief and Communal Consolation," in Snickers and Vondereau (eds.), *The YouTube Reader*, p. 231.
50. Michael Wesch and Alexandra Juhasz have both written thoughtfully on the challenges of discussion on YouTube, given the current comment function, which places all comments and response videos in one linear narrative and which makes it difficult to have a sustained or multivocal conversation. In the short term, however, it is of note that constructive inputs in the comments stream frequently responded directly to the most obstreperous, racist, or conspiratorially inclined negative comments.
51. Howard Rheingold, "Using Participatory Media and Public Voice to Encourage Civic Engagement," in W. Lance Bennett (ed.), *Civic Life Online: Learning How Digital Media Can Engage Youth* (Cambridge, MA: The MIT Press, 2008), p. 99, http://www.mitpressjournals.org/doi/pdf/10.1162/dmal.9780262524827.097.
52. See http://www.youtube.com/user/vlogbrothers.
53. See http://www.projectforawesome.com.
54. See http://thehpalliance.org/what-we-do.
55. See, in a different context, Livia Hinegardner's analysis of the value of solidarity videos in the context of Mexican activism: Livia Hinegardner, "Action, Organization and Documentary Film: Beyond a Communications Model of Human Rights Video," *Visual Anthropology Review* 25.2 (2009), pp. 172–85.
56. See "Egypt: Bloggers Open the Door to Police Brutality Debate," http://hub.witness.org/en/node/33.
57. Maggie Michael, "Video Shows Egypt Prisoner's Humiliation," *Washington Post*, January 21, 2007, http://www.washingtonpost.com/wp-dyn/content/article/2007/01/21/AR2007012100468.html.
58. They have commonalities in this with the "happy slapping" video genre, in which someone is caught by surprise and assaulted on camera.
59. See LiveLeak, "Brutal Behaviour Of Slovak Police Caught On Camera," April 8, 2009, http://www.liveleak.com/view?i=551_1239203220.
60. See "NA STAMATHSEI TO REZILIKI!!!" http://www.youtube.com/watch?v=gCc7xc8hxDQ.
61. Nelli Kambouri and Pavlos Hatzopoulos, "Making Violent Practices Public," in Geert Lovink and Sabine Niederer (eds.), *Video Vortex Reader: Responses to YouTube* (Amsterdam: Institute of Network Cultures, 2008), downloadable at http://networkcultures.org/wpmu/portal/publications/inc-readers/videovortex.
62. Jamais Cascio, "The Rise of the Participatory Panopticon vs. The Pentagon," May 10, 2004, http://www.worldchanging.com/archives/000680.html.
63. See Wael Abbas on YouTube, http://www.youtube.com/user/waelabbas.
64. See his blog, *3arabawy*, at http://www.arabawy.org.
65. Henry Jenkins, *Convergence Culture: Where Old and New Media Collide* (New York: New York University Press, 2006), p. 18.
66. Jonathan McIntosh, "Buffy vs. Edward: Twilight Remixed," June 20. 2009, http://www.

rebelliouspixels.com/2009/buffy-vs-edward-twilight-remixed.

67. See Jonathan McIntosh, "Avatar Equals Pocahontas," http://www.politicalremixvideo.com/2010/03/03/avatar-pocahontas, March 3, 2010.
68. See "Cassetteboy vs. Nick Griffin vs. Question Time," October 23, 2009, http://www.youtube.com/watch?v=_QAvkFS_cgk&feature=player_embedded.
69. See "One Whore—APNSW STAR WHORES Karaoke," http://blip.tv/sexworkerspresent/one-whore-apnsw-star-whores-karaoke-203321.
70. See "They Dont Care about Us—New Orleans Housing (In)Justice 4 Years after Katrina," September 12, 2009, http://www.youtube.com/watch?v=Bne5i90pPw4&feature=player_embedded.
71. See "East Timor—They Don't Really Care About Us," http://www.youtube.com/watch?v=bA4K1pNSc3s&feature=related, September 13, 2007.
72. See "Michael Jackson, Iran—They Don't Care about Us," http://www.youtube.com/watch?v=lm-FUQUKoXM&skipcontrinter=1.
73. Preamble to the Universal Declaration of Human Rights, http://www.un.org/Overview/rights.html.
74. See "Come Clean for the Congo," http://www.youtube.com/watch?v=JasbiUATEaE, May 8, 2009.
75. See "Pledge 2 Protect: The Campaign," http://www.standnow.org/campaigns/pledge2protect-campaign.
76. See "Pledge on Camera: How Anti-Genocide Student Activists are Ushering-In a New Era of Video Advocacy," November 4, 2009, http://hub.witness.org/STAND, and "WITNESS and STAND Partnership Spotlight: Pledge on Camera," December 3, 2009, http://hub.witness.org/STAND-SPOTLIGHT.
77. Tom Sherman, "Vernacular Video," n.d. www.noemalab.org/sections/ideas/ideas_articles/pdf/sherman_vernacular_video.pdf.
78. *Ibid.*, pp. 3, 2, 4.
79. See Jane Gaines "The Production of Outrage: The Iraq War and the Radical Documentary Tradition," *Framework* 48.2 (Fall 2007), pp. 36–55, for a set of observations on traditions of "image suspicion" that inform the phrase "bombarded with images."
80. For more on these two competing ways of understanding the new digital environment, see Mary Joyce, "Introduction: How to Think about Digital Activism," in Mary Joyce (ed.), *Digital Activism Decoded: The New Mechanics of Change* (New York: International Debate Education Association, 2010), pp. 1–14.
81. Yochai Benkler, *The Wealth of Networks: How Social Production Transforms Markets and Freedom* (New Haven: Yale University Press, 2006), p. 213.
82. Rheingold, "Using Participatory Media and Public Voice to Encourage Civic Engagement," in Bennett (ed.), *Civic Life Online*, p. 100.
83. See NetCentric Advocacy: Advocacy Strategy for the Age of Connectivity, "The Advocacy Side of Network-Centric Advocacy: Action of Delivering an Argument," http://www.network-centricadvocacy.net/2005/03/the_advocacy_si.html. Kearns coined the term "network-centric" approach. See "Network-Centric Advocacy," http://activist.blogs.com/networkcentricadvocacypaper.pdf.
84. See Netcentric Campaigns, "Lessons from the Obama Groundswell," February 19, 2008, http://netcentriccampaigns.org/node/138.
85. See Darfurian Voices, www.24hoursfordarfur.org.

86. See "ProCreate Your Own: Help Us Make Apple Green," http://www.greenpeace.org/apple/procreate-video.
87. See http://www.ushahidi.com.
88. See http://www.crowdvoice.org and http://www.storify.com.
89. See http://www.photosynth.net.
90. See, in this regard, the work of Nonny de la Peña and Peggy Weil in the related field of immersive journalism at the website Immersive Journalism: Using Virtual Reality and 3D Environments to Convey the Sights, Sounds and Feelings of the News, http://www.immersivejournalism.com.
91. For a fascinating case study of how this happened in another context, consider the flow between citizen journalism and the mainstream media of images and commentary during the November 2007 state of emergency in Pakistan, documented in a paper for the MIT Center for Future Civic Media, Huma Yusuf, "Old and New Media: Converging During the Pakistan Emergency (March 2007-February 2008)," Center for Future Civic Media MIT, 2009, http://civic.mit.edu/sites/civic.mit.edu/files/Old%20and%20New%20Media%20Pakistan%20Emergency.pdf.
92. Indeed, as this essay goes to press, many of these approaches have been utilized by citizen activists and human rights advocates participating in the "Arab Spring" of 2011 in Tunisia, Egypt, Libya, Yemen, Bahrain, Syria, and elsewhere.

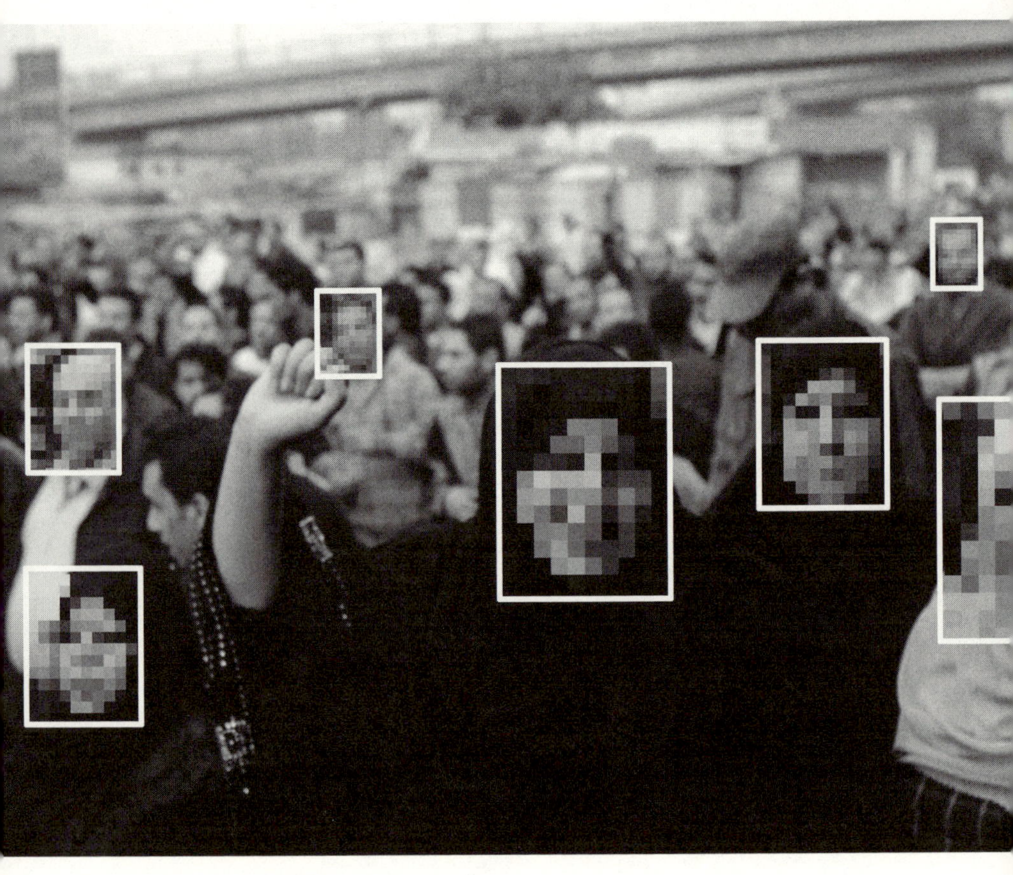

FIGURE 1 Mass protest in Egypt with visual anonymization applied (photo: Sarah Carr, under Creative Commons license, BY-NC-SA 2.0).

Human Rights Made Visible: New Dimensions to Anonymity, Consent, and Intentionality

Sam Gregory

Online video platforms and social-media networking sites have become part of the fabric of communication for human rights issues—platforms for demonstrating injustice and calling for action and opportunities to share powerful testimony and images in ways that were never possible before. In this essay, I will focus on largely undiscussed issues of human rights principles and practice that have been given additional prominence by visual media: issues of privacy, anonymity, informational self-determination, dignity, safety, consent, and intention that originate at the moment of filming and that reverberate through patterns of use and reuse of the visual media.[1] How does ubiquitous video update our understanding of privacy and of the ability to communicate anonymously?

Forty-eight hours of video are uploaded to YouTube every minute. A small, but significant percentage of this material is social-justice and human rights documentation and advocacy, on, from, or about human rights violations or crises. In "The Participatory Panopticon and Human Rights: WITNESS's Experience Supporting Video Advocacy and Future Possibilities" in this volume, I explore this human rights media ecosystem at length, but YouTube's news and politics editor, Steve Grove, supplies a useful brief summary reminder of the types of content creators who use such video-sharing spaces: "citizen reporters" shooting and uploading videos, clip cutters who grab the "salient moments" from news coverage, "mash-up artists, video bloggers, admakers and musicians" making video commentaries, "curators" who gather and discover interesting content and "embed, tweet, e-mail and share it on Facebook," and of course, a multitude of "viewers" who watch, rank, share and comment.[2] To these categories I would add the advocacy video creators who craft the material into narratives for action.

The possibilities of creating change via video have been vigorously promoted in the past few years, but the risks for those who do so in all the above categories also have been equally well demonstrated. Some of the most notable and most publicized examples include what happened during and after the Saffron Revolution in Burma and during the Syrian "Arab Spring" protests, when intelligence agents scrutinized photographs and video footage to identify demonstrators and bystanders, and in Iran, where the government took to crowd sourcing the identification of protestors via facial pictures grabbed from YouTube, which they then placed on a website with a request that the public identify them.

So what comes next? How do we ensure that the evolving online mobile and ubiquitous video environment becomes safer for human rights defenders and for those who experience or witness human rights abuses? At the heart of this challenge is the question of how we establish online and other participatory cultures that create and share social-justice and human rights material in a manner that balances the right to privacy (and the integrity of the person) with the right to freedom of expression for both those filmed and those doing the filming and that hold onto a consideration of the very real dangers to human rights defenders and victims or survivors.

How could support for human rights defenders be better integrated into the "terms of service" built into user interfaces and integrated into the institutional policies of online video platforms? What steps could online service providers and facilitators of video take to enable human rights content and to address key emerging concerns about anonymity, dignity, and avoiding revictimization? More broadly, how could we place key human rights values front and center as people film, share, comment, remix, and annotate footage from the front lines of human rights crises, large and small, in the Global North and the Global South?

The underlying challenge for any consideration of social-justice advocacy in ubiquitous video spaces is that most of the services used by the broader public are "public" spaces only insofar as their corporate owners permit it. As the Internet commentator Ethan Zuckerman has put it, "Hosting your political movement on YouTube is a little like trying to hold a rally in a shopping mall. It looks like a public space, but it's not—it's a private space, and your use of it is governed by an agreement that works harder to protect YouTube's fiscal viability than to protect your rights of free speech."[3] The implications of this corporate basis for online spaces become apparent in the context of business–social responsibility conflicts over potentially illegitimate legal requests from governments to reveal user identities or to take down content unless companies want to risk exclusion from markets or, more problematically, face criminal charges for their employees on the ground.

These private spaces largely make user interfaces as friction-free as possible, an approach that may be at odds with important considerations with human rights content such as issues of consent and contextualization. In general, the human rights user has been deprioritized as a consumer and user (and indeed, human rights is a minor category in terms of the relative quantity of postings) in relation to other users of these mass public platforms.[4] Yet any progress in addressing human rights questions must be informed by a dialogue between the closed, proprietary sector and the human rights and open-video communities, one that includes the technology providers of services, hardware, and software, in both the online and mobile arenas. Proprietary platforms dominate too much of the space and are used by too many of the grassroots activists and citizen documentors creating human rights video to be ignored in favor of niche or specialized spaces that seem more immediately aligned either ideologically or in terms of their noncorporate ownership or content focus.

THE HUMAN RIGHTS AT STAKE

At stake here are foundational principles found in the Universal Declaration of Human Rights (UDHR) and subsequent binding covenants such as the International Covenant on Civil and Political Rights (ICCPR). "Everyone has the right to freedom of opinion and expression; this right includes freedom to hold opinions without interference and to seek, receive and impart information and ideas through any media and regardless of frontiers," UDHR Article 19 declares, and "No one shall be subjected to arbitrary interference with his privacy, family, home or correspondence," UDHR Article 12 insists.[5] ICCPR Article 19 adds that restrictions on the right to freedom of opinion and expression "shall only be such as provided by law and are necessary: (a) For respect of the rights or reputations of others; (b) For the protection of national security or of public order (ordre public), or public health and morals."[6] Following from this and from the subsequent Johannesburg Principles on National Security, Freedom of Expression and Access to Information,[7] governments can limit the free flow of information only in order to protect certain narrowly determined interests such as national security and public morals. The World Summit on the Information Society reaffirmed the importance of the rights to freedom of opinion and expression as "an essential foundation of the information society."[8] International declarations on the rights of human rights defenders also emphasize the capacity to disseminate and receive information on human rights topics.[9]

A complement to the freedom of expression is the right to freedom from arbitrary and unlawful interference with one's privacy and correspondence, recognized both in Article 12 of the UDHR and in Article 17 of the ICCPR. The right to privacy is usually understood to include both the individual's right to a zone of autonomy within a "private sphere" such as the home and in personal choices within the public sphere.

It is in exercising such choices that problems arise. Critical to active rights to free expression and to privacy is the ability to choose to communicate anonymously. This is not an absolute right (since anonymity can also be used, for example to cover criminal activity), but the possibility of expressing one's opinions anonymously, with no a priori restrictions, enables freedom of expression and supports the right to privacy. Most contemporary discussions about anonymous communication on the Internet focus on online identity and data protection—on options for encryption or for using proxy servers and circumvention approaches such as the anonymizing network Tor[10] to conceal both the person communicating and the data being transmitted. This focus is based on concerns about the handover of user information to repressive governments (such as Yahoo in China providing the details of journalist Shi Tao) or about the ability of governments to access and track user personal data and communications. Alongside this, there is also a tendency to assert that privacy is a thing of the past online and that societal trends and social norms are moving away from assumptions of privacy and anonymity, as has been claimed, for example, by Mark Zuckerberg, CEO of Facebook.[11]

But with visual human rights media a predominant and largely unaddressed question involves the identification of people who speak and the people who appear, intentionally or not, in a video as it circulates from situations of individual or mass human rights violations. Consider, for example, the persecution later faced by bystanders and people who stepped in to film or assist Neda Agha-Soltan as she lay dying during the election protests in Iran in 2009.[12] Here, the current methods of enhancing privacy in electronic communications are largely inadequate—for example, concealing the IP address from which you sent a video. People in videos can be identified by old-fashioned investigative techniques, by crowd sourcing (as with the Iran example noted in the introduction), or by facial recognition tools. In addition, the metadata of location and creator is embedded in the image, and there are no ready options either in the capture of footage or the upload options to video-sharing and social-media platforms to anonymize or conceal the identity of those who speak out or those who are accidentally caught in "incriminating" circumstances. There are few options to preserve what we might term "visual privacy" and improve the choices we make about protecting our personal visual identity or holding onto "visual anonymity." "Visual anonymity" may sound like a contradiction in terms, but people often wish to speak out and to "be seen," but still wish to conceal their face, the background of their home, and so on. And in an era of increasing facial-recognition capabilities, the one time when you choose to say something politically unpopular, blow the whistle on an abuse or abuser, or speak out in some other manner can be correlated, whether you like it or not, with the other 99 percent of your online identity. Similarly, people caught in the background of a video often are unaware they are even being filmed at that moment. At the policy level, there is relatively limited discussion of either the right to one's visual identity or the right to informational self-determination over how that identity is disseminated and used.

In addition to the issues of the right to freedom of opinion and expression and to privacy, as recognized in international human rights law, other fundamental human rights and underlying human rights values are both promoted and problematized by the ubiquity of the new media. These include respect for individual dignity and personal integrity and the valorization of survivors of human rights violations and their intentions in speaking out in a world in which so many people are filming and in which the appropriation, remixing, and reuse of imagery and voices may conflict with these core values and even lead to psychological or physical revictimization.

Respect for human rights is grounded as a practice in a conception of the dignity, agency, worth and integrity of every person, each of whom is possessed of rights. "All human beings are born free and equal in dignity and rights," the Universal Declaration of Human Rights declares in Article 1, and the primary principle that every human being is possessed of "inherent dignity" runs through every right included in the UDHR. Human rights documentation processes place a heavy emphasis on both presenting and protecting the evidentiary or testimonial voice or experience of victims, survivors, and locally based advocates. Contemporary thinking about the nature of testimony, witnessing, and trauma also emphasizes the responsibility of the witness of abuse to represent it responsibly and with ethical integrity—to be, so to speak, the "ethical witness" who carries the responsibility to share the traumatic experience "in a manner that empathizes with, rather than violates, the silent victim."[13]

Both the principle of the integrity of the victim/survivor's experience and that of the role of the ethical witness are made problematic by the possibilities for remixing, reappropriation, and recirculation and by contemporary trends toward circulation, rather than distribution. As Henry Jenkins has noted, a key aspect of contemporary media practice that captures this distinction is the idea of spreadability. There is a "constant tension at this moment between wanting to lock down content . . . and wanting to empower consumers to help spread the word," and that for content today, "if it doesn't spread, it's dead."[14]

These possibilities of circulation, remixing, and reappropriation pull the material further and further from its source testifier and/or witness and from its original context, the event or violation being documented, and also away from the original intentions of its creators. As I note in "The Participatory Panopticon," video distribution in and of itself can also contribute to creating further layers of victimization. Here we encounter concerns about psychological revictimization and the preservation of individual human dignity, as distinguished from more collective terms of cultural dignity that intertwine for example with religious sensitivities.

We also confront the paradox that the misuse of material gathered in a specific setting may increase the chances that the footage will find an audience (even an unexpected one) that may be willing and able to respond to either the broader human rights context or even sometimes to the specific situation and intentions of its creator. Circulatory systems online now encourage such recontextualizations, reuses and remixes of video footage. Yet much human rights footage comes from specific locations where people have taken risk to speak out with a particular purpose in mind. How do we preserve their agency?

Within the broader universe of open video, one option might be a licensing system that recognizes intentionality, for example, "You may use this video in any way you like, provided you push for redress for human rights abuses in Burma." This would be of value to people concerned about how human rights video material is used who want to conceive of ways in which an item (often from a place of great crisis) can circulate and spread while still holding onto the motivations that generated the material in the first place. Such a system would add to approaches that recognize intellectual property rights (using copyright law) and/or creative commons approaches that offer choices of a degree of commercial or noncommercial use and remixing. Similarly, a system of embedded metadata or tagging created or added at the moment of filming, uploading, or contextualization might highlight key considerations of intention to be considered when reusing or circulating the footage or media item. A further dimension to the issue of how material is used in ways that are unanticipated by the creators or people featured is the issue of informed consent and how this translates for new visual cultures. In human rights organizations, there are strong traditions focused on the protection of victims and survivors, and the largest organizations, such as Amnesty and Human Rights Watch, have rededicated themselves to this tradition. WITNESS's own practice focuses on supporting the ability of individuals to make informed choices about if, how, where, and when their image is used. We have at times also tried to encourage use of a "worst-case scenario" model for consent. This is a digital-era adaptation of traditional consent approaches. It assumes that all media, once it is "out there," is infinitely copiable and circulatable. When Naw Paw Paw, a villager in Karen State, Burma, spoke out against the Burma military junta's abuses in a clip produced by a human rights organization from the refugee camps of the Thai-Burma border, could she anticipate that three years later, a million people on YouTube would have seen her? More importantly, could she also have anticipated that the successful circulation of the video probably means that the very same people responsible for the violations in her area will see the video and her challenge to

FIGURE 2 An activist working with WITNESS in Egypt, protected with ObscuraCam (photo: WITNESS).

their power? Indeed we should probably assume this with any video that makes claims of accountability.

However, this "worst-case scenario" model of consent is difficult enough to promote (and also heavily contested)[15] in the "professional" documentary world and in the mainstream news world and the human rights community. It is impossible to sustain in the online participatory culture of user-generated media if one anticipates that in ten years, 90 percent of human rights media shot and/or created will be made by nonprofessionals outside of the professional practices of human rights documentors, news journalists, or documentary makers. It is also increasingly difficult to sustain in its current form as questions of ethical responsibility transition from being part of binary relationship between documentor and subject to an ethics of an image in circulation being reused, combined, and framed in ways unexpected by the original creators and in contexts distant from the people who filmed and were filmed.[16]

So consent can never be assured in a world of uploaded content from relatively anonymous sources. However, there are potential technological approaches and innovations within these spaces that can help address challenges posed by the issues of consent, representation, and safety—balancing openness and transparency with an active response to real risks. As we move increasingly to a smart-phone-based mobile environment in which mobile phones are the primary visual documentation tools, we can investigate how devices could conceal faces and backgrounds, either during or shortly after shooting (as WITNESS has been doing with its ObscuraCam project [fig. 2; see also fig. 1])[17] and how server-based approaches could similarly support doing so in environments where on-the-fly visual anonymization is not possible. Just as a filming process conducted using an app can prompt for embedding metadata information about intention, so too, a filming app/platform approach can provide prompts on obtaining consent during those filming/upload processes. Alongside these tools, the development, promotion, and dissemination of learning materials and spreadable guides to security approaches could reinforce awareness of the need to safeguard the rights, dignity, and lives of those being filmed.

In mass online sharing spaces, the use of dedicated human rights categories and curation and the institution of enhanced governance and review policies for material that is placed within these categories can both help address the problems of unjustified take-downs of human rights material and help provide services for anonymization and protection, as was suggested by YouTube users in a moderated conversation that WITNESS and YouTube coordinated on this topic and explored further in a WITNESS report, "Cameras Everywhere."[18] However, these remedies might face the same problem that has afflicted dedicated social-justice spaces—they are more easily targeted and blocked because content self-selects or is placed into a space that is easier to censor, block, or knock down with a denial of service attack.[19]

A FRAMEWORK FOR SOLUTIONS TO HUMAN RIGHTS DILEMMAS

As I have suggested above, ways to reduce the downsides of increased human rights media production, sharing, and distribution will likely rely on combinations of approaches that are within the "quasi-public" spaces of online services, as well as on tools and apps that are created outside those spaces.

Importantly, they will also rely on finding ways to evaluate how existing ethical frameworks and approaches from established human rights and documentary practices are made accessible, relevant, and proximate to new online spaces, communities, and "digital natives," as well as to digital newcomers, since these questions are above all questions of digital media literacy. Just as important as the site architecture of YouTube or an autonomous tool that can blur faces is how existing traditions of informed consent are translated by online communities into new paradigms and standards. As trends in video production move toward direct live streaming, this further emphasizes the urgency not just of tools that are at the point of creation, but more so of norms concerning safety, security, and consent being reemphasized and regenerated anew.

Here, too, I hope that human rights organizations can play a role in supporting the focused aggregation and curation of human rights material, as WITNESS did with its Hub project, demonstrating within their own practice, via test-case projects, how to balance participation, openness, effectiveness, and safety. An additional open question is how well voluntary codes of conduct, sets of principles, and collaborations between civil society, human rights groups, and technology and communications companies such as the Global Network Initiative will further enhance self-regulation, the promotion of effective practices, internal innovation to address challenges, and stronger positions taken by the corporate online and mobile service providers and technologists themselves resisting government pressures.

All this needs to be done while retaining a clear understanding of the danger experienced on the ground in real-life spaces, and not in the apparently safer online environments. It is common to talk about a trend toward openness, transparency, and disclosure and a decline in expectations of privacy. Yet the realities of human rights risks on the ground where videos may be shot and distributed are not connected to these changing online norms, whether they may be real or imagined. It remains as risky as ever to challenge power or to speak out against injustice, and power holders continue to trample people's rights.

NOTES

This paper draws in part on material originally published in Sam Gregory, "Cameras Everywhere: Ubiquitous Video Documentation of Human Rights, New Forms of Video Advocacy, and Considerations of Safety, Security, Dignity and Consent," *Journal of Human Rights Practice* 2.2 (July 2010), pp. 191–207.

1. Among the rights that I do not address in this article are the rights of participation in cultural life and access to science and culture. Article 27(1) of the UN Declaration of Human Rights states: "Everyone has the right freely to participate in the cultural life of the community . . . and to share in scientific advancement and its benefits." For more on this in relation to intellectual property and media, see, for example, Lea Shaver, "The Right to Science and Culture," *Wisconsin Law Review* 2010.1 (March 6, 2009), p. 121, http://papers.ssrn.com/sol3/papers.cfm?abstract_id=1354788. I also do not address here questions of communication rights and the right to access the Internet. For example, legislation in Finland now makes access to broadband Internet a legal right. See "Finland Makes Broadband a 'Legal Right,'" BBC News, http://www.bbc.co.uk/news/10461048. Nor do I focus on the much-discussed questions of freedom of expression and Internet censorship. See Ronald Deibert, John Palfrey,

Rafal Rohozinski, and Jonathan Zittrain (eds.), *Access Denied: The Practice and Policy of Global Internet Filtering* (Cambridge, MA: The MIT Press, 2008), and Ronald Deibert, John Palfrey, Rafal Rohozinski, and Jonathan Zittrain (eds.), *Access Controlled: The Shaping of Power, Rights, and Rule in Cyberspace* (Cambridge, MA: The MIT Press, 2010). Many of these issues are already being addressed in advocacy spaces by tools providers such as the Tor Project, http://www.torproject.org, by academic research initiatives such as the Berkman Center for Internet and Society at the Harvard Law School, and by coalition initiatives such as the Dynamic Coalition on Internet Rights and Responsibilities (linked to the Internet Governance Forum), http://internetrightsandprinciples.org, and the Global Network Initiative (a "multi-stakeholder group of companies, civil society organizations [including human rights and press freedom groups], investors and academics"), http://www.globalnetworkinitiative.org.

2. Steve Grove, "YouTube's Ecosystem for News," Nieman Reports, Summer 2010, http://www.nieman.harvard.edu/reports/article/102417/YouTubes-Ecosystem-for-News.aspx.
3. Ethan Zuckerman, "Public Spaces, Private Infrastructure—Open Video Conference," October 1, 2010, http://www.ethanzuckerman.com/blog/2010/10/01/public-spaces-private-infrastructure-open-video-conference.
4. A number of other corollaries somewhat outside the limits of this essay result from the underlying basis for any commercial video-sharing platform. Many of these have been explored in depth by the Transmission network and others (see for example "Why NOT Just Use YouTube," http://transmission.cc/node/112). There is the inherent queasiness one feels when human rights imagery is exploited for commercial purposes (viewing on a commercial platform is subsidized by advertising). There are issues of surveillance by corporations and the state and of the handover of user information, as well as of an editorial and redress process that is not democratic or transparent in large part. Additionally, on a creative level, most commercial spaces are inflexible in their options for downloading, repurposing, and sharing and are navigating the uneasy relationship between intellectual property rights and freedom of expression that is at stake with new forms of cultural production and participation.
5. The Universal Declaration of Human Rights, http://www.un.org/en/documents/udhr.
6. International Covenant on Civil and Political Rights, http://www2.ohchr.org/english/law/ccpr.htm.
7. The Johannesburg Principles on National Security, Freedom of Expression and Access to Information, http://www.article19.org/pdfs/standards/joburgprinciples.pdf.
8. World Summit on the Information Society, Declaration of Principles: Building the Information Society—A Global Challenge in the New Millennium, Article A(4), http://www.itu.int/dms_pub/itu-s/md/03/wsis/doc/S03-WSIS-DOC-0004!!PDF-E.pdf.
9. See the UN Declaration on the Right and Responsibility of Individuals, Groups and Organs of Society to Promote and Protect Universally Recognized Human Rights and Fundamental Freedoms, March 8, 1999, particularly Article 6, http://www.unhchr.ch/huridocda/huridoca.nsf/(symbol)/a.res.53.144.en.
10. See https://www.torproject.org.
11. See, for example, this digest of responses— http://www.theatlanticwire.com/opinions/view/opinion/Facebook-Loses-Face-Over-Self-Serving-Privacy-Policy-2164—to Mark Zuckerberg's assertion in a January 2010 interview about privacy: http://www.ustream.tv/recorded/3848950
12. See Negar Azimi, "Iran in Pictures: Social Suffering and Three Sets of Images," in this volume.

13. Frances Guerin and Roger Hallas (eds.), "Introduction," in *The Image and the Witness: Trauma, Memory and Visual Culture* (London: Wallflower Press, 2007), p. 15.
14. Nikki Usher, "Why Spreadable Doesn't Equal Viral: A Conversation with Henry Jenkins," Nieman Journalism Lab online, November 23, 2010, http://www.niemanlab.org/2010/11/why-spreadable-doesnt-equal-viral-a-conversation-with-henry-jenkins.
15. See, for example, the discussion in Patricia Aufderheide, Peter Jaszi, and Mridu Chandra, "Honest Truths: Documentary Filmmakers on Ethical Challenges in Their Work," Center for Social Media, School of Communication, American University, Washington, D.C., 2009, http://www.centerforsocialmedia.org/making-your-media-matter/documents/best-practices/honest-truths-documentary-filmmakers-ethical-chall, or Brian Winston, *Lies, Damn Lies and Documentaries* (London: BFI Publishing, 2000).
16. For more on this, see Sam Gregory and Patty Zimmermann, "The Ethical Engagements of Human Rights Social Media," November 22, 2010, http://blog.witness.org/2010/11/the-ethical-engagements-of-human-rights-social-media.
17. ObscuraCam, a collaboration between WITNESS and the Guardian Project: http://www.witness.org/cameras-everywhere/witness-labs.
18. Sameer Padania and Steve Grove, *WITNESS Video for Change*, "Your Ideas on Human Rights and Free Expression on YouTube," September 21, 2010, http://blog.witness.org/2010/09/your-ideas-on-human-rights-and-free-expression-on-youtube, and Sameer Padania, Sam Gregory, Yvette Alberdingk-Thijm, and Bryan Nunez "Cameras Everywhere: Current Challenges and Opportunities at the Intersection of Human Rights, Video and Technology" (WITNESS, 2011), available at http://www.witness.org/cameras-everywhere/report-2011.
19. See Ethan Zuckerman, "Intermediary Censorship," in Deibert, Palfrey, Rohozinski, and Zittrain (eds.), *Access Controlled*, pp. 71–86, including the suggestion of applying common carrier status to online service providers.

Director Warwick Thornton, with Rowan Mcnamara as Samson and Marissa Gibson as Delilah, on the set of *Samson and Delilah*, 2008 (photo: Mark Rogers, courtesy of the filmmaker from http://samsonanddelilah.com.au/media.php, accessed July 13, 2010).

Indigenous Counterpublics: A Foreshortened History

Faye Ginsburg

In May 2007, a newspaper article in the *Australian* announced an indigenous protest in the real world concerning the virtual appropriation of a major Aboriginal sacred site into the trendy online world of Second Life 3D, created in 2003. Their concern was directed against Telstra, Australia's largest telecommunications corporation and creator of The Pond, a virtual island and popular destination representing things Australian on Second Life, including the part of the site objected to by the Anangu people, the indigenous owners of the famous sacred site of Uluru in South Australia. also well known to tourists and others by its English name, Ayers Rock. These Aboriginal owners were concerned about the possible desecration, albeit virtual, of the online representation of Uluru, Australia's dramatic geological formation and part of the Anangu sacred ancestral heritage. Although the online site, like its physical counterpart, includes barriers to discourage people from walking or flying over the virtual Uluru, "representatives of the traditional owners . . . warned that even with the restrictions, it may be possible to view sacred sites around [the virtual] Uluru."[1] In the physical world, since 1987, non-Aboriginal visitors face strict prohibitions against photography or filming without consent of the indigenous landowners due to Tjukurpa (Dreamtime) beliefs, because these areas are the sites of gender-linked rituals and are forbidden ground for Anangu of the opposite sex of those participating in the rituals in question. The photographic ban is intended to prevent Anangu from inadvertently violating this taboo by encountering photographs of the forbidden sites in the outside world.

Signs have been posted around the restricted areas to help visitors respect the request. They also warn visitors not to climb the rock, partly due to the fact that the path crosses a sacred Dreamtime track. Telstra's spokesperson confirmed that the company had not sought the permission of Uluru's landowners to use images of the site for commercial purposes.[2] The case heated up in September 2008, when

Uluru on the Second Life website.

Telstra Big Pond, the telecommunications corporation that hosts virtual Australia on Second Life, posted billboards advertising its Big Pond Internet service in front of the virtual version of Uluru and started serving grog—alcohol—at the Billabong Bar, a virtual pub just next to the digital Uluru. If the rules of the real world applied in Second Life, the bar would be right in the middle of the Mutitjulu community—a dry area. Telstra Big Pond removed the billboards after protests.[3] As one Australian blogger, Laurel Papworth, commented on her blog: "It might only be a virtual world, it might just be Second Life—but I believe we take our values with us. In-and-out of real world, virtual world, doesn't matter, we reveal who we are at all times."[4] And if you asked remote-living Aboriginal people how they feel, they might respond that in addition to their worries regarding violation of cultural protocols, they don't even have access to sufficient broadband to have access to Second Life.

In addition to the protest over Uluru's virtual violation, there is anxiety over the uneven distribution of broadband capacity to people living in remote areas, a point of emerging concern from the Arctic to the Amazon. This position was laid out clearly by the Igloolik Isuma collective in the initial FAQ section of Isuma TV, first launched in 2009, quoted below.[5]

> One danger to Inuit and other indigenous communities in the 21st century is the risk of getting stuck on the wrong side of the digital divide. Remote regions must gain full participation in the information economy or face falling forever farther behind. If IsumaTV succeeds, remote viewers will demand better quality reception. Increasing demand for larger bandwidth will help pressure governments, foundations and international agencies to ensure the indigenous world is included in hi-speed bandwidth networks, rather than left out.
>
> All future economy will be conducted and controlled digitally; leaving indigenous cultures long on pipelines but short on bandwidth ensures permanent second-rate inequality for generations to come. Indigenous investors must find the vision to invest in internet and new media development, film and television production and distribution, as if these were pipelines, airlines, or shipping companies, since in the new economy of the century before us, that's what they are.

These comments and the Second Life story seem profoundly contemporary in their concern with the stratification of virtual worlds, with the difficulties of containing cultural and intellectual property in a digital viral medium, and with issues of infrastructure access in a digital age when we are continually persuaded that it's a small world after all. Yet they are nonetheless emblematic of many of the epistemologically challenging issues that have been raised in the field of visual anthropology over the last three decades—if not longer—about the status and implications of indigenous media.[6] In this short history of debates in the field, the Second Life story and the concerns articulated by Isuma TV remind us that such issues are not only academic, but also, of course, have consequences in the lives of indigenous people themselves, many of whom are avid producers and consumers of visual media of all kinds. In the process, they have become increasingly aware of how dominant cultural protocols regarding media—valorizing free and open access—are at times very different from those in their own cultures, where certain forms of mediation are restricted in their circulation. Such recognitions shape some of the central and enduring concerns raised about indigenous media. These include questions of cultural difference that frame not only media representation and indigenous aesthetics, but also the very notion of what can or cannot be rendered visually accessible to those in or outside particular communities, a set of concerns that might fall under the rubric of "image ethics,"[7] and problems with control over the increasingly promiscuous circulation of images, with sacred objects, sites, and activities that should be witnessed only by initiated traditional owners offering an extreme case and the repatriation of archives another. They also include concerns about the ways in which both radical alterity—profound cultural, cosmological, political, and aesthetic difference from Western norms—and rights to represent indigenous realities are negotiated through contemporary media worlds, both on-screen and off-screen and the uptake of media practices as an extension of cultural and political activism in establishing the presence of indigenous lives within their own communities, in nation-states, and on the world stage.

These questions, which hover around concerns regarding who has the right to represent indigenous lives and landscapes in both old and new media, are not new. Indeed, they linger in the background of what is considered the foundational text in this field, Sol Worth and John Adair's classic study *Through Navajo Eyes*, first published in 1972.[8] That book inaugurated a paradigm shift in the field of visual anthropology, although its consequences took some time to be more fully articulated. While Worth and Adair's book focused on whether novice Navajo filmmakers would make films that embodied the radical alterity of other cultural perspectives when brought to a new medium—that is, whether their films would "be Navajo" in some fundamental way—the book also, perhaps unwittingly, opened the eyes of many Anglophone readers at the time who (with the exception of those familiar with the work of French anthropologist/filmmaker Jean Rouch) had not yet imagined that the camera might be put in the hands of those who had historically been objects of the anthropological gaze. The unexpected elegance of this idea—that this technology might allow many to encounter the native's point of view without the mediation of either the ethnographer or anthropological language—was exciting to some, but apparently threatening to others, who continued to try to police the legitimacy of indigenous media throughout the 1990s, arguing that the technology of the camera is fundamentally Western.[9]

The logical, if unintended consequence of Worth and Adair's interest in literally seeing other worldviews via film was to open people's minds as to who might have the right to represent other cultural worlds through a variety of media, including film, photography, and video. No longer could one assume that it is the exclusive domain of the anthropologist (or filmmaker) to make documentary or other photographic or moving-image representations of indigenous people who had so long been the disempowered object of the ethnographic gaze. At the same time, the fact that cameras were circulating into the hands of so many of the world's subaltern subjects did not necessarily undermine the legitimacy of ethnographic film, but rather put this genre into salutary dialogue with this other emerging field of representations, creating what I characterized in an article in 1999 as a cultural "parallax effect":

> This term was originally invented to describe the phenomenon that occurs when a change in the position of the observer creates the illusion that an object has been displaced or moved. In astronomy, this effect is harnessed to gain a greater understanding of the position and nature of stars and planets in the cosmos. In optics,

> the small parallax created by the slightly different angles of vision of each eye is recognized as that which enables us to judge distances accurately and see in three dimensions. Drawing on a similar principle, one might understand indigenous media as arising from a historically new positioning of the observed behind the camera so that the object—the cinematic representation of culture—appears to look different than it does from the observational perspective of ethnographic film. Yet, by juxtaposing these different but related kinds of cinematic perspectives on culture, one can create a kind of parallax effect; if harnessed analytically, these "slightly different angles of vision" can offer a fuller comprehension of the complexity—the three-dimensionality, so to speak–of the social phenomenon we call culture and those media representations that self-consciously engage with it. It is my argument that resituating ethnographic film in relation to related practices such as indigenous media can help expand the field's possibilities and revive its contemporary interest and purpose beyond a narrowly defined field. The parallax created by the different perspectives in these media practices is one that is particularly important now as anthropology struggles to position itself in relation to contemporary critiques.[10]

Now, more than a decade after I wrote that essay, it is clear that both fields—indigenous media and ethnographic film—have continued to develop in the context of the dizzying proliferation of media forms and images that distinguishes the contemporary era. From the vantage point of the early twenty-first century, it is hard to imagine that just over a decade ago, some scholars were assuming that the uptake of media in indigenous communities would be the death knell of "authentic cultural practices," despite considerable evidence to the contrary.[11] If anything, the opposite has turned out to be the case. Indigenous media work has shown itself to be a particularly robust form of contemporary cultural objectification. From small-scale video and local radio, to archival websites, to national television stations and feature films, indigenous media makers have found opportunities for cultural creativity of all sorts. These projects often support the maintenance or even revival of ritual practices and local languages while establishing forms of cultural labor that repair fraying intergenerational relationships and bring much-needed sources of productive activity and at times income into communities that suffer from high rates of poverty and unemployment.

The work has developed across a range of technologies and community or institutional bases. Most notably, these include small-format local productions originally produced in analog video in the 1980s and now increasingly on digital video local and regional television created over the last two decades, facilitated initially by the launch of communication satellites over remote areas, as with the Central Australian Aboriginal Media Association (CAAMA) and the Inuit Broadcasting Corporation (IBC) in Canada, and now by digital possibilities as inaugurated in 2009 with Isuma TV in Nunavut, Canada, by Igloolik Isuma.[12] They also include indigenously run national television stations, beginning with the Aboriginal People's Television Network (APTN) in Canada (1999), Maori TV in New Zealand/Aoteoroa (2003) (and a second channel for Maori speakers in 2007), Taiwan Indigenous Television (2005), and National Indigenous Television (NITV) in Australia (2007).

Indigenous media work in fiction filmmaking, including the production of approximately forty indigenously directed feature films worldwide, has contributed to indigenous film taking its place as a form of world cinema on the global stage, circulating not only through a lively circuit of indigenous film festivals worldwide, but also through mainstream venues such as Cannes, the Toronto International Film Festival, and the Sundance Film Festival, arenas that not only showcase such work, but in some cases help support its development. At these festivals, many indigenous features have gone on to win major prizes, which serve as important forms of cultural capital that can be turned into resources to continue to support their work.

Indigenous work in digital media that crosses platforms and epistemologies raises important questions that bring us back to some of the basic issues about representation and the materiality of different media, from the kind of virtual worlds (and problems) suggested in the opening example to other concerns about the increasing stratification of media practices that are dependent on literacy based media forms (such as computer interfaces) that undergird the shift to the digital from analog formats. For example, Isuma TV and its latest retooling, the Nunavut Independent TV Network (NITV), launched May 29, 2009, both exploit the possibilities of the digital for providing alternative ways of circulating indigenous media around the world to other communities whose very remoteness has made such access difficult through conventional means of distribution.[13]

Finally, indigenous archives based on the repatriation of ethnographic and other films and photographs made in earlier, often colonial/settler eras are an increasingly important and exciting social practice enhanced by mindful use of digital technologies, often created through deeply collaborative creative partnerships with technically skilled nonindigenous fellow travelers as they together imagine and invent new ways to build in cultural protocols and nonalphabetic language use, as in the groundbreaking work of the Ara̲ Irititja Project in Australia.[14]

INDIGENOUS MEDIA: MEDIATING CULTURE AND THE ACTIVIST IMAGINARY

While I cannot cover all these areas in depth given the constraints of length,[15] I will attempt to give a broad sense as to how these particular technologies have differentially shaped the development of Indigenous media under different media regimes. Since the 1980s, Indigenous media has attracted ongoing and sometimes intense scholarly attention.[16] Central to much of this work is a recognition that the uptake of new-media technologies by indigenous producers was often motivated—at least initially—by a desire to "talk back" to structures of power that have erased or distorted indigenous interests and realities. Many of the works and projects that have been produced might best be understood as forms of "cultural activism," a term I have used to underscore the intertwined sense of both political agency and cultural intervention that people bring to these efforts, part of a spectrum of practices of self-conscious mediation and mobilization of culture more generally that took on a particular shape and velocity beginning in the late twentieth century.[17] In the mid-1990s, George Marcus coined a related term, "the activist imaginary," to describe how subaltern groups turn to film, video, and other media not only to "pursue traditional goals of broad-based social change through a politics of identity and representation," but also out of a utopian desire for "emancipatory projects . . . raising fresh issues about citizenship and the shape of public spheres within the frame and terms of traditional discourse on polity and civil society."[18] Even as indigenous media practices have evolved in their sophistication and reach in many parts of the world, these central motivations continue to drive much of the work, whether from remote communities or urban centers, a point that is underscored in the writing about this work.

In two of the key locales, Canada and Australia, indigenous media first developed in response to the entry of mass media into the lives of First Nations people, primarily through the state's imposition of satellite-based commercial television on remote regions where more traditional populations lived, beginning in Canada in the late 1970s[19] and in Australia in the 1980s. Remote communities vigorously opposed the "dumping" of mainstream media into their lives without the opportunity to shape their own media to meet local concerns. At the same time, the increasing availability of inexpensive, user-friendly, small-format analog video presented an opportunity for these groups to produce their own work, which some indigenous activists imagined, metaphorically, as a shield of local manufacture that might fend off the invasion of these other signals from the dominant culture.

This happened with the early foundational case made famous by activist researcher Eric Michaels, a student of Sol Worth, who built on and transformed Worth's ideas when he was hired to study the impact of media on indigenous people living in the Central Desert of Australia. In the 1980s, he worked with Warlpiri people to help them develop their own analog video practices and low-power television—what he called "the Aboriginal invention of television in Central Australia"—created as an alternative to the onslaught of commercial television via the satellite.[20] Michaels's work was foundational for the emergence of indigenous media as a topic in visual anthropology. He showed how local indigenous media might be particularly well suited for anthropological inquiry. Small in scale and sustaining an alternative to the mass-media industries that dominate late-capitalist societies, these practices occupy a clear position of difference from dominant cultural assumptions about media aesthetics and practices. Thus, they provide a kind of natural laboratory for understanding the possibilities of radically different media practices that are "off the grid" of most media scholarship (which is largely Eurocentric) or research addressing indigenous lives, research in which media practices are too easily regarded as either epiphenomenal or insufficiently traditional. As Michaels pointed out in the 1980s, Aboriginal "art or video objects become difficult to isolate for analysis because the producer's intention is the opposite. Warlpiri artists demonstrate their own invisibility in order to assert the work's authority and continuity with tradition. They do not draw attention to themselves or to their creativity."[21] Building on this insight, I have pointed to the significance of "embedded aesthetics" in indigenous media being produced in traditional Aboriginal communities, where they maintain a system of evaluation that refuses a separation of textual production and circulation from broader arenas of social relations. Rather, the quality of a work is assessed according to its capacity to embody, sustain, and even revive or create certain social relations.

Indigenous media, then, can be seen as a new and complex object operating in a number of domains as an extension of collective self-production.[22] As another instance of this complex sense of aesthetics, Jennifer Deger's book on her work with Yolngu media making in northern Australia focuses on what one might call an indigenous Yolngu theory of "media effects" in which traditional concepts of the impact of revelation/witnessing/showing can be constitutive of identity, a kind of active viewing that empowers and catalyzes ancestral power, rendered evident even if it is not actually visible.[23] In other parts of the world, for example among the Aymara and Quechua filmmakers who make up the Bolivian indigenous media collective CEFREC, there is a refusal of authorship in the production of films and a "noncapitalist" economy that shapes the circuits of exhibition and exchange that are fundamental to the Andean indigenous-media world.[24]

Debates about such work contribute to and reflect the changing and sometimes contested status of "culture" in a globalizing world where culture is increasingly commodified, as well as in social/anthropological theory and, importantly, in the writings of indigenous filmmakers and intellectuals.[25] "Culture" is a category that is increasingly objectified and mediated as it becomes a source of claims for political and human rights, both within the nation-states encompassing indigenous people and on the world stage. As Terry Turner has shown regarding the work of Kayapo media makers, cultural claims "can be converted into political assets, both internally as bases of group solidarity and mobilization, and externally as claims on the support of other social groups, governments and public opinion all over the globe."[26]

THE POLITICS OF RESEARCH

Indigenous-media projects have often been a site for activist participation on the part of anthropologists and communications scholars such as Michaels and many others since then, because they and indigenous intellectuals alike have been quick to see the political promise and cultural possibilities of indigenously controlled media making. Such collaborations include work such as Harald Prins's advocacy-media productions with Micmac, Apache, and other groups,[27] my own work with Aboriginal Australians,[28] Terry Turner and Vincent Carelli's successful projects helping to launch Amazonian media,[29] and a host of others.[30] These collaborative research projects—what Jean Rouch called *anthropologie partagée* (shared anthropology)—have helped to produce and/or promote as well as analyze the making of film and video as part of indigenous projects of cultural revival, whether through recording traditional rituals or through the use of video, film, and media events as a persuasive tool for claims to political sovereignty. These scholars and others have actively supported indigenous-media production while recognizing the dilemmas that such work can present. Harald Prins, for example, who has helped to catalyze indigenous filmmaking for Native American claims to land and cultural rights, nonetheless points out "the paradox of primitivism," in which traditional imagery of indigenous people in documentaries about native rights, while effective (perhaps even essential) as a form of political agency, may also distort the cultural processes that indigenous peoples are committed to preserving.[31]

Often, when doing fieldwork among and sympathizing with dominated groups, anthropologists feel a responsibility to support projects by non-Western or postcolonial groups who are resisting the impositions of Western or global capitalist media. While the media we study may be off the map of dominant media cartographies, they are no less crucial to the transformations of the twenty-first century. Those studying indigenous media seek to grasp the ways in which media are integrated into communities that are parts of nations and states, as well as into the transnational networks and circuits produced in the worlds of late capitalism and postcolonial cultural politics. Our relations with those we study are changing as our cultural worlds grow closer in ways that push the boundaries of anthropology. It is difficult to exoticize others or to maintain fictions of bounded or untouched communities of difference when one includes media in one's purview, if only because it forces a recognition that "natives" are deeply engaged in establishing their own multiple representational strategies and objectifications on their own terms, through forms that are marked as resolutely modern, yet that are indigenized in multiple ways. Local uses and meanings of media and of comparative political economies of media production and consumption (including real constraints posed by the unreliability of electricity and the vicissitudes of poverty) suggest the persistence of difference and the importance of locality while highlighting the forms of inequality that continue to structure our world.

While anthropologists and media scholars debate the impact that media technologies might have on the communities with which they work and whence they come, indigenous media makers are busy using and rethinking the technologies for their own purposes. Activists are documenting traditional activities with elders and working with them to repatriate archival material; creating works to teach young people literacy in their own languages, using many forms, including the radically underappreciated, but deeply significant radio; engaging with dominant circuits of mass media and projecting political struggles through mainstream media as well as in alternative arenas; communicating among dispersed kin and communities on a range of issues; using video as legal documents in negotiations with states; presenting videos on state television to assert their presence televisually within national imaginaries; or creating award-winning feature films. When new technologies are embraced as powerful forms of collective self-production, they enable indigenous cultural activists to assert their presence in the polities that encompass them and to enter more easily into much larger movements for social transformation and for the recognition and redress of human and cultural rights, processes in which media play an increasingly important role.[32]

Perhaps the most articulate theorization of indigenous media has come from the work of the late Maori filmmaker and intellectual Barry Barclay, who coined the term "Fourth Cinema" in his book *Our Own Image*, published in 1990. In that publication and in almost all his writing until his death in 2008, he argued for indigenous filmmaking as a *hui*, the term for a Maori gathering or meeting, drawing on the power of community on and off the screen. As film scholar Stuart Murray explains *Images of Dignity: Barry Barclay and Fourth Cinema*, "In keeping with his developing ideas about Fourth Cinema, Barclay saw all of his features as comprising multiple elements—from the pre-production consultation with the communities to be filmed, to the actual detail of the shooting, and on to the questions of distribution, reception and film use." His emphasis on *korero*, or protocols, and on ensuring that the end product was appropriately returned to those who had given it, has established a notion of total filmmaking, an inclusive process of discussion and advice.[33]

As Barclay and others suggest, indigenous media worldwide represent a countercurrent to neoliberal trends that seek to deracinate and commodify culture.

Often working against the grain of a late-capitalist economy, indigenous producers seek to circulate their work for reasons other than profit. Instead, productions are understood to be based on embedded notions of reciprocity, cultural rights, and the need for communities to maintain guardianship over work so that circulation and archives are managed according to local protocols.

THE CASE OF INDIGENOUS TELEVISION

Given the prominence of experiments in television in the broader debates concerning indigenous media in visual anthropology, I want to explore the issues raised by this medium in some depth. Television—from low-power operations, to terrestrial national channels, to satellite TV—has been used for almost four decades by indigenous communities around the world, beginning with the launch of communications satellites over the Canadian Arctic in the 1970s that motivated Inuit communities to create their own productions with the Inuit Broadcasting Corporation in 1982.[34] Indigenous television experiments offer a powerful alternative to the notion of television as a "vast wasteland," the term coined and made famous in 1961 by Newton Minow in his first speech as chairman of the U.S. Federal Communications Commission. Rather, they show how the medium can be reimagined to promote and develop the cultural resurgence of minoritized communities, providing a provocative case study in terms of which the global impact of television can be reexamined and understood.

Over the last three decades, television has spread from centers to peripheries and from the earth to the sky, part of the rapidly changing landscape of television worldwide—what some call "Planet TV"[35]—as media technology has expanded from terrestrial TV to the more flexible range of satellite and small-format video and, increasingly, digital convergence with the Internet.[36] The localized possibilities in this form of globalization are especially apparent in the uptake of such media forms in First Peoples' communities throughout the world, creating: something new in the air,"[37] modes of communication that could be seen as having much longer histories that range from songlines to satellites[38] or from birchbark talk to digital dreamspeaking,[39] to use the poetics of some key studies. The capacity of such media to communicate the concerns of indigenous people to many audiences has created, some argue, a discursive space for an emergent indigenous public sphere,[40] while the most pessimistic suggest that these projects inevitably entail a corrupt relationship that involves "getting into bed with the state."[41]

These concerns about compromise haunt much of the early research and debate on indigenous television, echoing the suspicions of indigenous communities as they have struggled to imagine how they might turn the imposition of media technologies such as television—described early on by Inuit leader Rosemary Kuptana as a potential neutron bomb that kills the people and leaves structures intact—to their advantage.[42] Generally, this has involved recognition of the cultural possibilities of indigenously controlled media making as a way of rendering the nations that encompass them more aware of indigenous concerns while also strengthening internal intergenerational and intercommunity knowledge. When indigenous producers can control or even redesign the circumstances of production and circulation, indigenous activists have embraced television and other media as technologies that have allowed them some degree of agency and enhanced cultural expression, albeit within hegemonic forms of representation and often under less than ideal conditions.[43]

To some extent, indigenous concerns about compromise have benefited from the fact that many of the communication technologies they wanted to use initially were regarded as experimental and marginal. Indeed, the very idea of indigenous television was regarded as somewhat of an oxymoron, so that early projects often developed under the radar of state scrutiny, in many cases allowing this work to unfold at its own pace, in line with indigenously based ideas of what constitutes appropriate production and circulation practices, as well as aesthetics.[44] As indigenous television has started to play more of a role in the global mediasphere, some are concerned, once again, that it will be increasingly compromised by the homogenizing demands of broadcast standards.

Local indigenous television projects based in more traditional remote communities first emerged in Canada in the 1970s and in Australia in the 1980s, with other varieties of indigenous television emerging in the 1990s in the United States, Brazil, Bolivia, and Mexico. These included participation in highly localized low-power TV such as Radio y Video Tamix in Mexico or PAW TV in Yuendumu, Australia—what one scholar of Mexican indigenous media calls "television sin reglas" (television without rules)[45]—and regional remote networks such as the Central Australian Aboriginal Media Association. Urban Aboriginal activists, strongly identified with their heritage, but less traditional in their orientation, began their own projects with units affiliating with national television stations, such as the Indigenous Production Units inaugurated in 1988 as part of Australia's ABC and SBS stations, and established national stations underwritten by government support, as happened with the Aboriginal People's Television Network in Canada,[46] Maori TV in Aotearoa/New Zealand,[47] Taiwan Indigenous Television in Taiwan, and National Indigenous Television in Australia.

Following on the heels of broader movements for indigenous rights, activists in a number of locales pushed government bodies to allocate resources for their communities to produce and circulate representations of themselves, their histories, and their worldviews. Of particular concern was the capacity to create programming for all age groups in their local languages to combat the overwhelming effects of exposure to the dominant culture and its language through other forms of television, a debate that was active in the 1970s and that resurfaced in 2005 regarding language policy on Canada's APTN and New Zealand's Maori TV. Eventually, the indigenous appropriation of television was recognized as an important technology in the development of indigenous citizenship for those living in both remote and urban areas and for their recognition by the surrounding settler societies, as well. Significantly, these developments have also served as incubators of indigenous talent, as indigenous producers, directors, actors, and editors have had opportunities made available to them that never before existed. Increasingly, indigenous work from different parts of the world circulates internationally, forming a regular part of programming for these television stations.

Scholars and researchers have been attracted to indigenous television since the mid-1980s, seeking in it the empirical evidence of a kind of embedded cultural critique, an aesthetic and political alternative to mass media beholden to governmentality or late-capitalist interests This sense of possibility was first articulated in the mid-1980s in the work of Eric Michaels mentioned earlier, which showed the complex epistemologies surrounding image production in traditional Aboriginal life, including the significance of kin groups and cosmologies in the off-screen production of work as a source of authentication as to the truth value of the final product, as well as the extension of traditional linguistic taboos on the names of those who had died to prohibitions on circulating images of the dead.

As indigenous-media productions have developed under these regimes, the work made for such purposes increasingly circulates beyond the televisual moment of broadcast to other native communities through the circulation of tapes, films, DVDs, and Internet portals, as well as to non-Aboriginal audiences via regional, national, and even international television. The capacity of this work to have a life after television, so to speak, helps overcome the potential isolation of indigenous media to a particular channel or programming slot—what one scholar has identified as "media reservations."[48] More broadly, the telling and circulation of indigenous stories and histories through media forms that can circulate beyond the local has been an important force for constituting claims for land and cultural rights and for developing alliances with other communities.

Getting indigenous histories into mainstream media, as indigenous units situated in national broadcasters have done, has been a critical goal everywhere, because Aboriginal citizens feel their contributions to national narratives have largely been erased or ignored. As a case in point, the October 2008 broadcast in Australia of the seven-part indigenously directed series *First Australians* was widely regarded as a major breakthrough, offering a compelling counternarrative of the nation's history from an indigenous point of view. This extraordinary historical documentary series produced for Australian television (SBS I) focused on the history of Australia from an indigenous perspective, from the precontact period to the present. The prominent Indigenous filmmakers Rachel Perkins (Arrente/Kalkadoon) and Beck Cole (Yawura/Djarbera-Djarbera) directed four and three of the seven episodes, respectively. The series launch in October 2008 had a remarkable impact across the nation, with praiseworthy and lengthy coverage in the mainstream press. The words of one writer in one of Australia's newspapers of record, the *Age*, were typical of the critical reception, hailing *First Australians* as "one of the most significant documentary series in the history of Australian television. For the first time, the story of Aboriginal Australia has been condensed into a coherent narrative that begins with the mythological birth of humanity on this continent."[49] The series was accompanied by a book, *First Australians: A Visual History*, edited by Rachel Perkins and Marcia Langton, elaborating on the historical and visual archival sources that were used in the films.[50] In addition to its paradigm-changing effect on the Australian public sphere, the series also demonstrated the productivity of colonial archival film and photography when it is appropriated, resignified, and repurposed by indigenous media makers as visible evidence of their experiences told from their point of view.

Six months later, *The American Experience*, a show on the Public Broadcasting Service in the United States, televised its five-part series *We Shall Remain*, each episode focusing on a key moment in Native American history. Four of the five episodes were directed by established indigenous directors, including three by Chris Eyre (Cheyenne/Arapaho) and one by Dustinn Craig (Apache), along with a team of scholars with the expertise to guide each of the films. The project, as the series website proclaimed, created "a provocative multi-media project that establishes Native history as an essential part of American history."[51]

Perhaps one of the most innovative experiments in indigenous television was the launch of Nunavut Independent TV Network (NITV) on Isuma TV on May 29, 2009, by the longstanding and always groundbreaking remote Arctic Inuit media collective Igloolik Isuma. This is perhaps the best-known of indigenous media groups in the world, notably through the global success of their prize-winning film *Atanarjuat, The Fast Runner* (2000), the first Inuit feature film, created through their distinctive community-based production process. A subsequent film, *Before Tomorrow* (2008, Arnait women's collective), gathered prizes on its festival run. The group developed its video style in the 1980s and formed officially in 1990, turning televisual technologies into vehicles for the cultural expression of Inuit lives and histories, a counterpoint to the introduction of mainstream, satellite-based television into the Canadian Arctic. Headed by director Zacharias Kunuk, Isuma engages Igloolik community members, while Brooklyn-born filmmaker and Isuma partner Norman Cohn leads a support team in Montreal. Frustrated by the difficulty of showing their work to other Inuit communities, in 2008, they launched a groundbreaking alternative for indigenous distribution, Isuma TV, a free Internet video portal for global indigenous media available to both local audiences and worldwide viewers. NITV on Isuma TV is a digital distribution project, bringing a high-speed version of Isuma TV into remote Nunavut communities, where the bandwidth is often inadequate even to view YouTube. NITV allows films to be uploaded from anywhere, rebroadcast through local cable or low-power channels, or downloaded to digital projectors.

The bigger story here concerns the unanticipated possibilities presented to indigenous cultural activists at moments of media innovation. As Norman Cohn explains:

> We saw the historical technological "moment of opportunity" for the internet, the way we saw the analog video moment in 1970, and the Atanarjuat digital/film moment in 1998: the brief window in the technology of communication where marginalized users with a serious political and cultural objective, could bypass centuries of entrenched powerlessness with a serious new idea at a much higher level of visibility than usual in our top-down power-driven global politics. In 2007, internet capacity allowed us to end-run the film industry entirely and launch a video website that could take aspects of YouTube to a much higher level of thematic seriousness, and see what happens. So this is a serious experiment in the history of alternate media experiments since the early-70's, as Isuma has been from the start, helping viewers see indigenous reality from its own point of view.[52]

Projects such as NITV raise concerns about the increasing stratification of media practices dependent on literacy-based media forms that undergird the shift to the digital, although Web 2.0 innovations—web applications that facilitate participatory information sharing, interoperability, user-centered design, and collaboration—might arguably get around the literacy problem, opening up the capacity of this realm to orality in indigenous languages, a point to which I will return.

FIRST NATIONS/FIRST FEATURES

Feature film offers a different kind of practice, creating new opportunities for the recognition of the complex realities of a range of indigenous experiences, with stories emerging from the multiple legacies of settler colonialism that have shaped aboriginal lives everywhere, although some have been less clearly marked in public discourse until now. Many of the films made since the late 1980s offer alternative and complex accountings of histories and subjectivities, providing a site for a counterpublic articulation of a broader range of indigenous experience than the depleted repertoire of long-standing cinematic stereotypes.

What role do these films made by indigenous people—and especially feature films—play in reconceptualizing national imaginaries and destabilizing unified national narratives? Fundamentally, this work can be understood as part of broader efforts to "decolonize the screen." As the respected Maori filmmaker and writer Merata Mita put it, "Swimming against the tide becomes an exhilarating experience. It makes you strong. For 90 minutes or so, we have the capability of indigenizing the screen in any part of the world our films are shown. This represents power and is one reason that we make films that are uniquely and distinctly Maori."[53]

Their work also demonstrates that a textual analysis of what we see on-screen is not sufficient if it does not also take into account the cultural and political labor of indigenous activists whose interventions have made support for this possible, revealing how contemporary states and their indigenous citizens negotiate diversity. This problematic is central to current discussions of cultural citizenship, a topic that has gained considerable currency over the last decade in anthropology and other fields: in other words, citizenship is not just a legal status, defined by a set of rights and responsibilities, but also an identity, an expression of one's membership in a political community that must be accommodated and recognized within liberal democracies.

Indigenous filmmakers working in the field of cultural production who have wanted to develop their own capacities—their voices and visions—as well as the social and financial capital needed to enter into feature filmmaking have faced a far more complex and costly infrastructure than is needed by those who have been working in small-scale video. To understand works such as indigenously directed feature films, it is as important to attend to off-screen circumstances shaping cultural production as it is to understand the on-screen narratives, including, the cultural and institutional conditions that helped bring at least some of this work into being and provide the venues for its visibility and the crucial role played by indigenous cultural activists and their fellow travelers to get support for the programs and resources necessary to create the kind of films that can expand, if not transform a national cinema.

The histories of initiatives to develop indigenous feature film in different parts of the world, first launched in a systematic way in the 1980s with two groundbreaking films that debuted in 1987 (both at the Cannes Film Festival) by Maori director Barry Barclay, *Ngati*, and Sami director Nils Gaup, *Pathfinder*. In May 2009,

Samson and Delilah, a feature film by indigenous Australian director Warwick Thornton, won the Camera d'Or, the prize for the best first feature at the Cannes Film Festival. On getting the prize, Thornton spoke of the significance of filmmaking in his life:

> I grew up on the streets of Alice Springs, getting into trouble with the police. I needed direction and somehow I found cinema, or cinema found that direction for me. It saved my life. The original story came out of anger at the neglect of our children, not only by the government and wider society, but even by parents. So it came from a dark place. I had to think about it for a year in order to present something that wasn't angry, where people could just go on a journey with these children. I've got so many more stories to tell, what I believe are beautiful stories, that are fires inside me that I desperately need to show the world.[54]

These success stories are instructive as experiments in testing the limits of multicultural arts policies as works transcend the bounded world suggested by restricted funding categories, demonstrating their value on the world stage, as well as in local indigenous worlds. In particular, they raise questions about the impact of culturally restricted categories of support for this form of indigenous cultural production as, increasingly, these films circulate internationally, implicating such work in the nation's broader trade relations and political economies in which "culture" is increasingly caught up. For example, in his book discussing the Bolivian indigenous film collective CEFREC, Jeff Himpele argues that the circulation of indigenous video makers and their work is made possible in part by the wider international political shift in which "indigeneity" has become a valuable political image, as well as through transcontinental technologies, networks and resources.[55] The travels of indigenous films and filmmakers to the United States, Europe, and elsewhere are not just a form of cultural expansion and strength; an ever-expanding circuit of indigenous film festivals allows them to form significant alliances with native media makers across the world.

RETHINKING THE DIGITAL AGE

In her editor's introduction to the volume *Native on the Net*, Kyra Landzelius asks: "Can the info-superhighway be a fast track to greater empowerment for the historically disenfranchised? Or do they risk becoming 'roadkill': casualties of hypermedia and the drive to electronically map everything?"[56] Recent developments give some insight into what it might actually mean to enter the digital age for indigenous subjects in communities located in remote regions of the world where access to telephone landlines can still be difficult.[57]As Harald Prins has argued regarding the place of indigenous people in "Cyberia," "Although indigenous peoples are proportionally underrepresented in cyberspace—for obvious reasons such as economic poverty, technological inexperience, linguistic isolation, political repression, and/or cultural resistance—the Internet has vastly extended traditional networks of information and communication. . . . Together with the rest of us, they have pioneered across the new cultural frontier and are now surfing daily through Cyberia."[58] While indigenous use of digital technologies is uneven, at best, Prins points optimistically to the circumstances in which the cross-platformed use of digital technologies is being taken up in indigenous communities on their own terms, furthering the development of political networks and the capacity to extend their traditional cultural worlds into new domains.

Indigenous digital media have raised important questions about the politics and circulation of knowledge at a number of levels. Within communities, these questions may be about who has had access to and understanding of media technologies and who has the rights to know, tell, and circulate certain stories and images. Within nation-states, such media are linked to larger battles over cultural citizenship, racism, sovereignty, and land rights, as well as to struggles over funding, airspace and satellites, networks of broadcasting and distribution, access to archives, and digital broadband services that may or may not be available to indigenous communities. Norman Cohn, who has been working with the Nunavut-based media collective Igloolik Isuma for over two decades, articulates the dilemmas of this kind of hardware stratification while at the same time inventing new ways to put digital technologies to use—Web 2.0 in particular, which offers a technological boost over the problem of literacy—in radically different cultural circumstances.

> At present, Inuit and other Indigenous people are on the brink of being left out of the most important new communication technology since the printing press. Almost everything in the 21st century will be conducted at least partly by internet. Being left off, even for another decade or two, is like a linguistic, cultural and economic death sentence. Isuma's commitment to create IsumaTV even in the face of these disadvantages is our recognition of how access to the internet cannot be 'negotiable' for Indigenous communities struggling to survive. This is particularly the case since the new 2.0 multimedia internet actually offers a practical tool especially suitable for oral cultures in remote regions. Unlike the literary medium of print, or the 1.0 print-based internet which is all about reading, in which oral cultures traditionally have been disadvantaged by participating in their second languages, the 2.0 audio-visual internet advantages people using sophisticated aural and visual skill-sets in their own first languages.[59]

Efforts such as Igloolik Isuma's NITV are evidence of how indigenous-media projects formed over the last decades are now positioned at the conjuncture of a number of historical developments. These include the circuits opened by new-media technologies, ranging from satellites to compressed video and cyberspace, as well as the ongoing legacies of indigenous activism worldwide, most recently by a generation comfortable with media and concerned with making their own representations as a mode of cultural creativity and social action. They also represent the complex and differing ways in which encompassing settler states have responded to these developments—the opportunities of media and the pressures of activism—and have entered into new relationships with the indigenous nations that they encompass.

CONCLUSION

I conclude on a note of cautious optimism. The evidence of the growth and creativity of indigenous media over the last two decades, whatever problems may have accompanied them, is nothing short of remarkable, whether working out of grounded communities or broader regional or national bases. While indigenous-media activism alone certainly cannot unseat the power asymmetries that underwrite the profound inequalities continuing to shape their worlds, the issues and images that their media interventions raise about their cultural futures are on a continuum with broader issues of self-determination, cultural rights, and political sovereignty and may help bring some attention to these profoundly interconnected concerns.

While activism and policy concerns initially shaped much of indigenous media, it is important to acknowledge the current range of genres being produced: drama, current affairs, political analysis, humor, cooking shows, variety shows, music videos, and sports. Additionally, the media technologies being deployed range from low-format video to satellite, cable to Web 2.0, radio to feature film and television. As indigenous media have grown more robust over the last two decades—in part through the increasing convergence of media forms that makes it hard to know where to draw the boundaries between television, film, and web-based work—a remarkably diverse array of works suggest that this synthesis of media technology with new forms of collective self-production has much to offer indigenous communities as they redefine themselves and future generations in the twenty-first century.

NOTES

A version of this essay entitled "Native Intelligence: A Short History of Debates on Indigenous Media and Ethnographic Film" appears in Jay Ruby and Marcus Banks (eds.), *Made to Be Seen: Perspectives on the History of Visual Anthropology* (Chicago: University of Chicago Press, 2011). Many thanks to Jay Ruby and Marcus Banks, for pushing me to write this essay, and to Meg McLagan for her insightful comments and patience. This work is based on ongoing research that began in 1988 in Australia and that has continued since then in many locations. The work has been funded over the years by fellowships and grants from NYU, and the Guggenheim and Macarthur Foundations. I am indebted to a number of people for ongoing conversations that have informed this paper including Jane Anderson, Philip Batty, Sally Berger, Vincent Carelli, Norman Cohn, Jennifer Deger, Francoise Dussart, Samia Gaudie, Sara Hourez, Darlene Johnson, Frances Jupurrula Kelly, Merata Mita, Rachel Naninaaq Edwardson, Alanis Obamsawim, Frances Peters, Rachel Perkins, Jolene Rickard, Sally Riley, Beverly Singer, Juan Salazar, Wal Saunders, Ramesh Srinivasan, Loretta Todd, David Vadiveloo, Pegi Vail, Elizabeth Weatherford, Amalia Cordova, Michelle Raheja as well as current and former graduate students Lucas Bessire, Kristin Dowell, Danny Fisher, Aaron Glass, April Strickland, Lisa Stefanoff, Sabra Thorner, Ernesto de Carvalho, and Erica Wortham. As always, I am grateful to Fred Myers for his thoughtful comments and enthusiastic support.

1. Simon Canning, "Uluru Row Rocks Telstra," AustralianIT, http://australianit.news.com.au/story/0,24897,21786053-15306,00.html.
2. Canning, "Uluru Row Rocks Telstra."
3. Asher Moses, "BigPond Backs Down on Uluru Adverts," *The Age*, September 8, 2008, http://www.theage.com.au/news/biztech/bigpond-backs-down-on-uluru-advrts/2008/09/08/1220725906421.html.
4. Laurel Papworth, "Bigpond Brands Uluru," http://laurelpapworth.com/bigpond-brands-uluru.
5. The initial FAQ section is no longer available at Isuma TV, http://www.isuma.tv.
6. While the term "indigenous" can index a social formation "native" to a particular area (for example, *I Love Lucy* is "indigenous" to America), I use it here in the strict sense of the term, as interchangeable with the neologism "First Peoples" to indicate the original inhabitants of areas later colonized by settler states (Australia, the United States, New Zealand, Canada, most of Latin America). These people, an estimated 5 percent of the world's population, are struggling to sustain their own identities and claims to culture and land, surviving as internal colonies within encompassing nation-states. The last two or more decades of indigenous activism throughout the world, especially in the Americas, and the catalytic effect of the formation of groups such as the UN Working Group on Indigenous Populations in 1977 and the UN Decade of Indigenous People (1994–2004), part of the globalization of social life that has caught the attention of so many scholars and that has built significant networks for many of the players, have significantly influenced the uptake and development of media of all sorts in indigenous communities and the development of Fourth World theory, beginning in the mid 1970s. See Linda Tuhiwai Smith's important book *Decolonising Methodologies: Research and Indigenous Peoples* (London: Zed Books, 1999).
7. Larry Gross, John Katz, and Jay Ruby (eds.), *Image Ethics in the Digital Age* (Minneapolis: University of Minnesota Press, 2003); Steven Leuthold, *Indigenous Aesthetics* (Seattle: University of Washington Press, 1998).

8. Sol Worth, John Adair, and Richard Chalfen, *Through Navajo Eyes* (1972; Albuquerque: University of New Mexico Press, 1997).
9. Some anthropologists have expressed alarm at these developments. See, for example, James Faris, "Anthropological Transparency, Film, Representation and Politics," in Peter Ian Crawford and David Turton (eds.), *Film as Ethnography* (Manchester: University of Manchester Pres, 1992), pp. 171–82. They see indigenous media practices as destructive of cultural difference and the study of such work as "ersatz anthropology" (James Weiner, "Televisualist Anthropology: Representation, Aesthetics, Politics," *Current Anthropology* 38.2 [Spring 1997], pp. 197–236), echoing the concerns over the destructive effects of mass culture first articulated by intellectuals of the Frankfurt School. However, absolutely no evidence to support this position has ever been put forward. For this debate in the context of indigenous media, see the Spring 1997 issue of *Current Anthropology* and John Palatella, "Pictures of Us," *Lingua Franca* 8.5 (Spring 1998), pp. 50–57.
10. Faye Ginsburg, "The Parallax Effect: The Impact of Indigenous Media on Ethnographic Film," in Jane M. Gaines and Michael Renov (eds.), *Collecting Visible Evidence* (Minneapolis: University of Minnesota Press), p. 158.
11. The broader question this raised has haunted much of the research and debate on the topic of the cross-cultural spread of media: what I called in 1991 the "Faustian contract," whether indigenous people (or indeed minority or dominated subjects anywhere) can assimilate dominant media to their own cultural and political concerns or are inevitably compromised by its presence. See Faye Ginsberg, "Indigenous Media: Faustian Contract or Global Village?" *Cultural Anthropology* 6.1 (1991), pp, 92–112.
12. See the Central Australian Aboriginal Media Association, http://caama.com.au; the Inuit Broadcasting Corporation, http://www.inuitbroadcasting.ca/index.php; and Isuma TV, http://www.isuma.tv.
13. For a discussion of this project, see my "Beyond Broadcast: Launching NITV on Isuma TV," May 4, 2009, and commentary on it as part of a media commons discussion on indigenous media for the web-based In Media Res, http://mediacommons.futureofthebook.org/imr/2009/05/01/beyond-broadcast-launching-nitv-and-isuma-tv.
14. As their website explains, "Ara Irititja" means "'stories from a long time ago" in the language of Anangu (Pitjantjatjara and Yankunytjatjara people) of Central Australia. The aim of Ara Irititja is to bring back home materials of cultural and historical significance to Anangu. These include photographs, films, sound recordings, and documents. Ara Irititja has designed a purpose-built computer archive that digitally stores repatriated materials and other contemporary items. Anangu are passionate about protecting their archival past, accessing it today, and securing. See the Ara Irititja Project, http://www.irititja.com.
15. For other important work in this area, see Jane Anderson, *Knowledge, Culture: The Production of Indigenous Knowledge in Intellectual Property Law* (London: Edward Elgar Press, 2009); Ian Bryson, *Bringing to Light: A History of Ethnographic Filmmaking at the Australian Institute of Aboriginal and Torres Strait Islander Studies* (Canberra: Aboriginal Studies Press, 2002); Kim Christen, "Gone Digital: Aboriginal Remix in the Cultural Commons," *International Journal of Cultural Property* 12.3 (2005), pp. 315–44; Michael Christie, "Words, Ontologies and Aboriginal Databases," *Digital Anthropology* 116 (August 2005), pp. 52–63; Faye Ginsburg, "Rethinking the Digital Age," in Pamela Wilson and Michelle Stewart (eds.), *Global Indigenous Media: Cultures, Poetics, and Politics* (Durham: Duke University Press, 2008), pp. 287–306; Janet Lydon, *Eye Contact: Photographing Indigenous Australians* (Durham: Duke University Press, 2005);

Juan Fancisco Salazar, "Imperfect Media: The Poetics of Indigenous Media in Chile," Ph.D. dissertation, University of Western Sydney, 2004; Juan Francisco Salazar, "Indigenous Peoples and the Cultural Construction of Information and Communication Technology (ICT) in Latin America," in Laurel Dyson, Max Hendricks, and Stephen Grant (eds.), *Information Technology and Indigenous People* (London: Information Science Publishing, 2007), pp. 14–26; and Ramesh Srinivasan, Jim Enote, Katherine M. Becvar, and Robin Boast, "Critical and Reflective Uses of New Media Technologies in Tribal Museums," *Museum Management and Curatorship* 24.2 (2009), pp. 169–89.

16. See, for example, Timothy Asch, "The Story We Now Want to Hear Is Not Ours to Tell—Relinquishing Control Over Representation: Toward Sharing Visual Communication Skills with the Yanomamo," *Visual Anthropology Review* 7.2 (1991), pp. 102–106; Patricia Aufderheide, "The Video in the Villages Project: Videomaking with and by Brazilian Indians," *Visual Anthropology Review* 11.2 (1995), pp. 83–93; Vincent Carelli, "Video in the Villages," *Commission on Visual Anthropology Bulletin*, May 1988, pp 10–15; Kristin Dowell, "Honoring Stories: Aboriginal Media, Art, and Activism in Vancouver," Ph.D. dissertation, New York University, 2006; Kathleen Fleming, "Zacharias Kunuk: Videomaker and Inuit Historian," *Inuit Art Quarterly* (Summer 1991), 24–28; Ginsburg, "Indigenous Media: Faustian Contract or Global Village?"; Leuthold, *Indigenous Aesthetics*; Michael Meadows and Helen Molnar, *Songlines to Satellites: Indigenous Communications in Australia, the South Pacific, and Canada* (Annandale, New South Wales: Pluto Press, 2001); Hans Henrik Philipsen and Birgitte Markussen (eds.), *Advocacy and Indigenous Film-Making* (Højbjerg, Denmark: Intervention Press, 1995); Harold Prins, "American Indians and the Ethnocinematic Complex: From Native Participation to Production Control," in R. Boonzajer Flaes (ed.), *Eyes across the Water: The Amsterdam Conference on Visual Anthropology and Sociology, 1989* (Amsterdam: Het Spinhuis, Oudezids Achterburgwal, 1989), pp. 80–90; Lorna Roth, *Something New in the Air: Indigenous Television in Canada*. (Montreal: McGill Queens University Press, 2005); Salazar, "Imperfect Media"; Terence Turner, "The Social Dynamics of Video Media in an Indigenous Society: The Cultural Meaning and the Personal Politics of Video-Making in Kayapo Communities," *Visual Anthropology Review* 7.2 (1991), pp. 68–76; Terence Turner, "Representing, Resisting, Rethinking: Historical Transformations of Kayapo Culture and Anthropological Consciousness," in George W. Stocking (ed.), *Colonial Situations: Essays on the Contextualization of Ethnographic Knowledge* (Madison: University of Wisconsin Press, 1991), pp. 285–313; Terence Turner, "Defiant Images: The Kayapo Appropriation of Video," *Anthropology Today* 8.6 (1992), pp. 5–16; Terence Turner, "Representation, Collaboration, and Mediation in Contemporary Ethnographic and Indigenous Media," *Visual Anthropology Review* 11.2 (1995), pp. 102–106; Pegi Vail, "Producing America: The Native American Producer's Alliance," master's thesis, New York University, 1997; Elizabeth Weatherford, "Native Visions: The Growth of Indigenous Media," *Aperture* 119 (Summer 1990), pp. 58–61; Erica Cusi Wortham, "Narratives of Location: Televisual Media and the Production of Indigenous Identities in Mexico," Ph.D. dissertation, New York University, 2000.

17. Faye Ginsburg, "Aboriginal Media and the Australian Imaginary," *Public Culture* 5.2 (1993), pp. 557–78; Faye Ginsburg, "From Little Things, Big Things Grow": Indigenous Media and Cultural Activism, in Richard G. Fox and Orin Starn (eds.), *Between Resistance and Revolution: Cultural Politics and Social Protest* (New Brunswick: Rutgers University Press, 1997), pp. 118–44; Maureen Mahon, "The Visible Evidence of Cultural Producers," *Annual Review of Anthropology* 29 (2000), pp. 467–92.

18. George Marcus, "Introduction," in George Marcus (ed.), *Connected: Engagements with Media* (Chicago: University of Chicago Press, 1996), pp. 1–18.
19. Roth, *Something New in the Air*.
20. Eric Michaels, *The Aboriginal Invention of Relevision in Central Australia, 1982–1986: Report of the Fellowship to Assess the Impact of Television in Remote Aboriginal Communities* (Canberra: Australian Institute of Aboriginal Studies, 1986).
21. Eric Michaels, with Frances Jupurrurla Kelly, "The Social Organization of an Aboriginal Video Workplace," *Australian Aboriginal Studies* 1 (1984), p. 34.
22. Faye Ginsburg, "Embedded Aesthetics: Creating a Discursive Space for Indigenous Media," *Cultural Anthropology* 9.3 (1994), p. 368.
23. Jennifer Deger, *Shimmering Screens: Making Media in an Aboriginal Community* (Minneapolis: University of Minnesota Press, 2006).
24. Jeff Himpele, *Circuits of Culture: Media, Politics, and Indigenous Identity in the Andes* (Minneapolis: University of Minnesota Press, 2008).
25. Barry Barclay, *Our Own Image* (Auckland: Longman Paul, 1990); Marcia Langton, *Well, I Heard It on the Radio and I Saw It on the Television: An Essay for the Australian Film Commission on the Politics and Aesthetics of Filmmaking by and about Aboriginal People and Things* (Sydney: Australian Film Commission, 1993); Victor Masayesva, Jr., "The Emerging Native American Aesthetics in Film and Video, *Felix: A Journal of Arts and Media* 2.1 (1995), pp. 156–61; Merata Mita, "Opening Comments," *Felix: A Journal of Arts and Media* 2.1 (1995), pp. 152–53; Albert Muenala, "Cinema as an Instrument for Indigenous People's Identity," *Felix: A Journal of Arts and Media* 2.1 (1995), pp. 154–56; Michelle Raheja, *Reservation Reelism: Redfacing, Visual Sovereignty, and Representations of Native Americans in Film* (Lincoln: University of Nebraska Press, 2010); Beverly Singer, *Wiping the Warpaint off the Lens: Native American Film and Video* (Minneapolis: University of Minnesota Press, 2001); Smith, *Decolonising Methodologies*.
26. Terrence Turner, "Anthropology and Multiculturalism: What is Anthropology That Multiculturalists Should Be Mindful of It?" *Cultural Anthropology* 8.4 (1993), pp. 411–29.
27. Harald Prins, "Visual Media and the Primitivist Perplex: Colonial Fantasies, Indigenous Imagination, and Advocacy in North America," in Faye D. Ginsburg, Lila Abu-Lughod, and Brian Larkin (eds.), *Media Worlds: Anthropology on New Terrain* (Berkeley: University of California Press, 2002), pp. 58–74.
28. Ginsburg, "Indigenous Media," and Ginsburg, Abu-Lughod, Brian Larkin (eds.), *Media Worlds*.
29. Terrence Turner, "Representation, Politics, and Cultural Imagination in Indigenous Video: General Points and Kayapo Examples, in Ginsburg, Abu-Lughod, Brian Larkin (eds.), *Media Worlds*, pp. 75–89; Carelli, "Video in the Villages"; Aufderheide, "The Video in the Villages Project."
30. See Pam Wilson and Michelle Stewart (eds.), *Global Indigenous Media: Cultures, Practices, and Politics* (Durham: Duke University Press, 2008).
31. Prins, "Visual Media and the Primitivist Perplex."
32. Manuel Castells, *The Rise of the Network Society* (London: Blackwell, 1996).
33. Stuart Murray, *Images of Dignity: Barry Barclay and Fourth Cinema* (Wellington: Huia Publishers, 2008), p. 69.
34. Meadows and Molnar, *Songlines to Satellites*; Roth, *Something New in the Air*.
35. Lisa Parks and Shanti Kumar (eds.), *Planet TV: A Global Television Reader* (New York: New York University Press, 2002).

36. Henry Jenkins, *Convergence Culture: Where Old and New Media Collide* (New York: New York University Press, 2007).
37. Roth, *Something New in the Air*.
38. Meadows and Molnar, *Songlines to Satellites*.
39. Kathleen Buddle-Crowe, "From Birchbark Talk to Digital Dreamspeaking: A Partial History of Aboriginal Media Activism in Canada," Ph.D. dissertation, University of Ontario, 2001.
40. John Hartley and Alan McKee, *The Indigenous Public Sphere: The Reporting and Reception of Aboriginal Issues in the Australian Media* (Oxford: Oxford University Press, 2000).
41. Philip Batty, "Governing Cultural Difference: The Incorporation of the Aboriginal Subject into the Mechanisms of Government with Reference to the Development of Aboriginal Radio and Television in Central Australia," Ph.D. dissertation, University of South Australia, 2003.
42. Debbie Brisebois, "The Inuit Broadcasting Corporation," *Anthropologica* 25.1 (1983), pp. 107–15.
43. See Ginsburg, "Indigenous Media."
44. See Leuthold, *Indigenous Aesthetics*.
45. Erica Wortham, "Making Culture Visible: Indigenous Media in Mexico," Ph.D. dissertation, Department of Anthropology, New York University, 2002, p. 265.
46. Sigurjón Baldur Hafsteinsson, "Aboriginal Journalism Practices as Deep Democracy: APTN National News," in Sigurjón Baldur Hafsteinsson and Marian Bredin (eds.), *Indigenous Screen Cultures in Canada* (Winnipeg: University of Manitoba Press, 2010), pp. 63–58; Roth, *Something New in the Air*.
47. Faye Ginsburg and April Strickland, "The Latest in Reality TV?: MĐori Television Stakes a Claim on the World Stage," *Flow: A Critical Forum on Television & Media Culture* (July 22, 2005), http://flowtv.org/2005/07/maori-television-global-television-first-peoples-television.
48. Roth, *Something New in the Air*, p. 157.
49. Sacha Molitorisz, "The Story of Black Australia," *Age*, October 9, 2008, http://www.theage.com.au/articles/2008/10/08/1223145363254.html. The commentary on the series website, http://www.sbs.com.au/firstaustralians, was uniformly positive, with many people posting comments on how little they knew of Australia's black history.
50. Rachel Perkins and Marcia Langton, *First Australians: A Visual History* (Melbourne: Melbourne University Press, 2009).
51. For more information on this series, see http://www.pbs.org/wgbh/amex/weshallremain/the_films/index.
52. Quoted in Fay Ginsburg, "Beyond Broadcast: Launching NITV on Isuma TV," In Media Res, May 4, 2009, http://mediacommons.futureofthebook.org/imr/2009/05/01/beyond-broadcast-launching-nitv-and-isuma-tv.
53. Merata Mita, quoted in Kristin Dowell, "Indigenous Media Gone Global: Strengthening Indigenous Identity On- and Offscreen at the First Nations\First Features Film Showcase," *American Anthropologist* 108.2 (2006), p. 377.
54. Stephanie Bunbury, "Australian Love Story Wins Cannes Prize," *Age*, May 25, 2009, http://www.theage.com.au/news/entertainment/film/2009/05/25/1243103459083.html.
55. Jeff Himpele, "Film Distribution as Media: Mapping Difference in the Bolivian Cinemascape," *Visual Anthropology Review* 12.1 (2006), pp. 47–66.
56. Kyra Landzelius, (ed.), *Native on the Net: Indigenous and Diasporic Peoples in the Digital Age* (London: Routledge, 2006), p. 1.
57. In addition to sources cited in note 17 above, see Alopi S. Latukefu, "Remote Indigenous

Communities in Australia: Questions of Access, Information, and Self-Determination," in Landzelius (ed.), *Going Native on the Net*, pp. 1–42; and Jolene Rickard, "First Nation Territory in Cyber Space Declared: No Treaties Needed," CyberPowWow: An Aboriginally Determined Territory in Cyberspace, http://www.cyberpowwow.net/nation2nation/jolenework.html.

58. Harald Prins, "Digital Revolution: Indigenous Peoples in Cyberia," in William A. Haviland (ed.), *Cultural Anthropology*, 10th.ed. (Fort Worth: Harcourt College Publishers, 2001), pp. 306–308.

59. Norman Cohn, "Hi-Speed Internet in Low-Speed Communities," comment, May 13, 2009, on Faye Ginsburg, "Beyond Broadcast: Launching NITV on Isuma TV," In Media Res: A Media Commons Project, http://mediacommons.futureofthebook.org/imr/2009/05/01/beyond-broadcast-launching-nitv-and-isuma-tv.

White Band Day, July 2, 2005. White bands are collected and draped on a large sign reading Make Poverty History (photo: courtesy Make Poverty History).

The White Band's Burden: Humanitarian Synergy and the Make Poverty History Campaign

Leshu Torchin

In 2005, Bob Geldof announced Live 8, a set of concerts to take place worldwide on Saturday, July 2, in anticipation of the upcoming G8 Summit in Gleneagles, Scotland. Unlike Live 8's predecessor, Live Aid, two concerts that took place in the United States and the United Kingdom two decades prior, the Live 8 concerts were not benefit performances. In Geldof's words, the concerts "were not fundraisers but rallying points for the largest political constituency ever mobilised to call for justice for Africa and the world's poor."[1] The word choices—"rallying," "constituencies," and "justice"—introduced poverty as an object of politics and political action. The refrain of the campaign, "Justice, not charity" crystallized this viewpoint, moving global poverty into the field of economic rights. The Live 8 concerts sought to construct Habermasian publics—groups formed around the issue of economic justice—out of audiences, thereby providing a nearly literal theatre for the exchange of ideas and the formation of political actors. Meanwhile, the global broadcast of these concerts was intended to amplify both their discursive and their gathering power. The concerts aired on 140 television channels worldwide with the aid of live feeds from the BBC and MTV; they were also available on 400 radio stations and through the Internet—AOL provided free video streams, even to nonsubscribers. By increasing the audience, the broadcasts could increase the size of Geldof's desired political constituency.

The Live 8 concerts were only one component of a highly visible campaign designed to produce such constituencies, to draw public attention to the upcoming G8 Summit, and to apply pressure to decision makers—the convening world leaders. Live 8 and Bob Geldof advocated for the recommendations of the Commission for Africa, an organization set up by then Prime Minister Tony Blair in 2004.[2] And the campaign's messaging and branding were integrated with those of Make Poverty History in the UK and the ONE campaign against African poverty and disease in the United States, both of which endorsed the implementation of the United Nations Millennium Development Goals. The Millennium Development Goals, much like the Commission for Africa report, recommended such plans as debt relief, increased aid—particularly for African nations—and the establishment of international fair trade policies.[3] These coalitions of advocacy organizations that came together under The Global Call to Action against Poverty, which sought to alleviate global poverty. Although essentially separate organizations, sometimes with separate or distinct goals, the integrated branding and messaging of the campaign aided in publicizing the (occasionally) shared goals.[4] And it is the combination of advocacy and publicity that is the subject of this essay.

While the coalition provided numbers and strength for the campaign, its visibility was enhanced through a wider network of media platforms. People seeking concert tickets and concert information were directed to a website with further information on Live 8—The Long Walk to Justice and the Make Poverty History campaign (see fig. 1). Here, the visitor found multiple videos varying in length from the traditional thirty-sixty-ninety-second length of an advertisement or public-service announcement (PSA); these videos promoted this project as well as others dealing with crises of economic human rights.[5] The sites also informed visitors of a rally in Edinburgh, also taking place on July 2, 2005. Other media platforms calling attention to the Millennium Development Goals included the New Year's special of the BBC sitcom *The Vicar of Dibley*; the romantic comedy *The Girl in the Café*, an HBO-BBC coproduction set in a fictional G8 Summit; and a CNN-TV special hosted by Christiane Amanpour called *Can We Save Them?* Each media event bolstered the existence of the other. For instance, *Can We Save Them?* used clips from *The Girl in the Café* to illustrate the aims of the Make Poverty History campaign and to promote the upcoming airing. The multimedia performances enabled mutual benefits or synergies. CNN-TV, a sister company of HBO, could promote the film and the ideas. Indeed, these networked platforms produced shared visual strategies and crystallized talking points to solidify the message.

What follows maps out this campaign, in which multimedia performance and networking became a key mode of directing and sustaining attention to the program's goals. The multiple performances reframed poverty as a political concern by deploying discourses associated with human rights. In this way, they suggested poverty is a symptom of violation and subject to political and legal jurisdiction. Meanwhile, the deployment of celebrity amplified the publicity function: the celebrities became a fulcrum for campaign attention as they advanced popular personae beneficial for their careers. By working across media, the campaign built a focused message useful for conveying its talking points and aims. This study of the campaign combines analyses of campaign events and processes in order to flesh out the equation of exposure

Birhan Woldu and Bob Geldof on stage at Live 8 in Hyde Park, London, England (photo: courtesy Live 8).

to justice that underpins many approaches to politics and visual media—one characterized in B.V.A. Roling's statement "If mass violations become known, the world reacts."[6] Although contemporary visual-culture scholarship compels our recognition that media are not transparent delivery systems of information, the faith in exposure remains seductive.[7] However, through the reading of texts and practices, framing discourses and associated activities, one can identify and examine the hailing mechanisms that called upon the audiences to become publics.

ENTERTAINING ADVOCACY: NOTES ON THEORY AND METHOD

The intersection of entertainment media and politics is a longstanding phenomenon. From early on, media and performance have been deployed as a means of engaging audiences in the service of a humanitarian program. Slave testimony, both performed and published, was a common practice in the British and American abolitionist movements. And as soon as film came into being, relief organizations used the new medium, as well as its celebrities, to promote their goals.[8] Nevertheless, entertainment politics have increased dramatically in recent years. The development of global media circuitry has intensified the reliance of this combination in order to extend the reach of campaigns and to capitalize on the immediacy of time and space.

Through the ability to broadcast beyond state borders, media and media actors can hail transnational citizens or a cosmopolitan public subject to international human rights law, NGOs, or supranational organizations. Just as media once cultivated the imagined community of nations, they can now foster an imagined global citizenry. And indeed, the fostering of this new imaginary seems predicated on popular media. Celebrity diplomacy, with figures such as Bono, Angelina Jolie, Bill Gates, and George Soros, continues to blur the presumed boundaries between celebrity, entertainment, and politics.[9] Partnerships between NGOs, supranational organizations such as the UN, and popular film have become prevalent. NGOs and activists have taken up film, both popular features and documentaries, as a tool for advocacy.

Similar operations not only provided Make Poverty History with an institutional constituency and framework for mounting a campaign, they also supplied a discursive strategy of economic rights—one that was launched in global justice movements such as Jubilee 2000 and the World Trade Organization protests, and in film, as well. For instance, *Life and Debt* (Stephanie Black, 2001), explores the enforced poverty caused by both ongoing debt to the World Bank and International Monetary Fund (IMF) and the installation of free trade zones, which fail to pay workers a living wage. Indeed, the films and videos from this campaign are part of an overall rise in the development of an economic rights consciousness and cycle of filmmaking. Films have been used to call attention to the violation of political and civil rights such as genocide and torture, abuses that both inhabit the popular imagination and are readily visible as inscribed on the body. However, in more recent years, many films have cultivated an economic rights imaginary: they visualize the unseen systems of global capitalism and place poverty in the realm of politics and jurisprudence. These include such films as *Black Gold* (Mark and Nick Francis, 2006), about the international coffee business and the need for fair trade practices; *Darwin's Nightmare* (Hubert Sauper, 2004), which examines the effects of the Lake Victoria fishing industry on a local community; and Abderrahmane Sissako's *Bamako* (2006) which reenacts the proceedings of African civil society against the World Bank and IMF. Given the accelerating intersection of popular media and politics, on screen and off, it is more pressing than ever to examine how these forms of entertainment and visual culture are deployed within political campaigns.

Such an examination is additionally important in the face of heightened criticism, ready to find the intersection of politics and entertainment to be specious, given the latter's association with mass culture and the media consumer, and to dismiss such work altogether. Looking back to Theodor W. Adorno and at the work of critics as diverse as Jürgen Habermas, Daniel Boorstin, and Neil Postman, one sees a suspicion that popular or mass culture destroys high culture, critical thinking, and the political potential of the public sphere.[10] And in 2005, Clifford Bob suggested that promotional tactics and market-based approaches to transnational advocacy impede the moral agency of NGOs. Dismissive skepticism lingers in hybrid terms such as "charitainment," which James Poniewozik coined in response to celebrity activism and Live 8.[11]

The growing commercialization of the public sphere is a legitimate concern, to be sure. Corporate ownership poses a threat to democracy by regulating permissible discourse and minimizing participatory culture.[12] And, as Alison Brysk notes, globalization may well smuggle in new possibilities for abuse at the same time that it promises mechanisms of liberation and furthers social-justice movements. Indeed, this irony emerges particularly strongly in the study of media campaigns dealing with poverty: the networks of global media are frequently tied to the same corporations and systems responsible for the inequality. These critiques center on the continued imbalance of power relations, often viewing rights discourses as a new imperialism, a universal concept of humanity that disregards the diversity of local practices. They aver that the marketing of politics invariably transforms the citizen into a consumer or that by drawing on propaganda tactics, these media encourage false consciousness and erode agency.

The risks accumulate in high-profile mainstream media campaigns such as Live 8 and Make Poverty History. In a popular campaign that relies on systems of celebrity and publicity, the systems themselves can become the stars of the show. A campaign that effectively navigates media noise and produces a loud and sustained message can also drown out minor voices and smaller efforts. By promoting its own capacity to create change and mobilize action, a campaign can effect an almost recursive publicity: the campaign exists to promote itself. It can also fail to engage solidarity outside the comfort zone of mainstream or First World arenas. Meanwhile, the celebrity can act as a lightning rod attracting otherwise diffuse attention, effectively publicizing a campaign's mission, but conversely, the campaign becomes a vehicle to promote a celebrity persona. While this arrangement can provide mutual benefits, the heightened investment in the campaign can also lead to unfortunate competition in the activist domain: other solidarity movements are eclipsed, or even silenced in the process.[13]

All these risks must temper the analysis of a campaign, but they should not obviate the explorations of how popular-media channels—as opposed to alternative media—can produce what Meg McLagan has termed "witnessing publics," recipients of testimony who become poised to act.[14] Indeed, human rights activists, reliant on the notion of the exposure and making public of abuses, may benefit from lessons of publicity and marketing. As Patricia Aufderheide has observed, publicity and promotion are increasingly important for social documentarians.[15] Meanwhile, Liesbet Van Zoonen, Joke Hermes, and John Corner ask how popular culture encourages ideas of citizenship,[16] a membership in and obligation to a larger community no longer coterminous with the nation. And in her study of Make Poverty History, Kate Nash suggests that this campaign conducted both in and through the media "has much to teach us about the practical possibilities for a more cosmopolitan orientation to citizenship within and beyond national borders."[17] What follows builds on this work, exploring how the Live 8 concerts and the wider context of performance help the audience to entertain the political impulse in relation to poverty, as well as to publicize the aims of the campaign.

To answer, one looks not only at the events and the aesthetic strategies of cultivating emotional and political concern, but also at the channels of distribution and exhibition that work together to produce the coherent narrative that engages the citizen. Henry Jenkins's concept of transmedia storytelling provides the model for such exploration. "Transmedia storytelling," he writes, "represents a process where integral elements of a fiction get dispersed systematically across multiple delivery channels for the purpose of creating a unified and coordinated entertainment experience."[18] In the case of the Live 8 Concerts and the Make Poverty History campaign, one finds key concepts of the campaign and the Millennium Development Goals transmitted across an array of interlocking media platforms, although, as opposed to the immense complexity of the entertainment worlds, the goal here was to make the vast and often complicated political world comprehensible and open to participation. This process relies upon relationships cultivated through partnerships and synergies between grassroots organizations and media channels, which engage in processes of mutually beneficial promotion. The activities developed around Live 8 provide an excellent opportunity to examine how formal strategies travel across or work in tandem with other performance platforms (live performance, the Internet, television), in order to produce political claims, hail publics, and negotiate the often overwhelming media and political ecosystems. Such practices are not contrary to the activist impulse, which need not be limited to the more seemingly sober domains of the documentary, alternative media, or revolutionary art.

THE CONCERTS

In the earliest days, Live 8 concerts were planned for Philadelphia, London, Paris, Berlin, and Rome, locations firmly rooted in G8 nations. This was a reasonable decision, given both logistical concerns (the concerts were announced little over a month in advance of the concerts) and the goal: to mobilize political constituencies around the G8 summit and to apply pressure to G8 leaders. At the same time, this decision upheld Europe, America, and the G8 as the primary agents of change. Within days, additional venues in Barrie, Canada, Tokyo, Johannesburg, and Moscow were announced—decisions that expanded the global terrain, but ultimately maintained the global distribution of power (still in G8 nations) and absented Third World publics from the participatory dimensions of the campaign.

The original concert lineups reflected this dynamic. "Hideously white" is what London-based Black Information Ink called it, as First World artists mobilized on behalf of the third world. This shifted somewhat with the intervention of Peter Gabriel and WOMAD (World of Music Arts and Dance, an organization that Gabriel helped found in 1980) and the introduction of an additional concert: Africa Calling—Live 8 at The Eden Project in Cornwall. Although concert lineups in London and Paris, as well as Eden, featured noted Senegalese artist Youssou N'Dour, this overwork of his body—physical and signifying—might have conjured up the problematic economies that the concerts sought to redress.

Media circuitry played a key role in expanding the potential audience/constituency. In addition to the free video streams of the concerts that AOL provided to all Internet users, including nonsubscribers, XM Satellite Radio broadcast the concerts on an array of channels. Meanwhile, MTV Networks opened up their channels worldwide to broadcast the concerts and attendant commentary, providing an "unprecedented global platform."[19] No doubt this volunteerism provided the networks with excellent publicity. Reports marveled at the MTV network's global broadcast and willingness to provide live coverage of a televised event for eight hours. At the same time, critics questioned the impulse, wondering if the events functioned predominantly as PR for G8 leaders and corporate sponsors, rather than for the issues themselves.[20] According to Live 8 spokespeople, 85 percent of the world's population had access to these presentations, suggesting the capacity of audiovisual media technologies to heighten the visibility of the campaign. However, the subvention of global corporate structures tempers a sanguine outlook. This transnational corporatization may implicitly produce conditions of poverty and contribute to the limitation of access. Not all nations are wired, and not all people have access to these technologies, a fact that erased the extremely poor and various Third World publics from audiences, even as these publics haunted the stage as an "issue" or as photographs of starving, big-eyed children.

Onstage, Third World victims shared time with the political agents of the First World, in image, but also in person. At the Hyde Park performance, Bob Geldolf introduced Birhan Woldu, the Ethiopian girl of the CBC news report that had allegedly inspired Geldof to organize Live Aid. Before she took the stage, he spoke to the audience of the concerts twenty years earlier and the images that inspired their creation. He gestured to a large television screen—one that took up the stage area and whose images were also broadcast to screens positioned throughout the audience area. A montage of famine photographs and videos, made iconic by their

1980s coverage, took the screen, accompanied by the song "Drive" by the Cars, a soundtrack occasionally punctured by screams, wails, and coughs of the children depicted. The lyrics expressed the refusal to accept such poverty ("Can't go on") and asked after care ("who's going to drive you home?"). This performative sequence continued with Geldof's expression of dismay: poverty persists, with most of its victims being children. So why are they there, he asked. To answer, he gestured to a photograph of a little girl and explained that this girl once had ten minutes to live, but because there were concerts in the UK and the United States, she is still here. Don't let them tell us it doesn't work, he insisted, and with that, he introduced Woldu. She spoke to the audience, thanking Live Aid on behalf of Africa. She asked that everyone support Live 8.[21]

The combination of video and physical performance functioned not only as a reminder of African poverty, but also as a performance of the efficacy of the display. Her initial image had prompted Geldof to action; Live Aid had allowed her to live long enough to stand onstage with Madonna, who sang "Like a Prayer," the song choice itself a return to the religious sentiments that coded the coverage of the Ethiopian famine.[22] Such concerts work, both she and her presence asserted, refuting the criticisms of the 1980s humanitarian drive, often seen to have prolonged the conditions of the famine and the suffering attached. This concert, like the last one, could also produce beneficial change. She testified—not simply to poverty, but also to the potency of the performance.

A reminder of the concert's and the audience's roles in political mobilization graced the stage beyond these occasional performances. During the concerts, the various screens broadcast a list of names. These were signatories of the Live 8 List, a petition calling for the world leaders convening at the summit to provide 100 percent debt relief and increased aid to Africa. The Live 8 website provided visitors with the opportunity to sign. Audiences at the concerts could see their names, had they remembered to sign when visiting the site for tickets or information. Meanwhile, audiences at home could add their names as they watched the concerts, with new media supplying a participatory outlet for those not physically present. These names and the act of signing served to perform the political aims of the concerts, as well as to feed the romance of individual participation in political action. As display, they worked as both reminder and instruction: the audiences were part of a political constituency.

THE INTERNET

The Internet was central to the production and maintenance of a wider transnational constituency. The Live 8 website served as a portal to information and to the action that would be performed on stage or realized in the audience. While AOL provided streaming video of the live events, visitors to the Live 8—Long Walk to Justice / Make Poverty History site before and after the concerts were presented with textual and audiovisual information regarding the aims of the campaign and avenues of participation. The website was not only a source of tickets, but a place for people to sign petitions and to learn more about developing their own related events and activities that would continue the publicity work for the campaign.

Streaming video—offered for either broadband or dial-up connections—provided powerful means of inviting audiences into an affective community while providing information to aid in political responses. The launch offered Bob Geldolf's video press release announcing the concerts and their aims and introducing "Justice, not charity" as the campaign's refrain. Nelson Mandela's video partnered Make Poverty History and its aims with the past memory of antiapartheid movements, further focusing a political lens through which to view poverty. In the video, Mandela speaks directly to the camera while older footage of crowds shouting "Amandla!"—the rallying cry of the African National Congress—appears in the background. "Sometimes it falls upon a generation to be great," he explains to the viewer. "Poverty is a prison," he states, recalling his own political imprisonment and the revolutionary aspects of change. He tells the audience how poverty is man made and can be overcome by human action, each claim furthering the reframing of poverty as a political issue. This is no longer the domain of charity alone. Poverty is not simply an issue of natural conditions, as the droughts associated with past famines have often suggested. The human action required is clarified in his next statements: The G8 leaders have promised to focus on poverty, and there are clear steps to be taken: trade justice, debt relief, and increased aid. In other words, he advocates the implementation of the Millennium Development Goals as he promises this audience that they, too, can be part of something great, something historical, and something that will change the world. Such claims contributed to an emotional response different from pity or charity. They stressed the empowerment of the audience with the "denunciation of systemic injustice for which the appropriate emotion is indignation and the desire to bring about change."[23]

THE CLICK

On the broadcast, Bono, a key figure in Live Aid and Band Aid and a celebrity whose political activity almost ensures legitimacy, aids in the creation of an affective and political community. "You can relax, I'm not asking for your money," he begins, reminding the viewer of the new, political direction of the event. He wishes he had never seen the news report that prompted his political turn—a false wish that functions to remind us of how a display can mobilize sentiment and action. As Geldof did, he comforts the viewers, letting them know that what has happened to date has been helpful, thereby guarding against a compassion fatigue that might impede commitment. However, he tells us, poverty continues, because things widely available to the First World are not available in Africa, leading to death from the simplest of causes. This means that someone dies every three seconds, he explains, and to animate this loss, he clicks his fingers. With a beat, a pause, and a click, he begins a chant "Someone's mother; someone's daughter; another one." And like Mandela, he points out that world leaders are about to meet to discuss debt relief, increased aid, and trade justice. He, too, engages viewers in thinking about their historical agency and identity as a potentially great generation. "What will we be remembered for?"

Bono's speech, and most specifically, the gesture of the click, appeared across platforms, becoming a mantra for the campaign. The video ad "Click" (one public-service announcement of many to come) featured a montage of various celebrities (Brad Pitt, George Clooney, Colin Firth, Emma Thompson, Jamie Foxx), with each shot lasting three seconds, each incorporating a click of the fingers. Liam Neeson's voiceover explains: "A child dies, completely unnecessarily, as the result of extreme poverty, every three seconds. There we go. That's another one. Somebody's daughter. Somebody's son. All these deaths are avoidable." Performers at the concerts also followed this script. In addition to leading the Philadelphia audience in a sing-along to the theme song for *The Fresh Prince of Bel Air*, Will Smith led the audience in a collective clicking of fingers, helping to transform the abstract concept of distant poverty into (an admittedly limp) visceral experience. The collective action engaged a socially networked sensation while building brand recognition. The clicks would become a means of remembering the advocacy goals and the mission they all now shared.[24] This click, as I discuss later, was also deployed in the film *The Girl in the Café*.

VIDEOS

Videos presented the campaign's concerns with images of Africa. Toddlers animate "extreme poverty in action" with depictions of street children throughout the continent. Orphans of Nkandla offer clips from the documentary of the same name, directed by Brian Woods, which aired on both HBO and BBC4. The film depicts the impact of AIDS/HIV on three families in Zululand. However, it was *Drop the Debt*, directed by the late Anthony Minghella, that provided a departure from the standard images of Africa in crisis while still hewing to and promoting the principles of the campaign. This short subject takes place in an unidentified African village where people work hard to make a living. A song entitled "Hole in the Bucket" (credited to the Jubilee Debt Campaign) accompanies the efforts of a multigenerational family finding all manner of ways to earn money. The song begins "My family borrowed money from someone we never met. And every day we save up the little bits that we get." The lyrics continue, stating the wish "to live a simple life," but that "something's gone wrong." The film articulates the institutional inequality and injustice of the system by showing that the money borrowed (the money that has created the debt) was borrowed to rectify the damage done by colonialism and corporate globalization. At the end of the film, the family goes through a doorway into London, where they attempt to give back a few pounds to a family. "This is the money that we owe you," they explain.

In a matter of three minutes, the short depicts the demand for debt repayment as unjust and utterly shameful. The debt was incurred due to Western involvement and now seems to be a way of maintaining the same systems of colonial domination. Africans here are not simple victims, but active participants in their own development. However, with every moment spent working on this debt, how are they to develop their own countries? In visualizing this gross inequity—a family works all day and all night to bring a few pounds to one family across the world—Minghella forces us to question the concept of value at both an economic and a moral level: Can we live without these few pounds? The video animates the human face of these poverty issues without invoking the old and worn-out images of crisis.

THE WHITE BAND

Activities for applying pressure to decision makers went beyond the concerts themselves. In addition to the rally in Edinburgh on July 2 and a march scheduled for four days later, there were activities designed around "the white band," a concept that also provides this essay with its title. The white band was selected as the symbol of the global fight to end poverty and was deployed within the concerts and the rally. Participants at the rally were encouraged to wear white T-shirts so that the collective could form a human white band. Participants were also encouraged to wear white bands (fifty by seven centimeters—about twenty by three inches) that contained written messages to G8 Summit leaders and to hold special events in which friends, family, and their community came together to make these bands. "Invite the local media too," the website enjoined, suggesting that this performance of belonging could, in itself, become a media event and a means of publicizing the rally and the Millennium Development Goals.

There is something generative in approach. In this case, the rally, organized alongside the concerts for mutual publicity purposes, incorporates its own performative aspect—the human white band—to publicize its alliance with a political goal, and it offers ancillary pockets of activity to develop attention and build an activist base. It does not seem entirely outlandish to propose that this plan harnesses the participatory practices of the fan. These events are designed to invite publics into a broader structure of sympathy outside the event itself (the concert, the rally) that enforces its messages (implementation of the Millennium Development Goals).

The white band surfaced, stylistically speaking, in the "Click" PSA. The overall appearance is one of whiteness: each celebrity wears a white T-shirt; each shot is set against a white backdrop. The video is letterboxed, a gesture that seems puzzling, given the noncinematic exhibition setting. How could aspect ratio be an issue? The first impression is one of watching a GAP or CK One ad. However, the combination of the white T-Shirts, the white backdrop, and the aspect ratio conjures up a white band on screen. The celebrities may be selling their appeal to engage the alliance of the viewer, but they are inviting them into a partnership devoted to what is now a political cause.

COMPLEMENTARY TV PROGRAMS

Television joined the interconnected performance platforms that advocated the goals of the campaign through information, instruction, and affective engagement. Television screens populated the concert arenas. They stood in audience spaces to extend the reach of the live performance and onstage to facilitate dialogues between multiple spaces and multiple times—for instance, Bob Geldof's encounter with the images that prompted his action so many years ago.

However, television did not serve only as a channel for the concerts, but offered a platform for the promotion of the Make Poverty History campaign by means of TV shows that complemented the staging of the Live 8 concerts and their predecessor. A special New Year's Day episode of *The Vicar of Dibley* (BBC1) was written by Richard Curtis, cofounder of the campaign and Comic Relief, but better known for such films as *Four Weddings and a Funeral* and *Love, Actually*. The program served as a high-profile launch for the campaign, depicting the recognition by the lead character, Geraldine (Dawn French) of the twenty-year anniversary of Live Aid and her alarm at the present-day statistics around extreme poverty.

While Geraldine dons a white band at the end of the episode, a more direct promotion came in the form of a ninety-second campaign video that aired during this show's time slot.[25] An off-screen tie-in developed less than two weeks later, when, on January 13, 2005, six hundred women vicars wearing white bands convened in front of 10 Downing Street. There, a twelve-person delegation (including Richard Curtis, Dawn French, and ten clergy members) met with Prime Minister

Vicars' March—13th January 2005. Around 600 vicars from across the country join Dawn French to deliver a white band card at No 10 Downing Street where it is received by Tony Blair (photo: courtesy Make Poverty History).

Tony Blair (fig. 3) and "reiterated the challenges on debt, trade and aid laid down earlier... by the MPH campaign."[26]

Later that year, closer to the summit and the concerts, *The Girl in the Café* and *Can We Save Them?* would carry on the project of promoting the campaign and its related activities. Like the videos on the Make Poverty History website, they framed poverty as a political issue, equipped the viewer with talking points in favor of adopting the Millennium Development Goals, and encouraged participation by performing the efficacy of media advocacy and potential for change. These programs not only coordinated strategies, but they coordinated television channels, allowing networks to benefit in the project of joint endorsement.[27]

Written by Richard Curtis, *The Girl in the Café*, a television film and coproduction of HBO and the BBC aired on June 25, 2005, a week prior to the concerts. Dismissed by some as shameless propaganda, [28] the film demands attention for the storytelling modes deployed in its educational mission and for its place in an impressive network of media platforms serving to publicize the Make Poverty History campaign. The film tells the story of the relationship between Lawrence (Bill Nighy), a British civil servant who is an assistant to the chancellor of the exchequer, and Gina (Kelly McDonald), a young woman with no political affiliation and a clear stand-in for the audience, even those with no romantic designs on Nighy. Lawrence invites her to a fictional G8 summit in Reykjavik, where they engage in intimate discussions about the Millennium Development Goals. As their relationship develops, so, too, do Gina's political consciousness and advocacy tendencies. She interrupts parties and dinners with demands that the goals stay on the agenda and gives impassioned speeches as to why. Indeed, the genre, which may at first glance seem inappropriate to the subject, is entirely apt: there is transformation through human connection. Those who were once isolated—Lawrence is repeatedly cut off from others through framing and focus—come together, here with genuine affection and shared social commitment. They share conversations that facilitate this change. Much as in the romantic narrative, each encounter brings greater political fervor and possibility for commitment. Gina begins to read economic documents to pass the time. She gives an impassioned speech recalling the other paeans to love in Richard Curtis films. Gina was once apolitical, but becomes part of a greater cause on behalf of the world's poor. The film concludes with the British prime minister pledging his commitment to fair trade practices, debt relief, and aid in a grand speech (the DVD chapter title is "Most Magnificent Promises"), but without an explicit resolution to Lawrence and Gina's relationship. This, too, seems appropriate to both the genre and the mission: what happens at the meeting is a matter of securing pledges for future action. It remains to be seen whether this will play out in life.

The discussions of the Millennium Development Goals place extreme poverty in the arena of politics and human rights. Lawrence explains his role in the G8 Summit to Gina, receiving two loud instances of joking snores. Here, too, Gina functions as stand-in for the wider audience by treating economic politics as boring and divorced from her own sensibilities and worldview. However, Lawrence woos her into a political mind-set through the presentation of ideas in a clear and easy language. The Millennium Development Goals were part of a universal promise to halve extreme poverty by 2015. "This is poverty that kills," he explains. "We want to halve the number of children who die before they turn five; we want to halve the number of mothers who die in childbirth." These are, he tells her, "absolutely basic human rights." "We are fighting for something as big as the abolition of slavery," he states at another time, securing the link of "debt, trade, and aid" with a history of global activism for human rights and the necessity of political intervention. Lest this understanding be forgotten, the British prime minister reminds us in his "most magnificent promise," in which he avers, "We cannot allow this casual holocaust to take place on our watch for one more year." "'Holocaust" is a bold, yet effective word choice that reframes poverty as a question of rights or justice, not of charity. Poverty is a man-made problem with a solution located in human, political action.

Gina's developing political consciousness finds expression in the terminology and popular phrases of the Make Poverty History campaign. Lawrence explains, and she repeats later, that at the G8 Summit there were "eight men in one room who can change hundreds of millions of lives," an enforcement of political possibility (and reempowerment of the world's powerful) that appeared onstage at the concerts and in many of the Internet videos in the weeks prior. Her dinner party conversation echoes Bono's direct address, Bob Geldolf's rationale for the concerts, and other public-service announcements when she asks such questions as "Can it really be true that 800 million people are living on less than one dollar a day?" and "So lots more mothers die the day they give birth, lots more children die before they're five, lots and lots more die of diseases that are just a drop-by a-doctor for people like you and me?" By the end, her resolve fully formed, she gives a speech to the world leaders on behalf of the starving children. She demands the implementation of the Millennium Development Goals of trade justice, increased aid, and complete debt relief. "Eight men in one room could literally save hundreds of millions of lives," she states. And at the end of her speech, she draws upon a strategy to animate the loss. She clicks her fingers, pauses, and again, a click. "Every three seconds," she tells these world leaders, "someone succumbs to extreme poverty. There we go. . . . That was someone's daughter . . . someone's son." Even the film itself adopts the sonic aspect of the "Click" PSA when the credits run with a clicking noise punctuating the silence at three-second intervals. "You have the power to be great or to be ashamed," Gina says, offering the opportunity of the great generation found in Mandela's plea to world leaders while also deploying the human rights weapon of shame, a concept reliant on exposure, affect, morality, and public relations.

Gina serves multiple functions as audience stand-in. She provides a vector for the distillation of information and its dissemination, making the stakes of the G8 Summit comprehensible to viewers, and she serves as role model for a witness turned activist. Transformed through exposure to information, she evolves from unaware and jokingly bored—a constant trope and apparent anxiety for Curtis, who wrongly presumes the inherent dullness of politics—to aware and active. However, words are possibly not as effective as images, even in this promising story of development. At one point, Gina suggests that in order to make the reports "more real," official documents contain pictures of starving children drinking dirty water. Nevertheless, equipped with data, she develops and demonstrates the capacity to advocate—indeed, she can't shut up. She asks that the Millennium Development Goals not slip down the agenda. She reminds the leaders what is at stake. As the audience's surrogate, she reminds the audience of their role as citizens: to monitor their representatives at the conference, to apply pressure to the decision makers. When a leader explains to Gina, who requests the entire package of debt, aid, and trade, that it is his obligation to represent the interests of his country, she points out that the citizens may prefer saving the lives of children to their own interests. The claim echoes the *Drop the Debt* video, in which Britons are baffled and upset to receive the few pounds of debt repayment. In addition, she asserts the role of the citizen at the meeting: the G8 leaders are representatives, not autonomous agents acting on their own behalfs. Gina's absence at the point of the announcement indicates the power of the civilian to encourage change, even when not present. The pressure exists outside the meeting, where viewers, too, can now hope for implementation of the goals.

Promotional strategies further bolstered the aims of the TV film. Interviews with the stars, a typical component of publicity, yielded sound bites from the Make Poverty History campaign. "This film is an attempt to lobby the eight men who will sit in one room and could literally save hundreds of millions of lives," offered Bill Nighy in one such exchange.[29] Time Warner's ownership of HBO and CNN-TV allowed "corporate synergy" to facilitate "cross-platform marketing"[30] that mutually benefited corporate and campaign aims. HBO provided CNN-TV with twenty-five minutes from *The Girl in the Café* to be used in reportage and in the one-hour TV special on global poverty *Can We Save Them?*. Both channels benefited from the exchange. The television special incorporated a full ten-minute clip from the film, edited as a trailer or advertisement for the upcoming screening. And while HBO sought to "create a dialogue around the film,"[31] CNN found the film useful as a means to "make a complex issue comprehensible to the audience." The president of domestic operations explained that "we will be covering the summit and I'm not sure that many Americans know what it is, or care or understand why it matters. The movie is a phenomenal way of making the central issue of the G-8 summit accessible to Americans."[32] The simplification drew on the expressions cultivated by the public-service announcements of the campaign. Consumable details embedded in slogans echoed the Internet videos: people live on less than one dollar a day; a person dies every three seconds; eight men in one room, and so on.

As trailers go, this is a long one, running at ten minutes and practically functioning as substitute for the entire film outside the romantic comedy. The clip hits the talking points of the campaign for the viewer who might miss the full narrative experience. The viewer receives the consumable data of numbers, the framing of poverty as politics, and even the desired outcome: the British prime minister coming to the topic of the millennium development goals and refusing to endure any longer the casual holocaust of extreme poverty. The clip even manages to provide a narrative of Gina's development as an ideal viewer—an average person who can understand these goals and can pressure leaders into implementation of them.[33]

Politicized partners and audiences continued to proliferate. HBO found a sponsor in the Council on Foreign Relations, and the premiere screening of *The Girl in the Café* in Washington boasted both journalists and policy makers from Congress, the State Department, the International Monetary Fund, and the World Bank as its audience. Afterward, on June 22, 2005—three days prior to the television premiere—the Council on Foreign Relations hosted a talk about the film featuring Fareed Zakaria, editor of Newsweek International, moderated by Jeff Greenfield, senior analyst at CNN.[34]

SYNERGIES: MEDIA AND HUMANITARIAN POLITICS

In the Live 8 project and the Make Poverty History campaign, political actors thus also prove to be media consumers and part of the intended audience; at the same time, they serve a function within the production, promotion, and circulation of the information. On this field of political-cultural production, we find the synergies of an extraordinarily integrated cross-media marketing practice: CNN and the Council on Foreign Relations receive attention through the HBO film, and the discussion, in turn, promotes the film. At the same time, all these performances work together to create visibility for the G8 Summit, the Live 8 concerts, and the aims of the Make Poverty History campaign. This integrated transmedia display shapes popular knowledge about the Millennium Development Goals and possibly their urgency: these promises must not slip down the agenda; the world leaders must consider a joint package of debt, aid, and trade. What thus emerges with each closer look at the Live 8 campaign is a constellation of performance platforms that mutually support one another while bolstering the production and presentation of messages. The synergies draw together political, corporate, and entertainment entities in the service of each other and of the wider campaign.

These synergies were effective in realizing the goals of the Live 8 project. "The incredible level of public commitment and face-to-face lobbying was undoubtedly influential in ensuring global poverty was placed higher on the national and global agenda than ever before" begins Make Poverty History 's review of international policy changes in 2005, "2005: The Year of Make Poverty History."[35] Indeed, the G8 Summit yielded pledges for increased aid and some debt cancellation, while AIDS/HIV treatment for all was entered onto future agendas. This occurred in spite of the 7/7 bombings of the London Metro system, which hijacked the carefully designed media campaign and turned the issue to extreme poverty's chief opponent for agenda time: global security.[36] However, follow through on the promise has been less than forthcoming, and for this reason—among others—there has been no end to the campaigning from Live 8, Make Poverty History, DATA (formerly ONE), or the Global Call to Action against Poverty (GCAP).

The Live 8 website, www.live8live.com, continued to be updated and revised, particularly as they sought to monitor compliance with the pledge one year following and to increase attention to the 2006 G8 Summit in St. Petersburg. "Make Promises Happen" joined the "Make Poverty History" slogan. The site offered a media center with Geldolf's "report card," pictures, press releases, case studies, links, and further online resources. Videos continued to be updated, many still drawing on the "white band" thematic introduced a year prior. Although the updating appears to have stopped after 2006, the website remains: links aren't broken, and content still is available, including videos featuring Ricky Gervais, who calls attention to actions in 2006. In addition to basic information around the campaign, Gervais offers a plug for the upcoming series of his program *Extras*. Stephen Merchant, his writing partner, comes into the frame, chiding him for this self-promotion. The exchange draws on the criticism and potential of this synergistic mutual benefit, deploying irony to distance itself from the more distasteful aspects of the entertainment-based media campaign.

Once put in play, the forces generated by the conjunction of political, corporate, and entertainment interests linger beyond the actual occasion of their original conjunction. In the digital age, while some productions are ephemeral, many never really go away. Make Poverty History 's website, www.makepovertyhistory.org/takeaction, stayed active longer than Live 8's, providing updates on information, developments, and G8 Summits up until 2007. Nevertheless, with active links, the site still offers a media storehouse with information from the past years, as well as opportunities to find resources to action in the UK and abroad. Many of the videos used in the original campaign remain, with new ones joining, including a video, silent save for the three-interval click, with intertitles that encourage the viewer to continue their monitoring function: "Tell the G8 that every move they make, we'll be watching them." YouTube may provide a means for audiences to express this monitoring function: online, one can find numerous remixes of the videos produced and further distributed by audiences, thus enabling an amateur network to bolster the official advocacy circuits in place. With user-generated content, these witnessing publics can become witnessing publicists. That is, technology aids in the transformation of an audience into a political constituency and in the continued extension of this phenomenon.

ONE International, aka DATA, and GCAP maintain the most up-to-date sites, www.one.org/international and www.whiteband.org, proving comprehensive reports and updates on G8 Summits up until the most recent one at this writing. These sites do not include video, but supply guidance for activists, thus positioning themselves more as resources for political information than as means to move audiences to take political action.

"Media companies are learning how to accelerate the flow of media content across delivery channels to expand revenue opportunities, broaden markets, and reinforce viewer commitments," writes Henry Jenkins of the synergies that the combination of old and new media now provide.[37] The communications work of the Make Poverty History–Live 8 campaign shows how this model can be extended to a political framework. This campaign, already bolstered by a coalition membership of various organizations, offered a combination of multiple performance platforms, networked to cultivate sustained publicity for a basic goal: to pressure world leaders into implementing the Millennium Development Goals at the G8 Summit. No single event, performance, or airing worked in isolation, but instead, each was deployed to enhance the overall promotional potential of the integrated system that could continue to develop over time. The concerts, the websites, *The Girl in the Café*, and *Can We Save Them?* were part of a wide reaching transmedia campaign that shared rhetorical and infrastructural devices that enabled the mutual promotion and reinforcement of sponsors, both commercial (for example, Time-Warner and celebrity participants) and activist (Make Poverty History). With shared strategies, the network of performances cultivated political claims concerning the subject of poverty, outlining the stakes and providing solutions.

Contributing to a global consciousness-raising program, the campaign did more than call attention to the issue of poverty. It took essential steps in reframing the issue of extreme poverty as a political concern. Building on a network of existing organizations and on a coordinated rhetoric helped to cultivate a vision of global economic justice and to excite viewer commitment. The performances worked to activate political constituencies, equipping them with talking points and resources for action and boosting confidence by incorporating a message that traveled across all presentations: that change can happen through these encounters and activities. This message, combined with the ongoing presence of the campaign, albeit in different form, fosters sustainable potential for future engagement, or at least revitalizes the possibilities for political commitment.

Analyzing the campaign in this manner requires that efficacy be measured by an assessment of communication strategies and responses, rather than by the achievement of ultimate goals, such as ending or halving world poverty by 2015. From what can be seen, the coordinated effort created a robust scenario for promoting political messages and exciting political actors. However, there remain potential downsides. While extreme poverty received a significant place on the platform, so, too, did select celebrities who managed to enhance their public profiles with appearances onstage and in the videos. Moreover, the promotional strategies reenacted plays of First World agency and Third World victimhood. The white band project and the rallies encouraged solidarity and collective spirit, but the dominating themes and questions represented Africa as helpless. "Can we save them?" asked CNN, claiming Africa and the Global South as the responsibility of the saviors of the West and the Global North. "Take up the White Man's burden," Rudyard Kipling had exhorted colonizers in 1899. In 2005, this trope had morphed into the white band's burden as the refrain of "eight men in one room can change hundreds of millions of lives" reaffirmed the authority and power of the G8 nations. The efficiency of the delivery system armed nascent activists with clear slogans, chants, and talking points, but equally provided world leaders with the language to evade the demands and the follow-up questions.

Such drawbacks do not necessarily undo the gains of this campaign or, more to the point, this campaign's strategies. As I stated earlier, media are not transparent delivery systems, nor does showing necessarily lead to acting. Rather, rhetorical and aesthetic devices combine with exhibition and distribution practices in order to provide a sustained and clear message with a means to action. Moreover, such schemes need not be drawn solely from alternative media practices. There are methods and partners to be found in commercial media worlds. These create problematic bedfellows, to be sure. One cannot lose sight of the risks, but there are still gains to be found in practices and presentations geared to sustain attention and excite engaged publics.

NOTES

1. Bob Geldof, quoted in "Bob Geldof Launches Live 8—'The Long Walk To Justice,'" www.live-8live.com/docs/release_06_01.doc.
2. Information about the Commission for Africa can be found at http://www.commissionforafrica.info.
3. At the time, much of the activity was under the heading of either "Live 8—The Long Walk to Justice" or "The Make Poverty History Campaign." Since then, organizations have more clearly developed within their own. ONE has since merged with Debt, AIDS, Trade in Africa (DATA), an organization founded by Bono and Bobby Shriver.
4. Although Live 8 and Bob Geldof are affiliated with and mobilized for the recommendations of the Commission for Africa, the apparent public partnership with Make Poverty History integrates them into this study as much as the campaign. I do wish, however, to signal that these are two different organizations with occasionally differing recommendations.
5. Since 2005, the sites have split, although they do share videos, in particular, the "Click" videos discussed later in the chapter and Nelson Mandela's statement.

6. Cited in Thomas Keenan, "Mobilizing Shame," *South Atlantic Quarterly* 103.2/3 (Spring–Summer 2004), p. 438.
7. This optimistic faith in the immediate efficacy in exposure and revelation characterizes much of human rights scholarship. For instance, Helen Fein promotes the study of genocide in order "to expose the propaganda of the mobilizers of hate and to support counter-media, such as a human rights broadcasting network which could unmask disinformation and propaganda, unveil motives of agitators of hate and promote respect for human rights and peace." Helen Fein, "Testing Theories Brutally: Armenia (1915), Bosnia (1992) and Rwanda (1994)," in Levon Chorbajian and George Shirinian (eds.), *Studies in Comparative Genocide* (New York: St. Martin's Press 1999), p. 163. Thomas Keenan writes of this model in "Mobilizing Shame."
8. For example, in 1919, *Ravished Armenia*, a coproduction of the Selig Polyscope studio and humanitarian organization Near East Relief, was released to great fundraising success. The success of this film led to further film activism on the part of Near East Relief, with short films such as *Alice in Hungerland* and *Seeing Is Believing* reaching audiences. They later took on actor Jackie Coogan as a celebrity spokesperson, combining campaigns with popular film exhibition. I write about this in Leshu Torchin, "*Ravished Armenia*: Visual Media, Humanitarian Advocacy, and the Formation of Witnessing Publics," *American Anthropologist* 108.1 (March 2006), pp. 214–20.
9. In *Celebrity Diplomacy* (Boulder Paradigm Publishers, 2008), Andrew F. Cooper writes of this phenomenon, also noting the longstanding tradition of celebrity politics.
10. Jon Simons offers an excellent review of the scholarship in "Popular Culture and Mediated Politics: Intellectuals, Elites, and Democracy," in John Corner and Dick Pels (eds.), *Media and the Restyling of Politics: Consumerism, Celebrity, Cynicism* (London: Sage, 2003), pp. 171–89.
11. Clifford Bob, *The Marketing of Rebellion: Insurgents, Media, and International Activism* (Cambridge: Cambridge University Press, 2005); James Poniewozik, "The Year of Charitainment," in *Time*, December 26, 2005.
12. See Robert McChesney, *Rich Media, Poor Democracy: Communication Politics in Dubious Times* (Urbana: University of Illinois Press, 1999).
13. When I moved to Scotland, I learned of frustrations among certain media activists who found their efforts thwarted when faced with the juggernaut of the Make Poverty History campaign. Because the reports have been anecdotal and conveyed privately, I will not discuss this further, but accept this as a basis for meditating on possible risks.
14. Meg McLagan, "Human Rights, Testimony, and Transnational Publicity," *The Scholar and Feminist Online* 2.1, "Public Sentiments" (Summer 2003).
15. Pat Aufderheide, "Frameworks for Action: The Changing Business and Policy Environments," in *In the Battle for Reality: Social Documentaries in the U.S.* (Washington, D.C.: Center for Social Media, American University, 2003), pp. 69–85, http://www.centerforsocialmedia.org/sites/default/files/Battle_for_Reality3.pdf.
16. Corner and Pels (eds.), *Media and the Restyling of Politics*; Joke Hermes, "Hidden Debates: Rethinking the Relationship between Popular Culture and the Public Sphere," *Javnost—The Public* 13.4 (2006), pp. 27–44; Liesbet Van Zoonen, *Entertaining the Citizen: When Politics and Popular Culture Converge* (Oxford: Rowman and Littlefield, 2005).
17. Kate Nash, "Global Citizenship as Show Business: The Cultural Politics of Make Poverty History," *Media Culture & Society* 30.2 (2008), p. 167.
18. This phrasing comes from Henry Jenkins's blog *Confessions of an Aca-Fan*, http://www.henryjenkins.org/2007/03/transmedia_storytelling_101.html, which clarifies and updates ideas

outlined in *Convergence Culture: Where Old and New Media Collide* (New York: New York University Press, 2006).

19. "MTV Networks Music Services to Offer Unprecedented Global Platform for Upcoming Live 8 Concerts," MTV Think, Press Releases, June 22, 2005, http://www.mtv.com/thinkmtv/about/press_releases.jhtml.
20. Ann Talbot, "Live 8: Who Organised the PR campaign for Blair and Bush?" *World Socialist Website*, July 11, 2005, http://www.wsws.org/articles/2005/jul2005/live-j11.shtml.
21. The role of Live Aid in saving her life has been questioned in such articles as Jennie Bristow, "Who Saved Birhan Woldu's Life?" *Spiked-Online*, July 7, 2005, http://www.spiked-online.com/articles/0000000CAC4D.htm.
22. Pictures of a mother and child dominated, conjuring up either Madonnas or Piëtas. Meanwhile, desert landscapes of masses of starving people further contributed to this religious imagery, with reporters such as BBC's Michael Buerk speaking of a crisis of "biblical proportions."
23. Nash, "Global Citizenship as Show Business," p. 174. Nash observes that indignation is the affect mentioned in Luc Bolstanski's *Distant Suffering: Morality, Media, and Politics* (Cambridge: Cambridge University Press, 1999), one substantially different from the occasionally ethically challenged emotion of pity, which refuses equality and solidarity with the suffering subject.
24. This can backfire: My friend and colleague Mike Arrowsmith related a possibly apocryphal story. It seems Bono took the stage in Edinburgh and began the clicking. "Every time I click my fingers, a child dies," he said. "Well you better stop doing it then," someone called out from the audience. The activity can be made ludicrous—not too far a reach—and alternative perceptions of the celebrity spokesperson can be deployed. In this case, the joke particularly works for playing with Bono's seeming sense of power and self.
25. This inclusion, along with the absence of any disclosure of Curtis's leadership role in the campaign, were among the criticisms emerging in a BBC impartiality report two years later. This report charged *The Vicar of Dibley* with "breach[ing] the letter and spirit of four of the corporation's editorial guidelines" in its clear promotion of a single-issue campaign. Leigh Holmwood, "Dibley Criticised for Campaign Plug," *Guardian*, Monday, June 18, 2007. At the same time, the BBC maintains the webpage for the episode, http://www.bbc.co.uk/comedy/vicarofdibley/newyear.shtml, which directs its visitors to the Make Poverty History website.
26. "Female Clergy Join Fight Against Poverty," *Make Poverty History News Release*, January 13, 2005.
27. This mutual benefit may have helped to spur the aforementioned report of 2007, which expressed concern over how the rise of "celebrity-driven, single-issue campaigns presents the BBC with impartiality dilemmas, particularly in entertainment areas dealing with factual material." Holmwood, "Dibley Criticised for Campaign Plug." Such concerns did not emerge in the strictly commercial domains of CNN and HBO.
28. Peter Paterson, "Propaganda, Actually," *London Daily Mail*, June, 27, 2005, p. 49
29. Frazier Moore, "*Girl in the Café* Has Heart and Mission," AP Wire Report, June 21, 2005, http://www.highbeam.com/doc/1P1-110239385.html.
30. Lia Miller, "Corporate Synergy in Action: CNN Will Promote HBO Movie," *New York Times*, June 20, 2005.
31. President of HBO Films Colin Callendar, paraphrased in Miller, "Corporate Synergy in Action."
32. Jonathan Klein, cited in Miller, "Corporate Synergy in Action."
33. Reportedly, *The Girl in the Café* was given to Prime Minister Tony Blair to view prior to his interview with *Can We Save Them?* host Christiane Amanpour. The possible intentions

abound. Was this to inform Blair of the talking points of the campaign? After all, the film includes the arguments against aid and debt relief, as well as their rebuttal. Was it to alert him to what viewers in the UK and the United States would now assume about his duty? Or was it to educate him about his duty, hoping he would enact the role in real life of the prime minister as portrayed on the screen.

34. A transcript is available at the Council on Foreign Relations website in their publications and transcripts section, http://www.cfr.org/publication/8221/girl_in_the_caf.html?breadcrumb=%2Fpublication%2Fpublication_list%3Fgroupby%3D3%26type%3Dtranscript%26filter%3D2005%26page%3D4.

35. "2005: The Year of Make Poverty History," http://www.makepovertyhistory.org/docs/mph-lookback05.pdf.

36. Given that terrorist acts themselves are increasingly dependent on media for publicizing the events and the expression of discontent, the timing hardly seems coincidental. Suicide bombing or "martyrdom operations" offer a form of extreme testimony, and statements and events are often filmed and shipped to news organizations. This way, those outside the system may still find ways to make it work for them.

37. Henry Jenkins, *Convergence Culture: Where Old and New Media Collide* (New York: New York University Press, 2006), p. 18.

Hidden hives on a New York City rooftop (photo: John Jacen).

Honey in the City: Just Food's Campaign to Legalize Beekeeping in New York City

Charles Zerner

> Lithuania is smoky, Jordan is spiced with the tang of yellow star thistle. Japan's buckwheat soba honey is nearly as dark as soy and almost savory. The fat spherical jar of Israeli honey, with a comb in its amber liquid, exudes eucalyptus and sunlight. And what of this light yellow sample, thinner than most, with a haunting of mint? "Lower East Side of Manhattan," offers Andrew Cote . . . beekeeper. . . . "I'm trying to figure out which weeds grow in lots and alleys there near the rooftop hives to give it that distinctive taste."
>
> —Gerri Hershey, "Sharing a Taste of Honey, on an International Scale," *New York Times* November 28, 2008

The social organization, communicative capacities, and behavioral repertoire of honeybees have been sources of countless metaphors, analogies, and reflections on human politics, governmental forms, and social orders, from Aristotle's apicultural meditations to E. O. Wilson's entomological panegyrics and questionable sociobiological speculations on the lives of social insects.[1] The experimental physiologist and bee researcher Karl Von Frisch analyzed how the bee's dances convey precise information about the distance and direction of food sources.[2] Von Frisch's historic demonstration of the communicative content of his famous dance of the bees has, in its own right, become a source of inspiration, controversy, and reflection in the work of contemporary social theorists and historians, including cultural anthropologist Hugh Raffles, geographer Jake Kosek, and science historians Tania Munz and Paolo Palladino.[3]

Margaret Atwood, lyric poet and novelist, has placed apiculture, gardening, and environmental concerns at the center of many of her speculative fictions. In Atwood's novel *The Year of the Flood*, the state of communication between human beings and bees is emblematic of the precarious relationships between humans, nature, technology, and survival in a desolate, postapocalyptic world. In Atwood's dystopia, a community on the margins, God's Gardeners cultivate a thriving rooftop garden, buzzing with bees and flowers, amid a desolate landscape of industrial ruins. On the Gardeners' Rooftop Garden, a refugee named Toby who has sought sanctuary is introduced to the bees:

> One day, old walnut-faced Pilar—Eve Six—asked Toby if she wanted to know about bees. Bees and mushrooms—these were Pilar's specialties. Toby liked Pilar, who seemed kind, and who had a serenity she envied; so she said yes.
>
> "Good," said Pilar. "You can always tell the bees your troubles." . . .
>
> Pilar took her to visit the beehives, and introduced her to the bees by name. "They need to know you're a friend," she said. "They can smell you. Just move slowly," she cautioned as the bees coated Toby's bare arm like golden fur. "They'll know you next time." . . . She [Pilar] said you had to speak out loud because the bees couldn't read your mind precisely, any more than a person could. So Toby did speak, although she felt like a fool. What would anyone down there on the sidewalk think if they saw her talking to a swarm of bees?

According to Pilar, bees all over the world had been in trouble for decades. It was the pesticides, or the hot weather, or a disease, or maybe all of these—nobody knew exactly. But the bees on the Rooftop Garden were all right, in fact, they were thriving.[4]

While New York City is not Atwood's postapocalyptic urban ruin, its bees are certainly not thriving. This essay tracks the strategies of visibility by which Just Food, an NGO focused on food security and equitable access to food throughout New York City's neighborhoods, and its allies in apicultural advocacy and urban agriculture have sought to communicate the plight of the bees to a larger society and to mobilize New York City's policy makers and legislators to change the city's regulations prohibiting apiculture. Just Food and its allies are seeking to make visible the environmental situation of New York's honeybees, which face scarce urban habitats, colony-collapse disorder, and the situation of New York's beekeepers, who until very recently were liable for $2,000 fines if they were caught taking care of bees.

I use the phrase "strategies of visibility" as a broad-spectrum term encompassing the full gamut of human sensory capacities, portals, and surfaces—eyes, ears, noses, throats, and skins, among others—as well as the multiple nodes, networks, and sites of communication, lines of thinking, and modes of transmission and performance that Just Food volunteers, staff members, and allies have used to grab headlines, reach publics, mobilize constituencies, influence congressional representatives, and shape legislation to legalize apiculture in New York City. Just

Food's primary focus is on serving community gardeners throughout the city, and its closest allies in this effort have been Green Thumb and other groups in the metropolitan and Hudson River Valley region, including the New York Restoration Project and several land trusts.

In the course of their campaign, Just Food organizers used the Internet, audio programs, print media, word of mouth, words on fliers and words on petitions, web-linked images, political protests, access to members of Congress, and media-genic events. Just Food also used alliances with local governmental bodies and a variety of nongovernmental organizations linked to apiculture and the local-food movement, including the New York City Beekeepers Meetup Group, the New York City Beekeepers Association, the Gotham City Honey Cooperative, and hundreds of individual beekeepers to mobilize public opinion, obtain positive publicity, and exert pressure on City Hall. A variety of rhetorical strategies and strategic framings were part of Just Food's campaign to generate public support for bees, beekeepers, and legislative change.

During the 1920s and 1930s in New York city, beekeeping was a widespread, if not a commonplace practice. Hives were managed inside Radio City Music Hall, on the roof of the American Museum of Natural History[5] and inside buildings and on rooftops and in backyard gardens across the Bronx, Brooklyn, Queens, and Manhattan. In 1999, however, during the law-and-order regime of then mayor Rudolph W. Giuliani, the New York City Health Code prohibited the possession, keeping, harboring, and selling of "wild animals." Besides banishing an anomalous gaggle of animals including iguanas, ferrets, elephants, polar bears, cougars, alligators, and whales, the code banished bees, classifying them as "wild, ferocious, fierce, dangerous, or naturally inclined to do harm." Section 161.01 of the Health Code, subsection (b)(12), banned "all venomous insects, including but not limited to bee, hornet, and wasp." From 1999 until the spring of 2010, the good times for beekeepers, bees, pollination, and local honey production in New York City were over.

During the summer of 2009, Just Food, in conjunction with several local, regional, and national apiculture organizations, began a multifaceted campaign to mobilize support for the delisting of honeybees as dangerous, wild creatures and the decriminalization of New York citizens who practice apiculture in their backyards, on their roofs, and in abandoned lots. This campaign, like other recent campaigns of nongovernmental activism, was an assemblage of technical devices, infrastructures, and practices and employed forms of symbolic, cultural, and aesthetic mediation. So let us inquire what in assemblage of media tools has been used by Just Food and its allies during this campaign. What images, narrative strategies, performative means, sensory portals, electronic, print, and sonic channels have been used to mobilize support for legal change in this case?

Patrick Gannon with his bees (photo: Elizabeth Leitzell).

The Just Food campaign for the legalization of apiculture in New York City created performative events that included the Honey Festival in Union Square and the Beekeepers Ball in South Street Seaport. In order to understand these events and their origins, I interviewed Just Food executive director Jacquie Berger. I asked her to describe Just Food's agenda. She replied:

> Just Food advocates for local food and urban food systems and alliances with national, international, and local organizations. We initially sought to encourage people with our urban farming chicken program. Our chicken program is up and clucking. Bees increase the productivity of gardens and create an edible product. We wanted to do the bee program at the same time, but our researchers quickly discovered apiculture is illegal. While we dreamed up the bee program with Heifer International, the campaign to legalize apiculture was dreamed up in-house. We initially conducted research on why it was illegal, under whose jurisdiction it was. It didn't take long to discover that the regulations in the code could not be easily waved away by a magic wand.

I asked her how the apiculture campaign developed and who developed the visions for program development, planning, and communication. She explained:

We have a team of media professionals who are all volunteers. They serve on our communications committee. We told them about the campaign and asked: How do we raise the profile of the campaign? How do we attract attention of powerful people, groups, friendly supporters? How do we create a media-grabbing campaign? At one of our monthly meetings, we learned about National Pollinator Week.[6] It was only two months away, and we decided it was the perfect thing to work with. National Pollinator Week was developed in response to colony-collapse disorder, which threatens to drastically reduce the honeybee population nationally. The third National Pollinator Week was coming up. We did outreach with underground bee associations and the Just Food network to pull together a working group, and we got a tremendous response. Volunteers from all over the city, Brooklyn, the Lower East Side, all over, and groups including the New York City Beekeeper Meetup Group, the New York City Beekeepers Association, the Gotham City Honey Coop, the Meadery, and Silvermine Apiary up in Connecticut. We asked our groups: Do something more public!

We asked the Union Square Greenmarket if they would allow us to do the Honey Festival in Union Square — to do it in their space. We have some people who are theater professionals. People came dressed up in bee costumes. One guy on stilts with antennae sprouting from his forehead came to the square. Just Food set up tables with beekeeper associations. Although we can't legally sit at a table and collect petitions in Union Square, we can walk around and collect signatures, based on an agreement between the city and the Greenmarket and the Parks Department.

The Beekeepers Ball was emphatically the most dramatic, parodic, performatively polymorphous event staged by Just Food and company. Performed on the waterfront edge of Manhattan, the Beekeepers Ball overlooked the East River and was flanked by the Brooklyn Bridge to the north, facing out toward Brooklyn's leafy Promenade. Visual, auditory, aromatic, culinary, and chromatic stimuli exploded at the ball in ways that broadcast the message that bees, beekeeping, biodiversity, honey, hives, and urban agriculture are crucial and they are pleasures. Steven Stern, a *New York Times* reporter, offered this lively account in an article entitled "Hoping to Generate a Bit More Buzz":

The Beekeepers Ball, held Monday night at the Water Taxi Beach in the South Street Seaport, was, among other things, a lesson in coalition politics.

In attendance were New York City beekeepers, aspiring New York City beekeepers, beekeepers not from New York City, friends of beekeepers, friends of bees, people who like to dress as bees, people who like to dress their children as bees, bee-dressed children, one cross-dressing beekeeper, a couple of guys who spend much of their time dressed in armor, fans of honey, fans of local food and a team of French videographers.

> Bees may be sexy; signing petitions and phoning politicians is less so. But Jacquie Berger clearly knows the adage about vinegar and honey. And honey was certainly in evidence at the Water Taxi Beach: honey-coated pork ribs, hot dogs with honey mustard, and burgers in sliced honey-glazed doughnuts. The beer, provided by the Brooklyn brewery Kelso, was infused with city honey and whipped up specially for the occasion. A vendor sold delicious honey-strawberry ice pops. The proprietors of the Long Island Meadery were on hand, passing out samples of their syrupy honey wine. They usually market the stuff at Renaissance fairs and gatherings of armored reenactors. Though new to the locavore crowd, they were definitely used to serving costumed drinkers.[7]

However, as Stern also wrote in the *Times*,

> John Howe's beekeeping suit was not a costume: it was his beekeeping suit. As founder of the New York City Beekeeping Meetup Group, Mr. Howe provides an online home for beekeeping fans, and sponsors classes, bringing what he calls wanna-bees into the fold. When he started his first rooftop hive in 2002, he knew of two or three beekeepers in the city. Now, he knows of at least 40. Lately, he has been spending more time fielding calls from the news media.
>
> So has Andrew Coté, head of the New York City Beekeepers Association. He rattled off a list of other American cities with strong, legal beekeeping scenes and expressed indignation that New York was not among them: "We are not followers in this city!"

The Honey Festival in Union Square during National Pollinator Week was more directly political. As Jacquie Berger told me:

> We had volunteers walking around Union Square on market day, during the Honey Festival, getting people to sign the petition to legalize beekeeping. At the same time, the organic food advocacy group and gourmet restaurant Stone Barns, based up in the Hudson River Valley foodshed, came down and provided a demonstration hive and a honey tasting. People came into the square, walked up to the Stone Barns booth, and tasted these fantastic honey-and-cream whole wheat pancakes. And we asked people to go over and sign our petition.
>
> Food bloggers followed us for a whole week at the green market, reporting on cooking demonstrations in the Square as the cook made little whole wheat pancakes with honey and cream, rhubarb compote. So people were coming over for the food and asking the Barns people why they were there.[8]

Both the Honey Festival and the Beekeepers Ball are contemporary enactments of the Bahktinian carnivalesque—performative follies and enchantments appealing to the eye, the mouth, the nose, and the ears, and Just Food also made its own music with language in a move we might call the "narrative turn." While beetles, wasps, and praying mantises have often been portrayed in film and fiction as embodiments of the dangerous other, the foreign, and the frightening,[9] honeybees' literary and filmic legacies since Ovid have been much kinder. Bees have been portrayed as the epitome of the insect world's quintessential good citizens: industrious and productive, choreographically gifted, highly organized, and agriculturally indispensable. Just Food, in its online petition to legalize honeybee culture, asserts: "Honeybees are garden heroes! Honeybees help gardens grow more fruit and vegetables and produce sweet honey. They are nature's best pollinators and contribute to productive harvests in community gardens, public parks and nature centers."[10]

Just Food's casting of honeybees as heroes probably has less to do with bees' courage and much more to do with their homely, dependable, and crucial role in agriculture in both rural orchards and urban contexts. Nature, as William Cronon and Jennifer Price remind us, is in the city, on the High Line, on your porch, and in your kitchen flower pot.[11] And flowers need fertilization. In its petition, Just Food develops the conceit of urban bees as docile, productive, efficient citizens, rhetorically enfolded within the mantle of the productive human community.[12] While not asserting that bees are us or that they are significant others in the manner of Donna Haraway's notion of companion species,[13] Just Food does assert that honeybees are good ecological citizens, a special species that is recognized as important for utilitarian and aesthetic reasons, a species that should be supported, cared for, and cultivated, rather than criminalized, outlawed, or feared.

If a visit to Union Square or South Street Seaport was not enough to persuade New Yorkers of the goodness of honeybees, Just Food, on its website, invited New Yorkers to visit a bar in "real life" and engage in a virtual tour of beehives, beekeepers, and apicultural practices while sipping honey-laced mead and checking out the local customers: Jimmy's Bar No. 43. The invitation reads:

> Explore the incredible world of urban beekeeping without leaving your bar-stool. Learn about the ancient art of mead-making, while indulging in a mead tasting-you'll find out why this ancient beverage is known as the nectar of the gods. On this virtual tour, you'll visit rooftop, backyard, and community garden hives and hear the tales of intrepid beekeepers. Come to Jimmy's Bar No. 43 and find out what all the buzz is about.[14]

While Just Food is the organizing center for such events, it has worked in collaboration with local, regional, national, and, to a limited extent, international actors and at least one U.S. government agency. In addition to the organizations already mentioned, Just Food is also affiliated with a Norwalk, Connecticut, father-and-son business called Silvermine Apiary, which operates over two hundred hives in Fairfield County and Manhattan, and an international apicultural NGO called Bees without Borders (BWB), founded by Andre Coté of Silvermine Apiary.[15]

"Where has the campaign gone? What were the consequences? I asked Berger at the conclusion of our interview. "In the midst of Pollinator Week last summer," she said,

> we got a call from the New York City Department of Health to talk about collaboration. The Department of Health got our petitions. They represent one of the most densely populated vertical cities in the world. We are showing them apiculture practices in other urban settings. We are showing them what they can do to protect the populace. They will revisit the code in the fall. The City Health Department has the authority to change the code. They are talking with us. We are prepared to suggest legal language to improve the code and to regulate beekeeping. We can give them language to suggest best practices.
>
> There is a quiet hum of activity now within this small community of beekeepers and attorneys. They are going back and forth with Health Department people on what the policy should look like. What the code should look like and what people should say during the coming fall meetings of the board.

On March 16, 2010, the campaign achieved the victory it sought. As the *New York Times* blog announced:

> New York City Board of Health voted to lift a ban against beekeeping, legalizing the hives of hundreds of residents who have tended bees in defiance of the law.
>
> The unanimous vote amends the health code to allow residents to keep hives of Apis mellifera, the common, nonagresssive honeybee. Beekeepers will be required to register with the Department of Health and Mental Hygiene and to adhere to appropriate practices.[16]

What were our methods?" Berger asked rhetorically. "We used all possible methods!"

Just Food hoped that the bee campaign would not end with legalization. Since the legalization, Jacquie Berger suspects that there has been a surge in beekeeping throughout the city, and Berger hopes that the campaign can morph into a "beekeeping apprenticeship program, modeled on Just Food's Chicken Program." In that program Just Food picks grantees in New York City to develop chicken care, build chicken coops, and teaches New York City residents how to "keep chickens well and with a lot of community support." Because beekeeping practices change with the seasons, Just Food is contemplating year-long apprenticeship programs in beekeeping throughout the boroughs. Most importantly, beekeeping is important to Just Food's agenda because "Just Foods serves community gardeners to help them grow, market, and distribute more produce. Bees assist in pollination, and they are nonhuman partners in creating another product: honey."

For Just Food and New York City, there are also larger ecological and urban issues on the horizon. Relationships between food production and climate change have not been on New York City's environmental agenda. Just Food is "helping people plug into a food production system that has a low carbon footprint. Eating locally and organically is part of the picture in reducing urban carbon emissions. Food has not been part of the New York City government plans to reduce greenhouse gas emissions."[17] Just Food intends to make community gardening part of the New York City plan for greenhouse gas emissions and to put community gardening into the federal Farm Bill, up for renewal in 2012, in ways that link local gardens to global greenhouse gas emissions.

Just Food's beekeeping legalization campaign encompasses the multiple forms of mediation and networked communication that art historian W. T. J Mitchell envisions when he writes that "visual culture entails a meditation on blindness, the invisible, the unseen, the unseeable, and the overlooked; also on deafness and the visible language of gesture. It also compels attention to the tactile, the auditory, the haptic and it also compels attention to the phenomenon of synaesthesia."[18] Within Mitchell's expansive, sensuous conception of visual culture and its modalities, the taste and crunch of New York City honeycomb and the fragrance of Lower East Side mint in Silvermine Apiary's honey are palpable, as are the performative antics of beekeepers, their families, and friends, at spectacles such as the Honey Festival and the Beekeepers Ball.

Beyond uttering locavore victory slogans that echo the naive anarchism of the 1960s and the blue-green Whole Earth optimism of the 1970s environmental movement—"Down with the Code," "Long life for the wildflowers, weeds, beekeepers, and honeybees of New York City," "Honey in the city!"—ecological activists, media scholars, urban theorists, and landscape designers might use the story of New York City and its ten-year ban on honeybee culture as a critical metaphor for and indictment of urban policy, an example of the "desertification" of the city. While bees and pollen, nectar and flowers, weedy lots, flying seeds, and roofs of the city, constitute a seemingly small collection of organisms, sites, and relationships, they contain within them the power of the small.

On May 1, 2010, a thick, magnificently eclectic collection of writings, images, and imaginings on the future of culture/nature in the city appeared. Based on a remarkable conference organized by Mohsen Mostafavi, dean of the Harvard Graduate School of Design, this volume envisions a vibrant mulitiplicity of new ways of organizing the city. In these visions, the city is rethought and reorganized on a variety of scales to repair and remake urban landscapes that are "demineralized," well watered, green, and agriculturally productive. Mostafavi's introduction declares:

> The visionary Italian architect and urbanist Andrea Branzi has for many years espoused the advantages of a different approach toward the city—one that is not reliant on a compositional or typological approach. Rather, for Branzi, it is the fluidity of the city, its capacity to be diffuse and enzymatic in character, that merits accomplishment. . . . A key feature of this type of urbanism—like the agricultural territory—is its capacity to be reversible, evolving, and provisory. These qualities are necessary in response to the changing needs of a society in a state of constant reorganization.[19]

Even more striking is Mostafavi's analogy between the physiological effects of acupuncture techniques on the human body and the kinds of effects he imagines on the body urban:

> More specifically, the blurring of boundaries—real and virtual, as well as urban and rural—implies a greater connection and complementarity between the various parts of a given territory. Conceptually akin to acupuncture, the interventions in and transformation of an area often have a significant impact beyond perceived physical limits. Thinking simultaneously at small and large scales calls for an awareness that is currently unimaginable in many existing patters of legal, political, and economic activity.[20]

An acupunctural vision of the city, imagining the urban territory as a fluctuating mosaic, a multiscalar, temporally variegated landscape, is a conception of the urban landscape in which apicultural interventions, on a variety of scales and at a variety of sites, might flourish—on rooftops, in abandoned or underused lots, in community gardens, and on barges moored in rivers, with hidden connections and effloresences throughout the city.

It is time to invite nature into the city in ways variable and imaginative, in schemes that are recuperative, productive, and redemptive. Now that Just Food and its allies have succeeded in lifting the ban on apiculture, perhaps they will seek a wider network of allies, including landscape architects, urban planners, agriculturalists, aquaculturalists, legislators, and policy specialists to rethink and remake the fabric of New York City. In these emerging experiments in ecological urbanism, it is time to integrate honeybees into conceptions of the urban citizenry and to integrate honeybees' habitats, man-made and natural, in gardens, meadows, weedy edges, and wetlands into the visions of designers remaking, on multiple scales, the material and social worlds that are New York City.

NOTES

1. On questionable analogies between ant "supercolonies" and particular forms of human society in E. O. Wilson's only work of fiction, *Anthill* (Cambridge, MA: Harvard University Press, 2001), see Verlyn Klinkenborg, "Life Lessons, Taught by Insects," *New York Times*, April 8, 2010.
2. Tania Munz and Jake Kosek provided helpful clarifications on von Frisch's research findings. I am grateful to them both, and to Toby Volkman, for their helpful comments on this essay.
3. See Karl von Frisch, *The Dance Language and Orientation of Bees*, trans. Leigh E. Chadwick (1965; Cambridge, MA: Harvard University Press, 1993) for the classic account of Frisch's analysis of bee communication. Hugh Raffles discusses von Frisch's account of bees in Sina Najafi, "The Language of the Bees: An Interview with Hugh Raffles," *Cabinet* 25 (Spring 2007), http://www.cabinetmagazine.org/issues/25/raffles.php. Jake Kosek discussed the fashioning of bees as instruments of surveillance and homeland security in "The Natures of the Beast: On the New Uses of the Honeybee," paper presented at the Yale University Agrarian Studies Colloquium Series, November 20, 2009. On the interpretive controversies surrounding von Frisch's translations of the bee dance movements, see Tania Munz, "The Bee Battles: Karl von Frisch, Adrian Wenner and the Honey Bee Dance Language Controversy," *Journal of the History of Biology* 38.3 (November 2005), pp. 535–70. Paolo Palladino has discussed the figure of the insect and its uses in the construction of the human-animal distinction in "Becoming Human: Wasps, Bees and the Politics of Metaphor," paper delivered at conference Thinking with Insects, May 20, 2010, London School of Tropical Medicine and Health. On E. O. Wilson's comparisons and analogies between social insects and human societies, see E. O. Wilson and Burt Holldobler, *The Superorganism: The Beauty, Elegance, and Strangeness of Insect Societies* (New York: W. W. Norton, 2009).
4. Margaret Atwood, *The Year of the Flood* (New York: Doubleday, 2009), pp. 99–100.
5. Joshua Bustein, "Beekeepers Keep the Lid On," *New York Times*, June 19, 2009, http://nytimes.com/2009/06/21/nyregion/21ritual.html.
6. National Pollinator Week is sponsored by the Pollinator Partnership, http://www.pollinator.org/about.htm. According to its website, "Pollinator Partnership (P2) . . . works to protect the health of managed and native pollinating animals vital to our North American ecosystems and agriculture. Our website is a premiere source of information for consumers, gardeners, land managers, educators, resource managers, producers, and farmers to help pollinators, essential components for all of life." As one of its many projects, "P2 manages the North American Pollinator Protection Campaign (NAPPC) a collaborative group of over 120 organizations and individuals that promote and implement a continent-wide Action Plan to encourage activities to protect the numbers and health of all pollinating animals."
7. Steven Stern, "Hoping to Generate a Bit More Buzz," *New York Times*, June 23, 2009, http://www.nytimes.com/2009/06/24/dining/24bees.html.
8. The mission statement of Stone Barns emphasizes the organization's geographic proximity to New York City: "Stone Barns Center for Food and Agriculture is a farm, a kitchen, a classroom–an exhibit, a laboratory, a campus. The mission of this unique, nonprofit, member-driven collaboration is to celebrate, teach and advance community-based food production and enjoyment, from farm to classroom to table. . . . Stone Barns Center is within a 45-minute drive for the nearly 19 million residents of the New York metropolitan area." Stone Barnes

Center for Food and Agriculture website, http://www.stonebarnscenter.org/sb_about/mission.aspx.

9. On the demonic, alien, or simply awful images of the insect in visual culture and Western narratives, see Charlotte Sleigh, "Inside Out: The Unsettling Nature of Insects"; Nicky Coutts, "Portraits of the Nonhuman: Visualiations of the Malevolent Insect"; and Sarah Gordon, "Entomophagy: Representations of Insect Eating in Literature and Mass Media," all in Eric C. Brown (ed.), *Insect Poetics* (Minneapolis: University of Minnesota Press, 2009), pp. 281–97, 298–318, and 342–62, respectively. See also Erich Hoyt and Ted Schultz, *Insect Lives: Stories of Mystery and Romance from a Hidden World* (Cambridge, MA: Harvard University Press, 1999). In the military vein, see Jeffry Lockwood *Six-Legged Soldiers: Using Insects as Weapons of War* (Oxford: Oxford University Press, 2009).
10. Just Foods, "Legalize Beekeeping in NYC!" December 8, 2008, http://www.gopetition.com/petitions/legalize-beekeeping.html.
11. William Cronon, "The Trouble with Wilderness, or, Getting Back to the Wrong Nature," *Environmental History*, 1.1 (1996), pp. 7–55; Jennifer Price, *Flight Maps: Adventures with Nature in Modern America* (New York: Basic Books, 1999).
12. *New York Times* columnist Tammy Horn raises the bee to a status even higher than hero in her story entitled "Honey Bees: A History," April 11, 2008, http://topics.blogs.nytimes.com/2008/04/11/honey-bees-a-history: "Long known as angels of agriculture, honeybees have received global attention due to losses attributed to a combination of factors: Colony Collapse Disorder, mites, deforestation and industrial agriculture. Honey bees provide pollination for crops, orchards, and flowers; honey and wax for cosmetics, food, and medicinal-religious objects; and inspiration to artists, architects and scientists."
13. See Donna Haraway, *The Companion Species Manifesto: Dogs, People, and Significant Otherness* (Chicago: Prickly Paradigm Press, 2003).
14. Urban Gardens, "NYC Pollinator Week: Hidden Hives Tour Tonight!" http://www.urbangardensweb.com/2009/06/25/nyc-pollinator-week-hidden-hives-tour-tonight.
15. In 2005, Bees without Borders, in collaboration with the United States Agency for International Development, sent Coté to Iraq, where he documented the impact of the 1991 Gulf War on apiculture. "Before the Gulf War, there were an estimated half a million hives in Iraq. After the oil field fires and smoke, and the current war, there are about 20,000 beehives," Coté says. "Slowly, well-tended colonies of pollinators can help bring back devastated areas. And honey is always a miracle. It is the one food on earth that does not spoil. It can be eaten, traded, sold, and traded for just the tiniest edge to survive." Jerri Hershey, "Sharing a Taste of Honey, on an International Scale, *New York Times*, November 28, 2008, http://www.nytimes.com/2008/11/30/nyregion/connecticut/30colct.html.
16. Mireya Navarro, "Bring on the Bees," *New York Times*, March 16, 2010, http://cityroom.blogs.nytimes.com/2010/03/16/brin-on-the-bees
17. Jacquie Berger, conversation with the author.
18. W. T. J. Mitchell, "Showing Seeing: A Critique of Visual Culture," in Nicholas Mirzoeff (ed.), *The Visual Culture Reader*, 2nd ed. (London: Routledge, 2002), p. 90.
19. Mohsen Mostafavi, "Why Ecological Urbanism? Why Now," in Mohsen Mostafavi (ed.), with Gareth Doherty, *Ecological Urbanism* (Cambridge, MA: Harvard University Press, 2009), p. 30. Among the case studies in this visionary ecological urbanism are images of cybersimulacra, including Stefano Boeri's *Bosco Vertical* (Vertical forest), in which "high-rise buildings laden

with common green surfaces and spaces [are] inserted in the politics of demineralization of the city that combines ideally with projects of demographic densification and urban reforestation." Stefano Boeri, "Five Ecological Challenges for the Contemporary City," in *Ecological Urbanism*, p. 449. While Boeri's spectacular, delicate interlacing of vertical forestry and domestic dwellings in the sky constitutes a heaven-oriented solution to the greening and densification of the city, Michael Desvigne and Jena Novel's *Lisieres* project for Paris constitutes a series of lush, horizontally organized agricultural sites interspersed within and around cities. In landscape designer Dorothée Imbert's words, "The Desvigne and the Nouvel team devised an urban-agricultural codification for the periphery's *lisiere* (forest border and seam).... The *lisiere* between Paris and the surrounding agricultural zone becomes an 800-kilometer joint of varying width where traces of a long gone farming landscape articulate with a new type of productive open-space system. The hedges, ditches, thickets, and paths reappear within an infrastructure of greenhouses, allotment gardens, recycling, energy production, composting, and sports fields." Dorothée Imbert, "Aux Fermes Citoyens!" in *Ecological Urbanism*, p. 256.

20. Mostafavi, "Why Ecological Urbanism? Why Now," p. 30.

FIGURE 1 Michael Rakowitz, from "The worst condition is to pass under a sword which is not one's own," 2010 (courtesy the artist and Lombard-Fried Gallery).

The Market Is the Medium: Postcynical Strategies in the Work of Michael Rakowitz

Liza Johnson

> We're an empire now, and when we act, we create our own reality. And while you're studying that reality—judiciously, as you will—we'll act again, creating other new realities, which you can study too, and that's how things will sort out. We're history's actors . . . and you, all of you, will be left to just study what we do.
>
> —Senior aide to George W. Bush, 2004

Jean-Luc Godard's 1967 film *2 or 3 Things I Know about Her*, a standard-bearer for the genre of the essay film, is a rigorous meditation on the relationships between everyday life, commodity packaging, and the U.S. war in Vietnam. The film crystallizes important modernist assumptions about the ways that the consumer marketplace limits criticality and, by extension, participates in the production of violence and the continual recruitment of the consent of the governed. Godard's film is at once a tribute to pop art, constantly flashing primary-colored fragments of signage, and an amplification of pop's critical aspirations. Where Andy Warhol's treatments of products and packaging register a pop ambivalence, in Godard's film, their appealing surfaces ultimately become unambivalent technologies of amnesia. In the film's final scene, the camera pulls back to reveal a tableau of shiny grocery products laid out on the grass, arranged like buildings gridded onto city streets or plotted like markers in a cemetery (fig. 2). Godard's own voice whispers the narration, anchoring the packages to their role in his forgetting of reality: "I listen to commercials on my transistor. Thanks to ESSO, I serenely take the road to dreams and forget all else. I forget Hiroshima and Auschwitz. I forget Budapest. I forget Vietnam and minimum wages. I forget the housing crisis. I forget famine in India. I've forgotten it all except that it takes me back to zero. I have to start over from there."[1]

Caught in the double bind of his efforts to think critically, act politically, and remember historically in the face of amnesiac consumer pleasures, Godard's tone

FIGURE 2 Still from Jean-Luc Godard, *Two or Three Things I Know About Her*, 1967.

is melancholy and knowing. Throughout, the film masterfully engages modernist critical strategies that render this dilemma of knowingness. The film's protagonist, a middle-class prostitute named Juliette, speaks her self-reflexive opening lines as a direct address to the viewer: "Speak as though you are quoting the truth. Old man Brecht says it," directly demanding from the viewer the kinds of knowing self-awareness that Brecht's Epic Theater used with the hope of cutting through the complacency of modern life. Juliette, too, knows of her own complicit witnessing of the war, looking at photographs of Vietnamese people in magazines and pondering her safe distance from the front lines, from where the war is profoundly, materially felt: "It's strange that a person who is in Europe on August 17, 1966, can think of another who is in Asia." And, the film suggests, this person in Asia is presented in the same manner, through the same medium, as fashion items and brand-named grocery products.

To the extent that the film's narrator and its characters are aware of the dilemma presented by their desire to critique war and commodity culture while still engaged within a capitalist everyday, the film's logic is less a traditional critique of ideology than it is a thoughtful articulation of particular conditions of political melancholy, even depression. Godard and his characters are not the naive victims of false consciousness; they know they're prostitutes for candy-colored boxes. If not exactly enjoying their false consciousness, as Slavoj Žižek might claim, Godard and his characters are caught in the knowingness of the kind of double bind that Peter Sloterdjik called "cynical reason" or "enlightened false consciousness."[2] Framing cynical reason as a broad response to the aftermath of the social movements of the 1960s, Sloterdjik argues that contemporary subjects are less the duped victims of ideology than they are grudgingly knowing witnesses to the functioning of power, continually acting "against better knowledge."[3] Godard's 1967 knowingness suggests that the very period we often look to as filled with pre-cynical possibility was itself struck through with the complexities of knowing that one does not believe in what one is doing, but that one does it anyway, because there seems to be no alternative but to know and to act cynically. Certainly, then, the neoliberalizing projects predicted by Godard and the depressing triumphalism of post–Berlin Wall globalized capitalism have only made the proliferation of cynicism and political despair seem more reasonable by exaggerating the sense that there may be no alternative to the institutional, corporate, and governmental demands that citizens act against their better knowledge.

Cynical reason can be said to operate not only by and through commodity culture, but also as a broader political stance—and may be a stance not only for citizens, but for the state. The United States itself operates to a great extent in a mode of cynical simulationism—not only acting against a better knowledge of reality, but also actively simulating events and accounts that displace and supplant actual events and referents. The Persian Gulf War, critically noted for its so-called "virtuality,"[4] served only to widen the gap that Juliette speaks of between the images of war that circulate in media and their referents on the ground in an occupied foreign nation. By creating wild asymmetries in the material impact of violence, that action generated atrocious devastation on the ground in Iraq while leaving spectators and even some U.S. combatants to watch the violence on-screen.

Perhaps the pinnacle of U.S. state-sponsored cynical virtuality was the run-up to military action in Iraq in 2003, in which dissimulated claims of Iraq's possession of "weapons of mass destruction" were used to justify the U.S. invasion. Contested at the time by UN weapons inspectors and further undermined by later events, such as the Valerie Plame affair, the answer to the question of whether there was ever an on-the-ground referent to the "intelligence" concerning the WMDs remains both speculative and of dire consequence.[5] The Bush administration seemed to believe that the nation was so nursed on cynical reason it could be told directly that not only wasn't the administration acting based on the best of their knowledge, but that they could actually invent knowledge, as in an unnamed administration official's claim "We're an empire now, and when we act we create our own reality."[6] The administration seemed to rely on a nation that, as a whole, had severed the relationship between critical thought, political action, and historical memory. Many would be content to know—and tell each other—that the administration was lying.

The neoliberal organization of war functions efficiently because of its treatment of markets—including labor markets and information products. The state has exhibited managerial savvy by insisting on a "volunteer army" that differentially affects lower and middle classes while maintaining access to consumption for everyone else. Additionally, knowledge of the events of war depends on a news structure that is constituted by and through news formats that are themselves entertainment commodities. Given this, even to achieve a cynical stance of knowingness is not without effort and may well feel like a political act in and of itself. If it still takes some effort to know that you are being lied to, then the work of knowing may cause you to feel that possessing knowingness (cynical reason) constitutes a political act. But especially given the use of cynical strategies by the state itself, it makes sense to ask whether this is really the case. If a certain kind of cynical knowingness can now be described as a form of popular common sense, a status quo of political feeling, and even a governmental and corporate strategy, then it makes sense to ask questions about whether an aesthetics and politics of knowingness that putatively aspires to counter this status quo might in fact be critically defanged or outmoded.

Contemporary art practices have had a troubled relationship with the problem of political action, market logic, and cynical reason. David Joselit has noted that to be taken seriously as a critically potent artist, one must engage the problems of consumption, offering within one's artwork a critique of the marketplace. Yet he notes that even art that criticizes the marketplace for the most part depends "for its enunciation and dissemination on the market system itself."[7] Artists know this, yet seem paradoxically trapped, bound by limits that again suggest that knowing—knowingness—is enough, is itself a kind of action sufficient to politics. To navigate this dilemma, Joselit posits that artists might begin to "embrace markets more broadly and imaginatively as a medium,"[8] though he confesses that he has no idea what this might look like in practice. Artists have struggled with this dilemma by producing ephemeral or performative art that is hard to commodify or by producing works that, by circulating as commodities, themselves comment on the political economy of the sign, as in appropriation art. Using markets as a medium might also differ from forms of institutional or cultural critique that thematize markets by revealing obfuscated or mystified commodity relationships, as, for example, in the work of Hans Haacke. Joselit gestures toward ideas that might even differ from those that undergird the work of artists such as the Yes Men, whose amusing parodies imitate the market-driven rhetoric and appearance of the owners of capital—simulating the appearance of capital without actualizing new relationships of trade and exchange.

But what might it mean for Godard's commodity graveyard to be reanimated—less concerned with objects and their ability to prey on consumers and instead, redirected, postcynically, toward the entire set of market relationships, such as production, consumption, distribution, and exchange? Though Joselit worries that the dilemma he describes may be "easy to solve theoretically but difficult, if not impossible, to resolve practically," he still posits the possibility for a form of critical art practice that uses the inherent relationality of market trade and exchange as a medium. Might it be possible to work through markets without rejecting critiques of the marketplace and without making simple or naive claims to return to a fantastically unmediated version of reality?

I want to look at three projects by the artist Michael Rakowtiz that approach both the marketplace and the war in Iraq with a sensibility that I want to call "postcynical." By taking on the market as an artistic material, Rakowitz is able to consider Iraq without stalling in the position of cynical reason. Part of Rakowitz's wager is that in fact, we are not cynical subjects, knowing what we're doing is complicit with structures of power that harm us, but acting complicitly anyway. Rather, in crucial ways, we also do not know. Although we may be subjects of cynical and simulating governmental and corporate forms of partial knowledge, there are crucial ways in which we are not knowing. And it is from this perspective that this essay asks what kinds of knowledge can be produced by projects such as Rakowitz's Iraq-related artworks, which, by means of very specific new marketplaces, construct and reconstruct actual relations of social interdependency as these are constructed through the circulation of goods and images. Might such a project produce a different kind of knowledge, a knowledge that does not understand itself as a replacement for action, but nevertheless might produce new conditions for action? In this sense, might it be possible to work by way of the marketplace in a spirit that is beyond cynicism? I want to argue that through his refusal to disavow his participation in the marketplace, Rakowitz is able to mobilize a set of possibilities, ideas, and affects that differ crucially from those that are enabled on the one hand by state and corporate elocutions of the public sphere and, on the other, from art practices that disavow their dependence on market relationships for their own articulation.

Michael Rakowitz's project *Return* began during a moment of grocery shopping. At Sahadi's, a Brooklyn grocery story specializing in Middle Eastern imports, Rakowitz noticed a red-and-white can of date syrup, a brand he'd never seen before (fig. 3). "I was paying for it when Charlie Sahadi said, Your mother's going to love this; it's from Baghdad. . . . And he explained that the date syrup is actually pressed in Baghdad, then trucked in plastic vats to Syria, where it is canned in an aluminum facility before going over the border into Lebanon, where it receives a label saying product of Lebanon."[9]

The product spurred Rakowitz's inquiry into an unfolding series of facts and episodes related to Iraqi date production and trade. Dates are historically Iraq's

FIGURE 3 Iraqi date syrup, labeled "product of Lebanon."

most important export crop, a source of pride specific to Iraq's *terroir*, like Cuban tobacco or regional wine cultures. Importing from Iraq should have been possible after the "cessation of hostilities" in May 2003 and the beginning of U.S. efforts to "rebuild" Iraq. In practice, no products labeled "Product of Iraq" had entered the United States since the beginning of the Gulf War in 1990. Instead, products of Iraq such as date syrup, date cookies, and other agricultural products were repackaged and labeled as products of nearby countries such as Lebanon, Syria, and the United Arab Emirates, then shipped for global distribution. Even contemporary commodities may normally function as Marx describes, to mystify or obscure social relationships;[10] Rakowitz reminds us that the commodity is also still a hieroglyphic—one that became newly legible to him in this moment of consumption. This commodity and even its packaging are hardly empty, amnesiac pop signifiers—in fact, they register as overfull of meaning. Inspired by what the bottle of date syrup had revealed, Rakowitz decided to open his own market, with the single intention of importing dates from Iraq.

With the support of the public art organization Creative Time, Rakowitz opened a store. The quixotic mission of his enterprise would almost certainly have been bad business without cultural support, and this freedom to lose money is arguably one of the crucial ways in which Rakowitz was able to restructure market relationships and give them new meanings. He rented a storefront on Atlantic Avenue, a few blocks away from Sahadi's, and named the grocery Davison's and Co., after the import-export company that had been owned by his grandfather, an Iraqi Jew exiled in the 1940s. The store looked and functioned much like every other quotidian market on a street known for its Middle Eastern groceries, but with a reorganized, extremely limited offering of products and services. Rakowitz also offered free shipping to Iraq—another prospect that is generally prohibitively expensive without subsidy from cultural funding. He constituted a public for the piece by constituting a market for the store's goods and services. The storefront filled with customers, both random pedestrian traffic and more deliberate, purposeful visitors responding to Rakowitz's ad in *Aramica*, the leading Arab-American newspaper on the East Coast, or to journalistic coverage of the project eager to eat Iraqi dates or to ship things overseas.

Rakowitz began the process of importing Iraqi dates, and he also stocked his shelves with hybrid products such as the brand of Iraqi date syrup labeled as Lebanese—including items such as Iraqi mamoul date-filled cookies labeled as products of Syria or Saudi Arabia and Kraft cheese packaged for Arabic-speaking countries. A time line on one wall outlined a history of the Iraqi date. Since the date-importing process was lengthy, Rakowitz also offered for sale a substitute while waiting for their arrival—California dates grown from Iraqi seed, filling the large center table of his store. Rakowitz represented the Iraqi seed dates as one example of common forms of what he calls "cultural puncture"[11]—"the enemy within"—expressing as much as any of these hybrid products do the high degree of cultural interpenetration that "patriotic" fantasies of purity deny.

Rakowitz's market became a platform for a shifted conversation about Iraqi dates and Iraq more broadly. Many of the most interesting stories that circulated expressed a direct relationship to Iraq or Iraqis, a vernacular form of news reporting. For example, one customer brought a number of items to ship to Diwaniyah, Iraq, and talked to Rakowitz about why she wanted to ship them:

> Hana told me she needed to send these things because her niece had died of cancer in 2004, leaving behind a newborn baby. Her niece's husband had been a photographer with a studio in town. One evening he was working in the studio when a group of men walked in. They were extremists, and they said that photographing human subjects was unIslamic, and so they executed him. The baby was left an orphan and was taken in by relatives. Hana had gathered all the old toys and clothing and strollers and high chairs she had from raising her own three kids and decided to send it all to Iraq.[12]

These stories that circulated in Davison's and Co. did so in much different registers from the statistical or spectacular ones common to news and entertainment. Hana's account of her niece, for example, cuts against the numbing effects of statistical registers (as in "Eighty-one people were killed today by a car bomb"). It also dedramatizes the spectacle of violence—the convulsive moment of her nephew's execution necessarily returns to the everyday—by grounding it in the persistence of material objects: the need for highchairs and baby clothes.

The point of purchase is also the point of exchange for this representation. In this new discursive terrain, different accounts of contemporary Iraq could emerge, often spoken face to face: customer to customer, customer to Rakowitz, Rakowitz to customer, first-hand or second-hand, as in something like a barber shop or a cocktail party with strangers, with the store's material environment guiding the conversation in a particular direction. These exchanges functioned both as public art and as private enterprise; the exchange of information became part of or at least happened alongside the business transaction of exchanging money for food. Yet technically, the exchange of stories was not part of the market relationship. The new narratives and the flow of information were free, a variation on gossip. Although gossip normally takes place among parties who know each other, here, a sophisticated version of gossip and vernacular exchange among strangers becomes possible because it is structured through the very usual kinds of relationships that a transactional exchange offers. Blurring gossip and public speech by staging a privatized space of commerce enables an unexpected, in-between kind of utterance: gossip among strangers in an alternative sphere that both is and is not like a public sphere.

To begin the business of importing the dates, Rakowitz posted an ad on the Internet site of the Baghdad Business Center and through it made contact with a businessman named Bassam.[13] Bassam's efforts to complete the transaction became part of the store's narrative and would circulate to customers as part of the practice of their shopping. When customers would inquire about the progress of the dates, they would also learn the story of Bassam. Sometimes Bassam's reports would describe his visits to the date farmers or their efforts to design a package. Other times, his e-mails would describe his family fleeing to Jordan after witnessing a café bombing. Bassam's story of "business as usual" narrated the everyday under circumstances of crisis; details of the transaction were necessarily intermixed with stories of his family's personal danger, exile, and refugeeism. A fundamentally commercial form of contact was simultaneously a personal exchange narrated within the store—a relationship that undermined the nonrelationship and nonrecognition promoted by the state and by corporate media formats.

Once these two businesses had put the transaction in motion, farmers began sending pictures of the dates, and the exchanges of commerce circulated as exchanges of information within the store. The stories of the dates themselves also circulated in the store. In the beginning of October 2006, the crop was packaged and loaded onto a truck to drive from Baghdad to Amman, where they could be shipped by air to the United States. The road to Amman was at the time one of the most dangerous routes in the region—and also one of the busiest, overcrowded with Iraqis trying to flee to Jordan. At the border, the truck got caught up in a giant line that consisted mostly of Iraqis being turned away from Jordan, because Jordan had already admitted so many refugees from the recent war in Lebanon. The dates were stuck in the back of the truck, where the temperature could rise as high as 140 degrees. When they finally arrived at the border, they were sent back to Baghdad to be certified by the Ministry of Environment Radiation Protection Center to assure that they bore no trace of depleted uranium. When the certification was complete and the driver returned to the border, the shipment again was not allowed to cross into Jordan, this time for security reasons. He headed north to Syria and dropped the dates off at the airport, where the dates were briefly held by officials asking for bribes.

In Rakowitz's store in Brooklyn, agitated customers were eager for the arrival of the shipment. For example, one Moroccan man became exasperated, telling Rakowitz, "Do you know how long it took me to get to Brooklyn today, with the weekend trains?" When Rakowitz explained the dates had been stuck on the border behind thousands of refugees, the man's face changed, and he said, "The dates are like the people." Thus, the dates both were and were not a simile for people fleeing Iraq—a figure of speech, as well as being literally and substantially themselves, material objects. In this sense, the commodity becomes a different kind of ground for representation, since on one level the dates do not so much function representationally, but simply, substantially, and objectively are. On the other hand, they simultaneously in some degree substitute for the Iraqi people or represent conditions like those of people fleeing Iraq. This shift—between the goal of empathizing with an Iraqi subject and empathizing with an Iraqi object—is a significant one. As Rakowitz puts it, "We only forgive the innocent, and those dates never did anything to anyone."[14] The dates, then, become an unsentimental figure of innocence, one that by extension may enable empathy with conditions endured by Iraqi subjects or at least may enable customers in the store to feel the facts of the war in a new way.

One week later, Syria released the dates, and a representative of Bassam's company went to Damascus to arrange their flight. When he opened the boxes, he found that the skin was peeling away from the dates—though they were fine for human consumption, they looked terrible. The company sold them to a Damascus bakery and found a way to send a much smaller shipment—10 boxes instead of 200—directly from Baghdad.

When the dates finally arrived, Bassam's company had designed an expressive package. In addition to the history-making claim "Product of Iraq" written in bright yellow letters, the package showed a date palm pattern in the background and inset pictures of the Lion of Babylon and the reconstructed replica of the Ishtar Gates (see color plates). Far from being self-signifiying, empty of meaning, or amnesiac, the commodity and its package thus became technologies of remembering and articulating meaning, contextualizing the Iraqi date among other Iraqi national treasures, telling a story of cultural heritage and its loss.

The product, the package, and the reconfigured marketplace that produced and distributed it provided a platform for a redistribution of narrative, meaning, and affect around events and conditions that are routinely narrated differently in dominant cultural forms. Rakowitz's marketplace reorganized a set of relational practices that did something in addition to the (useful) traditional Marxist goal of restoring to a commodity the history of the labor relationships that produced it.[15] Instead, in this case, Rakowitz re-presents the relations of production themselves in order to make something else visible: the construction of the terms of what can be perceived about Iraq within a current U.S. political culture.

SPEAK AS THOUGH QUOTING THE TRUTH

"Stuff happens," said Defense Secretary Donald Rumsfeld in response to the April 2003 looting of Baghdad. Rumsfeld's remarks are the state's response to a violent event. They are citational, directing reference to a popular bumper sticker and away from the concrete referents in Iraq. The 1954 Hague Convention and the Geneva Convention both make clear that the protection of cultural patrimony is the responsibility of an occupying power. Given the considered work of scholars and activists to assess the threat to Iraq's cultural heritage, the U.S. actions can be described only as a knowing facilitation of the looting of Baghdad.[16] Rumsfeld's flippancy correctly summarizes U.S. indifference to Iraq's loss, at best presuming the disposability of Iraq's cultural history and at worst using the destruction of cultural property instrumentally, "as an act of psychological warfare."[17]

For the exhibition *The Invisible Enemy Should Not Exist*, Rakowitz and his studio assistants accessed websites filled with data about the looted objects, then used that information to fashion obsessively precise, dimensionally accurate replicas of the looted artifacts. They built these objects out of commodity packaging—in some cases, the exact same hybrid packages of mislabeled date syrup or mamoul cookies that were for sale at Davison's and Co. They recreated hundreds of small-scale, looted votive objects: small-scale human figures, doll-sized artifacts that may have lost their heads or arms, vases, small animal sculptures (see color plates). Rakowitz and his studio built these objects out of the disposable refuse of global exchange: cardboard boxes of molasses-flavored tobacco, wrappers from mamoul cookies made from "Saudi dates," tea containers packed for export to Irvine, California, boxes of Turkish delight, tins of Moroccan sardines, boxes of dates labeled for European export: "Frische Datteln," "Dattes Frisches Sans Agents." The materials also include Arab-language newspapers and magazines—the trash products of information culture.

The duplicate objects read as uncanny castoffs, resonating somewhere in the tonal realm of mourning and melancholia. The detailed work of replication seems obsessed with communicating as exactly as possible what the lost object is, but ends up exposing the failure to reproduce the object in its original substance. *Invisible Enemy* resonates with the impossibility of the project of copying objects that matter specifically for their authenticity, their provenance, and their auratic irreproducibility. This resonance is further complicated by the original objects—many of which were originally intended as votive sculptures, surrogates for the body that could, by substituting for the subject, make it possible not to turn one's back on the gods. In this sense, Rakowitz's objects are substitutes for votive objects, which are themselves substitutes for Mesopotamian subjects. The relay of signification is clear, grounded. Instead of the unmoored swirl of circulation common to the commodity—out of which the new sculptures are materially formed—the objects suggest a clear chain of reference back to concrete Iraqi artifacts and, before that, to embodied Mesopotamian persons.

Rakowitz again thus mobilizes market relationships as his medium. *The Invisible Enemy* presents its saleable objects in a way that reminds us that our everyday experience of the gallery is fundamentally similar to our everyday experience of the grocery—it is a space of consumption predicated on the possibility of ownership, consumption, possession. The viewer is implicated in the same kind of commodity desire that has transformed the artifacts from cultural-heritage properties into black-market commodities. In this sense, the piece provokes an awareness of the marketplace whether it is installed in a commercial gallery or in a nonprofit museum space. The exhibition's title is a translation of Aj-ibur-shapu, the name of the ancient Babylonian processional way that ran through the Ishtar Gate, which was excavated from 1902 to 1914 by the German archeologist Robert Koldewey and appropriated to Berlin's Pergamon Museum in the early part of the twentieth century—suggesting that the production of value around these one-of-a-kind objects has a long history, even in prewar formations of global exchange. One installation of Rakowitz's exhibition was planned for the Pergamon Museum, with the new substitute objects standing alongside the "real" Ishtar Gate. Ultimately, the museum deemed Rakowitz's work to pose questions about cultural patrimony, ownership, and the legal and illegal market for antiquities so forcefully that the exhibition was cancelled—causing Rakowitz to respond with a full-scale replica of the Ishtar Gate itself at Berlin's Haus der Kulturen der Welt.

Next to each object, Rakowtiz displays accession cards, mimicking the forms of museological guarantees of authenticity that secure an object's value. The cards describe an object's registrarial information: its dimensions, its materials, its origins and provenance. Also included on the cards are quotations from sources relevant to the looting. For example, this quote from Donald Rumsfeld appears on a card next to a vase: "Let me say one thing. The images you are seeing on television you are seeing over and over and over, and it's the same picture of some person walking out of some building with a vase, and you see it 20 times, and you think, 'My goodness, were there that many vases.' (Laughter) Is it possible that there were that many vases in the whole country?"[18]

Here, quotation functions neither as a technique for creating critical distance nor simply as a loose circulation of signs and images that don't land nearby any referent. Instead, relevant fragments of public information are collected in much the same way as other aspects of material culture, acknowledging that the discursive world in which the object exists becomes, meaningfully, part of the object's history—and in the sense of provenance, even a part of its value.

Market relationships are fundamentally relational—we trade and exchange, we fetishize commodities, we experience desire for objects. The so-called military-entertainment complex has worked to produce a unified, racialized, and profoundly distanced relation to people in Iraq as Arab/terrorist others, and that work may be crucial to the state violence enacted in Iraq. Various forms of nonrelationship (for example, "We don't negotiate with terrorists") result in a limit on thinking and feeling toward what Judith Butler has called the "ungrievable" subject.[19] Rakowitz's products ask us to substitute a relationship for a nonrelationship, to engage in the eminently relational practices of commodity desire, fetishism, and exchange. As with the dates in *Return*, the nonhuman objects again provide an unsentimental, but innocent figure that can be desired as a commodity or mourned or introjected as a lost object. The nonhuman commodity/object, as it circulates in the marketplace, must be relationally engaged by the spectator, which then, by a process of substitution, creates a relationship that actively contests dominant forms of nonrelationship.

The sculptures in *The Invisible Enemy* are surrounded by a series of narrative drawings, often installed in a linear time line on the walls of the gallery, mirroring museological displays of information meant to contextualize. The drawings constitute a clear, purposefully didactic, and occasionally eccentric history of Iraq's cultural patrimony and its destruction. Rakowitz's drawings render a version of Koldewey's excavation of the Ishtar Gate, of the destruction caused by Saddam Hussein's expansive reconstruction of that site during the 1980s, of the 1966 opening of the National Museum of Iraq and its collection of great artifacts of the ancient world, of the looting of that museum after the fall of Baghdad, and, most especially, of the efforts of Dr. Donny George, director general of the National Museum, to locate and recover the looted items. Quite unlike Godard's tentative, fragmentary mode of address, which always suggests the possibility of an alternative account, Rakowitz's images and their captions are instead frontal and decisive, organized in a mostly linear story that proceeds from the early part of the twentieth century up through the 2003 looting and its aftermath. If Rakowitz makes fewer gestures toward problematizing the authority of his narrator's account, it may be because he knows his is an oppositional account, in no danger of being understood as the only possible story or even as the dominant story. And it may be, additionally, that the relays of reference created in the piece, while in no way presuming some kind of direct or unmediated access to the real, nevertheless derive their meaning and tonal force from their interest in fact, in the truths of real people and objects, even if those people and objects are now lost or unavailable.

Toward that end, drawings in the show each describe real objects and events with an almost photographic or evidentiary intention—for example, we see an image of the National Museum of Iraq that is almost photorealistically drawn by Rakowitz in a style that suggests mechanical reproduction or printing separations. The captions are laden with facts, such as that the collection had included "the Warka Vase of Uruk, from the fourth millennium B.C., thousands of ancient stone cylinder seals, monumental Assyrian reliefs from royal palaces of the first millennium B.C., and a vast collection of inscribed clay tablets that are among the earliest examples of writing ever found."

Some of the panels appear less directly related to this fact-driven chronological history of Iraq's cultural heritage. Though they are identical in style and in narrative voice, some panels are clearly not generated by a supposedly neutral, chronological method of historical storytelling. For example, in one series, Rakowitz narrates elements from the life of Dr. Donny George in ways that suggest that history is both objectively "out there" and simultaneously constructed through Rakowitz's own rigorous authorial decision making. In this series, Rakowitz describes George's role as director general of the National Museum and creates a whole panel dedicated to showing George taking part in archaeological excavations "in order to avoid Ba'ath Party meetings."[20] These panels are expositional, telling us what happened to Dr. George, and when. They are also rhetorical, figuring Dr. George as reluctantly coexisting with the Ba'ath Party government, placing him nearby the other "innocent" elements that Rakowitz uses to problematize dominant narratives of Iraqi evil.

While these panels are easy to understand as part of these expositional and rhetorical strategies, the next panels are more surprising, almost humorous. Rakowitz depicts Dr. George behind a drum kit, since he had "sidelined as a drummer in a band called 99%—short for 99% of excellence—that specialized in covers of Deep Purple and Pink Floyd songs." The third panel of the series depicts the U.S. band Deep Purple, whose song "Smoke on the Water" "recalls a disastrous fire during a Frank Zappa and the Mothers of Invention concert at a casino in Montreux, Switzerland." The text drawn underneath Rakowitz's image panels describes a disaster that members of Deep Purple watched from "across lake Geneva in a mobile studio on loan from the Rolling Stones."[21] After this description of Dr. George's rock-and-roll experiences, the final two panels return to an expositional logic, showing the bullet that George received as a threat, motivating his flight to Syria in August 2006, and the seal of SUNY Stonybrook, where George accepted a teaching position in December 2006.

Rakowitz's decision to detail George's participation in a Deep Purple cover band could seem like a digression from the more usual facts of George's important work and eventual exile. Instead, the inclusion serves to highlight the high degree of cultural puncture in the worlds of the United States and Iraqi, worlds that have been made to seem falsely separate.

The work that Rakowitz does to remind us of the history of overlapping U.S. and Iraqi cultures also reminds us of the work that has been and must repeatedly be done to create the effect of separate cultures. Although these ideological effects have come to seem natural, Rakowitz encourages us to remember the labors at stake in making this so, giving the lie to hard-fought neoconservative efforts at cultural separation, ranging from the crass ideological force of naming an "Axis of Evil," as George W. Bush did in his 2002 State of the Union address, down to the daily work of policing culture, as in what George Lipsitz describes as the "new patriotism" of the 1980s. For example, in 1988, Lynne Cheney, then director of the National Endowment for the Humanities and wife of later Iraq War architect Dick Cheney, called for the replacement of social-science textbooks stressing "vacuous concepts" such as "the interdependence among people" with textbooks filled with "the magic of myths, fables, and tales of heroes. "[22] Rakowitz's panels function as the inverse of Cheney's platform—as a textbook designed to reverse the new patriotism, replacing its myths with fact-based narratives of cultural interdependence.

These drawings bring a specific narrative to bear on the exhibition's objects. The objects resonate with affective force, but with no single, obvious projective target for our identification. Instead, they propose a series of commodity desires and introjected losses related to the original objects (and commodities) for which Rakowitz's objects substitute. These objects also participate in an art marketplace in a way that reflects on and highlights the black market in antiquities that makes this work necessary. Within this narrative framework, the show's drawn panels

FIGURE 4 Dr. Donny George gives a tour of recreated antiquities in "The Invisible Enemy Should Not Exist," 2007.

allow Donny George to become a kind of protagonist in this story of lost objects. The drawings engage operations of identification and empathy for Dr. George in a realist vein that operates alongside the subjective pulls produced by the exhibition's objects. Because the relationships that the objects and images produce are so unexpected and on some level unthinkable or unfeelable within the dominant terms of U.S. discourse, the objects and images have the effect of reorienting affect and reconditioning the sensible. Viewers are allowed to feel the facts of the war in a fully unexpected way when they encounter through a photograph Dr. George giving tours of the only objects that remained available to him—Rakowitz's surrogate artifacts (fig. 4).

LIVING IN MODERN SOCIETY IS LIKE LIVING IN A COMIC STRIP

If Rakowitz understands the marketplace as a medium, then it follows that eBay is an important site for research. At the end of 2007, Rakowitz noticed that a U.S. soldier was selling a helmet from the Iraqi paramilitary unit Sadaam Fedayeen on eBay (fig. 5). Rakowitz found that these objects and other spoils of war are

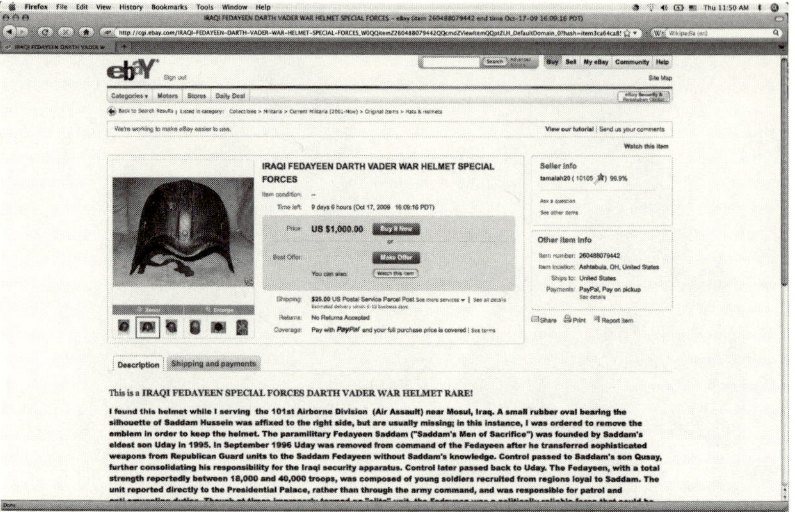

FIGURE 9 Fedayeed Helmet for sale on eBay.

routinely offered there, with soldiers assuming the role of broker. One soldier's statement read almost like a museum accession card, describing the quality, condition, and history of the object as it offered the helmet for auction under the heading "Iraqi Fedayeen Darth Vader War Helmet Special Forces."

> I found this helmet while I was serving the 101st Airborne Division (Air Assault) near Mosul, Iraq. A small rubber oval bearing the silhouette of Saddam Hussein was affixed to the right side, but are usually missing; in this instance, I was ordered to remove the emblem in order to keep the helmet. The paramilitary Fedayeen Saddam ("Saddam's Men of Sacrifice") was founded by Saddam's eldest son Uday in 1995. Uday was a fan of the Star Wars movies and thus the resemblance to the helmet worn by Darth Vader. . . . This is a GREAT DEAL! I also have other products listed, Please check them out.[23]

The commodity potential of this object, a Fedayeen helmet, was clear to the soldier who brokered it, as was the relevance of its condition, provenance, and history to its value. Equally clear to the soldier was the clear influence of U.S. popular culture. Rakowitz's exhibition *The Worst Condition Is to Pass Under a Sword Which Is Not One's Own*[24] is a sprawling, associative exploration of the history and meaning of this helmet and of related objects and stories, all of which underline the fact of cultural puncture and exchange and undermine the purity of the distinctness of U.S. and Iraqi identity upon which the "new patriotism" depends.

The show's use of the marketplace as a medium is shifted from the previous works, which in very direct senses are sited in literal marketplaces that sell objects. The gallery is still a marketplace for *The Worst Condition*, but the works in the show suggest a different mode of address. In *The Worst Condition*, what begins as a consideration of the Fedayeen helmet as a commodity follows a concrete chain of referentially grounded, research-driven facts to look at classically ideological images, objects, and narratives of both U.S. and Iraqi culture. The work, which can literally be circulated as a comic book or as pages in an art magazine at the same time as being offered for sale in the gallery, insists on treating the commodity-sign as material object, grounded in its on-the-ground referents and in its own role as such, possessed of direct material force. What does it mean that the costume from a George Lucas movie circulates not only as a sign, in the 1977 film *Star Wars*, and not just as a part of an ideological apparatus, but literally as a helmet, made of real material stuff by the Iraqi regime, a functional part of a repressive state apparatus?

Rakowitz considers Uday Hussein's Fedayeen helmet design as a cultural expression, along with many other examples of the ruling family's own forms of cultural production. Among these, he includes Saddam Hussein's monumental sculpture *Swords of Qādisīyah*, also known as *Hands of Victory* and *Victory Arch*, as well as the romance novel authored by Saddam Hussein in 2000, *Zabiba and the King*. Rakowitz implicitly and explicitly looks at the relationships between these cultural projects and the violent political projects in which the Husseins engaged. In this way, Rakowitz's exhibition is striking in its methodological similarity to the work of political theorist Michael Rogin in his 1987 study *Ronald Reagan, The Movie*.[25] In it, Rogin looks at the ways that cultural stories participated in the formation of Reagan as a subject, at the consequent effects of those stories on Reagan's political actions, and at the ultimate collapse of the differences between "us" and "them" that Reagan's thinking aspired to keep separated. Comparably, Rakowitz theorizes particular stories and images, showing their effects on the subject formation of Uday and Saddam Hussein and other relevant political actors, and considers their political force, at least partly, as an effect of the cultural force of these stories. And he does so by thinking by and through commodities—including cultural and entertainment commodities as well as their material effects. As in Rogin's work, the circulating images and products that Rakowitz considers break down any clear distinction between "us" and "them"—in this case, the U.S. and Iraq, between "the force" and "the dark side."

As he did in *The Invisible Enemy*, Rakowitz creates a sculptural replica, this time of Hussein's *Swords of Qādisīyah / Hands of Victory*. The original arch, as one of Rakowitz's accompanying drawings explains, was conceived by Saddam Hussein

> to commemorate Iraq's victory over Iran. Giant bronze casts of his hands wield the swords of Quaddisiya, which belonged to Sa'adibn Abi Waqqas, commander of the army that defeated the Persians in 636 A.D. The swords, made from steel melted down from the weapons of slain Iraqis, rise above the helmets of vanquished Iranians, which cascade around the base of each hand. The swords were cast by H+H Metalform, a German company partially acquired by Iraq to supply its ballistic missile program.[26]

Here, Rakowitz explicitly thematizes the state's aesthetic and cultural production. His re-creation of Saddam Hussein's sculpture is fashioned of papier-mâché made from the pages of Hussein's own romance novel, *Zabiba and the King*. Rakowitz mimics Hussein's gesture of melting down the helmets of vanquished Iranians by making his own replica helmets out of melted-down GI Joe toys—themselves products designed to circulate among American children and facilitate an interest in stories of military power. He also collects found examples of U.S. soldiers and military contractors photographing themselves with the *Hands of Victory*, which accumulate into a seemingly infinite wallpaper of examples of everyday people repurposing Hussein's sculpture toward their own meanings (fig. 6)—often nationalistically American in their own claims of victory, often also touristically goofy in a way that belies the military force that secures their playfulness.

As in *The Invisible Enemy Should Not Exist*, Rakowitz takes pains to keep the drawings grounded in researched fact, in "real" historical referents. Tonally, the exhibition's drawings partly function as "proof," documenting the circulation of other cultural products and narratives through the *Hands of Victory*. For example, one series shows the ways in which the sculpture is itself a copy or visual echo of Boris Vallejo's poster for the 1981 *Star Wars* sequel *The Empire Strikes Back*. Rakowitz's panels offer a formal comparison between Vallejo's image of Darth Vader holding crossed light sabers in each of his fists and drawings of the similarly crossed swords of the *Victory Arch*. Rakowitz offers detectivelike "proof" of the influence of *Star Wars* and science fiction fantasy culture, for example, by rendering an elaborate drawing of the first Iraqi screening of *Star Wars* at the Ba'ath Party headquarters, which, he writes, "most likely took place in March of 1980, nearly three years after its original U.S. release."

Facts thus serve as evidence for subjective experience. If facts have force, and we know for a fact that *Star Wars* was screened in the palace, what, exactly, did that screening do? We know that ultimately, a Fedayeen helmet was inspired. In a pair of Rakowitz's panels, Luke Skywalker stands against a desert landscape on the planet Tatooine, contemplating his destiny. In the next, Uday stands against a desert landscape near the palace in Baghdad. Rakowitz captions the image, "Did Uday, like every other boy of his generation, ever recreate that scene in his

FIGURE 6 Michael Rakowitz, from "The worst condition is to pass under a sword which is not one's own," 2010 (courtesy the artist and Lombard-Fried Gallery).

mind—standing outside his parents' house, the sun setting in the background, waiting for the future?" What happened in between the known *Star Wars* screening and the fact of Uday's design of the Vaderesque Fedayeen uniform? Rakowitz cannot know for sure, but he can observe the comparable landscapes, the imperial palaces, and the Oedipal dramas that the two figures unarguably have in common. In this way, Rakowitz shows us the profound ways that subjectivity itself—even the subjectivity of iconic political figures—is in part fashioned by the marketplace circulation of images, icons, and stories, and by extension, so is politics.

Other postcynical artists have also made efforts to uncover or imagine the subjective forces acting upon and within the iconic images of public figures who see themselves as history's actors. For example, Paul Chan describes a method of "radical empathy"[27] in works such as his 2002 video *RE: The Operation*. The unexpected forms of empathy he uses are precisely about refusing cynicism—willfully producing compassion for figures for whom modernist critical tradition might more strongly suggest dispassion and disidentification. In *RE: The Operation*, Chan begins with the fictional conceit that administration officials are physically located in the theater of war in Afghanistan. Chan uses public information to profile the members of George W. Bush's cabinet, then speculates wildly to project upon them imagined interior lives, creating a series of love letters to and from the public figures. For example, he creates this love letter from George W. Bush to Laura:

> I'm sorry I've not written you sooner. I miss you and the dogs. It feels like we are always in the middle of the operation, never the end. Maybe the end will never come. I don't know. I miss everything, even the wind. There is no wind here and when it does blow it brings only sand with the smell of people starving. I miss the clean wind back home. I miss you.[28]

Chan's projections ask the viewer to compare this imagined, intimate, interior life with existing discursive knowledge of this public figure. Is it possible that this figure could be poetic? Is it possible that he can smell people starving? Or that this smell would bother him? These extrapolations of empathy, feeling, and sentiment are structured to make clear that they are, precisely, speculative and attribute to the public figure's degrees of personal intimacy and intellectual sophistication that the public record does not suggest:

> How does one fight evil with a kind of terror that doesn't make one evil himself? I feel evil from the work and dirty from the pleasure of passivity that duty demands. Dick quotes Robespierre, saying virtue without terror is impotent. But is terror the only faith for justice? Didn't Robespierre become a kind of terror without justice? Isn't this what they call fearful symmetry?
>
> I love you. Send more jerky.[29]

In a comparable flight of compassionate speculation, Taylor Mac's *The Palace of the End* is a delirious reading of the actually existing romance novels authored by Saddam Hussein and Lynne Cheney. Mac sings his "romance epic song" while sitting on a stool, wearing a glittery, trash-influenced drag ensemble and playing his ukulele. His song describes the plot of the lesbian romance novel that really was written by Lynne Cheney and compares it to *Zabiba and the King*, the Saddam Hussein romance novel that serves as building material for Rakowitz's replica of the *Victory Arch*. Mac riffs off of these cultural documents, and after several verses of literary interpretation, Mac builds his own fiction on the cultural ground laid by Cheney and Hussein. In Mac's account, Lynne Cheney is a spectator at Saddam Hussein's execution. He sings, "Lynne is going for a photo op for a symbolic gesture of America being on top. She expects to be pleased when she sees Saddam die so violently." Mac's plot builds to a moment of eye contact between them at Hussein's execution: "But when she sits down across from the protective glass Saddam and Lynne make eye contact. And Lynne, caught off guard, allows her eyes to tell the story. All about her husband, Dick Cheney, and how he's away in an undisclosed location."[30]

Mac imagines a talk-show version of a therapeutic narrative for Cheney and Hussein, both victims of unfortunate Oedipal dramas and deserving of our projective sympathies: "Saddam never could give love cause Saddam never could get love. Lynne Cheney never could get love, so, Lynne Cheney never could give love. So Lynne saw Saddam, and Saddam saw Lynne, as he breathed the poison gas in. Lynne repents and falls in love with him."[31]

Both Mac and Chan offer examples of speculative projects that ask the viewer to identify with public images or historical persons, but they go beyond Brecht's characterization of a "crude" empathy that would use easy forms of identification to assimilate the other's experience into the self.[32] Instead, their works draw from the raw material of information encoded in corporate forms of public discourse and entertainment products, but they ask the viewer to overidentify with that information in such an impossible way that it begins to resemble disidentification.

Rakowitz's panels often suggest a similar degree of surprising identification, with the additional element that they are generally not speculative, but rather are anchored in fact in ways that are often hard to believe, but true. In one series, Rakowitz displays a drawing of a photograph of a soldier standing in front of the *Victory Arch* with his hands positioned to appear as if he is holding the giant bronze swords, his uniform displaying his last name, Slaughter (fig. 7). From this image, Rakowitz leaps to a consideration of the World Wrestling Federation character named Sergeant Slaughter and details the 1990s WWF narrative in which Slaughter teamed up with an Iranian wrestler (Hossain Khosrow) and an Iraqi wrestler (General Andan) to dramatize the Gulf War conflict in the context of pro wrestling. Rakowtiz's narrative unfolds the true story of the various ethnic identities each was asked to play within the WWF, then goes on to unfold the incredible backstory of Andan, who, after an early wrestling career in London as "The Shiek," was in 1969 summoned by Saddam Hussein himself to bring wrestling to Iraq, became hugely popular in his home country, and was then later forced to flee Iraq over Hussein's jealousy.

In addition to the consideration of celebrity icons and other kinds of well-known public information, *The Worst Condition* also mines stories that are part of the public record, yet remain largely unknown. For example, one narrative thread that spreads across several panels tells the story of "boy rocket scientist" Gerry Bull (fig. 8). The story begins on October 30, 1938, when "ten-year old Gerald Bull heard H. G. Wells's *The War of the Worlds* on the radio."[33] Rakowitz's narrative shows the influence of science fiction on Bull, who became Canada's chief

FIGURE 7 Michael Rakowitz, *Strike the Empire Back* series, 2009 (courtesy the artist and Lombard-Fried Gallery).

FIGURE 8 Michael Rakowitz, *Strike the Empire Back* series, 2009 (courtesy the artist and Lombard-Fried Gallery).

aerodynamicist, was commissioned by Canada and the United States to design a supergun, which became Project HARP. Project HARP was a giant gun that Bull had dreamed about since his encounter with Jules Verne. Though Project HARP was a failure, his ideas were revived in the 1980s by the Reagan administration in its *Star Wars* antiballistic-weapons project. Bull also went on to spend time in prison for an illegal weapons project for South Africa and eventually went to work directly for Saddam Hussein on a supergun project known as Project Babylon. Thus, cultural fantasies begun by Wells in the 1930s become materially realized as the concrete tools of repressive force. Rakowitz is at pains not simply to expose ideology that operates through entertainment narratives, but rather to elaborate the concrete, material effects of immaterial fantasy.

The story of Gerald Bull, while public information, is not generally well known, even though it adds a great deal to better-known accounts of Iraq's development of weapons of mass destruction. In this sense, Rakowitz is using details that are associatively linked to the material commodity with which he began, allowing those associations to bring to light forgotten or repressed aspects of history. These aspects of his work can be compared to that of other research-based artists such as Marc Lombardi, an artist whose work draws out the open secrets of public information that are always available, knowable, and yet remain generally and widely unknown because they don't circulate as official state accounts or as wide-market broadcast stories in news or entertainment.[34] Lombardi's drawing about the same Gerry Bull—*Gerry Bull, Space Research Corporation, and Armcor of Pretoria South Africa ca. 1972–1980*—crafts an elaborate flow chart that focuses less on Iraq or on biographical detail, but painstakingly maps out two years of relationships between arms developers in the United States, Canada, South Africa, and Israel. Like his other drawings, Lombardi's Gerry Bull drawing is imageless, faceless, a brilliant graphical rendering of public information that attempts no subjective treatment of Gerald Bull's character or subjectivity. Rakowitz's treatment of the same subject does a comparable amount of informational work about Bull's relationship to a later period, connecting the dots between science fiction, Gerry Bull, Reagan-era weapons projects, and the Iraqi regime. Both artists carefully reconstruct a series of relationships in a way that actually shifts the public account of what is known, and in this way, no presupposition or cynical stance of knowingness could make sense of them, because it is the works themselves that present the new knowledge, which, though already available, was previously not acknowledged as known. In Rakowtiz's panels, Bull is also embodied, given a face and a biography, and narrated as someone personally subject to the influence of Cold War ideology and science fiction entertainment, just as he is professionally subject to competing governmental claims and, ultimately, shadowy corporate or state assassination.

In this way, Rakowitz constantly refers to both fact and fiction as having realness—that Saddam Hussein and *Star Wars*, Jerry Bull and *The War of the Worlds*, while not all equally material in their substance, nevertheless circulate in the world and exert force. His narratives thus reconsider the discursive forces that constitute and police reality, which for Rakowitz is never located outside of ideology, narrative, or representation. By doing so, his works resist earlier suspicions of the critical potential of artwork that insists on its grounding in real social referents. At an earlier moment, such works that take an intense interest in their "content" were sometimes characterized of "privileging of the signified and . . . jettisoning the work of the signifier,"[35] as dangerously unmediated, or as somehow claiming to be "in reality, in truth, not in ideology."[36] In the present moment, it is only increasingly clear that the state and corporate logic that critical art is meant to criticize is itself often simulationist, citational, endlessly self-reflexive—that is to say, dangerous for precisely the opposite reasons, privileging the signifier and jettisoning the work of the signified and, at times, perhaps even the existence of some kind of material referent in reality.

Perhaps it is against this fundamentally cynical formation of government and corporate action that Barak Obama was elected, with his capacities to perform hope and reclaim the idea that words have meaning—whether or not he can or wants actually to shift these modes of state and corporate behavior and address. If governmental and corporate interests have only increasingly appropriated the strategies of historical critical modernism, perhaps these other, postcynical ways of negotiating realness and reality can be acknowledged as doing something other than short-circuiting signification. In this and in his other Iraq War projects, Rakowtiz is renegotiating the terms of what is legible, visible, and sensible about the current U.S. war in Iraq. In his 1967 film, Godard worried that the landscape was becoming littered with graphical advertisements and brand-name commodity logos and images, collapsing the distinction between word, image, the built environment, and reality. Melancholy, he whispers, "living in modern life is like living in a comic book." Rakowitz doesn't argue against this, but instead of reiterating this knowing observation, he takes on the form of the comic book itself and recirculates the images and icons that count as entertainment and political commodities, reshaping both the form and the content of the public record. By recognizing and working by means of marketplaces—a grocery store or a gallery, even electronic and mass-cultural marketplaces such as eBay, comics, and other spaces of exchange, Rakowitz uses packaging and pop elements to work toward a postcynical goal. Instead of the amnesiac form that modernist criticality might suggest, Rakowitz instantiates the possibility to think and feel the war differently.

POSTSCRIPT, 2011

In the time that has passed since the completion of this article in 2009, some changes have taken place in the historical world that is touched by Michael Rakowitz's works. It seems important to note a few developments that, like the artworks I describe here, have also created substantive shifts in the ways that what Donald Rumsfeld called the "knowns" and "unknowns" of the war in Iraq are shaped.

In April 2010, the Internet-based activist organization Wikileaks began to amplify their large-scale experiment in public information. Wikileaks undertook the publication of a series of documents about the U.S. wars in Afghanistan and Iraq. Their projects included the April 2010 release of the *Collateral Murder* video, showing Iraqi journalists being killed by an Apache helicopter, the July 2010 release of a group of 76,900 documents about the war in Afghanistan, the October 2010 release of over four hundred thousand documents in the *Iraq War Logs*, and the November 2010 release of diplomatic cables now commonly known as Cablegate. Mirroring forms of public cynicism, each Wikileaks release raised questions about whether the documents contained new information or simply documented what everyone already suspected. For example, when the *New York Times* published the Iraq materials, they claimed that the documents "provide no earthshaking revelations,"[37] even while acknowledging that the documents reveal or confirm important facts about the use of private contractors, Iraqi civilian casualties, and the use of torture and other abusive practices. That is to say, the revelation of important information is here framed as *already known*. By extension, the releases raised the question of whether the exposure of information would in fact create change, since the cynical stance forced upon the public was always to believe that governments knew the things they were revealed to have known. A full analysis of the Wikileaks releases is beyond the scope of my essay here, but it is clear that Wikileaks in some ways does shift the public stance of cynical knowingness by changing the terrain of what is known and by whom.

In March 2011, Dr. Donny George passed away at the age of sixty. Michael Rakowitz acknowledged George's passing with an e-mail tribute, crediting George with inspiring *The Invisible Enemy Should Not Exist* and highlighting George's courageous work in protecting Iraq's cultural heritage. The news of George's death also adds another layer of loss to a project that is itself about loss—just as there was a moment when Donny George was able to give tours only of Rakowtiz's surrogate artifacts, now, the tours of these surrogates must also be given by a surrogate for George. In his tribute to George, Rakowitz included this anecdote:

> In 1987, [George] was head of a field expedition in Babylon when Saddam Hussein paid a visit. "I met him and took him around. He was very calm. He was just listening. In one of the museums there, we had some inscriptions translated. In one, Nebuchadnezzar was saying that one of the gods had sent him to protect 'the black-headed people.' Saddam said, 'You should change that.' And I said, 'No, sir, it's scientific, we can't change it, this is exactly as it was said. It doesn't mean that people are black, it means "all the people." Because if you have a crowd of Iraqis, all you see are their black heads.' He wanted to change it to 'all the people.' And I said no. Later, one of his bodyguards took me aside and said, 'How can you say no to the leader?' And I said, 'It's science.' And he said, 'Well, good. God bless you. Otherwise, you would have vanished.'"[38]

This story, of George standing up to Saddam Hussein by forcing the recognition of "science," underscores the shared commitment of George and Rakowitz to the idea that empires cannot, in fact, make their own reality.

In October 2011, the United States announced that it would withdraw its troops in Iraq before the end of 2011.[39] While troops had been expected to remain in Iraq well into 2012, the withdrawal was directly hastened by the release of the

FIGURE 9 Michael Rakowitz, *Spoils*, 2011 (courtesy the artist and Lombard Fried).

Wikileaks cables; Iraqis refused to grant legal protections to U.S. soldiers after Wikileaks revealed the direct involvement of U.S. ground troops in the 2006 deaths of Iraqi civilians, including children.[40]

In September 2011, Michael Rakowitz opened a new project, *Spoils*, at the New York restaurant Park Avenue Autumn. *Spoils* interrogates the marketplace and uses it as the medium of the work in new ways. To experience the piece, a consumer of culture must order a special dish created by Rakowtiz and chef Kevin Lasko (fig. 9). Made from Iraqi date syrup and American venison, this "culinary intervention" is served on dishware from Saddam Hussein's palace—which itself included Wedgewood china from the palace of King Faisal II. The dishware suggests at once a bitter sense of the material spoils of war and the constant contest to control the meanings and symbols that swirled around Saddam Hussein's government. The piece acknowledges the china collectors from whom the plates are borrowed—and acknowledges them not just for their market position as owners of the spoils of war, but as organizers of meaning, "taking ownership of the symbols of his regime." Intriguingly, the plates were acquired from two different sources—Usama Alkhazraji, an Iraqi refugee now living in Michigan, and an active-duty U.S. Infantry soldier, Lorenzo Luna.[41] Like the other works that I describe here, *Spoils* emphasizes the idea of cultural puncture, combining the traditional taste of Iraqi date syrup with American ingredients and serving them to the customer in a way that the "complicated, even bitter history of the dishware" cannot be ignored. And in ways that arguably take Rakowitz's experiment with the marketplace one step further, the viewer becomes more than a viewer, but is positioned by the mode of address of the artwork as the most literal kind of consumer. Rakowitz reminds us that for now, the articulation of meaning rarely escapes the marketplace, and just as Rakowitz refuses to disavow these market relationships, so is the consumer of *Spoils* also implicated.

NOTES

1. Jean-Luc Godard, *2 or 3 Things I Know about Her* (1967).
2. Peter Sloterdijk, *Critique of Cynical Reason*, trans. Michael Eldred (Minneapolis: University of Minnesota Press, 1987), p. 5.
3. *Ibid*., p. 6.
4. This claim was perhaps most provocatively offered by Jean Baudrillard, whose account of this asymmetry, titled *The Gulf War Did Not Take Place*, applied his theories of simulation to the 1990 military action. See Jean Baudrillard, *The Gulf War Did Not Take Place*, trans. Paul Patton (Bloomington: Indiana University Press, 1995).
5. It can be intriguing to think about what kinds of cynicism and earnestness are performed by Donald Rumsfeld's remark in response to a question about whether there is intelligence linking WMDs to terrorist organizations: "There are known knowns. These are things we know that we know. There are known unknowns. That is to say, there are things that we know we don't know. But there are also unknown unknowns. There are things we don't know we don't know." Here, it seems that the spokesman for the government is simultaneously acknowledging a kind of cynical knowingness and asserting an earnest, and possibly disingenuous, anti-simulationist stance, acknowledging the importance of an external reality while at the same time creating a space in which to dissimulate new "knowledge" and create its own "knowns." U.S. Department of Defense, News Transcript, February 12, 2002.
6. Ron Suskind, "Without a Doubt: What Makes Bush's Presidency So Radical—Even to Some Republicans—Is His Faith-Infused Certainty in Uncertain Times," *New York Times Magazine*, October 17, 2004.
7. David Joselit, "Market Dissent," *October* 123 (Winter 2008), p. 88.
8. *Ibid*.
9. Liza Johnson, "Enemy Kitchen: An Interview with Michael Rakowitz," *Gastronomica* 7.3 (Summer 2007), p. 13.
10. Karl Marx, "The Fetishism of Commodity and Its Secret," from *Capital*, vol. 1, in Robert C. Tucker (ed.), *The Marx-Engels Reader* (New York: Norton, 1978), p. 322.
11. Steven Winn, "Michael Ratkowitz's 'Enemy Kitchen' Breaks Down Cultural Barriers," *San*

Francisco Chronicle, December 27, 2007, http://articles.sfgate.com/2007-12-27/entertainment/17274415_1_michael-rakowitz-iraqi-flag-kubba.

12. Johnson, "Enemy Kitchen," p. 13.
13. The businessman asked Rakowitz not to use his real name, and "Bassam" is not it.
14. Michael Rakowitz, unpublished interview with the author, November 2009.
15. Perhaps ironically, this critical practice has enjoyed increased visibility and circulation through recent forms of the marketing of organic and free-trade products. The uncovering of these mystified relationships then creates added value for foods whose production histories are known.
16. Zainab Bahrani, "Looting and Conquest," *Nation*, May 14, 2003, http://www.thenation.com/article/looting-and-conquest.
17. *Ibid.*
18. Donald Rumsfeld, as cited in Michael Rakowitz, *The Invisible Enemy Should Not Exist* (2007).
19. Judith Butler, *Precarious Life* (New York: Verso, 2004), p. 36.
20. Here, for example, Rakowitz is careful to position Donny George alongside the other figures of the innocent he creates.
21. Rakowitz, *Ballad of Donny George*, from the exhibition *The Invisible Enemy Should Not Exist*, 2007.
22. See George Lipsitz, *The Possessive Investment in Whiteness* (Philadelphia: Temple University Press, 2002), p. 82, citing Lynne Cheney, "Report" in *On Campus* 7.3 (November 1987), and Lynne Cheney, "Report to the President, the Congress, and the American People," *Chronicle of Higher Education* 35.4 (September 21, 1988), pp. A18–19.
23. Offering on eBay, "Iraqi Fedayeen Darth Vader War Helmet Special Forces," October 17, 2009.
24. This title quotes the invitation card for the opening ceremony for the sculpture *Swords of Qādisīyah / Hands of Victory* commemorating Saddam Hussein's declaration of victory over Iran in the Iran-Iraq war.
25. Michael Rogin, *Ronald Regan, The Movie, and Other Episodes in Political Demonology* (Berkeley: University of California Press, 1987).
26. Text from Rakowitz drawing *More Machine than Man*, in the *Worst Condition* series.
27. George Baker, "An Interview with Paul Chan," *October* 123 (Winter 2008), p. 212.
28. Paul Chan, *RE: The Operation* (2002).
29. *Ibid.*
30. Taylor Mac, *The Palace of the End* (2009), http://www.youtube.com/watch?v=6Q1-K1ht984.
31. *Ibid.*
32. Brecht describes this mistake in "A Short Organum for the Theater," writing that "it is the crudest form of empathy when the actor simply asks: what should I be like if this were to happen to me? What would it look like if I were to say this and do that?—instead of asking: have I ever heard anybody saying this and doing that?" John Willet, *Brecht on Theater* (London: Methuen, 1957), p. 195. I am influenced by Jill Bennett's work on empathy, which "moves away from the traps of 'crude empathy' to describe art that, by virtue of its specific affective capacities, is able to exploit forms of embodied perception in order to promote forms of critical inquiry." She writes, "The conjunction of affect and critical awareness may be understood to constitute the basis of an empathy grounded not in affinity (*feeling for* another insofar as we can imagine *being* that other) but on a *feeling for* another that entails an encounter with something irreducible and different, often inaccessible." Jill Bennett, *Empathic Vision: Affect,*

Trauma, and Contemporary Art (Stanford: Stanford University Press, 2005), p. 10.

33. Drawing, Michael Rakowitz, *The Worst Condition* series.

34. After 9/11, FBI agents even travelled to the Whitney Museum to consult one of Lombardi's drawings, *BCCI-ICIC &FAB, 1972–91*. Lombardi's drawing was made exclusively from public information, but was so assiduously researched and so unusually reorganized that it was able to play a role in this international version of police work. Robert Hobbs, *Marc Lombardi: Global Networks* (New York: Independent Curators International, 2003), p.11.

35. Rosalind Krauss, in Hal Foster, et al., "The Politics of the Signifier: A Conversation on the Whitney Biennial," *October* 66 (Autumn 1993), p. 21.

36. Hal Foster, *Return of the Real* (Cambridge, MA: The MIT Press, 1996), p. 174. Ondine Chavoya outlines arguments offered in a different context as critics reacted to the 1993 Whitney Biennial, UCLA's 1990 exhibition *Chicano Art: Resistance and Affirmation*, and other efforts of artists, especially artists of color, to negotiate signification and reference to the real. Chavoya suggests that these critics' lines of reasoning tempts "a strategy of social abjection wherein social content is attributed to the site of the 'real,'" and is then "rendered unspeakable." Chavoya reminds us that "in this sense, the real is relegated to the status of the unsymbolizable, but as Judith Butler has argued, that which is positioned as the real 'is always relative to a linguistic domain that authorizes and produces the foreclosure, and achieves that effect through producing and policing a set of constitutive exclusions.'" Judith Butler, *Bodies That Matter* (London: Routledge, 1993), cited in Ondine Chavoya, "Orphans of Modernism: Chicano Art and Urban Space in Southern California," Ph.D. dissertation, University of Rochester, 2007, pp. 121–22.

37. "The Iraq Archive: The Strands of a War," *New York Times*, October 23, 2010, p. A1, http://www.nytimes.com/2010/10/23/world/middleeast/23intro.html.

38. Nina Burleigh, "From Baghdad to the L.I.E.," *New York*, January 14, 2007, http://nymag.com/news/intelligencer/26585.

39. Mark Landler, "Last U.S. Soldiers To Exit From Iraq In 2011, Obama Says," *New York Times*, October 21, 2011, p. A1, http://www.nytimes.com/2011/10/22/world/middleeast/president-obama-announces-end-of-war-in-iraq.html.

40. CNN Wire Staff, "Obama: Iraq War Will Be Over by Year's End; Troops Coming Home," CNN U.S., October 22, 2011, http://articles.cnn.com/2011-10-21/middleeast/world_meast_iraq-us-troops_1_iraq-war-operation-new-dawn-iraq-and-afghanistan-veterans?_s=PM:MIDDLEEAST.

41. *Spoils* exhibition materials, 2011.

Contributors

BARBARA ABRASH is an independent film producer, writer, and curator with a focus on social-issue documentary. She is coauthor (with Jessica Clark) of *Social Justice Documentary: Designing for Impact* (2011).

NEGAR AZIMI is senior editor of *Bidoun*, an award-winning arts and culture magazine. Her essays have been published in *Artforum*, *Frieze*, *Harper's*, *The Nation*, *Slate*, and the *New York Times Magazine*, among other venues. She studied international relations and politics at Stanford and Harvard and is a lapsed doctoral student in anthropology at Columbia University.

ARIELLA AZOULAY teaches visual culture and political philosophy. Among her recent books are *Civil Imagination: The Political Ontology of Photography, from Palestine to Israel: A Photographic Record of Destruction and State Formation, 1947–1950* (2012) and *The Civil Contract of Photography* (Zone, 2008). She is the curator of the exhibitions *Potential History* (2012, STUK/Artefact, Leuven), *Untaken Photographs* (2010, Igor Zabel Award, Moderna Galerija, Lublin; Zochrot, Tel Aviv), *Architecture of Destruction* (Zochrot, Tel Aviv), *Everything Could Be Seen* (Um El Fahem Gallery of Art), and a director of documentary films, including *Civil Alliance, Palestine, 47–48* (2012), *I Also Dwell among Your Own People: Conversations with Azmi Bishara* (2004), and *The Food Chain* (2004).

AMAHL BISHARA is an assistant professor of anthropology at Tufts University, where she teaches and conducts research on the relationship between the media, the state, and human rights, especially in the context of the Israeli-Palestinian conflict. Her forthcoming book on the production of U.S. news in the West Bank during the second intifada is entitled *Back Stories: U.S. News Production and Palestinian Politics*.

JUDITH BUTLER is the Maxine Elliot Professor in the Departments of Rhetoric and Comparative Literature at the University of California, Berkeley. She is the author of *Subjects of Desire: Hegelian Reflections in Twentieth-Century France* (1987), *Gender Trouble: Feminism and the Subversion of Identity* (1990), *Bodies That Matter: On the Discursive Limits of "Sex"* (1993), *The Psychic Life of Power: Theories of Subjection* (1997), *Excitable Speech: A Politics of the Performative* (1997), *Antigone's Claim: Kinship between Life and Death* (2000), *Precarious Life: Powers of Violence and Mourning* (2004), *Undoing Gender* (2004), *Giving an Account of Oneself* (2005), *Who Sings the Nation-State?: Language, Politics, Belonging* (with Gayatri Spivak, 2007), *Frames of War: When Is Life Grievable?* (2009), and *Is Critique Secular?* (cowritten with Talal Asad, Saba Mahmood, and Wendy Brown, 2009).

EDUARDO CADAVA teaches in the Department of English at Princeton University, where he also is an associate member of the Department of Comparative Literature, the School of Architecture, the Program in Latin American Studies, and the Center for African American Studies. He is the author of *Words of Light: Theses on the Photography of History* (1997) and *Emerson and the Climates of History* (1997) and coeditor of *Who Comes After the Subject?* (with Peter Connor and Jean-Luc Nancy, 1991), *Cities without Citizens* (with Aaron Levy, 2003), and a special issue of the *South Atlantic Quarterly* entitled *And Justice for All?: The Claims of Human Rights* (with Ian Balfour, Spring–Summer 2004). He is currently completing a translation of Nadar's memoirs, *Quand j'étais photographe*, and a collection of essays on the ethics and politics of mourning entitled *Mourning Politics*. His book *Paper Graveyards: Essays on Art and Photography* is forthcoming in 2013.

JONATHAN CRARY is the Meyer Schapiro Professor of Modern Art and Theory at Columbia University. One of the founders of Zone Books, he is the author of *Techniques of the Observer: On Vision and Modernity in the Nineteenth Century* (1990) and *Suspensions of Perception: Attention, Spectacle, and Modern Culture* (1999).

ANN CVETKOVICH is the Ellen C. Garwood Centennial Professor of English and Professor of Women's and Gender Studies at the University of Texas at Austin. She is the author of *Mixed Feelings: Feminism, Mass Culture, and Victorian Sensationalism* (1992), *An Archive of Feelings: Trauma, Sexuality, and Lesbian Public Cultures* (2003), and *Depression: A Public Feeling* (2012). She coedited (with Janet Staiger and Ann Reynolds) *Political Emotions* (2010), and she has been coeditor, with Annamarie Jagose, of *GLQ: A Journal of Lesbian and Gay Studies*.

FAYE GINSBURG is the founder and ongoing director of the Center for Media, Culture, and History at New York University, where she is also the David Kriser Professor of Anthropology and codirector of the Center for Religion and Media and of the NYU Council for the Study of Disability. An award-winning author/editor of four books, including *Media Worlds: Anthropology on New Terrain* (2002), she is completing *Mediating Culture: Indigenous Media in the Digital Age* and currently carrying out research on cultural innovation and learning differences with Rayna Rapp.

SAM GREGORY is currently the program director at WITNESS and runs their Cameras Everywhere initiative. He teaches on human rights and participatory media as an adjunct lecturer at the Harvard Kennedy School. He blogs at http://blog.witness.org/author/sam and tweets at http://twitter.com/samgregory.

ZEYNEP DEVRIM GÜRSEL is a cultural anthropologist. She is the director and coproducer of *Coffee Futures* (2009). She received her Ph.D. in anthropology with a designated emphasis in film studies from the University of California, Berkeley. Her research focuses on how things become imaginable for both individuals and groups and how forms in which the past and today are narrated are also shaped by and in turn shape expectations of the future. She is currently completing a manuscript, *Image Brokers*, on the production, distribution, and circulation of international news images.

ROGER HALLAS is an associate professor of English and codirector of the LGBT Studies Program at Syracuse University. He is author of *Reframing Bodies: AIDS, Bearing Witness and the Queer Moving Image* (2009) and the coeditor (with Frances Guerin) of *The Image and the Witness: Trauma, Memory and Visual Culture* (2007). He is also codirector of the Illuminating Oppression Human Rights Film Festival in Syracuse.

ANDREW HERSCHER is an associate professor at the University of Michigan with appointments in the Taubman College of Architecture and Urban Planning, the Department of Slavic Languages and Literatures, and the Department of the History of Art. He is the author of *Violence Taking Place: The Architecture of the Kosovo Conflict* (2010).

SANDI HILAL is an architect based in Bethlehem. She is consultant with the United Nations Relief and Works Agency on its camp-improvement program and a visiting professor at Al-Quds University / Bard College in Abu Dis–Jerusalem. She is a founder member of DAAR. In 2006, she obtained a research doctorate in transborder policies for daily life from the University of Trieste. She is a coauthor of the research projects *Stateless Nation* (with Alessandro Petti) and *Border Devices* (with multiplicity.lab). Her publications include *Senza stato una nazione* (2003), "Living among the Dead" (*Domus*, April 2005), "Road Map" (*Equilibri*, August 2004), *La stanza dei sogni* (2004), and "Stateless Nation" (*Archis*, Preview no. 4, 2003). Her projects have been published in the *New York Times*, *The Guardian*, *Il Manifesto*, *Al Ayyam*, *Al-Quds*, *Artforum*, and *Archis*.

KIRSTEN JOHNSON works as a director and a cinematographer. She shared the 2010 Sundance Documentary Competition Cinematography Award with Laura Poitras for *The Oath*. Her cinematography is featured in the winner of the award for documentary at the 2008 Tribeca Film Festival, *Pray the Devil Back to Hell* and in the Sundance 2012 Audience Award winner, *The Invisible War*. Her cinematography also appears in *Fahrenheit 9/11*, in the Academy Award–nominated *Aslyum*, the Emmy-winning *Ladies First*, the multiple-award-winning *Women, War, and Peace* series, and in the Sundance premiere documentaries *Finding North, This Film Is Not Yet Rated, American Standoff*, and *Derrida*. As a director, she is currently cutting a documentary shot in Afghanistan. Her previous film, *Deadline* (codirected with Katy Chevigny), premiered at Sundance in 2004 and won the Thurgood Marshall Award.

LIZA JOHNSON is an artist and filmmaker. Her work has been exhibited internationally in museums, galleries, and film festivals, including the Museum of Modern Art, the Wexner Center for the Arts, and the Walker Art Center, as well as at the Cannes, New York, Berlin, and Rotterdam Film Festivals, among many others. She also writes about art and film. Johnson is a professor of art and chair of American Studies at Williams College.

THOMAS KEENAN teaches literary theory and human rights at Bard College, where he directs the Human Rights Project. He is the author of *Fables of Responsibility: Aberrations and Predicaments in Ethics and Politics* (1997), coeditor (with Wendy Chun) of *New Media, Old Media: A History and Theory Reader* (2006), and coauthor (with Eyal Weizman) of *Mengele's Skull: The Advent of a Forensic Aesthetics* (2012).

CARRIE LAMBERT-BEATTY is the John L. Loeb Associate Professor of the Humanities at Harvard University in the Department of Visual and Environmental Studies and the Department of History of Art and Architecture. She is the author of *Being Watched: Yvonne Rainer and the 1960s* (2008).

JALEN MANSOOR teaches at the University of British Columbia. She completed her Ph.D. at Columbia University in 2007 and has taught at the State University of New York at Purchase, Barnard College, Columbia University, and Ohio University. She works as a critic for *Artforum* and is a frequent contributor to *October, Texte zur Kunst*, and, more recently, *The Journal of Aesthetics and Protest*. She has written many catalog essays, including essays on Blinky Palermo for *Dia* (2009) and Agnes Martin, also for *Dia* (2011). She has also produced monographic studies on, among others, Piero Manzoni, Ed Ruscha, and Mona Hatoum. She coedited (with Beth Hinderliter) *Communities of Sense: Rethinking Aesthetics and Politics* (2010). She is preparing a book that addresses formal and procedural violence in the work of Alberto Burri, Lucio Fontana, and Piero Manzoni and another on bare life in the work of Santiago Sierra.

YATES MCKEE writes about art, politics, and ecology.

MEG MCLAGAN is an independent filmmaker and cultural anthropologist. She is the co-director (with Daria Sommers) of the feature documentary *Lioness* which won the Center for Documentary Studies Filmmaker Award at Full Frame Documentary Film Festival and aired on the PBS series Independent Lens. She also writes about media, architectures of activism, and the documentary form.

ALESSANDRO PETTI is an architect, researcher in urbanism, chair of the Urban Studies and Spatial Practices Program at Al-Quds University/Bard College in Palestine, and director of Campus in Camps, an experimental educational program centered in Dheisheh Refugee Camp, Bethlehem. He is also a founding member and director of DAAR. He has written extensively on the emerging spatial order dictated by the paradigm of security and control and has published several articles centered on DAAR artistic practices. He has cocurated research projects on the contemporary urban condition such as *Border Devices* (2002–2007) and *Uncertain States of Europe* (2001–2003) (with multiplicity.lab) and *Stateless Nation* (with Sandi Hilal).

HUGH RAFFLES teaches anthropology at the New School in New York City. His writing has appeared in a wide range of publications, including *Granta*, *Cabinet*, *Orion*, *Public Culture*, the *New York Times*, and the *Wall Street Journal*. His most recent book is *Insectopedia* (2010).

FELICITY D. SCOTT is director of the Program in Critical, Curatorial, and Conceptual Practices in Architecture at the Columbia University Graduate School of Architecture, Planning, and Preservation, where she also teaches architectural history and theory. Her research focuses on articulating genealogies of political and theoretical engagement with questions of technological transformation within modern and contemporary architecture, as well as within the discourses and institutions that have shaped and defined the discipline. She has published numerous articles in journals, magazines, and edited anthologies, and *Architecture or Techno-Utopia: Politics after Modernism* (2007). *Living Archive 7: Ant Farm* appeared on *ACTAR Editorial* in May 2008. She is also a founding coeditor of *Grey Room*, a quarterly journal of architecture, art, media, and politics.

KENDALL THOMAS is the Nash Professor of Law and Director of the Center for the Study of Law and Culture at Columbia University. He is the co-editor of *Critical Race Theory: The Key Writings that Founded the Movement* (1996) and *What's Left of Theory?* (2000).

LESHU TORCHIN is a lecturer in film studies at the University of St. Andrews, where she works on the subject of film, genocide, and human rights advocacy. She is the author of *Creating the Witness: Documenting Genocide in Film, Video, and the Internet* (and coeditor of *Film Festival Yearbook 4: Film Festivals and Activism* (2012). Her work also has appeared in *Third Text, Film & History*, and *American Anthropologist*.

EYAL WEIZMAN is an architect, a professor of visual cultures, and the director of the Centre for Research Architecture at Goldsmiths, University of London. Since 2011 he also has directed the forensic architecture project funded by the European Research Council on the place of architecture in international humanitarian law. He is a founding member of the architectural collective DAAR. His books include *Mengele's Skull: The Advent of a Forensic Aesthetics* (with Thomas Keenan, 2012), *Forensic Architecture* (2012), *The Least of All Possible Evils* (2011), *Hollow Land* (2007), *A Civilian Occupation* (2003), and the series *Territories 1, 2,* and *3, Yellow Rhythms*. He has worked with a variety of NGOs worldwide and was member of B'Tselem's board of directors. He is currently on the advisory boards of the Institute of Contemporary Arts in London, the Human Rights Project at Bard College, among other academic and cultural institutions.

BENJAMIN J. YOUNG is a Ph.D. candidate in the Department of Rhetoric at the University of California, Berkeley, completing a dissertation on the photo works of Allan Sekula. He has taught at U.C. Berkeley and at the School of Visual Arts. He is also managing editor of *Grey Room*.

HUMA YUSUF is a Pakistani columnist and investigative journalist. She writes for Pakistan's *Dawn* newspaper and for international publications such as *Foreign Policy*, the *Christian Science Monitor*, and Indian *Express*. She has won the All Pakistan Newspaper Society Best Column Award (2008 and 2010), the European Commission's Prix Lorenzo Natali for Human Rights Journalism (2006) and UNESCO's Gender in Journalism Award (2005). She was also the 2010–2011 Pakistan Scholar at the Woodrow Wilson International Center for Scholars in Washington, D.C., where she researched the independent news media's impact on Pakistani politics and society. She completed a master's degree in comparative media studies at the Massachusetts Institute of Technology

CHARLES ZERNER is the Barbara B. and Bertram J. Cohn Professor of Environmental Studies and director of Intersections: Border Zones in Environmental Studies, Arts, and Science, Technology, and Society at Sarah Lawrence College. Trained as a lithographer, he holds degrees in law and architecture.

D0225463

The World War
1939–1945

THE WORLD WAR 1939–1943

The cartoonists' vision

ROY DOUGLAS

ROUTLEDGE
London and New York

First published 1990 by Routledge
11 New Fetter Lane, London EC4P 4EE

Simultaneously published in the USA and Canada
by Routledge
a division of Routledge, Chapman and Hall, Inc.
29 West 35th Street, New York, NY 10001

Typeset in 10/12pt Sabon, Compugraphic
by Mayhew Typesetting, Bristol

Printed in Great Britain
by T.J. Press (Padstow), Cornwall

British Library Cataloguing in Publication Data
Douglas, Roy,
The world war 1939–1945: the cartoonists's vision.
1. Cartoons. Special subjects. World war 2
I. Title
741.5

Library of Congress Cataloging in Publication Data
also available

ISBN 0-415-03049-8

Contents

Acknowledgements

The author wishes to express his grateful thanks to people who have assisted materially in the work. His wife, Jean, checked the manuscript and provided many helpful suggestions about style and presentation. Professors Frank Healey and Bertram Pockney, and Mr John Taylor, all of Surrey University, checked through the author's translations from French, Russian, and German respectively, and provided a number of interesting sidelights which have found their way into the book.

The author also wishes to express his gratitude to the following: the University of Birmingham for access to, and permission to use, the *Krokodil* material; London Express Newspapers Feature Services for permission to use material from the *Daily Express* and *Sunday Express*; Syndication International (1986) Ltd for permission to use copyright material from the *Daily Mirror*; Solo Syndication & Literary Agency Ltd for permission to use material from the *Daily Mail*, *News Chronicle*, *Star*, and *Evening Standard*; *Punch* for copyright material reproduced by permission; The British Library for permission to reproduce material from the Newspaper Library; *The Washington Post* for permission to reproduce copyright material; *The Christian Science Monitor* for permission to reproduce the cartoon on p. 298; Society for Cultural Relations with the USSR for permission to reproduce the cartoons on pp. 94, 95, 126, 145, 149, 158, 161, 162, 175, 218, 220.

The author and publisher have made every effort to obtain permission to reproduce copyright material throughout this book. If any proper acknowledgement has not been made, or permission not received, we would invite any copyright holder to inform us of this oversight.

All of these cartoons have been reproduced from contemporary newspapers. The quality of the print was often poor – newsprint from the next page is still visible on some cartoons, for instance. The author apologises to the reader for these imperfections.

Introduction

The Second World War is sometimes seen as a more or less straightforward struggle between two opposing groups of states, each side seeking at all costs to defeat the other. On that view, the issue was essentially strategic, even though it had economic and ideological overtones, and was influenced from time to time by acts of personal courage or cowardice, wickedness or altruism.

That picture of the war will not withstand detailed examination. The more closely one examines the conflict, the more complex it is seen to be. No two countries, however closely allied, ever saw matters in quite the same way as each other. To every government, the interests of the particular country over which it ruled were primary. The loss of a thousand allies was much less serious than the loss of a thousand of its own nationals.

The different countries also had radically different perceptions of where the most crucial issues of the war lay. To most Britons, for example, the 'real' war was between Britain and Germany. British forces were certainly engaged against Italians and Japanese as well as Germans; but those conflicts were seen as sideshows, only of interest where personal friends were involved, or in so far as they might affect the outcome of the struggle against Germany. Even more, campaigns in which Britain's allies were engaged against Germany were seen as mere episodes in the 'real' war between Britain and Germany. By contrast, the Germans never saw Britain as their principal enemy, except perhaps for a few months in 1940–1. The Germans would probably have been pleased to reach a compromise with Britain, in order to concentrate their attention against others.

The Battle of France in May and June 1940 provides a useful illustration of how matters looked from different national angles. Four major countries were involved in the fighting: France and Britain on one side, Germany and Italy on the other. No two countries saw the issues in the same, or even in similar, lights. To Germany, the essential object was not so much to dominate France as to stop France – and if possible Britain as well – from interfering with German ambitions elsewhere. To most French people, the struggle was for their own homeland, and all other

issues in the war were peripheral. A Frenchman could quite easily and logically pass from a mood of vigorous defiance of the invading enemy to one of willingness to collaborate with that enemy in order to avert further, and apparently pointless, destruction.

The British government certainly regarded the Battle of France as very important, but they never saw it as the central battle of the whole war, on whose outcome everything depended. There were very serious debates at the highest level as to how far British forces should be engaged: whether, for example, the loss of a few British aeroplanes more or less in the struggle to save France might prove of vital importance in determining the fate of Britain herself in the weeks which were to follow. To the Italians, the Battle of France was even less vital than it was to the British. The most important question to them was whether certain French territories to which Italy laid claim could be added to their own country as another stage in the gradual process of national extension which had already been continuing for more than three-quarters of a century.

As the war progressed, relationships between different countries changed. Official propagandists and ordinary citizens alike were anxious to blot from their memories the attitudes which they had taken toward other belligerents in earlier times.

Nowhere is that point illustrated more clearly than in changing British attitudes towards the USSR. In August 1939, a Non-aggression Pact was made between Germany and the Soviet Union. Later in the year, both countries attacked Britain's ally, Poland, and the Soviet Union attacked Finland as well. Many people on the Allied side regarded the Soviet Union as a 'moral enemy' no less obnoxious than Nazi Germany itself. Conversely, Germany's erstwhile associates Italy and – even more so – Japan, found the German–Soviet arrangements extremely embarrassing, as also did the Soviet Union's political apologists in Allied countries.

Then relations between Germany and the Soviet Union gradually deteriorated, and from June 1941 onwards they were engaged in the most bloody conflict in the history of man. In that stage of the war, none of the belligerents on either side found it convenient to recall the attitudes those two countries had taken towards each other for the first year or so. Germany and the Soviet Union were obviously unwilling to recall their former friendship; while their respective associates did not care to remind them.

Just as the war looked different from different national angles, and sometimes from the same national angle at different times, so also were sharp differences sometimes perceptible within the same country at the same time. Nowhere is this point brought out more strikingly than in the United States during the first couple of years of the war, when America was nominally neutral. There were bitter differences about how much assistance the United States should give to the Allies, and how far

America should risk actual conflict with Germany. In the latter part of 1941 there was further controversy in the United States as to what attitude should be taken towards the conflict between Germany and the Soviet Union.

In this book, the medium of the cartoon is used to study how the course of the war looked from different national standpoints, and sometimes from different standpoints within a particular nation. The cartoonist, of course, exaggerates and oversimplifies situations, just as he exaggerates the physical features of his subjects; but the cartoon often preserves a vitality which has been lost from factual accounts of events. Why should the cartoon be such a useful vehicle for illustrating different attitudes to the war? There is, of course, the old cliché that a picture is worth a thousand words, and good cartoons often express ideas far more vividly and simply than speeches or books.

One question which seriously troubles thinking people too young to remember the war, is how millions of quite ordinary people in all major countries were prepared both to kill and to risk being killed. It is not enough to say that there was military conscription, and that various penalties, sometimes draconian, were imposed upon people who refused to do what was required of them. There can be little doubt that there was genuine popular support for the conflicting national causes throughout the war, and the cartoon often gives us a good idea of how that support was built up. It is useful to go behind the 'received wisdom' of our own day, and to look closely at attitudes which people and governments sometimes find it convenient to forget that they once entertained.

In some countries – the Soviet Union and Nazi Germany, for example – no wartime cartoon could be printed which expressed opinions dissenting from those of the government, and therefore cartoons also tell us what the country's government wanted people to think at the time. Yet even in totalitarian countries there were sometimes considerable differences in emphasis. One of the most marked characteristics of Nazi Germany was anti-Semitism, which reached its ultimate horror in the policy of genocide deliberately pursued from 1941 onwards. Some German periodicals – *Der Stürmer* is the extreme example – are full of viciously anti-Semitic cartoons. Others, like *Das Reich*, make little reference to Jews in their cartoons, except for occasional snide figures with putatively Semitic features. The reason is not difficult to understand; the former paper was targeted largely at an uninformed and unthinking readership, the latter at an educated clientele who would have reacted negatively to crude propaganda.

Inevitably, the author has drawn selectively on possible sources. His own complete ignorance of the language has excluded Japanese cartoons, which might have thrown useful light on the Far Eastern war. He encountered considerable difficulty in obtaining German material, and

even more in obtaining Soviet cartoons from the early phase of the war, save from the single source, *Krokodil*, which itself was not easy to track down. By contrast, the American press presented an *embarras de richesse*, and it was impossible to do more than skim the surface of an enormous amount of material.

Some rather striking differences will be seen between the cartoons of different countries. The most obvious of these is the contrast between cartoons of the democracies (in our western sense of the word) and all totalitarian countries. In the totalitarian countries, it is absolutely axiomatic that every opinion expressed or implied in a cartoon corresponded with the opinion which the country's government wished its people to hold; in the democratic countries that is certainly not the case. Once war was actually engaged, no substantial body of opinion formally opposed the prosecution of that war, and the minorities who did take such a view do not seem to have left any memorable cartoons. Yet there was much criticism of governments, some of which will be encountered in this book. There can be little doubt that the Soviet or German cartoonist had been given some close guidelines as to what he was required to say, while the British or American cartoonist had much greater discretion and freedom of expression.

Another contrast between cartoons of totalitarian and democratic countries is that the democracies never hesitated to portray their national leaders – sometimes in an admiring manner, although sometimes critically. The author can only recall having seen a single cartoon from a totalitarian country in which a national leader appears at all – a Soviet cartoon in which the nominal head of state, President Kallinin, appears in a non-controversial light. There certainly appears to be no portrayal of Stalin in a Soviet wartime cartoon or of Hitler in a German one, although both men occasionally appeared on official posters. Is it fanciful to suggest that nobody would have dared to draw them in a cartoon, however reverentially, lest in some way the portrait happened to give offence?

As the reader peruses the cartoons in this book, he may well conclude that they often evince some 'national' characteristics. These are at times rather subtle and difficult to define; but it would generally not be difficult to identify British and Soviet cartoons, even if dubbed in the same language and making the same point. The British cartoon, one might say, is making its point with a rapier in a rather gentle, guying, manner, while the Soviet cartoon uses a sledge-hammer. Again, there is a kind of wistful cynicism about a French cartoon which is seldom to be found in a German, Soviet, American or even British drawing.

1

The road to war

During the 1920s, great hopes had been pinned on international agreements, and on the League of Nations, as devices for averting future wars. 'No more war' was more than an optimistic slogan; it expressed what many people believed the future would be. But in the 1930s international relations deteriorated rapidly, and serious conflicts soon developed. There was fighting between Japan and China in 1931–2, which was renewed on a much larger scale from 1937 onwards. In 1935–6, Italy went to war against Abyssinia (Ethiopia). From 1936 until the early part of 1939 a civil war, characterized by much wanton savagery on both sides, raged in Spain. During that civil war, Italy and Germany gave assistance to one side, the Soviet Union to the other. Many people saw it as a sort of full-dress rehearsal for a much wider conflict. As the decade advanced, the general drift towards another major war became more and more obvious.

The relative importance of different countries was profoundly different in the 1930s from what it is today. The British Empire or Commonwealth – the two terms were used interchangeably – encompassed about a quarter of the land surface of the globe, and a similar proportion of the human race. The empires of the various countries of western Europe contained between them nearly all of Africa, most of southern Asia, the whole of Australasia and considerable parts of the Americas. International politics still turned largely on relations between the European Great Powers – Britain, France, Germany, and Italy – with Japan playing an increasingly important role in the Far East.

Britain and France, the principal European victors of the First World War, were 'satiated' or (to put it more euphemistically) 'peace-loving' Powers. Any great international change was likely to redound to their disadvantage. By contrast, Germany – the chief vanquished country of the earlier conflict – was naturally 'revisionist'. In 1933, Germany came under Nazi control. Two years later, she formally repudiated the disarmament clauses of the 1919 Treaty of Versailles, and began large-scale rearmament. Soon everybody else was rearming too.

The position of other important countries was much more uncertain. The United States had fought on the Allied side in the First World War

and shared the concern of Britain and France that major international changes, and particularly war, should be averted. The vast majority of Americans deplored the internal atrocities and aggressive international policy of Nazi Germany; but America had no serious fear of attack on her own mainland territory, and had no wish whatever to preserve the world empires of European countries. There was a very strong current of 'isolationism' – the view that the United States could, and should, have avoided involvement in the First World War, and should certainly avoid involvement in any new conflict which might arise.

Italy and Japan had both fought on the Allied side in the First World War, and had acquired substantial territories as a result. Before 1931, Japan seemed to be Britain's closest friend in Asia, and for most of the 1930s there were influential people in both countries who saw no good reason why that friendship should not be revived. But the Japanese attack on China in 1931, and the renewed attack in 1937, deeply offended a large body of opinion in Britain on moral grounds, and some people also suspected that Japan might have designs on British possessions in the Far East.

Italy came under the rule of Benito Mussolini as far back as 1922, and there had been early signs of a disposition by Fascist Italy to resort to force, in the Corfu incident of the following year. This was followed, however, by more than a decade in which Italy did not behave noticeably worse in international affairs than other Great Powers were wont to do. Italy had much reason to be apprehensive of the consequences of a German revival, and until the spring of 1935 Mussolini had opposed the rising power of Hitler's Germany as vigorously as anybody in Europe.

A complex chain of events drew Germany, Italy, and Japan together in the latter part of the decade. All had territorial designs against other countries, and many people considered that there were substantial similarities between their internal regimes. The word 'fascist' proved a useful, though inaccurate, term to cover them all. Other terms, like 'the dictatorships' and 'the Axis Powers' were also commonly used to describe them, but they too were objectionable for one reason or another. The belief that the 'fascist' countries had common interests was self-serving, and the 'democracies' Britain and France made remarkably little effort to drive wedges between them.

The role of the Soviet Union in the period between the two World Wars was the subject of deep discussion at the time, and has remained so ever since. The Bolshevik Revolution of 1917 was widely regarded, both by its supporters and by its enemies, as part of a design to bring about immediate world revolution, and therefore as a challenge to all existing political orders. In several countries, attempts were made to establish Bolshevik-type governments, while foreign enemies of the revolution organized wars of intervention against Soviet Russia. By the early 1920s,

however, it became apparent that there was no immediate prospect either of the Bolsheviks (now renamed Communists) promoting revolution elsewhere, or of their enemies defeating Communism in the Soviet Union. A *modus vivendi* was achieved, and other countries gradually came to establish economic and diplomatic links with the new Russia. Yet there was profound mutual suspicion, and the Soviet Union existed largely in isolation from the rest of the world: a state of affairs for which each side was disposed to blame the other, but which perhaps really suited both of them.

Communist parties were set up in most countries in about 1920. In some places they were made illegal. In some, like France, they were large and influential; in others, like Britain, they never won substantial support. In all countries, Communists followed exactly whatever line of opinion the Soviet government happened to be advocating. Any members who deviated were expelled. The Polish Communist leaders, who fell foul of their Soviet mentors, were invited to Moscow and liquidated.

When Hitler took power in Germany, he made no secret of his hostility both to German Communists and to the Soviet Union, and hinted broadly at military aspirations towards Soviet territory. In the middle 1930s, the Soviet government showed increasing concern to co-operate with others in resisting that threat, and mutual assistance treaties were concluded with France and Czechoslovakia in 1936. Yet this apparent thaw of diplomatic and military relations with the west coincided closely with a great tightening of political authority within the Soviet Union itself. It is now generally agreed (although many people angrily denied it at the time), that Stalin was operating a reign of terror on a gigantic scale in which innumerable innocent Soviet citizens, and something like two-thirds of the Red Army's high command, perished.

Out of all this some exceedingly difficult questions arose, which vexed many people who were deeply fearful of Hitler's Germany and whose natural disposition was to co-operate with the Soviet Union in resisting that threat. In the first place, was the internal regime in the Soviet Union one whit less repressive and tyrannical than the internal regime in Nazi Germany? In the second place, had the original Bolshevik desire to inaugurate world revolution been abandoned, and – if not – was Stalin's Russia any less a threat to the world order than the 'Fascist' Powers? Even if the Soviet government was no longer seriously plotting world revolution, did she still entertain designs against territory of her immediate neighbours, most particularly territory which before 1917 had belonged to Russia? And finally, even if all the earlier questions could be answered favourably for the Soviet Union, what sort of value could be placed on the military support of a country whose army was in such a state of turmoil, and where so many people were bitterly alienated from the government?

In Britain and France, profound debates were taking place in the late 1930s as to what policies should be adopted to deal with the deteriorating international position. There was something to be said for an attitude of passive defence and non-involvement in the quarrels of others. There was something to be said for selecting a 'principal enemy', and attempting to buy off other potential enemies in order to isolate that country. The two policies, however, which attracted most interest in government circles were appeasement and collective security.

The idea of appeasement was particularly associated with Neville Chamberlain, who became the British Prime Minister in May 1937. Chamberlain recognized that many changes were bound to occur in the world in the next few years. His overriding concern was to ensure that those changes took place peacefully as a result of agreements: agreements which might sometimes be distasteful but which, once made, would be kept scrupulously. Britain, whose influence was great and whose own interests were not directly threatened, was in a particularly strong position to bring about these agreements.

From the spring of 1938 to the spring of 1939, appeasement was put to the test. The German seizure of Austria in March 1938 took place so suddenly that there was no chance of effective resistance. Some Austrians – what proportion of the country is still a matter of argument – welcomed the change. Then Germany began to exert great pressure on Czechoslovakia. International engagements of France and the Soviet Union towards Czechoslovakia made war seem likely; but in the end conflict was averted by territorial concessions from the Czechs which were endorsed at the Munich conference of September 1938. Germany gave assurances that the truncated Czechoslovakia should remain in existence. Critics of appeasement in Britain and France represented Munich as a mere surrender to Hitler. There is evidence, however, that Hitler had hoped for a good deal more Czech territory than he received, and perhaps desired a short, triumphant war to demonstrate to others the invincibility of German arms. If that is so, then he too must have been far from pleased at the upshot.

On 15 March 1939, Germany seized the western provinces of Czechoslovakia, in flat defiance of the Munich settlement. Appeasement, at least so far as Germany was concerned, was abandoned, and the attention of the British government was immediately drawn to the alternative policy of 'collective security'.

'Collective security' was understood to mean that the countries who sought to resist international aggression should stand together, and should – in effect – threaten any aggressor with war against them all. In Britain, this policy was supported by most leading spokesmen of the Opposition parties – the Labour and Liberal Parties. The same view had been growing among supporters of the Conservative-dominated National

Government. Some Conservative rebels, of whom Winston Churchill was the most famous, had been advocating collective security for a long time, but some people within the government were leaning the same way, and when appeasement demonstrably failed, the British government immediately sought to establish the broadly-based alliance which its critics were recommending.

Which countries should be asked to join? France, certainly. It was widely believed that Poland had been marked out as Hitler's next major victim, and so Poland was also an obvious invitee. Nazi Germany had been complaining noisily that Poland had incorporated a slice of German territory after the First World War, and was demanding restoration of that territory – the so-called 'Polish Corridor'.

It was taken as no less axiomatic that the Soviet Union should be invited to participate, whatever apprehensions people might entertain about her long-term aims, and whatever they might think about her internal administration. Surely simple self-interest prescribed that the Soviet Union would wish to keep Nazi Germany well away from her own western borders?

Immediately, approaches were made to the three potential allies. Britain soon came to appreciate the profound mutual antagonism existing between the Soviet Union and Poland. Although the Soviet government was not making any immediate territorial claims against Poland, there was little doubt that they considered the existing frontier lay much too far to the east. The Poles were afraid that the Soviet Union would take any available opportunity to rectify the situation. Even if that were not the case, any alliance with the Soviet Union would be likely to enrage Hitler and so make a German attack more likely.

Long before these difficulties could be resolved, a new event forced the British government's hand. Rather dubious evidence emerged which suggested that Germany planned to take action against Poland in the immediate future. In order to forestall such an event, the British government issued a 'guarantee' to Poland on 31 March – just over a fortnight after the destruction of Czechoslovakia – promising that if Germany attacked Poland, Britain would go to her assistance. France already had a somewhat ambiguous commitment to go to Poland's assistance in the event of a German attack. Without asking too closely how France, still less Britain, could actually help the Poles in such an event, one might say that a kind of collective security now existed in Europe. For the time being, most people in politics, whether supporters or opponents of the British government, were satisfied with the gesture. The one serious voice of scepticism was that of Lloyd George, who had been Prime Minister in the second half of the earlier war; but few people paid much attention to him in the spring of 1939.

During most of the ensuing summer, attempts were made to extend the

alliance to include the Soviet Union, as had originally been intended. It gradually became apparent that there was no way of resolving the mutual antagonisms and fears of the Soviet Union and Poland. Negotiations between the Soviet government on one side and the British and French on the other continued, but the parties behaved less and less as if they expected any real agreement to emerge. The Russians feared, reasonably enough, that they would be left bearing the brunt of any fighting which might take place, particularly if they were not authorized to enter Poland, and perhaps certain other countries as well. The Poles feared, equally reasonably, that if the Red Army once entered Poland, it would prove inordinately difficult to remove. The British government wanted the Soviet alliance but could scarcely brush aside the fears of a country to which it had so recently issued a guarantee.

By this time, few people doubted that events were moving towards a final showdown. This did not necessarily mean war. Many people in the western countries thought that Hitler was bluffing, and his bluff would be called. Many people in Germany thought the same about Britain and France. But, if war did come, it was widely believed that there would be a close correspondence between political ideology and the international line-up. Italy and Japan were seen as Germany's natural friends and allies. Italy was in such a parlous economic state that she might well decide to stand aside, while Japan was already busy enough with China; but the moral support of both countries for Germany could be taken for granted.

On the other side stood another ideological bloc, the 'democracies'. Britain and France were apparently committed to go to war if Germany attacked Poland. The United States and the various parliamentary democracies of western and northern Europe might well not enter the war at once, but their moral support was taken for granted. How far the Soviet Union would assist the democracies was far from clear, but most people had little doubt that she would either be an active ally against Nazi Germany or, at worst, a sympathetic neutral.

2

The arrival of war

On 21 August 1939, the world was astonished to hear that a Non-aggression Pact between Germany and the Soviet Union was being prepared. A couple of days later the treaty was signed in Moscow. While, in theory, it was no more than an agreement that the two countries would not attack each other and would respect each other's interests, it was generally assumed that there was a great deal more in it.

The new agreement came as a profound shock to Britain and France. The Pact certainly meant that there was no prospect of military assistance from the Soviet Union should Poland be attacked by Germany. This made such an attack likely in the immediate future; and that attack would activate the British guarantee issued to Poland at the end of March. Many people guessed that there were secret clauses linked to the Pact which involved a division of spheres of influence in a large part of Europe between Germany and the Soviet Union. If that was the case, then trouble could be anticipated not only from Germany but from the Soviet Union as well.

The German–Soviet Non-Aggression Pact was followed on 1 September 1939 by the German invasion of Poland. The Poles resisted, so Britain and France were both now under Treaty obligations to go to war against Germany in Poland's defence. When the British cabinet met the same morning they were prepared to declare war, but they soon learnt that their French counterparts were requesting a period of delay.

In the next couple of days the British government did what it could to prod the French into action, while a growing body of opinion at home suspected – wrongly, as it happened – that Chamberlain was looking for possible ways of avoiding the obligation to go to war. In the end, the British cabinet resolved to declare war without waiting any longer for the French to make up their minds, and the declaration was issued in the morning of 3 September. The French declaration of war followed a few hours later.

On the outbreak of war, the British government was broadened to incorporate 'rebel' Conservatives like Winston Churchill; but members of the Opposition parties were still left out. There was no doubt, however, that both Labour and Liberal Parties were giving full support to the prosecution of the war.

Apart from some action at sea involving Britain, nearly all fighting in the first few weeks of war took place in Poland. The Polish army fell back rapidly in face of the German invasion. Then, on 17 September 1939, Soviet troops crossed the eastern frontier of Poland.

At first some Soviet sympathizers interpreted the Soviet invasion as a move designed to drive the Germans out of Poland, but it was soon clear that the invasions were collusive, for when the two armies met there was no hostility. Within a month of the German attack, Polish resistance was almost at an end, and on 28 September any lingering doubts about Soviet attitudes to Germany were removed by a joint declaration from the two countries, agreeing to recognize a line of demarcation dividing Poland between them. The German and Soviet governments even went to the point of issuing a joint demand for Britain and France to call off the war.

Cartoon 2.1 Les Revenants. *Le Canard Enchaîné*, Paris, 23 August 1939

The first cartoon, 'The Ghosts', is from a French satirical periodical, and was evidently drawn about mid-August 1939, a few days before the announcement of the German–Soviet Non-aggression Pact. Like most cartoons of the period, it assumed the widespread 'ideological' view of the international line-up. The two dictators Hitler and Mussolini were considered to have similar political ideologies, and also similar international interests.

Hitler and Mussolini are at a seance, attempting to conjure the 'spirit of Munich'. At this date, many critics of the British and French governments considered that those governments had made foolish and shameful concessions to Germany at the Munich conference of September 1938. The 'spirit of Munich', as understood by the cartoonist, therefore meant a willingness on the part of those countries to make further concessions to Germany and perhaps Italy as well. The 'spirit of Munich' is represented by an umbrella – which contemporary cartoonists usually drew in association with British Prime Minister Neville Chamberlain. The cartoonist appears to consider that Hitler and Mussolini are co-operating closely, and are preparing to work together to secure further concessions in the near future. This rather whimsical style of humour is often found in French satirical comment on social as well as political matters.

On the very day this cartoon appeared – 23 August 1939 – the German–Soviet Non-aggression Pact was signed, demonstrating that Hitler was willing to thrust Italy aside in favour of a different kind of alliance.

Cartoon 2.2 The retreat to Moscow. *News Chronicle*, London, 26 September 1939

"... if we had the Ukraine, National Socialist Germany would be swimming in surplus prosperity!"
[Hitler, Nuremberg, 1936

This cartoon appeared in the *News Chronicle* – theoretically Liberal, but in practice a forum for various kinds of anti-Government opinion. 'Vicky', the cartoonist here, was not a Party man but would rank as a socialist. Hitler, dressed as Napoleon, is retreating from his former designs against the Soviet Union. The parallel is drawn with the 'retreat from Moscow' in 1812, which is widely considered to represent the beginning of the end of Napoleon's power.

Before the Soviet–German Non-aggression Pact of August 1939, Hitler's speeches and writings had repeatedly expressed the deepest possible hostility to Communism, and the desire that Germany should acquire Soviet territory, particularly in the Ukraine. The quotation at the bottom of the picture is a good example of such statements.

The cartoonist is evidently trying to assure his readers that the German–Soviet Non-aggression Pact, which looked like a great diplomatic victory for Hitler, was really a massive defeat for him, for he has been compelled to abandon his former attitudes through fear of Soviet power. The torn papers behind Hitler's horse read 'Ideologies' – for Hitler was forsaking his opposition to Communism – 'Anti-Comintern' (which will be discussed in connection with the next cartoon), and 'Ukraine' – for the Non-aggresion Pact implied abandonment of Hitler's territorial aspirations in that direction.

Cartoon 2.3 But[t]erfly. *Le Canard Enchaîné*, Paris, 11 October 1939

In this French cartoon, the theme of Puccini's opera *Madame Butterfly* is invoked. Nazi Germany, as Lieutenant Pinkerton, departs with Russia as its new friend, leaving Japan, as the tragic heroine in the title-role, inconsolable on the shore.

The vessel in which Germany and Russia are departing is labelled 'Anti-Komintern'. The 'Anti-Comintern Pact' was set up in 1936 as an agreement between Germany and Japan, ostensibly for mutual defence against activities of the Communist International (Comintern), which centred on Moscow. Italy joined in the following year, and several other countries joined later.

The Comintern had been established in 1920, to co-ordinate the new Communist parties in various parts of the world in a common cause of world revolution. Long before 1939 it was generally realized that the Comintern had little immediate interest in world revolution, but was primarily concerned to advance the perceived diplomatic objectives of the Soviet Union, whatever these might happen to be.

Just as the Comintern had abandoned its original objectives, but remained in existence to serve quite different purposes, so also was the Anti-Comintern Pact widely considered to have real objectives very different from its nominal ones. On that view, the real aim of the Anti-Comintern Pact was to co-ordinate international aggression, whether against the Soviet Union or against others.

By forming the new Non-aggression Pact of 1939 with the Soviet Union, Germany abandoned both the nominal and the real objects of the Anti-Comintern Pact, and effectively jettisoned her close alliance with Japan and Italy. The Japanese made little secret about their dismay at this turn of events.

Cartoon 2.4 England – Frankreich. *Simplicissimus*, Munich, 8 October 1939

This cartoon appeared in *Simplicissimus*, a German satirical magazine aimed at readers who would be fairly conversant with international events.

An elderly and irascible John Bull – representing England – prods the French soldier with Chamberlain's umbrella. The French soldier seems to be standing on guard, ready to defend his own country against attack, but with no desire to go to war for any other reason. The words at the bottom are a parody of the beginning of the 'Marseillaise', suggesting that France is being pushed into war on Britain's behalf.

There was a measure of truth in that view. French opinion was by no means as unanimous as British opinion about the need to go to war after the German attack on Poland, and some people in the French government also had doubts on the matter. The British decision to go to war whether France joined in or not virtually forced the French hand.

It is important to remember that in 1939 the British – shielded by the Channel, which is shown in the cartoon – were in a far less vulnerable position than the French, many of whom still had vivid recollections of German invasions of their own soil in 1914 and 1870.

England-Frankreich

(Karl Arnold)

„Allons enfants pour les Anglais!"

Cartoon 2.5 More British frightfulness! *Daily Herald*, London, 6 September 1939

MORE BRITISH FRIGHTFULNESS!

This cartoon appeared in the *Daily Herald*, principal newspaper of the Labour Party, a few days after war began. Labour was the main 'Opposition' party at this period but gave strong support to the prosecution of war against Germany. The *Daily Herald* was aimed at the thinking working-class or lower-middle-class reader.

In the first phase of the war, there was little co-ordination between the three Allies, Britain, France, and Poland. The Poles were fighting with great bravery, but they were being rapidly overrun by the far more efficient German army. The British army was very small and it would take a long time to get what there was of it to France. The French military was not disposed to launch a major attack in the west which could give a breathing-space to Poland, for they were well aware that in that event nearly all the sacrifice would be made by Frenchmen.

Without access to Germany by land, and with an Air Force still considerably weaker than the German, Britain could do relatively little against Germany. However, British aircraft were used in 'leaflet raids', to drop propaganda leaflets on Germany. This action was based on the widespread British belief that Hitler was far from popular in his own country and would soon be undermined even further if Germans could only be told the truth about the disastrous effect of his policies. At this stage of the war, there was a strong disposition in many British publications to draw a sharp division between the Nazi leaders, who were hated, and the German people, who were 'Hitler's first victims'. As the war

proceeded, that distinction was made less and less frequently.

In this cartoon Dr Goebbels, German Minister of Propaganda, is shown to be furious about Britain's action in supplying Germans with 'the truth'. Right from the start there was considerable doubt about the effectiveness of this kind of propaganda, which came under almost daily discussion in the British Cabinet. After a short time it was discontinued.

The title of the cartoon is an ironic reference to the disposition of German propagandists (like propagandists of all belligerent countries) to accuse their enemies of 'frightfulness'.

Cartoon 2.6 Enter the Bear. *Daily Herald*, London, 18 September 1939

ENTER THE BEAR

The *Daily Herald* cartoon, 'Enter the Bear', appeared very soon after the Soviet invasion of Poland. It shows a wounded Polish soldier, defending himself desperately against the German eagle, being surprised in the rear by the Russian bear, which carries the features of Stalin. The cartoonist's sympathies are obviously with Poland against both assailants.

It is noteworthy that hostility towards the Soviet invasion was at least as strong in this Labour newspaper as in those elements of the British Press which supported the Conservatives. Many people in the Opposition parties who had shown considerable sympathy for the Soviet Union before the war regarded the Soviet–German Non-aggression Pact, and, *a fortiori*, the Soviet attack on Poland, as treachery against the common cause of resistance to Nazi Germany.

Cartoon 2.7 Dva perekhoda granitsy. *Krokodil*, Moscow, September 1939

Два перехода границы.

Cartoon 2.7 comes from the magazine *Krokodil*, the principal source of Soviet satirical comment. It is entitled 'Two crossings of frontiers'.

Most unfortunately *Krokodil* in this period was only dated by the month, and so it is not absolutely clear which was the frontier crossing illustrated in the first frame. It probably represents the Red Army crossing into Poland in the Soviet invasion which began on 17 September, but it is possible that it represents the German invasion of 1 September. Whichever is the case, the frontier post carrying the Polish white eagle has been knocked down by invading troops.

The meaning of the second frame is clear. As a result of the national invasion, Polish peasants have taken it into their hands to make their own 'invasion', and are taking over their landlord's estate. This seems to make it more likely that it was the Soviet invasion which was being represented in the first frame – the familiar Communist argument of the period being that the Red Army was not only defending the Soviet state but also assisting proletarian movements in other countries.

Cartoon 2.8 Syshchestvenni Moment. *Krokodil*, Moscow, no.25, September 1939

Another Soviet cartoon, 'Moment of Truth', to a similar effect. The Polish officer, in a state of great agitation, rides up to a group of peasants, shouting that they should take action because 'our country is in peril'. A peasant replies indifferently, 'We don't know about yours, but ours is completely safe.'

Presumably the attackers from whom the Poles are fleeing are the Soviet invaders. The reply is to the effect that the peasants' 'country' is the Soviet Union, not Poland. They have, therefore, no interest in fighting for Poland's defence. This cartoon is another illustration of the Soviet view, still maintained at this stage of the war, that the interests of workers and peasants lay in revolutionary, not in national, conflict, and that the Soviet Union was the spearhead of their interests.

Whichever country was truly the one to which the peasants owed loyalty, events less than two years later would show that it was by no means 'safe'.

СУЩЕСТВЕННЫЙ МОМЕНТ

- Панове наше отечество в опасности!
- Не знаем, как ваше, а наше теперь уже в полной безопасности.

Cartoon 2.9 Putting the lid on it! *Daily Mirror*, London, 2 October 1939

Putting the Lid on It!

At the end of September 1939, the German and Soviet governments followed their earlier Non-aggression Pact with an agreement to partition Poland. It was widely believed that this second agreement was accompanied by a division between the two countries of 'spheres of influence' over a large part of eastern Europe – in other words, each of them was contemplating further acts of aggression, with which the other would not interfere.

The new agreement between Germany and the Soviet Union was accompanied by a 'peace offer' – a joint demand by the two countries that the Allies should call off the war, with the threat that if the 'offer' were refused, Germany and Russia 'would consult together regarding the necessary measures to be taken'.

In this *Daily Mirror* cartoon, Hitler and Stalin offer 'peace' to Britain and France. Hitler displays a coffin, Stalin brings in the lid. The two men are actively co-operating in a common purpose. The Soviet government was seen by this stage of the war as no less a 'moral enemy' than Nazi Germany itself.

3

Scandinavia and the Baltic

During the winter of 1939–40, attention was directed to the Baltic and Scandinavia.

Almost immediately after the September agreement between Germany and the Soviet Union, the USSR began to lay claim to its own 'sphere of influence'. This included, among other places, the three little Baltic States – Estonia, Latvia, and Lithuania. Those countries had belonged to the Russian Empire before the First World War, but their populations were overwhelmingly non-Russian and they became independent in 1918. In the autumn of 1939 they were required by the Soviet Union to accept military garrisons, and their foreign policies came effectively under Soviet control. For the time being, however, their internal independence was allowed to continue.

Soviet pressure on the Baltic States was followed by similar pressure on Finland. In November 1939 the Soviet government demanded that the Finns should cede important territory in the south-east of the country, and accept military garrisons elsewhere. In return, the Finns were offered some territory further north, which would be of little use to them.

The Finns refused the Soviet demands, and at the end of November Soviet troops invaded Finland. In Britain and France, sympathy ran very strongly with the Finns. The same was true in most other countries, including Germany's recent associates Italy and Japan. Nazi Germany was one of the few countries which defended the action of the Soviet government, although even the German defence was somewhat half-hearted.

The Finns put up a tremendous resistance to the Soviet invasion during the winter of 1939–40. In the end, however, it was clear that the Russians would eventually be able to bring up overwhelming force, and would be able to destroy Finland unless the Finns came to terms. The terms which the Soviet Union offered were certainly onerous, for the Finns were required to cede the territory which the Soviet Union had demanded of them earlier, and to admit Soviet bases into the country. These terms were accepted by Finland on 12 March 1940. Against all the odds, however, the independence of the country had been preserved.

The USSR was not the only country which tried to advance its own interests in northern Europe during the winter of 1939-40. There were

huge deposits of iron ore in the north of Sweden and a large part of current production went to Germany, where it was very important for war industries. Some Allied experts were convinced that the Germans were so dependent on these supplies that Germany would lose her capacity to wage war if they were cut off.

At first the Allies tried to persuade Sweden to take action against Germany. The Swedes, who realized that the Allies could not possibly defend them adequately against the Germans, refused. Then the Allies hit on a new gambit. Efforts were made during the Russo-Finnish war to persuade Norway and Sweden to permit British and French troops to pass through those countries, with the ostensible object of helping Finland – but with the real aim of getting control of the orefields, which lay close to the route through which those troops must pass. The Scandinavians, who were appalled at the prospect of suffering the same fate as Finland, temporized. At one moment Sweden had good reason to fear attack from any of three quarters: from the Russians; from the Germans; or from the Allies. If for any reason one of those countries entered Sweden, it was likely that the others would do so as well. Sweden's only hope lay in strict neutrality.

When the Russo-Finnish war ended, the Allied interest in Scandinavia did not cease. The Swedish iron ore reached Germany by two main routes. In the summer, it was taken from Swedish ports at the head of the Gulf of Bothnia. In the winter, when the Gulf was frozen but the waters round Norway were ice-free, it was taken to Narvik, and from there down the Norwegian coast.

Early in April, the Allies attempted to stop the ore traffic by laying mines in Norwegian territorial waters. The Germans immediately countered by occupying Denmark and the principal towns of Norway. Britain and France landed troops in Norway at the Norwegians' request, and sought to drive the Germans out.

Meanwhile, the Western Front remained quiet.

Cartoon 3.1 Hésitation Stalinienne. *Le Petit Parisien*, 2 November 1939

When the Soviet Union had already absorbed eastern Poland, and had begun to exert pressure on the Baltic States, there was much speculation about Soviet objectives. This French cartoon, drawn several weeks before the attack on Finland, shows Stalin deliberating between two possible policies. On the left, the ghost of Tsar Peter the Great (1672–1725) advocates a military push towards other parts of Europe. On the right, the ghost of Lenin (who ruled Russia 1917–24) advocates 'Communism born from chaos' – implying that the Soviet Union should encourage others to fight rather than engage in war herself, confident that the chaos resulting from war would provide a breeding-ground for Communism. Either policy would have the most sinister implications for all European countries, Allied, neutral, and enemy alike.

It is unlikely that quite such a pointed cartoon would have been drawn in Britain at this time. The French were a good deal more apprehensive of the Soviet threat than were the British. There are several possible reasons for this. France's more vulnerable geographical position is a partial explanation. The French Communist Party, as we have seen, was far larger than its British counterpart. At the time of the Russian 'wars of intervention' during the 'revolutionary' period from 1917 onwards, France had played a more active part against the Bolsheviks than Britain, and was perhaps to that extent more fearful of Soviet revenge.

Cartoon 3.2 Under new management. *Evening Standard*, London, 30 November 1939

Cartoon 3.2 appeared on the first day of the Russo-Finnish war. The cartoonist, David (later Sir David) Low, was the most famous, and the most perceptive, of all British cartoonists of the period. His own politics were more or less Liberal, but he drew for the *Evening Standard*, which was controlled by Lord Beaverbrook. Lord Beaverbrook was a Conservative, but his views were often very independent and sometime embarrassing to his own party. He recognized Low's genius, and allowed him full rein to express his own ideas. At this time, however, there was probably little difference between the cartoonist and the newspaper proprietor.

Soviet Foreign Minister Molotov is driving a tank labelled 'Nazi technique' against the Finns. In this cartoon, as in many which were drawn in this period in Allied countries, emphasis is laid on the essential similarity of the German and Russian governments.

The cartoon draws particular attention to the similar techniques employed by Nazi Germany and the Soviet Union in their policies of international aggression. In both cases, territorial demands were first made against the victim. Then, if these demands were refused, there was a great volume of 'hate propaganda', designed to whip up feeling within the aggressor country. This was followed by 'wild accusations'. If all that failed to produce submission, a 'fake incident' was invented – some kind of action on the frontier which made the victim appear to be in the wrong. This was followed by 'shameless aggression'.

People who saw this cartoon would have recollected vividly the propaganda techniques used by Nazi Germany against Czechoslovakia in 1938, and against Poland in 1939, and could easily be reminded of the similarity between those cases and the current attitude of the Soviet Union towards Finland.

Cartoon 3.3 Gadalka. *Krokodil*, Moscow, nos. 35–6, December 1939

ГАДАЛКА (*Маннергейму*): — Линия, родимый, прерывается!.. Видно, недолго жить осталось.

In this Soviet cartoon, drawn very soon after the attack, the Finnish military leader Field-Marshal Mannerheim is consulting a fortune-teller. On his palm are the words 'Maginot Line'. This was the name of the French fortifications which had been built against the German frontier, but a similar line of fortifications, often called the 'Mannerheim Line', protected Finland from the Soviet Union. The fortune-teller asserts that the condition of the line indicates that his remaining life will not be long.

The cartoonist seeks to show his Soviet readers that Finnish resistance is futile. Probably most people in the Allied countries would have agreed with that assessment; but in the weeks that followed, the power and courage of the Finnish defence was astonishing.

The Russians were doubtless as surprised as anybody. Just after the 'Winter War' began, they set up a 'satellite' government of Finnish Communist *émigrés* under the leadership of Otto Kuusinen in the little town of Terijoki which they had occupied. The Soviet leaders were probably convinced not only that the Soviet army was much stronger than the Finnish army, but also that large numbers of Finnish workers sympathized with Communism and would desert the government in Helsinki as soon as they had the opportunity. In fact, nothing of the kind happened.

Cartoon 3.4 L'Addition. *Le Petit Parisien*, 5 March 1940

L'ADDITION

— « *400.000 tués ou blessés, 500 avions, 1.300 tanks...* » *Je l'avais bien dit que j'aurais Viborg « coûte que coûte ».*

Soviet losses in the Finnish campaign were enormous, and this military failure disposed the Soviet government to come to terms with Finland. In this French cartoon, 'The Bill', Stalin meditates on the cost: '400,000 killed or wounded, 500 aeroplanes, 1,300 tanks. . . Didn't I say I would take Viborg "at whatever cost"?'

This cartoon was drawn not long before the end of the 'Winter War'. By this time, most people had guessed what the outcome would be. Finland could not expect to continue indefinitely in her fight against the Red Army, which was numerically vastly superior to her own. On the other hand, the Finnish resistance had already cost the Soviet Union dearly, both in material and in propaganda terms, and would cost her a lot more if the war continued. Thus both sides were becoming disposed to accept a settlement which would rank as a Soviet victory but would nevertheless preserve Finnish independence.

The peace terms which were imposed on Finland a week after this cartoon appeared compelled her to cede a considerable amount of territory, including Viborg (Vipuri), the second town in the country. Yet the incompetence of the Red Army against a much smaller enemy was obvious for all to see. It is possible that Hitler was as much impressed as everyone else, and this may well have influenced his decision, more than a year later, to attack the Soviet Union.

Cartoon 3.5 Der schwedische Odysseus und die Sirenen. *Simplicissimus*, Munich, 4 February 1940

Der schwedische Odysseus und die Sirenen

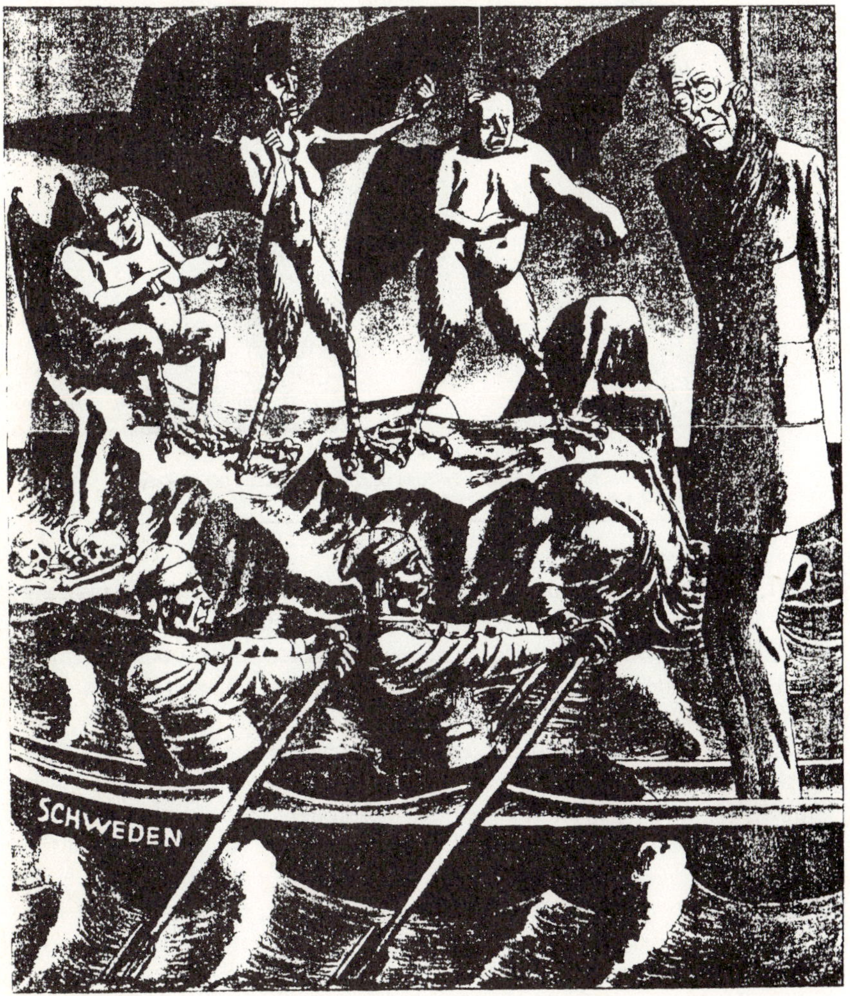

„Versuchen wir es mal mit Gesang, wenn er darauf nicht reinfällt, wollen wir schärfere Töne anschlagen!"

In this German cartoon, the aged King Gustav V of Sweden plays the part of Odysseus and guides the boat 'Sweden' past rocks on which Allied sirens are sitting and attempting vainly to lure her to destruction (see Homer, *Odyssey*, Bk xii, especially 165–200). The skulls at the feet of the

left-hand siren (possibly meant to represent Churchill, though the likeness is poor) would probably be seen by readers as an allusion to the fact that other countries, notably Czechoslovakia and Poland, had been destroyed when they relied on British assurances.

In the wording at the bottom of the cartoon, the leading Siren (Chamberlain, in the middle), declares that they will first try to achieve their purpose with a song (that is, by encouraging the Swedes); but, if that fails, they will sing a harsher tune (that is, they will use warlike measures against Sweden).

Cartoon 3.6 The starter's pistol? *Daily Mail*, London, 10 April 1940

Throughout the autumn and winter of 1939–40 there was very little action on the Western Front. This had puzzled many people, who had expected that the declaration of war against Germany would immediately be followed by heavy fighting on the Franco-German frontier. The cartoonist evidently considered that the commencement of fighting in Norway early in April 1940 would lead to immediate action on the Western Front as well. In fact this anticipation was wrong, and for another month not much warlike activity took place in Europe, except for Norway.

4

The Battle of France

Both the French and British governments came under serious attack in the first part of 1940, particularly from people who had been bitter critics of 'Appeasement' in pre-war days, and who remained far from convinced that those governments possessed either the capacity or the will to prosecute the war to a victorious conclusion. In March 1940, a crisis in France resulted in the fall of premier Edouard Daladier and his replacement by Paul Reynaud, who was widely regarded both in his own country and in Britain as a more determined leader.

Early in May there was a somewhat similar crisis in Britain. Deep concern over the Chamberlain government's conduct of the war surfaced rather unexpectedly in a Parliamentary debate. The government won a majority, but something like 100 of their nominal supporters either voted against them or deliberately abstained. Chamberlain realized that a much more broadly-based government was necessary if the war was to be brought to a victorious conclusion. At first he tried to bring the Opposition parties into his government; but they were not prepared to serve under him. So Chamberlain resigned, and was succeeded by Winston Churchill, who on 10 May was able to form a genuinely all-party coalition which remained in power until the summer of 1945. With the single exception of Lloyd George, every important British statesman either joined the government or soon accepted an important diplomatic mission abroad.

On the very day Churchill's government was formed, German armies invaded Belgium and the Netherlands, and soon swept into France. The Maginot Line, which followed the Franco-German frontier but did not run along the Franco-Belgian frontier, was bypassed. Within a few days, a great German 'bulge' divided the Allied armies. North of the bulge lay the Belgians, most of the British and some of the French. South of the bulge were most of the French. The prospect of a pincer-movement to cut off the bulge and reunite the Allies armies was debated, but never set into effect. On 28 May King Leopold III of the Belgians capitulated. Perhaps the position of Allied forces north of the bulge was hopeless even before that event; but afterwards there could be no doubt at all on the matter.

The evacuation of Allied soldiers from the Channel port of Dunkirk

had already commenced. Great numbers of vessels, most of them small craft never designed for belligerent use, sailed to Dunkirk and brought back to Britain all that could be rescued from the northern armies. In the end, more than a third of a million British, French, and Belgian soldiers were saved.

For most of June, the Battle of France was fought. On 10 June, Italy declared war on Britain and France. From a military point of view this did little immediate harm to the Allies. The French army, pressed desperately by the Germans further north, did well when fighting against the Italians. By the middle of the month it was evident that the Germans would eventually control the whole country if fighting continued.

The French cabinet then began to argue whether the country's government, and whatever troops could be saved, should be evacuated overseas – perhaps to French North Africa – or whether an armistice with Germany should be sought. Reynaud, who favoured resistance, resigned, and the 84-year old Marshal Pétain took over. Pétain had won great prestige in the First World War, both for his military capacity and for his skill and humanity in dealing with mutinous troops.

The new French government immediately sought an armistice. Negotiations were protracted, but on 22 June the armistice was arranged. The north and west of the country was to be set under German military occupation, but the south-east was left for the time being under the control of Pétain's government, which ruled from the town of Vichy. The French fleet was to be kept in certain ports, but was not seized. The French empire was not touched.

The wisdom and morality of nearly every major decision taken by the various Allies in this period was questioned at the time, and is still debated by historians today. This is not the place to answer such questions, but it is useful to ask them, because the existence of the debates had considerable influence on what happened during the later stages of the war, and afterwards. Cartoons of the period throw important light on how some of these debates looked to contemporaries.

Cartoon 4.1 One position that isn't going to be evacuated. *Evening Standard*, London, 8 May 1940

ONE POSITION THAT ISN'T GOING TO BE EVACUATED

Failure of the Allied expedition to Trondheim in central Norway was the ostensible reason for the British Parliamentary debate on 7–8 May, which eventually led to Neville Chamberlain's resignation from the premiership. This cartoon, published while the debate was still proceeding, shows Chamberlain (left) and other members of his government who have barricaded themselves in the cabinet room. The cartoon implies that, while they may evacuate military positions (as they had recently done in Norway), they have no intention of evacuating their political position and leaving office.

Chamberlain wields his famous umbrella as a weapon. The figure to the right of the cartoon, the Chancellor of the Exchequer, Sir John (later Viscount) Simon, seizes a bottle of ink to throw at the attackers. Simon was a famous lawyer as well as a politician, and in that sense ink was his natural weapon. The third defending figure is probably Sir Samuel Hoare, (later Viscount Templewood), Secretary of State for Air, who had long been subjected to very strong criticism by political opponents. It is noticeable that two men who occupied very important positions in the

government at the time this cartoon was drawn do not appear among the defenders. These are the Foreign Secretary, Viscount (later Earl) Halifax, and Winston Churchill, First Lord of the Admiralty, who had been the Minister primarily responsible for the Norwegian campaign. The reason for these striking omissions is that Halifax and (even more so) Churchill were admired by critics of the government. Both of them were seen as possible Prime Ministers in place of Chamberlain. Thus the cartoonist was trying to distance the Ministers of whom he disapproved from those of whom he approved.

The 'National Government', over which Chamberlain currently presided, had taken office in August 1931 – hence the words '8 years of dithering' on the papers behind the defenders. At the very beginning it looked like a genuine all-party coalition, but within a short time it became for most purposes a Conservative government, which nevertheless contained a number of individuals (including Simon) with different political antecedents.

In this period of the war, the National Government was coming under increasing criticism for a variety of reasons – some of them related to its pre-war foreign policy, others domestic. On the wall in the cartoon hangs a portrait of Chamberlain's immediate predecessor, Stanley Baldwin (Earl Baldwin), who was still alive, although in retirement. In his periods of office Baldwin had been quite popular among opponents as well as political supporters; but during the war he came under exceptionally bitter attack from critics of the government, and even from a considerable number of its supporters.

In the event, Chamberlain and his associates did not put up the 'last ditch' defence which the cartoonist suggested. A couple of days after the cartoon appeared, Chamberlain resigned the Premiership, and Churchill formed his Coalition Government. Chamberlain gave all the support he could to Churchill and took a leading part in the Churchill government until his health failed later in 1940.

Cartoon 4.2 Le père et le fils. *Marianne*, Paris, 5 June 1940

Le père et le fils

The Belgian government fled shortly after the German invasion, but King Leopold III remained behind with his army. On 28 May the King surrendered to the Germans. Many commentators in France and Britain reacted at the time with extreme bitterness, accusing Leopold of cowardice, treachery, or both.

Leopold was the son of King Albert of the Belgians, whose personal courage in the 1914 war attracted great admiration in Allied circles. In this French cartoon, the great silhouette on the left of the cartoon is of King Albert, who is seen resolutely facing the heat of battle; the craven little figure escaping to the right is King Leopold.

There was at the time, and there remains to this day, a deep controversy about the behaviour of Leopold. Some people have suggested that by insisting on remaining with his troops in Belgium when the country's government fled to Britain, he was showing marked courage, and that the decision to call on his troops to lay down their arms was prompted by genuine patriotism and a desire to avoid unnecessary loss of life among soldiers whose military position was impossible. Other commentators declare that he failed to give his Allies adequate notice of withdrawal from the conflict.

Cartoon 4.3 'This way, chum!' *Daily Mirror*, London, 1 June 1940

"This way, chum!"

This cartoon appeared during the Dunkirk evacuation, which took place at the end of May and the beginning of June 1940. The sailor carries the wounded soldier on his back, away from the flames of battle, to the small boat which will return him to Britain.

In two respects this cartoon is rather misleading. By no means all of the evacuation was conducted by the Navy – a very large part of it was achieved by civilian craft. The soldier still has his rifle; in fact, the great bulk of Allied weapons was left behind in northern France.

The importance of the Dunkirk evacuation would be difficult to overstate. The number of Allied soldiers saved was vastly greater than the British government thought possible at the beginning of the operation. Although most of the military equipment had been lost, it was soon replaced by supplies from the United States. Thus when the Germans contemplated invasion of Britain, just a few months later, there was a substantial army ready to meet them.

The soldier in the cartoon is obviously meant to be British. Large numbers of French, and some Belgian, troops were also rescued; but the British people, to whom this cartoon was addressed, were primarily interested in the fate of their own compatriots. Some French commentators suggested that the evacuation was carried out in a way which would deliberately select British troops in preference to those of other Allies; in effect, that the French were holding the line against the Germans not far from Dunkirk, while the British were being brought home. This criticism produced bitterness at the time, and the question – like the debate over the role of King Leopold – remains a matter of argument today.

Cartoon 4.4 The ghost of Matteotti. *Daily Herald*, London, 12 June 1940

THE GHOST OF MATTEOTTI: *"You're getting on, Mussolini. Once you were content to murder men for your own ends. Now you murder a nation."*

Cartoon 4.4 commemorates Mussolini's decision to enter the war on Germany's side on 10 June 1940, during the period of the Battle of France. Mussolini is seen driving a blindfolded Italy towards a mass of French bayonets. There is force in the comment. Many Italians were very reluctant to go to war, and the French fought with considerable success against the Italians. The blindfolding of Italy apparently implies that Mussolini's propaganda has prevented the Italians learning the truth about the war.

Matteotti, who reproves Mussolini, was an Italian socialist murdered by Mussolini's *fascisti* in 1924. At that time, the crime had attracted worldwide execration, by no means confined to people sharing Matteotti's political opinions, and it was still vividly remembered sixteen years later. In this cartoon, Matteotti's ghost is foretelling that Mussolini would lead their country to defeat.

For the first part of the war, Italy had been neutral, or rather – as Mussolini put it – 'non-belligerent'. The Italian government knew that the country was in no position to fight a prolonged war, was probably deeply offended by the Soviet-German Non-aggression Pact – and in any case was uncertain about the likely outcome of the war. The decision to join in was taken at a point where a German victory seemed extremely likely in the near future. Mussolini certainly sought whatever pickings Italy might acquire – Churchill's description of the Italian dictator as 'Hitler's jackal' had a large measure of justice. It is also quite likely that Mussolini was becoming alarmed at Hitler's strength and sought to convince the Germans that Italy was a force to be reckoned with.

In the event, Mussolini's calculations proved completely wrong. Even in the Battle of France, Italian troops fared poorly. As we shall see, Italy hopelessly over-extended herself, both in a military and in an economic sense. Matteotti's forecast in the cartoon proved correct.

Cartoon 4.5 Comme en 93. *Marianne*, Paris, 5 June 1940

This French cartoon, published as the Battle of France was becoming desperate, makes an appeal to the spirit of the French revolution – 'as in (17)93'. Marianne, who urges the French soldier forward, carries the *Tricolor*, bearing the slogan 'Liberty or death'.

The couplet from the 'Marseillaise', composed in 1792, seems very apposite:

> What seeks this horde of slaves,
> Traitors, conspiring kings?

In the immediate aftermath of the execution of Louis XVI in January 1793, France was threatened with invasion from many quarters, but the French raised an army themselves which espoused the cause of the Revolution with great enthusiasm, and proved immensely effective in the field. 'Conspiring kings' and their 'slave' soldiers played a large part in the general attack on France, and there were many French 'traitors' who wished to see them victorious.

The 'slaves' in 1940 are presumably the German invaders, enslaved by Hitler. 'Traitors' were playing a large part in undermining resistance to the invaders, as they had also done in Norway. 'Conspiring kings' may conceivably be an allusion to Leopold III of the Belgians, who, about a week earlier, had ordered his armies to cease fire. Perhaps the words were left in merely because the couplet was familiar and fitted in with the spirit of 1793. Although the French fought bravely against the invaders in 1940, there appears to have been little of the 'spirit of '93'.

Cartoon 4.6 V Perevode na Anglo-Frantsuski. *Krokodil*, Moscow, no. 7, April 1940

В ПЕРЕВОДЕ НА АНГЛО-ФРАНЦУЗСКИЙ

Когда же встанешь во весь рост
ты,
отдающий жизнь свою им!
Когда же в лицо им бросишь вопрос:
за что воюем!

This Soviet cartoon, 'Translation into Anglo-French', presents a very different view of the function of the Allied soldier. Despite the title, the ordinary soldier, the officer, and the Roman Catholic priest with his Rosary, all seem French rather than British.

So far from fighting for a revolutionary cause, the soldier is seen to be fighting for a reactionary one. He is being urged to stand up to his full height and fling off the priest, the high officer and (apparently) the capitalist who are in his way – asking them, 'What are we fighting for?' It implies that he would be better advised to fight against the 'class enemy' in his own country, rather than against the Germans.

This appeal to workers in Allied countries (though not, apparently, in Germany) to attend to 'class interests' rather than 'national interests' parallels the earlier Soviet cartoon of the Polish peasants (Cartoon 2.6). Very likely the Soviet propagandists at this stage of the war were still hoping that the conflict would lead to a widespread Communist revolt in all belligerent countries, which would draw its leadership and inspiration from Moscow.

Cartoon 4.7 A trump to beat his ace? *Daily Mail*, London, 17 June 1940

A trump to beat his ace?

—by Illingworth.

By mid-June, Paris had fallen. This was Hitler's 'ace'. The 'trump' by which Marianne is preparing to beat Hitler's ace is 'Roosevelt's Pledge'.

Franklin D. Roosevelt, President of the United States, sympathized strongly with the Allies. For some time the French Premier, Paul Reynaud, meditated sending a desperate appeal to Roosevelt to bring America into the war. For constitutional reasons if for no others, Roosevelt could not possibly have done this, whatever he thought of the matter. The British government had no illusions about Roosevelt's difficulties, and had strongly discouraged Reynaud from making an appeal to the American President which could only result in disappointment. Reynaud, probably feeling that he had nothing further to lose, persisted in his idea, and on 13 June formally appealed to Roosevelt.

The President sent a friendly, but non-committal, reply to Reynaud. Desperate people in France read into that reply what they wanted to read, and interpreted it as a 'pledge' from Roosevelt to do as Reynaud requested. It is perhaps a mark of how desperate the war looked in Britain too that Roosevelt's reply is called a 'pledge' in this cartoon.

By the time this cartoon was published, Reynaud had fallen, and on the very day it appeared the new Pétain government sought an armistice.

Cartoon 4.8 'Just agree, pal, and we can be one big happy family.' *Daily Herald*, London, 20 June 1940

"Just agree, pal, and we can be one big happy family."

Cartoons 4.8 and 4.9, by the same artist and in the same newspaper, at an interval of five days, show how swiftly people could revise their views at this stage of the war. In the first, Pétain, a dignified, soldierly figure, is being threatened at pistol-point by Hitler and Mussolini as he studies the proposed peace terms. The reader is evidently expected to sympathize with Pétain's plight.

Cartoon 4.9 Pétain: 'She says "I do".' *Daily Herald*, 25 June 1940

PETAIN: ***She says, "I do."***

In Cartoon 4.9, drawn shortly after the armistice had been accepted, Pétain is drawn as a doddering poltroon, father of the bride Marianne, who is gagged and bound at her marriage to 'Hitlerini' – a compound of Hitler and Mussolini. The reader is evidently expected to view Pétain with contempt, and to judge that if Marianne were free to speak for herself she would give a very different answer.

Available evidence suggests strongly that the overwhelming majority of French people agreed – at first – with what Pétain had done, although many had the gravest doubts later on.

5

Aftermath

Until June 1940, France was widely believed to be the strongest military power in Europe. Her sudden defeat posed immense problems for all countries – Allied, enemy, and neutral alike.

Germany was now supreme in western Europe, and it was difficult to envisage any circumstances in which Britain by herself could alter that state of affairs. Yet Britain was undefeated. With a great Navy and a sizeable and growing Air Force, she could reasonably hope to resist any German attempt to invade and conquer her. Indeed, why should Germany wish to invade and conquer Britain? The operation, whether successful or not, would be immensely costly for Germany and would bring her little positive benefit. Whatever view Hitler may have had of the distant future, his immediate wish was probably to conclude a negotiated peace.

Churchill and his associates made a profoundly important calculation. In the end, they decided, the logic of events would bring both the United States and the Soviet Union into the war on Britain's side, whatever the people of either country, or their rulers, might think of the matter at the moment. So Britain's immediate task was simply to hang on, for massive help would eventually come.

But there were great immediate problems. Although the armistice terms had not required France to surrender her navy, yet there was a serious danger that at some point in the future that navy might pass into enemy hands. If that happened, then Britain would be in the gravest peril. So the British government resolved to seize what it could of the French navy. Some ships were in British ports, and were easily taken. Others were in secure French ports, where capture was out of the question. Others still lay in less secure ports of French Africa. In July, a major naval operation was mounted at Mers-el-Kebir in Algeria (which was then French), to take or destroy some of those vessels. Thus in the early part of July serious fighting broke out between the two erstwhile Allies, in which many French sailors lost their lives.

The French National Assembly was convened as soon as this could be done after the armistice, and granted Pétain full powers by an overwhelming majority. Already, however, there existed another possible pole of attraction for the French people. During the Battle of France, a junior

General, Charles de Gaulle, escaped to Britain and set about organizing what became known as the 'Free French'. De Gaulle and his associates were clearly supported by the British, but they were not recognized as a 'government-in-exile' like the Poles, Norwegians, Dutch, and Belgians who had fled their countries after the German invasions. Many French people saw de Gaulle as the great hope for their country's future; but others regarded him as a traitor who had wilfully disobeyed orders. From the anomaly of de Gaulle's position, many serious inter-Allied problems would later arise.

When it became apparent that the British government did not propose to come to terms with Germany, plans were hastily devised for an invasion of Britain. During the summer of 1940 German aircraft sought to gain control of the skies over south-east England in preparation, but failed in the attempt. The land assault was postponed.

In the aftermath of the Battle of France, some profound questions were raised about the future of the European empires and spheres of influence in other parts of the world. The French colonies had the opportunity to decide between Vichy and the Free French, and several opted for the latter. There were considerable doubts about the long-term future of European possessions in the Far East. For the time being, however, Japan remained neutral in the European war, and was deeply embroiled with China.

Very important changes were taking place in eastern Europe. By the agreement with Germany reached in the autumn of 1939, the Soviet Union was allocated a sphere of influence which included the three Baltic States, Estonia, Latvia, and Lithuania, and also Bessarabia, an area of mixed population which Romania had taken from Russia during the Civil War period. Immediately after the fall of France, the Soviet government exerted massive pressure on the Baltic States, compelling them to join the Soviet Union as constituent republics.

At the same time, Soviet pressure was exerted on Romania, a country which traditionally had looked to France for protection. The Romanians were required to cede not only Bessarabia, but also the northern part of the province of Bukovina: territory which had never been Russian, but had belonged to Austro-Hungary before 1918. Bukovina had not been included in the earlier German–Soviet agreement and there were signs of distinct German disapproval. The Romanians, who probably feared that the Soviet Union might soon take over their whole country, turned to Germany in desperation as their only possible protector. The Germans, perhaps with some reluctance, complied. Romanian oil was a very important asset.

Under the 'Vienna Award' of August 1940, Germany extracted a considerable price from Romania. At the end of the 1914–18 war, Romania had received Transylvania from Hungary. Transylvania was of

mixed population, and the Hungarians bitterly resented its loss. By the new arrangement Romania was required to return a large part of the province to Hungary.

Romania was not the only country aggrieved by the 'Vienna Award'. Just as Germany had resented the seizure of northern Bukovina, so now did the Russians resent the character of the 'Vienna Award', considering that they should have been involved as well as Germany. These disputes, both apparently capable of easy resolution, were scarcely noticed by the world at large; but they may now be seen as the first signs of a developing gulf between Germany and the Soviet Union.

Cartoon 5.1 'Very well, alone.' *Evening Standard*, London, 18 June 1940

"VERY WELL, ALONE" (Copyright in All Countries.)

This cartoon was published on the day of the French cease-fire. The cartoonist emphasizes Britain's determination to continue the war in the new circumstances, even though some kind of attack was expected from across the Channel in the near future. That was certainly the view of the British government, and within a short time became the view of the overwhelming majority of ordinary British people.

Cartoon 5.2 Mars. . . *Das Reich*, Berlin, 28 July 1940

Mars: „Nun, mein lieber Freund Churchill, immer noch auf der Suche nach neuen Kriegsschauplätzen? Wie wär's mit diesem hier?“
Im Felde gezeichnet von Soldat Erich Freyer

This cartoon is said to have been drawn by a German soldier. The war-god Mars playfully congratulates Churchill on seeking new areas for fighting, and suggests another one – England. When it became plain that Britain would not come to terms, plans were made for a German invasion.

From the beginning of the war, German propaganda had declared that the war was essentially 'Britain's war'; that not only Germany herself but also Britain's allies, like Poland, Norway, and France, had been involved because of British interests rather than their own, and had suffered dire consequences as a result. Churchill had long been picked out by German propagandists as Britain's principal 'warmonger', and this cartoon suggests that he was now about to suffer the natural and just consequences of his own policies – for Britain was to become the battlefield, and would be defeated.

Wartime propaganda in all countries suggested that the country concerned was the innocent victim of the machinations and conspiracies of others, and Nazi Germany was no exception to this rule.

Cartoon 5.3 V Anglii. *Krokodil*, Moscow, no. 13, June 1940

Вчера Чембдерлен в палате гарантиробал нам победу.
Неужели гарантировал? Тогда мы пропали.

In Britain, civilians were enrolled into the Local Defence Volunteers – later the Home Guard – in preparation for the anticipated invasion. In this Soviet cartoon, 'In England', one man assures the other that Chamberlain, in a speech, had recently guaranteed victory. The other man replies, 'Did he guarantee that? Then we are finished.'

The older man is a stereotype of the pipe-smoking, bowler-hatted Englishman. The LDV was at first very short of uniforms; members paraded in civilian clothes, with arm-bands, and with as much proper uniform as happened to be available. The sandbags in the background were very characteristic of British towns in this period.

Just as the previous cartoon illustrates German preoccupation with Churchill as the principal enemy, so does this one illustrate the particular Soviet animus against Neville Chamberlain, whose pre-war policies were blamed for the current predicament in Europe. It is noteworthy that the former Prime Minister, despite the ministerial changes of May 1940, remained a member of the government, and his utterances were still of international interest.

Cartoon 5.4 Britannia waives the rules. *Daily Herald*, London, 5 July 1940

BRITANNIA WAIVES THE RULES

This is a remarkably flippant and insensitive cartoon about a peculiarly tragic occasion: the British attempt to seize, or to destroy, parts of the French fleet in case they should fall into German hands. Pétain, the aged waiter, is attempting to serve Hitler with the French fleet, which Britannia seizes with her trident, to the great joy of Free France.

Almost everything in this cartoon is wrong. Hitler was a vegetarian. The very last thing that Pétain wished to do was to surrender the French fleet. Even if he had little hope of an eventual Allied victory, that fleet was an extremely important bargaining-counter in dealing with the Germans. The Free French can hardly have felt much pleasure at an incident in which many French sailors lost their lives, and which can hardly have helped their popularity in their own country; while the British government was certainly distressed at the action which it felt compelled to take.

Cartoon 5.5 Churchill: Je ne vous reconnais pas. . .
La Gerbe, Paris, 11 July 1940

CHURCHILL – Je ne vous reconnais pas . . . vous êtes trop Francais.
PÉTAIN – Mais, moi, je vous reconnais . . . vous êtes bien Anglais.

This cartoon appeared in *La Gerbe*, a periodical published in Paris while the Germans were in occupation.

Churchill, using the word 'recognize' in its diplomatic sense, tells Pétain, 'I don't recognize you – you are too French.' Pétain, using 'recognize' in its popular sense, retorts bitterly, 'But I recognize you – you are so English.'

The people producing *La Gerbe* were French Fascists, who were strongly sympathetic with the Nazi view of events. It is important to note that Fascists, like Communists, were much more numerous in France than they were in Britain, and quite a lot of the journal's readers would have been disposed to agree with its views. At a later date, *La Gerbe* became critical of Pétain, whom it did not regard as sufficiently pro-German.

Most people in Britain probably did not distinguish clearly at this stage between different kinds of 'Vichy-ites'. In fact, however, there was a very wide range of opinion at Vichy, from people who wanted the Allies to win but considered that they had little chance of doing so, through neutralists who regretted that France had been brought into the war at all, to pro-Germans who hoped later to 'switch the war' and re-enter the conflict on Germany's side.

Cartoon 5.6 Freedom speaks all languages! *Daily Mirror*, London, 30 August 1940

Freedom Speaks All Languages!

The French Colony of Chad Is to Fight for Freedom Under General de Gaulle

Some French colonies, particularly those which were closely linked geographically and economically to British possessions, had a real choice between allegiance to Vichy and allegiance to de Gaulle's Free French. Early in August 1940, the New Hebrides – an Anglo-French condominium – decided for the Free French. Later in the same month, the French colony of Chad, whose Governor was a Negro, did the same. Chad, which lay between the British colony of Nigeria and the Anglo-Egyptian Sudan, was conveniently placed for taking such a decision. Other French colonies followed later.

Cartoon 5.7 Spravedlivost' prezhde bcevo. *Krokodil*, Moscow, no. 9, May 1940

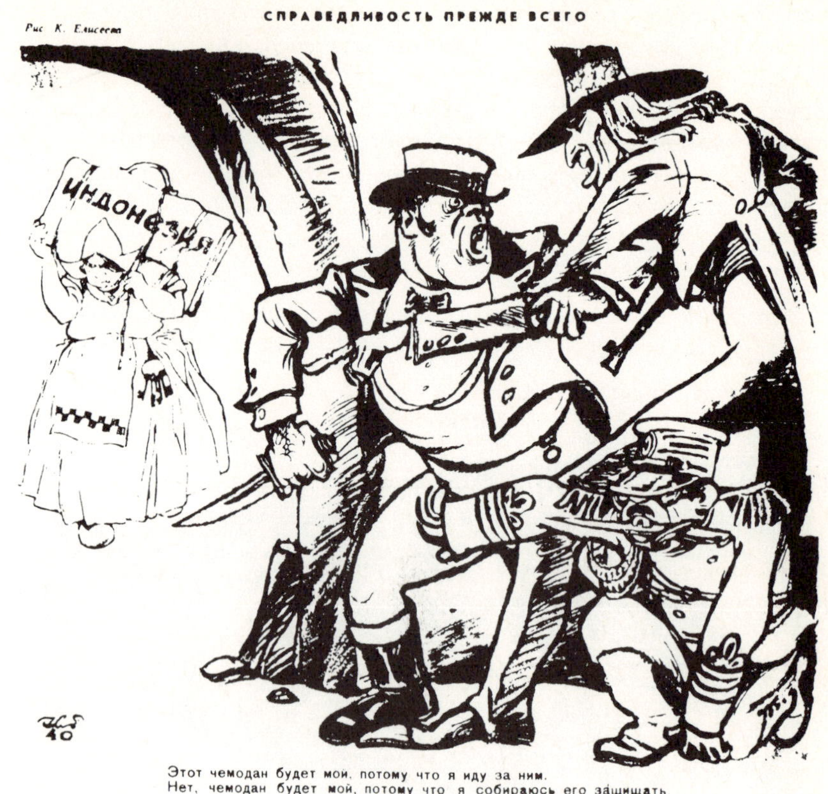

In 1940 the Netherlands collapsed even more rapidly than France or Belgium. This raised important questions about the future of Dutch overseas possessions, particularly the Dutch East Indies – now Indonesia. In this Soviet cartoon, 'Fairness above all', a rather unpleasant-looking woman in Dutch costume – possibly meant to represent Queen Wilhelmina – carries a large suitcase labelled 'Indonesia' and a bunch of keys – which seems to suggest that the East Indies are kept in servitude. British and American robbers each seek to steal the suitcase for themselves, and are quarreling bitterly. The dialogue reads:

> 'That suitcase will be mine because I am going for it.'
> 'No, the suitcase will be mine because I am getting ready to defend it.'

Meanwhile a third robber, with Japanese features, prepares to spring upon the Dutch woman and seize the suitcase to his own advantage.

Soviet propaganda in this period contended that the conflict was an 'imperialist war', which was really concerned not with ideologies but with colonies and markets. On that view, the British and Americans would both be expected to attempt to seize Dutch possessions, now that the Netherlands government was seriously weakened. Quarrels between the various 'imperialist' powers in the area – notably the British, the Americans, and the Japanese – would be expected to occur. In fact, no attempt was made by either Britain or the United States to take over Dutch colonies. The East Indies remained in the hands of the Netherlands government-in-exile until the Japanese attack at the end of 1941.

Cartoon 5.8 Na semeynom prazdnike. *Krokodil*, Moscow, no. 21, November 1940

НА СЕМЕЙНОМ ПРАЗДНИКЕ

Сожалеем, что несколько задержались, но мы только что освободились.

A Soviet view of the seizure of the Baltic States. Three girls, whose sashes are labelled respectively Latvia, Lithuania, and Estonia, are welcomed to a feast by young people wearing national costumes of other Soviet republics. The caption means, roughly, 'Family celebration'; the banner welcomes them to the 'friendship of the peoples of the Soviet Union'.

The mechanism by which the Baltic States were seized is relevant to an understanding of this cartoon. Enormous pressure was exerted to bring down the existing governments in the three countries and replace them by Soviet sympathizers. 'Elections' were then held, at which only Communists and Communist sympathizers were allowed to stand. The new Parliaments then applied for incorporation in the Soviet Union – a request which was granted a few weeks later.

The official Soviet view, illustrated in Krokodil, was that the Baltic States had voluntarily acceded to the Soviet Union. They had belonged to the Russian Empire before the Revolution, when they became independent. So, in the cartoon, they are seen as returning to a community to which they had previously belonged. The woman speaking on behalf of the other Republics greets them with the words, 'We are sorry that you are somewhat late, but are glad that you have been rescued.'

Cartoon 5.9 . . .And the east wind blew stronger!
Daily Mirror, London, 29 June 1940

This cartoon refers to the difficulties of Romania in the immediate aftermath of the French collapse. King Carol II of Romania is on the steeple and is being blown by storm clouds bearing the features of Hitler and Stalin. The king looks with particular alarm at the eastern wind – Stalin. The Soviet Union was at that moment exerting massive pressure on Romania to cede the province of Bessarabia and the northern part of Bukovina.

Whether Hitler was 'blowing' as well, as this cartoon suggests, is more doubtful. The Romanians, who had traditionally looked to France for help, were turning reluctantly to Germany as their only possible protector against further Soviet aggression. Germany certainly had an economic interest in Romania, whose oil was extremely important for the Nazi war machine, but was probably reluctant at this point to enter serious rivalry against the Soviet Union.

Early in September, a government more sympathetic towards the Germans than was King Carol, took office in Romania. Carol fled the country and his son Michael became king.

6

Autumn 1940

By the end of September 1940, it was evident that a German invasion of Britain was no longer possible that year. In the ensuing autumn and winter, the Germans conducted a great deal of 'terror bombing' against Britain. The object was to shatter civilian morale; the effect was the reverse. A wave of public fury was generated against the assailants, and with it a determination to prosecute the war against Germany at all costs. Government propaganda seems to have played little part in this surge of opinion.

At midsummer, there had been reason for thinking that the war in Europe would soon end. By the early autumn, it was clear that it would continue for a considerable time to come. Thus all countries needed to make long-term plans which had not seemed necessary a few months earlier.

Towards the end of September a new agreement was reached between Germany, Italy, and Japan. This arrangement, the so-called Tripartite Pact, effectively reconstituted the pre-war Anti-Comintern Pact, which had been shattered by the German–Soviet agreements of the previous year. This alliance did not bring Japan immediately into the war, but represented a sort of division of worldwide spheres of influence between the three countries. Apparently efforts were made to link the Soviet Union with the Pact, but these failed because of disagreements over the Balkans.

In the late summer and autumn, Italy tried to seize what she could. It is interesting to speculate how far this behaviour was prompted by avarice, and how far by fear that her ally Germany was becoming dangerously powerful. British Somaliland was easily taken. Italy now prepared an assault on Egypt.

Egypt was not a British possession, but was under strong British influence. Under a Treaty made in 1936, Britain was authorized to maintain troops in Egypt to defend the Suez Canal, and larger numbers of soldiers in event of war. The Suez Canal was extremely important to maintain sea communications with India and other British territories in Asia, and with Australasia. A decision was taken to defend Egypt strongly, in spite of the risk that British troops might suddenly be required at home to deal with a German invasion. In the middle of September, an

attack was launched against Egypt from Libya, then an Italian colony. At first the Italians cut far into Egypt, but soon the tide of war turned. By the end of the year the British had begun to invade Libya, and had captured great numbers of Italian prisoners.

At the end of October, Italy launched an attack on Greece. Most people expected Greece to be overrun; but the Greeks turned at bay, inflicted serious defeats on the Italians, and before the year was out had advanced well into Albania.

Thus in the closing months of 1940 the war was taking on a new character. Germany was supreme in most of northern and western Europe. Italy, however, was everywhere on the retreat.

Cartoon 6.1 Thirty days had September. . . *Daily Herald*, London, 30 September 1940

THIRTY DAYS HAD SEPTEMBER...

The most important question of all in the late summer of 1940 was whether there would be a German invasion of the British Isles. As summer passed into autumn, conditions became increasingly unsuitable for an invasion. In this cartoon Goebbels, German Minister of Propaganda, keeps postponing the date for 'the balloon to go up' – for Hitler to invade Britain – to the confusion of his domestic audience. There are several punctures in the balloon 'Invasion'. By the time this cartoon was drawn, it was virtually certain that no serious invasion could be launched until the following spring – if at all. Meanwhile, Britain was accumulating more and more weapons, particularly small arms from the United States.

This cartoon was drawn by the same artist as an earlier one (Cartoon 2.5), which had suggested that the Nazis were very vulnerable to German public opinion, which would respond to 'the truth' revealed by British leaflets. In the present case, the German audience seems to have complete sympathy with Hitler's objective, although it is becoming restive at the Führer's failure to achieve that objective. By the second half of 1940, little distinction, if any, was being made in British propaganda between 'the Nazis' and 'the Germans'.

Cartoon 6.2 Orders and decorations. *Evening Standard*, London, 4 October 1940

As a result of the Tripartite Pact of September 1940, Mussolini, Hitler, and the representative of Japan have received their 'Orders and Decorations' – their spheres of influence – as Lords of Africa, Europe, and Asia respectively. To the left of the picture, Stalin has evidently protested to the German Foreign Minister, Joachim von Ribbentrop, that he is receiving nothing under the arrangements. Ribbentrop assures Stalin that Hitler will soon have a 'New Order' for him.

The Nazis had declared that they were establishing a 'New Order' in Europe, and there is a pun on the word 'Order'. Ribbentrop is implying that Hitler has hostile intentions against the Soviet Union in the not-too-distant future. This cartoon is remarkably perceptive: indeed, it seems to have anticipated Hitler's actual decision by a couple of months. Yet it was a fair inference from observed events. If the Soviet Union and Germany

could not agree about spheres of influence, then sooner or later war between them was predictable.

Josef Stalin was often spoken of in the west as 'Joe' or 'Uncle Joe'. Later in the war, Churchill frequently referred to him as 'U.J.' in messages to President Roosevelt. The use of first names in cartoons, writing and popular speech was curious and irregular. Stalin was the only Soviet leader mentioned in this way. Churchill was universally known in Britain as 'Winston' and Hitler as 'Adolf'. Few if any other British public figures were then commonly known by their Christian names, and – of the German leaders – Hermann Göring was the only one granted the same familiarity as the Führer. Roosevelt was seldom called 'Franklin' by the general public, either in Britain or in his own country.

Mussolini, as 'Lord of Africa', appears to be chief of a primitive tribe. Even enlightened Europeans at that time generally took a very patronizing view of people from other parts of the world, and the cartoonist's readers probably visualized most Africans as savages.

Hitler, as 'Lord of Europe', is drawn as a Germanic barbarian of the first millennium AD. He wears a blonde wig, although his real hair was dark. Nazi internal propaganda laid much stress on the 'racial superiority' of 'Aryans' and – among the Aryans – the tall, fair-haired, blue-eyed 'Nordic' people: a type which neither Hitler himself nor most of the Nazi leaders resembled. The word 'Aryan' (which is really a linguistic and not an ethnological term) was used in contrast with other groups of people – e.g. the 'Semitic' people, and was exploited to support the persecution of Jews, gipsies, and others whom the Nazis considered not merely 'non-Aryan' but 'Untermenschen' – 'sub-humans'.

The Nazis never allowed this bizarre theory to obstruct their diplomacy. The Japanese were in no sense 'Aryan' at all, but Hitler welcomed the Japanese as associates and eventually as allies against the ('Aryan') British. It is striking to note that the Italian Fascists did not entertain the preposterous racial theories of the Nazis.

Cartoon 6.3 'All mine!' *Daily Mirror*, London, 9 August 1940

"All Mine!"

Shortly after the fall of France, Italy attacked the colony of British Somaliland, in east Africa, and after a short time succeeded in overrunning it. This cartoon suggests that the triumph over which Mussolini is rejoicing was more or less worthless.

Cartoon 6.4 Mediterranean outlook – visibility bad.
Evening Standard, London, 7 October 1940

The Italian attack on Egypt commenced in mid-September 1940, at a time when a German invasion of Britain was seen as an immediate possibility. At first, Marshal Graziani made considerable progress, but then halted, apparently because of supply difficulties. This cartoon suggests that it was the presence of the British navy which made it impossible for Mussolini to give the necessary assistance to Graziani. For a long time, little change took place in North Africa; but early in December the British were able to counter-attack.

Mussolini, who is attempting without success to gain sight of 'victorious Graziani' through his periscope across the hull of a great British warship, is being accosted by Hitler, who shows irritation at the slow progress being made.

Cartoon 6.5 O. . .prostates ton Mikron. *Eleftheron Vema*, Athens, 2 November 1940

The Italian invasion of Greece was launched on 28 October 1940. This Greek cartoon was drawn a day or two later. Mussolini, ironically described as 'the protector of the small' is astonished that little Greece is resisting his designs. He says, 'Hey, there, my boy, I am seeking your good!' Behind Mussolini stand the bound figures of Italian possessions: Libya, Ethiopia (Abyssinia), Albania, and the Dodecanese.

Two of these possessions would have been of particular interest to Greek readers. Albania, which had been seized by Italy in 1939, was the base for the Italian attack, and a considerable proportion of its population was Greek in language and culture. The Dodecanese – the 'twelve islands' in the Aegean – had been Turkish until 1912, when they were acquired by Italy. The population, however, was overwhelmingly Greek. The Greeks had a long history of conflict with the Italians, of which all readers of this cartoon would have been aware.

Cartoon 6.6 Appearances are sometimes deceptive.
New York Herald Tribune, 9 November 1940

The Greeks rapidly counter-attacked against the Italians, with considerable success. In this American cartoon, Mussolini first tells a sympathetic Hitler that he proposes to attack the Greek soldier; but, once battle is joined, finds himself in difficulty with his intended victim and cries to Hitler for assistance.

It now seems unlikely that Hitler ever encouraged an Italian attack on Greece – from which Germany could gain nothing. Mussolini was probably more interested in forestalling Hitler than in helping him, and can hardly have wished for German 'assistance' because of a few early reverses.

Cartoon 6.7 Meta ton vomvardismon tes Kerkuras.
Eleftheron Vema, Athens, 27 December 1940

Μετὰ τὸν βομβαρδισμὸν τῆς Κερκύρας

ΗΡΩΔΗΣ: Μ' ἔφαγες, Μπενίτο!...

The Italian bombardment of Kerkyra (Corfu Town) on Christmas Day 1940 was an act of terrorism which horrified opinion in many countries. In this Greek cartoon, which appeared on the day before the Feast of the Holy Innocents, the ghost of King Herod indicates his approval of Mussolini's own 'massacre of the innocents'.

Current events in Corfu were a poignant reminder to Greeks of the island's past history. The population was mainly Greek, but for many years, down to the late eighteenth century, it had belonged to Venice. For part of the nineteenth century, Corfu and the other Ionian Islands were British, but on the strong advice of Gladstone the wishes of the people of the islands to join Greece were respected, and they were handed over voluntarily in 1864. In 1923 the Italians bombarded, and for a time occupied, Corfu, before evacuating it in response to pressure from the League of Nations. Thus recent events in Corfu recalled to Greeks both their historic friendship with Britain and the imperialist ambitions of Italians.

Cartoon 6.8 Musseum piece. *Daily Express*, London, 17 December 1940

MUSSEUM PIECE

ADOLF: "Now explain this one!"

By mid-December 1940, Italy was in great difficulties. British Commonwealth forces swung to the attack in North Africa, and the Greeks had advanced well into Albania. The cartoon title is a pun on the name of Mussolini – commonly called 'Musso' in Britain. Hitler, looking far from pleased, demands an explanation from Mussolini, the museum official, of several items. 'Abyssinian pottery' refers to the risings which Britain was currently fomenting in Abyssinia. The 'Grecian vase' shows Greek soldiers driving the corpulent figure of Mussolini out of Albania. Hitler is particularly disturbed at the 'Egyptian decoration'.

Sidi Barrani, on the Egyptian coast, represented the furthest advance of the Italians in September. On 11 December it was recaptured by the British – the 'decoration' represents an Australian soldier, a British seaman, and RAF aeroplanes. Great numbers of Italian prisoners, including staff officers, were taken. 'The Key' suggests that this victory was the key to the whole military situation in North Africa.

Hitler's annoyance is easy to understand. A decisive Allied victory either in the Balkans or in North Africa would have widespread strategic implications for Germany as well as Italy. As the inscription in the bottom right hand corner suggests, further Allied victories over Italy seemed likely in the near future. By the date of the cartoon, Italy was more of a liability than an asset to Hitler.

Cartoon 6.9 Woodman, don't spare that tree! *Daily Mail*, London, 19 March 1941

WOODMAN, DON'T SPARE THAT TREE!

—by Illingworth.

Cartoon 6.9, drawn in March 1941, shows the *denouement* so far as Mussolini's ambitions were concerned. The British woodman, wielding an axe carrying the Union Jack, is cutting down 'Musso[lini]'s African Empire', among whose leaves sits the Italian dictator. The chips carry the names of places in British Somaliland, Italian Somaliland and the Italian colony of Eritrea which had recently been captured, or recaptured, by British forces.

This cartoon, like the previous one, implies that further Allied (and particularly British) victories were likely in the near future.

7

The Neutrals

When 1941 began, Britain, Germany, and Italy were still the only major Powers engaged in the conflict; but none of them was in any position to deliver a 'knock out blow' against the other side, and it looked as if the eventual upshot would be determined by the behaviour of countries which were still neutral.

A few countries were destined to remain neutral throughout the war. Eire was still part of the British Commonwealth in those days, but did not enter the war in 1939 when other Commonwealth countries did so. Spain, on the other hand, was expected by many people to enter the war on Germany's side, but also remained neutral. So did Turkey, although her participation on either side seemed possible at different points in the war and could have exerted a great influence on events.

In the first few months of the year, a great deal was happening in the Balkans. Until the middle of 1940, it had suited the purposes of all major Powers to leave south-eastern Europe alone. In the second half of that year, however, the Soviet Union, Germany, Italy, and finally Britain – as the ally of Greece – had become involved in Balkan affairs.

The Italian failure in Greece, and the concomitant risk that the Allies would secure a firm foothold in the southern Balkans, presented an intolerable threat to Hitler. If the Italians could not deal with the Greeks, then the Germans must do so. Access to Greece, however, was difficult for Germany, who had no maritime presence in the Mediterranean. Hungary and Romania, though not really German allies at this stage, were under strong German influence; but neither of them shared a common frontier with Greece. The only feasible route for Germany to intervene was through Bulgaria or Yugoslavia.

After great German pressure, Bulgaria yielded, but Yugoslavia was a different proposition. The government was disposed, though reluctantly, to come to terms with Germany. The leaders of the country's armed forces thought differently. On 25 March, Yugoslav representatives signed an alliance with Germany and Italy. Two days later there was a *coup d'état* in Belgrade. The young King Peter II, just a few months short of his eighteenth birthday and legal majority, was declared to be of age, and the power of the Regent, Prince Paul, was ended. The country could

now be regarded as firmly pro-Allied in its orientation.

Germany exerted strong pressure on the Greeks to come to terms with Italy. British 'official' opinion was by no means united as to whether Greek resistance was advisable; but in the end the Greeks decided to stand against the new challenge. On 6 April, Germany invaded both Yugoslavia and Greece, and within a very few weeks had occupied the mainlands of both countries, although some guerilla resistance persisted in remote areas. Crete held out for some time, but the Germans were in control there too by the end of May.

Cartoon 7.1 The riddle of the Sphinxes. *New York Times*, 26 January 1941, copying *Manchester Dispatch*

"THE RIDDLE OF THE SPHINXES"

Butterworth in The Manchester Dispatch

A cartoon drawn very early in 1941. The many neutral 'sphinxes' look with great suspicion at each other, while the world ponders the question – or questions – which they pose. Among those neutrals were still numbered the United States, the Soviet Union, and Japan, as well as smaller, but still very significant, countries like Turkey, Yugoslavia, Spain, and Vichy France.

Bulgaria, Turkey, and Japan all look with particular apprehension in the direction of Stalin, perhaps because all of them were worried about the possibility of a Soviet attack. 'Uncle Sam' shows particular concern about Japan. The Americans were perturbed about growing Japanese strength in the Pacific.

Cartoon 7.2 'What a curious fellow. He says he does know a better 'ole.' *The Star*, London, 4 October 1940

Hitler, Mussolini and a Japanese officer are in a shell hole, with 'ruin' blasting around them. Franco, dictator of Spain, has left the hole and is looking for safety elsewhere.

Franco's victory in the Spanish civil war of 1936–9 was attributable to German and Italian assistance, and many people expected Spain to enter the war on the German side. If she had done so in 1940, this might have posed great difficulties for Britain in the Mediterranean.

The inclusion of a Japanese in the shell hole at this stage of the war is striking. Japan was not yet involved in the 'main' war, although she had been fighting a war of her own against China for several years. Many people continued to regard her as a 'moral enemy', and this disposition may have played a substantial part in encouraging policies which eventually brought her into war on Germany's side.

The caption alludes to a very famous First World War cartoon by Bruce Bairnsfather. A young soldier and an older one – 'Old Bill' – are in a shell hole similar to the one portrayed here. The younger man complains about the hole; his companion retorts that if he knows a 'better 'ole' he should go to it.

Cartoon 7.3 In the Balkan web. *Punch*, London, 19 February 1941

IN THE BALKAN WEB

Hitler, the spider, has ensnared Hungary and Romania (not quite true at this date), while Bulgaria is in great difficulties (more accurate). Yugoslavia – where there were considerable altercations between pro-German and pro-Allied elements – is shaking the web. Greece, which has a visible sting in its tail, seems likely soon to break free. A much larger insect – Stalin – has blundered into the web, and is preparing even more trouble for the spider. Whether Stalin should be regarded as a potential victim or as another spider is an interesting point of speculation. Mussolini is not even acknowledged; in the Balkans he scarcely mattered by February 1941.

Cartoon 7.4 The lively corpse. *Daily Express*, London, 31 March 1941

THE LIVELY CORPSE

"YOU HAVE SPOILT A BEAUTIFUL FUNERAL! I DEMAND AN EXPLANATION!"

This cartoon was drawn after the Yugoslav *coup d'état* which repudiated alliance with Germany, but before the German attack on the country. Hitler, von Ribbentrop, Göring and Goebbels are the undertakers who had bound Yugoslavia, and were preparing to inter the country in the coffin 'Axis Pact'. The Yugoslav has untied his bonds and escaped from the coffin. The newspaper he is reading contains an overstated reference to a recent Italian reverse in the Mediterranean. The valley of the River Vardar, marked in the cartoon, provided an important communication through southern Yugoslavia into Greece. In the bottom right hand corner of the cartoon, the Japanese representative at the funeral prepares to depart. This point will be discussed later.

Cartoon 7.5 'I think we're being watched, mein Fuehrer'. *News Chronicle*, London, 9 April 1941

Between the Yugoslav *coup d'état* and the German attack, the Soviet Union concluded a treaty of friendship and non-aggression with Yugoslavia. This was a signal that any German move in that direction would meet strong disapproval in Moscow. The close association between Germany and the Soviet Union was clearly over.

In this cartoon Hitler is discussing his 'Drang nach dem Osten' – the traditional German policy of pressure towards the east – with one of his military leaders, and the names of possible objectives litter the ground. Propaganda Minister Goebbels warns Hitler that they are being 'watched'. The gigantic figure of Stalin looms over the hills.

Cartoon 7.6 The glory that is Greece. *Daily Express*, London, 15 April 1941

THE GLORY THAT IS GREECE

This cartoon commemorates the Greek decision to resist German pressure and to defend the country against attack from that quarter. The Greek soldier treads on the *fasces*, symbol both of ancient Rome and of Mussolini's Italy, and is prepared for whatever may come from the direction of the German swastika on the hills.

Cartoon 7.7 Beim Delphischen Orakel. *Das Reich*, Berlin, 4 May 1941

Allied writings and speeches at the time of the Italian, and later the German, attack on Greece made frequent allusions to Greece's classical past. This German cartoon, drawn shortly after the Germans secured control of the Greek mainland, also makes a classical reference – in this case to the celebrated ambiguity of the Delphic Oracle.

Prime Minister Churchill and Foreign Secretary Anthony Eden are making what is presumably a second visit to the Oracle. Churchill upbraids the priestess for having foretold wrongly that strangers entering Greece would be driven out. The priestess retorts 'Well, and. . .?' implying that her prophecy had really been fulfilled. It was the British (who had sent forces to aid the Greeks), and not the German invaders, who were the 'strangers' whom she had in mind.

It is now known that Churchill had been markedly less eager than Eden to encourage the Greeks to resist Germany in the first place – appreciating that Britain was in no position at that stage to give the Greeks adequate assistance. The cartoonist cannot have known that fact.

Cartoon 7.8 Der Spuk im St.-James Palast. *Das Reich*, Berlin, 22 June 1941

This German cartoon of June 1941, 'The ghosts in St James's Palace', reflects on the military and diplomatic position in Europe at that time. A considerable number of European countries had defended themselves unsuccessfully against German attack in the previous couple of years, and now had 'governments-in-exile' in London or elsewhere under British protection. Churchill is addressing a meeting of the 'ghosts' representing those countries. Foreign diplomats in Britain were (and are) accredited to the 'Court of St James'. The message is clear: all countries which had relied upon Britain thus far had been destroyed, and the same fate awaits any who may be so rash as to place similar reliance in the future.

8

The Soviet Union, 1939–41

At the beginning of the war, the Soviet Union had been seen in Britain and other Allied countries as a 'moral enemy', closely associated with Germany. The Soviet invasion of eastern Poland finally broke the resistance of a fighting ally. The 'winter war' against Finland was regarded as clear proof both of the rapacity and of the military incompetence of the USSR. These views had been held not just by the political 'right' but by people of most shades of opinion. In Britain at any rate, people were motivated much more by the role which the Soviet Union seemed to be playing in the war than by considerations of ideology.

At the time of the Battle of France there were some signs that the Allies were seeking a *rapprochement* with the Soviet Union, and in the aftermath – as we have seen – British leaders decided that eventually Germany and Russia would go to war. Every effort was therefore made to avoid attitudes which would hinder that development. There was little British protest, for example, at the seizure of the Baltic States in the late summer of 1940. In the latter part of 1940 and the early months of 1941, there were various signs which suggested that relations between the Soviet Union and Germany were less close than they had been in the autumn of 1939, although there were few indications of any active Soviet desire to improve relations with the Allies.

A curious sign of growing Soviet apprehensions about Germany appeared in the spring of 1941. Yosuke Matsuoka, the Japanese Foreign Minister, was to visit Germany for discussions. At that time, the only practical way of making the journey was by rail across the Soviet Union. In March 1941, Matsuoka stopped at Moscow, and there had talks with Soviet leaders. No agreement emerged, and he proceeded on his way. On Matsuoka's return journey in the following month, he had further talks, and this time a Non-aggression Pact was concluded between the two countries. This development, like many events in international diplomacy, admitted of more than one interpretation; but one possible explanation was that the Soviet government had some idea that Germany planned to attack the USSR, and was anxious to avoid war with Japan simultaneously.

On 22 June 1941, Germany invaded the Soviet Union, and in the next

few days Italy, Romania, Finland, and Hungary joined in the war against the USSR on Germany's side. Japan decided, soon afterwards, to adhere to her recent Non-aggression Pact and remain neutral.

The British response was immediate. On the night of the German attack, Churchill broadcast a strong message of support for the Soviet Union. With considerable difficulty, Britain even persuaded the Polish government-in-exile in London and the Soviet Union to reach an agreement which enabled a Polish army to be organized on Soviet soil. The United States, which had been giving Britain every assistance short of war, gave similar help to the Soviet Union.

At first, many people had anticipated a swift and complete German victory. As the summer wore on, German armies advanced great distances into the Soviet Union and by the beginning of December had reached the outer suburbs of Moscow. Enormous numbers of casualties were inflicted on the Red Army and great numbers of prisoners were taken; but there was no sign of a Soviet collapse.

A considerable number of European countries gave more or less assistance to the Germans in their war against the Soviet Union. Finland and Romania were mainly concerned to recover territory which the Soviet Union had annexed from them in the previous year. Other countries of central and eastern Europe, which had come under German military domination, had little alternative but to do as they were required. 'Collaborationist' regimes, often composed of people who were sympathizers with Nazi ideology long before the war, had been set up in occupied countries of western Europe, and these also sent contingents.

Cartoon 8.1 The bargain. *News Chronicle*, London, 15 April 1941

When Matsuoka, the Japanese Foreign Minister, paid his second visit to Moscow, in April 1941, agreement was speedily reached for a Non-aggression Pact between the two countries. The papers which Matsuoka and his Soviet counterpart Molotov are holding behind their backs seem to represent the substance of the agreement.

The Soviet-Japanese agreement has not received the attention it deserves, and its importance would be difficult to overstate. When Germany attacked the Soviet Union just over two months later, Japan did not enter the conflict on Germany's side, and, in fact, the two countries were at peace until August 1945. This saved the Soviet Union from a two-front war. The German-Soviet war was a 'close-run thing'; a simultaenous attack from Japan might well have proved fatal.

The Japanese, freed from immediate risk on the Soviet front, were able to develop their interests further south: interests which eventually brought them into conflict with Britain and the United States. There are curious parallels between the effects of the two Soviet Non-aggression Pacts. The pact of 1939 enabled Germany to concentrate her attention first on Poland and later on France without fear of Soviet intervention; the pact of 1941 enabled Japan to concentrate first on China and later on the western democracies.

Cartoon 8.2 Forgive me comrade. . . *Daily Mail*, London, 23 June 1941

For a considerable time relations between the Soviet Union and Germany had been deteriorating, and Hitler's action in stabbing Stalin was by no means as unexpected as this cartoon rather implies.

In the background, German soldiers and aeroplanes advance towards the Soviet wheatfields and power supplies. At that moment, neither the cartoonist nor his readers were likely to have much sympathy with Stalin's plight; but they could see a common interest in frustrating Hitler's designs.

The cartoon suggests that Hitler's attack was likely to prove fatal. Many people in Britain and the United States appear to have expected that result.

Cartoon 8.3 Khorosha shapka! *Krokodil*, Moscow, no. 12, June 1941

Хороша шапка! Одна беда: по ней русские уже раз давали.

An early Soviet reaction to the invasion. Hitler is trying on the costume of Napoleon. He is pleased with the 'nice hat' which is the title of the cartoon, but regrets his predecessor's bad fortune in Russia. In the looking-glass, Hitler sees his own death.

Soviet cartoons in the wartime period were constantly depicting the monstrous character of the invaders, and predicting their doom. Many of those cartoons drew parallels either with Napoleon's disastrous campaign of 1812 or with the German invasion during the 1914 war.

There were constant allusions to Russia's historical past; to military leaders like Peter the Great and Suvarov, and to literary figures like the poet Pushkin. Every effort was made to glorify past feats of Russian arms. Revolutionary themes were played down completely. No doubt Stalin and his advisers were well aware that many Soviet citizens were deeply alienated from the Communist regime, but could be expected to respond to an appeal to traditional 'patriotism'.

Cartoon 8.4 Daily Express, London, 30 June 1941

Japan did not come to Hitler's assistance in the war against the Soviet Union. If she had done, the intervention might have proved decisive.

This cartoon considers Japan's bewilderment immediately after the invasion commenced. In 1936, Hitler had appealed for Japan to join an Anti-Comintern Pact, whose nominal enemy was 'international Communism' sponsored by the Soviet Union. Japan complied. Then, in 1939, Hitler concluded her Non-aggression Pact with Russia . Japan was nonplussed, but eventually followed the new German lead and concluded her own Non-aggression Pact with the Soviet Union in April 1941.

When Germany went to war with the Soviet Union two months later, the Japanese refused to follow, preferring to stick to their recent treaty.

The Japanese appreciated that their own interests were by no means indissolubly bound up with those of Nazi Germany. We have already noted the shocked reaction of Japan to the German–Soviet Non-aggression Pact of 1939 (Cartoon 2.3). In the summer of 1941, the disparity of Japanese and German policies was equally clear; it is astonishing that the Allies made little effort to exploit that fact on either occasion.

Cartoon 8.5 Let us hope. *Chicago Tribune*, 5 December 1941

Cartoon 8.6 Not geography, but – FACT. *Daily Herald*, 16 September 1941

Not geography, but—FACT.

Cartoons 8.5 and 8.6 present two radically different views of how the democratic countries should behave towards the German–Soviet conflict. Both views were put forward in Britain and in the United States. The *Chicago Tribune*, the leading neutralist and anti-Soviet newspaper in the United States, argued that the best course was to leave the two antagonists to destroy each other.

The *Daily Herald* expressed the opposite view. At the end of the summer of 1941, Leningrad was just beginning to endure an enormously long and terrible siege from the advancing Germans. The cartoonist suggests that if Leningrad (which symbolized the resistance of the Soviet Union) should fall, then London would become the front line; while if London should fall, then New York would be threatened.

Cartoon 8.7 Cupid. *News Chronicle*, 25 June 1941

CUPID

The British government had anticipated the German attack on the Soviet Union for some time and had prepared its response. On the night of the invasion, Churchill made a broadcast statement to the effect that Britain would give what help she could to the Soviet Union. The United States, though still technically neutral, was already giving massive assistance to Britain, and as soon as the Soviet Union was attacked gave similar help there.

In this cartoon, Hitler, as Cupid, stirs the affections of President Roosevelt and Winston Churchill towards Stalin. There was never any real question of the advice which the *Chicago Tribune* implied in the earlier cartoon being followed by either the British or the American government. 'The enemy of my enemy is my friend' was the general view.

Cartoon 8.8 Gegenseitige Hilfeleistung. *Das Reich*, Berlin, 27 July 1941

In July 1941 the British and Soviet governments made a Mutual Assistance Pact, agreeing that neither would conclude a separate peace agreement with Germany or her allies. This cartoon, 'Reciprocal assistance', presents a German view of the new agreement. Churchill and Stalin, who are both drowning and shouting 'Help!' clasp each other desperately.

At that point of the war, there was something to be said for this assessment of the situation. The Soviet Union was suffering great military reverses. Britain was not at that moment suffering similar reverses, but had failed to retain any 'fighting ally' for very long. Neither Britain nor the Soviet Union was able to give much immediate help, either directly or indirectly, to the other.

Cartoon 8.9 Blunting the Blitz. *Daily Express*, London, 28 July 1941

BLUNTING THE BLITZ.

The German attack against the Soviet Union surged forward. Enormous areas of Soviet territory were occupied; but neither the Red Army nor the Soviet state showed signs of collapse. As Churchill pointed out, what mattered at that stage was not so much where the Eastern Front lay, but that the Eastern Front continued to exist.

Five weeks or so after the attack began, the German army was constantly advancing and the Red Army was constantly retreating. Yet the 'Blitzkrieg' threat – the threat of a 'lightning war' which would destroy the enemy through one massive attack – had failed.

In this cartoon the German tank continues to advance and the Soviet tank continues to retreat; but the 'Blitzkreig' arrow is blunted and turned against Hitler, who becomes increasingly frantic in each successive drawing.

Cartoon 8.10 Our debt piles up! *Daily Mirror*, London. 30 October 1941

Our debt piles up!

As the struggle continued, the British and American public began to receive some idea of the enormous casualty lists, and the vast amount of destruction, in the Soviet Union. A great sense of admiration for the Soviet people was generated, and a lot of fellow-feeling too; Britain had proved that she could 'take it' in 1940; the Soviet Union was doing the same, but on a much larger scale, in 1941.

This *Daily Mirror* cartoon shows a growing pile of 'Russian losses', with the suggestion that these losses imposed a debt of honour on Britain.

Just as Soviet propaganda was playing down any kind of 'revolutionary' appeal in favour of a 'patriotic' appeal, so also was British propaganda emphasizing the heroism and the effectiveness of Soviet resistance – discounting any suggestion that Britain might perhaps 'contract out' of the war, leaving Germany and the Soviet Union to fight it out.

The British mood became increasingly one of frustration, not through defeat but through incapacity to play an active part in the war, for Britain was obviously far too weak at that point to take military action which would have much effect on the German campaign in the Soviet Union. The feeling of moral debt, however, induced a growing disposition to accommodate Soviet diplomatic interests.

Cartoon 8.11 A good clean up. *Daily Express*, London, 28 August 1941

A GOOD CLEAN UP

The only place where Britain and the Soviet Union were able to co-operate directly in military action in 1941 was Iran – then generally known as Persia.

There was evidence of Nazi influence which the Iranian government would not – or could not – effectively counter. This cartoon was drawn at the end of July 1941, when the two Allies were beginning to put pressure on Iran, but it represents more appropriately the position a month later, when Soviet troops entered Iran from the north and British troops entered from the south.

The Persian carpet is being cleaned of unpleasant 'Nazi tourists' by the rifles of the Allies. Germans who were ostensibly holiday-making tourists had established themselves in various other countries from time to time in preparation for a military take-over. The carpet-beater of the Iranian who sits baffled on the ground was inadequate for the task.

Cartoon 8.12 La Dernière Croisade. *La Gerbe*, Paris, 16 October 1941

LA DERNIÈRE CROISADE

– Litvinov! Litvinov! . . . Ne vois tu pas, au loin, poindre L'Américain?
– Hélas, Petit Père, sur la steppe qui poudrais, je ne vois . . . que L'Europe! . . .

How important were Nazi Germany's European allies in the war against the Soviet Union? One view is expressed in this French 'collaborationist' cartoon. A desperate Stalin in a beleagured city – presumably Moscow – addresses his look-out man, Maxim Litvinov (former Soviet Foreign Minister who became Ambassador to the United States), asking whether he can see, in the distance, the Americans coming – that is, coming to give assistance to the Soviet Union in her dire straits. Litvinov replies that he can see nothing coming across the steppe except Europe. Contingents bearing various European flags are coming from the distance, intent on destroying Stalin. Litvinov addresses Stalin with the epithet 'Little Father' – a term respectfully applied by Russians before the Revolution to the Tsar. The 'Great Father' was God, to Whom the Tsar was considered next in rank.

The conversation has literary echoes, and its metre is somewhat reminiscent of the *alexandrin* used by writers like Racine. The language is also an imitation of the French classical style.

There is a perceptible difference between German cartoons, which make little reference to the role of the European collaborators, and the cartoons of a journal like *La Gerbe*, which maintained the 'romantic' view that the war against the Soviet Union was indeed the 'last Crusade' in which – as in the medieval Crusades – European nations which had often been in conflict with each other joined forces against a common enemy.

Cartoon 8.13 Fashistskaya Psarnya. n.d.

ФАШИСТСКАЯ ПСАРНЯ

Cartoon 8.14 Triumf Pobeditelya. n.d.

Both from *Sovyetskii Masteri Satira, 1941–45*. (*Soviet Masters of Satire, 1941–45*), Moscow/Leningrad, 1946

ТРИУМФ ПОБЕДИТЕЛЯ

Гитлеровская „аллея побед"

These two Soviet cartoons express complete contempt not merely for the behaviour of Hitler's European allies but for their military value.

In the first cartoon, 'Fascist kennel', Mussolini of Italy, Horthy of Hungary, Tiso of Slovakia*, Mannerheim of Finland, and Antonescu of Romania – the countries which actually declared war on the Soviet Union – wait hungrily by, while Hitler gnaws on the bone. Nazi Germany alone is profiting; the dogs have given nothing, and are deriving no benefit from the relationship.

In the second cartoon, Hitler and his Minister of Propaganda, Goebbels review the 'Hitlerite "Allies for Victory"'. Various 'collaborationist' leaders, including Mussert of the Netherlands, Quisling of Norway, and Pétain of France, stand on plinths bearing white flags of surrender with legends like 'Capitulation of Holland on the 5th day', 'Capitulation of Norway on the 21st day', 'Capitulation of France on the 35th day', referring to the brief periods for which their respective countries contrived to fight against the attacking Germans. Rather strangely, Denmark, which did not fight at all against the invaders, is omitted. More significantly, there is no Polish representative; Poland produced no 'collaborationist' leader at all. Perhaps the Nazis, who regarded the Poles as *Untermenschen* – sub-humans – made no attempt to find such a person during the brief Polish campaign of 1939.

Hitler carries a whip, whose implication is obvious. Hitler's Propaganda Minister, Goebbels, a short man who is often presented as a simian figure, wears a tail which matches Hitler's whip.

In both cartoons, no distinction is made as to the circumstances in which Hitler's associates came into their predicaments. In the first cartoon, for example, Mannerheim and Antonescu, who had joined the war primarily in order to recover territory which the Soviet Union had recently seized from them, are not distinguished from Mussolini or Tiso who had no such grievance. In the second cartoon, willing collaborators like Mussert and Quisling are not distinguished from Pétain, who reluctantly accepted the part he played after the French military defeat of 1940.

* When Czechoslovakia was destroyed in March 1939, the western provinces of Bohemia and Moravia became a German protectorate, and the far-eastern province of Ruthenia was annexed by Hungary. Slovakia, in the middle, became nominally independent.

9

Atlantic partnership, 1939 – 41

At the beginning of the war in Europe, the United States was neutral. Public opinion polls were frequently held in America, and at this stage of the conflict certain very clearly defined views emerged. Practically everybody hoped that the Allies rather than the Germans would be victorious. Large majorities believed that the United States should keep out of the conflict. Some people, however, were persuaded that the United States would eventually become involved on the Allied side whatever was done, and that the sooner America took the plunge the better. It would seem likely that President Franklin D. Roosevelt eventually came to hold that view, though whether he did so at the very beginning is less certain.

The President had been in office since early 1933. His party, the Democratic Party, held substantial majorities both in the Senate and in the House of Representatives, as it had done since 1932. Matters of finance and legislation, as well as the final decision whether to go to war, rested in the hands of Congress. It could not be assumed that a Party in Congress would follow a President of the same persuasion in important matters to the degree that a British Prime Minister can normally expect members of his own Party to follow him in Parliament, and Congressmen were deeply conscious that their constituents were strongly opposed to American participation if this could possibly be avoided.

At the outbreak of the European war, a Neutrality Act was operative in the United States. This prescribed, among other things, that war materials should not be sent to belligerent countries. Many Americans wished, for reasons ranging from the selfish to the altruistic, to send arms to the Allies, though few wished to confer a similar favour on the Germans. The dilemma was met rather neatly. In November 1939, Congress modified the Neutrality Act, permitting belligerents to collect arms from the United States in their own vessels, but still forbidding American vessels to carry arms to belligerents. As the British navy was far too effective for a German vessel to be able to cross the Atlantic, collect arms, and then return home, the effect of the repeal was to enable the Allies but not the Germans to obtain war material from the United States.

In the course of 1940, German U-boat attacks on Allied shipping in the North Atlantic mounted. This represented the gravest risk of all to Britain, for half of her food, as well as great quantities of raw materials and weapons, came by sea. If the German grand strategy of the Battle of the Atlantic were to succeed, then Britain would be forced into submission.

To counter this fearful risk, the British and American governments reached an agreement in August 1940 to the effect that a large quantity of American war material, including fifty over-age destroyers, should be transferred to Britain; while, in return, the Americans should be authorized to establish wartime bases in certain British possessions on and near the American continent. Both elements of this agreement were very valuable for Britain. The destroyers would be very helpful against submarines; while the Americans would be assisting greatly in the defence of British territories without interfering with their sovereignty.

In November of the same year an American Presidential election was held. Custom, though not strict law, prescribed that a President should not stand for a third term, but Roosevelt decided to ignore that custom. His Republican opponent, Wendell Willkie, was very far indeed from the 'isolationist' wing of his own Party; indeed, his line on questions of foreign policy was difficult to distinguish from that of Roosevelt himself. In the end, the President was re-elected for a further four years.

During 1941, the Americans moved further and further from strict neutrality. In the early part of the year there was considerable controversy in the United States over the President's proposals for 'lend-lease'. The principle was that American material should be loaned to Britain for the duration, and its return made in kind after the war. Isolationist minorities in both Parties resisted the proposal in Congress, but it was eventually carried. When the Soviet Union entered the war against Germany a few months later, similar lend-lease facilities were extended to her.

In 1941 the German U-boat campaign was stepped up. This led to an even closer 'Atlantic partnership' between Britain and the United States. American naval vessels would accompany British merchant ships to the mid-Atlantic, and notify them of German vessels. In the eastern Atlantic British naval vessels would take over and conduct them for the remainder of their journey.

Cartoon 9.1 Uncomfortable grandstand. *Evening Standard*, London, 22 September 1939

UNCOMFORTABLE GRANDSTAND (*Copyright in All Countries.*)

Americans sit in the grandstand 'Neutrality', which carries the Stars and Stripes on its roof – observing the war, but not participating. Bombs and shells are whizzing around them. President Roosevelt turns concernedly to his Secretary of State, Cordell Hull. The cartoonist implies that neutrality was an untenable position; that the United States would sooner or later be forced into the conflict. That view was widely held in Britain at the time, but had fewer adherents in America.

Quite a lot of people in Britain, and perhaps this cartoonist, felt a measure of indignation against the United States for not immediately intervening on the Allied side.

Cartoon 9.2 Adolf locked out! *Daily Herald*, London, 8 November 1939

ADOLF LOCKED OUT!
(With profound apologies to Mrs. Anna Lea Merritt's famous picture, "Love Locked Out," in the Tate Gallery.)

On 4 November 1939, Congress repealed those clauses of the Neutrality Act which prohibited the sale of American arms to belligerents, but insisted that those belligerents must collect weapons in their own vessels. The door to the USA arsenal is locked by the British navy – that is, British warships make it impossible for Germany to carry arms across the Atlantic. The cup 'Blitzkrieg' lies shattered on the ground – implying that the Allies will in future be able to obtain enough weapons from the United States to destroy Hitler's capacity to defeat them in a 'Blitzkrieg' – a 'lightning war'.

Cartoon 9.3 Chelovekolyubee Dyadi. *Krokodil*, Moscow, no. 34, December 1939

ЧЕЛОВЕКОЛЮБИВЫЕ ДЯДИ

Рис. К. Елисеева

— Я охотно продам вам оружие. Только, умоляю вас, не пользуйтесь им во вред людям.

This Soviet cartoon, 'Uncle's [i.e. Uncle Sam's] Benevolence', is bitterly critical of Congress's recent modifications to the Neutrality Act. Uncle Sam is selling weapons to the Allied representatives. Behind him is a placard, 'Fresh Daily!', listing various weapons of war. The notice on the bench reads 'Credit spoils relationships' – meaning that only cash will be accepted. Uncle Sam tells the purchasers that he will be willing to let them have the weapons, but hypocritically enjoins them not to hurt people with those weapons.

In English slang of the period, 'uncle' meant a pawnbroker, which carried overtones of meanness and of capacity to drive a hard bargain against defenceless clients. Perhaps this idiom did not exist in Russian; but, if it did, this would provide an added point to the cartoon.

Cartoon 9.4 In a hurry, Mister? *Washington Post*, 23 June 1940

In A Hurry, Mister?

During the Battle of France, President Roosevelt had spoken very explicitly in support of the Allies – although he had not been able to satisfy the French Premier Paul Reynaud's plea that America should enter the war forthwith on the Allies' side.

This American cartoon shows the President hastening along 'Intervention Avenue' – in other words, moving as fast as he can towards American participation in the war. In his hurry he has knocked down Congress, which was proceeding at a more leisurely pace in the same direction, and is resentful of Roosevelt's haste and bad manners.

Cartoon 9.5 U posteli Dzhona Bulya. *Krokodil*, Moscow, no. 11, May 1940

Soviet cartoonists in this period had little sympathy either with Britain in her plight or with the United States for rendering assistance to Britain. This *Krokodil* cartoon shows the very sick John Bull visited by Uncle Sam in the character of a doctor. Uncle Sam murmurs, 'He must live! He owes me so much!' There is a light pun on the Russian word 'dolzhen', which means 'must' in the first sentence and 'owes' in the second.

The implication of the cartoon is that American assistance for Britain was prompted, not by idealistic sympathy with her cause, but by fear that, unless Britain survives, there will be no way in which the United States can recover the extensive British debts.

John Bull's bed is grandly bedecked, contrasting his opulent past with his precarious physical plight.

Cartoon 9.6 'Democracy is just a big fake!'
Evening Standard, London, 4 November 1940

The American Presidential elections were held on 5 November 1940. This cartoon, which appeared on the previous day, comments on the essential similarity of the opinions of the two candidates on the most vital issue of the day – the country's attitude to Nazi Germany. Both men held views very far removed from the 'isolationists' who could be found in both Parties, but particularly among the Republicans.

Although the candidates made no secret of their sympathy for the Allies, and of their desire to assist the Allies by means short of war, each of them also maintained that they would do what lay in their power to avoid American involvement in the conflict.

There seems to be a scintilla of reason in the complaint which the cartoonist attributes to Hitler. However they voted, the American electors had no real choice on the most important question facing their country – whether the United States should pursue a course of foreign policy designed to counter Nazi Germany at all costs, even at risk of war. Most British readers probably hoped that Roosevelt would win, but Willkie would be an acceptable alternative.

Cartoon 9.7 What more could we ask for?
Washington Post, 1 February 1941

What More Could We Ask For?

These cartoons were both drawn during the acute phase of the lend-lease controversy in the United States, and represent two widely different American views of available policies towards the war.

The first suggests what might happen if America did not give the fullest possible help to the Allies, even at some risk of the United States becoming involved in war themselves. The world would be organized to fit the will of Hitler, and the United States completely cut off. The 'appeasolationists' – a compound word from 'appeasers' and 'isolationists' – foolishly congratulate Uncle Sam on the decision he has taken to avoid involvement.

Cartoon 9.8 Our bombproof shelter with the reinforced roof. *Chicago Daily Tribune*, 6 March 1941

The second cartoon, from the isolationist *Chicago Daily Tribune*, reflects bitterly on the recent Presidential election campaigns and the policies which had been developed in the short period since then. Roosevelt, the Democratic Party candidate, and Willkie, the Republican candidate, had both made promises to try to keep America out of the war. In the current lend-lease controversy, both were supporting the government's proposals, which (the cartoonist implies) will be likely to lead to American involvement in the war.

Cartoon 9.8 suggests that the election promises of the two candidates have been shattered by bombs delivered from the 'War Bloc' – that is. from people in both Parties who favoured warlike policies. The '50 million voters', who had supported one or other candidate in reliance on their 'Platform Promises', are bemused among the ruins.

Cartoon 9.9 Opening the flood-gates. *Daily Mail*, London, 10 March 1941

In Britain, passage of the Lend-Lease Bill through Congress was almost universally welcomed. In this cartoon, President Roosevelt winds up the lock-gate 'American Aid to Britain' through the Lease and Lend Bill – thus letting in the flood which will swamp the Nazi leaders assembled at the 'New Order Picnic'. Ribbentrop, Hitler, Goebbels, and Göring are shown. The expression 'New Order' derives from a Nazi declaration that they were building a 'New Order in Europe'.

As the United States edged more and more closely towards involvement in the war, Roosevelt became an increasingly popular figure in Britain.

Cartoon 9.10 Thumbs down on Hitler. *News Chronicle*, London, 18 May 1941

THUMBS DOWN ON HITLER

Not long after the Lease-Lend Bill had passed through Congress, the American administration worked out a system in response to the German submarine campaign, under which American naval vessels would convoy shipping which carried supplies for Britain to the mid-Atlantic, where British vessels would take over.

President Roosevelt, who has already endorsed the Lend-Lease Bill and 'Neutrality Patrols', is preparing to give his final authorization to the convoys system by pressing the appropriate button in a 'thumbs down' gesture against the Nazis. The papers by the President's left hand allude to various indications that American public opinion was supporting his policy of increasing toughness towards Germany.

The reference to 'Stimson's speech' among the papers on the President's desk concerns Henry L. Stimson, a lifelong Republican but a strong supporter of aid for the Allies, whom Roosevelt had appointed Secretary for War in 1940, emphasizing the bipartisan character of his foreign policy. Other papers on the desk allude to the growing American sympathy with a 'tough' policy towards Germany, as evidenced in public opinion polls.

Cartoon 9.11 Die Platten des Herrn Roosevelt. *Das Reich*, Berlin, 10 August 1941

Die Platten des Herrn Roosevelt: „Nein, zum Totlachen, was man so in kurzer Zeit zusammenredet!"

By the latter part of 1941, the Germans had accepted that the United States was a 'moral enemy'. This cartoon of August 1941 was drawn shortly before the 'Atlantic Charter' meeting between Churchill and Roosevelt, which will be discussed in the next chapter.

President Roosevelt listens with cynical amusement to gramophone records of his own speeches. 'I will keep the USA out of the war!' – which probably comes from the 1940 Presidential election campaign – contrasts with the current situation, where the United States is moving more and more closely towards war. 'Stalin is the murderer of all culture, traditional and moral' contrasts with the much more recent 'We will assist Stalin to the best of our ability.'

10

Japan, 1939 – 41

In the early part of the war, it was far from clear that Japan and Germany would eventually become allies, however widely the war might extend. Japan had been at war with China for a long time. The Americans strongly favoured China for both economic and altruistic reasons. The British people felt much less closely involved in the conflict, so long as no assault was made on British possessions in the Far East.

As the European war developed, the Americans began also to intervene in the Far Eastern war. In September 1940 an embargo was imposed on certain American exports to Japan, which affected Japanese oil supplies. Japan could still get oil from the Dutch East Indies (Indonesia); but these supplies could easily become blocked.

The Soviet–Japanese Non-aggression Pact of April 1941 meant that Japan need no longer worry about her north-western defences, and from that point onwards she became increasingly interested in south-east Asia. Three months later, she made a further agreement with Vichy France for more bases in Indo-China. These new bases, unlike the ones she had acquired in the previous year, appeared to have little relevance to the war against China, but seemed designed to threaten British, Dutch, and American possessions in the general area of south-east Asia. It is quite possible that the Japanese had no plans of conquest at that stage, but were merely seeking economic influence. Whatever Japan's intentions may have been, the Americans responded immediately with an announcement that Japanese assets in the United States would be frozen. The British soon followed suit. This practically blocked trade with Japan.

As the economic measures began to bite against Japan, the country was compelled either to come to terms with the United States and Britain, or else to go to war against them. Japan would almost certainly have far preferred to make terms – if for no other reason than because she was deeply engaged in China and did not wish for another conflict with immensely stronger antagonists. By late November it was clear that Japan could not secure the economic relaxation she required. So she turned to the alternative, and set in operation plans for war.

On 7 December 1941, Japan attacked the American Pacific Fleet and air base at Pearl Harbor in Hawaii, and invaded the British possession of

Malaya. Later in the day, war was formally declared on both Britain and the United States. A few days later, Germany and Italy also declared war on the United States.

Thus the whole character of the war was changed. The 'Grand Alliance' of which Churchill had dreamed in the darkest part of 1940 had come into existence eighteen months later, for Britain, the United States, and the Soviet Union were all engaged in war against Germany and Italy. Perhaps he had not contemplated war against Japan as well at that moment; but it was a price which Churchill was certainly willing to pay in order to secure eventual victory against what he saw as the principal enemy.

Cartoon 10.1 'Scram!' *Daily Mirror*, London, 2 August 1940

"SCRAM!"

Towards the end of July 1940, the United States cut off supplies of certain kinds of fuel to countries outside the western hemisphere, in order to make it more difficult for Japan to wage her war against China. This represented an important step in the deterioration of American-Japanese relations.

In this British cartoon, Uncle Sam, the petrol attendant, rudely refuses supplies to the Japanese tank driver.

Cartoon 10.2 The dragon moves again. *Daily Express*, London, 21 October 1940

THE DRAGON MOVES AGAIN

By the middle of 1940, Japanese action made it very difficult for military supplies to reach China by sea. An important route for those supplies continued to run through the British colony of Burma. The Japanese set pressure on Britain to close the 'Burma Road'. Britain, who was in no position to refuse in the immediate aftermath of the fall of France, complied for a three-month period. The Americans mounted counter-pressure for Britain to reopen the Road once the three-month period was over, and in October Britain complied.

The decision to do this appears to have been generally popular in Britain. In this cartoon, a convoy of war materials, in the shape of the Chinese dragon, speeds into China along the reopened Road.

Britain had been compelled to choose between antagonizing the Americans, whose support was vital in the war against Germany, and embarking on a course of increasing hostility towards Japan, with the growing risk of a new war in the Far East for which she was ill-prepared.

Cartoon 10.3 'When are you coming in, Matsuoka?. . .'
Daily Express, London, 10 July 1941

"WHEN ARE YOU COMING IN, MATSUOKA? I'VE ALREADY ENTERED MY THIRD WEEK IN RUSSIA."
"WHAT'S THE HURRY, ADOLF? WE'VE JUST ENTERED OUR FIFTH YEAR IN CHINA."

Before the Japanese–Soviet Non-aggression Pact of April 1941, there had been a long period of hostility between the two countries. When Germany attacked the Soviet Union two months later, Japan had to choose whether to adhere to the recent Non-aggression Pact or to take advantage of the Soviet preoccupation with Germany and join in the attack. After some hesitation, the Japanese decided to stick to their treaty.

This cartoon suggests that Hitler was embarrassed and angry as a result of the Japanese decision. Japanese Foreign Minister Matsuoka points out blandly that his own country has long been engaged in war in China (without help from Germany, one might add) – and was too busy to assist.

The heat was taken off the Soviet Union; but the Japanese were now free to give their attention to the rich European and American possessions of south-east Asia and beyond.

Cartoon 10.4 Jap.: 'But I was invited in. . .'
Daily Express, London, 1 August 1941

JAP.: "BUT I WAS INVITED IN BY HONOURABLE HOST."

French Indo-China included modern Vietnam, Laos, and Cambodia. After the fall of France, the colony remained loyal to the Vichy government. The Japanese, however, immediately set pressure on the French to allow them to occupy military bases within the colony which were important for the war against China, and the French complied.

A year later, the Japanese applied pressure for further bases in Indo-China, which seemed to have nothing to do with the campaign against China but were likely to prove important if Japan later decided to attack British and American possessions in the Far East.

In this cartoon, the Japanese, laden with loot, is apprehended by John Bull and Uncle Sam as policemen – but points out that he was 'invited in'. Admiral Darlan, who at that time was particularly influential at Vichy, does not dispute the Japanese assertion. The French, indeed, had no particular reason for concern at the Japanese presence in their colony, for it was not they, but the British and Americans, who were threatened. Thus the Japanese miscreant could truthfully point out that the French permitted him to be in their property, but the British and American policemen were still deeply apprehensive of his motives.

The words 'Good Sea View' refer to Indo-China's strategic position, commanding much of the tropical area of the Pacific Ocean.

Cartoon 10.5 Sitting not so pretty. *News Chronicle*, London, 28 July 1941

SITTING NOT SO PRETTY

The American and British response to the Japanese move in Indo-China was to freeze Japanese assets in their own countries. The object – as the cartoon suggests – was to make the path of the Japanese economy so slippery that it would be forced to jettison the gigantic burden of 'Imperialism'. The Japanese – so it was hoped – would be forced to relax their grip on China and desist from threats against other countries, because they would be unable to obtain supplies of oil and other essential war materials.

The practical result was very different. Both the Japanese on one side and the Anglo-Americans on the other had every reason to avoid conflict – not least because of the other wars in which they were respectively interested; but they were rapidly drifting towards war with each other.

This cartoon, like many others drawn in Britain and the United States during the second half of 1941, demonstrates the growing hostility with which the governments of those countries were coming to regard Japan, who was by then perceived as an enemy second only to Germany in importance.

Cartoon 10.6 The War of Nerves. *Washington Post*, 20 August 1941

In August 1941, Roosevelt and Churchill met at Placentia Bay, in Newfoundland. The most famous product of their meeting was the 'Atlantic Charter' – a high-sounding declaration of war aims which was soon adopted (though with various mental reservations) by the other Allies. The 'Eight Points' of the Charter were soon eroded by various qualifications, and in the latter part of the war little was heard of it. The most remarkable feature of the Charter itself was the fact that it was supported both by Churchill and by the head of a country which was still, technically, neutral.

Roosevelt and Churchill clearly had not ventured on the dangerous and time-consuming journey to Newfoundland merely in order to issue a declaration like the Atlantic Charter. As this cartoon suggests, Hitler must fully have appreciated that the 'Eight Points' of the Atlantic Charter were supplemented by various other 'points' which were weapons of war directed against him.

Cartoon 10.7 Mystère et discretion. *La Gerbe*, Paris, 14 August 1941

— Chut ! J'ai pu venir sans qu'ils s'en doutent…
— Les Allemands ?
— Non : mes électeurs !

A French 'Collaborationist' view of the Roosevelt–Churchill meeting. Roosevelt greets his friend Churchill, remarking that he, the President, has been able to slip away without 'them' realizing it. Churchill assumes that Roosevelt means the Germans; Roosevelt corrects him and explains that he means his own electors. Churchill wears a lifebelt marked 'S.O.S.', and the British vessel is in a state of disrepair – indicating that Britain was in a parlous condition and was deeply dependent on American support.

For obvious reasons of security, the meeting had not been announced in advance. Yet it was also politically advantageous for the meeting to take place unannounced, for American isolationists would doubtless have protested noisily if they had known beforehand, fearing (with some justification) that the two men would devise ways of bringing the United States closer to participation in war.

Cartoon 10.8 'Enough in the tank. . .?' *Evening Standard*, London, 8 August 1941

The Anglo-American decision of July 1941 to freeze Japanese credits made it exceedingly difficult for Japan to get oil for her war machine. The question for the robbers in the armoured car was whether they had enough oil to get to the Dutch East Indies (Indonesia), where they could then seize all their requirements. In other words, did Japan possess sufficient oil reserves to fight her way to control of the East Indies, whereafter her oil problems would be at an end?

Cartoon 10.9 Somebody's getting the bird. *Daily Mirror*, London, 7 November 1941

Somebody's getting the bird!

For a substantial part of 1941, two very important sets of discussions were taking place. The first set of discussions was among the Japanese themselves, who were considering whether or not to go to war with the United States and Britain. The two sides were fairly evenly divided. Ultimately the matter turned on the fate of the other discussions – the 'Washington conversations' between representatives of the Japanese and American governments, where the Japanese sought to reach a tolerable compromise with the Americans about the future of Japanese credits and therefore the availability of goods from the United States and the Allies.

Eventually Sabure Kurusu, a particularly experienced Japanese diplomat, was sent to Washington to take charge of the conversations. As this British cartoon suggests, the gesture was not greeted with much enthusiasm.

'Noah', who is despatching the very warlike dove, is General Tojo, Prime Minister of Japan. The surrounding waters are turbulent and beset by German submarines, and the 'ark' is heavily armed. The firm impression is conveyed that the cartoonist neither expected nor wished the Kurusu mission to succeed.

Cartoon 10.10 United States. *News Chronicle*, London, 10 December 1941

The Kurusu mission to Washington failed to produce an acceptable compromise, and the Japanese probably thought – correctly – that the Americans were simply playing for time. Japan made active preparations for immediate war. On 7 December came the Japanese attack on the American base at Pearl Harbor and the British possession of Malaya.

Pearl Harbor produced an immediate and violent reaction in the United States and Britain, for the 'Washington conversations' were still in progress and there had been no Japanese declaration of war. Within a few hours, both countries were at war with Japan. The Allies were not only shocked at their losses, but furiously resentful of the circumstances of the attack.

The *News Chronicle* cartoon alludes to the almost complete national unity which the Japanese action produced in the United States; for after Pearl Harbor critics of American participation in the war were of negligible importance. Roosevelt heads the marchers, supported by his erstwhile Republican opponent, Wendell Willkie. Fiorello La Guardia was the pugnacious and charismatic Mayor of New York. Herbert Hoover had been Roosevelt's Republican predecessor at the White House, and was still politically active. John L. Lewis was a celebrated Trade Union leader, who at times proved a considerable thorn in the flesh of the government. Hearst was proprietor of a chain of hitherto isolationist newspapers, including the *Chicago Tribune*. Lindbergh had originally won fame as an aviator, but in more recent years had sometimes expressed considerable sympathy with the European dictators.

Although Hitler is one of the two figures in the bottom left-hand corner of the picture, the United States was not yet at war with Germany when this cartoon appeared.

Cartoon 10.11 From *Urok Istoryi (Lesson of History)*, Moscow, 1942

On 11 December 1941, the 'Grand Alliance' against Germany and Italy was completed by the German and Italian declarations of war against the United States. The reason remains far from clear, for it is hard to see what advantage Hitler or Mussolini could have envisaged for their own countries by involving them in war against a powerful enemy which might otherwise have been far too busy in the Pacific to trouble them much for a long time to come.

Whatever the motives of Hitler and Mussolini may have been, the practical result was to weld together the so-called 'Big Three' Allies – Britain, the United States, and the Soviet Union – in war against Germany and Italy.

In this Soviet cartoon, arms bearing the insignia of the 'Big Three' Allies are thrusting a stone marked 'Wartime friendship USSR, England, USA' on Hitler and Mussolini. There is no Japanese representative in the cartoon, for Japan and the Soviet Union remained at peace until August 1945. Soviet propagandists, who at this time had no wish to bring Japan into the war against them, were very circumspect about the Japanese.

China, which had been fighting against Japan since 1937, is seldom regarded as a major ally even in British cartoons of the period.

11

The Far East, 1941 – 2

At first, the Japanese attack was enormously successful. A great part of the American Pacific fleet was destroyed at Pearl Harbor on 7 December 1941, and within a short time the most important British vessels in the Pacific had been sunk as well. Japanese armies advanced with astonishing speed, and were soon in control of the British possessions, Malaya, Hong Kong and Burma, the Dutch East Indies, and the Philippines – then a possession of the United States. In February 1942, the Japanese were so close to Australia that they were able to bomb Port Darwin with aircraft whose range was, by modern standards, very short. Soon they seemed poised to invade either Australia, or India, or both.

The Japanese threat to India forced the British government to give urgent consideration to that country's political future. For many years there had been intermittent disorders in the subcontinent, where the very influential Congress Party had long demanded independence. Important constitutional legislation for India had been passed by the British Parliament a year or two before the war, but had not yet come into full operation. India's declaration of war against Germany in 1939 had been delivered by the Viceroy, after very little consultation with Indian leaders, but Congress refused to support this action. Now, in 1942, there was serious danger that a large number of Indians would co-operate actively with the Japanese if they invaded the country.

The British cabinet resolved to offer Dominion status to India after the war, provided that the Indians were prepared to co-operate in the war, and also that acceptable safeguards could be provided for the Moslem minority. Sir Stafford Cripps, who had by that time relinquished his diplomatic post in Moscow, was despatched to make this offer to the Indian leaders.

The Cripps mission failed to produce the agreement which the government desired. The cause of its failure was mainly the deep fears which Moslems entertained about their own likely fate in a predominantly Hindu India. Yet, once the offer had been made, no British government could henceforth treat the idea of Dominion status for India as unrealistic.

In the event, no major Japanese attack was made on India, although a small part of the country was invaded later in the war. By the middle of

1942, there were signs that the general Japanese advance was being contained. The battle of Midway Island in early June is sometimes considered to have been decisive. In August, a major Allied counter-attack commenced in the Solomon Islands. A very long time would elapse before defeat of Japan could be confidently predicted; but the early Japanese initiative had been lost.

Cartoon 11.1 Shades of an old fable. *Washington Post*, 2 January 1942

Shades Of An Old Fable

The extremely rapid Japanese advances at the end of 1941 and the beginning of 1942 led to bitter cartoon criticisms of alleged government unpreparedness, both in Britain and in the United States.

This *Washington Post* cartoon alludes to a children's story, familiar both in Britain and in the United States. Japan, as the 'Big Bad Wolf', has approached the straw house of the first of the Three Little Pigs, and is 'huffing and puffing and blowing the house down'. The house in the cartoon is the Philippines – islands which at that time formed an American colony.

Even at the date of this cartoon – a little over three weeks after Pearl Harbor – the Japanese were making huge inroads in the Philippines. The cartoonist attributes the American failure to unpreparedness.

Cartoon 11.2 Arms for the East. *Punch*, London, 31 December 1941

ARMS FOR THE EAST

"How about shipping this thing now?"

L. S. Amery, Secretary of State for India in the British government and a noted 'imperialist', has marked the cargo 'Dominion Status for India' with the label 'Not to be sent till after the war'. Churchill suggests that it should be despatched at once.

This cartoon carries strong political overtones. Amery had long been noted for his strong imperialist views. So, indeed, had Churchill, who, in the early 1930s, had been a most intransigent opponent of Indian self-government.

When war came, however, Churchill was willing to support any kind of action which seemed likely to advance the Allied cause. If Dominion status (i.e. effective independence) for India was likely to mobilize the Indians against Japan, the Prime Minister would be sure to support it. Churchill did not support the idea of immediate Dominion status, as this cartoon suggests, and it is not certain that at the date of the cartoon he was even convinced about the necessity for Dominion status after the war. He certainly came to the view by the early part of 1942 that eventual Dominion status for India was a worthwhile price to pay for Indian support in the war, and the 'Cripps mission' was sent to India with a conditional offer of eventual independence if the Indians would co-operate in the war.

Cartoon 11.3 Dangerous tune. *News Chronicle*, London, 18 February 1942

DANGEROUS TUNE

As soon as the question of India's future came under close study, a new difficulty was appreciated. Most people in Britain had long assumed that the 'issue' in India lay between Britons on one side and Indians on the other. As the debate proceeded, it became increasingly clear that Moslems in India were very apprehensive about what would happen to their own people if the country came under the rule of the Hindu majority.

This *News Chronicle* cartoon shows three snake-charmers: Nehru, of the predominantly Hindu Congress Party, which was the largest political group in India and a strong force in support of Indian independence; Jinnah, the leading personality of the Indian Moslem League, and the British Secretary for India, Amery. All of them are adopting equally dangerous attitudes of intransigence. Instead of drawing from the basket a small snake which will dance to one or other of their respective tunes, they are conjuring from the undergrowth a gigantic Japanese serpent which threatens to destroy them all.

Cartoon 11.4 Qui est donc ce mendiant? *La Gerbe*, Paris, 9 April 1942

Mahatma Gandhi was the most influential of all the Indian politicians in the campaign for independence; but his relationship with the Congress Party was at times very tenuous.

This cartoon from *La Gerbe* shows Gandhi enquiring of another Indian who the beggar is who has approached them. He is informed that the beggar is 'the Ambassador Extraordinary of His Very Gracious Majesty'. That was Sir Stafford Cripps, who had just been sent by the British Government on his 'Mission' to India.

The implication of the cartoon is that Cripps has nothing to give to the Indians, but is desperate for favours from India.

Cartoon 11.5 Der Indische Trick. *Das Reich*, Berlin, 5 April 1942

DER INDISCHE TRICK

„Herrschaften, vor Ihren eigenen Augen läßt der Illusionist aus dem Nichts einen prächtigen Kletterbaum entstehen, sodann läßt er seinen behenden Gehilfen daran hochklettern, um schließlich beides, Kletterbaum und Gehilfen, spurlos verschwinden zu lassen . . . !!"

This German cartoon alludes to the well-known illusion, the 'Indian rope trick'. It suggests that the offer of Dominion status for India is purely verbal and illusory. Churchill has invented the idea and despatched Cripps to make the offer. Once it has produced its effect, the Prime Minister will blow it away – and Cripps, incidentally, will disappear as well.

Cartoon 11.6 Daily Mail, London, 16 July 1942

This is a bitter reflection on the failure of the Cripps mission and its aftermath. Gandhi, in 'Congress Cloud-Cuckoo Land', contemplates a 'new crack-brained scheme of helping the United Nations by revolt against the British'. The Japanese cynically rejoice that they will be the beneficiaries of Congress's schemes.

The term 'United Nations' was coming into use about this time as a collective name for the Allies. At the end of the war, when nearly all significant countries which were not actually on the enemy side had declared war on Germany, it gradually turned into the designation of the international organization which the Allies were establishing for post-war purposes.

Cartoon 11.7 The new star. . . *Daily Express*, London, 18 November 1942

THE NEW STAR (NOVA PUPPIS) RECENTLY DISCOVERED, WAS ALSO OBSERVED IN TOKYO.
—News item

Military events later in 1942 greatly reduced the Japanese threat to India – and suggested that Japanese conquests had reached their limit.

The Japanese naval officer in this cartoon has already been hit by the battles of the Coral Sea (May) and Midway (June) which checked the Japanese advance in the Pacific area.

The 'new star' refers to operations in the Solomon Islands. These islands, which lie to the east of New Guinea, were a British possession but had been occupied by the Japanese early in 1942. The Japanese presence posed a considerable strategic threat to Australia. In the second part of the year, American and Australian forces landed in the Solomon Islands and commenced an extremely tough and bloody operation which gradually pushed the Japanese out. Tokyo is 'observing' the event with consternation.

It is often a matter of argument which battles are 'decisive', but many historians consider that Midway represented the turning-point in the Far Eastern war, while the protracted campaign in the Solomons was widely seen as evidence that the tide had already turned.

12

The German war in 1942

As the winter of 1941–2 approached, the Red Army was able to counterattack and recover large tracts of territory which had been seized in the summer and early autumn. From December 1941 onwards, a very sharp contrast could be drawn between the fate of the western Allies, who were meeting disaster everywhere in the Pacific, and the resilient Soviet forces who were driving back those German armies which practically all Britons, and most Americans, saw as the main enemy.

In the warmer months of 1942, the Germans again seized the initiative in the Soviet Union, and by the autumn were established close to the Caucasus. As in 1941, however, there was at no point any suggestion of a Soviet collapse. In mid-October, the great battle of Stalingrad commenced. By early 1943 the Germans had been defeated at Stalingrad, with enormous losses. Many writers are disposed to regard Stalingrad as *the* decisive battle of the war.

In Britain there was a growing public demand for a 'Second Front' – a term commonly understood to mean a major military attack in western Europe from bases in Britain, designed eventually to squeeze Nazi Germany out of existence between Anglo-Americans and the Soviet forces. This Second Front pressure could be sustained whatever the military situation might be at a particular moment. If the Red Army was doing well, then this was an argument for knocking Germany off balance while she was reeling from Soviet attacks; if the Red Army was doing badly, this was an argument for relieving the German pressure by an attack in the west.

There was an uncomfortable realization that Soviet losses were incomparably greater than Anglo-American losses, and there was also a growing impatience with the privations of war – 'Let's get the job finished.' Finally, there was a suspicion in some left-wing circles (which appears to have had little foundation in fact) that western governments were quite willing to allow Germany and the Soviet Union to destroy each other, and then intervene at the end to 'clear up the mess'.

The overriding reason why no Second Front was launched in 1942 was the success of the German U-boat campaign in the North Atlantic. Any attack which was to have hope of success would require great numbers

of American troops and great quantities of supplies from across the Atlantic. While the U-boats were not able to starve Britain out, they were able greatly to reduce the amount of material and the number of men who could be brought to Britain. There was, however, one serious military operation across the Channel: the Dieppe Raid of August 1942. A force mainly of Canadians was landed in France, with the primary aim of testing invasion technique. The results were not encouraging.

Cartoon 12.1 Axis war dance! *Daily Mirror*, London, 12 December 1941

Axis war dance!

This cartoon was drawn in December 1941, just a very few days after Japan entered the war. It draws the contrast between the jubilant Japanese, flushed with their great early victories against the Allies, and Hitler, furious at the Russian successes as winter approached.

The word 'Axis', which appears in the title, was originally applied in the late 1930s to the association between Germany and Italy ('Rome–Berlin Axis'), but it was later extended to include Japan as well. From about 1941 onwards, it was used to include all enemy countries.

Cartoon 12.2 Retribution, Surrender, Victory, Peace!
Daily Mirror, London, 18 March 1942

Retribution, Surrender, Victory, Peace!

This cartoon, like the preceding one, appeared in the London *Daily Mirror*. That newspaper, which had a huge readership among the Forces, was becoming increasingly critical of the government on a variety of counts. In this cartoon of March 1942 a Soviet soldier is holding an invitation card, appealing to the British Parliament for 'co-operation' – that is, for a Second Front, with the clear implication that this course will accelerate the common victory.

Cartoon 12.3 'The price of petrol. . .' *Daily Mirror*, London, 6 March 1942

"The price of petrol has been increased by one penny"—Official

This is yet another cartoon from the *Daily Mirror*. The message which the cartoonist apparently sought to put over was that the privations of sailors attempting to bring supplies to Britain – like the shipwrecked mariner in this picture – bore no comparison with the minor cost and inconvenience sustained by civilians at home. Churchill drew a totally different message, interpreting the cartoon as an attempt to build up a 'defeatist', peace-at-any-price attitude to the war, and even meditated action to ban the *Daily Mirror* from publication.

However the cartoon is seen, there is no doubt that the artist was drawing attention to the enormous human cost of the Battle of the Atlantic, and the great destruction which U-boats were wreaking on Allied shipping.

By this stage of the war, petrol was strictly rationed and was not obtainable for pleasure purposes. Cars were in any case far less common than they are today.

Cartoon 12.4 Atlantic sea serpent. *Washington Post*, 21 January 1942

Atlantic Sea Serpent

This American cartoon of early 1942 sees another aspect of the German Atlantic submarine menace. 'Uncle Sam', preoccupied with the Battle of the Pacific against Japan – which was going extremely badly at that moment – is forced to turn to the even more immediate menace of the U-boats, which, unless successfully countered, would destroy him.

As the United States fronts both the Atlantic and the Pacific, it was almost inevitable that Americans living in the west of the country should be, on the whole, more concerned about the Japanese war, while Americans living in the east were more concerned about the German war. At one point there was real fear of a Japanese landing on the western seaboard, and great numbers of people of Japanese extraction were removed inland from California as security risks. The major American newspapers did not (and do not) enjoy the nationwide distribution of their British counterparts. The great majority of readers of the *Washington Post* lived on the eastern side of the country, and therefore would have been disposed to accept the newspaper's view.

President Roosevelt – also an easterner – was of the same mind on this matter, and agreed with Churchill that the German war must take priority over the Japanese war. It is interesting to ponder what the results might have been if Roosevelt had thought otherwise.

Cartoon 12.5 Au revoir! *Daily Herald*, London, 21 August 1942

A U R E V O I R !

The one serious attempt which the western Allies made in 1942 to test the strength of German defences in Europe was the Dieppe Raid, conducted mainly by Canadian troops based in Britain against that French port.

This cartoon was drawn so soon after the Dieppe raid that the extent of Allied losses was probably not appreciated at the time. The picture of soldiers contentedly watching the devastation they have wrought on the enemy as they return safely to their home base is, to put it mildly, a cosily optimistic view, for the cost to the Allies was great in comparison to the military benefits received. The message of the cartoon is that the Allies would return to the French channel ports later. That, no doubt, was the general intention; but the experience of the Dieppe raid did not suggest that the return visit – the Second Front – could take place for a very long time.

Cartoon 12.6 Est' na Volge utes. . . *Krokodil*, Moscow, no. 39, October 1942

Есть на Волге утес!

'There is a crag on the Volga. . .' Great waves of German soldiers and armaments assail the 'crag', over which waves the flag labelled 'Stalingrad'. The battle for Stalingrad, at the turn of 1942–3, was sufficiently protracted to permit cartoons to be drawn, charting its course.

Soviet wartime cartoons had, if anything, an even stronger propaganda element than those of most other countries. The message is constantly stated: that the enemy is not only evil, but foredoomed to certain defeat.

Cartoon 12.7 General-Fel'dmarshal Paulyus popal v Istoriyu. *Krokodil*, Moscow, no. 7, February 1943

Генерал-фельдмаршал Паулюс попал в историю

This Soviet cartoon, 'General-Field Marshal Paulus passes into history', was drawn at the end of the Stalingrad campaign. The book 'Plan of the Stalingrad Operation' is slammed shut by a hand representing the Red Army. Von Paulus, the German officer in command, is trapped between its pages, waving the white flag of surrender tied to his Field Marshal's baton. The box in which the baton was stored, carrying the signature 'Adolf Hitler', lies by the book.

Von Paulus, who held the rank of General for most of the campaign, was promoted Field Marshal by Hitler just before the end. This was not so much a compliment to his military skill as an instruction that he should fight to the death, for there was a tradition that no German Field Marshal had ever been taken alive. The hint was not taken; von Paulus, perceiving that the situation was hopeless and that no good would be done to his shattered army by requiring it to fight on, surrendered.

13

War and the changing world

Before 1939, five European countries would have ranked as 'Great Powers'. Four of those countries entered the war more or less voluntarily in the first twelve months of its course. By the end of 1941, France and Italy could hardly be accounted 'Great Powers' at all, while three enormously important countries, two of them wholly non-European and the other partly so, had become involved in the conflict. Whatever happened, whoever won, the original belligerents would certainly not be in a position to decide the future without reference to these 'outsiders'. Thus in the course of 1941 an essentially European conflict had broadened into a real world war. That war is today called the Second World War, and the name is too firmly fixed for anyone to shift; but it was truly the first and only World War. Europe had ceased to be the nerve-centre of the human race.

Each of the three great countries who entered the war in 1941 exerted a gigantic effect not merely on military events but on the whole course of human ideas and political assumptions. As we have seen, the ideas generated by the Russian revolution of 1917 had either inspired or terrified great numbers of people in all social classes and in all countries. When the German attack came in 1941, the Soviet government – and, indeed, the governments of the other Allied countries – tried desperately hard to play down the revolutionary role of Soviet Communism and to concentrate attention on the military and national issues at stake. The general public in Britain and in many occupied countries found the distinction less easy to make, and there were many signs of a swing in opinion: in some places towards overt Communism, but in countries like Britain towards a kind of democratic socialism. Propaganda in the European 'Axis' countries, on the other hand, laid great stress on the continuance of a 'Bolshevik menace', and several European countries which had no quarrel with Britain or the United States were mobilized into the war against the Soviet Union.

The United States exerted an effect of a different kind. Technologically, America was far ahead of all other Allies. It is difficult to see how Britain could have withstood the crisis of mid-1940 and the ensuing Battle of the Atlantic without American material and financial assistance, and the hope

of much more to come. It may well be that the Soviet Union also could not have survived without American help.

As the United States rose, so did Britain decline. Allied propaganda from late 1941 onwards constantly emphasized the idea of Britain, the United States, and the Soviet Union as the 'Big Three' – with China perhaps making it the 'Big Four'. Those countries were conceived as equals in the war, who were to remain equals in determining the future peace. Yet it was very soon clear that Britain could not possibly provide the essentials of war on the same scale as either the United States or the Soviet Union, while the financial debt to America was bound to affect her post-war position. Propaganda in enemy countries challenged the 'Big Three' view, contending that Britain was becoming increasingly subservient to the United States, while both of them were facing a gigantic and growing threat from the Soviet Union.

The impact of Japan was more indirect. We have already noted the rapid Japanese advances through British colonies in south-east Asia, and the perceived threat to India and even Australia. Japan was destined to go down in defeat; but the colonial peoples of Asia perceived that the Europeans were not invincible. This was a lesson they would never forget, and its effect in undermining the prestige of the British Empire is incalculable. Although most Britons probably saw the Far Eastern war as little more than an irritating diversion from the 'real' war against Germany, yet it was Japan much more than Germany who determined Britain's wartime and post-war international decline.

Cartoon 13.1 Vstrecha nad Berlinom. n.d.

The Soviet cartoon-poster on p. 149 is not dated but probably comes from late 1941, before the United States was fully engaged in the war. The caption reads 'Meeting over Berlin', and the Soviet and British airmen shake hands. The poem underneath may be roughly translated: 'The brotherly countries fixed/A meeting over the enemy city/From this handshake/No benefit will come to Germany.'

The message is one of wartime unity, with no hint of ideological differences between the two countries. They are seen as equals, whose mutual co-operation is essential for the common purpose. The bombs raining upon Berlin issue from the handshake, not from the respective aeroplanes.

The cartoonist gloats over the destruction which is about to befall Germany. This represents a striking change of attitude since the earliest phase of the Soviet-German conflict. One of the first Soviet cartoons on the subject appeared in *Krokodil* in June 1941. It showed pictures of Hitler, Göring and Goebbels with the caption 'Enemies of the Soviet people', followed by the same pictures with the caption 'Enemies of the German people'. As in Britain, the distinction between the Nazi leaders who were the enemy, and the German people with whom there was no quarrel, was made less and less clearly in cartoons from the Soviet Union as the war proceeded.

Cartoon 13.2 Von Stufe zu Stufe. *Das Reich*, Berlin
30 November 1941

Von Stufe zu Stufe

German propaganda made much of Britain's decline relative both to the United States and the Soviet Union. This cartoon, 'From step to step', traces the changing relationship between Churchill and Roosevelt. In the first frame Churchill, the chief, invites Roosevelt to become an associate in the firm 'British Empire & Co.' By the second stage, Roosevelt has become chief, and in the third frame a dejected-looking Churchill has been relegated to the job of porter in the firm, now renamed 'Greater USA, formerly British Empire'.

Cartoon 13.3 'Anthony. . .' *Das Reich*, Berlin, 11 January 1942

„Anthony, um Himmels wille gesetzt der Fall, es gelänge d den Koloß ins Rollen zu bringe wie willst du ihn denn wied aufhalten?!"

Eden: „Aber Liebling, ich hab an alles gedacht, sieh vorn d Tafel!"

As the war developed, German propaganda insisted even more strongly that the Soviet Union was becoming a threat to the Allies as well as themselves. Stress was laid on the argument that the 'Bolshevik menace' confronted everybody; that Germany and her associates were the only people countering the menace, and that the Allies were irresponsibly letting it loose upon the world.

In December 1941, British Foreign Secretary Anthony Eden visited Moscow for conversations with Stalin. It is now known that the meeting was not an immediate success from the point of view of either party; but the cartoonist probably did not realize this, and drew the picture shortly after Eden's return. The lady – presumably his wife – warns Eden of the danger of giving a push to the great stone which carries the Soviet insignia, because of the damage it will do to Britain as it rolls downhill. Eden foolishly replies that he has put up a notice telling the stone to stop at a certain point: 'England begins here.'

Cartoon 13.4. Washington: Neujahr 1942. *Das Reich*, Berlin, 4 January 1942

At the turn of 1941–2, while Eden was visiting Moscow to meet Stalin, Churchill travelled to Washington to meet Roosevelt and co-ordinate war plans between the two countries.

In this German cartoon the two leaders sanctimoniously sing New Year hymns together, while each is trying to pick the other's pocket. The implication is that each is attempting to obtain all kinds of dishonest advantages at the expense of the other.

Cartoon 13.5. The old, old story. *The Star*, London, 13 January 1942

This cartoon was drawn at a very early stage of the war in the Far East. 'Complacency, Blunder and Muddle' from British colonial days are leaving the unfortunate British soldier alone to face the huge Japanese tiger lurking in the undergrowth. The cartoon probably refers to the fighting in Malaya, where Japan was making exceedingly rapid advances even in January 1942.

The point which the cartoonist evidently seeks to make is that the current predicament of Allied forces in the Far East is the natural consequence of past failures, and that it is urgently necessary to rectify those errors, wherever possible, in order to contain the position in future.

This, however, is not the only implication which may be drawn. Not only did the Japanese find their early victories astonishingly easy – probably much easier than they had anticipated – but the colonial peoples could see the weakness of the Imperialists' position, and were almost certain to draw morals which nobody had intended from those events.

Cartoon 13.6 Japanese propaganda cartoon for Philippines. n.d. From A. Rhodes, *Propaganda, the Art of Persuasion*, 1976

The Japanese invaders of countries in south-east Asia behaved with considerably more intelligence towards the people whom they had overrun than the Germans evinced in most of conquered Europe. They maintained at least the facade of being 'liberators' of the Asian peoples from European and American imperialism. In this cartoon issued by the Japanese in the occupied Philippines, the people of Asia, with the Japanese flag floating above them, are rescuing Juan, the Filipino, from the shark- and crocodile-infested waters of 'American imperialism' and 'racial prejudice', with the words 'Philippine independence' at the top of the cliff.

The Philippines were an American colony, but the Japanese adopted similar policies towards other occupied countries which had belonged before the war to the British or the Dutch. Local regimes, nominally independent, were set up under Japanese suzerainty. People in these countries began to think what some Indians had been thinking for a long time: that in the future they might become completely independent both of the former Imperial Powers and of the the Japanese as well.

14

North Africa and France, 1942–3

In the autumn of 1942, the protracted struggle in Libya and Egypt at last turned decisively in the Allies' favour, with the second battle of El Alamein. From that date the Axis forces in north Africa were in general retreat, though by no means routed. The victory at El Alamein was followed in a very few days by large-scale British and American landings in French North Africa, designed to drive enemy forces completely from the southern shores of the Mediterranean.

These landings brought to a head some exceedingly difficult and long-standing diplomatic problems. As we have seen, the British had encouraged General de Gaulle's Free French, but refused to grant them the full status of a government-in-exile. There was often considerable acrimony between Churchill and de Gaulle. The Americans, who were not at war when the Free French were first established in 1940, kept in full diplomatic contact with Vichy and gave no sort of acknowledgement to the Free French. The situation did not change much when the United States entered the war at the end of 1941. The Americans believed for a long time that many of the Vichyites could, with proper handling, eventually be brought on to the Allied side.

Not long before the landings in French North Africa, the Americans began to co-operate with another pro-Allied French General, Giraud: a man militarily senior to de Gaulle but far less charismatic. For security reasons, however, it was considered necessary to keep all the French in the dark about the projected landings until the very last moment – a matter which de Gaulle resented bitterly.

Soon after the landings took place, the invading Allies made contact with a major Vichy personality, Admiral Darlan, who happened to be in Algiers visiting his sick son. Darlan contrived to produce a cease-fire by the Vichy French forces in north Africa, and thus the risk of serious fighting between the Allies and Frenchmen was averted. Darlan was repudiated by Pétain, but the Germans took the occasion to occupy that part of France which had been left to Vichy administration in 1940. The Germans also made a serious attempt to capture the French fleet which had been impounded at Toulon after the armistice, but this was frustrated when the fleet scuttled itself.

The French scene was now immensely complicated. Giraud and de Gaulle were on bad terms with each other, and both detested Darlan. Pétain was at loggerheads with Darlan and the Allies, but plainly not trusted by the Germans. Second in rank at Vichy was the very ambitious and unscrupulous Pierre Laval, who had intrigued savagely against Pétain in the past. Laval was a much more willing collaborationist, but – unlike Pétain – had little prestige in his country and therefore was of limited value to the Germans.

The Anglo-Americans soon established themselves in French North Africa, and in early 1943 a great pincer movement began in which the German and Italian forces were caught between Allied armies moving from opposite ends of the North African coastline. By the end of May, the Allies were in complete control of north Africa.

Cartoon 14.1 Romans v Pustyne. From *Hitler i evo Svora* (*Hitler and his Dogs. Caricatures 1942–1943*), Moscow/Leningrad, 1943

РОМАНС В ПУСТЫНЕ

Роммель (своему итальянскому союзнику). «Не жди меня, я не вернусь».

In the early autumn of 1942, the British began a general advance in the Western Desert, first driving the enemy from El Alamein in Egypt, and then rapidly pursuing them into Libya.

In this Soviet cartoon, 'Romance in the Desert', Field-Marshal Erwin Rommel, the German commander, retreats in precipitate haste, shouting at the Italian who is trying to catch him up, 'Don't wait for me, I shall not return.' The words are an obvious parody on a popular Russian song of the period, 'Wait for me, I shall return.'

The hat and shorts of the Italian are on fire: an allusion, apparently, to the success of the British military operation.

Theoretically, the Germans had gone to north Africa to help out their Italian allies. In practice they showed little interest in the welfare of the Italians.

Cartoon 14.2 Keeping company with the twins!
Washington Post, 12 July 1942

This cartoon appeared in July 1942. The United States still had full diplomatic relations with the Vichy government, but clearly had much more sympathy with those French people who were actively supporting the Allies, as is shown by the expressions on the faces of 'Uncle Sam' and the two girls.

The cartoon is, nevertheless, a considerable oversimplification. Although some of the Vichyites were pro-Nazi – as the swastika on the cap of 'Vichy France' suggests – by no means all of them were. American diplomats were well aware that in certain places, notably north Africa, most Vichyites had pro-Allied sympathies. Relations between the Americans and the Free French were certainly not as close as the cartoon indicates.

Cartoon 14.3 Needs must – *Daily Herald*, London, 12 November 1942

NEEDS MUST —

Who copied from whom? As the Soviet cartoon opposite is undated, it is difficult to know.

Very soon after the Anglo-American invasion of North Africa began, the Germans moved into the part of France which had been left unoccupied by the terms of the armistice of July 1940. In both cartoons, Hitler passes across the human bridge from 'Occupied France' into 'Unoccupied France'. Pétain is present in both 'bridges', but in the Soviet cartoon he is joined by Laval. The British cartoon makes the extra points that Hitler is being impelled across the bridge by United Nations (i.e. Allied) initiative, and is tearing up the 1940 armistice terms.

Cartoon 14.4 'Vishachy Most'. From *Chyorny po Belomy (Black on White)*, Moscow, 1945

«ВИШАЧИЙ МОСТ»

Висячий мост «Лаваль — Петэн»
Или иначе — «Мост измен».

The poem of the Soviet cartoon reads 'The hanging bridge – "Laval-Pétain"/Or otherwise "The bridge of treason".' The caption seems to be a pun on the similarity between the Russian words for 'hanging' (visyachy) and for 'Vichyite' (Vishachy).

As in many Soviet cartoons, the point is hammered home, while the British cartoon leaves more to the imagination of the reader.

Cartoon 14.5 Tulon! From *Hitler i evo Svora* (*Hitler and his Dogs. Caricatures 1942–1943*), Moscow/Leningrad, 1943

ТУЛОН!

Попытка Гитлера захватить французский военный флот в Тулоне сорвалась. Французские моряки потопили все корабли, жертвуя своей жизнью

Французские корабли глубоко опустились, но высоко поднялся флаг Сражающейся Франции

A Soviet comment on the fate of the French fleet at Toulon. Hitler and Goebbels, in naval uniform, accompanied by another German (probably the Secret Police (Gestapo) chief, Himmler), arrive at Toulon harbour. As in another Soviet cartoon, Goebbels wears a monkey's tail. Laval has just hoisted the Nazi flag to greet them. As the Germans arrive, the French fleet disappears beneath the waters, waving the Tricolor as a defiant gesture. The Germans, and Laval, are appalled.

The wording at the top of the cartoon explains what has happened; the wording at the bottom reads 'The French fleet bravely scuttles itself, but proudly waves the flag of Fighting France.'

If the French fleet at Toulon had passed into German hands, the consequences for the Allies could have been very serious.

Cartoon 14.6 Somebody's Darlan? *Punch*, London, 9 December 1942

SOMEBODY'S DARLAN?

The position of Admiral Darlan remained anomalous in the extreme. The Anglo-Americans mistrusted him profoundly, not just as a 'Vichyite', but as a man who was at one time suspected of seeking to 'switch the war' and bring France in on Germany's side. The Free French, whether associated with de Gaulle or with Giraud, could only regard him as a dangerous and untrustworthy rival. The Vichyites perceived his behaviour as the immediate cause of the German occupation of south-east France. The Germans deplored his co-operation with the Allies. Whether, as this punning cartoon suggests, he was nevertheless 'somebody's darling', seemed a matter of great doubt.

On Christmas Eve, 1942, Darlan was assassinated. Officially, his murderer was said to be a young French royalist, who was brought to secret trial and executed with great speed. It is easy to point out a considerable number of people who had a motive to kill Darlan; but who was really guilty remains a mystery.

Cartoon 14.7 Freie Franzosen. *Das Reich*, Berlin, 17 January 1943

Churchill and Roosevelt met at Casablanca, in Morocco, in January 1943, and a feature of the conference was a formal handshake between their respective Free French protégés de Gaulle and Giraud – although disputes among the Free French continued for a long time.

This German cartoon, drawn at the time of the Casablanca conference, shows two Free French officers, one with a bag of British pounds and the other with a bag of American dollars. Each furiously accuses the other of having sold his country.

Neither group of Free Frenchmen was in a position to do much without large subventions from major Allied countries.

Cartoon 14.8 Ironing them out. *Daily Express*, London, 31 March 1943

IRONING THEM OUT

The Eighth Army – the British army of the Western Desert – moved rapidly through Libya in early 1943 and soon entered the French colony of Tunisia. General Montgomery ('Monty'), its commander, irons out the German tanks and Rommel's defences as his forces sweep westwards. Meanwhile, other Allied forces were advancing into Tunisia from Algeria.

15

The war in 1943

It was in 1943 that it became really evident that the Allies would probably win the war.

Progress on the Russian front was particularly impressive. After the battle of Stalingrad, at the turn of 1942–3, the Red Army began to sweep westwards. Its progress was not unchallenged, and there were some severe reverses. It is sometimes said that Stalingrad made it clear that Germany could not win, but the Soviet victory at the great tank battle of Kursk in the ensuing summer made it likely that the Allies would eventually secure a total victory.

War in the Mediterranean region also ran strongly in the Allies' favour. When German and Italian forces had been cleared from north Africa, the British and Americans prepared an assault on Italy, which Churchill once called 'the soft under-belly of the Axis'.

The first stage of the operation was to invade Sicily from newly acquired bases in Tunisia. The campaign began on 10 July 1943 and the capture of the island was completed in mid-August. As a kind of bonus, Mussolini was driven from office on 25 July, and promptly arrested. Government of Italy passed effectively to the King, Victor Emmanuel III, and to Marshal Badoglio. For the time being, Italy remained at war with the Allies. Even at this stage, Italy was scarcely a free agent in the matter, for large numbers of German troops were in the country and were playing a very important part in the defence of Sicily.

On 3 September the Allies commenced an invasion of the Italian mainland across the Straits of Messina, and what was to prove a very slow progress up the peninsula began. Five days later, the Italian government formally surrendered. The Germans immediately countered by seizing strategically important places and forcibly disarming Italian troops. In September, the Germans rescued Mussolini from captivity, and the former dictator soon set up what was called the 'Italian Social Republic' under German suzerainty in the German-occupied part of the country. Meanwhile the Victor Emmanuel–Badoglio government prepared a complete switch of sides, and in October 1943 declared war on Germany.

The position of Victor Emmanuel and Badoglio was already anomalous, and soon became more so. The King had long been an

ineffectual figure, but he had backed Mussolini for more than twenty years. Badoglio had been the Italian military leader in the war against Abyssinia in 1935–6. Thus neither of them had a record about which the Allies could feel much enthusiasm. Churchill was disposed to back Victor Emmanuel, not out of any regard for the King but in the belief that his presence might determine the loyalties of Italian officers. Roosevelt was more dubious. In the end, it was arranged that the King should pass over the functions of monarchy to his son, while retaining the Royal title. This was done when the Allies at last entered Rome – which did not take place until June 1944.

The fighting in Italy continued almost to the end of the European war, but after 1943 was subsumed by much greater events elsewhere. Of the two Italian 'governments', one was plainly a satellite of the Germans and the other a satellite of the Allies. Neither the discredited and ailing Mussolini nor the unimpressive King and Marshal could inspire much enthusiasm among Italians, who could hardly be expected to fight with vigour for either side while their country was being shattered by the military operations of both.

The year 1943 also saw a radical change in the 'Battle of the Atlantic'. In the spring, the Allies began to take such a fearful toll of German U-boats that submarine operations against convoys were suspended. This meant that American supplies and forces could be brought across the Atlantic far more easily than hitherto, and the build-up of forces for an eventual Second Front in western Europe was able to begin in earnest.

The war in the Far East also began to turn visibly in the Allies' favour. As we have seen, this process had begun before the end of 1942. The nature of the terrain precluded the great land-battles which characterized the war in north Africa and in the Soviet Union; but gradually Japanese forces were cleared from outlying territories by operations which often involved active co-operation between United States and British Commonwealth forces. This was not only a lengthy and tedious process, largely conducted in tropical conditions, but also an exceptionally bloody one. European soldiers would normally surrender when defeat was a military certainty, for officers would not order their men to continue fighting when no useful purpose could be served by so doing; but the Japanese tradition held that surrender was disgraceful, and they would often fight almost to the last man, whatever the military position.

Cartoon 15.1 Nemets predpolagaet. . . *Krokodil*, Moscow, nos 38–9, 1943

НЕМЕЦ ПРЕДПОЛАГАЕТ...

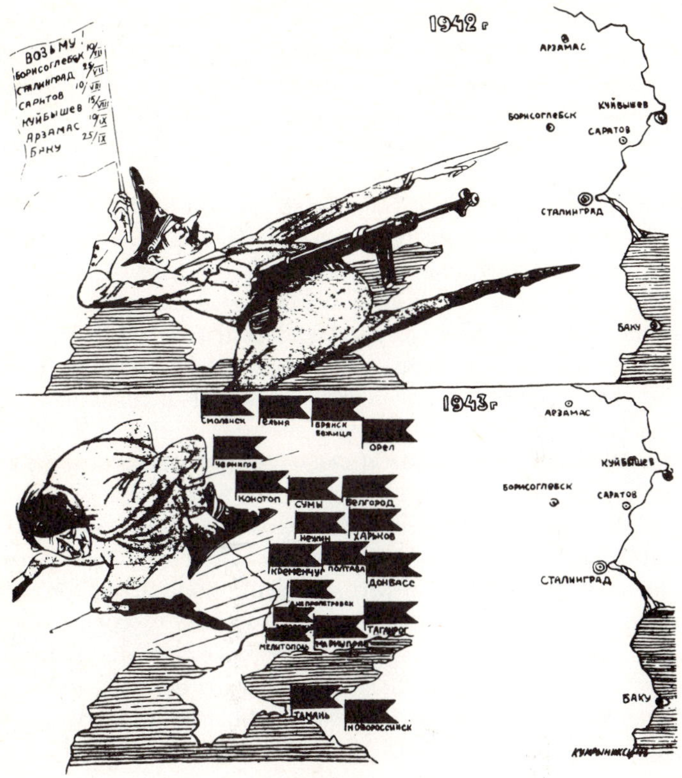

...А РУССКИЙ РАСПОЛАГАЕТ!

A Soviet cartoon of 1943, commenting on the changed military situation on the Soviet front. In 1942, Hitler had been striding forward towards Stalingrad, and the banner he carries declares his intention to seize places even further away. The text at the top of the cartoon refers to a statement by Stalin to the effect that actual dates had been found on a German officer indicating when the Germans expected to capture the towns in question. In 1943, however, Hitler is in precipitate retreat. The banners mark towns which the Red Army has recaptured.

The words of the caption and at the foot mean roughly 'The German proposes, but the Russian disposes.' In Russian, as in English, the words for 'proposes' and 'disposes' are similar ('predpolagaet. . . raspolagaet').

In 1943, the Soviet authorities had good reason to feel confident in eventual victory, and this confidence had a profound effect on Soviet diplomacy as well as military behaviour.

Cartoon 15.2 There's a battering at the gate! *St Louis Star-Times*, copied by *New York Times*, 18 July 1943

THERE'S A BATTERING AT THE GATE!

The Anglo-American invasion of Sicily is seen in this *New York Times* cartoon as the 'battering at the gate' which might eventually give the Allies access to Nazi-controlled Europe.

The term 'Fortress Europe' (Festung Europa) was widely used at the time by Nazi propaganda – a reference to the undeniably strong defences which protected the continent from all likely points of Allied invasion. Down to the invasion of Sicily, the most difficult military problem for the western Allies was how to gain an initial foothold. This cartoon seems to recognize that even if the Allies secured control of Sicily, the gatehouse, they would still face tremendous problems in their assault on the main fortress.

Cartoon 15.3 L'arrivo dei liberatori. An Italian cartoon reproduced in Arrigo Petacco, *Seconda Guerra Mondiale*, (1977–82) vol. 9

An Italian view, probably from the spring or summer of 1943. The Allied 'liberators' arrive from a troopship at an Italian port.

Allied propaganda constantly stressed that the Allies were entering European countries not as conquerors but as liberators. This line of argument might be expected to have a particularly strong appeal in Italy. Even before the Allied invasion began, the country was largely under German occupation, and later the Germans behaved even more oppressively. By contrast, a great many Italians had relatives and friends in the United States, and there was a strong tradition of friendship with Britain. Thus Italian propagandists had a serious task in countering the 'liberator' appeal of the Allies.

In this cartoon, a grim-faced Anglican ecclesiastic carries a sheaf of papers, 'People to convert'. An officer wearing the Soviet star in his cap (although Soviet troops played no part in the invasion) carries a sadistic-looking whip, and papers with the words 'Italians to oppress'. The third 'liberator' carries housebreaking implements and papers with the words 'Museums to plunder'. Italians were well aware that many national treasures had already found their way into Britain, America, and other foreign countries. The guard-of-honour includes a feeble-looking British soldier, an Indian with disaffection showing clearly on his face, a rather sloppy cigarette-smoking Australian and a Negro. The suggestion seems to be that the 'liberators' have behaved oppressively towards people under their imperial control, and are not likely to behave any better towards the Italians.

In this cartoon, appeals are being made simultaneously to Catholic religious feeling, fear and hatred of Communism, anger against foreign plunderers of Italian art-treasures and resentment against British imperialism. The Americans, who might be more difficult to satirize, are absent from this picture.

Cartoon 15.4 Krokodil, Moscow, no. 29, 1943

The fall of Mussolini. Three Atlantes had supported the pediment of the temple 'Fascism'. The central figure, Mussolini, has just fallen. Hitler remains in place on the right, and a complex of minor figures – apparently politicians from the various European countries which had been giving Hitler support in the war – remain on the left; but the whole edifice is rapidly collapsing.

In Russian, as in English, the word 'Fascism' came to be used loosely to label various enemy regimes, and the Nazi swastika is used on the left-hand plinth as a convenient emblem for all of them.

This cartoon suggests that the disruption of 'Fascism' had already reached a very advanced stage by the summer of 1943. This was certainly true of Fascism in Italy; but enemy regimes elsewhere still had great resources on which to draw.

Cartoon 15.5 Al Teatro. . . Treviso, Museo Civico, Collezione Salce. From Arrigo Petacco, *Seconda Guerra Mondiale*, vol. 9

After the Italian armistice of September 1943, a number of prominent Italians co-operated with the Allies. They are seen in this Italian cartoon as mere puppets, manipulated by Churchill and Roosevelt, with Stalin looking on. Churchill operates Badoglio and King Victor Emmanuel III. Roosevelt (who had considerable reservations about Churchill's policy towards the King and the Marshal) operates Benedetto Croce and Count Sforza, two anti-Fascist Italian politicians.

Cartoon 15.6 Celui qu'on n'attendait pas. . . *La Gerbe*, Paris, 23 September 1943

CELUI QU'ON N'ATTENDAIT PAS...
— *Buondi, signori!... Vous trinquiez à ma santé?...*

Two very different views of Mussolini's dramatic release from prison, and the subsequent establishment of the 'Italian Social Republic' (September 1943).

In the French 'collaborationist' cartoon, 'The unexpected guest', Churchill, Roosevelt, Badoglio, and King Victor Emmanuel have been celebrating the Italian armistice. A stalwart and vigorous-looking Mussolini suddenly appears in the doorway, to their visible consternation, and taunts them by enquiring whether 'you were drinking to my health'.

In the Soviet cartoon, 'Firm support for the Ministerial chair', a bound, tattered and miserable-looking Mussolini has been hauled up by Nazi hands into the seat which carries the banner 'Prime Minister'. He clutches the *fasces*, but is completely powerless and dependent on German support.

Cartoon 15.7 Krepkaya privyazannost'. . . From *Sovetsky Mastery Satiri, 1941–45* (*Soviet Masters of Satire, 1941–45*), Moscow/Leningrad, 1946

Крепкая привязанность к министерскому креслу

The Soviet view is closer to the truth. By this time Mussolini was in poor physical and perhaps mental shape. Allusion to this is made in the text set in small print set at the top of the Soviet cartoon. His 'Social Republic' had no independent authority in Italy. Even many Fascists had deserted him; it was the decision of the Fascist Grand Council which led to his removal from office in July 1943.

Cartoon 15.8 Comparative values. *Evening Standard*, London, 1 July 1943

Another pair of contrasting cartoons – this time both by the same artist and in the same newspaper, at an interval of three months.

The first cartoon was drawn at a time when Allied bombardment of Rome seemed a military possibility, but some critics were urging that the city should be spared for its artistic and architectural importance. The cartoonist brushes that argument aside, arguing that 'human freedom' is far more important.

Cartoon 15.9 'These fellows are sheer barbarians.' *Evening Standard*, 4 October 1943

Cartoon 15.9 was drawn when the Germans were in occupation of the city and were thought to be contemplating its destruction in order to impede the Allied advance. Even the 'ancient Vandal' – the Vandals sacked Rome in 455 AD – is appalled at the prospect.

The 'ancient Vandal' is presented, quite erroneously, as a sort of stone-age savage. The state of his apparel is curiously similar to that of the figure who rejoices over the destruction of Rome in the earlier cartoon. The cartoonist evidently believed that a course of action which might be morally imperative if operated by one side would constitute an unforgiveable crime against humanity if operated by the other.

Fortunately for the people of Italy, and for the whole world, neither side committed much destruction in Rome.

Cartoon 15.10 Crash-dive! *Daily Mail*, London, 21 June 1943

Crash-dive ! —by Illing

British aeroplanes sink 'Germany's U-boat hopes'. Hitler scurries to escape, while the sailor on the British naval vessel rejoices at the Führer's plight.

About a month before this cartoon appeared, Grand-Admiral Dönitz had suspended U-boat operations against convoys. Whether the cartoonist knew of this order or not, it was certainly clear to him and to his readers that great numbers of U-boats had been destroyed in recent months, and that operations against convoys had been greatly reduced.

Victory in the Battle of the Atlantic could not be as sharp and clear-cut as victory in land battles, but the results were no less important. The U-boat threat was the greatest single danger which Britain faced in both World Wars, for her very survival depended on great quantities of food and raw materials reaching the country from abroad. The relaxation of that threat in 1943 was of enormous importance in permitting the western Allies to build up forces and weapons in preparation for a major attack on continental Europe.

Cartoon 15.11 The roll back. *Daily Express*, London, 16 July 1943

THE ROLL BACK

The rays of Japan's Rising Sun are being rolled back by British Commonwealth and American forces in the Pacific, and great numbers of Japanese are being caught in the process.

The main phase of Japanese expansion was over (although in some places the Japanese continued to seize new territory, even into 1944). The 'roll back' encountered furious and often fanatical opposition, exceedingly costly in lives both for attackers and for defenders. Despite the optimism of this cartoon, it seemed likely in 1943 that the Japanese war would involve an extremely lengthy process of 'island-hopping', with huge casualty lists.

16

Inter-Allied problems, 1943

The speed of Allied military progress in 1943 compelled the 'Big Three' to give urgent consideration to a number of difficult diplomatic questions which had hitherto been left unresolved.

To set these problems in context, it is necessary to consider a long-standing military question. In 1942, the Soviet Union began to call with increasing insistence for the British and Americans to launch a Second Front in western Europe, to match their own continuing struggle in the east. The Dieppe Raid of August 1942 suggested that any major attack at that moment would have been enormously costly in lives, and would have ended in military calamity. Be that as it may, the British and American governments did believe that a Second Front would be feasible in 1943, and Churchill went so far as to promise this to Stalin.

The western Allies were unable to redeem this promise. The overwhelming reason why there was no Second Front in 1943 on the scale demanded appears to have been the continuing damage wrought by U-boats on shipping, which made it impossible to bring enough men and materials across the Atlantic to launch the attack with realistic hope of success. Whether that judgement was correct continues to be a matter of serious argument among military historians to this day. In the spring of 1943, the U-boat threat was substantially reduced; but it took some time to be sure that this change was permanent, and by then it was too late to organize a Second Front that year.

Whatever view we may entertain on the Second Front question, there can be no doubt that great numbers of Britons and Americans at all levels felt bitter disappointment and frustration, and also a sense of profound moral obligation to the Red Army and the Soviet civilian population who were sustaining losses on a staggering scale. The campaigns in north Africa and later in Italy were widely seen as poor substitutes for a full-scale Second Front in western Europe. The Soviet view that the western Allies were pulling less than their full weight, and the western apprehension that this judgement might be correct, produced important international consequences, for the British government in particular was prepared to make diplomatic concessions as a token of sympathy for the Soviet Union in its military ordeal. An early sign of these diplomatic changes arose in unexpected circumstances.

In April 1943, the Germans, who were still in occupation of large parts of the Soviet Union, announced the discovery of thousands of graves of Polish officers who had been taken as prisoners-of-war by the Red Army in 1939. These officers, the Germans claimed, had been murdered by the Soviet authorities in 1940 and had been buried at Katyn Forest, not far from Smolensk. Predictably, the Soviet government furiously denied the charge and accused the Germans of the crime. Today, there does not seem much doubt that the Soviet authorities were the culprits, but at the time this was far less clear.

The Polish government-in-exile in London urged that the International Red Cross should investigate the charges and counter-charges. Very embarrassingly, the Germans promptly offered to extend the necessary facilities. Here was a crime of which the Nazis were apparently innocent, and exposure of the criminals might deflect a lot of attention from many crimes of which they were undeniably guilty.

Relations between the Polish and Soviet governments had long been poor, and the Soviet authorities seized on the Katyn question to break diplomatic relations with the Poles. Churchill and Roosevelt attempted desperately, but ineffectively, to stop them. We may now decide that the Soviet government had reasons for wishing to break relations with the Poles which had nothing to do with Katyn; but that Katyn provided a convenient excuse. Obviously neither Churchill nor Roosevelt, whatever their private views on the matter, was going to support the German view of who committed the massacre at Katyn.

The dispute between the Soviet government and the Polish government-in-exile had deep roots which had little to do with Katyn. The whole future of Poland, both geographically and politically, was at stake. In 1939, it will be recalled, the Soviet Union had seized the eastern half of Poland – the area which the Poles call the *kresy*. This territory was formally incorporated in the Soviet Union soon afterwards. When the Polish–Soviet agreement was reached in July 1941, both governments found it prudent to leave the question of the future of the *kresy* undecided. At various times, right from Eden's visit to Moscow in December 1941 onwards, a number of questions concerning future European frontiers had been raised by the Soviet authorities, but it was in 1943 that the matter of Poland's future began to appear high on the agenda of inter-Allied discussions.

Current military developments made it likely that the Red Army would soon enter the *kresy*, and the future of the area could not be left unsettled for much longer. The Soviet government gradually made its own view of the matter clear. They insisted on the incorporation of most of the *kresy* in the Soviet Union, although they were open to discussion about details. They were willing to assist the Poles to take over large areas of eastern Germany in compensation; but the likely extent of this German territory was not clearly formulated until considerably later.

There was also a very important political and military issue at stake in the Polish–Soviet dispute. The Polish government sought to restore a Poland which would be completely free in its conduct of internal politics and international relations. The Soviet government seems, even at this stage, to have envisaged a Poland which would be in close military alliance with themselves, and whose government – while perhaps not necessarily Communist – would certainly have a 'left wing' political orientation.

The importance of Poland for all of the 'Big Three' Allies would be difficult to overstate. The Soviet Union recalled that the most dangerous foreign invasions of Russia in recent centuries had passed through Poland, and therefore saw a 'friendly' Poland as essential for its own security. The British could not forget that they had gone to war in 1939 in defence of Polish independence, and would find it exceedingly embarrassing to countenance a large truncation of Polish territory and a great reduction in the country's effective independence. The Americans were conscious that millions of their fellow-citizens were of Polish extraction. They constituted a vociferous group whose political weight could well prove decisive in a country where the balance between two great parties was fairly even.

In July 1943, the Polish question received an unexpected twist with the death of General Wladyslaw Sikorski in an air crash near Gibraltar. Sikorski had functioned both as Prime Minister of the Polish government-in-exile and as Commander-in-Chief of the substantial Polish forces overseas. German propaganda declared that Sikorski had been murdered at the instigation of the British secret service, in order to remove a diplomatic embarrassment. This seems unlikely, but the mystery has never been completely cleared up. Stanislaw Mikolajczyk, who succeeded to Sikorski's political role, and General Sosnkowski who succeeded to his military functions, were both considerably less impressive figures.

Difficulties of a different kind affected relations between the major Allies and Yugoslavia. After the German invasion of 1941, King Peter and his government went into exile, but General Draza Mihajlovic organized the guerrilla resistance of the so-called Cetniks. Not long after the Soviet Union entered the war, another resistance organization, the Partisans of Josip Broz-Tito, appeared. Relations between the various armed and irregular forces in Yugoslavia – Allied and enemy alike – were confused. Britain was giving most assistance to Yugoslavia, and in the course of 1943 the British gradually reached the conclusion that Tito was, from a military point of view, more useful than Mihajlovic, and thereafter gave assistance to the Partisans rather than the Cetniks. It is striking to note that the decision to transfer military assistance was taken by the British alone, apparently without prompting from the Soviet government. Thereafter attempts were made – with indifferent success – to secure

reconciliation between the Yugoslav government-in-exile and Tito's Partisans.

Another question affecting the Soviet Union and worldwide Communism was raised in 1943 which had even wider implications. Did the Soviet government still see itself as an instrument for fostering world revolution? Or could it be regarded as a typical 'Great Power' in the eighteenth- or nineteenth-century sense of the term: a Power with 'ambitions' which might well run counter to the interests of others, but prepared in the last analysis to come to terms with other Powers?

It was easy to provide abundant evidence from the writings not only of Lenin and the old Communist authorities, but also from the works of Stalin himself, which declared that long-term accommodation between Communism and other political systems was impossible; that the Soviet Union was necessarily cast into the role of the instigator of world revolution. If that view was still held in Moscow, then the other Allies were bound to regard the Soviet Union as a potential enemy no whit less dangerous than Nazi Germany itself.

In 1943, a significant gesture was made by the Soviet Union which suggested that the 'world revolution' view was obsolete. As we have seen, the Moscow-based 'Comintern', or 'Communist International', which openly aimed at co-ordinating the world's Communist parties towards world revolution, had been established in 1920. The Comintern was still in existence, although it was a rather ineffectual body, and many people much doubted whether its still adhered to its old revolutionary ideas. In 1943 a formal decision was taken to dissolve the Comintern. Did this represent a real change of heart, or was the Soviet Union merely biding its time for tactical reasons? Perhaps this looks like a very hypothetical question; but all relations between the Soviet Union and other countries were largely related to the answer which diplomats and statesmen were disposed to give.

Just as military events in the Soviet Union compelled the Allies to begin serious thinking about the aftermath of war, so also did these events have an important effect on German thinking about the future. Down to the time of Stalingrad, there had been all signs of confidence that Germany and her associates could meet and destroy any combination of enemies which might arise. In 1943 it became clear, even to the most sanguine Nazis, that Germany was by no means sure of victory. German propaganda began to develop on a different line. The Soviet Union was singled out as a unique menace to the world, which had by no means abandoned its original intention to destroy everyone else. In the Nazi view, the great crime of the other Allies was their association with that menace – which Germany and her associates were trying desperately to destroy.

The Nazis, of course, had every reason for pushing this line of

propaganda, whether they believed in it or not. Defeat was likely if the Allies stuck together, but might perhaps be avoided if a wedge could be driven between them. Emphasis on Soviet 'frightfulness' was also of value in domestic propaganda, and for persuading the Germans to continue resisting the enemy. Meanwhile Allied propagandists were disposed to treat any kind of controversy within their own camp, and any kind of public criticism of the Soviet Union, as folly, or even treachery, against the common cause.

The British and American governments appear to have taken the same view. Towards the end of 1943, a series of important inter-Allied discussions took place, culminating with the first 'Big Three' Conference, attended by Churchill, Stalin and Roosevelt at the unlikely venue of Tehran. Many important military plans were made by the Allied leaders, including the inauguration of a Second Front in north-western Europe in 1944. There were also considerable discussions about the future of Poland, and tacit agreement to the effect that most of the *kresy* should go to the Soviet Union, while Poland should receive compensation in the west at the expense of Germany.

Cartoon 16.1 Die Pest aus dem Osten. *Das Reich*, Berlin, 14 March 1943

DIE PEST AUS DEM OSTEN

Aus Lenin: Die nächsten Aufgaben der Sowjets: „Die Herrschaft der Sowjets kennt weder Freiheit noch Gerechtigkeit. Diese Herrschaft beruht auf Unterdrückung und Vernichtung jedes individuellen Willens.“

ERZBISCHOF VON CANTERBURY: *„Laßt uns eine besondere Fürbitte für die sowjetische Armee tun!“*

This German cartoon was drawn not long after the battle of Stalingrad, when – for the first time – it became clear to many Germans that victory over the Soviet Union was by no means a foregone conclusion. 'The Plague from the East' is composed of great numbers of savages, presumably meant to be Russians, preparing to spring on Germany and very likely other countries as well. Lenin is quoted saying 'The power of the Soviets knows neither freedom nor justice. This power is based on suppression and annihilation of all individual wills.' By contrast, the current Archbishop of Canterbury, William Temple, is quoted saying 'Let us pray especially for the Soviet Army.'

This cartoon seems to allude not only to the current perceived threat from Communism, but also to a much older idea. Around the turn of the nineteenth and twentieth centuries there was a good deal of interest in Germany (and to some extent in other European countries as well) in the idea that Europe would eventually face a great threat – sometimes called the 'Yellow Peril' – from Asia. The Soviet Union was represented as the embodiment, or perhaps as the harbinger, of that threat.

The message which the German reader is presumably intended to take is that the alternative to victory in the war against the Soviet Union is total destruction. The other Allies, and even their Christian leaders, are actually supporting the 'plague'.

Cartoon 16.2 The wedge. *Evening Standard*, London, 29 April 1943

THE WEDGE

A British cartoonist's view of the Katyn question. The artist probably believed at the time that the Germans were responsible for the massacre – or so the newspaper marked '"Polish graves" frame-up' suggests.

Whatever his opinion on that matter, however, his real interest is not in responsibility for the massacre, but in the current behaviour of the Poles. A Polish officer, with his cap pulled down over his eyes to obscure his vision, and bearing the words 'Shortsighted Diplomacy' on his jacket, holds a great wedge against the tree 'British-Russian-American Unity'. Goebbels prepares to hammer in the wedge.

This cartoon appeared about a week after the Soviet Union had broken diplomatic relations with the Poles. There is no hint that the Soviet authorities might bear any share of responsibility either for the original crime or for the subsequent diplomatic furore, which undeniably rebounded to the benefit of German propaganda.

Cartoon 16.3 'Bruder!' *Das Reich*, Berlin, 25 April 1943

A German view of Katyn and more recent events. A British airman stands on the ruins of Antwerp, which has recently been bombarded. He embraces a Red Army man whose holster drips with blood from the Katyn Forest. They salute each other as 'Brother!'

Like wartime cartoonists of all countries, the artists of *Das Reich* showed great moral indignation about the real or alleged atrocities of the other side, but were silent or forgiving when the crimes had been committed by their own compatriots.

Cartoon 16.4 Sole mourner. *Daily Mail*, London, 24 May 1943

Two views of the Soviet decision to dissolve the Comintern. In the *Daily Mail* cartoon, the coffin of the defunct Comintern which 'died naturally' is being escorted quietly to its grave by an indifferent-looking Stalin. Goebbels is the sole mourner, deploring the effect which the demise of the Comintern will have on German propaganda. The argument that the Comintern was a threat to all countries and governments has completely lost effect, and there is now no reason why other Allies should not co-operate to the full with the Soviet Union.

Cartoon 16.5 Nach der Häutung. *Das Reich*, Berlin, 13 June 1943

NACH DER HÄUTUNG

„So — jetzt kann aber niemand mehr etwas sagen — jetzt ist sie garantiert ungefährlich!"

Das Reich sees the matter completely differently. John Bull and Uncle Sam trail the Soviet serpent on a lead, as if it were a pet. The animal has just sloughed its skin, 'Third International' – i.e. Comintern. The American assures his British companion that 'now it is guaranteed safe'. The serpent is preparing to swallow both of them. In the German view, the dissolution of the Comintern was a mere tactical move, and the original aim of worldwide Communism directed from the Soviet Union is unaltered.

Cartoon 16.6 Well and truly laid. *Daily Express*, London, 28 May 1943

WELL AND TRULY LAID

Another pair of contrasting cartoons, one British and one German. These consider the implications of the closer relations between Britain and the Soviet Union which were developing in 1943.

Soon after the dissolution of the Comintern, a 'Twenty Year Treaty' was concluded between Britain and the Soviet Union. In form, it was a diplomatic signal of good will, and an expression of intention that this good will should continue long after the war. The *Daily Express* cartoon shows Churchill and the Soviet Foreign Minister Molotov co-operating in laying the Treaty as a foundation-stone of future co-operation, which is crushing Göring, Hitler, and Ribbentrop.

Yet there was an aspect of the Treaty of which the British public – and, indeed most parliamentarians – were unaware. In the course of discussions with Molotov in the previous year, Foreign Minister Eden had virtually acknowledged that Britain accepted the Soviet view that the three Baltic States which had been seized in 1940 should remain part of the Soviet Union after the war, whatever their peoples might think on the matter.

Cartoon 16.7 Die Lady Tanzt. *Das Reich*, Berlin, 1 August 1943

The German cartoon suggests that 'Miss Britannia', besotted by her lascivious-looking Soviet lover, has wantonly stripped off all clothing as she dances before him. The last garment, which she is tearing apart, is labelled 'Atlantic Charter'. That document, concluded between Churchill and Roosevelt as recently as August 1941, included an assertion of the 'right of all peoples to choose the form of government under which they will live'. The cartoon implies that this principle has already been abandoned by Britain in order to please the Soviet Union. Almost certainly the cartoonist knew nothing of Eden's action over the Baltic States, but he may well have realized that the British government was inclining to the view that much of the *kresy* should remain in the Soviet Union, whether the people living there wished it or not.

Cartoon 16.8 Realities in Yugoslavia. *Evening Standard*, London, 23 December 1943

A comment on the British government decision to transfer military support in Yugoslavia from the Cetniks to the Partisans. Partisans are fighting in the Yugoslav mountains and receiving assitance from the 'United Nations' – that is, from the Allies, and particularly from the British. A representative of the Yugoslav government-in-exile, currently seated in Cairo, warns that 'Tito is a rebellious red trouble-maker', and draws an unexpected response from the British officer.

Cartoon 16.9 Sikorski und Peter. *Das Reich*, Berlin, 23 January 1944

A gruesome German comment on the death of Sikorski and the current dispute over Yugoslavian assistance. The ghost of Sikorski who – according to the German view – had been murdered by the British at the Gibraltar air crash in July 1943, appears in front of King Peter of Yugoslavia. Peter is portrayed as a child, although in fact he was a a young man. Sikorski advises Peter not to accept any British government aeroplane. The Yugoslav government-in-exile was currently being 'advised' by the British to come to terms with Tito.

17

Western Europe, 1944

In 1943, the German campaign of submarine warfare in the north Atlantic was effectively met, and in the following months a gradual build-up for the 'Second Front' in western Europe began. During the early part of 1944, the Red Army pressed towards, and in places across, the western frontiers of the Soviet Union; while the slow advance of the British and Americans into Italy continued.

There was no secret that the great military operation planned for the late spring of 1944 was an Anglo-American invasion of western Europe across the English Channel. On 6 June – 'D-day' – the first landings were made in Normandy. Once a bridgehead had been established, progress was rapid, though by no means uninterrupted. On 25 August, the German garrison in Paris surrendered. Much of Belgium was liberated in the course of 1944, although the Germans retained a foothold in the south which proved an important obstacle to Allied progress. On 11 September the first troops from the western Allies penetrated into Germany itself.

As 1944 advanced, it became apparent to most observers that the Germans had lost the war. Was it possible, nevertheless, that they might escape with something less than the unconditional surrender which the Allies were demanding? There were two possible ways in which Germany might win terms. The first was by sowing dissent between Allies, particularly between the western Allies and the Soviet Union, and then contriving to make peace with one to the exclusion of the other. The other way was by demonstrating to the Allies that the price of the total victory which they sought would prove so great that it was better to reach an accommodation. This might be done by fighting so desperately that the cost in blood became unacceptable, or by unleashing new weapons of extreme frightfulness. These German hopes, which can never have been very realistic, gradually vanished as time went on and the Allies began to close in.

The Allied military advances in France posed great political problems. After the confusion of command during the French North African campaign of 1942–3, the original Free French gave place to a new French Committee of National Liberation – over which, however, de Gaulle soon

achieved control. Yet even at D-day the Committee was not recognized by major Allies as a 'government in exile'.

As the Allied troops advanced, however, the Vichy regime and its local supporters gradually collapsed, sometimes yielding place to local anarchy. It became important to the Anglo-Americans that some kind of civil authority should be established in France, and it was apparent that only de Gaulle possessed the prestige to head such an authority. With considerable reluctance Churchill and Roosevelt accepted the need to afford full recognition to de Gaulle's administration, which was at last granted towards the end of October.

Meanwhile, progress of the western Allies on the Italian front also continued, and also brought political problems in its wake. On 4 June – two days before D-day – Allied troops entered Rome. On the following day King Victor Emmanuel, without formally abdicating, ceded power to his son Umberto, who became 'Lieutenant of the Realm'. By this time the King had become a figure of ridicule, frequently lampooned in cartoons of Germans and Allies alike. The curious status both of the country's head of state and of its government – technically at war with Germany without yet having concluded formal peace with the Allies – generated confusion, and there was much doubt about the future of various once-Italian territories currently in occupation either by the Allies or by the Germans, to which there were rival claimants.

Cartoon 17.1 TrUmped! *Daily Herald*, London, 11 May 1944

TRUMPED!

The success of any major military operation by the Allies in western Europe depended on their capacity to bring men and supplies across the Atlantic.

As this cartoon suggests, Allied shipping losses were being steadily reduced, and German U-boat losses steadily increased, in the spring of 1944. Any lingering doubts about the Second Front would very soon be removed. The theme of a game of cards, for high stakes, appears repeatedly in cartoons of different countries.

Cartoon 17.2 The new Bayeux Tapestry. *Daily Mail*, London, 9 June 1944

The *Daily Mail* cartoon celebrates the beginning of the Second Front in Normandy as a sort of Norman Conquest in reverse, demanding a 'new Bayeux Tapestry'. Commandos land on the beaches and penetrate the 'Vallum Occidens' – dog-Latin for the West Wall – protecting Nazi-occupied Europe. Hitler, the 'Führer Teutonicus' and his associates regard their approach with dismay.

Cartoon 17.3 They storm the West Wall. *Chicago Daily Tribune*, 7 June 1944

THEY STORM THE WEST WALL

The *Chicago Daily Tribune*, which had adopted an isolationist stance in the early part of the war but was by this time enthusiastically supporting American participation, rose to the drama of the occasion. The figure of 'History', frequently used in that newspaper's cartoons, commemorates the 'most decisive hour' and prepares to inscribe the new conflict among the list of decisive battles of the past.

Cartoon 17.4 Wir bringen Ihnen Freiheit. . . *Das Reich*, Berlin, 25 June 1944

„Wir bringen Ihnen Freiheit, Frieden und Wohlstand!"
„Sehr schön, — meinen Sie Freiheit wie in Bessarabien, Frieden wie am Balkan und Wohlstand wie in Süditalien? . . ."

Das Reich, predictably, takes a less sympathetic view of the invasion, although – like the two Allied newspapers – it notes a parallel with the past. Europa, eponymous heroine of Europe, is accompanied by the bull in whose guise Zeus wooed her. Representatives of the major Allies approach her with a cornucopia (which, however, is empty, and which the Soviet representative is apparently attempting to ignite). They greet her with the words, 'We bring you freedom, peace and prosperity!' Europa cynically enquires whether they mean 'freedom as in Bessarabia, peace as in the Balkans, and prosperity as in southern Italy'. These are allusions respectively to the Soviet seizure of Bessarabia, the chronic instability and warfare of the Balkans, and the grinding poverty of southern Italy. From the motions of its tail, the bull appears to be in an angry mood.

Cartoon 17.5 Overshadowed. *Daily Mail*, London, 29 July 1944

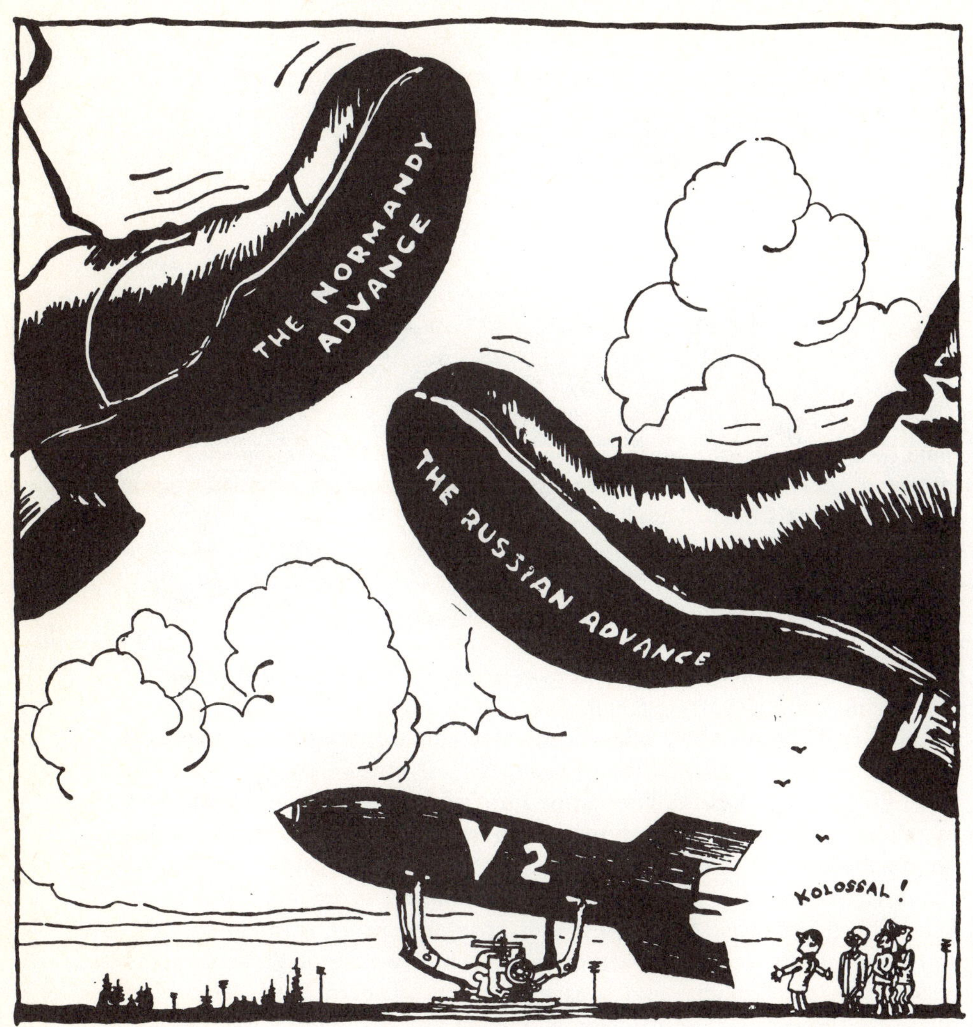

German propaganda had long maintained that Germany had 'secret weapons' in her armoury which would prove of critical importance in the war. Not long after D-day, one kind of these new weapons – the so-called 'V-1s' – were launched against targets in south-eastern England from bases close to the Channel coast. The V-1 weapons were unmanned aeroplanes (commonly known as 'flying bombs', 'buzz-bombs' or 'doodle-bugs') whose engines suddenly cut out, whereupon the weapon fell to earth and exploded. The V-2 weapons had not yet been launched when this cartoon was drawn; they were large rockets which also exploded on impact. The British people, who had rather assumed that the worst of their privations were over, were considerably shocked at the damage and suffering the V-weapons caused.

It became a matter of importance to capture the V-weapon bases as soon as possible. This cartoon, which appeared late in June 1944, shows Hitler and other Nazis admiring the V-2 weapons which were about to be delivered, while feet – representing the invading armies – were poised to crush bombs and Nazis alike.

This view proved somewhat sanguine. It was not until well into 1945 that the last V-weapon bases were captured by the Allies and the attacks finally ceased.

Cartoon 17.6 Sinking at the dock. *San Francisco Chronicle*, 29 June 1944

Sinking at the Dock

Cartoon 17.7 Panique aux greniers. *L'Aube*, Paris, 1 September 1944

Panique aux greniers

The Germans had allowed the Vichy regime to continue during the period of occupation, but its authority had long been crumbling. In the American cartoon, the rats 'Laval and his gang', seek to escape from Vichy to the Nazi harbour, but their route is blocked by an impassable obstacle. Pierre Laval was an astonishingly supple French politician, viewed by the Allies with especial hatred.

The French cartoon, 'Panic in the granaries', drawn shortly after the liberation of Paris, also sees the Nazis and their French associates as 'rats' who are fleeing desperately in face of the Allied invasion. They have feasted well on the corn – that is, they have flourished at the expense of France and the other occupied countries. Now their obesity hinders flight.

Cartoon 17.8 La dernière arme secrète. *Le Canard enchaîné*, Paris, 6 September 1944

La dernière arme secrète

A light-hearted French cartoon about 'secret weapons'. Pétain wields the *francisque*, or battle axe, emblem of the *Etat Francais*, commonly known as Vichy France. The weapon is an obvious anachronism – useful, no doubt, for the historic Franks but useless in twentieth-century warfare. Thus the weapon symbolizes the totally ineffective character of the regime over which Pétain still nominally presided.

Whether Pétain in this cartoon intended to assist or to threaten Hitler is not clear. In either event, the Führer is not impressed by the gesture of the Marshal – by then aged 88 – whom he evidently considers to be senile. Perhaps the expression on Hitler's face suggests a mixture of anxiety for his own likely fate and a sort of pitying contempt for Pétain.

Cartoon 17.9 Une opération réussie. *L'Aube*, Paris, 20 September 1944

Une opération réussie

By September 1944, when this cartoon appeared, the western Allies were already well established in France. 'A successful operation' shows the British, Soviet, and American surgeons who have just restored Marianne to health.

Cartoon 17.10 Salute the soldier? *Daily Mail*, London, 2 June 1944

SALUTE THE SOLDIER? —*by Illingworth.*

This cartoon was drawn shortly before D-day. General de Gaulle, carrying 'Plans for democratic France' with his portfolio, greets British Foreign Secretary Anthony Eden and American Secretary of State Cordell Hull in the street. They are uncertain whether to return his salute.

Bitter arguments had raged both in Britain and in the United States as to whether de Gaulle's 'French Committee of National Liberation' should be afforded full diplomatic recognition as the government of France, entitled to take over control of French territory as soon as it was liberated. Roosevelt and – to a somewhat lesser extent – Churchill were opposed to recognition. Their respective Foreign Ministers were less adamant on the matter.

'Salute the Soldier' was the name of a much-publicized war savings campaign. The title was meant to imply that people who were saving money instead of spending it were thereby giving positive assistance to the war effort.

Cartoon 17.11 Ah! Mon cher Général!. . . *Evening Standard*, London, 24 October 1944

As the Allies advanced into France, the need to establish some credible civil authority composed of Frenchmen, which would maintain control of liberated areas, became a matter of considerable urgency.

De Gaulle's 'French Committee of National Liberation' was the obvious candidate for that function, but much argument on the matter continued in Allied circles. On 23 October 1944, formal recognition was at last granted.

In this cartoon, which appeared on the following day, the 'Big Three' leaders welcome de Gaulle with somewhat unconvincing bonhomie. De Gaulle, who knew much about the political and diplomatic wrangles which had been going on behind the scenes, is uncertain how to respond.

Cartoon 17.12. 'Your Missus would give you. . .' *Daily Express*, London, 11 October 1944

"Your missus would give you 'Vive La Belgique' if she was to come round the corner"

An early Giles cartoon, very much in the spirit of those he is still drawing more than forty years later. As in most of his work, there is much warm humanity and astonishing detail.

Allied troops had already penetrated far into Belgium by this date, and were generally greeted with considerable enthusiasm by the civilian population – as in France.

Cartoon 17.13 New horizon. *Daily Herald*, London, 6 June 1944

NEW HORIZON

This cartoon, which actually appeared on D-day, celebrates the recent Allied capture of Rome, with the implication that 'the industrial North of Italy' was now in sight for the British soldier.

In the event, progress up the Italian peninsula continued to be rather slow.

Cartoon 17.14 I have a comrade – I hope! *Daily Mail*, London, 24 July 1944

I have a comrade—I hope! —*by Illingworth.*

By July 1944, the Allies were advancing on Germany from various directions, and many highly-placed Germans perceived that the war was irretrievably lost. The longer fighting continued, the worse it would be for Germany. Hitler and his immediate associates, however, would never make peace – if for no other reason than because they were certain to be brought to trial for their many crimes, and executed in the aftermath.

This appreciation led to the 'Generals' plot': an attempt by senior German officers to kill Hitler by a bomb on 20 July 1944. The 'plot' miscarried, and the culprits were executed.

This cartoon visualizes what might have happened if one of the 'Generals' contrived to escape as far as the Soviet lines and attempted to make his own peace with the Red Army. The Soviet authorities were tolerant of German officers who acknowledged defeat. Field Marshal von Paulus, who had led the Germans at Stalingrad but eventually surrendered to the Red Army early in 1943, was accepted into honourable captivity.

The title of the cartoon alludes to a German soldiers' song, with which the officer would certainly have been familiar.

18

Eastern Europe, 1944

By the end of 1943, there were abundant signs that the Red Army would soon cross the pre-war frontiers of the Soviet Union in pursuit of the retreating enemy. Enormous problems, military and diplomatic, were presented to all the belligerents by these events, and the way those problems were handled has had immense repercussions right down to the present.

Most difficult of all was the question of Poland's future, both territorial and political. Very early in 1944, the Red Army entered the *kresy*, which was treated as a newly recovered area of the Soviet Union. Yet the Soviet authorities desired some kind of acknowledgement for their 1939 conquests from Britain and the United States, and diplomatic discussions about the future of the area continued.

In the summer of 1944, the Red Army pressed west of the so-called 'Curzon Line', which divided the *kresy* from the area which all Allies agreed should be Polish after the war. Here the question of political administration was more acute and immediate. The Polish government-in-exile naturally considered that it should be permitted to return to Polish soil once the Germans had been effectively driven out; but as the Soviet Union refused to recognize its legality, this was out of the question. For the time being, an administration – soon to be known as the 'Lublin Committee' – was set up in the area of Soviet occupation, consisting of Poles who were sympathetic towards the Soviet authorities. Even the Russians, however, did not claim that the Lublin Committee was the legitimate government of Poland, and discussions about the country's future continued.

At the end of July the Red Army was close to Warsaw, and the Polish underground movement in the capital was urged by the Soviet radio to revolt against the occupying Germans. When the revolt had been in operation for a few days, the Red Army encountered a military check. Very soon the Soviet authorities roundly condemned the insurrection, and even refused permission to aeroplanes from the western Allies who had been supplying the Warsaw insurgents and sought to land on Soviet-controlled territory. Eventually, after strong pressure from Roosevelt and Churchill, this rule was somewhat relaxed; but by then the insurrection was already

doomed. It finally collapsed early in October 1944, after more than two months of heroic fighting. Behind the tragic history of the Warsaw rising there clearly lay diplomatic and political questions between the major Allies about Poland's future which were still unresolved, and which certainly would not disappear of their own accord.

Almost every country in eastern Europe, whether Allied, enemy or neutral, presented its own problems, and in no two of them were the issues quite the same. The difficulties of Yugoslavia have already been considered in part. For the mid-war period, Yugoslavia had been primarily the concern of Britain, and it was the British who had decided which Yugoslav guerrillas to support and on what terms. By the autumn of 1944, however, the Red Army seemed poised to enter the country from the north-east, and there was reason for thinking that the western Allies would eventually invade from the north-west, via Italy. There were dangers of serious disputes between the Soviet Union and the western Allies, as well as bitter conflicts between rival Yugoslavs.

In Greece, as in Yugoslavia, there had been problems with rival resistance organizations. There was the important difference, however, that the Greek Communists and their sympathizers (ELAS) had been a good deal less valuable to the Allies than their Yugoslav counterparts. Here it was the British who stood poised to invade in the early autumn of 1944; but the Soviet Union was undeniably in a position to influence the behaviour of ELAS once the invasion occurred, and this might, in some circumstances, prove very embarrassing for Britain.

The countries which had sided with Germany at the time of the attack on the Soviet Union, and which lay on the Soviet line-of-march in 1944, presented the Allies with problems of different kinds.

The position of Finland was particularly tragic. When she was attacked by the Soviet Union in 1939, most countries showed strong sympathy for her plight. The peace settlement of March 1940 cut off substantial areas of the country, and their loss was naturally resented by the Finns. In 1941 the Soviet Union attacked Finland again – perhaps anticipating a German thrust from that direction. As the conflict developed, Finland secured German assistance. The main Finnish 'war aim' was to recover territory which had been taken in 1940, although some Finns began to dream of a 'Greater Finland', which would extend to the White Sea.

Romania also had lost territory in 1940, but she had come under German influence thereafter and joined in the attack on the Soviet Union. Her principal aim was to recover Bessarabia and northern Bukovina, but Romanian troops co-operated with the Germans as far afield as Stalingrad. Hungary, whose main territorial quarrel was with Romania, had no aspirations to Soviet territory but was brought into the war shortly afterwards, perhaps by German trickery.

The two-and-a-half year German siege of Leningrad ended in January

1944, after enormous sufferings and well over a million civilian deaths. Thereafter, great Soviet pressure was put on Finland, and in March peace negotiations were attempted, but failed. About the same time Hungary sought to make peace, but this attempt also failed and the Germans took control of the country.

In the late summer of 1944, Soviet military advances led to renewed peace negotiations. In August, Romania withdrew from the war, and almost immediately re-entered it on the Allied side. Not long after, the Red Army occupied Bucharest. A Soviet armistice with Finland was concluded in September.

Bulgaria was in an anomalous position. War had been declared on the western Allies in 1941, but there was deep-rooted friendship for Russia, and the government did not declare war on the Soviet Union. The country was nevertheless compelled to permit German troops to pass through. Early in September, almost as soon as the Red Army reached the Bulgarian frontier, the Soviet Union declared war, to which the Bulgarians replied by immediately seeking armistice terms.

In nearly all of these countries, the British, the Russians, and the Americans had strong interests – military, economic, political, territorial, and sometimes emotional as well. The task of harmonizing those interests was of considerable urgency by the early autumn of 1944. The Nazis appear to have clung on to the hope that inter-Allied differences would prove so profound that one or other group of enemies would be prepared to come to terms in order to thwart the other. This was never a realistic possibility; but both long-term and short-term difficulties were enormous, and there was – on the face of it – everything to be said for holding a major 'Big Three' conference about that time.

There was one overriding reason why no such conference could be held: the American elections. The United States constitution required a Presidential election in November 1944. The power vested in the President is in some respects enormous, and until the contest was over nobody could speak with much authority for the United States. Roosevelt, who had broken all precedent by seeking – and winning – a third four-year term in 1940, was currently seeking a fourth term. Once the elections were over, a substantial further period had to elapse, for the formal inauguration of the elected candidate could not take place before January 1945. Thus it happened that in 1944, when it was peculiarly important to all countries that a clear voice should be heard from the United States, no such voice could be discerned.

Britain and the Soviet Union had to improvise as well as they could. In October 1944 a conference – sometimes known by its code-name 'Tolstoy' – was held in Moscow, attended by Churchill and Stalin. Mikolajczyk was summoned as well, and an earnest attempt was made to secure agreement about the political and territorial future of Poland. The Polish Prime

Minister, however, was in no position to commit his colleagues, and no agreement emerged. Agreement, however, was reached about most countries in south-eastern Europe, at least for the immediate future. This was expressed in percentages. In Romania, the Soviet Union was to have 90 per cent of influence and the western Allies 10 per cent. In Greece it would be the opposite way round. In Hungary and Bulgaria the balance would be 80:20 in favour of the Soviet Union; in Yugoslavia the influence would be equal.

A cartoon [right] which, at first sight, appears to have little to do with the affairs of eastern Europe, but which is in fact highly relevant.

The US Democratic Party is shown as the rather agitated-looking mother of four sons of various ages, all of whom show a close resemblance to President Roosevelt. They are labelled 'First term', 'Second term', etc. and refer to the various periods of his presidency. The elephant, on the other side of the street, is the symbol of the opposition Republican Party, and wears a look of disapproval.

At the time this cartoon was drawn, Roosevelt was nearing the end of the third term of his presidency and was considering running for a fourth. The cartoon appeared in January 1944. Election campaigns were certain to preoccupy American politicians right down to the elections of November. While attention would certainly be given to the task of fighting the war, most of the vital diplomatic questions would almost certainly be shelved by the American government until the elections were over. Roosevelt, as a candidate actively seeking re-election, would certainly not be willing to leave the United States for an international conference in 1944. Thus the major diplomatic decisions affecting eastern Europe were taken between the Soviet Union and Britain, or else were postponed until the elections were over.

Cartoon 18.1 Those things sort of get to be a habit.
New York Herald Tribune, 17 January 1944

Cartoon 18.2 'And this is the limit.' *Evening Standard*, London, 15 February 1944

After the siege of Leningrad was relieved towards the end of January 1944, Finland showed considerable interest in coming to terms with the Soviet Union. In this cartoon, Ryti and Tanner, two leading Finnish politicians, discuss the political situation in the light of Germany's retreat, while Mannerheim, the military leader, looks through binoculars into the distance. The notice 'Finland's "Limited War"' refers to the comparatively restricted geographical area of Finland's interest. The Finns wished to drive the Red Army out of Finland; they had no interest in helping Germany conquer the Soviet Union. The Finnish soldier retorts, 'And this is the limit', indicating that he was anxious to withdraw from the war altogether.

Finland's position was anomalous in many ways. At the time of the 'Winter war' of 1939–40, she had had general international sympathy. When, in 1941, she was forced into war on Germany's side, that sympathy largely remained. Finland was the only country with a democratic political constitution, in the western sense of the term, who did fight on the German side. The British Foreign Secretary, Eden, had great difficulty in persuading Churchill to countenance a British declaration of war against Finland, and the United States never declared war on Finland.

The peace moves to which this cartoon refers proved unsuccessful; a Soviet–Finnish armistice was not achieved until September 1944.

Cartoon 18.3 Daily Express, London, 3 March 1944

This cartoon appeared in March 1944, about the time of the abortive Soviet–Finnish peace negotiations. Finland has escaped from the German 'Satellite Quarters', to the annoyance of the Nazi gaoler. Other satellites have looks of studied innocence on their faces, suggesting that they are contemplating similar actions as soon as they get a chance.

The inclusion of Bulgaria among the satellites is interesting. Bulgaria had not entered the war against the Soviet Union on Germany's side in 1941, although she was at war with Britain and the United States, and had seized territory from Yugoslavia. The country's geographical location, however, made it impossible for her to resist German pressure for military occupation.

Cartoon 18.4 Fashistski Zoougolok 1944 goda. From *Sovetski Masteri Satiry, 1941–45* (*Soviet Masters of Satire, 1941–45*), Moscow/Leningrad, 1946

ФАЩИСТСКИЙ ЗООУГОЛОК 1944 ГОДА

Невинная голубица, кроткая овечка, безобидный зайчик, ласковый теленок

Soviet propaganda made no distinction between the circumstances in which different countries had joined the fight against the USSR.

In this cartoon, 'Fascist Zoopark, 1944', the words at the bottom read 'The innocent dove, the gentle sheep, the inoffensive hare, the tender calf'. Harmless-looking wooden figures have been set up, but behind them sinister figures lurk in ambush. Hitler himself hides behind the dove 'Romania', Admiral Horthy behind the sheep 'Hungary'. Behind the hare 'Finland' a figure – probably meant to be Mannerheim – sits on a paper carrying the words 'Great Finland' – an allusion to the aspirations which some Finns entertained for territory which would extend to the White Sea.

Behind the calf 'Spain' crouches General Franco, with the flag 'Blue Division' on his bayonet. Spain, though technically not at war with the Soviet Union, despatched the 'Blue Division' which assisted the German invaders. Just as the main Allies took very different views of Finland, so also did they take different views of Spain. None of them had sympathy with the political regime of Franco. The western Allies, however, recalled that Spain had not entered the war on Germany's side in 1940, even though she must have been under considerable temptation and pressure to do so. Such intervention could have done incalculable damage to the Allied cause.

Cartoon 18.5 Shila v meshke ne utaish'. From *Sovetski Masteri Satiry, 1941–45* (*Soviet Masters of Satire, 1941–45*), Moscow/Leningrad, 1946

Болгарское правительство ввело „нейтралитет" для того, чтобы дать возможность немцам укрыться в Болгарии от преследований союзников

(*Из газет*)

Шила в мешке не утаишь

This cartoon, 'The spikes in the bag are not hidden', was probably drawn about the time of the Soviet declaration of war on Bulgaria in September 1944.

One Bulgarian politician displays the white sheet 'Bulgarian neutrality', and another tries unsuccessfully to conceal a large gun with his hat. Behind the sheet are seen German soldiers and a tank, while the bayonets of other Germans project through it.

The Soviet cartoon implies that the Bulgarians are guilty of naïve hypocrisy and is evidently designed to justify the Soviet decision to attack the country, even though the Bulgarians played no part in the German attack on the Soviet Union. That view is supported by the Soviet news item in small print, which declares that the Bulgarian government was pretending neutrality in order to give the Germans a chance to escape from the Allies.

Cartoon 18.6 'Frei' Übungen bei Michaels. *Das Reich*, Berlin, 24 September 1944

On 12 September 1944, the armistice with Romania was signed in Moscow. Frontiers were to follow those existing at the end of June 1940. Romania would lose Bessarabia and northern Bukovina to the Soviet Union, but would recover from Hungary the part of Transylvania ceded under the 'Vienna Award'. The Romanians were also required to provide troops to fight Germany and Hungary, and to pay reparations to the USSR. King Michael had played a substantial part in events of the previous month which led to Romania changing sides.

In this German cartoon, the King and senior officials at his court are practicing the Communist clenched-fist salute, in recognition of Romania's new role as a close associate of the Soviet Union. One official explains to another that they are training their muscles for forced labour. This implies that the Romanians will soon be required to act as slave-workers for the USSR.

Cartoon 18.7 Some rats. . . *Daily Mirror*, London, 17 October 1944

Some rats don't know when a ship is sinking!

Admiral Miklós Horthy – his rank derived from the time of the Dual Monarchy – had been Regent of Hungary since 1920. Although Hungary had been at war with the Soviet Union since 1941, Horthy was on bad terms with Hitler, and in October 1944 attempted to obtain a separate peace with the Allies. The Germans kidnapped Horthy's son and threatened to shoot him. Horthy capitulated to this pressure, but the pro-Nazi 'Arrow Cross' movement seized power in Budapest, and Horthy was imprisoned.

In this cartoon, Horthy, who is in a tattered and wounded condition, is advancing to the microphone to broadcast an appeal for terms from the Allies. He is overwhelmed, however, by the 'rats', one of whom shouts 'Heil Hitler' into the microphone.

Cartoon 18.8 La carte polonaise. *La Gerbe*, Paris, 17 August 1944

— Pardon, Messieurs, c'est moi qui suis maitre !...

Three views of the Warsaw Rising of August–October 1944.

In the French 'collaborationist' cartoon, Churchill and Roosevelt have just played the card 'Poland' against Stalin; but he retorts by beating their Queen with an ace bearing the hammer and sickle. *La Gerbe* would very soon cease publication, for the Allies enterd Paris about a week after this cartoon appeared.

Cartoon 18.9 Bobby Winston und der Polenklau.
Das Reich, Berlin, 10 September 1944

BOBBY WINSTON UND DER POLENKLAU

Das Reich takes a different view of inter-Allied relations in 'Bobby Winston and the pillager of Poland'. Stalin carries the body of Poland in a sack; Churchill, the policeman, is either too stupid to realize what has happened, or condones the crime.

The *Evening Standard* cartoon shows the Polish rebels in 'tragic Warsaw' looking with dismay at the Polish officer, with 'Political Ineptness' on his uniform, who is apparently shouting to the world the facts about Warsaw's fate and the circumstances which have brought it about.

Cartoon 18.10 Unhelpful friend. *Evening Standard*, London, 7 September 1944

UNHELPFUL FRIEND

(Copyright in All Countries.)

Probably none of these cartoons was very close to the facts of the situation. There is little reason for thinking that Churchill and Roosevelt had had much part in playing 'the Polish card' by encouraging the insurgents in Warsaw to rise against the occupying Germans at that moment. They were certainly appalled at some features of Soviet behaviour, but this was not because Stalin had frustrated designs of their own. 'Bobby Winston' knew perfectly well what the 'Polenklau' was doing, and tried (without much success) to prevent it. There is little to suggest that the Poles fighting in Warsaw in any way disapproved of the decision of their government-in-exile to blurt out the facts of the Warsaw Rising, which in no way damaged their own hopeless position but reflected little credit on the Soviet government.

The German cartoon illustrates that measure of hypocrisy which is so commonly found in wartime cartoons of all countries. The 'Polenklau', whose activities it appears to deplore, had been started on his career by the German-Soviet Non-aggression Pact of 1939.

19

Yalta

On 7 November 1944, Franklin D. Roosevelt was re-elected President of the United States. A couple of months later he was formally inaugurated for a fourth term. Everything was now ready for the second 'Big Three' Conference, which was held at Yalta, in the Crimea, from 4 to 11 February 1945.

In the period immediately before Yalta, some serious inter-Allied problems developed. The most difficult of these concerned Poland. At the 'Tolstoy' Conference in Moscow in October 1944, both Churchill and Stalin had set strong pressure on Mikolajczyk to accept drastic territorial changes, and to reach an accommodation with the 'Lublin Committee'. The Polish Prime Minister explained that he was in no position to commit either his country or his government. On his return to London, it transpired that Mikolajczyk's colleagues were not prepared to go even as far as he was in the matter, and he resigned. The successor was Tomasz Arciszewski. Churchill lost all patience with the Polish government, and even publicly upheld Soviet claims to the overwhelmingly Polish city of Lwów (now known as Lvov). At the turn of the year, the Soviet Union formally recognized the 'Lublin Committee' of Edward Osobka-Morawski as the *de jure* government of Poland.

The position had now become absurd. In name, there were two 'Polish Governments' in existence, each engaged in war against Nazi Germany. One government was recognized by Britain and the United States, the other by the Soviet Union. Neither had any chance of governing Poland without the backing of at least one major Ally. Nobody knew what the people of Poland thought about either the territorial or the political questions involved.

In Yugoslavia the position was not much better. Partisans, Cetniks, Germans, Italians, and the Croatian Ustashi were fighting against, or allying with, each other in various combinations in different places, while there was the prospect that Soviet troops would soon enter the country from one side and the Anglo-Americans from another. In theory, a kind of reconciliation – the 'Tito–Subasic agreement' – had been reached in November 1944 between the Partisans and the Yugoslav government-in-exile. However, Subasic – technically Prime Minister of the exiled

government – was playing very much his own hand, and the agreement (which was of very dubious legality) was repudiated by King Peter. Meanwhile, Tito prepared to dispense with the King and Subasic alike.

Allied armies were closing in on Hitler's Europe. In some places it was fairly obvious which one would arrive first, but in others matters looked like developing into a race between diffrent Allied armies. Nobody was very clear how the Anglo-Americans and the Red Army would behave towards each other when they met, while in some places pro-Allied forces among the local population had their own ideas. Still less was it clear what should happen to the various parts of Europe in the immediate aftermath of war.

A sort of tacit agreement already existed about Germany and Austria before Yalta, to the effect that they would be occupied completely by the Allies for the indefinite future; but there was no agreement about the long-term future of those countries. Indeed, there is little indication that any of the 'Big Three' had really made up their own minds as to what was wanted.

At Yalta, apparent agreement was reached between Churchill, Roosevelt and Stalin on some of these problems. The lines of eventual military demarcation were agreed, but while fighting continued the Allied armies would take 'maximum surrender' – effectively, each would occupy as much territory as it could, and the agreed demarcations would be adopted later. Germany and Austria, originally proposed for occupation by the 'Big Three' only, were also to receive French zones of occupation. The eastern borders of Poland were agreed, and would follow roughly the Curzon Line – as the Russians wished. As for the 'liberated countries' of Europe, they would eventually have the opportunity of deciding their own kinds of governments. There was also agreement about the outline of the new form of the 'United Nations' which would continue into the post-war period as a peace-keeping force.

There was a highly secret agreement at Yalta that, within three months of the end of the European war, the Soviet Union would enter the conflict against Japan. Neither Stalin nor the western leaders appear to have been troubled in the least by the fact that this would necessarily constitute a breach of the Soviet–Japanese Non-aggression Pact of 1941. To the western Allies, Soviet intervention offered the prospect of exacting unconditional surrender from Japan with much less loss of life than would otherwise be the case. To the Soviet Union it offered the prospect of rich pickings in territory or influence in Asia.

Cartoon 19.1 Break through. *Daily Herald*, London, 9 November 1944

BREAK THROUGH

The re-election of Roosevelt as President of the United States in November 1944 was welcomed in Britain, and probably in the Soviet Union as well. This was partly a mark of appreciation for a man who was regarded as a great leader of his country both in peace and war; but there was also an enormous sense of relief that the long campaign, with its attendant uncertainties, was at last over.

In this British cartoon, Roosevelt, mounted on an American tank, coasts through the block of 'election hold-up'.

Cartoon 19.2 Taking the plunge. *Daily Herald*, London, 24 January 1945

TAKING THE PLUNGE

(King Peter of Jugoslavia has dismissed his Ministers without consulting the Allied Governments)

The 'Tito-Subasic Agreement' of November 1944 was reached under strong pressure from the British government. King Peter, who had never received the consultation to which he was entitled, perceived it as a device for getting rid of himself, and doubted the pledges of political and religious freedom which it contained. Eventually he issued a public statement condemning the agreement and foreseeing – correctly, as it turned out – that the eventual upshot would be a Tito dictatorship. Shortly afterwards, the Ministers who had acted without authority were dismissed by the King.

This cartoon is a reflection on King Peter's action. Churchill and Eden, as swimming instructors, are dismayed at Peter's decision to dive from the deep end of the swimming bath into the waters of 'internal strife'.

The 'internal strife' already existed, and would doubtless continue to exist whatever the King might do. The British grievance was really that the King insisted on bringing the whole matter into the open, instead of allowing it to pass without comment. The British government's authority to act as 'instructors' in a matter which concerned another country would probably be challenged by all Yugoslavs, on whatever side they happened to find themselves in the current controversy. Certainly there was no altruism in the British position so far as Peter was concerned. Earlier in January, Churchill had written that the 'Tito–Subasic Agreement' 'gives him a very poor chance of ever seeing his native land again, whether as King or subject'.

Cartoon 19.3 King of the castle. *Daily Herald*, London, 20 December 1944

KING OF THE CASTLE

At the end of 1944, while King Peter of Yugoslavia was being pushed aside for reasons related much more to international diplomacy than either to military requirements or to ideology, King George II of Greece was experiencing a totally different fate. The 'Tolstoy' arrangements set Greece under British tutelage, at least for the time being, and the British government had no compunction in giving general support, including military assistance, to the exiled King and his government.

In this cartoon, King George of Greece rides in a British tank, declaring that he will neither abdicate nor submit to a regency, and defies the 'Greek Resistance'.

The suggestion that the 'Greek Resistance' was unanimous in its dislike for the monarchy is simplistic in the extreme. ELAS, unlike its Yugoslav counterparts, appears to have done relatively little against the occupying enemy but had preserved its weapons – aiming at a take-over in Athens after the fighting against the Germans was over. A report by a delegation from the British TUC early in 1945 indicated the 'universal opinion' of British troops that 'had they not been ordered into action against ELAS there would have been wholesale massacre in Athens'.

Yet there was little justice in the different fates of the two monarchs. George, like his ELAS opponents, had done little to advance the Allied cause, and his support for the Metaxas dictatorship in his country in pre-war times was widely resented. Peter's only important action as effective sovereign of his own country was in 1941, at British instigation, to overthrow the government which had concluded a deal with the Germans, and thus line up Yugoslavia firmly on the Allied side.

Cartoon 19.4 Open wider, please. *Evening Standard*, London, 29 August 1944

In theory, the old League of Nations was still in existence until some time after the end of the Second World War, but nobody doubted that it was practically useless in current circumstances. For a very long time critics of the League had complained that it had no 'teeth' – in other words, that it had no power to enforce its opinions and compel countries to act as it required.

At the Dumbarton Oaks Conference of August-October 1944, representatives of the 'United Nations' – that is, the countries which were in alliance against Germany – considered means of establishing a 'League with teeth', and eventually decided to continue the organization of the United Nations as a post-war peace-keeping body. At Yalta in February 1945 the decisions of Dumbarton Oaks were ratified and extended.

In this cartoon, the US representative Edward R. Stettinius and Sir Alexander Cadogan, Civil Service head of the British Foreign Office, join with an unidentified Soviet colleague at the 'Dumbarton Oaks Dentistry' in equipping the League with a set of teeth.

When this cartoon was drawn, Stettinius had no political role, but not long afterwards he became US Secretary of State.

Cartoon 19.5 Weltwährungskonferenz. *Das Reich*, Berlin 18 June 1944

WELTWÄHRUNGSKONFERENZ

„Meine Herren, Sie sind so mager, machen wir es doch in Zukunft so, daß Sie mir das bißchen Fett, das Sie noch haben, abgeben!" Sturtzkopf

The Bretton Woods Conference of July 1944 was another inter-Allied conference of the pre-Yalta period, which would prove of considerable importance in shaping the post-war world. It led to the establishment of the World Bank and the International Monetary Fund (IMF), and made arrangements for post-war currency convertibility.

In this German cartoon, the American dollar smugly assures the European currencies that he is so fat, and they are so thin, that they might as well give in to his demands. This implies that the Bretton Woods arrangements – not yet completed at the time the cartoon was drawn – would prove an unqualified victory for American finance over all others.

Cartoon 19.6 Vorbereitung. . . *Das Reich*, Berlin
28 January 1945

Vorbereitung für eine neue „Dreier-Konferenz" —

Another German view of inter-Allied arrangements, this one drawn shortly before the Yalta Conference.

In the 'Preparation for a new "Triple Conference"' a servant gets the seating arrangements ready. The United States and the Soviet Union receive impressive chairs – Britain a mere footstool for the convenience of the others. German propaganda had long maintained that Britain had already been reduced to a position much inferior to that of her great Allies.

Cartoon 19.7 Parait qu'il ne fait pas. . . *Le Canard enchaîné*, Paris, 7 February 1945

— Parais qu'il ne fait pas partie des trois grands.

There had been some discussion about the possibility that France might be represented at the Yalta conference, but this was never taken very seriously by the 'Big Three'.

Two men stand by the conference room as de Gaulle – a very tall man – passes by. One reflects to the other 'It looks as if he won't be one of the Big Three.'

Cartoon 19.8 The rock. *Daily Herald*, London, 13 February 1945

THE ROCK

At the end of the Yalta Conference, Roosevelt, Churchill, and Stalin constitute 'The Rock', with the words 'Complete Agreement' written across them. The receding Nazi waves are completely ineffective against that rock.

By this stage of the war, the only remaining Nazi hope was that some profound and irresolvable dispute would appear between the 'Big Three', which would enable Germany to make some kind of peace with one or two of them to the exclusion of the other. If there was 'complete agreement' between them, then they would certainly press successfully for Germany's unconditional surrender.

Cartoon 19.9 The Wailing Wall. *Daily Express*, London, 14 February 1945

THE WAILING WALL

Germans read 'The Crimea [Yalta] Declaration: the text of the Big Three Communiqué', and show dismay at its contents.

Himmler, head of the notorious Gestapo (Secret Police) declares, 'It is brute force.' Goebbels, the Minister of Propaganda, who had so often directed 'hate campaigns' against various intended victims, cries, 'This is a plan of hate.' Two unidentified but rather prosperous-looking Germans embrace each other with the words 'Reparation Commission in Moscow!! It is unpossible [*sic*].' They evidently fear that they would be compelled to pay for damage done to the Soviet Union. Hitler screams, 'My Nazi Party to be wiped out!! It's murder!' The reader would reflect on the many murders for which the Nazis were responsible. Göring, head of the German Air Force, says 'No more Luftwaffe to bomb with! – Why, it's not human!' A military leader considers that the 'end of the General Staff' would be 'uncivilised', while a small Nazi is horrified at what the 'Big Three' propose for 'the defenders of Europe'.

The title, 'The Wailing Wall' for the structure on which the Declaration is exhibited is an intentionally ironic reference to the 'Wailing Wall' in Jerusalem where Jews traditionally prayed, and perhaps hints that the Nazis are about to experience some of the sufferings of Jews whom they have persecuted.

Cartoon 19.10 Yalterations! *Daily Herald*, London 20 February 1945

YALTERATIONS!

Tomasz Arciszewski, Prime Minister of the Polish government in London, deplores the changes to his own country which had been agreed at Yalta. Almost half of pre-war Poland was to be incorporated in the Soviet Union. Poland was to receive a smaller area of German territory in 'compensation', but would be militarily dependent on the Soviet Union to keep it. The Polish government in London would cease to be recognized by Britain and the United States. For reasons which will be considered later, a considerable time was to elapse before all of these changes took effect.

Scant sympathy is shown for Arciszewski's plight, even though he was a socialist, and the *Daily Herald*, in which the cartoon appeared, was a Labour newspaper.

20

The end of the war in Europe

By the time of the Yalta Conference in February 1945, the Allies had established a firm foothold in most of the occupied countries and had penetrated Germany itself from both east and west. There was still much hard fighting ahead, and there were occasional German counter-attacks, but the Allied progress was relentless.

In April, the German collapse became rapid. On the 26th of the month, Soviet and American troops entering Germany from opposite sides made contact. Two days later, Mussolini was captured and shot by Italian partisans. On 30 April, Hitler committed suicide in a bunker at the Reich Chancellery in beleaguered Berlin.

Grand Admiral Karl Dönitz became, briefly, the second and last Führer of the German Reich. On 7 May the unconditional surrender of Germany was formally signed, and the following day was celebrated as 'VE' – Victory in Europe – Day. At the moment of surrender, German troops still held most of Denmark and Norway, parts of the Netherlands, Czechoslovakia, Yugoslavia, and Italy, and patches of territory in Germany and Austria. In some places there was still some resistance by German troops after the formal surrender, but this was quickly extinguished.

As the Allies penetrated into the heart of Hitler's Europe, they reached the Nazi concentration camps and extermination camps. For years, there had been little secret about the Nazi intention to achieve the 'final solution' of the 'Jewish problem' – that is, to exterminate the whole Jewish people. Other groups, such as gypsies and the mentally ill, as well as political or religious opponents of Nazism, were destined for similar treatment. No less horrible than the policy were the means applied to implement it. The victims were not just murdered; in vast numbers of cases they were starved or tortured to death, and treated with every kind of degradation their guards could devise. Soldiers who were familiar enough with the horrors of war found these atrocities almost beyond belief. Enormous numbers of prisoners who survived to the moment of liberation were in such poor physical condition that they died in the days which followed. In some places, incredulous German civilians were paraded through the camps to see for themselves what had happened.

Cartoon 20.1 The last throw. *News Chronicle*, London
20 December 1944

THE LAST THROW

The last major German offensive of the Second World War was the attack in the Ardennes, headed by Generals Rundstedt and Model. The attack began in mid-December but had petered out before the end of the month. The ultimate object, we may surmise, had been to induce the Anglo-Americans invading from the west to conclude a separate peace.

In this cartoon, Rundstedt is shown hurling tanks and aeroplanes into battle, as Germany's 'last throw': her last hope to defeat the western Allies, or at least to convice them that complete victory was not worth the cost, and that it was better to come to terms.

Cartoon 20.2 The big roll-up. *Daily Express*, London 2 April 1945

THE BIG ROLL-UP

By the early spring of 1945, the final and total destruction of Nazi Germany was certain. In this cartoon of early April 1945, Allied soldiers, wearing British, American, and Soviet uniforms, are seen operating the 'big roll-up', as the map of Nazi-occupied Europe is pushed from two directions. Hitler and his military leaders view the situation with mounting despair. One senior officer seems to be leaving the others, with the intention of making his own arrangements for surrender.

Carton 20.3 'The whole German people. . .' *Evening Standard*, London, 19 April 1945

The public reaction to revelations about conditions in German concentration and extermination camps in the closing phase of the war was intense. Everybody in the Allied countries had long known of their existence, and that many horrible things were done inside them; but the extent of the atrocities was not generally appreciated until Allied troops actually arrived.

The 'gut reaction' of the British civilian reading the news in this cartoon is extreme, but similar views were certainly expressed. The reproof of the inmate is unanswerable.

Cartoon 20.4 My obvenyaem. *Krokodil*, Moscow, no. 20. 1945

Мы обвиняем!..

The starving inmates of concentration and extermination camps – men, women and children – tower over the barbed wire of their compounds. The title means 'We accuse!'. They silently charge Nazi leaders with the terrible crimes they have perpetrated. Göring and Himmler, but not Hitler, are among the accused, so the cartoon was apparently drawn between Hitler's death on 30 April 1945 and Himmler's suicide on 27 May. The expressions on the Nazis' faces suggest that they were by that time prisoners themselves. Himmler, who was in charge of the concentration camp system, was the object of special execration. The victims carry labels bearing names of some of the camps: Majdanek, Treblinka, Auschwitz (Oświecim), Buchenwald.

Cartoon 20.5 The Himmler salute. *News Chronicle*, London, 30 April 1945

THE HIMMLER SALUTE

This cartoon comments on Himmler's attempts, in the last stages of the European war, to negotiate a German surrender. The title is a parody on the 'Hitler salute', which was famous throughout the world.

Himmler salutes with his hands held up in surrender, but in so doing displays the blood which covers them. At his feet lie the starved, tortured victims of Himmler's own activities. A cleaver, struck into a butcher's block, holds down the 'Last bid to split Allies'.

It is conceivable, though unlikely, that Himmler hoped at this late date to negotiate terms which would be acceptable to some Allies but not to others, and thus to drive a wedge between them. That is what the cartoon seems to suggest his motives were. It seems much more likely that he hoped, by accelerating the German surrender, to earn a measure of gratitude from the Allies, who would perhaps overlook his own monstrous crimes.

Cartoon 20.6 '*Me* sir? *looting* sir?' *Daily Express*, London 9 April 1945

Allied troops entering Germany in the spring of 1945 behaved as victorious soldiers have done in comparable circumstances from time immemorial: they looted. The destruction of German towns had been very extensive, and in many cases the lawful owners of looted goods were dead or had fled in advance of the invaders. Some kinds of property, such as good cameras and watches, which had been difficult to obtain during the war and were easily portable, were particularly vulnerable to the solders' attentions.

In this Giles cartoon, the artist plainly feels some sympathy with the soldier who has taken household goods and food, and is suddenly arraigned before Authority. In Service slang, the word 'liberate' took on a new meaning. Newspapers and radio had repeatedly used it to refer to Allied conquests ('The liberation of Belgium has been completed', etc.). A soldier might say, 'I have just liberated a watch.'

Cartoon 20.7 Here endeth another lesson. *Daily Mirror*, London, 1 May 1945

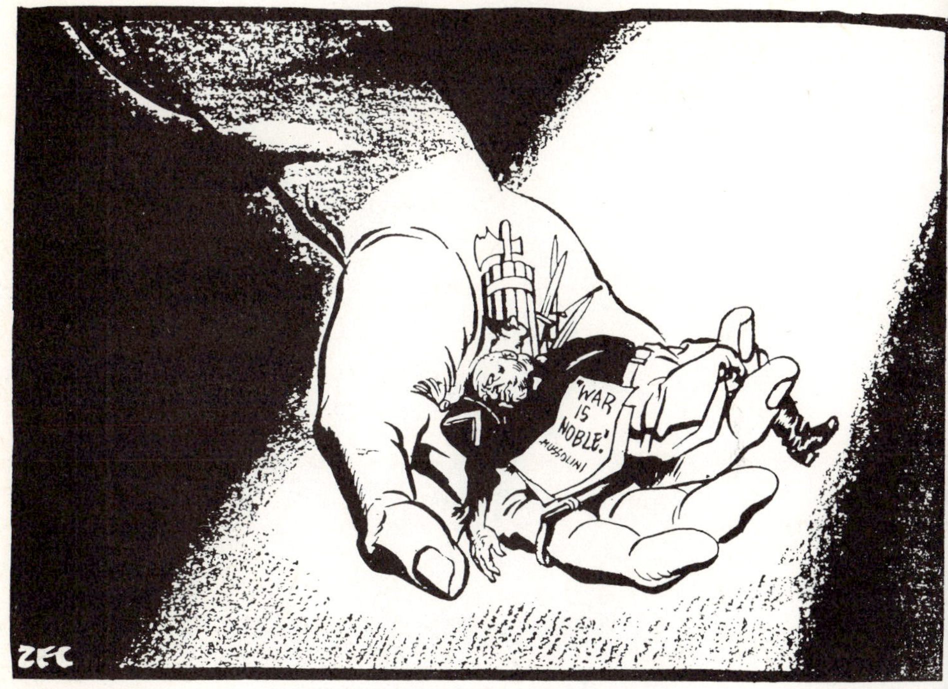

Here endeth another lesson

This cartoon commemorates the death of Mussolini, who was killed along with his mistress by Italian partisans on 28 April 1945, and whose body was then taken to a public square where it was exhibited to the contempt and insults of the Milanese mob (many of whom, no doubt, had cheered him not long before).

The quotation, 'War is noble', is probably authentic; Mussolini sometimes used to speak in that sort of way in earlier times. He lies crumpled with the *fasces* in what is presumably meant to be the hand of God. With Mussolini are also a number of bayonets. One of his boasts at the time of the Abyssinian war had referred to the decisive effect which was to be achieved by Italian 'bayonets'.

Cartoon 20.8 The last chapter. *Daily Express*, London, 30 April 1945

The boot of the Allied soldier is treading on a volume of the Führer's own book, *Mein Kampf*, in which – years before he took power – Hitler adumbrated his plans of conquest. Hitler himself is being crushed between its pages. The cartoonist could not have anticipated this, but the very day on which the drawing appeared witnessed Hitler's suicide.

Heinrich Himmler waves the white flag of surrender, while a rat flees into the distance. This is a comment on Himmler and others who were apparently trying to save their own skins by engineering speedy capitulation.

The similarity between this cartoon and Cartoon 12.7 is difficult to explain as mere coincidence.

Cartoon 20.9 'Il laisse. . .?' *Le Canard enchaîné*, Paris, 9 May 1945

Il laisse des orphelins?
Oui . . . de 20 à 30 millions!

The lady is reading in her newspaper of Hitler's death. A bystander asks whether he left any orphans. The reply is, 'Yes. . . between 20 and 30 millions!' This is a comment on the incredible number of children in many countries whose parents died as a result of the war, for which Hitler was primarily to blame.

Cartoon 20.10 'Here you are. . .' *Daily Mirror*, London, 8 May 1945

"Here you are—don't lose it again"

A cartoon for 'VE Day'. The wounded Allied soldier has just retrieved the laurels, 'Victory and peace in Europe' from the wreckage and carnage of war. His expression suggests irritation with those who lost those laurels earlier, and which he and his comrades have recovered at such cost.

During the Second World War, it was treated almost as a truism in Britain that the Allied countries had 'won the 1914–18 war but lost the peace' – in other words, that the recrudescence of German aggression in the 1930s and 1940s was only able to take place because of the culpable folly of political leaders in countries which had been among the victors of 1918.

The cartoonist is perhaps making this point with an eye to Britain's immediate political future: a point which will be brought out further in a later chapter.

21

Inter-Allied relations, 1945

Long before fighting was over, there were abundant signs that the 'complete agreement' at Yalta was largely illusory and that profound problems remained between the major Allied governments.

The Yalta 'agreement' over Poland was certainly illusory. It very soon appeared that Churchill and Stalin had left Yalta with completely different ideas of the kind of government which was to be set up in the country. By mid-March, a month or so after Yalta, Churchill had decided that, even if Stalin's interpretation was correct, the Soviet government was not keeping the agreement but was strengthening the Osobka-Morawski 'government' which had been installed at Warsaw. Thus it was becoming exceedingly difficult for any Poles from the west – moderates like Mikolajczyk as well as intransigents – to be admitted into that 'government'. The Americans more or less followed Churchill's view. Unless and until some working arrangement could be achieved with the Soviet government on the matter, the British and American governments found themselves unable to recognize the Osobka-Morawski regime and therefore constrained, *faute de mieux*, to continue recognizing the Arciszewski 'government-in-exile' whose behaviour in many ways they deplored.

Poland was the most serious issue between the Anglo-American governments on one side and the Soviet Union on the other, but it was by no means the only issue. There was a growing feeling that the Soviet government was not keeping its undertakings in relation to other countries within the area of its military occupation but was foisting communist-type regimes upon them, without consulting the local people on the matter.

At this moment, an unforeseen event added to the confusion. On 12 April, President Roosevelt died suddenly. He was succeeded by the Vice-President, Harry S. Truman. Truman was little known outside his own country. Worse, his predecessor had kept him in the most scandalous ignorance of both military and diplomatic affairs. The story of how Truman first heard of the atomic bomb after succeeding to the Presidency is well known; but he also had to find his feet very suddenly in the unfamiliar field of international politics.

Plans had long existed for the establishment of the United Nations Organization in its new form at an inaugural conference in San Francisco

in the latter part of April. Two days beforehand, there were furious altercations between the new American President and Molotov. At one moment it looked as if the western Allies' refusal to recognize the Osobka-Morawski government as representative of Poland at the conference would cause the Soviet Union to walk out.

Thus stood matters between the governments of the major Allies even before the end of war in Europe. Within a week of Germany's surrender, Churchill was sending blood-curdling messages to Truman, warning of the enormous Soviet military strength in Europe, and using for the first time the expression 'Iron Curtain' to describe the barrier in communications between the Allies.

Some of the inter-Allied disputes were settled without too much public controversy. The question of the Polish government was resolved by a sort of compromise, though one which certainly came much closer to the Soviet point of view than that of the western countries. A few 'London Poles', including Mikolajczyk, were accepted into the Soviet-sponsored 'government', and the British and American governments then transferred formal recognition from Arciszewski to the modified regime now in power in Warsaw.

There remained one further area on which some kind of agreement between the great Allies was imperative: the immediate future of Germany. This was the main topic of discussion at the last 'Big Three' Conference, held at Potsdam, in the suburbs of Berlin, at the end of July and the beginning of August 1945. There was, of course, already agreement about the zones of occupation, but a good deal more had to be decided. The frontier between Germany and Poland was, in theory, a matter which required resolution at a post-war Peace Conference, but some kind of tacit agreement was necessary for the meantime. The line drawn accorded with Soviet wishes, following the rivers Oder and Neisser. There were also agreements over reparations and demilitarization, and a measure of agreement over the country's immediate economic future.

Many of the matters which had been in dispute between the 'Big Three' during the spring and summer of 1945 were quite unknown to the ordinary citizens of Allied countries. Some secondary political figures in both Britain and the United States had publicly expressed their doubts about the Yalta settlement, and fragments of information about the continuing wrangles over Poland seeped through to the more politically conscious members of the public. Yet the mass of people in Allied countries knew and cared little about such matters. In this ignorance, and the fatuous illusion that all was well between the major governments, they were eagerly assisted by most of the available media.

Thus propaganda of the major Allied governments, and of the newspapers which gave general support to those governments, sought

to gloss over the disputes between them and to pretend that only inveterate mischief-makers could discern differences between the 'Big Three'. It was 'legitimate' for Allied cartoonists to lampoon relatively minor characters like King Peter of Yugoslavia, King George of Greece, or Tomasz Arciszewski of Poland, but it was not generally possible for them to point out the much more serious and general questions at stake between major Allies. Thus cartoons drawn during the wartime period provide only occasional glimpses of those questions; though the glimpses they do provide are sometimes very revealing.

Cartoon 21.1 Salvation Army. *Daily Mail*, London, 23 February 1945

SALVATION ARMY —by Illingworth

About the time of Yalta, the 'Big Three' made it plain that only countries which were at war with Germany would be permitted to become founder-members of the United Nations Organization. As membership was considered to carry considerable benefits, there was marked eagerness among countries which had hitherto been neutral to declare war on Germany.

This cartoon draws a comparison between the Allies' disposition to enrol new associates in the war against Germany with the religious proselytizing activities of the Salvation Army. The hymn-playing band, which includes leaders of various Allied countries, stands outside the doors of a Salvation Army 'citadel'. Churchill encourages various neutrals to enter the hall. Some are eagerly doing so. The man to the right, who looks away with a sour face, is De Valera, Prime Minister of Eire. Southern Ireland was resolutely neutral throughout the war.

Cartoon 21.2 Polish diplomacy. *Evening Standard*, London, 15 February 1945

In the immediate aftermath of Yalta, there was some appreciation that serious difficulties remained in connection with Poland. The general disposition was to blame the Poles.

In this Low cartoon, Tomasz Arciszewski, representing the Polish government in London, firmly repudiates the 'Big Three' decisions at Yalta affecting his country. Stanislaw Mikolajczyk, who was by this time outside the London Polish government but whose claims to inclusion in a future Polish government at Warsaw were backed by the British, expresses scepticism about this policy.

It is difficult to see what else Arciszewski, or anybody else claiming to derive authority from the Polish people, could have done in the circumstances. The Yalta agreement meant that about half of the territory of pre-war Poland, including towns like Lwów with overwhelmingly Polish populations, were to pass to the Soviet Union, and great numbers of serving Polish soldiers would find themselves foreigners in their birthplaces. Yet it is also easy to understand why Arciszewski's position appeared unrealistic to Mikolajczyk and to outside observers. There was no way in which the Poles could hope to revise the Yalta settlement.

Cartoon 21.3 Officer Stalin's idea of policing the world. *Chicago Sunday Tribune*, 18 February 1945

The Hearst press in the United States (which included the *Chicago Tribune*) was among the small group of organs of publicity in Allied countries which expressed, right from the start, profound doubts about the Yalta settlement, and particularly its provisions affecting Poland.

Stalin, in police uniform, helps Russia to enter a victim's house. The victim calls for assistance, and his cries are heard by another policeman who rushes across the street from the 'World League Police Station'. Stalin assures the second policemen that there is nothing to worry about.

The theme of this cartoon is remarkably similar to that of 'Bobby Winston und der Polenklau' (Cartoon 18.9). A few months earlier, Allied cartoonists would probably have hesitated to draw such cartoons, for fear of giving encouragement to the enemy; but by February 1945 the outcome of the war in Europe was not in doubt, and it was perceived as legitimate to look beyond the immediate conflict to problems bearing on the future.

Cartoon 21.4 Ne syckat' drugovo slova. *Izvestiya*, Moscow, 21 April 1945

Не сыскать другого слова

Передовая статья, помещенная в газете Херста «Дейли миррор», опасается установления при встрече дружественных отношений между американскими солдатами и бойцами Красной Армии.

(Из телеграмм).

«Фронт советский недалече,
Наша встреча с ним близка.
Будут рады этой встрече
Наши славные войска!»

Так в Нью-Йорке, в Вашингтоне
Речи честные звучат.
Но в другом, враждебном, тоне
Твари в херстовском загоне
Воют, хрюкают, рычат.

— Фронт советский! Осторожно! —
Указательный свой перст
Угрожающе-тревожно
Поднимает грязный Херст.

В страхе, потный — рожа скокла! —
Дичь неся про русский фронт,
Сквозь фальшивейшие стекла
Смотрит Херст на горизонт.

Чертыхнется, смотрит слова.
Прёт из Херста без покрова
Профашистских чувств основа
Крокодилий зев разверзт.
Не сыскать другого слова
Омерзительней, чем — Херст!

Д. БОЕВОЙ.

Soviet cartoons replied in kind to criticisms from the *Chicago Tribune* and its associated newspapers. In this *Izvestiya* cartoon, 'No need to say more', which appeared in April 1945, Hearst carries a bottle of poison labelled 'Hearst ink', while from his mouth droplets bearing Nazi swastikas emerge. The label stuck into the bottle reads 'Warning: Red Army!' The ink and spittle are being scattered between the American and Soviet flags, which represent American and Soviet troops entering Germany from opposite directions. The passage above the cartoon quotes from a leading article in one of the other Hearst newspapers, the New York *Daily Mirror* (no connection with the British newspaper of the same title), warning against fraternization between American and Soviet troops.

The Soviet cartoon's 'line' is clear. No criticism is made against the United States or its government. There is, however, a very strong implication that Hearst and those holding similar views are attempting maliciously to damage relations between the two countries.

Cartoon 21.5 Ironing out the creases. *Evening Standard*, London, 10 April 1945

Molotov, the Soviet Foreign Minister, Stettinius, the American Secretary of State, and Eden, the British Foreign Secretary, are portrayed as three laundresses, ironing 'clean sheets for 'Frisco' – i.e. co-operating in getting everything ready for the inaugural meeting of the United Nations Organization at San Francisco later in April 1945. 'Poland', represented by Arciszewski, is seen to be impeding their work.

This cartoon seems to imply that the London Poles, who objected to the way in which the 'Big Three' proposed to dispose of their country, are making gratuitous difficulties which are damaging international co-operation.

The cartoonist either did not know of, or preferred to ignore, the much more general difficulties which had already arisen between the major Allies.

Cartoon 21.6 Krokodil, Moscow, no. 25, 30 July 1945

An even later Soviet cartoon, again emphasizing the theme of inter-Allied unity.

This cartoon appeared at the time of the Potsdam conference. The large cars, carrying the United States, Soviet, and British flags, presumably carried senior dignitaries to the conference hall. The drivers, in military uniforms of the three countries, chat together as friends.

Cartoon 21.7 Philadelphia Record, April 1945, reprinted in *New York Times*, 15 April 1945

Doyle in The Philadelphia Record

The sudden death of President Roosevelt on 12 April 1945 came as a great shock to all the Allied countries, and it was widely felt that he was irreplaceable. His American supporters felt the loss most deeply, and he was widely remembered not just as a great wartime leader but also as the man who had played a vital part in leading his country from the Great Depression of the 1930s.

This American cartoon shows the flags of the Allied countries, ringing the globe, all at half-mast in mourning. Yet the clouds in the background are clearing; for it was evident that the war was approaching its end.

Cartoon 21.8 San Francisco Chronicle, 25 April 1945

San Francisco was host to the inaugural meeting of the United Nations in its new form, in late April 1945.

American soldiers killed in the two World Wars, and a small boy, symbolic of the future, look down on a vista of San Francisco, all hoping that its deliberations and action will bring a peaceful future.

22

British wartime politics

Many countries experienced political changes during the war years. Most of those changes were due to the fortunes of war itself. The one striking exception was the British General Election of July 1945, which resulted in a profound change in composition of the House of Commons and the return of a Labour government. This election may only be understood in the context of developments which had been taking place throughout the wartime years.

During the Second World War, as in the 1914–18 conflict, an electoral truce was arranged between the three main political parties. By-elections continued to be held when vacancies arose in the House of Commons, but the principal parties did not contest each other's seats. There was, however, the opportunity for minor parties to intervene, and at times to upset other people's calculations.

In the first phase of the war, a few Communist and Fascist candidates appeared, in both cases fighting on a more or less 'stop-the-war' programme, but all of them fared very badly. After the formation of Churchill's Coalition in May 1940 – which has already been discussed – there followed a period of genuine 'party unity', coinciding with what was – from Britain's point of view – the most acute and dangerous phase of the war.

In the early part of 1942, there were signs of deep public discontent. That mood appears to have received no encouragement at the time from any of the three main Parties, or even from the Communists, who in this phase of the war were overwhelmingly anxious to avoid any action which might embarrass the government in prosecuting the war as an ally of the Soviet Union. Yet in the first six months of the year four Conservative seats were captured by Independent candidates.

The same mood persisted, though on a reduced scale, for the remainder of the European war. Conservative seats were usually targeted – sometimes by Independents, sometimes by members of a new political movement known as Common Wealth. One Labour seat was captured in a late stage of the war by a Scottish Nationalist.

While it is easy to ascertain what critics were saying, it is much more difficult to determine why they were receiving such an eager response.

The Conservative-dominated National Government of the 1930s had long been criticized bitterly by political opponents both for its social policies and for its international policies. There was, however, a very marked disposition on the critics' part to distinguish between Churchill, whom they admired, and the Conservative Party which he was currently leading.

In December 1942, the celebrated Beveridge Report on the social services appeared. It proposed an amalgamation and large extension of those services, and promulgated the doctrine of 'Full Employment'. By this it was meant, not that everybody should always have a job, but that it should be a major objective of government policy to ensure that there were normally more jobs available than there were people seeking jobs. The eponymous author of the Report, Sir William Beveridge, was not at the time a politician at all, but an academic – although he later sat briefly in Parliament as a Liberal MP.

The Beveridge Report attracted enormous public interest. The government perceived that a serious public controversy was developing, and tried to play the whole thing down as a divisive issue which would distract attention from the war effort; but the division which followed in the House of Commons produced the most substantial revolt in the whole lifetime of the Coalition.

Soon after the end of the European war, a General Election was set in progress. Until the results were known, a 'Caretaker' government – effectively, a revival of the old National Government – would hold office.

The conditions of the election were curious. The previous General Election had been nearly ten years earlier. There were many anomalies with the voting registers. Some constituencies had become enormously populous, others had tiny, shrunken electorates. Ordinary Party activities had been largely abandoned during the war, and all Party organizations were in a weak condition. Vast numbers of voters were in the Services overseas.

Winston Churchill, who became leader of the Conservative Party not long after he succeeded to the Premiership in 1940, was unquestionably the most charismatic political figure, and was greeted with great enthusiasm wherever he went. It is now evident that many of the people who welcomed the Prime Minister did so because of his wartime record, and had no intention of voting for the Party which he led.

The political stance of the media in the 1945 General Election was important, and probably had a substantial effect on the results. Television played no part. Television broadcasting had commenced only a short time before the war and was suspended in wartime. Most families had radio sets, and sound broadcasting was the monopoly of the BBC, which attempted to preserve a stance of objective impartiality. Of the popular daily newspapers, the *Daily Mail* was Conservative. The *Daily Express* was Conservative as well, but more idiosyncratic. The *Daily Herald* was

avowedly Labour. The *News Chronicle*, officially Liberal, in practice leaned more towards Labour. The *Daily Mirror* was giving strong support to Labour. As it had a massive readership among Service people, it was probably very influential. There were three London evening newspapers, all with a large readership in south-east England. The *Star* was counterpart to the *News Chronicle*, the *Evening News* to the *Daily Mail*. The *Evening Standard* was counterpart to the *Daily Express*, but David Low, its very perceptive political cartoonist, was strongly anti-Conservative.

Polling Day was 5 July 1945, but a further three weeks elapsed before votes from the forces overseas could be counted. The results were eventually declared in the late stages of the Potsdam Conference. Labour won a huge majority of seats, although – as is nearly always the case with British elections – no Party won an overall majority of the popular vote. Clement Attlee, leader of the Labour Party, succeeded to the premiership, and was able to take charge of the British delegation at Potsdam. Thus two of the acknowledged 'Big Three' leaders had changed within the space of four months.

Cartoon 22.1 Upsetting the queue. *News Chronicle*, London, 5 May 1942

UPSETTING THE QUEUE

This cartoon appeared in the spring of 1942. It comments on the results of three recent by-elections in which apparently safe Conservative seats had been captured by Independent candidates. The Labour and Liberal Parties, which would normally be expected to profit from Conservative unpopularity, were prevented from advancing candidates because of the 'party truce' arrangements which they had made.

The queue – queueing had developed to a great extent during wartime – consists of Conservatives who hoped to be returned to Parliament without a serious contest whenever a suitable vacancy arose. This explains the notice over the cashier's desk. An Independent, however, is winning the support of the people. The heading over the door is a parody on a famous whisky advertisement and alludes to the exceptionally long time which had elapsed since the previous General Election.

Cartoon 22.2 After the Blitz. *Daily Express*, London, 3 July 1942

After the run of anti-government by-elections in the spring of 1942, the critics overreached themselves by moving a hostile resolution in the House of Commons in July 1942. The result was an overwhelming victory for the Coalition Government.

This cartoon recalls damage done to the British House of Commons by an enemy bomb earlier in the war. Churchill stands triumphant amid the rubble.

Cartoon 22.3 Tackling the first giant. *Daily Herald*, London, 2 December 1942

This cartoon appeared in the *Daily Herald* soon after the Beveridge Report was published. The Report had referred to Want, Ignorance, Disease, Squalor, and Idleness as 'the five giants on the road to reconstruction'. Sir William Beveridge is seen, sword in hand, attacking the first 'giant'.

When the Report came to be debated in the House of Commons a few months later, the official attitude of the Coalition Government was to discourage any firm commitment to the Beveridge proposals, although a number of members of the government undoubtedly felt personal sympathy with the ideas. In the division which followed the debate, the great majority of those Labour and Liberal MPs who were not prevented from so doing by membership of the government voted for the Report in defiance of the advice of their own leaders.

Cartoon 22.4 '. . .I tell you they're *not* publicly owned!'. *Evening Standard*, London, 28 February 1944

Labour members of the government were inhibited from pushing their Party's traditional social and economic policies during the lifetime of the Coalition. They must have felt considerable mortification when members of a new political movement, Common Wealth, which did not acknowledge the 'party truce', began to capture Conservative seats which otherwise might have been expected to fall to Labour in Parliamentary by-elections. The policy of Common Wealth was in many ways similar to the traditional Labour policy. Sir Richard Acland, leader of Common Wealth, had originally been elected as a Liberal, but gradually broke with his former party.

Cartoon 22.5 'I didn't know it was loaded!' *Daily Mirror*, London, 24 May 1945

"*I didn't know it was loaded!*"

At the end of the war with Germany, Churchill presented the Labour Party members of the Coalition Government with the choice of either keeping the Coalition alive until the end of the Japanese war or facing an immediate General Election. The Ministers concerned opted for an immediate election, and the Coalition was dissolved.

This *Daily Mirror* cartoon sees the choice set before the Labour people as an 'ultimatum' from Churchill. It may be read to suggest that the effect was very different from that which Churchill had intended – or, alternatively, that Churchill was trying to excuse himself from blame for destroying the Coalition.

Cartoon 22.6 Applicants for the caretaking job. *Evening Standard*, London, 25 May 1945

APPLICANTS FOR THE CARETAKING JOB

The 'Caretaker' government which was set up to hold office until results of the General Election were known was composed mainly of Conservatives, but it also included some members of the Liberal National Party which had broken from the Liberals in 1931 and could, for most purposes, be regarded as a section of the Conservative Party.

Two of these 'Liberal Nationals' are being interviewed by Churchill for posts in the 'Caretaker' government. They are Ernest Brown (left), and Leslie Hore-Belisha. The cartoonist may have thought (wrongly, as it happened) that one of them would get Ernest Bevin's wartime post as Minister of Labour and National Service. Both carry equipment appropriate for an office caretaker.

The notice on the back of the seat is signed by Bevin and implies, correctly, that he would soon return to high office. In the event, Bevin became Foreign Secretary in the eventual Labour government. Brown and Hore-Belisha both tremble at the prospect of the return of the formidable Bevin.

Cartoon 22.7 'Long live the forward march. . .'
News Chronicle, London, 5 July 1945

"Long live the forward march of the common people in all the lands, towards their just and tru inheritance . . ." ***Winston Churchill,*** **October 21, 1940**

A typical 'opposition' cartoon from the 1945 General Election. The 'common people' whom Churchill had invoked are pressing home their attack, while the phantoms of the 'Men of Munich' vanish. Criticism of the foreign policy of the pre-war National Government played a substantial part in 'opposition' propaganda, even though Churchill himself had been one of the foremost critics of the 'Munich' policy.

Cartoon 22.8 'How about knocking these things down now?' *Daily Mail*, London, 11 June 1945

'How about knocking these things down now?'

Churchill and his supporter Lord Beaverbrook suggest that the wall 'War time restrictions and controls' which had been erected during the war to protect 'Great Britain House' from the blast of enemy bombs has outlived its purpose and should be demolished. The Labour leaders Attlee (whom Churchill is addressing), Morrison and Bevin, however, are contemplating 'Plans for bigger & better blast walls' – that is, for more restrictions and controls.

Cartoon 22.9 Everything but freedom! *Daily Mail*, London, 27 June 1945

EVERYTHING BUT FREEDOM!

Supporters of the Conservatives and their associates argued that the return of a Labour government would mean loss of liberty. Here is a typical example of that kind of argument. The various 'benefits' promised by the Labour Party's programme are seen as features which characterize life in a prison. The warders are Clement Attlee, Herbert Morrison, and (controlling the prisoners) Ernest Bevin.

Over the door across the courtyard are the words 'Governor Laski'. Harold Laski, Chairman of the Labour Party, was not a parliamentarian; but some of his utterances implied that a Labour government would be subject to the instructions of the extra-Parliamentary Labour Party. During the election, some Conservative newspapers made a considerable feature of Laski's remarks, which could have been highly embarrassing to the Labour leadership. In the event the newspapers probably overplayed their hand, and their insistence on the menace of the obscure Laski became something of a joke. It is also likely that even Conservative readers found it difficult to visualize Labour leaders who had played a major part in the war against Germany as potential 'prison guards'.

Cartoon 22.10 'Your "freedom" is in danger!'
Daily Mirror, London, 23 June 1945

"Your 'freedom' is in danger!"

This is an Opposition answer to the 'freedom' argument. The Conservative supporter is lecturing the bound 'Public' about the danger to its 'freedom'. The 'Public' is clearly not free at all in current conditions.

The word 'Tory' has been deleted and the word 'National' substituted on the placard which the propagandist is holding. At the 1945 General Election, candidates supporting the Churchill government commonly described themselves as 'National', perhaps because they suspected that 'Conservative' or 'Tory' would prove unpopular names with the electors.

Cartoon 22.11 The third chair. *Daily Mail*, London, 15 June 1945

THE THIRD CHAIR

Stalin and Truman are in conference, and a third chair, meant for Britain, is ranged beside them. Attlee, climbing on the backs of Bevin and Morrison, attempts to assume that chair. All three of them are seen as absurd, diminutive, Disneyesque characters, palpably unfit for such an important position. Stalin regards them with unconcealed contempt, Truman looks puzzled at the whole episode.

The argument here is a 'national' one. Only Churchill is fit to defend Britain's interests in the councils of the world. The Labour leaders are simply not up to the job.

Cartoon 22.12 The Big Three. *News Chronicle*, London, 25 June 1945

THE BIG THREE

This cartoon sets the 'Big Three' argument of the previous cartoon in a different context, and effectively stands it on its head. The 'Big Three' who are met in conference are three of the main advocates of the Conservative campaign: Churchill, Brendan Bracken, and Lord Beaverbrook. On the table are papers referring to themes which they have invoked during the campaign. 'Gestapo bogey' refers to an ill-advised speech by Churchill in which he suggested that a Labour government would be bound to introduce some features of the Nazi secret police into Britain. 'Savings scare' refers to a suggestion that small savings would be jeopardized by Labour policies. 'Laski stunt' refers to the matter discussed in connection with Cartoon 22.9.

Behind the small figures of the three Conservatives are three much bigger men, representing what the cartoonist considered the 'real' issues of the election: the housing problem (demolishing slums, and building houses to replace those destroyed in the war); social security (ensuring adequate social services) and employment (the Beveridge 'full employment' question).

Cartoon 22.13. 'Waiting for something to come up'
Daily Express, London, 23 July 1945

'WAITING FOR SOMETHING TO COME UP'

This cartoon comments on the long period of delay between polling and the declaration of results. The citizen – cartoonist Strube's 'Little Man' – has planted the 'New Parliament Seeds' from the ballot box in his wheelbarrow, but germination will take a long time. The figures looking over the fence are (from left to right): General Franco of Spain; an unidentified Latin American; 'Uncle Sam'; Stalin; Lord Beaverbrook; Attlee; Churchill; the Liberal leader, Sir Archibald Sinclair.

The point being made is that the results of the election will be important for all those people in various ways. In 1945, world attention really was to some extent riveted on British domestic politics.

Lord Beaverbrook, who features in the line on the fence, was not comparable in importance with the others, but he was proprietor of the *Daily Express* in which the cartoon appeared, and a much more colourful personality than any other newspaper owners of the period. Beaverbrook attracted attention from cartoonists of all political persuasions and seems to have cared little how they portrayed him, provided that they did not ignore him.

Cartoon 22.14 News Chronicle, London, 27 July 1945

This cartoon comments on the results of the 1945 General Election. Not only did Labour win a large majority of seats, but they also drove from Parliament several senior MPs belonging to the Conservative Party and its associates.

Ernest Bevin, who had been Minister of Labour during the Coalition period (and therefore responsible for employment policy), sits grinning as the clerk at the Employment Exchange (Job Centre). In the queue for work are a number of men who until recently had held high office. Heading the queue is Brendan Bracken (First Lord of the Admiralty in the 'Caretaker' government). Behind him is Ernest Brown (Minister of Aircraft Production), then Leslie Hore-Belisha (Minister of National Insurance), L. S. Amery (Secretary of State for India and Burma), Sir Edward Grigg (Minister resident in the Middle East), Duncan Sandys (Minister of Works), Richard Law (Minister of Education), Geoffrey Lloyd (Minister of Information) and Sir Walter Wormersley (Minister of Pensions). Another remarkable defeat – not in the queue, perhaps because he was not at the time a Minister) – was Harold Macmillan.

Cartoon 22.15 Excusez-moi. . . *Le Canard enchaîné*, Paris, 1 August 1945

A French comment on the British change of government. The British lion apologizes to the American eagle and the Russian bear for his brief departure from the Potsdam Conference, explaining that he had been away to change his hat. He now wears a worker's cloth cap, signalling the 'working class' orientation of the new Labour government.

When the results of the British General Election were declared, Attlee and Churchill had to return briefly to London to go through the formalities of a change of government. On his return, Attlee took charge of the British delegation for the last day or two of the conference.

Cartoon 22.16 Giddap, Napoleon! *New York Herald Tribune*, 6 August 1945

Giddap, Napoleon!

An American view of the change. The gigantic figure 'Postwar Problems' has mounted the horse 'English Labor Party', leaving the Conservative Party to graze. The new mount regards its burden with apprehension.

United States commentators, like many external observers, constantly used the word 'English' where 'British' or 'United Kingdom' would be appropriate.

23

The end of the Far Eastern war

At Potsdam, Stalin and Truman each imparted some very important information to the other delegates. Stalin reported that the Japanese government had made representations to Moscow, seeking terms. Truman revealed that a new bomb, based on a completely new scientific principle, had been tested by the United States. This, of course, was the first, experimental, atomic bomb. The Potsdam Conference ended on 2 August 1945. In the next fortnight, events moved very rapidly.

The problem with Japan was not to procure the country's defeat – for that was already assured – but to bring about the unconditional surrender which the Allies demanded. Ordinary Japanese soldiers showed a disposition, unmatched in the Allied armies, to fight to the death in militarily impossible situations, considering that any other course would be dishonourable, and worse than death. There was a prospect that the task of exacting unconditional surrender would prove so costly in Allied lives that it would have to be abandoned, with unforeseeable consequences.

During the Potsdam period, and in the few days which followed, massive air raids using 'conventional' weapons were launched against Japanese cities. Then, on 6 August, the first atomic bomb was launched against Hiroshima, with the loss of something like 80,000 dead. Two days later, the Soviet Union declared war on Japan. On the following day, 9 August, the second atomic bomb was used against Nagasaki. After a few days of intense negotiations, Japan accepted the Allied demand for unconditional surrender on 14 August. The following day was celebrated as 'VJ Day' (Victory over Japan).

It is useful to reflect on the circumstances which led to Soviet intervention in the Japanese war on 8 August. This intervention followed, almost to the day, the three-month period after the end of the German war which Stalin had promised at Yalta.

At the time of Yalta, both the western Allies and the Soviet Union had good reason to desire an arrangement of that kind. The atomic bomb was far from ready, and there was considerable doubt among experts as to whether it would work. Without a decisive weapon of that kind, the Anglo-Americans faced the prospect of either reaching a settlement with Japan which fell far short of unconditional surrender, or, in the

alternative, a long struggle, exceedingly costly in lives. If, however, the Soviet Union joined in as well, the campaign would probably be much shorter and less costly.

The Soviet Union also saw advantages from participation, for this would give her an important say in the eventual Far Eastern settlement. There was not much Japanese territory which she sought for herself – the southern part of the island of Sakhalin was the most significant – but she desired economic and political influence in the Japanese 'satellite', Manchuria, the Japanese possession Korea, and perhaps more besides.

After the successful test of the atomic bomb, the position had changed. The British still desired Soviet intervention; the Americans seem to have been considerably more doubtful. If the war would be decided by the atomic bomb, and Soviet participation would have little effect on the upshot, then why invite the Soviet Union to assume the role of a major Power in the north Pacific region? By the same token, it was important for the Soviet government that they should become participants and, at small cost, acquire this important new area of influence.

Cartoon 23.1 Birds of a feather. *Washington Post*, 29 July 1945

BIRDS OF A FEATHER

On 26 July, during the Potsdam Conference, a formal demand was issued by the governments of the United States, Britain, and China, for Japan to surrender unconditionally forthwith. The Soviet Union, which was not at that time at war with Japan, could not be party to the demand.

The Allied appeal was rebuffed, even though the Japanese could have had no doubt that they were bound to be defeated if the war continued, and this cartoon suggests a possible reason. The Japanese may have believed that dissension might yet be sown between the Soviet Union and the western Allies which would keep the USSR out of the war against them, and perhaps set the different Allied countries even more deeply at loggerheads.

If that could all happen, then Japan might well be able to obtain terms which were well short of unconditional surrender. Thus – as this American cartoon suggests – the Japanese and the American 'Russophobes' were both 'working the same side of the street', and tending, for utterly different reasons, to encourage the same kind of effect.

The title 'Son of Heaven', mentioned on the Japanese poster, was borne by the Japanese Emperor, who was considered divine.

Cartoon 23.2 'I didn't speak.' *Daily Herald*, London, 25 July 1945

"I didn't speak."
"I thought you growled."

Japanese soldiers are defending home territory against the Allies. Coming from behind them is a Russian bear. The Soviet intention to enter the war against Japan, though known to the Allied leaders, had not been disclosed to the public. The cartoonist, however – like many people at the time – guessed that a Soviet attack would be made on Japan in the near future.

The 'Rising Sun' flag beside the soldiers was the Emperor's standard, and would not have been used by troops as this cartoon implies.

Cartoon 23.3 Berlin i Tokio. *Pravda*, Moscow, 11 August 1945

Берлин и Токио

«...Основные цели, которые заставили Японию и Германию взяться за оружие, были одни и те же...»

Японская газета «Ниппон таймс» (декабрь 1944 г.).

Рис. Кукрыниксы.

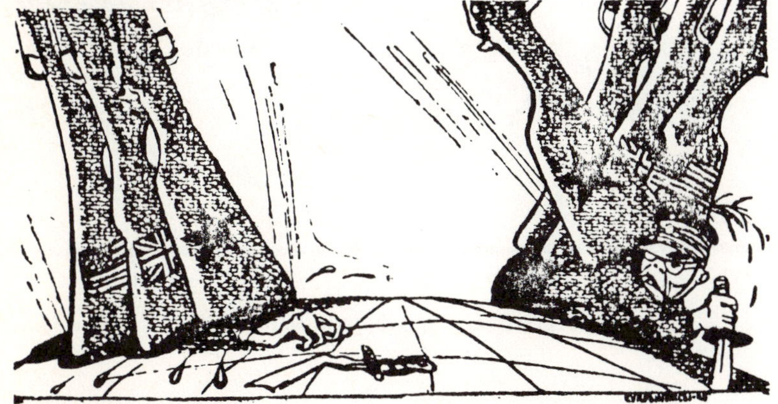

Они сознались, что имели
Одни намеренья и цели:

Они свою ковали ось,
Чтоб шар земной проткнуть насквозь.

Но разлучилась эта пара...
Один исчез не так давно
И на коре земного шара
Оставил грязное пятно.

Теперь другой узнал на деле,
Что грозный суд неотвратим,
Что одинаковые цели
Ведут к последствиям одним.

За преступления жестокие
Враги дадут ответ одни.
Приехал к финишу Берлин,
За ним последует и Токио.

С. МАРШАК.

During the long and terrible Soviet–German struggle, Japan had been neutral. The Soviet government decided to go to war with Japan soon after that struggle was finished, but it was necessary to explain to the Soviet people why they were being required to take up arms again, this time against a country which had honoured its Non-aggression Pact throughout the conflict, in spite of strong temptations to do otherwise.

Essentially, the argument was that Germany and Japan had similar policies, and for that reason there could be no secure peace until both were defeated. This *Pravda* cartoon, which appeared a very few days after the Soviet declaration of war against Japan, is an example of that argument. The text is a quotation from the Japanese newspaper *Nippon Times* of December 1944: 'The essential consideration which compelled Japan and Germany to take up arms was one and the same.'

The cartoon suggests what that consideration was. In the top picture, Hitler and a Japanese military leader are shown carving up the world – i.e. the consideration was greed for conquest. But the bottom picture foretells the consequences. Rifles carrying the Soviet, British, and American insignia have already crushed Hitler. The British and American rifles, plus a third – presumably the Chinese – already weigh heavily on the Japanese. Now a fourth rifle, the Soviet one, is being brought into position, and will shortly deliver the *coup de grâce*.

The poem at the foot is by S. Marshak, author of a number of wartime Russian poems. In this period, poetry tends to play a much larger part in Soviet propaganda than in the propaganda of most countries.

Cartoon 23.4 Posledny oblomok fashistskoi osi. *Izvestiya*, Moscow, 12 August 1945

Последний обломок фашистской оси

Японский милитаризм прибывает к месту назначения... Рис. Бор. Ефимова.

This *Izvestiya* cartoon, which also appeared in the short space between Soviet intervention in the Far Eastern war and the Japanese surrender, is entitled 'The last fragment of the fascist axle' (i.e. 'Axis'), and the words at the bottom read 'Japanese militarism arrives at its appointed place.'

Most of the chariot 'Hitler's New Order' lies in ruins at the foot of the cliff, and vultures fly near by. Japanese militarism, with a sword between his teeth, and clutching desperately to the broken axle, is being pushed remorselessly towards the cliff edge by the weapons of the 'Big Three' and China.

Cartoon 23.5 The last enemy. *Daily Mail*, London, 15 August 1945

THE LAST ENEMY

The Japanese Emperor leads his people who bow before the American, British, and Soviet soldiers. In the middle distance are the ruins of bomb-shattered Japan, with smoke still pouring from the rubble. Mount Fujiyama and the sun – presumably setting rather than rising – are in the distance.

Cartoon 23.6. Za Tualetom. *Krokodil*, Moscow, 30 August 1945

A Soviet comment on the end of the Japanese war. The world is shaving itself with a razor carrying the emblems of the 'Big Three'. Stubble in the form of swastikas lies in a heap of foam on the table. The last fragments of stubble are being cleared from the Japanese islands.

Cartoon 23.7 Sure, we can use him. *New York Herald Tribune*, 16 August 1945

A feature of the end of the Japanese war which attracted adverse comment in some quarters was the Allies' decision to permit Emperor Hirohito to remain on the throne. Hirohito's personal influence on events appears to have been slight, and – when it was exercised – was on the side of moderation. His quasi-religious role in Japanese society, however, was such that the people of his country would be far more willing to ackowledge defeat if he remained on the throne than otherwise.

This American cartoon defends the decision to retain the Emperor. It sees the United Nations as an old-fashioned street organ-grinder, and Hirohito as the monkey who traditionally accompanied an organ-grinder. The monkey is carrying the cup in which passers-by put coins. The implication is that Hirohito could do no harm, and would probably do a certain amount of good by making the Japanese more willing to accept Allied peace terms.

Cartoon 23.8. 'Be funny if the siren. . .' *Sunday Express*, London, 19 August 1945

"Be funny if the siren went now, wouldn't it?"

A whimsical comment on 'VJ Day' in a British town. A jolly crowd joins in street celebrations. The scene is typical of many such celebrations, and is realistic. Many people are doing things which they would not normally consider doing – certainly not with several policemen near by. The balloon vendor muses to the policeman that it would 'be funny if the siren went now'. Sirens were used to give warning of air raids, so that people could take cover.

As in many Giles cartoons, the detail is as funny and as perceptive as the general drawing.

24

The remaining problems

The Second World War, like most conflicts, did not so much settle the world's problems as change the questions.

Europe was no longer the centre of world events. Germany and Italy were destroyed, France was a shadow of its former self. Britain was still generally acknowledged to be one of the 'Big Three', whose voices would determine the future; but perceptive observers could see that her glories lay in the past. Two new 'Super-powers', both of which had stood largely on the sidelines of world events during the inter-war period, had been brought to the centre of decision-making.

Various territorial problems arising out of the war itself were still unresolved. In Europe, the most serious of these concerned Venezia Giulia, the area at the head of the Adriatic: a region where the rural population was overwhelmingly South Slav but the town dwellers were largely Italian. The area was currently disputed between Italy, backed rather hesitantly by the Anglo-Americans, and Yugoslavia, which was then regarded as more or less a client of the Soviet Union. Some people saw a serious risk that the dispute could lead to a 'shooting war', into which major Allies might be drawn on opposite sides.

The situation at the end of the war in the Far East was much more confused than it had been in Europe, for there had been no prior agreement about areas of occupation, and their were many claimants. Britain, the United States, the Soviet Union, China, France, the Netherlands, the Chinese Communists and a variety of national and rebel movements all had demands to make on territory which at the end of the war was in Japanese possession.

The Allies did not contest each other's claims for restitution of territory which Japan had taken from them during the war, but nationalist movements in places like the Dutch East Indies, and the Chinese Communists, had ideas of their own about their countries' futures. In some places held by Japan at the end of the war, and most notably in Korea, forces of different Allied countries stood poised to occupy the territory, and arbitrary arrangements had to be made between them. Such arrangements would prove of great importance in the next few years.

Ordinary men and women in many countries had begun to ask

searching questions about their own social and economic structures. We have already seen how some of these questions were asked in Britain, whose home territory had never been occupied by the enemy. Comparable questions took a more acute form elsewhere. Many Frenchmen, for example, asked why their country, which had appeared so strong, had collapsed so quickly, and what lessons the answer implied for the future. Asian countries, who had witnessed the astonishingly rapid advances of Japan, could never again take for granted the permanent superiority of European colonialists.

The emergence of the 'Big Three' during the war implied new problems for the aftermath. These problems became increasingly acute as the rapid disintegration of the British Empire soon turned the wartime 'Big Three' into the 'Big Two' super-powers, whose conflicting political and economic ideologies rapidly polarized the world into the framework of a 'Cold War'.

Finally, the technology of wartime posed problems of an even more durable nature. The most immediately important of those problems was the atomic bomb and the whole issue of nuclear energy, in both warlike and peaceful forms. Documents circulating at the highest levels of government in Britain and the United States leave us in no doubt that some of the risks were perceived, and even exaggerated, within days of the destruction of Hiroshima. Yet inventions and discoveries had been made, or existing knowledge had been developed under the compulsion of war, in many other fields, whose effects would be almost as revolutionary: long-range heavy aeroplanes; jet propulsion; antibiotics; new pesticides; radar and sonar; new plastics.

Cartoon 24.1 Careful! *Daily Mail*, London, 16 May 1945

This cartoon appeared about a week after the end of the European war. An allegorical figure – perhaps 'Peace' – holds a bomb-detector over Trieste, and shouts a warning to the soldiers who accompany her.

Trieste was the most important town of Venezia Giulia, an area which had received comparatively little attention during most of the war but which was suddenly perceived to be of great importance. Anglo-American forces moving northwards through Italy, and Yugoslav partisans, arrived in Venezia Giulia almost simultaneously, shortly before the end of the war. The Yugoslavs laid claim to it. No doubt the ultimate fate of Venezia Giulia would be decided by the eventual Peace Treaties, but in such a case possession was likely to be nine points of the law.

Such a problem might once have been 'solved' by a simple assessment of the relative strength of armies in the vicinity, in which case the western Allies would doubtless have had the final say. Matters, however, were less simple than that. The Yugoslav government was rapidly passing into Communist control, and in 1945 most people assumed that 'Communist' and 'pro-Soviet' meant more or less the same thing. If that was so, then Soviet interests and those of the western Allies might be directly engaged.

The course of Italian politics was closely linked to this problem. The Italian Communists were a large and influential body, and at one point it seemed by no means unlikely that they would become the government of Italy in the fairly near future. Yet most Italians felt a strong 'national' interest in Venezia Giulia, and particularly Trieste. If the western Allies could be seen to be taking a strong line against Yugoslav claims to Trieste, then sympathizers with the Italian Communists would be forced to choose between their communism and their nationalism, and many would probably choose the latter.

Any course of action by the western Allies was fraught with huge risks. To deny the Yugoslav claim to Trieste involved a risk of fighting, and perhaps eventual Soviet intervention; to acknowledge the Yugoslav claim would greatly increase the risk of Italy going communist, and perhaps other countries doing the same, which would tilt the world balance very seriously. 'Peace', in this cartoon, was justified in experiencing a sense of alarm at what seemed to be a simple question. Various temporary expedients were used to 'de-fuse' the problem, but no permanent solution was reached until nine years later.

Cartoon 24.2 Le Canard enchaîné, Paris, 4 July 1945

— Léopold III
— Et moi, Marianne III . . .

The scene is a third-class railway waiting room, and the joke is based on the recurrence of the number three. King Leopold of the Belgians introduces himself as 'Léopold III'. Marianne – the French Republic – returns the courtesy 'And I am Marianne III'.

The fate both of King Leopold and of the French Third Republic were under searching review in their respective countries. King Leopold was accused by some people of having surrendered Belgian troops unncessarily to the Germans in 1940, and there was much debate in Belgium about whether or not he should remain king. Leopold eventually abdicated in 1951, in favour of his son.

The French Third Republic, established after the Franco-Prussian War of 1870–1, had been formally replaced by Pétain's 'French State' after the 1940 defeat, but the Free French did not acknowledge the change and when de Gaulle's regime was recognized by the Allies in 1944 it claimed to be in effect a continuance of the Third Republic. At the end of the war, however, the constitutional structure of France came under searching review, and in 1946 the Third Republic was replaced by a Fourth Republic.

Cartoon 24.3 People's Car. *Evening Standard*, London, 7 August 1945

Just after the Potsdam Conference, Stalin, Attlee and Truman muse on prospects of the 'new Germany', with '7,000,000 outcasts from the East, etc.' The figure given was probably a considerable underestimate.

Before 1938, there had been great numbers of *Volksdeutsch* – people of German speech and culture – living in various countries of central and eastern Europe, including millions in Czechoslovakia and Poland. The alleged plight of *Volksdeutsch* in those two countries had been used by Hitler as an excuse for German aggression. At the end of the war, the Germans living there were expelled. In addition, large areas of pre-war Germany were for practical purposes given to Poland at Potsdam, and nearly all the Germans had probably already been expelled from those places even before the conference. The problem of German refugees was further compounded when many people living in the Soviet zone of occupation fled to the west of the country.

The name 'People's Car' arose before the war. At a time when cars were considered expensive luxuries, far beyond the reach of most people, the German government claimed to have plans for the production of great numbers of 'people's cars' and obtained large sums of money from citizens for that purpose. The cars never materialized, but the money was used for military purposes.

The 'new Germany' car in this picture is clearly weighed down with the 'outcasts'.

Cartoon 24.4 For good or evil. *Punch*, London, 15 August 1945

FOR GOOD OR EVIL

Cartoon 24.5 Unofficial delegate. *Christian Science Monitor*, Boston, Mass., 11 August 1945

Cormack in The Christian Science Monitor © 1945 TCSPS

Cartoon 24.6 World: Have you thought out your last words yet? *Daily Express*, London, 10 August 1945

WORLD: HAVE YOU THOUGHT OUT YOUR LAST WORDS YET?
MARS: HAVE YOU?

Cartoons 24.4–24.6 are three of many to the same general effect, which appeared in the immediate aftermath of the detonation of atomic bombs on Hiroshima and Nagasaki. They make a point which thoughtful people throughout the world came to appreciate in August 1945. The atomic bomb had altered the whole character of warfare permanently and irrevocably. It was bound to have enormous repercussions on international relations; while the physical principles involved in the bomb's manufacture would probably revolutionize the character of peaceful industry as well.

At that moment, the capacity to utilize nuclear energy in weapon manufacture was confined to the United States and, to some extent, Britain; but others already knew enough of the essential principles to prepare their own atomic bombs in the near future. Nobody in the United States or Britain knew how far others, and particularly the Soviet Union, had already progressed in the direction of atomic bomb manufacture. There was every reason, furthermore, for thinking that atomic bombs much more powerful than those which had destroyed the Japanese cities would soon be made.

Cartoon 24.7 And now to work. *Evening Standard*, London, 17 August 1945

The scale of destruction in the Second World War vastly exceeded that of any other conflict in human history. It is impossible to assess the number of dead with any confidence, but the figure of fifty millions may not be far wrong. Innumerable others had suffered physical or mental injuries which would shorten, or blight, their lives. Most belligerents had sustained great material damage, and all had sustained massive economic loss. The fact that different kinds of wartime loss had fallen to varying extents on different countries had already altered radically the balance of their importance and influence by 1945. A great many of the general assumptions of 1939 – whether social, economic, political, scientific, technological, or cultural – had already gone for ever. The tasks of reconstruction which confronted the young people shown in this cartoon were boundless.

Series design by Julie Fry
Typesetting by Meighan Gale
Image placement and production by Julie Fry
Printed and bound by Thomson-Shore, Inc.